Travel Discount Coupon

This coupon entitles you to special discounts when you book your trip through the

GLOBAL TRAVEL NETWORK®
RESERVATION SERVICE

Hotels ♦ Airlines ♦ Car Rentals ♦ Cruises
All Your Travel Needs

Here's what you get: *

- ♦ A discount of $5 **or more for two
- ♦ A discount of or more for one person
- ♦ Free membersh e miles on enrollment ravel Network Miles-to-Go® frequent-traveler program. Earn one mile for every dollar spent through the program. Redeem miles for free hotel stays starting at 5,000 miles. Earn free roundtrip airline tickets starting at 25,000 miles.
- ♦ Personal help in planning your own, customized trip.
- ♦ Fast, confirmed reservations at any property recommended in this guide, subject to availability.***
- ♦ Special discounts on bookings in the U.S. and around the world.
- ♦ Low-cost visa and passport service.
- ♦ Reduced-rate cruise packages and special car rental programs worldwide.

Visit our website at http://www.travelnetwork.com/Frommer or call us globally at 201-567-8500, ext. 55. In the U.S., call toll-free at 1-888-940-5000, or fax 201-567-1838. In Canada, call at 1-905-707-7222, or fax 905-707-8108. In Asia, call 60-3-7191044, or fax 60-3-7185415.

* To qualify for these travel discounts, at least a portion of your trip must include destinations covered in this guide. No more than one coupon discount may be used in any 12-month period, for destinations covered in this guide. Cannot be combined with any other discount or promotion.

**These are U.S. dollars spent on commissionable bookings.

***A $10 USD fee, plus fax and/or phone charges, will be added to the cost of bookings at each hotel not linked to the reservation service. Customers must approve these fees in advance. If only hotels of this kind are booked the traveler(s) must also purchase roundtrip air tickets from Travel Network for the trip.

Valid until December 31, 1998. Terms and conditions of the Miles-to-Go® program are available on request by calling 201-567-8500, ext 55.

CAR234

"Amazingly easy to use. Very portable, very complete."

—*Booklist*

♦

"The only mainstream guide to list specific prices. The Walter Cronkite of guidebooks—with all that implies."

—*Travel & Leisure*

♦

"Complete, concise, and filled with useful information."

—*New York Daily News*

♦

"Hotel information is close to encyclopedic."

—*Des Moines Sunday Register*

Frommer's® 98

Caribbean

by Darwin Porter &
Danforth Prince

Macmillan • USA

About the Authors

A native of North Carolina, **Darwin Porter** was a bureau chief for the *Miami Herald* when he was 21, and later worked in television advertising. A veteran travel writer, he is the author of numerous best-selling Frommer's guides, notably to England, France, Italy, and Spain. He is assisted by **Danforth Prince,** formerly of the Paris Bureau of the *New York Times.* They have been frequent travelers to the Caribbean for years, and are intimately familiar with what's good there and what isn't. They have also written *Frommer's Caribbean Cruises,* the most candid and up-to-date guide to cruise vacations on the market. In this guide, they share their secrets and discoveries with you.

MACMILLAN TRAVEL

A Simon & Schuster Macmillan Company
1633 Broadway
New York, NY 10019

Find us online at **http://www.frommers.com** or
on America Online at Keyword: **Frommers**

ISBN 0-02-861656-1
ISSN 1044-2375

Editor: Philippe Wamba
Special thanks to Alicia Scott
Design by Michele Laseau
Digital Cartography by Roberta Stockwell and Ortelius Design

Special Sales

Bulk purchases (10+ copies) of Frommer's and selected Macmillan travel guides are available to corporations, organizations, mail-order catalogs, institutions, and charities at special discounts and can be customized to suit individual needs. Existing editions can be produced with custom cover imprints such as corporate logos. For more information write to: Special Sales, Macmillan General Reference, 1633 Broadway, New York, NY 10019.

Manufactured in the United States of America

Contents

List of Maps

An Invitation to the Reader

In researching this book, we discovered many wonderful places—hotels, restaurants, shops, and more. We're sure you'll find others. Please tell us about them, so we can share the information with your fellow travelers in upcoming editions. If you were disappointed with a recommendation, we'd love to know that, too. Please write to:

Darwin Porter & Danforth Prince
Frommer's Caribbean '98
Macmillan Travel
1633 Broadway
New York, NY 10019

An Additional Note

Please be advised that travel information is subject to change at any time—and this is especially true of prices. We therefore suggest that you write or call ahead for confirmation when making your travel plans. The authors, editors, and publisher cannot be held responsible for the experiences of readers while traveling. Your safety is important to us, however, so we encourage you to stay alert and be aware of your surroundings. Keep a close eye on cameras, purses, and wallets, all favorite targets of thieves and pickpockets.

What the Star Means

✪ Frommer's Favorites

Our favorite places and experiences—outstanding for quality, value, or both.

The following abbreviations are used for credit cards:

AE American Express
DC Diners Club
DISC Discover
MC MasterCard
V Visa

The following abbreviations are used in hotel listings:

MAP (Modified American Plan) usually means room, breakfast, and dinner, unless the room rate has been quoted separately, and then it means only breakfast and dinner.

AP (American Plan) includes your room plus three meals.

CP (Continental Plan) includes room and a light breakfast.

EP (European Plan) means room only.

Find Frommer's Online

Arthur Frommer's Outspoken Encyclopedia of Travel (www.frommers.com) offers more than 6,000 pages of up-to-the-minute travel information—including the latest bargains and candid, personal articles updated daily by Arthur Frommer himself. No other website offers such comprehensive and timely coverage of the world of travel.

1

Choosing the Perfect Island: The Best of the Caribbean

In the Caribbean, you can hike through national parks and scuba dive along underwater mountains. But perhaps your idea of the perfect island vacation is to plunk yourself down on the sands with a frosted drink in hand. Whether you want a veranda with a view of the sea or a plantation house set in a field of sugarcane, this chapter will help you choose the lodgings that best suit your needs. If you're looking for a rum-and-reggae cruise or an utterly quiet evening, read on.

For a thumbnail portrait of each island, see "The Islands in Brief," in chapter 2.

1 The Best Beaches

Good beaches with soul-warming sun, crystal-clear waters, and fragrant sea air can be found on virtually every island of the Caribbean, with the possible exceptions of Saba (which has rocky shores) and Dominica (where the few beaches have dramatically black sands that reflect the hot sun).

- **Seven Mile Beach** (Grand Cayman): It's really about 5½ miles long, but who's counting? Lined with condos and plush resorts, this beach is known for its array of water sports and its translucent aquamarine waters. Australian pines dot the background, and the average winter temperature of the water is a perfect 80°F. See chapter 4.
- **Luquillo Beach** (Puerto Rico): This crescent-shaped public beach, 30 miles east of San Juan, is the local favorite. Much photographed because of its white sands and coconut palms, it also has tent sites and picnic facilities. The often-fierce waters of the Atlantic are subdued by the coral reefs protecting the crystal-clear lagoon. See chapter 5.
- **Trunk Bay** (St. John): Protected by the U.S. National Park Service, this beach is one of the Caribbean's most popular. A favorite with cruise-ship passengers, it's known for its underwater trail, where markers guide beachcombers along the reef just off the white sandy beach. See chapter 6.
- **Cane Garden Bay** (Tortola): One of the Caribbean's more spectacular stretches of beach, Cane Garden Bay extends for 1½ miles of white sand and is a jogger's favorite. It's a much better choice than the more obvious (and crowded) Magens Bay beach on neighboring St. Thomas. See chapter 7.

The Caribbean Islands

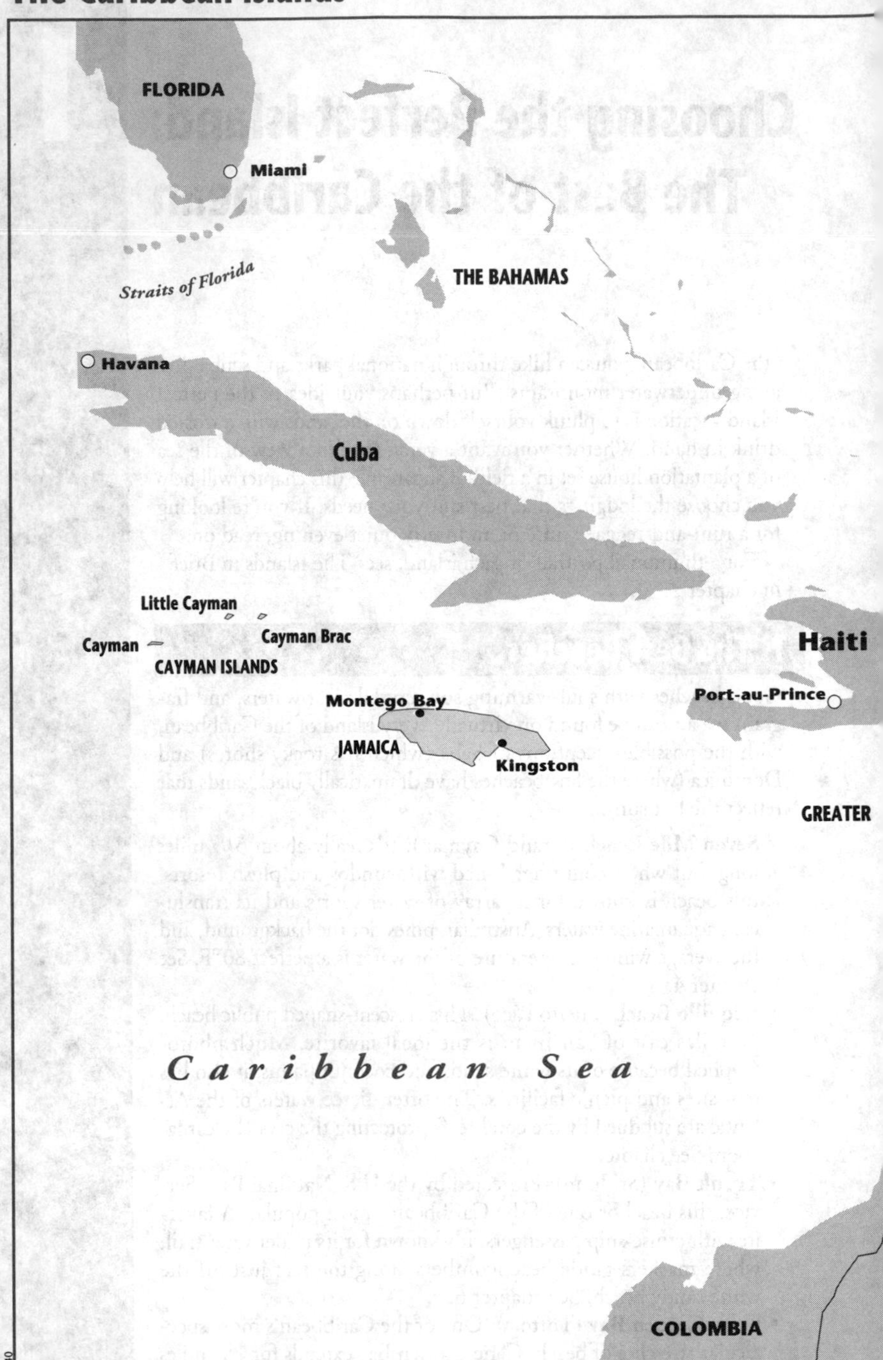

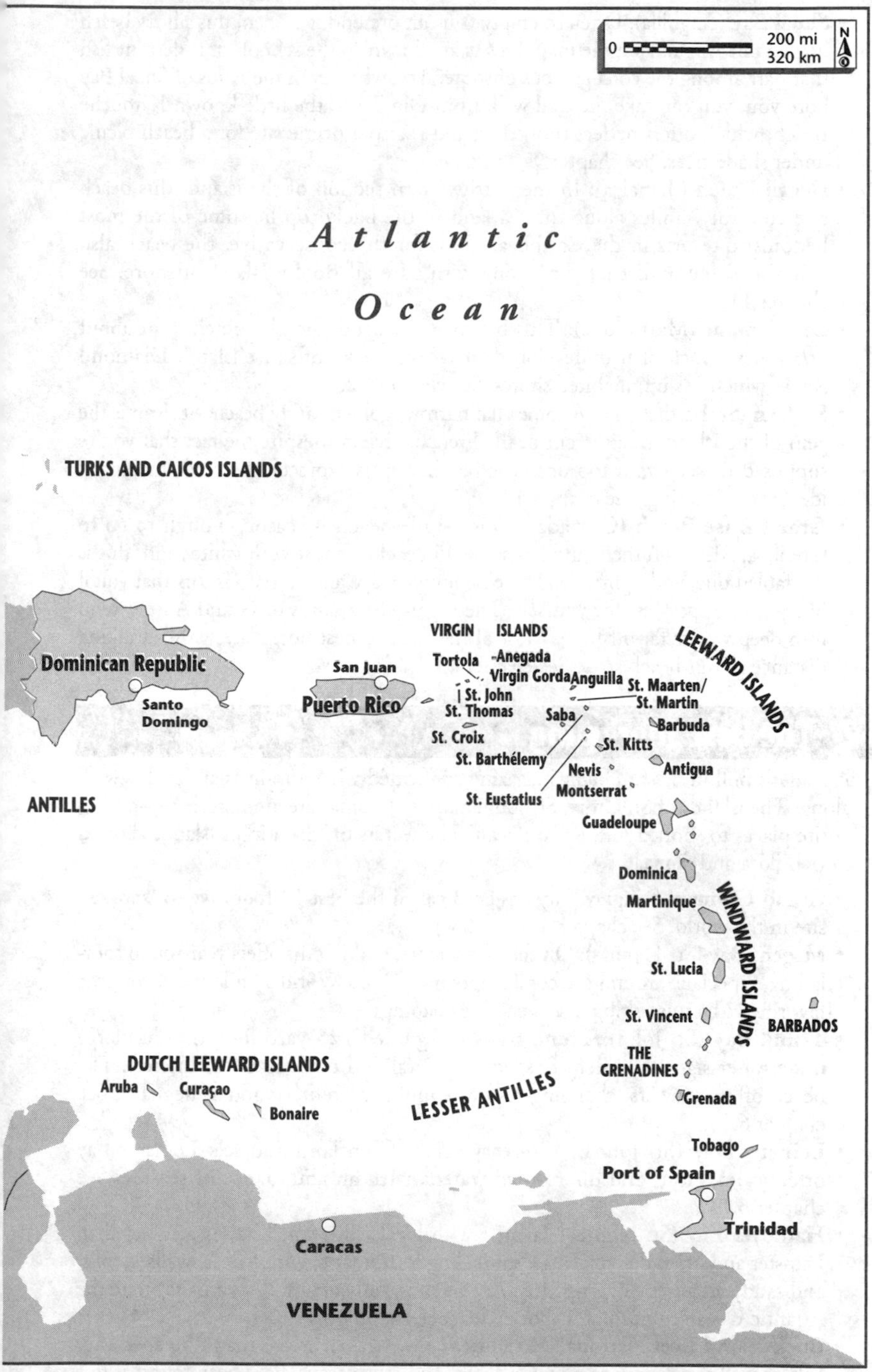

0
200 mi
320 km
N
Atlantic
Ocean
TURKS AND CAICOS ISLANDS
Dominican Republic
Santo
Domingo
ANTILLES
San Juan
Puerto Rico
VIRGIN ISLANDS
Tortola
Anegada
Virgin Gorda
St. John
St. Thomas
St. Croix
St. Barthélemy
St. Eustatius
Anguilla
St. Maarten/
St. Martin
Saba
Barbuda
St. Kitts
Nevis
Antigua
Montserrat
LEEWARD ISLANDS
Guadeloupe
Dominica
Martinique
WINDWARD ISLANDS
St. Lucia
St. Vincent
BARBADOS
THE
GRENADINES
Grenada
DUTCH LEEWARD ISLANDS
Aruba
Curaçao
Bonaire
LESSER ANTILLES
Tobago
Port of Spain
Trinidad
Caracas
VENEZUELA

- **Shoal Bay** (Anguilla): Often so empty you can pretend it's Eden, this silvery beach helped put Anguilla on the map. Divers are drawn to the schools of iridescent fish that dart among the coral gardens offshore. And when even the sands of Shoal Bay bore you, you can take the trail walk from Old Ta to the little-known Katouche Beach, which offers perfect snorkeling and is also a prime site for a beach picnic under shade trees. See chapter 9.
- **Negril Beach** (Jamaica): In the northwestern section of the island, this beach stretches for 7 miles along the sea, and in the backdrop lie some of the most hedonistic resorts in the Caribbean. Not for the conservative, the beach also contains some nudist patches along with bare-all Booby Island offshore. See chapter 11.
- **Le Diamant** (Martinique): This bright white sandy beach stretches for about $6^1/_2$ miles, much of it undeveloped. It faces a rocky offshore island, Diamond Rock, which has uninhabited shores. See chapter 12.
- **St. Jean** (St. Barthélemy): A somewhat narrow, golden sandy beach, St. Jean is the gem of the island, reminiscent of the French Riviera (despite the fact that you're supposed to keep your top on). The beach strip is protected by reefs, making it ideal for swimming. See chapter 12.
- **Grand Anse Beach** (Grenada): This 2-mile beach is reason enough to go to Grenada. Although the island has some 45 beaches, most with white sand, this is the fabled one, and rightly so. There's enough space and so few visitors that you'll likely find a spot just for yourself. The sugar-white sands of Grand Anse extend into deep waters far offshore. Most of the island's best hotels are within walking distance of this beach strip. See chapter 13.

2 The Best Snorkeling

A reader's poll in *Scuba Diving* magazine confirmed what Virgin Islanders knew all along: The islands of St. Croix, St. John, and St. Thomas are among the top-five favorite places to snorkel in the Caribbean. The waters off the Virgin Islands abound in rich flora and fauna.

- **Grand Cayman:** Stingray City has been called the best 12-foot dive (or snorkel) site in the world. See chapter 4.
- **Magens Bay** (St. Thomas): On the north shore, Coki Point offers year-round snorkeling, especially around the coral ledges near Coral World's underwater tower, a favorite with cruise-ship passengers. See chapter 6.
- **Trunk Bay** (St. John): Trunk Bay's self-guided 225-yard-long trail has large underwater signs that identify species of coral and other items of interest. The beach offers showers, changing rooms, equipment rentals, and a lifeguard. See chapter 6.
- **Leinster Bay** (St. John): With easy access from land and sea, Leinster Bay offers calm, clear, and uncrowded waters, with an abundance of sea life. See chapter 6.
- **Haulover Bay** (St. John): A favorite with locals, this small bay is rougher than Leinster and often deserted. The snorkeling is dramatic, with ledges, walls, nooks, and sandy areas set close together. At this spot, only about 200 yards separate the Atlantic Ocean from the Caribbean Sea. See chapter 6.
- **Buck Island Reef National Monument** (St. Croix): More than 250 species of fish, as well as a variety of sponges, corals, and crustaceans, have been found at this 850-acre island and reef system, 2 miles off St. Croix's north shore. The reef is strictly protected by the National Park Service. See chapter 6.

- **Cane Bay** (St. Croix): One of the island's best diving and snorkeling sites is off this breezy north-shore beach. On a clear day, you can swim out 150 yards and see the Cane Bay Wall that drops off dramatically to deep waters below. Multicolored fish and elkhorn and brain coral are in abundance here. See chapter 6.
- **Tobago:** The shallow, sun-flooded waters off the Latin American coastline boast enormous colonies of marine life. Buccoo Reef on Tobago offers many opportunities for snorkeling, and many local entrepreneurs take water enthusiasts out for junkets. See chapter 15.
- **Bonaire:** All the attributes that make Bonaire a world-class dive destination apply to its snorkeling, too. Snorkelers can wade from the shores off their hotels to the reefs and view an array of coral and a range of colorful fish. The reefs just off Klein Bonaire and Washington/Slagbaai Park receive especially rave reviews. See chapter 16.
- **Curaçao Underwater Park** (Curaçao): In contrast to Curaçao's sterile terrain, the marine life that rings the island is rich and spectacular. The best-known snorkeling sites stretch for 12½ miles along Curaçao's southern coastline (the Curaçao Underwater Park), although there are many other highly desirable sites. Sunken ships, gardens of hard and soft coral, and millions of fish are a snorkeler's treat. See chapter 16.

3 The Best Dive Sites

All the major islands offer diving trips, lessons, and equipment, but here are the top picks:

- **Grand Cayman:** This island has been called "the best-known dive destination in the Caribbean—if not the world," by *Skin Diver* magazine. There are 34 dive operations on Grand Cayman (plus five more on Little Cayman, and three on Cayman Brac). A full range of professional dive services are available, including equipment sales, rentals, and repairs; instruction at all levels; underwater photography; and video schools. See chapter 4.
- **St. Croix:** Increasingly known as a top diving destination, St. Croix hasn't overtaken Grand Cayman yet, but it has a lot going for it. Beach dives, reef dives, wreck dives, nighttime dives, wall dives—they're all here. But the highlight is the underwater trails of the national park at Buck Island, off St. Croix's mainland. Other desirable sites include the drop-offs and coral canyons at Cane Bay and Salt River. Davis Bay is the location of the 12,000-foot-deep Puerto Rico Trench, the fifth-deepest body of water on earth. See chapter 6.
- **Virgin Gorda:** Many divers plan their entire vacations around exploring the famed wreck of the HMS *Rhone,* off Salt Island. This royal mail steamer, which went down in 1867, is the most celebrated dive site in the Caribbean. See chapter 7.
- **Saba:** Islanders can't brag about its beaches, but Saba is blessed with some of the Caribbean's richest marine life. It's one of the premier diving locations in the Caribbean, with 38 official dive sites. The unusual setting includes underwater lava flows, black sand, large strands of black coral, millions of fish, and underwater mountaintops submerged under 90 feet of water. See chapter 10.
- **Bonaire:** The highly accessible reefs that surround Bonaire have never suffered from poaching or pollution, and the island's environmentally conscious dive industry will ensure that they never do. Diving is possible 24 hours a day throughout the year. Created from volcanic eruptions, the island is an underwater mountain. As such, fringe reefs await right off the beach of every hotel on any part of the island. See chapter 16.

4 The Best Sailing

Virtually any large-scale hotel in the Caribbean will provide small sailboats (especially Sunfish, Sailfish, and small, one-masted catamarans) for its guests. For larger craft, the Virgin Islands and the Grenadines come instantly to mind for their almost-ideal sailing conditions. These two regions offer many options for dropping anchor at secluded coves surrounded by relatively calm waters. Both areas are spectacular, but while the Virgin Islands offer more dramatic, mountainous terrain, the Grenadines offer insights into island cultures little touched by the modern world.

Other sailing venues in the Caribbean include Antigua, Barbados, St. Martin, and the French-speaking islands. But if you plan on doing a lot of sailing, know in advance that the strongest currents (and biggest waves) usually occur on the northern and eastern sides of most islands—the Atlantic, as opposed to the Caribbean, side.

- **The Virgin Islands:** Perhaps because of their well-developed marina facilities (and those of the nearby United States), the Virgin Islands receive the lion's share of really devoted yachties. The reigning capital for sailing is Tortola, the largest island of the British Virgins. On site are about 300 well-maintained sailing craft available for bareboat rentals, and perhaps 100 charter yachts.

  The largest of the Caribbean's yacht chartering services is **The Moorings** (☎ **800/535-7289;** fax 813/530-9747). Run by Ginny and Charlie Cary, this yachting charter center is described more fully in chapter 7, "The British Virgin Islands." If you'd like sailing lessons, consider Steve Colgate's **Offshore Sailing School** (☎ **800/221-4326** for more information) or Tortola's **Treasure Isle Hotel** (☎ **800/334-2435** in the U.S., or 809/494-2501), which offers courses in seamanship year-round. (One of their programs is exclusively on how to sail catamarans.) On the island of Virgin Gorda, in the British Virgin Islands, the best bet for both boat rentals and accommodations, as well as for a range of instruction, is the **Bitter End Yacht Club** (☎ **809/494-2746**).

  Some of the biggest charter business in the Caribbean is conducted on St. Thomas, especially at **American Yacht Harbor,** Red Hook (☎ **809/775-6454**), which offers bareboat and fully crewed charters. Other reliable rental agents include **Charteryacht League,** at Flagship (☎ **800/524-2061** or 809/774-3944).

  On St. Croix, boating is less a factor in the local economy than it is on St. Thomas or in the British Virgins.
- **The Grenadines:** Boating is a way of life in the Grenadines, partly because access to many of the remote islands is difficult or impossible by airplane. Although boats that belong to a yacht charterer might be scattered at any of several ports (Union Island, Bequia, Mayreau, or Mustique), the corporate entity that actually owns the boats is often located on nearby St. Vincent. One of the most visible of these is **Nicholson Yacht Charters** (☎ **800/662-6066** in the U.S., or 809/460-1530 in St. Vincent). On Bequia, Mustique, Petit St. Vincent, and Union Island, all the hotels can put you in touch with local entrepreneurs who rent sailing craft.

5 The Best Golf Courses

Some of the world's most famous golf architects, including Robert Trent Jones (both junior and senior), Pete Dye, Gary Player, and others, have designed challenging courses in the Caribbean.

- **El Conquistador** (Puerto Rico; ☎ **800/468-5228** in the U.S., or 787/863-1000): Its fairways meander over the rolling hills that surround one of Puerto Rico's most fabled resorts. The par-72 layout was designed by Robert Von Hagge in 1967, and redesigned by Arthur Hills & Associates (who flattened some of the more daunting slopes). Golfers, who must be guests of the El Conquistador resort, enjoy sweeping views of the sea. The winds are tricky and change frequently, adding to the challenge. See chapter 5.

- **Hyatt Dorado Beach Hotel** (Puerto Rico; ☎ **800/233-1234** in the U.S., or 787/796-1234): This resort maintains two golf courses, both set on what were originally citrus and coconut plantations. Both courses were designed by Robert Trent Jones Sr. No one can agree on which of the two courses is the more interesting, but the elegance of both is breathtaking. If you're an absolute golf glutton, the Hyatt's companion resort, the Cerromar, a short drive down the coastal road, offers an additional pair of golf courses. See chapter 5.
- **Palmas del Mar** (Puerto Rico; ☎ **800/468-3331** in the U.S., or 787/852-6000): Designed by Gary Player, this par-72 golf course near Humacao is one of the most noteworthy anywhere. Its botanical highlights include thousands of mature palm trees and carefully maintained sections of tropical rain forest. The course is so good that many golf-playing retirees have bought homes adjacent to the fairways. The most challenging holes? Numbers 11 through 16, although many beginners have lost their tempers over no. 18 as well. Lessons are offered to players of all different levels. See chapter 5.
- **Teeth of the Dog and The Links at Casa de Campo** (Dominican Republic; ☎ **800/877-3643** in the U.S. and Canada, or 809/523-3333): Hispaniola's most challenging golf course, Teeth of the Dog, is one of designer Pete Dye's masterpieces. Seven holes are set adjacent to the sea, whereas the other 11 are confoundedly labyrinthine. The resort also has a second golf course, The Links, which some claim is even more difficult. See chapter 8.
- **The Four Seasons** (Nevis; ☎ **800/332-3442** in the U.S., 800/268-6282 in Canada, or 809/469-1111): We consider this our personal favorite in all of the Caribbean, and so do readers of *Caribbean Travel & Life*. It was carved out of a coconut plantation and tropical rain forest in the 1980s, and its undulating beauty is virtually unequaled. Designed by Robert Trent Jones Jr., the course begins at sea level, rises to a point midway up the slopes of Mount Nevis, then slants gracefully back down near the beachfront clubhouse. Electric carts carry golfers through a labyrinth of well-groomed paths, some of which skirt steep ravines. See chapter 9.
- **Tryall** (Montego Bay, Jamaica; ☎ **809/956-5660**): This is the finest golf course on an island known for its tricky breezes. The site, now occupied by the Tryall Golf, Tennis, and Beach Club, was once the home of one of Jamaica's best-known sugar plantations; the only remnant is a ruined waterwheel. The promoters of Johnny Walker Scotch, who know a lot about golfing, selected this place for their most prestigious competition. During the winter season, the course is usually open only to guests of the Tryall Beach Club. See chapter 11.
- **Wyndham Rose Hall Resort** (Rose Hill, Jamaica; ☎ **809/953-2650**): This is one of the top five courses in the world, even though it faces other tough competition in Montego Bay. The signature hole is no. 8, which doglegs onto a promontory and a green that thrusts about 200 yards into the sea. The back nine, however, is the most scenic and most challenging, rising into steep slopes and deep ravines on Mount Zion. See chapter 11.
- **Golf de St-François** (Guadeloupe; ☎ **590/88-41-87**): Six of its 18 holes are ringed with water traps, the winds are devilishly unpredictable, and the par is a sweat-inducing 71. This fearsome course displays the wit and skill of its designer,

Robert Trent Jones, Sr. Most of the staff are multilingual, and because it's owned by the local municipality, it's a lot less snobby than you might expect. See chapter 12.

6 The Best Tennis Facilities

- **El Conquistador** (Puerto Rico; ☎ **800/468-5228** in the U.S., or 787/863-1000): Facilities at this megaresort include seven Har-Tru tennis courts, a resident pro, and a clubhouse with its own bar. If you're looking for a partner, the hotel will find one for you. Only guests of the hotel can use the courts, some of which are illuminated for night play. See chapter 5.
- **Hyatt Regency Cerromar Beach/Hyatt Dorado Beach** (Puerto Rico; ☎ **800/233-1234** in the U.S.): These twin beachfront resorts are within a 15-minute walk of one another. There are 20 Laykold tennis courts, some lit, some ringed with stadium seats; all are administered by a tennis pro who gives lessons. If you want pointers on improving your serve or strokes, someone will be on hand to videotape you. See chapter 5.
- **Wyndham Sugar Bay Resort** (St. Thomas; ☎ **800/927-7100** in the U.S., 809/777-7100): Some tennis buffs are deserting the Buccaneer on St. Croix for this new challenger at Estate Smith Bay. The resort offers the U.S. Virgin Islands' first stadium tennis court, with a capacity of 220 spectators. In addition, it offers about half a dozen Laykold courts, each of which is lit for night play. There's an on-site pro shop and lessons are available. See chapter 6.
- **The Buccaneer** (St. Croix; ☎ **800/255-3881** in the U.S., or 809/773-2100): Hailed as having the best tennis facilities in the Virgin Islands, this resort is the venue for several tournaments every year. There are eight all-weather Laykold courts, two of which are illuminated at night. There's also a pro shop. Nonguests can play here for a fee. See chapter 6.
- **Casa de Campo** (Dominican Republic; ☎ **809/523-3333**): There are so many facilities at this 7,000-acre resort that tennis might come as an afterthought. But if you're a tennis devotee, the facilities here include 13 clay courts (half are lighted, and two are ringed with stadium seating), four all-weather Laykold courts, a resident pro, ball machines, and tennis pros who are usually available to play with guests. During midwinter, residents and clients of Casa de Campo have first crack at court time. See chapter 8.
- **Curtain Bluff** (Antigua; ☎ **800/672-5633** or 809/462-8400): It's small, select, and carefully run by people who love tennis. It's also the annual site of a well-known spring tournament. The courts are set in a low-lying valley. See chapter 9.
- **Half Moon Golf, Tennis, and Beach Club** (Montego Bay, Jamaica; ☎ **800/626-0592** in the U.S., or 809/953-2211): This resort sprawls over hundreds of acres; amid the expanse are about a dozen tennis courts and at least four squash and/or racquetball courts. Jamaica has a strong, British-based affinity for tennis, and Half Moon keeps the tradition alive. See chapter 11.

7 The Best Honeymoon Resorts

More and more couples are exchanging their vows in the Caribbean. Many resorts will arrange everything from the preacher to the flowers, so we've included in the following list some outfits that provide wedding services. For more information about the various options and the legal requirements for marriages on some of the more popular Caribbean islands, see chapter 3, "Planning a Trip to the Caribbean."

- **Hyatt Regency Grand Cayman** (Grand Cayman; ☎ **800/233-1234** or 809/949-1234): Hands down, this is the most glamorous and best-landscaped resort in the Cayman Islands. Honeymooners can buy a package that includes champagne and wine, a room with an oversize bed, a one-day Jeep rental, a romantic sundowner sail on a 65-foot catamaran, and discounts at clothing stores, the resort's restaurants, and a golf course. They'll even present you with a honeymoon memento for your home. See chapter 4.
- **El Conquistador** (Puerto Rico; ☎ **800/468-5228** in the U.S., or 787/863-1000): A complex of hotels set on a forested bluff overlooking the sea, this is one of the most lavish resorts ever built in the Caribbean. The architecture incorporates Moorish gardens and Andalusian fortresses. You'll find hammocks for two on the resort's offshore private island, as well as about a dozen private Jacuzzis artfully concealed by vegetation throughout the grounds. See chapter 5.
- **Petit St. Vincent Resort** (the Petit St. Vincent, in the Grenadines; ☎ **809/458-8801**): If your idea of a honeymoon is to run away from everybody except your new spouse, this is the place. It takes about three planes and a boat to reach it, but the effort to get here is worth it—that is, if you want total isolation and privacy. Even the staff doesn't bother you unless you raise a flag for room service. If the honeymoon's going well, you may never have to leave your stone cottage by the beach. See chapter 13.
- **The Buccaneer** (St. Croix; ☎ **800/255-3881** in the U.S., or 809/773-2100): Posh and discreet, this resort boasts some of the most extensive vacation facilities on St. Croix—three beaches, eight tennis courts, a spa and fitness center, an 18-hole golf course, and 2 miles of carefully maintained jogging trails. The accommodations include beachside rooms with fieldstone terraces leading toward the sea. The resort's stone sugar mill (originally built in 1658) is one of the most popular sites for weddings and visiting honeymooners on the island. See chapter 6.
- **Biras Creek Estate** (Virgin Gorda, B.V.I.; ☎ **800/608-9661** in the U.S., or 809/494-3555): If you're eager to escape your in-laws and bridesmaids after a wedding ceremony, this is the place. It's a quintessential mariner's hideaway, reached only by a boat ride of several miles across the open sea. Perched on a narrow promontory jutting into the Caribbean, it's an intensely private retreat set on 150 acres with a crisscrossing network of signposted nature trails. Honeymooners get better acquainted in the spacious open-air walled showers in each bathroom. See chapter 7.
- **St. James's Club** (Antigua; ☎ **800/274-0008** in the U.S., or 809/460-5000): There are enough diversions available at this very posh, British-style resort to keep a honeymoon couple up and about for weeks. Breakfast, lunch, and dinner are included along with unlimited drinks. Among the perks is a private, candlelit dinner for two in a romantic setting. Seven-night packages begin at $3,500 per couple in high season, at $3,010 off-season. See chapter 9.
- **Four Seasons** (Nevis; ☎ **800/332-3442** in the U.S., 800/268-6282 in Canada, or 809/469-1111): Though not as historic as some of the island's plantation-style inns, the Four Seasons rules without peer as the most deluxe hotel on the island, with the most extensive facilities. Set in a palm grove adjacent to the island's finest beach, it has the atmosphere of a supremely indulgent country club. The Four Seasons can offer you a four-day wedding package with a choice of wedding venues (in a church, on a beach; with a judge or with a civil magistrate). Your wedding cake will be individually designed by the resort's pastry chef, and music, photographs, flowers, legalities, and virtually anything else you want can be arranged by the staff. See chapter 9.

- **Sandals** (Jamaica; ☎ **800/SANDALS**): There are half a dozen members of this resort chain in Jamaica alone (plus two others on St. Lucia). Each one prides itself on providing an all-inclusive (cash-free) environment where meals are provided in abundance to any couple. Enthusiastic members of the staff bring heroic amounts of community spirit to whatever knot-tying rituals happen to be celebrated on-site. Sandals will provide everything from a preacher to petunias (as well as champagne, a cake, and all the legalities) for you to get hitched on-site. Any of these resorts can provide a suitable setting, but one of the most appealing is Sandals Royal Jamaican, outside Montego Bay, Jamaica. See chapter 11.
- **The SuperClubs of Jamaica** (☎ **800/859-SUPER**): These all-inclusive properties are for upscale honeymooners who can afford a little more elegance and luxury. They operate somewhat like Sandals, but have far more style and a higher price tag. Prices are high in winter, but when mid-April arrives, rates plummet. SuperClubs, such as Grand Lido and Sans Souci Lido, are scattered between Ocho Rios and Negril. If you pay for the food and room packages, the hotel chain will throw in the wedding for free—they'll provide the license, the witnesses, the minister, and even a two-tier wedding cake. They'll see that you're married in the garden or on a white sandy beach. See chapter 11.
- **Sandy Lane** (Barbados; ☎ **800/225-5843** in the U.S. and Canada, or 809/432-1311): A satisfying sense of ritual pervades this venerable British-inspired hotel. Four-day honeymoon packages begin at $2,450 and include a bottle of champagne, a breakfast, tennis, a lunch or dinner cruise, and a candlelit dinner. See chapter 14.

8 The Best Romantic Hideaways

- **Horned Dorset Primavera Hotel** (Puerto Rico; ☎ **800/633-1857** or 787/823-4030): This resort, on the western side of Puerto Rico, has a main clubhouse that's reminiscent of an Iberian villa. Great care is lavished on the sophisticated continental/California cuisine, and drinks are served in a well-stocked library. The accommodations are comfortable and dignified, and contain oversize mahogany beds and large private verandas with views of lushly planted hillsides sloping down to a narrow sandy beach. See chapter 5.
- **Peter Island Resort and Yacht Harbour** (B.V.I.; ☎ **809/495-2000** or 800/346-4451): Romantics appreciate its isolation on a 1,800-acre private island south of Tortola and east of St. John. (Reaching it requires a 30-minute waterborne transfer, which many urban refugees consider part of the fun.) It's very laid-back—bring a companion and/or a good book, and enjoy the comings and goings of yachts at the island's private marina. See chapter 7.
- **Rawlins Plantation** (St. Kitts; ☎ **800/346-5358** in the U.S., or 809/465-6221): Surrounded by 25 acres of carefully clipped lawns and tropical shrubbery, and set on a panoramic hillock about 350 feet above sea level, this hotel evokes a 19th-century plantation with its rugs of locally woven rushes and carved four-poster beds. You'll be separated from the rest of the island by hundreds of acres of sugarcane, and there are few phones and no televisions. See chapter 9.
- **The Golden Lemon** (St. Kitts; ☎ **800/633-7411** in the U.S., or 809/465-7260): It started its life as a French manor house during the 17th century, but by the time its present owners began restoring it, it was decidedly less glamorous. It required the refined tastes of Arthur Leaman, a former editor at *House & Garden*, to bring it to its full potential. Today the Golden Lemon is an authentic Antillean

retreat—luxurious, laid-back, and romantic—set in an isolated fishing village loaded with charm. See chapter 9.

- **Cap Juluca** (Anguilla; ☎ **800/323-0139** in the U.S., or 809/497-6666): A unique resort in the Caribbean, it utilized the skills of top postmodern architects, a couple of million dollars, and a thrillingly beautiful beach to create just the right atmosphere. The result: Something like a Saharan Casbah whose domed villas seem to float against the scrubland and azure sky. You'll always have the feeling that someone very famous is enjoying a romantic off-the-record tryst behind the sheltering walls of this extremely stylish resort. See chapter 9.
- **Trident Villas and Hotel** (Port Antonio, Jamaica; ☎ **800/993-2705** in the U.S., or 809/993-2602): This is a retreat straight out of *Lifestyles of the Rich and Famous.* Perhaps you'll opt for a studio cottage or tower, or a room within the hotel's antique-filled main building. Imperial suites are the ultimate in luxury. The white-gloved waiters with their silver service and crystal evoke the heyday of the British Empire. See chapter 11.
- **Anse Chastanet Beach Hotel** (St. Lucia; ☎ **800/223-1108** in the U.S., or 758/459-7000): Offering panoramic views of mountains and jungle, this hotel is a winner with romantics. With its small size, it offers a lot of privacy and rustic charm. See chapter 13.
- **Petit St. Vincent (PSV) Resort** (The Grenadines; ☎ **800/654-9326** in the U.S., or 809/458-8801): The sheer distance of PSV from the United States makes it the most secluded and discreet of the Caribbean's luxury hideaways. Located on a privately owned island, the artfully built clubhouses and bungalows were crafted from tropical woods and local stone. The results are simultaneously rustic and lavish. Your bungalow is designed in such a way that if you don't put on any clothes until dinnertime, no one will see you au naturel except your companion. See chapter 13.
- **The Cotton House** (The Grenadines; ☎ **800/826-2809** in the U.S., or 809/456-4777): Cosmopolitan and evoking fashionable London, this hotel was built on the tiny island of Mustique during the 18th century as a cotton warehouse. Richly overhauled in the 1970s by one of Britain's most tasteful designers, it houses 27 airy accommodations. Although the glamour that was associated with the Cotton House in the 1970s has dissipated as its illustrious guests have found new haunts, recent renovations have brought back its undeniable charm and romance. See chapter 13.

9 The Best Places to Get Away from It All

- **Little Cayman Beach Resort** (Cayman Islands; ☎ **800/327-3835** in the U.S. and Canada, or 345/948-1033): The only way to reach the 10-square-mile island where this resort is located is by airplane. Snorkelers will marvel at some of the most spectacular and colorful marine life in the Caribbean. The resort has the most complete water sports facilities on the island, and bikes are available for exploring. See chapter 4.
- **Biras Creek Estate** (Virgin Gorda, B.V.I.; ☎ **800/608-9661** in the U.S., or 809/494-3555): The only access to this resort is by private launch. The sea air and the views over islets, cays, and deep blue waters will relax you in your charming guest room. The nautical atmosphere will quickly remove all thoughts of the nine-to-five job you left behind. See chapter 7.
- **Guana Island Club** (B.V.I.; ☎ **800/544-8262** in the U.S., or 809/494-2354): One of the most secluded hideaways in the entire Caribbean, this resort occupies

a privately owned 850-acre bird sanctuary with nature trails. Head here for views of rare plant and animal life, and for several excellent uncrowded beaches, but remember that there's no nightlife. See chapter 7.

- **Ottley's Plantation Inn** (St. Kitts; ☎ **800/772-3039** in the U.S., or 809/465-7234): As you approach, its dignified verandas appear majestically at the crest of 35 acres of impeccably maintained lawns and gardens. It's one of the most charming plantation house inns anywhere in the world, maintained with style and humor by its expatriate American owners. The food is the best on the island, and the setting will soothe your tired nerves within a few hours after your arrival. See chapter 9.

10 The Best Family Resorts

- **Hyatt Regency Cerromar Beach Hotel** (Puerto Rico; ☎ **800/233-1234** or 787/796-1234): This is the best place for kids on the whole island. The big attraction is a water playground that contains the world's longest freshwater swimming pool: a 1,776-foot fantasy pool with five different depths, five interconnected free-form pools, and 14 waterfalls with tropical landscaping. If that weren't enough, Hyatt also offers Camp Hyatt, a day camp for ages 3 to 13. See chapter 5.
- **El Conquistador** (Puerto Rico; ☎ **800/468-5228** in the U.S., or 787/863-1000): Children aren't forgotten amid the glamour and hoopla of this fabulous resort. Camp Coquí provides daycare for children 3 to 12 every day between 9am and 3pm, at a price of $38 per child per day. Activities include fishing, sailing, arts and crafts, and nature treks. Baby-sitting services are available, and children 11 and under stay free in a room with their parents. See chapter 5.
- **Doubletree Sapphire Beach Resort and Marina** (St. Thomas; ☎ **800/524-2090** in the U.S., or 809/775-6100): More than any other hotel on St. Thomas, this well-designed resort caters to both adults and children. There are supervised activities for preteens at the Little Gems Kids Klub, and a baby-sitting service for children under four. Other activities can include the entire family. The white sandy beaches are among the safest and most desirable on the island. See chapter 6.
- **The Buccaneer** (St. Croix; ☎ **800/255-3881** in the U.S., or 809/773-2100): Posh, upscale, and offering extremely good service, this hotel is a longtime favorite that occupies a 300-acre former sugar estate. Its kids' programs (for ages 5 to 12) include a half-day sailing excursion to Buck Island Reef and guided nature walks that let kids touch, smell, and taste tropical fruit. See chapter 6.
- **Chenay Bay Beach Resort** (St. Croix; ☎ **800/548-4457** in the U.S., or 809/773-2918): The owners of this West Indian cottage colony designed a "Cruzan Kids" program, with activities based on the experiences of their own children. Programs are generally sports oriented, including tennis, swimming, and kayaking, and are heavily featured during midsummer and again at Christmastime. See chapter 6.
- **Four Seasons** (Nevis; ☎ **800/332-3442** in the U.S., 800/268-6282 in Canada, or 809/469-1111): The staff of the Kids for All Seasons day camp are kindly, matronly souls who work well with children. During the adult cocktail hour, when parents might opt for a romantic sundowner, kids attend a supervised "children's hour" that resembles a really good birthday bash. Other activities include tennis lessons, water sports, and storytelling. See chapter 9.
- **Boscobel Beach** (Ocho Rios, Jamaica; ☎ **800/859-7873** in the U.S., or 809/975-7330): This all-inclusive hotel (with lots of facilities—even a petting zoo!) is

one of the few anywhere that specifically markets itself to parents with young children. A vast array of activities are planned for children under 14, including painting classes, computer fun, and parties. See chapter 11.

- **FDR** (Runaway Bay, Jamaica; ☎ **800/654-1FDR** in the U.S., or 809/973-4591): FDR gives you a suite with its own kitchen, and a so-called "Girl Friday" whose duties include baby-sitting. Neither its beach nor its pool is the most appealing on Jamaica, but the price is right, and the baby-sitting is part of the all-inclusive price. Programs for children include dress-up parties, donkey rides, basketball, tennis, and snorkeling. See chapter 11.
- **Sandy Beach Hotel** (Barbados; ☎ **246/435-8000**): Set amid lots of fast-food and family-style restaurants on the southwest coast, this family-oriented hotel offers one- and two-bedroom suites. Each unit has a kitchen so you can cook for yourself and save money. The beach is a few steps away, and the ambience is informal. If you bring the kids, they'll have plenty of playmates. See chapter 14.
- **Hyatt Regency Aruba** (Aruba; ☎ **800/233-1234** in the U.S. and Canada, or 297/8-61234): Designed like a luxurious hacienda, with award-winning gardens, this resort is the most upscale on Aruba. There are supervised activities for children 3 to 12 that include games and contests such as crab races and hula-hoop competitions. See chapter 16.

11 The Best Inns

- **Villa Madeleine** (St. Croix; ☎ **800/548-4461** or 809/778-7377): This recently built, almost perfect re-creation of a 19th-century Great House occupies the summit of a scrub-covered ridge. The food is among the best on St. Croix. Accommodations include richly furnished hideaway suites with sweeping views over the coastline. See chapter 6.
- **Drake's Anchorage Resort Inn** (Mosquito Island, B.V.I.; ☎ **800/624-6651** in the U.S., or 809/494-2254): Set off the northeastern coast of Virgin Gorda, this simple, austere 12-room inn is the only establishment of any kind on Mosquito Island. Guests can enjoy the island's 126 acres of forest and scrubland, and snorkeling opportunities abound offshore. The island has a restaurant, a bar frequented by yachters, and a kind of roguish charm. Don't expect luxurious amenities—everything is almost studiously simple here. But if you want an insight into the way the Caribbean used to be, this is the place. See chapter 7.
- **The Admiral's Inn** (Antigua; ☎ **800/223-5695** in the U.S., or 268/460-1027): The most historically evocative corner of Antigua is Nelson's Dockyard, which was originally built in the 1700s to repair His Majesty's ships. The brick-and-stone inn that flourishes here today was once a warehouse for turpentine and pitch. In the late 1960s it was transformed into a well-designed and very charming hotel. (If you're trying to escape from urban pressures, you might be bothered by the sometimes-raucous scene in the hotel's bar and restaurant.) See chapter 9.
- **Romantik Montpelier Plantation Inn** (Nevis; ☎ **869/469-3462,** or 212/599-8280 in the U.S.): Style and grace are the hallmarks of this former 18th-century plantation, now converted to an inn and set on a 100-acre estate. Guests have included the Princess of Wales. Cottage rooms are spread across 10 acres of ornamental gardens. Swimming, horseback riding, windsurfing, a private beach, and "ecorambles" fill the agenda. See chapter 9.
- **Hermitage Plantation** (Nevis; ☎ **800/682-4025** in the U.S., or 869/469-3477): Guests stay in clapboard-sided cottages separated by carefully maintained bou-gainvillea and grasslands. The beach is a short drive away, but this slice of

19th-century plantation life (complete candlelit dinners amid the antiques and polished silver of the main house) is decidedly romantic. See chapter 9.

- **François Plantation** (St. Barthélemy; ☎ **800/932-3222** in the U.S., or 590/27-78-82): At this inn, about a dozen pastel-colored bungalows are scattered among the lushest gardens on St. Barts. The mood is discreet, permissive, and fun (as long as you don't bother any of the other guests). The food is French-inspired and served on a wide veranda decorated in a whimsical colonial style. See chapter 12.
- **Frangipani Hotel** (Bequia, the Grenadines; ☎ **809/458-3255**): This is the century-old homestead of the Mitchell family, whose most famous scion later became prime minister of St. Vincent. Today it's a small, very relaxed inn. It's fun to watch the yachts making their seaward forays from the nearby marina. See chapter 13.
- **Spice Island Inn** (Grenada; ☎ **800/223-9815** in the U.S., or 809/444-4258): Each of this hotel's 56 accommodations is a suite (with Jacuzzi) either beside the beach (one of Grenada's best) or near a swimming pool. Friday nights feature live music from the island's most popular bands. See chapter 13.
- **Avila Beach Hotel** (Curaçao; ☎ **599/9/614377**): This hotel's historic core, built in 1780 as the "country house" of the island's governor, retains its dignity and lack of excess ornamentation. Although it has functioned as a hotel since the end of World War II, a new owner added 40 bedrooms in motel-like outbuildings and upgraded the sports and dining facilities in the early 1990s. Today the Avila provides a sandy beach and easy access to the shops and distractions of nearby Willemstad. See chapter 16.

12 The Best Destinations for Serious Shoppers

Since the American government allows U.S. citizens to take (or send) home more duty-free goods from the U.S. Virgins than from other ports of call, the U.S. Virgin Islands remain the shopping bazaar of the Caribbean. U.S. citizens may carry home $1,200 worth of goods untaxed, as opposed to only $400 worth of goods from most islands in the Caribbean. (The only exception to this rule is Puerto Rico, where any purchase, regardless of the amount, can be carried tax free back to the U.S. mainland.)

- **Cayman Islands:** Goods are sold tax free from a daunting collection of malls and minimalls throughout Grand Cayman. Most of these are along the highway that parallels Seven Mile Beach; you'll need a car to shop around. There are also lots of stores in George Town, which you can explore on foot, poking in and out of some large emporiums in your search for bargains. See chapter 4.
- **Puerto Rico:** For U.S. citizens, there's no duty on anything (yes, anything) you buy in Puerto Rico. That doesn't guarantee that prices will be particularly low, however. Jewelry and watches abound, often at competitive prices, especially in the island's best-stocked area, Old San Juan. Also of great interest are such Puerto Rican handcrafts as charming folkloric papier-mâché carnival masks. See chapter 5.
- **St. Thomas:** Many of its busiest shops are in restored warehouses that were originally built in the 1700s. Charlotte Amalie, the capital, is a shopper's town. However, despite all the fanfare, real bargains are hard to come by. Regardless, the island attracts hordes of cruise-ship passengers on a sometimes-frantic hunt for bargains, real or imagined. The number of stores in Charlotte Amalie is staggering—they're stocked with more merchandise than anywhere else in the entire Caribbean.

Look for two local publications, *This Week* and *Best Buys;* either might steer you to the type of merchandise you're seeking. If at all possible, try to avoid shopping when more than one cruise ship is in port—the shopping district is a madhouse on those days. See chapter 6.

- **St. Croix:** This island is a poor stepchild of St. Thomas, but there's still much to interest the "born-to-shop" visitor here, and merchandise has never been more wide-ranging than it is today. Even though most cruise ships call at Frederiksted, a colorful but isolated town near the island's western tip, most of shops are found in Christiansted, the island's capital. You'll see many of the same shops and chains on St. Croix that you find on St. Thomas, including such omnipresent names as Little Switzerland. Prices are about the same as on St. Thomas. See chapter 6.
- **Dominican Republic:** The island's best buys include handcrafts, amber from Dominican mines, and the distinctive pale-blue semiprecious gemstone known as larimar. The amber you buy from a street-side vendor might be nothing more than orange-colored, transparent plastic; buy only from well-established shops if your investment is a large one. Other charming souvenirs might include a Dominican rocking chair (remember the one JFK used to sit in?), which is sold boxed, in pieces. Shopping malls and souvenir stands abound in Santo Domingo, in Puerto Plata, and along the country's northern coast. See chapter 8.
- **Jamaica:** The shopping was better in the good old days before new taxes added a 10% surcharge. Despite that, Jamaica offers a wealth of desirable goods, including flavored rums, Jamaican coffees, handcrafts (such as woodcarvings, woven baskets, and sandals), original paintings and sculpture, and cameras, wristwatches, and VCRs. Unless you're a glutton for handmade souvenirs (which are available on virtually every beach and street corner), you'd be wise to limit most of your purchases to bona fide merchants and stores. See chapter 11.
- **Sint Maarten/St. Martin:** Although there's no duty on any purchases you'll make on either side of the island's Dutch/French border, goods are not especially cheap. Merchants have been suspected of fixing prices on both sides of the border, and after a few days, you might grow exceedingly tired of displays of electronic gadgets. It's best to arrive on the island as a well-educated consumer, with a firm grip on what is and what isn't a favorable price for whatever you really need. Phillipsburg, capital of the island's Dutch side, is the best place to shop. See chapters 10 and 12.
- **Barbados:** Local shops seem to specialize in all things English. Merchandise includes bone china from British and Irish manufacturers, wristwatches, jewelry, and perfumes. There's also a wide array of other goods. Bridgetown's Broad Street is the shopping headquarters of the island, although some of the stores represented here maintain boutiques (with similar prices but with a less extensive range of merchandise) at many of the island's hotels and in shopping malls along the congested southwestern coast. Except for cigarettes and tobacco, duty-free items can be hauled off by any buyer as soon as they're paid for. Duty-free status is extended to anyone showing a passport or ID and an airline ticket with a date of departure from Barbados. See chapter 14.
- **Aruba:** The wisest shoppers on Aruba are cost-conscious souls who have carefully checked the prices of comparable goods before leaving home. Duty is relatively low (only 3.3%). Much of the European china, jewelry, perfumes, wristwatches, and crystal has a disconcerting habit of reappearing in every shopping mall and hotel boutique on the island, so after you determine exactly which brand of watch or china you want, you can comparison-shop. See chapter 16.

- **Curaçao:** Curaçao has been a mercantile center since the 1700s. In the island's capital, tidy and prosperous Willemstad, hundreds of merchants will be only too happy to cater to your needs. A handful of malls lie on Willemstad's outskirts, but most shops are clustered within a few blocks of the center of town. During seasonal sales, goods might be up to 50% less than comparable prices in the States; most of the year, you'll find luxury goods (porcelain, crystal, watches, and gemstones) priced at about 25% less than in the States. Technically, you'll pay import duties on virtually everything you buy, but rates are so low you might not even notice. See chapter 16.

13 The Best Nightlife

It's sleepy time on the following islands: The British Virgins, Montserrat, Nevis, Anguilla, St. Eustatius, Saba, St. Barthélemy, Dominica, Bonaire, St. Vincent, and all of the Grenadines. The serious partier will probably want to choose the following destinations:

- **Puerto Rico:** Puerto Rico contains all the raw ingredients for great nightlife, including casinos, endless rows of bars and bodegas, cabaret shows with girls and glitter, and discos that feature everything from New York imports to some of the best salsa and merengue anywhere. If you're a really serious partier, you'll have lots of company in Puerto Rico. Be prepared to stay out very late; you can recover from your Bacardi hangover on a palm-fringed beach the next day. See chapter 5.
- **St. Thomas:** The Virgin Islands' most active nightlife is found here. Don't expect glitzy shows like those in San Juan's Condado area, or any kind of casino. The resort with the strongest emphasis on music is Marriott's Frenchman's Reef, whereas the Hard Rock Café in Charlotte Amalie is best for nightly rock 'n' roll. Nearby, the Greenhouse Restaurant features recorded music, live concerts, and golden-oldies nights. See chapter 6.
- **St. Croix:** It's very similar to St. Thomas, but with fewer options. A consistently good choice is the Buccaneer Hotel, which stages limbo/folkloric shows, reggae players, and concerts by local stars. Otherwise, the funky clubs and hole-in-the-wall bars of Christiansted dominate the nightscape. See chapter 6.
- **Dominican Republic:** Large resort hotels in the Dominican Republic evoke a Latino version of Las Vegas reminiscent of Batista's Cuba. And if cabaret shows aren't your thing, there are casinos, and enough discos to keep a soca or hip-hop enthusiast busy for weeks. However, Santo Domingo is not the safest place to be out at night, so take a cab back to your hotel. See chapter 8.
- **Jamaica:** Many visitors are drawn here by a love for the island's distinct musical forms. Foremost among these are reggae and soca, both of which are performed at hotels, resorts, and raffish dives throughout the island. Hotels often stage folkloric shows that include entertainers who sing, dance, swallow torches, and walk on broken glass. There are also plenty of indoor/outdoor bars where you might actually be able to talk to people. Local tourist boards in Negril and Montego Bay sometimes organize weekly beach parties called "Boonoonoonoos." See chapter 11.
- **Sint Maarten/St. Martin:** This island has a rather cosmopolitan nightlife and contains the densest concentration of restaurants in the Caribbean, each with its own bar. Discos are often indoor/outdoor affairs. Hotel casinos abound, and if you're addicted to the jingle of slot machines and roulette wheels, you won't lack for company. See chapters 10 and 12.

- **Barbados:** Bridgetown is home to at least two boats (the *Bajan Queen* and the *Jolly Roger*) that embark at sundown for rum-and-reggae cruises, as well as oversize music bars like the Warehouse and Harbour Lights. Otherwise, a host of bars, British-style pubs, dozens of restaurants, and discos (both within and outside of large hotels) beckon from St. Lawrence Gap or the crowded southwest coast. See chapter 14.
- **Aruba:** This island has 10 casinos, each with its own unique decor and each with a following of devoted gamblers. Some offer their own cabaret or comedy shows, dance floors with live or recorded music, restaurants of all degrees of formality, and bars. See chapter 16.

14 The Best Gambling

- **Puerto Rico:** The country's gaming headquarters lies along the Condado in San Juan, although there are also casinos in megaresorts scattered throughout the island. The casinos here are the most fun in the Caribbean, and also some of the most spectacular. Each contains lots of sideshows (restaurants, merengue bars, art galleries, piano bars, shops) that can distract you from the roulette and slots. Puerto Ricans take pride in dressing well at their local casinos, which enhances an evening's glamour. No drinking is permitted at the tables, and tight controls are exerted by U.S. gaming authorities. See chapter 5.
- **Dominican Republic:** The tourist areas of Puerto Plata and Santo Domingo are sprinkled with casinos, and the island's ever-developing north shore contains its share of jingle-jangle too. Our favorite is the casino in the Jaragua Hotel in Santo Domingo, which offers floor shows, live merengue concerts, a wraparound bar, and at least five different restaurants. See chapter 8.
- **Sint Maarten:** Gambling is illegal on the island's French side (St. Martin), so the casinos are the exclusive domain of the Dutch. The gaming halls have an atmosphere of nonchalance, which might appeal to you if you dislike gaming halls with high stakes and lots of intensity. There are about seven casinos on Sint Maarten, usually in large resort hotels. Hotels on the French side sometimes arrange gambling junkets to the Dutch side. See chapter 10.
- **Aruba:** After dark, visitors throng to the island's 10 casinos. The casinos are big, splashy, colorful, and, yes, people even occasionally win. Drinks are usually free while you play. Conveniently, the legal tender in most of Aruba's casinos is the U.S. dollar. See chapter 16.
- **Curaçao:** The canny merchants of Curaçao have known how to make a guilder since the early colonial days. There are at least a dozen casinos beckoning from strategic points throughout the island. See chapter 16.

2 Getting to Know the Caribbean

Golden beaches shaded by palm trees and crystalline waters teeming with colorful sea creatures—it's all just a few hours' flight from the east coast of the United States. Dubbed the "Eighth Continent of the World," the Caribbean islands have an amazing variety of terrain that ranges from thick rain forests to haunting volcanoes, from white- to black-sand beaches. Spicy food, spicier music, and the gentle, leisurely lifestyle of the islands draw millions of visitors each year, all hoping to find the perfect place in the sun. We'll help you choose yours in the pages that follow.

1 The Islands in Brief

ANGUILLA (British Leewards) Although it's developing rapidly as sunseekers discover its 12 miles of arid but spectacular beaches, Anguilla is still quiet, sleepy, and relatively free of racial tensions. A flat, coral-based island, it maintains a maritime tradition of proud fisherfolk who, until the recent tourist-related boom, eked out a living from the sea. Although some moderately priced accommodations are available, Anguilla is increasingly known for upscale resorts.

ANTIGUA (British Leewards) Antigua is famous for having a different beach for each day of the year. Some British traditions (including a passion for cricket) linger on though the nation became independent in 1981. The island has a population of 80,000, mostly descended from the African slaves of plantation owners. There are isolated and conservative but very glamorous resorts, horribly maintained highways, and some of the most interesting historic naval sites in the British maritime world. Antigua is politically linked to the sparsely inhabited and largely undeveloped island of Barbuda, about 30 miles north. In spite of its small size, Barbuda has two resorts that are pockets of posh, with lethal prices to match.

ARUBA (Dutch Leewards) Until its beaches were "discovered" in the late 1970s, Aruba was an almost forgotten outpost of Holland, mostly valued for its oil refineries and salt factories. Today it's favored for the lunar landscapes of its desertlike terrain, spectacular beaches, constant sunshine, and an almost total lack of racial tensions. Its population of 70,000 is culturally diverse, with roots in Holland, Portugal, Spain, Venezuela, India/Pakistan, and Africa. A building boom in the 1980s has transformed this gambling-conscious island into a pale version of Las Vegas and created some of the most aggressive marketing campaigns in Caribbean history.

BARBADOS For generations, this Atlantic outpost was one of the most staunchly loyal members of the British Commonwealth. Originally devoted to a plantation economy that made its aristocracy rich, the island is the most easterly in the Caribbean, floating in the mid-Atlantic like a great coral reef and ringed with beige-sand beaches. Cosmopolitan Barbados has the densest population of any island in the Caribbean, a sports tradition that avidly pursues cricket, and a loyal group of return visitors who appreciate its many stylish, medium-size hotels. Service is usually extremely good, a by-product of its British mores, which have flourished since the turn of the century. Topography varies from rolling hills and savage waves on the eastern (Atlantic) coast, to densely populated flatlands, rows of hotels and apartments, and sheltered beaches in the southwest.

BONAIRE Its strongest historical and cultural links are to Holland, and although it has always been a poor relation of nearby Curaçao, Bonaire boasts better scuba diving and better bird life than any of its larger and richer neighbors. The terrain is as dry and inhospitable as anything you'll find in the Caribbean, a desert landscape whose sparseness is offset by a wealth of marine life above the island's miles of offshore reefs.

BRITISH VIRGIN ISLANDS (B.V.I.) Still a British Crown Colony, this lushly forested chain contains about 50 mountainous islands (depending on how many rocks, cays, and uninhabited islets you want to include). Superb for sailors, the B.V.I. are less densely populated, less developed, and have fewer social problems than the U.S. Virgin Islands. Tortola is the main island, followed by Virgin Gorda, which boasts some of the poshest hotels in the West Indies. Anegada, a coral atoll geologically different from the other members of the B.V.I., mainly attracts the yachting set.

CAYMAN ISLANDS This is a trio of islands set near the southern coast of Cuba. Flat and prosperous, this tiny nation is dependent on Britain for its economic survival and attracts millionaire expatriates from all over because of its lenient tax and banking laws. Relatively unattractive, these islands are covered with scrubland and swamp, but boast more than their share of upscale (and horrendously expensive) private homes and condominiums. Until recently, Grand Cayman enjoyed one of the most closely knit social fabrics in the Caribbean, although with recent prosperity, some of it is beginning to unravel. Because of the marine life above the offshore reefs, scuba divers seek out the Caymans almost as avidly as tax exiles. Greater numbers of hotels have begun lining the sands of the nation's most famous sunspot, Seven Mile Beach.

CURAÇAO (Dutch Leewards) Since much of the island's surface is an arid desert that grows only cactus, its canny Dutch settlers ruled out farming and developed Curaçao into one of the Dutch Empire's busiest trading posts. Until the post–World War II collapse of the oil refineries, Curaçao was a thriving mercantile society with a capital (Willemstad) that somewhat resembled Amsterdam and a population with a curious mixture of bloodlines (including African, Dutch, Venezuelan, and Pakistani), reflected in the range of languages spoken here: Dutch, Spanish, English, and, the lingua franca, Papiamentu, a mixture of African and European dialects. Tourism began to develop during the 1980s, and many new hotels have been built. Overall, Curaçao is more than just a hotel industry: It's a well-defined society in its own right.

DOMINICA (British Windwards) An English-speaking island set midway between Guadeloupe and Martinique, Dominica (*Doh-mi-NEE-kah*), the largest and most mountainous island of the Windwards, is not to be confused with the Dominican Republic (see below). A mysterious, little-visited land of waterfalls, rushing streams, and rain forests, it has only a few beaches, which are mainly lined with black volcanic sand. But if you like the offbeat and unusual, you may find this the lushest and most fascinating island in the Caribbean. Some 82,000 people live here, including 2,000 remaining descendants of the once-fierce Carib Indians. The capital is Roseau. Dominica is one of the poorest islands in the Caribbean, and has the misfortune of lying directly in the hurricane belt.

DOMINICAN REPUBLIC Occupying the eastern two-thirds of Hispaniola, the island it shares with Haiti, the mountainous Dominican Republic is the second-largest country of the Caribbean. Long-time victim of an endless series of military dictatorships, it now has a more favorable political climate and offers some of the least expensive vacation options in the entire Caribbean. Its crowded capital is Santo Domingo, with a population of two million. The island offers lots of Hispanic color, zesty merengue music, and many opportunities to dance, drink, and party. The contrast between the wealth of foreign tourists and the poverty of locals is especially obvious here, and it's not the safest of the islands.

GRENADA (British Windwards) The southernmost nation of the Windward Islands, Grenada (*gre-NAY-dah*) is one of the lushest in the Caribbean. Extravagantly fertile, it's one of the largest producers of spices in the western hemisphere, a result of a gentle climate, volcanic soil, and a number of islanders who make a living cultivating nutmeg and cloves. There's a lot of very appealing local color on Grenada, particularly since the political troubles of the 1980s seem, at least for the moment, to have ended. The beaches are white and sandy, and the populace (a mixture of English expatriates and islanders of African descent) is friendly. Once a British Crown Colony but now independent, the island nation also incorporates two smaller islands: Carriacou and Petit Martinique, neither of which has many tourist facilities. Grenada's capital, St. George's, is one of the most raffishly charming towns in the Caribbean.

GUADELOUPE (French West Indies) It isn't as sophisticated or cosmopolitan as the two outlying islands over which it holds administrative authority (Saint Barthélemy and the French section of St. Martin). Despite that, there is a lot of natural beauty in this *département* of mainland France. With a relatively low population density (only 340,000 people live here, mostly along the coast), butterfly shaped Guadeloupe is actually two distinctly different volcanic islands separated by a narrow saltwater strait, the Rivière Salée. It's ideal for scenic drives and Creole color, offering an unusual insight into the French colonial world. At its worst, Guadeloupe can combine the least attractive aspects of mainland France with some of the worst apathy in the Caribbean. At its best, it can be absolutely charming.

JAMAICA A favorite of North American honeymooners, Jamaica is a mountainous island rising abruptly from the sea 90 miles south of Cuba and about 100 miles west of Haiti. One of the most densely populated nations in the Caribbean, with a vivid sense of its own identity, Jamaica has a history rooted in the plantation economy, and some of the most turbulent and impassioned politics in the western hemisphere. Despite a regrettable increase in crime and harassment of tourists by vendors in such resorts as Ocho Rios, Jamaica is one of the most successful black democracies in the world. The island is large enough to allow the more or less peaceful coexistence of all kinds of people within its beach-lined borders, including everything from expatriate English aristocrats to dyed-in-the-wool Rastafarians. Overall, and despite its long history of social unrest and increasing crime, Jamaica is a fascinating island.

MARTINIQUE (French West Indies) One of the most exotic French-speaking destinations in the Caribbean, Martinique was the site of a settlement demolished by volcanic activity (St. Pierre, now only a pale shadow of a once-thriving city). Like Guadeloupe and St. Barts, Martinique is legally and culturally French (certainly many islanders drive with a Gallic panache—read: very badly), although many Creole customs and traditions continue to flourish. The beaches are beautiful, the Créole cuisine is full of flavor and flair, and the island has lots of tropical charm.

MONTSERRAT (British Leewards) This tiny pear-shaped "Emerald Isle" (only 11 miles long and 7 miles wide) lies 27 miles southeast of Antigua. It's a British Crown Colony with a deep-rooted respect for conservative church-going values. Long a favorite with British rock stars, Montserrat has fertile volcanic soil, beaches of both black and white sand, and a distinct sense of lying off the beaten path of Caribbean tourism. Its population numbers only 12,500 residents, most of African descent. Unless you rent one of the island's private villas, tourist facilities are limited, although clean and tidy.

PUERTO RICO Home to 3.3 million people whose primary language is Spanish, the Commonwealth of Puerto Rico is under the jurisdiction of the United States. It's one of the most urbanized islands of the Caribbean, with lots of traffic, glittering casinos, relatively high crime, and a more-or-less comfortable mix of Latin culture with imports from the U.S. mainland. The island's interior is filled with ancient volcanic mountains; the coastline is ringed with sandy beaches. The commonwealth also includes a trio of small offshore islands: Culebra, Mona, and Vieques (the last has the most tourist facilities). San Juan, the island's 16th-century capital, has some of the most extensive and best-preserved Spanish colonial neighborhoods in the New World, lots of things to see and do, and a steady flow of cruise-ship passengers who keep the stores and casinos filled throughout much of the year.

SABA (Dutch Windwards in the Leewards) Saba is a cone-shaped extinct volcano that rises abruptly and steeply from the watery depths of the Caribbean. There are no beaches to speak of, but the local Dutch- and English-speaking populace has traditionally made a living from fishing, trade, and needlework rather than tourism. Hotel choices are limited, and are often designed in the traditional Saban style of stone foundations terraced into sloping hillsides with white walls and red roofs. The thrifty seafaring folk of Saba can offer insights into the old-fashioned lifestyle of the Antilles. There's only one road on the island, and unless you opt to hike away from its edges, all island traffic proceeds along its narrow, winding route.

ST. BARTHÉLEMY (also called St. Barts or St. Barths; French West Indies) Part of the French département of Guadeloupe, lying 15 miles from Sint Maarten, St. Barts is a small, hilly island with a population of 3,500 people who live on 13 square miles of verdant terrain ringed by pleasant white-sand beaches. A small number of African descendants live harmoniously on this chic Caribbean island with descendants of Norman and Breton mariners and a colony of more recent expatriates from Europe's mainland. An expensive and exclusive stamping ground of the rich and famous, with a distinctive seafaring tradition and a decidedly French flavor, St. Barts has a "storybook" capital at Gustavia.

SINT EUSTATIUS (known as Statia; Dutch Windwards in the Leewards) During the 1700s this Dutch-controlled island ("The Golden Rock") was one of the most important trading posts in the Caribbean. During the U.S. War of Independence, a brisk arms trade helped to bolster the local economy, but the glamour ended in 1781, when British Admiral Romney sacked the port, hauled off most of the island's wealth, and propelled Sint Eustatius onto a path of obscurity, where, until the advent of tourism, it remained for almost 200 years. Today the island is among the poorest in the Caribbean, with 8 square miles of arid landscape, beaches that have strong and sometimes-dangerous undertows, a population of around 1,700 people, and a sleepy capital whose name is Oranjestad. Out of desperation, the island is very committed to maintaining its political and fiscal links to the Netherlands.

ST. KITTS & NEVIS (British Leewards) These two islands, with a rich sense of British maritime history, form a single nation despite their separation by a 2-mile strait. St. Kitts (also known as St. Christopher, with 68 square miles) and Nevis (with 36 square miles) both enjoyed some of the richest sugarcane economies of the plantation age, and the boiling rooms and Great Houses have in many cases been transformed into quaint inns. Both islands lie somewhat off the beaten tourist track, and both have a very appealing small-scale charm.

ST. LUCIA (British Windwards) St. Lucia (*LOO-sha*), 24 miles south of Martinique, is the second largest of the Windward Islands, with a population of around 150,000. Although in 1803 Britain eventually won control of the island, French influence is still evident in the Creole dialect. A volcanic island with lots of rainfall and great natural beauty, it has both white- and black-sand beaches, bubbling sulfur springs, and beautiful mountain scenery. Most tourism is concentrated on the island's northwestern tip, near the capital (Castries), but the arrival of up to 200,000 visitors a year has definitely altered the old agrarian lifestyle throughout the island.

SINT MAARTEN/ST. MARTIN (Dutch Windwards in the Leewards/French West Indies) Lying 144 miles east of Puerto Rico, this scrub-covered island has been divided between the Dutch (Sint Maarten) and the French (St. Martin) since 1648. Regardless of how you spell it, it's the same island, although both sides of the unguarded border are quite different. The Dutch side contains the island's more important airport, more shops, and more tourist facilities, while St. Martin has some of the poshest hotels. (The French side generally has superior food, as well.) There's a lot to do on this island, especially dining and drinking options, as the recent tourist boom proves. Both sides of the island are modern, urbanized, and cosmopolitan. And both suffer from traffic jams, a lack of parking space in the capitals, tourist-industry burnout (especially on the Dutch side), and a disturbing increase in crime.

ST. VINCENT & THE GRENADINES (British Windwards) Despite its natural beauty and its population of 105,000 people (of mostly African descent), this miniarchipelago has only recently been discovered by tourists, though it has always been known to divers and the yachting set, who consider its north-to-south string of cays and coral islets one of the most beautiful sailing regions in the world. St. Vincent, 18 miles long and 11 miles wide, is by far the largest and most fertile island in the country. Its capital is the sleepy, somewhat-dilapidated town of Kingstown (not to be confused with Kingston, Jamaica). Stretching like a pearl necklace to the south of St. Vincent are some 32 neighboring islands called the Grenadines. These include the charming boatbuilding community of Bequia and Mustique, where Princess Margaret has a home. Less densely populated islands in the chain include the tiny outposts of Mayreau, Canouan, Palm Island, and Petit St. Vincent, which was mostly covered with scrub until hotel owners planted much-needed groves of palm and hardwood trees.

TRINIDAD & TOBAGO The southernmost of the West Indies, this two-island nation lies just 7 miles off the coast of Venezuela. Both islands once had sugar-plantation economies and enjoyed fantastic wealth during the 18th century. Trinidad is the most industrialized island in the Caribbean, with oil deposits and a polyglot population derived from India, Pakistan, Venezuela, Africa, and Europe. Known for its calypso music and carnivals, Trinidad is one of the most culturally distinctive nations in the Caribbean, with a landmass of more than 1,800 square miles, a rich artistic tradition, a bustling capital (Port-of-Spain), and an impressive variety of exotic flora and fauna.

About 20 miles northeast of Trinidad, tiny Tobago (9 miles wide and 26 miles long) is calmer and less heavily forested, with a rather dull capital (Scarborough) and an impressive array of white-sand beaches. While Trinidad seems to consider tourism only one of many viable industries, Tobago is absolutely dependent on it.

U.S. VIRGIN ISLANDS Formerly Danish possessions, these islands became part of the United States in 1917. Originally based on a plantation economy, St. Croix is the largest and flattest of the U.S. Virgins, whereas St. Thomas and St. John are more mountainous. St. Thomas and, to a lesser degree, St. Croix possess all the diversions, facilities, and amusements you'd find on the U.S. mainland, including bars, restaurants, and lots of modern resort hotels. St. Thomas, which is way overbuilt, is sometimes referred to as the shopping mall of the Caribbean, and cruise-ship passengers constantly pass through. Much of the surface of St. John is devoted to a national park, a gift from Laurance Rockefeller to the national park system. All three islands offer sailing, snorkeling, and unspoiled vistas. Crime is on the increase, however—an unfortunate fly in the ointment of what would otherwise be a U.S.-owned corner of paradise.

2 A Taste of the Islands

AN OVERVIEW

Hotel chefs throughout the Caribbean prepare presentable American and continental cuisine, but in recent years hotels have placed a greater emphasis on local dishes. Even so, it's often better to order a $15 meal at a local restaurant than it is to have a $50 dinner in a so-called gourmet restaurant at some deluxe resort.

FRUITS, VEGETABLES & SIDE DISHES The abundance of fruit in the islands is obvious; at breakfast you'll usually find freshly sliced fruit, not always ripe enough. Coconut is used in everything from breads to soups. Soursop ice cream appears on some menus, and guava might turn up in anything from juice to cheese. Papaya is called *papaw,* and it will most often be your melon choice at breakfast. Mango is ubiquitous, used not only in chutney but also in drinks and desserts. The avocado, most often called *pears,* is used in fresh seafood salads and often stuffed with fresh crabmeat.

Most visitors know that the plantain (which is similar to a banana) is not eaten raw. It's usually served as a cooked side dish, the way Americans present french fries. Puerto Ricans eat dried plantains, called *tostones,* instead of potato chips.

Two staples of the Caribbean islands have always been rice and pigeon peas. Balls of cornmeal, called *fungi,* often accompany a salt-pork main dish known as *mauffay.* Sometimes these cornmeal concoctions will appear on the menus of local restaurants as *coo coo.*

One of the most common vegetables in the islands is *christophine* (sometimes called *foo foo*), a green, prickly gourd that tastes somewhat like zucchini. *Breadfruit,* introduced to the islands by Captain Bligh (of *Bounty* fame), is green and round and used like a potato. Potatoes and yams are also local favorites. The leafy *callaloo* is like spinach and is often served with crab, salt pork, and fresh fish (with floating fungi as a garnish).

In a true local restaurant in the Caribbean, you'll see hot peppers placed on the table. Be sparing. A selection of hot-pepper pastes is called *sambal.*

SEAFOOD Throughout the islands, warm-water lobster is the king of the sea and the most sought after (and most expensive) main course to order. The catch of the day is most likely to be red snapper or grouper, but could also be shark or barracuda.

Caution is urged in eating barracuda, which have been known to contain copper deposits. Fish caught north of Antigua and also along the Cayman Islands and Cuba are said to be at risk. The barracuda in south-lying Barbados are fine and usually very healthy.

Dolphin may also appear on the menu, but don't worry, this dolphin is a fish and not the playful mammal you saw in *Flipper.*

DRINKS Since the late 16th century, rum has been associated with slavery, Yankee traders, pirates, and bootlegging. A whole series of rum barons arose, with names that became famous around the world: Bacardi, Gonzalez, Myers, and Barcelo, to name only a few. "Kill-devil," as rum was once called, is of course the favorite drink of the islands. Distilled easily from sugarcane, rum played a major role in the history of the West Indies. Today the rusted machinery and tumble-down ruins of distilleries are tourist stopovers on dozens of Caribbean islands.

Planter's punch is still the most popular drink in the islands, but the average bar in the Caribbean offers a bewildering array of other rum-based drinks as well. Sure, these frosty drinks are pastel-colored and come with cute umbrellas, but they'll get you drunk on very short notice because of their elevated sugar content, as well as the hot climate.

Don't think that the only beer you'll be able to find will be imported from Milwaukee or Holland. Of course, Heineken is ubiquitous, as is Amstel, especially in the Dutch islands, but Red Stripe from Jamaica is the most famous.

Water is generally safe throughout the islands, but many tourists get sick from drinking it simply because it's different from the water they're accustomed to. If it's available, order bottled water.

ISLAND SPECIALTIES

ANGUILLA Order spiny lobsters if you can get them; they're very good and invariably fresh. Seafood lovers will also enjoy the crayfish, whelk, yellowtail, and red snapper. Some local restaurants serve some of the most elegant continental fare in the West Indies, although they're generally forced to work with frozen ingredients imported from elsewhere, often Miami.

ANTIGUA & BARBUDA At most restaurants and in most resorts catering to tourists, you get typical American or continental fare. But a host of French restaurants have opened in the past few years on Antigua. Local food, when it's available on either island, tends to be spicy, with sauces often based on Creole recipes or even on East Indian curry dishes. That means pepperpot stew, spareribs, curried goat, and the like. A British heritage lingers in some of the island's blander dishes. If fresh seafood is on the menu, try it.

ARUBA A few of Aruba's restaurants serve *rijstaffel,* the multidish Indonesian "rice table," or *nasi goreng,* a minirijstaffel. In addition, many Chinese restaurants operate in Oranjestad. More and more Aruban specialties are beginning to appear on menus. Although not always suited to the tropics, these include *keshi yena,* Edam cheese filled with a mixture of chicken or beef and flavored with onions, pickles, tomatoes, olives, and raisins. *Sopito de pisca* is a savory fish chowder made with a bouquet of spices. *Funchi,* like a cornmeal pudding of the Deep South, accompanies many regional dishes. French is the cuisine of choice for many of the island's top chefs.

BARBADOS The famous flying fish appears on every menu, and when prepared right, it's a delicacy—moist and succulent, nutlike in flavor, approaching the subtlety of brook trout. Bajans boil it, steam it, bake it, stew it, fry it, and stuff it.

Try the sea urchin, or *oursin,* which you may have already sampled on Martinique and Guadeloupe. Bajans often call these urchins "sea eggs." Crab-in-the-back is another specialty, as is *langouste,* the Barbadian lobster. Dolphin and salt fish cakes are other popular items. *Cou-cou,* a side dish made from okra and cornmeal, accompanies fish. Yams, sweet potatoes, and eddoes (similar to yams) are typical vegetables. Luscious Barbadian fruits include papaya, passion fruit, and mango.

If you hear that any hotel or restaurant is having a *cohobblopot* (or more commonly, a Bajan buffet), call for a reservation. This is a Barbadian term that means to "cook up," and it inevitably will produce an array of local dishes.

BONAIRE Bonaire's food is generally acceptable, though nearly everything has to be imported. Your best bet is fresh-caught fish and an occasional rijstaffel, the traditional Indonesian "rice table," or local dishes. Popular foods are conch cutlet or stew, pickled conch, red snapper, tuna, wahoo, dolphin, fungi (a thick cornmeal pudding), rice, beans, *sate* (marinated meat with curried mayonnaise), goat stew, and Dutch cheeses.

THE BRITISH VIRGIN ISLANDS The food is relatively simple and straightforward, with fresh fish the best item on the menu. Most other items, including meat and poultry, are shipped in frozen. In most major restaurants and hotels, an American or continental cuisine (with Caribbean influences) prevails. For a taste of authentic island foods, go where the locals go (we'll recommend several good bets in each chapter). Locals give colorful names to the various fish brought home for dinner, everything from "ole wife" to "doctors." "Porgies and grunts," along with yellowtail, kingfish, and bonito, show up on many tables. Fish is usually boiled in a lime-flavored brew seasoned with hot peppers and herbs, and is commonly served with a Créole sauce of peppers, tomatoes, and onions, among other ingredients. Salt fish and rice is another low-cost dish, the fish flavored with onion, tomatoes, shortening, garlic, and green pepper.

Conch Creole is a tasty stew, flavored with onions, garlic, spices, hot peppers, and salt pork. You might also order a plate of succulent conch fritters if you get the chance. A favorite local dish is chicken and rice, made with Spanish peppers. Curried goat, the longtime "classic" West Indian dinner, is made with herbs, including cardamom pods and onions. The famous johnnycakes that accompany many of these fish and meat dishes are deep-fried in fat or baked.

THE CAYMAN ISLANDS American and continental cooking predominates, although there's also a cuisine known as Caymanian, which features specialties made from turtle. (Environmental groups in the States consider this species to be endangered; however, in the Cayman Islands it is bred for food, as opposed to being caught in the wild at sea.) Fresh fish is the star, and conch is used in many ways. Local lobster is in season from late summer through January. Since most dining places have to rely on imported ingredients, prices tend to be high.

CURAÇAO The basic cuisine is Dutch, but there are many specialty items, particularly Latin American and Indonesian. The cuisine strikes many visitors as heavy for the tropics, so you may want to have a light lunch and order the more filling concoctions, such as *rijstaffel,* in the evening. You may want to finish your meals with Curaçao, the liqueur that made the island famous.

Ertwensoep, the well-known Dutch pea soup, is a popular dish, as is *keshi yena,* which is Edam cheese stuffed with meat and then baked. *Funchi,* a Caribbean cornmeal pudding, accompanies many local dishes. *Sopito,* fish soup often made with coconut water, is an especially good local dish, and conch is featured in curries and many other dishes.

DOMINICA The local delicacy is the fine flesh of the *crapaud* (a frog), called "mountain chicken." Freshwater crayfish is another specialty, as is *tee-tee-ree,* fried cakes made from tiny fish. Stuffed crab back is usually a delight—the backs of red and black land crabs are stuffed with delicate crabmeat and Creole seasonings. The fresh fruit juices of the island are divine, and no one spends a day without at least one rum punch.

DOMINICAN REPUBLIC The national dish is *sancocho,* a thick stew made with meats (maybe seven kinds), vegetables, and herbs, especially marjoram. Another national favorite is *chicharrones de pollo,* pieces of fried chicken and fried green bananas flavored with pungent spices. One of the most typical dishes is *la bandera* (the flag), made with red beans, white rice, and stewed meat. Johnnycakes and *mangu,* a plantainlike dish, are frequently eaten. Johnnycakes can be bought on the street corner or at the beach, but you must ask for them as *vaniqueques.*

A good local beer is called Presidente. Wines are imported, so prices tend to run high. Dominican coffee compares favorably with that of Colombia and Brazil.

GRENADA We've found the food on Grenada better than on the other British Windward Islands. Many of the chefs are European or European trained, and local cooks are also on hand to prepare Grenadian specialties, such as conch (called *lambi* here), lobster, callaloo soup (with greens and crab), and soursop or avocado ice cream. Turtle steaks appear on many menus, although this is an endangered species. The national dish, called "oil down," consists of breadfruit and salt pork covered with dasheen leaves and steamed in coconut milk (it's not the favorite of every visitor). Some 22 kinds of fish, including fresh tuna, dolphin, and barracuda, are caught off the island's shores, and most are good eating. Naturally, the spices of the island, such as nutmeg, are used plentifully. Meals are often served family style in an open-air setting with a view of the sea.

GUADELOUPE The Creole cuisine of Guadeloupe is similar to Martinique's, and we think it's the best in the Caribbean. The island's chefs have been called "seasoned sorcerers." Creole cooking has African roots and is based on seafood. Out in the country, every cook has his or her own herb garden, since the cuisine makes great use of herbs and spices. Except in the major hotels, most restaurants are family run, offering real homemade cooking. Best of all, you usually get to dine al fresco.

Stuffed, stewed, skewered, or broiled spiny lobsters, as well as clams, conch, oysters, and octopus, are presented to you with French taste and subtlety. Every good chef knows how to make *colombo,* a spicy rich stew of poultry, pork, or beef served with rice, herbs, sauces, and a variety of seeds. Another Creole favorite is *calalou* (callaloo in English), a soup made with spinachlike callaloo greens and flavored with savory herbs. Yet another traditional French Caribbean dish is *blaff,* fresh seafood poached in clear stock and usually seasoned with hot peppers.

JAMAICA There is great emphasis on seafood. Rock lobster appears on every menu—grilled, thermidor, cold, hot. *Ackee and saltfish,* the national dish, is a concoction of salt cod and a brightly colored vegetable that looks and tastes something like scrambled eggs. *Escovitch* (marinated fish) is usually fried and then simmered in vinegar with onions and peppers. Curried mutton and goat are popular, as is pepperpot stew, all highly seasoned.

Jerk pork is found everywhere, but is best in country areas, where it's barbecued slowly over wood fires until crisp and brown. Rice and peas (really red beans) are usually served with onions, spices, and salt pork. Vegetables are exotic: breadfruit, imported by Captain Bligh in 1723; callaloo, rather like spinach, used in pepperpot soup; *cho-cho,* served boiled or stuffed; and green bananas and plantains, fried or boiled and served with almost everything. Then there's pumpkin, which goes into a soup or is served on the side, boiled and mashed with butter. Sweet potatoes appear with main courses, but there's also a sweet-potato pudding made with sugar and coconut milk, flavored with cinnamon, nutmeg, and vanilla.

You'll come across dishes with really odd names: *stamp and go* are saltfish cakes eaten as appetizers; *dip and fall back* is a salty stew with bananas and dumplings; and *rundown* is mackerel cooked in coconut milk, often eaten for breakfast. *Patties* (meat pies) are another staple snack; the best on the island are in Montego Bay. Boiled corn, roast yams, roast saltfish, fried fish, soups, and fruits are all sold at roadside stands.

In some parts of Jamaica, "tea" is used to describe any nonalcoholic drink, a tradition dating from plantation days. *Fish tea* is actually a bowl of hot soup made from freshly caught fish. *Skyjuice,* a favorite with Jamaicans on hot afternoons, is sold by street vendors from not-always-sanitary carts. It consists of shaved ice with sugar-laden fruit syrup and is sold in small plastic bags with a straw. Coconut water is a refreshing drink, especially when you stop by the road to have a local vendor chop open a fresh coconut.

Rum punches are everywhere, and the local beer is Red Stripe. The island produces many liqueurs, the most famous being Tía Maria, made from coffee beans. Rumona is another good one to take home with you. *Bellywash,* the local name for limeade, will supply the extra liquid you may need to counteract the heat. Blue Mountain coffee is the best, but tea, cocoa, and milk are usually available to round off a meal.

MARTINIQUE See Guadeloupe, above.

MONTSERRAT Some of the best fruits and vegetables in the Caribbean are grown in the rich, volcanic soil of Montserrat. The island is known for its tomatoes, carrots, and mangoes. *Goat water* (a mutton stew) is the most popular local dish. Another island specialty is *mountain chicken,* otherwise known as frogs' legs.

PUERTO RICO Although Puerto Rican cooking has similarities to Cuban, Spanish, and Mexican cuisine, it has its own unique style, using such indigenous seasonings and ingredients as cilantro, papaya, cacao, nispero, apio, plantains, and yampee.

Cocina Criola (Creole cooking) was initiated by the Arawaks and Taínos, the original inhabitants of the island. Long before Columbus arrived, these peaceful people thrived on a diet of corn, tropical fruits, and seafood. When Ponce de León arrived with Columbus in 1508, the Spanish added beef, pork, rice, wheat, and olive oil to the island's foodstuffs. Soon after, the Spanish began planting sugarcane and importing slaves from Africa, who brought with them okra and taro, known in Puerto Rico as *yauita.* The mingling of flavors and ingredients from different ethnic groups created Puerto Rican cuisine.

Lunch and dinner generally begin with sizzling hot appetizers such as *bacalaitos* (crunchy cod fritters), *surullitos* (sweet, plump cornmeal fingers), and *empanadillas* (crescent-shaped turnovers filled with lobster, crab, conch, or beef). Next, a bowl of steaming *asopao* (a hearty gumbo soup with rice and chicken or shellfish) may be followed by *lechón asado* (roast suckling pig), *pollo en vino dulce* (succulent chicken in wine), or *bacalao* (dried salted cod mixed with various roots and tubers and fried). No matter the selection, main dishes are served with salted *tostones* (deep-fried plantains or green bananas) and plentiful portions of rice and beans.

The aroma that wafts from kitchens throughout Puerto Rico comes from *adobo* and *sofrito*—blends of herbs and spices that give many of the native foods their distinctive taste and color. Adobo, made from peppercorns, oregano, garlic, salt, olive oil, and lime juice or vinegar, is rubbed into meats before they are roasted. Sofrito, a potpourri of onions, garlic, and peppers browned in olive oil or lard and colored with *achiote* (annatto seeds), imparts a bright-yellow color to the island's rice, soups, and stews.

Dessert is usually *flan* (custard) or perhaps *nisperos de batata* (sweet-potato balls made with coconut, cloves, and cinnamon). Finish your meal with Puerto Rican coffee—strong, black, and aromatic.

Rum is the national drink, and you can buy it in almost any shade. On Puerto Rico it's quite proper to order a cold beer before even looking at the menu; one local choice is India, famous for its pure water. However, most Puerto Ricans drink a golden brew known as Medalla.

SABA No one visits for the food. Caribbean and continental dishes prevail, but there is no really outstanding restaurant. Most of the food is imported.

ST. BARTS This is one of the few islands in the Caribbean where haute cuisine prevails. Perhaps it's somewhat incongruous in a tropical setting, but some excellent continental cuisine is served. There are almost no local dishes, except fresh fish and lobster. Sometimes, however, dishes are given Caribbean flavor, as in chicken breast served with mango sauce or perhaps panfried prawns Creole style. Antillean stuffed crab is a regular feature, as is a *colombo* of lamb (stew flavored with curry and roasted bananas). But chances are that the chef will serve you sole with champagne sauce or filet of beef in pepper sauce, as in France.

ST. EUSTATIUS Often called Statia, this Dutch island isn't going to produce any gourmet cookbooks. Most of the food is imported, and restaurants are adequate, not exciting. Some restaurants make a stab at preparing a French cuisine with generally frozen ingredients. Local bistros serve some regional cooking such as stewed conch, salt fish with johnnycakes, or curried goat.

ST. KITTS & NEVIS On St. Kitts, most guests eat at their hotels, but the island has a number of good restaurants where you can find spiny lobster, crab back, pepperpot stew, breadfruit, and curried conch. The drink of the island is Cane Spirit Rothschild (CSR), a pure sugarcane liqueur developed by Baron Edmond de Rothschild. Islanders mix it with Ting, a bubbly grapefruit soda.

On Nevis, the local food is good. Suckling pig is roasted with many spices, and eggplant is used in a number of tasty ways, as is avocado. (You may see turtle on some menus, but remember that this is an endangered species.)

ST. LUCIA Try to break free of your hotel and dine in one of St. Lucia's little character-loaded restaurants (we'll make suggestions in chapter 13). The local food is excellent and reflects the years of French and British occupation. St. Lucia's marketplace offers the ingredients for local dishes, including callaloo soup (fresh greens, dumplings, and salted beef), *pouile dudon* (a sweet, zesty chicken dish), and breadfruit cooked on open hot coals. Pumpkin soup, flying fish, lobster, and *tablette* (a coconut sugar candy that resembles white coral) round out the menu choices.

SINT MAARTEN/ST. MARTIN This island, part Dutch, part French, has a truly excellent cuisine, in spite of its heavy reliance on imported ingredients. Here you'll find classic French cuisine, as well as American and continental, with a touch of West Indian spice and flavors. All the French classics are served, including frogs' legs and escargots, but Caribbean offerings, inspired by Martinique, include *crabes farcis* (stuffed crab), *blaff* (seafood poached and seasoned with peppers), and curried *colombo* (a stew with chicken, mutton, or goat).

Nearby Anguilla supplies a never-ending basket of spiny lobsters, the most delectable dish on the island. Dutch specialties are rare, although there's plenty of tasty Dutch beer. A lot of good French wine, served by either the bottle or the carafe, is also shipped into the island.

ST. VINCENT & THE GRENADINES Most dining takes place in the hotels, although there are a few local bistros serving such West Indian food as fish Creole style and callaloo soup. But mostly locals try to serve what they've heard foreigners like, including frozen steak flown in from Chicago, frozen shrimp from Latin America, and frozen french fries from who-knows-where. And anyway, what is served often doesn't matter after diners have had a few rum punches before dinner—local bartenders take pride in the variety of their rum punches as well as their lethal effects.

TRINIDAD & TOBAGO The food on these islands is as varied and cosmopolitan as the islanders themselves. Although this was a British colony for years, English cuisine never made much of an impression. Red-hot curries testify to Trinidad's strong East Indian influence, and some Chinese dishes are about as good here as any you'll find in Hong Kong. Creole and Spanish fare, as well as French, are also to be enjoyed. A typical savory offering is a roti, a king-size crepe, highly spiced and filled with chicken, shellfish, or meat. Of course, you may prefer to skip such local delicacies as opossum stew and fried armadillo. Naturally, your fresh rum punch will have a dash of Angostura Bitters. In Trinidad there is a tendency to deep-fry everything—you can avoid this by careful menu selections.

Tobago has fewer dining choices than Trinidad. In Tobago your best bet is local fish dishes, such as stuffed kingfish in Creole sauce. Local crayfish is also good, and lobster appears on some menus, perhaps stuffed into a crepe. One island favorite that appears frequently is seafood casserole with ginger wine. Some typical Tobago dishes include baby shark marinated in lime and rum and conch stewed with coconut and rum.

THE U.S. VIRGIN ISLANDS Although a lot of the food is imported (often from Miami or Puerto Rico) and frozen, St. Thomas, and to a lesser extent St. Croix and St. John, serve some of the finest American and continental cuisine in the Caribbean. Very experienced chefs, especially from Europe, are often brought in during the winter season to tempt your taste buds. A whole range of ethnic restaurants exist too, including Chinese and Mexican. Italian food is also commonplace.

The most famous soup of the islands is kallaloo, or *callaloo,* made in an infinite number of ways from a leafy green vegetable similar to spinach. This soup is flavored with salt beef, pig mouth, pig tail, ham bone, fresh fish, crabs, or perhaps conch, along with okra, onions, and spices. Many soups are sweetened with sugar, and putting fruits in soups is common. The classic red-bean soup made with pork or ham, various spices, and tomatoes, is sugared to taste. Tannia soup is made from the root of the so-called Purple Elephant Ear. Salt-fat meat and ham, along with tomatoes, onions, and spices, are added to the tannias.

Souse is an old-time favorite made with the feet, head, and tongue of the pig, and flavored with a lime-based sauce and various spices. Salt-fish salad is traditionally served on Holy Thursday or Good Friday, as well as at other times. It's made with boneless salt fish, potatoes, onions, boiled eggs, and an oil-and-vinegar dressing.

Herring gundy is an old-time island favorite made with salt herring, potatoes, onions, sweet and hot green peppers, olives, diced beets, raw carrots, herbs, and boiled eggs. Seasoned rice is popular with Virgin Islanders, who often serve several starches at one meal. Most often rice is flavored with ham or salt pork, tomatoes, garlic, onion, and shortening. *Fungi* is a simple cornmeal dumpling that can be made more interesting with the addition of various ingredients, such as okra. Sweet fungi becomes a dessert, with sugar, milk, cinnamon, and raisins.

Okra (often spelled *ochroe* in the islands) is a mainstay vegetable, often accompanying beef, fish, or chicken. It's fried in an iron skillet after being flavored with hot pepper, tomatoes, onions, garlic, and bacon fat or butter. *Accra,* another popular dish, is made with okra, black-eyed peas, salt, and pepper. It's dropped into boiling fat and fried until golden brown.

The classic vegetable dish—some families serve it every night—is peas and rice, made with pigeon peas flavored with ham or salt meat, onion, tomatoes, herbs, and sometimes slices of pumpkin.

For dessert, sweet-potato pone is a classic, made with sugar, eggs, butter, milk, salt, cinnamon, raisins, and chopped almonds. The exotic fruits of the islands lend themselves to various homemade ice creams, including mango. Orange-rose sherbet is made by pounding rose petals into a paste and flavoring it with sugar and orange juice. Guava ice cream is a delectable flavor, as are soursop, banana, and papaya. Sometimes dumplings are served for dessert, made with guava, peach, plum, gooseberry, cherry, or apple.

3

Planning a Trip to the Caribbean

This chapter is devoted to the where, when, and how of your Caribbean trip—the advance-planning issues that need resolving before you leave home. But before we begin, we'd like to make a recommendation: Since the islands are so culturally and ethnically diverse, we encourage you to island-hop rather than to stay in one place if you have the time, money, and energy. It's easy to fly within the region, and island-hopping will enrich your Caribbean vacation.

1 Visitor Information, Entry Requirements, Customs & Money

VISITOR INFORMATION

All the major islands have tourist representatives whom you can contact for information before you go; we'll list each one in the appropriate chapter. **The Caribbean Tourism Organization,** 20 E. 46th St., New York, NY 10017 (☎ **212/682-0435**), can also provide a brochure containing brief descriptions on what to see and do on the islands, as well as general information.

You may also want to contact the U.S. State Department for background bulletins. Contact the Superintendent of Documents, **U.S. Government Printing Office,** Washington, DC 20402 (☎ **202/512-1800**). A free catalog of books and background notes is available. Background bulletins are available for Caribbean nations including Antigua and Barbados, the Dominican Republic, Grenada, Jamaica, St. Lucia, St. Kitts and Nevis, St. Vincent and the Grenadines, and Trinidad and Tobago.

A good **travel agent** can also provide information, but make sure the agent is a member of the American Society of Travel Agents (ASTA). If you have a complaint, write to **ASTA Consumer Affairs,** 1101 King St., Alexandria, VA 22314 (☎ **703/706-0387**).

If you have Internet access, "City.net" (**http://www.city.net/regions/caribbean/**) is a great site that will point you toward a wealth of Caribbean travel information on the Web. One of the best Caribbean sites they list, especially if you're aiming for a resort or plan to take a cruise, is "Caribbean-On-Line" (**http://www.webcom.com/earleltd/**), a series of virtual guidebooks full of information on hotels, restaurants, and shopping, along with sights and detailed maps of the islands and their major towns and ports. The site also includes links to travel agents and cruise lines that are up on the Web.

ENTRY REQUIREMENTS

Even though the Caribbean islands are, for the most part, independent nations and thereby classified as international destinations, passports are not generally required (see the individual island chapters for specific requirements). You do, however, have to have identity documents, and a passport is the best form of identification and will speed you through Customs and Immigration. Other acceptable documents include an ongoing or return ticket, plus a current voter registration card or a birth certificate (the original or a copy that has been certified by the U.S. Department of Health). You will also need a photo ID, such as a driver's license or an expired passport; however, driver's licenses are not acceptable as a sole form of ID. Visas are usually not required, but some countries may require you to fill out a tourist card (see the individual island chapters for details).

Before leaving home, make two copies of your documents, including your passport and your driver's license, your airline ticket, and any hotel vouchers. If you're on medication, you should also make copies of prescriptions.

CUSTOMS

Each island has specific requirements. Generally, you're permitted to bring in items intended for your personal use, including tobacco, cameras, film, and a limited supply of liquor, usually 40 ounces.

U.S. CUSTOMS The U.S. government generously allows U.S. citizens $1,200 worth of duty-free imports every 30 days from the U.S. Virgin Islands; those who go over their exemption are taxed at 5% rather than 10%. The limit is $400 for such international destinations as the French islands of Guadeloupe and Martinique, and $600 for many other islands. If you only visit Puerto Rico, you don't have to go through Customs at all, since it's an American commonwealth.

Joint Customs declarations are possible for members of a family traveling together. For instance, if you are a husband and wife with two children, your exemptions in the U.S. Virgin Islands become duty free up to $4,800! Unsolicited gifts of $100 per day from the U.S. Virgin Islands (or $50 a day from the other islands) can be sent to friends and relatives. U.S. citizens, or returning residents at least 21 years of age, traveling directly or indirectly from American Samoa, Guam, or the U.S. Virgin Islands are allowed to bring in free of duty 1,000 cigarettes, 5 liters of alcohol, and 100 non-Cuban cigars. Duty-free limitations on articles from other countries are generally 1 liter of alcohol, 200 cigarettes, and 200 cigars.

Collect receipts for all purchases made abroad. Sometimes merchants suggest a false receipt to undervalue your purchase, but be aware that you might be involved in a sting operation—the merchant might be an informer for U.S. Customs. You must also declare on your Customs form the nature and value of all gifts received during your stay abroad. It's prudent to carry proof that you purchased expensive cameras or jewelry on the U.S. mainland. If you purchased such an item during an earlier trip abroad, you should carry proof that you have previously paid Customs duty on the item.

For more specifics, write to the **U.S. Customs Service,** 1301 Constitution Ave., P.O. Box 7407, Washington, DC 20044, (☎ **202/927-6724**) and request the free pamphlet *Know Before You Go.*

CANADIAN CUSTOMS For total clarification, write for the booklet *I Declare,* issued by **Revenue Canada,** 2265 St. Laurent Blvd., Ottawa, K1G 4K3, (☎ **800/**

461-9999 or 613/993-0534). Canada allows its citizens a $300 exemption, and they are permitted to bring back duty free 200 cigarettes, 2.2 pounds of tobacco, 40 imperial ounces of liquor, and 50 cigars. In addition, they are allowed to mail gifts to Canada from abroad at the rate of Can$60 a day, provided the gifts are unsolicited and are not alcohol or tobacco (write on the package: *unsolicited gift, under $60 value*). All valuables should be declared on Form Y-38 before departure from Canada, including serial numbers, as in the case of expensive foreign cameras you already own. *Note:* The $300 exemption can be used only once a year and only after an absence of seven days.

BRITISH CUSTOMS On returning from the Caribbean, if you either arrive directly in the United Kingdom or arrive via a port in another European Community (EC) country where you did not pass through Customs controls with all your baggage, you must go through U.K. Customs and declare any goods in excess of the allowances. These are: 200 cigarettes or 50 cigars or 250 grams of tobacco; 2 liters of still table wine and 1 liter of spirits or strong liqueurs over 22% volume, or 2 liters of fortified or sparkling wine or other liqueurs, or 2 liters of additional still table wine; 60cc (ml) of perfume; 250cc (ml) of toilet water; and £145 worth of all other goods, including gifts and souvenirs. (No one under 17 years of age is entitled to a tobacco or alcohol allowance.) Only go through the green "nothing to declare" line if you're sure that you have no more than the Customs allowances and no prohibited or restricted goods. For further details on U.K. Customs, contact **H.M. Customs and Excise Office,** Dorset House, Stamford St., London SE1 9PY (☎ **0171/202-4510**).

MONEY

CASH/CURRENCY The U.S. dollar is widely accepted on many of the islands, and is the legal currency of the U.S. Virgin Islands, the British Virgin Islands, and Puerto Rico. Many islands use the Eastern Caribbean dollar, even though your hotel bill will most likely be presented in U.S. dollars and U.S. currency is accepted by many merchants. French islands (Martinique and Guadeloupe) use the French franc, although many hotels often quote their prices in U.S. dollars.

For details, see "Fast Facts" in the individual island chapters.

TRAVELER'S CHECKS It's getting easier each year to find ATMs all around the world that will allow you to access your bank account while you're on the road, and that is certainly true of the more heavily touristed islands covered in this book. But you may be headed for a more remote destination or want the security of carrying traveler's checks so that you can obtain a refund if your checks are stolen (if you've properly documented the serial numbers). Most large banks sell traveler's checks, charging fees averaging between 1% and 2% of the value of the checks you buy, although some out-of-the-way banks, in rare instances, have charged as much as 7%.

American Express (☎ **800/221-7282** in the U.S. and Canada, with many regional representatives around the world) is one of the largest issuers of traveler's checks. No commission is paid by members of AAA providing checks are purchased at AAA offices. American Express platinum card holders get traveler's checks issued commission free at American Express offices or through the American Express service number (☎ **800/553-6782**). Gold card holders can get commission-free checks only through the American Express service number; other cardholders pay a commission.

Citicorp (☎ **800/645-6556** in the U.S. and Canada, or 813/623-1709, collect, from other parts of the world) is another major issuer. **Thomas Cook** (☎ **800/223-7373** in the U.S. and Canada, or 609/987-7300, collect, from other parts of the

The U.S. Dollar & the British Pound

The U.S. dollar is commonly used throughout the Caribbean, except on the French islands of Martinique and Guadeloupe. It is widely accepted even on islands that print their own currency. British travelers will want to convert their pounds sterling into dollars, even for use on islands that are British Crown Colonies.

The British pound trades at an average of around 62 pence = U.S.$1. Stated another way, U.S.$1.60 = £1. The chart below gives a rough approximation of conversion rates you're likely to find at the time of your trip, but confirm before you make transactions.

U.S.$	U.K.£	U.S.$	U.K.£
.25	.16	15.00	9.38
.50	.31	20.00	12.50
.75	.47	25.00	15.63
1.00	.625	50.00	31.25
2.00	1.25	75.00	46.88
3.00	1.88	100.00	62.50
4.00	2.50	150.00	93.75
5.00	3.13	200.00	125.00
6.00	3.75	250.00	156.25
7.00	4.38	300.00	187.50
8.00	5.00	350.00	218.75
9.00	5.63	400.00	250.00
10.00	6.25	500.00	312.50

world) issues MasterCard traveler's checks, and **Interpayment Services** (☎ **800/221-2426** in the U.S. and Canada, or 212/858-8500, collect, from other parts of the world) sells Visa traveler's checks.

CREDIT & CHARGE CARDS Credit and charge cards are widely used in the Caribbean. Visa and MasterCard are the major cards used, although American Express and, to a lesser extent, Diners Club, are also popular. We've noted which cards are accepted at each hotel and restaurant recommended throughout this book.

ATM NETWORKS Plus, Cirrus, and other automated-teller machine (ATM) networks operate in the Caribbean. Before departing, check to see if your PIN number must be reprogrammed for use at Caribbean ATMs to withdraw money on either your ATM or credit card. ATMs are found in such places as Puerto Rico and St. Thomas; however, don't count on this service being available at one of the remote islands such as Mustique in the Grenadines.

Always determine what the frequency limits for withdrawals and cash advances are on your bank or credit card. For locations of Cirrus abroad, call ☎ **800/424-7787** in the U.S. For Plus usage abroad, dial ☎ **800/843-7587.** ATMs give a better exchange rate than banks, but some ATMs exact a service charge on every transaction.

MONEYGRAMS So you've run out of money while you're still on the road. Assuming you have friends or relatives who will advance you the money, a new service sponsored by American Express might be able to help you out of your jam. **Moneygram,** 6200 S. Quebec St. (P.O. Box 5118), Englewood, CO 80155-5118 (☎ **800/926-9400**), is the fastest-growing money-wiring service in the world. Funds can be transferred from one individual to another in less than 10 minutes from any of thousands of locations to any of thousands of other locations throughout the world. An American Express phone representative will give you the names of four or five offices near you. (You don't have to go to an American Express office; some locations are pharmacies or convenience stores in small communities.) Acceptable forms of payment include cash, Visa, MasterCard, or Discover, and occasionally, a personal check. Service charges collected by AmEx are $10 for the first $300 sent, with a sliding scale of commissions after that (sending $5,000 costs about $200 in fees). Included in the transfer is a 10-word telex-style message (say, "I love you but pay me back"). The deal also includes a free three-minute phone call to the recipient. Funds are transferred within 10 minutes, and can then be retrieved by the beneficiary at the most convenient location when proper photo ID is presented, and in some cases, a security code established by whoever provides the funds.

The program is now in place on Antigua/Barbuda, Barbados, the Dominican Republic, Grenada, Jamaica, Puerto Rico, St. Lucia, St. Vincent and the Grenadines, Trinidad and Tobago, and the U.S. Virgin Islands.

2 When to Go

CLIMATE

The temperature variations in the Caribbean are surprisingly slight, averaging between 75° and 85°F in both winter and summer, although it can get really chilly, especially in the early morning and at night. The Caribbean winter is usually like a perpetual northern American May. Overall, the mid-80s prevail throughout most of the region, and trade winds make for comfortable days and nights, even without air-conditioning.

The humidity and bugs can be a problem here year-round. However, more mosquitoes come out during the rainy season, which traditionally occurs in the autumn.

THE HURRICANE SEASON The curse of Caribbean weather, the hurricane season lasts from June 1 to November 30 (at least officially). But there's no cause for panic. Satellite forecasts give adequate warnings so that precautions can be taken.

To get a weather report before you go, call the nearest branch of the National Weather Service, listed in your phone directory under the "U.S. Department of Commerce." You can also call Weather Trak; for the telephone number for your particular area, dial ☎ **900/370-8725** (a taped message gives you the three-digit access code for the place you're interested in; the call costs 75¢ for the first minute and 50¢ for each additional minute).

THE "SEASON"

The Caribbean has become a year-round destination. The "season" runs roughly from mid-December to mid-April. Hotels charge their highest prices during the peak winter period, which is generally the driest season; however, it can be a wet time in mountainous areas, and you can expect showers especially in December and January on Martinique, Guadeloupe, Dominica, St. Lucia, on the north coast of the Dominican Republic, and in Jamaica's northeast section.

For a winter vacation, make reservations two to three months in advance—even earlier for trips at Christmas and in February.

THE "OFF-SEASON"

Dollar for dollar, you'll spend less money by renting a summer house or self-sufficient unit in the Caribbean than you would on Cape Cod, Fire Island, Laguna

Beach, or the coast of Maine. Sailing and water sports are better too, because the West Indies are protected from the Atlantic on their western shores, which border the calm Caribbean Sea.

The off-season in the Caribbean is roughly from mid-April to mid-December (although this varies from hotel to hotel) and amounts to a summer sale. In most cases, hotel rates are slashed a startling 20% to 60%.

After the winter hordes have left, a less-hurried way of life prevails. You'll have a better chance to appreciate the food, the culture, and the local customs. Swimming pools and beaches are less crowded, and you'll enjoy more immediate access to sports facilities. Resort boutiques often feature summer sales, hoping to clear the merchandise they didn't sell in February. You can often walk in unannounced at a top restaurant and get a seat for dinner, and you'll get better service. The atmosphere is more cosmopolitan because of the influx of Europeans; you'll no longer feel as if you're at a Canadian or American outpost. Airfares are lower, and tickets and accommodations are much easier to obtain.

3 Adventure Tours

BIRDING **Victor Emanuel Nature Tours** (☎ **800/328-8368**) offers week-long bird-watching trips led by a biologist in Trinidad and Tobago, costing approximately $1,825 per person. The trip is based at the Asa Wright Nature Center, which has 150 of the more than 400 species of birds found in Trinidad. Discussion sessions on the symbiosis between plant and bird life are offered, along with field trips.

The company also operates weeklong birding trips to Jamaica (home to some 30 species of birds found nowhere else in the world), costing $1,250 per person. Trips are conducted by a Jamaican ornithologist.

HIKING Unlike many of its neighboring islands, Jamaica offers mountain peaks of up to 7,400 feet. The flora, fauna, waterfalls, and panoramas of those peaks have attracted increasing numbers of hikers and hill climbers, each determined to experience the natural beauty of the island firsthand. One outfit that caters to these needs is the **Jamaica Alternative Tourism Camping and Hiking Association,** whose members include three tour operators. Foremost among them is **SENSE Adventures Ltd.,** P.O. Box 216, Kingston 7, Jamaica (☎ **809/927-2097;** fax 809/929-6967), whose owner, Pauline Stuart, offers individually designed, islandwide driving and hiking tours of Jamaica, including the Blue Mountains and canoe trips along its rivers. Her crew of Jamaican guides can accompany participants on expeditions ranging from one to several days. Each tour can be completely customized, and groups are limited to from six to eight people. The cost for one of these guides is between $35 and $150 a day, depending on the guide's level of expertise, plus tips, food, and accommodation for the guide. Camping gear can be rented. Many participants opt for all-inclusive packages priced at $55 to $90 per person per day, depending on the number of participants.

Unique Destinations, 307 Peaceable St., Ridgefield, CT 06877 (☎ and fax **203/431-1571**), specializes in Caribbean holidays off the beaten track. The emphasis is on adventure, nature, wildlife, culture, history, sports, local cuisine, and unusual accommodation choices. Programs include activities on the islands Dominica, Jamaica, Saba, St. Kitts, Nevis, St. Vincent and its satellite Grenadines including Bequia. Properties range from remote nature resorts to jungle and river lodges, even restored sugar plantation ruins. Activities include rain forest hiking, scuba diving, sailing, snorkeling, sea kayaking, horseback riding, art workshops, and naturalist-guided ecology and conservation-oriented tours.

In Search of the Big Wahoo

Some of the world's premier fishing grounds are found in the Caribbean—they're teeming with a spectacular variety of deep-sea game fish, including wahoo, sailfish, tuna, marlin, and dolphin (the fish, not the mammal). Among the shallow-water fish are tarpon, bonefish, pompano, and barracuda.

Spring through autumn is the best time to fish, although the sport is still practiced during the winter.

Puerto Rico is the fishing capital of the Caribbean—some 30 world records have been set there. Charters are plentiful in San Juan and Palmas del Mar.

Some of the other excellent fishing grounds are in the Cayman Islands, whose offshore waters are filled with tuna, yellowtail, and other catches; and the Dominican Republic, which attracts anglers in pursuit of sailfish, and bonito.

Those in search of marlin head for the north coast of Jamaica from September to April, whereas the south coast is favored in winter. Port Antonio is Jamaica's major fishing center.

The U.S. Virgin Islands are popular with vacationers pursuing Allison tuna, bonito, marlin, and wahoo. Red Hook on St. Thomas is the major charter center, although St. John and St. Croix lure anglers as well.

Ex-Ec Hikes and Tours of Dominica (☎ **800/667-3932**) specializes in week-long excursions to Dominica. Hiking is the main attraction, but side adventures entail scuba diving, whale watching, mountain bicycling, and snorkeling. The trips feature scenic drives through Carib Indian territory. The company also offers trips to St. Vincent.

Nature Expeditions (☎ **800/869-0639**) runs the best nine-day excursions to Trinidad and Tobago, going for $1,990 per person. Trip participants are based at the Asa Wright Nature Center, a 200-acre reserve on a former coffee plantation. Guests stay in individual cabins or in the center's guest house.

KAYAKING **Arawak Expeditions,** P.O. Box 853, Cruz Bay, St. John (☎ **800/238-8687** in the U.S., or 809/693-8312), is the only outfitter in the Virgin Islands offering overnight sea-kayaking/island-camping excursions. Full- and half-day trips are also available. You cruise through the island somewhat as the Arawaks did, except that they used dugout canoes. Today's vessels are two-person fiberglass kayaks complete with a foot-controlled rudder. The outfit provides kayaking gear, healthy meals, camping equipment, and two experienced guides. The cost of a full-day trip is $65, a half-day trip is $40, and multiday excursions range in price from $750 to $1,095.

SAILING (FOR WOMEN) A program for women of all ages and levels of nautical expertise is offered by **Womanship,** The Boat House, 410 Severn Ave., Annapolis, MD 21403 (☎ **800/342-9295** in the U.S., or 410/267-6661). It offers expert sailing instruction by women for a maximum of six students with two instructors. Tortola is the primary port of departure for the Caribbean trips, and sailing instruction takes place in the British Virgin Islands. Most courses last a full week from Sunday to Saturday, year-round except during August. Trips can be arranged for couples and families as well.

CRUISES FOR NATURALISTS The best wildlife cruises are packaged by **Oceanic Society Expeditions,** Fort Mason Center, Building E, San Francisco, CA 94123

(☎ **800/326-7491** in the U.S., or 415/441-1106). Whale-watching jaunts and some research-oriented trips are also a feature. You can swim with hump-backed whales in the Dominican Republic, or be part of the research swim with dolphins in The Bahamas. Another specialist in this field is **Tropical Adventures,** 111 Second Ave. N., Seattle, WA 98109 (☎ **800/247-3483** in the U.S., or 206/441-3483), which offers terrific packages to Saba.

4 Getting Married in the Caribbean

See also "The Best Honeymoon Resorts," in chapter 1, for specific resorts that offer wedding and honeymoon packages. **Club Med** (☎ **800/CLUB-MED**), and **Sandals** (☎ **800/SANDALS**) are two chains that have helped many couples tie the knot.

If you yearn to take the plunge on a sun-dappled island, here are some wedding basics on the islands:

ANGUILLA Couples need to file a license application on Anguilla, which takes approximately 48 hours to process. Presentation of a passport or a birth certificate and photo ID, and, if applicable, proof of divorce or death certificate of deceased spouse must be shown. The fee for the license and stamp duty is $284. For further information, contact Ms. Carmencita Davis, Registrar of Births, Deaths and Marriages, Judicial Department, The Valley, Anguilla, B.W.I. (☎ **809/497-2377**). A local wedding service, **Sunshine Lady Productions,** Box 85, The Valley, Anguilla, Leeward Islands, B.W.I. (☎ **809/497-2911;** fax 809/497-3884), will make the arrangements.

ANTIGUA There is a 24-hour waiting period for marriages on Antigua. A couple appears at the Ministry of Justice in the capital of St. John to complete and sign a declaration before a marriage coordinator and pays a $150 license fee. The coordinator will arrange for a marriage officer to perform a civil ceremony at any of Antigua's hotels or another venue selected by the couple. The fee for the marriage officer is $50. Several hotels and resorts offer wedding/honeymoon packages. For more information on civil or religious wedding ceremonies, contact the **Antigua Department of Tourism,** 610 Fifth Ave., Suite 311, New York, NY 10020 (☎ **212/541-4117**).

ARUBA Civil weddings are possible on Aruba only if one of the partners is an Aruban resident. However, visiting couples can arrange Roman Catholic, Protestant, and Jewish weddings on the island. For more information about planning a wedding on Aruba, contact the **Aruba Tourism Authority,** 1000 Harbor Blvd., Weehawken, NJ 08707 (☎ **800/TO-ARUBA** in the U.S., or 201/330-0800).

BARBADOS Couples can now marry the same day they arrive on Barbados, but must first obtain a marriage license from the **Ministry of Home Affairs** (☎ **246/228-8950**). Bring either a passport or a birth certificate and photo ID, $50 (U.S.) in fees, and $12.50 for the revenue stamp that can be obtained at the local post office, a letter from the authorized officiant who will perform the service, plus proof, if applicable, of pertinent deaths or divorces of a former spouse(s). A Roman Catholic wedding on Barbados carries additional requirements. For more information, contact the **Barbados Tourism Authority,** 800 Second Ave., New York, NY 10017 (☎ **800/221-9831** or 212/986-6516).

BONAIRE To get married on Bonaire, the bride and/or groom must have a temporary residency permit, obtained by writing a letter to the governor of the Island Territory of Bonaire, Wilhelminaplein 1, Kralendijk, Bonaire, N.A. The letter, submitted within two months of departure for Bonaire, should request permission to marry on Bonaire, apply for temporary residency, as well as inform the governor of your arrival and departure dates and the date you wish to marry. The partner who applies for residency must be on island for seven days before the wedding. A special dispensation must be issued by the governor if there is less than a 10-day time period between the announcement of the marriage and getting married. In addition, send three passport photos, copies of the bride's and groom's passports, birth certificates, and proof of divorce or in the case of widows and widowers, the death certificate of the deceased spouse.

If you desire, you can arrange your wedding on Bonaire through **Multro Travel and Tours,** Kaya Amazon 27B (P.O. Box 237), Bonaire, Dutch Antilles, Attn: Mrs. Marvel Tromp, (☎ **599/7-8334;** fax 599/7-8834), or check with the hotel where you're planning to stay. Some hotels arrange weddings on special request. For further information, contact the **Bonaire Tourist Office** (☎ **800/826-6247** in the U.S., or 212/956-5911).

BRITISH VIRGIN ISLANDS There is no requirement of island residency, but a couple must apply for a license at the attorney general's office, and stay in the British Virgin Islands for three days while the application is processed. You'll need to present a passport or original birth certificate and photo identification, plus certified proof of your marital status, plus any divorce or death certificates that apply to a former spouse(s). Two witnesses must accompany the couple. The fee is $110. Marriages can be performed by the local registrar or by the officiant of your choice. Contact the **Registrar's Office,** P.O. Box 418, Road Town, Tortola, B.V.I. (☎ **809/494-3701** or 809/494-3492).

CAYMAN ISLANDS Arrangements with a marriage officer must be made before arrival in the Cayman Islands in order to name the individual who will be officiating on the application. The application for a special marriage license, which costs $200, can be obtained from the **Deputy Secretary's Office,** Third Floor, Government Administration Building, George Town (☎ **345/949-7900**). There is no waiting period. Present a birth certificate plus the embarkation/disembarkation cards issued by the island's immigration authorities, along with divorce decrees or proof of a spouse's death (if applicable). Complete wedding services and packages are offered by **Cayman Weddings of Grand Cayman,** which is owned and operated by Caymanian marriage officers Vernon and Francine Jackson. For more information contact them at P.O. Box 678, Grand Cayman (☎ **345/949-8677;** fax 345/949-8237). A brochure, ***Getting Married in the Cayman Islands,*** is available from Government Information Services, Broadcasting House, Grand Cayman (☎ **345/949-8092;** fax 345/949-5936).

CURAÇAO Couples must be on the island two days before applying for a marriage license, for which there is a 14-day waiting period. Passport, birth certificate, return ticket, and divorce papers (if applicable) are required. The fee is subject to change, so call in advance. For further information, contact the **Curaçao Tourist Board,** 475 Park Ave. S., Suite 2000, New York, NY 10016 (☎ **212/683-7660;** fax 212/683-9337).

JAMAICA In high season, some Jamaican resorts witness several weddings a day. Many of the larger Jamaican resorts can arrange for an officiant, a photographer, and even the wedding cake and champagne. Some resorts, however, will even throw in your wedding with the cost of your honeymoon at the hotel. Both the Jamaican Tourist Board and your hotel, perhaps one of the many Sandals resorts in Jamaica, will assist you with the paperwork. Participants must reside on Jamaica for 24 hours before the ceremony. Bring birth certificates and affidavits saying you've never been married before, or, if you've been divorced, bring copies of your divorce papers, or in the case of widows and widowers, a copy of the deceased spouse's death certificate. The cost of the license and stamp duty is $200. The cost of the ceremony can range from $50 to $200, depending on how much legwork you want to do yourself. You may apply in person at the **Ministry of National Security and Justice,** 12 Ocean Blvd., Kingston, Jamaica (☎ **809/922-0080**).

PUERTO RICO There are no residency requirements. You'll need parental consent if either party is under 18. Blood tests are required, although a test conducted within 10 days of the ceremony on the U.S. mainland will suffice. A doctor in Puerto Rico must sign the license after conducting an examination of the bride and groom. For complete details, contact the **Commonwealth of Puerto Rico Health Department,** Demographic Register, 171 Quisaueya St., Hato Rey, PR 00917 (☎ **787/767-9120**).

ST. LUCIA Both parties must have remained on the island for 48 hours prior to the ceremony. Present your passport or birth certificate, plus (if either participant has been widowed or divorced) proof of death or divorce from the former spouse(s). Before the ceremony, it usually takes about two days to process all the paperwork. Fees usually run around $150 for a lawyer (one is usually needed for the application to the governor-general), $25 for the registrar to perform the ceremony, and $37.75 for the stamp duty and the license. Some resorts and vacation properties also offer wedding packages that include all the necessary arrangements for a single fee. For more information, contact the **St. Lucia Tourist Board,** 820 Second Ave., 9th Floor, New York, NY 10017 (☎ **212/867-2950;** fax 212/370-7867).

U.S. VIRGIN ISLANDS No blood tests or physical examinations are necessary, but there is a $25 license fee, a $25 notarized application, and an eight-day waiting period, which is sometimes waived, depending on circumstances. Civil ceremonies before a judge of the territorial court cost $200 each; religious ceremonies performed by clergy are equally valid. Fees and schedules for church weddings must be negotiated directly with the officiant. More information is available from the **U.S. Virgin Island Division of Tourism,** 1270 Avenue of the Americas, New York, NY 10020 (☎ **212/332-2222**).

The guide *Getting Married in the U.S. Virgin Islands* is distributed by U.S.V.I. tourism offices; it gives information on all three islands, including wedding planners, places of worship, florists, and limousine services. The guide also provides a listing of island accommodations that offer in-house wedding services.

Couples can apply for a marriage license for St. Thomas or St. John by contacting the **Territorial Court of the Virgin Islands,** P.O. Box 70, St. Thomas, U.S.V.I. 00804 (☎ **809/774-6680**). For weddings on St. Croix, applications are available by contacting the Territorial Court of the Virgin Islands, Family Division, P.O. Box 929, Christiansted, St. Croix, U.S.V.I. 00821-929 (☎ **809/778-9750**).

5 Health & Insurance

STAYING HEALTHY Finding a good doctor in the Caribbean is not a problem, and most speak English. See the "Fast Facts" section in each chapter for specific names and addresses on each individual island. Before you leave home, you can obtain a list of English-speaking doctors from the **International Association for Medical Assistance to Travelers (IAMAT),** in the United States at 417 Center St., Lewiston, NY 14092 (☎ **716/754-4883**); in Canada, at 40 Regal Rd., Guelph, ON N1K 1B5 (☎ **519/836-0102**).

If you have a chronic medical problem, always talk to your doctor before leaving home. For conditions such as epilepsy, a heart condition, diabetes, or an allergy, wear a **Medic Alert Identification Tag;** Medic Alert's 24-hour hotline enables a foreign doctor to obtain your medical records. For a lifetime membership, the cost is a well-spent $35 to $70, plus a $15 annual fee. To join, contact Medic Alert Foundation, 2323 Colorado Ave., Turlock, CA 95382 (☎ **800/825-3785**).

If you'd like more health information before you go to the Caribbean, write **Centers for Disease Control and Prevention (CDC),** 1600 Clifton Rd., NE, Atlanta, GA 30333. Some information is also available from the CDC Traveler's Hot Line at ☎ **404/332-4559,** or on the Internet at http://www.cdc. gov.

Although tap **water** is generally safe to drink, it's better to drink mineral water. Also, avoid iced drinks. Stick to beer, hot tea, or soft drinks.

If you experience **diarrhea,** moderate your eating habits and drink only mineral water until you recover. If symptoms persist, consult a doctor.

The Caribbean sun can be brutal. Wear sunglasses and a hat and use **sunscreen** liberally. Limit your time on the beach the first day. If you do overexpose yourself, stay out of the sun until you recover. If your exposure is followed by fever or chills, a headache, or a feeling of nausea or dizziness, see a doctor.

One of the biggest menaces are the "no-see-ums," which appear mainly in the early evening. You can't see these **gnats,** but you sure can "feel-um." Screens can't keep these critters out, so carry your favorite bug repellent.

Mosquitoes are a nuisance. Malaria-carrying mosquitoes in the Caribbean are confined largely to Haiti and the Dominican Republic. If you're visiting either, consult your doctor for preventive medicine at least eight weeks before you leave. Dengue fever is prevalent in the islands, most prominently on Montserrat, Antigua, St. Kitts, Dominica, and the Dominican Republic. Once thought to have been nearly eliminated, it has made a comeback. To date, no satisfactory treatment has been developed; visitors are advised to avoid mosquito bites—as if that were possible.

Vaccinations are not required to enter the Caribbean if you're coming from the United States, Britain, or Canada.

Infectious hepatitis has been reported on such islands as Dominica, Haiti, and Montserrat. Consult your doctor about the advisability of getting a gamma-globulin shot before you leave.

If you're staying in a regular Caribbean hotel, few preventive measures are generally needed. Take along an adequate supply of any **prescription drugs** that you need and a written prescription that uses the generic name of the drug, not the brand name. You may want to pack first-aid cream, insect repellent, aspirin, Band-Aids, and all that good stuff.

INSURANCE Review your present policies before traveling internationally; you may already have adequate coverage between them and what's offered by credit/charge-card companies if the trip tickets were purchased with their card. Fraternal organizations sometimes can provide policies that protect members in case of sickness or accident abroad.

Many homeowners' insurance policies cover theft of luggage during foreign travel and loss of documents (for instance, your airline ticket), although coverage is usually limited to about $500.

Some policies (and this is the type you should have) provide cash advances or transferal of funds so that you won't have to dip into your precious travel funds to settle medical bills.

If you've booked a charter flight, you'll probably have to pay a cancellation fee if you cancel a trip suddenly, even if you cancel because of an unforeseen crisis. It's possible to get insurance that will cover such a fee, either through travel agencies or through a credit/charge-card company, when such insurance is written into tickets paid for by the card.

Companies offering special travel insurance policies include the following: **Travel Guard International,** 1145 Clark St., Stevens Point, WI 54481 (☎ **800/826-1300** outside Wisconsin, or 715/345-0505), offers a comprehensive travel protection policy that covers lost luggage, emergency assistance, accidental death, trip cancellation, and medical coverage abroad. Package costs start at $40 and are based on your total trip cost. Children under 16 are automatically covered if accompanying adults have purchased a policy.

Travelers Insurance PAK, Travel Insured International, P.O. Box 280568, East Hartford, CT 06128 (☎ **800/243-3174** or 860/528-7663), offers illness and accident coverage costing from $10 for 6 to 10 days. For lost or damaged luggage, $500 worth of coverage costs $20 for 6 to 10 days. Trip cancellation insurance is $5.50 per $100 of coverage to a limit of $10,000 per person.

World Access Service Corporation, 6600 W. Broad St., P.O. Box 11188, Richmond, VA 23230 (☎ **800/284-8300** or 804/285-3300), is one of the nation's largest travel insurance and emergency assistance providers. Its toll-free hotline is staffed 24 hours. Services include trip cancellation/interruption, travel delay, emergency medical, lost baggage or baggage delay, bankruptcy/default protection, travel accident coverage, emergency medical evacuation, and legal assistance when traveling. Another feature of its medical assistance program is its on-site hospital payment. Plan prices start at $34.

Mutual of Omaha (Tele-Trip), Mutual of Omaha Plaza, Omaha, NE 68175 (☎ **800/228-9792**), offers insurance packages priced from $49 per person for a cruise or tour valued at $1,000, including travel-assistance services, and financial protection against trip cancellation, trip interruption, flight and baggage delays, accident-related medical costs, accidental death and/or dismemberment, and medical evacuation coverages. An application for insurance can be arranged over the phone with a major credit or charge card.

6 Tips for Travelers with Special Needs

FOR TRAVELERS WITH DISABILITIES You can obtain a free copy of ***Air Transportation of Handicapped Persons,*** published by the U.S. Department of Transportation. Write for Free Advisory Circular No. AC12032, Distribution Unit, U.S. Department of Transportation, Publications Division, 3341Q 75th Ave., Landover, MD 20785 (☎ **301/322-4961;** fax 301/386-5394). Only written requests are accepted.

For names and addresses of operators of tours specifically for visitors with disabilities, and other relevant information, contact the **Society for the Advancement of Travel for the Handicapped (SATH),** 347 Fifth Ave., Suite 610, New York, NY 10016 (☎ **212/447-7284;** fax 212/725-8253). Yearly membership dues in the society are $45, $25 for senior citizens and students. Send a self-addressed, stamped envelope and $5. SATH will also provide you with hotel/resort accessibility for Caribbean destinations.

The **Information Center for Individuals with Disabilities,** Fort Point Place, 27–43 Wormwood Place, Boston, MA 02210 (☎ **617/727-5540,** or 800/462-5015 in Massachusetts), is another good source. It has lists of travel agents who specialize in tours for persons with disabilities, and provides travel-tip fact sheets for Caribbean destinations.

For the blind or visually impaired, the best source of information is the **American Foundation for the Blind,** 11 Penn Plaza, Suite 300, New York, NY 10001

(☎ **800/232-5463** to order information kits and supplies, or 212/502-7600). It acts as a referral source for travelers and can offer advice on the transport and border formalities for seeing-eye dogs.

One of the best organizations serving the needs of persons with disabilities is **Flying Wheels Travel,** 143 West Bridge (P.O. Box 382), Owatoona, MN 55060 (☎ **800/535-6790** or 507/451-5005). It offers customized, all-inclusive vacation packages in the Caribbean.

For a $25 annual fee, consider joining **Mobility International USA,** P.O. Box 10767, Eugene, OR 97440 (☎ **541/343-1284** voice and TDD). It answers questions on various destinations and also offers discounts on its programs, videos, and publications. Their quarterly newsletter, *Over the Rainbow,* provides information on Caribbean hotel chains, accessibility, and transportation.

TIPS FOR BRITISH TRAVELERS The **Royal Association for Disability and Rehabilitation (RADAR),** Unit 12, City Forum, 250 City Rd., London, ECIV 8AF (☎ **0171/250-3222**), publishes holiday "fact packs," three in all, which sell for £2 each or all three for £5. The first one provides general information, including planning and booking a holiday, insurance, finances, and useful organization and holiday providers. The second outlines transportation available when going abroad and equipment for rent. The third deals with specialized accommodations.

FOR GAY & LESBIAN TRAVELERS Some of the islands are more gay friendly than others. These would include all the U.S. possessions, notably Puerto Rico, which is hailed as the "gay capital of the Caribbean," and offers gay guest houses, nightclubs, bars, and discos. To a lesser extent, much of St. Thomas, St. John, and St. Croix are welcoming, though they have nowhere near the number of gay-oriented establishments as Puerto Rico.

The French islands—St. Barts, St. Martin, Guadeloupe, and Martinique—are technically an extension of mainland France, and the French have always regarded homosexuality with a certain blasé tolerance. The Dutch islands of Aruba, Bonaire, and Curaçao are quite conservative, so discretion is suggested.

Gay life is fairly secretive in many of the sleepy islands of the Caribbean. There are even some islands with repressive laws, including Jamaica and Barbados. Homosexuality is illegal in Barbados, and there is often a lack of tolerance here in spite of the large number of gay residents and visitors. Jamaica is the most homophobic island in the Caribbean, with harsh antigay laws, even though there is a large local gay population. One local advised that it's not smart for a white gay man to wander the streets of Jamaica at night.

Many all-inclusive resorts, notably the famous Sandals of Jamaica, have discriminatory policies. Although Sandals started off welcoming "any two people in love," they quickly switched to allowing only male-female couples. Gays are definitely excluded from their love nests. However, not all all-inclusives practice such blatant discrimination. Hedonism II, a rival of Sandals in Negril, is a "couples-only" resort, but any combination will do here. The Grand Hotel Lido, a more upscale all-inclusive in Negril, will welcome whatever combination shows up (even singles, for that matter).

Men can order *Spartacus* ($32.95), the international gay guide, or *Odysseus, The International Gay Travel Planner* ($25), an annually published guide to international gay accommodations. Both lesbians and gay men might want to pick up a copy of *Gay Travel A to Z* ($16), which specializes in general information, as well as listings of bars, hotels, restaurants, and places of interest for gay travelers throughout the world. These books and others are available from **Giovanni's Room,** 1145 Pine St., Philadelphia, PA 19107 (☎ **215/923-2960**).

Our World, 1104 N. Nova Rd., Suite 251, Daytona Beach, FL 32117 (☎ **904/441-5367**), is a magazine devoted to options and bargains for gay and lesbian travel worldwide. It costs $35 for 10 issues. ***Out and About,*** 8 W. 19th St., Suite 401, New York, NY 10011 (☎ **800/929-2268**), has been hailed for its "straight" reporting about gay travel. It profiles the best gay or gay-friendly hotels, restaurants, gyms, clubs, and other places, with coverage of destinations throughout the world. The cost is $49 a year for 10 information-packed issues, plus four events calendars. It aims for the more upscale gay male and lesbian traveler, and has been praised by everybody from *Travel and Leisure* to the *New York Times.* Both these publications are also available at most gay and lesbian bookstores.

The **International Gay Travel Association (IGTA),** P.O. Box 4974, Key West, FL 33041 (☎ **800/448-8550**), encourages gay and lesbian travel worldwide. With around 1,200 member agencies, it specializes in networking, providing the information travelers would need to link up with the appropriate gay-friendly service organization or tour specialist. It offers quarterly newsletters, marketing mailings, and a membership directory that's updated four times a year. Travel agents who are IGTA members will be tied into this organization's vast information resources.

FOR SENIORS Write for a free booklet called *101 Tips for the Mature Traveler,* available from Grand Circle Travel, 347 Congress St., Suite 3A, Boston, MA 02210 (☎ **800/221-2610** or 617/350-7500). This tour operator offers extended vacations, escorted programs, and cruises that feature unique learning experiences for seniors at competitive prices.

SAGA International Holidays, 222 Berkeley St., Boston, MA 02116 (☎ **800/343-0273**), books senior citizens on cruises to the Caribbean, offering them good value. To participate, persons must be 50-plus. Medical insurance is included in the net price of the cruise-ship booking.

7 Flying to the Caribbean

All the biggest islands have regularly scheduled airline service from North America, and the smaller islands are tied into this vast network through their own carriers. For details of how to reach each island, see the "Getting There" sections in the individual island chapters.

If you fly in summer, spring, and fall, you'll see substantial reductions on airfares to the Caribbean. It's usually cheaper to fly Monday to Thursday. Also, consider air-and-land packages, which offer reduced rates.

SOURCES FOR DISCOUNT TICKETS

BUCKET SHOPS (CONSOLIDATORS) Consolidators exist in many shapes and forms. In its purest sense, a bucket shop acts as a clearinghouse for blocks of tickets that airlines discount and consign during normally slow periods of air travel. In the case of the Caribbean, that means from mid-April to mid-December.

Tickets are sometimes, but not always, discounted 20% to 35%. Terms of payment can vary, anywhere from 45 days prior to departure to the last minute. Discounted tickets can also be purchased through regular travel agents, who usually mark up the ticket 8% to 10%, maybe more, thereby greatly reducing your discount.

A survey conducted of flyers who use consolidator tickets found only one major complaint: You can't arrange for advance seat assignment. The survey revealed that *most* flyers received a savings off the regular price. But, and here's the hitch, many flyers reported no savings at all, as the airlines will sometimes match the consolidator ticket with a promotional fare. The situation calls for some careful investigation on your part to determine just how much you're saving.

Bucket shops abound from coast to coast. Look for their ads in your local newspaper's travel section.

In New York, try **TFI Tours International,** 34 W. 32nd St., 12th Floor, New York, NY 10001 (☎ **800/745-8000** outside New York State, or 212/736-1140). This tour company offers services to 177 cities worldwide.

CHARTER FLIGHTS Many of the major carriers offer charter flights at rates that are sometimes 30% (or more) off the regular airfare. There are some drawbacks, however. Advance booking of up to 45 days or more may be required, and there are hefty cancellation penalties, although you can take out insurance against emergency cancellations.

Since charter flights are so complicated, it's best to ask a good travel agent to explain the problems and advantages. Sometimes charters require ground arrangements, such as the prebooking of hotel rooms.

Council Travel (☎ **800/226-8624**) occasionally offers reduced fares to the Caribbean. Call for the office nearest you.

REBATORS To confuse the situation even more, rebators have also begun to compete in the low-cost airfare market. These outfits pass along to the passenger part of their commission, although many of them assess a fee for their services. They're not the same as travel agents, but they sometimes offer roughly similar services, such as discounted land arrangements, including hotels and car rentals. Most rebators offer discounts averaging anywhere from 10% to 25% (but this could vary from place to place), plus a handling charge.

Travel Avenue, 10 S. Riverside Plaza, Suite 1404, Chicago, IL 60606 (☎ **800/333-3335** in the U.S., or 312/876-6866), is one of the oldest agencies of its kind. It offers up-front cash rebates on every airline ticket over $300 it sells. It sells airline tickets to independent travelers who have already worked out their travel plans. Also available are tour and cruise fares, plus hotel bookings.

Another major rebator is **The Smart Traveller,** 3111 SW 27th Ave. (P.O. Box 330010), Miami, FL 33133 (☎ **800/448-3338** in the U.S., or 305/443-3544; fax 305/443-3544). This agency offers discounts on package tours, Caribbean cruises, dive packages, and villa and condo rentals.

TRAVEL CLUBS Travel clubs supply an unsold inventory of tickets that are discounted from 20% to 60%. After you pay an annual fee, you're given a "hotline" number to call to find out what discounts are available. Some discounts become available a few days in advance of actual departure, some a week in advance, and some as much as a month. Of course, you're limited to what's available, so you have to be flexible. Some of the best of these clubs are listed below.

Moment's Notice, 7301 New Utrecht Ave., Brooklyn, NY 11204 (☎ **212/486-0500** or 718/234-6295), charges $25 per year for membership, which allows spur-of-the-moment participation in dozens of tours. Its discounted air-and-land packages to all Caribbean islands sometimes represent substantial savings over what you'd have paid through more conventional channels. Members can call the hotline (☎ **212/873-0908**) to learn what options are available. Most of the company's best-valued tours depart from JFK, LaGuardia, and Newark airports.

Travelers Advantage, 3033 South Parker Rd., Suite 900, Aurora, CO 80014 (☎ **800/TEL-TRIP**), offers a three-month trial offer for $1 and an annual membership fee for $49. This includes the Half Price HotelCard, granting you 50% off regular published room rates at more than 3,000 participating hotels, both foreign and domestic. Travelers Advantage is a full service travel agency. For membership information, call ☎ **800/548-1116.**

Another club, **Encore Travel Club,** 4501 Forbes Blvd., Lanham, MD 20706 (☎ **800/638-8976** in the U.S.), charges $49.95 a year for membership, which offers up to 50% discounts at more than 4,000 hotels. It also offers discounts on airfare, cruises, and car rentals through its volume purchase plans. Membership includes a travel package outlining the company's many services, and use of a toll-free phone number for advice and information.

8 Cruises

Here's a brief rundown of some of the major cruise lines and cruise specialists serving the Caribbean. For more detailed information, pick up a copy of *Frommer's Caribbean Cruises,* 2nd Edition, and *Frommer's Caribbean Ports of Call,* 1st Edition.

How should you book your cruise and get to the port of embarkation before the good times roll? If you've developed a dialogue over the years with a favorite travel agency, by all means, leave the details to the tried and true. Many agents will propose a package deal from the principal airport closest to your residence to the airport nearest to the cruise-departure point. It's possible to purchase your air ticket on your own and book your cruise ticket separately, but in most cases, you'll save money by combining the fares into a package deal. You're likely to save money, sometimes lots of money, by contacting a specialist whose past successes have focused on booking cruises. He or she will be likely to match you with a cruise line whose priorities and style are compatible with your needs and wants, and also steer you toward any of the special promotions that come and go as frequently as Caribbean rainstorms.

Some of the most likely contenders include the following: **Ambassador Tours,** 120 Montgomery St., Suite 400, San Francisco, CA 94104 (☎ **800/989-9000** or 415/981/5678); **Cruises Inc.,** 5000 Campuswood Dr. E., Syracuse, NY 13057 (☎ **800/854-0500** or 315/463-9695); **Cruises of Distinction,** 2750 S. Woodward Ave., Bloomfield Hills, MI 48304 (☎ **800/634-3445** or 810/332-3030); **Cruise Fairs of America,** Century Plaza Towers, 2029 Century Park East, Suite 950, Los Angeles, CA 90067 (☎ **800/456-4FUN** or 310/556-2925); **Kelly Cruises,** 1315 W. 22nd St., Suite 105, Oak Brook, IL 60521 (☎ **800/837-7447** or 708/990-1111); and **Hartford Holidays Travel,** 626 Willis Ave., Williston Park, NY 11596 (☎ **800/828-4813**). Any of these stay tuned to last-minute price wars brewing between such megacarriers as Carnival, Princess, Royal Caribbean, Holland America, as well as such low-budget contenders as Dolphin and Commodore.

Regardless of the line you opt for, there's a strong possibility that your cruise will depart from Miami, a city that within the last 20 years has succeeded at defining itself as the cruise capital of the world. To a somewhat lesser extent, vessels also depart for Caribbean waters from San Juan, New York, Port Everglades, Tampa, and New Orleans. Europeans can board ships in Europe, and then sail transatlantic on their way to ports in the Caribbean.

Most of the cruise ships travel at night, arriving the next morning at the day's port of call. Once their ship is anchored, passengers can go ashore for sightseeing, shopping, swimming/snorkeling, and snacking. Cruise prices vary widely. Sometimes the same route with the same ports of call carries different fares, according to the amenities and level of luxury featured aboard the cruise ship.

American Canadian Caribbean (☎ **800/556-7450** or 401/247-0955) is a Rhode Island–based cruise outfit whose shallow-draft, small-scale coastal cruisers have been studied with almost obsessive interest by most of their competitors. They embark on

7- to 12- day excursions through complicated shoals, near Caribbean landmasses where larger ships cannot go. Although itineraries at this small-scale outfitter, whose level of repeat passengers is exceptionally high, are likely to change, at least one of its trio of ships spends part of its winter cruising around The Bahamas, the Virgin Islands, the Panama Canal, and the coasts of Central America.

Carnival Cruise Lines (☎ **800/438-6744** or 305/599-2600), a specialist in the maintenance of some of the biggest and most brightly decorated ships afloat, is the richest, boldest, brashest, and most successful mass-market cruise line in the world. Eight of its megavessels depart from Florida or Caribbean ports that include Miami, Tampa, and San Juan, and four of them specialize in seven-day tours that feature stopovers at selected ports in the U.S. Virgin Islands, and other ports that include Aruba, San Juan, Guadeloupe, Grenada, Grand Cayman, and Jamaica. Of those four, the one that's likely to attract special notice in 1998 is the supermegaship *Destiny,* which at 101,000 tons is the largest cruise ship in the world. Most cruises offer good value, last from three to seven nights, and feature nonstop activities, lots of glitter, and the hustle and bustle of armies of clients and crew members embarking and disembarking at every port. Cuisine and party-colored drinks are plentiful, although with vessels of this size, might convey a hint of being mass produced. The overall atmosphere is comparable to a floating theme park with hordes of visitors, loaded with whimsy and with lots of emphasis on partying in a style you might have expected in Atlantic City. Lots of single passengers, some of them with gleams in their eye, opt for this line, and some actually get lucky. The average onboard age is a relatively youthful 42, although ages range from 3 to 95.

Celebrity Cruises (☎ **800/437-3111** or 305/262-8322) maintains five newly built, medium-to-large size ships offering cruises of between 7 and 17 nights. In addition to stops at such ports as Key West, San Juan, Grand Cayman, Ocho Rios, Antigua, and Curaçao, among others, at least four of its ships dock in St. Thomas, at least for a day. The niche this line has created is unpretentious but classy, several notches above mass-market, but with pricing that's nonetheless relatively competitive. Accommodations are roomy and well equipped, and cuisine is among the most intensely cultivated of any of its competitors afloat.

Costa Cruise Lines (☎ **800/462-6782** or 305/358-7325), the U.S.-based branch of a cruise line that has thrived in Italy for about a century, maintains hefty to megasize vessels that are newer than those of many other lines afloat. Two of these offer virtually identical jaunts through the western and eastern Caribbean on alternate weeks, departing from Fort Lauderdale. Ports of call during the eastern Caribbean itineraries of both vessels include stopovers in St. Thomas, Serena Cay (a private island off the coast of the Dominican Republic known for its beaches), Grand Cayman, Jamaica, and in some cases, Key West and Cozumel. There's an Italian flavor and lots of Italian design on board here, and an atmosphere of relaxed indulgence. The ships—*CostaRomantica* and *CostaVictoria*—feature tame versions of ancient Roman Bacchanalia as well as such celebrations as *Festa Italiana,* and focaccia and pizza parties by the pool.

Clipper Cruise Line (☎ **800/325-0010**) has ships that are small, conservative, and lack most of the amenities offered aboard the emerging crop of megavessels. The ambience is all-American, middle-American, and not as cheap as you might have thought, considering the price you'll pay for stripped-down amenities and a sometimes inexperienced staff. The ports of call these small ships visit, however, tend to be somewhat more exotic than those visited by larger ships, and include Dominica and such Grenadine outposts as Bequia, Mustique, and Petit St. Vincent. Some of the vessels make transits of the Panama Canal and visit coastal resorts in Costa Rica.

Club Med Cruises (☎ **800/4-LESHIP**), as its name implies, is basically Club-Med-at-sea, and if you like what you saw at a land-based Club Med, you'll appreciate the Gallic summer camp for adults you're likely to find aboard this outfit's ships, one of which sails the Caribbean. Its vessels are the largest cruise ships with sails, but frankly, they're in use less often than you might hope for, and no one aboard shows any qualms about motoring, instead of sailing, between such ports of call as St. Barts, St. Kitts, St. Lucia, and scattered ports in the Virgin Islands and Venezuela. The venue encourages a sense of *laissez rouler les bons temps* ("let the good times roll") and stresses its French- and English-speaking sense of lighthearted internationalism. Onboard cuisine is a lot less glamorous than you might have expected from a France-based outlet, served in ample but straightforward portions.

Commodore Cruise Line (☎ **800/237-5361** or 954/967-2100) has only one ship, a solid and seaworthy vessel, but it's much less competitive than many of the newer vessels being launched by more affluent lines. Clients who embark for jaunts through the western Caribbean usually spend three full days at sea, visiting ports in Jamaica, the Cayman Islands, and Honduras. The ship has a relative lack of state-of-the-art facilities, but its low rates make an almost impossible dream—participation in a Caribbean cruise—a reality for many first-time cruisers without a lot of cash.

Cunard (☎ **800/221-4770**), despite whirlwinds of recent fiscal and managerial problems, is famous for its British flair and its ownership of the legendary *QE2.* The line's smallest and most opulent vessels are *Sea Goddess I* and *II,* which resemble small but choice, and extremely expensive, private yachts when compared to a Carnival megaship. Both of these ships define St. Thomas, and to a lesser degree, Barbados, as their home port during part of each winter. From here, they begin transits through the Panama Canal and visit ports throughout the central and southern Caribbean. Onboard ambience is high-priced, high-class, and although occasionally somewhat staid, the venue is usually very grand.

Dolphin Cruise Lines (☎ **800/222-1003** or 305/358-5122) bases its success on low-cost, relatively unglittery cruises aboard a trio of much-renovated older vessels with somewhat outmoded amenities that are anything but cutting-edge. Nothing is particularly fancy, but no one seems to mind in view of the good value. Cruise bargain-hunters and retirees often make up the passenger list. One of the ships, *SeaBreeze,* spends more time in the eastern Caribbean than the others, making regular stops on alternate weeks in Puerto Rico and the U.S. Virgin Islands, usually with three days at sea in between.

Holland America Line—Westours (☎ **800/426-0327** or 206/281-3535) is the most high-toned of the mass-market cruise lines, with eight respectably hefty and good-looking ships that represent one of the great maritime nations, the Netherlands. Cruises, which stop at deepwater, relatively mainstream ports throughout the Caribbean, last for an average of seven days. They usually offer solid value, with very few jolts or surprises, and an overall sense of squeaky-clean thrift and value. Expect a solid, well-grounded clientele of mature travelers on board who expect (and get) returns for their dollar. Cruise stopovers, among others, include Key West, Grand Cayman, St. Maarten, St. Lucia, Curaçao, Barbados, and St. Thomas. Late-night revelers and serious partiers might want to book cruises on other lines such as Carnival.

Norwegian Cruise Line (☎ **800/327-7030** or 305/445-0866) appeals to all ages and income levels, with Scandinavian officers, an international staff, and a pervasive modern Viking theme. Two of the company's five ships (the relatively informal *Seaward* and the line's dignified flagship, *Norway*) make it a point to stop in St. Thomas as part of circuits that encompass visits to such other points as Santo Domingo,

St. Lucia, and St. Kitts. Others focus on visits to Norwegian Cruise Line's private Bahamian island, Great Stirrup Cay, St. Maarten, St. Kitts, and St. Lucia. One of the ships (*Seaward*) defines its home port as San Juan, a fact that places participants within the heart of Caribbean action sooner than vessels that depart from South Florida. The company's largest ship and corporate symbol (the *Norway*) offers the best amenities and services. Between visits in port, the line administers a snappy array of onboard activities and, in many cases, a revolving array of international sports figures for game tips and lectures.

Princess Cruises (☎ **800/421-0522** or 310/553-1770) has a large and far-flung fleet, at least five members of which sail in Caribbean and Bahamian waters. The company is one of the very few in the world offering luxury accommodations and upscale service aboard its megaships. These usually carry a smaller number of passengers than similarly sized vessels on less elegant lines. Cruises last 7 to 11 days, and visit both major and minor islands. The clientele is upscale, with an average passenger age of 55 or over. A respectable percentage of the staff is British. One of its newest megaships, *Dawn Princess,* launched in spring 1997, stops at St. Thomas once every two weeks as part of seven-day circuits from San Juan through the eastern Caribbean. This state-of-the-art ship, patterned on its megaliner prototype, *Sun Princess,* is one of the most regal of the Princess fleet.

Radisson Seven Seas Cruises (☎ **800/477-7500**) is noted for the level of glamour and prestige that permeates its cruises, and it sends only one of its ships, the *Radisson Diamond,* into the Caribbean on a regular basis. Designed along lines distinctly different from every cruise line afloat, it's a relatively slow but stable ship floating atop submerged pontoons similar to those used by catamarans or oil-drilling platforms in the North Sea. Despite the fact that its design is not likely to be duplicated anytime soon within the cruise industry, passengers appreciate it for its fine cuisine, upscale service, and suitability for corporate conventions at sea. Cruises are relatively expensive compared to those offered by less-prestigious lines. They last from 7 to 15 days, usually focusing on ports within Costa Rica, and stop en route at Curaçao, Aruba, Grand Cayman, Cayman Brac, Cartagena, and Cozumel.

Royal Caribbean Cruise Line (RCCL) (☎ **305/539-6000**) leads the industry in the development of megaships. Most of this company's dozen or so vessels weigh in at around 73,000 tons, are among the largest of any line afloat, and represent a roster of floating hardware that's more impressive than that of many national navies. Marketed as a mainstream, mass-market cruise line whose components have been fine-tuned through endless repetition, the line encourages a house-party theme that's somehow a bit less frenetic than that found aboard the megaships of other cruise lines. The company is well run, and there are enough onboard activities to suit virtually any taste and age level. Though accommodations and accouterments are more than adequate, they are not upscale, and cabins aboard some of the line's older vessels tend to be a bit more cramped than the industry norm. Using either Miami or San Juan as their home port, RCCL ships call regularly at such oft-visited ports as St. Thomas, San Juan, Ocho Rios, St. Maarten, Grand Cayman, and Curaçao. RCCL is the only cruise line in the business that owns, outright, two tropical beaches whose sands and watersports facilities are the focus of many of the company's cruises. They're sited in isolated areas of Haiti and The Bahamas, and, according to rumors, the company is in the market to soon acquire a third.

Royal Olympic Cruises (☎ **800/872-6400** or 212/397-6400), formed in 1995 from a merger between Sun Lines and Epirotiki Cruises, is a well-respected Greek shipping line that operates the only Greek-registered ship in the Caribbean, the comfortable but aging and well-maintained *Stella Solaris.* Most stopovers at Caribbean ports (Trinidad, St. Vincent, Bequia, Barbados, and Curaçao) are configured as visits en route to either the Amazon or the Panama Canal. Despite the age of the ship, its many restorations and the cheerfulness of one of the best staffs of any vessel afloat make this a consistently popular ship.

Seabourn Cruise Line (☎ **800/929-9595** or 415/391-7444) is a desirable, upscale, and expensive outfit whose *Seabourn Pride* offers cruises of from 10 to 14 days in unabashed luxury. It's the *ne plus ultra* of seagoing elegance. Cruises last from 7 to 16 days, and, depending on the itinerary, might include stops at such islands as St. Thomas, Jost Van Dyke, Virgin Gorda, and the French part of St. Martin en route to and from the Panama Canal. There are more activities than you'd expect aboard such a relatively small ship (10,000 tons), and an absolutely amazing amount of onboard space per passenger. Cuisine is superb, served within a dining room that's unapologetically formal. Throughout every venue, the emphasis is on topnotch service, luxury, discretion, and impeccably good taste.

Seawind Cruises (☎ **800/356-5566** or 305/573-3222) operates only one ship, the seaworthy but not particularly glamorous *Seawind Crown,* the only major cruise ship based in the southern Caribbean port of Aruba. Although it's a large ship, it carries only 624 passengers, allowing lots of room for wandering and relaxing. Most of its cruises last seven nights, and focus on southern Caribbean islands that are too far from south Florida to be efficiently visited by most major cruise ships. They include Trinidad and Tobago, as well as Martinique, Curaçao, and St. Lucia. The line is adept at arranging land-based holidays, sometimes at startlingly low rates, either before or after a cruise, at hotels on Aruba, St. Lucia, or Martinique.

Star Clippers (☎ **800/442-0553** or 305/442-0550) owns vessels that were built as the hobby (some say obsession) of a Swedish industrialist who lavished more than $40 million on each of the two replicas of the fastest sailing vessels ever constructed, the 19th-century clipper ships. The vessels manage to be both radical and traditional at the same time, based on the best shipbuilding principles of the 19th century along with computer-enhanced space-age materials. By anyone's point of view, they are astonishingly accurate improvements upon the original clipper ships of long ago. Aboard each ship, only 10 deckhands are needed to hoist sails that aboard the original clippers would have required four dozen. In winter, one of the line's two vessels operates from bases in Antigua and Barbados, and includes week-long jaunts that stop in St. Vincent, Grenada, Carriacou, and Martinique.

Tall Ship Adventures (☎ **800/662-0090** or 303/755-7983) has only one ship—a tall-masted reconfiguration of a circa-1917 schooner that was originally built to carry copper ore from the coast of Chile to the Baltic ports of Germany. Today, after extensive refittings, it carries sailing ship aficionados on meandering trips through the Virgin Islands. It focuses more intently on the waters and scattered islets of the British Virgin Islands than any other cruise line, spending most of its winter exploring such relatively remote outposts as Peter Island, Norman Island, Cooper Island, Marina Cay, Long Bay, and sites on or slightly offshore from Virgin Gorda. Cruises last a week, begin and depart from Road Town, on Tortola, and make absolutely no excuse for the bare-boned but invigorating experiences they are.

Windjammer Barefoot Cruises (☎ **800/327-2601** or 305/672-6453) is similar in ambience to the above-mentioned Tall Ship Adventures and operates seven sailing ships, most of which are faithful renovations of antique schooners or sail-driven private yachts. Most have illustrious antecedents, including stints as the private getaway ships of sometimes notorious billionaires or wannabes. They're proud of their role as some of the least formal boats afloat, with few passengers ever bringing more than a roster of shorts and T-shirts for their time aboard. The armada goes to rarely visited outposts, with special emphasis on the scattered reefs and cays of the Virgin Islands and the Grenadines. If you're looking for something a bit more staid, consider the fleet's durable but not very exciting supply ship, *Amazing Grace,* a freighter-style vessel that carries provisions and supplies for the company's other (sailing) ships. At least some of the stops *Amazing Grace* makes are within the Virgin Islands, covered as part of its sweeping 13-day peregrinations between Freeport, The Bahamas, and Trinidad.

Windstar Cruises (☎ **800/258-7245** or 206/281-3535) has a fleet of sailing ships that utilize adaptations of 19th-century designs and 21st-century materials. In fall, winter, and spring, its look-alike vessels make seven-day excursions that include stops at St. Thomas, Jost Van Dyke, Virgin Gorda, Saba, French St. Martin (*Wind Spirit*), Barbados, Nevis, St. Barts, Bequia, and the rarely visited Ile des Saintes off Guadeloupe. An experience aboard this ship is unlike that offered by any diesel-driven cruise ship, and quite a bit more stylish (with the possible exception of Star Clippers; see above) than aboard the other sailing ships listed within this overview.

9 Chartering Your Own Boat

Experienced sailors and navigators can charter "bareboat," a rental with a fully equipped boat but with no captain or crew. You're on your own, and you'll have to prove your qualifications before you're allowed to rent such a craft. Even an experienced skipper may want to take along someone familiar with local waters, which may in some places be tricky.

You can also charter a boat with a skipper and crew. Charter yachts, varying from 50 to more than 100 feet, can accommodate four to a dozen people.

Most yachts are rented on a weekly basis, with a fully stocked bar, plus equipment for fishing and water sports. The average charter carries four to six passengers, and usually is reserved for a week.

The Moorings, 19345 U.S. 19 North, 4th Floor, Clearwater, FL 34624 (☎ **800/535-7289** in the U.S. and Canada, or 813/535-1446; fax 813/530-9747), operates one of the largest charter yacht operations in the Caribbean, with its main branch located in the British Virgin Islands. Other Caribbean and Bahamian branches are in St. Martin, Guadeloupe, Martinique, St. Lucia, and Grenada, to name a few, and each has a regatta of yachts, some of which are available for chartering. Depending on their size, yachts are rented to up to four couples at a time. Arrangements can be made either for bareboating (qualified sailors only) or for renting yachts with a full crew and cook. Depending on circumstances, the vessels come equipped with a barbecue, snorkeling gear, a dinghy, and linens, and the boats are serviced by an experienced staff of mechanics, electricians, riggers, and cleaners. If you're going out on your own, you'll get a thorough briefing about Caribbean waters, reefs, and anchorages. Seven-night combined hotel-and-crewed-yacht packages can run $675 to $1,195 per person.

Nicholson Yacht Charters, 78 Bolton St., Cambridge, MA 02140-3321 (☎ **800/662-6066** in the U.S., or 617/661-0555; fax 617/661-0554), or P.O. Box 103, St. John's, Antigua, W.I., is one of the best in the business, handling charter yachts for use throughout the Caribbean basin, particularly the route between Dutch-held Sint Maarten and Grenada and the routes around the U.S. Virgin Islands and British Virgin Islands and Puerto Rico. The company features boats of all sizes, and it can arrange rentals of motor or sailing yachts up to 298 feet long. Especially popular are arrangements where two or more yachts, each sleeping eight guests in four equal double cabins, race each other from island to island during the day, anchoring near each other in secluded coves or at berths in Caribbean capitals at night. The price for renting a yacht depends on the number in your party, the size of the vessel, and the time of the year. Weekly rates range from $3,500 up to $50,000 or so. You can get a really splendid vessel for $12,000 to $25,000 weekly, and at that price, why not?

Sunsail, 980 Awald Rd., Suite 302, Annapolis Landing Marina, Annapolis, MD 21403 (☎ **800/327-2276** in the U.S., or 410/280-2553), specializes in yacht chartering from its bases in the British Virgin Islands, Antigua, St. Lucia, the French West Indies, and The Bahamas. More than 30 bareboat and crewed yachts between 30 and 56 feet are available for cruising these waters, offering programs such as Caribbean racing and regattas, flotilla sailing, skippered sailing, and one-way or stay-and-sail barefoot cruises. The company usually requires a deposit of 25% of the total rental fee; arrangements should be made four to six months in advance. Clients with flexible schedules need only reserve a month in advance. Sunsail also offers charter flights from the United States to the Virgin Islands.

10 Package Tours

To save time comparing the price and value of all the package tours out there, call **TourScan,** P.O. Box 2367, Darien, CT 06820 (☎ **800/962-2080** or 203/655-8091). Every season, the company gathers and computerizes the contents of about 200 brochures containing 10,000 different vacations in the Caribbean, The Bahamas, and Bermuda. TourScan selects the best value at each hotel and condo. Two catalogs are printed each year, which list every hotel and condo on almost every Caribbean island, in all price ranges (the scope of the islands and resort hotels is amazing). Write to TourScan to request their $4 catalogs, the price of which is credited to any TourScan vacation. Founded in 1987, the company is also a full-service travel agency, specializing in the Caribbean.

Another good deal might be a combined land-and-air package offered by one of the major U.S. carriers. Call their toll-free numbers for more information: **American Airlines Fly-Away Vacations** (☎ **800/433-7300**), and **Delta's Dream Vacations** (☎ **800/872-7786**). **TWA Getaway Vacations** (☎ **800/GETAWAY**) specializes only in packages to Jamaica and San Juan, and **United Airlines Vacations** (☎ **800/328-6877**) covers only San Juan.

Other tour operators include the following:

Caribbean Concepts Corp., 575 Underhill Blvd., Syosset, NY 11791 (☎ **800/423-4433** in the U.S., or 516/496-9800; fax 516/496-9880), offers all-inclusive low-cost air-and-land packages to the islands, including apartments, hotels, villas, or condo rentals.

AIB Tours, 2500 NW 79th Ave., Suite 211, Miami, FL 33122 (☎ **800/242-8687** outside Florida, or 305/715-0056), offers tours to Aruba, Bonaire, Curaçao, and Santo Domingo. Tour packages include land, air, transfers, and hotel taxes.

Other options for general independent packages include:

Renaissance Vacations, 2655 Lejeune Rd., Suite 400, Coral Gables, FL 33134 (☎ **800/874-0027** in the U.S.), offering all-inclusive deals to Ocho Rios (Jamaica), St. Thomas, Santo Domingo, and Grenada. **Horizon Tours,** 1010 Vermont Ave. NW, Suite 202, Washington, DC 20005 (☎ **888-SUN-N-SAND** in the U.S., or 202/393-8390; fax 202/393-1547), specializes in all-inclusive upscale resorts on the islands of The Bahamas, Jamaica, Antigua, Aruba, Barbados, St. Lucia, Puerto Rico, Martinique, and Dominica.

Club Med (☎ **800/258-2633** in the U.S.) has various all-inclusive options throughout the Caribbean and The Bahamas for families and singles.

Globus, 5301 South Federal Circle, Littleton, CO 80123 (☎ **800/851-0728,** ext. 518), gives escorted tours of the Caribbean. The trips, which are island-hopping expeditions to three of four islands, focus on the historical and cultural aspects of the West Indies.

Finally, **Liberty Travel,** 69 Spring St., Ramsey, NJ 07446 (☎ **201/934-3500**), advertises more packages to The Bahamas and the Caribbean than any other agency.

PACKAGES FOR BRITISH TRAVELERS Package tours can be booked through **British Virgin Islands Holidays,** 11–13 Hockerill St., Bishop's Stortford, Herts CM23 2DH (☎ **01279/656111**). This company is the major booking agent for all the important hotels in the British Virgin Islands. Stays can be arranged in more than one hotel if you'd like to visit more than one island. The company also offers staffed yacht charters and bareboat charters.

Caribbean Connection, Concorde House, Forest Street, Chester CH1 1QR (☎ **01244/341131**), offers all-inclusive packages (airfare and hotel) to the Caribbean and customizes tours for independent travel. Other Caribbean specialists operating out of England include **Kuoni Travel,** Kuoni House, Dorking, Surrey RH5 4AZ (☎ **01306/740888**), and **Caribtours,** 161 Fulham Rd., London SW3 6SN (☎ **0171/581-3517**), a small, very knowledgeable outfit that focuses on Caribbean travel and tailors individual itineraries.

11 Renting Your Own Villa or Condo

Even Princess Margaret rents out her private villa on Mustique in the Grenadines, providing you have the proper references. Throughout the Caribbean you can secure good deals by renting privately owned villas and condos, and not all of them charge royal rates.

Many villas have a staff, or at least a maid who comes in a few days a week, and they also provide the essentials for home life, including linens and housewares. Condos usually come with a reception desk and are often comparable to life in a suite in a big resort hotel. Nearly all condo complexes have swimming pools (some more than one).

Agencies specializing in these rentals include the following:

Villas of Distinction, P.O. Box 55, Armonk, NY 10504 (☎ **800/289-0900** in the U.S., or 914/273-3331), offers private villas with one or six bedrooms and a swimming pool. Domestic help is often included. They have offerings on St. Martin, Anguilla, Mustique, Barbados, the U.S. and British Virgins, the Cayman Islands, St. Lucia, Antigua, St. Barts, and Jamaica.

At Home Abroad, 405 E. 56th St., Suite 6-H, New York, NY 10022-2466 (☎ **212/421-9165**), has a roster of private upscale homes for rent on Antigua, Barbados, Jamaica, Mustique, Montserrat, Nevis, St. John, St. Martin, St. Thomas, Tortola, and Virgin Gorda, most with maid service included.

Caribbean Connection Plus Ltd., P.O. Box 261, Trumbull, CT 06611 (☎ **203/261-8603;** fax 203/261-8295), offers many apartments, cottages, and villas in the Caribbean, especially on St. Kitts, Nevis, and Montserrat, but also on some of the more obscure islands such as St. Eustatius, Tobago, St. Vincent, Dominica, and Nevis. Caribbean Connection specializes in island-hopping with **InterIsland Air,** and offers especially attractive deals for U.S. West Coast travelers. This is one of the few reservations services whose staff has actually been on the islands, so members can talk to people who really know the Caribbean.

VHR, Worldwide, 235 Kensington Ave., Norwood, NJ 07648 (☎ **800/633-3284** in the U.S. and Canada, or 201/767-9393), offers the most comprehensive portfolio of luxury villas, condominiums, resort suites, and apartments for rent not only in the Caribbean, but also in The Bahamas, Mexico, and the United States. The company can also arrange for airfare and car rental. The company's more than 4,000 homes and suite resorts are hand-picked by the staff, and these accommodations are generally less expensive than comparable hotel rooms.

Hideaways International, 767 Islington St., Portsmouth, NH 03801 (☎ **800/843-4433** in the U.S., or 603/430-4433; fax 603/430-4444), publishes *Hideaways Guide,* a pictorial directory of home rentals throughout the world, including the Caribbean, especially the British Virgin Islands, U.S. Virgin Islands, and Cayman Islands, with full descriptions so you know what you're renting. Rentals range from cottages to staffed villas to whole islands! On most rentals you deal directly with owners. At condos and small resorts, Hideaways offers member discounts. Other services include yacht charters, cruises, airline ticketing, car rentals, and hotel reservations. Annual membership is $99; a four-month trial membership is $39.

Heart of the Caribbean Ltd., 17485 Penbrook Dr., Brookfield, WI 53045 (☎ **414/783-5303**), is a villa wholesale company offering travelers a wide range of private villas and condos on several islands, including Sint Maarten/St. Martin and Barbados. Accommodations range from one to six bedrooms, and from modest villas and condos to palatial estates. Homes have complete kitchens, and maid service can be arranged. Discounts on cars and airfare can also be provided.

Rent-a-Home International, 7200 34th Ave. NW, Seattle, WA 98117 (☎ **206/789-9377;** fax 206/789-9379), maintains an inventory of several thousand properties, specializing in condos and villas with weekly rates ranging from $700 to $30,000. It arranges bookings for week-long stays or longer. For their color catalog including prices, descriptions, and pictures, send $15, which will be applied to your next rental.

Sometimes local tourist offices will also advise you on vacation-home rentals if you write or call them directly.

The Cayman Islands

4

Don't go to the Cayman Islands expecting fast-paced excitement. Island life focuses on the sea. Snorkelers will find a paradise; beach lovers will relish the powdery sands of Seven Mile Beach; but party-hungry travelers in search of urban thrills might be disappointed.

The Caymans, 480 miles due south of Miami, consist of three islands: Grand Cayman, Cayman Brac, and Little Cayman. Despite its name, Grand Cayman is only 22 miles long and 8 miles across at its widest point. The other islands are considerably smaller, of course, and contain very limited tourist facilities, in contrast to well-developed Grand Cayman. George Town on Grand Cayman is the capital, and is therefore the hub of government, banking, and shopping.

English is the official language of the islands, although it's often spoken with an English slur mixed with an American southern drawl and a lilting Welsh accent.

GETTING THERE

The Cayman Islands are easily accessible. Flying time from Miami is 1 hour 20 minutes; from Houston, 2 hours 45 minutes; from Tampa, 1 hour 40 minutes; and from Atlanta, 3 hours 35 minutes. Only a handful of nonstop flights are available from the heartland of North America to Grand Cayman, so many visitors use Miami as their gateway.

Cayman Airways (☎ **800/422-9626** in the U.S. and Canada, or 345/949-2311 locally), offers the most frequent service to Grand Cayman, with three daily flights from Miami, four flights a week from Tampa, three flights weekly from Atlanta (with a stopover in Tampa), and three nonstop flights a week from Houston. Once in the Caymans, the airline's subsidiary, Island Air Ltd., operates frequent flights between Grand Cayman and Little Cayman and Cayman Brac. Round-trip fares between Grand Cayman and Cayman Brac begin at $94.

Many visitors also fly to Grand Cayman on **American Airlines** (☎ **800/433-7300**), which operates three daily nonstop flights from Miami. **Northwest Airlines** (☎ **800/447-4747**) flies to Grand Cayman from Detroit, and from Memphis via Miami. **US Airways** (☎ **800/428-4322**) operates one daily flight from Charlotte, North Carolina, to Grand Cayman.

FAST FACTS: The Cayman Islands

Business Hours Normally, banks are open Monday to Thursday from 9am to 2:30pm and on Friday from 9am to 1pm and 2:30 to 4:30pm. Shops are usually open Monday to Saturday from 9am to 5pm.

Currency The legal tender is the Cayman Islands dollar (CI$), currently valued at U.S.$1.25 (U.S.$1 equals 80¢ CI). Canadian, U.S., and British currencies are accepted throughout the Cayman Islands, but you'll save money if you exchange your U.S. dollars for Cayman Islands dollars. The Cayman dollar breaks down into 100 cents. Coins come in 1¢, 5¢, 10¢, and 25¢. Bills come in denominations of $1, $5, $10, $25, $50, and $100 (note that there is no CI$20 bill). Most hotels quote rates in U.S. dollars. However, many restaurants quote prices in Cayman Islands dollars, which might lead you to think that food is much cheaper. Unless otherwise noted, quotations in this chapter are in U.S. dollars, rounded off.

The cost of living in the Cayman Islands is about 20% higher than in the United States.

Documents No passports are required for U.S. or Canadian citizens, but entering visitors must have proof of citizenship (voter registration card or birth certificate) and a return ticket.

Electricity It's 110 volts AC (60 cycles), so American and Canadian appliances will not need adapters or transformers.

Emergencies For medical or police emergencies, dial 911.

Fax **The Cable and Wireless,** Anderson Square, George Town, on Grand Cayman (☎ **345/949-7800**), is open from 8:15am to 5pm Monday to Friday, on Saturday from 9am to 1pm, and on Sunday from 9am to noon.

Hospitals On Grand Cayman, the only hospital is **George Town Hospital,** Hospital Road (☎ **345/949-8600**). On Cayman Brac, the only hospital is the 18-bed **Faith Hospital** (☎ **345/948-2243**).

Information The **Cayman Islands Department of Tourism** has the following offices in the United States: 9525 W. Bryn Mawr, Suite 160, Rosemont, IL 60018 (☎ **847/678-6446**); Two Memorial City Plaza, 820 Gessner, Suite 170, Houston, TX 77024 (☎ **713/461-1317**); 3440 Wilshire Blvd., Suite 1202, Los Angeles, CA 90010 (☎ **213/738-1968**); 6100 Blue Lagoon Dr., Suite 150, Miami, FL 33126 (☎ **305/266-2300**); and 420 Lexington Ave., Suite 2733, New York, NY 10170 (☎ **212/682-5582**). In Canada, contact Earl B. Smith, **Travel Marketing Consultants,** 234 Eglinton Ave. E., Suite 306, Toronto, ON M4P 1K5 (☎ **416/485-1550**). In the United Kingdom, the contact is **Cayman Islands,** 6 Arlington St., London, SW1A 1RE (☎ **0171/491-7771**).

Taxes A government tourist tax of 10% is added to your hotel bill. Also, a departure tax of CI$8 ($10) is collected when you leave the Caymans.

Telephone A modern automatic telephone system enables Cayman operators to dial numbers worldwide 24 hours; international direct dialing is also possible. The Cayman Islands are no longer part of the 809 area code. Now the area code is **345.**

Time U.S. eastern standard time is in effect all year; daylight saving time is not observed.

Tipping Most restaurants add a 10% to 15% charge in lieu of tipping. Hotels also add a 10% service charge to your bill.

The Cayman Islands

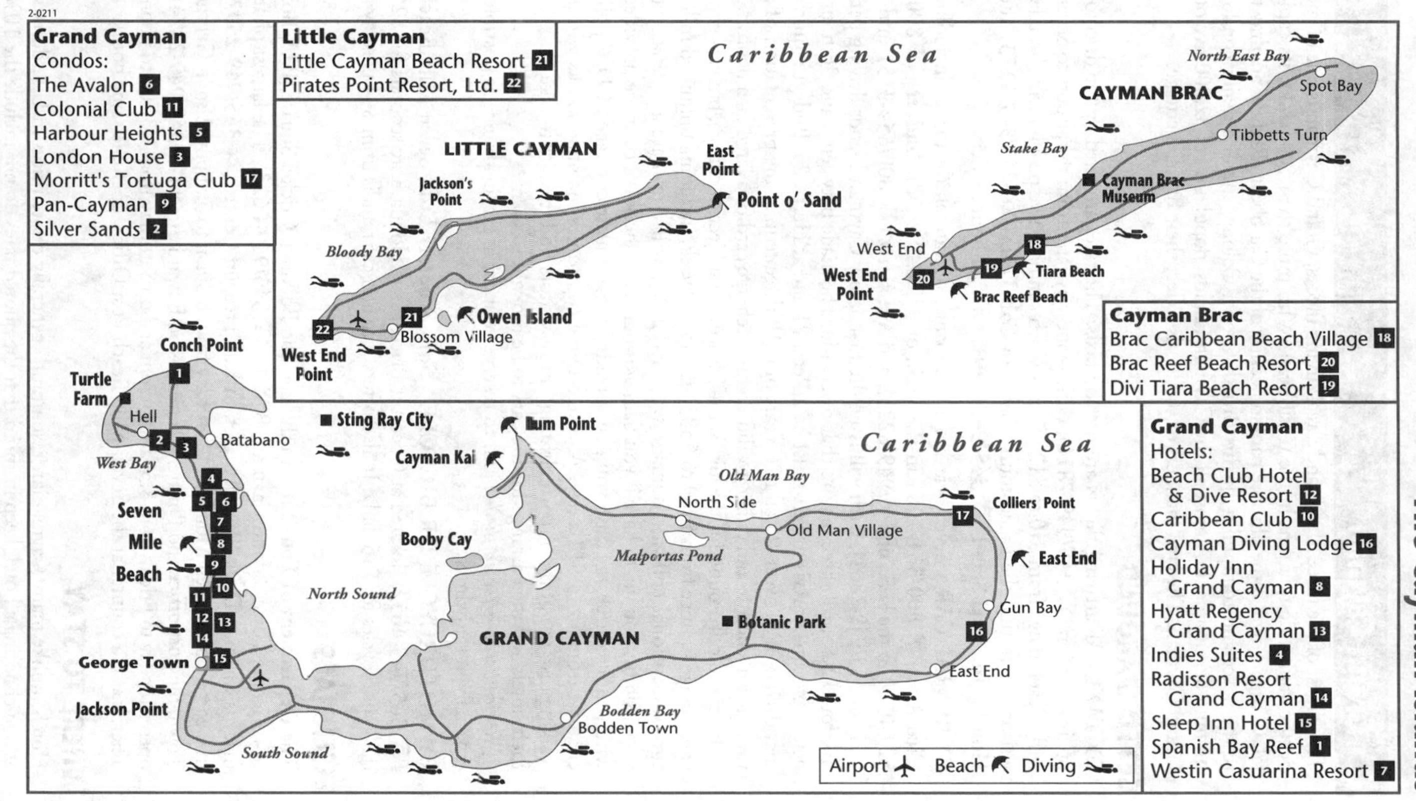

1 Grand Cayman

The largest of the three islands and a real diving mecca, Grand Cayman is one of the hottest tourist destinations in the Caribbean. With more than 500 banks, its capital, George Town, is the offshore banking center of the Caribbean. Retirees are drawn to the peace and tranquillity of this British Crown Colony, site of a major condominium development. Almost all the Cayman Islands' population of 32,000 live on Grand Cayman. The civil manners of the locals reflect their British heritage.

GETTING AROUND

BY TAXI All arriving flights are met by taxis. The rates are fixed by the director of civil aviation (☎ **345/949-7811**); typical one-way fares from the airport to Seven Mile Beach range from $10 to $12. Taxis (which can hold five people) will also take visitors on around-the-island tours. **Cayman Cab Team** (☎ **345/947-1173**) and **Holiday Inn Taxi Stand** (☎ **345/947-4491**) offer 24-hour service.

BY RENTAL CAR Several car-rental companies operate on the island, including **Cico Avis** (☎ **800/331-1084** in the U.S., or 345/949-2468), **Budget** (☎ **800/527-0700** in the U.S., or 345/949-8223), and **Ace Hertz** (☎ **800/654-3131** in the U.S., or 345/949-7861). Each will issue the mandatory Cayman Islands driving permit for U.S.$5. All three require that reservations be made between 6 and 36 hours before pickup. At Avis drivers must be at least 21 and at Hertz, 25. Budget requires that drivers be between 25 and 70 years old. All three require the presentation of a valid driver's license and either a valid credit or charge card or a large cash deposit.

It pays to call around for the lowest rate. Prices are subject to change, but cars generally range in price from $259 to $385 and up per week, including unlimited mileage. An optional collision-damage waiver (CDW) will eliminate any financial responsibility you might have if you damage your car. (Check the coverage provided with your credit/charge card; you may already have adequate coverage.) CDW policies cost from $9 to $12 a day. All three rental companies maintain kiosks within walking distance of the airport, although most visitors find it easier to take a taxi to their hotels and then arrange for the cars to be brought to them.

Remember to drive on the left and to reserve your car as far in advance as possible, especially in midwinter.

BY MOTORCYCLE OR BICYCLE **Soto Scooters Ltd.,** Seven Mile Beach (☎ **345/945-4652**), located at Coconut Place, offers Honda Elite scooters for $25 daily, or bicycles for $15 daily. It also offers Jeep and car rentals from $44 per day.

ESSENTIALS

The **Department of Tourism** is in the Pavilion Building, Cricket Square (P.O. Box 67), George Town, Grand Cayman, B.W.I. (☎ **345/949-0623**). The largest pharmacy is **Cayman Drug,** Panton Street, in Kirk Freeport Centre (☎ **345/949-2597**) in George Town, open Monday to Saturday from 8:30am to 5:30pm. Also in George Town, the **post office** and Philatelic Bureau is on Edward Street (☎ **345/949-2474**), open Monday to Friday from 8:30am to 5pm and on Saturday from 8:30am to noon. There's also a counter at the Seven Mile Beach Post Office, open the same hours.

WHERE TO STAY

Hotels, unlike many Caymanian restaurants, generally quote prices in U.S. dollars. When choosing a hotel, keep in mind that the quoted rates do not include the 10% government tax and the 10% hotel service tax.

VERY EXPENSIVE

Caribbean Club. West Bay Rd. (P.O. Box 30499), Grand Cayman, B.W.I. ☎ **345/947-4099.** Fax 345/947-4443. 18 villas. A/C TV TEL. Winter, $275–$410 one-bedroom villa; $325–$440 two-bedroom villa. Off-season, $175–$290 one-bedroom villa; $210–$315 two-bedroom villa. Children under 10 not accepted in winter. AE, MC, V.

Located right at the midpoint of Seven Mile Beach, the Caribbean Club is an exclusive compound of well-furnished one- and two-bedroom villas, each with a full-size living room, dining area, patio, and kitchen. When the owners are away, the units are rented to guests. The look is very Bermudian. Although it has a long list of faithful repeat visitors who would stay nowhere else, it's not as elegant as some hotels in its price range. The pink villas are 3 miles north of George Town, either on or just off the beach; the six oceanfront units are always more expensive, of course. Accommodations are furnished in each owner's individual taste (which may not be your own). The club was last renovated in 1994, but refurbished in 1996. At the core of the colony, the two-story club center, with tall, graceful arches, has picture windows that look out onto the grounds, which are planted with palm trees and flowering shrubs. The staff is one of the best and most helpful on the island.

Dining/Entertainment: Lantanas, the dining room, is open for lunch and dinner (see "Where to Dine," below).

Services: Room service during open hours of Latanas (breakfast not available), free guest laundry.

Facilities: Tennis court.

✪ **Hyatt Regency Grand Cayman.** West Bay Rd. (P.O. Box 1588), Grand Cayman, B.W.I. ☎ **800/233-1234** or 345/949-1234. Fax 345/949-8528. 236 rms, 50 villas. A/C MINIBAR TV TEL. Winter, $305–$425 double, $510 Regency Club double; $550 one-bedroom villa; $685–$825 two-bedroom villa. Off-season, $190–$310 double, $380 Regency Club double; $315 one-bedroom villa; $440–$570 two-bedroom villa. AE, CB, DC, DISC, MC, V.

This $80 million resort is the best-managed and most stylish hotel in the Cayman Islands. Two miles north of George Town, the hotel is a major component in the 90-acre Britannia Resort community, which includes the Britannia Golf Course. Two acres front Seven Mile Beach, and provide the setting for all kinds of water sports. The hotel's design combines neoclassicism with modern art and a sort of British colonial airiness. Dozens of Doric arcades are festooned with flowering vines that cascade beneath reflecting pools and comfortable teakwood settees. Low-rise buildings surround a large landscaped courtyard that contains gardens, waterfalls, and the swimming pool.

The Hyatt offers luxury rooms with private verandas. The rooms are only moderate in size and were last renovated in 1995. Two buildings and 44 rooms are devoted to the Regency Club, which has concierge service from 5am to 11pm daily. The hotel also offers one- and two-bedroom luxury villas along the Britannia Golf Course or waterway, which have fully equipped kitchens and easy access to the resort's facilities. Guests in the villas have their own private pool, whirlpool, laundry room, cabaña, and patio area.

This is definitely the choice for kids with well-heeled parents. The wide range of accommodations can meet the needs of families of almost any size.

Dining/Entertainment: The resort offers several dining choices, including the Garden Loggia Café, which serves breakfast or dinner (and a buffet champagne brunch on Sunday), with Asian and Italian cuisine. There's a seafood restaurant, Hemingway's (see "Where to Dine," below), and you can also have lunch or dinner daily at the Britannia Golf Club and Grille, a few steps away from the first tee. Hyatt's own ferry will take you on a 40-minute cruise to Rum Point where you can have lunch or dinner.

Services: Room service, baby-sitting, laundry. A Camp Hyatt program for children 3 to 12 costs $25 to $62.50 per day and has an activity-filled agenda.

Facilities: The most complete array of water sports in the Caymans (see "Water Sports, Beaches & Other Outdoor Pursuits," below, for more information on the Hyatt's Red Sail Sports facility and its offerings), health club, huge swimming pool (with a whirlpool and swim-up bar), the Britannia Golf Course, tennis courts.

Westin Casuarina Resort. Seven Mile Beach (P.O. Box 30620), Grand Cayman, B.W.I. ☎ **800/WESTIN-1** or 345/945-3800. Fax 345/949-5825. 339 rms, 4 suites. A/C MINIBAR TV TEL. Winter, $315–$495 double; from $850 one-bedroom suite; from $1,300 two-bedroom suite. Off-season, $195–$325 double; $600 one-bedroom suite; from $800 two-bedroom suite. AE, MC, V.

Desirable land on Seven Mile Beach is so sought-after that when Westin wanted to build a luxury hotel, the largest on the island, it had it demolish the old Galleon Beach Hotel to make room for this $50 million investment. Completed late in 1995, and designed by eminent architect Edward D. Stone Jr., with a postmodern gray facade and turquoise roofs, it was conceived as a direct competitor of the nearby Hyatt. Unlike the Hyatt, it lies directly on the sands of the beach on eight acres of landscaped gardens; it has beautiful swimming pools and lots of sports facilities. The bedrooms are in five-story wings, each outfitted in a soothing color scheme. Most have French doors leading onto balconies, and all have in-room safes and ceiling fans.

Dining/Entertainment: The most upscale of the restaurants is Casa Havana, a dinner-only restaurant that evokes the glamour of pre-Castro Cuba. Ferdinand's is a middle-bracket restaurant serving breakfast, lunch, and dinner. Salads and sandwiches are served at the Courtyard Café poolside restaurant.

Services: 24-hour room service, concierge, limited programs for children, massage.

Facilities: One of the largest pools and poolside decks (5,000 square feet) in the Caymans, appealingly lined with palm and date trees, and centered around a swim-up bar. Swimming pools, designed as lazy ovals or lagoons, flank the north and south sides of the hotel, each with its own cascade/waterfall. Illuminated tennis courts, and an on-site branch of Red Sail Watersports for scuba and sailing. Gift shop, hair and beauty salon, car rentals. An 18-hole championship golf course, The Links at Safehaven, is across the street from the resort.

Expensive

Holiday Inn Grand Cayman. West Bay Rd. (P.O. Box 904), Grand Cayman, B.W.I. ☎ **800/421-9999** in the U.S., or 345/947-4444. Fax 345/945-4213. 215 rms. A/C MINIBAR TV TEL. Winter, $238–$338 double, triple, or quad. Off-season, $178–$248 double, triple, or quad. AE, MC, V.

Some 3 miles north of George Town and 5 miles from the airport, this modern beachfront hotel boasts bedrooms done in floral prints with bright, tropical flair. Its reputation as the largest and best hotel on the island ended in 1986 with the opening of the Hyatt. Most rooms have sitting areas, and all have baths with dressing rooms. Ocean-view and oceanfront rooms are more expensive. This is an ideal choice for families, since rooms can house three to four guests at no extra charge for the third or fourth occupant. Note that this inn attracts groups on package tours. In general, the hotel is short on island charm and the service overall isn't very efficient, but it's a solid choice for those who want to be where the action is.

Dining/Entertainment: Breakfast buffets are served in the Verandah, and the Ten Sails Pub offers English pub-style meals, such as steak-and-kidney pie, along with draft beer. After a swim, kids flock to the Sweet Tooth, which offers ice cream and yogurt treats.

Services: Room service, baby-sitting, laundry.

Facilities: Lagoonlike swimming pool with arched bridges, poolside cocktails available, fully equipped dive shop, fitness room, sailing, snorkeling, waterskiing, deep-sea fishing.

Indies Suites. Foster Dr., off West Bay Rd. (P.O. Box 2070), Grand Cayman, B.W.I. ☎ **800/654-3130** in the U.S. and Canada, or 345/945-5025. Fax 345/945-5024. 38 one-bedroom suites, 2 two-bedroom suites. A/C TV TEL. Winter, $255 one-bedroom suite; $305 two-bedroom suite. Off-season, $170 one-bedroom suite; $200 two-bedroom suite. Rates include continental breakfast. AE, MC, V.

Built in 1990 and set at the more tranquil end of Seven Mile Beach (but across the road), this three-story establishment offers some of the most comfortable accommodations on the island, although the design is cookie-cutter. The motel-like units surround a landscaped swimming pool. Each unit contains a kitchen and has a pastel decor, and some are sold as time-share units. On the premises are coin-operated laundry facilities, a freshwater pool and Jacuzzi, a scuba facility (Indies Divers), a bohío-style (open air with a palm-thatched roof) poolside bar, and a gift shop. There's no hotel restaurant, although there are a lot of places to dine within a short drive; many of the long-term guests prefer to cook in their own kitchens. On Wednesday night there's a barbecue with live music around the pool. In general, the resort is for self-sufficient types who don't mind the lack of catering facilities or staying slightly away from the beach. Don't expect a lot of attention from the staff, but there is regular hotel-style maid service.

Radisson Resort Grand Cayman. West Bay Rd. (P.O. Box 30371), Grand Cayman, B.W.I. ☎ **800/333-3333** or 345/949-0088. Fax 345/949-0288. 311 rms, 4 suites. A/C TV TEL. Winter, $165–$450 double; from $450 suite. Off-season, $140–$250 double; from $450 suite. AE, DC, MC, V.

Opened in 1990, this five-story hotel has an enviable location beside Seven Mile Beach, a five-minute drive (2 miles) north of George Town. It's a favorite with large package tour groups, and has good water sports facilities. Its red-roofed, vaguely colonial design resembles a cluster of balconied town houses. Bedrooms were refurbished in the winter of 1996–97.

Dining/Entertainment: Serving a standard international cuisine, an oceanfront restaurant offers three meals a day, offering guests a choice of dining inside or else out in the open air overlooking the water. Choose this place more for the beach out front than for the cuisine.

Services: Room service, laundry, baby-sitting.

Facilities: Swimming pool ringed with a beach bar/cabaña and sun parasols (located a few steps from the famous beach), fully equipped dive shop, whirlpool, spa, beauty shop, health club, full range of water sports with good snorkeling 50 feet offshore.

MODERATE

Beach Club Hotel & Dive Resort. West Bay Rd. (P.O. Box 903G), Grand Cayman, B.W.I. ☎ **345/949-8100.** Fax 345/947-5167. 41 rms. A/C TV TEL. Winter, $160–$305 double. Off-season, $113–$185 double. MAP $45 per person extra. Children 12 and under stay free in parents' room. Honeymoon and dive packages available. AE, DC, MC, V.

Set 3 miles north of George Town, the Beach Club is one of the oldest and best-located hotels on the island. Built in the early 1960s in a plain single-story building along Seven Mile Beach, it established a scuba-diving center and has since attracted a loyal repeat clientele (although some guests complain that you pay a lot for what you get here). When cruise-ship passengers are in port, however, the beach space is overcrowded.

Designed like a large colonial plantation villa, it has a formal Doric portico, lots of lattices, and a popular bar that separates the hotel from the beach. Here, calypso music and rum flow freely for guests who seem to live in their bathing suits all day. The divers who opt for week-long scuba packages usually take one of the tile-floored villas clustered amid trees at the edge of the beach. Otherwise, most accommodations are simple, nondescript, but comfortable bedrooms in the main hotel. The best units are the ocean-view rooms with four-poster beds. Each room comes with a veranda and furniture ranging from Caribbean rattan to reproductions of English Sheraton. Housekeeping can be improved.

Sleep Inn Hotel. West Bay Rd. (P.O. Box 30111), Grand Cayman, B.W.I. ☎ **345/949-9111.** Fax 345/949-6699. 115 rms, 6 suites. A/C TV TEL. Winter, $115–$185 double; $155–$195 junior suite for 2. Off-season, $105–$115 double; $145 junior suite for 2. Children 12 and under stay free in parents' room. AE, DC, DISC, MC, V.

Opened in 1992, the Sleep Inn is the closest hotel on Seven Mile Beach to the center of George Town. On rather bleak grounds, it lies 250 feet from the sands and about a five-minute drive from the international airport. It's one of the more reasonably priced hotels on the island, with great value for your money, and a good choice for families.

A franchise of Choice Hotels International, it offers both smoking and nonsmoking rooms and units that are accessible for persons with disabilities. Furnishings are rather nondescript and simple. The rooms have modern tropical furnishings, TVs with built-in radios and alarm clocks, and a small safe for valuables; the suites contain kitchenettes.

Features include the Dive Shop, with a full-service dive and water-sports program, a swimming pool and Jacuzzi, a pool bar, and a pool grill, where barbecues are held regularly.

Spanish Bay Reef. West Bay Rd. (P.O. Box 30867), Grand Cayman, B.W.I. ☎ **800/482-3483** in the U.S., 800/424-5500 in Canada, or 345/949-3765. Fax 345/947-5167. 50 rms. A/C TV TEL. $178–$265 double. All-inclusive 4-day/3-night package: Winter, $622–$1,021 diver, $523–$911 nondiver. Off-season, $547–$827 diver, $418–$738 nondiver. AE, MC, V.

A small, intimate, long-established resort set in an isolated location amid the scrublands of the northwestern tip of Grand Cayman, this was the island's first all-inclusive establishment. Rather informally run, the pale-pink, two-story stucco units are a favorite with divers who appreciate the marine life of the offshore reefs. The casual furnishings are in a Caribbean motif. The accommodations, which are rather simple, have balconies or patios with garden or ocean views.

The package rates quoted above include all meals and beverages, island sightseeing, entertainment, use of bicycles, introductory scuba and snorkeling lessons, unlimited snorkeling or scuba diving from the shore (including tanks and weight belt), round-trip transfers, taxes, and service. If you're a diver, ask about Certified Divers Packages when making your reservations. Facilities include a private coral beach, freshwater pool, and Jacuzzi. Guests lounge around Calico Jack's Poolside Bar, and later enjoy an array of food (with lots of fish) in the Spanish Main Restaurant. There's also a disco.

INEXPENSIVE

Cayman Diving Lodge. Pirate's Cove, East End (P.O. Box 11), Grand Cayman, B.W.I. ☎ **800/852-3483** or 345/947-7555. 10 rms. A/C. Year-round, 2-tank dives, $494 double for 3 nights,

$840 double for 5 nights, $1,186 double for 7 nights. Three-tank dives, $554 double for 3 nights, $960 double for 5 nights, $1,366 double for 7 nights. Rates are all-inclusive. AE, MC, V.

This casual, informal, laid-back place caters to experienced divers and is in the southeast corner of the island, 20 miles east of George Town. The horseshoe-shaped lodge is a two-story, half-timbered building set amid tropical trees on a private coral-sand beach with a live coral barrier reef just offshore. Diving and snorkeling equipment are available for unlimited shore diving. Scuba and snorkeling trips include a daily two-tank morning dive of 3½ hours. The resort owns two 45-foot Garcia dive boats that are very comfortable.

In the rooms, the view of the ocean is better than the somewhat worn decor and furnishings. Linoleum floors, shower-only baths, and jalousies set the tone. A few units have balconies. Caymanian chefs serve abundant meals and specialize in fish dishes; vegetarian food is also available. Guests can also rent bikes to tour relatively flat Grand Cayman. This place is an exceptional value for the money.

CONDOS

The Avalon. West Bay Rd. (P.O. Box 31236), Grand Cayman, B.W.I. ☎ **345/947-4171.** Fax 345/947-4189. 15 condos. A/C TV TEL. Winter, $575 apt for 4; $640 apt for 6. Off-season, $390 apt for 4; $455 apt for 6. AE, MC, V.

One of Cayman's newest and best condo complexes is the Avalon, occupying prime real estate on Seven Mile Beach. It consists of 27 oceanfront three-bedroom/three-bath units, 15 of which can be rented. Only a short distance from restaurants, about a five-minute drive from George Town, it has an architectural style and grace that's lacking in many beachfront properties. The well-appointed, spacious units have a tropical motif. Each condo has a fully equipped open kitchen and a large, screened lanai that overlooks a stretch of the beach. Oversize tubs and separate shower stalls are in each bathroom. Facilities include a tennis court, fitness center, swimming pool, and Jacuzzi. As a luxury touch, each condo unit has a private garage. Rooms have maid service every day but Tuesday.

Colonial Club. West Bay Rd. (P.O. Box 320W), Grand Cayman, B.W.I. ☎ **345/947-4660.** Fax 345/945-4839. 24 condos. A/C TEL. Winter, $364–$416 apt for 2; $416–$468 apt for 3 or 4; $468–$520 apt for 5 or 6. Off-season, $230–$280 apt for 2; $280–$330 apt for 3 or 4; $330–$380 apt for 5 or 6. Minimum stay 5 nights Dec 16–Apr 15. AE, MC, V.

Although smaller than the hostelries flanking it, the pastel-pink Colonial Club occupies a highly desirable stretch of the famous Seven Mile Beach. Built in 1985, it's a three-story and rather standard condominium development about 4 miles north of George Town and some 10 minutes from the airport. First-class maintenance, service, and accommodations are provided in the apartments, all with kitchen fans, maid service, and laundry facilities.

Usually only 10 of the 24 apartments are available for rent—the rest are privately owned and occupied. You have a choice of units with two bedrooms and three baths or units with three bedrooms and three baths. Facilities include a tennis court (lit at night), a Jacuzzi, and a freshwater pool. There's no on-site restaurant.

Harbour Heights. West Bay Rd. (P.O. Box 30624), Grand Cayman, B.W.I. ☎ **345/947-4295.** Fax 345/945-4522. 20 condos. A/C TV TEL. Winter, $295 apt for 2; $315 apt for 3; $335 apt for 4. Off-season, $185 apt for 2; $195 apt for 3; $205 apt for 4. Additional person $20 extra. Minimum stay 7 days in winter. AE, MC, V.

You can stay in style and comfort by the day, week, or month in this three-story beachfront complex 6 miles north of George Town. You're on your own for meals, but there's a good-size recreation area and a large free-form swimming pool with a surrounding tile terrace filled with white lounge furniture. The apartments are of generous size and can accommodate one to four guests. Each has a living room and dinette, an attractive and complete kitchen, two bedrooms, two baths, ample closet space, and a balcony or patio. The furnishings are all in white tropical designs with decorative fabrics and accent rugs. Daily maid service is included. Since the units at ground level don't have water views, try for a condo on the second or third floor. All units but one have a dishwasher.

London House. Seven Mile Beach, Grand Cayman, B.W.I. ☎ **345/947-4060.** Fax 345/947-4087. 21 condos. A/C TV TEL. Winter, $295 one-bedroom apt; $335 one-bedroom minipenthouse; $315–$375 two-bedroom apt; $900 three-bedroom penthouse. Off-season, $255 one-bedroom apt; $285 one-bedroom minipenthouse; $275–$330 two-bedroom apt; $500 three-bedroom penthouse. Extra person $20 per day. AE, MC, V.

At the more tranquil northern end of Seven Mile Beach, this hotel is an enduring favorite for those seeking apartment living. The units have fully equipped kitchens, spacious living and dining areas, and private patios or balconies overlooking the water. Each was last renovated in 1996. Floral prints and rattan set the decorating tone in most units. Ceiling fans supplement the air-conditioning, and daily maid service is available. The complex has its own seaside swimming pool. Try to get a room away from the pool if you're bothered by noise, because sometimes house parties are staged on the patio. Many restaurants are nearby, although there's a stone barbecue for private poolside cookouts.

Morritt's Tortuga Club. East End (P.O. Box 496GT), Grand Cayman, B.W.I. ☎ **800/447-0309** or 345/947-7449. Fax 345/947-7669. 145 condos. A/C TV. Winter, $175–$205 studio; $230–$295 one-bedroom apt; $295–$375 two-bedroom townhouse; $325–$405 two-bedroom penthouse. Off-season, $145–$155 studio; $160–$185 one-bedroom apt; $225–$250 two-bedroom townhouse; $255–$280 two-bedroom penthouse. AE, MC, V.

Set on the grounds of the famed Tortuga Club, which was destroyed in 1989 by Hurricane Hugo, this condo cluster was built in the Antillean plantation style from the wreckage of the former hotel. The property sits on 8 beachfront acres on the East End, known for some of the island's best diving. Profiting from its position near offshore reefs teeming with marine life, it's the site of Cayman Windsurfing, which offers snorkeling, windsurfing, and the rental of sailing craft and catamarans. Tortuga Divers, also on the premises, offers resort courses.

About a 26-mile drive from the airport, the club is composed of clusters of three-story beachfront condos opening onto the water. Many are rented as time-share units. There's also a swim-up bar around a swimming pool. Each of the comfortably furnished one- and two-bedroom apartments has a fully equipped kitchen, although many clients opt instead for meals in the complex's restaurant. The club's buildings and facilities are well maintained.

Pan-Cayman. West Bay Rd. (P.O. Box 440GT), Grand Cayman, B.W.I. ☎ **345/945-4002.** Fax 345/945-4011. 10 condos. A/C TV TEL. Winter, $305 two-bedroom apt; $390 three-bedroom apt. Off-season, $165–$185 two-bedroom apt; $245 three-bedroom apt. Additional person $35–$45 extra. DISC, MC, V.

The Georgian-style facade of this popular beachfront choice was altered to suit its Caribbean setting, 4 miles north of George Town. It was last renovated in 1995. Each apartment has its own fully equipped kitchen, a private balcony or patio with an unrestricted view of the sea, and comfortable summer furniture. Hotel-type maid service is provided. This place is popular in winter, so reserve well in advance. The atmosphere is homey and welcoming, and people come for peace and tranquillity.

Silver Sands. West Bay Rd. (P.O. Box 205GT), Grand Cayman, B.W.I. ☎ **800/327-8777** in the U.S., 800/424-5500 in Canada, or 345/949-3343. Fax 345/949-1223. 19 condos. A/C TV. Winter, $360–$370 two-bedroom apt; $440 three-bedroom apt. Off-season, $205–$210 two-bedroom apt; $290 three-bedroom apt. Additional person $20 extra. Children 10 and under stay free in parents' unit. Minimum stay 7 nights in winter, 3 off-season. AE, MC, V.

A good choice for families, this modern eight-building complex is arranged horseshoe fashion on the beach 7 miles north of George Town. The well-maintained apartments are grouped around a freshwater pool. The eight apartment blocks contain either two-bedroom/two-bath or three-bedroom/three-bath units. The two-bedroom unit can hold up to six people, and the three-bedroom unit can house up to eight guests. Each apartment comes with a balcony, a fully equipped kitchen, and maid service. The resident manager will point out the two tennis courts and the utility rooms with washer-dryers. In all, this is a smoothly run operation, which in spite of its costs, satisfies most clients.

WHERE TO DINE

Make sure you understand which currency the menu is printed in. If it's not written on the menu, ask the waiter if the prices are in U.S. dollars or Cayman Island dollars. It will make a big difference when you get your final bill.

EXPENSIVE

✪ **Chef Tell's Grand Old House.** Petra Plantation, S. Church St. ☎ **345/949-9333.** Reservations required. Main courses CI$16.95–CI$28 ($21.20–$35). AE, MC, V. Mon–Fri 11:45am–2:30pm and 6–10pm, Sat–Sun 6–10pm. Closed Sun June–Nov. AMERICAN/CARIBBEAN/PACIFIC RIM.

This mansion is a former plantation house that was constructed at the turn of the century by a Bostonian coconut merchant. It lies amid venerable trees 1 mile south of George Town, past Jackson Point. Built on bedrock near the edge of the sea, it stands on 129 ironwood posts that support the main house and a bevy of gazebos. The Grand Old House is the island's premier caterer and hosts everything from lavish weddings and political functions to informal family celebrations.

German-born Tell Erhardt, a TV celebrity chef, is generally conceded to be the finest on the island, although many savvy locals dispute that, having their own favorite dives. His appetizers remain among the most delectable on the island, including a country venison pâté with pistachio, home-smoked marlin and salmon, or coconut beer-battered shrimp. Dig into the lobster and scallops in a Pernod sauce, the sesame-seared tuna with Asian stir-fry vegetables, and most definitely the catch of the day prepared Cayman style with tomatoes, peppers, and onions.

Hemingway's. In the Hyatt Regency Grand Cayman, West Bay Rd. ☎ **345/949-1234.** Reservations recommended. Main courses CI$16–CI$34 ($20–$42.50). AE, CB, DC, DISC, MC, V. Daily 11:30am–2:30pm and 6–10pm. SEAFOOD/INTERNATIONAL.

The finest seafood on the island can be found 2 miles north of George Town at Hemingway's, which is named after the novelist and inspired by Key West, his one-time residence. You can dine in the open air with a view of the sea. The menu is among the more imaginative on the island. Appetizers include pepperpot soup—a reputed favorite of Papa's—and gazpacho served with a black-bean relish. The catch of the day, perhaps snapper or wahoo, emerges from the grill to your liking. You can also order conch steak with lime butter or roast rack of lamb served on a fruit compote with caramelized-onion mashed potatoes. Want something more imaginative? Try grouper stuffed with crabmeat, mahimahi with a sweet-potato crust and topped with a roasted-tomato dressing, or macadamia-crusted pork with mango juice.

✪ **Lantanas.** In the Caribbean Club, West Bay Rd. ☎ **345/947-5595.** Reservations required. Main courses CI$17–CI$31 ($21.25–$38.75). AE, DISC, MC, V. Daily 5:30–10pm. CARIBBEAN/AMERICAN.

In the middle of Seven Mile Beach is one of the best dining choices on Grand Cayman. The restaurant is named for the tiny lantana flower, whose pink and orange petals grow not only in the arid Cayman Islands but in parts of the United States. The menu is arguably the most imaginative on the island. Begin, for example, with a quesadilla filled with barbecued lobster, guacamole, and roasted red bell pepper in sour cream or else the roasted-garlic soup. The fish dishes are generally excellent, as exemplified by blackened or grilled dolphin with pepper Alfredo or the tropical coconut shrimp in a Cuban honey-rum sauce. The kitchen will even prepare an island-style jerk pork tenderloin with rice, black beans, plantains, and mango salsa. About the only indication that chef Fred Schrock is Austrian is his Viennese apple strudel. The upstairs has a view of Seven Mile Beach, and the downstairs has a Caribbean tropical decor.

Ottmar's Restaurant and Lounge. West Bay Rd. (entrance adjacent to the rear entrance of the Clarion Grand Pavilion). ☎ **345/947-5879.** Reservations recommended. Main courses CI$13.95–CI$20 ($17.40–$25); Sun brunch CI$30 ($37.50). AE, DISC, MC, V. Daily 6–10:30pm. INTERNATIONAL.

One of the island's top restaurants, Ottmar's is outfitted in a French Empire motif with lots of paneling, rich upholstery, and plenty of space between tables. There's a formal bar/lounge area decorated with deep-sea fishing trophies. This is the domain of an Austrian expatriate, Ottmar Weber, who has long abandoned the kitchen of his youth to roam the world, taking culinary inspiration wherever he finds it. The results are usually pleasing. There's a professional welcome and attentive service. You can order such dishes as Bavarian cucumber soup, bouillabaisse, French pepper steak, and Wiener schnitzel. Our favorite dish is chicken Trinidad, stuffed with grapes, nuts, and apples rolled in coconut flakes, sautéed golden brown, and served in orange-butter sauce. There's an array of sophisticated desserts, plus a selection of vegetarian dishes. Lunch is served at the Waterfall Restaurant.

Ristorante Pappagallo. At Villas Pappagallo, Conch Point, Barkers (near the northern terminus of West Bay Rd. and Spanish Cove, 8 miles north of George Town). ☎ **345/949-1119.** Reservations required. Main courses CI$14.95–CI$29 ($18.70–$36.25). AE, MC, V. Daily 6–10:30pm. NORTHERN ITALIAN/SEAFOOD.

One of the island's most memorable restaurants lies on a 14-acre bird sanctuary overlooking a natural lagoon, 15 minutes north of George Town. Its designers incorporated Caymanian and Aztec weaving techniques in its thatched roof. Glass doors, black marble, and polished brass mix a kind of Edwardian opulence with a Tahitian decor. You dine on black tagiolini with lobster sauce, fresh crab ravioli with asparagus sauce, lobster in brandy sauce, or perhaps Italian-style veal and chicken dishes. An occasional dish may be beyond the reach of the chef to prepare well, but the veal and seafood are generally good bets. The place strikes some diners as too pricey for what you get; we like to stop in for a nightcap.

MODERATE

The Almond Tree. N. Church St. (near the corner of Eastern Ave.). ☎ **345/949-2893.** Reservations recommended. Main courses CI$14.95–CI$21.95 ($18.70–$27.45). AE, MC, V. Daily 5:30–10pm. SEAFOOD/INTERNATIONAL.

Likable and unpretentious, this restaurant is supported by poles and branches, and lined with reeds and thatch rising into a peak. It contains a bar area accented with Trader Vic's–style artifacts and a garden lined with palmettos and flowering shrubs. Many guests prefer to dine in the garden; others like a table in the building's interior. Uncomplicated and straightforward cuisine is served, including mango chicken, conch steak, catch of the day, lobster, and filet mignon. This is not the most imaginative array of dishes ever offered, but the kitchen concentrates on what it does well. If you've never ordered it (because it's banned Stateside), this might be the place to request turtle steak. It's grown commercially in the Caymans and not taken from the wild.

Benjamin's Roof. Coconut Place (off West Bay Rd.). ☎ **345/945-4080.** Reservations recommended. Main courses CI$9.95–CI$29.50 ($12.45–$36.90). AE, MC, V. Daily 3–10:30pm. AMERICAN/INTERNATIONAL.

Set on the upper floor of a shopping center, this restaurant is decorated like the interior of a greenhouse, with a wealth of verdant plants. There's a bar set up in the corner of the place, and an accommodating staff serves food and drink to the accompaniment of live piano music and a singer/guitarist. Menu items might include blackened alligator tail, lobster bisque, a mixed grill of seafood, Austrian-style Wiener schnitzel, lobster fettuccine, blackened shrimp, and grilled lamb with herbs. This is a wholesome, family type place, featuring a children's menu. Nothing is too spicy or overseasoned (a few dishes are even bland). But for the most part, the cookery is first-rate and well prepared.

Crow's Nest Restaurant. South Sound. ☎ **345/949-9366.** Reservations recommended. Main courses CI$11.95–CI$21.95 ($14.95–$27.45). AE, MC, V. Mon–Sat 11:30am–2pm and 5:30–10pm, Sun 5:30–10pm. CARIBBEAN.

With a boardwalk and a terrace jutting onto the sands, this informal restaurant has a view of both Sand Cay and a nearby lighthouse. The restaurant is on the southwesternmost tip of the island, a four-minute drive from George Town. It's one of those places that evokes the Caribbean "the way it used to be." There's no pretense here—you get good, honest Caribbean cookery, including grilled seafood, at great prices. Many dishes are spicy, especially their signature appetizer, fiery coconut shrimp. Try one of the daily specials or perhaps sweet, tender lobster. Other dishes might include grilled tuna steak with ackee or Jamaican chicken curry with roast coconut. For dessert, try the banana toffee pie.

Hog Sty Bay Café and Pub. N. Church St. ☎ **345/949-6163.** Reservations recommended in winter. Main courses CI$14.50–CI$18.95 ($18.10–$23.70). AE, MC, V. Daily 8am–10pm (last order). (Bar open till midnight.) CARIBBEAN/ENGLISH.

On a plot of seafront land near the beginning of West Bay Road, the Hog Sty Bay Café and Pub has developed a loyal clientele. In a low-slung cottage whose verandas are vivid shades of pink, blue, and yellow, the place is the creative statement of Pennsylvania-born Tom Keagy, and divides its time and attention between an amusingly decorated pub and a Caribbean-inspired dining room open to a view of the harbor.

In the pub, you can order such British staples as fish and chips or cottage pie, and such drinks as a Snake Bite (equal parts of hard English cider and English lager). Also available are all the foamy tropical drinks you'd expect.

The food is competently prepared and satisfying, though not a lot more. Dining choices include a Caesar salad topped with marinated conch or Cajun chicken, fresh catch of the day, shrimp, pastas, and seafood pastry stuffed with lobster, shrimp, and scallops, all of which are great values for the money. Don't overlook this as a possible site for breakfast, where you can devour huevos rancheros.

Lobster Pot. N. Church St. ☎ **345/949-2736.** Reservations required in winter. Main courses CI$10.50–CI$25 ($13.10–$31.30). AE, MC, V. Mon–Fri 11:30am–2:30pm and 5:30–10pm, Sat–Sun 5:30–10pm. SEAFOOD.

One of the island's best-known restaurants, the Lobster Pot overlooks the water from its second-floor perch. It's situated at the western perimeter of George Town near what used to be Fort George. True to its name, it offers lobster prepared in many different ways: Cayman style, bisque, and salad. Conch schnitzel and seafood curry are on the menu, together with turtle steak grown commercially at Cayman Island kraals. Sometimes the seafood is a bit overcooked for our tastes, but most dishes are right on the mark. The place is also known for its prime beef steaks. For lunch, you might like the English fish and chips or perhaps seafood jambalaya or a pasta. The Lobster Pot's pub is a pleasant place for a drink—you may find someone up for a game of darts, too.

The Wharf. West Bay Rd. ☎ **345/949-2231.** Reservations recommended. Main courses CI$18–CI$26 ($22.50–$32.50). AE, MC, V. Mon–Fri noon–2:30pm and 6–10pm, Sat–Sun 6–10pm. CARIBBEAN/CONTINENTAL.

About 2 miles north of George Town, the 375-seat Wharf has been everything from a dinner theater to a nightclub. In 1989 it became a leading restaurant on the island. Try to catch the traditional 9pm feeding of the tarpon, which are kept in a large tank on the premises. It's quite a show. The restaurant is decorated in soft pastels and offers dining inside, out on an elevated veranda, or on a beachside terrace. The sound of the surf mingles with music from the strolling Paraguayan harpist and pan flute player and chatter from the Ports of Call Bar, located on the premises. Many diners begin with a Wharf salad of seasonal greens; others prefer the homemade black-bean soup or the home-smoked salmon. The main dishes feature everything from Cayman green-turtle steak (when available) to pepper steak Madagascar. The seafood potpourri includes lobster, shrimp, and scallops in a mild curry sauce, and the veal Martinique features medallions of tender veal in a zesty citrus sauce. The kitchen makes a laudable effort to break away from the typical, dull menu items, and for the most part they succeed.

INEXPENSIVE

✪ **Big Daddy's Restaurant and Sports Bar.** West Bay Rd. ☎ **345/949-8511.** Reservations recommended at dinner. Main courses CI$4.95–CI$14.50 ($6.20–$18.10). AE, MC, V. Mon–Sat 8–11am, noon–4pm, and 5–10pm; Sun 4pm–midnight. INTERNATIONAL.

Set on the upper level of a building whose ground floor is devoted to a liquor store under the same management, this is a bustling, big-windowed emporium of food and drink. One area is devoted to a woodsy, nautically decorated bar area, where TV screens broadcast either CNN or whatever sports events might be of interest to the informal crowd. Three separate dining areas, more or less isolated from the activities at the bar, serve well-prepared food. Menu items include deli sandwiches, half-pound burgers, garlic shrimp, T-bone steaks, barbecued ribs, fresh catch of the day, and pasta dishes. The food is often better than the location or ambience would suggest.

Island Taste. S. Church St. ☎ **345/949-4945.** Reservations recommended. Main courses CI$9–CI$21.50 ($11.30–$26.90). AE, MC, V. Mon–Sat 10:30am–4:30pm and daily 6–10pm. CARIBBEAN/MEDITERRANEAN.

Set beside the harbor front in George Town, this restaurant sits across from the headquarters of the *Atlantis* submarine. There's an indoor and outdoor bar area and indoor tables, but the most popular seating area is on the wraparound veranda, one floor above street level. The restaurant has one of the largest "starter" selections on the island. Soups include both white conch chowder and turtle soup. Appetizers feature fresh oysters, Mexican ceviche, and calamari Vesuvio. At least seven pasta dishes are on the dinner menu, including linguine with small clams. You can also order T-bone steak and chicken parmigiana. However, most of the menu is devoted to seafood dishes. Dolphin is served in different ways and perennial favorites include the turtle steak and spiny lobster. Every night the chef offers all-you-can-eat deep-fried shrimp for only CI$15.75 ($19.70) per person. This place caters more to large appetites than to picky gourmets, and offers great value for the money.

Whitehall Bay. The Waterfront, N. Church St. ☎ **345/949-8670.** Reservations recommended Sat–Sun. Main courses CI$9.50–CI$21.50 ($11.90–$26.90). AE, MC, V. Daily 11am–10pm. CARIBBEAN.

Most of this restaurant's dining tables overlook the coral reef and piers that jut out into the sea. It's a short walk north of George Town's center and housed in a gingerbread Caribbean-style building. An inner room provides additional tables, a bar, and an unusual collection of photographs depicting early Cayman Islanders. Menu items include salads, sandwiches, marinated conch, catch of the day, crab backs, curried chicken, steaks, turtle stew, and Cayman-style lobster. The kitchen turns out typical West Indian fare, and it does so with some charm.

WATER SPORTS, BEACHES & OTHER OUTDOOR PURSUITS

What they lack in nightlife, the Caymans make up for in water sports—the fishing, swimming, waterskiing, and diving are among the finest in the Caribbean. In fact, *Skin Diver* magazine called Grand Cayman "the largest single island in the Caribbean for dive tourism." Coral reefs and coral formations encircle the islands and are filled with lots of marine life, which scuba divers are forbidden to disturb.

It's easy to dive close to shore, so boats aren't necessary, but there are plenty of boats and scuba facilities available. On certain excursions we recommend a trip with a qualified dive master. The island has lots of dive shops, but they won't rent scuba gear or supply air to a diver unless he or she has a card from one of the national diving schools, such as NAUI or PADI. Most hotels also rent diving equipment to their guests, as well as arrange snorkeling and scuba-diving trips.

Grand Cayman is the headquarters of **Red Sail Sports,** in the Hyatt Regency Grand Cayman, West Bay Road (☎ **800/255-6425** or 345/945-5965), universally regarded as the most up-to-date and best-equipped water-sports facility in the Cayman Islands. Red Sail has a wide range of offerings, from deep-sea fishing to sailing, diving, and more, and can also arrange waterskiing for $75 per half hour (the cost can be divided among several people) and parasailing for $45 per ride. Other locations are at the Westin Casuarina (☎ **345/949-8732**) and at Rum Point (☎ **345/947-9203**).

What follows are the best options for a gamut of outdoor activities, arranged by subject.

BEACHES One of the finest in the Caribbean, Grand Cayman's ✪ **Seven Mile Beach,** which begins north of George Town, has sparkling white sands rimmed with Australian pines. Beaches on the **east and north coasts** are also fine, as they're protected by an offshore barrier reef. In winter the average water temperature is 80°F; it rises to 85° in summer.

FISHING Grouper and snapper are most plentiful for those who bottom-fish along the reef. Deeper waters turn up barracuda and bonito. Sports people from all over the world come to the Caymans for the big ones: tuna, wahoo, and marlin. Most hotels can make arrangements for charter boats and experienced guides are also available. **Red Sail Sports,** in the Hyatt Regency Grand Cayman, West Bay Road (☎ **800/255-6425** or 345/947-5965), offers deep-sea-fishing excursions in search of tuna, marlin, and wahoo on a variety of air-conditioned vessels with an experienced crew. Tours depart at 7am and 1pm, last half a day, and cost $500 (a full day costs $700). The fee can be split among four to six people.

Into the Deep: Submarine Dives

So scuba diving's not enough for you? You want to see the real undiscovered depths of the ocean? On Grand Cayman, you have two options: the Atlantis reef dive, or the Atlantis deep dive, which takes you beyond the limits of scuba diving, down to 800 feet.

One of the island's most popular attractions is the ***Atlantis XI,*** Goring Avenue (☎ **800/887-8571** or 345/949-8296), a submersible that's 65 feet long, weighs 80 tons, and was built at a cost of $3 million to carry 48 passengers. You can view the reefs and colorful tropical fish through the 26 large viewpoints two feet in diameter, as the vessel cruises at a depth of 100 feet through the maze of coral gardens at a speed of 1 1/2 knots; a guide keeps you informed.

There are three types of dives. The premier dive, *Atlantis* Odyssey, features such high-tech extras as divers communicating with submarine passengers by wireless underwater phone and moving about on underwater scooters. This dive, operated both day and night, costs $82. On the *Atlantis* Expedition dive, you'll experience the reef and see the famous Cayman Wall; this dive lasts 55 minutes and costs $72. The *Atlantis* Discovery, which costs $55, lasts 40 minutes and introduces viewers to the marine life of the Caymans. Children 4 to 12 are charged half price (no children under 4 allowed). *Atlantis XI* dives Monday to Saturday, and reservations are recommended 24 hours in advance.

Atlantis also operates two deep-diving research submersibles, each of which carries two passengers and one pilot at a time. The submarines go as deep as 800 feet, although their limit is 1,000 feet. Grand Cayman is the top of an underwater mountain, whose side—known as the Cayman Wall—plummets straight down for 500 feet before becoming a steep slope falling away for 6,000 feet to the bottom of the ocean. These trips last just more than an hour and allow passengers to see the variety of sea life at different levels of the dive. Weather permitting, each dive goes down to the wreck of the *Kirk Pride,* a cargo ship that sank in 1976 and was lodged on a rock ledge at 780 feet. These deep dives cost $295 per person, and are available to anyone over the age of eight. Reservations should be made as early as possible, as availability is severely limited.

GOLF The major golf course on Grand Cayman is at the **Britannia Golf Club,** next to the Hyatt Regency on West Bay Road (☎ **345/949-8020**). The course, the first of its kind in the world, was designed by Jack Nicklaus and is unique in that it incorporates three different courses in one: a 9-hole championship layout, an 18-hole executive setup, and an 18-hole Cayman course. The last was designed for play with the Cayman ball, which goes about half the distance of a regulation ball. The Britannia charges $50 to $80 for greens fees in season, $40 to $65 off-season, depending on the configuration of the course you intend to play. Cart rentals go for $15 to $25; club rentals, $25. Hyatt guests can reserve 48 hours in advance, but everyone else can reserve no more than 24 hours in advance. Guests of the Hyatt receive a discount off the above rates.

SAILING **Red Sail Sports** (see "Fishing," above) rents 16-foot Prindle cats for $40 per hour, depending on the time of day. One of the best-designed sailing catamarans in the Caribbean is berthed in a canal a short walk from the water-sports center. Some 65 feet in length, with an aluminum mast 75 feet tall, it's fast, stable, and exhilarating. A 10am to 2pm sail to Stingray City, with snorkeling equipment and lunch included in the price of $60.50 per person, leaves once daily. A sunset sail from 5 to 7pm, with hors d'oeuvres, costs $27.50 per person. A romantic 3½-hour dinner sail costs $62.

SCUBA DIVING Established in 1957, the best-known dive operation in the Cayman Islands is **Bob Soto's Diving Ltd.** (☎ **800/262-7686** to make reservations, or 345/949-2022). Owned by Ron Kipp, the operation has grown to include full-service dive shops at Treasure Island, the SCUBA Centre on North Church Street, and Soto's Coconut in the Coconut Place Shopping Centre. A resort course, designed to teach the fundamentals of scuba to beginners who know how to swim, costs $90. This requires a full day: The morning is spent in the pool and the afternoon is a one-tank dive from a boat. All necessary equipment is included. Certified divers can choose from a wide range of one-tank ($40 to $45) and two-tank ($60 to $65) boat dives daily on the west, north, and south walls, plus shore diving from the SCUBA Centre. A full certification course costs $375. Nondivers can take advantage of daily snorkel trips ($20), including tours of Stingray City. The staff is helpful and highly professional.

Red Sail Sports (see "Fishing," above) offers beginners' scuba diving as well as excursions for the experienced. A two-tank morning dive includes exploration of two different dive sites at depths ranging from 50 to 100 feet, and costs $66. Beginners can take advantage of a course offered daily that costs $99 per person. A full certification course, requiring a maximum of five days, costs $440.

EXPLORING THE ISLAND

The capital, **George Town,** can easily be explored in an afternoon; it's known for its restaurants and shops (and banks!), but not sights. The town does offer a clock monument to King George V, as well as the oldest government building in use in the Caymans today, the post office on Edward Street. Stamps sold here are sought by collectors.

The island's premier museum, the **Cayman Islands National Museum,** Harbour Drive, in George Town (☎ **345/949-8368**), is in a much-restored clapboard-sided antique building directly on the water. The veranda-fronted building once served as the island's courthouse. The formal exhibits include a collection of Caymanian artifacts collected by Ira Thompson, beginning in the 1930s. Today the museum incorporates a gift shop, theater, cafe, and exhibits portraying the natural, social, and cultural history of the Caymans. Admission is CI$4 ($5) for adults, CI$2 ($2.50) for students and senior citizens, and free for children six and under. It's open Monday to Friday from 9am to 5pm and on Saturday from 10am to 2pm (last admission is half an hour before closing).

Elsewhere on the island, you might want to go to **Hell!** That's at the north end of West Bay Beach, a jagged piece of rock named Hell by a former commissioner. Here the postmistress will stamp "Hell, Grand Cayman" on your postcard to send back to the States.

The ✪ **Cayman Turtle Farm,** Northwest Point (☎ **345/949-3894**), is the only green-sea-turtle farm of its kind in the world, and is also, with some 250,000 visitors annually, the most popular land-based tourist attraction in the Caymans. Once the islands had a multitude of turtles in its surrounding waters (which is why Columbus called the islands "Las Tortugas"). Today these creatures are sadly few in number; the green sea turtle is an endangered species. The turtle farm has a twofold purpose: To provide the local market with edible turtle meat and to replenish the waters with hatchling and yearling turtles. Visitors today can look at 100 tanks in which these sea creatures can be observed in every stage of development; the hope is that one day their population in the sea will regain its former status. Turtles here range in size from 6 ounces to 600 pounds. At a snack bar and restaurant, you can sample turtle dishes. You cannot bring turtle products into the United States. The turtle farm is open daily from 8:30am to 5pm. Admission is $6 for adults, $3 for children 6 to 12, free for children 5 and under.

At **Botabano,** on the North Sound, fishers tie up with their catch, much to the delight of photographers. You can buy lobster (in season), fresh fish, and even conch. A large barrier reef protects the sound, which is surrounded on three sides by the island and is a mecca for diving and sports fishing.

If you're driving, you might want to go along **South Sound Road,** which is lined with pines and, in places, old wooden Caymanian houses. After leaving the houses behind, you'll find good spots for a picnic. On the road again, you'll reach **Bodden Town,** once the largest settlement on the island. At Gun Square, two cannons commanded the channel through the reef. They're now stuck muzzle-first into the ground.

On the way to the **East End,** just before Old Isaac Village, you'll see onshore sprays of water shooting up like geysers. These blowholes sound like the roar of a lion. Later, you'll spot the fluke of an anchor sticking up from the ocean floor. As the story goes, this is a relic of the famous "Wreck of the Ten Sails" in 1788. You can also see a modern wreck: the *Ridgefield,* a 7,500-ton Liberty ship from New England, which struck the reef in 1943.

Old Man Bay is reached by a road that opened in 1983. From here, you can travel along the north shore of the island to **Rum Point,** which has a good beach and is a fine place to end the tour. After visiting Rum Point, you can head back toward Old Man Village, where you can go south along the cross-island road through savannah country, where royal palms sway in the breeze. You might even spot the green Cayman parrot. The road will eventually lead you back to George Town.

The offshore waters of Grand Cayman are home to one of the most unusual (and ephemeral) underwater attractions in the world, **Stingray City.** Set in the sun-flooded, 12-foot-deep waters of North Sound, about 2 miles east of the island's northwestern tip, the site originated in the mid-1980s when local fishers cleaned their catch and dumped the offal overboard. They soon noticed scores of stingrays (which usually eat marine crabs) feeding on the debris, a phenomenon that quickly attracted local divers and marine zoologists. Today, between 30 and 50 relatively tame stingrays hover in the waters around the site for daily handouts of squid and ballyhoo from increasing hordes of amateur snorkelers and scuba enthusiasts.

Interestingly, most of the stingrays that feed here are females, the males preferring to remain in deeper waters offshore. To capitalize on the phenomenon, about half a dozen entrepreneurs lead expeditions from points along Seven Mile Beach, traveling around the land mass of Conch Point to the feeding grounds. One well-known outfit is **Treasure Island Divers** (☎ **800/872-7552** or 345/949-4456), which charges divers $45 and snorkelers $25. The trip is made on Monday, Wednesday, Friday, and Sunday at 1:30pm.

Be warned that stingrays possess deeply penetrating and viciously barbed stingers capable of inflicting painful damage on anyone who mistreats them. (Above all, the divers say, never try to grab one by the tail.) Despite the dangers, divers and snorkelers seem adept at feeding and petting the velvet surfaces of these creatures without incident.

An annual event, **Cayman Islands Pirates' Week** is held in late October. It's a national festival in which cutlass-bearing pirates and sassy wenches storm George Town, capture the governor, throng the streets, and stage a costume parade. The celebration, which is held throughout the Caymans, pays tribute to the nation's past and its cultural heritage. For the exact dates, contact the Pirates Week Festival Administration (☎ **345/949-5078**).

On 60 acres of rugged wooded land off Frank Sound Road, North Side, the **Queen Elizabeth II Botanic Park** (☎ **345/947-9462**) offers visitors a one-hour walk through wetland, swamp, dry thicket, mahogany trees, orchids, and bromeliads. The trail is 8/10 mile long. You'll likely see hickatees, the fresh-water turtles found only on the Caymans and in Cuba. Occasionally you'll spot the rare Grand Cayman parrot, or perhaps the anole lizard, with its cobalt-blue throat pouch. Even rarer is the endangered blue iguana. There are six rest stations with visitor information along the trail. The park is open daily from 7:30am to 5:30pm. Admission is $2.50 for adults, $1 for children, free for children five and under.

In 1996 a visitor center opened here, with changing exhibitions, plus a canteen for food and refreshments. It's set in a botanic park adjacent to the woodland trail and includes a heritage garden with a re-creation of a traditional Cayman home, garden, and farm; a floral garden with 1 1/2 acres of flowering plants, and a 2-acre lake, with three islands, home to many native birds.

One of the newest attractions in the Cayman Islands is the **Mastic Trail,** a restored 200-year-old footpath through a two-million-year-old woodland area in the heart of the island. The trail lies west of Frank Sound Road, about a 45-minute drive from the heart of George Town. Named for the majestic mastic tree, the trail showcases the reserve's natural attractions, including a native mangrove swamp, traditional agriculture, and an ancient woodland area, home to the largest variety of native plant and animal life found in the Cayman Islands. Guided tours, lasting 2 1/2 hours and limited to eight participants, are offered Monday to Friday at 8:30am and at 3pm, and again on Saturday at 8:30am. Reservations are required, and the cost is CI$25 ($31.25) per person. The hike is not recommended for children under six, the elderly, or persons with physical disabilities. Wear comfortable, sturdy shoes and carry water and insect repellent. For reservations, call ☎ **345/949-1996** Monday to Friday from 10am to 3pm.

SHOPPING

The duty-free shopping in George Town encompasses silver, china, crystal, Irish linen, British woolen goods, and such local crafts as black-coral jewelry. However, we've found the prices on many items to be similar to U.S. prices. Don't purchase turtle products—they cannot be brought into the United States. What follows is an A to Z list of the best shopping George Town has to offer.

Artifacts Ltd. Harbour Dr. (across from the cruise-ship dock), George Town. ☎ **345/949-2442.**

The premier outlet for some of the rare stamps issued by the Caymanian government, this shop is managed by Charles Adams, one of the country's philatelic authorities. Stamps range in price from 17¢ to $900, and the inventory includes the rare War Tax Stamp issued during World War II. Other items for sale include antique Dutch and Spanish coins unearthed from underwater shipwrecks, enameled boxes, and antique prints and maps.

Black Coral and . . . Fort St., George Town. ☎ **345/949-0123.**

Connoisseurs of unusual fine jewelry and unique objets d'art are drawn to the stunning black-coral creations of an internationally acclaimed sculptor, Bernard K. Passman, displayed here. He produced the Cayman Islands' wedding gift to Prince Charles and Lady Diana: a 97-piece cutlery set of sterling silver with black-coral handles, although who knows which party kept it in the divorce settlement. Another commission for the Cayman Islands was the creation of a black-coral horse and corgi dogs for Queen Elizabeth and Prince Philip. The gallery on Fort Street is a sightseeing attraction. Signed, limited-edition pieces are excellent investments.

English Shoppe. Harbour Dr. (in front of the cruise-ship landing), George Town. ☎ **345/949-2457.**

Watches, black- and pink-coral jewelry, and 14- and 18-karat jewelry are offered, all with prices quoted in U.S. dollars. The shop is divided into two sections, one selling fine jewelry and the other hawking souvenirs.

The Jewelry Centre. Fort St., George Town. ☎ **345/949-0070.**

A virtual department store of jewelry, this outlet has the largest selection of jewelry on the island. In a two-story building in the center of town, it contains six departments specializing in loose or set diamonds, gold (sold as chains or as ornaments, including coins found in shipwrecks offshore), black coral, colored gemstones, and caymanite, the pinkish-brown striated rock found only on the Caymans.

Kennedy Gallery. West Shore Centre, George Town. ☎ **345/949-8077.**

This gallery opened in 1993 in a shopping center on Seven Mile Beach. Specializing in watercolors by local artists (including Joanne Sibley and Lois Brezinski) as well as copies and originals of works by the establishment's founder, Robert Kennedy, it sells artworks ranging from $15 to as much as $7,000.

Kirk Freeport Plaza. Cardinal Ave. and Panton St., George Town. ☎ **345/949-7477.**

The largest store of its kind in the Caymans, Kirk Freeport Plaza contains a treasure trove of gold jewelry, watches, china, crystal, perfumes, and cosmetics. The store holds a Cartier franchise for the island and has handbags, valises, and perfumes priced 15% to 35% below suggested retail prices Stateside. Also stocked are crystal and porcelain from Wedgwood, Waterford, Lladró, and Baccarat, priced 30% to 50% less than recommended retail prices Stateside.

Sunflower Boutique. S. Church St. (directly on the waterfront), George Town. ☎ **345/949-4090.**

The largest of its type in the Cayman Islands, this boutique sells hand-painted skirts and blouses; T-shirts and shorts for men and women; jewelry fashioned from black, pink, and white coral; an assortment of gift items; and Caribbean paintings.

GRAND CAYMAN AFTER DARK: PUBS & CLUBS

The Cracked Conch. West Bay Rd., near Turtle Bay Farm. ☎ **345/947-5217.**

Although primarily a restaurant, this popular seafood eatery, known for its conch fritters and conch chowder, is also becoming known as a drinking and entertainment center. It offers karaoke and also shows classic dive films. Its happy hour with free hors d'oeuvres Tuesdays through Friday evenings is one of the best values on the island.

Lone Star Bar & Grill. West Bay Rd. ☎ **345/945-5175.**

It's like a transplanted corner of the Texas Panhandle. You can enjoy juicy hamburgers in the dining room or head directly for the bar in back. Here, beneath murals of Lone Star beauties, you can watch several sports events simultaneously on 15 different TV screens and sip lime and strawberry margaritas. Monday and Thursday are fajita nights, all-you-can-eat affairs, whereas Tuesday is all-you-can-eat lobster night, virtually unheard of in the Caribbean. There's a new volleyball court free for any client's use.

The Planet. West Bay Rd. ☎ **345/949-7169.** Cover $4 Tues, Thurs; $5 Wed, Fri–Sat.

About a block inland from West Bay Road, this dance club is adjacent to the island's only cinema. It's the largest dance floor with the biggest indoor stage on the island, containing a total of four bars dispensing reasonably priced drinks along with bar food. The mix of locals and tourists form a wide age range—from 18 to 50. Thursday is retro music night, with tunes from the 70s. Monday night is devoted to watching football games and there's no cover.

Ten Sails Pub and Coconuts Comedy Club. In the Holiday Inn Grand Cayman, West Bay Rd. ☎ **345/947-4444.** Cover: Pub, free during the day; comedy club, CI$12 ($15), plus a 2-drink minimum.

During the day, this place functions as an English-style pub. Several nights a week, however, the premises are transformed into the comedy club Coconuts, with comedic talents imported from all over the world. After the show, you can try your talents at karaoke, if you must. Murals of swashbuckling pirates and their treasure adorn the walls. A few steps from the pub's entrance, beside the hotel pool, a local musician and his band play island music throughout the evening.

2 Cayman Brac

The "middle" island of the Caymans was given the name Brac (Gaelic for bluff) by 17th-century Scottish fishers who settled here. The bluff for which the 12-mile-long island was named is a towering limestone plateau rising to 140 feet above the sea, covering the eastern half of Cayman Brac. Caymanians refer to the island simply as Brac, and its 1,400 inhabitants, a hospitable bunch of people, are called Brackers. Perhaps their laid-back lifestyle speaks to the laissez-faire attitudes of their predecessors: In the early 18th century the Caymans were occupied by pirates, and Edward Teach, the infamous Blackbeard, is supposed to have spent quite a bit of time around Cayman Brac. The island is about 89 miles east of Grand Cayman.

The big attraction of the Brac bluff today isn't new, in fact it's ancient. There are more than 170 caves honeycombing its limestone height. Some of the caves are at the bluff's foot whereas others can be reached only by climbing over jagged limestone rock. One of the biggest of them is Great Cave, which has a number of chambers. Harmless fruit bats cling to the roofs of the caverns.

On the south side of the bluff you won't see many people, and the only sounds are the sea crashing against the lavalike shore. The island's herons and wild green parrots are seen here. Most of the Brackers live on the north side, many in traditional wooden seaside cottages, some built by the island's pioneers. The islanders must all have green thumbs, as attested to by the variety of flowers, shrubs, and fruit trees in many of the yards. On Cayman Brac you'll see poinciana trees, bougainvillea, Cayman orchids, croton, hibiscus, aloe, sea grapes, cactus, and coconut and cabbage palms. The gardeners grow cassava, pumpkins, breadfruit, yams, and sweet potatoes.

There are no actual towns on the island, only settlements, such as Stake Bay (the "capital"), Spot Bay, the Creek, Tibbitt's Turn, the Bight, and West End, where the airport is located.

GETTING THERE

Flights from Grand Cayman to Cayman Brac are operated by **Cayman Airways** (☎ **800/422-9626** in the U.S. and Canada, or 345/949-2311). The airline uses relatively large 737 jets. There are three daily flights, plus a morning return. The cost is $154 for an overnight round-trip, or $99 for a day trip.

WHERE TO STAY

Brac Caribbean Beach Village. P.O. Box 4, Stake Bay, Cayman Brac, B.W.I. ☎ **800/791-7911** or 345/948-2265. Fax 345/948-1111. 16 condos. Year-round, $165 apt for 2; $220 apt for 4; $1,000 apt for 2 adults for 7 nights. Scuba packages from $275 for 6 dives. MC, V.

The largest condo project on the island offers 16 two-bedroom/two-bath or two-bedroom/three-bath condos on a white sandy beach, along with a pool and scuba-diving program. Accommodations come with full-size refrigerator with ice maker, microwave, and coffeemaker, and 12 of them open onto a private balcony. A variety of items, including breakfast food, are stocked before your arrival. The master bedroom is furnished with a queen-size bed, the guest bedrooms with twin beds, and there's a cable TV in the living room. Maid service costs an extra $35 per day. The bedrooms are rather simply furnished in a Caribbean tropical motif, with rattan and chintz. The hotel offers some of the best dining on the island (see Captain's Table, below).

Brac Reef Beach Resort. P.O. Box 56, Cayman Brac, B.W.I. ☎ **800/327-3835** in the U.S. and Canada, or 345/948-1323. 40 rms. A/C TV. Winter, $468–$517 per person double for divers, $358–$407 per person double for nondivers. Off-season, $462 per person double for divers, $352 per person double for nondivers. Rates are for 3-night packages and include MAP and 2 days of diving; additional packages available. AE, DC, DISC, MC, V.

On a sandy plot of land on the south shore 2 miles east of the airport, near some of the best snorkeling in the region, this resort contains motel-style units comfortably furnished with carpeting, ceiling fans, and modern baths. Once the location was little more than a maze of sea grapes, a few of whose venerable trunks still rise amid the picnic tables, hammocks, and boardwalks. On the premises are the rusted remains of a Russian lighthouse tower that was retrieved several years ago from a Cuban-made trawler.

Dining/Entertainment: Lunches are informal affairs, whereas dinners are most often served buffet style under the stars. The food is not quite as good as that at the Divi Tiara (see below).

Services: Laundry, maid service, baby-sitting.

Facilities: Pool, Jacuzzi, Reef Divers (a full-service operation providing instruction for both beginning and advanced divers, and the use of all rental gear, including masks, snorkels, fins, regulators, and weight belts).

Divi Tiara Beach Resort. P.O. Box 238, Cayman Brac, B.W.I. ☎ **800/367-3484** in the U.S. and Canada, or 345/948-1553. Fax 345/948-7564. 52 rms, 13 suites. A/C TV TEL Winter, $125–$200 double; $245–$255 suite. Off-season, $95–$140 double; $180 suite. Children 15 and under stay free in parents' room. MAP $41 per person extra. AE, DISC, MC, V.

Part of the Divi Divi hotel chain, the Tiara, about 2 miles east of the airport, attracts divers and honeymooners to its beachfront. Many newcomers respond at once to the landscaping, which incorporates croton, bougainvillea, and palms. All the rather basic accommodations are housed in motel-like outbuildings; 13 of the units are time-shares, each with an ocean view, Jacuzzi, and king-size bed.

Dining/Entertainment: At the bar guests gaze out to sea while sipping their drinks before heading to the Poseidon dining room to enjoy Caribbean and American cuisine. There's entertainment at the hotel twice a week.

Services: Laundry.

Facilities: An excellent Peter Hughes Dive Tiara operation; a swimming pool raised above a white-sand beach where boardwalks run beneath groves of palms; tennis court lit for night play.

WHERE TO DINE

Captain's Table. Brac Caribbean Beach Village, Stake Bay. ☎ **345/948-2265.** Reservations recommended. Main courses $11.25–$22.50; lunch from $12. MC, V. Daily 11:30am–3pm and 6–9:30pm. AMERICAN.

The decor is Caribbean cliché, vaguely nautical with oars over and around the bar and pieces of boats forming the restaurant's entryway. In the same building as a scuba shop and the reception desk, the restaurant offers both indoor and air-conditioned seating, along with outside dining by the pool. Begin with a captain's cocktail of shrimp and lobster or else conch fritters, then follow with one of the soups such as black bean. Main dishes include everything from the catch of the day, often served panfried, to barbecue ribs. At lunch you can order a selection of burgers and sandwiches.

FUN ON & OFF THE BEACH

The biggest lure to Cayman Brac is the variety of **water sports:** swimming, fishing, snorkeling, and some of the world's best diving and coral reef exploration. There are undersea walls on both the north and south sides of the island, with stunning specimens lining their sides. The best dive center is **Peter Hughes Dive Tiara** at the Divi Tiara Beach Resort (see "Where to Stay," above).

History buffs might check out the **Cayman Brac Museum,** in the former Government Administration Building, Stake Bay (☎ **345/948-2622**), which has an interesting collection of Caymanian antiques, including pieces rescued from shipwrecks and items from the 18th century. Open Monday to Friday from 9am to noon and 1 to 4pm, Saturday from 9am to noon, and Sunday 1 to 4pm. Admission is free.

3 Little Cayman

The smallest of the Cayman Islands, cigar-shaped Little Cayman has only about 40 permanent inhabitants. Little Cayman is 10 miles long and about a mile across at its widest point. It lies about 75 miles northeast of Grand Cayman and some 5 miles from Cayman Brac. The entire island is coral and sand.

The islands of the Caymans are mountaintops of the long-submerged Sierra Maestra Range, which runs north and into Cuba. Coral formed layers over the underwater peaks, eventually creating the islands. Beneath Little Cayman's Bloody Bay is one of the mountain's walls—a stunning sight for snorkelers and scuba divers.

The island seems to have come into its own now that fishing and diving have taken center stage; this is a near-perfect place for such pursuits. The waters around the little island were hailed by the late Philippe Cousteau as one of the three finest diving spots in the world. The flats on Little Cayman are said to offer the best bonefishing in the world, and a brackish inland pool can be fished for tarpon. Even if you don't dive or fish, you can row 200 yards off Little Cayman to isolated and uninhabited Owen Island, where you can swim at the sandy beach and picnic by a blue lagoon.

There may still be pirate treasure buried on the island, but it's in the dense interior of what is now the largest bird sanctuary in the Caribbean. Little Cayman is also home to a unique species of lizard that predates the iguana. It's the oldest species of New World reptile, and there are only 50 specimens in the world.

Blossom Village, the island's "capital," is on the southwest coast.

GETTING THERE

Most visitors fly from Grand Cayman to Little Cayman. **Island Air** (☎ **800/949-0241** or 345/949-5252), a charter company, charges $154 round-trip. Call Island Air directly.

WHERE TO STAY & DINE

Little Cayman Beach Resort. Blossom Village, Little Cayman, Cayman Islands, B.W.I. ☎ **800/327-3835** in the U.S. and Canada, or 345/948-1033. Fax 345/948-1040. 40 rms. A/C TV. Winter, $573–$674 per person double for divers, $422–$523 per person double for nondivers. Off-season, $518–$618 per person double for divers, $368–$469 per person double for nondivers. Rates are for 3-night packages and include MAP. Longer packages are available. AE, MC, V.

The governor of the Cayman Islands flew in to open this largest-ever resort on Little Cayman. The first part opened in 1992, the second half in 1993. Lying on the south coast, the resort is close to many of the island's diving and sporting attractions, including bonefishing in the South Hole Sound Lagoon, and this place is popular with fisherfolk, divers, bird-watchers, and adventure-oriented travelers. The hotel, owned by the Tibbetts family, lies only 3/4 mile from the Edward Bodden Airport (really a grass airstrip), and it has a white-sand beach fringing a shallow, reef-protected bay. Nonsmoking units are available, and the rooms have ceiling fans and air-conditioning. They are divided into two pastel coral two-story buildings with gingerbread trim. The most desirable units are the four luxurious oceanfront rooms which go fast, since, in spite of their added comfort, they're booked at the same rate as the less preferred rooms. The hotel has a tennis court and a swimming pool overlooking the sea and a Jacuzzi, along with complete water-sports facilities including a dive shop. Its bar and restaurant are among the most popular on the island.

Pirates Point Resort, Ltd. Little Cayman, Cayman Islands, B.W.I. ☎ **345/948-1010.** Fax 345/948-1011. 10 rms. Winter, $215 per person double for divers, $150 per person double for nondivers; $195 per person triple for divers, $140 per person triple for nondivers. Off-season, $195 per person double for divers, $135 per person double for nondivers; $175 per person triple for divers, $125 per person triple for nondivers. Rates all-inclusive (nondiver rates do not include bar tab). Children 5 and under not accepted. MC, V.

For water activities or just relaxing, this resort near West End Point offers a family environment with gourmet cuisine. The owner and manager, Gladys Howard, a graduate of Cordon Bleu in Paris who has studied with such stars as Julia Child and the late James Beard, has written several cookbooks. In her menus, she uses fresh fruits and vegetables grown locally, as well as local seafood.

The place has four remodeled and air-conditioned rooms, and a family cottage of two large rooms, each suitable for three or four people. In addition, it has four recently built seaside cottages, with air-conditioning and balconies overlooking Preston Bay. The resort offers package holidays, including room, three excellent meals per day with appropriate wines and all alcoholic beverages, and two-tank boat dives daily featuring tours of the Bloody Bay Wall, the Cayman trench, and Jackson Reef. Nondiving activities include snorkeling, bird watching, and exploring. Recent facilities added include a swimming pool and Jacuzzi. Bonefishing, tarpon fishing, and an Owen Island picnic are available for an additional charge. Prince Charles himself, sailing by on his yacht, selected Owen Island for a picnic.

5 Puerto Rico

No one has ever suffered from boredom on Puerto Rico, which offers a vast array of resorts, activities, and entertainment. It has hundreds of beaches, a mind-boggling array of water sports, acres of golf courses, miles of tennis courts, and casinos galore. It has more discos than any other place in the Caribbean, and shopping bargains to equal St. Thomas.

Lush, verdant Puerto Rico is only half the size of New Jersey and is located some 1,000 miles southeast of the tip of Florida. With 272 miles of Atlantic and Caribbean coastline, and a culture dating back 2,000 years, Puerto Rico is a formidable attraction. Old San Juan is its greatest historic center, with 500 years of history, as reflected in its restored Spanish colonial architecture.

It's also a land of contrasts. There are 79 cities and towns on Puerto Rico, each with a unique charm and flavor. The countryside is dotted with centuries-old coffee plantations, sugar estates still in use, a fascinating tropical rain forest environment, and foreboding caves and enormous boulders with mysterious petroglyphs carved by the Taíno peoples, the original settlers.

Accommodations have also been greatly improved in recent years, even in some of the smaller cities such as Ponce and Mayagüez. *Paradores* (government-sponsored inns) are sprinkled across the island for visitors who want a more intimate experience than that provided by the more impersonal hotels of San Juan.

Dorado Beach, Cerromar Beach, and Palmas del Mar are the chief centers for those who've come for golf, tennis, and beaches. San Juan's hotels on the Condado/Isla Verde coast also have, for the most part, a complete array of water sports. The continental shelf, which surrounds Puerto Rico on three sides, contributes to an abundance of coral reefs, caves, sea walls, and trenches for scuba diving and snorkeling.

San Juan is the world's second-largest home port for cruise ships. The old port of San Juan recently underwent a $90 million restoration.

In this chapter, we start out in San Juan, and then move west, counterclockwise around the island, until we reach Ponce. Then we'll turn our attention to attractions east of San Juan, and head clockwise around the island. Keep in mind that you can base yourself at one resort and still do a lot of exploring elsewhere if you don't mind driving for a couple of hours. It's possible to branch out and see a lot of the island even if you're staying in San Juan.

GETTING THERE

Puerto Rico is by far the most accessible of the Caribbean islands, with frequent airline service. **American Airlines** (☎ **800/433-7300**) has designated San Juan as its hub for the entire Caribbean. American offers 39 nonstop daily flights to San Juan from Baltimore, Boston, Chicago, Dallas–Fort Worth, Hartford, Miami, Newark, New York (JFK), Orlando, Philadelphia, Tampa, Fort Lauderdale, and Washington (Dulles), plus flights to San Juan from both Montréal and Toronto with changes in Chicago or Miami. There are also at least two daily flights from Los Angeles to San Juan that touch down in Dallas or Miami.

American, because of its wholly owned subsidiary, **American Eagle,** also is the undisputed leader among the short-haul local commuter flights of the Caribbean. It usually flies in propeller planes carrying between 42 and 64 passengers. Collectively, American Airlines/American Eagle take passengers to 38 destinations on 30 islands of the Caribbean, far more than any other carrier.

Delta (☎ **800/221-1212**) has four daily nonstop flights from Atlanta Monday to Friday, nine nonstop on Saturday, and seven nonstop on Sunday. It also offers one daily nonstop flight to San Juan from Orlando. Flights into Atlanta from around the world are frequent, with excellent connections from points throughout Delta's network in the South and Southwest.

United Airlines (☎ **800/241-6522**) has daily nonstop flights from Chicago to San Juan. **Northwest** (☎ **800/447-4747**) has daily connecting flights via Detroit to San Juan and one daily nonstop flight from Detroit. They also have Saturday and Sunday nonstop service from Memphis and Minneapolis to San Juan. **TWA** (☎ **800/892-4141**) has three daily nonstop flights in winter from New York to San Juan, dropping down to two in the off-season. There are also daily nonstop flights from St. Louis to San Juan in winter, but none in summer. **US Airways** (☎ **800/428-4322**) also competes, with one weekly direct flight from Baltimore to San Juan.

Smaller airlines include **Carnival** (☎ **800/824-7386**), a Florida-based airline owned by the Carnival Group of cruise-line fame. The line offers a nonstop flight from New York to Aguadilla and Ponce, and connecting flights through New York's JFK and Newark. They also have flights from Miami and Los Angeles to San Juan.

Tower Air (☎ **800/221-2500,** or 800/452-5531 in New York City) has a daily nonstop flight from New York to San Juan every day except Tuesday and Saturday.

British travelers wanting to visit San Juan can take a **British Airways** (☎ **800/247-9297**) weekly flight direct from London to San Juan on Sunday; **Lufthansa** (☎ **800/645-3880**) passengers can fly on Saturday (one weekly flight) from Frankfurt to San Juan via Condor (a subsidiary operating the flight); and **Iberia** (☎ **800/772-4642**) has two weekly flights from Madrid to San Juan, leaving on Thursday and Sunday.

GETTING AROUND THE ISLAND

FLIGHTS WITHIN PUERTO RICO **American Eagle** (☎ **787/749-1747**) flies from Luís Muñoz International Airport to Mayagüez, which can be your gateway to the west of Puerto Rico. Fares vary widely according to the season, the restrictions associated with your ticket, and whatever special promotion might be in effect at the time of your booking, but expect to pay between $69 and $130 round-trip, per person, and try to book your passage as early as possible prior to your flight.

RENTAL CARS Some local car-rental agencies may tempt you with slashed prices, but if you're planning to tour the island, you won't find any local branches should you run into car trouble. And some of the agencies advertising low-cost deals don't take credit or charge cards and want cash in advance. You also have to watch out for

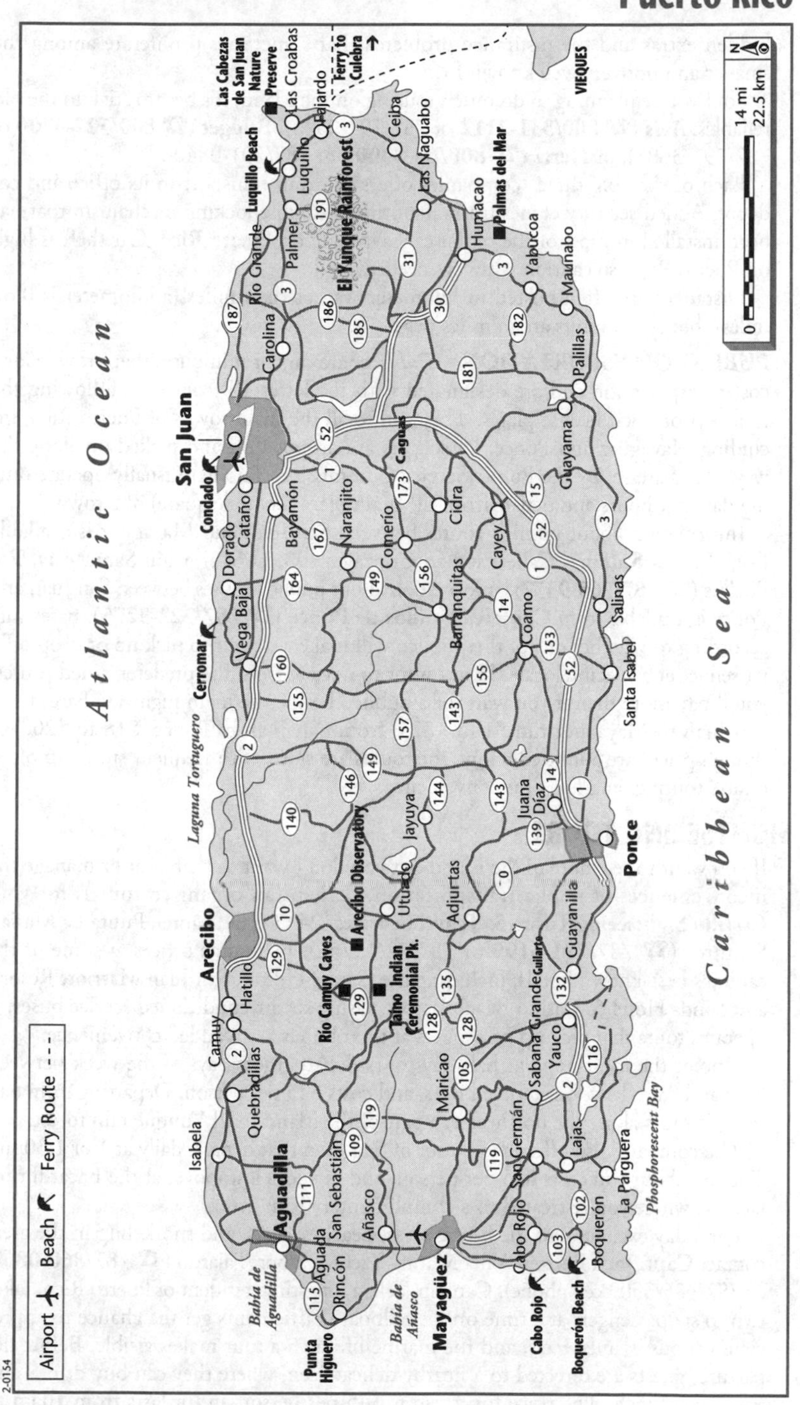
2-0154
Airport
Beach
Ferry Route
Atlantic Ocean
Caribbean Sea
San Juan
Condado
Ponce
Mayagüez
Aguadilla
Arecibo
Cerromar
Laguna Tortuguero
Luquillo Beach
Las Cabezas de San Juan Nature Preserve
Ferry to Culebra
El Yunque Rainforest
Palmas del Mar
VIEQUES
Arecibo Observatory
Río Camuy Caves
Taíno Indian Ceremonial Pk.
Punta Higuero
Bahía de Aguadilla
Bahía de Añasco
Cabo Rojo
Boquerón Beach
Phosphorescent Bay
Isabela
Quebradillas
Camuy
Hatillo
Vega Baja
Dorado
Cataño
Bayamón
Carolina
Río Grande
Palmer
Luquillo
Fajardo
Las Croabas
Ceiba
Naguabo
Humacao
Yabucoa
Maunabo
Patillas
Guayama
Salinas
Santa Isabel
Coamo
Cayey
Cidra
Caguas
Comerío
Naranjito
Barranquitas
Juana Díaz
Jayuya
Utuado
Adjuntas
Guayanilla
Yauco
Sabana Grande
San Germán
Lajas
La Parguera
Boquerón
Maricao
Rincón
Aguada
San Sebastián
Añasco
14 mi
22.5 km

hidden extras and the insurance problems that sometimes proliferate among the smaller and not very well known firms.

So if you're planning to do much touring on the island, it's best to stick to the old reliables: **Avis** (☎ **800/331-2112** or 787/791-2500), **Budget** (☎ **800/527-0700** or 787/791-3685), or **Hertz** (☎ **800/654-3001** or 787/791-0840).

Each of the "big-three" companies offers minivan transport to its office and car depot. Added security comes from an antitheft double-locking mechanism that has been installed in most of the rental cars available on Puerto Rico. Car theft is high on Puerto Rico, so caution is always needed.

Distances are often posted in kilometers rather than miles (a kilometer is 0.62 miles), but speed limits are in miles per hour.

PUBLIC TRANSPORTATION ***Públicos*** are cars or minibuses that provide low-cost transportation and are designated with the letters "P" or "PD" following the numbers on their license plates. They run to all the main towns of Puerto Rico, including Mayagüez and Ponce. Passengers are dropped off and picked up along the way. Rates are set by the Public Service Commission. Públicos usually operate during daylight hours and depart from the main plaza (central square) of a town.

Information about público routes between San Juan and Mayagüez is available from **Lineas Sultana,** Calle Esteban González 898, Urbanización Santa Rita, Rio Piedras (☎ **787/765-9377**). Information about público routes between San Juan and Ponce is available from **Choferes Unidos de Ponce** (☎ **787/722-3275**). Fares vary according to whether or not the público will make a detour to pick up or drop off a passenger at a specific locale. If you want to deviate from the predetermined routes, you'll pay more than if you wait for a público beside the main highway. Fares from San Juan to Mayagüez run $10 to $25; from San Juan to Ponce, $18 to $20. Although prices are admittedly low, the routes are slow, with frequent stops, an often erratic routing, and lots of inconvenience.

SIGHTSEEING TOURS

If you want to see more of the island but you don't want to rent a car or manage the inconveniences of public transportation, perhaps an organized tour is for you. **Castillo Sightseeing Tours & Travel Services,** 2413 Calle Laurel, Punta La Marias, Santurce (☎ **787/791-6195** or 787/726-5752), maintains offices at some of the capital's best-known hotels, including the Caribe Hilton, San Juan Marriott Resort, and Sands Hotel & Casino Beach Resort. Using six air-conditioned service buses, it operates tours that pick up passengers at their hotels as an added convenience.

One of the most popular half-day tours departs most days of the week between 8:30 and 9am, lasts four to five hours, and costs $25 per person. Departing from San Juan, it tours along the northeastern part of the island to El Yunque rain forest.

The company also offers a city tour of San Juan that departs daily at 1 or 1:30pm. The four-hour trip costs $25 per person, and includes a stopover at the Bacardi rum factory, where you're treated to a complimentary rum drink.

For a day excursion to the best islands, beaches, reefs, and snorkeling in the area, contact **Capt. Jack Becker,** Villa Marina Yacht Harbor, Fajardo (☎ **787/860-0861,** or 787/385-3509 cell phone). Captain Jack, a long-time resident of Puerto Rico, takes two to six passengers at a time on his sailboat. Participants get the chance to appreciate various islands, reefs, and the marine life such a tour makes visible. Before departure, guests are directed to a nearby delicatessen, where they can buy drinks and a package lunch. The price for a trip is $45 per person and it lasts from 10am to 3:30pm. Reservations can be made at any hour.

ECOTOUR PACKAGES

Puerto Rico's varied and often hard-to-reach natural treasures have been conveniently packaged into a series of ecotours, operated by **Tropix Wellness Tours** (☎ **787/268-2173;** fax 787/268-1722). Four major tours are offered, including the exploration of sea turtles' nesting sites in Culebra, the phosphorescent bay in Vieques, the Río Camuy cave system in Camuy, and the dry, desertlike forest in Guanica.

The **Happy Turtle Tour** on Culebra includes a half-day kayaking/snorkeling expedition and a visit to the sea turtles' nesting sites during the spring/summer season. The cost includes four days/three nights of accommodations at a villa with a view and air-conditioning. The tour starts at Rivas Dominici Airport in Miramar and interisland air transportation to Culebra Airport is included. Rates are $473 per person, based on double occupancy, and include continental breakfast, three boxed lunches, and equipment for escorted expeditions.

Vieques, Puerto Rico's other offshore island, is the focus of the **Bioluminescent Bay Tour,** which includes an expedition to the Isla Nena, home to one of the most panoramic bioluminescent bays in the world. Additional attractions on Vieques include reefs, bird sanctuaries, and deserted sandy beaches. The tour includes four days/three nights of accommodations at the Crows Nest and interisland air transportation to Vieques. Rates are $388.75 per person, based on double occupancy, and include full breakfast, three boxed lunches, and equipment.

The **Caveman Tour** in Camuy includes an expedition through one of the largest underground cave river systems in the world. Miles of natural waterways are surrounded by stalagmites, stalactites, sunless vegetation, and 20 different species of marsupials. The tour includes three days/two nights of accommodations at the Paragor Guajatacai in Cebradija. Rates are $243 per person, based on double occupancy, and include two full breakfasts, one full lunch, and equipment.

The **Express Tour** in Maricao includes a full-day hiking expedition in the mountains and natural spring-water pools of the area. The Express Tour costs $243 per person, including three days/two nights double occupancy at the Hacienda Juanita, a restored coffee plantation turned hotel.

The **Wet & Dry Tour** in Guanica includes two expeditions: A dry forest hike and mangrove kayaking at sunset. Southwestern Puerto Rico is home to the world's largest remaining tract of tropical dry coastal forest. This part of the island also features miles of mangrove channel systems. Visitors can explore these waterways by kayak as they are led to secluded Caribbean beaches. The tour includes four days/three nights of accommodations at the Copamarina Hotel. Rates are $518 per person, based on double occupancy, and include three full breakfasts and equipment.

Tropix Wellness Tours will customize an itinerary for those traveling to Puerto Rico alone, or for groups of six or more. "Add-ons" to the fixed tours, such as body-rafting expeditions through underground cave rivers and hiking excursions, can also be arranged.

FAST FACTS: Puerto Rico

American Express American Express–related services are handled by Travel Network, at 1035 Ashford Ave., Condado (☎ **787/725-0960**). The office is open Monday to Friday from 9am to 5pm and on Saturday from 9 to 11:30am.

Banks All major U.S. banks have branches in San Juan, and are open Monday to Friday from 8:30am to 2:30pm.

Currency The **U.S. dollar** is the coin of the realm. Canadian currency is accepted by some big hotels in San Juan, although reluctantly.

Documents Since Puerto Rico is part of the United States, American citizens do not need a passport or visa. Canadians, however, should carry some form of identification, such as a birth certificate. Citizens of the United Kingdom should have a passport.

Electricity The electricity is 110 volts AC (60 cycles), as it is in the continental United States and Canada.

Emergencies In an emergency, call 911, or else the local **police** (☎ **787/343-2020**), **fire department** (☎ **787/343-2330**), **ambulance** (☎ **787/343-2550**), or **medical assistance** (☎ **787/754-3535**).

Information Out in the island, it's best to go to the local city hall for tourist information. Ask for a copy of ***Qué Pasa,*** the official visitors' guide.

For information before you leave home, contact one of the following **Puerto Rico Tourism Company** offices: 575 Fifth Ave., New York, NY 10017 (☎ **800/223-6530** or 212/599-6262); 3575 W. Cahuenga Blvd., Suite 405, Los Angeles, CA 90068 (☎ **800/874-1230** or 213/874-5991); or 901 Ponce de León Blvd., Suite 604, Coral Gables, FL 33134 (☎ **800/815-7391** or 305/445-9112).

In Canada you can stop by 41–43 Colbourne St., Suite 301, Toronto, ON M5E 1E3 (☎ **800/667-0394** or 416/368-2680) for information.

Language English is understood at the big resorts and in most of San Juan. Out in the island, Spanish is still *numero uno.*

Safety Use common sense and take precautions. Muggings have been reported on the Condado and Isla Verde beaches in San Juan, so you might want to confine your moonlit-beach nights to the fenced-in and guarded areas around some of the major hotels. The countryside of Puerto Rico is safer than San Juan, but caution is always the rule. Avoid small and narrow little country roads and isolated beaches, either by night or day.

Taxes There's a government tax of 7% in regular hotels or 9% in hotels with casinos. The airport departure tax is included in the price of your ticket.

Time Puerto Rico is on Atlantic standard time year-round, making it one hour ahead of U.S. eastern standard time. In winter, when it's noon in Miami, it's 1pm in San Juan. But from April until late October (during daylight saving time on the East Coast), Puerto Rico and the East Coast keep the same time.

Tipping Some hotels add a 10% service charge to your bill. If they don't, you're expected to tip for services rendered. Tip as you would in the United States (15% to 20%).

Weather Puerto Rico is cooler than most of the other Caribbean islands because of its northeast trade winds. Sea, land, and mountain breezes also help keep the temperatures at a comfortable level. The climate is fairly stable all year, with an average temperature of 76°F. The only variants are found in the mountain regions, where the temperature fluctuates between 66° and 76°F, and on the north coast, where the temperature ranges from 70° to 80°F.

1 San Juan

San Juan, the capital of Puerto Rico, is a major city—actually an urban sprawl of several municipalities that lie along the island's north coast. Its architecture ranges from classic colonial buildings that recall the Spanish empire to modern beachfront hotels reminiscent of Miami Beach.

ESSENTIALS

ARRIVING If you're not traveling on a package deal that includes transfers to your hotel, you'll see lots of options after landing at the San Juan airport. A wide variety of vehicles refer to themselves as *limosinas* (their Spanish name).

One outfit with a sign-up desk in the arrivals hall of the international airport, near the American Airlines arrival facilities, is the **Airport Limousine Service** (☎ **787/791-4745**). It offers minivan transport from the airport to various neighborhoods of San Juan for prices that are lower than for similar routings offered by taxis. Whenever 8 to 10 passengers can be accumulated, the fare for transport, with luggage, to any hotel in Isla Verde is $2.50 per person; to the Condado, $3 per person; and to Old San Juan, $3.50 per person.

For conventional limousine service, **Bracero Limousine** (☎ **787/253-5466**) offers upholstered cars with drivers to meet you and your entourage at the arrivals terminal of the airport for luxurious and strictly private transport to your hotel. Transport anywhere in San Juan ranges from $105 to $145, depending on your destination, and should be arranged in advance of your arrival.

ORIENTATION San Juan breaks down into several divisions: **San Juan Island,** containing the city center and the old walled city (Old San Juan); **Santurce,** a large peninsula that's linked to San Juan Island by causeway; **Condado,** a narrow peninsula that stretches between San Juan Island and Santurce; **Puerto de Tierra,** the section east of Old San Juan that contains many government buildings; **Miramar,** a lagoon-front section south of Condado; and **Isla Verde,** which is detached from the rest of San Juan by an isthmus.

VISITOR INFORMATION Tourist information is available at the **Luís Muñoz Marín Airport** (☎ **787/791-1014**). Another office is at **La Casita,** Pier 1, Old San Juan (☎ **787/722-1709**).

GETTING AROUND

BY TROLLEY The best way to save your feet in Old San Juan is to board one of the free open-air trolleys that slowly make their way through the narrow, often cobblestoned, old streets. You can board a trolley at any point along its route, or go to the marina or La Puntilla for departures.

BY BUS The **Metropolitan Bus Authority** (☎ **787/767-7979**) operates buses in the greater San Juan area. Bus stops are marked by upright metal signs or yellow posts, reading "*parada.*" Bus terminals in San Juan are in the dock area and at Plaza de Colón. A typical fare is 25¢ to 50¢. The higher fee is for the faster buses that make less stops. Call for more information about routes and schedules.

BY TAXI Taxis, operated by the **Public Service Commission** (☎ **787/756-1919**), are metered in San Juan—or should be. Make sure your driver turns on and uses the meter. The initial charge is $1, plus 10¢ for each 1/10 mile and 50¢ for every suitcase. A minimum fare is $3. Call the PSC to request information or report any irregularities. Taxi Turisticos is a fleet designed especially for visitors; taxis are painted white with an official logo on their doors. Their rates, ranging between $6 and $16, are fixed, and these cabs go between Old San Juan and the Condado, or else to Isla Verde.

BY FERRY The ***Agua Expreso*** (☎ **787/751-7055**) connects the old town of San Juan with the industrial and residential communities of Hato Rey and Cataño, across the bay. Ferries depart daily every 30 minutes from 6am to 9pm. The one-way fare is 75¢ to Hato Rey (till 6:40pm) and 50¢ to Cataño (till 8pm). Departures are from the San Juan Terminal at the pier in Old San Juan. However, avoid rush hours, as locals who work in town use this ferry connection by the hundreds. Rides last about 20 minutes. Call for more information.

FAST FACTS: SAN JUAN

One of the most centrally located **drugstores** is the Puerto Rico Drug Co., Calle San Francisco 157 (☎ **787/725-2202**), in Old San Juan; it's open Monday to Friday from 7am to 9:30pm, Saturday from 8am to 9:30pm and on Sunday from 8:30am to 7:30pm. Walgreen's, 1130 Ashford Ave., Condado (☎ **787/725-1510**), is a 24-hour pharmacy. In a **medical emergency,** call ☎ **787/721-2116.** Ashford Memorial Community Hospital, 1451 Ashford Ave. (☎ **787/721-2160**) maintains 24-hour emergency rooms.

GREAT DISCOUNTS THROUGH THE LELOLAI VIP PROGRAM

For $10, the cost of membership in Puerto Rico's ✪ **LeLoLai VIP** (Value in Puerto Rico), visitors can enjoy the equivalent of up to $200 in travel benefits. Admission to folkloric shows and discounts on guided tours of historic sites and natural attractions, as well as on lodgings, meals, shopping, sports activities, and more, add up to significant savings.

The *paradores puertorriqueños,* the island's modestly priced network of country inns, give cardholders 10% to 20% lower room rates Monday to Thursday. Discounts of 10% to 20% are offered at many restaurants, from San Juan's toniest hotels to several *mesones gastronómicos,* government-sanctioned restaurants out on the island serving Puerto Rican fare. Shopping discounts are offered at many stores and boutiques and, best yet, cardholders get 10% to 20% discounts at many island attractions.

The card also entitles you to free admission to folkloric musical shows, including *Noches de Puerto Rico* Thursday at 10pm (adults only) at Sands Hotel Casino & Beach Resort. The pass also works for another show, *Jolgorio* at the Caribe Terrace of the Caribe Hilton on Wednesday at 8:30pm. For more information about this card, call ☎ **787/723-3125.**

WHERE TO STAY

All hotel rooms on Puerto Rico are subject to a 7% to 9% tax, which is not included in the rates listed in this chapter. Most hotels also impose a 10% service charge.

IN OLD SAN JUAN

El Convento. 100 Cristo St. ☎ **800/525-4800** or 787/723-9020. Fax 787/721-2877. 57 rms, 4 suites. A/C TV TEL. Winter, $285–$380 double; off-season, $195–$320 double. Suite from $500 year-round. AE, MC, V. Bus A7, T1, or 21.

Puerto Rico's most famous (but not the best) hotel had been allowed to deteriorate to a shabby version of its former self but it came back to life in 1996 when it was restored and reopened. Built in 1651, this hotel in the heart of the old city was once the New World's first Carmelite convent. Over the years El Convento played many roles when it ceased being a convent—everything from dance hall to flop house. By 1953, it had been turned into a parking lot for garbage trucks. Rescued from ruin, it opened as a hotel in 1962 but didn't make money and was seized by the government for back taxes.

Now restored at the cost of around $275,000 per room, El Convento offers accommodations on its third to fifth floors, with a concierge-style reception and check-in and a club lounge. Handcrafted in Spain, room furnishings are in traditional Spanish style, with mahogany beams and handmade tile floors.

The lower two floors feature artists and artisans in residence, with galleries, specialty shops, restaurants, and cafes. The interior courtyard is again open to the sky, as it was in the 1600s. Breakfast is served in an outdoor garden terrace. There's also a swimming pool, Jacuzzi, indoor fitness center, and massage facilities, plus an intimate casino.

Gallery Inn at Galería San Juan. Calle Norzagaray 204–206, San Juan, PR 00901. ☎ **787/722-1808.** Fax 787/724-7360. 9 rms, 13 suites. Year-round, $95–$300 double; $200–$350 suite. Rates include continental breakfast. AE, MC, V. Bus: A7, T1, or 21.

Set on a hilltop in the old town, with a sweeping view of the sea, this unusual hotel contains a maze of verdant courtyards. In the 1700s it was the home of an aristocratic Spanish family. Today it's one of the most whimsically bohemian hotels in the Caribbean. The guest house is run by its Connecticut-born owner, Jan D'Esopo, a noted painter, sculptor, and silk-screen artist. She is assisted by her husband, Manuco Gandía. All courtyards and rooms are adorned with hundreds of sculptures, silkscreens, or original paintings, usually for sale. The Library Room and the Stevy Room have no air-conditioning. There are three free parking spaces; other parking is available on street.

✪ **Wyndham Old San Juan Hotel & Casino.** 101 Calle Marina, 00901 San Juan, PR. ☎ **800/996-3426** or 787/721-5100. Fax 787/721-1111. 200 rms, 40 suites. A/C MINIBAR TV TEL. Winter, $305 double; from $375 suite. Off-season, $250 double; from $325 suite. AE, CB, DISC, DC, MC, V.

Opened in 1997, this nine-story hotel was built on one of the only parcels of land remaining within the historic core of San Juan. It was conceived as part of a $100 million renovation of San Juan's cruise port facilities, and as such is jointly owned by the Puerto Rican government, the construction company that built it, and Wyndham Hotels. Its position between buildings erected by the Spanish monarchs in the 19th century and the city's busiest and most modern cruise-ship terminals is one of the most unusual and desirable in Puerto Rico.

Great care was taken to create a pastel-colored building whose iron railings and exterior detailing convey a sense of colonial San Juan, an effect heightened with the addition of $1.5 million worth of mahogany trim inside the hotel. Its triangular floor plan encircles an inner courtyard that floods light into the tasteful and comfortable, beige-and-white bedrooms, each of which has two phone lines and a modem connection for laptop computers. Everything about the place is designed as an enhancement for the nearby cruise-ship facilities and the attractions of historic San Juan.

Dining/Entertainment: About 80% of the lobby level is devoted to a 10,000 square foot casino, where facilities for five-card stud poker, recently legalized, compete with 240 slot machines and roulette tables. Because of the nearby availability of all the restaurants of Old San Juan, the hotel has only one restaurant, an upscale, fine dining emporium that also functions as the breakfast area. Two bar/lounges, one with live music, round out the entertainment venue.

Services: 24-hour room service, concierge.

Facilities: A conference center, within an early 20th-century historic building known as *Isla Bonita,* is connected to the hotel by an aerial catwalk. A swimming pool, health club, and Jacuzzi on the 9th floor overlook the harbor and cruise-ship docks.

San Juan Accommodations

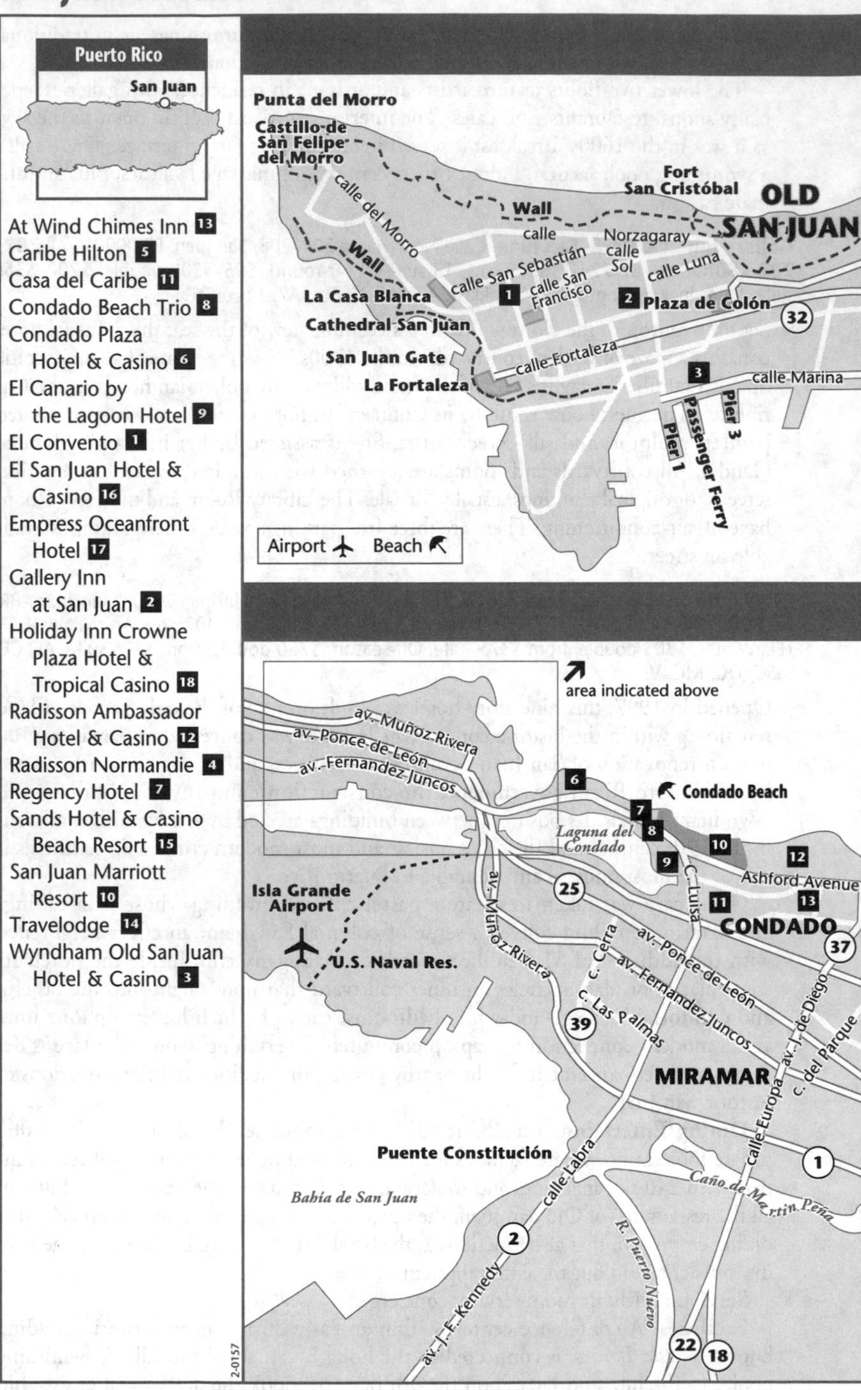

Puerto Rico
San Juan
At Wind Chimes Inn 13
Caribe Hilton 5
Casa del Caribe 11
Condado Beach Trio 8
Condado Plaza Hotel & Casino 6
El Canario by the Lagoon Hotel 9
El Convento 1
El San Juan Hotel & Casino 16
Empress Oceanfront Hotel 17
Gallery Inn at San Juan 2
Holiday Inn Crowne Plaza Hotel & Tropical Casino 18
Radisson Ambassador Hotel & Casino 12
Radisson Normandie 4
Regency Hotel 7
Sands Hotel & Casino Beach Resort 15
San Juan Marriott Resort 10
Travelodge 14
Wyndham Old San Juan Hotel & Casino 3
Punta del Morro
Castillo de San Felipe del Morro
calle del Morro
Wall
Fort San Cristóbal
OLD SAN JUAN
calle Norzagaray
calle Sol
calle Luna
calle San Sebastián
calle San Francisco
La Casa Blanca
Plaza de Colón
Cathedral San Juan
San Juan Gate
calle Fortaleza
La Fortaleza
calle Marina
Pier 1
Passenger Ferry
Pier 3
Airport
Beach
area indicated above
av. Muñoz Rivera
av. Ponce de León
av. Fernandez Juncos
Condado Beach
Laguna del Condado
Ashford Avenue
C. Luisa
CONDADO
Isla Grande Airport
U.S. Naval Res.
c. Cerra
c. Las Palmas
c. del Parque
av. J. de Diego
MIRAMAR
calle Europa
Puente Constitución
Caño de Martin Peña
Bahía de San Juan
calle Labra
R. Puerto Nuevo
av. J. F. Kennedy
2-0157

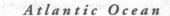

OLD SAN JUAN & PUERTO DE TIERRA

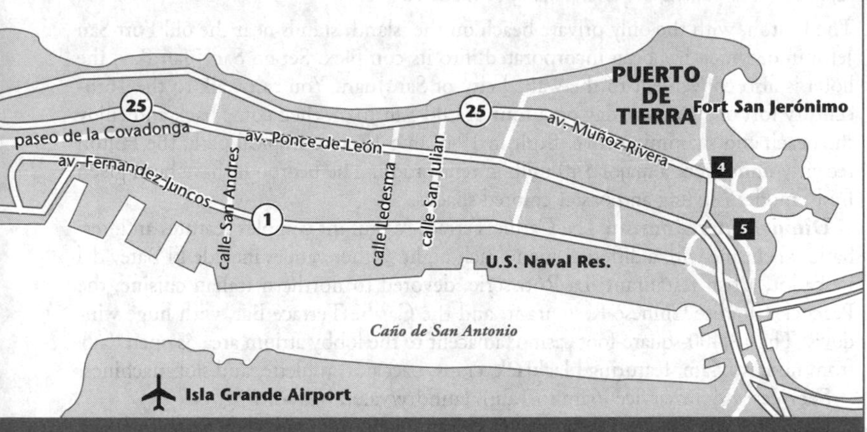

MIRAMAR, CONDADO, SANTURCE, OCEAN PARK & ISLA VERDE

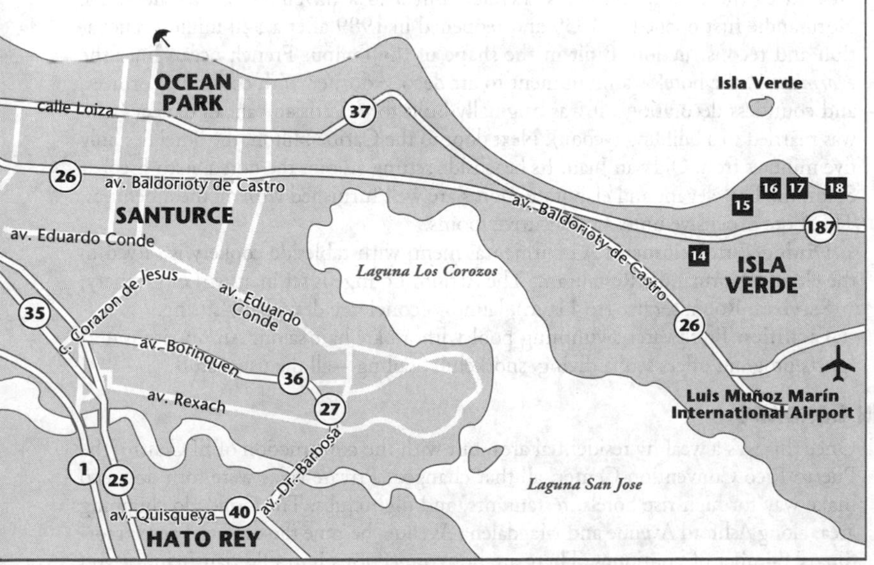

In Puerto de Tierra

Caribe Hilton. Calle Los Rosales, San Juan, PR 00902. ☎ **800/HILTONS** in the U.S. and Canada, or 787/721-0303. Fax 787/724-6992. 622 rms, 49 suites. A/C MINIBAR TV TEL. Winter, $299–$449 double. Off-season, $185–$349 double. Year-round, $500–$1,300 suite. Children 15 and under stay free in parents' room (maximum 4 people per room). AE, CB, DC, DISC, MC, V. Self-parking $7; valet parking $14. Bus: A7.

The Hilton, with the only private beach on the island, stands near the old Fort San Jerónimo, which has been incorporated into its complex. Set on San Juan Bay, the hotel is also convenient to the walled city of San Juan. You can walk to the 16th-century fort or spend the day on a tour of Old San Juan, then come back and enjoy the beach and swimming cove. Built in 1949 in a 17-acre tropical park, the Hilton recently underwent a major $40 million renovation. The bedrooms have been given fresh, modern styling and pastel-colored shades.

Dining/Entertainment: The Caribe Terrace restaurant complex features an international cuisine with a different menu each night. Other venues include El Batey del Pescador, a fish restaurant; La Rôtisserie, devoted to northern Italian cuisine; the Peacock Paradise Chinese Restaurant; and the Caribe Terrace Bar, with huge windows. The 12,400-square-foot casino, adjacent to the lobby atrium area, is open daily from noon to 4am, featuring blackjack, craps, baccarat, roulette, and slot machines.

Services: Room service (6am to 1am), laundry/valet, baby-sitting.

Facilities: Spa Caribe, two freshwater swimming pools, health club, aerobics, beach activities, children's playground, play room, six lighted tennis courts, business center.

Radisson Normandie. Avenida Muñoz-Rivera (at the corner of Calle Los Rosales), San Juan, PR 00902. ☎ **800/333-3333** in the U.S., or 787/729-2929. Fax 787/729-3083. 177 rms, 3 suites. A/C MINIBAR TV TEL. Winter, $220–$250 double; $490 suite. Off-season, $175–$205 double; $410 suite. Rates include full American breakfast. AE, DC, DISC, MC, V. Outdoor parking $5. Bus: A7.

Geared to the upscale business traveler, but also a haven for vacationers, the Normandie first opened in 1939 and reopened in 1989 after a $20 million renovation and reconstruction. Built in the shape of the famous French ocean liner the *Normandie,* the hotel is a monument to art deco. Adorned with columns, cornices, and countless decorations, it was originally built for a Parisian cancan dancer (who was married to a building tycoon). Next door to the Caribe Hilton, the hotel lies only five minutes from Old San Juan. Its beachside setting adjoins the noted Sixto Escobar Stadium. The elegant and elaborate rooms are well furnished with all the amenities. The more expensive units are executive rooms.

Dining/Entertainment: A continental menu with tableside cookery is served in the elegant Normandie Restaurant. The Atrium Lounge is set in a swirl of greenery.

Services: Room service (to 11pm), laundry, concierge desk, baby-sitting.

Facilities: Freshwater swimming pool with a bar, hair salon. An on-site watersports program offers scuba diving, snorkeling, sailing—all the usual stuff.

In Condado

Once this was a wealthy residential area, but with the construction of El Centro, the Puerto Rico Convention Center, all that changed. Private villas were torn down to make way for high-rise hotels, restaurants, and nightclubs. The Condado shopping area, along Ashford Avenue and Magdalena Avenue, became the center of an extraordinary number of boutiques. There are bus connections into Old San Juan, or you can take a taxi.

Very Expensive

✪ Condado Plaza Hotel & Casino. 999 Ashford Ave., San Juan, PR 00907. ☎ **800/468-8588** in the U.S., or 787/721-1000. Fax 787/253-0178. 540 rms, 15 suites. A/C MINIBAR TV TEL. Winter, $285–$400 double; $1,200 suite. Off-season, $255–$370 double; $335–$850 suite. AE, CB, DC, DISC, MC, V. Valet parking $15. Bus: A7.

This is one of the busiest hotels on Puerto Rico, with enough facilities, restaurants, and distractions to keep a visitor busy for weeks. The Hilton is its major rival, but we prefer this one's style and flair. Although not the most intimate of San Juan's hotels, it is the most visible, set on a strip of beachfront at the beginning of the Condado. The original buff-colored structure is linked by an elevated passageway above Ashford Avenue to its annex, the Laguna Wing, which has its own lobby with direct access from the street.

All units have private terraces. The complex's most deluxe section, the Plaza Club, contains 75 units, five duplex suites, a VIP lounge reserved exclusively for the use of its guests, and private check-in/check-out service.

The hotel is owned by the same consortium that owns the somewhat more upscale El San Juan Hotel & Casino. Use of the facilities at one hotel can be charged to a room at the other.

Dining/Entertainment: The Lotus Flower is one of the island's leading Chinese restaurants. Ristorante Capriccio has northern Italian cuisine. Las Palmas and Tony Roma's are other dining choices. La Posada, next to the casino and open 24 hours a day, is known for its prime beef and seafood. For nighttime entertainment, La Fiesta offers live Latin music.

Services: 24-hour room service, fresh towels at beach and pools, laundry.

Facilities: Five swimming pools, water sports, fitness center in the Laguna Wing, two lit Laykold tennis courts.

Radisson Ambassador Hotel & Casino. 1369 Ashford Ave., San Juan, PR 00907. ☎ **800/468-8512** in the U.S., or 787/721-7300. Fax 787/723-6151. 146 rms, 87 suites. A/C TV TEL. Winter, $235–$265 double; from $325 suite. Off-season, $220–$250 double; from $270 suite. AE, CB, DC, DISC, MC, V. Self-parking $6; valet parking $10. Bus: A7.

In the heart of the Condado, but a short walk from the beach, the Ambassador emerged as a star-studded hotel after entrepreneur Eugene Romano poured more than $40 million into its restoration in 1990. The hotel offers theatrical drama and big-time pizzazz, with Czech and Murano chandeliers; hand-blown wall sconces; Turkish, Greek, and Italian marble; and yards of exotic hardwoods. What's missing (especially at these prices) are the resort amenities associated with the Hilton and the Condado Plaza.

Accommodations are in a pair of high-rise towers, one of which is devoted to suites. The decors are inspired variously by 18th-century Versailles, 19th-century London, imperial China, and art deco California. Each unit has pay-per-view movies and a balcony with outdoor furniture.

Dining/Entertainment: La Scala's northern Italian cuisine is the hotel's culinary highlight. But the newest treat is Sweeney's, a "Scotch & Sirloin" grill for those who like to eat like Jackie Gleason did back in the '50s. The casino (open noon to 4am) has more slot machines than any other on the Condado, and a singer/pianist performs from a quiet corner bar. There are four bar/lounges, one of which has live local dance music.

Services: Room service (6:30am to midnight), baby-sitting, laundry, 24-hour concierge, VIP floors with extra amenities and enhanced services, a social programmer who offers a changing array of daily activities.

Facilities: Penthouse-level fitness and health club, beauty salon, rooftop swimming pool, Jacuzzi, business center (staffed with typists, translators, guides, and stenographers).

San Juan Marriott Resort. 1309 Ashford Ave., San Juan, PR 00907. ☎ **800/228-9290** or 787/722-7000. Fax 787/289-6006. 525 rms, 13 suites. A/C MINIBAR TV TEL. Winter, $265–$380 double; from $525 suite. Off-season, $153–$330 double; from $500 suite. AE, DC, DISC, MC, V. Parking $8.

It's the tallest building on the Condado, a 21-story landmark that Marriott spent staggering sums to renovate and enlarge. It reopened in a radically different format after a tragic fire gutted the premises in 1989. The new entity packs lots of postmodern style, and one of the best beaches on the Condado lies right outside. Furnishings in the soaring lobby were inspired by the Chippendale salon of a high-style hotel. If there's a flaw, it's the decor of the comfortable but bland bedrooms whose pastel themes look washed out when compared to the rich mahoganies and jewel tones of the bedrooms in the rival Condado Plaza Hotel. Nonetheless, the rooms boast one of the most advanced telephone networks on the island, carefully maintained security and fire-prevention systems, safes, and in-room VCRs. About half of them occupy a new nine-story, pink-and-turquoise wing that Marriott added during the hotel's reconfiguration and rebuilding.

Dining/Entertainment: There's live music in the lobby every evening from 6 to 9pm; two bands perform there Thursday to Saturday from 9pm to 3am. Dining options include Tuscany's (see "Where to Dine," below); La Vista, whose buffet lunches and dinners are worth a detour; and a poolside grill that serves tropical drinks, sandwiches, and salads.

Services: 24-hour room service, concierge, beauty salon, shopping kiosks, tour desk, car-rental facilities.

Facilities: The Stellaris Casino, which isn't as glitzy as some of its competitors, is next to the hotel's main lobby. There are two tennis courts and two swimming pools (whose mosaic bottoms glow luminously when viewed from the hotel's observatory-style 21st floor), and a health club with many massage and spa treatments.

Moderate

El Canario by the Lagoon Hotel. Calle Clemenceau 4, San Juan, PR 00907. ☎ **800/533-2649** in the U.S., or 787/722-5058. Fax 787/723-8590. 40 rms. A/C TV TEL. Winter, $100–$110 double. Off-season, $80–$90 double. Rates include continental breakfast and morning newspaper. AE, DC, DISC, MC, V. Bus: A7 or 2.

A European-style hotel operated by the Olsons, El Canario is in a quiet residential neighborhood just a short block from Condado Beach. The attractive but small rooms all have their own balconies, rattan furniture, refrigerators, and safes. The hotel has a guest laundry and an in-house tour desk. A relaxing, informal atmosphere prevails, and the hotel provides excellent value for the money.

Inexpensive

At Wind Chimes Inn. Calle Taft 53, Condado, San Juan, PR 00911. ☎ **800/946-3244** or 787/727-4153. Fax 787/726-5321. 12 rms, 1 suite. A/C TV TEL. Winter, $65–$75 double; from $85 suite. Off-season, $55–$65 double; $75 suite. Rates include continental breakfast. AE, DISC, MC, V. Bus: M8, A7, T1, 21, or 2.

This restored and renovated Spanish manor is one of the best Puerto Rican guest houses on the Condado, with great value at affordable rates. Upon entering a tropical patio, you'll find tile tables surrounded by palm trees and bougainvillea. There's plenty of space on the deck and a covered lounge for relaxing, socializing, and eating breakfast. Dozens of decorative wind chimes add melody to the daily breezes. The rooms offer a choice of size, beds, and kitchens; all contain ceiling fans and air-conditioning. The location is one short block from the beach and 3 1/2 miles from the airport.

Casa del Caribe. Calle Caribe 57, San Juan, PR 00907. ☎ **787/722-7139.** Fax 787/725-3995. 9 rms. A/C TV TEL. Winter, $65–$85 double. Off-season, $55–$75 double. Rates include continental breakfast. AE, DISC, MC, V. Bus: A7, T1, or 2.

Formerly known as Casablanca, this renovated guest house lies in the heart of the Condado. Built in the 1940s, it was later expanded, then totally refurbished with a tropical decor late in 1995. A very Puerto Rican ambience has been created, with emphasis on Latin hospitality and comfort. On a shady side street just off Ashford Avenue, behind a wall and garden, you'll discover Casa del Caribe's wraparound veranda. The cozy guest rooms have ceiling fans and air conditioners, and most of them feature original Puerto Rican art. The front porch is a social center for guests. Don't expect the Ritz, but if you're looking for a bargain on the Condado, this is it.

In Isla Verde

Beach-bordering Isla Verde is closer to the airport than the other sections of San Juan, but farther from Old Town. Some of the most deluxe hotels of the Caribbean are located here. If you don't mind the isolation and want access to the fairly good beaches, then consider one of the following hotels.

Very Expensive

✪ **El San Juan Hotel & Casino.** 6063 Isla Verde Ave. Carolina, San Juan, PR 00979. ☎ **800/468-2818** or 787/791-1000. Fax 787/253-2003. 372 rms, 20 suites. A/C MINIBAR TV TEL. Winter, $370–$470 double; from $960 suite. Off-season, $255–$370 double; from $775 suite. AE, DC, DISC, MC, V. Self-parking $8; valet parking $13.

For dozens of reasons, this is the best hotel on Puerto Rico—some say it's the best in the entire Caribbean basin. Built in the 1950s, it was restored with an infusion of $45 million. The beachfront hotel is surrounded by 350 palms, century-old banyans, and gardens. Its 700-yard-long sandy beach is the finest in the San Juan area. The hotel's river pool, with its currents, cascades, and lagoons, evokes a jungle stream. The lobby is the most opulent and memorable in the Caribbean. Entirely sheathed in red marble and hand-carved mahogany paneling, the public rooms stretch on almost endlessly.

The accommodations have intriguing touches of high-tech. Each contains a dressing room, three phones, and a VCR. A few feature Jacuzzis. About 150 of the accommodations, designed as comfortable bungalows, are in the outer reaches of the garden. Known as *casitas,* they include Roman tubs, atrium showers, and access to the fern-lined paths of a tropical jungle a few steps away.

The hotel is a great choice for families, with more activities for children than any other on Puerto Rico.

Dining/Entertainment: La Veranda Restaurant, near the beach, is open 24 hours. Yamato, a Japanese restaurant, is one of the best at the hotel. Good Italian food is served for lunch and dinner at La Piccola Fontane. Or you can promenade down a re-creation of a Hong Kong waterfront to a Chinese restaurant, Back Street Hong Kong. The in-house casino is open daily from noon to 4am.

Services: 24-hour room service, dry cleaning, baby-sitting, massage service. The supervised Kids Klub has daily activities ranging from face painting to swimming lessons—all for children 5 to 12 years old.

Facilities: Rooftop health club, spa, two swimming pools, water sports, steam room, sauna, tennis court, table tennis.

Sands Hotel & Casino Beach Resort. 187 Isla Verde Ave., Isla Verde, PR 00979. ☎ **800/443-2009** in the U.S., or 787/791-6100. Fax 787/791-8525. 403 rms, 9 suites. A/C TV TEL.

Winter, $299–$349 double; from $700 suite. Off-season, $205–$250 double; from $500 suite. AE, DC, DISC, MC, V. Self-parking $5; valet parking $10. Bus: A7, M7, or T1.

Originally built around 33 years ago as the Americana, this hotel received a new lease on life in 1987, when it was overhauled into a Caribbean version of the Sands Hotel in Atlantic City. It is, of course, outclassed by the far swankier El San Juan Hotel next door, but, amid tropical gardens and with a beachfront setting, it enjoys a high occupancy rate and the attentions of many tour operators. The comfortable bedrooms have balconies and terraces. The most desirable are in the Plaza Club, a minihotel within the hotel that sports a private entrance, concierge service, complimentary food and beverage buffets, and suite/spa and beach facilities.

Dining/Entertainment: The hotel's most upscale restaurant is Giuseppe, serving northern Italian cuisine. Equally appealing is the Ruth's Chris Steak House, and Tucano's, a tropical theme restaurant serving seafood and Caribbean cuisine. Simple beachfront dining is offered in the Boardwalk Grill. The in-house nightclub offers revue-style spoofs of Hollywood legends and glittery Vegas-inspired shows, depending on bookings. The in-house casino is also popular.

Services: Room service (6am to 2pm and 5pm to 2am), baby-sitting, laundry, limousine service, massage service.

Facilities: The resort boasts the Caribbean's largest free-form swimming pool, complete with waterfalls, rockscapes, and a swim-up bar; business center; scuba diving.

Expensive

Holiday Inn Crowne Plaza Hotel & Tropical Casino. Rte. 187, km 1.5 Isla Verde, San Juan, PR 00979. ☎ **800/2-CROWNE** in the U.S. and Canada, or 787/253-2929. Fax 787/253-0079. 254 rms, 22 suites. A/C TV TEL. Winter, $199–$219 double; $239–$369 suite. Off-season, $169–$179 double; $229–$269 suite. AE, DC, DISC, MC, V. Self-parking $6; valet parking $10. Bus: T1.

This is the easternmost of the grand modern hotels of San Juan, and the leading Caribbean showcase of the Holiday Inn chain. Set on a landscaped plot of beachfront close to the airport, the hotel incorporates tropical themes and colors in its decor. Rising 12 stories above a great beach, the resort has gathered a loyal clientele from North America and the Caribbean since it opened in 1991.

You register in a large but simple lobby sheathed with beige marble. The bedrooms each offer some kind of ocean view and are decorated in pastel shades. The bathrooms, which contain both marble and tile, have hair dryers and phones. Each accommodation is double-insulated against noises from the nearby airport.

Dining/Entertainment: The premier dining outlet is Windows on the Sea, an oceanfront emporium serving international and Puerto Rican food. An acceptable (but not great) Italian cuisine is offered at La Dolce Vita. There's also a large casino.

Services: Room service (6:30am to midnight daily), baby-sitting, laundry. On floors devoted to enhanced facilities and services, a concierge staff provides free continental breakfasts and complimentary early evening hors d'oeuvres.

Facilities: A large free-form swimming pool with swim-up bar, a sandy beachfront studded with palm trees and sea grapes, car-rental facilities, a tour desk, children's games room, children's pool, fitness center, an in-house gift shop, and both a sports club and a beach club devoted to land and water sports.

Moderate

Empress Oceanfront Hotel. 2 Amapola St., Isla Verde, PR 00913. ☎ **800/678-0757** in the U.S., or 787/791-3083. Fax 787/791-1423. 30 rms. A/C TV TEL. Winter, $148–$168 double. Off-season, $88–$128 double. AE, DC, MC, V. Bus: T1.

Set on $2^1/_2$ acres of rocky headlands jutting out from the coastline, this four-story pink-sided hotel is efficiently run by an Anglo-Latino family that immigrated from

Brooklyn. From its enclosed swimming pool terrace, you'll enjoy sweeping views of the high-rise hotels and valuable real estate nearby.

On the premises is a popular bar, the Blue Dolphin, and a likable restaurant, Sonny's Oceanfront Place for Ribs. A Jacuzzi is near the pool. The pleasantly airy decor is inspired by the tropics.

Travelodge. Avenida Isla Verde (P.O. Box 6007, Loiza Station), Santurce, PR 00914. ☎ **800/468-2028** or 787/728-1300. Fax 787/727-7150. 88 rms, 2 suites. A/C TV TEL. Winter, $137 double; $175 suite. Off-season, $91 double; $160 suite. AE, MC, V.

Rising eight stories above the busy traffic of Isla Verde, this chain hotel offers comfortable bedrooms furnished simply with bland modern furniture. Many guests carry a tote bag to the beach across the street, then patronize the bars, restaurants, and swimming facilities of the expensive hotels nearby. There's only one restaurant (the Country Kitchen), one swimming pool, and one bar (the Escort Lounge) at Travelodge. Don't expect tons of personal service from the desk personnel or staff. There is live dance music by the pool Monday through Saturday nights.

WHERE TO DINE

In Old San Juan

Expensive

✪ **Chef Marisoll.** Calle del Cristo 202. ☎ **787/725-7454.** Reservations required. Main courses $22–$32. AE, MC, V. Tues–Sat noon–2:30pm and 7–10:30pm, Sun 7–10:30pm. CONTEMPORARY.

Marisoll Hernández is the finest female chef in San Juan. Trained in Hilton properties, including one in London, she broke away to become an independent restaurateur in the Old Town of San Juan. In a Spanish colonial building, with a courtyard patio for dining, her eight-table restaurant is warm and intimate. Servicc is low key and slightly formal. You could, of course, have a sandwich for lunch, but few would want to settle for that when they can sample one of the chef's imaginative dishes. Two of her soups are worthy of appearing in *Gourmet* magazine, including a cream of exotic wild mushrooms with an essence of black truffles, and her butternut-squash soup with crisp ginger. There's usually a catch of the day, or you can try her risotto with shrimp, lobster, and scallops in a saffron sauce. A truly elegant and beautifully flavored tenderloin with foie gras is another specialty.

Il Perugino. Calle del Cristo 105. ☎ **787/722-5481.** Reservations required. Main courses $18–$23. AE, MC, V. Tues–Wed 7–10:30pm, Thurs–Sat noon–3pm and 6:30–11pm. TUSCAN/UMBRIAN.

This is one of the most elegant Italian restaurants in San Juan. It's located in a 200-year-old town house, a short walk uphill from the town's cathedral. The courtyard contains covered dining tables. The entire setting is painted in shades of ochre and umber reminiscent of Perugia, the homeland of owner/chef Franco Seccarelli. Assisted by his Puerto Rican wife, Luzalma, he serves a well-prepared menu that concentrates on the standard Umbrian dishes. Examples include shrimp salad (usually a mundane dish, but quite special as prepared here), a carpaccio of scallops, and a perfectly marinated fresh salmon. Want something more adventurous? Try the "black pasta" with crayfish and baby eels. Daily specials sometimes add variety to the menu.

✪ **La Chaumière.** Calle Tetuán 367. ☎ **787/722-3330.** Reservations recommended. Main courses $20.50–$29.50. AE, DC, MC, V. Mon–Sat 6pm–midnight. Closed July–Aug. Bus: A7, T1, or 2. FRENCH.

Behind the famous Tapía Theater, this restaurant with a cafelike decor has a loyal following of foodies drawn to its classic cuisine—the kind of dishes that you might find in a roadside tavern somewhere deep in France. The setting is appropriate, a bit flowery like a greenhouse. You might begin with a rather heartily flavored country pâté, then follow with a rack of baby lamb Provençale. A tender chateaubriand is served only for two. Those old standbys, veal Oscar and oysters Rockefeller, also regularly appear.

Yukiyu. Calle Recinto Sur 311. ☎ **787/721-0653.** Reservations recommended. Main courses $14–$19; fixed-price teppanyaki dinners $20–$35; sushi $2.50–$10.50 apiece. AE, DISC, MC, V. Mon–Fri noon–2:20pm and 5–11pm, Sat noon–2:20pm and 7–11pm. Bus: A7, T1, or 2. JAPANESE.

Traditional Japanese and other Asian cooking techniques are combined in this restaurant in Old Town. Its sushi bar is acclaimed as the best in the Caribbean, and tabs can mount quickly. Sushi is available at both lunch and dinner, although the teppanyaki grill at the front, where your own personal chef will attend to you, is offered only at dinner. The dining room itself is postmodern and monochromatic.

Against this backdrop, the various chefs tempt you with hibachi chicken or chicken with scallops and sesame seeds. You might begin with miso soup or steamed pork dumplings, then go on to a shrimp-and-vegetable tempura, or perhaps fillet of sole with capers. Fresh yellowfin tuna with teriyaki is a favorite, as is the chicken teriyaki.

Moderate

Al Dente. Calle Recinto Sur 309. ☎ **787/723-7303.** Reservations recommended. Main courses $10–$15. AE, MC, V. Mon–Fri noon–2pm and 5:30–10pm; Sat noon–10:30pm. Bus: A7, T1, or 2. SICILIAN.

Located in the heart of Old San Juan, this unpretentious restaurant has a decor that might remind you of some trattoria you enjoyed in Palermo. Both the dress code and the ambience are relaxed and casual. You might sample the scallops on a bed of spinach sautéed in cream, or gnocchi with pesto, fettuccine maestro, ravioli, or well-seasoned calamari. The chef also makes his own desserts, including cheesecake, tiramisu, and chocolate tortes. Nearly all dishes are genuinely satisfying and the restaurant delivers quality food at a reasonable price. Brochettes of fresh tuna laced with pepper and Mediterranean herbs is an excellent choice.

✪ **Amadeus.** Calle San Sebastián 106 (across from the Iglesia de San José). ☎ **787/722-8635.** Reservations recommended. Main courses $13.50–$19.50. AE, MC, V. Tues–Sun noon–2am (kitchen closes at 12:30am). Bus: M2, M3, or T1. CARIBBEAN.

Housed in a brick-and-stone building that was constructed in the 18th century by a wealthy merchant, Amadeus offers Caribbean ingredients with a nouvelle twist. The appetizers alone are worth the trip here, especially Amadeus dumpling with guava sauce and arrowroot fritters. The chef will even prepare a smoked salmon and caviar pizza. While receiving a cordial welcome, you can enjoy dishes *de la tierra* (from the land) or *del mar* (from the sea), including a fresh catch of the day. One zesty specialty is pork scaloppini with sweet and sour sauce.

El Patio de Sam. Calle San Sebastián 102 (across from the Iglesia de San José). ☎ **787/723-1149.** Reservations not required. Main courses $7.95–$21.95. AE, DC, DISC, MC, V. Sun–Thurs 11am–midnight, Fri–Sat 11am–1:30am. Bus: A7, T1, or 2. AMERICAN/PUERTO RICAN.

This is a popular gathering spot for American expatriates, newspeople, and shopkeepers, and is known for having the best burgers in San Juan. Even though the dining room is not outdoors, it has been transformed into a patio. You'll swear you're dining al fresco: Every table is placed near a cluster of potted plants, and canvas panels and awnings cover the skylight. For a satisfying lunch, try the black-bean soup, followed by the burger platter, and top it off with a key lime tart. Except for the hamburgers, some other items on the menu have not met with favor among many visitors, who have written us that the food was overpriced and the service confused. Nevertheless, it remains Old Town's most popular dining room. They now have live entertainment, Monday through Saturday, with a guitarist playing Spanish music some nights, giving way to a classical pianist on other nights.

Inexpensive

Butterfly People Café. Calle Fortaleza 152. ☎ **787/723-2432.** Reservations not required. Main courses $5.50–$9.50. AE, DC, MC, V. Mon–Sat 11am–5pm. Bus: A7, T1, or 2. CONTINENTAL/AMERICAN.

This restaurant is on the second floor of a restored mansion in Old San Juan. Next to the world's largest gallery devoted to butterflies, you can dine in the cafe, which overlooks a courtyard and has 15 tables inside. The cuisine is tropical and light European fare made with fresh ingredients. You might begin with gazpacho or vichyssoise, follow with quiche or one of the daily specials, and finish with chocolate mousse or the tantalizing raspberry chiffon pie with fresh raspberry sauce. A full bar offers tropical specialties such as piña coladas, fresh-squeezed Puerto Rican orange juice, and Fantasias, a frappe of seven fresh fruits. Wherever you look, framed butterflies will delight you.

Hard Rock Café. Calle Recinto Sur 253. ☎ **787/724-7625.** Reservations not required. Main courses $5.95–$15.95. AE, MC, V. Daily 11am–midnight. (Bar, daily 11am–2am.) Bus: A7, T1, or 2. AMERICAN.

Filled with rock 'n' roll memorabilia, this cafe lies in a historic district of Old Town. Serving a "classic" American cuisine against a backdrop of loud rock music, the Hard Rock is here to stay, packing in the crowds for drinks, burgers, and T-shirts. Check out the artifacts from the rock 'n' roll hall of fame, ranging from a wig worn by Elton John to a jacket that encased the torso of John Lennon. There's also a Pink Floyd guitar and Phil Collins's drumsticks. Throughout the day well-stuffed sandwiches and juicy burgers are served, although many prefer to head here for dinner, filling up on fajitas, barbecued chicken, pork ribs, or even the catch of the day. The chili will set you ablaze.

La Bombonera. Calle San Francisco 259. ☎ **787/722-0658.** Reservations recommended. Main courses $5.75–$15.90. AE, DISC, MC, V. Daily 7:30am–8pm. Bus: M2, M3, or T1. PUERTO RICAN.

This favorite, which offers exceptional value at affordable prices, was established in 1902, and ever since it has been offering homemade pastries and endless cups of coffee amid traditional colonial decor. Its sandwiches are some of the best in town. For decades it was a rendezvous for the island's literati and for Old San Juan families, but now it has been discovered by foreign visitors. The food is authentic and inexpensive. The regional dishes include rice with squid, roast leg of pork, and seafood asopao. For dessert, you might select an apple, pineapple, or prune pie, or one of many types of flan. Service is polite, if a bit rushed, and the place fills up quickly at lunchtime.

La Mallorquina. Calle San Justo 207. ☎ **787/722-3261.** Reservations not accepted at lunch, recommended at dinner. Main courses $13.95–$29.95 at dinner. AE, MC, V. Mon–Sat 11:30am–10pm. Bus: A7, T1, or 2. PUERTO RICAN.

San Juan's oldest restaurant was founded in 1848. It's in a three-story, glassed-in courtyard with arches and antique wall clocks. Even if you've already eaten, you might want to stop by for a drink at the old-fashioned wooden bar. The chef specializes in the most typical Puerto Rican rice dish: asopao, which some readers find too salty. You can have it with either chicken, shrimp, or lobster and shrimp. *Arroz con pollo* (rice with chicken) is almost as popular. Begin with garlic soup or gazpacho. Other recommended main dishes are grilled pork chop with fried plantain, beef tenderloin Puerto Rican style, and assorted seafood stewed in wine. Lunch is busy; dinners are sometimes quiet. The food seems little changed over the decades; visit here for tradition and exceptional value rather than innovation.

In Condado

Very Expensive

La Scala. In the Radisson Ambassador Plaza Hotel & Casino, 1369 Ashford Ave. ☎ **787/721-7300.** Reservations recommended. Main courses $16.95–$35. AE, MC, V. Tues–Fri noon–3pm, Sun–Thurs 6–1:30pm, Fri–Sat 6pm–midnight. Bus: A7. NORTHERN ITALIAN.

One of the most sophisticated Italian restaurants in San Juan caters to discerning diners who appreciate the nuances of fine cuisine and service. The decor includes neutral colors, stucco arches, and murals. The menu lists just about the entire repertoire of northern Italian cuisine. You'll find a specialty version of Caesar salad, fresh mushrooms in garlic sauce, and a succulent half-melted version of fresh mozzarella in carozza. The fresh fish and seafood are flown in from New York and Boston. Most meals here are memorable, and the cookery, for the most part, is creative and delicate. Service is attentive.

✪ **Los Faisanes.** Avenida Magdalena 1108. ☎ **787/725-2801.** Reservations required. Main courses $19.95–$39.95. AE, MC, V. Sun–Fri noon–3pm and 6:30–11:30pm, Sat 6:30–11:30pm. Bus: A7, T1, or 2. INTERNATIONAL/SPANISH/CARIBBEAN.

On a relatively quiet corner of the Condado, Los Faisanes is one of the finest and most discreetly elegant restaurants in San Juan, with a restrained decor that makes this feel like a sedate private home. You'll be offered a selection of dishes inspired by the cuisines of France, Italy, and the Hispanic world. Several different preparations of pheasant are usually available, as well as a changing selection of chicken, beef, veal, and seafood dishes, several of them prepared at your table. Fresh fillet of tuna is prepared Hemingway style, with onions, Chardonnay, lemon juice, and olive oil. The roast duck, flavored with cinnamon and guava, is a winner. There's a fresh, assertive taste to the food, backed up by a good wine cellar.

✪ **Ramiro's.** Avenida Magdalena 1106. ☎ **787/721-9049.** Reservations recommended off-season, required in winter. Main courses $23–$35; 5-course fixed-price meal $56.95. AE, DC, MC, V. Mon–Thurs noon–3pm and 6:30–10:30pm, Fri noon–3pm and 6:30–11pm, Sat 6:30–11pm, Sun noon–3pm and 6–10pm. Bus: A7, T1, or 2. SPANISH/INTERNATIONAL.

In a half-century-old building near La Concha Hotel, you'll find a refined cuisine and a touch of Old Spain. One of the most distinguished dining places on Puerto Rico, this restaurant prepares "New Creole" cooking, a style pioneered by owner and chef Jesús Ramiro. The menu is the most imaginative on the Condado. You might begin with breadfruit mille-feuille with local crabmeat and avocado. For your main course, any fresh fish or meat can be charcoal-grilled for you on request. Rack of lamb is one of the specialties; you can also have fresh filet of grouper. Among the many homemade desserts are caramelized mango on puff pastry with strawberry-and-guava sauce, and "four seasons" chocolate.

Ristorante Capriccio. On the mezzanine level of the Condado Plaza Resort, 999 Ashford Ave. ☎ **787/721-1000.** Reservations recommended. Main courses $16.50–$35. AE, DISC, DC, MC, V. Daily noon–11pm. ITALIAN.

Despite the superb service of an international staff, this restaurant is surprisingly unpretentious. Much of this is because of the tact and charm of its Provence-born director, Roger Duperray, whose Italian cuisine is among the best in Puerto Rico.

This is the kind of place where big business deals are clinched. On the mezzanine level, tables overlook an ocean view that seems to stretch all the way to Spain. Soft lighting, stiff drinks, and well-chosen wines add to the ambience. There are at least 14 kinds of pastas, including versions with vodka, and a specialty version (linguine Roger) made with fresh spinach, mushrooms, onions, and smoked salmon that's particularly delectable. There's also an ultrafresh fish of the day prepared in any of three different ways, lobster Fra Diavola, grilled salmon with hollandaise sauce, and a succulent version of cioppino Genovese. Veal, chicken, and beef dishes range from the standard (saltimbocca Romana) to the idiosyncratic (medallions of filet steak Atilla, prepared with anchovy-flavored garlic, cognac, and cream sauce).

Expensive

Chart House. 1214 Ashford Ave. ☎ **787/724-0110.** Reservations recommended Mon–Fri, required Sat–Sun. Main courses $16.50–$40. AE, DC, DISC, MC, V. Sun–Thurs 5–11:30pm, Fri–Sat 5pm–12:15am. Bus: A7, T1, or 2. STEAK/SEAFOOD.

Chart House, part of a chain of restaurants based in California and one of the best spots on the island, attracts hundreds of locals on any night. It's housed in a lattice-trimmed villa built in 1910. Today the heavy ceiling beams have been exposed, track lighting installed, and paintings added to create a warm ambience. The food is well prepared, and prime rib is a specialty. You can also order tuna fillet, seafood pasta, top sirloin, live Nicaraguan lobster, Alaskan king crab, and a copious salad.

Chayote. In the Olimpo Hotel, Avenida Miramar 603. ☎ **787/722-9385.** Reservations recommended. Main courses $16–$19.95. AE, MC, V. Mon–Fri noon–2:30pm and 7–10pm, Sat 7–10:30pm. PUERTO RICAN/INTERNATIONAL.

Chayote's cuisine is among the most innovative in San Juan. It draws local business leaders, government officials, and film stars such as Sylvester Stallone and Melanie Griffith. The setting is a modern, basement-level, peach-colored enclave in a surprisingly obscure hotel (the Olimpo). Some aspects of the place might remind you of an artsy bistro in Washington, D.C., or New York.

The restaurant changes its menu every three months, so we can't predict what you're going to be offered. However, chances are you'll find such appetizers as a yuca turnover stuffed with crab meat and served with a mango and papaya chutney or corn tamales with shrimp in a coconut sauce. A ripe plantain stuffed with chicken and served with a fresh tomato sauce is yet another starter. For a main dish, you might try a red snapper filet with a citrus vinaigrette made of passion fruit, orange, and lemon. An exotic touch appears in the pork filet seasoned with dried fruits and spices in a tamarind sauce and served with a green banana and taro root timbale. There's nothing better than the mango flan served with macerates strawberries to finish off the meal.

✪ **Compostela.** Avenida Condado 106. ☎ **787/724-6088.** Reservations required. Main courses $16–$32.95. AE, DC, MC, V. Mon–Fri noon–3pm and 6:30–10:30pm, Sat 6–11pm. Bus: 2. SPANISH/PUERTO RICAN.

This restaurant's formality is largely derived from the battalion of well-dressed waiters whose manners evoke Old Spain. Established by a Galician-born family, the pine-trimmed restaurant has gained a reputation as one of the best in the capital.

The chef made his name on his roast peppers stuffed with salmon mousse. Equally delectable is duck with orange and ginger sauce or baby rack of lamb with fresh herbs. Of course, any shellfish grilled in a brandy sauce is a sure winner. The chef also makes two different versions of paella, both savory. The wine cellar, comprised of some 10,000 bottles, is one of the most impressive in San Juan.

Martino's. In the Dutch Inn Hotel & Casino, Avenida Condado 55. ☎ **787/722-5256.** Reservations recommended. Main courses $17–$38. AE, DC, MC, V. Daily 5:30pm–midnight. Bus: A7. NORTHERN ITALIAN.

Martino's offers some of the finest service on the Condado and a classic Italian cuisine. It's the domain of chef and owner Martin Acosta. His restaurant's picture windows open onto views of the Atlantic and the night lights of the Condado. Appetizers include hot seafood antipasti and Caesar and spinach salads. You can order one of the homemade pasta dishes for a main course or else roam the menu, finding such appetizing dishes as seafood supreme, vitello Martino (with shrimp), gnocchi with cream sauce and Parmesan, and filet mignon Monnalisa, which is flambéed at your table. In fact, almost any dish can receive a tableside flambé if you want. Good and reasonably priced wines add to the dining pleasure.

✪ **Pikayo.** In the Tanama Princess Hotel, 1 Calle Joffre. ☎ **787/721-6194.** Reservations recommended. Main courses $22–$34. AE, MC, V. Mon–Sat 6–10:30pm. Closed 2 weeks in Oct. PUERTO RICAN/CAJUN.

This is the best place to go for the new generation of Puerto Rican cookery, with a touch of Cajun thrown in for spice and zest. This place not only keeps up with the latest culinary trends, it often sets them. Set on the lobby level of a hotel on the Condado, this restaurant occupies a dining room lined with mahogany, varnished cherry, and light pastel shades of turquoise and green. Formal but not stuffy, it configures itself as a specialist in the *criolla* cuisine of colonial Puerto Rico, emphasizing the Spanish, Indian, and African elements that contributed to its unusual recipes. A staff member, perhaps chef Wilo Benet or his wife, Lorraine, will advise you on such traditional dishes as *mofongo* (plantains layered with shrimp and served with saffron-flavored broth); *viandas* (mashed tropical tubers); *tostones* (fritters made from green plantains) stuffed with codfish or cheese, or crabmeat stew. Most main courses are accompanied with the staff of life in the *criolla* world, *arroz y habichuelas coloradas* (white rice and beans). Especially delicious is seared yellowfin tuna with fresh onions.

Tuscany's. In the San Juan Marriott Resort, 1309 Ashford Ave. ☎ **787/722-7000.** Reservations and jackets for men recommended. Main courses $18.50–$26. AE, DC, DISC, MC, V. Daily 6–11pm. NORTHERN ITALIAN.

Richly accessorized with mahogany and granite, this is the showcase restaurant of one of the most elaborate hotel reconstructions in the history of Puerto Rico. In 1995, its team of chefs swept most of the first prizes at the annual Culinary Exposition, a contest held by the Puerto Rico Tourism Association. You'll have lots of choices here, including a range of gourmet pizzas prepared in a wood-burning oven tucked into one corner.

The chef doesn't skimp on ingredients, and prepares such elegant selections as a veal chop with a Brunnelo Tuscan red-wine sauce or seafood casserole with shrimp, scallops, and prawns with tomato sauce. There are several appealing pastas, such as ravioli filled with lobster and herbs (served with a leek and saffron sauce), or a trio of risottos that can be ordered as an appetizer or main course. Sirloin steak Florentine style arrives perfectly cooked.

Moderate

Ajili Mójili. 1052 Ashford Ave. (at the corner of Calle Joffre). ☎ **787/725-9195.** Reservations recommended. Main courses $12–$22. AE, MC, V. Mon–Thurs 6:30–10pm, Fri–Sat 6:30–11pm, Sun 5–10pm. PUERTO RICAN/CREOLE.

This is the only restaurant in San Juan's tourist zone that's devoted exclusively to *la cucina criolla,* the starchy, sometimes greasy cuisine that developed on the island a century ago. It's set in the heart of the tourist facilities of the Condado, across from the Convention Center. Despite the relative modernity of the building that contains it, look for artfully battered replicas of the kind of crumbling brick walls you'd expect in Old San Juan, and a bar that looks like something you'd have found in a colony of Spain a century ago. The staff will willingly describe menu items in colloquial English. Locals come here for a taste of the food they enjoyed at their mother's knee, and a meal here might afford insights into the island's culture. Examples include *mofongos* (green plantains stuffed with veal, chicken, shrimp, or pork), *arroz con pollo* (stewed chicken with saffron rice), *medallones de cerdo encebollado* (pork loin sautéed with onions), *lechon asado con maposteado* (roast pork with rice and beans), and *carne mechada* (beef rib eye stuffed with ham). The preferred accompaniment for this hearty island fare? Ice-cold bottles of local beer, such as Medalla.

Urdin. Avenida Magdalena 1105. ☎ **787/724-0420.** Reservations recommended. Main courses $11.95–$24.95. AE, MC, V. Mon–Sat noon–3am, Sun noon–midnight. PUERTO RICAN/ INTERNATIONAL.

Urdin is proud of the reputation it's built as one of the bright new restaurants in the capital. It occupies a low-slung, stucco-covered house set near a slew of competitors near the Condado. Inside, a fanciful decor of postmodern, Caribbean-inspired accents and cut-out metal sculpture bring a touch of Latino New York.

The food is innovative and flavorful; it's the staff that can diminish (if they're sulky) or enhance (if they're welcoming) a meal here. The food is strong, opinionated, and earthy, filled with authentic Spanish flavor that's not necessarily geared to the palates of timid diners. For starters, there are baby eels Bilbaina style or a Castilian lentil soup. Preferred main dishes include roast duck with a blueberry sauce, and a roast veal chop in its own juice, with eggplant, spinach, and cheese. Opinion was divided at our table over the shrimp with mango and ginger sauce. One always-pleasing dish is piquillo peppers stuffed with a seafood mousse and black-olive sauce. Savvy locals finish their meal with a slice of sweet-potato cheesecake.

Inexpensive

Oasis. 1043 Ashford Ave. ☎ **787/724-2005.** Reservations not required. Main courses $6.50–$32. AE, DC, DISC, MC, V. Daily 11:30am–11:30pm. Bus: A7, T1, or 2. CUBAN/ INTERNATIONAL.

This lone budget eatery manages to hold its own along an expensive Condado beachfront strip where prices are sometimes lethal. Most dishes here are very reasonable in price, except shellfish (especially lobster). The family-style dining room has a large array of "Cuban Creole" dishes, along with international specialties and Puerto Rican selections. The tables in back open onto views of the ocean.

Caldo Gallego, that richly flavored soup of beans and greens with meat and sausage, is a hearty opener, perhaps followed by stuffed Cornish game hen, oxtails in a Creole sauce, breaded red snapper fillet, or lobster asopao. Paella for two is another specialty. Good value, good food (and plenty of it), and an informal, relaxed atmosphere keep this place going year after year.

Tony Roma's. In the Condado Plaza Hotel, 999 Ashford Ave. ☎ **787/721-1000,** ext. 2123. Reservations not accepted. Main courses $7.50–$17.95. AE, DC, MC, V. Daily noon–midnight. Bus: A7. BARBECUE.

Efficient and unpretentious, this is Puerto Rico's busiest branch of an international chain of eateries. It's one of the least expensive restaurants in the Condado, and as such, is well appreciated for its spicy barbecued food (the honey barbecue is not as fiery). Menu items include a wide range of barbecued dishes, such as chicken and several different varieties of ribs, as well as hamburgers and the famous Tony Roma onion ring loaves.

In Santurce

✪ La Casona. Calle San Jorge 609 (at the corner of Avenida Fernández Juncos). ☎ **787/727-2717.** Reservations required. Main courses $23–$44. AE, DC, MC, V. Mon–Fri noon–11pm, Sat 6–11pm. Bus: 1. SPANISH/INTERNATIONAL.

One of the finest restaurants in Puerto Rico, La Casona offers the kind of dining usually found in Madrid, complete with a strolling guitarist. Since 1972 the chefs here have dispensed their special dishes in a turn-of-the-century mansion surrounded by gardens. The much-renovated but still-charming place draws some of the most fashionable diners on Puerto Rico. Paella marinara, prepared for two or more, is a specialty, as is zarzuela de mariscos (seafood medley). Or you might select filet of grouper in Basque sauce, octopus vinaigrette, rabbit stew, or a rack of lamb. The cuisine has flair and flavor, and is served with much effort and expense.

In Isla Verde

Expensive

Back Street Hong Kong. In El Juan Hotel & Casino, Isla Verde Ave. ☎ **787/791-1224.** Reservations recommended. Main courses $17.95–$32.95; fixed-price menus $35–$55. AE, MC, V. Daily 6pm–midnight. Bus: M4 or T1. MANDARIN/SZECHUAN/HUNAN.

To reach this restaurant, you head down a re-creation of a backwater street in Hong Kong—disassembled from its original home at the 1964 New York World's Fair, it was rebuilt here with its original design intact. A few steps later you enter one of the best Chinese restaurants in the Caribbean. Beneath a soaring redwood ceiling, you can enjoy pineapple fried rice served in a real pineapple, a version of scallops with orange sauce, Szechuan beef with chicken, or a Dragon and Phoenix (lobster mixed with shrimp).

La Piccola Fontana. In El San Juan Hotel & Casino, Isla Verde Ave. ☎ **787/791-1000,** ext. 1271. Reservations required. Main courses $19–$29.95. AE, MC, V. Daily 6pm–midnight. Bus: T1. NORTHERN ITALIAN.

Right off the luxurious Palm Court in the El San Juan Hotel (see above), this restaurant arguably serves the finest classic northern Italian cuisine in Puerto Rico. From its white linen to its classically formal service, it enjoys a worldwide reputation. Small and intimate, it's an octagonal neo-Palladian room with crystal chandeliers. Look for the daily specials, such as the fish of the day (depending on the catch), or you might try one of the eight classic veal dishes. From the sea come such main courses as hot seafood supreme or calamari marinara. Many diners prefer one of the pasta dishes as a main course, perhaps the homemade manicotti or baked ziti. For openers, there are such temptations as hot seafood antipasti and a Caesar salad. The chocolate cheesecake, a chef's specialty, is a smooth finish.

Inexpensive

Sonny's Oceanfront Place for Ribs. In the Empress Oceanfront Hotel, 2 Amapola St. ☎ **787/791-3083.** Reservations not required. Main courses $8.95–$14.95. AE, DC, DISC, MC, V. Daily 8am–11pm. Bus: T1. AMERICAN.

This restaurant overlooks the sea and the hotel's terraced swimming pool. The cuisine is unpretentious and guaranteed to satisfy hunger pangs for American food with burgers, several different types of barbecued ribs, pastas, chicken, omelets, and steak, including filet mignon. Swordfish can be grilled, broiled, or fried and brushed with lemon.

In Miramar

Augusto's Cuisine. In the Hotel Excelsior. 101 Ave. Ponce de León, Miramar. ☎ **787/725-7700.** Reservations recommended. Main courses $25–$30. Set menu $65–$80. AE, MC, V. Tues–Fri noon–3pm, Tues–Sat 7–9:30pm. FRENCH/INTERNATIONAL.

This restaurant succeeds at configuring itself firmly within the upper tier of the most elegant and glamorous restaurants of Puerto Rico, with a decidedly European texture that's hard to reproduce within larger, more anonymous restaurants. Austrian-born owner and chef Augusto Schreiner, assisted by a partly French-born staff, operates from a gray-and-green dining room set on the lobby level of a 15-story hotel in Miramar, a suburb near the island's main airport. Menu items are concocted from strictly fresh ingredients, and include such dishes as lobster Rockefeller (cooked au gratin with spinach, bacon, and Parmesan cheese); rack of lamb with aromatic herbs and fresh garlic; an oft-changing cream-based soup of the day (one of the best is corn and fresh oyster soup), and a succulent version of medallions of veal Rossini-style, prepared with foie gras and Madeira sauce. The wine list is as extensive as that within any other restaurant on the island.

BEACHES, WATER SPORTS & OTHER OUTDOOR PURSUITS

IN & AROUND SAN JUAN

BEACHES With some 300 miles of coastline, both Atlantic and Caribbean, Puerto Rico obviously has plenty of beaches. Odds are, you'll want to choose a hotel on or near a good beach, so we've tried to mention nearby beaches in each hotel review.

Some public stretches of shoreline around San Juan are overcrowded, especially on Saturday and Sunday; others are practically deserted. If you find that secluded, hidden beach of your dreams, proceed with caution. On unguarded beaches you'll have no way to protect yourself or your valuables should you be approached by a robber or mugger, which has been known to happen. For more information about the island's many beaches, call the **Department of Sports and Recreation** (☎ **787/722-1551**).

All beaches on Puerto Rico, even those fronting the top hotels, are open to the public, although you will be charged for parking and for use of *balneario* facilities, such as lockers and showers.

The best Condado beach is the one that fronts the Marriott; the best beach at Isla Verde is at the Hotel El San Juan.

The public beaches on the north shore of San Juan at **Ocean Park** and **Park Barbosa** are good and sandy, and can be reached by bus. **Luquillo,** on the north coast, is some 30 miles east of San Juan. Public beaches shut down on Monday; if Monday is a holiday, the beaches are open for the holiday but close the next day, Tuesday. Beach hours are 9am to 5pm in winter, to 6pm off-season. All three of these have changing rooms and showers; Luquillo also has picnic tables.

DEEP-SEA FISHING It's top-notch! Allison tuna, white and blue marlin, sailfish, wahoo, dolphin, mackerel, and tarpon are some of the fish that can be caught in Puerto Rican waters, where 30 world records have been broken. Charter arrangements can be made through most major hotels and resorts.

Capt. Mike Benitez, who has chartered out of San Juan for more than 40 years, was listed in 1993 by the *Sports Fishing Tournament Guide* as one of the 15 most qualified sport-fishing captains in the world. Past clients have included, among others, ex-President Carter. Benitez Fishing Charters can be contacted directly at P.O. Box 9066541, Puerto de Tierra, San Juan, PR 00906 (☎ **787/723-2292** until 9pm). The captain offers a 45-foot air-conditioned deluxe Hateras, the *Sea Born.* Fishing tours for parties of up to six cost $450 for a half-day excursion and $750 for a full day, with beverages and all equipment included.

HORSE RACING Great thoroughbreds and outstanding jockeys compete all year at **El Comandante,** Avenida 65 de Infantería, Route 3, kilometer 15.3, at Canovanas (☎ **787/724-6060**), Puerto Rico's only racetrack, a 20-minute drive east of the center of San Juan. Post time varies from 2:15 to 2:45pm on Monday, Wednesday, Thursday, Friday, and Sunday. A restaurant is open on race days from 12:30 to 4:30pm. Entrance to the clubhouse costs $3 per person, although no admission is charged for the grandstand. Call ahead for luncheon reservations; most credit and charge cards are accepted.

SCUBA/SNORKELING In San Juan, the best-recommended option for underwater diving is **Karen Vega's Carib Aquatic Adventures,** P.O. Box 2470, San Juan Station, San Juan, PR 00902 (☎ **787/729-2929,** ext. 240). Most of its activities revolve around its dive shop in the rear lobby of the Radisson Normandie Hotel. The company offers diving certification from both PADI and NAUI as part of 40-hour courses priced at $465 each. A resort course for first-time divers costs $97. Also offered are kayak rentals (single or double) at $17 or $34 per hour, windsurfing (see below), and a choice of full-day diving expeditions to various reefs off the east coast of Puerto Rico or in San Juan. Private charter cruises of San Juan Bay start at $55 per person, with a maximum boat capacity of 35 people on a 60-foot motor yacht, *San Antonio.*

TENNIS In San Juan, the **Caribe Hilton & Casino** and the **Condado Plaza Hotel & Casino** have tennis courts. Nonguests can use these hotel courts if they make a reservation. Also, there's a **public court** at the old navy base, Isla Grande, Miramar. The entrance is from Avenida Fernández Juncos at Stop 11.

WINDSURFING The sheltered waters of the Condado Lagoon in San Juan is a favorite spot. Throughout the island, many of the companies featuring snorkeling and scuba diving also offer windsurfing equipment and instruction, and dozens of hotels offer facilities on their own premises.

One of the best places in San Juan to go windsurfing is at **Karen Vega's Carib Aquatic Adventures,** with its main branch in the rear lobby of San Juan's Radisson Normandie Hotel (☎ **787/729-2929,** ext. 240). Rentals cost $25 per hour, with a lesson costing $45.

STEPPING BACK IN TIME: EXPLORING THE HISTORIC SIGHTS OF SAN JUAN

The streets are narrow and teeming with traffic, but a walk through Old San Juan (in Spanish, El Viejo San Juan) is like a stroll through five centuries of history. You can do it in less than a day. In a seven-square-block landmark area in the westernmost part of the city you can see many of Puerto Rico's chief historical attractions, and do some shopping along the way.

The Spanish moved to Old San Juan in 1521, and the city played an important role as Spain's bastion of defense in the Caribbean. Once the city was called Puerto Rico (Rich Port), as the whole island was once called San Juan.

CHURCHES

Capilla de Cristo. Calle del Cristo (directly west of Paseo de la Princesa). Free admission. Tues 10am–2pm. Bus: T1.

The Cristo Chapel was built to commemorate what legend says was a miracle. In 1753 a young rider lost control of his horse in a race down this very street during the fiesta of St. John's Day and plunged over the precipice. Moved by the accident, the secretary of the city, Don Mateo Pratts, invoked Christ to save the youth, and had the chapel built when his prayers were answered. Today it's a landmark in the old city and one of its best-known historical monuments. The chapel's

Campèche paintings and gold and silver altar can be seen through its glass doors. Since the chapel is open only one day a week, most visitors have to settle for a view of its exterior.

Catedral de San Juan. Calle del Cristo 153 (at Caleta San Juan). ☎ **787/722-0861.** Free admission. Daily 8:30am–4pm. Bus: T1.

The San Juan Cathedral was begun in 1540 and has had a rough life. Restoration today has been extensive, so it hardly resembles the thatch-roofed structure that stood here until 1529, when it was wiped out by a hurricane. Hampered by lack of funds, the cathedral slowly added a circular staircase and two adjoining vaulted Gothic chambers. But then in 1598 along came the Earl of Cumberland to loot it, and a hurricane in 1615 to blow off its roof. In 1908 the body of Ponce de León was disinterred from the nearby Iglesia de San José and brought here. The cathedral faces Plaza de las Monjas (the Nuns' Square), a shady spot where you can rest and cool off.

Iglesia de San José. In Plaza de San José, Calle del Cristo. ☎ **787/725-7501.** Free admission. Church and Chapel of Belém, Mon–Wed and Fri 7am–2:30pm, Sat 7am–1pm. Bus: T1.

Initial plans for this church were drawn in 1523, and Dominican friars supervised its construction in 1532. Before entering, look for the statue of Ponce de León in the adjoining plaza—it was made from melted-down British cannons captured during Sir Ralph Abercromby's unsuccessful attack on San Juan in 1797.

Both the church and its monastery were closed by decree in 1838, and the property was confiscated by the royal treasury. Later, the Crown turned the convent into a military barracks. The Jesuits restored the badly damaged church. This was the place of worship for Ponce de León's descendants, who are buried here under the family's coat-of-arms. The conquistador, killed by a poisoned arrow in Florida, was interred here until his removal to the Catedral de San Juan in 1908.

Although badly looted, the church still has some treasures, including *Christ of the Ponces,* a carved crucifix presented to Ponce de León, four oils by José Campéche, and two large works by Francisco Oller. Many miracles have been attributed to a painting in the Chapel of Belém, a 15th-century Flemish work called *The Virgin of Bethlehem.*

FORTS

✪ **Fort San Cristóbal.** In the northeast corner of Old San Juan (uphill from Plaza de Colón on Calle Norzagaray). ☎ **787/729-6960.** Free admission. Daily 9am–5pm. Bus: T1 or M3; then the free trolley from Covadonga station to the top of the hill.

This huge fortress, begun in 1634 and re-engineered in the 1770s, is one of the largest ever built in the Americas by Spain. Its walls rise more than 150 feet above the sea, a marvel of military engineering. San Cristóbal protected San Juan against attackers coming by land as a partner to El Morro, to which it is linked by a half mile of monumental walls and bastions filled with cannon-firing positions. A complex system of tunnels and dry moats connects the center of San Cristóbal to its "outworks," defensive elements arranged layer after layer over a 27-acre site. You'll get the idea if you look at the scale model on display. Like El Morro, the fort is administered and maintained by the National Park Service. Be sure to see the Garita del Diablo, or the Devil's Sentry Box, one of the oldest parts of San Cristóbal's defenses, and famous in Puerto Rican legend. The devil himself, it is said, would snatch away sentinels at this lonely post at the edge of the sea. In 1898, the first shots of the Spanish-American War in Puerto Rico were fired by cannons on top of San Cristóbal during an artillery duel with a U.S. Navy fleet. Check at the guard house at the entrance for the schedule of special activities and fort tours led by park rangers for that day.

✪ **Castillo San Felipe del Morro.** At the end of Calle Norzagaray. ☎ **787/729-6960.** Free admission. Daily 9am–5pm. Bus: T1 or M3.

Called "El Morro," this fort stands on a rocky promontory dominating the entrance to San Juan Bay. Constructed in 1540, the original fort was a round tower, which can still be seen deep inside the lower levels of the castle. More walls and cannon-firing positions were added, and by 1787 the fortification attained the complex design you see today. This fortress was attacked repeatedly by both the English and the Dutch. The National Park Service protects the fortifications of Old San Juan, which have been declared a World Heritage Site by the United Nations. With some of the most dramatic views in the Caribbean, you'll find El Morro an intriguing labyrinth of dungeons, barracks, vaults, lookouts, and ramps. Historical and background information is provided in a video in English and Spanish shown to fort visitors. The nearest parking to the historic fort is the underground facility beneath the Quincentennial Plaza at the Ballajá barracks (Cuartel de Ballajá) on Calle Norzagaray.

Fort San Jerónimo. East of the Caribe Hilton, at the entrance to Condado Bay. ☎ **787/724-1844.** Free admission. Wed–Sat 9am–3pm. Bus: T1.

Completed in 1608, this fort was damaged in the English assault of 1797. Reconstructed in the closing year of the 18th century, it has now been taken over by the Institute of Puerto Rican Culture. Anyone wanting to see the view from the inside must call the Caribe Hilton; security here will open the gate to let you inside, but a special request has to be made.

OTHER HISTORIC SIGHTS

The **city walls** around San Juan were built in 1630 to protect the town against both European invaders and Caribbean pirates. The thickness of the walls averages 20 feet at the base and 12 feet at the top, with an average height of 40 feet. Between Fort San Cristóbal and El Morro, bastions were erected at frequent intervals. You can start seeing the walls from your approach from San Cristóbal on your way to El Morro. Bus: T1.

San Juan Gate, Calle San Francisco and Calle Recinto Oeste, built around 1635, just north of La Fortaleza, several blocks downhill from the cathedral, was the main gate and entry point into San Juan—that is, if you arrived by ship in the 18th century. The gate is the only one remaining of the several that once pierced the fortifications of the old walled city. Bus: T1.

Plazuela de la Rogativa, Caleta de las Monjas, basks in legend. In 1797 the British across San Juan Bay at Santurce held the Old Town under siege. However, that same year they mysteriously sailed away. Later, the commander claimed he feared that the enemy was well prepared behind those walls—he apparently saw many lights and believed them to be reinforcements. Some people believe that those lights were torches carried by women in a *rogativa,* or religious procession, as they followed their bishop. An artfully stylized bronze statue of a bishop, trailed by a trio of torch-bearing women, was donated to the city on its 450th anniversary. Bus: T1.

El Arsenal. La Puntilla. ☎ **787/724-5949.** Free admission. Wed–Sun 8:30am–4:30pm. Bus: T1.

The Spaniards used a shallow craft to patrol the lagoons and mangroves in and around San Juan. Needing a base for these vessels, they constructed El Arsenal at the

Old San Juan

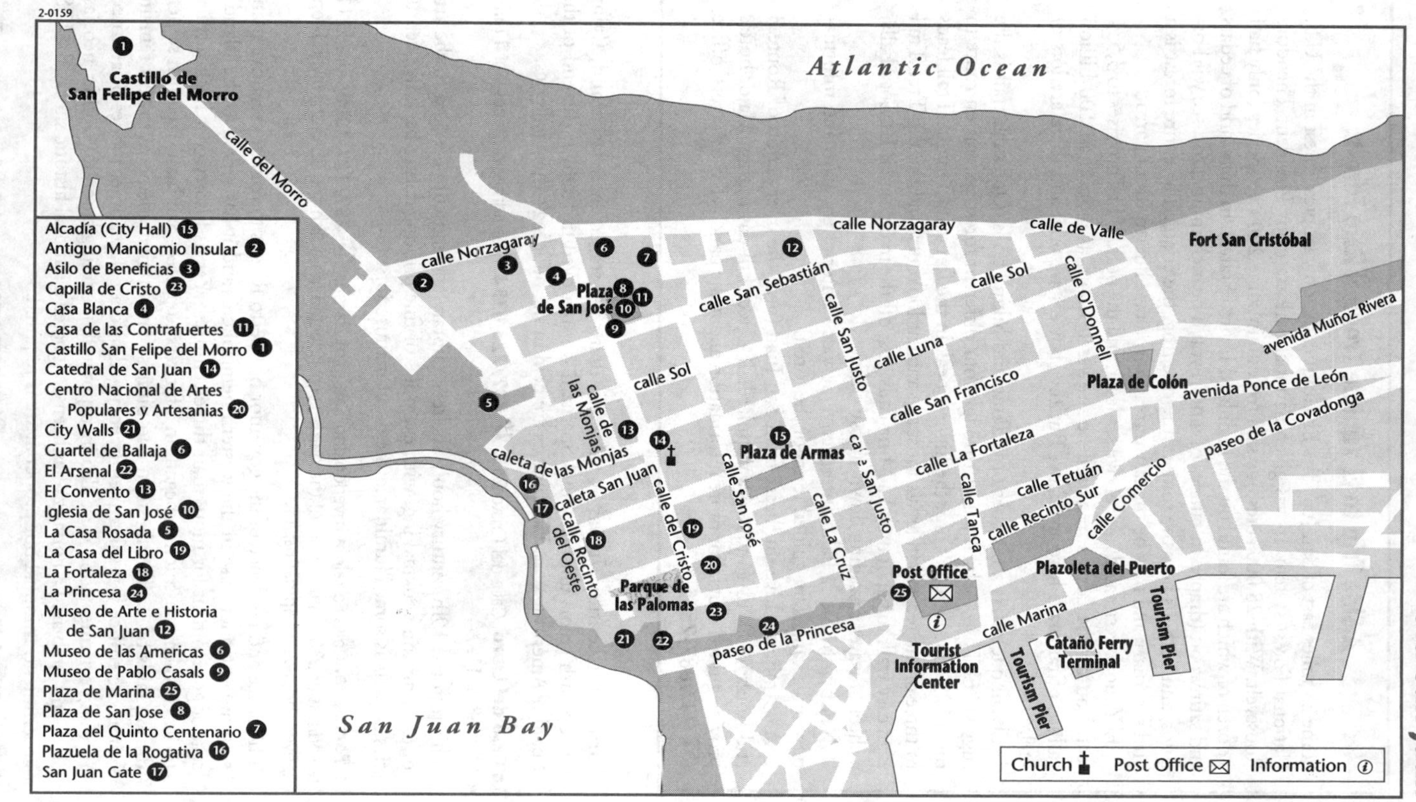

2-0159
Atlantic Ocean
San Juan Bay
Castillo de San Felipe del Morro
Fort San Cristóbal
Plaza de San José
Plaza de Armas
Plaza de Colón
Parque de las Palomas
Post Office
Tourist Information Center
Plazoleta del Puerto
Cataño Ferry Terminal
Tourism Pier
Tourism Pier
calle del Morro
calle Norzagaray
calle de Valle
calle San Sebastián
calle Sol
calle O'Donnell
calle Luna
calle San Francisco
calle La Fortaleza
calle Tetuán
calle Recinto Sur
calle Comercio
calle Marina
paseo de la Princesa
calle San Justo
calle Tanca
calle La Cruz
calle San José
calle del Cristo
calle de las Monjas
caleta de las Monjas
caleta San Juan
calle Recinto del Oeste
avenida Muñoz Rivera
avenida Ponce de León
paseo de la Covadonga
Church
Post Office
Information
Alcadía (City Hall) 15
Antiguo Manicomio Insular 2
Asilo de Beneficias 3
Capilla de Cristo 23
Casa Blanca 4
Casa de las Contrafuertes 11
Castillo San Felipe del Morro 1
Catedral de San Juan 14
Centro Nacional de Artes Populares y Artesanias 20
City Walls 21
Cuartel de Ballaja 6
El Arsenal 22
El Convento 13
Iglesia de San José 10
La Casa Rosada 5
La Casa del Libro 19
La Fortaleza 18
La Princesa 24
Museo de Arte e Historia de San Juan 12
Museo de las Americas 6
Museo de Pablo Casals 9
Plaza de Marina 25
Plaza de San Jose 8
Plaza del Quinto Centenario 7
Plazuela de la Rogativa 16
San Juan Gate 17

A Side Trip to El Yunque Tropical Rain Forest

Some 25 miles east of San Juan lies El Yunque, the only tropical forest in the U.S. National Forest system. It was given national park status by President Theodore Roosevelt. With 28,000 acres, it's said to contain some 240 tree species (only half a dozen of which are found on the mainland United States). In this world of cedars and satinwood (draped in tangles of vines), you'll hear chirping birds, see wild orchids, and perhaps hear the song of the tree frog, the coquí. The entire forest is a bird sanctuary and may be the last retreat of the rare Puerto Rican parrot.

El Yunque is situated high above sea level, and the peak of El Toro rises to 3,532 feet. You can be fairly sure you'll be showered upon, as more than 100 billion gallons of rain falls here annually. But the showers are brief and there are lots of shelters.

El Yunque offers a number of walking and hiking trails. One such trail is the rugged "El Toro," which passes through four different forest systems en route to the 3,523-foot Pico El Toro, the highest peak in the forest. El Yunque Trail leads to three of the recreation area's most spectacular lookouts, and the Big Tree Trail is an easy walk to panoramic La Mina Falls. Just off the main road is La Coca Falls, a sheet of water cascading down mossy cliffs.

Nearby, the Sierra Palm Interpretive Service Center offers maps and information and arranges for guided tours of the forest.

A 45-minute drive southeast from San Juan (near the intersection of Route 3 and Route 191), El Yunque is a popular half-day or full-day outing. Major hotels provide guided tours. For more information about the park, call the rangers' office (☎ **787/887-2875**).

turn of the century. It was at this base that they staged their last stand, flying the Spanish colors until the final Spaniard was removed in 1898, at the end of the Spanish-American War. Exhibitions are held in the building's three galleries.

La Casa del Libro. Calle del Cristo 255. ☎ **787/723-0354.** Free admission. Tues–Sat 11am–4:30pm. Bus: T1.

This restored 19th-century house shelters a library and museum devoted to the arts of printing and bookmaking, with examples of fine printing dating back five centuries, as well as some illuminated medieval manuscripts.

La Fortaleza. Calle Fortaleza, overlooking San Juan Harbor. ☎ **787/721-7000,** ext. 2211. Free admission. 30-minute tours of the gardens (conducted in English and Spanish) given Mon–Fri, every hour 9am–4pm. Bus: T1.

The office and residence of the governor of Puerto Rico is the oldest executive mansion in continuous use in the western hemisphere, and it has served as the island's seat of government for more than three centuries. Yet its history goes back farther, to 1533 when construction began on a fortress to protect San Juan's Spanish settlers during raids by Carib tribesmen and pirates. The original medieval towers remain, but as the edifice was subsequently enlarged into a palace, other modes of architecture and ornamentation were also incorporated, including baroque, Gothic, neoclassical, and Arabian. La Fortaleza has been designated a national historic site by the U.S. government. Informal but proper attire is required.

Alcaldía (City Hall). Calle San Francisco. ☎ **787/724-7171,** ext. 3070. Free admission. Tours by appointment Mon–Fri 9am–3pm. Closed holidays. Bus: T1.

The City Hall, with its double arcade flanked by two towers resembling Madrid's City Hall, was constructed in stages from 1604 to 1789. Still in use, this building is more than a historical site—it's a unique place full of monuments and legends.

Casa Blanca. Calle San Sebastián 1. ☎ **787/724-4102.** Admission $1 adults, 50¢ children. Tues–Sat 9am–noon and 1–4:30pm. Bus: T1.

Ponce de León never lived here, although construction of the house (built in 1521) is sometimes attributed to him. The house was erected two years after the explorer's death, and work was ordered by his son-in-law, Juan García Troche. The parcel of land was given to Ponce de León as a reward for services rendered to the Crown. Descendants of the explorer lived in the house for about 2$^{1}/_{2}$ centuries until the Spanish government took it over in 1779 for use as a residence for military commanders. The U.S. government also used it as a home for army commanders. On the first floor, the Juan Ponce de León Museum is furnished with antiques, paintings, and artifacts from the 16th through the 18th century.

Casa de los Contrafuertes (House of the Buttresses). Plaza de San José, Calle San Sebastián 101. ☎ **787/724-5477.** Free admission. Tues–Sat 8:30am–4:30pm. Bus: T1.

Adjacent to the Museo de Pablo Casals, this building, which has thick buttresses, is believed to be the oldest residence remaining in El Viejo San Juan. The complex also contains a **pharmacy museum,** which documents the history of a 19th-century pharmacy in the town of Cayey. Upstairs you'll find a **graphic arts museum,** displaying prints and paintings by local artists.

MUSEUMS

Museo de las Americas. Cuartel de Ballajá. ☎ **787/724-5052.** Free admission. Tues–Fri 10am–4pm, Sat–Sun 11am–5pm.

One of the major new museums of San Juan, the Museo de las Americas, showcases the artisans of North, South, and Central America, featuring everything from carved figureheads from New England whaling ships to dugout canoes carved by Carib Indians in Dominica. Also on display is a changing collection of paintings by artists from throughout the Spanish-speaking world, some of which are for sale, and a permanent collection called "Puerto Rican Santos," which includes a collection of wood saints (carved wooden depictions of saints) donated by Dr. Ricardo Alegría.

Museo de Pablo Casals. Plaza de San José, Calle San Sebastián 101. ☎ **787/723-9185.** Admission $1 adults, 50¢ children. Tues–Sat 9:30am–5:30pm. Bus: T1.

Adjacent to the Iglesia de San José, this museum is devoted to the memorabilia left to the people of Puerto Rico by the musician Pablo Casals. The maestro's cello is here, along with a library of videotapes (played upon request) of some of his festival concerts. This small 18th-century house also contains manuscripts and photographs of Casals. The annual Casals Festival draws worldwide interest and attracts some of the greatest performing artists; it's still held during the first two weeks of June.

Museo de Arte e Historia de San Juan. Calle Norzagaray 150. ☎ **787/724-1875.** Free admission. Mon–Fri 8am–noon and 1–4pm; Sat 9am–noon and 1–5pm. Bus: T1 to Old San Juan terminal; then a trolley car from the terminal to the museum.

Located in a Spanish colonial building at the corner of Calle MacArthur, this cultural center was the city's main marketplace in the mid-19th century. Local art is displayed in the east and west galleries, and audiovisual materials reveal the history of the city. Sometimes major cultural events are staged in the museum's large courtyard. English- and Spanish-language audiovisual shows are presented Monday to Friday every hour on the hour from 9am to 4pm.

Museum of the University of Puerto Rico. Avenida Ponce de León, Recinto de Río Piedras. ☎ **787/764-0000,** ext. 2452. Free admission. Mon–Fri 9am–4:30pm, Sat–Sun 9am–4pm. Closed holidays. Take the bus marked "*río piedras*" from Plaza de Colón in Old San Juan to stop 36.

Here you'll find good collections of paintings by Puerto Rican artists, including Francisco Oller and José Campéche, the first important artist of the country (18th century). There's also a large collection of pre-Columbian Puerto Rican native artifacts from the Ingeri, sub-Taíno, and Taíno civilizations.

SHOPPING

U.S. citizens don't pay duty on items brought back to the United States. And you can still find great bargains on Puerto Rico, where the competition among shopkeepers is fierce. Even though the U.S. Virgin Islands are duty free, many readers report finding far lower prices on many items in San Juan than on St. Thomas.

The streets of **Old Town,** such as Calle San Francisco and Calle del Cristo, are the major venues for shopping. Note, however, that most stores in Old San Juan are closed on Sunday.

Native handcrafts can be good buys. Look for *santos* (hand-carved wooden religious figures), needlework, straw work, ceramics, hammocks, *guayabera* shirts for men, papier-mâché fruits and vegetables, and paintings and sculptures by Puerto Rican artists.

The biggest and most up-to-date shopping plaza in the Caribbean Basin is **Plaza Las Americas,** which lies in the financial district of Hato Rey, right off the Las Americas Expressway. The complex, with its fountains and advanced architecture, has more than 200 mostly upscale shops.

ANTIQUES

José E. Alegria & Associates. Calle del Cristo 152–154. ☎ **787/721-8091.**

This shop opposite the Gran Hotel Convento is housed in an adjacent pair of Spanish colonial buildings dating from the 1520s, with rooms opening onto patios and courtyards. It sells antique furniture and paintings, with an emphasis on the 18th century. The collection is the finest in San Juan. An array of furniture from modern Spain is also for sale. Prices are high, but so is the quality.

ART

Galería Botello. Calle del Cristo 208. ☎ **787/723-2879.**

A contemporary Latin American art gallery, Galería Botello is a living tribute to the late Angel Botello, one of Puerto Rico's most outstanding artists. Born in a small village in Galicia, Spain, after the Spanish Civil War he fled to the Caribbean and spent 12 years in Haiti. His paintings and bronze sculptures, evocative of his colorful background, are done in a style uniquely his own. This *galería* is his former home, and he restored the colonial mansion himself. Today it's a setting to display his paintings and sculptures, and it also offers a large collection of Puerto Rican antique *santos.* The gallery not only sells works by Botello, but showcases many outstanding local artists as well.

Galería Palomas. Calle del Cristo 207. ☎ **787/724-8904.**

This and the also recommended Galería Botello are the two leading art galleries of Puerto Rico. Works range from $70 to $35,000, include some of the leading painters of the Latin American world, and are rotated every two to three weeks. The setting is a 17th-century colonial house. Of special note are works by such local artists as Homer, Moya, and Alicea.

Haitian Souvenirs. Calle San Francisco 206. ☎ **787/723-0959.**

This is our favorite of the three stores in San Juan specializing in Haitian art and artifacts. Its walls are covered with framed versions of primitive Haitian landscapes, portraits, crowd scenes, and whimsical visions of jungles where lions, tigers, parrots, and herons take on quasihuman personalities and forms. Most paintings range from $80 to $350, although prices can usually be bargained down a bit. Look for the brightly painted wall hangings crafted from sheets of metal (priced at around $120 each).

Beach Wear

W. H. Smith. In the Condado Plaza Hotel, 999 Ashford Ave. ☎ **787/721-1000,** ext. 2094.

This outlet sells mostly women's clothing, everything from bathing suits and beach attire to jogging suits. For men, there are shorts, bathing suits, and jogging suits. There's also a good selection of books and maps.

Butterflies (Mounted)

Butterfly People. Calle Fortaleza 152. ☎ **787/723-2432.**

Butterfly People is a gallery and cafe in a handsomely restored building in Old San Juan. Butterflies, sold here in artfully arranged boxes, range from $20 for a single mounting to thousands of dollars for whole-wall murals. The butterflies are preserved and will last forever. The dimensional artwork is sold in limited editions and can be shipped worldwide. Most of these butterflies come from farms around the world, some of the most beautiful coming from Indonesia, Malaysia, and New Guinea.

Fashion

Lindissima Shop. Calle Fortaleza 300. ☎ **787/721-0550.**

This is the finest, most tasteful, and most elegant women's shop in Old Town, one of only three or four that cater to the supremely well-dressed. If you feel underdressed, or lack an outfit for a special formal night aboard ship, this shop has what you need. Garments range from $59 to $700. Some of the most dazzling items are beaded bolero blazers that go well with clingy skirts and halter tops crafted from black crepe chiffon.

London Fog. Calle del Cristo 156. ☎ **787/722-4334.**

The last thing you need in steamy San Juan is a winter overcoat or parka, but the prices at this factory outlet of London Fog are usually so low that a purchase is often well worth it. Prices are between 30% and 35% less than for equivalent garments on the U.S. mainland. Men's, women's and children's garments are displayed on two floors of a colonial house.

Nono Maldonado. 1051 Ashford Ave. ☎ **787/721-0456.**

Named after its owner, a Puerto Rico–born designer who worked for many years as the fashion editor of *Esquire* magazine, this is one of the most fashionable and upscale haberdashers in the Caribbean. Selling both men's and women's clothing, it contains everything from socks to dinner jackets, as well as ready-to-wear versions of Maldonado's twice-a-year collections. Both ready-to-wear and couture are available here. Although this is the designer's main store (midway between the Condado Plaza and the Condado Beach Trio), there is also a Maldonado boutique in the El San Juan Hotel in Isla Verde.

Polo Ralph Lauren Factory Store. Calle del Cristo 201. ☎ **787/722-2136.**

It's as stylish and carefully orchestrated as anything you'd expect from one of North America's leading clothiers. Even better, its prices are 35% to 40% less than the cost of equivalent garments sold retail on the U.S. mainland. You can find even greater discounts on irregular or slightly damaged garments. The store occupies two floors of a pair of colonial buildings, with one upstairs room devoted to home furnishings. Men's sizes larger than a 42 waist are almost never in stock.

Gifts & Handcrafts

Anaiboa. Calle San Francisco 100. ☎ **787/724-8017.**

It occupies a cubbyhole that opens onto a pedestrians-only stretch adjacent to Calle del Cristo. Run by a married team of artists (Edgard Rodriguez and Marianne Ramirez), it sells one-of-a-kind artifacts including ceramic boxes, hat racks, mirrors, serving trays, and small-scale furniture accented with whimsical drawings of faces, plants, and animals. Many objects sell for as little as $15.

Bared & Sons. Calle Fortaleza 65 (at the corner of Calle San Justo). ☎ **787/724-4811.**

Now in its fourth decade, this is the main outlet of a chain of at least 20 upper-bracket jewelry stores on Puerto Rico. There's a worthy inventory of gemstones, gold, diamonds, and wristwatches on the street level that does a thriving business with cruise-ship passengers. But the real value of this store lies one floor up, where a monumental collection of porcelain and crystal is packed, in claustrophobic proximity, for display. It's a great source for hard-to-get and discontinued patterns (priced at around 20% less than at equivalent outlets Stateside) from Christofle, Royal Doulton, Wedgwood, Limoges, Royal Copenhagen, Lalique, Baccarat, and Daum.

El Artesano. Calle Fortaleza 314. ☎ **787/721-6483.**

If your budget doesn't allow for an excursion to the Andes, head for this shop. You'll find Mexican and Peruvian icons of the Virgin Mary; charming depictions of fish and Latin American birds in terra-cotta and brass; all kinds of woven goods; painted cupboards, chests, and boxes; and mirrors and Latin dolls.

Galería Bóveda. Calle del Cristo 209. ☎ **787/725-0263.**

This long narrow space is crammed with exotic jewelry, clothing, wall hangings, and elaborately detailed masks from Sri Lanka, Ghana, India, and Thailand. Most of the clothing is designed for women.

Olé. Calle Fortaleza 105. ☎ **787/724-2445.**

Browsing this store is a learning experience. Practically everything comes from Puerto Rico or Latin America. If you want a straw hat from Ecuador, hand-beaten Chilean silver, Christmas ornaments, or Puerto Rican *santos,* this is the place.

Puerto Rican Arts & Crafts. Calle Fortaleza 204. ☎ **787/725-5596.**

Set in a 200-year-old colonial building, this unique store is one of the premier outlets on the island for authentic artifacts. Of particular interest are papier-mâché carnival masks (from $20 to $250) from Ponce, whose grotesque and colorful features were originally conceived to chase away evil spirits. Taíno designs inspired by ancient petroglyphs are incorporated into most of the sterling-silver jewelry (from $12 to $60) sold here. There's an art gallery in back, with silk-screened serigraphs by local artists. The outlet has recently added a gourmet Puerto Rican food section with items like coffee, rum, and hot sauces for sale.

Jewelry

Barrachina's. Calle Fortaleza 104 (between Calle del Cristo and Calle San José). ☎ **787/725-7912.**

The birthplace, in 1963, of the piña colada, Barrachina's is a favorite of cruise-ship passengers. It offers one of the largest selections of jewelry, perfume, and gifts in San Juan. There's a patio for drinks where you can order (what else?) a piña colada. There's also a Bacardi rum outlet, a costume-jewelry department, a gift shop, and a section for authentic silver jewelry.

The Gold Ounce. Plaza los Muchachos, Calle Fortaleza 201. ☎ **787/724-3102.**

This is the direct factory outlet for the oldest jewelry factory on Puerto Rico, the Kury Company. Most of the output is shipped Stateside. Don't expect a top-notch jeweler here: Many of the pieces are replicated in endless repetition. But don't overlook the place for 14-karat-gold ornaments. Some of the designs are charming, and prices are about 20% less than at retail stores on the North American mainland.

Joyería Riviera. Calle La Cruz 205. ☎ **787/725-4000.**

Some consider this emporium of 18-karat gold and diamonds the Puerto Rican equivalent of Tiffany's. Adjacent to Plaza de Armas, the shop has an impeccable reputation. Its owner, Julio Abislaiman, stocks his store at such diamond centers as Antwerp, Tel Aviv, and New York. This is the major distributor of Rolex watches on Puerto Rico, although other brands are also sold. Prices range from $250 into the tens of thousands of dollars—at these prices, it's a good thing you can get "whatever you want," according to the owner.

200 Fortaleza. Calle Fortaleza 200 (at the corner of Calle La Cruz). ☎ **787/723-1989.**

Known as a leading cost-conscious place to buy fine jewelry in Old San Juan, this shop has 14-karat Italian gold chains and bracelets that are measured, fitted, and sold by weight. You can purchase watches or beautiful gems in modern settings in both 14- and 18-karat gold.

Vergina Gallery. Calle del Cristo 202. ☎ **787/721-0592.**

The most exotic jewelry emporium in San Juan, this is the only outlet in the Caribbean showcasing the neo-Byzantine and ancient Greek designs of Zolotos, one of Greece's most spectacular jewelers. Most of the pieces are made of hammered 18- and 22-karat gold, inset with colorful glittering gemstones. There's also an inventory of streamlined platinum jewelry from Germany, and worthy reproductions of medieval Greek and Russian icons, priced from $10 to $3,000.

Yas Mar. Calle Fortaleza 205. ☎ **787/724-1377.**

This shop sells convincing, glittering fake diamonds for those who don't want to wear the real thing. It also stocks real diamond chips, emeralds, sapphires, and rubies.

LEATHER

Leather & Pearls. Calle Tanca 252 (at the corner of Calle Tetuán). ☎ **787/724-8185.**

Majorca pearls and fine leather garments, bags, shoes, and accessories (including Gucci, Mark Cross, Fendi, and Paloma Picasso) are sold here.

LINENS

The Linen House. Calle Fortaleza 250. ☎ **787/721-4219.**

This unpretentious store specializes in napery, bed linens, and lace. Inventories include embroidered shower curtains selling for around $35 each, and lace doilies, bun warmers, place mats, and tablecloths that seamstresses took weeks to complete. Some astonishingly lovely items are available for as little as $30. The aluminum/pewter serving dishes have strikingly beautiful Spanish-colonial designs. Prices here are sometimes 40% lower than on the North American mainland.

SAN JUAN AFTER DARK

THE PERFORMING ARTS

Qué Pasa, the official visitor's guide to Puerto Rico, lists cultural events, including music, dance, theater, film, and art exhibits. It's distributed free by the tourist office.

Centro de Bellas Artes. Avenida Ponce de León 22. ☎ **787/724-4747,** or 787/725-7334 for the ticket agent. Tickets $12–$60, depending on the show; 50% discounts for seniors. Bus: 1.

In the heart of Santurce, the Performing Arts Center is a six-minute taxi ride from most of the Condado hotels. It contains the Festival Hall, Drama Hall, and the Experimental Theater. Some of the events here will only be of interest to Spanish-speakers; others attract an international audience.

El Teatro. In El Centro, at the Condado Beach Trio, Ashford Ave. ☎ **787/722-8433.** Tickets usually $28, but can vary with the show. Bus: A7.

In San Juan's convention center, part of the previously recommended Condado Beach Trio complex of hotels and restaurants, this locale is known for having the most spectacular revues in San Juan, usually with colorful costumes, Latin music, and dancing. A "taste of the tropics" is promised and ultimately delivered. However, the room is also used for special events, so call to find out what's happening at the time of your visit. Shows are at 9pm Monday through Wednesday and Saturday, and at both 9 and 10pm on Friday. Friday night shows include LeLoLai at 9pm and Ole Latino at 10pm.

Teatro Tapía. Avenida Ponce de León. ☎ **787/723-2079.** Tickets $10–$30, depending on the show.

Standing across from Plaza de Colón is one of the oldest theaters in the western hemisphere, built about 1832. Much of Puerto Rican theater history is connected with the Tapía, named after the island's first prominent playwright, Alejandro Tapía y Rivera. Various productions, some musical, are staged here throughout the year and include drama, dances, and cultural events. You'll have to call the box office (open Monday to Friday from 9am to 4pm) for specific information.

THE CLUB & MUSIC SCENE

Amadeus Disco. In El San Juan Hotel & Casino, Isla Verde Ave., Isla Verde. ☎ **787/791-1000.** Cover $8 Wed–Thurs and Sun, $10 Fri–Sat. Bus: A7, T1, or 2.

Its conservative art deco interior attracts the rich and beautiful, the merely rich, and the gaggle of onlookers pretending to be both. The Amadeus Disco is in the most exciting hotel in San Juan, so you can also stop in at the adjacent casino and gawk at the best-decorated lobby on Puerto Rico. The duplex area has one of the best sound systems in the Caribbean. Closed Monday and Tuesday.

Copa. In the Sands Hotel & Casino, Isla Verde Ave., Isla Verde. ☎ **787/791-6100.** Cover (including 2 drinks) $28, but could vary. Bus: A7, T1, or 2.

This is one of the major showrooms for revues along the San Juan beachfront strip. Although we can't predict what show will be featured when you visit, one previous revue was *Legends live at the Copa,* with impersonators appearing as Marilyn Monroe, Elvis, and Barbra Streisand. The show might also feature a major Las Vegas–type headliner from the mainland such as Whitney Houston or Diana Ross. Performances are Monday through Wednesday at 9 and 11pm and Friday and Saturday at 10:30pm.

Egypt. Avenida Roberto H. Todd 1. ☎ **787/725-4664.** Cover (including 1 or 2 drinks) $5–$10.

This busy nightclub attracts young, upwardly mobile singles. There's a dance floor well worn by years of boogying, although many visitors just come for drinks at the long and very accommodating bar. The decor is inspired by ancient Egypt. There's live music every Thursday and usually on Friday. The club is on two floors: normally one devoted to disco, the other to Latin music. No jeans are allowed on Thursday, Friday, or Saturday. The transformation from a bar to a crowded disco usually occurs around 9pm.

Laser. Calle del Cruz 251. ☎ **787/725-7581.** Cover $8–$10.

Set in the heart of the old town, this disco has shifted its focus from straight to gay and, since late in 1996, back again to mostly straight, at least according to its owners. Once inside, you can wander over the three floors of its historic premises, listening to whatever music happens to be hot in New York at the time of your visit, with lots of additional Latino merengue and salsa thrown in as well. Although the only regularly scheduled nights for business at this club are Thursday, Friday, and Saturday, its owners and staff are alert to the arrivals of cruise ships in the nearby harbor, and open their doors whenever a ship happens to pull into port. In that event, expect for the place to be packed, both with locals and cruisers, and as such, radically affect the composition of its otherwise regular clientele. Usually, it's open from 8pm to 4am.

The Bar Scene

Fiesta Bar. In the Condado Plaza Hotel & Casino, 999 Ashford Ave. ☎ **787/721-1000.**

This bar lures in a healthy mixture of local residents and hotel guests. The margaritas are appropriately salty, the rhythms are hot and Latin, and the free admission usually helps you forget any losses you might have suffered in the nearby casinos.

Palm Court. In the El San Juan Hotel & Casino, Isla Verde Ave., Isla Verde. ☎ **787/791-1000.**

This is the most beautiful bar on the island—perhaps in the entire Caribbean. Set in an oval wrapped around a sunken bar area, amid marble and burnished mahogany, it offers a view of one of the world's largest chandeliers. After 9pm Monday to Saturday, live music emanates from an adjoining room (El Chico Bar).

Shannon's Irish Pub. Calle Bori 496, Río Piedras. ☎ **787/281-8466.**

Ireland and its ales meet the tropics at this pub with a Latin accent. A sports bar, it's the regular watering hole of many university students, a constant supplier of high-energy rock 'n' roll and 10 TV monitors. There's live music Wednesday through Sunday—everything from rock to jazz to Latin. There are pool tables, and a simple cafe serves inexpensive lunches Monday through Friday.

Violeta's. Calle Fortaleza 56 (2 blocks from the Gran Hotel Convento). ☎ **787/723-6804.**

Stylish and comfortable, Violeta's occupies the ground floor of a 200-year-old beamed house. Sometimes a pianist performs at the oversize grand piano. An open courtyard out back provides additional seating for sipping margaritas.

Hot Nights in Gay San Juan

The Barefoot Bar. 2 Calle Vendig. ☎ **787/724-7230.**

This, along with the bar at the Atlantic Beach Hotel, just across the street, is the most informed and most tuned-in gay bar in Puerto Rico. It occupies a blue building whose terrace extends out over the sands of the same beach shared by the Marriott Hotel, which lies almost next door. At least 98% of the clientele is gay and male, and includes goodly numbers of whatever transient workers from the local airlines and cruise ships happen to be in port at the time of your arrival. Simple lunches, consisting mostly of sandwiches and salads, are served from noon till around 4pm; after that the food service ends in favor of drinking and dialogue.

The Beach Bar. In the Atlantic Beach Hotel, 1 Calle Vendig. ☎ **787/721-6900.**

Its indoor/outdoor format, and its position adjacent to a terrace that extends out over the sands of the beach, are roughly equivalent to the facilities at the Barefoot Bar, which is just across the street. Together, they form a complex of bars and terraces that appeal to a clientele that's mostly male and mostly gay. A restaurant within the hotel serves breakfast and lunch, but not dinner, to a clientele that shows up between 11am and 1am every day of the week.

Cups. Calle San Mateo 1, Santurce. ☎ **787/268-3570.**

Its venue is that of a Latino tavern, and its premises are valued as the only place in San Juan that caters almost exclusively to lesbians. Men of any sexual persuasion, in almost every case, aren't particularly welcome, a fact appreciated within a scene that reminds many lesbians of a tropical version of one of the bars they left behind in New York. Although music plays, the venue encourages quiet conversation over beer or wine, diversions that are pursued every night from 9pm to midnight.

Krash. 1257 Ponce de León, Santurce. ☎ **787/722-1131.** Admission $10 Fri–Sat, and includes 2 free drinks; otherwise, free.

Any gay male employed by any of the cruise lines that dock in San Juan's harbor overnight will almost invariably head for the flashing lights and up-to-date music of Puerto Rico's largest and busiest gay disco. It was renovated in 1996 in an ancient Greek/Egyptian motif, and occupies two levels of a building in an urban neighborhood in the Santurce district. Looking for a night on the town? Consider beginning it with a drink at either of the two gay bars on Calle Vendig (see above), then walking the 15-minute stroll to reach Krash. The average age of clients is around 28. Rum-based drinks, merengue, and whatever music is favored in New York at the time are popular, and most of the flirting, dancing, and conversations here begin after around 10:30pm. Open Wednesday through Sunday from 9pm to 5am.

CASINOS

These are one of the island's biggest draws. Many visitors come here on package deals and stay at one of the posh hotels at the Condado or Isla Verde, just to gamble.

You can try your luck at the **Caribe Hilton** (one of the better ones), the **Condado Beach Trio, El San Juan Hotel & Casino** on Isla Verde Avenue in Isla Verde, and the **Condado Plaza Hotel & Casino.** There are no passports to flash or admissions to pay, as in European casinos. The **Radisson Ambassador Plaza Hotel and Casino** is another deluxe hotel noted for its casino action. The **Dutch Inn Hotel & Casino,** Avenida Condado 55, also has a gambling emporium. One of the most recent casinos to open on the island is at the **Holiday Inn Crowne Plaza Hotel and Tropical Casino** on Route 187. The Stellaris Casino at the **San Juan Marriott Resort** is also one of the island's newest.

One of the largest casinos on the island is the **Sands Casino** at the Sands Hotel & Casino Beach Resort, on Isla Verde Avenue in Isla Verde. Open from noon to 4am daily, this 10,000-square-foot gaming facility is an elegant rendezvous. One of its Murano chandeliers is longer than a bowling alley. The casino offers 207 slot machines, 16 blackjack tables, three dice tables, four roulette wheels, and a minibaccarat table.

The best casinos "out in the island" are those at the **Hyatt Regency Cerromar Beach** and **Hyatt Dorado Beach.** In fact, you can drive to either of these from San Juan to enjoy their nighttime diversions. There are also casinos at **Palmas del Mar** and at **Westin Rio Mar at Palmer** and yet another at the **Mayagüez Hilton** in western Puerto Rico. Puerto Rico's "second city," Ponce, now has a major casino following the opening of the **Ponce Hilton and Casino.**

Most casinos are open daily from noon to 4pm and again from 8pm to 4am. Jackets for men are sometimes requested.

2 Dorado

The name itself evokes a kind of magic. Along the north shore of Puerto Rico, about a 40-minute (22-mile) drive west of San Juan, a world of luxury resorts and villa complexes unfolds. The big properties of the Hyatt Dorado Beach Hotel and Hyatt Regency Cerromar Beach Hotel sit on the choice white sandy beaches here.

Many guests of these hotels only pass through San Juan on arrival and departure. Others, particularly first-timers, may want to spend a day or so sightseeing and shopping in San Juan before heading for one of these complete resort properties, since, chances are, once at the resort they'll never leave the grounds. The hotels are self-contained, with beach, swimming, golf, tennis, dining, and nightlife activities.

If you don't have a car and need to use public transportation, call **Dorado Transport Corp.** (☎ **787/796-1214**) in San Juan. It offers shuttle service to the area from the airport daily from 10am to 10pm. The charge is only $15 per passenger, but a minimum of three must take the trip.

WHERE TO STAY

Either Hyatt resort is a good choice for families. These Dorado twins offer "family getaway" packages at Camp Coquí, the Puerto Rican version of Camp Hyatt, featuring professionally supervised day and evening programs for children ages 3 to 12. Children also receive a 50% discount on meals.

✪ **Hyatt Dorado Beach Hotel.** Dorado, PR 00646. ☎ **800/233-1234** in the U.S., or 787/796-1234. Fax 787/796-2022. 298 rms, 17 casitas. A/C MINIBAR TV TEL. Winter, $495–$645 double; from $770 casita. Spring and fall, $240–$315; from $450 casita. Summer, $170–$240 double; from $365 casita. MAP (mandatory in winter) $64 extra for adults, $32 extra for children. AE, DC, DISC, MC, V.

The Hyatt sprawls across a plantation filled with palms, pine trees, and purple bougainvillea, and a 2-mile sandy ocean beach. We think it's superior to its sibling, the Cerromar (see below), and more tranquil. Located 22 miles west of San Juan, the Dorado Beach is a low-rise building. Two side-by-side 18-hole championship golf courses, designed by Robert Trent Jones Sr., are its big draw, along with a slew of other sports facilities. The present hotel, originally a Rockefeller playground, opened in 1958, and many repeat guests, including celebrities, have been coming back ever since.

The Hyatt Hotels Corporation has spent millions on improvements. The renovated bedrooms have marble baths and terra-cotta flooring throughout. Rooms are available on the beach or in villas tucked in and around the lushly planted grounds. The casitas are a series of private beach or poolside houses.

Dining/Entertainment: Breakfast can be taken on your private balcony and lunch on an outdoor ocean terrace. Dinner is served in a three-tiered main dining room where you can watch the surf. Hyatt Dorado chefs have won many awards, and the food at the hotel restaurants and Su Casa Restaurant (not included in the MAP) is among the finest in the Caribbean. The Beach Grill and Pro Shop are for casual meals. And don't forget the casino.

Services: Room service (7am to midnight), baby-sitting, laundry/dry cleaning.

Facilities: Two 18-hole golf courses, seven all-weather tennis courts, a full-service spa, two swimming pools, children's camp, one of the best windsurfing schools in Puerto Rico.

✪ **Hyatt Regency Cerromar Beach Hotel.** Dorado, PR 00646. ☎ **800/233-1234** or 787/796-1234. Fax 787/796-4647. 504 rms, 43 suites. A/C MINIBAR TV TEL. Winter, $325–$420 double; from $745 suite. Spring and fall, $225–$265 double; from $570 suite. Summer, $175–$210 double; from $435 suite. MAP $64 extra for adults, $32 extra for children. AE, DC, DISC, MC, V.

Near the more elegant Hyatt Dorado Beach Hotel, this Hyatt stands on its own beach and boasts a wealth of sports facilities and resort amenities. The name Cerromar is a combination of two words—*cerro* (mountain) and *mar* (sea)—and true to its name, it's surrounded by mountains and ocean. Approximately 22 miles west of San Juan, the high-rise hotel shares the 1,000-acre former Livingston estate with the Dorado, so guests can enjoy the Robert Trent Jones Sr. golf courses as well as the other sports facilities at the next-door hotel; a shuttle bus runs back and forth between the two resorts every half hour.

All rooms have first-class appointments and are well maintained; the majority have private balconies. The floors throughout are tile and the furnishings are casual tropical, in soft colors and pastels. All rooms have honor bars and in-room safes.

Dining/Entertainment: The outdoor Swan Café has three levels connected by a dramatic staircase; some tables overlook a lake populated by swans and flamingos. Other dining choices include Sushi Wong's and the hotel's pride and joy, Medici's. The Flamingo bar offers a wide, open-air expanse overlooking the sea and the water playground.

Services: 24-hour room service, laundry/dry cleaning, baby-sitting.

Facilities: The water playground contains the world's longest freshwater swimming pool: a 1,776-foot-long fantasy pool with a riverlike current in five connected free-form pools. It takes 15 minutes to float from one end of the pool to the other. There are also 14 waterfalls, tropical landscaping, a subterranean Jacuzzi, water slides, walks, bridges, and a children's pool. A full-service spa and health club provide services for both body and skin care, including Swedish massages and a Powercise machine that "talks" to you. In addition to 21 tennis courts, there's also a children's day camp for guests 3 to 12, open year-round and known as Camp Hyatt.

WHERE TO DINE

El Malecón. Rte. 693, km 8.2. ☎ **787/796-1645.** Reservations not required. Main courses $7.95–$33.50. AE, MC, V. Sun–Thurs 11am–10pm, Fri–Sat 11am–11pm. PUERTO RICAN.

If you'd like to discover an unpretentious local place serving good Puerto Rican cuisine, then head for El Malecón, a simple concrete structure one minute from a small shopping center. It has a cozy family ambience and is especially popular on weekends. Some members of the staff speak English, and the chef is best with fresh seafood, which most diners order. The chef might also prepare a variety of items not listed on the menu.

Medici's. In the Hyatt Regency Cerromar. ☎ **787/796-1234,** ext. 3240. Reservations required. Main courses $17.50–$32. AE, DC, DISC, MC, V. Daily 6:30–9:30pm. INTERNATIONAL/ITALIAN.

Frequented by an upscale clientele, Medici's is an elegant 340-seat dining room. Tables sit on tiers at several levels, each of which has been angled for views of the gardens. The staff sets the mood of relaxed formality, the music is classical, and the wine cellar is diversified. Guests can take their pick—from steak to spa cuisine, from osso buco to Caribbean flavors. The kitchen also turns out a northern Italian cuisine, and most items, including pastas, are available as appetizers or main or side dishes. Try the prosciutto with melon or spinach with fried calamari as an appetizer, followed by a delectable grilled swordfish with peppercorn sauce and cioppino (shrimp, lobster, and mussels in a light tomato basil sauce).

✪ **Su Casa.** In the Hyatt Dorado Beach Hotel. ☎ **787/796-1234.** Reservations required. Main courses $24–$39. AE, MC, V. Daily 7pm–midnight. SPANISH/CARIBBEAN.

Set in the 19th-century Livingston family home, this Spanish colonial building has been a favorite for the rich and famous since the Rockefellers entertained guests at their posh Dorado Beach hideaway. Diners sit at candlelit tables and enjoy the serenade of strolling entertainers. The chef produces an innovative cuisine, using Puerto Rican fruits and vegetables whenever possible, including plantain, spinach, and eggplant. The elegant food is the best at Dorado, and the atmosphere rather chic. Many dishes have been lightened to suit contemporary appetites. Menus change frequently but include dishes concocted from the area's finest products plus those shipped in—everything from juicy tender filet mignon to succulent lobsters. Try, for example, the rack of lamb. Don't plan to rush through a meal at Su Casa—allow yourself enough time to enjoy your dinner.

SPORTS

GOLF A golfer's dream, Puerto Rico has some splendid courses, and eight major ones. The **Hyatt Resorts Puerto Rico** at Dorado (☎ **787/796-1234**), with 72 holes of golf, offers the greatest number of options in the Caribbean. The 18-hole Robert Trent Jones Sr.–designed courses at the Hyatt Regency Cerromar and the Hyatt Dorado Beach match the finest anywhere. The courses were built between 1959 and 1970. The two original courses (east and west) were carved out of a jungle and offer tight fairways bordered by trees and forests, with lots of ocean holes. The somewhat newer, and less frequently televised north and south courses feature wide fairways with well-bunkered greens and an assortment of lakes, water traps, and tricky wind factors. Each of the four has a 72 par. The longest course is the south course at 7,047 yards. Scheduling of tee-off times is almost always easier if you're a resident of one of the Hyatt resorts. For the north and south courses, Hyatt residents pay $80 for greens fees, whereas nonresidents are charged $120. At the east and west courses, Hyatt residents are charged $120 for greens fees, rising to $140 for nonresidents. The pro shop is open daily from 7am to 5:30pm. Nonguests who call ahead can play these courses, too.

TENNIS Again, the twin Hyatt resorts of **Dorado** and **Cerromar** (☎ **787/796-1234**) have the monopoly, with a total of 21 courts between them. The charge is $15 an hour, rising to $18 from 6 to 8pm. Lessons are available for $55 per hour. Nonguests can't use the courts, however.

WINDSURFING The best place on the island's north shore is along the well-maintained beachfront of the Hyatt Dorado Beach Hotel. Here, **Lisa Penfield Watersports** (☎ **787/796-1234,** ext. 3768, or 787/796-2188) offers 90-minute lessons for $55 each; board rentals cost $60 per half day. Well supplied with a wide array of Windsurfers, including some designed specifically for beginners and children, the school benefits from the almost uninterrupted flow of the north shore's strong, steady winds and an experienced crew of instructors. A kayaking/snorkeling trip, lasting 1 1/2 hours, costs $45. Two-tank boat dives go for $119 per person. Waverunners can be rented for $55 per half hour, a Sunfish for $50 an hour.

3 Highlights in Northwestern Puerto Rico

Dubbed "an ear to heaven," the **Arecibo Observatory** (☎ **787/878-2612**) contains the world's largest and most sensitive radar/radiotelescope. The telescope features a 20-acre dish or radio mirror set in an ancient sinkhole. It's 1,000 feet in diameter and 167 feet deep, and allows scientists to examine the ionosphere, the planets, and the moon with powerful radar signals and to monitor natural radio emissions from distant galaxies, pulsars, and quasars. It's being used by scientists as part of the Search for Extraterrestrial Intelligence (SETI). This research effort speculates that advanced civilizations elsewhere in the universe might also communicate via radio waves. The 10-year, $100 million search for life in space was launched on October 12, 1992, the 500-year anniversary of the New World's discovery by Columbus.

Unusually lush vegetation flourishes under the giant dish—ferns, wild orchids, and begonias. Assorted creatures like mongooses, lizards, and dragonflies have also taken refuge there. Suspended in outlandish fashion above the dish is a 600-ton platform that resembles a space station.

Free self-guided tours are available at the observatory Tuesday to Friday from 2 to 3pm and on Sunday from 1 to 4:30pm. There's a souvenir shop on the grounds. The observatory lies a 90-minute drive west of San Juan, outside the town of Arecibo. From Arecibo, it's a 35-minute drive via Routes 22, 134, 635, and 625 (the site is signposted).

Río Camuy Cave Park, 1 hour and 20 minutes west of San Juan on Route 129, at kilometer 18.9 (☎ **787/898-3100**), contains the third-largest underground river in the world. It runs through a network of caves, canyons, and sinkholes that have been cut through the island's limestone base over the course of millions of years. Known to the pre-Columbian Taíno peoples, the caves came to the attention of speleologists in the 1950s. They were opened to the public in 1986.

Visitors first see a short film about the caves, then descend into the caverns in open-air trolleys. The trip takes you through a 200-foot-deep sinkhole and a chasm where tropical trees, ferns, and flowers flourish, along with birds and butterflies. The trolley then goes to the entrance of Clara Cave of Epalme, one of 16 in the Camuy caves network, where visitors begin a 45-minute walk, viewing the majestic series of rooms rich in stalagmites, stalactites, and huge natural "sculptures" formed over the centuries. The park has added the Tres Pueblos Sinkhole and the Spiral Sinkhole to its slate of attractions.

The caves are open Tuesday to Sunday from 8am to 4pm. Tickets are $10 for adults, $7 for children 2 to 12; senior citizens pay $5. Parking is $2. For more information, phone the park.

4 Rincón

At the westernmost point of the island, Rincón, 6 miles north of Mayagüez, has one of the most exotic beaches on the island, which draws surfers from around the world. In and around this small fishing village are some unique accommodations.

GETTING THERE

If you rent a car at the San Juan airport, it will take approximately 2½ hours to drive here via the busy northern Route 2, or 3 hours via the scenic mountain route (no. 52) to the south. We recommend the southern route through Ponce.

In addition, there are five flights each weekday, and three each on Saturday and Sunday, from San Juan to Mayagüez on **American Eagle** (☎ **800/433-7300**). These flights take 45 minutes. From the Mayagüez airport, Rincón is a 30-minute drive to the north on Route 2 (turn left, or west, at the intersection with Route 115). Round-trip fares range from $69 to $130 per person.

WHERE TO STAY

✪ **Horned Dorset Primavera Hotel.** Rte. 429 (P.O. Box 1132), Rincón, PR 00677. ☎ **800/633-1857** or 787/823-4030. Fax 787/823-5580. 22 rooms, 9 suites. A/C. Winter, $340 double; $440–$650 suite for 2. Off-season, $224 double; $324–$525 suite for 2. MAP $71.25 per extra person. AE, DC, MC, V. From the Mayagüez airport, take Route 2 north 1/2 mile to the Anasco intersection; turn left onto Route 115 toward Rincón for 4 miles; after El Coche Restaurant, take a sharp left onto Route 429 and go about a mile; the hotel is on the left, at distance marker km 3.

This is the most sophisticated hotel on Puerto Rico, and one of the most exclusive and elegant small hostelries anywhere in the Caribbean. Established in 1987, it was built on the massive breakwaters and seawalls erected by a local railroad many years ago, and was named after a successful hotel (the Horned Dorset), which its owners still maintain in upstate New York.

The hacienda evokes an aristocratic Spanish villa, with wicker armchairs, hand-painted tiles, ceiling fans, seaside terraces, and cascades of flowers. Management does not allow children under 12, most pets, radios, or televisions—this is really a restful place. Accommodations are in a series of suites that ramble uphill amid lush gardens. The decor is tasteful, with four-poster beds and brass-footed tubs in marble-sheathed bathrooms.

In 1996, the hotel completed a $1.4 million addition, the eight-suite Casa Escondida villa. Set at the edge of the property, adjacent to the sea, it is decorated with an accent on teakwood and marble. Some of the units have private plunge pools, others offer private verandas or sundecks. Each contains high-quality reproductions of colonial furniture by Baker.

Dining/Entertainment: The hotel's restaurant is one of the finest on Puerto Rico (see "Where to Dine," below). There's a bar open throughout the day that serves delectable rum punches. Guitarists and singers often perform during cocktail and dinner hours.

Services: Room service (at breakfast and lunch only), concierge, laundry, massage, limousine and touring services.

Facilities: The best hotel library on Puerto Rico (books on art, music, comparative literature, and poetry), swimming pool, secluded semiprivate beach, deep-sea fishing; tennis courts, golf, and scuba diving available nearby.

Parador Villa Antonio. Rte. 115, km 12.3 (P.O. Box 68), Rincón, PR 00677. ☎ **800/443-0266** in the U.S., or 787/823-2645. Fax 787/823-3380. 55 apts. A/C TV TEL. $74.90–$107 double. AE, DC, MC, V.

Ilia and Hector Ruíz offer apartments by the sea in this privately owned and run parador. The beach outside is a nice one, but we've seen litter here; it's not kept as clean as it should be by the local authorities, probably because of budget constraints. Facilities include a children's playground, games room, two tennis courts, and a swimming pool. Surfing and fishing can be enjoyed just outside your front door, and you can bring your catch right into your cottage and prepare a fresh seafood dinner in your own kitchenette (there's no restaurant). Be aware that the air-conditioning doesn't work properly here, and in general better maintenance is needed. Room prices are based on the view, not the size. From Rincón, take Route 2 to Route 22; stay on 22 until you see the sign Hatillo-Arecibo. At this point, bear left and get back on no. 2 and stay on it until you see a sign, ANASCO NO. 109 LEFT, RINCÓN NO. 115

RIGHT. Take no. 115 until you reach El Bambino Restaurant. After passing the restaurant, take a hard left and in about 200 feet make a right turn.

WHERE TO DINE

✪ **Horned Dorset Primavera.** Rte. 429. ☎ **787/823-4030.** Reservations recommended. Fixed-price dinner $56. AE, MC, V. Daily noon–2:30pm, with dinner seatings at 7, 8, and 9pm. CLASSIC FRENCH/CARIBBEAN.

This place reigns without equal as the finest restaurant in western Puerto Rico. It's so alluring that diners sometimes journey out from San Juan for an intimate dinner. It's the counterpart of an award-winning restaurant in Leonardsville, New York, the Horned Dorset. Meals are served beneath soaring ceilings. A masonry staircase sweeps from the garden to reach the second-floor precincts.

The chef is never better than in preparing medallions of lobster in an orange-flavored beurre-blanc (white butter) sauce, although the grilled breast of duckling with bay leaves and raspberry sauce is also delectable. Dorado (mahimahi), on another occasion, was grilled and served with a ginger-cream sauce on a bed of braised Chinese cabbage. It was delicious, as was baby hen with foie gras. This restaurant serves people who eat at the best places in the world, and it pleases even their discriminating palates.

HITTING THE BEACH (& THE LINKS)

One of Puerto Rico's most outstanding surfing beaches, comparable to the finest surfing spots in the world (according to competitors in the 1988 World Surfing Championship held there), is at **Punta Higuero,** on Route 413 near Rincón. In the winter months especially, uninterrupted Atlantic swells with perfectly formed waves averaging five to six feet in height roll shoreward, and rideable swells sometimes reach 15 to 25 feet.

Punta Borinquén Golf Club (☎ **787/890-2987**), at Aguadilla, the former Ramey Air Force Base, has an 18-hole public course, open daily from 7am to 7pm. Greens fees are $10 for an all-day pass, plus an additional $10 for use of an electric cart.

5 Mayagüez

Puerto Ricans have nicknamed their third-largest city the "Sultan of the West." This port city, not architecturally remarkable, was once the needlework capital of the island. There are still craftspeople who sew fine embroidery.

Mayagüez is the honeymoon capital of Puerto Rico. The tradition dates from the 16th century; it's said that when local fathers needed husbands for their daughters, they kidnapped young Spanish sailors who were en route to Latin America.

GETTING THERE

American Eagle (☎ **800/433-7300**) flies six times daily throughout the year between San Juan to Mayagüez. Flight time is 25 minutes, although there are often delays on the ground at either end of the itinerary. Depending on restrictions and the season you book your flight, round-trip passage ranges from $69 to $130 per person.

If you rent a car at the San Juan airport and want to drive to Mayagüez, the faster, and more efficient route is the northern route that combines sections of the newly widened route 22 with the older Route 2. Estimated driving time for a local resident is about 90 minutes, although newcomers usually take about 30 minutes longer. The southern route, which combines the modern Route 52 with a transit across the outskirts of historic Ponce, and a final access into Mayagüez via the southern section of Route 2, requires a total of about three hours and affords some worthwhile scenery across the island's mountainous interior.

WHERE TO STAY

Best Western Mayagüez Resort & Casino. Rte. 104 (P.O. Box 3629), Mayagüez, PR 00709. ☎ **800/981-3954** or 787/831-7575. Fax 787/265-3020. 141 rms, 8 suites. A/C MINIBAR TV TEL. Year-round, $135–$175 double; $250 suite. AE, MC, V. Parking $4.50.

For at least 30 years after its construction in 1964, this hotel functioned as Hilton's outpost on western Puerto Rico, an isolated branch of the worldwide chain whose five-story T-shaped hotel contained western Puerto Rico's busiest and most animated casino. In 1995, it was bought by a consortium of local investors, who poured 5.5 million much-needed dollars into a radical renovation. Since its opening in 1996, the hotel has benefited more than ever from its redesigned casino, its country-club format, and its position on 20 acres of tropical gardens at the northern approach to the city, 3 miles from the airport. Its carefully landscaped grounds have been designated as an adjunct to the nearby Mayagüez Institute of Tropical Agriculture by the U.S. Department of Agriculture. There are five species of palm trees, eight kinds of bougainvillea, and numerous species of rare flora, set adjacent to the Institute's collection of tropical plants. The hotel's well-designed bedrooms open onto views of the swimming pool, and many units have private balconies.

Dining/Entertainment: For details about El Castillo, the hotel's restaurant, see "Where to Dine," below. The hotel functions as one of the entertainment centers of Mayagüez. Its casino, renovated along with the rest of the hotel in 1995–96, has free admission and is open daily from noon to 4am. You can drink and dance at the Victoria Lounge Wednesday to Sunday from 8:30pm to 3am; entrance is free.

Services: Room service (6:30am to 11pm), laundry, baby-sitting.

Facilities: Olympic-size swimming pool, children's pool, playground, Jacuzzi, minigym, three tennis courts, deep-sea fishing, skin-diving, surfing and scuba diving can be arranged. A golf course lies within a 30-minute drive from the hotel.

Holiday Inn & Tropical Casino. 2701 Rte. 2, km 149.9, Mayagüez, PR 00680-6328. ☎ **800/HOLIDAY** in the U.S. and Canada, or 787/833-1100. Fax 787/833-1300. 147 rms, 5 suites. A/C TV TEL. $131–$151 double; from $200 suite. AE, DC, MC, V.

This is one of the two most mainstream hotels of western Puerto Rico, an establishment that competes directly with the Best Western Mayagüez Resort & Casino in almost every way. Set 2 miles north of Mayagüez's city center, behind a parking lot and a well-maintained lawn that simply isn't as dramatically landscaped as the Mayagüez Resort's surrounding acreage, it's a six-story hotel that opened in 1993. Clean, contemporary, and comfortable, it has a marble-floored, high-ceilinged lobby, an outdoor swimming pool with its own waterside bar, and a generously sized casino outfitted in glittering shades of green with touches of pink. Bedrooms are comfortably but functionally outfitted in motel style. The establishment's social center is Holly's bar and restaurant, an airy, stylish eatery that's open daily for breakfast, lunch, and dinner.

Hotel Parador El Sol. Calle Santiago Riera Palmer, 9 Este, Mayagüez, PR 00680. ☎ **787/834-0303.** Fax 787/265-7567. 52 rms. A/C TV TEL. $60 double; $70 triple. Rates include continental breakfast. AE, MC, V.

This hotel provides some of the most reasonable and hospitable accommodations in this part of Puerto Rico, although it's far more geared to the business traveler than to the tourist, with no-frills furnishings. Central to the shopping district and to all highways, two blocks from the landmark Plaza del Mercado in the heart of the city, the seven-floor restored hotel offers up-to-date facilities that include cable TV, a restaurant, and a swimming pool.

WHERE TO DINE

El Castillo. In the Best Western Mayagüez Resort & Casino, Rte. 104. ☎ **787/831-7575.** Breakfast buffet $11.25. Buffet lunch (Mon–Sat) $14, Sun brunch buffet $21.95. Main courses $12–$25. AE, MC, V. Daily 6:30am–11pm. INTERNATIONAL.

This is the most professionally managed and large-scale dining room in western Puerto Rico, the main gastronomic outlet for the largest hotel and casino in the western part of the island. Ringed with paneling and known as the venue for copious lunchtime buffets, it serves only à la carte items at nighttime. These include such dishes as seafood stew served on beds of linguine with marinara sauce; grilled salmon with a mango-flavored Grand Marnier sauce; and fillets of sea bass with a cilantro, white wine, and butter sauce. Steak and lobster are served on the same platter, if you want it. The food has real flavor and flair and isn't the typical bland hotel fare so often dished up.

EXPLORING THE AREA: SURFING BEACHES & TROPICAL GARDENS

Along the western coastal bends of Route 2, north of Mayagüez, lie the best surfing **beaches** in the Caribbean. Surfers from as far away as New Zealand come to ride the waves. You can also check out panoramic **Punta Higuero** beach, nearby on Route 413, near Rincón.

South of Mayagüez is **Boquerón Beach,** one of the island's best.

For golfers, the **Mayagüez Hilton** at Mayagüez (☎ **787/831-7575**) makes arrangements for guests to play at a nine-hole course at a nearby country club.

The chief sight is the **Tropical Agriculture Research Station** (☎ **787/831-3435**). At the administration office, ask for a free map of the tropical gardens, which contain a huge collection of tropical species useful to people, including cacao, fruit trees, spices, timbers, and ornamentals. The location is on Route 65, between Post Street and Route 108, adjacent to the University of Puerto Rico at Mayagüez campus and across the street from the **Parque de los Próceres** (Patriots' Park). The grounds are open free, Monday to Friday from 7am to 5pm.

Mayagüez might also be the jumping-off point for a visit by chartered boat to **Mona Island,** "the Galapagos of the Caribbean," which enjoys many legends of pirate treasure and is known for its white-sand beaches and marine life. The island is virtually uninhabited, except for two policemen and a director of the institute of natural resources. The island attracts hunters seeking pigs and wild goats, along with big-game fishers. But mostly it's intriguing to anyone who wants to escape civilization. Playa Sardinera on Mona Island was a base for pirates. On one side of the island, at Playa de Pajaros, are caves where the Taíno people left their mysterious hieroglyphs. Camping is available at $1 per night. Everything needed, including water, must be brought in, and everything, including garbage, must be taken out. For further information, call the **Puerto Rico Department of Natural Resources** at ☎ **787/724-3724.**

Encantos Ecotours (☎ **800/272-0005**) offers a four-day/three-night tour of Mona on the second Friday of each month for $599 per person. The price includes ground transportation to and from San Juan, sea transportation departing from Cabo Rojo, all diving/snorkeling, spelunking, and camping gear, and all meals and fees.

6 Ponce

Puerto Rico's second-largest city, Ponce ("The Pearl of the South") was named after Loíza Ponce de León, grandson of Ponce de León. Today it's Puerto Rico's principal shipping port on the Caribbean Sea. The city is well kept and attractive, as reflected by its many plazas, parks, and public buildings. It somewhat has the air of a provincial Mediterranean town. Look for the *rejas* (framed balconies) of the handsome colonial mansions.

Maps and information can be found at the **tourist office,** on the second floor of the Citibank Building on Plaza de las Delicias (☎ **787/841-8160**).

GETTING THERE

Ponce lies 75 miles southwest of San Juan and is reached by Route 52.

American Eagle (☎ **800/433-7300**) offers daily flights between San Juan and Ponce (flight time: 40 min.) for $69 to $90 round-trip, depending on the ticket. However, prices are known to fluctuate, so call for last-minute details.

WHERE TO STAY

Hotel Meliá. Calle Cristina 2, Ponce, PR 00731. ☎ **787/842-0260.** Fax 787/841-3602. 78 rms. A/C TV TEL. $70–$80 double. Rates include continental breakfast. AE, DC, MC, V. Parking $3.

A city hotel with southern hospitality, the Meliá, which has no connection with the international hotel chain, often attracts businesspeople. The location is a few steps away from the Cathedral of Our Lady of Guadalupe and from the Parque de Bombas (the red-and-black firehouse). Although this old and somewhat tattered hotel was long ago outclassed by the Hilton, many of its admirers who could afford more upscale accommodations still prefer to stay here for its old-time atmosphere and aura. The lobby floor and all stairs are covered with Spanish tiles of Moorish design. The desk clerks speak English. The rooms are comfortably furnished and pleasant enough, and most have a balcony facing either busy Calle Cristina or the old plaza. Breakfast is served on a rooftop terrace with a good view of Ponce, and the Hotel Meliá Restaurant plods along under separate management. You can park your car in the lot nearby.

✪ **Ponce Hilton and Casino.** Avenida Santiago de los Caballeros 14 (P.O. Box 7419), Ponce, PR 00732. ☎ **800/HILTONS** in the U.S. and Canada, or 787/259-7676. Fax 787/259-7674. 153 rms, 8 suites. A/C MINIBAR TV TEL. Year-round $190–$210 double; $400 suite. Additional person $45 extra. AE, CB, DC, DISC, MC, V. Self-parking $4.50; valet parking $10.

Opened in 1993 on an 80-acre tract of land right on the beach at the western end of Avenida Santiago de los Caballeros, about a five-minute (7-mile) drive from the center of Ponce, this is the most glamorous hotel in southern Puerto Rico. Designed like a miniature village, with turquoise-blue roofs, white walls, and lots of tropical plants, ornamental waterfalls, and gardens, it welcomes conventioneers and individual tourists alike. Accommodations contain tropically inspired furnishings, ceiling fans, terraces or balconies, and several luxurious extra amenities.

Dining/Entertainment: The most glamorous of the hotel's three restaurants is La Cava (see "Where to Dine," below). Other choices include Terrazza, overlooking the sea, and the less formal El Bohemio. There's also a casino open daily from noon to 4am. Breakfasts, served from an elaborate buffet, are the best in Ponce.

Services: Room service, laundry, baby-sitting (if arranged in advance).

Facilities: A lagoon-shaped pool ringed with gardens, business center, fitness center, video arcade, bike rentals, playground, summer camp for children; water sports available.

WHERE TO DINE

El Ancla. Avenida Hostos Final 9, Playa Ponce. ☎ **787/840-2450.** Reservations not required. Main courses $5.95–$35. AE, DC, MC, V. Sun–Thurs 11am–10pm, Fri–Sat 11am–midnight. PUERTO RICAN/SEAFOOD.

Established by members of the Lugo family in 1978, this place ranks among the best restaurants of Ponce. Much of its appeal derives from its location south of the city on soaring piers that extend from the rocky coastline out over the surf. As you dine, the sound of the sea rises literally from beneath your feet.

Specialties, made with the catch of the day, might include red snapper served with a pumpkin flan, dorado in a tomato-brandy sauce, seafood casserole, and broiled lobster. Steak, veal, and chicken dishes are also available. The dishes have real Puerto Rican zest and flavor.

✪ **La Hacienda/La Cava de la Hacienda.** In the Ponce Hilton, Avenida Santiago de los Caballeros 14. ☎ **787/259-7676.** Reservations recommended. Main courses $17–$29. AE, DC, MC, V. Daily 6:30–10:30pm. INTERNATIONAL.

These restaurants are the most elegant and stylish dining rooms in Ponce. Designed like a network of interconnected rooms in a 19th-century coffee plantation, they offer impeccable service and a dignified formality. The menu at both restaurants is the same, only the ambience is different. La Hacienda is a high-ceilinged octagon, with plenty of room between tables and lots of exposed paneling. La Cava de la Hacienda resembles an underground wine cellar. There's also a pair of private dining rooms for groups of 6 to 10 diners.

Menu items change every two weeks, but might include snails in a Pinot Noir sauce, cheese fondue for two, a paillard of salmon with sorrel sauce, veal medallions, minted lamb chops, and lobster-stuffed ravioli. Desserts might include a flamed baked Alaska or créme brûlée. Although it's rare for dishes to scale the heights, each is competently prepared with the freshest ingredients.

La Montserrate. Sector Las Cucharas, Rte. 82. ☎ **787/841-2740.** Reservations not required. Main courses $14–$29. AE, DC, DISC, MC, V. Daily 10am–10pm. PUERTO RICAN/SEAFOOD.

Beside the seafront, in a residential neighborhood about 4 miles west of the town center, this restaurant draws a loyal clientele from the surrounding houses. A culinary institution in Ponce, it occupies a large, airy, modern building divided into two different dining areas. The first of these is slightly more formal than the next. Most visitors, however, head for the large room in back, where windows on three sides encompass a view of some offshore islands. Specialties, concocted from the catch of the day, might include octopus salad, four different kinds of asopao, a whole red snapper in Creole sauce, or a selection of steaks and grills. Nothing is innovative or magical here, but the cuisine is typical of the south of Puerto Rico, and it's a family favorite. The fish dishes are better than the meat selections.

SEEING THE SIGHTS

A $40 million restoration project is restoring more than 1,000 buildings in town to their original turn-of-the-century charm. Architectural styles that combine neoclassical with "Ponce Creole" and art deco give the town a distinctive ambience.

Any of the Ponceños will direct you to their **Museo de Arte de Ponce,** Avenida de las Americas 25 (☎ **787/848-0505**), which has the finest collection of European and Latin American art in the Caribbean. Among the nearly 400 paintings, sculpture, and artwork on display are exceptional pre-Raphaelite and Italian baroque paintings. The building was designed by Edward Durell Stone, and it has been called the

"Parthenon of the Caribbean." It's open daily from 10am to 5pm. Adults pay $3; children 11 and under are charged $1.

Most visitors head for the **Parque de Bombas,** Plaza de las Delicias (☎ **787/284-3338**), the main plaza of Ponce. This fantastic old black-and-red firehouse was built for a fair in 1883. Open Monday and Wednesday through Friday from 9:30am to 6pm.

Around the corner from the firehouse, the trail will lead to the **Cathedral of Our Lady of Guadalupe,** Calle Concordia/Calle Union (☎**787/842-0134**). Designed by architects Francisco Porrata Doría and Francisco Trublard in 1931, featuring a pipe organ installed in 1934, it remains an important place for prayer. It's open Monday to Friday from 6am to 3:30pm and on Saturday and Sunday from 6am to noon and 3 to 8pm.

El Museo Castillo Serrallés, El Vigía 17 (☎ **787/259-1774**), the largest and most imposing building in Ponce, was built high on a hilltop above town by the Serrallés family (owners of a local rum distillery) in the 1930s. This is one of the architectural gems of Puerto Rico and the best evidence of the wealth produced by the turn-of-the-century sugar boom. Guides will escort you through the Spanish Revival house, where Moorish and Andalusian details include panoramic courtyards, a baronial dining room, and a small cafe and souvenir shop. It's open Tuesday to Sunday from 10am to 5pm. Admission is $3 for adults, $2 for senior citizens over 62, and $1.50 for children 15 and under and students.

The oldest cemetery in the Antilles, excavated in 1975, is near Ponce on Route 503 at kilometer 2.7. The **Tibes Indian Ceremonial Center** (☎ **787/840-2255**) contains some 186 skeletons, dating from A.D.300, as well as pre-Taíno plazas from A.D. 700. The museum is open Wednesday to Sunday from 9am to 4pm. Admission is $2 for adults and $1 for children. Guided tours in English and Spanish are conducted through the grounds. Shaded by trees are seven rectangular ball courts and two dance areas. The arrangements of stone points on the dance grounds, in line with the solstices and equinoxes, suggest a pre-Columbian Stonehenge. A re-created Taíno village includes not only the museum but also an exhibition hall where you can see a documentary about Tibes; you can also visit the cafeteria and souvenir shop.

The **Hacienda Buena Vista,** Route 10, kilometer 16.8 (☎ **787/284-7020**), is a 30-minute drive north of Ponce. Built in 1833, it preserves an old way of life, with its whirring waterwheels and artifacts of 19th-century farm production. Once it was one of the most successful plantations on Puerto Rico, producing coffee, corn, and citrus. It was a working coffee plantation until the 1950s, and 86 of the original 500 acres are still part of the estate. The rooms of the hacienda have been furnished with authentic pieces from the 1850s. **Tours,** lasting two hours, are conducted Wednesday to Sunday at 8:30am, 10:30am, 1:30pm, and 3:30pm (in English only at 1:30pm). Reservations are required; contact the **Conservation Trust of Puerto Rico** (☎ **787/722-5882**) Monday to Friday; otherwise, call the hacienda directly. Tours cost $5 for adults, $2 for children. The hacienda lies in the small town of Barrio Magüeyes, on Route 10 between Ponce and Adjuntas.

7 Las Croabas & Luquillo Beach

Now that we've covered the western portion of Puerto Rico, we'll begin heading east from San Juan. From the capital, Route 3 leads toward the fishing town of Fajardo, where you'll turn north to Las Croabas, about 31 miles from the capital.

You'll be near **Luquillo Beach,** one of the island's best and most popular public stretches of sand.

WHERE TO STAY

✪ **El Conquistador Resort & Country Club.** Las Croabas (P.O. Box 70001, Fajardo), PR 00738. ☎ **800/468-5228** in the U.S., or 787/863-1000. Fax 787/253-0178. 918 rms, 50 suites. A/C MINIBAR TV TEL. Winter, $395–$595 double; from $1,200 suite. Off-season, $310–$545 double; from $970 suite. Children 15 and under stay free in parents' room. Additional bed for 3rd or 4th occupant $40 extra. MAP $75 extra per adult, $37.50 extra per child 12 and under. AE, DC, DISC, MC, V. Parking $10. Limousine from the San Juan airport about $25.

One of the most impressive hostelries anywhere in the tropics, El Conquistador is a destination unto itself, with an incredible array of facilities. Rebuilt in 1993 at a cost of $250 million by Kumagai/Mitsubishi, it incorporates a million dollars' worth of art and five hotels into 500 acres of forested hills whose edges slope down to the sea. The architecture drew its inspiration from the Mediterranean. All the far-flung elements of the resort are interconnected by serpentine, landscaped walkways, and by a railroad-style funicular that makes frequent trips up and down the hillside. Throughout, gardens mingle with murals, paintings, and sculptures. The accommodations are outfitted with comfortable and stylish furniture, soft tropical colors, and about half a dozen unexpected amenities (such as bathrobes and ironing boards).

Dining/Entertainment: The resort contains 16 different restaurants and lounges, one of which is a 24-hour tropical deli; some of the others are highlighted in "Where to Dine," below. A casino offers gambling as well as live music from a nearby piano bar. The array of bars and nightlife include Drake's Library, outfitted with books, mahogany, and a billiards table, and the disco, Amigos Bar and Lounge, with live merengue and salsa.

Services: Room service, baby-sitting, men's and women's beauty salon, laundry/dry cleaning, massages, spa services. There's a special activities area and games room just for kids. Camp Coquí provides for children 3 to 12 daily for $38 per day (9am to 3:30pm). Activities may include fishing, sailing, or arts and crafts.

Facilities: The hotel is sole owner of a "fantasy island" (Palomino Island), with caverns, nature trails, horseback riding, and a wide choice of such water sports as scuba diving, windsurfing, and snorkeling. About half a mile offshore, the island is connected by private ferries to the main hotel at frequent intervals. There's also a 25-slip marina where some of the boats are for rent, six swimming pools, many different Jacuzzi tubs, a fitness center, and state-of-the-art conference facilities. Tennis courts are lit for night play, and there's an 18-hole championship golf course designed by Arthur Hills with "unbelievable views"; greens fees are $125 per person. Plus, there's an arcade of 22 retail shops.

✪ **Westin Rio Mar Beach Resort & Country Club.** P.O. Box 2006, 6000 Rio Mar Blvd., Palmer, PR 00721. ☎ **800/4 RIO MAR** or 787/888-6000. Fax 787/888-6600. 528 rms, 72 suites. A/C MINIBAR TV TEL. Winter, $325–$500 double; from $550 suite. Off-season, $205–$420 double; from $450 suite. AE, CB, DC, DISC, MC, V. Lies 19 miles east of Luis Muñoz Marin International Airport (entrance off Puerto Rico Hwy. 3).

Marking Westin's debut entry into the Caribbean, this $180 million, 481-acre resort opened in 1996 onto Luquillo Beach. Almost overnight, Westin has become a major new player in the Caribbean sweepstakes. The centerpiece of this sprawling resort is a Spanish/Caribbean–style hotel and conference center at the base of El Yunque National park. Between beach and hotel are swimming pools, grottoes, fountains, and tropical gardens. More than half of the guest rooms look out over palm trees to the Atlantic. Other accommodations open onto El Yunque. The style is Spanish hacienda, with dark woods, archways, and tile floors. Each room has a balcony or terrace. Muted earth tones, wicker, rattan, and painted wood furniture add to the ambience.

Dining/Entertainment: You'll never go hungry here. The resort boasts 12 restaurants and lounges, everything from Marbella (its indoor/outdoor terraced all-day dining restaurant), to Palio, its upmarket Italian trattoria. There's also a beachfront pool grill and bar. In the evening, many guests gather to enjoy the music in an outdoor nightclub, or else they try their luck at the hotel's casino.

Services: 24-hour room service, laundry/dry cleaning.

Facilities: The resort encompasses the Rio Mar Country Club and its championship golf course designed by George and Tom Fazio, with a second 18-holer under development. There are also 13 tennis courts, with a beach club, and an array of water sports and other sporting activities that include horseback riding, hiking, deep-sea game fishing, and sailing and boating. There's also a kids' club, plus a health club and a comprehensive spa.

WHERE TO DINE

✪ **Isabela's Grill.** In El Conquistador Resort. ☎ **787/863-1000.** Reservations recommended. Main courses $14–$36; Sun buffet lunch $39.50 per person. AE, DISC, MC, V. Mon–Sat 6–10pm, Sun 11:30am–3pm and 6pm–midnight. SPANISH/INTERNATIONAL.

Of all the restaurants in El Conquistador Resort, this is the premier venue. The severe Spanish baroque room was inspired by an aristocratic monastery in Spain. The massive gates are among the most spectacular pieces of wrought iron on Puerto Rico. The service is impeccable, and the food is among the finest on the island.

The chef's talents have reached new heights as reflected by the appetizers, which range from seafood ceviche to wild mushrooms baked in a phyllo with a goat-cheese dressing. Special care is taken with the beef dishes, even though the meat has to be imported frozen. Treats range from an extra thick cut of veal chop to a prime rack of lamb. Prime rib of beef is a feature, as are New York strip and porterhouse. You might opt for the seafood, everything from grilled fillet of salmon in a pink peppercorn sauce to grilled tuna flavored with ginger and tomato salsa for some island zest.

Otello's. In El Conquistador Resort. ☎ **787/863-1000.** Reservations required in winter, recommended off-season. Main courses $19.95–$37.95. AE, DISC, MC, V. Daily 6pm–midnight. NORTHERN ITALIAN.

Here you can dine by candlelight in the old-world tradition, with a choice of both indoor and outdoor seating. The decor is neo-Palladian. You might begin with one of the soups, perhaps pasta fagioli, or select one of the zesty Italian appetizers, such as clams Posillipo. Pastas can be ordered as a half-portion appetizer or as a main dish, and they include the likes of homemade gnocchi or fettuccine with shrimp. The chef is known for veal dishes. A selection of poultry and vegetarian food is offered nightly, along with several shrimp and fish dishes. When we dined here, the grilled swordfish with a bell pepper sauce had beautiful accents, as did the veal chop in an aromatic herb sauce.

TO THE LIGHTHOUSE: EXPLORING LAS CABEZAS DE SAN JUAN NATURE RESERVE

Better known as **El Faro** or "The Lighthouse," this preserve in the northeastern corner of the island, north of Fajardo off Route 987, is one of the most beautiful and important areas on Puerto Rico—a number of different ecosystems flourish in the vicinity.

Surrounded on three sides by the Atlantic Ocean, the 316-acre site encompasses forestland, mangroves, lagoons, beaches, cliffs, offshore cays, and coral reefs. El Faro serves as a research center for the scientific community. It's home to a vast array of flora and fauna, including sea turtles and other endangered species.

The nature reserve is open Wednesday to Sunday; reservations are required, so call before going. For reservations throughout the week, call ☎ **787/722-5882;** for reservations on Saturday and Sunday, call ☎ **787/860-2560** (reservations on weekends can be made only on the day of your intended visit). Admission is $5 for adults, $2 for children 11 and under, $2.50 seniors. Guided tours are conducted at 9:30am, 10am, 10:30am, and 2pm (in English at 2pm).

8 Palmas del Mar

Called the "Caribbean side of Puerto Rico," the residential resort community of Palmas del Mar lies on the island's eastern shore, 45 miles from San Juan, outside the town of Humacao. It's about an hour's drive from the San Juan airport.

You'll find plenty to do: golf, tennis, scuba diving, sailing, deep-sea fishing, horseback riding, whatever. Hiking on the resort's grounds is another favorite activity. There's a forest preserve with giant ferns, orchids, and hanging vines. There's even a casino. In fact, the resort has one of the most action-packed sports programs in the Caribbean.

The Humacao Regional Airport is 3 miles from the northern boundary of Palmas del Mar. Its 2,300-foot strip will accommodate private planes; no regularly scheduled airline currently serves the Humacao airport.

Palmas del Mar will arrange minivan or bus transport from Humacao to the San Juan airport for $16 to $25 each way. Call the resort if you want to be met at the airport.

WHERE TO STAY

Lying on 2,700 acres, **Palmas del Mar,** P.O. Box 2020, Humacao, PR 00791 (☎ **800/468-3331** or 800/725-6273 in the U.S., or 787/852-6000), is a former coconut plantation that includes a stretch of the Caribbean coastline. Guests are housed in villas built around a marina, the beach, a tennis complex, and a championship golf course. You have a choice of either rooms or villas, depending on your space needs. In the same complex are some privately owned condominium homes that the owners make available to guests when they're not living in them. In addition to the villas, guests can stay at the luxurious Palmas Inn or the Candelero Hotel. Most guests book into Palmas del Mar on a package plan, such as a golf package. Most packages are for seven days/six nights in winter and four days/three nights in summer.

Once you arrive at Palmas del Mar, you can depend on the free hotel shuttle service to get you to any of the hostelries recommended below.

The complex offers families an activities program in June and July for children aged 3 to 13, with supervised activities including swimming, handcrafts, and water polo. And kids will love the 3 miles of beaches, of course.

Candelero Hotel. Palmas del Mar (P.O. Box 2020), Humacao, PR 00792. ☎ **800/725-6273** in the U.S., or 787/852-6000. Fax 787/852-6320. 101 rms. A/C TV TEL. Winter, $192–211 double. Off-season, $138 double. MAP $55 per person extra in winter, $34.50 extra off-season. AE, DC, MC, V.

The rooms here come in a variety of sizes, some with king-size beds. High cathedral ceilings accentuate the roominess that is further extended by patios on the ground floor. Some of the superior accommodations have private balconies. The beach, tennis center, and golf course are close at hand.

Palmas Inn. Palmas del Mar (P.O. Box 2020), Humacao, PR 00792. ☎ **800/725-6273** in the U.S., or 787/852-6000. Fax 787/852-6320. 23 junior suites. A/C TV TEL. Winter, $298–$328 double. Off-season, $208 double. Rates include American breakfast. MAP $55 per person extra in winter, $34.50 extra off-season. AE, DC, MC, V.

This branch contains only junior suites, their views of the sea partially blocked by palm trees. The decor here evokes that of a Mediterranean villa, evoking a spacious, airy feeling; accommodations are decorated in a Spanish antique style. If you want a tranquil hideaway, you might want to come in June, when it's relatively quiet, although the lack of service is the trade-off. The inn also houses the Palm Terrace Restaurant.

Villa Suites. Palmas del Mar (P.O. Box 2020), Humacao, PR 00792. ☎ **800/468-3331** in the U.S., or 787/852-6000. Fax 787/852-2230. 135 villa suites. A/C TV TEL. Winter, $288–$430 one-bedroom villa; $389–$565 two-bedroom villa; $508–$710 three-bedroom villa. Off-season, $192–$258 one-bedroom villa; $259–$339 two-bedroom villa; $338–$426 three-bedroom villa. MAP $55 per person extra in winter, $34.50 extra off-season. Three- to 5-night minimum booking in winter. AE, DC, MC, V.

Adjacent to the Candelero Hotel, this complex of red-roofed, white-walled, Iberian-inspired villas would be a good choice for a family vacation. Each of the villas, furnished and decorated according to the taste of its absentee owner, contains a fully working kitchen and plenty of privacy. Prices depend on the villa's proximity to the beachfront or golf course; an additional handful of villas built against a steep hillside overlook the 20 tennis courts.

WHERE TO DINE

Dining possibilities in Palmas del Mar come in a wide variety, depending on which "village" you're staying in. The Palm Terrace Restaurant is arguably the best, serving continental food, but the choice is vast. Currently, modified American plan (MAP) guests can select from a choice of two specialty restaurants on the grounds.

All the restaurants are open during the winter season; however, in summer only three or four may be fully functional.

Chez Daniel/Le Grill. Marina de Palmas del Mar. ☎ **787/850-3838.** Reservations required. Main courses $19–$29.50. AE, MC, V. Mon and Wed–Thurs 6:30–10pm, Fri–Sun noon–3pm and 6:30 10pm. Closed June. FRENCH.

It's French, it's nautical, it's fun, and it's the preferred venue for occupants of the yachts moored at the adjacent pier. Daniel Vasse, the executive chef, presents a menu that might begin with fish soup or stuffed mussels, followed by such main courses as lobster and chicken sautéed with butter in tarragon and lemon sauce. Filet mignon in a Roquefort sauce is another delectable dish, as are fillet of salmon or roast rack of lamb. For dessert, you can order a soufflé Cointreau.

Toco Coco's. In the Candelero Hotel. ☎ **787/852-6000**, ext. 50. Reservations required only for groups of 6 or more. Main courses $18–$27. AE, DC, DISC, MC, V. Daily 6:30–11am, noon–2:30pm, and 6–10:30pm. INTERNATIONAL.

Cooled by trade winds, this restaurant overlooks a courtyard and swimming pool. It's an ideal choice for any casual meal. Lunch always includes sandwiches and burgers; if you want heartier fare, ask for the Puerto Rican specialty of the day, perhaps red snapper in garlic butter, preceded by black-bean soup. Dinner is more elaborate. Begin with stuffed jalapeños or chicken tacos, followed by Caribbean lobster, New York sirloin, paella, or the catch of the day. The cooking, although of a high standard, is never quite gourmet—it's just good hearty food. Every night in winter is a virtual theme night here, ranging from an Italian festival on Monday to a Puerto Rican night on Saturday.

SPORTS, ON & OFF THE WATER

Nonguests of the Palmas del Mar resorts can still use these hotel facilities, but should call ahead first.

DEEP-SEA FISHING Some of the best year-round fishing in the Caribbean is found in the waters just off Palmas del Mar, the resort complex on the southeast coast of Puerto Rico. Here, **Capt. Bill Burleson,** P.O. Box 8270, Humacao, PR 00792 (☎ **787/850-7442**), operates charters on his fully customized 46-foot sport-fishing yacht, *Karolette,* which is electronically equipped for successful fishing. Burleson prefers to take fishing groups to Grappler Banks, 18 nautical miles away. The banks are two sea mounts, rising to about 240 feet below the surface and surrounded by depths of 6,000 to 8,000 feet. They lie in the migratory paths of the wahoo, tuna, and marlin. A maximum of six people are taken out, costing $450 for four hours, $600 for six hours, and $800 for nine hours. He also offers snorkeling expeditions to Vieques Island at $75 per person for up to five hours.

GOLF The **Golf Club** at Palmas del Mar (☎ **787/852-6000,** ext. 54) is one of the leading courses on Puerto Rico. On the southeast coast, it has a par-72, 6,803-yard layout designed by Gary Player. Crack golfers consider holes 11 to 15 the toughest five successive holes in the Caribbean. The pro shop is open daily from 7am to 5pm.

HORSEBACK RIDING The Equestrian Center at Palmas del Mar (☎ **787/852-6000,** ext. 12721) has 42 horses, including English hunters for jumping, plus a variety of trail rides and instruction for all levels of ability. The land set aside for equestrian pursuits abuts the resort's airstrip and is bounded on one side by a stream. Trail rides skirt this creek and follow paths through the coconut plantation and jungle. A trail ride costs $22 per person for one hour and $40 for two hours.

SCUBA DIVING **Coral Head Divers & Water Sports Center,** P.O. Box 10246, Humacao, PR 00792 (☎ **800/635-4529** in the U.S., or 787/850-7208), operates out of a building on the harbor at the Palmas del Mar Resort. The dive center owns two fully equipped boats, measuring 26 and 48 feet. The center offers daily two-tank open-water dives for certified divers, plus snorkeling trips to Monkey Island and Vieques. The two-tank dive includes tanks, weights, and computer for $75. A snorkeling trip to Monkey Island includes use of equipment and a beverage for $45 per person. A scuba resort lesson costs $45.

TENNIS The **Tennis Center** at Palmas del Mar (☎ **787/852-6000,** ext. 51), the largest on Puerto Rico, features 20 courts. Court fees for hotel guests are $18 per hour during the day and $22 at night. Special tennis packages are available, including accommodations. Call for more information.

PALMAS DEL MAR AFTER DARK

The hot nightspot in Palmas del Mar is the **Palm Terrace Restaurant & Lounge,** near the casino. Here guests can drink and dance to the latest rhythms Wednesday to Sunday from 8pm to 2am (perhaps later on Friday and Saturday). The $7 minimum includes your first drink.

The **casino** in the Palmas del Mar complex, near the Palmas Inn (☎ **787/852-6000,** ext. 10142), is near the reception area. It has 12 blackjack tables, two roulette wheels, a craps table, and dozens of slot machines. The casino is open daily year-round, Sunday through Thursday from 6pm to 2am and Friday and Saturday from 6pm to 3am. Under Puerto Rican law, drinks cannot be served in a casino, but you can enjoy one in the Palm Terrace Lounge.

The U.S. Virgin Islands

6

The U.S. Virgin Islands are known for their sugar-white beaches, which are among the finest in the world. The most developed island in the chain is **St. Thomas,** which has the largest concentration of shopping in the Caribbean in its capital, Charlotte Amalie. With a population of some 50,000, tiny St. Thomas isn't exactly a secluded tropical retreat; you'll hardly have its beaches to yourself. The place abounds in bars and restaurants, including fast-food joints, and has a vast selection of hotels in all price ranges.

St. Croix is bigger, but more tranquil. A favorite with cruise-ship passengers (as is St. Thomas), St. Croix touts its shopping and has more stores than most islands in the Caribbean, especially in and around Christiansted, although it's not the shopping mecca Charlotte Amalie is. Its major attraction is Buck Island, a national park that lies offshore. The place is peppered with inns and hotels and is condo heaven.

St. John, the smallest of the three islands, is also the most beautiful and the least developed. Lying a few miles east of St. Thomas, it has only two big hotels. Some two-thirds of the island is a national park. Even if you visit only for the day while based on St. Thomas, you'll want to sample the island's dream beach, Trunk Bay.

The U.S. Virgin Islands lie in two bodies of water: St. John is entirely in the Atlantic Ocean, St. Croix is entirely in the Caribbean Sea, and St. Thomas separates the Atlantic and the Caribbean. These islands enjoy one of the most perfect year-round climates in the world. They lie directly in the belt of the subtropical, easterly trade winds. At the eastern end of the Greater Antilles and the northern tip of the Lesser Antilles, the U.S. Virgins are some 60 miles east of Puerto Rico and 1,100 miles southeast of Miami.

For much of late 1995 and early 1996, St. Thomas seemed to be visited more by carpenters than by tourists. Hurricane Marilyn struck the island in mid-September 1995; with winds of 140 to 150 m.p.h., it dealt a devastating blow to St. Thomas, shutting down most of its hotels. Since the island economy is almost wholly tourist-based, this was a major disaster. Hotels rushed to bounce back from the blow. Some were able to open in time for the winter season of 1995 and 1996; others announced opening dates in 1996. Even in 1997 some properties had not fully recovered from the devastating effects of Marilyn.

St. Croix, which still has lingering memories of Hurricane Hugo's destruction of 1989, escaped Marilyn with far less damage and bounced back quickly, picking up the lost business from St. Thomas. St. John sustained damage in part but also recovered quickly, with some notable exceptions here and there.

GETTING THERE

Nonstop flights to the U.S. Virgin Islands from either New York or Atlanta usually take 3 3/4 and 3 1/2 hours, respectively. The flight time between St. Thomas and St. Croix is only 20 minutes. Flying to San Juan from mainland cities and changing planes may save you money over the APEX nonstop fare.

American Airlines (☎ **800/433-7300**) offers frequent service into St. Thomas and St. Croix from the U.S. mainland, with five daily flights from New York to St. Thomas. Summer flights can vary; call for more information. Passengers originating in other parts of the world are usually routed to St. Thomas through American's hubs in Miami or San Juan, both of which offer nonstop service (often several times a day) to St. Thomas. Connections from Los Angeles or San Francisco to either St. Thomas or St. Croix are usually made through New York, San Juan, or Miami. American can also arrange discount packages that include both airfare and hotel. Flights from Puerto Rico to the U.S. Virgin Islands are on American's partner, **American Eagle** (☎ **800/433-7300**), which has about 10 to 15 flights daily.

Delta (☎ **800/221-1212**) offers two daily nonstop flights between Atlanta and St. Thomas, the first departing in the morning and the second in the afternoon. The latter flight also provides an air link to St. Croix. **TWA** (☎ **800/221-2000**) flies into San Juan two or three times daily nonstop from JFK. A flight from St. Louis touches down at JFK before going to Puerto Rico. In San Juan connections are made to St. Thomas. **US Airways** has two flights from Baltimore to St. Thomas daily—one nonstop from Baltimore, the other originating in Philadelphia and stopping in Baltimore before flying on to St. Thomas. **Prestige Airways** (☎ **800/299-U.S.V.I.**), originating out of Washington, D.C., offers flights every Thursday and Sunday from Miami and on to St. Thomas and St. Croix.

It's now easier than ever before to travel between St. Thomas and St. Croix. **American Eagle** (☎ **809/778-1140**) has seven flights a day, costing $60 per person one way. In addition, **Virgin Islands Seaplane** (☎ **809/777-4491**), offers eight round-trip flights daily, going for $50 per person one way. Flight time is only 30 minutes. It's also possible to take **Fast Cat** (☎ **809/773-3278**), a catamaran that goes from St. Thomas to St. Croix three times a day, costing $50 round-trip for adults and $30 for children under 12. One-way passage is $25 for adults or $15 for children.

A new ferry service from St. Thomas to Puerto Rico, with a stop in St. John, is available once every two weeks, maybe more if demand merits it. The trip from Puerto Rico to Charlotte Amalie takes about two hours, costing $60 one way, including ground transportation to the San Juan airport or Condado. For more information, call ☎ **809/776-6282.**

FAST FACTS: The U.S. Virgin Islands

Currency The **U.S. dollar** is the unit of currency in the Virgin Islands.

Customs Every U.S. resident can bring home $1,200 worth of duty-free purchases, including a gallon of alcoholic beverages per adult. If you go over the $1,200 limit, you pay a flat 5% duty, up to an additional $1,000. You can also mail home gifts valued at up to $100 per day, which you don't have to declare. (At other spots in the Caribbean, U.S. citizens are limited to $400 or $600 worth of merchandise and a single bottle of liquor.)

Documents U.S. and Canadian citizens are required to present some proof of citizenship to enter the Virgin Islands, such as a voter registration card or a birth certificate. A passport is not strictly required, but carrying one is a good idea.

Driving Remember to drive *on the left.* This comes as a surprise to many visitors, who expect that U.S. driving practices will hold here. Of course, obey speed limits, which are 20 m.p.h. in towns, 35 m.p.h. outside.

Electricity It's the same as on the mainland: 120 volts AC (60 cycles). No transformer, adapter, or converter is needed for American appliances.

Information Before you go, contact the **U.S. Virgin Islands Division of Tourism,** 1270 Ave. of the Americas, New York, NY 10020 (☎ **212/332-2222**). Branch offices are at: 225 Peachtree St. NE, Suite 260, Atlanta, GA 30303 (☎ **404/688-0906**); 500 N. Michigan Ave., Suite 2030, Chicago, IL 60611 (☎ **312/670-8784**); 2655 Le Jeune Rd., Suite 907, Coral Gables, FL 33134 (☎ **305/442-7200**); 3460 Wilshire Blvd., Suite 412, Los Angeles, CA 90010 (☎ **213/739-0138**); and 900 17th St. NW, Suite 500, Washington, DC 20006 (☎ **202/624-3590**). Offices outside the United States are found at 3300 Bloor St. West, Suite 3120, Centre Tower, Toronto, ON M8X 2X3, Canada (☎ **416/233-1414**), and at 2 Cinnamon Row, Plantation Wharf, York Place, London SW11 3TW, England (☎ **0171/978-5262**).

Mail The Virgin Islands are part of the U.S. Postal Service, so postage rates are the same as on the mainland.

Safety The U.S. Virgin Islands have more than their share of crime. St. John is safer than St. Thomas or St. Croix. But even on St. John there is crime—possessions that are left unattended are likely to be stolen. Travelers should exercise extreme caution both day and night when wandering the backstreets of Charlotte Amalie on St. Thomas and both Christiansted and Frederiksted on St. Croix—muggings are commonplace. Avoid night strolls or drives along quiet roads. Never go walking on the beaches at night.

Time The U.S. Virgins are on Atlantic standard time year-round, which places the islands an hour ahead of U.S. eastern standard time. When the U.S. East Coast goes on daylight saving time, the Virgin Islands have the same time.

Tipping As a general rule, it's customary to tip 15% as in the States. Some hotels add a 10% to 15% surcharge to cover service, so check before you wind up paying twice.

Water There's ample water for showers and bathing in the Virgin Islands, but you are asked to conserve. Hotels will supply you with all your drinking water. Many visitors drink the local tap water with no harmful aftereffects. Others, more prudent or with more delicate stomachs, should stick to bottled water.

Weather From November to February, temperatures average about 77°F. The average temperature divergence is 5° to 7°F. Sometimes in August the temperature peaks in the high 80s, but the subtropical breezes keep it comfortably cool in the shade. The temperature in winter may drop into the low 60s, but this happens rarely.

1 St. Thomas

The busiest cruise-ship harbor in the West Indies, rivaled only by San Juan, St. Thomas is the second largest of the U.S. Virgins; it's about 40 miles north of St. Croix. St. Thomas, with the U.S. Virgins' capital at Charlotte Amalie, is about 12 miles long and 3 miles wide. The capital is also the shopping center of the Caribbean. Hotels on the north side of St. Thomas face the Atlantic, and those on the south side front the calmer Caribbean.

Vacationers discovered St. Thomas right after World War II, and they've been flocking back ever since. Shopping, sights, and sun prove a potent lure. Tourism has raised the standard of living here; it's now one of the highest in the Caribbean. Condos have grown up over the debris of bulldozed shacks.

St. Thomas is a boon for cruise-ship shoppers, who flood Main Street, the shopping center, which is basically three to four blocks in the center of town. However, this center, which gets very crowded, is away from all beaches, major hotels, most restaurants, and entertainment facilities. At a hotel "out on the island," you can still find seclusion.

If you're visiting in August, make sure you carry along mosquito repellent.

GETTING AROUND

BY RENTAL CAR St. Thomas has many leading North American car-rental firms at the airport, and competition is stiff. The big companies, however, tend to be easier to deal with in cases of billing errors. Before you go, compare the rates of the "big three": **Avis** (☎ **800/331-1084**), **Budget** (☎ **888/227-3359**), and **Hertz** (☎ **800/654-3001**). There is no tax on car rentals in the Virgin Islands.

St. Thomas has a high accident rate: Many visitors are not used to driving on the left, the hilly terrain shelters blind curves and entrance ramps, and some motorists drive after too many drinks. In many cases, the roads are narrow and the lighting is poor; we recommend collision-damage insurance. It costs $13 to $14 per day extra, depending on the fine print, but be alert to the fact that even if you purchase it, you might still be responsible for a whopping deductible if you have an accident. The company with the least attractive insurance policies is Hertz. The Hertz deductible is the full value of the car, while the Avis deductible is only $250 if you pay an additional $8.95 in liability insurance. Budget has no deductible at all. Ask about insurance coverage and your financial responsibilities before you rent. The minimum age requirement for drivers at all three companies is 25. The cheapest car rentals begin at around $235 per week with unlimited mileage.

BY TAXI The chief means of transport around the island is the taxi, which is unmetered; agree on the fare with the driver before you get into the car. Taxi fares are $30 for two passengers for two hours of sightseeing; each additional passenger pays another $12. For 24-hour radio-dispatch service, call ☎ **809/774-7457.** Many taxis transport 8 to 12 passengers in vans to multiple destinations.

BY BUS St. Thomas has the best public transportation of any island in the U.S. chain. Administered by the government, **Vitran buses** (☎ **809/774-5678**), depending on their route, serve Charlotte Amalie, its outlying neighborhoods, and the countryside as far away as Red Hook. Vitran stops are found at intervals beside each of the most important traffic arteries on St. Thomas, including the edges of Veterans Drive in the capital. You rarely have to wait more than 30 minutes during the day, and they run between 5:30am and 10:30pm. A one-way ride costs 75¢

St. Thomas Accommodations/Sports

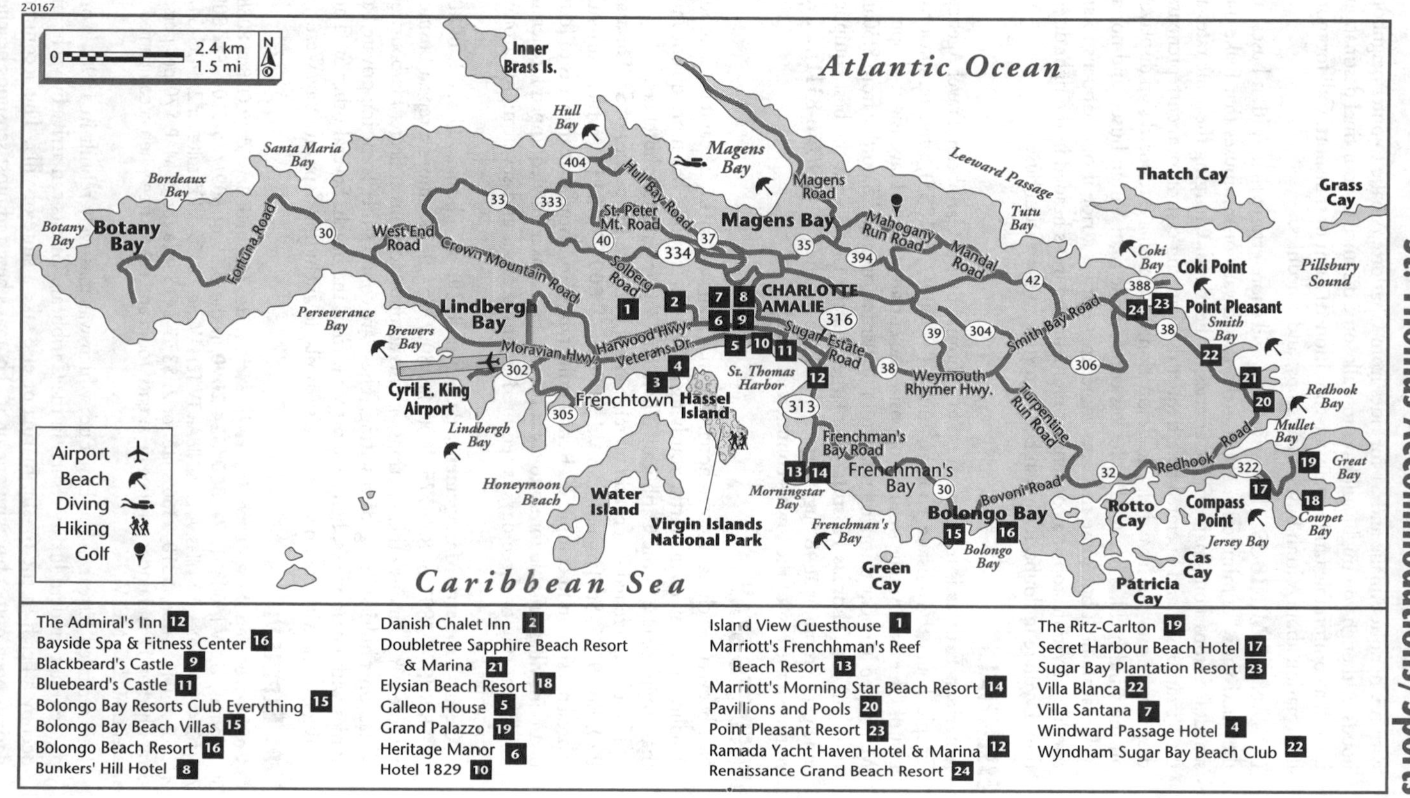

within Charlotte Amalie and $1 for rides from Charlotte Amalie to outer neighborhoods. Although you might still have to walk some distance to your final destination, it's still a comfortable (and usually air-conditioned) form of transport. Call for more information about Vitran buses, their stops, and schedules.

BY VAN OR MINIBUS Less structured and more erratic than Vitran buses are the **"taxi vans,"** a miniflotilla of privately owned vans or minibuses that make unscheduled stops along major traffic arteries of the island. Charging the same rates as the Vitran buses, and operated by a frequently changing cast of local entrepreneurs, they may or may not have their end destination written on a cardboard sign displayed on the windshield. They tend to be less comfortable than Vitran buses, and not as well maintained, but some residents sometimes opt for a ride if one happens to arrive near a Vitran stop at a convenient moment and if it's headed in the right direction. If you're in doubt, it's much better to stick to the Vitran buses.

ESSENTIALS

American Express is represented on St. Thomas by the Caribbean Travel Agency/Tropic Tours, 9716 Estate Thomas, Suite 1 (☎ **809/774-1855**), a five-minute drive east of Charlotte Amalie's center, opposite the entrance to the Havensight Shopping Mall (open Monday through Friday from 8:30am to 5pm and Saturday from 8:30am to noon). **St. Thomas Hospital,** the largest on the island with the best-equipped emergency room, is at 48 Sugar Estate, Charlotte Amalie (☎ **809/776-8311**), a five-minute drive east of the town's commercial center.

WHERE TO STAY

Nearly every beach has its own hotel. You may want to stay in the capital, Charlotte Amalie, or at any of the farther outlying points. St. Thomas has more quaint inns than anyplace else in the Caribbean. There's an 8% government hotel tax.

If you're interested in a condo rental, contact **Paradise Properties of St. Thomas,** P.O. Box 9395, St. Thomas, U.S.V.I. 00801 (☎ **809/775-3115**), which currently represents six condo complexes. Rental units range from studio apartments to four-bedroom villas suitable for up to eight people. Each has a fully equipped kitchen. A minimum stay of three days is required in any season, and seven nights around Christmas.

Ocean Property Management, P.O. Box 8529, St. Thomas, U.S.V.I. 00801 (☎ **800/874-7897** or 809/775-2600; fax 809/775-5901), enjoys a repeat business of some 60%. Among other offerings, it rents accommodations at Secret Harbourview Villas, on a hillside in a garden setting. These are condo suites featuring private balconies with ocean views, lying a short walk from the beach. Several other St. Thomas locations with condo suites are also available, including Sapphire Bay West.

VERY EXPENSIVE

✪ **Doubletree Sapphire Beach Resort & Marina.** Rte. 36, Smith Bay Rd. (P.O. Box 8088), St. Thomas, U.S.V.I. 00801. ☎ **800/524-2090** in the U.S., or 809/775-6100. Fax 809/775-4024. 114 suites, 57 villas. A/C MINIBAR TV TEL. Winter, $355–$405 suite for 2; $435–$475 villa for 2. Off-season, $310–$360 suite for 2; $375–$415 villa for 2. MAP $70 per person extra. Children 12 and under stay free in parents' room and eat for free when accompanied by a parent. AE, DC, MC, V.

This secluded retreat in the East End, which was massively rebuilt in 1996, is one of the finest modern luxury resorts in the Caribbean. Guests can arrive by yacht and occupy a berth in the 67-slip marina or else take a suite or villa. The accommodations open onto a bay with one of St. Thomas's best and most sensuous beaches, and exude casual elegance. The beaches are two crescents broken by the coral-reef peninsula of Prettyklip Point. The suites have fully equipped kitchens and microwaves, bedroom areas, living/dining rooms with queen-size sofa beds, and large, fully tiled outdoor galleries with lounge furniture. The villas are on two levels: The main one contains the same amenities as the suites, whereas the upper level includes a second full bath, a bedroom and sitting area with a queen-size sofa bed, and a sun deck with outdoor furniture. The suites accommodate one to four guests; the villas are suitable for up to six guests. The configuration of the accommodations and the children's program make this a good choice for families.

Dining/Entertainment: The Seagrape is one of the island's finest eating places. Sometimes a five-piece band is brought in for dancing under the stars. For more casual dining, the hotel has the Sailfish Café.

Services: Beach towels, daily chamber service, guest-services desk, baby-sitting. The resort also offers supervised activities for children at the Little Gems Kids Klub.

Facilities: A 1-acre freshwater pool, snorkeling equipment, Sunfish sailboats, windsurfing boards, four all-weather tennis courts, waterfront pavilion with snack bar, complete diving center.

Elysian Beach Resort. 6800 Estate Nazareth, Cowpet Bay, St. Thomas, U.S.V.I. 00802. ☎ **800/753-2554** or 809/775-1000. Fax 809/776-0910. 175 units. Winter, $225–$285 double; from $315 suite. Off-season, $175–$210 double; from $225 suite. Special honeymoon packages available. Rates include continental breakfast. AE, DC, DISC, MC, V.

This time-share resort on Cowpet Bay in the East End has a European kind of glamour, and it's within a 20-minute drive of Charlotte Amalie. The thoughtfully planned bedrooms have balconies, and 14 offer sleeping lofts reached by a spiral staircase. The decor is tropical, with white ceramic tile floors, rattan and bamboo furnishings, and natural-wood ceilings. The rooms are in a bevy of four-story buildings connected to landscaped gardens. Many of the rooms can be broken up into various combinations, with doors locked or shut, depending on the needs of a client. Of the various units, 43 can be converted into one-bedroom suites, 43 into two-bedroom suites, and 11 into three-bedroom suites.

Dining/Entertainment: The hotel offers elegant international dining at its Palm Court Restaurant, plus weekly barbecues on the terrace. Other dining options include the Oasis, which serves light fare right on the beach. Drinks can be ordered at the pool bar or in a first-class lounge. In season, live entertainment is offered.

Services: Open-air shuttle to town, room service, masseur, baby-sitting.

Facilities: Fitness center, swimming pool, snorkel gear, canoes, Sunfish, tennis court.

✪ **Marriott's Morning Star Beach Resort.** Frenchman's Reef Beach Resort, Flamboyant Point, Charlotte Amalie, St. Thomas, U.S.V.I. 00802. ☎ **800/232-2425** or 809/776-8500. Fax 809/776-3054. 96 rms. A/C MINIBAR TV TEL. Winter, $325–$395 double. Off-season, $185–$235 double. MAP $58 per person extra. AE, DC, MC, V.

Both its public areas and its plushly outfitted accommodations are among the most outstanding on the island, but Hurricane Marilyn forced a major refurbishment in 1995. The resort was built on the landscaped flatlands near the beach of the well-known Marriott's Frenchman's Reef Beach Resort (see below), and there's a wide array of water sports. The resort has five buildings, each containing between 16 and 24 units. Guests have the amenities and attractions of the large hotel nearby, yet maintain the privacy of the more exclusive enclave. Each accommodation has rattan furniture and views of the garden, beach, or the lights of Charlotte Amalie.

Dining/Entertainment: Caesar's Ristorante, located on Morning Star Beach, serves lunch and dinner, and rather standard cuisine. More alluringly, the Oriental Terrace features Japanese exhibition cookery on a teppanyaki grill. The Raw Bar is an ideal spot for sunset cocktails, and a variety of restaurants and bars are also available at the adjoining Marriott's Frenchman's Reef Beach Resort.

Services: Room service, baby-sitting, valet, plus all the services provided by the Frenchman's Reef next door.

Facilities: Two giant swimming pools; four tennis courts; water-sports program including parasailing, dive shop, Jacuzzi, and private beach, one of the island's best, shared with the Frenchman's Reef.

Renaissance Grand Beach Resort. Rte. 38, Smith Bay Rd. (P.O. Box 8267), St. Thomas, U.S.V.I. 00801. ☎ **800/468-3571** in the U.S., or 809/775-1510. Fax 809/775-2185. 297 rms, 23 suites. A/C MINIBAR TV TEL. Winter, $325–$435 double; $595 one-bedroom suite; $895 two-bedroom suite. Off-season, $225–$325 double; $450 one-bedroom suite; $550 two-bedroom suite. MAP $60 per person extra. AE, DC, MC, V.

Perched on a steep hillside above a small but fine beach 7 miles northeast of Charlotte Amalie, this resort, which has a wide array of sports facilities, occupies 34 acres on the northeast shore of St. Thomas. Following hurricane damage in 1995, the newly renovated accommodations are in two separate areas: poolside and hillside. The two-story town-house suites and one- or two-bedroom suites have whirlpool spas, and all units are stylishly outfitted. Each accommodation has satellite color TV with HBO and Spectravision, a hair dryer, a robe, a safe, and an open balcony or patio.

Dining/Entertainment: You can enjoy beachfront breakfast, lunch, and dinner at Baywinds, which features continental and Caribbean cuisine. Dinner and Sunday brunch are served in Smugglers Bar and Grill. There's a poolside snack bar and live entertainment and dancing in the Baywinds Lounge.

Services: Concierge, daily children's program, round-the-clock baby-sitting, laundry service, tropical garden tour, 23-hour room service, twice-daily chamber service, newspaper and coffee with wake-up call. The year-round children's program is free for guests 3 to 14 and directed by counselor-supervised, trained personnel.

Facilities: Two swimming pools (and a kiddie pool); daily scuba and snorkel lessons; free Sunfish sailboats, kayaks, Windsurfers, snorkel equipment; on-site full-service dive shop; water-sports center, where you can arrange for day sails, deep-sea fishing, and other island excursions; six lit tennis courts; exercise facility; newsstand, gift shop, beauty salon. There's an 18-hole golf course 10 minutes away.

✪ **The Ritz-Carlton.** Great Bay, St. Thomas, U.S.V.I. 00802. ☎ **800/241-3333** or 809/775-3333. Fax 809/775-4444. 148 rms, 4 suites. Winter, $400–$525 double; $925 suite. Off-season, $200–$395 double; from $475 suite. AE, DC, DISC, MC, V.

St. Thomas went "ritzy" almost overnight when this chic hotel chain took over the Grand Palazzo, which had opened in 1992 on a 15-acre oceanfront estate at the island's eastern tip. Immediately the Ritz, 4½ miles southeast of Charlotte Amalie, set amid landscaped gardens and fronted by white-sand beaches, became St. Thomas's toniest property, edging out Sapphire Beach, Elysian, and Marriott.

Accommodations are in half a dozen three-story villas designed with Italian Renaissance motifs and Mediterranean colors. Guests register in a reception *palazzo,* whose arches and accessories were inspired by a Venetian palace. From the monogrammed bathrobes to the digital in-room safes, the accommodations have more amenities than those at any other hotel on the island.

Dining/Entertainment: The restaurant offers panoramic views and serves an exceptional international menu. There's also an outdoor cafe for more casual dining, plus weekly live local entertainment.

Services: Concierge, 24-hour room service, valet, in-room massages, hair salon.

Facilities: Private beach with windsurfing, Sunfish and Hobie Cat sailing, and snorkeling; 125-foot free-form pool; complete fitness center; four lighted tennis courts; cruises on private catamaran. Diving and deep-sea fishing excursions arranged.

Secret Harbour Beach Hotel. 6280 Estate Nazareth, Nazareth Bay, St. Thomas, U.S.V.I. 00802. ☎ **800/524-2250** or 809/775-6550. Fax 809/775-1501. 7 studios, 47 one-bedroom suites, 6 two-bedroom suites. A/C TV TEL. Winter, $265 studio double; $295 one-bedroom suite; $495 two-bedroom suite. Off-season, $169–$189 studio double; $199–$219 one-bedroom suite; $299–$319 two-bedroom suite. Rates include continental breakfast. AE, MC, V.

A favorite with honeymooners, this all-suite resort is on the beach at Nazareth Bay, right outside Red Hook. In the wake of devastation caused by Hurricane Marilyn, renovations were completed in the summer of 1997. The four contemporary buildings face southwest, affording great views of spectacular sunsets. Each unit has a private deck or patio and a full kitchen. There are three kinds of accommodations: studio apartments with a bed/sitting-room area, patio, and dressing-room area; one-bedroom suites with a living/dining area, a separate bedroom, and a sundeck; and, the most luxurious, a two-bedroom suite with two baths and a private living room.

Dining/Entertainment: The Sea Side Restaurant serves both a continental and Caribbean cuisine, and the Secret Harbour Beach Café is a more informal place for breakfast and lunch on an outdoor terrace or in the gazebo. At a beachfront bar a manager's cocktail party is held weekly.

Services: Baby-sitting, daily maid service.

Facilities: Five-star PADI dive center and water-sports facility on the beach, catamaran for sail charters, two all-weather tennis courts, fitness center, freshwater pool, and Jacuzzi.

EXPENSIVE

Bluebeard's Castle. Bluebeard's Hill (P.O. Box 7480), Charlotte Amalie, St. Thomas, U.S.V.I. 00801. ☎ **800/524-6599** in the U.S., or 809/774-1600. Fax 809/774-5134. 160 rms. A/C TV TEL. Winter, $195–$235 double. Off-season, $140–$175 double. Additional person $25 extra. MAP $50 per person extra. AE, DC, MC, V.

Bluebeard's is a popular resort lying on one side of the bay overlooking Charlotte Amalie. In the 1930s, the U.S. government turned what had been a private home into a hotel that once hosted Franklin D. Roosevelt. Its former position as the number-one hotel of the island has long been surpassed by deluxe East End resorts such as the Ritz-Carlton and Sapphire Beach.

The hill surrounding the hotel is now heavily built up with everything from offices to time-shares. Many guests prefer the rooms in the old tower, especially no. 139 or 140. Some 50 rooms in the newer unit, which also includes meeting rooms, have less charm. The guest rooms come in a wide variety of shapes and sizes—all pleasantly but blandly decorated. After Hurricane Marilyn, the hotel reconfigured its rooms to give them a more suitelike appearance by replacing two beds with one queen-size bed, turning the rest of the space into a sitting room.

Dining/Entertainment: The Terrace Restaurant commands a panoramic view and offers many delectable American and Caribbean specialties, open-air brunch, lunch, and late-night dining. Other dining choices include A Room with a View and Entre Nous (see separate recommendation below).

Services: Free transportation to famous Magens Bay Beach, a 15-minute drive away.

Facilities: Freshwater swimming pool, two whirlpools, championship tennis courts.

Bolongo Beach Club. 7150 Bolongo, St. Thomas, U.S.V.I. 00802. ☎ **800/524-4746** or 809/775-1800. Fax 809/775-3208. 75 rms, 8 villas. A/C TV TEL. Winter, $235 double; $290 one-bedroom villa for up to 4 occupants; $390 two-bedroom villa for up to 6 occupants. Off-season, $195 double; $210 one-bedroom villa; $255 two-bedroom villa. AE, MC, V.

Few other hotels in St. Thomas have experimented as frequently as this one, or reconfigured its corporate structure as often. After unsuccessful linkages with nearby hotels, and devastation during the 1995 hurricanes, it finally reverted to the same beach-fronted, self-enclosed configuration that earned it its initial success as one of the first hotels on the eastern side of St. Thomas. You'll find a half-moon-shaped beach, and a cement-sided, pink-walled series of two- and three-story buildings plus some motel-like units closer to the sands, and a social center consisting of a smallish swimming pool and a raffish-looking beachfront bar replete with palm fronds. Most clients check in on the semi-inclusive plan that only includes breakfast plus use of nonmotorized sports equipment. To a lesser degree, others opt for all-inclusive plans that include all meals, drinks, a sailboat excursion to St. John, and some use of scuba equipment. Accommodations are simple, summery, and filled with undistinguished furniture appropriate to the unpretentious, often barefoot format of this resort. Villas (that is, apartment-style condos with full kitchens) lie within a three-story building.

You can also stay here on package deals, a winter semi-inclusive deal costing $235 per couple, or a package for $195 semi-inclusive and $400 all-inclusive. The semi-inclusive package includes a continental breakfast and use of all nonmotorized water sports. The all-inclusive package features three meals, unlimited drinks from the bar, use of all nonmotorized water sports, an outing to St. John, a half-day cruise, a scuba class, and use of scuba equipment.

Dining/Entertainment: The resort includes a relatively formal venue, Lord Rumbottom's, serving two-fisted portions of prime rib, as well as the less formal, bistro-style Coconut Henry's, where burgers, sandwiches, and salads mix with party-colored drinks. Although either venue serves drinks, there's another option for drinking at Iggie's Sing-Along and Sports Bar.

Services: Baby-sitting can be arranged. The gift shop (Beach Traders) on site is a registered outlet for Budget Rent-a-Car.

Facilities: Fitness Center, three swimming pools, two tennis courts, professional volleyball, basketball court. St. Thomas Diving Club (an independent outfit) is on their premises; *Heavenly Days,* a 49-passenger catamaran docked right on the hotel's beach, makes frequent cruises to St. John, depending on demand.

Marriott's Frenchman's Reef Beach Resort. Flamboyant Point (P.O. Box 7100), Charlotte Amalie, St. Thomas, U.S.V.I. 00801. ☎ **800/524-2000** in the U.S., or 809/776-8500. Fax 809/776-3054. 421 rms, 18 suites. A/C MINIBAR TV TEL. Winter, $275–$310 double; from $750 suite. Off-season, $160–$175 double; from $350 suite. MAP $60 per person extra. AE, DC, DISC, MC, V.

Frenchman's Reef, 3 miles east of Charlotte Amalie, has an excellent location facing south on a projection of land overlooking both the harbor and the Caribbean. Not suited for those seeking cozy island ambience, this is a full-service American-style megaresort that will undergo a $30 million renovation in the 1997 off-season. It's a tour group favorite, and the darling of conventioneers, but also a popular honeymooners' choice. Everywhere you look are facilities devoted to the good life.

To reach the private beach, you take a glass-enclosed elevator. The bedrooms vary greatly, but in general are traditionally furnished in upper bracket motel style and are quite comfortable, though we find the rooms at the hotel's neighbor, Morning Star, to be more luxurious.

Dining/Entertainment: Seafood with a continental flair is served at Windows on the Harbor, which resembles the inside of a cruise ship and has a view of the harbor. The Lighthouse Cafe was once an actual lighthouse. Caesar's Ristorante offers Italian cuisine, and the Oriental Terrace features Japanese cooking. The Raw Bar serves light meals daily. At night the Wahoo Bar offers live entertainment.

Services: Room service (7am to 10:30pm), laundry, baby-sitting.

Facilities: Two swimming pools with poolside bar, tennis courts, water sports (snorkeling, scuba diving, sailing, deep-sea fishing).

Point Pleasant Resort. 6600 Estate Smith Bay, St. Thomas, U.S.V.I. 00802. ☎ **800/777-1700** or 809/775-7200. Fax 809/776-5694. 130 rms. A/C TV TEL. Winter, $255–$360 double. Off-season, $170–$240 double. AE, DC, DISC, MC, V.

This is a very private, unique resort on Water Bay, on the northeastern tip of St. Thomas, a five-minute walk from Stouffer's Beach. It's a series of condo units rented when the owners are not in residence. The complex is set on a 15-acre bluff with flowering shrubbery, century plants, frangipani trees, secluded nature trails, old rock formations, and lookout points. From your living-room gallery, you can look out on a collection of islands: Tortola, St. John, and Jost Van Dyke. Some of the villa-style accommodations have kitchens, and the furnishings, mostly featuring rattan and floral fabrics, give the rooms a light and airy feel.

Dining/Entertainment: The restaurant, Agavé Terrace, is one of the finest on the island and offers three meals a day. The cuisine, featuring seafood, is a blend of nouvelle American dishes with Caribbean specialties. Local entertainment is provided several nights a week.

Services: Complimentary use of a car four hours per day, shopping and dinner shuttle.

Facilities: Three freshwater swimming pools, lit tennis courts, snorkeling equipment, Sunfish sailboats.

Wyndham Sugar Bay Beach Club. 6500 Estate Smith Bay, St. Thomas, U.S.V.I. 00802. ☎ **800/927-7100** in the U.S., or 809/777-7100. Fax 809/777-7200. 291 rms, 9 suites. A/C TV TEL. Winter, $250 double; $270–$290 suite. Off-season, $150 double; $170–$190 suite. Rates include all meals and drink, plus nonmotorized activities. AE, DC, MC, V.

In a neck-and-neck race with the Renaissance Grand Beach Resort (see above), this hostelry is in the East End of St. Thomas, a five-minute ride from Red Hook. It was built in 1992 as an upscale Crowne Plaza Holiday Inn, but is now under the Wyndham wing. It's well located for panoramic views, and the bedrooms have balconies to take in those vistas. The rooms are often decorated with rattan pieces and pastel color schemes inspired by the tropics. They contain such amenities as dataports, room safes, and hair dryers.

Dining/Entertainment: The main restaurant, Manor House, offers breakfast and dinner daily, with tables affording views of St. John and the British Virgin Islands. Casual meals are served poolside, entertainment is offered nightly, and there's an ice-cream parlor in the Main Grove Café.

Services: Room service (until 11pm), Kids Klub, baby-sitting, tour desk.

Facilities: Tennis, water sports, a secluded beach (that's really too small for a resort of this size), three connected freshwater pools with a waterfall, a fitness center; nearby golf.

Moderate

Blackbeard's Castle. Blackbeard's Hill (P.O. Box 6041), Charlotte Amalie, St. Thomas, U.S.V.I. 00804. ☎ **800/344-5771** in the U.S., or 809/776-1234. Fax 809/776-4321. 18 rms, 3 junior suites, 3 full suites. A/C TV TEL. Winter, $140 double; $170 junior suite for two; $190 full suite for two. Off-season, $95 double; $120 junior suite for two; $145 full suite for two. Rates include continental breakfast. AE, MC, V. From the airport, turn right onto Rte. 30; when you get to Rte. 35, take a left turn and travel 1/2 mile until you see the sign pointing left to the hotel.

Once a private residence, this hotel has been transformed into a genuinely charming inn that enjoys one of the finest views of Charlotte Amalie and the harbor, thanks to its perch high on a hillside above the town. Hurricane Marilyn shut the hotel in 1995, but it bounced back partially for the 1996 winter season. In 1679 the Danish governor erected a soaring tower of chiseled stone here as a lookout for unfriendly ships. Legend says that Blackbeard himself lived in the tower half a century later. Each bedroom has a semisecluded veranda, a flat-weave Turkish kilim, terra-cotta floors, simple furniture, and a private bath. Guests enjoy use of a swimming pool, and the establishment's social center is the bar and grill. In the winter of 1997, the hotel opened Cafe Lulu, featuring a cross-cultural cuisine with dishes from the Caribbean, Mediterranean, and Asia. On weekends, live music is performed and a Sunday brunch is available. Magens Beach, a 15-minute taxi ride from the hotel, is the nearest beach.

Hotel 1829. Kongens Gade (P.O. Box 1567), Charlotte Amalie, St. Thomas, U.S.V.I. 00804. ☎ **800/524-2002** in the U.S., or 809/776-1829. Fax 809/776-4313. 14 rms, 1 suites. A/C MINIBAR TV TEL. Winter, $90–$180 double; from $230 suite. Off-season, $70–$130 double; from $165 suite. Rates include continental breakfast. AE, DISC, MC, V.

Now a national historic site, this inn has more Caribbean charm and flavor than any other on the island (it's a 15-minute ride from Magens Beach, though). Built by a French sea captain for his bride, it was designed by an Italian architect in a Spanish motif, with French grill work, Danish bricks, and sturdy hardwood doors from the Netherlands. Danish and African labor completed the structure in 1829 (hence the name). After a major renaissance, this once-decaying historical site has become one of the leading small hotels in the Caribbean, attracting a small percentage of stylish gay clients. Right in the heart of town, it stands about three minutes from Government House. On a hillside with many levels and many steps (no elevator), it's reached by a climb. The 1829 has been a hotel since the 19th century and has entertained everybody from Edna St. Vincent Millay to Mikhail Baryshnikov.

Amid a cascade of flowering bougainvillea are the upper rooms, which overlook a central courtyard with a miniature swimming pool. The rooms, some of which are boxlike and small, are well designed, comfortable, and attractive; most face the sea. During the restoration, the old was preserved wherever possible, and some rooms have antiques.

Villa Blanca. 4 Raphune Hill, Rte. 38 (P.O. Box 7505), Charlotte Amalie, St. Thomas, U.S.V.I. 00801. ☎ **809/776-0749.** Fax 809/779-2661. 16 rms. TV. Winter, $115–$135 double. Off-season, $75–$95 double. Honeymoon packages available. AE, DC, MC, V.

Small, intimate, and charming, this small-scale hotel lies 1 1/2 miles east of Charlotte Amalie on three secluded acres of panoramic hilltop land. Owner Blanca Terrasa Smith converted her private residence (once the home of Dodge heiress Christine Cromwell) into a hotel. Each of the rooms contains a ceiling fan and/or air-conditioning, a well-equipped kitchenette, and a private balcony or terrace with sweeping views either eastward to St. John or westward to Puerto Rico and the harbor of Charlotte Amalie. On the premises is a freshwater swimming pool. The closest beach is Morningstar Bay, about a 20-minute drive.

Inexpensive

Galleon House. Government Hill (P.O. Box 6577), Charlotte Amalie, St. Thomas, U.S.V.I. 00804. ☎ **800/524-2052** in the U.S., or 809/774-6952. Fax 809/774-6952. 14 rms, 12 with bath. A/C TV TEL. Winter, $69 double without bath, $89 double with bath. Off-season, $59 double without bath, $69 double with bath. Rates include continental breakfast. AE, DISC, MC, V.

At the east end of Main Street, about a block from the main shopping section of St. Thomas, Galleon House is reached after a climb that is especially difficult in sweltering heat. Nevertheless, its rates are among the most competitive in town, if you don't mind a place operated without state-of-the-art maintenance and a staff attitude many readers have lodged complaints about. Nevertheless, it's an acceptable choice if your demands aren't too high. You walk up a long flight of stairs to reach a concrete terrace doubling as the reception area. Rooms are scattered in several hillside buildings, each with a ceiling fan, cable TV with HBO, and adequate air-conditioning. There's a small freshwater pool and a sun deck. Breakfast is served on a veranda overlooking the harbor, and Magens Beach is 15 minutes from the hotel by car or taxi.

Island View Guesthouse. 11-C Contant (P.O. Box 1903), St. Thomas, U.S.V.I. 00803. ☎ **800/524-2023** for reservations only, or 809/774-4270. Fax 809/774-6167. 10 rms, 8 with bath; 1 suite. TV TEL. Winter, $65 double without bath, $95 double with bath; $115 suite. Off-season, $50 double without bath, $70 double with bath; $95 suite. Rates include continental breakfast. AE, MC, V. From the airport, turn right to Rte. 30; then cut left and continue to the unmarked Scott Free Rd. where you go left and look for the sign.

Island View is located in a hilly neighborhood of private homes and villas about a 7-minute drive west of Charlotte Amalie and a 20-minute drive from the nearest beach at Magens Bay. Set 545 feet up Crown Mountain, it has sweeping views over Charlotte Amalie and the harbor. Family owned and managed, it was originally built in the 1960s as a private home. Enlarged in 1989, it contains main-floor rooms (two without private bath) and some poolside rooms, plus six units in a recent addition (three with kitchens and all with balconies). The bedrooms are cooled by breezes and fans, and the newer ones have optional air-conditioning. Furnishings in the rooms are very basic, although a major restoration was completed in 1997, following damage from Hurricane Marilyn. A self-service open-air bar on the gallery operates on the honor system.

Villa Santana. Denmark Hill, St. Thomas, U.S.V.I. 00802. ☎ and fax **809/776-1311.** 7 suites. TV TEL. Winter, $125–$195 suite for 2. Off-season, $85–$135 suite for 2. AE.

This all-suite whitewashed property was built by Gen. Antonio López de Santa Anna of Mexico in the 1850s and boasts a panoramic view of Charlotte Amalie and the St. Thomas harbor. It's a five-minute walk from the shopping district in Charlotte Amalie and a 15-minute drive from Magens Beach. The unique country villa consists of converted rooms from the general's estate; guests can sleep in his former library, wine cellar, or old pump house. All rooms have fully equipped kitchens, private baths, and ceiling fans, but no air-conditioning. Your best bet is La Mansion suite, which has a loft and sitting room, along with a queen-size bed and bath, plus a living room, kitchen, and bath downstairs. The decor is of a Mexican design with clay tiles, rattan furniture, and stonework. The property includes a small pool, sundeck, and small garden with hibiscus and bougainvillea.

Where to Dine

The cuisine on St. Thomas is among the best in the entire West Indies. Prices, unfortunately, are high, and many of the best spots can only be reached by taxi. With a few exceptions, the finest and most charming restaurants aren't in Charlotte Amalie, but are out on the island.

In Charlotte Amalie

Beni Iguana's Sushi Bar. In the Grand Hotel Court, Veteran's Dr. ☎ **809/777-8744.** Reservations recommended. Sushi $4.50–$6 per portion (2 pieces); salads $8.95–$12.45; main courses $6–$13.75; combo plates for 4 to 5 diners $25–$60 each. AE, MC, V. Daily 11:30am–10pm. JAPANESE.

It's the only Japanese restaurant on St. Thomas, a change of pace from the Caribbean, steak, and seafood restaurants nearby. Along with a handful of shops, it occupies the sheltered courtyard and an old cistern across from Emancipation Square Park. Select a table outside, or pass through wide Danish colonial doors into a red- and black-lacquered interior devoted to a sushi bar and a handful of simple tables. Most meals begin with a selection of sushi (freshwater eel, tuna, yellowtail, or amberjack), which the chefs dub "edible art," and this is followed by a salad or a roll of seafood wrapped in rice. A perennial favorite is the "13" roll, stuffed with spicy crabmeat, salmon, lettuce, cucumbers, and scallions. Todd Reinhard, an American carefully trained in the art of Japanese cuisine, is your host.

Chart House Restaurant. Villa Olga, Frenchtown. ☎ **809/774-4262.** Reservations recommended. Main courses $16.95–$29.95; fixed-price dinner until 6:30pm $16.75. AE, DC, MC, V. Daily 5:30–10pm. STEAKS/SEAFOOD.

The stripped-down 19th-century villa that contains the Chart House was the Russian consulate during the island's Danish administration. It lies a short distance beyond the most densely populated area of Frenchtown village. The dining gallery is a spacious open terrace fronting the sea. Cocktails start daily at 5pm, when the bartender breaks out the ingredients for his special drink known as a Bailey's banana colada.

The Chart House features the best salad bar on the island, with a choice of 30 to 40 items, and comes with dinner. Menu choices range from Hawaiian chicken to Australian lobster tail. This chain is known for serving the finest cut of prime rib anywhere. Calamari, pasta dishes, coconut shrimp, and fresh fish are part of the expanded menu. For dessert, order the famous Chart House "mud pie."

Entre Nous. In Bluebeard's Castle, Bluebeard's Hill. ☎ **809/776-4050.** Reservations recommended. Main courses $18.50–$31. AE, MC, V. Tues–Sun 6–9:30pm. Closed Sept. CONTINENTAL.

This long-established restaurant operates under independent management in one of St. Thomas's most famous hotels and serves some of the island's best cuisine. Although relying heavily on French and Italian cuisines, the food is increasingly eclectic, with an emphasis on visual presentation. An open-air restaurant, it offers candlelit dinners and a sweeping view of the faraway harbor. Caesar salad will be created at your table, followed by Caribbean lobster prepared any way you like, perhaps simply with garlic butter. The seafood mélange with a fresh selection of fish and shellfish is one of the most appetizing main dishes, especially when coated with garlic butter. The seasame-crusted salmon comes swimming in a vanilla bean sauce, and confit of duck leg is surrounded by crisp duck breast in a wild berry compote. Desserts are a specialty, especially old-fashioned ones such as baked Alaska, which is flambéed right at your table.

Greenhouse. Veterans Dr. ☎ **809/774-7998.** Main courses $9.95–$19.95; breakfast $3.95–$4.95. AE, DISC, MC, V. Daily 8am–2am. AMERICAN/CARIBBEAN.

Fronted by big sunny windows, this waterfront restaurant attracts cruise-ship passengers who have shopped and need a place to drop. The food is not the island's best, but it's perfectly satisfying if you're not too demanding. A breakfast menu of eggs, sausages, and bacon segues into the daily specialties, including much American fare and some Jamaican-inspired dishes. A pretty good freshly grilled mahimahi is served here with a Florida key lime ginger butter and Jamaican jerk seasoning, or you might order one of the delectable specialties such as barbecued pork ribs, again with Jamaican jerk spices. Happy hour is daily from 4:30 to 7pm. This is one of the safest places to be in Charlotte Amalie after dark.

Hard Rock Café. 5144 International Plaza, the Waterfront, Queen's Quarter. ☎ **809/777-5555.** Reservations not accepted. Main dishes $7.95–$16.95. AE, MC, V. Mon–Sat 10am–9pm, Sun 10am–3pm. AMERICAN.

Occupying the second floor of a pink-sided mall whose big windows overlook the ships moored in Charlotte Amalie's harbor, this restaurant is a member of the international Hard Rock chain. Entire walls are devoted to the memorabilia of such artists as John Lennon, Eric Clapton, and Bob Marley. Throughout most of the day the place functions as a restaurant, serving barbecued meats, salads, sandwiches, burgers, fresh fish, and steaks. Its burgers are the best in town, but people mainly come for the good times. Music is provided by a live band on Friday night, and by a DJ on Thursday and Saturday.

✪ **Hervé Restaurant & Wine Bar.** Government Hill. ☎ **809/777-9703.** Reservations needed. Main courses $17.75–$24.75; lunch $14.75–$16.75. AE, MC, V. Mon–Sat 11:30am–2:30pm and 6–10pm. CONTINENTAL/AMERICAN/CARIBBEAN.

Located right next to Hotel 1829 (see below), Hervé has quickly become the hot new restaurant of St. Thomas, surpassing all competition in town, including its next door neighbor. A panoramic view of Charlotte Amalie and a historic setting are minor benefits—it's the cuisine here that matters. Hervé P. Chassin, whose experience has embraced such stellar properties as the Hotel du Cap d'Antibes, is a restaurateur with a vast, classical background. Here in his own unpretentious setting, he offers high-quality food at reasonable prices.

Study the menu in a room decorated with classic black-and-white photographs of St. Thomas at the turn of the century. There are two dining areas: a large open-air terrace and a more intimate wine room. Contemporary American dishes are served with the best of classic France, along with Caribbean touches. Start with the pistachio-encrusted brie, shrimp in a stuffed crab shell, or conch fritters with mango chutney. From here, you can let your taste buds march boldly forward with such temptations as red snapper poached with white wine, or a delectable black-sesame-crusted tuna with a ginger/raspberry sauce. Well-prepared nightly specials of game, fish, and pasta are featured. Desserts here are equally divine—you'll rarely taste a creamier crème caramel or a lighter, fluffier mango or raspberry cheesecake.

Hotel 1829. Kongens Gade (at the east end of Main St.). ☎ **809/776-1829.** Reservations recommended, but not accepted more than one day in advance. Main courses $19.50–$32.50; fixed-price dinner $28.50. AE, DISC, MC, V. Daily 6–11pm. CONTINENTAL.

Hotel 1829 is graceful and historic, and its restaurant serves some of the finest food on St. Thomas. Guests head for the attractive bar for a before-dinner drink. Dining is on a terrace or in the main room, whose walls are made from ships' ballast. The floor is made of 200-year-old Moroccan tiles. The cuisine has a distinctively European twist, with many dishes prepared and served from trolleys beside your table.

This is one of the few places in town that serves the finest of caviar; otherwise, diners settle for a selection of appetizers including goat-cheese bruschetta with roasted-red-pepper hummus. A ragout of swordfish is made more inviting with pine-nut/basil pesto, and the sautéed snapper in brown butter is always a reliable choice. Mint-flavored roast rack of lamb and chateaubriand for two are other possibilities.

Virgilio's. 18 Dronningens Gade (entrance on a narrow alleyway running between Main St. and Back St.). ☎ **809/776-4920.** Reservations recommended. Main dishes $8.95–$19.95. AE, MC, V. Mon–Sat 11:30am–10:30pm. NORTHERN ITALIAN.

The best northern Italian restaurant in the Virgin Islands, Virgilio's neo-Baroque interior is sheltered under heavy ceiling beams and brick vaulting. A well-trained staff attends to the tables. Owner Virgilio del Mare serves meals against a backdrop of stained-glass windows, crystal chandeliers, and soft Italian music. Everything appears on the menu from stuffed grape leaves to a delectable house special: *cinco peche,* clams, mussels, scallops, oysters, and crayfish simmered in a saffron broth. The lobster ravioli here is the best there is, and such classic dishes as rack of lamb are served with a distinctive flair, this one filled with a porcini mushroom stuffing and glazed with a roasted garlic aioli. The marinated grilled duck is served chilled, and you can even order an individual pesto pizza. Fresh fish is also served.

In Frenchtown

Alexander's. Rue de St. Barthélemy. ☎ **809/776-4211.** Reservations recommended. Main courses $12–$24.95. AE, MC, V. Mon–Sat 11:30am–10pm. AUSTRIAN/GERMAN.

Alexander's, west of town, will accommodate you at one of its 12 tables in air-conditioned comfort with picture windows overlooking the harbor. The Teutonic dishes are the best on the island. There's a heavy emphasis on seafood, and the menu includes conch schnitzel on occasion. Other dishes include a mouth-watering Wiener schnitzel, goulash, and homemade pâté. For dessert, try the homemade strudel, either apple or cheese. Lunch consists of a variety of crepes, quiches, and a daily chef's special. At both lunch and dinner, the menu offers 10 to 13 different pasta dishes, although we prefer the ones at Virgilio. Alexander's also has a Bar and Grill, open daily from 11am to midnight; Epernay, a wine bar open Monday through Friday from 4pm to 1am (until 2am on weekends); and a Frenchtown Deli & Coffeeshop, selling meat and cheese by the pound. It's open daily from 10am to 8pm, with the coffee shop featuring pastries and drinks from 7am to 8pm.

✪ **Craig & Sally's.** 22 Estate Honduras, Frenchtown. ☎ **809/777-9949.** Reservations recommended. Main courses $12.50–$27.50. AE, MC, V. Tues–Sat 11:30am–3pm, Tues–Sun 5:30–10pm. INTERNATIONAL.

Set in an airy, open-sided pavilion in Frenchtown, this Caribbean cafe is operated by a husband-wife team who escaped from the snowbelt. All the eclectic cuisine is created by Sally, who maintains a firm grip in the kitchen. Craig is the greeter and coordinator and he confides that the food is not "for the faint of heart, but for the adventurous soul." His affection for fine wines has led him to create the most extensive and sophisticated wine list on St. Thomas. Views of the sky and sea are complemented by a cuisine that ranges from pasta to seafood, with influences from Europe and Asia. Roast pork with clams, filet mignon with macadamia nut sauce, and grilled swordfish with a sauce of fresh herbs and tomatoes are examples from a menu that changes every day. The lobster-stuffed twice-baked potatoes are examples of creative cuisine at its most inspired.

On the North Coast

Agavé Terrace. Point Pleasant Resort, 6600 Estate Smith Bay. ☎ **809/775-4142.** Reservations recommended. Main courses $17.50–$38. AE, MC, V. Daily 6–10pm. CARIBBEAN.

Perched high above a steep and heavily forested hillside on the eastern tip of St. Thomas, this restaurant, one of the island's best, offers a sweeping panorama and matchless romantic atmosphere. The house drink, created by the bartender, is Desmond Delight, a combination of Midori, rum, pineapple juice, and a secret ingredient.

Following one or more Delights, you might opt for dinner. The house appetizer is an Agavé sampler prepared for two, which includes portions of crabmeat, conch fritters, and chicken pinwheel. For a main course, the preferred chef's specialty is seafood cardinale, served with lobster-flavored cream and fresh tomato sauce on a bed of angel-hair pasta. Usually six different types of fish turn up in the catch of the day; the fish can be prepared in seven different ways, including grilled, and is served with nine different sauces. There is an extensive wine list. A live steel drum band draws listeners Tuesday and Thursday nights.

Eunice's Terrace. 66–67 Smith Bay, Rte. 38. ☎ **809/775-3975.** Reservations not accepted. Main courses $5.25–$18.95. AE, MC, V. Mon–Sat 11am–10pm, Sun 5–10pm. Take the Red Hook bus. WEST INDIAN/AMERICAN.

A 30-minute taxi ride east of the airport, just east of the Coral World turnoff, is one of the best-known West Indian restaurants, which is devoid of a romantic atmosphere but oozes with lots of local color. Locals and tourists alike crowd into its confines for savory platters of island food served in generous portions. Eunice Best and her restaurant made news around the world on January 5, 1997, when Bill and Hillary Clinton showed up unexpectedly for lunch. Surrounded by secret service men, they shared a conch appetizer, then Mrs. Clinton went for the vegetable plate, and the president for the catch of the day, a fish called "Old Wife," which Clinton declared he loved. At the news, Mrs. Best just "went to pieces" and wept. A popular concoction called a Queen Mary (tropical fruits laced with dark rum) is a favorite starter, and dinner specialties include conch fritters, broiled or fried fish (especially dolphin), sweet-potato pie, and a number of specials usually served with fungi, rice, or plantain. A bottle of hot yellow sauce enhances flavors. On the lunch menu are fish burgers, sandwiches, and such daily specials as Virgin Islands doved pork or mutton. (Doving, pronounced *"DOUGH-ving,"* involves baking sliced meat while basting with a combination of its own juices, tomato paste, Kitchen Bouquet, and island herbs.) Key lime pie is a favorite dessert.

✪ **Romano's Restaurant.** 97 Smith Bay Rd. ☎ **809/775-0045.** Reservations recommended. Main courses $22.95–$26.95; pastas $15.95–$18.95. AE, MC, V. Mon–Sat 6:30–10:30pm. Closed 1 week in Apr for Carnival and Aug. Take the Vitran bus. ITALIAN.

Located on the sandy-bottomed flatlands near Coral World, this chef-owned hideaway of New Jersey–born Tony Romano is decorated with exposed brick and well-stocked wine racks. The chef specializes in the flavorful and herb-laden cuisine that some diners yearn for after a constant diet of Caribbean cooking. Specialties include linguine con pesto, a four-cheese lasagna, osso buco, scallopini marsala, and broiled salmon. All desserts are made on the premises. The place always seems full of happy diners, who find something a little different and special here.

In & Around Red Hook

Blue Marlin at Piccola Marina. 6300 Estate Smith Bay. ☎ **809/775-6350.** Main courses $15.50–$18.50. AE, MC, V. Daily 6–10pm and Sun 10:30am–2:30pm. Bar opens at 3pm. Take the Red Hook bus. INTERNATIONAL.

A popular eatery, this place has a casual, laid-back atmosphere. It's conveniently located right beside the ferry dock to St. John. The food is good, and much more imaginative than you might think. Everything is homemade, and fresh ingredients are used whenever possible. The kitchen doesn't turn out magic, but it's far better than your average, merely acceptable fare. Only fresh fish is used, and the kitchen makes its own oils, including orange-pepper oil, basil oil, and various vinaigrettes. One of the more intriguing dishes is grilled wahoo with a pineapple and cucumber sambal, or grilled salmon over baby greens. Grilled New York strip, along with Caribbean chicken and baby back ribs with a zesty sauce, are also served. On site is an ice-cream parlor and a pastry shop.

East Coast. In Red Hook Plaza, Rte. 38. ☎ **809/775-1919.** Main courses $6.75–$21.75. AE, MC, V. Daily 5:30–11pm. (Bar, daily 4:30pm–4am.) Take the Red Hook bus. CARIBBEAN.

Across the street from Red Hook Plaza, East Coast packs in a nightly crowd of visiting and local sports fans, who cheer their favorites playing on TV. What's not readily apparent is that the adjacent restaurant serves very good meals. Put your name on the list and enjoy a beer at the bar while waiting for a table. You can dine in a denlike haven or on an outdoor terrace in back. The fish of the day is prepared the way you like it: grilled, blackened, or in a teriyaki sauce. The selections might include tuna, wahoo, dolphin, swordfish, or snapper, which is best in a garlic-cream sauce. The kitchen also turns out Cajun shrimp and their famous "Coast burgers." There's live music on Saturday nights.

Palm Court. In the Elysian Beach Resort, 6800 Estate Nazareth, Cowpet Bay. ☎ **809/775-1000.** Reservations recommended. Main courses $19.95–$25; lunch $6.95–$12.95; Sun brunch $10.95 adults, $12.95 children. AE, DC, DISC, MC, V. Mon–Sat 7:30–10:30am, Sun 7:30–10am; daily 11:30am–2:30pm and 6:30–9:30pm. INTERNATIONAL.

On the premises of a luxury resort, this restaurant offers cuisine, decor, and service that achieve a more subtle, European-style glamour than any other on St. Thomas. At dinner tempt yourself with the shrimp cocktail or the savory conch fritters, followed by such main dishes as Caribbean lobster tail, swordfish, rack of lamb, and an intriguing angel-hair pasta studded with shrimp and flavored with ginger. Saturday is Caribbean night, with a live steel band and a generous buffet that includes everything from steaks to conch in lemon butter. The cost is $22.95 for adults and $11.50 for children.

Windjammer Restaurant. 41 Frydenhoj, Compass Point, off Rte. 32. ☎ **809/775-6194.** Reservations recommended. Main courses $7.75–$19.75. AE, MC, V. Mon–Sat 6–10pm. Closed Sept. SEAFOOD/GERMAN.

This restaurant at the easternmost tip of the island, 1 mile west of Red Hook, was destroyed by Hurricane Marilyn, but it's bounced back to become better and fresher than before. The food remains as good as ever, maybe even better. The Windjammer was rebuilt much as it was in its prestorm days, including the mahogany bar and paneling. The oil lamps make for romantic dining and a tropical *Gemüichkeit.* The extensive menu continues to reflect a German heritage, with a strong emphasis on seafood. Fresh fish arrives daily, including those all-time favorites, mahimahi, wahoo, and grouper. The fish is prepared in several different ways. Our preference is "island style"—that is, in lime and ginger *buerre blanc* (white butter) sauce. The chef's specialty is chicken à la Bremen, a boneless breast of chicken wrapped in bacon in a casserole with mussels, shrimp, and asparagus. Appetizers are likely to include those continental favorites, escargots in garlic butter and veal soup. Save room for the yummy devil's food cake, which has lots and lots of chocolate.

On Sapphire Beach

Seagrape. In the Doubletree Sapphire Beach Resort & Marina, Rte. 6, Smith Bay Rd. ☎ **809/775-6100.** Reservations recommended. Main courses $12.95–$24.95; Sun brunch

$9.50–$15.95. AE, MC, V. Mon–Sat 7:30–10:30am, 11am–3pm and 6–10pm, Sun 11am–3pm (brunch) and 6–10pm. CONTINENTAL/AMERICAN.

Counted among the finest dining rooms along the east coast of St. Thomas, Seagrape is open to the sea breezes of one of the most famous beaches in the Virgin Islands. The restaurant's attractions are the sounds of the waves, a well-trained staff, and fine-quality food. The lunch menu includes the grilled catch of the day and freshly made salads, and a children's menu is also available. The dinner menu includes traditional items like teriyaki chicken breast, veal marsala, and New York strip steak, but dishes are prepared with style and flair. The rib eye comes with mashed potatoes laced with garlic for added flavor. The chicken breast is made more delightful with a mushroom salsa. The well-attended Sunday brunches include such favorites as Grand Marnier French toast and Belgian waffles with fresh fruit.

NEAR THE SUB BASE

Barnacle Bill's. At the Crown Bay Marina, 16 Sub Base. ☎ **809/774-7444.** Reservations not required. Main courses $3–$15. AE, MC, V. Mon–Sat 11:30am–midnight. INTERNATIONAL.

Established by hardworking entrepreneur Bill Grogan, this restaurant is best known as a bar with live music. Its fans, however, also enjoy its view of one of the island's most prestigious marinas (Crown Point) and its food, which includes some of the best pizzas in St. Thomas. Portions, large and well prepared, include everything from steaks to lobsters, with lots of burgers, sandwiches, pastas, and salads as well. The setting is a pastel-colored, clapboard-sided house with lots of outdoor terraces and decks overlooking the yachts moored in the nearby marina.

L'Escargot. 12 Sub Base. ☎ **809/774-6565.** Reservations recommended. Main courses $15–$24. AE, MC, V. Daily 11:45am–2:30pm and 6–10pm. FRENCH.

This place has been in and out of fashion for so long it's a virtual island legend for its sheer endurance. But it also serves a first-rate cuisine. Its focal point is a low-slung semioutdoor terrace with close-up views of Crown Bay Marina. Menu items include the standard repertoire of French dishes, including rack of lamb with rosemary sauce, scampi in pesto sauce with linguine, grilled swordfish with spicy mango sauce, lobster thermidor, onion soup, fresh mushroom salad, and chocolate mousse.

Victor's New Hide Out. 103 Sub Base, off Rte. 30. ☎ **809/776-9379.** Reservations recommended. Main courses $9.95–$29.95. AE, MC, V. Mon–Sat 11:30am–3:30pm and 5:30–10pm, Sun 5:30–10pm. SEAFOOD/CARIBBEAN.

Victor's is operated by Victor Sydney, who comes from Montserrat. You never know who's going to show up here—maybe Bill Cosby, perhaps José Feliciano. Victor's has some of the best local dishes on the island, but first you have to find it—this hilltop perch is truly a place to hide out. If you're driving, call for directions; otherwise, take a taxi. Its dishes have much sophisticated flair and zest, as opposed to the more down-home cookery found at Eunice's Terrace, and this place is an excellent value for your money. This large, airy restaurant serves fresh lobster prepared Montserrat style (that is, in a creamy sauce) or grilled in the shell. You might also ask for a plate of juicy barbecued ribs. For dessert, try the coconut, custard, or apple pie.

BEACHES, WATER SPORTS & OTHER OUTDOOR PURSUITS

BEACHES Chances are, your hotel will be right on the beach, or very close to one, and this is where you'll plop down on the sands for most of your stay. All the beaches in the Virgin Islands are public, and most lie anywhere from 2 to 5 miles from Charlotte Amalie.

High Society on the High Seas: Chartering Your Own Yacht for the Day

The biggest charter business in the Caribbean is done by Virgin Islanders. On St. Thomas most of the business centers around the Red Hook and Yacht Haven marinas.

Perhaps the easiest way to go to sea is to charter "your yacht for the day" from **Yacht *Nightwind,*** Sapphire Marina (☎ **809/775-4110,** 24 hours a day) for only $90 per person. You're granted a full-day sail starting with breakfast and including a champagne buffet lunch and an open bar aboard this 50-foot yawl. You're also given free snorkeling equipment and instruction and you visit St. John and the outer islands.

New Horizons, 6501 Red Hook Plaza, Suite 16, Red Hook (☎ **809/775-1171**), offers windborne excursions amid the cays and reefs of the Virgin Islands. This two-masted 60-foot ketch has circumnavigated the globe and has been used as a design prototype for other boats. Owned and operated by Canadian Tim Krygsveld, it contains a hot-water shower, serves a specialty drink called a New Horizons Nooner (with a melon-liqueur base), and carries a complete line of snorkeling equipment for adults and children. A full-day excursion, with a "hot buffet Italian al fresco" and an open bar, costs $90 per person. Children 2 to 12, when accompanied by an adult, are charged $45. Excursions depart daily, weather permitting, from the Doubletree Sapphire Beach Resort & Marina. Call ahead for reservations and information. The outfitter has recently expanded with another vessel, *New Horizons II,* a 44-foot custom-made speed boat taking you to some of the most scenic highlights of the British Virgin Islands, costing $100 for adults or $55 for children (2 to 12) for the all-day trip. New Horizons also operates Power Trip next door, renting out 25-foot Wellcrafts for $245 per day for up to eight people. The boats have fuel-efficient engines and can make it to any of the 10 islands in the vicinity of St. Thomas. The outfitter also offers dive and fishing equipment and will supply a captain upon request.

THE NORTH SIDE Less than a mile long, ✪ **Magens Bay** lies between two mountains 3 miles north of the capital. Named one of the world's 10 most beautiful beaches, it charges $1 per person and $1 per car. Changing facilities are available, and snorkeling gear and lounge chairs can be rented, as can paddle boats and kayaks. There is no public transportation to reach it; from Charlotte Amalie, take Route 35 north all the way. The gates to the beach are open daily from 6am to 6pm (after 4 o'clock you'll need insect repellent). The beach is terribly overcrowded on cruise-ship days (which is virtually any day), but the crowds thin in the midafternoon. If you'd like to flash your wares, as many locals do, you can follow a marked trail to **Little Magens Bay,** a separate beach reserved for nude bathers.

In the northeast near Coral World, **Coki Beach** is good, but gets terribly crowded when cruise ships are in port. Snorkelers are attracted here, as are pickpockets, so protect your valuables. Concessions at the beach can arrange everything from waterskiing to parasailing. An East End bus runs to Smith Bay and lets you off at the gate to Coral World and Coki.

Also on the north side is **Renaissance Grand Beach Resort,** one of the island's most beautiful. Many water sports are available at this beach, which opens onto

You can avoid the crowds by sailing aboard the ***Fantasy*** (☎ **809/775-5652**), which is at 6700 Sapphire Village, no. 253, and departs from the American Yacht Harbor at Red Hook at 9:30am daily. It sails to St. John and nearby islands, allowing a maximum of six passengers to go swimming, snorkeling, beachcombing, and trolling. Snorkel gear with expert instruction is provided, as is a champagne lunch. An underwater camera is available. The cost of a full-day trip is $95 per person. A full-day trip to Jost Van Dyke is also offered for $90 per person, including a B.V.I. Customs charge of $15 (no lunch). A half-day sail, morning or afternoon, lasts three hours and costs $55. Sunset tours are also popular, with an open bar and hors d'oeuvres, costing $45 per person.

Remember Grace Kelly and Bing Crosby crooning a duet in *High Society?* The ***True Love,*** 6501 Red Hook Plaza, Suite 54 (☎ **809/775-6547,** 24 hours a day), a sleek coast guard–certified 54-foot Malabar schooner, is the very same yacht featured in the classic 1956 film. No longer just for lovers, the craft sails daily from Sapphire Marina for $90 per person, or $85 if you use traveler's checks. Included in the price is a gourmet lunch, open bar, snorkeling equipment, and lessons.

American Yacht Harbor, Red Hook (☎ **809/775-6454**), offers both bareboat and fully crewed charters. It does so from a colorful yacht-filled harbor set against a backdrop of Heritage Gade, a reproduction of a Caribbean village. The harbor is home to numerous boat companies, including day trippers, fishing boats, and sailing charters. There are also five restaurants on the property, serving everything from continental to island cuisine.

You may want to check out the ***Yachtsman's Guide to the Virgin Islands,*** available at major marine outlets, bookstores, through catalog merchandisers, or direct from **Tropic Isle Publishers,** P.O. Box 610938, North Miami, FL 33261-0938 (☎ **305/893-4277**). The guide, revised annually and costing $15.95, is supplemented by charts and photographs.

Smith Bay and is near Coral World. The beach lies right off Route 38, and fronts the previously recommended hotel.

THE SOUTH SIDE On the south side near Marriott's Frenchman's Reef Beach Resort, **Morningstar** lies about 2 miles east of Charlotte Amalie. This is where you can wear your most daring swimwear, as do many of the habitués who flock here. They're often young people (a large percentage gay) who work on the cruise ships. You can rent sailboats, snorkeling equipment, and lounge chairs. The beach can easily be reached by a cliff-front elevator at Frenchman's Reef.

Limetree Beach is a classic for those who like a serene stretch of sand. You can feed hibiscus blossoms to iguanas, and rent snorkeling gear and lounge chairs. There is no public transportation, but the beach can easily be reached by taxi from Charlotte Amalie.

One of the most popular beaches, **Brewer's** lies in the southwest near the University of the Virgin Islands and can be reached by the public bus marked "*fortuna*" heading west from Charlotte Amalie Road.

Near the airport, **Lindberg Beach** has a lifeguard, toilet facilities, and a bathhouse. It, too, lies on the Fortuna bus route heading west from Charlotte Amalie.

THE EAST END Small and special, **Secret Harbour** lies near a collection of condos whose owners you'll meet on the beach. With its white sand and coconut palms, it's a living cliché of Caribbean charm. The snorkeling near the rocks here is some of the best on the island. No public transportation stops here, but it's an easy taxi ride east of Charlotte Amalie heading toward Red Hook.

One of the finest on St. Thomas, ✪ **Sapphire Beach** is set against the backdrop of the desirable Sapphire Beach Resort & Marina complex, where you can lunch or order drinks. Windsurfers like it a lot, and snorkeling gear and lounge chairs can be rented. A large reef is found close to the shore, and there are good views of offshore cays and St. John. The beach of fine white coral sand opens onto beautiful views of the bay. To reach it, you can take the East End bus from Charlotte Amalie, going via Red Hook. Ask to be let off at the entrance to Sapphire Bay; it's not too far to walk from there to the water.

DEEP-SEA FISHING Fishing is very good in the U.S. Virgins, and 19 world records have been set here in recent years (eight for blue marlin). Sports fishing is offered on the ***Fish Hawk*** (☎ **809/775-9058**). Captain Al Petrosky sails from Fish Hawk Marina Lagoon at the East End on his 48-foot diesel-powered craft, which is fully equipped with rods and reels. All equipment (but no lunch) is included in the rate of $400 per half day for up to six passengers. A full-day excursion, depending on how far the boat goes out, ranges from $700 to $800.

GOLF On the north shore, **Mahogany Run,** at the Mahogany Run Golf Course, Mahogany Run Road (☎ **800/253-7103** or 809/777-6006), is an 18-hole, par-70 course. Designed by Tom and George Fazio, this is one of the most beautiful courses in the West Indies, rising and dropping like a roller coaster toward the sea where cliffs and crashing waves are the ultimate hazards at the 13th and 14th holes. For 18 holes, greens fees are $85, $70 in the late afternoon. From May through September, greens fees are $55, rising to $85 the rest of the year. Cart fees cost $15 year-round. No cut-offs, tank tops, or swimwear are allowed in the clubhouse or on the golf course.

KAYAK TOURS **Virgin Island Ecotours** (☎ **809/779-2155** for information) offers kayak trips through a mangrove lagoon on the southern coastline. Lasting 2 1/2 hours and costing $50 per person, the tour is led by professional naturalists who allow enough time for 30 minutes of snorkeling.

SCUBA & SNORKELING With 30 spectacular reefs just off St. Thomas, the U.S. Virgins are rated as one of the "most beautiful areas in the world" by *Skin Diver* magazine.

St. Thomas Diving Club, 7147 Bolongo Bay (☎ **800/538-7348** or 809/776-2381), is a full-service PADI five-star IDC center, the best on the island. An open-water certification course, including four scuba dives, costs $330. An advanced open-water certification course, including five dives that can be accomplished in two days, goes for $275. Every Thursday participants are taken on an all-day scuba excursion that includes a two-tank dive to the wreck of the HMS *Rhone* in the British Virgin Islands, costing $110. A scuba tour of the 350-foot wreck of the *Witshoal* is featured every Saturday for experienced divers only. You can also enjoy local snorkeling for $25.

DIVE In!, in the Sapphire Beach Resort & Marina, Smith Bay Road, Route 36 (☎ **809/775-6100**), is a well-recommended and complete diving center offering some of the finest diving services in the U.S. Virgin Islands, including professional instruction (beginner to advanced), daily beach and boat dives, custom dive packages, underwater photography and videotapes, snorkeling trips, and a full-service PADI dive center. An introductory course costs $55, with a one-tank dive going for $50, two-tank dives for $70. An open-water certification course with four dives in three days costs $350, and a six-dive pass is $185.

TENNIS The best tennis on the island is at the **Wyndham Sugar Bay Beach Club,** 6500 Estate Smith Bay (☎ **809/777-7100**), which has the Virgin Island's first stadium tennis court, seating 220, plus six additional Laykold courts lit at night. There's also a pro shop.

Another good resort for tennis is the **Bolongo Bay Beach Resort,** Bolongo Bay (☎ **809/775-1800**), which has two tennis courts that are lit until 10pm. They are free to members and hotel guests.

At **Marriott's Frenchman's Reef Tennis Courts,** Flamboyant Point (☎ **809/776-8500,** ext. 444), four courts are available, and nonresidents are charged $10 a half hour per court. Lights stay on until 10pm.

WINDSURFING This increasingly popular sport is available at the major resort hotels and at some public beaches, including Brewer's Bay, Morningstar Beach, and Limetree Beach. The **Renaissance Grand Beach Resort,** Smith Bay Road, Route 38 (☎ **809/775-1510**), is the major hotel offering windsurfing. Hotel guests are granted a lesson for $25 and use of the equipment for free. If you're a nonresident, the cost goes up to $35 per hour.

SEEING THE SIGHTS

IN CHARLOTTE AMALIE

The capital of St. Thomas, Charlotte Amalie, where most visitors begin their sightseeing on this small island, has all the color and charm of an authentic Caribbean waterfront town. In days of yore, seafarers from all over the globe flocked to this old-world Danish town, as did pirates and members of the Confederacy, who used the port during the American Civil War. (Sadly, St. Thomas was the biggest slave market in the world.)

The old warehouses once used for storing pirate goods still stand and. for the most part, house today's shops. In fact, the main streets (called "Gade," because of the islands' Danish heritage) are now a virtual shopping mall and are usually packed. (See "Shopping," below, for our specific recommendations.) Sandwiched among these shops are a few historic buildings, most of which can be covered on foot in about two hours. Before starting your tour, stop off in the so-called Grand Hotel, near Emancipation Park. No longer a hotel, it contains, along with shops, a **visitor center,** Tolbod Gade 1 (☎ **809/774-8784**), that's open Monday to Friday from 8am to 5pm and on Saturday from 8am to noon.

Fort Christian. In the town center. ☎ **809/776-4566.** Free admission. Mon–Fri 8:30am–4:30pm, Sat 9:30am–4pm, Sun noon–2pm.

Most visitors explore Charlotte Amalie to shop rather than to look at historic buildings; however, they can't miss this imposing structure dating from 1672 and dominating the center of town. Named after the Danish king, Christian V, the fort has been everything from a governor's residence to a jail. The fort became a national historic landmark in 1977, but still functioned as a police station, court, and jail until 1983. Now a museum, the fort houses displays detailing the history of the island culture and its people, including the Danish settlement. Cultural workshops and turn-of-the-century furnishings are just some of the exhibits. A museum shop features local crafts, maps, and prints.

Seven Arches Museum. Government Hill. ☎ **809/774-9295.** Admission $5. Tues–Sat 10am–3pm or by appointment.

Browsers and gapers like to flood in here to take a look at the private home of longtime residents Philibert Fluck and Barbara Demaras. This is an 18th-century Danish house, completely restored to its original condition and furnished with West Indian antiques. You can walk through the yellow ballast arches and visit the great room with its view of the busiest harbor in the Caribbean. There are night-blooming cacti and iguanas on the roof of the slave quarters. The admission of $5 includes a cold tropical drink served in a walled garden filled with flowers.

St. Thomas Synagogue. Synagogue Hill. ☎ **809/774-4312.** Free admission. Mon–Fri 9am–4pm.

This synagogue (its full name is Beracha Veshalom U'Gemilut Hasidim, which translates as Blessing, Peace, and Loving Deeds) is the oldest one in continuous use under the American flag and the second oldest in the western hemisphere. It still maintains the tradition of keeping sand on the floor, commemorating the exodus from Egypt. Erected in 1833 by Sephardic Jews, it was built of local stone, ballast brick from Denmark, and mortar made of molasses and sand. To reach the synagogue, make the steep climb from Main Street up to Krystal Gade.

ELSEWHERE ON THE ISLAND

West of Charlotte Amalie, Route 30 (Veterans Drive) will take you to **Frenchtown** (turn left at the sign to the Admirals Inn). This was settled by French-speaking people who were uprooted when the Swedes invaded and took over their homeland on St. Barts. They were known for wearing *cha-chas,* or straw hats. Some of the people who live here today are the direct descendants of those long-ago immigrants.

This colorful village, many of whose residents engage in fishing, contains several interesting restaurants and taverns. Now that Charlotte Amalie has been deemed a dangerous place to be at night, Frenchtown has picked up the business, and it's the best choice for nighttime dancing, entertainment, and drinking.

✪ **Coral World Marine Park & Underwater Observatory.** 6450 Coki Point. ☎ **809/775-1555.** Admission $16 adults, $10 children, but prices are subject to change in 1997. Daily 9am–6pm.

This aquarium, a 20-minute drive from downtown off Route 38, is St. Thomas's number-one tourist attraction. It was destroyed by Hurricane Marilyn in 1995, but is being rebuilt and should be fully functional sometime in 1997. The marine complex features a three-story underwater observation tower 100 feet offshore. Through windows you'll see sponges, fish, coral, and other underwater life in its natural state. In the Marine Gardens Aquarium, saltwater tanks display everything from sea horses to sea urchins. An 80,000-gallon reef tank features exotic marine life of the Caribbean; another tank is devoted to sea predators, with circling sharks and giant moray eels, among other creatures. The entrance is hidden behind a waterfall of cascading water.

The latest addition to the park is a semisubmarine that lets you enjoy the panoramic view and the underwater feeling of a submarine without truly submerging. Coral World's guests can take advantage of adjacent Coki Beach for snorkel rental, scuba lessons, or simply swimming and relaxing. Lockers and showers are available.

Also included in the marine park are the Tropical Terrace Restaurant, duty-free shops, and a tropical nature trail. Activities include daily fish and shark feedings and exotic bird shows.

Paradise Point Tramway. ☎ **809/774-9809.** Admission $10 per person round-trip, children half-price. Daily 9am–5pm.

This tramway, opened in 1994, affords visitors a dramatic view of Charlotte Amalie harbor on a ride to a 697-foot peak, although you'll pay dearly for the privilege. The tramway operates four cars, each with a 10-person capacity, for the 15-minute round-trip ride. The tramways, similar to those used at ski resorts, transport customers from the Havensight area to Paradise Point, where riders disembark to visit shops and the popular restaurant and bar.

Estate St. Peter Greathouse Botanical Gardens. At the corner of Rte. 40 (6A St. Peter Mountain Rd.) and Barrett Hill Rd. ☎ **809/774-4999.** Admission $8 adults, $4 children. Daily 9am–5pm.

This estate consists of 11 acres set at the foot of volcanic peaks on the northern rim of the island. It's laced with self-guided nature walks that will acquaint you with some 200 varieties of West Indian plants and trees, including an umbrella plant from Madagascar. From a panoramic deck you can see some 20 of the Virgin Islands, including Hans Lollick, an uninhabited island between Thatched Cay and Madahl Point. The house itself is worth a visit, its interior filled with art by locals. The $8 admission is perhaps a little steep for what you actually get.

UNDER THE SEA

A major attraction is the ✪ ***Atlantis* submarine** (☎ **809/776-5650**), which takes you on a one-hour voyage to depths of 90 feet, unfolding a world of exotic marine life. You'll gaze on coral reefs and sponge gardens through two-foot windows on the air-conditioned sub, which carries 30 passengers. To board the submarine, you take a surface boat from the West Indies Dock, right outside Charlotte Amalie, to the *Atlantis,* which lies near Buck Island (the St. Thomas version, not the more famous Buck Island near St. Croix). The fare is $72 per person. Children 4 to 12 pay $27, and teens (13 to 17) are charged $36. Children 3 and under are not permitted. The *Atlantis* operates daily from November to April and Tuesday to Saturday from May to October. Reservations are imperative. Hours and days vary depending on the arrival of cruise ships. For tickets, go to the Havensight Shopping Mall, Building 6, or call for reservations.

SHOPPING

Shoppers not only have the benefits of St. Thomas's liberal duty-free allowances, but they'll also find well-known brand names at savings of up to 40% off U.S. mainland prices. However, to find true value, you often have to plow through a lot of junk. Many items—binoculars, stereos, watches, cameras—can be matched in price at your hometown discount store. Therefore, you need to know the prices back home to determine if you're making a savings.

Most of the shops, some of which occupy former pirate warehouses, are open Monday to Saturday from 9am to 5pm; some stay open later. Nearly all stores close on Sunday and major holidays, unless a cruise ship is in port. Friday is the biggest cruise-ship visiting day at Charlotte Amalie (one day we counted eight at one time), so try to avoid shopping then.

Nearly all the major shopping on St. Thomas is located along the harbor of Charlotte Amalie. Cruise-ship passengers mainly shop at the **Havensight Mall** where they disembark at the eastern edge of Charlotte Amalie. The principal shopping street is called **Main Street** or Dronningens Gade (its old Danish name). North of this street is another merchandise-loaded street called **Back Street** or Vimmelskaft.

Many shops are also spread along the **Waterfront Highway** (also called Kyst Vejen). Between these major streets or boulevards are a series of side streets, walkways, and alleys, all filled with shops. Major shopping streets are Tolbod Gade, Raadets Gade, Royal Dane Mall, Palm Passage, Storervaer Gade, and Strand Gade.

All the major stores on St. Thomas are located by number on an excellent map in the publication *St. Thomas This Week,* distributed free to all arriving plane and boat passengers.

If you want to combine a little history with shopping, go into the courtyard of the old **Pissarro Building,** entered through an archway off Main Street. The Impressionist painter lived here as a child, and the old apartments have been turned into a warren of interesting shops.

It's illegal for most street vendors to ply their trades outside a designated area called **Vendors Plaza,** at the corner of Veterans Drive and Tolbod Gade. Hundreds converge at 7:30am, remaining there usually no later than 5:30pm, Monday to Saturday. (Very few remain in place on Sunday, unless a cruise ship is scheduled to arrive.)

When you completely tire of French perfumes and Swiss watches, head for **Market Square** as it's called locally, or more formally, Rothschild Francis Square. Here under a Victorian tin roof, locals with machetes will slice open fresh coconuts for you so you can drink the milk, and women wearing bandannas will sell ackee, cassava, or breadfruit they harvested themselves.

Art Galleries & Fine Crafts

✪ **Bernard K. Passman.** 38A Main St. ☎ **809/777-4580.**

Bernard K. Passman is the world's leading sculptor of black coral art and jewelry, famous for his "Can Can Girl" and his four statues of Charlie Chaplin. On Grand Cayman he learned to fashion exquisite treasures from black coral found 200 feet under the sea. After being polished and embellished with gold and diamonds, some of Passman's work has been treasured by royalty. There are also simpler and more affordable pieces for sale.

Camille Pissarro Building Art Gallery. Caribbean Cultural Centre, 14 Dronningens Gade. ☎ **809/774-4621.**

In the house where Pissarro, dean of Impressionism, was born in 1830, this art gallery—reached by climbing a flight of stairs—honors the illustrious painter. In three high-ceilinged and airy rooms, you'll discover all the available Pissarro paintings relating to the islands. Many prints and note cards of local artists are also available. The gallery also sells original batiks, alive in vibrant colors.

✪ **Jim Tillett Art Gallery & Silk Screen Print Studio.** Tillett Gardens, 4126 Anna's Retreat, Tutu. ☎ **809/775-1929.** Take Rte. 38 east from Charlotte Amalie.

Since 1959 Tillett Gardens, once an old Danish farm, has been the island's arts and crafts center. Including an art gallery and a screen-printing studio, this tropical compound is a series of buildings housing arts and crafts studios, galleries, and an outdoor garden restaurant and bar. Prints in the galleries start as low as $10. The best work of local artists is displayed here—originals in oils, watercolors, and acrylics. The Tillett prints on fine canvas are all one of a kind, and the famous Tillett maps on fine canvas are priced from $30. If you're not interested in buying any art, perhaps you'd prefer watching the daily iguana feedings in the garden.

Bags

Coki. Compass Point Marina. ☎ **809/775-6560.**

Coki of St. Thomas has a factory 1½ miles from Red Hook amidst a little restaurant row, so you might want to combine a gastronomic tour with a shopping expedition. From the factory's expansive cutting board come some of the most popular varieties of shoulder tote bags in the Virgin Islands. These include pieces of canvas and elegant cotton prints converted to beach bags, zip-top bags, and draw-string bags. All Coki bags are 100% cotton, stitched with polyester sailmaker's thread.

BRIC-A-BRAC

Carson Company Antiques. Royal Dane Mall, off Main St. ☎ **809/774-6175.**

Its clutter and eclecticism might appeal to you, especially if you appreciate small spaces loaded with merchandise, tasteless and otherwise, from virtually everywhere. Much of it is calibrated to appeal to the tastes of cruise-ship passengers looking for bric-a-brac that usually accumulates on shelves back on the U.S. mainland. Bakelite jewelry is cheap and cheerful, and the African artifacts are often especially interesting.

ELECTRONICS

✪ **Royal Caribbean.** 33 Main St. ☎ **809/776-4110.**

This is the largest camera and electronics store in the Caribbean. This store and its outlets carry Nikon, Minolta, Pentax, Canon, and Panasonic products. It's a good source for watches, including such brand names as Seiko, Movado, Corum, Fendi, and Zodiac. They also have a complete collection of Philippe Charriol watches, jewelry, and leather bags, and a wide selection of Mikimoto pearls, 14- and 18-karat jewelry, and Lladró figurines.

There are additional branches at 23 Main St. (☎ **809/776-5449**) and Havensight Mall (☎ **809/776-8890**).

FASHION

Cosmopolitan. Drakes Passage and the waterfront. ☎ **809/776-2040.**

Since 1973, this store has drawn a lot of repeat business. Its shoe salon features Bally of Switzerland, and Bally handbags are a popular addition. In swimwear, it offers one of the best selections of Gottex of Israel for women and Gottex, Hom, Lahco of Switzerland, and Fila for men. A men's wear section offers Paul & Shark from Italy, and Burma Bibas sports shirts. The shop also features ties by Gianni Versace and Pancaldi of Italy (priced at least 30% less than on the U.S. mainland), and Nautica sportswear for men discounted at 10%.

FRAGRANCES

Tropicana Perfume Shoppe. 2 Main St. ☎ **800/233-7948** or 809/774-0010.

This store at the beginning of Main Street is billed as the largest perfumery in the world, and it offers all the famous names in perfumes, skin care, and cosmetics. They carry Lancôme and La Prairie among other products. Men will also find Europe's best colognes and aftershave lotions here.

GIFTS

✪ **A. H. Riise Gift & Liquor Stores.** 37 Main St. at A. H. Riise Gift & Liquor Mall (perfume and liquor branch stores at the Havensight Mall). ☎ **800/524-2037** or 809/776-2303.

St. Thomas's oldest outlet for luxury items such as jewelry, crystal, china, and perfumes is still the largest. It also offers the widest sampling of liquors and liqueurs on the island. Everything is displayed in a 19th-century Danish warehouse, extending from Main Street to the waterfront. The store boasts a collection of fine jewelry and watches from Europe's leading craftspeople, including Vacheron Constantin, Bulgari, Omega, and Gucci, as well as a wide selection of Greek gold, platinum, and precious gemstone jewelry.

Imported cigars are stored in a climate-controlled walk-in humidor. Delivery to cruise ships and the airport is free. A. H. Riise offers a vast selection of fragrances for both men and women, along with the world's best-known names in cosmetics and treatment products. Waterford, Lalique, Baccarat, and Rosenthal, among others, are featured in the china and crystal department. Specialty shops in the complex sell Caribbean gifts, books, clothing, food, art prints, note cards, and designer sunglasses.

Caribbean Marketplace. Havensight Mall (Building III). ☎ **809/776-5400.**

The best selections of Caribbean handcrafts are found here, in addition to some distinctively Caribbean food items, including Sunny Caribbee products, a vast array of condiments (ranging from spicy peppercorns to nutmeg mustard). There's also a wide selection of Sunny Caribbee's botanical products. Other items range from steel-pan drums from Trinidad to wooden Jamaican jigsaw puzzles, from Indonesian batiks to bikinis from the Cayman Islands. Do not expect very attentive service.

Down Island Traders. Veterans Dr. ☎ **809/776-4641.**

The aroma of spices will lead you to these markets, which have Charlotte Amalie's most attractive array of spices, teas, seasoning, candies, jellies, jams, and condiments, most of which are packaged from natural Caribbean products. The owner carries a line of local cookbooks, as well as silk-screened T-shirts and bags, Haitian metal sculpture, handmade jewelry, Caribbean folk art, and children's gifts. Be sure to ask for their collection of tropical coconut-mango bath and body products and the Calypso Spa Sun Care line.

Little Switzerland. 5 Main St. ☎ **809/776-2010.**

A branch of this shop seems to appear on virtually every island in the Caribbean. Its concentration of watches, including Omega and Rolex, is topped by no one. It also sells a wide variety of other objects as well, including cuckoo clocks and music boxes. Its china, especially the Royal Worcester and Rosenthal collection, is outstanding, as are its crystal and jewelry. The store also maintains the official outlets for Hummel, Lladró, and Swarovski figurines. There are several other branches of this store on the island, especially at the Havensight Mall, but the main store has the best selection.

Jewelry

Blue Carib Gems and Rocks. 2 Back St. (behind Little Switzerland). ☎ **809/774-8525.**

For a decade, the owners of this shop scoured the Caribbean for gemstones, and these stones have been brought directly from the mines to you. The raw stones are cut, polished, and then fashioned into jewelry by the lost-wax process. On one side of the premises you can see the craftspeople at work, and on the other, view their finished products. A lifetime guarantee is given on all handcrafted jewelry. Since the items are locally made, they are duty free and not included in the $1,200 Customs exemption.

✪ **Cardow Jewelers.** 39 Main St. ☎ **809/776-1140.**

Often called the Tiffany's of the Caribbean, Cardow Jewelers boasts the largest selection of fine jewelry in the world. This fabulous shop, where more than 20,000 rings are displayed, offers savings because of its worldwide direct buying, large turnover, and duty-free prices. Unusual and traditional designs are offered in diamonds, emeralds, rubies, sapphires, Brazilian stones, and pearls. Cardow has a whole wall of

Italian gold chains, and also features antique-coin jewelry. The Treasure Cove, a discount area within the store, has cases of fine gold jewelry all priced under $200.

Colombian Emeralds International. Havensight Mall. ☎ **809/774-2442.**

The Colombian Emeralds stores are renowned throughout the Caribbean for offering the finest collection of Colombian emeralds, both set and unset. Here you buy direct from the source, cutting out the middleperson, which can mean significant savings for you. In addition to jewelry, the shop stocks fine watches. There's another outlet on Main Street.

H. Stern Jewellers. Havensight Mall. ☎ **800/524-2024** or 809/776-1223.

This international jeweler is one of the most respected in the world, with some 175 outlets. In a world of fake jewelry and fake everything, it's good to know that there's still a name you can count on. Stern is Cardow's (see above) leading competitor on the island. Colorful gem and jewel creations are offered at Stern's locations on St. Thomas. There are two on Main Street, this one at the Havensight Mall, and branches at Marriott's Frenchman's Reef. Stern gives worldwide guaranteed service, including a one-year exchange privilege.

Irmela's Jewel Studio. In the Old Grand Hotel, at the beginning of Main St. ☎ **800/524-2047** or 809/774-5875.

Irmela's has made a name for itself in the highly competitive jewelry business on St. Thomas. Here the jewelry is unique, custom designed by Irmela, and handmade by her studio or imported from around the world. Irmela has the largest selection of cultured pearls in the Caribbean, including freshwater Biwa, South Sea, and natural-color black Tahitian pearls. Choose from hundreds of clasps and pearl necklaces. Irmela also has a large selection of unset stones.

Leather

The Leather Shop. 1 Main St. ☎ **809/776-0290.**

Here you'll find the best selection from Italian designers such as Fendi, Longchamp, De Vecchi, Furla, and Il Bisonte. There are many styles of handbags, belts, wallets, briefcases, and attaché cases. Some of these items are very expensive, of course, but there is less expensive merchandise like backpacks, carry-ons, and Mola bags from Colombia. If you're looking for a bargain, ask them to direct you to the outlet store on Back Street, selling close-outs at prices that are sometimes 50% cheaper than on the U.S. mainland.

Linens

The Linen House. A. H. Riise Mall. ☎ **809/774-1668.**

The Linen House is considered the best store for linens in the West Indies. You'll find a wide selection of place mats, decorative tablecloths, and many hand-embroidered goods, much of it handmade in China. Other branches are at Havensight Mall (☎ **809/774-0868**), and 7A Royal Dane Mall (☎ **809/774-8117**).

St. Thomas After Dark

St. Thomas has more nightlife than any other of the Virgin Islands, but it's not as extensive as you might think. The big hotels seem to offer the most varied programs.

The Performing Arts

Reichhold Center for the Arts. University of the Virgin Islands, 2 John Brewer's Bay. ☎ **809/693-1550.** Tickets $12–$40.

This artistic center, the premier venue in the Caribbean, lies west of Charlotte Amalie. Call the theater or check with the tourist office to see what's on at the time of your visit. The lobby displays a frequently changing free exhibit of paintings and sculptures by Caribbean artists. A Japanese-inspired amphitheater is set into a natural valley, with seating space for 1,196. The smell of gardenias adds to the beauty of the performances. Several different repertory companies of music, dance, and drama perform here. Performances begin at 8pm (call the theater to check).

The Club & Music Scene

Barnacle Bill's. At the Crown Bay Marina, in the Sub Base. ☎ **809/774-7444.** No cover, except $3 on "Limelight Mondays," when several different bands are featured.

A restaurant during the day, this is one of the best nightclubs on St. Thomas in the evening. Beginning around 9pm, a parade of local and imported musical talent plays to full houses until at least 1am. Although the bar is open nightly, live music is presented January through March from Thursday through Saturday. This place has especially cheap beer.

Cabaña Lounge. Blackbeard's Castle, Blackbeard's Hill. ☎ **809/776-1234.**

This lounge is one of the friendliest and most *simpatico* places to gather in St. Thomas any night but Monday from 5pm "until." Your hosts, Bob Harrington and Henrique Konzen, Blackbeard's owners, provide a limited but choice menu (nothing over $12) and an inviting atmosphere. On some nights, activities such as games are featured, sometimes there are movie nights, and there's even an Ides of March toga party. After Hurricane Marilyn destroyed much of the property, this bar and pool area was converted into the Cabaña. Before that, it had been used strictly by Bob and Henrique as an extension of their own living quarters.

Epernay. Rue de St. Barthélemy, Frenchtown. ☎ **809/774-5348.**

Adjacent to Alexander's Restaurant, this stylish watering hole with a view of the ocean adds a touch of Europe to the neighborhood. You can order glasses of at least six different brands of champagne, and vintage wines by the glass. Appetizers cost $6 to $10 and include sushi and caviar. You can also order tempting main courses, plus desserts, such as chocolate-dipped strawberries.

Greenhouse. Veterans Dr. ☎ **809/774-7998.** No cover Thurs–Tues, $5 Wed (including the first drink).

Set directly on the waterfront, this bar and restaurant is one of the few nightspots we recommend in Charlotte Amalie. You can park nearby and walk to the entrance. Each night a different entertainment is featured, ranging from reggae to disco. Wednesday night is the "big blast."

Iggie's Bolongo. Bolongo Beach Resort, 7150 Bolongo. ☎ **809/779-2844.**

During the day, Iggie's premises function as an informal, open-air restaurant serving hamburgers, sandwiches, and salads. After dark, however, it turns into an entertainment venue featuring karaoke and occasional live entertainment. Call to find out what's happening.

Turtle Rock Bar. In the Mangrove Restaurant at the Wyndham Sugar Bay Beach Club, 6500 Estate Smith Bay. ☎ **809/777-7100.** No cover.

Set a few minutes' drive west of Red Hook, this is a popular bar where live music, steel bands, and karaoke provide diversions. Although there's lots of space on the premises if anyone should get the urge to dance, very few clients ever seem to take the opportunity, preferring instead to listen to the steel-pan bands (which play from 2pm to closing every night), or the more elaborate bands that play on Tuesday,

Sunday, and other nights, according to availability. Thursday night is devoted to karaoke (for those of you who simply must—or those of you who want to stay away). If you're hungry, burgers, salads, steaks, and grilled fish are available at the Mangrove Restaurant a few steps away. Entrance to the complex is free, and happy hour (when most drinks are half price) is 4 to 6pm every night.

Walter's. 3 Trompeter Gade. ☎ **809/774-5025.** No cover Sun–Thurs, $3 Fri–Sat.

Dimly and rather flatteringly lit, this two-level watering hole attracts locals (often gay men) in season, drawing more off-island visitors in winter. Located about 100 yards from the island's famous synagogue (see above), in a clapboard town house built around 1935, Walter's cellar bar features an intimate atmosphere with music from the 1950s, 1960s, and 1970s.

2 St. John

The smallest and least populated of the U.S. Virgin Islands, St. John is known for its lush, unspoiled beauty. More than half of its land, as well as its shoreline, was set aside and protected as the Virgin Islands National Park in 1956.

Ringed by a rocky coastline, crescent-shaped bays, and white-sand beaches, the island contains an array of bird- and wildlife that's the envy of ornithologists and zoologists around the world. Miles of winding hiking trails lead to panoramic views and the ruins of 18th-century Danish plantations. Mysterious geometric petroglyphs incised into boulders and cliffs can be pointed out by island guides; of unknown age and origin, the figures have never been deciphered.

The yachting set seeks out its dozens of sheltered coves for anchorage and swimming. The hundreds of underwater coral gardens that surround St. John's perimeter are protected by the National Park Service as rigorously as the land surface. Any attempt to damage or remove coral from these waters is punishable by large and strictly enforced fines.

About 3 to 5 miles east of St. Thomas, St. John lies just across Pillsbury Sound. The island is about 7 miles long and 3 miles wide, with a total land area of some 20 square miles.

GETTING THERE

The easiest and most common way to get to St. John is by **ferryboat** (☎ **809/776-6282**), which leaves from the Red Hook landing pier on St. Thomas's eastern tip; the trip takes about 20 minutes each way. Beginning at 6:30am, boats depart more or less every hour, with minor exceptions throughout the day. The last ferry back to Red Hook departs from St. John's Cruz Bay at 11pm. Because of such frequent departures, even cruise-ship passengers temporarily anchored in Charlotte Amalie for only a short stay can visit St. John for a quickie island tour. The one-way fare is $3 for adults, $1 for children 10 and under. Schedules can change without notice, so call in advance before your intended departure.

To reach the ferry, take the Vitran bus from a point near Market Square (in Charlotte Amalie) directly to Red Hook. The cost is $1 per person each way. In addition, privately owned taxis will be willing to negotiate a price to carry you from virtually anywhere to the docks at Red Hook.

It's also possible to board a **boat** for St. John directly at the Charlotte Amalie waterfront for a cost of $7 each way. The ride takes 45 minutes. The boats depart from Charlotte Amalie at 9am and continue at intervals of between one and two hours until the last boat departs around 7pm. (The last boat to leave St. John's Cruz Bay for Charlotte Amalie departs at 5:15pm.) Call for more information.

GETTING AROUND

BY PUBLIC TRANSPORTATION The most popular way to get around is by **surrey-style taxi** (☎ **809/776-8294**). Typical fares are $3 to Trunk Bay, $3.50 to Cinnamon Bay, or $7 to Mahoe Bay. Between midnight and 6am fares are increased by 40%. Call for more information.

BY CAR OR JEEP The roads are undeveloped and uncluttered, and offer panoramic vistas. Because of these views, many visitors opt to rent a car (sometimes with four-wheel drive) to tour the island. You might consider one of the open-sided Jeep-like vehicles. Most people need a car for only a day or two. During the busiest periods of midwinter, there's sometimes a shortage of cars, so try to reserve early.

Gasoline is almost never included in the price of a rental. You're likely to be delivered a car with an almost-empty tank, just enough to get you to one of the island's two gas stations. (A third gas station on the island dispenses gas only to government vehicles.) Because of the distance between gas stations, it's never a good idea to drive around St. John with less than half a tank of gas.

The two largest car-rental agencies on St. John are **Hertz** (☎ **800/654-3001** or 809/776-6412) and **Avis** (☎ **800/331-2112** or 809/776-6374); Budget is not represented. If you want a local firm, try **St. John Car Rental,** across from the post office in Cruz Bay (☎ **809/776-6103**). Its stock is limited to Jeep Wranglers, Jeep Cherokees, and Suzuki Sidekicks.

ESSENTIALS

In a medical emergency, dial 911. Otherwise, go to **St. John Myrah Keating Smith Community Health Clinic,** 28 Sussanaberg (☎ **809/693-8900**). A leading drugstore is **St. John Drugcenter,** in the Boulon Shopping Center, Cruz Bay (☎ **809/776-6353**), which also sells film, cameras, magazines, and books; it's open Monday to Saturday from 9am to 6pm and on Sunday from 10am to 2pm.

The **St. John Tourist Office** (☎ **809/776-6450**) is located near the Battery, a 1735 fort that's a short walk from where the ferry from St. Thomas docks. It's open Monday to Friday from 8am to noon and 1 to 5pm.

WHERE TO STAY

RESORTS

✪ **Caneel Bay.** Virgin Islands National Park, St. John, U.S.V.I. 00831. ☎ **800/928-8889** or 809/776-6111. Fax 809/693-8280. 166 rms. MINIBAR. Dec 20–Mar, $350–$750 double. Off-season, $250–$550 double. AE, DC, MC, V. MAP $75 per person extra.

Caneel Bay was the dream and creation of megamillionaire Laurance S. Rockefeller in 1956 when it became the original ecoresort. The resort is actually part of the national park, containing some 350 species of trees. Long reigning as one of the premier resorts of the Caribbean, Caneel Bay is definitely not one of the most luxurious. One of its devoted fans once told us, "It's like living at summer camp." That means no phones, no air-conditioning, and no TV sets in the rooms. Nevertheless, the movers and shakers of the world have descended on this place, whereas younger people tend to head elsewhere. To attract more of a family audience, young children are now allowed at the resort, which can annoy some of the older guests.

In 1995 Hurricane Marilyn swept across the resort, canceling its winter season, but it reopened in November 1996. Operated by Rosewood Hotels and Resorts, it lies on a 170-acre portion of the national park, offering a choice of seven beaches. The main buildings are strung along the bays, with a Caribbean lounge and dining room at the core.

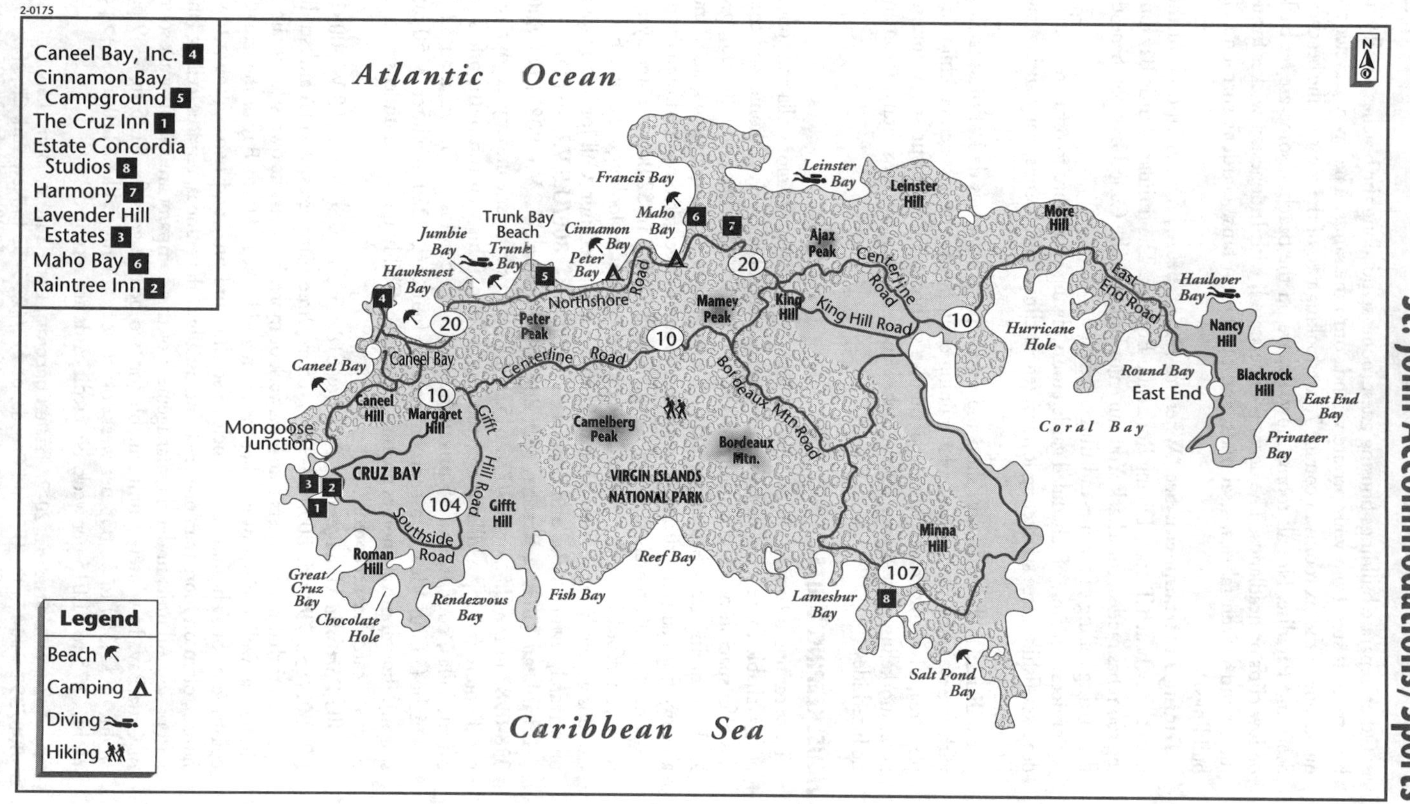
2-0175
Caneel Bay, Inc. 4
Cinnamon Bay Campground 5
The Cruz Inn 1
Estate Concordia Studios 8
Harmony 7
Lavender Hill Estates 3
Maho Bay 6
Raintree Inn 2
Legend
Beach
Camping
Diving
Hiking
Atlantic Ocean
Caribbean Sea
Coral Bay
Francis Bay
Leinster Bay
Leinster Hill
More Hill
Maho Bay
Trunk Bay Beach
Jumbie Bay
Cinnamon Bay
Trunk Bay
Peter Bay
Hawksnest Bay
Northshore Road
Peter Peak
Mamey Peak
King Hill
Ajax Peak
Centerline Road
King Hill Road
East End Road
Haulover Bay
Nancy Hill
Blackrock Hill
Hurricane Hole
Round Bay
East End
East End Bay
Privateer Bay
Caneel Bay
Caneel Hill
Margaret Hill
Mongoose Junction
CRUZ BAY
Gifft Hill Road
Gifft Hill
Camelberg Peak
Bordeaux Mtn Road
Bordeaux Mtn.
VIRGIN ISLANDS NATIONAL PARK
Minna Hill
Southside Road
Roman Hill
Great Cruz Bay
Chocolate Hole
Rendezvous Bay
Fish Bay
Reef Bay
Lameshur Bay
Salt Pond Bay
10
20
104
107

Other, separate buildings housing guest rooms stand along the beaches, so all you have to do is step from your private veranda onto the sands. The savvy traveler requests one of the six rooms in cottage 7, overlooking two of the most idyllic beaches, Scott and Paradise. Not all rooms, however, are on the beaches; some are set back on low cliffs or headlands. The decor is understated, with Indonesian wicker furniture, hand-woven fabrics, sisal mats, and plantation fans. Gardens surround all buildings.

Dining/Entertainment: See "Where to Dine," below, for descriptions of the Caneel Bay Beach Terrace Dining Room and Equator. The intimate Turtle Bay dining room has made a comeback. You can enjoy drinks at the Caneel Bay Bar, beneath the soaring ceiling of a stone-and-timber pavilion.

Services: An array of scheduled garden tours, diving excursions to offshore wrecks, deep-sea fishing, free snorkeling lessons, tennis clinics and lessons, baby-sitting, valet laundry.

Facilities: Full-service dive shop and water-sports activities desk, fitness facility with free weight and cardiovascular training equipment, business center, children's play area, 11 tennis courts, free use of Sunfish sailboats and Windsurfers, swimming pool, snorkeling gear, kayaks, seven beaches, endless hideaways for solitary or romantic interludes.

Housekeeping Units

Villa vacations are on the rise on St. John, and there are actually more villa and condo beds available for rent on St. John than there are hotel beds. Private homes and condos offer spaciousness and comfort, as well as privacy, and come with fully equipped kitchens, dining areas, bedrooms, and such amenities as VCRs and patio grills. Rentals range from large multiroom resort homes to simply decorated one-bedroom condo apartments. Villa rentals typically average about $1,200 to $2,000 per week year-round, an affordable option for multiple couples or families looking for a large house. Condos generally range from $105 to $360 per night per unit. Call for information on privately owned **villas and condos** on St. John (☎ **800/U.S.V.I.-INFO**).

Caribbean Villas & Resorts, P.O. Box 458, St. John, U.S.V.I. 00831 (☎ **800/338-0987** in the U.S., or 809/776-6152), the island's biggest company, is your best bet if you're seeking a villa or a condo on St. John. This well-run outfit offers 76 private villas, condos, and 45 private homes. Most condos go for less than $210 per night (a Cruz View two-bedroom unit for four costs $220 in winter, $150 off-season), though private homes are more expensive. Children five and under stay free; no credit cards are accepted.

Villa Portfolio Management, P.O. Box 618, Cruz Bay, St. John, U.S.V.I. 00831 (☎ **800/858-7989** or 809/693-9100), offers three complexes of villas and studio apartments that many renters take for a week or more. Each has its own self-contained kitchen, as well as views over either the town and harbor of Cruz Bay or the faraway coastline of St. Thomas. Units include studios and one- and two-bedroom town houses, often on more than one level, and usually with verandas, terraces, ceiling fans, and patios. All units under the management of this company are a short walk south of Cruz Bay. In winter, a unit suitable for two people goes for $175 to $269 per night, or $1,330 to $2,033 per week; off-season, it's more like $110 to $145 per night, $875 to $1,015 per week. No credit cards are accepted.

Estate Concordia Studios. 20–27 Estate Concordia, Coral Bay, St. John, U.S.V.I. 00830. ☎ **800/392-9004** in the U.S. and Canada, or 212/472-9453 in New York City. Fax 212/861-6210 in New York City. 9 studios, 5 tents. Winter, $135–$190 studio for 2; $95 ecotent for 2. Off-season, $95–$150 studio for 2; $60 ecotent for 2. Additional person $15 extra. MC, V.

Opened in 1993, this environmentally sensitive, 51-acre development project was widely praised for its integration with the local ecosystem. The elevated structures were designed to coexist with the stunning southern edge of St. John. Nestled on a low cliff above a salt pond, surrounded by hundreds of acres of pristine national park, the secluded location is recommended for those with a rental vehicle. Each building was designed to protect mature trees, and is connected to its neighbors with boardwalks. The nine studios are contained in six postmodern cottages. Each comes with kitchen, bathroom, balcony, and ceiling fan. Some units have an extra bedroom or a larger-than-expected private bathroom. The five ecotents, which are solar and wind powered and equipped with large screened-in windows to lend a "tree house" atmosphere, are a newer addition. Tents have two twin beds in each bedroom, one or two twin mattresses on a loft platform, and a queen-size fold-out couch, allowing the tent-cottages to sleep five or six comfortably. Each kitchen comes with a stove and a running-water sink. Each tent also has a toilet and private shower.

Estate Concordia also features a hillside swimming pool and guest laundry facilities. On-site management assists with activity suggestions.

Harmony. P.O. Box 310, Cruz Bay, St. John, U.S.V.I. 00831. ☎ **800/392-9004** in the U.S. and Canada, 212/472-9453 in New York City, or 809/776-6226. Fax 809/776-6504, or 212/861-6210 in New York City. 12 studios. Winter, $150–$180 studio for 2. Off-season, $95–$125 studio for 2. Additional person $25 extra. Seven-night minimum stay in winter. MC, V.

Built on a hillside above the Maho Bay Campground, this is a small-scale cluster of 12 luxury studios in six two-story houses with views sweeping down to the sea. Designed to combine both ecological technology and comfort, it's one of the few resorts in the Caribbean to operate exclusively on sun and wind power. Its construction was adopted as part of the U.S. National Park Service *Handbook for Sustainable Design.* Most of the building materials are derived from recycled materials, including reconstituted plastic and glass containers, newsprint, old tires, and scrap lumber. The managers and staff are committed to offering educational experiences, as well as the services of a small-scale resort. Guests are taught how to operate a user-friendly computer telling them how their studio's energy is being spent.

The studios contain queen-size sofa beds and/or twin beds, tile bathrooms, kitchenettes, dining areas, and outdoor terraces. Guests can walk a short distance downhill to use the restaurant, grocery store, and water-sports facilities at the Maho Bay campground.

Lavender Hill Estates. P.O. Box 8306, Lavender Hill, Cruz Bay, St. John, U.S.V.I. 00831-8306. ☎ **800/562-1901** or 809/779-4647. Fax 809/776-6969. 10 condo apts. TV TEL. Winter, $235 one-bedroom apt; $295 two-bedroom apt. Off-season, $140 one-bedroom apt; $175 two-bedroom apt. $20 extra per person. DISC, MC, V.

This outfit offers some of the best condominium values on the island, with a swimming pool with lounging deck and a tropical setting. It's a short walk to the shops, markets, restaurants, and safari buses of Cruz Bay. Compared to other accommodations in the area, the rates are midway between the campgrounds and inns and the upscale properties of Virgin Grand and Caneel Bay. The units, built in 1984, overlook Cruz Bay Harbor, and each one has a spacious central living/dining area opening onto a tiled deck, along with a fully equipped kitchen and one or two bedrooms. Laundry facilities are available. Units are furnished in a modern Caribbean style.

GUEST HOUSES

Let's face it. Except for the campgrounds recommended next, the tabs at most of the establishments on St. John are far beyond the pocketbook of the average traveler. If you'll settle for just the basics, the following places are just fine.

The Cruz Inn. P.O. Box 566, Cruz Bay, St. John, U.S.V.I. 00831. ☎ **800/666-7688** in the U.S., or 809/693-8688. Fax 809/693-8590. 4 rms (2 with bath), 3 two-bedroom suites, 3 one-bedroom apt, 1 two-bedroom apt. Winter, $55 double without bath, $75 double with bath; $90 two-bedroom suite; $95 one-bedroom apt; $105 two-bedroom apt. Off-season, $50 double without bath, $65 double with bath; $75 two-bedroom suite; $85 one-bedroom apt; $95 two-bedroom apt. Rates include continental breakfast. Additional person $15 extra. Three night minimum stay in apt. AE, DISC, MC, V.

This is hardly the most refined or elegant accommodation on St. John, but it is admired by travelers who seek clean, reasonably comfortable accommodations at a fair price. Overlooking Enighed Pond, the inn is on par with Raintree Inn (see below) and is a bit rustic. Cruz Inn recently finished remodeling, and now all its rooms have a private bath. The studios and suites also have a refrigerator and are air-conditioned, while all the apartments have kitchenettes and two are also air-conditioned. Three two-bedroom suites and one of the studios are in the main building. The Papaya Suite is airy, has a wraparound deck, and sleeps up to six. Lying a few blocks from the Cruz Bay Dock, the inn has a convivial bar, a low-cost restaurant serving standard food, and an outdoor deck.

Raintree Inn. P.O. Box 566, Cruz Bay, St. John, U.S.V.I. 00831. ☎ **800/666-7449** or 809/693-8590. Fax 809/693-8590. 8 rms, 3 efficiencies. A/C TEL. Winter, $87–$92 double; $133.50 efficiency. Off-season, $70–$80 double; $111.60 efficiency. Three-day minimum stay in efficiencies. AE, DISC, MC, V.

One block from the ferry stop, next to the Catholic church, the Raintree Inn has simple no-smoking double rooms, some with high ceilings. Linen, towels, and soap are supplied upon request. The three efficiencies have full kitchens, and two twin beds are in a slightly cramped loft. A small deck is attached. The inn adjoins a reasonably priced restaurant next door, the Fish Trap (see "Where to Dine," below). Laundry service is available on the premises.

CAMPGROUNDS

Cinnamon Bay Campground. P.O. Box 720, Cruz Bay, St. John, U.S.V.I. 00831. ☎ **800/539-9998** in the U.S., or 809/776-6330. Fax 809/776-6458. 126 units, none with bath. Winter, $95–$105 cottage for 2; $75 tent site; $17 bare site. Off-season, $63–$68 cottage for 2; $48 tent site; $17 bare site (5-day minimum). Additional person $15 extra. AE, MC, V.

Established by the National Park Service in 1964, this is the most complete campground in the Caribbean, although security is minimal. The site is directly on the beach, and thousands of acres of tropical vegetation surround you. Life is simple here, and you have a choice of three different kinds of accommodations: tents, cottages, and bare sites. Bare sites must be reserved at least eight months in advance and can be secured by a credit card. At the bare campsites, nothing is provided except a picnic table and charcoal grill. The canvas tents are 10 by 14 feet. Cottages are 15 by 15 feet and consist of a room with two concrete walls and two screen walls. They contain four twin beds, and the maximum allowed in a cottage is four. Cooking facilities are also supplied. Lavatories and showers are in separate buildings nearby. Linen is changed weekly, and camping is limited to a two-week period in any given year. Near the road is a camp center office, with a grocery and a cafeteria.

✪ **Maho Bay.** P.O. Box 310, Cruz Bay, St. John, U.S.V.I. 00831. ☎ **800/392-9004,** 809/776-6226, or 212/472-9453 in New York City. Fax 809/776-6504, or 212/861-6210 in New York City. 114 tent-cottages, none with bath. Mid-Dec to Apr, $95 tent-cottage for 2 (minimum stay of 7 nights required). May to mid-Dec, $60 tent-cottage for 2 (no minimum stay). Additional occupant (regardless of age) $15 extra. MC, V.

Maho Bay is an interesting concept in ecology vacationing, where you camp close to nature, but in considerable comfort. Only problem is, the place is so popular you need to book a year in advance if you'd like to camp here in winter. Defined as a deluxe campground, it's located an 8-mile drive northeast from Cruz Bay on a hillside above the beach surrounded by the Virgin Islands National Park. To preserve the existing ground cover, all tent-cottages are on platforms above a thickly wooded slope. Utility lines and pipes are hidden under wooden boardwalks and stairs.

The tent-cottages are covered with canvas and screens. Each unit has two movable twin beds, a couch, electric lamps and outlets, a dining table, chairs, a propane stove, and an ice chest (cooler). That's not all—you're furnished with linen, towels, and cooking and eating utensils. There's a store where you can buy supplies, and you can do your own cooking or eat at the camp's outdoor restaurant. Guests share communal bathhouses. It's a great choice for families.

Maho Bay has an open-air Pavilion Restaurant, which always serves breakfast and dinner. Lunches are offered in winter, and the international dinner menu is changed nightly depending on what food is fresh. Both meat and vegetarian selections are offered. The Pavilion also functions as an amphitheater and community center where various programs are featured. The camp has an excellent water-sports program.

WHERE TO DINE

VERY EXPENSIVE

Caneel Bay Beach Terrace Dining Room. In the Caneel Bay Hotel. ☎ **809/776-6111.** Reservations required for dinner. Main courses $28–$38; Mon night grand buffet $50; lunch buffet $22. AE, DC, MC, V. Daily 11:30am–2:30pm and 7–9pm. INTERNATIONAL/SEAFOOD.

Right below the Equator (see below) is an elegant dining choice with open-air tables overlooking the beach. The self-service buffet luncheon is one of the best in the Virgin Islands. Appetizers might include papaya with prosciutto, and the salads are good as well, including a marinated green bean salad and a tossed garden greens mimosa salad. Main dishes are likely to include baked fillet of red snapper or roast prime rib of blue-ribbon beef carved to order with natural juices. For dessert, try strawberry cheesecake or Boston cream pie. Menus change nightly. Although we've found the cuisine here variable over the years, the professional standards remain high. The resort caters to palates that have been tempted by all the great restaurants of the world. It uses only first-rate, quality products, and in most cases handles them deftly.

EXPENSIVE

✪ **Asolare.** Cruz Bay. ☎ **809/779-4747.** Reservations required. Main courses $20–$29. AE, MC, V. Daily 5:30–9:30pm. FRENCH/ASIAN.

This is the most beautiful and elegant restaurant in St. John, with the hippest and best-looking staff. Set in a spot where some of the British Virgin Islands can be viewed in silhouette, Asolare sits on top of a hill overlooking Cruz Bay. It's a homey old plantation, with a big fireplace in the dining room that never sees the need to be lit. The word *Asolare* translates to "the leisurely passing of time without purpose," and that's what many diners prefer to do here. Chef Carlos Beccar Varela roams the world for inspiration, and cooks with flavor and flair, using some of the best ingredients available on the island. To get you going, try the prawn and coconut milk soup, a spicy tuna tartare wrapped in somen noodles, or, most definitely, the Peking roasted quail. Salmon is awakened from its sleep with a zesty Szechuan pepper crust, or else you may prefer the roasted rack of lamb served tantalizingly with baby bok choy. The chef's special is Asolare pat-thai, a medley of rice noodles, shrimp, chicken, and black soy beans. It's worth swimming across the channel to try the frozen mango guava soufflé or the chocolate pyramid cake with warm white chocolate ice cream hearts.

Ellington's. Gallows Point, Cruz Bay. ☎ **809/693-8490.** Reservations required only for seating upstairs. Main dishes $13–$28. AE, MC, V. Daily 4:30–10pm. CONTINENTAL.

Ellington's is set near the neocolonial villas of Gallows Point, to the right after you disembark from the ferry. Its exterior has the kind of double staircase, fan windows, louvers, and low-slung roof found in an 18th-century Danish manor house. Drop in at sunset for a drink on the panoramic upper deck where an unsurpassed view of St. Thomas and its neighboring cays unfolds. The establishment is named after a local radio announcer ("The Fat Man"), a raconteur and mystery writer whose real-estate developments helped transform St. John into a stylish enclave for the American literati of the 1950s and 1960s. Named Richard "Duke" Ellington (not to be confused with the great musician), he entertained his friends, martini in hand, around a frequently photographed table painted with a map of St. John. The tabletop today is a centerpiece at the sunset lounge.

The dinner menu changes often to accommodate the freshest offerings of the sea—sometimes it includes wahoo or mahimahi with Cajun spices. Some other favorites include conch fritters, swordfish scampi, chilled mango soup, and chicken Martinique. The South American sea bass is especially zesty. It's a romantic setting at night.

✪ **Equator.** In the Caneel Bay Hotel, Caneel Bay. ☎ **809/776-6111.** Reservations required. Main courses $12–$27. AE, MC, V. Winter, daily 6:30–10pm. Off-season, Wed–Thurs and Sun 6:30–10pm. CARIBBEAN/LATIN/THAI.

This restaurant lies behind the tower of an 18th-century sugar mill, where ponds with water lilies fill former crystallization pits for hot molasses. A flight of stairs leads to a monumental circular dining room, with a wraparound veranda and sweeping views of a park. In the center rises the stone column that horses and mules once circled to crush sugarcane stalks, and alongside it is a giant poinciana-like Asian tree of the *Albizia lebbeck* species. Islanders call it "woman's tongue tree."

The cuisine is the most daring on the island, and, for the most part, the chefs manage to pull off their transcultural offerings. The teriyaki tuna comes with a pickled lobster roll and tempura vegetables. The pepper-cured tandoori lamb with Egyptian-style couscous is another tasty winner, as is the wok-fried catfish with Polynesian ponzu and fried rice. The service could be improved, however.

Le Château de Bordeaux. Junction 10, Centerline Rd., Bordeaux Mountain. ☎ **809/776-6611.** Reservations recommended. Main courses $18–$28. MC, V. Mon–Sat with 2 nightly seatings, 5:30–6:30pm and 7:30–8:45pm. Closed Sun–Mon in summer. CONTINENTAL/CARIBBEAN.

Set 5 miles east of Cruz Bay near the geographical center of the island, and close to one of its highest points, this restaurant is known for its eastward-facing vistas and some of the best high-altitude views on St. John. A lunch grill on the patio serves burgers and drinks Monday through Saturday from 10am to 4:30pm. In the evening, amid a Victorian decor with lace tablecloths, you can begin with a house-smoked chicken spring roll, or a velvety carrot soup. After that, move on to one of the saffron-flavored pastas or a savory West Indian seafood chowder. Smoked salmon and filet mignon are a bow to the international crowd, although the wild-game specials are more unusual. The well-flavored and -seasoned roast rack of lamb is notable. There's a changing array of cheesecakes, among other desserts. The specialty drink is a passion fruit daiquiri.

✪ **Paradiso.** Mongoose Junction. ☎ **809/693-8899.** Reservations recommended. Main courses $15–$25. AE, MC, V. Thurs–Tues 6–9:30pm. (Bar, daily 5–10pm.) ITALIAN/AMERICAN.

The most talked-about restaurant on St. John, other than Asolare, and the only one that's air-conditioned, is located in the island's most interesting shopping center, Mongoose Junction. The decor includes lots of brass, glowing hardwoods, and nautical antiques. Paradiso has the most beautiful bar on the island, crafted from mahogany, purpleheart, and angelique.

The Italian food here is the best on the island, including a selection of pastas. To get you going, opt for the Caesar salad. A platter of smoked seafood is a winning selection, followed by seafood puttanesca, mussels and shrimp with tomatoes, capers, and garlic in a marinara sauce with linguini. Featured in *Bon Apétit,* chicken Picante Willie is a spicy, creamy picante sauce over crispy chicken with linguini and ratatouille. The house drink is Paradiso Punch, the bartender's version of plantation punch.

✪ **Saychelles.** 4 Cruz Bay, Wharfside Village. ☎ **809/693-7030.** Reservations recommended in winter. Main courses $15.50–$24.50. AE, DC, MC, V. Daily 6–10pm. Closed Oct 1–15. SEAFOOD/CARIBBEAN.

Evoking a Riviera bistro, this hip hangout attracts a chic international crowd in winter, likely to turn up wearing just about anything. Fortunately Chef Keith Seidner doesn't just depend on the view of the bay for inspiration. His delectable cuisine is first-rate, and he is one of the most creative chefs on island. Chefs come and go rather quickly around here, so we hope Keith will still be here when you show up. After watching the sunset, dip into the beef carpaccio, calamari salad, or tuna tartare before working up an appetite for a main dish. Make it the chef's specialty: sesame-seared tuna with wasabi and teriyaki sauce. Save room for the mango cheesecake or one of the freshly made sorbets such as papaya, guava, or lime served in a waffle basket.

MODERATE

Café Roma. Cruz Bay. ☎ **809/776-6524.** Reservations not required. Main courses $8–$17. MC, V. Daily 5–10pm. ITALIAN.

Diners climb a flight of steps to reach this restaurant in the center of Cruz Bay. You might arrive early and have a strawberry colada, then enjoy a standard pasta, veal, seafood, or chicken dish. On most evenings, there are 30 to 40 vegetarian items on the menu, much better than at most restaurants. The owner claims with good reason that his pizzas are the best on the island, praised by New Yorkers and Chicagoans who know their pizza. Ask for their white pizza, made without the red sauce. This is not a place for great finesse in the kitchen, but it's a long-standing favorite, and has pleased a lot of diners seeking casual, informal meals, not grand Italian cuisine. Paradiso (see above) is better, but then again, it's much more expensive. Italian wines are sold by the glass or bottle, and you can end the evening with an espresso.

INEXPENSIVE

The Fish Trap. In the Raintree Inn, Cruz Bay. ☎ **809/693-9994.** Reservations not accepted except for parties of 6 or more. Main courses $7.95–$22.95. AE, DISC, MC, V. Tues–Fri 11am–3pm and 4:30–9:30pm, Sat–Sun 10:30am–2:30pm and 4:30–9:30pm. SEAFOOD.

The Fish Trap attracts both locals and vacationers. It's known for its wide selection of fresh fish, but it also caters to the vegetarian and burger crowd. In the midst of coconut palms and banana trees, most diners begin with one of the night's appetizers, such as seared scallops with stir-fried vegetables, before moving on to a main course. We recently enjoyed an herb-crusted snapper with a Dijon tarragon cream sauce, and on another occasion, blackened swordfish with roasted red pepper aioli was the crowd-pleasing choice. Another good choice is the grilled escolar and shrimp with papaya and kiwi salsa. Obviously, this is not just another fish-and-chips joint.

Mongoose Restaurant and Deli. Mongoose Junction. ☎ **809/693-8677.** Reservations required during winter. Main dishes $13.95–$18.95. AE, MC, V. Daily 8am–10pm. (Bar, daily 8am–10pm.) CARIBBEAN.

Some visitors compare the soaring interior design here to a large Japanese birdcage, because of the strong vertical lines and the 25-foot ceiling. Set among trees and built above a stream, it looks like something you might find in Northern California. Some guests perch at the open-centered bar for a drink and sandwich, whereas others sit on an adjacent deck where a canopy of trees filters the sunlight. The bar offers more than 20 varieties of frothy island libations.

Lunches include soups, well-stuffed sandwiches, salad platters, burgers, and pastas. Dinner is more formal, with such specialties as grilled steaks, fresh catch of the day, and surf and turf. The fresh fish is served in different ways, including grilled and blackened. Of course, you've ordered food such as this at many other places, and probably better versions of it, but the setting, locale, long hours, and reasonable prices make this a winning choice. The Sunday brunch is mobbed with St. Johnians, who make eggs Benedict the most popular dish.

Morgan's Mango. Cruz Bay. ☎ **809/693-8141.** Reservations recommended. Main courses $6.95–$21.95. AE, MC, V. Daily 6–10pm. Bar opens at 5:30pm. CARIBBEAN.

The chefs at this restaurant across from the National Park dock roam the Caribbean for tantalizing flavors that they adapt for their dishes served here. The restaurant is easy to spot, with a big canopy that is a visible landmark and its only protection from the elements. The bar wrapping around the main dining room offers some 30 frozen drinks. Thursday is Margarita Night, when a soft rock duo plays. Although some critics claim the kitchen "overreaches" in trying to do too much with the overly ambitious menu on any given night, the Morgan's kitchen staff does emerge with some zesty flavors—everything from Anegada lobster cake to a spicy Jamaican pickapepper steak. Try flying fish served as an appetizer, followed by Haitian voodoo snapper pressed in Cajun spices, then grilled and served with fresh fruit salsa. Equally delectable is mahimahi in a Cruzan rum and mango sauce. You can also order more standard steak, chicken, and vegetarian dishes. The knockout dessert is the mango-banana pie.

Pusser's. Wharfside Village, Cruz Bay. ☎ **809/693-8489.** Reservations recommended. Main courses $9.95–$24.95. AE, DISC, MC, V. Daily 11am–3pm and 6–10pm. INTERNATIONAL/CARIBBEAN.

A double-decker, air-conditioned store and pub in Cruz Bay, Pusser's overlooks the harbor and is near the ferry dock. These stores are unique to the Caribbean, and they serve Pusser's Rum, a blend of five West Indian rums that the Royal Navy has served to its men for three centuries. You face a choice of three bars: the Beach Bar, where you can enjoy food while still in your bathing suit, the Oyster Bar (the main dining area), and the Crow's Nest. The same food is served at each bar. Here you can enjoy traditional English fare, including steak and ale. Try the jerk tuna fillet, the jerk chicken with a tomato basil sauce over penne, or the spaghetti with lobster cooked in rum, wine, lemon juice, and garlic. Caribbean lobster is the eternal favorite, or else you might be seized with island fever and order the chicken Tropical, which features coconut encrusted, pan-seared chicken served up with a rum and banana sauce with macadamia nuts. Finish your meal with Pusser's famous "mud pie." The food is satisfying, competent, and not a lot more, but after all that Pusser rum, who can judge?

✪ **Shipwreck Landing.** 34 Freeman's Ground, Rte. 107, Coral Bay. ☎ **809/693-5640.** Reservations requested. Main courses $9.75–$15.25; lunch from $10. AE, MC, V. Daily 11am–10pm. (Bar, daily 11am–11pm.) SEAFOOD/CONTINENTAL.

Eight miles east of Cruz Bay on the road to Salt Pond Beach, Shipwreck Landing is run by Pat and Dennis Rizzo. You dine amid palms and tropical plants on a veranda overlooking the sea. The intimate bar specializes in tropical frozen drinks. Lunch isn't ignored here, and there's a lot more than sandwiches, salads, and burgers—try a pan-seared blackened snapper in Cajun spices, or conch fritters to get you going. The chef shines brighter at night though, offering a pasta of the day along with such specialties as a rather tantalizing Caribbean blackened shrimp. A lot of the fare is routine, including New York strip steak and fish and chips, but the grilled mahimahi in lime butter is worth the trip. Entertainment, including jazz and reggae, is often featured in winter (but only on Friday in summer).

BEACHES, WATER SPORTS & OTHER OUTDOOR PURSUITS

Don't visit St. John expecting to play golf. Come for some of the best snorkeling, scuba diving, swimming, fishing, hiking, sailing, and underwater photography in the Caribbean. The island is known for its coral-sand beaches, winding mountain roads, hidden coves, and trails that lead past old, bush-covered sugarcane plantations.

BEACHES The best one, hands down, is ✪ **Trunk Bay,** the biggest attraction on St. John and a beach collector's find. To miss its great white sweep would be like touring Europe and skipping Paris. Trouble is, even though it's a beautiful stretch of sand, the word is out. It's likely to be overcrowded, and there are pickpockets. The beach has lifeguards and offers rentals, such as snorkel gear. Beginning snorkelers in particular are attracted to its underwater trail near the shore.

At Trunk Bay, you can take the ✪ **National Park Underwater Trail** (☎ **809/776-6201**), stretching for 650 feet, allowing you to identify what you see, everything from false coral to colonial anemones. You'll pass lavender sea fans and schools of silversides. Equipment rental costs $4, and rangers are on hand to provide information.

If you're coming from St. Thomas, both taxis and "safari buses" to Trunk Bay meet the ferry from Red Hook when it docks at Cruz Bay.

As mentioned, **Caneel Bay,** the stamping ground of the rich and famous, has seven beautiful beaches on its 170 acres. Among them is **Hawksnest Beach,** a little gem of white sand, beloved by St. Johnians. The beach is a bit narrow and windy, but beautiful, as filmmakers long ago discovered. Close to the road are barbecue grills, and there are portable toilets. Safari buses and taxis from Cruz Bay will take you along North Shore Road.

The campgrounds of **Cinnamon Bay** and **Maho Bay** (see "Where to Stay," above) have their own beaches where forest rangers sometimes have to remind visitors to put their swimming trunks back on. Snorkelers find good reefs here, and changing rooms and showers are available.

Salt Pond Bay is known to locals, but often missed by visitors. The remote bay here is tranquil and there are no facilities. The Ram Head Trail beginning here and winding for a mile leads to a panoramic belvedere overlooking the bay.

BIKING Bicycles are available for rent, at $25 per day, from the **Cinnamon Bay Watersports Center** on Cinnamon Bay Beach (☎ **809/776-6330**). Whereas St. John's steep hills and off-road trails can challenge the best of riders, cyclists in search of more moderate rides can visit the ruins at Annaberg or the beaches at Maho, Francis, Leinster, or Watermelon Bay.

BOAT CHARTERS You can take half- and full-day boat charters, including trips to the Baths at Virgin Gorda on Tuesday. The cost of this full-day adventure is $80 per person. On Wednesday and Friday an "Around St. John Snorkel Excursion" costs $40 per person, and a sunset cocktail cruise also goes for $50 per person. Call **Vacation Vistas and Motor Yachts** (☎ **809/776-6462** or 809/771-3996) for more details.

HIKING St. John's U.S. National Park is laced with a wide choice of clearly marked **walking paths.** At least 20 of these originate from North Shore Road (Route 20) or from the island's main east-west artery, Centerline Road (Route 10). Each is marked at its starting point with a pre-planned itinerary; the walks last 10 minutes to 2 hours.

Another series of **hikes** traversing the more arid eastern section of St. John originate at clearly marked points along the island's southeastern tip, off Route 107. Many of the trails wind through the grounds of 18th-century plantations, often past ruined schoolhouses, rum distilleries, molasses factories, and Great Houses, many of which are covered with lush, encroaching vines and trees.

Because of the island's semiwild state, with terrain ranging from arid and dry (in the east) to moist and semitropical (in the northwest), many hikers and trekkers consider a visit here among the most rewarding in the Virgin Islands. The island boasts more than 800 species of plants, 160 species of birds, and more than 20 hiking trails maintained in fine form by the island's crew of park rangers.

Maps of the island's hiking trails are available from the national park headquarters at Cruz Bay, but one of our favorite tours requires only about a half-mile stroll (about 30 minutes, round-trip, not including stops to admire the views) and departs from clearly marked points along the island's north coast, near the junction of routes 10 and 20. Identified by the National Park Service as Trail no. 10, the **Annaberg Historic Trail** is a self-guided tour that includes the partially restored ruins of a manor house built during the 1700s and overlooking the island's north coast. Signs along the way give historical and botanical data.

If you want to prolong your hiking experience, the **Leinster Bay Trail** (Trail no. 11) begins near the point where Trail no. 10 ends. Following the edge of Watermelon Bay, it leads past mangrove swamps and coral inlets rich with plant and marine life, often with markers identifying some of the plants and animals.

The **National Park Service** (☎ **809/776-6330** or 809/776-6201) provides a number of free, ranger-led activities in the park. One of the most popular is the 2½-mile Reef Bay hike. A park ranger leads the hike down the Reef Bay Trail interpreting the natural and cultural history along the way. Included is a stop at the only known petroglyphs on the island and a tour of the sugar mill ruins. Reservations are required for this hike and can be made by phone. Visitors are encouraged to stop by the Cruz Bay Visitor Center where you can pick up the park brochure, which includes a map of the park, and the *Virgin Islands National Park News,* which has the latest information on activities in the park.

TENNIS **Caneel Bay** (☎ **809/776-6111**) has 11 courts and a pro shop, but these courts aren't lit at night and are used exclusively by guests. There are two public courts at Cruz Bay, however.

WATER SPORTS GALORE The most complete line of water sports available on St. John is offered at the **Cinnamon Bay Watersports Center** on Cinnamon Bay Beach (☎ **809/776-6330**). For the adventurous, there's windsurfing, kayaking, and sailing.

The windsurfing here is some of the best anywhere, for either the beginner or the expert. High-quality equipment is available for all levels, even for kids. You can rent a board for $15 an hour; a two-hour introductory lesson costs $40.

Want to paddle to a secluded beach, explore a nearby island with an old Danish ruin, or jump overboard anytime you like for snorkeling or splashing? Then try a sit-on-top kayak; one- and two-person kayaks are available for rent for $10 to $17 per hour.

You can also sail away in a 12- or 14-foot Hobie monohull sailboat, which can be rented for $20 to $30 per hour.

Snorkeling equipment can be rented from the Watersports Beach Shop for $7.

Divers can ask about scuba packages at **Low Key Watersports,** Wharfside Village (☎ **800/835-7718** or 809/693-8999). All wreck dives are two-tank/two-location dives. A one-tank dive costs $55 per person, with night dives going for $65. Snorkel tours are also available at $25 per person, and parasailing is available at $50. The center uses its own custom-built dive boats and also offers and specializes in water-sports gear, including masks, fins, snorkels, and "dive skins." It also arranges day sailing charters, kayaking tours, and deep-sea sport fishing.

Cruz Bay Watersports, P.O. Box 252, Palm Plaza, St. John, U.S.V.I. 00831 (☎ **800/835-7730** or 809/776-6234), is a PADI and NAUI five-star diving center on St. John. Certifications can be arranged through a dive master, for $225 to $350. Certification classes start daily, as well as two-tank reef dives with all the dive gear for $70 to $78. Beginner scuba lessons start at $68, and wreck dives (Wednesday and Friday), night dives, and dive packages are available at accommodations that range from budget to first class. Snorkel tours are available daily as well as trips to the British Virgin Islands (bring your passport).

SEEING THE SIGHTS

The best way to see St. John in a nutshell, and rather quickly, especially if you're on a cruise-ship layover, is to take a 2-hour taxi tour. The cost is $30 for one or two passengers, or $12 per person for three or more riders. Almost any taxi at Cruz Bay will take you on these tours, or else you can call **Virgin Island Taxi** (☎ **809/774-4550**). For complaints, problems, or information, you can also call the **Taxi Commission** (☎ **809/776-8294**).

Many visitors like to spend a lot of time at **Cruz Bay,** where the ferry docks. In this West Indian village there are interesting bars, restaurants, boutiques, and pastel-painted houses. It's pretty sleepy, but it's relaxing after the fast pace of St. Thomas. The **Elaine Ione Sprauve Museum** (☎ **809/776-6359**) at Cruz Bay isn't big, but it does contain some local artifacts. It's at the public library and can be visited Monday to Friday from 9am to 5pm; admission is free.

Most cruise-ship passengers dart through Cruz Bay and head for the island's biggest attraction, the **Virgin Islands National Park** (☎ **809/776-6201**). See "Beaches, Water Sports & Other Outdoor Activities," above, for information on organized park activities. Established in 1956, the park totals 12,624 acres, including submerged lands and water adjacent to St. John. The park has more than 20 miles of biking trails to explore.

If time is limited, try to visit the **Annaberg Ruins** on Leinster Bay Road, where the Danes maintained a thriving plantation and sugar mill after 1718. It's located off North Shore Road east of Trunk Bay on the north shore. On certain days of the week (dates vary) guided walks of the area are given by park rangers.

Trunk Bay is one of the world's most beautiful beaches. It's also the site of one of the world's first marked underwater trails (bring your mask, snorkel, and fins). It lies to the east of Cruz Bay along North Shore Road. The beach can get crowded, so beware of pickpockets.

Fort Berg (also called Fortsberg), at Coral Bay, dating from 1717, played a disastrous role during the 1733 slave revolt—it served as the base for soldiers who brutally crushed the rebellion.

SHOPPING

Compared to St. Thomas, St. John's shopping isn't much, but what's here is intriguing. The boutiques and shops of Cruz Bay are individualized and quite special. Most of the shops are clustered at **Mongoose Junction,** in a woodsy area beside the roadway, about a five-minute walk from the ferry dock. We've already recommended restaurants in this complex (see "Where to Dine," above), and it also contains shops of merit.

Before you set sail for St. Thomas, you'll want to visit **Wharfside Village,** just a few steps from the ferry-departure point on the waterfront, opening onto Cruz Bay. Here in this complex of courtyards, alleys, and shady patios is a mishmash of all sorts of boutiques, along with some restaurants, fast-food joints, and bars.

Bamboula. Mongoose Junction. ☎ **809/693-8699.**

Bamboula has an unusual and very appealing collection of gifts from the Caribbean, Haiti, India, Indonesia, and Central Africa. Its exoticism is unexpected and very pleasant. The store has added clothing for both men and women under its own label—hand-batiked soft cottons and rayons made for comfort in a hot climate. Many locally crafted items, ideal as gifts, are also sold.

The Canvas Factory. Mongoose Junction. ☎ **809/776-6196.**

The Canvas Factory produces its own handmade, rugged, and colorful canvas bags in the "factory" at Mongoose Junction. Their products range from sailing hats to soft-sided luggage to cotton hats.

The Clothing Studio. Mongoose Junction. ☎ **809/776-6585.**

The Caribbean's oldest hand-painted clothing studio has been in operation since 1978. You can watch talented artists create original designs on fine tropical clothing, including swimwear, and daytime and evening clothing, mainly for babies and women, with a few items for men.

Coconut Coast Studios. Frank Bay. ☎ **809/776-6944.**

A five-minute stroll from the heart of Cruz Bay (follow along the waterfront bypassing Gallows Point) will lead you to the studios of Elaine Estern and Lucinda Schutt. One of the best watercolorists on the island, Elaine is especially known for her Caribbean landscapes, and is the official artist for Westin Resorts, St. John. Lucinda is the artist for Caneel Bay. Note cards begin at $8, with unmatted prints costing $15 to $275.

Donald Schnell Studio. Mongoose Junction. ☎ **809/776-6420.**

In this working studio and gallery, Mr. Schnell and his assistants have created one of the finest collections of handmade pottery, sculpture, and blown glass in the Caribbean. The staff can be seen working daily and are especially noted for their rough-textured coral work. Water fountains are a specialty item, as are house signs. The coral-pottery dinnerware is unique and popular. The studio will mail works all over the world. Go in and discuss any particular design you may have in mind.

Fabric Mill. Mongoose Junction. ☎ **809/776-6194.**

This shop features silk-screened and batik fabrics from around the world. Vibrant rugs and bed, bath, and table linens add the perfect touch to your home if you like a Caribbean flair. Whimsical soft sculpture, sarongs, scarves, and handbags are also made in this studio shop.

Pusser's of the West Indies. Wharfside Village, Cruz Bay. ☎ **809/693-8489.**
This link in a famous chain was previously recommended for food and drink. The store offers a large collection of classically designed old-world travel and adventure clothing along with unusual accessories. It's a unique shopping trip for the island. Clothing for women, men, and children is displayed, along with T-shirts emblazoned with the Pusser's emblem.

R and I Patton Goldsmithing. Mongoose Junction. ☎ **809/776-6548.**
On the island since 1973, this is one of the oldest tourist businesses here, and three-quarters of its merchandise is made on St. John. It has a large selection of island-designed jewelry in sterling silver, gold, and precious stones. Also featured are the works of goldsmiths from outstanding American studios, plus Spanish coins.

ST. JOHN AFTER DARK

Bring a good book. St. John is not St. Thomas after dark, and everybody here seems to want to keep it that way. Most people are content to have a long leisurely dinner and then head for bed.

Among the popular bars of Cruz Bay, **Pusser's** (see above) at Wharfside Village has the most convivial atmosphere. The **Caneel Bay Bar,** at the Caneel bay resort (☎ **809/776-6111**), presents live music nightly from 8:30 to 11pm. The most popular drinks include a Cool Caneel (local rum with sugar, lime, and anisette) and the trademark of the house, a Plantation Freeze (lime and orange juice with three different kinds of rum, bitters, and nutmeg).

All of the places recommended above are very touristy. If you'd like to go where the locals go for drinking and gossiping, try **JJ's Texas Coast Café,** Cruz Bay (☎ **809/776-6908**), a real local dive lying across the park from the ferry dock. Your Texan host, JJ Gewels, makes everybody feel welcome—at least if he likes you. The Tex-Mex food here is the island's best, and the margaritas are called lethal, and deservedly so!

Another Cruz Bay hot spot is **Bad Art Bar** (☎ **809/693-8666**), which is aptly named. You'll agree that whoever selected this funky art had no taste at all, unless you're the type to go for a velvet Elvis (several locals claim to have spotted him on St. John, especially when they've had one drink too many). Find yourself a Day-Glo table and devour one of the frozen drink specials, especially the "Witches Tit" and "Busted Nut." Live entertainment is presented two nights a week, and if you go between 6 and 8pm daily you can order two-for-one frozen drink specials. The location is above the Purple Door Restaurant.

Also at Cruz Bay, check out the action at **Fred's** (☎ **809/776-6363**), which brings in island bands on Wednesday, Friday, and Sunday nights. The most laid-back bar on the island, it's also the best place to go to dance, at least on those nights. It's just a little hole-in-the-wall and can get crowded fast. The location is across from The Lime Inn.

The best sports bar on the island is **Skinny Legs,** Emmaus, Coral Bay, beyond the fire station (☎ **809/779-4892**). It's only a shack made out of tin and wood, but it serves the best hamburgers in St. John. The chili dogs aren't bad either. The yachting crowd likes to hang out here, and it often seems like the richer they are, the poorer they dress—many of them look as if they're refugees, although in fact they're disembarking from $1.5 million yachts. The bar has a satellite dish to televise major sporting events. Live music is presented at least once a week; otherwise it's the dartboard or horseshoe pits for you.

As a final option, check out **Sea Breeze,** 4F Little Plantation, Coral Bay on Salt Pond Road (☎ **809/693-5824**), where you can not only drink and enjoy live entertainment, but can order three meals a day. Each night a different chef demonstrates his/her specialties. The Sunday brunch is an island highlight. A local dive and popular hangout, this place is very laid-back. Try the barbecued beef sandwich, the best on the island.

3 St. Croix

Even though seven different flags have flown over St. Croix, it's the nearly 2½ centuries of Danish influence that still permeates the island and its architecture.

At the east end of St. Croix, which, incidentally, is the easternmost point of the United States, the terrain is rocky and arid. The west end is lusher, with a rain forest of mango and mahogany, tree ferns, and dangling lianas. Rolling hills and upland pastures characterize the area lying between the two extremes. African tulips are just one of the species of flowers that add a splash of color to the landscape, which is dotted with stately towers that once supported grinding mills. The island is 84 square miles.

St. Croix has some of the best beaches in the Virgin Islands, and ideal weather. It doesn't have the nightlife of St. Thomas, nor would its permanent residents want that.

See "Getting There" at the beginning of the chapter for details on flights to St. Croix.

GETTING AROUND

BY TAXI At Alexander Hamilton Airport you'll find official taxi rates posted. Per person rates require a minimum of two passengers; a single person pays double the posted fares. Expect to pay about $10 for one or two riders from the airport to Christiansted and about $8.50 for one or two from the airport to Frederiksted. As the cabs are unmetered, agree on the rate before you get in.

The **St. Croix Taxicab Association** (☎ **809/778-1088**) offers door-to-door service.

BY BUS Air-conditioned buses run between Christiansted and Frederiksted about every 30 minutes daily between the hours of 5:30am and 9pm. Beginning at Tide Village, to the east of Christiansted, buses go along Route 75 to the Golden Rock Shopping Center. Then they make their way to Route 70, with stopovers at the Sunny Isle Shopping Center, La Reine Shopping Center, St. George Village Botanical Garden, and Whim Plantation Museum, before reaching Frederiksted. Bus service is also available from the airport to each of the two towns. Fares are $1 or 55¢ for senior citizens. For more information, call ☎ **809/773-7746.**

BY RENTAL CAR Okay, we've warned you: The roads are often disastrous. Sometimes the government smoothes them out before the big season begins, but don't count on it.

Car-rental rates on St. Croix are reasonable. However, because of the island's higher than usual accident rate (which is partly because many tourists aren't used to driving on the left), insurance costs are higher than on the mainland.

Budget (☎ **800/626-4516** or 809/778-9636), **Hertz** (☎ **800/654-3001** or 809/778-1402), and **Avis** (☎ **800/331-2112**) all maintain their headquarters at the island's airport, with kiosks near the baggage-claim areas.

Reminder: Driving is on the left.

2-0178
0
3 mi
5.1 km
N
Legend
Beach
Golf
Diving
Hiking
Buck Island
Green Cay
Salt R. Bay
Cane Bay
Hams Bluff
Davis Bay
Northside
Butler Bay
Sprat Hole
Scenic Road
Mahogany Road
North Shore Road
River Road
Canaan Road
Peppertree Road
Rattan Road
Sion Hill Road
Fredensborg
Bethlehem
Kingshill
FREDERIKSTED
Centerline Road
Alexander Hamilton Airport
Manning Bay
Limetree Bay
Longford
Long Pt.
Sandy Pt.
Christiansted Harbor
Protestant Cay
Gallows Bay
Cheney Basy
CHRISTIANSTED
(see inset)
Lowry Hills Road
7 Hills Road
East End Road
Southgate
Teague Bay
Cottongarden Pt.
Point Udall
Turners Hole
South Shore Road
Grass Pt.
Great Pond Bay
CARIBBEAN SEA
CHRISTIANSTED
Christiansted Harbor
Wharf
Caravelle Arcade
Pan Am Pavilion
Comanche Walk
King's Alley
Strand Street (Strandgade)
(Kongens Gade)
King Street
King Cross Street (Kongens Tvaergade)
Cross Street (Dronningens Tvaergade)
Company Street
Queen Street
(Compagnietsgade)
Church Street (Kirkegade)
Hospital Street (Hospitalgade)
(Dronningens Gade)
Hill Street
Anchor Inn 16
Buccaneer 11
Cane Bay Reef Club 4
Caravelle 15
Chenay Bay Beach Resort 12
Colony Cove 8
Cormorant Beach Club 5
Danish Manor Hotel 18
The Frederiksted 1
Hibiscus Beach Hotel 6
Hilty House 7
Hotel on the Cay 10
King Christian Hotel 17
Pink Fancy 14
Sugar Beach Condominiums 9
Villa Madeleine 13
The Waves at Cane Bay 3
Westin Carambola Beach Resort 2

BY BIKE **St. Croix Bike and Tours,** 5035 Cotton Valley, Christiansted (☎ **809/773-5004**), offers bike rentals and guided bicycle tours. The outfitter rents 21-speed mountain bikes, which are suitable for the rugged terrain of St. Croix. In addition to these rentals, they feature two tours of varying ability levels, including a Rainforest Mountain Bike Tour for the experienced rider, covering 14 to 18 miles of tropical forests and scenic hillsides. The less strenuous Coastal Bike Tour is centered around the island's natural beauty. Call for more information.

ESSENTIALS

The **American Express** representative is Southerland, Chandler's Wharf, Gallows Bay (☎ **800/260-2682** or 809/773-9500). For medical care, try the **St. Croix Hospital,** 6 Diamond Bay, Christiansted (☎ **809/778-6311**).

WHERE TO STAY

All rooms are subject to an 8% hotel room tax, which is *not* included in the rates given below.

If you're interested in a villa or condo rental, contact **Island Villas,** Property Management Rentals, 6 Company St., Christiansted, St. Croix, U.S.V.I. 00820 (☎ **800/626-4512** or 809/773-8821; fax 809/773-8823), which offers some of the best properties on St. Croix. The outfit specializes in villa and condo rentals, really private residences with pools; many are on the beach. The range goes from one-bedroom units to six-bedroom villas, with prices of $1,200 to $5,500 per week.

VERY EXPENSIVE

✪ **Buccaneer.** Rte. 82 (P.O. Box 25200), Gallows Bay, St. Croix, U.S.V.I. 00824. ☎ **800/255-3881** in the U.S., or 809/773-2100. Fax 809/778-8215. 150 rms. A/C TEL. Winter, $210–$575 double. Off-season, $170–$240 double. Rates include continental breakfast. AE, DC, DISC, MC, V.

A large, luxurious, family-owned resort in operation since 1948, the Buccaneer is 2 miles east of Christiansted. Its 240 acres contain three of the island's best beaches, and it offers the best sports program on St. Croix. The property was once a cattle ranch and a sugar plantation, and its first estate house, dating from the mid–17th century, stands near a freshwater swimming pool. Pink and patrician, the hotel offers a choice of accommodations in its main building or in one of the beachside properties. The baronially arched main building has a lobby opening on drinking or viewing terraces, with a sea vista on two sides and Christiansted to the west. The accommodations effectively use tropical furnishings to provide fresh, comfortable bedrooms, which range from standard to deluxe (some of the standard rooms are a bit small).

Dining/Entertainment: Breakfast and dinner are served at the Terrace Dining Room and at the Little Mermaid Restaurant. Lunch is also served at the Mermaid and the Grotto. Dino's, long a popular St. Croix institution, has also opened here. There is entertainment nightly at the Terrace Lounge, with a variety of music ranging from jazz to island steel drums.

Services: Trips to Buck Island can be arranged.

Facilities: Swimming pool, eight championship tennis courts, fitness center and health spa, 18-hole golf course, 2-mile jogging trail.

Cormorant Beach Club. 4126 La Grande Princesse, St. Croix, U.S.V.I. 00820. ☎ **800/548-4460** or 809/778-8920. Fax 809/778-9218. 34 rms, 4 suites. A/C TEL. Winter, $210–$230 double; $250–$265 triple; $295 suite. Off-season, $140–$190 double; $165–$230 triple; $300 suite. Dive, golf, honeymoon packages available. AE, DC, DISC, MC, V.

On a 12-acre site about 3 miles northwest of Christiansted on Route 75, this resort strikes a perfect balance between seclusion and accessibility. Long Reef, one of the better-known zoological phenomena of the Caribbean, lies a few hundred feet from the hotel's sandy beachfront. The hotel's social life revolves around a wood-sheathed, high-ceilinged clubhouse, whose walls were removed to give guests a firsthand taste of the salty air. Off the central core are a library, the largest freshwater pool on St. Croix, and an airy dining room that had to be rebuilt in the wake of Hurricane Marilyn.

The rooms are located in well-maintained outbuildings. Each contains a spacious bath, a tasteful decor of cane and wicker furniture, and bouquets of seasonal flowers. In winter, children under 5 are politely discouraged.

Dining/Entertainment: You can stay here on the Cormorant Beach Club (CBC) meal plan including breakfast, complete lunch, and all drinks until 5pm for only $37.50 per person per day. The All-Inclusive Plan (AIP) adds to the CBC plan an open dinner menu and all beverages until closing for $77.50 per person per day. Thursday night is Caribbean Grill Night with a buffet and entertainment, and the Sunday brunch is well attended.

Services: Laundry; arrangements for golf, horseback riding, sailing, and scuba diving.

Facilities: Freshwater swimming pool, two tennis courts, snorkeling, dive shop, croquet, library just off the lobby.

Villa Madeleine. Teague Bay (P.O. Box 3109), St. Croix, U.S.V.I. 00822. ☎ **800/548-4461** or 809/778-7377. Fax 809/773-7518. 43 villas. A/C TV TEL. Winter, $425 two-bedroom villa. Off-season, $300 two-bedroom villa. AE, DC, DISC, MC, V.

Eight miles east of Christiansted, Villa Madeleine was built in 1990 on 6½ acres and remains the island's poshest property. It's very independent of everything else on St. Croix. People arrive here and aren't heard from again until they show up at the airport to leave. Many of the well-heeled occupants are living here full time as retirees. The focal point is the Great House, whose Chippendale balconies and proportions emulate the Danish colonial era. Inside, a splendidly conceived decor incorporates masses of English chintz and mahogany paneling, like something you'd find in *Architectural Digest.*

The hotel rents two-bedroom villas, each with its own privacy wall and plunge pool. Decorated with style, each unit has a four-poster bed, marble bathroom, and kitchen. The villas comprising the resort are individually owned, and different management companies handle some of them. Service and standards, it should be noted, can vary greatly depending on the villa you're assigned. Therefore, don't expect the standards and service of a typical Caribbean luxury resort. Beach-lovers willingly travel the third of a mile to the nearest beaches, Reef and Grapevine. Parents are discouraged from bringing children 11 and under.

Dining/Entertainment: On the premises is the Café Madeleine, a continental restaurant, with a piano bar and nautical accessories. No breakfast is served. A second restaurant, The Turf Club, is a New York–style steak house decorated with horse-racing memorabilia. The Turf allows any kind of tobacco smoking, including cigars.

Services: Concierge, laundry, maid service every three days, baby-sitting (with advance notice).

Facilities: Small library with writing tables, games room for cards and billiards, laundry room; tennis courts, golf course below the property, good beach five minutes away.

Westin Carambola Beach Resort. P.O. Box 3031, Kingshill, St. Croix, U.S.V.I. 00851. ☎ **800/WESTIN-1** in the U.S. and Canada, or 809/778-3800. Fax 809/778-1682. 150 rms, 1 suite.A/C MINIBAR TV TEL. Winter, $245–$330 double; $540 suite. Off-season, $165–$250 double; $380 suite. AE, CB, DC, DISC, MC, V.

Set on 28 acres above Davis Bay, on the island's sparsely populated north shore, a 30-minute drive from Christiansted, this hotel reopened in 1993 after renovations and an ill-fated three-year closing. It had originally opened with much fanfare in 1987, but was closed by Hurricane Hugo in 1989 and later damaged by the hurricanes of 1995. Today it's owned by the Kentucky-based Sargasso Corporation and has been operated since 1995 as a Westin. The island's only chain hotel, and one of the largest hostelries on St. Croix, it's adjacent to an outstanding golf course designed by Robert Trent Jones Sr.

Guests are housed in red-roofed, two-story outbuildings, each of which contains six units. The accommodations are furnished in rattan and wicker, with pastel colors, each has a balcony partially concealed from outside view, overlooking either the garden or sea.

Dining/Entertainment: Diners face a trio of choices, and the dining rooms are open to nonresidents. The Saman Room offers breakfast and lunch daily, with dinner served either here or at the Mahogany Room. Sandwiches and salads are offered daily in the New York Deli. The hotel's Sunday brunch is already becoming an island tradition. Friday night is a pirate's buffet.

Services: 24-hour room service, baby-sitting, concierge who can arrange tours, car rentals.

Facilities: A large swimming pool, four hard-court tennis courts, 18-hole golf course.

MOD ERATE

Anchor Inn. 58 King St., Christiansted, St. Croix, U.S.V.I. 00820. ☎ **800/524-2030** in the U.S., or 809/773-4000. Fax 809/773-4408. 30 rms. A/C MINIBAR TV TEL. Winter, $115–$145 double; $135–$165 triple. Off-season, $90–$105 double; $110–$125 triple. Additional person $20 extra. Scuba packages available. AE, DC, DISC, MC, V.

One of the few hotels in town directly on the waterfront, the Anchor Inn is set in a courtyard near Government House, in the heart of the national historic district and shopping belt. The space is so compact and intimate that you might not believe it holds 30 comfortably furnished, though somewhat drab, rooms, each with refrigerator, radio, bath, and a small porch. A few rooms (without porches) have king- and queen-size beds and dressing rooms.

Directly on the waterfront is a sundeck and small swimming pool, as well as the Anchor Inn's own boardwalk, where catamarans and glass-bottom boats embark on daily cruises to Buck Island. There are also deep-sea-fishing boats, a scuba-dive shop, and honeymoon and family package tours are available. Dining is at Antoine's, on the harbor (see "Where to Dine," below). To reach the nearest beach, you can take a $3 round-trip ferry ride across the harbor.

Hibiscus Beach Hotel. 4131 La Grande Princesse, St. Croix, U.S.V.I. 00820. ☎ **800/442-0121** or 809/773-4042. Fax 809/773-7668. 36 rms, 1 two-bedroom efficiency. A/C MINIBAR TV TEL. Winter, $180–$190 double; $290 efficiency. Off-season, $130–$140 double; $220 efficiency. Honeymoon, dive, and golf packages available. AE, DISC, MC, V.

On one of the island's best beaches—lined with palm trees, next to the Cormorant—this is one of the most appealing properties to have opened in the mid-1990s. Its rates are also comfortably affordable, and the hotel has attracted a lively clientele. Each of its beachfront rooms is complete with patios or balconies, and ceiling fans aid the air-conditioning. Furnishings are in the standard Caribbean motel style. Other amenities include an in-room safe and fresh flowers every day. Located 10 minutes from Christiansted, the hotel also has a seaside swimming pool and a beachfront restaurant and bar, which offers good value theme buffets. Complimentary snorkeling equipment is provided.

Hilty House. P.O. Box 26077, Questa Verde Rd., Gallows Bay, St. Croix, U.S.V.I. 00824. ☎ and fax **809/773-2594.** 4 rms, 2 cottages. Winter, $110 double; $115–$135 cottage. Off-season, $95 double; $100–$110 cottage. Rates for regular rooms include continental breakfast. Honeymoon packages available. No credit cards.

Jacquie and Hugh Hoare-Ward own and manage this bed-and-breakfast in a 200-year-old building that was once a rum distillery. Hilty House is located on the east side of St. Croix atop a hill off Queste Verde Road, above Christiansted, surrounded by mountains and hills. The airport, 7 miles away, is a 15-minute drive; the nearest beach is at Christiansted, a 10-minute drive. Upon their arrival, guests pass through a shaded courtyard to a set of iron gates that lead through the inn's gardens to the main house.

The plantation-style house is beautifully appointed with hand-painted Italian tiles throughout. The interior has a high-ceilinged living room and an enormous fireplace that houses a spit. The bedrooms are individually decorated, and some even have chandeliers. There are also two self-catering cottages that can be rented with a required minimum stay of three nights. The Danish Kitchen, one of the cottages, has an enclosed porch, TV, and telephone.

Dinner, a buffet meal with a set price of $25, is only served on Monday night. Guests can swim in the large pool decorated with hand-painted tiles. The atmosphere is very homey, and the place gives off a warm feeling. Children 11 and under are not permitted, and no more than two people can stay in each room.

Hotel on the Cay. Protestant Cay, Christiansted, St. Croix, U.S.V.I. 00820. ☎ **800/524-2035** or 809/773-2035. Fax 809/773-7046. 52 rms, 3 suites. A/C TV TEL. Winter, $160 double; $190 suite. Off-season, $105 double; $135 suite. Additional person $25 extra. AE, DC, MC, V.

With its buff-colored stucco, archways, and terra-cotta tiles, this rather sterile looking hotel evokes Puerto Rico or the Dominican Republic, and is the most prominent building on a three-acre island in the middle of Christiansted's harbor. Reaching it requires a four-minute boat ride from a well-marked quay in the town center. (Hotel guests ride free; nonguests pay a $3 ferryboat charge, round-trip.) Its position in the clear waters of the harbor is both its main allure and its main drawback: Its wide sandy beaches provide the only pollution-free swimming in the town center, but it's the first hotel to be wiped off the map whenever a hurricane strikes. In theory, this place should be a lavishly landscaped, upscale retreat; unfortunately, what you'll find doesn't quite meet those high expectations. But despite some drawbacks, it provides simple, unfrilly, and clean accommodations near the beach. Someone is always working on upgrading the landscaping around this place, even though the hotel has suffered for many years from setbacks and a series of fiscal downturns.

Dining/Entertainment: Breakfast, lunch, and tropical drinks are served daily from 7am to 5pm beneath a shed-style restaurant, the Harbormaster. The only dinner ever served is on Tuesday night, from 7 to 10:30pm, when the place is the most crowded in town, thanks to the beach barbecue, steel band, and "Moko Jumbi" floor show, priced at $23.50 per person.

✪ **King Christian Hotel.** 59 King's Wharf (P.O. Box 3619), Christiansted, St. Croix, U.S.V.I. 00822. ☎ **800/524-2012** in the U.S., or 809/773-2285. Fax 809/773-9411. 39 rms. A/C TV TEL. Winter, $100 economy double, $140 superior double. Off-season, $85 economy double, $107 superior double. AE, DC, DISC, MC, V.

This three-story hotel is right in the heart of everything, directly on the waterfront. Before its transformation into a hotel in the early 1960s, it had been a warehouse for 300 years. It was recently restored, and all its front rooms have two double beds, a bathroom, cable color TV, refrigerator, room safe, and private balcony overlooking the harbor, and they're among the largest in town. The no-frills economy-wing rooms have a bath and two single beds or one double bed, but no view or balcony. Still, it's one of the best values in town.

You can relax on the sundeck or shaded patio, or in the freshwater pool. The staff will make arrangements for golf, tennis, horseback riding, and sightseeing tours, and there's a beach just a few hundred yards across the harbor, reached by ferry. Mile Mark Charters water-sports center offers daily trips to Buck Island's famous snorkeling trail as well as a complete line of water sports. You can park in a public lot off King Street.

Pink Fancy. 27 Prince St., Christiansted, St. Croix, U.S.V.I. 00820. ☎ **800/524-2045** in the U.S., or 809/773-8460. Fax 809/773-6448. 13 rms. A/C TV TEL. Winter, $75–$120 double. Off-season, $65–$90 double. Extra person $15. Rates include continental breakfast. Children 11 and under stay free in parents' room. AE, MC, V.

This small, unique private hotel is located one block from the Annapolis Sailing School. The oldest part of the four-building complex is a 1780 Danish town house, now one of St. Croix's historic landmarks. Years ago the building was a private club for wealthy planters. Fame came when Jane Gottlieb, the Ziegfeld Follies star, opened it as a hotel in 1948. In the 1950s the hotel became a mecca for writers and artists, including, among others, Noël Coward. The spacious efficiency rooms, with ceiling fans, are in four buildings clustered around the swimming pool. The bigger rooms contain a kitchenette with a two-burner stove and refrigerator. Other than the complimentary breakfast, you're on your own for meals.

INEXPENSIVE

✪ **Danish Manor Hotel.** 2 Company St., Christiansted, St. Croix, U.S.V.I. 00820. ☎ **800/524-2609** in the U.S., or 809/773-1377. Fax 809/773-1913. 34 rms, 2 suites. A/C TV. Winter, $69–$115 double; $115–$150 suite. Off-season, $59–$89 double; $89–$110 suite. Rates include continental breakfast. AE, DC, DISC, MC, V.

This is the best of the inexpensive hotels in the heart of Christiansted, painted in vivid shades of pink, blue, and violet, with hand-painted tropical friezes around the postage stamp swimming pool, plus art and mementos strewn about the courtyard bar. The only drawback is that there's no view of the sea from most rooms. However, some rooms on the top (third) floor overlook the sands of Protestant Cay. An L-shaped three-story addition stands in the rear, with spacious but sterile rooms with air-conditioning, ceiling fans, and cable TV with HBO. The entrance to the courtyard is through old arches. You can park in a public lot off King Street. The hotel has a courtyard for guests where cool drinks and wine coolers are available, and the popular Italian/seafood restaurant, Tutto Bene (see "Where to Dine," below), fronts the hotel. Guests can swim at the beach in Christiansted Harbor, about a five-minute ferry ride from the hotel.

The Frederiksted. 20 Strand St., Frederiksted, St. Croix, U.S.V.I. 00840. ☎ **800/595-9519** in the U.S., or 809/772-0500. Fax 809/772-0500. 40 rms. A/C TV TEL. Winter, $95–$105 double. Off-season, $85–$95 double. AE, DC, DISC, MC, V.

For those who'd like to stay in the "second city" of St. Croix, historic Frederiksted, this contemporary four-story inn is the answer. The location is about a 10-minute ride from the airport in the center of Frederiksted. Much of the activity takes place in the outdoor tiled courtyard, where guests enjoy drinks and listen to live music on Friday and Saturday nights. There's also a small swimming pool here. The average-size bedrooms, a bit tattered, are done in a tropical motif of pastels and are equipped with small refrigerators for drinks as well as a wet bar. The best (and most expensive) bedrooms are those with an ocean view, even though they're subject to street noise. A full breakfast is served at the poolside patio, and the bar is popular in the evening, as guests order rum punches. The nearest beach is Dorch Beach, a 1-mile walk along the water from the hotel or a 5-minute drive.

CONDOS

In general, condominiums are rented at half or a third of the going hotel rates, and if you wait until after April 15, prices are lowered even more.

Cane Bay Reef Club. P.O. Box 1407, Kingshill, St. Croix, U.S.V.I. 00851. ☎ **800/253-8534** in the U.S., or 809/778-2966. Fax 809/778-2966. 7 suites. A/C. Winter, $140–$180 suite for 1 or 2. Off-season, $95–$115 suite for 1 or 2. Additional person $15 extra. MC, V.

This is one of the little gems of the island, offering large suites, each with a living room, a full kitchen, a bedroom, a bath, and a balcony overlooking the water. The decor is breezily tropical, with cathedral ceilings, overhead fans, and Chilean tiles. The location is on the north shore of St. Croix, about a 20-minute taxi ride from Christiansted, fronting the rocky Cane Bay Beach near the Waves at Cane Bay (see below). Guests enjoy the pool, and local rum drinks are served at the patio bar.

Chenay Bay Beach Resort. Rte. 82, East End Rd. (P.O. Box 24600), St. Croix, U.S.V.I. 00824. ☎ **800/548-4457** in the U.S., or 809/773-2918. Fax 809/773-2918. 50 cottages. A/C TV TEL. Winter, $195–$240 cottage for 1 or 2. Off-season, $140–$175 cottage for 1 or 2. Additional person $25 extra; children under 18 stay free. $65 per person extra for all meals, drinks, and water sports. AE, MC, V.

With a quiet and barefoot-casual ambience, these West Indian–style cottages, new or newly renovated, are nestled on a 30-acre beach, with an open-air swimming pool. With one of the island's finest beaches for swimming, snorkeling, and windsurfing, Chenay Bay is just 3 miles east of Christiansted and is a terrific choice for families. Each cottage contains a fully equipped kitchenette, private bath, and ceiling fan. The 20 original cottages are smaller and more time worn than the newer duplexes. The Beach Bar and Grille is open for Caribbean dining daily from 8am to 9pm. The hotel has a popular Tuesday West Indian buffet and pig roast and a Saturday night "Caribbean kaleidoscope" with a mélange of West Indian cuisine and entertainment. The resort also has one of the island's best children's programs during the summer and holiday periods. Tennis courts and kayaking are available.

Colony Cove. 3221 Estate Golden Rock, St. Croix, U.S.V.I. 00820. ☎ **800/828-0746** in the U.S., or 809/773-1965. Fax 809/773-5397. 60 condos. A/C TV TEL. Winter, $185 apt for 1 or 2, $210 apt for 4. Off-season, $125 apt for 1 or 2, $150 apt for 4. Children under 6 free. Additional person $20 extra in winter, $10 in summer. AE, MC, V. Travel east on Route 75 going toward Christiansted as far as Five Corners, and then turn left and pass Mill Harbor; Colony Cove is the next driveway to the left.

Of all the condo complexes on St. Croix, Colony Cove is the most like a full-fledged hotel. About a mile west of Christiansted next to a palm-dotted beach, it's composed of four three-story buildings that ring a swimming pool. Each apartment contains a washer and dryer (rare for St. Croix), a kitchen, an enclosed veranda or gallery, two air-conditioned bedrooms, and a pair of bathrooms. There's an on-site water-sports center, plus two tennis courts.

Sugar Beach Condominiums. 3245 Estate Golden Rock, St. Croix, U.S.V.I. 00820. ☎ **800/524-2049** in the U.S., or 809/773-5345. Fax 809/773-1359. 46 studios and apts. A/C TV TEL. Winter, $180 studio; $225 one-bedroom apt; $275 two-bedroom apt; $350 three-bedroom apt. Off-season, $110 studio; $145 one-bedroom apt; $180 two-bedroom apt; $250 three-bedroom apt. Maid service extra. AE, DISC, MC, V.

This row of modernized studios and one-, two-, and three-bedroom apartments is strung along 500 feet of sandy beach on the north coast off North Shore Road. Its location near a housing development, however, is a turn-off for some visitors. When you tire of the sand, you can swim in the free-form freshwater pool nestled beside a sugar mill where rum was made three centuries ago. Under red-tile roofs, the apartments with enclosed balconies are staggered to provide privacy. All apartments open toward the sea, are tastefully decorated, and have completely equipped kitchens. The property has two Laykold tennis courts, and the Carambola golf course is minutes away.

The Waves at Cane Bay. Cane Bay (P.O. Box 1749, Kingshill), St. Croix, U.S.V.I. 00851. ☎ **800/545-0603** in the U.S., or 809/778-1805. Fax 809/778-4945. 12 rms. A/C TV. Winter, $140–$195 double. Off-season, $85–$125 double. Additional person $20 extra. AE, CB, MC, V. From the airport, go left on Rte. 64 for 1 mile, turn right on Rte. 70 for 1 mile, go left at the junction with Rte. 75 for 2 miles, and then drive left at the junction with Rte. 80 for 5 miles.

This intimate and tasteful property run by Suzanne and Kevin Ryan is about 8 miles from the airport, midway between the island's two biggest towns. It's set on a well-landscaped plot of oceanfront property on Cane Bay, the heart of the best scuba and snorkeling at Cane Bay Beach, which is rocky and tends to disappear at high tide. There's a PADI dive shop on the property. Accommodations are in two-story units with screened-in verandas, all directly on the ocean. The rooms are high-ceilinged, with fresh flowers, well-stocked kitchens, private libraries, and thick towels. A two-room villa next to the main building has a large oceanside deck. The social center is a beachside bar. A restaurant on the premises is open six nights a week.

WHERE TO DINE

IN CHRISTIANSTED

Expensive

✪ **Indies.** 55–56 Company St. ☎ **809/692-9440.** Reservations recommended. Main courses $16–$21. AE, DISC, MC, V. Mon–Fri 11:30am–2:30pm and 6–9:30pm, Sat–Sun 6–9:30pm. CARIBBEAN/INTERNATIONAL.

Catherine Plav-Drigger is one of the most superlative chefs in the Caribbean, and at her restaurant you're likely to get your finest meal on St. Croix. Set in a 19th-century courtyard lined with antique cobblestone, Indies is a welcoming retreat. Catherine's fresh ingredients are first-rate, and her menu reflects the produce and flavors of the tropics. You dine adjacent to a carriage and cookhouse from the 1850s in a sheltered courtyard protected from the noise of the street outside.

The menu changes depending on what's fresh. The beautiful fresh fish and lobster are caught in Caribbean waters, and local seasonal fruits and vegetables are featured. The Thai green curry grilled shrimp with banana, chutney, and scallions has a savory flavor, as does the lobster and corn quesadilla, both sometimes served as an appetizer. For a soup you often face a choice of an excellent island pumpkin-ginger soup with coconut or a West Indies–style seafood chowder. Main courses are likely to be anything—a superb grilled wahoo with a pepper sauce and grilled scallions, or perhaps a spicy Caribbean chicken with a fresh pineapple chutney. Sushi, with a special emphasis on a delectable version of local tuna, is a featured specialty two nights a week.

✪ Kendricks. 12 Chandlers Wharf, Gallows Bay. ☎ **809/773-9199.** Reservations required at dinner upstairs. Main courses $14–$26; lunch $7–$17. AE, MC, V. Daily 11:30am–3pm and 6–9pm. FRENCH/CONTINENTAL.

This, the island's toniest restaurant, has moved out to Gallows Bay, but its local fans have followed it to its new location overlooking Christiansted Harbor. It has both upstairs and downstairs dining rooms. The downstairs is more informal, serving lunch as well as dinner. Some of its recipes have been featured in *Bon Appétit,* and deservedly so. You'll immediately warm to some of the specialties, especially homemade eggplant ravioli with a tomato-basil butter or grilled filet mignon with black truffle in a bordelaise sauce. One dish—almost a signature, actually—is seared scallops and artichoke hearts in a lemon-cream sauce, which is an appetizer. Another dish that explodes with flavor is the pecan-crusted roast pork loin with a ginger mayonnaise. The downstairs lunch features baby back ribs, salads, and pastas. Friday is oyster and clam night, and there is live entertainment (also on Saturday too). Sunday is football day on TV and buffalo wings are served.

Top Hat. 52 Company St. (opposite Market Sq.). ☎ **809/773-2346.** Reservations recommended. Main courses $20–$34, including access to a salad bar. AE, CB, DC, DISC, MC, V. Mon–Sat 6–10pm. Closed May–June. CONTINENTAL/DANISH.

Set on the second floor of an 18th-century merchant's house, two blocks inland from Christiansted's wharves, this is the only Danish restaurant in the Virgin Islands. A bit bourgeois and staid, it's a long-enduring favorite, in spite of its rather standard cuisine. Operated since 1970 by Bent and Hanne Rasmussen, two Scandinavians, it offers well-prepared dishes such as crisp roast duck prepared in the Danish style with apples, prunes, red cabbage, sugar-brown Irish potatoes, and demiglace sauce; gravlax, herring, chilled cucumber soup, local dolphin simply sautéed with butter and lime; and a version of Wiener schnitzel. This may be the only place around where you can order smoked eel and scrambled eggs, as well as frikadeller, those Scandinavian meatballs. The Top Hat platter comes with herring, roast beef, pâté, frikadeller, cheese, and fried fish.

Moderate

Antoine's. 58A King St. ☎ **809/773-0263.** Reservations required in winter. Main courses $13–$20. AE, MC, V. Daily 7:30am–2:30pm, and 6:30–9:30pm. CARIBBEAN/INTERNATIONAL.

Set directly on King's Wharf, on the second floor of a building overlooking Christiansted's harbor and marina, this restaurant is an institution. Many visitors come just for the bar, which dispenses more than 35 different kinds of frozen drinks, and the island's largest selection of beer. In addition to the covered terrace, there's a satellite bar in back (the Aqua Lounge) decorated with a Windsurfer suspended from the ceiling, and a cubbyhole Italian restaurant (Pico Bello) serving lunch and dinner daily. Regardless of where you decide to consume your meal, a range of pastas and veal dishes is available, as well as such Teutonic specialties as goulash, knockwurst salad, roulade of beef, and Wiener schnitzel. Local dishes like fish chowder, lobster, and a choice of seafood are also on hand. In spite of the fame of this place, the dinners are only mediocre. Antoine's is more of a tradition for breakfast, when you can try one of the "creative" alpine omelets.

Tutto Bene. 2 Company St. ☎ **809/773-5229.** Reservations accepted only for parties of 6 or more. Main courses $12.95–$19.75. AE, V. Dinner only, daily 6–10pm. ITALIAN.

In the heart of town, Tutto Bene has more the allure of a bistro-cantina than of a full-fledged restaurant. The Connecticut-born owner, Tony Cerruto, believes in simple, hearty, and uncomplicated *paysano* dishes, the kind mammas fed their sons in the old country. At lunch you can enjoy bistro-style veggie frittatas, a chicken pesto sandwich, or spinach lasagna. If you don't feel like eating, there's a large mahogany bar in back that does a brisk business of its own. You'll dine on wooden tables covered with painted tablecloths, amid warm colors and often lots of hubbub. Menu items are written on a pair of oversize mirrors against one wall. A full range of delectable pastas is offered nightly, and great care goes into the seafood dishes. Fish might be served parmigiana, or you can order seafood Genovese with mussels, clams, and shrimp with a white wine/pesto sauce over linguine.

Inexpensive

Annabelle's Tea Room. 51-ABC Company St. ☎ **809/773-3990.** Reservations recommended. Sandwiches, salads, and platters $6.50–$12. No credit cards. Mon–Sat 9am–3pm. INTERNATIONAL.

This restaurant occupies a quiet gingerbread courtyard filled with tropical plants, and surrounded by clapboard-sided buildings whose iron railings evoke New Orleans. Don't expect grand cuisine—what you get is a shady place to rest your feet, a warm welcome from Anna Deering or a member of her staff, a sense of Cruzan history, and a simple but refreshing assortment of sandwiches, salads, soups, and platters. Dolphin (the fish) in herb-flavored butter sauce, Cubano or "Lazy Virgin" sandwiches ("all vegetables and cheese, with no meat"), and conch Créole are ongoing favorites.

✪ **Camille's Café.** Queen Cross St. at 53B Company St. ☎ **809/773-2985.** Reservations not required. Main courses $10.95–$15.95; fixed-price dinner $15.95. MC, V. Mon–Sat 7:30am–3pm and 5–10pm. MEDITERRANEAN.

Across from Government House, Camille's, a wine bar, serves New York deli-type food during the day, along with a selection of Mediterranean dishes at dinner. It's one of the best dining values in town, especially for its fixed-price dinner. Salads are featured, or you might begin with a homemade soup. Sandwiches are also available for lunch. The menu includes such dishes as fresh fish, filet mignon, prime rib, lobster, and chicken. The place is a neighborhood enclave frequented by convivial locals. Its brick walls and beamed ceilings were originally part of an 18th-century guest house.

Harvey's. 11B Company St. ☎ **809/773-3433.** Main courses $7–$10. No credit cards. Mon–Wed 11:30am–6pm, Thurs–Sat 11:30am–9pm. CARIBBEAN/CONTINENTAL.

The setting might be a back room in Truman Capote's "House of Flowers," no great compliment. Forget the plastic and the flowery tablecloths that give this place its 1950s aura, and try to grab one of a dozen tables. If you do, you can enjoy the thoroughly zesty cooking of island matriarch Sarah Harvey, who takes joy in her work and definitely means to fill your stomach with her basic but good food. There's plenty of it, too, beginning with one of her homemade soups, including callaloo or chicken. She'll even serve you conch in butter sauce as an appetizer. Main dishes are the type of food she was raised on: barbecue chicken, barbecue spareribs (barbecue is big here), boiled fillet of snapper, and even lobster when they can get it. Fungi comes with virtually everything. For dessert, try one of her delectable tarts made form guava, pineapple, or coconut.

Nolan's Tavern. 5A Estate St. Peter, Christiansted East. ☎ **809/773-6660.** Reservations recommended only for groups of 6 or more. Burgers $7–$8.50; main courses $12.75–$16.25. AE, DISC, MC, V. Kitchens open daily for dinner 5–9pm, bar at 3pm. INTERNATIONAL/WEST INDIAN.

It's the first place people in the know think of when you ask them for a warm, cozy, Antillean tavern with absolutely no social pretensions. It lies 2 miles east of

Christiansted's harbor front, across from the capital's most visible elementary school, the Pearl B. Larsen School. Your host is Nolan Joseph, a Trinidad-born chef and greeter who makes a special point of welcoming guests, and offering "tasty food and good service." No one will mind if you stop in just for a drink. Mr. Joseph, referred to by some diners as "King Conch," prepares the mollusk in at least half a dozen ways, including versions with curry, Creole sauce, and garlic-pineapple sauce. He reportedly experimented for three months to perfect a means of tenderizing the tough mollusk without artificial chemicals, and you'll be able to assess his progress. His ribs are also worthy—like Sinatra, he prepares them "my way." Many guests come here to fill up on steak, ribs, and chicken.

IN FREDERIKSTED

Le St. Tropez. Limetree Court, 67 King St. ☎ **809/772-3000.** Reservations recommended. Main courses $13.50–$22.50. AE, DISC, MC, V. Mon–Fri 11:30am–2:30pm and 6–10pm, Sat 6–10:30pm. FRENCH/MEDITERRANEAN.

At the most popular bistro in Frederiksted, you can dine on a covered terrace, presided over by Danielle and André Ducrot. Since it's small, it's always better to call ahead for a table. If you're visiting for the day, make this bright little cafe your luncheon stopover, and enjoy crepes, quiches, soups, or salads in the sunlit courtyard. At night the atmosphere glows with candlelight, and assumes more *joie de vivre.* Try the Mediterranean cuisine, beginning with mushrooms aioli, escargots Provençale, or one of the freshly made soups. Main dishes are likely to include medallions of beef with two mushrooms, the fish of the day, or a magret of duck. Ingredients are always fresh and well prepared; look for the daily specials, perhaps coq au vin.

Pier 69. 69 King St. ☎ **809/772-0069.** Reservations not accepted. Sandwiches and platters $4.25–$17. AE, DC, DISC, MC, V. Mon–Thurs 10am–midnight, Fri–Sun 10am–4pm. AMERICAN/CARIBBEAN.

Although you can get a worthy but unfussy platter of food here, this place is far more interesting for its resemblance to a funky bar in New York's Greenwich Village than for its reputation as a culinary citadel. New York–born Unise Tranberg is the earth-mother/matriarch of the place, which looks like a warm and somewhat battered combination of a 1950s living room with a nautical bar sheathed in varnished tropical woods. Regardless of when you opt to arrive, someone will probably be deep into his or her second or third drink, so if you imbibe a bit, you won't be alone. Counterculture fans from Christiansted make this their preferred hangout, sometimes opting for a mango colada or a lime lambada. If you're stepping off a ship and want something to eat, menu items include a predictable array of salads, sandwiches, and platters, which draw their inspiration from the United States, the Caribbean, and everywhere in between.

AROUND THE ISLAND

✪ **Dino's Bistro.** In the Buccaneer, Gallows Bay. ☎ **809/773-2100.** Reservations recommended. Main courses $16–$30. AE, CB, DC, DISC, MC, V. Thurs–Mon 6–9:30pm. ITALIAN/MEDITERRANEAN.

In 1995, this successful Italian restaurant moved from independent premises to a location within St. Croix's most favored resort. Set close to the lobby, the restaurant offers views of the sea as well as of the lights of Christiansted. Chef Dino DiNatale is back, zestier and better than ever. He serves the best and most flavorful Italian cuisine on the island, including hallmarks of modern Italian cookery. You might, for example, begin with an array of antipasti delectably prepared from fresh ingredients, and that old favorite of every Sicilian *paysano,* black linguine with squid, is given an original touch here. Mushroom fettuccine is another noteworthy choice, as is the local fish du jour prepared in several different ways—one of our favorites is with cilantro, tomato, and ginger. An innovative pasta dish is fettuccine Caribbean, with chicken, rum, black beans, ginger, cilantro, and both sweet and hot peppers.

Duggan's Reef. East End Rd., Teague Bay. ☎ **809/773-9800.** Reservations required for dinner in winter. Main courses $14.50–$29; pastas $10–$24. AE, MC, V. Daily noon–3pm and 6–9:30pm. (Bar, daily 11am–11:30pm.) Closed for lunch in summer. CONTINENTAL/CARIBBEAN.

Set only 10 feet from the still waters of Reef Beach, and open to the sea breezes, Duggan's Reef is an ideal perch for watching the Windsurfers and Hobie cats careening through the nearby waters. The restaurant, owned for more than a decade by Boston-born Frank Duggan, is the most popular on St. Croix—all visitors seemingly dine here at least once during their stay on the island. At lunch, a simple array of salads, crepes, and sandwiches is offered. At night a more elaborate menu contains the popular house specialties: Duggan's Caribbean lobster pasta and Irish whiskey lobster. The local seafood is fresh and depends on the day's catch; in other words, it's fresh fish or no fish. That catch of the day can be baked, grilled, or blackened in the Cajun style, as you like it. It also can be served island style (with tomato, pepper, and onion sauce). Begin with fried calamari or a conch chowder before sampling a pasta dish such as seafood Diavolo. Main dishes include New York strip steak or veal piccata. The cuisine remains consistently reliable.

The Galleon. East End Rd., Green Cay Marina, 50 Estate Southgate. ☎ **809/773-9949.** Reservations recommended. Main courses $15.50–$36. AE, MC, V. Daily 6–10pm. Proceed east on Rte. 82 from Christiansted for 5 minutes; after going a mile past the Buccaneer, turn left into Green Cay Marina. FRENCH/NORTHERN ITALIAN.

Overlooking the ocean, the Galleon is a local favorite, and deservedly so. The best cooking in Europe is found in northern Italy and France, and that's what's offered here, including osso buco, just as good as that served in Milan. Freshly baked bread, two fresh vegetables, and rice or potatoes accompany main dishes. The menu always includes at least one local fish, such as wahoo, tuna, swordfish, dolphin, or even fresh Caribbean lobster. Or you might order a perfectly done rack of lamb, which will be carved right at your table. An extensive listing of wines is sold by the glass. Music from a baby grand accompanies your dinner.

✪ **The Mahogany Room.** Carambola Beach Resort. ☎ **809/778-3800.** Reservations recommended. Main courses $36–$60. AE, DC, DISC, MC, V. Winter, Tues–Thurs and Sat 6–10pm. Off-season, Sat only 6–10pm. INTERNATIONAL.

An exclusive enclave in this previously recommended hotel, the setting for this restaurant is elegant, with wooden beams and stone walls. The restaurant seats 100 under a vaulted cathedral ceiling with mahogany and teak furniture. Tables lit by softly glowing lamps have a 190° view that includes the ocean. Ambience is important here, but it is the cuisine that continues to lure the upmarket patrons. Although chefs come and go here at an alarming rate, the food remains of consistently high quality. The menu changes, but dishes tend to evoke the better aspects of the nouvelle cuisine craze of the '80s, but without the excesses of those times. For example, grilled wahoo appears here with a roasted pepper couscous, char-grilled scallions, and a Hoisin sesame glaze. For a touch of island flavor, tuna is quick seared and served with a papaya and mango chutney. Steaks are handled with care, and lamb and veal, although flown in frozen, still emerge tasty from the kitchen, although it might be a case of gilding the lily to serve veal tenderloin with lobster medallions *and* lump crabmeat. Appetizers are tangy and flavorful. Even a jumbo prawn cocktail appears with black-bean salsa instead of the usual tomato guck.

Sprat Hall Beach Restaurant. Rte. 63. ☎ **809/772-5855.** Reservations not required. Lunch $7–$15. No credit cards. Daily 9am–4pm (hot food 11:30am–2:30pm). CARIBBEAN.

One mile north of Frederiksted, this restaurant is an informal spot on the western coast of St. Croix near Sprat Hall Plantation. It's the best place on the island to combine lunch and a swim. The restaurant has been in business since 1948, feeding both locals and foreign visitors. Try such local dishes as conch chowder, pumpkin fritters, tannia soup, and the fried fish of the day. These dishes have authentic island flavor, perhaps more so than at any other place on the island. If you'd like more standard fare, they also do salads and burgers. The bread is home-baked daily. The place is directed by Cruzan-born Joyce Merwin Hurd and her husband, Jim, who charge $2 for use of the showers and changing rooms.

✪ **The Terrace Restaurant.** At the Buccaneer, Gallows Bay. ☎ **809/773-2100.** Reservations recommended. Main courses $10–$30. AE, DC, DISC, MC, V. Daily 6–10pm. INTERNATIONAL.

For years this was a humdrum hotel dining room with a predictable and not very noteworthy menu that virtually never changed. All that changed in the mid-1990s, however, when the management poured time and energy into making a more creative statement in this open-air, sea-view area where tones of eggshell blue and sea green, and a prominent bar off in one corner, create a soothing decorative theme. Menu items vary with the availability of the ingredients, but are likely to include fried local lobster cakes, a warm spinach salad, a selection of pasta dishes (bow-ties with Caribbean lobster meat and broccoli is a favorite), freshly caught fish, grilled steaks, and a molasses glazed plank roast fillet of salmon with a saffron-accented ginger-pineapple coulis. Lighter fare includes a selection of pizzas, nachos with all the traditional garnishes, and cheeseburgers. There is also a full children's menu. Every Friday night Tommy Romano, a Trinidad-born bandleader, performs from 8 to 11pm with four other musicians. The music includes calypso, blues, and jazz.

BEACHES, WATER SPORTS & OTHER OUTDOOR PURSUITS

BEACHES Beaches are St. Croix's big attraction. The drawback is that getting to them from Christiansted, home to most of the hotels, isn't always easy. It can also be expensive, especially if you want to go back and forth every day of your stay. Of course, you can always rent one of those housekeeping condos right on the water.

In Christiansted, if you want to beach it, head for the **Hotel on the Cay.** You'll have to take a ferry to this palm-shaded island.

Cramer Park, at the northeastern end of the island, is a special public park operated by the Department of Agriculture. Lined with sea grape trees, the beach also has a picnic area, a restaurant, and a bar.

We highly recommend **Davis Bay** and **Cane Bay**—they're the type of beaches you'd expect to find on a Caribbean island, with palms, white sand, and good swimming and snorkeling. Cane Bay adjoins Route 80 on the north shore. Snorkelers and divers are attracted to this beach, with its rolling waves, coral gardens, and drop-off wall. No reefs guard the approach to Davis Beach, which draws bodysurfers but doesn't have changing facilities. It's on the North Shore, in the vicinity of the Carambola Beach Resort.

Windsurfers like **Reef Beach,** which opens onto Teague Bay along Route 82, East End Road, a half-hour ride from Christiansted. Food can be ordered at Duggan's Reef. On Route 63, a short ride north of Frederiksted, **Rainbow Beach** beckons with its white sand and ideal snorkeling conditions. In the vicinity, also on Route 63, about five minutes north of Frederiksted, **La Grange** is another good beach. Lounge chairs can be rented, and there's a bar nearby.

At the **Cormorant Beach Club** about 5 miles west of Christiansted, some 1,200 feet of white sands are shaded by palm trees. Since a living reef lies just off the shore, snorkeling conditions are ideal. **Grapetree Beach** offers about the same footage of clean white sand on the eastern tip of the island (Route 60). Follow the South Shore Road to reach it. Water sports are popular here.

Two more beaches on St. Croix include **Buccaneer Beach,** 2 miles west of Christiansted, and **Sandy Point,** directly south of Frederiksted, the largest beach in all the U.S. Virgin Islands. Its waters are shallow and calm, perfect for swimming. Jutting out from southwestern St. Croix like a small peninsula, Sandy Point is reached by taking the Melvin Evans Highway (Route 66) west from the Alexander Hamilton Airport.

FISHING The fishing grounds at **Lang Bank** are about 10 miles from St. Croix. Here you'll find kingfish, dolphin, and wahoo. Light-tackle boats along the reef tend to catch jack or bonefish. At **Clover Crest,** in Frederiksted, Cruzan anglers fish right from the rocks.

Serious sports fishers can board the ***Shenanigans*** (☎ **809/773-7165** during the day, or 809/773-0917 at night), a 42-foot Ocean Super Sport convertible, available for four-, six-, or eight-hour charters with bait and tackle included. It's anchored at the St. Croix Marina, Gallows Bay. Phone for reservations.

GOLF St. Croix has the best golfing in the U.S. Virgins. In fact, guests staying on St. John and St. Thomas often fly over for a day's round on the island's two 18-hole and one 9-hole golf courses.

The ✪ **Carambola Golf Course,** on the northeast side of St. Croix (☎ **809/778-0747**), was designed by Robert Trent Jones Sr., who called it "the loveliest course I ever designed." The course, formerly the Fountain Valley and the site of "Shell's Wonderful World of Golf," has been likened to a botanical garden. Its collection of par-3 holes is known to golfing authorities as the best in the tropics. Carambola's course record of 65 was set by Jim Levine in 1993. Greens fees are $77 per person for a day in winter ($47.50 in summer), which allows you to play as many holes as you like. Rental of a golf cart is mandatory at $12.50 per 18 holes.

The other major course, at the **Buccaneer** (☎ **809/773-2100,** ext. 738), 2 miles east of Christiansted (see "Where to Stay," above), is a challenging 5,810-yard, 18-hole course with panoramic vistas that allows the player to knock the ball over rolling hills right to the edge of the Caribbean. In winter, greens fees are $25 for 9 holes or $40 for 18 holes, with a cart rental going for $14.

A final course is the **Reef,** at Teague Bay (☎ **809/773-8844**), a 3,100-yard, nine-hole course, charging greens fees of $10 to $14, with carts renting for $5 to $8. On the east end of the island, its longest hole is a 579-yard par 5.

HORSEBACK RIDING Specializing in nature tours, **Paul and Jill's Equestrian Stables,** Sprat Hall Plantation, Route 58 (☎ **809/772-2880**), is the only equestrian stable in the Virgin Islands. Set on the sprawling grounds of the island's oldest plantation Great House, it's operated by Paul Wojcie and his wife, Jill Hurd, one of the daughters of the establishment's original founders. The stables are known throughout the Caribbean for the quality of the horses and the scenic trail rides through the forests, past ruins of abandoned 18th-century plantations and sugar mills, to the tops of the hills of St. Croix's western end. All tours are accompanied by the operators, who give running commentaries on island fauna, history, and riding techniques. Beginners and experienced riders alike are welcome.

A two-hour trail ride costs $50 per person. Tours usually depart daily in winter at 10am and 4pm and off-season at 5pm, with slight variations according to demand. Reservations at least a day in advance are important.

TENNIS Some authorities rate the tennis at the **Buccaneer** (☎ **809/773-2100,** ext. 736) as the best in the West Indies. This hotel (see "Where to Stay," above) offers a choice of eight courts, two lit for night games, all open to the public. Nonguests pay $12 per person per hour; however, you must call to reserve a court. A tennis pro is available for lessons, and there's also a pro shop.

A notable selection of recently restored courts can also be found at the **Carambola Golf Club** (☎ **809/778-0747**), which has five clay courts open to the public. The charge is $25 per hour for nonguests. Courts are no longer lit for night games. Both a pro shop and a tennis pro offering lessons are available.

WATER SPORTS Sponge life, black-coral trees (the finest in the West Indies), and steep drop-offs into water near the shoreline have made St. Croix a diver's dream.

Buck Island, with an underwater visibility of more than 100 feet, is the site of an underwater nature trail, and it's the major diving target (see "A Side Trip to Buck Island: Unspoiled Nature and World-Class Snorkeling," later in this chapter). All the minor and major agencies offer scuba and snorkeling tours to Buck Island. St. Croix is home to the largest living reef in the Caribbean, including the fabled north-shore wall that begins in 25 to 30 feet of water and drops, sometimes straight down, to 13,200 feet. There are 22 moored sites, allowing the dive boats to tie up without damaging the reef. Favorite scuba-diving sites include the historic **Salt River Canyon,** the gorgeous coral gardens of **Scotch Banks,** and **Eagle Ray,** the latter so named because of the rays that cruise along the wall there. **Pavilions** is yet another good dive site, with a virgin coral reef that's in pristine shape.

Dive St. Croix, 59 King's Wharf (☎ **800/523-DIVE** in the U.S., or 809/773-3434), operates the 38-foot dive boat *Reliance.* The staff offers complete instruction from resort courses through full certification, as well as night dives. A resort course is $75, with a two-tank dive going for $70. Scuba trips to Buck Island are offered for $65, and dive packages begin at $190 for six dives.

V.I. Divers Ltd., in the Pan Am Pavilion on Christiansted's waterfront (☎ **800/544-5911** or 809/773-6045), is the oldest (established in 1971) and one of the best dive operations on the island. In fact, *Rudales Scuba Diving* magazine rated its staff as among the top 10 worldwide. A full-service PADI five-star facility, it offers daily two-tank boat dives, guided snorkeling trips to Green Cay, night dives, and a full range of scuba-training programs from introductory dives through dive master. Introductory dives, which require no experience, are $95 for a two-tank dive, including all instruction and equipment. The outfitter offers a six-dive package for $195 and a 10-dive package for $295. A two-tank or beach dive is priced at $75, with night dives going for $55. A two-hour guided snorkel tour costs $25, or $35 for the boat snorkeling trip to Green Cay.

WINDSURFING The best place for this increasingly popular sport is the **St. Croix Water Sports Center** (☎ **809/773-7060**), located on a small offshore island in Christiansted Harbor and part of the Hotel on the Cay. They give lessons and are open daily from 9am to 5pm in winter and 10am to 5pm in off-season. Windsurfing rentals are $25 per hour. They also offer Sea Doos, which seat two and can be rented for $50 per half hour, parasailing for $50 per person, and snorkeling equipment for $12 per day.

EXPLORING THE RAIN FOREST

Unlike the rest of St. Croix, a verdant parcel in the island's western district is covered with dense forest, a botanical landscape very different from the scrub-covered hills on other parts of the island. Set amid the sparsely populated terrain of the island's northwestern corner, north of Frederiksted, the area grows thick with mahogany trees, kapok (silk-cotton) trees, turpentine (red birch) trees, samaan (rain) trees, and all kinds of ferns and vines. Sweet limes, mangos, hog plums, and breadfruit trees, which have sown themselves in the wild since the plantation era, are woven among the forest's larger trees. Bird life includes crested hummingbirds, pearly eyed thrashers, green-throated caribs, yellow warblers, and perky banana quits.

Although technically the district is not a tropical rain forest, it's known by virtually everyone as the Rain Forest. How best to experience its botanical charms? Some visitors opt to drive along Route 76 (which is also known as Mahogany Road, the most mysterious road on St. Croix), stopping the car beside any of the footpaths that meander off the highway into dry riverbeds and glens on either side. (It's advisable to stick to the best-worn of the foot trails to avoid losing your way, and retrace your steps after a few moments of admiring the local botany.)

Equally feasible is a hike beside those highways of the island's western sector where few cars ever venture. Three of the most viable include the Creque Dam Road (Routes 58/78), the Scenic Road (Route 78), and the Western Scenic Road (Routes 63/78). Consider beginning your trek near the junction of Creque Dam Road and Scenic Road. (Although passable by cars, it's likely you'll only see a few along these roads during your entire walking tour.)

Your trek will cover a broad triangular swath, beginning at the above-mentioned junction, heading north and then west along Scenic Road. First the road will rise, then descend toward the coastal lighthouse of the island's extreme northwestern tip, Hamm's Bluff. Most trekkers will decide to retrace their steps after about 45 minutes of northwesterly walking, returning to their parked cars after admiring the land and seascapes. Real diehards, however, will continue trekking all the way to the coastline, then head south along the coastal road (Butler Bay Road), then head east along Creque Dam Road to their parked car at the junction of Creque Dam Road and Scenic Road. Embark on this longer expedition only if you're really prepared for a prolonged trek (about five hours) and some serious nature-watching.

EXPLORING THE SIGHTS

Taxi tours are the ideal way to explore the island. For one or two passengers, the cost is often $30 for two hours or $40 for three hours. All prices should be negotiated and agreed upon in advance. For more information, call the **St. Croix Taxi Association** at ☎ **809/778-1088.**

IN CHRISTIANSTED

The picture-book harbor town of the Caribbean, Christiansted is an old, handsomely restored (or at least in the process of being restored) Danish port. On the northeastern shore of the island, on a coral-bound bay, the town is filled with Danish buildings erected by prosperous merchants in the booming 18th century. These red-roofed structures are often washed in pink, ocher, or yellow. Arcades over the sidewalks make ideal shaded colonnades for shoppers. The whole area around the harbor front has been designated a historic site, including **Government House,** which is looked after by the National Park Service.

You can begin at the **visitors' bureau** (☎ **809/773-0495**), a yellow-sided building with a cedar-capped roof near the harbor front. It was originally built as the Old Scalehouse in 1856 to replace a similar, older structure that burned down. In its heyday, all taxable goods leaving and entering the harbor were weighed here. The scales that once stood could accurately weigh barrels of sugar and molasses up to 1,600 pounds each.

Steeple Building. On the waterfront off Hospital St. ☎ **809/773-1460.** Admission $2 (also includes admission to Fort Christiansvaern). Mon–Fri 9:30am–noon, 1–3pm; hours can vary because the staff depends on volunteers.

This building's full name is the Church of Lord God of Sabaoth, and it was completed in 1753 as St. Croix's first Lutheran church, now a major island attraction. It, too, stands near the harbor front, reached by going along Hospital Street. It was embellished with a steeple in 1794–96, and today houses exhibits relating to island history and culture. The building was deconsecrated in 1831, and served at various times as a bakery, a hospital, and a school.

Fort Christiansvaern. ☎ **809/773-1460.** Admission included in the ticket to the Steeple Building. Mon–Thurs 8am–5pm; Fri–Sat 9am–5pm.

This fortress overlooking the harbor is the best-preserved colonial fortification in the Virgin Islands. The fort is maintained as a historic monument by the National Park Service. Its original four-pronged star-shaped design was in accordance with the most advanced military planning of its era. The fort is also the site of the St. Croix Police Museum, which traces police work on the island from the late 1800s to the present. Photos, weapons, and artifacts capture the police force's past.

St. Croix Aquarium. Caravelle Arcade. ☎ **809/773-8995.** Admission $4.50 adults, $2 children. Tues–Sat 11am–4pm.

This aquarium moved here from Frederiksted, and has expanded with many new exhibits, including one devoted to "night creatures." In all it houses some 40 species of marine animals and more than 100 species of invertebrates. With constant rotation, each creature can adjust easily back to its natural habitat, as hundreds pass through the tanks each year. A touch pond contains starfish, sea cucumbers, brittle stars, and pencil urchins. The aquarium allows you to become familiar with marine life before you see it while scuba diving or snorkeling.

In Frederiksted

This former Danish settlement at the western end of the island, about 17 miles from Christiansted, is a sleepy port town that comes to life only when a cruise ship docks at its shoreline.

In 1994, a 1,500-foot pier opened to accommodate the largest cruise ships (the old pier had suffered damage from Hurricane Hugo in 1989). The pier facility is designed to accommodate two large cruise vessels and two minicruise ships simultaneously.

Frederiksted was destroyed by a fire in 1879, and the citizens rebuilt it with wood frames and clapboards on top of the old Danish stone and yellow-brick foundations.

Most visitors begin their tour at russet-colored **Fort Frederik,** next to the cruise-ship pier (☎ **809/772-2021**). Some historians claim that this was the first fort to sound a foreign salute to the U.S. flag, in 1776. It was here on July 3, 1848, that Gov.-Gen. Peter von Scholten emancipated the slaves in the Danish West Indies. The fort, at the northern end of Frederiksted, has been restored to its 1840 appearance. You can explore the courtyard and stables, and a local history museum has been installed in what was once the Garrison Room. Admission is free, and it's open Monday through Saturday from 8:30am to 4:30pm.

Just south of the fort, the Customs House is an 18th-century building with a 19th-century two-story gallery. Here you can go into the **visitors' bureau** (☎ **809/772-0357**) and pick up a free map of the town.

Nearby, privately owned **Victoria House,** on Market Street, is a gingerbread-trimmed structure built after the fire of 1879.

Along the waterfront Strand is the **Bellhouse,** once the Frederiksted Public Library. One of its owners, G. A. Bell, ornamented the steps with bells. Today the house is an arts-and-crafts center and a nursery. Sometimes a local theater group presents dramas here.

The **Danish School,** on Prince Street, was adapted in the 1830s into a building designed by Hingelberg, a well-known Danish architect. Today it's the police station and Welfare Department.

Two churches are of interest: **St. Paul's Anglican Church,** 28 Prince St., was founded outside the port in the late 18th century; the present building dates from 1812. **St. Patrick's Catholic Church,** 5 Prince St., was built in the 1840s.

Around the Island: From Nature Reserves to Rum Factories

North of Frederiksted you can drop in at **Sprat Hall,** the island's oldest plantation, or else continue along to the rain forest, which covers about 15 acres, including the 150-foot-high **Creque Dam.** The terrain is private property, but the owner lets visitors go inside to explore. Most visitors come here to see the jagged estuary of the northern coastline's **Salt River.** The Salt River was where Columbus landed on November 14, 1493, the only known site where the explorer ever landed on what is now U.S. territory. Marking the 500th anniversary of Columbus's arrival, then-Pres. George Bush signed a bill creating the 912-acre **Salt River Bay National Historical Park and Ecological Preserve.** The land mass includes the site of the original Carib village explored by Columbus and his men, including the only ceremonial ball court ever discovered in the Lesser Antilles.

The park contains the largest mangrove forest in the Virgin Islands, sheltering many endangered animals and plants, plus an underwater canyon attracting scuba divers from around the world.

At the Carib settlement, Columbus's men liberated several Taíno women and children who were being held as slaves. On the way back to their vessels, the Spaniards faced a canoe filled with hostile Caribs, armed with poison-tipped arrows. One Spanish soldier was killed, and perhaps six Caribs were either slain or captured. This is the first documented case of hostility between invading Europeans and the Native Americans. Sailing away, Columbus named this part of St. Croix "Cape of the Arrows."

The **St. Croix Environmental Association,** 3 Arawak Building, Gallows Bay (☎ **809/773-1989**), conducts tours of the area and can be called for details. Tours cost $15 for adults, $12 for children under 12.

St. George Village Botanical Garden of St. Croix. 127 Estate St., Kingshill. ☎ **809/692-2874.** Admission $5 adults, $1 children 12 and under; donations welcome. Nov–May, daily 9am–5pm; June–Oct, Tues–Sat 9am–4pm.

Just north of Centerline Road, 4 miles east of Frederiksted at Estate St. George, is a veritable 16-acre Eden of tropical trees, shrubs, vines, and flowers. Built around the ruins of a 19th-century sugarcane workers' village, the garden is a feast for the eye and the camera, from the entrance drive bordered by royal palms and bougainvillea to the towering kapok and tamarind trees. There's a gift shop and rest rooms, and self-guided walking-tour maps are available at the entrance to the garden's Great Hall.

Cruzan Rum Factory. W. Airport Rd., Rte. 64. ☎ **809/692-2280.** Admission $3. Tours given Mon–Fri 9–11:30am and 1–4:15pm.

This factory distills the famous Virgin Islands rum, which is considered by residents to be the finest in the world. Guided tours depart from the visitors' pavilion; call for reservations and information. There's also a gift shop.

Estate Whim Plantation Museum. Centerline Rd. ☎ **809/772-0598.** Admission $5 adults, $1 children. Mon–Sat 10am–4pm.

About 2 miles east of Frederiksted, this museum was restored by the St. Croix Landmarks Society and is unique among the many sugar plantations whose ruins dot the island of St. Croix. This Great House is different from most in that it's composed of only three rooms. With three-foot-thick walls made of stone, coral, and molasses, the house is said by some to resemble a luxurious European château.

A division of Baker Furniture Company used the Whim Plantation's collection of models for one of its most successful reproductions, the "Whim Museum–West Indies Collection." A showroom in the museum sells these reproductions, plus others from the Caribbean, including pineapple-motif four-poster beds, cane-bottomed planters' chairs with built-in leg rests, and Caribbean adaptations of Empire-era chairs with cane-bottomed seats.

Also on the museum's premises is a woodworking shop (that features tools and techniques from the 18th century), the estate's original kitchen, a museum store, and a servant's quarters. The ruins of the plantation's sugar-processing plant, complete with a restored windmill, remain.

SHOPPING

IN CHRISTIANSTED

In Christiansted, where the core of our shopping recommendations are found, the emphasis is on hole-in-the-wall boutiques selling one-of-a-kind merchandise; the selection of handmade items is especially strong. Knowing that it can't compete with Charlotte Amalie, Christiansted has forged its own creative statement and has now become the chic spot for merchandise in the Caribbean. All the shops are within half a mile or so.

Following the hurricanes of 1995, a major redevelopment of the waterfront at Christiansted was launched. **King's Alley Complex** (☎ **809/778-8135**) opened as a pink-sided compound, filled with the densest concentration of shopping options on St. Croix. You might want to drop in, at least for some window shopping.

Caribbean Clothing Co. 41 Queen Cross St. ☎ **809/773-5012.**

This outlet sells hip sports clothing by top name U.S. designers in all the latest styles. They carry Calvin Klein, Guess, Polo, and Dockers, among others. You not only get casual wear such as jeans, but some evening clothes for women as well. They also sell a small stock of shoes for both men and women, along with a good selection of jewelry, belts, scarves, and purses.

Colombian Emeralds. 43 Queen Cross St. ☎ **809/773-1928.**

Along with stunning emeralds, called "the rarest gemstone in the world," rubies and diamonds also dazzle here. The staff will show you their large range of 14-karat-gold jewelry, along with the best buys in watches, including Seiko quartz. Even though fake jewelry is peddled throughout the Caribbean, Colombian Emeralds is the genuine thing.

Crucian Gold. 57A Company St. ☎ **809/773-5241.**

In this small West Indian cottage, you encounter the unique gold creations of island-born Brian Bishop. He designs all the gold jewelry himself, and cheaper versions of his work come in sterling silver. The most popular item is the Crucian bracelet, which contains a "True Lovers' Knot" in its design. The outlet also sells hand-tied knots (bound in gold wire), rings, pendants, and earrings.

Elegant Illusions Copy Jewelry. 55 King St. ☎ **809/773-2727.**

This branch of a hugely successful chain based in California sells convincing fake jewelry. The look-alikes range in price from $9 to $1,000, and include credible copies of the baroque and antique jewelry your great-grandmother might have worn.

If you want the real thing, you can go next door to **King Alley Jewelry** (☎ **809/773-4746**), which is owned by the same company and specializes in fine designer jewelry, including Tiffany and Cartier.

Estate Mount Washington Antiques. 2 Estate Mount Washington. ☎ **809/772-1026.**

This place is a remarkable discovery: the best treasure trove of colonial West Indian furniture and "flotsam" in the Virgin Islands. Try to arrive on Sunday when owners Tony and Nancy Ayer are on site to provide professional guidance and commentary. After browsing through their shop and perhaps making a purchase, you can walk around the grounds of an 18th-century sugar plantation under restoration.

Folk Art Traders. 1B Queen Cross St. ☎ **809/773-1900.**

Since 1985, the operators of this store have traveled throughout the Caribbean ("in the bush") to acquire a unique collection of local art and folk-art treasures, not only carnival masks, pottery, ceramics, and original paintings, but also handwrought jewelry. The assortment is wide-ranging, including batiks from Barbados and high-quality iron sculpture from Haiti. There's nothing else like it in the Virgin Islands.

Gone Tropical. 55 Company St. ☎ **809/773-4696.**

About 60% of the merchandise in this unique shop is made in Indonesia (usually Bali). The prices of new, semiantique, or antique sofas, beds, chests, tables, mirrors, and decorative carvings are the same as or less than those of similar pieces you might have bought new at more conventional furniture stores. The store also sells worthy art objects (which can be shipped wherever you want) ranging in price from $5 to $5,000, as well as jewelry, batiks, candles, and baskets.

Green Papaya. Caravella Arcade no. 15. ☎ **809/773-8848.**

The shopkeepers here have assembled a unique collection of accessories for home interiors, including picture frames, lighting fixtures, and baskets. There are two rooms, one displaying these wares, another dedicated to their new interior design service, with fabrics on display.

Harborside Market & Spirits. 59 King's Wharf. ☎ **809/773-8899.**

This outlet sells one of the island's best selections of duty-free liquors, wine, and beer. The location is also one of the most convenient in town, and saves you a trip to Woolworth's, which also has good prices in liquor but is inconveniently located outside of town.

Java Wraps. In the Pan Am Pavilion, Strand St. ☎ **809/773-3770.**

Known for its resort wear for women, men, and children, this shop is a kaleidoscope of colors and prints. You expect Dorothy Lamour, star of all those *Road* pictures, to appear at any minute. In fact, today's Dorothy (actually a local salesperson) demonstrates how to wrap and tie beach pareos and sarongs. Men's shirts display a collection of tropical and ethnic prints, and there's also a children's selection. The outlet also carries Javanese and Balinese art and antiquities.

Larimar. The Boardwalk/King's Walk. ☎ **809/692-9000.**

Everything sold in this shop is produced by the largest manufacturer of larimar gold settings in the world. Discovered in the 1970s, larimar is a pale-blue pectolyte prized for its sky-blue color. It's extracted from mines in only one mountain in the world, which is located on the southwestern edge of the Dominican Republic, near the Haitian border. Objects range in price from $25 to $1,000. Although other shops sell the stone in imaginative settings, this emporium has the widest selection.

Little Switzerland. 1108 King St. ☎ **809/773-1976.**

This store has branches throughout the Caribbean and is the island's best source for crystal, figurines, watches, china, perfume, flatware, leather, and lots of fine jewelry. It specializes in all the big names, such as Paloma Picasso leather goods. For luxuries like a Rolex watch, an Omega, or heirloom crystal such as Lalique, Swarovski, and Baccarat, this is the place. At least a few items are said to sell for up to 30% less than on the U.S. mainland, but don't take anyone's word for that unless you've checked prices carefully.

Many Hands. In the Pan Am Pavilion, Strand St. ☎ **809/773-1990.**

Many Hands sells Virgin Islands handcrafts exclusively. The merchandise includes West Indian spices and teas, shellwork, stained glass, hand-painted china, pottery, and handmade jewelry. Their collection of local paintings is intriguing, as is their year-round "Christmas tree."

Only in Paradise. 5 Company St. ☎ **809/773-0331.**

It's the largest store of its kind in Christiansted, and filled with merchandise you'll absolutely never need during your visit, but which you might want as intriguing dust collectors after you return home. The inventory includes cunningly crafted boxes, jewelry, and accessories for fashionable evenings out on the town. The outlet also sells a curious mix of leather products and lingerie. The taste is bourgeois and plush. Don't expect attentive service, however, as the staff seems rather inexperienced.

The Royal Poinciana. 1111 Strand St. ☎ **809/773-9892.**

This is the most interesting gift shop on St. Croix. In what looks like an antique apothecary, you'll find such Caribbean-inspired items as hot sauces ("fire water"), seasoning blends for gumbos, island herbal teas, Antillean coffees, and a scented array of soaps, toiletries, lotions, and shampoos. There's also a selection of museum-reproduction greeting cards and calendars. Also featured are fun and educational gifts for children.

St. Croix Perfume Center. 53 King St. ☎ **800/225-7031** or 809/773-7604.

Here you'll find the largest duty-free assortment of men's and women's fragrances on St. Croix, usually at 30% below U.S. mainland prices. For a minimum charge of $5, this store will ship perfumes anywhere in the world. The center recently added Iman cosmetics for women of color.

Sonya Ltd. 1 Company St. ☎ **809/778-8605.**

Sonya Hough is the matriarch of a cult following of local residents who wouldn't leave home without wearing one of her bracelets. She's most famous for her sterling-silver or gold (from 14- to 24-karat) interpretations of the C-clasp bracelet. Locals communicate discreet messages by how it's worn: If the cup of the C is turned toward your heart, it means you're emotionally committed. If the cup of the C is turned outward, it means you're available to whomever strikes your fancy. Prices range from $20 to $2,500. She also sells rings, earrings, and necklaces.

Urban Threadz/Tribal Threadz. 52C Company St. ☎ **809/773-2883.**

It's the most comprehensive clothing store in Christiansted's historic core, with a two-story, big-city scale and appeal that's different from the tropical-boutique aura of nearby T-shirt shops. It's the store where island residents prefer to shop, because of the clothing's hip, urban styles. Garments for men are on the street level, women's garments are upstairs, and the inventory includes everything from Bermuda shorts to lightweight summer blazers and men's suits. They carry Calvin Klein, Nautica, and Oakley, among others.

Violette Boutique. In the Caravelle Arcade, 38 Strand St. ☎ **809/773-2148.**

A small department store carrying lines known worldwide, Violette stocks many exclusive fragrances and hard-to-find toiletry items. It also has the latest in Cartier, Fendi, Pequignet, and Gucci. A wide selection of famous cosmetic names is featured, and Fendi has its own area for bags and accessories. A selection of gifts for children is also carried. Many famous brand names found here aren't available elsewhere on the island, though they are definitely found elsewhere in the Caribbean.

Woolworth's. In the Sunny Isle Shopping Center, Centerline Rd. ☎ **809/778-5466.**

Although primarily a department store, this retail outlet contains the largest supply of duty-free liquor on the island. Cruzan rum is in plentiful supply, along with a vast array of other brand-name liquors and liqueurs.

ST. CROIX AFTER DARK

St. Croix doesn't have the nightlife of St. Thomas, so to find the action, you might have to hotel- or bar-hop or consult ***St. Croix This Week.***

Try to catch a performance of the **Quadrille Dancers,** the cultural treat of St. Croix. Their dances have changed little since plantation days; the women wear long dresses, white gloves, and turbans, and the men are attired in flamboyant shirts, sashes, and tight black trousers. When you've learned their steps, you're invited to join the dancers on the floor. Ask at your hotel if and where they're performing.

THE PERFORMING ARTS

Island Center. Sunny Isle. ☎ **809/778-5272.** Tickets $5–$25.

This 1,100-seat amphitheater, half a mile north of Sunny Isle, continues to attract big-name entertainers to St. Croix. Its program is widely varied, ranging from jazz, nostalgia, and musical revues to Broadway plays such as *The Wiz.* Consult *St. Croix This Week* or call the center to see what's being presented. The Caribbean Community Theatre and Courtyard Players perform regularly. Call for performance times.

THE CLUB & MUSIC SCENE

Blue Moon. 17 Strand St. ☎ **809/772-2222.**

This little dive, which is also a good bistro, is the hottest and hippest spot in Christiansted on Thursday and Friday nights. On Thursdays pianist Bobby Page (the Bobby Short of St. Croix) takes over the keys, and on Friday a five-piece ensemble provides the entertainment. The good news is that there is no cover, so you'll only have to spend money on drinks. Stick around to try some of the food from an eclectic menu that samples flavors from the Bayou Country to Asia.

Hondo's Nightclub. 53 King St. ☎ **809/773-5855.** Cover $5.

Simply called "Hondo's" by the regulars, this local dive is a hot spot with mostly recorded music, although they occasionally "heat up" with live reggae, calypso, Latino, and international music. It's always party night here, and locals usually outnumber the tourists. Exercise caution going through the streets late at night to reach this joint.

The Marina Bar. In the King's Alley Hotel, King's Alley/The Waterfront. ☎ **809/773-0103.**

This bar occupies a panoramic position on the waterfront, on a shaded terrace overlooking the sea and Protestant Cay. Although the place remains open throughout the day, the real festivities begin right after the last seaplane departs for St. Thomas (around 5:30pm) and continue energetically until 8:30pm. Sunset-colored cocktails made with rum, mangos, bananas, papaya, and grenadine are the libations of choice. You can stave off hunger pangs with burgers, sandwiches, and West Indian–style platters. The bar has live entertainment most nights, usually steel bands. On Monday you can bet on crab races.

Mt. Pellier Hut Domino Club. Montpellier. ☎ **809/772-9914.**

This one-of-a-kind club came into being as a battered snack shack established to serve players of a never-ending domino game. Gradually it grew into a drinking and entertainment center, although the game is still going strong. Today, the bar boasts a beer-drinking pig (Miss Piggy), and has a one-man band, Piro, who plays on Sunday. The bartender will also serve you a lethal rum-based Mamma Wanna.

The Terrace Lounge. In the Buccaneer, Rte. 82, Estate Shoys. ☎ **809/773-2100.** Cover $5 for those who aren't staying in the hotel.

Every night this lounge off the main dining room of one of St. Croix's most upscale hotels welcomes some of the Caribbean's finest entertainers, often including a full band.

The Wreck Bar. 5-AB Hospital St., Christiansted. ☎ **809/773-6092.**

The margaritas are "absolutely habit-forming," and the decor in this hole-in-the-wall, featuring a retractable awning that extends over the open-air dance floor whenever it rains and an indoor-outdoor space full of bamboo and thatch, is directly inspired by *Gilligan's Island.* The place has a sense of irreverent fun, especially when it offers live reggae.

A SIDE TRIP TO BUCK ISLAND: UNSPOILED NATURE & WORLD-CLASS SNORKELING

The crystal-clear water and the white coral sand of Buck Island, a satellite of St. Croix, are legendary. Some visitors, including Arthur Frommer, have called it "the single most important attraction of the Caribbean." In years past the island was frequented by the swashbuckling likes of Morgan, LaFitte, Blackbeard, and even Captain Kidd. Now the National Park Service has marked an underwater snorkeling trail in the waters offshore, attracting a new generation of Caribbean seafarers. The park covers about 850 acres, including the land area, which has a sandy beach with picnic tables and barbecue pits, as well as restrooms and a small changing room. There are two major underwater trails for snorkeling on the reef, plus many other labyrinths and grottoes for more serious divers. You can also take a hiking trail through the tropical vegetation that covers the island. Despite the fact that access to Buck Island is only via chartered tours and boat trips, the numbers of visitors here make this one of the most-visited rock spits in the Caribbean.

Only $^1/_3$ mile wide and a mile long, Buck Island lies $1^1/_2$ miles off the northeastern coast of St. Croix. A barrier reef shelters many reef fish, including queen angelfish and the smooth trunkfish. The attempt to return the presently uninhabited Buck

Island to nature has been successful—even the endangered brown pelicans are producing young here.

Small boats run between St. Croix and Buck Island, and snorkeling equipment is supplied. You head out in the morning, and nearly all charters allow for 1$^1/_2$ hours of snorkeling and swimming.

You can have a memorable ramble through sun-flooded and shallow waters off the rocky coastline. A couple of warnings, though: Bring protection from the sun's sometimes-merciless rays; and even more important, don't rush to touch every plant you see. The island's western edge has groves of poisonous machineel trees, whose leaves, bark, and fruit cause extreme irritation if they come into contact with human skin.

Circumnavigating the island on foot will take about two hours. Buck Island's trails meander from several points along its coastline to its sun-flooded summit, affording views over nearby St. Croix.

Buck Island's greatest attraction is its **underwater snorkeling trail,** which rings part of the island. Equipped with a face mask, swim fins, and a snorkel, you'll be treated to some of the most beautiful underwater views in the Caribbean. Plan on spending at least two-thirds of a day at this extremely famous ecological site.

Mile Mark Watersports, in the King Christian Hotel, 59 King's Wharf, Christiansted (☎ **800/523-DIVE** or 809/773-2628), conducts twice-daily tours of Buck Island. They offer two ways to reach the reefs. One is a half-day tour aboard a glass-bottom boat departing from the King Christian Hotel. Tours are daily from 9:30am to 1pm and 1:30 to 5pm, and cost $35 per person; all snorkeling equipment is included. A more romantic half-day journey is aboard one of the company's sailboats, which, for $45 per person, offers the sea breezes and the thrill of harnessing the wind's power to reach the reef. A full-day tour, offered daily from 10am to 4pm on the company's 40-foot catamaran, can take up to 20 participants to Buck Island's reefs. Included in the tour are a West Indian barbecue picnic on the isolated sands of Buck Island's beaches and plenty of opportunities for snorkeling. The full-day tour costs $60.

Captain Heinz (☎ **809/773-3161** or 809/773-4041) is an Austrian-born skipper with more than 22 years of sailing experience. His trimaran, *Teroro II,* leaves Green Cay Marina "H" Dock at 9am and 2pm, never filled with more than 24 passengers. The snorkeling trip costs $45 in the morning or $40 in the afternoon. All gear and safety equipment are provided. The captain is not only a skilled sailor but is also a considerate host. He will even take you around the outer reef, which the other guides do not, for an unforgettable underwater experience.

The British Virgin Islands

7

With their small bays and hidden coves, the British Virgin Islands are among the world's loveliest cruising grounds. Strung over the northeastern corner of the Caribbean, about 60 miles east of Puerto Rico, are some 40 islands, although that's including some small, uninhabited cays or spits of land. Only three of the British Virgins are of any significant size: Tortola ("dove of peace"), Virgin Gorda (the "Fat Virgin"), and Jost Van Dyke. Remote Norman Island is said to have been the inspiration for Robert Louis Stevenson's *Treasure Island.* On Deadman Bay, a rocky cay, Blackbeard marooned 15 pirates and a bottle of rum, which gave rise to the ditty.

Columbus came this way in 1493, but the British Virgins apparently made little impression on him. Although the Spanish and Dutch contested it, Tortola was officially annexed by the English in 1672. Today these islands are a British colony, with their own elected government and a population of about 17,000.

The vegetation is varied and depends on the rainfall. In some parts, palms and mangos grow in profusion, whereas other places are arid and studded with cactus.

There are predictions that mass tourism is on the way, but so far the British Virgins are still a paradise for escapists.

GETTING THERE

BY PLANE There are no direct flights from New York to the British Virgin Islands, but you can make connections from San Juan and St. Thomas to Beef Island/Tortola. (See chapter 5, "Puerto Rico," and chapter 6, "The U.S. Virgin Islands," for information on flying to these islands.)

Your best bet to reach Beef Island/Tortola is to take **American Eagle (☎ 800/433-7300** in the U.S.), the most reliable airline in the Caribbean, with at least four daily trips from San Juan to Beef Island/Tortola.

Another choice, if you're on one of Tortola's neighboring islands, is the much less reliable **Leeward Islands Air Transport (LIAT)** (**☎ 809/462-0701**). This Caribbean carrier makes the short hops to Tortola from St. Kitts, Antigua, St. Maarten, St. Thomas, and San Juan in small planes not known for their frequency or careful scheduling. Reservations are made through travel agents or through the larger U.S.-based airlines that connect with LIAT hubs.

Area Code Change Notice

Please note that, effective October 1, 1997, the area code for the British Virgin Islands will change from **809** to **284.** All of the B.V.I. area codes in this book are listed as **809.** You will be able to dial 809 until April 1, 1998.

Beef Island, the site of the major airport serving the British Virgins, is connected to Tortola by the one-lane Queen Elizabeth Bridge.

BY FERRY You can travel from Charlotte Amalie (St. Thomas) by public ferry to West End and Road Town on Tortola, a 45-minute voyage along Drake's Channel through the islands. Boats making this run include **Native Son (☎ 809/495-4617)**, **Smith's Ferry Service (☎ 809/495-4495)**, and **Inter-Island Boat Services (☎ 809/776-6597)**. The latter specializes in a somewhat obscure routing—that is, from St. John to the West End on Tortola.

FAST FACTS: The British Virgin Islands

American Express Local representatives include Travel Plan, Waterfront Drive (**☎ 809/494-2347**), in Tortola; and Travel Plan, Virgin Gorda Yacht Harbour (**☎ 809/495-5586**), in Virgin Gorda.

Area Code As of October 1, 1997, the area code in the B.V.I. will be **284,** not **809.** When calling from outside the islands, you must then dial **49** before all British Virgin Island numbers.

Banks Banks are generally open Monday through Thursday from 9am to 3pm, Friday from 9am to 5pm. To cash traveler's checks, try **Bank of Nova Scotia,** Wickhams Cay (**☎ 809/494-2526**) or **Barclays Bank,** Wickhams Cay (**☎ 809/494-2171**), both near Road Town on Tortola.

Cameras and Film The best place for supplies and developing on Tortola is **Bolo's Brothers,** Wickhams Cay (**☎ 809/494-2867**).

Crime Crime is rare here; in fact, the British Virgin Islands are among the safest places in the Caribbean. Still, you should take all the usual precautions you would anywhere, and don't leave items unattended on the beach.

Currency The U.S. dollar is the legal currency, much to the surprise of British travelers.

Customs You can bring items intended for your personal use into the British Virgin Islands. For U.S. residents, the duty-free allowance is only $400, providing you have been out of the country for 48 hours. You can bring unsolicited gifts home if they total less than $50 per day to any single address. You don't pay duty on items classified as handcrafts, art, or antiques.

Dentist For dental emergencies, contact **Dental Surgery (☎ 809/494-3474)**, which is in Road Town, Tortola behind the Skeleton Building and next to the *BVI Beacon,* the local newspaper.

Doctor See "Hospitals," below.

Drug Laws Drugs, including use, possession, and sale, are strictly prohibited, and penalties are stiff.

Drugstores The best place to go is **J. R. O'Neal,** Main Street, Road Town (**☎ 809/494-2292**), in Tortola; closed Sunday.

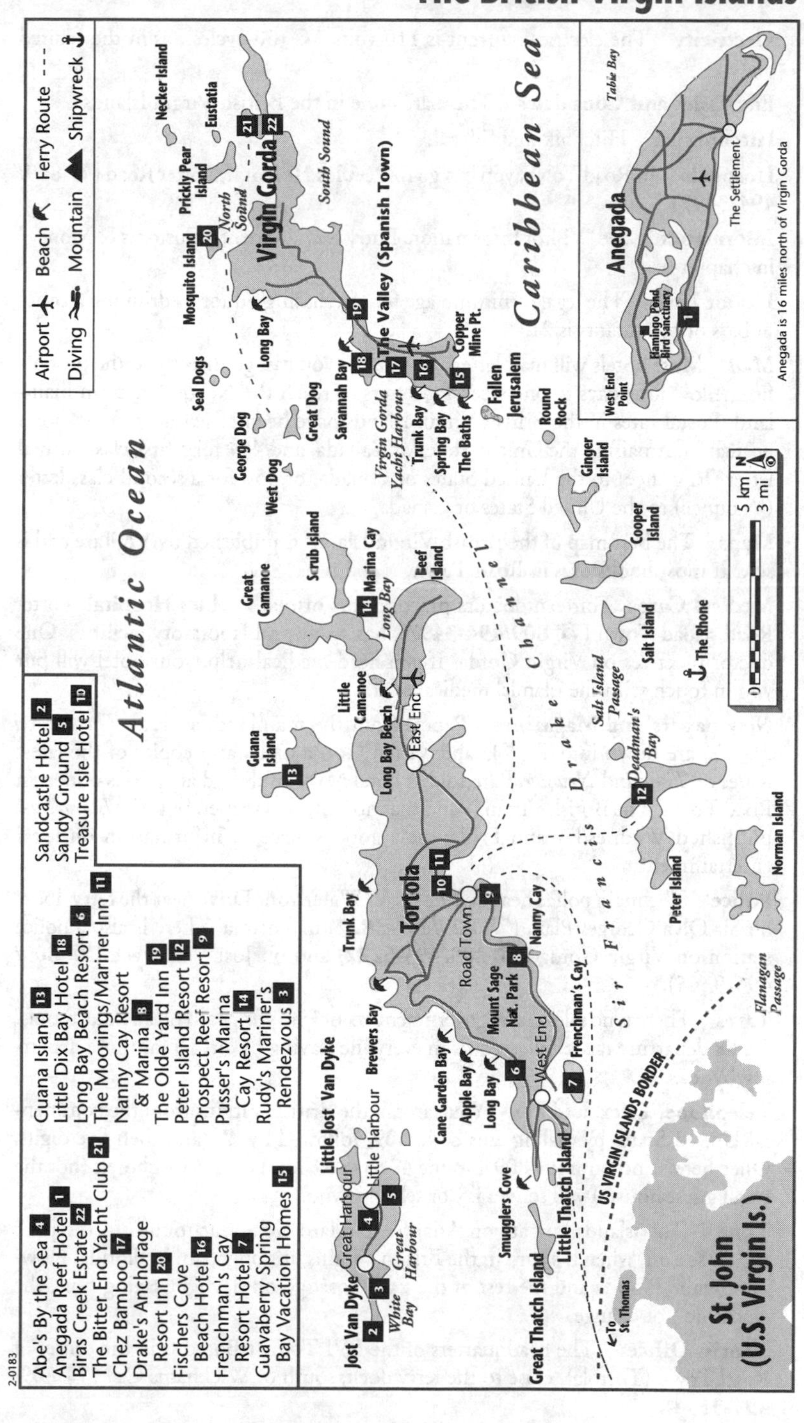
2-0183
Abe's By the Sea 4
Anegada Reef Hotel 1
Biras Creek Estate 22
The Bitter End Yacht Club 21
Chez Bamboo 17
Drake's Anchorage Resort Inn 20
Fischers Cove Beach Hotel 16
Frenchman's Cay Resort Hotel 7
Guavaberry Spring Bay Vacation Homes 15
Guana Island 13
Little Dix Bay Hotel 18
Long Bay Beach Resort 6
The Moorings/Mariner Inn 11
Nanny Cay Resort & Marina 8
The Olde Yard Inn 19
Peter Island Resort 12
Prospect Reef Resort 9
Pusser's Marina Cay Resort 14
Rudy's Mariner's Rendezvous 3
Sandcastle Hotel 2
Sandy Ground 5
Treasure Isle Hotel 10
Airport
Beach
Ferry Route
Diving
Mountain
Shipwreck
Atlantic Ocean
Caribbean Sea
Sir Francis Drake Channel
Jost Van Dyke
White Bay
Great Harbour
Little Harbour
Little Jost Van Dyke
Great Thatch Island
Little Thatch Island
Smugglers Cove
Long Bay
Apple Bay
Cane Garden Bay
Brewers Bay
West End
Mount Sage Nat. Park
Frenchman's Cay
Road Town
Nanny Cay
Trunk Bay
Tortola
Long Bay Beach
East End
Guana Island
Little Camanoe
Great Camanoe
Long Bay
Marina Cay
Scrub Island
Beef Island
West Dog
George Dog
Great Dog
Seal Dogs
Virgin Gorda Yacht Harbour
Savannah Bay
Long Bay
The Valley (Spanish Town)
Trunk Bay
Spring Bay
The Baths
Copper Mine Pt.
Mosquito Island
North Sound
Prickly Pear Island
Virgin Gorda
South Sound
Eustatia
Necker Island
Fallen Jerusalem
Round Rock
Ginger Island
Cooper Island
Salt Island
The Rhone
Salt Island Passage
Deadman's Bay
Peter Island
Norman Island
Flanagan Passage
US VIRGIN ISLANDS BORDER
To St. Thomas
St. John (U.S. Virgin Is.)
0 5 km 3 mi
N
Anegada
Tabic Bay
The Settlement
West End Point
Flamingo Pond Bird Sanctuary
Anegada is 16 miles north of Virgin Gorda

Electricity The electrical current is 110 volts AC (60 cycles), as in the United States.

Embassies and Consulates There are none in the British Virgin Islands.

Hitchhiking Hitchhiking is illegal.

Hospitals In Road Town, you can go to **Peebles Hospital,** Porter Road (☎ **809/494-3497**).

Information See "Visitor Information, Entry Requirements, Customs & Money" in chapter 3.

Liquor Laws The legal minimum age for purchasing liquor or drinking alcohol in bars or restaurants is 21.

Mail Most hotels will mail letters for you, or you can go directly to the post office. Allow four days to one week for letters to reach the North American mainland. Postal rates in the British Virgin Islands have been raised now to 30¢ for a postcard (airmail) to the United States or Canada, and 45¢ for a first-class airmail letter (1/2 ounce) to the United States or Canada, or 35¢ for a second-class letter (1/2 ounce) to the United States or Canada.

Maps The best map of the British Virgin Islands is published by **Vigilate** and is sold at most bookstores in Road Town.

Medical Care Thirteen doctors practice on Tortola; **Peebles Hospital,** Porter Road, Road Town (☎ **809/494-3497**), has X-ray and laboratory facilities. One doctor practices on Virgin Gorda. If you need medical help, your hotel will put you in touch with the islands' medical staff.

Newspapers and Magazines Papers from the mainland, such as *The Miami Herald,* are flown into Tortola and Virgin Gorda daily, and copies of the latest issues of *Time* and *Newsweek* are sold at hotel newsstands and at various outlets in Road Town. The British Virgin Islands has no daily newspaper, but *The Island Sun,* published Wednesday and Friday, is a good source of information on local entertainment.

Police The main police headquarters is on Waterfront Drive near the ferry docks on Sir Olva Georges Plaza (☎ **809/494-3822**) in Tortola. There is also a police station on Virgin Gorda (☎ **809/495-5222**) and on Jost Van Dyke (☎ **809/495-9345**).

Taxes There is no sales tax. A government tax of 7% is imposed on all hotel rooms. An $8 departure tax is collected from everyone leaving by air, $5 for those departing by sea.

Telephone, Telex, and Fax You can call the British Virgins from the continental United States by dialing area code **809,** followed by **49,** and then five digits. Once here, omit both the 809 and the 49 to make local calls. Most hotels (not the small guest houses) will send a fax or telex for you.

Time The islands operate on Atlantic standard time year-round. In the peak winter season, when it's 6am in the British Virgins, it's only 5am in Florida. However, when Florida and the rest of the East Coast go on daylight saving time, the clocks do not change.

Tourist Offices The headquarters of the BVI Tourist Board is in the center of Road Town (Tortola), close to the ferry dock, south of Wickhams Cay (☎ **809/494-3134**).

1 Tortola

On the southern shore of this 24-square-mile island is **Road Town,** the capital of the British Virgin Islands. It's the seat of Government House and other administrative buildings, but it feels more like a small village than a town. The landfill at Wickhams Cay, a 70-acre town center development and marina in the harbor, has lured a massive yacht-chartering business here and has transformed the sleepy capital into more of a bustling center.

The entire southern coast, including Road Town, is characterized by rugged mountain peaks. On the northern coast are white sandy beaches, banana trees, mangos, and clusters of palms.

Close to Tortola's eastern end, **Beef Island** is the site of the main airport for passengers arriving in the British Virgins. The tiny island is connected to Tortola by the one-lane Queen Elizabeth Bridge, which the queen dedicated in 1966. On the north shore of Beef Island is Long Bay Beach.

Because Tortola is the gateway to the British Virgin Islands, the information on how to get here is covered above.

GETTING AROUND

BY TAXI Taxis meet every arriving flight. Government regulations prohibit anyone from renting a car at the airport—visitors must take a taxi to their hotels. The fare from the Beef Island airport to Road Town is $15 for one to three passengers. Your hotel can call a taxi for you. A **taxi tour** lasting 2½ hours costs $45 for one to three people. To call a taxi in Road Town, dial ☎ **809/494-2322;** on Beef Island, ☎ **809/495-2378.**

BY RENTAL CAR Because of the volume of tourism to Tortola, you should reserve a car in advance, especially in winter. A handful of local companies rent cars, but we recommend using one of the U.S.-based chains, even if the cost is slightly higher. On Tortola, **Budget** (☎ **800/527-0700** or 809/494-5150) is at 1 Wickhams Cay, Road Town. **Avis** (☎ **800/331-2112** or 809/494-3322) maintains offices opposite the police headquarters in Road Town. **Hertz** (☎ **800/654-3001** or 809/495-4405) has offices outside Road Town, on the island's West End, near the ferryboat landing dock. Rental companies will usually deliver your car to your hotel. All three companies require a valid driver's license and a temporary B.V.I. driver's license, which the car-rental company can sell you for $10; it's valid for three months.

Remember to **drive on the left.** Because island roads are narrow, poorly lit, and have few, if any, lines, driving at night can be tricky. It's a good idea to rent a taxi to take you to that difficult to find beach, restaurant, or bar.

BY BUS **Scato's Bus Service** (☎ **809/494-5873**) operates from the north end of the island to the west end, picking up passengers who hail it down. Fares for a trek across the island are $1 to $3.

VISITOR INFORMATION

There is a **B.V.I. Tourist Board Office** (☎ **809/494-3134**) at the center of Road Town near the ferry dock. You'll find information about hotels, restaurants, tours, and more. Pick up a copy of *The Welcome Tourist Guide,* which has a useful map of the island. If you have Internet access, the tourist board has a Web site at **www.bviwelcome.com.**

WHERE TO STAY

None of the island's hotels is as big, splashy, and all-inclusive as the hotels in the U.S. Virgin Islands, and that's just fine with most of the islands' repeat visitors. All rates are subject to a 10% service charge and a 7% government tax on the room.

EXPENSIVE

Frenchman's Cay Resort Hotel. West End (P.O. Box 1054), Tortola, B.V.I. ☎ **800/235-4077** in the U.S., 800/463-0199 in Canada, or 809/495-4844. Fax 809/495-4056. 9 villas. Winter, $220 one-bedroom villa; $330 two-bedroom villa. Off-season, $125 one-bedroom villa; $190 two-bedroom villa. MAP $45 per person extra. AE, DISC, MC, V. From Tortola, cross the bridge to Frenchman's Cay, turn left, and follow the road to the eastern tip of the cay.

This intimate resort is tucked away at the windward side of Frenchman's Cay, a little island connected by bridge to Tortola. The 12-acre estate enjoys delightful year-round breezes and views of Sir Francis Drake Channel and the outer Virgins. The individual one- and two-bedroom villas—actually a cluster of condos—are well furnished, each with a shady terrace, full kitchen, dining room, and sitting room. The two-bedroom villas have two full baths, a vacation in and of itself for families looking to escape the morning bathroom line.

Dining/Entertainment: The Clubhouse Restaurant and lounge bar is located in the main pavilion. The menu features a continental and Caribbean cuisine.

Facilities: Beach with snorkeling, freshwater swimming pool, tennis court, Sunfish sailboats, kayaks, Windsurfers; day-sail trips, horseback riding, scuba diving, island tours, and car rentals can be arranged.

✪ **Long Bay Beach Resort.** Tortola, B.V.I. ☎ **800/729-9599** in the U.S. and Canada; 800/898-379 in Britain, or 809/495-4252. Fax 914/833-3318 in Larchmont, N.Y. 62 rms, 20 villas. A/C. Winter, $220–$330 double; $450–$500 two-bedroom villa; $650–$700 three-bedroom villa. Off-season, $120–$195 double; $260–$350 two-bedroom villa; $360–$485 three-bedroom villa. MAP $40 per person extra. AE, MC, V.

On the north shore, about 10 minutes from the West End, is the only full-service resort on the island: a low-rise hotel resort complex set in a 52-acre estate with a mile-long white-sand beach. The accommodations include hillside rooms and studios, the smallest and most basic with the simplest furnishings, and deluxe beachfront rooms and cabanas with either balconies or patios that overlook the ocean. In addition the resort offers two- and three-bedroom villas complete with kitchen, living area, and a large deck with a gas grill. Beachfront deluxe rooms and villas have cable TV. If you're not staying right on the beach, you'll still enjoy an ocean view from any of the other accommodations.

Dining/Entertainment: The Beach Café offers breakfast and lunch as well as informal à la carte suppers. In the ruins of an old sugar mill the restaurant serves regular evening buffets with live entertainment. The Garden Restaurant has dinner by reservation only and offers a tantalizing variety of local and international dishes in a more elegant, alfresco setting.

Services: Daily maid service, laundry, baby-sitting, car rental; chef available on request for villa renters.

Facilities: Oceanside freshwater swimming pool, two championship tennis courts and one regular court, beach bar, shops, summer children's activity program (ages three to eight).

The Sugar Mill. Apple Bay (P.O. Box 425, Road Town), Tortola, B.V.I. ☎ **800/462-8834** or 809/495-4355. Fax 809/495-4696. 20 units, 1 villa. A/C. Winter, $190–$265 double; $280 triple; $295 quad; $585 two-bedroom villa. Off-season, $150 double; $195 triple; $210 quad; $400 two-bedroom villa. AE, MC, V. Closed Aug–Sept.

Tortola

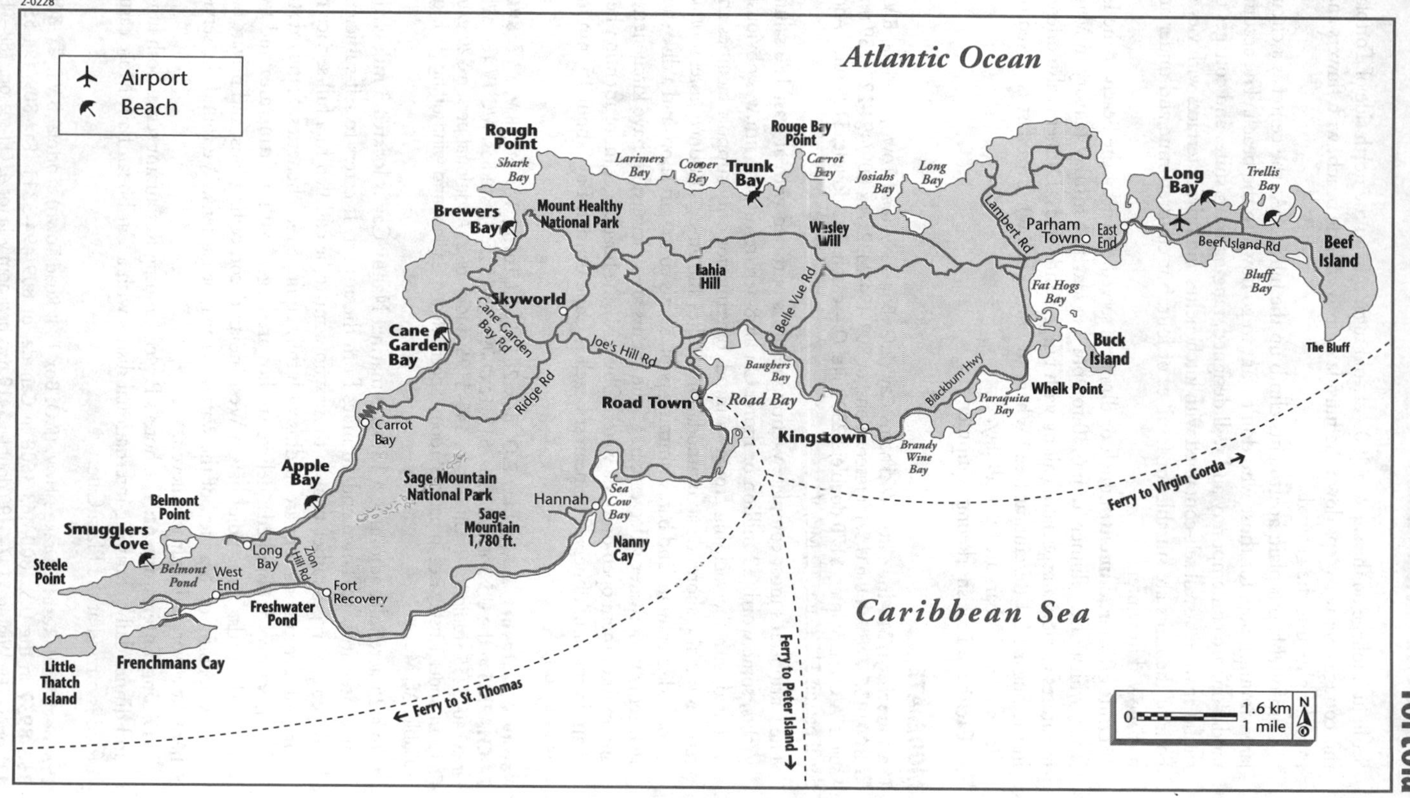

2-0228
Airport
Beach
Atlantic Ocean
Rough Point
Shark Bay
Larimers Bay
Cooper Bay
Trunk Bay
Rouge Bay Point
Carrot Bay
Josiahs Bay
Long Bay
Long Bay
Trellis Bay
Brewers Bay
Mount Healthy National Park
Wesley Will
Lambert Rd
Parham Town
East End
Beef Island Rd
Beef Island
Lahia Hill
Belle Vue Rd
Bluff Bay
Skyworld
Cane Garden Bay Rd
Fat Hogs Bay
Cane Garden Bay
Joe's Hill Rd
Buck Island
The Bluff
Baughers Bay
Blackburn Hwy
Whelk Point
Ridge Rd
Road Town
Road Bay
Paraquita Bay
Carrot Bay
Kingstown
Brandy Wine Bay
Apple Bay
Sage Mountain National Park
Hannah
Sea Cow Bay
Ferry to Virgin Gorda →
Belmont Point
Sage Mountain 1,780 ft.
Smugglers Cove
Long Bay
Zion Hill Rd
Nanny Cay
Steele Point
Belmont Pond
West End
Fort Recovery
Freshwater Pond
Caribbean Sea
Frenchmans Cay
Little Thatch Island
← Ferry to St. Thomas
Ferry to Peter Island →
0
1.6 km
1 mile
N

Set in lush foliage on the site of a 300-year-old sugar mill on the north side of Tortola, this cottage colony sweeps down the hillside to its own little beach, with flowers and fruits brightening the grounds.

Comfortable but plain apartments climb up the hillside. At the center is a circular swimming pool for those who don't want to go down to the beach. The accommodations are contemporary and well designed, ranging from suites and cottages to studio apartments, all self-contained with kitchenettes and private terraces with views. Four of the units are suitable for families of four, but children nine and under are not allowed in winter.

Dining/Entertainment: Lunch or dinner is served down by the beach at the Islands, which offers dinner from 6:30 to 9pm Tuesday to Saturday January to May; it features Caribbean specialties along with burgers and salads. Dinner is also offered in the Sugar Mill Restaurant (see "Where to Dine," below). Breakfast is served on the terrace. The bars are open all day.

Facilities: Free snorkeling equipment.

MODERATE

The Moorings/Mariner Inn. Wickhams Cay (P.O. Box 139, Road Town), Tortola, B.V.I. ☎ **800/435-7289** in the U.S. for reservations, or 809/494-2332. Fax 809/494-2226. 39 rms, 4 suites. A/C TEL. Winter, $170 double; $230 suite. Off-season, $95 double; $125 suite. Additional person $15 extra. AE, MC, V.

The Caribbean's most complete yachting resort is outfitted with at least 180 sailing yachts, some worth $2 million or more. On an 8-acre resort, the inn was obviously designed with the yachting crowd in mind, offering not only support facilities and services but also shoreside accommodations (suites and air-conditioned hotel rooms), a dockside restaurant and bar, swimming pool, tennis court, gift shop, and a dive shop that rents underwater video cameras. The rooms are spacious; all have kitchenettes, and most of them open onto the water. Obviously the boaties get more attention here than do the landlubbers. The nearest beach is Cane Garden Bay, about 15 minutes away by car.

Nanny Cay Resort & Marina. P.O. Box 281, Road Town, Tortola, B.V.I. ☎ **800/74-CHARMS** in the U.S., or 809/494-2512. Fax 809/494-0555. 42 studios. A/C TV TEL. Winter, $140–$255 studio for 2. Off-season, $45–$195 studio for 2. Additional person $20 extra. Children under 12 stay free in parents' room. Special diving, sailing, and windsurfing packages available. AE, MC, V.

On a 25-acre inlet adjoining a 180-slip marina, Nanny Cay is located 3 miles from the center of Road Town and 10 miles from the airport. It caters to self-sufficient, independent types rather than to those who want to be coddled in a full-service resort. All accommodations are studios with fully equipped kitchenettes. Standard studios have two double beds; deluxe studios are larger, with a sitting area and two queen-size beds. The studios have a West Indian decor, ceiling fans, and private balconies opening onto a view of the water, marina, or gardens. We found the service here, however, to be rather uneven.

Dining/Entertainment: The hotel's Pegleg Landing Restaurant serves both lunch and dinner daily, featuring international dishes with a Caribbean flair. More casual food is offered at the Plaza Café.

Prospect Reef Resort. Drake's Hwy. (P.O. Box 104, Road Town), Tortola, B.V.I. ☎ **800/356-8937** in the U.S., 800/463-3608 in Canada, or 809/494-3311. Fax 809/494-5595. 131 units. TEL. Winter, $147–$190 double; $410 two-bedroom villa for 4. Off-season, $88–$117 double; $274 two-bedroom villa for 4. AE, MC, V.

Built by a consortium of British investors in 1979, this is the largest resort in the British Virgin Islands. It rises above a small, private harbor in a series of two-story concrete buildings scattered over 44 acres of steeply sloping, landscaped terrain. The panoramic view of Sir Francis Drake Channel from the bedrooms is one of the best anywhere, but there's no beach to speak of at this hotel.

Each of the resort's buildings contains up to 10 individual accommodations and is painted in hibiscus-inspired shades of pink, peach, purple, or aquamarine. Initially designed as condominiums, there are unique studios, town houses, and villas, in addition to guest rooms. All include private balconies or patios; larger units have kitchenettes, good size living and dining areas, plus separate bedrooms or sleeping lofts. About one-third of the rooms are air-conditioned; others are cooled by ceiling fans and the trade winds. All rooms are wired for TVs, which you can rent.

Dining/Entertainment: Food at the hotel's Callaloo Restaurant (see below), offering a combination of continental specialties and island favorites, was praised by *Gourmet* magazine. There's a live lobster tank, and the callaloo beef Wellington, although likely to be a first for you, is sublime. Light meals are served on the terrace of the Scuttlebutt Bar and Grill or around the Seapool Bar and Grill.

Facilities: Five pools including sand-terraced sea pools for snorkeling, plus a narrow, artificial beach by one of the pools. Six tennis courts are available, as well as a health and fitness center and a pitch-and-putt course. Guest services staffers can fill you in on what's available from the harbor: day sailing, snorkeling, scuba diving, and sport fishing.

Treasure Isle Hotel. Pasea Estate, east end of Road Town (P.O. Box 68, Road Town), Tortola, B.V.I. ☎ **800/334-2435** in the U.S. for reservations, or 809/494-2501. Fax 809/494-2507. 39 rms, 2 suites. A/C TV TEL. Winter, $170 double; $230 suite. Off-season, $95 double; $125 suite. Additional person $15 extra. AE, DISC, MC, V.

The most central resort on Tortola was built at the edge of the capital on 15 acres of hillside overlooking a marina (not on the beach). The core of the hotel is a rather splashy and colorful lounge and swimming-pool area. The motel-like rooms are on two levels along the hillside terraces; a third level is occupied by more elegantly decorated suites at the crest of a hill.

Dining/Entertainment: Adjoining the lounge and pool area is a covered open-air dining room overlooking the harbor. The cuisine is respected here, with barbecue and full à la carte menus offered at dinner. On Wednesday the hotel puts on a West Indian "grill out," complete with live entertainment and dancing.

Services: Complimentary transportation to the nearest beach.

Facilities: The hotel has a fully equipped dive facility that handles beginning instruction up to full certification courses.

WHERE TO DINE

EXPENSIVE

✪ **Brandywine Bay Restaurant.** Brandywine Estate. ☎ **809/495-2301.** Reservations required. Main courses $20–$28. AE, MC, V. Mon–Sat 6–9:30pm. Closed Aug–Oct. Drive 3 miles east of Road Town (toward the airport) on South Shore Rd. NORTHERN ITALIAN.

This restaurant is set on a cobblestone garden terrace along the south shore, overlooking Sir Francis Drake Channel. It's the most elegant choice for romantic dining. Davide Pugliese, the chef, and his wife, Cele, the hostess, have earned a reputation on Tortola for their outstanding Florentine fare. Davide changes his menu daily, based on the availability of fresh produce. Typical dishes include beef carpaccio, homemade pasta, his own special calves' liver dish (the recipe is a secret), the typical bistecca alla fiorentina, and homemade mozzarella with fresh basil and tomatoes. Their skillful cookery ranges from the classic to the inspired. If you feel like indulging in game, you can order either pheasant or venison.

Callaloo. Prospect Reef Resort, Drake's Hwy. ☎ **809/494-3311.** Reservations recommended. Main courses $10–$28.50. AE, MC, V. Daily 7am–11pm. INTERNATIONAL.

One of the better hotel restaurants, this place gets rather romantic at night, especially if it's a balmy evening and the tropical breezes are blowing. It's the kind of cliché Caribbean setting that is forever a turn-on, and the food is quite good too. The menu is hardly imaginative, but the chefs do well with their limited repertoire. Begin with the conch fritters or shrimp cocktail, and don't pass on the house salad which has a zesty papaya dressing. Main dishes include fresh lobster when available (not as good as the Maine variety though) and also fresh fish like tuna, swordfish, or mahimahi. For dessert, make it the orange bread pudding if featured. If not, then the Key lime pie. Downstairs is the less expensive Scuttlebutt Bar and Grill.

Skyworld. Ridge Rd., Road Town. ☎ **809/494-3567.** Reservations required. Main courses $16.50–$29. AE, MC, V. Daily 11am–3pm and 5:30–8:30pm. INTERNATIONAL.

Under new management, Skyworld continues to be all the rage, one of the worthiest dining excursions on the island. On one of Tortola's loftiest peaks, at a breezy 1,337 feet, it offers views of both the U.S. Virgin Islands and the British Virgin Islands. Completely renovated, the restaurant is now divided into two sections—one more upscale with a dress code for men (shirts with collars and long trousers) and an enclosed garden section where you can dine in shorts. Both sections offer the same menu.

The fresh pumpkin soup is an island favorite, but you can also begin with seafood au gratin or, our favorite, mushrooms stuffed with conch. The fresh fish of the day is your best bet (we prefer to skip the steak with port and peaches). The best Key lime pie on the island awaits you at the end of the meal, unless you succumb to chocolate fudge ice cream pie.

Sugar Mill Restaurant. Apple Bay. ☎ **809/495-4355.** Reservations required. Main courses $16–$28. AE, MC, V. Daily noon–2pm and 7–8:30pm. Closed Aug–Sept. From Road Town, drive west for about 7 miles, take a right turn over Zion Hill going north, and then at the T-junction opposite Sebastians, turn right; Sugar Mill lies about 1/2 mile down the road. CALIFORNIAN/CARIBBEAN.

Here, you'll dine in an informal room that was transformed from a three-century-old sugar mill (see "Where to Stay," above). Colorful works by Haitian painters hang on the old stone walls, and big copper basins once used in distilling rum have been planted with tropical flowers. Before going to the dining room, once part of the old boiling house, visit the open-air bar on a deck that overlooks the sea.

Your hosts, the Morgans, know a lot about food and wine. Jinx Morgan supervises the dining room and is an imaginative cook herself. One of their most popular creations, published in *Bon Appétit,* is a curried-banana soup. You may also begin with smoked conch pâté. Jamaican jerk pork roast with a green-peppercorn salsa or ginger-lime scallops with pasta and toasted walnut sauce is a likely choice for dinner. Lunch can be ordered by the beach at the second restaurant, **Islands,** where dinner is also served Tuesday to Saturday from 6:30 to 9pm from January to May. Try jerk ribs or stuffed crabs here.

Moderate

Mrs. Scatliffe's Restaurant. Carrot Bay. ☎ **809/495-4556.** Reservations required (call before 5:30pm). Fixed-price meal $20–$27. No credit cards. Daily 7–8pm (no later). WEST INDIAN.

Mrs. Scatliffe's offers home-cooked meals on the deck of her island home, and some of the vegetables come right from her garden, although others might be from a can. You'll be served soup (maybe spicy conch), which will be followed by curried goat, "old wife" fish, or perhaps chicken in a coconut shell. After dinner your hostess and her family will entertain you with a fungi-band performance (except on Sunday) or gospel singing. Be duly warned: This entertainment isn't for everyone, including one reader who compared the hymns to a "screeching caterwaul." Service, usually from an inexperienced teenager, is not exactly efficient.

You might be exposed to Mrs. Scatliffe's gentle and often humorous form of Christian fundamentalism. A Bible reading and a heartfelt rendition of a gospel song might be served up with a soft custard dessert. She often serves lunch in winter but call ahead just to be sure.

Pusser's Landing. Frenchman's Cay, West End. ☎ **809/495-4554.** Reservations recommended. Main courses $13–$25. AE, DISC, MC, V. Daily 11am–10pm. CARIBBEAN/ENGLISH PUB/MEXICAN.

This second Pusser's (see below for the first) is even more desirably located in the West End, opening onto the water. Amongst this nautical setting you can enjoy fresh grilled fish, or perhaps an English-inspired dish, like shepherd's pie. Begin with a hearty bowl of homemade soup and follow it with filet mignon, West Indian roast chicken, or a filet of mahimahi. "Mud pie" is the classic dessert here, or else you can try Pusser's rum cake. Some dishes occasionally miss the mark, but on the whole this is a good choice. Happy hour is daily from 4 to 6pm.

INEXPENSIVE

✪ **Capriccio di Mare.** Waterfront Dr., Road Town. ☎ **809/494-5369.** Reservations not accepted. Main courses $5–$12. No credit cards. Daily 8–10:30am and 11am–9pm. ITALIAN.

Small, casual, and laid-back, this local favorite was created by the owners of the Brandywine Bay restaurant (see above) on a whim. It's the most authentic-looking Italian cafe in the Virgin Islands (U.S. or British). In the morning, many locals stop in for a delectable Italian pastry and a cappuccino. You can come back for lunch or dinner. In the evening, you might precede dinner with a mango Bellini, a variation of the famous cocktail (made with fresh peaches) served at Harry's Bar in Venice. Begin with such appetizers as *tiapina,* flour tortillas with various toppings, and move on to fresh pastas with succulent sauces, well-stuffed sandwiches, or the best pizzas on the island—our favorite is the pizza topped with freshly grilled eggplant. Some nights, you may discover specials like lobster ravioli in a rosé sauce. Their freshly made salads are consistently good—we go for the *insalata mista* with large leafy greens and slices of fresh Parmesan.

Pusser's Road Town Pub. Waterfront Dr. and Main St., Road Town. ☎ **809/494-3897.** Reservations not accepted. Main courses $7–$20. AE, DISC, MC, V. Daily 10am–10pm. CARIBBEAN/ENGLISH PUB/MEXICAN.

Standing on the waterfront across from the ferry dock, Pusser's serves Caribbean fare, English pub grub, and tasty pizzas. This is not as fancy or as good as the previously recommended Pusser's, but it's a lot more convenient and has faster service. The complete lunch and dinner menu includes shepherd's pie and deli-style sandwiches. *Gourmet* magazine published the recipe for the chicken-and-asparagus pie. They have John Courage ale on draft, but the drink of choice is the famous Pusser's Rum, the same blend of five West Indian rums that the Royal Navy has served its men for more than 300 years. Thursday is nickel beer night.

FUN ON & OFF THE BEACH

An organized tour may be the best way to see Tortola. **Travel Plan Tours,** Romasco Place, Wickham's Cay 1, Road Town (☎ **809/494-2872**), will pick you up at your hotel (a minimum of four required) and take you on a 2½-hour tour of the island for $25 per person. They also offer 2½-hour snorkeling tours for $35 per person and glass-bottom boat tours, also 2½ hours, for $25 per person.

BEACHES Beaches are rarely crowded on Tortola unless a cruise ship is in port. You can rent a car or a Jeep to reach them, or take a taxi (but arrange for a time to be picked up).

Tortola's finest and most accessible beach is ✪ **Cane Garden Bay** (see "A Side Trip to Cane Garden Bay," below), which some beach buffs have compared to the St. Thomas' famous Magens Bay Beach. It's directly west of Road Town, up and down some steep hills, but it's worth the effort to get there. Beware of big crowds in high season.

Surfers like **Apple Bay,** west of Road Town, and a hotel there, Sebastians, caters to them. January and February are the ideal time for a visit here.

Brewers Bay, site of a campground, is northwest of Road Town at the end of a long and bumpy road. Both snorkelers and surfers rave about beach. It's also a great place to enjoy walks in the early morning or at sunset.

Smugglers Cove is at the extreme western end of Tortola, opposite the offshore island of Great Thatch and just north of St. John. It's a picturesque crescent of white sand, and the turquoise waters are calm. Snorkelers like this beach, which is sometimes called Lower Belmont Bay.

Long Bay Beach is on Beef Island, east of Tortola. Cross the Queen Elizabeth Bridge to reach this mile-long beach; take the dirt road to the left before you come to the airport. It's a great beach for swimming. From Long Bay you'll have a good view of Little Camanoe, one of the rocky offshore islands around Tortola.

EXPLORING AN ANCIENT RAIN FOREST No visit to Tortola is complete without a trip to ✪ **Mount Sage,** a national park rising 1,780 feet. Here you'll find traces of a primeval rain forest, and you can enjoy a picnic while overlooking neighboring islets and cays. Go west from Road Town to reach the mountain.

Before you head out, go by the tourist office and pick up a brochure called *Sage Mountain National Park.* It has a location map, directions to the forest (where there's a parking lot), and an outline of the main trails through the park.

Covering 92 acres, **Sage Mountain National Park** was established in 1964 to protect the remnants of Tortola's original forests not burned or cleared during the island's plantation era. From the parking lot, a trail leads to the main entrance. The two major trails are the Rain Forest Trail and the Mahogany Forest Trail.

HORSEBACK RIDING **Shadow's Ranch,** Todman's Estate (☎ **809/494-2262**), offers horseback rides through Sage Mountain National Park or down to the shores of Cane Gardens Bay. Call for details, Monday to Saturday from 9am to 4pm. The cost is $25 per hour.

SAILING OFFSHORE The British Virgin Islands is the headquarters of the **Offshore Sailing School,** Prospect Reef Resort, Road Town (☎ **809/494-3311**). This school offers sailing instruction year-round. For information before you go, write or contact Offshore Sailing School, 16731 McGregor Blvd., Fort Myers, FL 33908 (☎ **941/494-3311**).

SNORKELING If you plan on snorkeling by yourself, exercise due caution and consider driving to **Marina Cay,** off Tortola's East End, which is known as a good

The Wreck of the *Rhone* & Other Top Dive Sites

The one site in the British Virgin Islands that lures divers over from St. Thomas is the wreck of the **HMS *Rhone,*** which sank in 1867 near the western point of Salt Island. *Skin Diver* magazine called this "the world's most fantastic shipwreck dive." It teems with marine life and coral formations and was featured in the 1977 movie *The Deep,* starring Nick Nolte and Jacqueline Bisset.

Although it's no *Rhone,* ***Chikuzen*** is another intriguing dive site off Tortola. It's a 270-foot steel-hulled refrigerator ship, which sank off the island's east end in 1981. The hull, still intact under about 80 feet of water, is now home to a vast array of tropical fish, including yellowtail, barracuda, black-tip sharks, octopus, and drum fish.

The best way for novice and expert divers to see these and other great dive sites is with one of the following outfitters:

Baskin in the Sun, a PADI five-star facility (☎ **800/233-7938** in the U.S., or 809/494-5854) on Tortola, is a good choice with two different locations at the Prospect Reef Resort, near Road Town, and at Soper's Hole, on Tortola's West End. Baskin's most popular trip is the supervised "Half-Day Scuba Diving" experience for $95, catered to beginners, but there are trips for all levels of experience. Daily excursions are scheduled to the HMS *Rhone,* as well as "Painted Walls" (an underwater canyon, the walls of which are formed of brightly colored coral and sponges), and the "Indians" (four pinnacle rocks sticking out of the water, which divers follow 40 feet below the surface).

Underwater Safaris (☎ **800/537-7032** in the U.S., or 809/494-3235) takes you to all the best sites, including the HMS *Rhone,* "Spyglass Wall," and "Alice in Wonderland." It has two offices: "Safari Base" in Road Town and "Safari Cay" on Cooper Island. Get complete directions and information when you call. The center, connected with The Moorings (see below), offers a complete PADI and NAUI training facility. An introductory resort course and one dive costs $95, and an open-water certification, with four days of instruction and four open-water dives, goes for $385, plus $40 for the instruction manual.

snorkeling beach, or **Cooper Island,** across Sir Francis Drake Channel. Underwater Safaris (see box above) leads dives and snorkel expeditions to both sites, weather permitting.

YACHT CHARTERS Tortola boasts the largest fleet of bareboat sailing charters in the world. The best place for this is **The Moorings,** Wickhams Cay (P.O. Box 139, Road Town), British Virgin Islands (☎ **800/535-7289** in the U.S., or 809/494-2332), whose 8-acre waterside resort is also recommended in "Where to Stay," above. This outfit, along with a handful of others, makes the British Virgins the cruising capital of the world. Charlie and Ginny Cary started the first charter service in the British Virgin Islands. You can choose from a fleet of sailing yachts, which can accommodate up to four couples in comfort and style. Depending on your nautical knowledge and skills, you can arrange a bareboat rental (with no crew) or a fully crewed rental with a skipper, a staff, and a cook. Boats come equipped with a portable barbecue, snorkeling gear, dinghy, linens, and galley equipment.

The Moorings has an experienced staff of mechanics, electricians, riggers, and cleaners. In addition, if you're going out on your own, you'll get a thorough briefing session about Virgin Island waters and anchorages.

SHOPPING

Remember that there's no duty-free-port shopping in the British Virgin Islands. British goods are imported without duty, and the wise shopper will be able to find some good buys among these imported items, especially in English china. Most of the shops on Tortola are on Main Street, Road Town.

Caribbean Corner Spice House Co. Soper's Hole. ☎ **809/495-4498.**

This has the finest selection of spices and herbs on the island, along with a selection of local handcrafts and botanical skin-care products, most of which you'll find useful in the fierce Caribbean sun. There's also a selection of Cuban cigars, but you'll have to smoke them on the island, as U.S. Customs does not allow their importation.

Caribbean Fine Arts Ltd. Main St., Road Town. ☎ **809/494-4240.**

This store has one of the most unusual collections of art from the West Indies. Not only does it sell original watercolors and oils, but also offers limited-edition serigraphs and sepia photographs from the dawn of the century. It also sells pottery and primitive art.

Caribbean Handprints. Main St., Road Town. ☎ **809/494-3717.**

This store features island handprints, all hand-done by local craftspeople on Tortola. It also sells colorful fabric by the yard.

Flamboyance. Soper's Hole. ☎ **809/495-4699.**

This is the best place to shop for duty-free perfume. Fendi purses are also sold here.

Fort Wines Gourmet. Main St., Road Town. ☎ **809/494-3036.**

For the makings of a picnic you'd have to fly to the mainland to top, stock up on provisions here, partaking of everything from Petrossian caviar to French champagne. Sample its full line of Hediard pâté terrines along with a wide selection of chocolates, including some of the best from Paris. There's also an elegant showcase of glassware, lacquered boxes, and handmade Russian filigree items plated in 24-karat gold.

J. R. O'Neal. Upper Main St., Road Town. ☎ **809/494-2292.**

Across from the Methodist church, this is a decorative and home accessories store, with the most extensive collection of items on the island. You'll find terra-cotta pottery, wicker and rattan home furnishings, Mexican glassware, Dhurrie rugs, baskets, and ceramics. There's also a collection of fine crystal and China.

Little Denmark. Main St., Road Town. ☎ **809/494-2455.**

Little Denmark is your best bet for famous names in gold and silver jewelry and china: Spode and Royal Copenhagen. Here you'll find many of the well-known designs from Scandinavian countries. It also offers jewelry made in the British Virgin Islands, and there's a collection of watches. The outlet offers a large selection of fishing equipment. They also sell Cuban cigars, which can't be brought back into the United States, but have to be smoked before you return.

Pusser's Company Store. Main St., Road Town. ☎ **809/494-2467.**

There's a long, mahogany-trimmed bar accented with many fine nautical artifacts and a line of Pusser's sports and travel clothing and upmarket gift items. Pusser's Rum is one of the best-selling items here, or perhaps you'd prefer a Pusser's ceramic flask as a memento of your visit.

Sunny Caribbee Herb and Spice Company. Main St., Road Town. ☎ **809/494-2178.** This old West Indian building was the first hotel on Tortola, and its shop specializes in Caribbean spices, seasonings, teas, condiments, and handcrafts. You can buy two world-famous specialties here: West Indian Hangover Cure and Arawak Love Potion. A Caribbean cosmetics collection, Sunsations, is also available and includes herbal bath gels, island perfume, and sunshine lotions. Most of the products are blended and packaged in an adjacent factory. With its aroma of spices permeating the air of the neighborhood, this factory is an attraction in itself. There's a daily sampling of island products, perhaps tea, coffee, sauces, or dips. In the Sunny Caribbee Art Gallery, adjacent to the spice shop, you'll find an extensive collection of original art, prints, metal sculpture, and many other Caribbean crafts.

TORTOLA AFTER DARK

Ask around to find out which hotel might have entertainment on any given evening. Steel bands and fungi or scratch bands (African-Caribbean musicians who improvise on locally available instruments) appear regularly, and nonresidents are usually welcome. Pick up a copy of ***Limin' Times,*** an entertainment magazine listing what's happening locally (usually available at your hotel).

✪ **Bomba's Surfside Shack,** Cappoon's Bay (☎ **809/495-4148**), is the oldest, most memorable, and most uninhibited nightlife venue on the island, known for its hedonistic bashes, called "Full Moon Parties." It sits on a 20-foot-wide strip of unpromising coastline near the West End. By anyone's standards this is the junk palace of the island; it's covered with Day-Glo graffiti and laced into a semblance of structure with wire and scraps of plywood, driftwood, and abandoned rubber tires. Despite its appearance, the shack has the sound system to create a really great party. The place is at its wildest on Wednesday and Sunday nights, when there's live music and a $7 all-you-can-eat barbecue. Open daily from 10am to midnight (or later, depending on business).

A SIDE TRIP TO CANE GARDEN BAY

If you've decided to risk everything and navigate the roller-coaster hills of the British Virgin Islands, then head to Cane Garden Bay, one of the choicest pieces of real estate on the island, as discovered long ago by the sailing crowd. Its white sandy beach, with sheltering palms, is a living example of Caribbean charm.

Rhymer's, Cane Garden Bay (☎ **809/495-4639**), is the place to go for food and entertainment. Skippers of any kind of craft are likely to stock up on supplies here, but you can also order cold beer and refreshing rum drinks. If you're hungry, try the conch or whelk, or the barbecued spareribs. The beach bar and restaurant is open daily from 8am to 9pm and serves breakfast, lunch, and dinner. On Thursday night a steel-drum band entertains the mariners. Ice and freshwater showers are available (you can rent towels). Ask about renting Sunfish and Windsurfers from concessions on the beach. American Express, MasterCard, and Visa are accepted.

2 Virgin Gorda

In 1493, on his second voyage to the New World, Columbus named this island Virgin Gorda or "fat virgin" (from a distance, the island looks like a reclining woman with a protruding stomach). The second-largest island in the cluster of British Virgin Islands, Virgin Gorda is 10 miles long and 2 miles wide, with a population of some 1,400. It's 12 miles east of Road Town and 26 miles from St. Thomas.

The island was a fairly desolate agricultural community until Laurance S. Rockefeller established the Little Dix Bay Hotel in the early 1960s, following his success with the Caneel Bay resort on St. John in the 1950s. He envisioned a "wilderness beach" here where privacy and solitude would reign. As a result, he is credited with putting Virgin Gorda on the map. In 1971 the Virgin Gorda Yacht Harbour opened. Operated by the Little Dix Bay Hotel, it accommodates 120 yachts today.

GETTING THERE **Air St. Thomas** (☎ **809/776-2722**) flies to Virgin Gorda daily from St. Thomas. A one-way trip (40 minutes) costs $63; round-trip, $129.

Speedy's Fantasy (☎ **809/495-5240**) operates a ferry service between Road Town and Virgin Gorda. Five ferries a day leave from Road Town Monday to Saturday, reduced to two on Sunday. The cost is $10 one way or $19 round-trip. From St. Thomas to Virgin Gorda, there is service three times a week (on Tuesday, Thursday, and Saturday), costing $25 one way or $45 round-trip.

ESSENTIALS The local **American Express representative** is Travel Plan, Virgin Gorda Yacht Harbour (☎ **809/495-5586**).

WHERE TO STAY

VERY EXPENSIVE

✪ **Biras Creek Estate.** North Sound (P.O. Box 54), Virgin Gorda, B.V.I. ☎ **800/608-9661** in the U.S., or 809/494-3555. Fax 809/494-3557. 32 suites, 1 two-bedroom villa. A/C. Winter, $495–$695 suite for 2; $795 villa for 2, $995 villa for 4. Off-season, $350–$425 suite for 2; $550 villa for 2, $575 villa for 4. Rates include all meals. AE, DISC, MC, V. Take the private motor launch from the Beef Island airport.

This private and romantic resort stands at the northern end of Virgin Gorda like a hilltop fortress, opening onto a decent beach, much of which is man-made. Acquired by a former guest, Bert Houwer, the hideaway has vastly improved after a several-million-dollar facelift. On a 150-acre estate with its own marina, it occupies a narrow neck of land flanked by the sea on three sides. To create their Caribbean hideaway, Norwegian shipping interests carved this resort out of the wilderness, but wisely protected the natural terrain. Cooled by ceiling fans and air-conditioning, units have well-furnished bedrooms and divan beds with a sitting room and private patio, plus a refrigerator. Children 5 and under not allowed.

Dining/Entertainment: The food has won high praise, and the wine list is also excellent here. The two restaurants and drinking lounge are quietly elegant, and there's always a table with a view. A barbecued lunch is often served on the beach.

Services: Laundry, baby-sitting, taxi service for guests arriving in Virgin Gorda to the hotel's motor launch, free trips to nearby beaches.

Facilities: Swimming pool, snorkeling, Sunfish, paddleboards, tennis courts, kayaks, Hobie waves, and unlimited use of motor dinghies.

✪ **The Bitter End Yacht Club.** John O'Point, North Sound (P.O. Box 46), Virgin Gorda, B.V.I. ☎ **800/872-2392** in the U.S. for reservations, or 312/944-2860. Fax 312/944-2860. 46 beachfront villas, 38 Commodore Club suites, 9 hillside villas, 3 Freedom 30 Live-Aboard yachts. Winter (double occupancy), $520 beachfront villa; $570 Commodore Club Suite; $480 hillside villa; $480 Freedom 30 yacht. Off-season (double occupancy), $420 beachfront villa; $470 Commodore Club suite; $380 hillside villa; $350 Freedom 30 yacht. Rates include meals. AE, DC, MC, V.

This rendezvous point for the yachting set has hosted the likes of treasure hunter Mel Fisher and Jean-Michel Cousteau, but less well-known sailors or just lovers of the sea have also been drawn to this family operated resort for the past 30 years. It opens onto one of the most unspoiled and secluded deep-water harbors in the Caribbean, offering the finest water-sports program in the U.S. or British Virgin Islands. Guests have unlimited use of the resort's million-dollar fleet, the Nick Trotter Sailing and

Windsurfing School. The Bitter End offers an informal yet elegant experience, as guests settle into one of the hillside chalets or well-appointed beachfront and hillside villas overlooking the sound. Only the Commodore Suites are air-conditioned.

For something novel, you can stay aboard one of the 30-foot yachts, yours to sail, with dockage and daily maid service, meals in the Yacht Club dining room, and overnight provisions.

Dining/Entertainment: Dining is in the Clubhouse Steak and Seafood Grille, the English Carvery, or the Pub. Evening entertainment is provided by "The Reflections," a steel-drum band who has performed for Princess Diana. On other nights, local reggae and soca bands perform.

Services: Laundry, free trips to nearby islands, ferry service from the Beef Island airport at Tortola.

Facilities: Unlimited use of Lasers, Sunfish, Rhodes 19s, windsurfing equipment, J-24s, Boston whalers, and outboard skiffs; reef snorkeling; scuba diving; sport fishing; fitness center; expeditions to neighboring cays; marine science participation; swimming pool.

Little Dix Bay Hotel. On the northwest corner of the island (P.O. Box 70), Virgin Gorda, B.V.I. ☎ **800/928-3000** in the U.S., or 809/495-5555. Fax 809/495-5661. 98 rms, 4 suites. TEL. Winter, $475–$725 double; $1,300 suite. Off-season, $250–$450 double; $650–$900 suite. Rates include breakfast. Additional person $50 extra. MAP $75 extra. AE, DC, MC, V. Take the private ferry service from the Beef Island airport to the resort.

Completely renovated in 1996, this 1964 hotel is now run by the Dallas-based Rosewood chain of luxurious hotels. An embodiment of understated luxury, the Little Dix Bay Hotel is a resort discreetly scattered along a half-mile crescent-shaped private bay on a 500-acre preserve. Many guests find this resort pricey and stuffy, infinitely preferring the more casual elegance of Biras Creek Estate and the Bitter End Yacht Club (see above). It has the same quiet elegance as Caneel Bay on St. John in the U.S. Virgins.

All rooms, built in the woods, have private terraces with views of the sea or of gardens. Trade winds come through louvers and screens, and the units are further cooled by ceiling fans or air-conditioning (in 44 of the rooms). Some units are two-story rondavels raised on stilts to form their own breezeways. All the guest rooms have been renovated with new furnishings and fabrics, evoking a Southeast Asian style with wicker or reed furniture, bamboo beds, Balinese boxes and baskets, along with ceramic objects of art. Telephones have also been added to each room.

Dining/Entertainment: Four interconnected pyramids that face the sea comprise the roof of the Pavilion, the hotel venue for lunch buffets, afternoon teas, and candlelit dinners. The cuisine is international, with Caribbean seafood specialties like red snapper with ratatouille drizzled with a curry infusion. For drinks, guests can sit on the restaurant's terrace where a band performs nightly. The Sugar Mill is elegant but casual, specializing in fresh grilled fish, lobster, and steaks. On the edge of the beach, the Beach Grill serves light lunches and dinners.

Services: Unequaled service with a "one-to-one" staff-guest ratio.

Facilities: Seven all-weather outdoor Laykold tennis courts, Sunfish sailboats, kayaks, snorkeling, scuba diving, waterskiing, boat rentals, deep-sea fishing, diving excursions, and the Virgin Gorda Yacht Harbor, half a mile from the resort (owned and operated by Little Dix Bay). The lack of a pool may bother some guests, but there is a fitness center.

MODERATE

✪ **Fischers Cove Beach Hotel.** The Valley (P.O. Box 60), Virgin Gorda, B.V.I. ☎ **809/495-5252.** Fax 809/495-5820. 12 studio hotel rms, 8 studio cottages. A/C. Winter, $145–$150 studio hotel rm; $170–$285 studio cottage. Off-season, $100 studio hotel rm; $125–$205 studio cottage. MAP $40 per person extra. AE, MC, V.

There's swimming at your doorstep in this group of units nestled near the sandy beach of St. Thomas Bay. Erected of native stone, each cottage is self-contained, with one or two bedrooms and a combination living/dining room with a kitchenette. At a food store near the grounds you can stock up on provisions if you're doing your own cooking. There are 12 pleasant but simple rooms with views of Drake Channel. Each has its own private bath (hot and cold showers) and private balcony. Jeep rentals are available, and there's a playground on the premises. Live entertainment is often presented.

The Olde Yard Inn. The Valley (P.O. Box 26), Virgin Gorda, B.V.I. ☎ **800/653-9273** or 809/495-5544. Fax 809/495-5986. 14 rms. Winter, $195 double; $220 triple; $245 quad. Off-season, $110 double; $130 triple; $150–$190 quad. MAP $50 per person extra. Honeymoon packages available. AE, MC, V.

This little charmer is a mile from the airport. Near the main house are two long bungalows with large renovated bedrooms, each with its own bath and patio. Four of the rooms are air-conditioned, and all have ceiling fans. Three of the rooms also contain minirefrigerators. You can go for a sail on a yacht or embark on a snorkeling adventure at one of 16 beaches.

Dining/Entertainment: Served under a cedarwood roof, the French-accented meals are one of the reasons for coming over here. Lunch is served poolside at the Sip and Dip Grill. Dinners are from 6:30 to 8:30pm. There's live entertainment three times a week in the dining room.

Facilities: Off-site sailboat rentals, Jacuzzi, modern health club, one of the best hotel libraries in the Caribbean, huge freshwater pool, complimentary shuttle service to Savannah Bay Beach (a 20-minute walk).

INEXPENSIVE

Guavaberry Spring Bay Vacation Homes. Spring Bay (P.O. Box 20), Virgin Gorda, BVI. ☎ **809/495-5227.** Fax 809/495-5283. 18 houses. Winter, $142 one-bedroom house for 2; $200 two-bedroom house for 4. Off-season, $95 one-bedroom house for 2; $140 two-bedroom house for 4. Additional person $15–$20 extra. No credit cards.

Staying in one of these hexagonal white-roofed redwood houses built on stilts is like living in a tree house, with screened and louvered walls to let in those sea breezes. Each home, available for daily or weekly rental, has one or two bedrooms, and all have a private bath, small kitchenette, dining area, and elevated sundeck overlooking Sir Francis Drake Passage. Within a few minutes of the cottage colony is the beach at Spring Bay, and the Yacht Harbour Shopping Centre is 1 mile away. It's also possible to explore The Baths, a popular natural attraction nearby.

The owners will make arrangements for day charters for scuba diving, snorkeling, or fishing, and will also arrange for island Jeep tours and sailing excursions.

WHERE TO DINE

Bath and Turtle Pub. Virgin Gorda Yacht Harbour, Spanish Town. ☎ **809/495-5239.** Reservations recommended. Main courses $16–$25. AE, MC, V. Daily 7am–midnight. INTERNATIONAL.

At the end of the waterfront shopping plaza in Spanish Town sits the most popular pub on Virgin Gorda, packed with locals during happy hour from 4 to 6pm. Even if you don't care about food, you might join the regulars over midmorning guava coladas or peach daiquiris. There's live music every Wednesday in summer only from

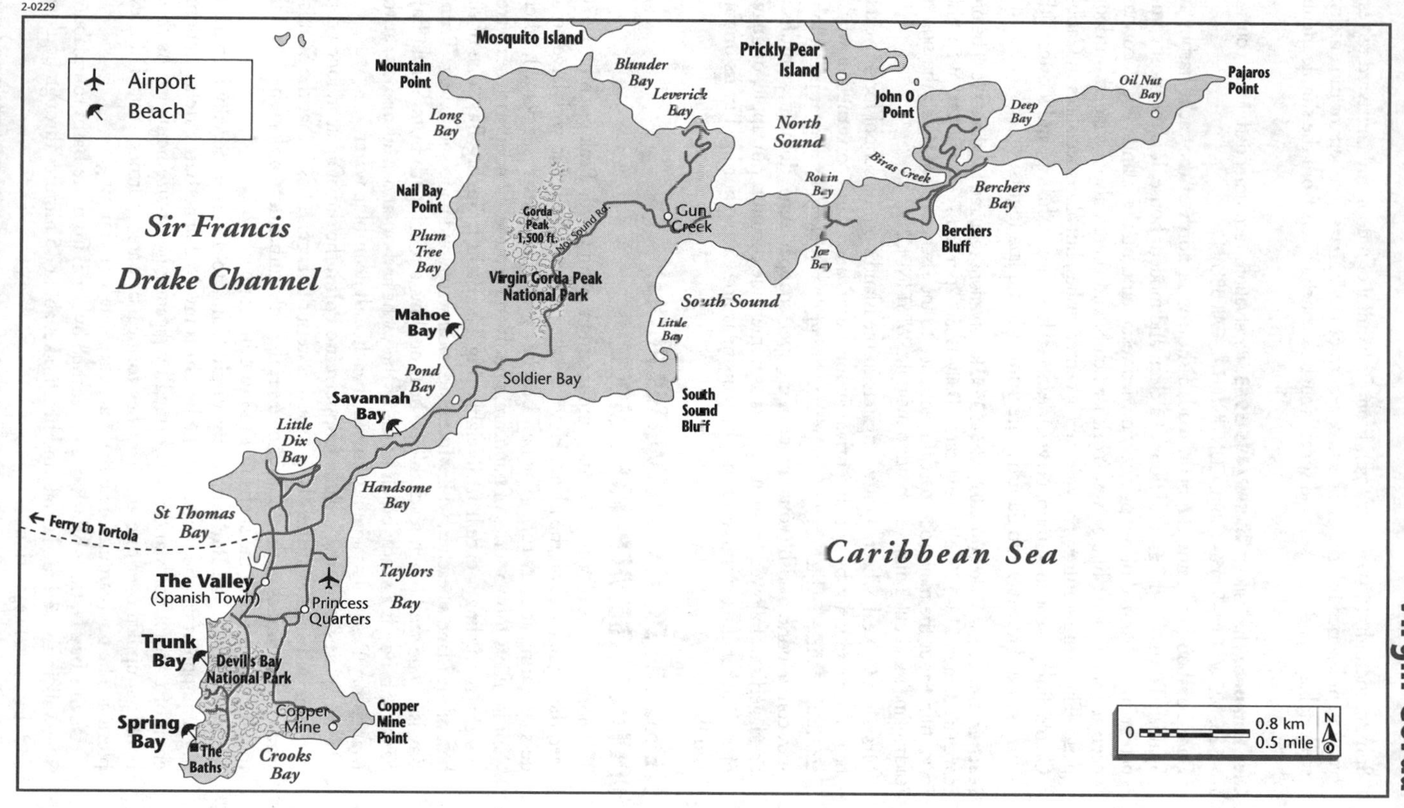
2-0229
Airport
Beach
Mosquito Island
Mountain Point
Long Bay
Nail Bay Point
Plum Tree Bay
Sir Francis
Drake Channel
Mahoe Bay
Pond Bay
Savannah Bay
Little Dix Bay
Blunder Bay
Leverick Bay
Prickly Pear Island
John O Point
North Sound
Gorda Peak 1,500 ft.
No Sound Rd.
Virgin Gorda Peak National Park
Gun Creek
Robin Bay
Jaw Bay
Biras Creek
Deep Bay
Oil Nut Bay
Pajaros Point
Berchers Bay
Berchers Bluff
South Sound
Little Bay
South Sound Bluff
Soldier Bay
Handsome Bay
St Thomas Bay
Ferry to Tortola
The Valley
(Spanish Town)
Princess Quarters
Taylors Bay
Trunk Bay
Devils Bay National Park
Spring Bay
The Baths
Copper Mine
Copper Mine Point
Crooks Bay
Caribbean Sea
0
0.8 km
0.5 mile
N

8pm to midnight (no cover charge). From its handful of indoor and courtyard tables, you can order fried fish fingers, nachos, very spicy chili, pizzas, Reubens or tuna melts, steak, lobster, and daily seafood specials such as conch fritters from the simple menu here.

Chez Bamboo. The Valley. ☎ **809/495-5963.** Reservations recommended. Main courses $16–$28. MC, V. Tues–Sun 6–10pm. CONTINENTAL/CARIBBEAN.

Chez Bamboo lies beside the main road, a short walk north of the yacht harbor at Spanish Town. On the ground floor of a clean and modern house, it is the most competent and urbanized of the privately owned restaurants on the island. The decor has been redone to look like a New York jazz club, and there's also a shaded outdoor patio. The menu features many French-accented dishes, but also specializes in Carib-Creole dining—conch gumbo, New Orleans–style barbecue shrimp, and lobster with curry sauce. Thursday and Saturday are prime rib and jazz nights.

Teacher Ilma's. The Valley. ☎ **809/495-5355.** Reservations required for dinner (call before 3pm). Full dinners $18–$25. No credit cards. Daily 12:30–2pm and 7:30–9:30pm. At Spanish Town, turn left at the main road past the entrance to the Fischers Cove Hotel; the sign to Teacher Ilma's is about 2 minutes ahead to the right. WEST INDIAN.

Mrs. Ilma O'Neal, who taught youngsters in the island's public school for 43 years, began her restaurant by cooking privately for visitors and island construction workers. Main courses, which include appetizers, might be chicken, local goat meat, lobster, conch, pork, or fish (your choice of grouper, snapper, tuna, dolphin, swordfish, or triggerfish), followed by such desserts as homemade coconut, pineapple, or guava pies. Teacher Ilma emphasizes that her cuisine is not Creole but local in its origins and flavors.

SEEING THE SIGHTS: SALTWATER POOLS, BOULDER-STREWN PARKS & MORE

The northern side of Virgin Gorda is mountainous, with Gorda Peak reaching 1,370 feet, the highest spot on the island. However, the southern half is flat, with large boulders appearing at every turn. The best **beaches** are at **The Baths** (see below), where giant boulders form a series of panoramic pools and grottoes flooded with sea water (nearby snorkeling is excellent). Neighboring The Baths is **Spring Bay,** one of the best of the island's beaches, with white sand, clear water, and good snorkeling. **Trunk Bay** is a wide sand beach reachable by boat or along a rough path from Spring Bay. **Savannah Bay** is a sandy beach north of the yacht harbor, and **Mahoe Bay,** at the Mango Bay Resort, has a gently curving beach with neon-blue water.

Other places of interest include **Coppermine Point,** the site of an abandoned copper mine and smelter at the island's southeastern tip. Legend has it that the Spanish worked these mines in the 1600s; however, the only authenticated document reveals that the English sank the shafts in 1838 to mine copper.

You'll find ✪ **The Baths** on every Virgin Gorda to-do list, especially if snorkeling (equipment can be rented on the beach) is involved. The Baths are a phenomenon of tranquil pools and caves formed by gigantic house-size boulders. As these boulders toppled over one another, they formed saltwater grottoes, suitable for exploring. The pools around The Baths are excellent for swimming.

Devil's Bay National Park can be reached by a trail from the Baths roundabout. The walk to the secluded coral-sand beach takes about 15 minutes through boulders and dry coastal vegetation.

The Baths and surrounding areas are part of a proposed system of parks and protected areas in the B.V.I. The protected area encompasses 682 acres of land, including sites at Little Fort, Spring Bay, the Baths, and Devil's Bay on the east coast.

The best way to see the island if you're over for a day trip is to call **Andy Flax** at the Fischers Cove Beach Hotel. He runs the **Virgin Gorda Tours Association** (☎ **809/495-5252**), which will give you a tour of the island for $20 per person. The tour leaves twice daily. You can be picked up at the ferry dock if you give them 24-hour notice.

Kilbrides Underwater Tours is located at the Bitter End Resort at North Sound (☎ **800/932-4286** in the U.S., or 809/495-9638). Today Kilbrides offers the best diving in the British Virgin Islands at 15 to 20 dive sites, including the wreck of the ill-fated HMS *Rhone.* Prices range from $80 to $90 for a two-tank dive on one of the coral reefs. A one-tank dive in the afternoon costs $60. Equipment, except wet suits, is supplied at no charge, and videos of your dives are available.

SHOPPING

There isn't much here. Your best bet is the **Virgin Gorda Craft Shop** at Yacht Harbour (☎ **809/495-5137**), which has some good arts and crafts, especially straw items. Some of the more upscale hotels have boutiques, notably the **Bitter End Yacht Club's Reeftique** (☎ **809/494-2745**), with its selection of sports clothing, including sundresses and logo wear. You can also purchase a hat here to protect you from the sun. You might also check out the **Boutique at Little Dix Bay** (☎ **809/495-5555**), with its selection of locally produced crafts along with the inevitable T-shirts that are displayed with some rather pricey sportswear.

VIRGIN GORDA AFTER DARK

There's isn't a lot of action at night, unless you want to make some of your own. The previously recommended **Bath & Turtle Pub** (☎ **809/495-5239**) at Yacht Harbour brings in local bands for dancing. Most evenings in winter the also recommended **Bitter End Yacht Club** (☎ **809/494-2745**) has live music. Call to see what's happening at the time of your visit.

The biggest venue for island nightlife is **Andy's Chateau de Pirate,** at Fischer's Cove Beach Hotel, The Valley (☎ **809/495-5252**). Built from poured concrete in 1985, this sprawling, sparsely furnished local hangout has a simple stage, a very long bar, and huge oceanfront windows that almost never close. Admission is free most nights, $5 Friday through Sunday. The complex also houses the Lobster Pot Restaurant, the Buccaneer Bar, and the nightclub EFX. The Lobster Pot is open from 7am to 10pm.

The place is a famous showcase for the island's musical groups, which perform Wednesday through Sunday from 8pm to midnight; lots of people congregate to listen and kibitz.

3 Jost Van Dyke

This rugged island off the west side of Tortola was named for a Dutch settler. In the 1700s a Quaker colony settled here to develop sugarcane plantations. One of the colonists, William Thornton, won the worldwide competition to design the U.S. Capitol in Washington, D.C. Smaller islands surround the place, including Little Jost Van Dyke, the birthplace of Dr. John Lettsome, founder of the London Medical Society.

About 150 people live on the 4 square miles of this mountainous island. On the south shore, White Bay and Great Harbor are good beaches. Whereas there are only a handful of places to stay, there are several dining choices, as it's a popular stopping-over point not only for the yachting set, but also for many cruise ships, including Club Med and Cunard (and often some all-gay cruises). The peace and tranquillity of yesteryear often disappear unless you're here when the cruise ships aren't.

GETTING THERE Take the ferry from either St. Thomas or Tortola. (Be warned that departure times can vary widely throughout the year, and at times don't adhere very closely to the printed timetables.) Ferries from St. Thomas depart from Red Hook three days a week (Friday, Saturday, and Sunday) about twice a day. More convenient (and more frequent) are the daily ferryboat shuttles from Tortola's isolated West End. The latter departs three times a day on the 25-minute trip, and costs $8 each way, $15 round-trip. Call the **Jost Van Dyke Ferryboat service** (☎ **809/494-2997**) for information about departures from any of the above-mentioned points. If all else fails, carefully negotiate a transportation fee with one of the handful of privately operated water taxis.

WHERE TO STAY

Very casual types consider the simple accommodations offered by Rudy's under "Where to Dine," below.

Sandcastle Hotel. White Bay, Jost Van Dyke, B.V.I. ☎ **809/690-1611.** Fax 809/775-3590. 4 cottages. Winter, $160–$175 double. Off-season $95–$115 double. MAP $40 per person extra. Additional person $35–$45 extra. Four-night minimum. MC, V. Take the private motor launch from Tortola; it's a 20-minute ride.

A retreat for escapists who want few neighbors and absolutely nothing to do, these four cottages are surrounded by flowering shrubbery and bougainvillea and have wonderful views. You mix your own drinks at the beachside bar, the Soggy Dollar, and keep your own tab. Visiting boaters often drop in to enjoy the beachside informality and order a drink called a "Painkiller." A line in the guest book proclaims "I thought places like this only existed in the movies."

For reservations and information, call or write the Sandcastle, Suite 201, Red Hook Plaza, St. Thomas, USVI 00802-1306 (☎ 809/775-5262). Don't send mail to Jost Van Dyke, as it could take months to reach there.

Sandy Ground. East End (P.O. Box 594, West End), Tortola, B.V.I. ☎ **809/494-3391.** Fax 809/495-9379. 8 villas. Winter, $1,400 per week villa for 2. Off-season, $980 per week villa for 2. Additional person $250 extra in winter, $150 extra off-season. MC, V. Take a private water taxi from Tortola or St. Thomas.

These self-sufficient housekeeping units are on a 17-acre hill site on the eastern part of Jost Van Dyke. The complex rents two- and three-bedroom villas. One of our favorites was constructed on a cliff that seems to hang about 80 or so feet over a small beach. If you've come all this way, you might as well stay a week, which is the way the rates are quoted. The airy villas, each privately owned, are fully equipped with refrigerators and stoves. Villa interiors vary widely, from rather fashionable to bare bones. The managers help guests with boat rentals and water sports. Diving, day sails, and other activities can also be arranged, and there are dinghies available. Snorkeling and hiking are among the more popular pastimes, and the beach is private.

WHERE TO DINE

Abe's by the Sea. Little Harbour. ☎ **809/495-9329.** Reservations recommended for groups of 5 or more. Dinner $12–$30; nightly barbecue $20. MC, V. Daily 8–11am, noon–3pm, and 7–10pm. Take a private motor launch or boat from Tortola; as you approach the east side of the harbor you'll see Abe's on your right. WEST INDIAN.

In this local bar and restaurant, sailors are satisfied with a simple menu of fish, lobster, conch, and chicken. Usually, the best item to order is West Indian steamed fish with onion and sweet pepper in a lime-flavored butter sauce. The barbecued spareribs are also the best in the area. Prices are low too, and it's money well spent. For the price of the main course, you get peas and rice, along with coleslaw, plus dessert. On Wednesday night in season, Abe's has a festive pig roast.

Rudy's Mariner's Rendezvous. Great Harbour. ☎ **809/495-9282.** Reservations required by 6:30pm. Dinner $12–$25. MC, V. Daily 7pm–midnight. WEST INDIAN.

Rudy's, at the western end of Great Harbour, serves good but basic West Indian food and plenty of it. The place looks and feels like a private home with a waterfront terrace for visiting diners. A welcoming drink awaits sailors and landlubbers alike, and the food that follows is simply prepared and inexpensive. Conch always seems to be on the menu, and there's always a catch of the day.

The Sandcastle. On White Bay. ☎ **809/690-1611.** Reservations required for dinner by 4pm. Fixed-price dinner $32; lunch main courses $5–$8. MC, V. Daily 9:30am-3pm and 1 seating at 7:30pm. INTERNATIONAL/CARIBBEAN.

This hotel restaurant (see "Accommodations," above) serves food that has often been frozen, but, even so, the flavors remain consistently good. Lunch is served in the open-air dining room, whereas lighter fare and snacks are available at the Soggy Dollar Bar. Dinner is by candlelight, featuring four courses, including such dishes as mahimahi Martinique (marinated in orange-lemon-lime juice and cooked with fennel, onions, and dill). Sandcastle hen is another specialty likely to appear on the menu: It's a Cornish hen marinated in rum, honey, lime, and garlic before being grilled. But, we'd skip all that for the sesame snapper. Desserts are luscious, including a piña colada cheesecake or a mango mousse. Meals are served with seasonal vegetables and fresh pasta, along with a variety of salads and homemade desserts.

4 Anegada

The most northerly and isolated of the British Virgins, 30 miles east of Tortola, Anegada has a population of about 250, none of whom has found the legendary treasure from the more than 500 wrecks lying off its notorious Horseshoe Reef. It's different from the other British Virgins in that it's a coral-and-limestone atoll, flat, with a 2,500-foot airstrip. Its highest point reaches 28 feet, and it hardly appears on the horizon if you're sailing to it.

At the northern and western ends of the island are some good beaches, which might be your only reason for coming here. This is a remote little corner of the Caribbean: Don't expect a single frill, and be prepared to put up with some hardships, such as mosquitoes.

Most of the island has been declared off-limits to settlement and reserved for birds and other wildlife. The B.V.I. National Parks Trust has established a flamingo colony in a bird sanctuary, which is also the protected home of several different varieties of heron as well as ospreys and terns. It has also designated much of the interior of the island as a preserved habitat for Anegada's animal population of some 2,000 wild goats, donkeys, and cattle. Among the endangered species being given a new lease on life here is the rock iguana, a fierce-looking but quite harmless reptile that can grow to a length of five feet. Although rarely seen, these creatures have called Anegada home for thousands of years.

GETTING THERE The only carrier flying from Tortola to Anegada, **Gorda Aero Service** (☎ **809/495-2271**), uses six- to eight-passenger prop planes. It operates four times a week, on Monday, Wednesday, Friday, and Sunday, charging $56 per person round-trip. In addition, **Fly B.V.I.** (☎ **809/495-1747**) operates a charter/sightseeing service to and from Anegada from Beef Island off Tortola. The one-way cost is $125 for two to three passengers.

GETTING AROUND Limited **taxi** service is available on the island—not that you'll have many places to go. **Tony's Taxis,** which you'll easily spot when you arrive, will take you around the island. It's also possible to rent bicycles; ask around.

SHOPPING Hardly the reason to visit Anegada, but once you're here drop in at **Pat's Pottery** (☎ **809/495-8031**), where islanders sell some interesting crafts, including dishes, plates, pitchers, and mugs in whimsical folk art patterns.

WHERE TO STAY & DINE

The Anegada Reef Hotel is the only major accommodation on the island. Neptune's Treasure, below, rents tents.

Anegada Reef Hotel. Setting Point, Anegada, B.V.I. ☎ **809/495-8002.** Fax 809/495-9362. 16 rms. A/C. Winter, $200–$230 double. Off-season, $180–$215 double. Rates include all meals. MC, V.

The only major hotel on the island is 3 miles west of the airport, right on the beachfront. It's one of the most remote places in this guide—guests who stay here are in effect hiding out. It's a favorite of the yachting set, who enjoy the hospitality provided by Lowell Wheatley. He offers motel-like and very basic rooms with private porches, with either a garden or ocean view. Go here for tranquillity, not for pampering.

You can arrange to go inshore fishing, deep-sea fishing, or bonefishing (there's also a tackle shop); they'll also set up snorkeling excursions and secure taxi service and Jeep rentals. There's a beach barbecue nightly, the house specialty is lobster, and many attendees arrive by boat. Reservations for the 7:30pm dinner must be made by 4pm. Dinners begin at $16.50, $30 if you order the generous portion of lobster. Nonguests are also welcomed at breakfast or lunch. If you're visiting just for the day, you can use the hotel as a base. Call and they'll have a bus meet you at the airport.

Neptune's Treasure. Between Pomato and Saltheap points. VHF Ch. 16 or 68, or **809/495-9439.** Reservations required only for dinner. Breakfast $4–$7; lunch $6–$30; dinner $12–$30. AE, MC, V. Daily 8am–11pm. SEAFOOD.

While on Anegada, you may want to visit this seaside restaurant that serves fresh fish and lobster caught by the owners. They also serve burgers, sandwiches, baby back ribs, and chicken. The family that runs the restaurant helpfully explains how to explore the island. They also rent tents with single or double mattresses. Tents range from $15 to $25 a night, a bare site costing only $7. Tent rentals come with sheets, pillow cases, and solar showers. You can take a taxi to one of their sandy beaches and go snorkeling along their reefs.

5 Marina Cay

Near Beef Island, Marina Cay is a private 6-acre islet. Its only claim to fame was as the setting of the 1953 Robb White book *Our Virgin Isle,* which was later filmed with Sidney Poitier and John Cassavetes. For 20 years after Robb White's departure, the island lay uninhabited until the hotel (see below) opened. The hotel has recently been taken over by Pusser's, the famous Virgin Islands establishment, which means that you'll always be able to sip the "Pusser's Painkiller." The island lies five minutes away by launch from Tortola's Trellis Bay, adjacent to Beef Island International Airport. The ferry running between Beef Island and Marina Cay is free. There are no cars on the island. We only mention the tiny cay at all because of the Marina Cay Hotel.

WHERE TO STAY & DINE

Pusser's Marina Cay Resort. Marina Cay (mailing address: P.O. Box 626, Road Town, Tortola), B.V.I. ☎ **809/494-2174.** Fax 809/494-4775. 4 rms, 2 villas. Winter, $125–$150 double; $350 villa. Off-season, $75–$95 double; $195 villa. Rates include continental breakfast. AE, MC, V. Take the private launch from Beef Island.

This small cottage hotel, opened in 1960 and extensively renovated in 1995, attracts the sailing crowd. It houses guests in simply furnished double rooms with king-size beds, all overlooking a reef and Sir Francis Drake Channel, dotted with islands. Each room has a private balcony. Marina Cay is a tropical garden.

Dining is casual in a beachside restaurant, with a cuisine featuring continental and West Indian dishes. Activities include snorkeling, windsurfing, scuba diving (with certification courses taught by a resident dive master), castaway picnics on secluded beaches, kayaking, underwater safaris, and deep-sea fishing.

6 Peter Island

Half of this island, boasting a good marina and docking facilities, is devoted to the yacht club. The other part is deserted. Beach facilities are found at palm-fringed Deadman Bay, which faces the Atlantic but is protected by a reef. All goods and services are at the one resort (see below).

The island is so private that except for an occasional mason at work, about the only company you'll encounter will be an iguana or a feral cat whose ancestors were abandoned generations ago by shippers (the cats are said to have virtually eliminated the island's rodent population).

GETTING THERE A hotel-operated ferry, **Peter Island Boat** (☎ **809/495-2000**), picks up any overnight guest who arrives at the Beef Island airport. It departs from the pier at Trellis Bay, near the airport. A round-trip costs $25. Other boats depart eight or nine times a day from Baughers Bay in Road Town. Passengers must notify the hotel two weeks before their arrival so transportation can be arranged.

WHERE TO STAY & DINE

✪ **Peter Island Resort.** Peter Island (P.O. Box 211, Road Town, Tortola), B.V.I. ☎ **800/346-4451** or 809/495-2000. Fax 809/495-2500. 50 rms, 3 villas. A/C MINIBAR TEL. Winter, $395–$545 double; $695–$895 Hawk's Nest two-bedroom villa; $3,950 Crow's Nest four-bedroom villa. Off-season, $195–$385 double; $525–$675 Hawk's Nest two-bedroom villa; $1,400–$3,950 Crow's Nest four-bedroom villa. MAP $75 per person extra. Crow's Nest rates include all meals. AE, MC, V.

This 1,800-acre tropical island is solely dedicated to Peter Island Resort guests and yacht owners who moor their crafts here. The island's tropical gardens and hillside are bordered by five private beaches, including Deadman's Beach (in spite of its name, it's often voted one of the world's most romantic beaches in travel magazine reader polls).

The resort contains 30 rooms facing Sprat Bay and Sir Francis Drake Channel (ocean-view or garden rooms) and 20 larger rooms on Deadman's Bay Beach (beachfront). Designed with a casual elegance, they have a balcony or terrace, ceiling fan, coffeemaker, clock radio, and hair dryer. The Crow's Nest, a luxurious four-bedroom villa, overlooks the harbor and Deadman Bay and features a private swimming pool, full kitchen, maid, gardener, personal steward, and island vehicle. The Hawk's Nest villas are two two-bedroom villas situated on a tropical hillside.

Dining/Entertainment: The Tradewinds Restaurant serves breakfast and dinner throughout the year in fine Caribbean tradition. For a more casual setting, the

Deadman's Beach Bar and Grill serves sandwiches and salads beside the ocean. The main bar, Drakes Channel Lounge, is also open throughout the day and evening.

Services: Room service (breakfast only), laundry, massage, baby-sitting, launch transport to/from Beef Island airport.

Facilities: Fitness center, gift shop, freshwater pool with a stunning view of the sea, four tennis courts (two lit for night play), scuba-diving base, library, spa, conference facility, basketball, mountain bikes; complete yacht marina with complimentary use of Sunfish, snorkeling gear, sea kayaks, Windsurfers, and 19-foot Squib day-sailers.

7 Mosquito Island (North Sound)

Sandy, 125-acre Mosquito Island, just north of Virgin Gorda, wasn't named for those pesky insects—it took its name from the Mosquito (or Moskito) tribe, who were the only known inhabitants of the small island before the Spanish conquistadors arrived in the 15th century. Archaeological relics of these peaceful people and their agricultural pursuits have been found here. To get here, take a plane to the Virgin Gorda airport and Speedy's Taxi from there to Leverick Bay Dock. The taxi driver will radio ahead, and a boat will be sent from Drake's to take you on the five-minute ride from the dock to the resort.

WHERE TO STAY

Drake's Anchorage Resort Inn. North Sound (P.O. Box 2510, Virgin Gorda), B.V.I. ☎ **800/624-6651,** 809/494-2254, or 617/969-9913 in Massachusetts. 4 rms, 4 suites, 2 villas. Winter, \$505–\$526 double; \$575–\$615 suite; \$695 villa. Off-season, \$350–\$425 double; \$485–\$515 suite; \$595 villa. Rates include all meals. AE, MC, V.

The privately owned island is uninhabited except for Drake's Anchorage Resort Inn, which many patrons consider their favorite retreat in the British Virgins. The hotel has comfortable rooms and suites with private baths and sea-view verandas. The resort's restaurant, attractively tropical in design, faces the water and offers a cuisine featuring local and continental dishes, including lobster and a fresh fish of the day.

Guests have free use of Windsurfers, snorkeling equipment, and bicycles. For additional fees, you can go scuba diving, deep-sea fishing, sailing, or to The Baths on Virgin Gorda. The snorkeling and scuba here are so good that members of the Cousteau Society spend a month each year exploring local waters. There are four beaches on the island, each with different wave and water conditions.

8 Guana Island

This 850-acre island, a nature preserve and wildlife sanctuary, is one of the most private hideaways in the Caribbean. Don't come here looking for action; rather, consider vacationing here if you want to retreat from the world. This small island right off the coast of Tortola offers seven virgin beaches and nature trails ideal for hiking and abounds in unusual species of plant and animal life. Head up to the 806-foot peak of Sugarloaf Mountain for a panoramic view. Arawak relics have been found on the island. It's said that the name of the island came from a jutting rock that resembled the head of an iguana. The Guana Island Club will send a boat to meet arriving guests at the Beef Island airport (trip time is 10 minutes).

WHERE TO STAY

Guana Island Club. P.O. Box 32, Road Town, Tortola, B.V.I. ☎ **800/544-8262** in the U.S., or 809/494-2354. 15 rms, 1 cottage. For reservations, write or call the Guana Island

Reservations Office, 10 Timber Trail, Rye, NY 10580 (☎ 800/544-8262 in the U.S., or 914/967-6050; fax 914/967-8048). Winter, $675 double; $1,290 cottage. March 16–Aug, $515 double; $925 cottage. Rent the island, $8,700–$11,000. Rates include all meals. No credit cards. Closed Sept–Oct. Take the private launch from Tortola.

Guana Island, the sixth or seventh largest of the British Virgin Islands, was bought in 1974 by Henry and Gloria Jarecki, dedicated conservationists who run this resort as a nature preserve and wildlife sanctuary. Upon your arrival on the island, a Land Rover will meet you and transport you up one of the most scenic hills in the region, in the northeast of Guana.

The cluster of white cottages were built as a private club in the 1930s on the foundations of a Quaker homestead. The stone cottages never hold more than 30 guests (and only two telephones), and since the dwellings are staggered along a flower-dotted ridge overlooking the Caribbean and the Atlantic, the sense of privacy is almost absolute. The entire island can be rented by groups of up to 30. Although water is scarce on the island, each airy accommodation has a shower. The decor is of rattan and wicker, and each unit has a ceiling fan. North Beach cottage, the most luxurious, is like renting a private home. The panoramic sweep from the terraces is spectacular, particularly at sunset.

Dining/Entertainment: Guests will find a convivial atmosphere at the rattan-furnished clubhouse. Casually elegant dinners by candlelight are served on the veranda, with menus that include homegrown vegetables and continental and Stateside specialties. A buffet lunch is served every day. The self-service bars operate on the honor system.

Services: Laundry.

Facilities: Seven beaches (some of which require a boat to reach), two tennis courts (one clay and one all-weather), fishing, snorkeling, windsurfing, kayaks, small sailboats, waterskiing.

8 The Dominican Republic

Sometimes called "the fairest land under heaven" because of its sugar-white beaches and mountainous terrain, the Dominican Republic has long attracted visitors not only for its natural beauty but also for its rich colonial heritage. At the same time, many travelers shy away from this region, because of its not-so-fair reputation for high crime, poverty, and social unrest. But despite these social and political issues, the Dominican Republic has become one the fastest-growing destinations in the Caribbean. Its Latino flavor sharply contrasts the character of many nearby islands, especially the British- and French-influenced ones.

The 54-mile-wide Mona Passage separates the Dominican Republic from Puerto Rico, and many poverty-stricken Dominicans risk their lives crossing this channel every day, hoping to slip into Puerto Rico and then illegally into the United States. Crime, especially muggings and robberies of visitors, is on the rise. But still, the island holds such fascination that visitors often return again and again. Canadians are especially fond of the Dominican Republic because their dollar buys more here than on any other Caribbean island.

The Dominican Republic, although often mistakenly referred to as "just a poor man's Puerto Rico," has its own distinctive cuisine and cultural heritage.

Columbus sighted its coral-edged Caribbean coastline on his first voyage to the New World and pronounced: "There is no more beautiful island in the world." The first permanent European settlement in the New World was founded here on November 7, 1493, and its ruins still remain near Montecristi in the northeast part of the island. Natives called the island Quisqueya, "Mother Earth," before the Spaniards arrived to butcher them.

Nestled amid Cuba, Jamaica, and Puerto Rico, the island of Hispaniola (Little Spain) consists of Haiti, on the westernmost third of the island, and the Dominican Republic, which has a lush land mass equal to that of Vermont and New Hampshire combined. In the Dominican interior, the fertile Valley of Cibao (rich sugarcane country) ends its upward sweep at Pico Duarte, formerly Pico Trujillo, the highest mountain peak in the West Indies, which soars to 10,417 feet.

Much of what Columbus first saw still remains in a natural, unspoiled condition, but that may change: The country is building and expanding rapidly. In the heart of the Caribbean archipelago, the country has an 870-mile coastline, about a third of which is devoted to beaches (the best are in Puerto Plata and La Romana), and near-perfect weather year-round. So why did it take so long for the Dominican Republic to be discovered by visitors? The answer is largely political. The country has been steeped in misery and bloodshed almost from its beginning, and it climaxed with the infamous reign of Rafael Trujillo (1930–61) and the civil wars that followed.

Today the Dominican Republic is being rebuilt and restored, and it offers visitors a chance to enjoy the sun and sea as well as to learn about the history and politics of a developing society.

GETTING THERE

American Airlines (☎ **800/433-7300**) offers the most frequent service, at least a dozen flights daily from cities throughout North America to either Santo Domingo or Puerto Plata. Flights from hubs like New York's JFK, Miami International, or San Juan's Luis Muñoz Marin airports are usually nonstop. You can also make connections to the Dominican Republic from Boston, Chicago, Los Angeles, and other cities through Miami, New York's JFK, or San Juan). Flights from New York's LaGuardia are usually routed through either Miami or San Juan.

If you're heading to one of the Dominican's smaller airports, your best bet is to catch a connecting flight with **American Eagle** (☎ **800/433-7300**), the American-affiliated local carrier. Its small-scale (around 60 passenger) planes depart every day from San Juan (with connecting flights from Mayagüez) for airports throughout the Dominican Republic, including Santo Domingo, Puerto Plata, La Romana, and Punta Cana.

Continental Airlines (☎ **800/525-0280** in the U.S.) flies daily from New Jersey's Newark airport to Santo Domingo. **TWA** (☎ **800/221-2000** in the U.S.) flies nonstop from New York's JFK to Santo Domingo every evening. Flights usually depart at 6pm, arriving on the island at 10:50pm. In addition, **Carnival** (☎ **800/824-7386**), flies daily to Santo Domingo from Miami, Orlando, and New York.

A Traveler's Advisory: Arriving at Santo Domingo's Las Américas International Airport is confusing and chaotic. Customs officials tend to be rude and overworked and give you a very thorough check! Stolen luggage is not uncommon here; beware of "porters" who offer to help with your bags. Arrival at La Unión International Airport, 23 miles east of Puerto Plata on the north coast, is generally much smoother and safer, but you should still be cautious.

For information on flights into Casa de Campo/La Romana, see section 2 of this chapter.

GETTING AROUND

This is not always easy if your hotel is in a remote location. The most convenient modes of transport are taxis, rental cars, *públicos* (multipassenger taxis), or *guaguas* (public buses).

BY TAXI Taxis aren't metered, and determining the fare in advance (which you should do) may be difficult if you and your driver have a language problem. Taxis can be hailed in the streets, and you'll definitely find them at the major hotels and at the airport. The minimum fare within Santo Domingo is $6, but most drivers try to get more. Don't get into an unmarked street taxi. Many visitors, particularly in Santo Domingo, have been assaulted and robbed by doing just that.

BY RENTAL CAR The best way to see the Dominican Republic is to drive; island buses tend to be erratic, hot, and overcrowded. If you want seat belts, you have to ask.

Your Canadian or American driver's license is suitable documentation, along with a valid credit or charge card or a substantial cash deposit. Unlike many Caribbean islands, you **drive on the right** here. Although major highways are relatively smooth, the country's secondary roads, especially those in the east, are covered with potholes and ruts. Roads also tend to be badly lit and badly marked in both the city and the countryside. Drive carefully and give yourself plenty of time when driving between island destinations. Watch out for policemen who flag you down and accuse you (often wrongly) of some infraction. Many locals give these low-paid policemen a $5 *regalo,* or gift "for your children," and are then free to go.

The high accident and theft rate in recent years has helped to raise car-rental rates here. Prices vary, so call around for last-minute quotes. Make sure you understand your insurance coverage (or lack thereof) before you leave home. Your credit- or charge-card issuer may already provide you with this type of insurance; contact the issuer to find out.

For reservations and more information, call the rental companies at least a week before your departure: **Avis** (☎ **800/331-1084**), **Budget** (☎ **800/527-0700**), and **Hertz** (☎ **800/654-3001**) all operate in the Dominican Republic.

BY PUBLIC TRANSPORTATION ***Públicos*** are unmetered multipassenger taxis that travel along main thoroughfares, stopping often to pick up people waving from the side of the street. A público is marked by a white seal on the front door. You must tell the driver your destination when you're picked up to make sure the público is going there. A ride is usually 15¢.

Public buses, often in the form of minivans or panel trucks, are called ***guaguas.*** For about the same price they provide the same service as públicos, but they're generally more crowded. Larger buses provide service outside the towns. Beware of pickpockets on board.

FAST FACTS: The Dominican Republic

Currency The Dominican monetary unit is the **peso (RD$),** made up of 100 centavos. Coin denominations are 5, 10, 25, and 50 centavos, and 1 peso. Bill denominations are RD$5, RD$10, RD$20, RD$50, RD$100, RD$500, and RD$1,000. Price quotations in this chapter appear sometimes in American and sometimes in Dominican currency, depending on the policy of the establishment. The use of any currency other than Dominican pesos is technically illegal, but few seem to bother with this mandate. At press time, we got about RD$13.20 to U.S.$1. (RD$1 equals about 7.5¢). Bank booths at the international airports and major hotels will change your currency at the prevailing free-market rate. You'll be given a receipt for the amount of foreign currency you've exchanged. If you have remaining pesos at the end of your trip, present this receipt at the Banco de Reservas booth at the airport and you can trade in your pesos for American dollars.

Documents To enter the Dominican Republic, citizens of the United States and Canada need only proof of citizenship, such as a passport or an original birth certificate. However, citizens may have trouble returning home without a passport—a reproduced birth certificate is not acceptable. Upon your arrival at the airport in the Dominican Republic, you must purchase a tourist card for U.S.$10. You can avoid waiting in line by purchasing this card when checking in for your flight to the island.

Electricity The country generally uses 110 volts AC (60 cycles), so adapters and transformers are usually not necessary for U.S.-made appliances.

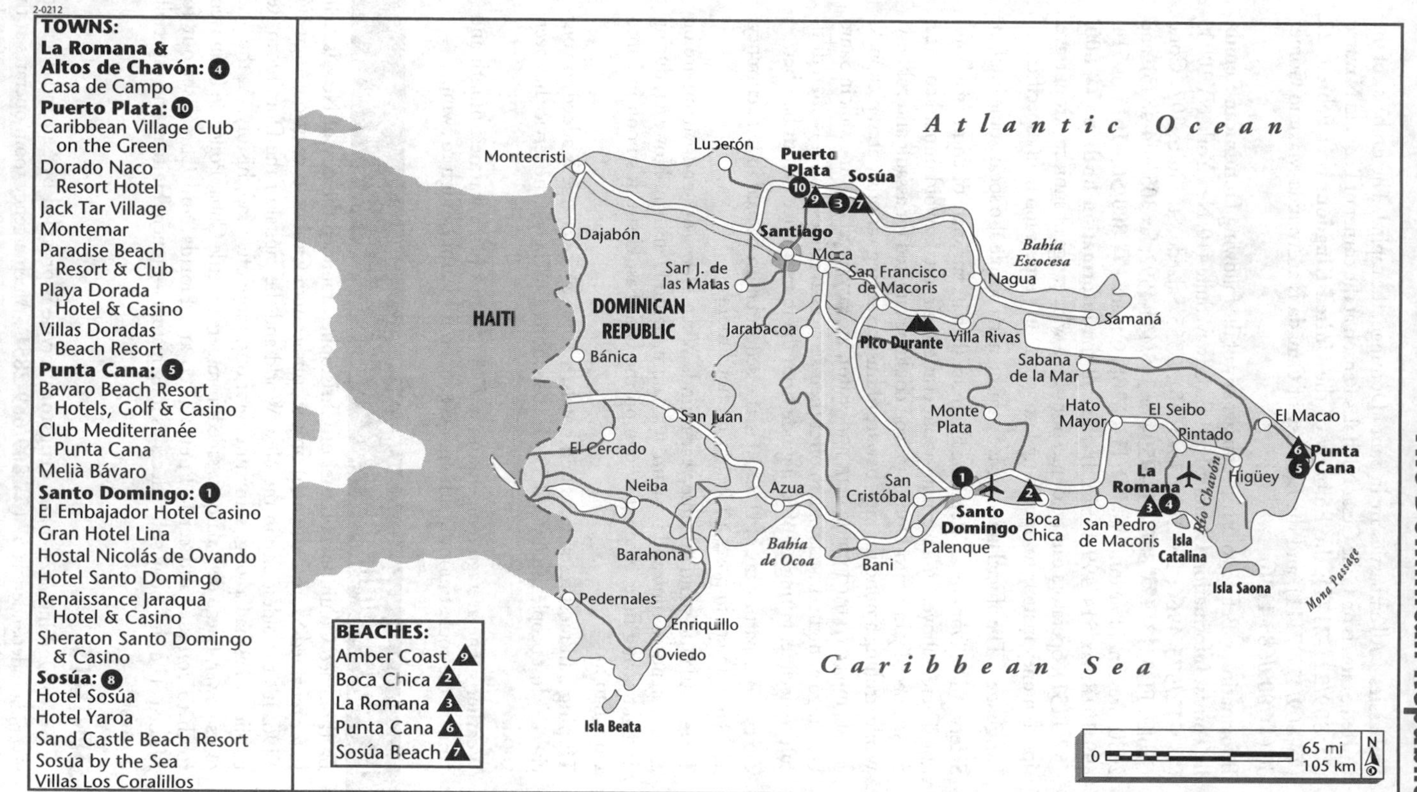

2-0212
TOWNS:
La Romana & Altos de Chavón: 4
Casa de Campo
Puerto Plata: 10
Caribbean Village Club on the Green
Dorado Naco Resort Hotel
Jack Tar Village
Montemar
Paradise Beach Resort & Club
Playa Dorada Hotel & Casino
Villas Doradas Beach Resort
Punta Cana: 5
Bavaro Beach Resort Hotels, Golf & Casino
Club Mediterranée Punta Cana
Meliã Bávaro
Santo Domingo: 1
El Embajador Hotel Casino
Gran Hotel Lina
Hostal Nicolás de Ovando
Hotel Santo Domingo
Renaissance Jaraqua Hotel & Casino
Sheraton Santo Domingo & Casino
Sosúa: 8
Hotel Sosúa
Hotel Yaroa
Sand Castle Beach Resort
Sosúa by the Sea
Villas Los Coralillos
Atlantic Ocean
Montecristi
Luperón
Puerto Plata
Sosúa
Dajabón
Santiago
Moca
Bahía Escocesa
San J. de las Matas
San Francisco de Macoris
Nagua
HAITI
DOMINICAN REPUBLIC
Jarabacoa
Samaná
Pico Durante
Villa Rivas
Bánica
Sabana de la Mar
San Juan
Monte Plata
Hato Mayor
El Seibo
El Macao
El Cercado
Pintado
Punta Cana
La Romana
Higüey
Neiba
Azua
San Cristóbal
Santo Domingo
Boca Chica
San Pedro de Macoris
Isla Catalina
Río Chavón
Barahona
Bahía de Ocoa
Bani
Palenque
Isla Saona
Mona Passage
Pedernales
Enriquillo
Oviedo
BEACHES:
Amber Coast 9
Boca Chica 2
La Romana 3
Punta Cana 6
Sosúa Beach 7
Caribbean Sea
Isla Beata
0
65 mi
105 km
N

Embassies All embassies are in Santo Domingo, the capital. The Embassy of the **United States** is on Calle Cesar Nicholas Penson at the corner of Leopold Navarro (☎ **809/221-2171**); the Embassy of the **United Kingdom** is at Febrero 27 (☎ **809/472-7111**), and the Embassy of **Canada** is at Avenida Máximo Gómez 30 (☎ **809/685-1136**).

Information Before your trip, contact any of the following **Dominican Republic Tourist Information Centers:** 1501 Broadway, Suite 410, New York, NY 10036 (☎ **212/575-4966;** fax 212/575-5448); 2355 Salzedo St., Suite 307, Coral Gables, FL 33134 (☎ **888/358-9594** or 305/444-4592; fax 305/444-4845); and 2080 Crescent St., Montréal, PQ, H3G 2B8, Canada (☎ **800/563-1611** or 514/499-1918; fax 514/499-1393). If you call the **information hotline** (☎ **800/752-1151**), operators can field questions on a wide range of subjects, from travel tips to money matters to upcoming festivals. Don't expect too many specifics.

Language The official language is Spanish; many people also speak some English.

Safety The Dominican Republic has more than its fair share of crime (see "Getting There," above, for a warning about crime at airports). Avoid unmarked street taxis, especially in Santo Domingo; you could be targeted for assault and robbery. While strolling around the city, beware of hustlers selling various wares; pickpockets and muggers are common here, and visitors are easy targets. Don't walk in Santo Domingo at night. Locals like to offer their services as guides, and it is often difficult to decline. Hiring an official guide from the tourist office is your best bet.

Taxes A departure tax of U.S.$10 is assessed and must be paid in U.S. currency. The government imposes a 13% tax on hotel rooms.

Time Atlantic standard time year-round. When New York and Miami are on eastern standard time and it's 6am, it's 7am in Santo Domingo. However, during daylight saving time, when it's noon on the U.S. East Coast, it's noon in Santo Domingo too.

Tipping In most restaurants and hotels, a 10% service charge is added to your check. Most people usually add 5% to 10% more, especially if the service has been good.

Weather The average temperature is 77°F. August is the warmest month and January the coolest month, although even then it's warm enough to swim.

1 Santo Domingo

Bartholomeo Columbus, brother of Christopher, founded the city of New Isabella (later renamed Santo Domingo) on the southeastern Caribbean coast on August 4, 1496. It's the oldest city in the New World and the capital of the Dominican Republic. It has had a long, sometimes glorious, more often sad, history. At the peak of its power, Diego de Valásquez sailed from here to settle Cuba, Ponce de León went forth to conquer and settle Puerto Rico and Florida, and Cortés set out for Mexico. The city today still reflects its long history—French, Haitian, and especially Spanish.

ESSENTIALS

In Santo Domingo, **24-hour drugstore** service is provided by San Judas Tadeo, Avenida Independencia 57 (☎ **809/689-2851**). An emergency room operates at the **Centro Médico Universidad,** Avenida Máximo Gómez 68, on the corner of Pedro Enrique Urena (☎ **809/221-0171**). For the **police,** call ☎ **911.**

WHERE TO STAY

Even the most expensive hotels in Santo Domingo might be classified as moderately priced in other parts of the Caribbean. However, remember that taxes and service charges will be added to your bill, which will make the rates 23% higher. When making reservations, ask if they're included in the rates quoted—usually they aren't.

EXPENSIVE

El Embajador Hotel Casino. Avenida Sarasota 65, Santo Domingo, Dominican Republic. ☎ **800/457-0067** or 809/221-2131. Fax 809/532-5306. 300 rms, 15 suites. A/C MINIBAR TEL TV. $85–$115 double on standard floor; from $130 junior suite on executive floor. Rates include continental breakfast. AE, DC, MC, V.

Trujillo, the former military strongman, had a personal luxury penthouse installed in this concrete-and-glass deluxe hotel, which still retains the aura of his 1950s heyday. Three miles southwest of the city center, it was built on the grounds of a horse-racing track. Today modern high-rise structures occupy the land where playboys and potentates played polo in the Trujillo era. The seven-story building has bedrooms decorated in French provincial style, with both king- and queen-size beds, walk-in closets, and private terraces. It was last remodeled in 1995, but more work remains to be done.

Dining/Entertainment: Among the best restaurants in Santo Domingo are the Jade Garden, featuring Chinese cuisine, and the Embassy Club, a deluxe restaurant and nightclub with an international cuisine marked by its flambé dishes. La Terraza is more informal, and you can drink and dance in La Fontana lounge. The casino is described in "Santo Domingo After Dark: Rolling the Dice," below.

Services: Room service, laundry, baby-sitting, medical auxiliary.

Facilities: Eight tennis courts, swimming pool, terrace with refreshments available, sauna, Turkish bath, Jacuzzi, and massage facilities.

✪ **Hotel Santo Domingo.** Avenida Independencia (at the corner of Abraham Lincoln), Santo Domingo, Dominican Republic. ☎ **800/877-3643** or 809/221-1511. Fax 809/535-4050. 220 rms, 5 suites. A/C MINIBAR TV TEL. $125 double; $140 Excel Club double; $200 executive suite. Rates include American breakfast. AE, MC, V.

Run by Premier Resorts & Hotels, the Santo Domingo has a tasteful extravagance without the glitzy overtones of the Jaragua. This ocher stucco structure opens onto the sea and sits on 14 tropical acres, 15 minutes from the downtown area. The prestigious address often attracts Latin American diplomats.

Oscar de la Renta helped design the interior. The average-sized rooms occupy two three-story structures, framed by latticework loggias, one that contains orange trees. Most of the rooms have views of the water, but some face the garden, which is quite charming. The superior Excel Club rooms offer ocean-view balconies and other amenities, plus Excel guests also have access to a private lounge featuring continental breakfast each morning and afternoon hors d'oeuvres and cocktails.

Dining/Entertainment: Guests can enjoy dinner at El Alcázar (see "Where to Dine," below) or El Cafetal; you can also enjoy a poolside lunch at Las Brisas. The piano bar, Las Palmas, draws a lively crowd at night.

Services: 24-hour room service, laundry, baby-sitting, rental cars.

Facilities: Three professional tennis courts (lit at night), Olympic-size swimming pool, sauna.

✪ **Renaissance Jaragua Hotel & Casino.** Avenida George Washington 367, Santo Domingo, Dominican Republic. ☎ **800/228-9898** in the U.S. and Canada, or 809/221-2222. Fax 809/686-0528. 289 rms, 11 suites. A/C MINIBAR TV TEL. $150 double; from $450 suite. MAP $46.50 per person extra. AE, DC, MC, V.

Often referred to as the "the pride of the Dominican Republic," this hotel was built on the 14-acre site of the old Jaragua (*ha-RA-gwa*) hotel, which was popular in Trujillo's day. Officially opened in 1988, it is a splashy, candy-pink waterfront palace that doesn't quite have the dignity and class of the Hotel Santo Domingo (though it does have the island's finest gym and spa facilities). Instead the Jaragua has a more ostentatious and flashy Latino flavor, and was appropriately featured on *Lifestyles of the Rich and Famous*. Located off the Malecón, and convenient to the city's major attractions and shops, this Las Vegas–style hotel consists of two separate buildings: the 10-story Jaragua Tower and the two-level Jaragua Gardens Estate.

The luxurious rooms are the largest in Santo Domingo and feature marble bathrooms with large makeup mirrors and hair dryers, multiple phones, refrigerators, and other posh amenities, all at a rather inexpensive (comparatively speaking) price.

Dining/Entertainment: The Jaragua boasts the largest casino in the Caribbean and a 1,000-seat Las Vegas–style showroom. Guests are also entertained at its cabaret theater, La Fiesta, and the Jubilee Disco. For dining, there's the Manhattan Grill, Figaro, and Latino; see "Where to Dine," below for details on these options. Lotus is a Chinese restaurant with unusual specialties, including seafood, and there's a 24-hour deli.

Services: 24-hour room service, laundry and dry cleaning, doctor on 24-hour call.

Facilities: Swimming pool with 12 private cabanas, snack bar, and outdoor bar; one of the best tennis centers in Santo Domingo, with four clay courts (lit at night) and a pro shop; beauty parlor and barber. The hotel's Spa and Health Club is the finest in the Dominican Republic.

MODERATE

Gran Hotel Lina. Avenidas Máximo Gómez and 27 de Febrero, Santo Domingo, Dominican Republic. ☎ **800/942-2461** or 809/563-5000. Fax 809/686-5521. 200 rms, 17 suites. A/C MINIBAR TV TEL. $111 double; from $130 suite. Rates include breakfast. AE, DC, MC, V.

Rising 15 floors in a sterile cinder block building, the Lina offers a wide range of services and facilities and has a more gracious and welcoming interior than its facade suggests. Situated in the heart of the capital, the hotel has hosted celebrities and dignitaries, from Julio Iglesias to David Rockefeller to several Latin American presidents. All the somewhat plain bedrooms contain refrigerators and full-size beds; at least 30% of the accommodations overlook the Caribbean. The best units are the executive rooms on the 11th floor.

Dining/Entertainment: The hotel's Lina Restaurant boasts one of the best-known restaurants in the Caribbean (see "Where to Dine," below), plus a cafeteria, snack bar, and piano bar.

Service: 24-hour room service, laundry, masseur, hairdresser.

Facilities: Swimming pool, Jacuzzi, solarium, gym, sauna, shopping arcade.

Sheraton Santo Domingo & Casino. Avenida George Washington 365, Santo Domingo, Dominican Republic. ☎ **800/325-3535** in the U.S., or 809/221-6666. Fax 809/687-8150. 240 rms, 18 suites. A/C MINIBAR TV TEL. Winter, $125–$160 double; $180–$210 suite. Off-season, $85–$120 double; $125–$180 suite. AE, DC, MC, V.

The Sheraton is an 11-story high-rise set back from the Malecón and perched at the end of a tree-lined drive. Upon arrival, you enter the vast lobby that's actually a solarium. The fair-sized bedrooms are equipped with hair dryers, and except for those on the third floor, all have ocean views. Some are equipped for travelers with disabilities. Service here can be hit or miss.

Dining/Entertainment: The plant-filled Petit Café overlooks the lobby, and Yarey's Lounge is a piano bar. Breakfast, lunch, and dinner are available at La Terraza coffee shop, which has a terrace surrounding a large pool that opens onto views of the sea. Other venues include La Canasta (featuring Dominican food), the Omni Disco, and a casino.

Services: 24-hour room service, baby-sitting, laundry, dry cleaning, 24-hour medical service, in-room safe.

Facilities: Complete business center, health club, outdoor pool, tennis courts, gift shop, sundries shop, clothing and jewelry boutique, tour desk; there's a golf course nearby.

INEXPENSIVE

Hostal Nicolás de Ovando. Calle Las Damas 53 (at Calle Las Mercedes), Santo Domingo, Dominican Republic. ☎ **809/688-9220.** Fax 809/221-4167. 43 rms. A/C TEL. $60 double. Rates include American breakfast. Additional person in room $10 extra. No credit cards.

Located in the shop-studded La Atarazana area (in the old town), this hostelry consists of two converted, 15th-century mansions (named after the governor of Hispaniola, who lived here from 1502 to 1509) that were designed as a fortified house, complete with an observation tower overlooking the Ozama River.

Set in the colonial zone, the *palacio* is said to be the oldest hotel in the New World. This hotel is not for resort lovers, but for those who want to be in the heart of old Santo Domingo. Its spartan bedrooms are small and unpretentious, but clean. The public rooms have heraldic tapestries, bronze mirrors, and colonial furnishings. Be careful when walking around this area at night.

WHERE TO DINE

Most of Santo Domingo's restaurants stretch along the seaside-bordering Avenida George Washington, popularly known as the Malecón. Some of the best restaurants are in hotels. It's safer to take a taxi when dining out at night, rather than wandering alone through the city's dark, and often dangerous, streets.

In most restaurants, casual dress is fine, although shorts are frowned upon at the fancier, more expensive spots. Many Dominicans prefer to dress up when dining out, especially in the capital.

EXPENSIVE

Figaro. In the Renaissance Jaragua Hotel & Casino, Avenida George Washington 367. ☎ **809/221-2222.** Reservations recommended. Main courses RD$155–RD$240 ($11.65–$18). AE, DC, DISC, MC, V. Tues–Sun 6:30pm–midnight. ITALIAN.

Vegetable lasagna and other homemade pastas may lure you to Figaro, which features northern and southern Italian fare, along with delectable pastries and cappuccino. Set on the lobby level of this previously recommended hotel, Figaro is one of the best Italian restaurants in Santo Domingo. Cured ham with fresh mozzarella is our favorite dish. Other specialties include lobster Fra Diavolo, eggplant parmigiana, and sirloin steak. Although the place is a bit mass-market and tends to lack innovation in its cuisine, it is nevertheless consistently reliable. The atmosphere resembles an Italian trattoria, with an open kitchen, bright tiles, and hanging wheels of cheese.

La Briciola. Calle Arzobispo Merino 152-A at Calle Padre Bellini. ☎ **809/688-5055.** Reservations recommended. Main courses RD$150–RD$280 ($11.25–$21). AE, DC, MC, V. Daily 7–11pm. ITALIAN/INTERNATIONAL.

This restaurant was established in 1994 as the Dominican branch of a chain of restaurants based in Milan. It occupies a once rundown trio of colonial houses whose 16th-century foundations were built very close to the Catedral de Santa María la Menor. Careful renovations retained the buildings' historic character and produced one air-conditioned dining room with a vaulted ceiling and a series of arcade-covered dining rooms, cooled by ceiling fans. Each overlooks an interior courtyard whose masonry and accessories evoke colonial Spain.

The menu represents all of Italy's culinary regions, with an emphasis on fresh pastas and the classics, including tortellini with pesto cream sauce, gnocchi, flavorful risottos, osso bucco, and plenty of fresh fish and meat entrees. Chances are you'll rarely be disappointed when sampling these savory viands.

✪ **Lina Restaurant.** In the Gran Hotel Lina, Avenidas Máximo Gómez and 27 de Febrero. ☎ **809/563-5000,** ext. 7250. Reservations recommended. Main courses RD$95–RD$170 ($7.15–$12.75). AE, DC, DISC, MC, V. Daily noon–4pm and 6:30pm–1am. INTERNATIONAL.

The Lina, lying one floor above street level in this previously recommended hotel, is one of the most prestigious restaurants in the Caribbean. Spanish-born Lina Aguado originally came to Santo Domingo as the personal chef of the dictator Trujillo, who she served until opening her own restaurant.

Today four master chefs, to whom Dona Lina taught her secret recipes, rule the kitchen of this modern hotel restaurant. The cuisine is international with an emphasis on Spanish dishes, and the service is first rate. Try the paella valenciana, the sea bass flambéed with brandy, or perhaps mixed seafood au Pernod, cooked casserole-style. Old-timers say that these new chefs don't have Lina's magical culinary touch, but that's hard to prove unless you were around in her day. We found the cooks to be extremely professional in both their preparation and presentation of meals. Lina's cuisine even wins the approval of visiting and hard-to-please Madrileños we know who are a bit contemptuous of Spanish food served outside Spain.

Pappalapasta. Calle Dr. Baez 23. ☎ **809/689-4849.** Reservations recommended. Main courses RD$95–RD$285 ($7.15–$21.40). AE, DC, MC, V. Tues–Sun noon–midnight. ITALIAN.

Housed within an 80-year-old building that was once a private home, this restaurant is just a short walk from the presidential palace, and so is known for its chaotic lunch scene. The yellow dining rooms are accented with modern art, cut-glass windows, and varnished hardwoods. Here, you can order from a variety of Italian dishes. Frankly, the staff is not as attentive as they should be, which is ironic considering the restaurant's high-powered clientele of lawyers and other professionals. The food, when it finally arrives, is far better than the service. Menu items might include dishes like sea bass, grilled with Creole sauce or meunière (lightly floured and sautéed in butter); fillet of beef with a brandy and mushroom-flavored cream sauce; red snapper with garlic, olives, and capers; and an assortment of pastas, gnocchis, and raviolis in savory sauces.

Reina de España. Calle Cervantes 103. ☎ **809/685-2588.** Reservations required Fri–Sat. Main courses RD$160–RD$300 ($12–$22.50). AE, MC, V. Daily noon–midnight. SPANISH/CREOLE/INTERNATIONAL.

One of the best independent (nonhotel) restaurants in Santo Domingo, the Reina de España lies near the Sheraton Santo Domingo & Casino in a once-private villa said to have belonged to an intimate friend of Trujillo. The chef draws inspiration from many regions of Spain, including roast suckling pig from Castile. The paellas are excellent, frogs' legs are prepared à la Romana, and the quail stew with herbs is as fine as that served in Toledo. However, the roast duck with mango sauce and the Dominican shrimp soup are definitely locally inspired. Lobster is prepared almost any way you like it, and most fish dishes are solid, including the seafood casserole. Meals here are among the most expensive in the capital, but patrons are usually satisfied. Imported meat is used.

✪ **Vesuvio I.** Avenida George Washington 521. ☎ **809/221-3333.** Reservations recommended Fri–Sat. Main courses RD$95–RD$325 ($9.40–$26.25). AE, DC, MC, V. Daily noon–1am. ITALIAN.

Along the Malecón, this is most famous Italian restaurant in the Dominican Republic, drawing crowds of visitors and local businesspeople. Ordering is always a problem here, as the Neapolitan owners, the Bonarelli family, have worked hard since 1954 to enlarge and perfect their menu. Most of their dishes rely on home-grown produce and every item is made to order. Their homemade soups are bubbling kettles of flavor. Their fresh red snapper, sea bass, and oysters are prepared in sauces that enhance, rather than smother, natural flavors. Recently, there have been some menu changes. They now offer dishes like papardelle al Bosque (with porcini mushrooms, rosemary, and garlic), kingfish carpaccio, and black tallarini with shrimp à la crema. Other outstanding newcomers include agnollotti alla Salvia (spinach and chicken in a creamy sage sauce), lobster Mediterráneo (chopped cold lobster with fresh tomatoes, onion, olive oil, and basil), and risotto tricolor (sun-dried tomatoes, basil, and mozzarella). Dominican crayfish is served in many ways here; our favorite is à la Vesuvio, topped with garlic and bacon.

The owner claims to be the pioneer of pizza in the Dominican Republic, and next door in **Pizzeria Vesuvio,** he makes a yard-long pizza! If you want to try their other Italian place, go to **Vesuvio II,** Avenida Tiradentes 17 (☎ **809/562-6060**).

MODERATE

El Alcázar. In the Hotel Santo Domingo, Avenida Independencia at Avenida Abraham Lincoln. ☎ **809/221-1511.** Reservations required. Fixed-price lunch buffet RD$150 ($11.25). AE, MC, V. Daily 11am–2pm. INTERNATIONAL.

Dominican designer Oscar de la Renta created El Alcázar in a Moroccan motif, with aged mother-of-pearl, small mirrors, and lots of fabric. The buffets are always good, at times even excellent, and they're one of the best dining buys in the city (at present only lunch is offered). The menu is likely to offer Chinese, Mexican, Italian, and Dominican food as well as fresh seafood; the chefs here specialize in zesty sauces. Presentation and service are two of the best reasons to dine here.

Jardín de Jade. In the Hotel Embajador, Avenida Sarasota 65. ☎ **809/221-2131.** Reservations recommended. Main courses RD$85–RD$195 ($6.40–$14.65). AE, DC, DISC, MC, V. Daily noon–3pm and 7:30–11pm. CHINESE.

The Jade Garden, 3 miles southwest of the center of town, is clearly a front-runner on Santo Domingo's Chinese restaurant scene. The management even sent its cooks to Hong Kong to learn secret Peking and northern Chinese recipes. The result is a delectable cuisine featuring dishes like minced pigeon, soybean chicken, sweet-corn soup (which is superb), lemon duck (even better!), sweet-and-sour pork, and walnut chicken with a soybean sauce. The pièce de résistance is the Peking duck, which the chef roasts in an open-fire stove. Finish with a toffee banana.

La Bahía. Avenida George Washington 1. ☎ **809/682-4022.** Main courses RD$125–RD$250 ($9.40–$18.75). AE, MC, V. Daily 9am–2am. SEAFOOD.

You'd never know that this unassuming place on the Malecón serves some of the best and freshest seafood in the Dominican Republic. One predawn morning, we passed by here and found fishermen waiting to sell the chef their latest catch. Rarely will you find a restaurant in the Caribbean with such diverse seafood options. For your appetizer, you might prefer ceviche, sea bass marinated in lime juice, or lobster cocktail. The soups always have big chunks of lobster and shrimp. House specialties include kingfish in coconut sauce, sea bass Ukrainian style, and baked red snapper, and the chef loves to play with conch. Overall, the cuisine is marked by hearty and robust flavors. Desserts are superfluous, and the restaurant stays open until the last customer finishes.

INEXPENSIVE

Fonda La Atarazana. Calle Atarazana 5. ☎ **809/689-2900.** Reservations recommended. Main courses RD$95–RD$270 ($7.15–$20.25). AE, DC, MC, V. Mon–Sat 10am–1am. CREOLE/INTERNATIONAL.

This patio restaurant, which opened in 1972, serves regional food in a colonial atmosphere. Just across from the Alcázar (see above), it's a convenient stop if you're shopping and strolling in the old city. The dishes here have robust country flavor, and are more true to the local cuisine than almost any other restaurant we've mentioned. One cheap, but delicious dish is *chicharrones de pollo,* tasty fried bits of Dominican chicken. Or you might try fresh fish prepared in a Creole sauce. Sometimes the chef cooks lobster thermidor and Galician-style octopus. If you don't mind waiting half an hour, you can order the *sopa de ajo* (garlic soup). Many fans return here for the fricasseed pork chops.

BEACHES & OUTDOOR ACTIVITIES

BEACHES The Dominican Republic has some great beaches, but they aren't in Santo Domingo. The principal beach resort near the capital is at **Boca Chica,** less than 2 miles east of the international airport and about 19 miles from the center of Santo Domingo. Clear, shallow blue water laves the fine white-sand beach, and there's a natural coral reef too. The east side of the beach, known as "St. Tropez," is popular with Europeans.

GOLF The **Santo Domingo Country Club** is an 18-hole course available to guests of most of the major hotels and resorts (a hotel staff member has to make the arrangements). The rule here is members first, which means tee times are almost impossible to get on weekends.

TENNIS The major hotels have good courts—especially the Santo Domingo Sheraton, Embajador, and Gran Hotel Lina—that even nonguests can use. Guests at the Renaissance Jaragua Resort & Casino and the Hotel Santo Domingo also enjoy excellent facilities. Some courts are lit for night games.

THE RELICS OF COLUMBUS & A COLONIAL ERA

Santo Domingo, a treasure trove of historic, but sometimes crumbling, buildings, is undergoing a major government-sponsored restoration. The old town is still partially enclosed by remnants of its original city wall. The narrow streets, old stone buildings, and forts resemble no other town or city in the Caribbean, except perhaps Old San Juan, whose restoration is far more complete.

Old and modern Santo Domingo meet at the **Parque Independencia,** a big city square marked by its Altar de la Patria, a shrine dedicated to Duarte, Sanchez, and Mella, who are all buried here. These men led the country's fight for freedom from Haiti in 1844. As in provincial Spanish cities, the square is a popular family gathering point on Sunday afternoon. At the entrance to the plaza is **El Conde Gate,** named for count (El Conde) de Penalva, who resisted the forces of Admiral Penn, the leader of a British invasion. It was also the site of the March for Independence in 1844 and holds a special place in Dominican hearts.

In the shadow of the Alcázar, **La Atarazana** is a fully restored section of town that once centered around one of the New World's finest arsenals. It extends for an entire city block—a catacomb of shops, art galleries, boutiques, and some good restaurants.

Just behind river moorings is the oldest street in the New World, **Calle Las Damas** (Street of the Ladies). Lined with colonial buildings, dome visitors assume that this was a bordello district, but it wasn't—the elegant ladies of the viceregal court used to promenade here in the evening.

Just north is the chapel of **Our Lady of Remedies,** where the first inhabitants of the city attended mass before the cathedral was erected.

Try to see the **Puerta de la Misericorda;** part of the original city wall, this "Gate of Mercy" was once a refuge for colonists fleeing hurricanes and earthquakes. To reach it, head west along Calle Padre Billini and turn left onto Calle Palo Hincado.

The **Monastery of San Francisco** is but a mere ruin; that any part of it is still standing is a miracle. It was destroyed by earthquakes, pillaged by Drake, and bombarded by French artillery. To reach the ruins, which are lit at night, go north on Calle Hostos and across Calle Emiliano Tejera. Continue up the hill and about midway along you'll see the ruins.

For a glimpse of Dominican life, head east along **Calle El Conde** from the Parque Independencia to **Columbus Square,** which has a large bronze statue honoring the discoverer, made in 1882 by a French sculptor, and the **Catedral de Santa María la Menor** (see below).

Below are some other must-see attractions:

Alcázar de Colón. Calle Emiliano Tejera, at the foot of Calle Las Damas. ☎ **809/689-4363.** Admission RD$10 (75¢). Mon and Wed–Fri 9am–5pm, Sat 9am–4pm, Sun 9am–1pm.

The most outstanding structure in the old city is the Alcázar, a palace built for Diego, the son of Columbus, and his wife, the niece of Ferdinand, king of Spain. Diego became the colony's governor in 1509, and Santo Domingo rose as the hub of Spanish commerce and culture in the Americas. Constructed of native coral limestone, it stands on the bluffs of the Ozama River. For more than 60 years it was the center of the Spanish court and entertained such distinguished visitors as Cortés, Ponce de León, and Balboa. After its heyday, it experienced two disastrous centuries as invaders pillaged it. By 1835 it lay in virtual ruin, and it was not until 1957 that the Dominican government finally restored it to its former splendor. The nearly two dozen rooms and open-air loggias are decorated with paintings and period tapestries, as well as 16th-century antiques.

✪ **Catedral de Santa María la Menor.** Calle Arzobispo Meriño, on the south side of Columbus Sq. ☎ **809/682-6595.** Free admission.

The oldest cathedral in the Americas was begun in 1514 and completed in 1540. With a gold coral limestone facade, it's a stunning example of the Spanish Renaissance style, with elements of gothic and baroque. The cathedral, visited by Pope John Paul II in 1979 and again in 1984, was the center for a celebration of the 500th anniversary of the European Discovery of America in 1992. You can view an excellent art collection of *retablos* (votive offerings), ancient wood carvings, furnishings, funerary monuments, and silver and jewelry of the Treasury. Open Monday to Saturday from 9am to 4pm. On Sunday masses begin at 6am.

El Faro a Colón (Columbus Lighthouse). Avenida España, on the water side of Los Tres Ojos near the airport (Sans Souci district). ☎ **809/591-1492.** Admission RD$10 (75¢) adults, RD$5 (40¢) children 11 and under. Tues–Sun 10am–5pm.

Built in the shape of a pyramid cross, the towering monument is both a sightseeing attraction and a cultural hub. In the heart of the structure is a chapel containing the tomb of Columbus and perhaps his mortal remains. The "bones" of Columbus were moved here from the Cathedral of Santa María la Menor (see above). (Other locations, including the cathedral of Seville, also claim to possess his remains.) Adjacent to the chapel is a series of museums representing more than 20 countries, plus a museum dedicated to the history of Columbus and the lighthouse itself. The most outstanding and unique feature is the lighting system, composed of high-tech searchlights and a beam that circles out for nearly 44 miles. When illuminated, Friday through Sunday, the lights project a gigantic cross in the sky that can be seen for miles beyond, even as far as Puerto Rico.

The lighthouse was inaugurated on October 6, 1992, the day Columbus's "remains" were transferred from the cathedral. The multimillion-dollar monument stands 688 feet tall (taller than the Washington Monument) and 131 feet wide.

Museo de las Casas Reales (Museum of the Royal Houses). Calle Las Damas, at the corner of Calle Las Mercedes. ☎ **809/682-4202.** Admission RD$10 (75¢). Mon–Fri 9am–5pm, Sat 10am–5pm.

Through artifacts, tapestries, maps, and re-created halls, including a courtroom, this museum traces Santo Domingo's history from 1492 to 1821. Gilded furniture, arms and armor, and other colonial artifacts make it the most interesting of all the museums of Old Santo Domingo. It contains replicas of the three ships commanded by Columbus, and one exhibit is said to hold part of the ashes of the famed explorer. You can see, in addition to pre-Columbian art, the main artifacts of two galleons sunk in 1724 on their way from Spain to Mexico, along with remnants of another 18th-century Spanish ship, the *Concepción.*

Other Sights

In total contrast to the colonial city, modern Santo Domingo dates from the Trujillo era. A city of broad, palm-shaded avenues, its seaside drive is called **Avenida George Washington,** more popularly known as the **Malecón.** This boulevard is filled with restaurants, as well as hotels and nightclubs. Use caution at night: There are pickpockets galore.

We also suggest a visit to **Paseo de los Indios,** a sprawling 5-mile park with a restaurant, fountain displays, and a lake.

About a 20-minute drive from the heart of the city, off the autopista de las Américas on the way to the airport and the beach at Boca Chica, is **Los Tres Ojos** or "three eyes," a trio of lagoons set in scenic caverns, with lots of stalactites and stalagmites. One lagoon is 40 feet deep, another 20 feet, and yet a third, known as "Ladies Bath," only 5 feet deep. A Dominican Tarzan will sometimes dive off the walls of the cavern into the deepest lagoon. The area is equipped with walkways.

Jardín Botánico. Avenida Republica de Colombia (corner of de los Proceres). ☎ **809/567-6211.** Admission RD$10 (75¢) adults, RD$5 (40¢) children. Tour by train RD$15 ($1.15) adults, RD$7 (55¢) children. Tues–Sun 9am–5pm.

In the northern sector of Arroyo Hondo, the 445-acre Botanical Gardens are the biggest in all of Latin American and contain the flowers and lush vegetation of the Dominican Republic. Seek out, in particular, the Japanese Park, the Great Ravine, and the floral clock. You can also tour the grounds by horse carriage or take a train.

Museo de Arte Moderno. Plaza de la Cultura, Calle Pedro Henríquez Ureña. ☎ **809/685-2153.** Admission RD$20 ($1.50). Tues–Sun 9am–5pm.

The former site of the Trujillo mansion, Plaza de la Cultura has been turned into a park and the Museum of Modern Art, which displays national and international works.

Also in the center are the **National Library** (☎ **809/688-4086**) and the **National Theater** (☎ **809/687-3191**), which sponsors, among other events, folk dances, opera, outdoor jazz concerts, traveling art exhibits, classical ballet, and music concerts.

ORGANIZED TOURS

Touring the far-flung monuments of Santo Domingo can sometimes be awkward and difficult to do on your own. Street signs aren't always clear, and it's often tough to get directions because of the language barrier. Throw in the afternoon heat and the city's crime rate, and traipsing around the city suddenly isn't so appealing. Some of these problems can be avoided by taking a guided tour.

Prieto Gray Line Tours of Santo Domingo, Avenida Francia 125 (☎ **809/685-0102**), one of the capital's leading tour operators, offers a three-hour tour of the Colonial Zone, leaving every day at 9am and again at 3pm; the cost is $28 per person. On Wednesday and Friday, the company offers a six-hour tour for $45 that includes lunch and visits to the Colonial Zone, the Columbus Lighthouse, the Aquarium, and the city's modern neighborhoods; entrance to several well-known museums and monuments is covered. About an hour of the tour is devoted to shopping.

They also offer a $75 full-day sailing excursion to the Isla Saona, an unspoiled island near La Romana, on Thursday and Sunday.

SHOPPING

The best buys in Santo Domingo are handcrafted native items, especially **amber jewelry.** Amber deposits, petrified tree resin that has fossilized over millions of years, were only fairly recently discovered in the Dominican Republic, but it has already become the national gem.

Look for pieces of amber with trapped objects, such as insect wings and spiders, inside. Colors range from a bright yellow to black, but most of the gems are golden in tone. Fine-quality amber jewelry, along with lots of plastic fakes, is sold throughout the country.

A semiprecious stone of light blue (sometimes a dark-blue color), **larimar** is the Dominican turquoise. It often makes striking jewelry and is sometimes mounted with wild boar's teeth.

Ever since the Dominicans presented president John F. Kennedy with what became his favorite rocker, visitors have wanted to take home a **rocking chair.** To simplify transport, these rockers are often sold unassembled.

Other good buys include Dominican rum, hand-knit articles, macramé, ceramics, and crafts in native mahogany. Always haggle over the price, particularly in the open-air markets; no stallkeeper expects you to pay the first price asked. The best shopping streets are **El Conde,** the oldest and most traditional shop-flanked avenue, and **Avenida Mella.**

In the colonial section, **La Atarazana** is filled with galleries and gift and jewelry stores, charging inflated prices. Duty-free shops are found at the airport, in the capital at the Centro de los Héroes, and at both the Hotel Santo Domingo and the Hotel Embajador.

Ambar Marie. Caonabo 9, Gazcue. ☎ **809/682-7539.**

In case you're worried that the piece of amber you like may be plastic, you can be assured of the real thing at Ambar Marie, where you can even design your own setting for your chosen gem. Look especially for the beautiful amber necklaces, as well as the earrings and pins.

Ambar Tres. La Atarazana 3. ☎ **809/688-0474.**

In the colonial section of the old city, Ambar Tres sells jewelry made from amber and black coral, as well as mahogany carvings, watercolors, oil paintings, and other Dominican products.

✪ **El Mercado Modelo.** Avenida Mella.

Head first for the National Market, filled with stall after stall of crafts and spices, fruits, and vegetables. The merchants will be most eager to sell, and you can easily get lost in the crush. Remember to bargain. You'll see a lot of tortoiseshell work here, but exercise caution, since many species, especially the hawksbill, are on the endangered-species list and could be impounded by U.S. Customs if discovered in your luggage. Rockers are for sale here, as are mahogany ware, sandals, baskets, hats, clay braziers for grilling fish, and so on.

Galería de Arte Nader. At Lupero and Duarte. ☎ **809/687-6674.**

In the center of the most historical section of town is a well-known gallery that sells so many Latino paintings that they're sometimes stacked in rows against the walls. Many of these paintings appear quite worthy, and works by some leading artists are displayed here. But others, especially those shipped in by the truckload from Haiti, seem to be mere tourist junk. In recent years, the focus has shifted away from Haiti. Today you get a more diversified collection of art, including some from such other Latin American countries as Colombia, Venezuela, and even Cuba. Don't miss the ancient courtyard in back if you want a glimpse of how things looked in the Spanish colonies hundreds of years ago.

Novo Atarazana. La Atarazana 21. ☎ **809/689-0582.**

Although the name implies that it's new, this is actually one of the best-established shops in town. If you don't have time to survey a lot of shops looking for local art and crafts, you'll find a wide cross section here. You can purchase pieces of amber, black coral, leather goods, wood carvings, and Haitian paintings.

Plaza Criolla. At the corner of Avenidas 27 de Febrero and Anacaona.

A modern shopping complex, Plaza Criolla has shops set amid gardens with tropical shrubbery and flowers, facing the Olympic Center. The architecture makes generous use of natural woods, and a covered wooden walkway links the stalls together.

Tu Espacio. Avenida Cervantes 102. ☎ **809/686-6006.**

One of the most charming shops in the capital is crammed with all sorts of goodies, including Taíno art (hand-carved reproductions, of course), Dominican and European antiques, monumental bamboo furniture, and odds and ends that Victorians used to clutter their homes with. If you're looking for that special trinket, you're likely to find it here. The merchandise is always changing.

SANTO DOMINGO AFTER DARK: ROLLING THE DICE

Santo Domingo has several major casinos, all of which are open nightly till 4 or 5am. The most spectacular is the **Renaissance Jaragua Resort & Casino,** Avenida George Washington 367 (☎ **809/221-2222**), whose brightly flashing sign is the most dazzling light along the Malecón at night. The most glamorous casino in the country is fittingly housed in the capital's poshest hotel and offers blackjack, baccarat, roulette, and slot machines. You can gamble in either Dominican pesos or U.S. dollars.

Other casinos include **El Embajador Casino,** Avenida Sarasota 65 (☎ **809/221-2131**), where the popular games of blackjack, craps, and roulette are offered. In between gaming sessions, you can have a drink at La Fontana, their casual bar where hors d'oeuvres are served. Another casino is at the **Hispaniola Hotel,** Avenida Independencia (☎ **809/221-7111**).

One of the most stylish casinos is the **Omni Casino,** in the Sheraton Santo Domingo Hotel & Casino, Avenida George Washington 361 (☎ **809/221-1511**).

Its bilingual staff will help you play blackjack, craps, baccarat, and keno, among other games. There's also a piano bar.

2 La Romana & Altos de Chavón

On the southeast coast of the Dominican Republic, La Romana was once a sleepy sugarcane town that specialized in cattle raising. Visitors didn't come near the place, but when Gulf and Western Industries opened a luxurious tropical paradise resort, the Casa de Campo, La Romana soon began drawing the jet set. Just east of Casa de Campo is Altos de Chavón, a village built specially for artists.

GETTING THERE

BY PLANE The easiest air routing to Casa de Campo from almost anywhere in North America is through San Juan, Puerto Rico (see "Getting There," in chapter 5). **American Eagle** (☎ **800/433-7300** in the U.S.) operates at least two (and in busy seasons, at least three) daily nonstop flights to Casa de Campo/La Romana from San Juan. Each flight takes a little over an hour and departs late enough in the day to permit transfers from other flights.

BY CAR If you're already in Santo Domingo, you can drive here in about an hour and 20 minutes from the international airport, along Las Américas Highway. (Allow another hour if you're in the center of the city.) Of course, everything depends on traffic conditions. Watch for speed traps—low-paid police officers openly solicit bribes whether you were speeding or not.

LA ROMANA

WHERE TO STAY

✪ **Casa de Campo.** La Romana, Dominican Republic. ☎ **800/877-3643** in the U.S., Canada, Puerto Rico, and the Virgin Islands, or 809/523-3333. Fax 809/523-8548. 280 casitas, 150 villas. A/C MINIBAR TV TEL. Winter, $200–$225 casita for 2; $445–$650 two-bedroom villa. Off-season, $145 casita for 2; $260 two-bedroom villa. MAP $49 per person extra. AE, MC, V.

Translated as "House in the Country," Casa de Campo is the greatest resort in the entire Caribbean, and that's pretty stiff competition. It brings a whole new dimension to a holiday. Gulf and Western took a vast hunk of coastal land, more than 7,000 acres in all, and carved out this chic resort, today owned and operated by Premier Resorts & Hotels and known as one of the best golf resorts in the world. Ubiquitous Miami architect William Cox helped create it, and Oscar de la Renta provided the style and flair. Tiles, Dominican paintings, louvered doors, and flamboyant fabrics decorate the interior.

The resort divides its accommodations into red-roofed, two-story casitas near the main building and more upscale villas that dot the edges of the golf courses, the gardens near the tennis courts, and the Atlantic shoreline. Some, within La Terrazza, are clustered in a semiprivate hilltop compound with views overlooking the meadows, the sugarcane, and the fairways down to the distant sea.

The resort lures many types of travelers, including families, in part because of its numerous recreational facilities and programs. Children's programs (ages 3 to 12) include full-day camping with horseback riding, aerobics, swimming, sack races, and treasure hunts.

Dining/Entertainment: Around the four swimming pools, each on a different level, are thatch huts on stilts serving beverages and light meals. La Caña is the two-level bar and lounge, with a thatch roof but no walls. For dinner, guests enjoy some of the best food in the Dominican Republic on a rustic roofed terrace. Sometimes, they'll have a pig roast right on the beach; most of the beef used is raised on the plains of La Romana. Other dining choices include El Patio, a glamorized coffee shop with substantial daily specials, and the Lago Grill, serving breakfast and lunch daily. See "Where to Dine," below, for a review of Tropicana.

Services: Room service (7am to midnight), laundry, baby-sitting.

Facilities: One of the most complete fitness centers on the island, with weight and exercise machines, whirlpool and sauna, aerobics classes, and masseuses. See "Beaches and Sports Galore at Casa de Campo," below, for details on golf, tennis, water sports, fishing, and polo and horseback-riding facilities.

Where to Dine

Tropicana. In Casa de Campo. ☎ **809/523-3333,** ext. 3000. Reservations required. Main courses RD$150–RD$250 ($11.25–$18.75). AE, MC, V. Daily 6–11pm. CARIBBEAN.

One of the most glamorous restaurants in the Casa de Campo complex, the Tropicana is a breezy pavilion known for its innovative Caribbean flair and a wide range of seafood and exotic West Indian dishes. Lying behind the main lobby area, it sometimes offers a seafood bar in winter.

Beaches & Sports Galore at Casa de Campo

At La Romana, on 7,000 acres of lush turf, you'll find three Pete Dye golf courses, a stable of horses for polo (three times a week), a private marina with deep-sea and river trips, snorkeling on live reefs, and 13 tennis courts. The facilities at **Casa de Campo** (☎ **809/523-3333**) are open to nonguests, but you should call ahead if you want to come out for the day, since guests have first dibs.

BEACHES A large, palm-fringed sandy crescent, **Bayahibe** is a 20-minute launch trip or a 30-minute drive from La Romana. In addition, **La Minitas** is a tiny but immaculate beach and lagoon. Transportation is provided on the bus, or you can rent a horse-drawn buckboard. Finally, **Catalina** is a beach on a deserted island just 45 minutes away by motorboat and surrounded by turquoise waters.

GOLF The Casa de Campo courses are known to dedicated golfers everywhere; in fact, *Golf* magazine declared it "the finest golf resort in the world." The course called **Teeth of the Dog** has also been called "a thing of almighty beauty," and it is. The ruggedly natural terrain has seven holes skirting the ocean. Opened in 1977, **the Links** is the inland course, built on sandy soil away from the beach. Most golf passes are sold as unlimited memberships for either three days ($165), or seven days ($330). Extra days cost $55 each. Golf-cart rentals are $20 per person per round. To play 18 holes, the cost is $100 for Teeth of the Dog, $85 for the Links (including cart). Open 7am to 7pm daily.

HORSEBACK RIDING Trail rides at Casa de Campo cost $19 for one hour, $32 for two. Lessons go for $39 per hour.

POLO Ever since the grand days when Dominican playboy Porfirio Rubirosa (see box above) mounted some of the finest horses in the world, the Dominican Republic has been a mecca for polo players. Today Casa de Campo is the ideal venue in the Caribbean for playing, learning, and watching the fabled sport. There are three full-size polo fields (one for practice only), a horse-breeding farm, and scores of polo ponies, as well as a small army of veterinarians, grooms, and polo-related employees. If a polo match is scheduled during your visit, by all means go.

Most serious polo players arrive with their own equipment, but beginners learn by watching more experienced players and participating in trail rides (which last one to three hours), as well as taking riding lessons at the resort's dude ranch. If polo players are present, they can play polo for $45 per player per match per chukker. Polo lessons are $45 per hour.

TENNIS Some 13 clay courts at Casa de Campo are lit for night play. The courts are available daily from 7am to 10pm. Charges are $15 per hour during the day or $18 at night. Tennis lessons are $50 per hour with a tennis pro, $42 with an assistant pro, and $35 with a junior pro.

WATER SPORTS & FISHING Casa de Campo has one of the most complete water-sports facilities in the Dominican Republic. Reservations and information on any seaside activity can be arranged through the resort's concierge. You can charter a boat for snorkeling or deep-sea fishing—the resort maintains eight charter vessels, with a minimum of eight people required per outing. Only three can fish at a time. Patrons interested in river fishing on the Chavón can arrange trips there through the hotel as well. Some of the biggest snook ever recorded have been caught here. Wednesday to Monday, full-day snorkeling trips to Isla Catalina cost $30 per snorkeler. Deep-sea fishing costs $300 for four hours (8:30am to 12:30pm or 1:30 to 5:30pm) or $400 for eight hours (9am to 5pm).

ALTOS DE CHAVÓN: AN ARTISTS' COLONY

In 1976, a sparsely populated plateau 100 miles east of Santo Domingo was selected by Charles G. Bluhdorn, then chairman of Gulf and Western Industries, as the site for a remarkable project. Dominican stone cutters, woodworkers, and ironsmiths began the task that would produce Altos de Chavón, today a flourishing Caribbean art center set above the canyon of the River Chavón and the Caribbean Sea.

A walk down one of the cobblestone paths of Altos de Chavón reveals at every turn architecture reminiscent of another era. Coral block and terra-cotta brick buildings house artists' studios, craft workshops, galleries, stores, and restaurants. Mosaics of black river pebbles, sun-bleached coral, and red sandstone spread out to the plazas. The **Church of St. Stanislaus** is centered on the main plaza, with its fountain of four lions and panoramic views.

The **School of Design at Altos de Chavón** has offered a two-year Associate in Applied Science degree, in the areas of communication, fashion, environmental studies, product design, and fine arts/illustration since its inauguration in 1982. The school is affiliated with the Parsons School of Design in New York and Paris.

The **galleries** at Altos de Chavón boast a varied and engaging mix of exhibits. The Principal Gallery, the Rincón Gallery, and the Loggia all showcase the work of well-known and emerging Dominican and international artists. The gallery has a consignment space where finely crafted silk-screen and other works are available for sale.

Altos de Chavón's ***talleres*** (craft ateliers) are the site of local artisans who have been trained to produce ceramic, silk-screen, and woven-fiber products. From the clay apothecary jars with carnival devil lids to the colored tapestries of Dominican houses, the richness of island myth and legend, folklore, and handcraft tradition is much in evidence. The posters, note cards, and printed T-shirts that come from the silk-screen workshops are among the most sophisticated in the Caribbean. All the products of Altos de Chavón's talleres are sold at La Tienda, the foundation's village store.

Thousands of visitors annually come to the **Altos de Chavón Regional Museum of Archeology,** which houses the objects of Samuel Pion, an amateur archaeologist and collector of treasures from the vanished Taíno tribes, the island's first settlers. The timeless quality of some of the museum's objects makes them seem strangely contemporary in design; some of the sculptural forms recall the work of Brancusi or Arp. The museum is open daily from 9am to 9pm.

At the heart of the village's performing-arts complex is the 5,000-seat open-air amphitheater. Since its inauguration by Frank Sinatra and Carlos Santana, the **amphitheater** has hosted renowned concerts, symphonies, theater, and festivals, including concerts by Julio Iglesias and Gloria Estefan. The annual **Heineken Jazz Festival** has brought together here such diverse talents as Dizzy Gillespie, Toots Thielmans, Tania Maria, and Randy Brecker.

WHERE TO DINE

Café de Sol. Altos de Chavón. ☎ **809/523-3333,** ext. 2346. Reservations not required. Pizza $8–$12. AE, MC, V. Daily 11am–11pm. PIZZA/AMERICAN.

The pizzas at this stone-floored indoor/outdoor cafe are the best on the south coast, including one made for vegetarians. The favorite seems to be *quattro stagioni,* made with tomato, mozzarella, mushrooms, artichoke hearts, cooked ham, and olives. You can also order such antipasti as a Mediterranean salad with tuna and ratatouille or a pasta primavera. The chef makes a soothing minestrone in the true Italian style, served with homemade bread. To reach the cafe, climb the stone steps to the rooftop of a building whose ground floor houses a jewelry shop.

Casa del Río. Altos de Chavón. ☎ **809/523-3333,** ext. 2345. Reservations required. Main courses $14–$22. AE, MC, V. Daily 6–11pm. FRENCH/CARIBBEAN.

The most romantic restaurant at Altos de Chavón occupies the basement of an Iberian-style 16th-century castle whose towers, turrets, tiles, and massive stairs are entwined with strands of bougainvillea. Inside, brick arches support oversize chandeliers, suspended racing sculls, and wine racks. Piano music might accompany your meal. Amid this bucolic atmosphere, you can indulge in some of the best seafood dishes on the south coast. Although the food has a slight French flair, and often a few Thai twists, everything tastes and looks firmly West Indian. Any of the seafood dishes, perhaps a lobster lasagna, is worthy of your attention. Lobster might also appear glazed with a vanilla vinaigrette that tastes a lot better than it sounds. You'll encounter innovative taste sensations here, especially in dishes involving lemongrass or coriander. We can't seem to forget the hearts of palm vichyssoise we once ordered here.

3 Punta Cana

Continuing east from La Romana, you reach Punta Cana, site of several major vacation developments, including Club Med, with more scheduled to arrive in the near future. Perhaps this easternmost tip of the Dominican Republic will one day rival Puerto Plata.

Known for its white-sand beaches and clear waters, Punta Cana is an escapist's retreat. Most resorts compete for the number of organized activities they provide for guests on their premises.

When you've had enough sun, head inland to the typical Dominican city of Higüey, 27 miles from Punta Cana, which has yet to be built up for tourism's sake. Here, you can see the **Basilica Nuestra Señora de la Altagracia,** with the largest carillon in the Americas.

Higüey was founded in 1494 by the conqueror of Jamaica, Juan de Esquivel, with immigrants brought in between 1502 and 1508 by Ponce de León to populate the land. It was from the castle he built here that the tireless seeker of the Fountain of Youth set out in 1509 to conquer Puerto Rico and in 1513 to check out Florida.

Toward the southern coast is **Saona Island,** where some 1,000 people live on 80 square miles of land, surviving primarily by fishing and hunting for pigeons and wild hogs. It must be a healthy way to live, for Saona has the lowest mortality rate in the Dominican Republic.

GETTING THERE

American Eagle (☎ **800/433-7300**) maintains between two and four daily nonstop flights to Punta Cana from San Juan; flight time is an hour and 10 minutes, departing late enough in the day to connect with dozens of flights to San Juan. We recommend that you reserve and pay for your tickets in advance. You can also opt for one of American Eagle's two or three (depending on the season) daily flights from San Juan to La Romana and then make the 90-minute drive to Punta Cana.

WHERE TO STAY & DINE

Bavaro Beach Resort Hotels, Golf & Casino. Apdo. Postal 1, Punta Cana, Higüey, Dominican Republic. ☎ **800/879-9698** in the U.S., or 809/686-5797. Fax 809/686-5680. 1,891 rms, 64 junior suites. A/C TV TEL. Winter, \$125–\$150 per person double; \$175 per person junior suite. Off-season, \$95–\$135 per person double; \$155 per person junior suite. Rates include MAP and taxes. \$25–\$40 for children 2–12 occupying parents' room. AE, DC, MC, V.

This is one of the most ambitious resort colonies in the Dominican Republic, a project whose scope hasn't been equaled here since the early days of Casa de Campo. Built between 1985 and 1996, it occupies almost 4½ square miles of land, including a 2-mile beach considered to be some of the best seafront property on the island. Developed by the Barcelos Group, a group of Spanish hotel investors, it consists of five separate low-rise hotels: Bavaro Beach Hotel, Bavaro Garden Hotel, Bavaro Golf Hotel, Bavaro Casino Hotel, and the newest contender, the Bavaro Palace Hotel. Arranged in the shape of a horseshoe, all but a few of the buildings lie parallel to the beachfront for maximum exposure to the sun. The overall effect is an unhurried, somewhat anonymous, and sometimes disorganized vacation village dotted with recreational facilities.

Accommodations in all five hotels are roughly equivalent and are outfitted in simple, summery furniture, with private verandas or terraces (the Bavaro Palace's rooms are somewhat more comfortable than the others). Most clients check in on the MAP plan, although a bewildering array of packages (including versions that focus on golf or all-inclusive dining and drinking) are also available. The clientele consists primarily of chartered tour groups from Italy, Spain, Germany, and South America, especially Argentina. Despite the resort's vast size and abundant recreational and dining facilities, expect the sense that the complex is evolving and growing; it never really seems to be either finished or particularly well staffed.

Dining/Entertainment: The resort contains 14 restaurants and 19 bars. Although all of them participate in the resort's MAP program, you might be charged extra for particularly costly items. Every evening, two of the bars become nightclubs, one specializing in disco, the other in Latino music. The resort has one of the largest casinos in the region, open every evening from 5pm until the last casino chip hits the roulette table.

Services: Laundry, baby-sitting, massage.

Facilities: Four swimming pools, an 18-hole golf course, daily aerobics sessions, scuba diving, snorkeling, sailing, windsurfing, waterskiing, deep-sea fishing, tennis, horseback riding, beauty salon, whirlpool baths big enough for 30 people at a time, medical facilities, on-site bank.

Club Mediterranée Punta Cana. Apdo. Postal 106, Provincia La Altagracia, Dominican Republic. ☎ **800/CLUB-MED** in the U.S., 809/686-5500, or 212/750-1670 in New York. Fax 809/687-2896. 334 rms. A/C. Christmas and New Year's holiday, \$1,505 per person per week double. Midsummer, \$785 per person per week double. Rates at other times vary between these figures, depending on the particular week. Rates include all meals. Children under 11 stay in parents' room for $980 per week in winter, $560 per week or else free during certain weeks of summer. Every guest is charged an annual membership fee of $50 per adult, $20 per child, plus a one-time initiation fee of $30 per family. AE, MC, V.

Some 145 miles east of Santo Domingo, this family-oriented Club Med opened in 1981 and put the far-eastern tip of the island of Hispaniola on the tourism map. The village lies along a reef-protected white-sand beach, off of which are some spectacular dive sites. It was here that the crews of the *Niña*, *Pinta*, and *Santa Maria* are believed by some to have put ashore. Three-story clusters of bungalows are strung along the beach; each contains twin beds and opens either onto the beach or onto a coconut grove. All rooms have private safes.

Dining/Entertainment: The heart of the village is a combined dining room/bar/dance floor and theater complex facing the sea. There are also three restaurants and a disco beside the sea. You get the usual Club Med activities here, including picnics, boat rides, nightly dancing, shows, and optional excursions.

Services: Laundry.

Facilities: Sailing, windsurfing, snorkeling, waterskiing, swimming, archery, 10 tennis courts (four lit at night); Mini-Club for juniors four to six, or Kids club 7 to 11, highlighting circus training and other activities.

Meliá Bávaro. Playa El Cortecito, Punta Cana, Higüey, Dominican Republic. ☎ **800/336-3542** or 809/221-2311. Fax 809/686-5427. 80 junior suites. Christmas–New Year's holidays, $215 suite for 2. Other times, $77–$140 suite for 2. MAP $45 per person extra. AE, MC, V.

The most glamorous addition to the resort scene in Punta Cana when it opened in 1992, this hotel transformed all of its rooms into junior suites in 1995. The Spanish-born architect who designed it (Alvaro Sanz) created an oasis for both vacationers and the many species of birds that call the resort their home. He retained most of the palms and mangrove clusters on the property and installed freshwater reservoirs. Owned by Meliá Hotels, the Spain-based giant, this resort drew at least part of its architectural inspiration from the company's successful hostelry in Bali.

All accommodations are suites that lie within earshot of the resort's mile-long private beach. About 100 of them occupy a compound of two-story bungalows; the rest sit adjacent to the resort's headquarters: a high-ceilinged, open-air pavilion.

Dining/Entertainment: El Trapiche, a seafood restaurant, is on an island in the middle of one of the swimming pools. An international restaurant, El Licey, sits on a pier jutting above a freshwater lake, adjacent to an open-air disco. The resort's main restaurant serves an array of buffets. There are a handful of bars, one is a soundproof music pub/disco floating atop a lake, another a swim-up pool bar.

Services: 24-hour room service, concierge, baby-sitting, car or scooter rentals.

Facilities: Two swimming pools, land and water-sports facilities, shopping arcade, four lit tennis courts.

4 Puerto Plata

Columbus wanted to establish a city at Puerto Plata and name it La Isabela. Unfortunately, a tempest detained him, and it wasn't until 1502 that Nicolás de Ovando founded Puerto Plata, or "port of silver," which lies 130 miles northwest of Santo Domingo. The port became the last stop for ships going back to Europe, their holds laden with treasures taken from the New World. Puerto Plata appeals to a mass-market crowd that shuns those pricey, pampering hotels in favor of the less expensive all-inclusive resorts that keep popping up here; some hotels are booked solid almost year-round. Some excellent restaurants have been forced to close because of the all-inclusive trend; in fact, the most popular dining choice along the coast now is Pizza Hut.

Most of the hotels are not actually in Puerto Plata itself but in a special tourist zone called Playa Dorada. It rains a lot in Puerto Plata during the winter (whereas the southern region and Punta Cana are drier). This zone consists of major hotels, a scattering of secluded condominiums and villas, a Robert Trent Jones–designed golf course, and a riding stable with horses for each of the major properties.

GETTING THERE

BY PLANE The international airport is actually not in Puerto Plata but is east of Playa Dorado on the road to Sosúa. For information about flights from North America, see "Getting There" at the beginning of this chapter.

BY CAR From Santo Domingo, the 3½-hour drive directly north on autopista Duarte passes through the lush Cibao Valley, home of the country's tobacco industry and Bermudez rum, and through Santiago de los Caballeros, the second-largest city in the country, 90 miles north of Santo Domingo.

GETTING AROUND

For information on renting a car, see "Getting Around" at the beginning of this chapter. You might find that a motor scooter will be suitable for transportation in Puerto Plata or Sosúa, although the roads are potholed.

BY TAXI Agree on a fare with the driver before you go anywhere, as taxis are not metered. You'll find taxis on Central Park at Puerto Plata. At night it's wise to rent your cab for a round-trip. It's also not a bad idea to do this during the day if you take a taxi to any of the other beach resorts or villages.

BY MOTOCONCHO The cheapest way of getting around is on a *motoconcho*, found at the major corners of Puerto Plata and Sosúa. These motorcycle "conchos," or taxis, can take you just about anywhere in town. You can also go from Puerto Plata to Playa Dorada (where the hotels are). Fares range from RD$10 to RD$25 (75¢ to $1.90).

BY MINIVAN Minivans are another means of transport, especially if you're traveling outside of town. They leave from Puerto Plata's Central Park and will take you all the way to Sosúa. Determine the fare before getting in. Usually a shared ride between Puerto Plata and Sosúa costs RD$10 (75¢) per person. Daily service is from 6am to 9pm.

BY ORGANIZED TOUR If your vacation in the Dominican Republic involves a flight in and out of Puerto Plata, and you want to see more of the country than just the beaches and tourist zones around your hotel, consider a guided tour. One of the best local tour operators is **Apollo Tours,** Calle John F. Kennedy 15 (☎ **809/586-6610**), which conducts tours of Puerto Plata and the surrounding sights on minivans or buses; tours cost RD$230 ($17.25) per person and are scheduled regularly from 8:30am to 1:30pm. On Wednesday and Friday, they offer an all-day city tour of Santo Domingo (RD$600, $45 per person), leaving Puerto Plata at 6am, and returning around 7pm.

ESSENTIALS

Round-the-clock **drugstore** service is offered by Farmacía Deleyte, Calle John F. Kennedy 89 (☎ **809/586-2583**). **Emergency 24-hour medical service** is provided by Clinica Dr. Brugal, Calle José del Carmen Ariza 15 (☎ **809/586-2519**). To summon the **police** in Puerto Plata, phone ☎ **809/586-2331.**

WHERE TO STAY

EXPENSIVE

Jack Tar Village. Playa Dorada (Apdo. Postal 368), Puerto Plata, Dominican Republic. ☎ **800/999-9182** in the U.S., or 809/320-3800. Fax 809/320-4161. 283 rms, 3 suites. A/C TV TEL. Winter, $310–$360 double; $620–$720 one-bedroom suite for 4, $980–$1,180 three-bedroom suite for 6. Off-season, $220–$260 double; $515 one-bedroom suite for 4, $860 three-bedroom suite for 6. Rates are all-inclusive. Children 2–12 sharing their parents' room $65 in winter, $60 off-season; children under 2 free. AE, MC, V.

This is not everyone's favorite resort, but some people like its consistency and reliability. It's often sold out for a surprisingly large number of weeks in winter. Owned by an investment group from Texas, this all-inclusive resort is east of the airport, at the edge of the sea. Accommodations are clustered around two swimming pools and the rooms, all of which have private patios or verandas, are decorated in typical American-motel style—conventional, but comfortable. Regrettably, only the suites, which are usually reserved for the casino's high rollers, have ocean views. Drinks, all meals, most water sports, and entertainment are part of the standard package, so you never have to leave the grounds. In the center of the resort, you'll find dozens of adults and children playing shuffleboard, cards, table tennis, and volleyball. If you prefer to linger beside one of the indoor/outdoor bars, where all your drinks are free, you'll have plenty of company. If you're more energetic, many water and land sports are offered.

Dining/Entertainment: In 1990 the resort opened a large, plush casino, one of the largest in the country, and a disco. Two nights a week, dinners are sit-down affairs in a high-ceilinged dining room with frequent musical entertainment. The rest of the time, and often at lunch, meals are buffet style. Drinks are free at the indoor and outdoor bars.

Services: Laundry, baby-sitting.

Facilities: Two swimming pools, sailing, windsurfing, snorkeling, scuba lessons, boogie boarding, inner tubing, volleyball, water aerobics, horseback riding, basketball, bicycling, shuffleboard, horseshoes, board and table games, three tennis courts, casino, activity-filled Kids Klub, and Robert Trent Jones–designed golf course.

MODERATE

Caribbean Village Club on the Green. Playa Dorada, Puerto Plata, Dominican Republic. ☎ **809/320-1111.** Fax 809/320-5386. 336 rms, 144 suites. A/C TV TEL. Winter, $95 per person double or suite; off-season, $75 per person double or suite. Rates are all-inclusive. AE, MC, V.

Upgraded in 1996 by a hotel chain, this is a modern low-rise property set near a cluster of competitors east of the airport. The hotel offers comfortable but simple bedrooms, and the price of accommodations includes three meals a day, all beverages, and some water sports. Surprisingly, the so-called suites aren't that much different from the regular doubles and don't cost any more either.

Dining/Entertainment: Standard Dominican and international food is offered at El Pilon, Italian pastas at Firenze, and fresh fish and seafood and local beef on the continental menu at La Miranda (sample some of the excellent Chilean vintages here, all at reasonable prices).

Services: Laundry, baby-sitting.

Facilities: Water sports, seven all-weather tennis courts, gym, sauna, swimming pool with swim-up bar.

Dorado Naco Resort Hotel. Playa Dorada (Apdo. Postal 162), Puerto Plata, Dominican Republic. ☎ **800/322-2388** in the U.S., or 809/320-2019. Fax 809/320-3608. 133 rms, 77 suites. A/C TV TEL. $107–$117 per person double; $131 per person suite. Third and 4th person $77 each. Off-season, $78–$93 per person double; $90–$100 per person suite. Third and 4th person $70 each. Rates are all-inclusive. Children 2–12 $32 a day; children under 2 stay free in parents' room. AE, DC, MC, V.

When the Dorado Naco was built east of the airport in 1982, there was only one other hotel in the entire Playa Dorada area. After registering, you'll be ushered past the poolside bar and restaurant complex, down a series of flowered walkways into your room. Each suite contains comfortable furniture, a kitchen, and a creative interior space. Many of the units are clustered along parapets or around well-planted atriums, and some of the larger ones include duplex floor plans and enough space and luxury to satisfy any vacationer. Two-bedroom suites and the penthouse can sleep up to four.

Dining/Entertainment: A wide array of entertainment is available, and a full range of activities is planned throughout the week in season. A beach bar and grill lie a short walk from every room. A nightly buffet is spread under a portico near the pool, and à la carte meals are available in the Flamingo Gourmet Restaurant and Valentino's Italian restaurant. Consider dining at the Flamingo even if you're not a resident of the hotel. It's one of the best in the area, serving a continental menu. The hotel has live music every night and live shows twice weekly.

Services: Room service (7am to 11pm), laundry, baby-sitting

Facilities: Swimming pool, tennis court, water-sports center (for scuba diving, snorkeling, waterskiing, and sailing).

✪ **Paradise Beach Resort & Club.** Playa Dorada (Apdo. Postal 337), Puerto Plata, Dominican Republic. ☎ **800/752-9236** or 809/586-3663. Fax 809/320-4858. 266 rms, 174 suites. A/C TV TEL. Winter, $110 per person double; $130 per person suite. Off-season, $90–$100 per person double; $110 per person suite. Rates are all-inclusive. AE, DC, MC, V.

This all-inclusive resort is the largest and best-positioned of all the Playa Dorada hotels. It's also superior when it comes to amenities and boasts an ecofriendly design: a cluster of Caribbean-Victorian low-rises with white-tile roofs and lattice-laced balconies. Brick paths cut through the well-manicured, tropical grounds. This hotel is far more successful today than it was during its tenure as the Eurotel Playa Dorada, which opened in 1985 and never seemed to take off. Accommodations are neatly furnished with tile floors and baths, twin or double beds, refrigerators (in most cases), and large closets.

Dining/Entertainment: The food (under the all-inclusive plan) is above average for the Playa Dorada area, and there's always plenty of it. Bars seem to be in all the right places, and there's also a disco.

Facilities: 18-hole golf course, horseback riding, water sports center, two tennis courts.

Playa Dorada Hotel & Casino. Playa Dorada (Apdo. Postal 272), Puerto Plata, Dominican Republic. ☎ **809/586-3988.** Fax 809/320-1190. 351 rms. A/C TV TEL. Year-round, $95 per person double. Rates are all-inclusive. Additional person $80 extra. AE, MC, V.

This theatrically designed hotel east of the airport is one of the few in all the Caribbean that can boast nearly full occupancy during most of the year. Rooms recently received a long overdue renovation. The reception area is an air-conditioned oasis of Victorian latticework set beneath the soaring ceiling. The bedrooms are arranged along rambling corridors. More than two-thirds of the hotel's units are set in red-roofed wings that face the $1\frac{1}{2}$-mile-long beach. The hotel also has specially designed rooms for travelers with disabilities. A sports package is included in the rates, so all the facilities are free.

Dining/Entertainment: In addition to La Palma restaurant, the many bars and entertainment facilities include a cocktail lounge and disco. Las Brisas and Mar Azul are two other restaurants. Around the swimming pool, the management hosts barbecues, buffet suppers, and weekly entertainment, including singers and dancers known throughout the Spanish-speaking world.

Services: Baby-sitting, laundry, valet.

Facilities: Boating, water sports, golf, three tennis courts (lit at night), swimming pool.

Villas Doradas Beach Resort. Playa Dorada (Apdo. Postal 1370), Puerto Plata, Dominican Republic. ☎ **809/320-3000.** Fax 809/320-4790. 244 rms. A/C TV TEL. $90 per person double year-round. Rates are all-inclusive. AE, MC, V.

This collection of town houses east of the airport is arranged in landscaped clusters, usually around a courtyard. There's no beachfront here. Each unit is pleasantly furnished with louvered doors and windows. Personal service from the lackadaisical staff seems minimal here.

Dining/Entertainment: A focal point of the resort is the restaurant Las Garzas, where night shows entertain guests every evening beneath the soaring pine ceiling. The management also puts on barbecues around the pool area, where a net is sometimes set up for volleyball games. El Pescador is a fish restaurant open for dinner beside the beach, and Pancho serves Mexican dishes. For Chinese food, Jardín de Jade is another option. The cone-shaped, thatch-roofed pool bar is extremely popular.

Services: Laundry, baby-sitting.

Facilities: Swimming pool, tennis, horseback riding, kiddie pool; sand beaches and a golf course within walking distance.

INEXPENSIVE

Montemar. Avenida Las Hermanas Mirabal (Apdo. Postal 382), Puerto Plata, Dominican Republic. ☎ **809/586-2800.** Fax 809/586-2009. 60 rms. A/C MINIBAR TV TEL. RD$450 ($33.75) double. AE, DC, MC, V.

Remodeled in 1995, the Montemar complex east of the airport plays a dual role: It's one of the pioneer resorts in the area, and it houses the local hotel school. The distinctive lobby has large bamboo chandeliers and a mural behind the reception desk. Most of the accommodations have views of palms and the sea. Some of the rooms are air-conditioned. Your needs will be cared for by a battalion of well-meaning, but poorly trained students.

A lounge nearby usually features a merengue band, which plays every night beside the illuminated palms. There are two tennis courts. Laundry, baby-sitting, and room service are provided. Three times a day a shuttle bus from the hotel takes guests to the beach. No meals, not even breakfast, are served.

WHERE TO DINE

EXPENSIVE

Another World/Otro Mundo. Km. 7, Highway Puerto Plata–Sosúa. ☎ **809/320-4400** or 809/543-8019. Reservations recommended. Main courses RD$85–RD$275 ($6.40–$20.65). DC, MC, V. Daily 6pm–midnight. INTERNATIONAL.

This is the most prosperous and unusual independent restaurant in Puerto Plata; it even attracts diners from the nearby all-inclusive hotels. About a mile east of Playa Dorada, in a green-sided Victorian building, it has a benign resident ghost that some readers claim to have spotted, an indoor/outdoor format accented with tropical touches, and an ersatz zoo whose residents (a tiger, monkeys, a honey bear, and wild birds) were all once abused before finding a home with the restaurant's kind-hearted owner, Stuart Ratner, a New York–born singer and actor who appeared in some productions during the 1970s with Barbra Streisand. Precede a meal here with a *cocolobo,* containing about four times the alcohol in a standard cocktail—it's "guaranteed to make you fly." Move on to frogs' legs, deep-water Caribbean crab, river prawns, chateaubriand, or beef Wellington. You can also choose a fresh local fish entree, such as snapper. Live music is often an added bonus here.

MODERATE

✪ **Jardín de Jade.** In the Villas Doradas Beach Resort, Playa Dorada. ☎ **809/586-3000.** Reservations recommended. Main courses RD$80–RD$275 ($6–$20.65). AE, DC, MC, V. Daily 7–11pm. CHINESE.

A high-ceilinged, airy, modern restaurant, the Jardín de Jade offers the finest Chinese food in the area. It's also one of the best dining values at the resort. Typical menu items include barbecued Peking duck, sautéed diced chicken in chile sauce, and fried crab claws. The chefs specialize in Cantonese and Szechuan cuisine. You've probably eaten these dishes before in better-prepared versions, but at least this restaurant provides a change of pace among other spots that tend to overcook and especially overfry. Because it's located in a solidly booked resort, it has a captive audience, yet it remains a reliable choice. Staff attitude and service could use some work, however.

INEXPENSIVE

Porto Fino. Avenida Las Hermanas Mirabal. ☎ **809/586-2858.** Main courses RD$45–RD$190 ($3.40–$14.25). AE, MC, V. Daily 10am–11pm. ITALIAN.

In this popular Italian restaurant, just across from the entrance of the Hotel Montemar in Puerto Plata, chicken Parmesan, eggplant Parmesan, ravioli, spaghetti, and pizzas are served in generous portions. You'll get off cheap if you order only pizza. Locals and visitors mingle freely here. This is a place to go for a casual meal in casual clothes, and not for some memorable gastronomic experience.

Roma II. Calle Beiler at Emilio Prud'homme. ☎ **809/586-3904.** Reservations not required. Main courses RD$60–RD$275 ($4.50–$20.65); pizza RD$50–RD$100 ($3.75–$7.50). AE, MC, V. Daily 11am–midnight. INTERNATIONAL.

This air-conditioned restaurant in the center of town is staffed by an engaging crew of well-mannered young employees who work hard to converse in English. You can order from a selection of 13 varieties of pizza, topped with tempting combinations like cheese, shrimp, and garlic. Seafood dishes include paella and several preparations of lobster and sea bass. The menu is unfussy, as is the presentation. Don't look for any new taste sensations (except for octopus vinaigrette, one of the chef's specialties). The meat dishes, such as filet mignon, are less successful than the seafood items.

Valentino's. In the Dorado Naco Resort Hotel, Playa Dorada. ☎ **809/320-2019.** Reservations required. Main courses RD$90–RD$385 ($6.75–$28.90). AE, DC, MC, V. Daily 6–11pm. ITALIAN.

This restaurant continues to be a staple on the dining scene. Located in the heart of the tourist zone, this ristorante and pizzeria offers homemade pasta, such as lasagna verdi al forno, and brick-oven pizza that's surprisingly good. Against an elegant backdrop, with fountains and pink marble, it serves a savory cuisine. Have a drink on the terrace, perhaps the bartender's special called a Bloody Mary antipasto; then follow with one of the main dishes, such as risotto primavera with grilled chicken Venetian style.

BEACHES, WATER SPORTS & OTHER OUTDOOR PURSUITS

The north coast is the site of the densest concentration of water-sports activities in the Dominican Republic, although the sea here tends to be rough. Snorkeling is popular, and the windsurfing is among the best in the Caribbean. Concessions for renting equipment come and go on the beach, but you're sure to find something. The resort of Cabarete, east of Puerto Plata, hosts an annual windsurfing tournament.

BEACHES You'll find superb but often wind blown beaches to the east and west of Puerto Plata. Among the better known are Playa Dorada, Sosúa, Long Beach, Cofresi, Jack Tar, and Cabarete.

GOLF Robert Trent Jones Jr. designed the par-72, 18-hole **Playa Dorada** championship golf course (☎ **809/320-4262**), which surrounds the resorts and runs along the coast. Even nongolfers can sip a cocktail and enjoy the views at the clubhouse. It's best to make tee times at your hotel's activities desk. Greens fees are RD$350 ($26.25) for 18 holes, RD$ 175 ($13.15) for 9 holes. You can hire a caddy for RD$135 ($10.15) for 18 holes, RD$75 ($5.65) for 9 holes. Cart rental costs RD$350 ($26.25) for 18 holes, RD$220 ($16.50) for 9 holes.

TENNIS Nearly all the major resort hotels have tennis courts. If yours doesn't, there are seven all-weather tennis courts at the Caribbean Village Club on the Green (see "Where to Stay," above), although guests at the resort have first dibs at court times.

SEEING THE SIGHTS

Fort San Felipe, the oldest fort in the New World, is a popular attraction. Philip II of Spain ordered its construction in 1564, a task that took 33 years to complete. Built with eight-foot-thick walls, the fort was virtually impenetrable, and the moat surrounding it was treacherous. The Spaniards sharpened swords and embedded them in coral below the surface of the water to discourage anyone from crossing the moat. The doors of the fort are only four feet high, another deterrent to swift passage. During Trujillo's rule, Fort San Felipe was used as a prison. Standing at the end of the Malecón, the fort was restored in the early 1970s. Admission is RD$10 (75¢). It's open Thursday through Tuesday from 8am to 4pm.

Isabel de Torres (☎ **809/586-2325**), a tower with a fort built when Trujillo was in power, affords a panoramic view of the Amber Coast from a point near the top, 2,595 feet above sea level. You reach the observation point by *teleférico* (cable car), a seven-minute ascent. Once here, you're also treated to seven acres of botanical gardens. The round-trip costs RD$80 ($6) for adults, RD$20 ($1.50) for children 12 and under. The aerial ride is operated on Monday, Tuesday, and Thursday to Sunday from 8am to 5pm. Be warned that there's often a long wait in line for the cable car, and at certain times it's likely to be closed for repairs, so check at your hotel before going there.

SHOPPING

The **Plaza Turisol Complex,** the largest shopping center on the north coast, has about 80 different outlets. Each week, it seems a new store opens. You may want to head here for a sampling of Puerta Plata merchandise before going to a specific shop. The plaza lies about five minutes from the centers of Puerto Plata and Playa Dorada, on the main road heading east. Nearby is a smaller shopping center, **Playa Dorada Plaza,** with about 20 shops, selling handcrafts, clothing, souvenirs, and gifts. Both centers are open daily from 9am to 9pm.

The **Centro Artesanal,** Calle John F. Kennedy 3 (☎ **809/586-3724**), is a non-profit school for the training of future Dominican craftspeople, and it's also a promotion center for local crafts and jewelry. Selected student projects are for sale.

The **Plaza Isabela,** in Playa Dorada about 500 yards from the entrance to the Playa Dorada hotel complex, is a collection of small specialty shops constructed in the Victorian gingerbread style, although much of the inventory has Spanish flair. Here you'll find the main branch of Dominican Republic's premier jeweler, **Harrison's,** Plaza Isabela, Playa Dorada (☎ **809/586-3933**). Established in 1980 by Boston-born Robert Harrison, the shop specializes in platinum, working it into configurations in which gemstones (usually diamonds or the local larimar), slide, pivot, or twist in unique ways. Most objects range from $300 to $1,200. Madonna, Michael Jackson, Keith Richards of the Rolling Stones, and actor Patrick Swayze have all donned Harrison's jewelry. Oddly, although there are almost two dozen branches of Harrison's within the Dominican Republic—there's another branch in the Playa Dorada Shopping Plaza in the Playa Dorada Hotel Complex—the chain has yet to expand to other parts of the world.

CASINOS: THE HOT TICKET IN PUERTO PLATA AFTER DARK

The following venues are open daily until 5am:

Jack Tar Village. Playa Dorada. ☎ **809/320-3800.**

Jack Tar joins the gaming flock with a casino and disco, along with a European-style restaurant. It's built in Spanish Mediterranean colonial style with a terra-cotta roof. Between bouts at the gaming tables, guests quench their thirst at one of five bars. There's also an entertainment center that includes a 90-seat restaurant and a disco for 250 dancers.

Playa Dorada Casino. In the Playa Dorada Hotel, Playa Dorada. ☎ **809/586-3988.**

The casino's entrance is flanked by columns and leads to an airy garden courtyard. Inside, mahogany gaming tables are reflected in the silver ceiling. No shorts are permitted inside the premises after 7pm, and beach attire is usually discouraged.

5 Sosúa

About 15 miles east of Puerto Plata is one of the finest beaches in the Dominican Republic, Sosúa Beach. A strip of white sand more than half a mile wide, it's tucked in a cove sheltered by coral cliffs. The beach connects two communities, which together make up the town known as Sosúa. But, regrettably, you may not be able to enjoy a day on the beach in peace, as vendors, and often beggars, frequently pursue visitors aggressively.

At one end of the beach is **El Batey,** an area with residential streets, gardens, restaurants, shops, and hotels. Real-estate transactions have been booming in El Batey and its environs, where many streets have been paved and villas constructed.

At the other end of Sosúa Beach lies **Los Charamicos,** a sharp contrast to El Batey. Here you'll find tin-roofed shacks, vegetable stands, chickens scrabbling in the rubbish, and warm, friendly people. This community is a typical Latin American village, recognizable through the aromas, sights, and sounds in the narrow, rambling streets.

Sosúa was founded in 1940 by European Jews seeking refuge from Hitler. Trujillo invited 100,000 of them to settle in his country on a banana plantation. But only 600 or so Jews were actually allowed to immigrate, and of those, only about a dozen or so remained. However, there are some 20 Jewish families living in Sosúa today, and for the most part they are engaged in the dairy and smoked-meat industry the refugees began during the war. There's a local one-room synagogue, where biweekly services are held. Many of the Jews intermarried with Dominicans, and the town has taken on an increasingly Spanish flavor; women of the town are often seen wearing both the Star of David and the Virgin de Altagracia. Nowadays many German expatriates are also found in the town.

GETTING THERE FROM PUERTA PLATA

Taxis, charter buses, and *públicos* from Puerto Plata and Playa Dorada let passengers off at the stairs leading down from the highway to Sosúa beach. Take the autopista east for about 30 minutes from Puerto Plaa. If you venture off the main highway, anticipate potholes that fall all the way to China.

WHERE TO STAY

Hotel Sosúa. Calle Dr. Alejo Martínez, El Batey, Sosúa, Dominican Republic. ☎ **809/571-2683.** Fax 809/571-2180. 40 rms. A/C TEL TV. $50 double. Rates include continental breakfast. AE, MC, V.

This has been one of the best and most likely choices for cheap sleeps in Sosúa for at least a decade, and it got even better in 1995 when the owners completely renovated the interior. It's located in a suburban community about a two-minute drive from the center of town. The simple and attractive layout includes a reception area designed to conceal a flagstone-rimmed pool from the street. The bedrooms are strung along a wing extending beside the pool and contain simple furniture, ceiling fans, a minifridge, and an occasional balcony. On the premises are a restaurant (La Tortuga, which is reviewed below), a minigym, a bar, and a boutique.

Hotel Yaroa. El Batey, Sosúa, Dominican Republic. ☎ **809/571-2651.** Fax 809/571-3814. 24 rms. A/C TEL. $54 double. MAP $10 per person extra. AE, MC, V.

Opened in 1986 and named after a native village that once stood nearby, the Yaroa has views of the surrounding trees. Inside you'll find an atrium illuminated by a skylight, lots of exposed wood and stone, and a well-designed garden ringing a sheltered swimming pool. Each bedroom has a Spanish-style *mirador* (sheltered balcony) with pine louvers for privacy, terra-cotta floors, a planter filled with local ferns, and lots of airy space. Two of the accommodations are designed like private cabanas at poolside. Breakfast, light lunches, and dinners featuring French cuisine are served at Verena (see "Where to Dine," below).

Sand Castle Beach Resort. Puerto Chiquito, Sosúa, Dominican Republic. ☎ **800/446-5963** in the U.S., or 809/571-2420. Fax 809/571-2000. 140 rms, 80 suites. A/C MINIBAR TV TEL. Winter, $90 double; from $100 suite. Off-season, $70 double; from $80 suite. MAP $35 per person extra. AE, MC, V.

This multilevel apartment-hotel was created in 1989 for an upscale clientele. The most luxurious accommodations along the north shore open onto views of the Atlantic and Puerto Chiquito Beach. Rooms are generally spacious and comfortable, and the luxurious decor features stained glass, detailed mahogany work, and 10-foot-long full-length mirrors in every bathroom. The most desirable units have views of the small, crescent beach below. There are two swimming pools and a Jacuzzi on the grounds.

Dining choices include the Sahara Gourmet (the best) and the Guarapo (more informal) serving buffets. The hotel is known for its recreational and entertainment facilities (included in the price): horseback riding, windsurfing, snorkeling, tennis, bicycling, a daily program of entertainment, nightly shows, sailing, and entrance to the disco.

Sosúa by the Sea. Sosúa Beach, Sosúa (Apdo. Postal 361, Puerto Plata), Dominican Republic. ☎ **809/571-3222.** Fax 809/571-3020. 46 studios, 35 apts. A/C MINIBAR TV TEL. $73–$75 studio; $92 apt. AE, MC, V.

The main blue-and-white building here is softened by its inviting wooden lattices. The pool area opens onto Sosúa Bay, and the resort stands on a coral cliff above the beach. From the open-air rooftop lounge you have a stellar view of Mount Isabel de Torres. The accommodations lie along meandering paths through tropical gardens. Reached by elevator, the airy but rather basic bedrooms are either studios or one-bedroom apartments, all with safes.

A formal restaurant serves both Dominican specialties and an international cuisine with live entertainment, and you can have lunch at the poolside bar and grill. The hotel has many amenities, including a massage facility and a beauty salon.

Villas Los Coralillos. Calle Alejo Martínez 1, Sosúa (Apdo. Postal 851, Puerto Plata), Dominican Republic. ☎ **809/571-2645.** Fax 809/571-2095. 48 studios, 5 villas. A/C. Winter, $56 double; $120 villa. Off-season, $40 double; $100 villa. Rates include breakfast. AE, DC, MC, V.

The well-furnished accommodations here lie in a series of terra-cotta-tiled Iberian villas cantilevered over a bougainvillea-draped hillside. The action centers around the pool and main restaurant overlooking Sosúa Bay. The views from some of the villas are among the most panoramic in Sosúa. Each standard unit has twin beds and a small veranda.

Dining is at the hotel's El Coral Restaurant (see "Where to Dine," below). The hotel has added yet another restaurant, La Bahía, serving pizzas, and it's open daily from 8am to 3am. Los Coralillos is the only hotel in town with direct access to the main Sosúa beach; if you tire of the pool, you can stroll to the sea through century-old mahogany and almond trees.

WHERE TO DINE

El Coral. El Batey. ☎ **809/571-2645.** Reservations recommended. Main courses RD$90–RD$300 ($6.75–$22.50). AE, DC, MC, V. Daily 7am–10:30pm. CARIBBEAN.

The best and arguably the most pleasant restaurant in town is El Coral, in a Spanish-style building roofed with red tiles and set at the bottom of the garden near the end of the Sosúa beach. It offers a spacious dining area with terra-cotta tiles, wooden accents, and stark-white walls opening onto a panoramic view of the ocean. There's a bar in a room adjoining the dining room. Savory specialties include conch or octopus Creole, pork chops with pineapple, and shrimp with garlic. The cooks fine tuned their cooking long ago, and they prefer to stick with what they do best rather than experiment.

La Tortuga. In the Hotel Sosúa, Calle Dr. Alejo Martinez, El Batey, Sosúa. ☎ **809/571-2683.** Reservations not required. Main courses $8–$18; fixed-price menus $10–$15. AE, MC, V. Daily 7am–11pm. DOMINICAN/ITALIAN.

Known for its pleasant atmosphere, this restaurant in the Hotel Sosúa received a radical facelift in 1994. The dining room overlooks a swimming pool and a small but charming garden. Set in a residential neighborhood a short walk from the resort's center, it serves a medley of inexpensive Italian wines that go well with such dishes as tortellini, spaghetti (with either meat or shellfish sauce), paella, and veal parmigiana. Main courses include four different preparations of chicken and beef. These dishes are perfectly acceptable and well prepared, but they tend to lack imagination.

Morua Mai. Pedro Clisante 5, El Batey. No phone. Reservations not required. Main courses RD$85–RD$275 ($6.40–$20.65). AE, MC, V. Daily 8am–midnight. CONTINENTAL/DOMINICAN.

The patio here, which faces a popular intersection in the center of town, is the closest thing to a European sidewalk cafe in town. Inside, where occasional live entertainment is a key draw, is a high-ceilinged, double-decked, and stylish space filled with neo-Victorian gingerbread touches, upholstered banquettes, and wicker furniture. Consider this place for a sun-washed drink or cup of afternoon tea in the side courtyard, where a cabana bar serves drinks from beneath a palm-thatched roof. Pasta, pizzas, and sandwiches, along with light meals, are served at lunch. Full dinners include such dishes as charcoal-grilled lobster and lots of fresh fish. An excellent paella is filled with lobster and shrimp, and one of the most popular dishes is surf and turf. The cookery isn't outstanding, but it's solidly good.

Restaurant Yaroa. In the Hotel Yaroa, El Batey. ☎ **809/571-2651.** Reservations recommended. Main courses RD$90–RD$225 ($6.75–$16.90). AE, MC, V. Daily 7am–11pm. DOMINICAN/ITALIAN.

The menu here is not large, but concentrates on a mixture of Dominican and Italian food that usually pleases the hotel's mostly Mediterranean clientele. Typical fare consists of lasagna or other pastas with salad, many different preparations of fish, grilled meats, and vegetarian platters. Filet mignon might be prepared with a Roquefort sauce; poached kingfish with a beurre blanc sauce. The restaurant sits in a land-locked garden adjacent to the resort's swimming pool, about a 5-minute walk from Sosúa Beach.

Sunset Place Restaurant. At Sosúa by the Sea, Sosúa. ☎ **809/571-3222.** Reservations required in winter. Main courses RD$125–RD$450 ($9.40–$33.75). AE, MC, V. Daily 7:30–11am, noon–4pm, and 6:30–10:30pm. INTERNATIONAL/DOMINICAN.

Rooftop gourmet dining with a continental chef entices both guests and nonguests of this previously recommended hotel. The restaurant serves soups, salads, and sandwiches at lunch, although dinner is when the chef's talents really shine. After watching the sun go down, choose from a selection of appetizers that might include soup, pâté, or perhaps vol-au-vent seafood pastry shell or a Caesar salad. Main dishes usually feature grilled lobster or tuna with bacon and mushrooms. You might also try the pepper steak, spaghetti carbonara, or chicken with pineapple, each of which had a zesty flavor on our last visit. For dessert, choose from a collection of fresh pastries or order a continental favorite like crêpes Suzette or sabayon.

The British Leeward Islands

9

A string of islands that form a crescent, the British Leewards consist of Antigua and Barbuda, Montserrat, the twin state of St. Kitts and Nevis, and little Anguilla. Of them all, Antigua, with its many beaches and resorts, is the best equipped for mass tourism. However, relatively new hotels are drawing thousands to Montserrat, Nevis, and to more remote Anguilla, which has become a chic getaway.

1 Antigua & Barbuda

Antiguans boast that they have a different beach for every day of the year (which is a bit of an exaggeration). The beaches are pretty spectacular; most are protected by coral reefs, and the sand is often sugar white. For most visitors, these beaches are reason enough to visit, but Antigua is also known for its sailing facilities, centered at English Harbour. Most hotels, restaurants, beach bars, and water-sports facilities lie north of the capital of St. John's in the northwest.

Antigua, Barbuda, and Redonda form the independent nation of Antigua and Barbuda, within the Commonwealth of Nations. Redonda is an uninhabited rocky islet of less than a square mile located 20 miles southwest of Antigua. Sparsely populated Barbuda is covered at the end of this section. Independence has come, but Antigua is still British in many of its traditions.

FAST FACTS: Antigua & Barbuda

Banking Hours Banks are usually open Monday to Thursday from 8am to 1pm and on Friday from 8am to 1pm and 3 to 5pm.

Currency The **Eastern Caribbean dollar (EC$)** is used on these islands. However, nearly all hotels bill you in U.S. dollars, and only certain tiny restaurants present their prices in EC dollars. Make sure you know which dollars are referred to when you inquire about a price. The EC dollar is worth about 37¢ in U.S. currency (EC$2.70 = U.S.$1). Unless otherwise specified, rates quoted in this chapter are given in U.S. dollars.

Customs Arriving visitors are allowed to bring in 200 cigarettes and 1 quart of liquor, plus 6 ounces of perfume.

Documents A valid passport is preferred when U.S. and Canadian nationals are visiting the island. However, an original birth certificate accompanied by a photo ID is also acceptable. Citizens of the United Kingdom need a passport, and all arriving visitors must have a departing ticket.

Electricity Most of the island's electricity is 220 volts AC (60 cycles), meaning that American appliances need transformers. However, the Hodges Bay area and some hotels are supplied with 110 volts AC (60 cycles).

Emergencies In an emergency, contact the police (☎ **268/462-0125**), the fire department (☎ **268/462-0044**), or an ambulance (☎ **268/462-0251**). In addition, you can also call ☎ 911 or 999 for any type of emergency.

Information Contact the **Antigua and Barbuda Department of Tourism,** 610 Fifth Ave., Suite 311, New York, NY 10020 (☎ **212/541-4117**); or 25 SE Second Ave., Suite 300, Miami, FL 33131 (☎ **305/381-6762**). In **Canada,** contact the Antigua and Barbuda Department of Tourism & Trade, 60 St. Clair Ave. E., Suite 304, Toronto, ON, M4T 1N5 (☎ **416/961-3085**). In the **United Kingdom,** information is available at Antigua House, 15 Thayer St., London W1M 5LD (☎ **0171/486-7073**).

Language The official language is English.

Taxes and Service Charges A departure tax of U.S.$11 is imposed, and an 8.5% government tax is added to all hotel bills. Most hotels also add a 10% service charge.

Time Antigua is on Atlantic standard time year-round, so it's one hour ahead of U.S. eastern standard time. When daylight saving time takes over in the States, then Antigua's time is the same as in the eastern United States.

Water Tap water is generally safe to drink here, but many visitors prefer to only drink bottled water.

Weather The average year-round temperature ranges from 75° to 85°F.

ANTIGUA

From its beginnings as a poverty-stricken island of sugar plantations, Antigua has risen to become a 20th-century vacation haven. American millionaires seeking British serenity under a tropical sun turned Antigua into an elegant destination around the exclusive Mill Reef Club (where you'll only be accepted if you're recommended by a member). The island has now developed a broader base of tourism and now attracts middle- and lower-income travelers in addition to the jet setters.

The landscape of rolling, rustic Antigua (*an-TEE-gah*) is dotted with stone towers that were once sugar mills. The inland scenery isn't as dramatic as what you'll find on St. Kitts, but, oh, those beaches!

The **summer carnival** takes place during the week preceding the first Tuesday in August. This festival includes a beauty competition and calypso and steel-band competitions. Carnival envelops the streets in exotic costumes that recall the people's African heritage. The spring highlight is Antigua's annual **sailing week** in late April or early May.

The capital is **St. John's,** a large, neatly laid-out town 6 miles from the airport and less than a mile from Deep Water Harbour Terminal. The port is the focal point of commerce and industry, as well as the seat of government and shopping. Trade winds keep the streets fairly cool, and they were built wide just to capture these breezes. Protected within a narrow bay, the port city consists of cobblestone sidewalks and weather-beaten wooden houses with corrugated iron roofs and louvered Caribbean verandas.

In September 1995, Hurricane Luis came to call on Antigua, whipping the island with 140-m.p.h. winds. It left devastation in its wake, forcing some hotels to close for renovations during the 1995–96 winter season. A popular T-shirt sold on the island told the story: "Hurricane Luis—you dangerous, you ferocious, you terrible, you too damn wicked!" The island has now bounced back from one of its worst disasters, at least until another hurricane hits.

Getting There

The major airline flying to Antigua's V. C. Bird Airport is **American Airlines** (☎ **800/433-7300** in the U.S.), which offers two daily nonstop flights to Antigua from its Caribbean hub in San Juan, Puerto Rico; flight time is about 1 1/2 hours. Each of these flights departs late enough in the day to allow easy transfers from other flights. One of these flights from San Juan is the continuation of a nonstop flight from New York's JFK, so passengers originating in New York can remain on the same aircraft during the flight's brief touchdown on Puerto Rico. Most vacations on Antigua will cost less if you book your air transport simultaneously with a hotel reservation; American's tour desk can provide these arrangements for you.

British Airways (☎ **800/247-9297** in the U.S.) offers flights to Antigua four times a week from London's Gatwick Airport.

Air Canada (☎ **800/268-7240** in Canada, **800/776-3000** in the U.S.) offers regularly scheduled flights from Toronto to Antigua on Saturday only.

BWIA (☎ **800/327-7401** in the U.S.) is an increasingly popular means of reaching Antigua. From Miami there are four flights weekly, and from Toronto there are two flights weekly. There are also five flights weekly from Kingston, Jamaica, plus connections from Europe—two flights a week from London and two flights weekly from Frankfurt.

Getting Around

BY TAXI Transportation isn't hard to find. Taxis meet every airplane, and drivers wait outside the major hotels. In fact, if you're going to be on Antigua for a few days, you may find that a particular driver has "adopted" you. The typical one-way fare from the airport to St. John's is $12, but to English Harbour it's $25 and up. The government of Antigua fixes the rates, and the taxis have no meters.

While it's costly, the best way to see Antigua is by private taxi as the drivers also act as guides. Most taxi tours cost $16 and up per hour.

BY RENTAL CAR Newly arrived drivers quickly (and ruefully) learn that the island's roads are among the worst, most potholed, and most badly signposted in the Caribbean. Many visitors prefer to rent a taxi whenever they want to go somewhere. Hotels and restaurants on the island will summon one for you. Considering that you have to *drive on the left* and are often tempted to have one piña colada too many, renting a car on Antigua is usually not a great idea.

If you insist on driving, you must obtain an Antiguan driver's license, which costs an overpriced $20. To obtain one, you must produce a valid driver's license from home. Most car-rental firms are authorized to issue you an Antiguan license, which they usually do without a surcharge.

Several different car-rental agencies operate on Antigua, although they're sometimes precariously financed local operations with cars best described as "battered." The best of them are affiliated with major car-rental companies in the United States. **Avis** (☎ **800/331-2112** in the U.S.) and **Hertz** (☎ **800/654-3131** in the U.S.) are both represented on Antigua, each offering pickup service at the airport. They charge

$10 per day for a collision-damage waiver; however, you'll still be liable for the first $1,000 worth of damage. Without it you'll be liable for up to the full value of any accidental damage to the vehicle.

BY BUS Buses are not recommended for the average visitor, although they do exist and are cheap. Service is erratic and undependable along impossibly bumpy roads. Officially, buses operate between St. John's and the villages daily from 5:30am to 6pm, but don't count on it. In St. John's, buses leave from the West Bus Station for Falmouth and English Harbour and from the East Bus Station to other parts of the island. Most fares are $1.

ESSENTIALS

Antigua is generally safe, but that doesn't mean you should go wandering alone at night on the practically deserted streets of St. John's. Don't leave valuables unguarded on the beach.

The **Antigua and Barbuda Department of Tourism,** at Thames and Long streets in St. John's (☎ **268/462-0480**), is open Monday to Thursday from 8am to 4:30pm and on Friday from 8am to 3pm.

The principal medical facility is **Holberton Hospital,** on Queen Elizabeth Highway (☎ **268/462-0251**). Telephone calls can be made from hotels or from the office of **Cable & Wireless,** 42–44 St. Mary's St., in St. John's (☎ **268/462-0840**). Faxes and telegrams can also be sent from here.

WHERE TO STAY

Antigua's hotels are among the best and most plentiful in the eastern Caribbean, and generally they're small—a 100-room hotel is rare on the island. Check summer closings, which often depend on the caprice of the owners, who may decide to shut down if business isn't good. Incidentally, air-conditioning, except in first-class hotels, isn't as common as some visitors think it should be. Chances are, your hotel will be on a beach. You can also rent an apartment or cottage if you want to cook for yourself.

Reminder: An 8.5% government tax and 10% service charge are added to your hotel bill, which makes quite a difference in your final tab.

Very Expensive

✪ **Curtain Bluff.** Old Road (P.O. Box 288, St. John's), Antigua, W.I. ☎ **800/672-5833** or 268/462-8400. Fax 268/462-8409. 51 rms, 12 suites. Dec 19–Apr 14, $655–$825 double; $925–$1,655 suite for two. Apr 15–May 14 and Oct 12–Dec 18, $525–$695 double; $775–$1,400 suite for two. Rates include all meals, wine by the glass, liquor, beer, soft drinks, tennis, water sports, and deep-sea fishing. AE. Closed May 15 to mid-Oct.

This oasis of serenity and comfort is the home of *Sailing Week* and is the island's premier resort, with good sports facilities. It lies on the southwest shore 15 miles from the airport, in the village of Old Road, the most lushly tropical section of the island. Once a pilot for Texaco, founder Howard W. Hulford discovered his Shangri-la back in the 1950s while flying over it, and established the hotel in 1961.

In a setting that resembles a subtropical forest, the resort offers beautifully furnished accommodations, including deluxe units with king-size beds, deluxe rooms with two double beds, a terrace room with a king-size four-poster bed, plus suites. Ceiling fans and trade winds keep the rooms cool, and individual terraces open onto the water.

Dining/Entertainment: Some guests come largely for the superb food. Swiss-born Ruedi Portmann keeps his continental menu limited, so that all the food will be freshly prepared and artistically arranged. The Curtain Bluff restaurant boasts the most extensive wine selection in the Caribbean, including all major red Bordeaux.

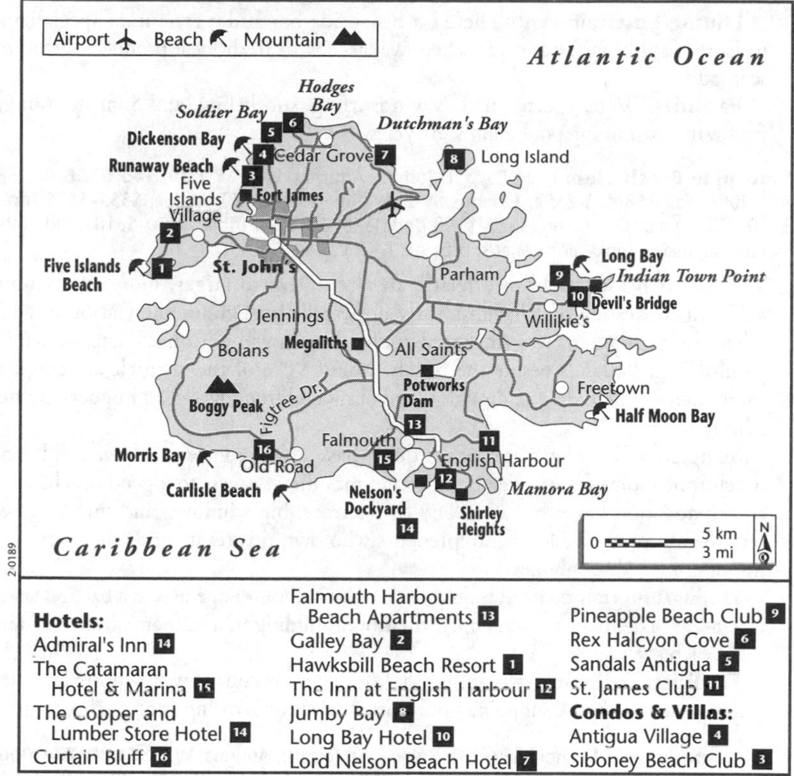

After dinner, guests can dance under the stars to a live band. Once a week the resort hires a steel band to entertain guests.

Services: Room service (8am to 9pm), baby-sitting.

Facilities: Sailing, waterskiing, skin diving, deep-sea fishing, scuba diving (for certified divers only), tennis (four championship courts plus a pro shop and a full-time pro), squash, exercise room, aerobics classes—all at no extra charge. In lieu of a swimming pool, there are two beautiful sand beaches, one opening onto more turbulent Atlantic waters, the other calm as the Caribbean Sea.

Galley Bay. Five Islands (P.O. Box 305, St. John's), Antigua, W.I. ☎ **800/345-0356,** 268/462-0302, or 561/994-5640. Fax 561/994-6344. 22 Gauguin cottages, 10 superior beachfront rms, 29 deluxe beachfront rms. Winter, $460 Gauguin cottage; $520 superior beachfront; $560 deluxe beachfront. Off-season, $360 Gauguin cottage; $420 superior beachfront; $460 deluxe beachfront. Rates include all meals, water sports, and land activities. AE, MC, V. Leave St. John's on the harbor road south, pass through Five Islands Village, turn right onto Galley Bay Road, and follow it for 5 miles.

A retreat set on 40 acres along a half mile of palm-fringed beach, Galley Beach reopened early in 1997, having bounced back from the hurricane's massive destruction of 1995. The place looks better than ever and is a true Caribbean refuge set between the beach and a lagoon. A variety of accommodations, all with ceiling fans, shower, hair dryer, refrigerator, and in-room safe, are available. The most charming are the grass-roofed Gauguin cottages. The other rooms open directly onto the beach and, as accurately advertised, are "only four seconds from bed to sea."

Dining/Entertainment: There's a beachside bar and a restaurant specializing in Euro-Caribbean food, made when available with fresh local produce, including seafood.

Facilities: Water sports (such as windsurfing, snorkeling, and Sunfish sailing), freshwater swimming pool, tennis, bicycles.

Pineapple Beach Club. Long Bay, St. John's, Antigua, W.I. ☎ **800/345-0356** or 268/463-2006. Fax 268/463-2452. 131 rms. A/C. Winter, $390–$470 double; $555–$595 triple; $680–$720 quad. Off-season, $320–$390 double; $465–$500 triple; $570–$610 quad. Rates include all meals, drinks, and water sports. AE, MC, V.

This resort prides itself on offering an alternative to larger, more anonymous all-inclusive resorts that have recently appeared throughout the Caribbean. It's a low-slung colony of two-story, red-roofed buildings built on 25 acres of sandy, palm-dotted flatlands beside the beach. About 90% of the clientele are couples, sometimes with children, although very young children (ages 5 and under) are not admitted.

Standard and garden-view rooms don't have any sea view at all; waterside and beachfront rooms feature views and sometimes direct access to a good beach. Each accommodation has either a balcony or a terrace, big windows, and simple (often rattan) furniture. The local entrepreneurs who own this resort pride themselves on not offering TVs or phones.

Dining/Entertainment: A hilltop aerie (the Outhouse) operates as a bar and snack restaurant. The main bar stays open till around midnight, and there's live entertainment each evening.

Facilities: Freshwater swimming pool, four tennis courts, water-sports facilities, fitness center, in-house shopping boutique, an electronic casino (slot machines only).

✪ **St. James's Club.** Mamora Bay (P.O. Box 63, St. John's), Antigua, W.I. ☎ **800/274-0008** in the U.S., 268/460-5000, or 212/486-2575 in New York City. Fax 268/460-3015. 85 rms, 20 suites, 73 2-bedroom villas. A/C TV TEL Winter, $360–$415 double; $465 suite for 2; from $585 two-bedroom villa for 2. Off-season, $215–$245 double; $270 suite for 2; from $330 two-bedroom villa for 2. Rates are all-inclusive. Children 5 and under stay free in parents' room. AE, DC, MC, V.

The St. James's Club, a luxurious but remote resort on Mamora Bay, offers elegant ocean-view rooms and suites. Pricey villas and hillside homes are also rented. The resort's sports facilities are among the best in the Caribbean.

Dining/Entertainment: The best of local and international dishes, freshly caught seafood, salads, barbecue grills, and tropical fruit are accompanied by cool white wine or dark rum cocktails. You can relax in elegant surroundings in the Rainbow Garden Restaurant or eat al fresco by candlelight at the Docksider Café overlooking Mamora Bay, enjoying lobster, barbecued chicken, or ribs. The Jacaranda nightclub will top off an evening for more active guests. Many enjoy gambling in the high-ceilinged but small European-style casino.

Services: Room service, laundry, baby-sitting. There are daily activity programs for children lasting one to three hours, including afternoon donkey rides three times a week. A children's playhouse and playground are also available.

Facilities: Water sports, including sailboats (Sunfish and Hobie cats), sailboards, aqua bikes, deep-sea fishing, waterskiing, snorkeling, scuba diving (with a scuba school offering American and European certification); seven hard tennis courts (two lit for night play), with a center court for tournaments; complete Universal-equipped gymnasium; Jacuzzi; massage facility; beauty salon; croquet court; three swimming pools; two beaches; a playground and playhouse for children.

Expensive

✪ **The Copper and Lumber Store Hotel.** Nelson's Dockyard, English Harbour (P.O. Box 184, St. John's), Antigua, W.I. ☎ **268/460-1058.** Fax 268/460-1529. 3 rms, 11 suites. Winter, $195–$275 double; $215–$325 suite. Off-season, $85–$145 double; $95–$175 suite. MAP $40 per person extra. AE, MC, V. From St. John's, follow the signs southeast to English Harbour.

As its name suggests, this charming 18th-century building was originally a store that sold wood and copper for repairing British sailing ships. The store and its adjacent harbor structures are built of brick once used as ships' ballast (a heavy material used to stabilize sailing). Each of the brick-lined period units has its own design and is filled with fine Chippendale and Queen Anne reproductions, antiques, brass chandeliers, hardwood paneling, and hand-stenciled floors. Even the showers look like those in a sailing vessel, with their thick panels of mahogany accented with polished brass fittings. All suites have kitchens, private baths (with showers only), and ceiling fans.

Dining/Entertainment: A traditional English pub adjoins the hotel and offers food daily from 10:30am to midnight. The Wardroom serves dinner nightly.

Services: Room service, laundry, baby-sitting.

Hawksbill Beach Resort. Five Islands Village (P.O. Box 108, St. John's), Antigua, W.I. ☎ **800/223-6510** in the U.S., or 268/462-0301. Fax 268/462-1515. 112 rms, 1 suite. Winter, $375–$450 double; $1,800 suite for 3 to 6. Off-season, $276–$325 double; $1,300 suite. Rates include MAP. AE, MC, V.

Taking its name from an offshore rock that locals say resembles a hawksbill turtle, this 37-acre resort, 10 miles west of the airport and 4 miles southwest of St. John's, has a former sugar mill that's been turned into a boutique. Set on four brown-sand beaches (one reserved for those who want to go home *sans* tan lines), it caters to the sporting set and is also popular for weddings and honeymoons. The hotel revolves around an open-air, breezy central core and offers comfortably furnished although rather small bedrooms with ceiling fans and showers. The least expensive accommodations open onto a garden. The rooms have no phones, TV sets, or air-conditioning. Three bedrooms suitable for three to six occupants are in the Great House.

Dining/Entertainment: There are two restaurants (one on the beach) and two bars. It's usually lively here if the crowd is right, with entertainment such as limbo dancers and calypso singers three nights a week in season.

Services: Laundry, baby-sitting.

Facilities: Swimming pool, tennis court, Sunfish sailing, windsurfing, snorkeling, waterskiing (for a nominal charge).

✪ **The Inn at English Harbour.** English Harbour (P.O. Box 187, St. John's), Antigua, W.I. ☎ **268/460-1014.** Fax 268/460-1603. 28 rms. Winter, $270–$390 double. Off-season, $135–$200 double. MAP $55 per person extra. AE, MC, V. Closed Sept 10 to mid-Oct. From St. John's, head south, through All Saints and Liberta, until you reach the south coast.

In a corner of Freeman's Bay, this small hotel offers guests (mainly Brits) a choice of pleasantly furnished rooms on the beach or in hillside cottages. Amenities include hair dryers, wall safes, balconies, ceiling fans, and small refrigerators. The inn occupies one of the finest sites on Antigua, with terrace views over Nelson's Dockyard and English Harbour, and is an exceptional value for the money.

Dining/Entertainment: Have a before-dinner drink in the old-style English Bar, with its stone walls and low overhead beams. Lunch is served both at the beach house and in the main dining room. The inn is known for the quality of its cooking, and there is live entertainment in winter.

Services: Room service, laundry, baby-sitting.

Facilities: Complimentary water sports (including Sunfish sailing, windsurfing, snorkeling, and rowing); daytime water taxi to Nelson's Dockyard; tennis courts (lit) nearby; waterskiing and day sailing available at an extra cost. Deep-sea fishing, scuba diving, golf, and horseback riding can be arranged.

Long Bay Hotel. Long Bay (P.O. Box 442, St. John's), Antigua, W.I. ☎ **800/291-2005** in the U.S., or 268/463-2005. Fax 268/463-2439. 18 rms, 6 cottages. Winter, $365–$380 double; $365–$435 cottage for 2. Off-season, $255–$280 double; $255–$350 cottage for 2. Rates include MAP. AE, MC, V.

Lying on a remote spit of land between the open sea and a sheltered lagoon, Long Bay, hard hit by Hurricane Luis, is on the eastern shore 1 mile beyond the hamlet of Willikie's. It faces one of the best beaches on the island, as well as a lagoon that has no reef and is safe for water sports. Owned and operated by the Lafaurie family since 1966, it's more an inn than a large-scale hotel. It features breeze-filled rooms as well as six furnished cottages for more reclusive guests.

Dining/Entertainment: The resort is centered around a clubhouse with the stone-walled Turtle Restaurant. The bar provides a relaxing environment. The hotel has a library and games room, plus a beach-house restaurant and bar.

Services: Room service, laundry, baby-sitting, special dinner seating for children.

Facilities: Championship tennis court, complete scuba facilities, sailboats, Windsurfers, snorkeling; golf nearby. Fishing can be arranged.

Rex Halcyon Cove. Dickenson Bay (P.O. Box 251, St. John's), Antigua, W.I. ☎ **268/462-0256.** Fax 268/462-0271. 195 rms, 15 suites. Winter, $190–$380 double; $380 suite. Off-season, $130–$315 double; $315 suite. MAP $50 per person extra. AE, DC, DISC, MC, V.

Halcyon Cove is 5 miles west of the airport and 3 miles north of St. John's, about a 15-minute taxi ride. It's a favorite with the package-tour crowd from both the United States and Europe, and many guests manage to stay here at lower rates than those listed above (ask the hotel or a travel agent about available packages). Most of the bedrooms have a balcony or terrace, and most are set at beach level. The rooms range from garden to superior to poolside deluxe rooms. The most expensive are called "oceanfront deluxe" and "oceanfront suites," the latter with color TV, mini-refrigerator, and a separate bedroom, living room, sitting area, and dressing area. Some of the units are air-conditioned.

Dining/Entertainment: The Arawak Terrace, the hotel's main dining room, is open for breakfast and dinner. You can also lunch or dine on the elongated Warri Pier, which stands on stilts 200 feet from the shore. There's also a beach barbecue for lunch. Frostie's Deli offers a coffee-shop menu.

Services: Room service, laundry, baby-sitting.

Facilities: Half-mile beach (often filled with aggressive vendors), freshwater swimming pool, snorkeling, windsurfing, pedal boats, waterskiing, volleyball, sailing, scuba diving, four all-weather tennis courts (lit for night play).

Sandals Antigua. Dickenson Bay, St. John's, Antigua, W.I. ☎ **800/SANDALS** in the U.S. and Canada, or 268/462-0267. Fax 268/462-4135. 191 rms, 34 junior suites, 17 rondaval suites, 12 honeymoon suites, 30 studio suites. A/C TV TEL Winter, $1,775–$2,065 double; $2,240 junior suite; $2,460 rondaval suite; $2,570 honeymoon suite; $2,365 studio suite. Off-season, $1,640–$1,905 double; $2,065 junior suite; $2,270 rondaval suite; $2,370 honeymoon suite; $2,180 studio suite. All rates are for an all-inclusive 7-night stay. AE, MC, V.

This is one of the latest additions to the Jamaica-based Sandals chain, and it has bounced back following a $12 million renovation after it was struck by Hurricane Luis. The resort only caters to male-female couples, and a large percentage of the guests are honeymooners (most in their 20s). Set on the island's northwestern coast, a 15-minute drive from St. John's, Sandals occupies the site of an older hotel that was redesigned. Most accommodations are in two-story motel-like units, many facing the beach. The most desirable units are a series of 17 circular one-room rondavals. Each unit offers a balcony or patio, a king-size bed, hair dryer, and safety-deposit box.

Dining/Entertainment: There are four restaurants, devoted to southwestern, Caribbean, Italian, and Japanese food, respectively; four bars (including one swim-up bar in the pool and a beach bar); and a disco. The extroverted staff actively encourages guests to participate in group activities.

Services: Organized tours to island attractions.

Facilities: Five pools, sandy beach, two tennis courts, five Jacuzzis, complete array of land and water sports (most included in the all-inclusive price), fitness center, saunas, volleyball.

Moderate

✪ **Admiral's Inn.** English Harbour (P.O. Box 713, St. John's), Antigua, W.I. ☎ **800/223-5695** in the U.S., or 268/460-1027. Fax 268/460-1534. 14 rms, 1 suite. Winter, $108–$132 double; $144–$154 triple; $220 suite for 2, $350 suite for 4. Off-season, $78–$94 double; $110–$116 triple; $130 suite for 2, $220 for 4. MAP $44 per person extra. AE, MC, V. Closed Sept to mid-Oct. Take the road southeast from St. John's, following the signs to English Harbour.

Designed in 1785, the year Nelson sailed into the harbor as captain of the HMS *Boreas*, and completed in 1788, this building once housed a dockyard. Today it's the most atmospheric inn on Antigua, set right in the heart of the island's major sightseeing attraction, Nelson's Dockyard, and offers great value at reasonable rates. Loaded with West Indian charm, the hostelry is constructed of brick brought from England as ships' ballast and features a terrace opening onto the harbor. The ground floor, with brick walls, giant ship beams, and island-made furniture, has a tavern atmosphere, with decorative copper, boat lanterns, old oil paintings, and wrought-iron chandeliers.

Some of the best rooms are on the ground floor in a tiny brick building on the site of a provisions warehouse for Nelson's troops. The small chambers on the top floor have the lowest rates. All rooms have twin beds and ceiling fans, and eight are air-conditioned.

Dining/Entertainment: For the inn's restaurant, see "Where to Dine," below. On Saturday night a live band plays.

Services: Room service, laundry, baby-sitting, free transportation to two nearby beaches, either Pigeon Point, a five-minute drive away, or Freeman's Bay Beach, across the harbor from the hotel.

Facilities: Snorkeling equipment, Sunfish craft.

Falmouth Harbour Beach Apartments. English Harbour Village, Yacht Club Rd. (P.O. Box 713, St. John's), Antigua, W.I. ☎ **268/460-1094.** Fax 268/460-1534. 24 studios. Winter, $120–$134 studio for 2; $144–$158 studio for 3. Off-season, $88–$94 studio for 2; $144–$158 studio for 3. Children 15 and under can share parents' studio for $15. AE, MC, V. Take the road southeast from St. John's and follow the signs to English Harbour.

This relatively simple place might be what you're looking for if you'd like to be near historic English Harbour. Situated just above a small sandy beach, it offers an informal Antiguan atmosphere. Twin-bedded studio apartments are available. Each unit has a ceiling fan, electric stove, refrigerator, oven, and terrace overlooking the water, but no phone, air-conditioning, or TV. A dozen studios are directly on the beach, whereas the others lie on a hillside just behind. The beach is sheltered, making it suitable for kids. An even better beach lies a three- or four-minute shuttle bus ride away.

You can dine at the nearby Admiral's Inn (see "Where to Dine," below). There are also other restaurants nearby, along with a supermarket, bank, post office, boutiques, and galleries, all within half a mile. Temo Sports, with tennis and squash facilities, is just next door, and there's a dive operation in the dockyard, with many sailing and fishing-boat charters. Bus service runs daily to and from St. John's, so it's possible to be self-sufficient without having to go to the expense of renting a car.

Rex Blue Heron. Johnson's Point Beach (P.O. Box 1715, St. John's), Antigua, W.I. ☎ **800/255-5859** or 305/471-6170 in the U.S., or 268/462-8564. Fax 268/462-8005, or 305/471-9547 in the U.S. 40 rms. Winter, $120–$153 single or double; $202 triple. Off-season, $102–$136 single or double; $187 triple. MAP $50 per person extra. Children 11 and under stay free in parents' room. AE, DC, DISC, MC, V.

On the most beautiful beach on Antigua, about 15 miles from either St. John's or the airport, this hotel attracts tranquillity seekers. Casually comfortable, it crowns Johnson's Point. This complex consists of two-story white stone buildings whose rooms overlook either well-kept gardens, the swimming pool, or the beachfront. In the lifetime of this edition the hotel might add two dozen more accommodations. The superior and beachfront units have air-conditioning, ceiling fans, TVs, and hair dryers, whereas the standard rooms offer only ceiling fans. Each room, however, has a patio or balcony. Along with two bars, there's an intimate on-site restaurant serving West Indian meals at affordable prices. A full range of water sports is available, including complimentary windsurfing, snorkeling equipment, and Sunfish sailing. Deep-sea and offshore scuba diving is also offered. There's live entertainment most evenings. The hotel appeals to couples and honeymooners.

Inexpensive

The Catamaran Hotel & Marina. P.O. Box 958, Falmouth Harbour, St. John's, Antigua, W.I. ☎ **800/223-6510** in the U.S., 800/424-5500 in Canada, or 268/460-1036. 16 units. Year-round, $65 double; $80 double efficiency; $120 double deluxe rooms; $150 Captain's Cabin for 2. Children under 10, $15 extra. (EP rates.) AE, MC, V. Closed Sept.

This is a longtime favorite on Antigua. At Falmouth Harbour, a 2-mile drive from English Harbour, the Catamaran opens onto a palm-lined beach. When we first discovered the property years ago, a film crew had taken it over while making a movie about pirates of the West Indies. Management had to post a sign: "Today's 'pirates' must wear bathing suits on the beach." It's not as wild around here any more, and peace and tranquility prevail.

On the second floor are eight self-contained rooms, each with a four-poster bed, a queen-size mattress, and a balcony opening onto the water. The most luxurious and spacious rental is called the Captain's Cabin. The standard rooms are quite small but well maintained and adequately comfortable, and the efficiencies at water's edge can be rented by one person or two. Each efficiency has a balcony and an equipped kitchen. Boaters will like its location at the 30-slip Catamaran Marina. You can purchase supplies at a nearby grocery store, or else enjoy the hotel's own reasonably priced meals. Sportfishing and diving can be arranged, and the hotel offers Sunfish dinghies and rowboats.

Lord Nelson Beach Hotel. Dutchman's Bay (P.O. Box 155, St. John's), Antigua, W.I. ☎ **268/462-3094.** Fax 268/462-0751. 17 rms. Winter, $100–$115 double. Off-season, $70–$80 double. Third person in room $30 in winter, $25 off-season. AE, MC, V. Closed Sept–Oct.

This hotel originally built just before World War II is on Antigua's isolated northeast coast, 5 miles east of St. John's. Once a beach club for American army officers, it was acquired by the Fuller family, expatriate Americans, in 1949. Today it's a more substantial concrete structure, with a dining room capped with timbers that were salvaged from warehouses destroyed during the hurricanes of 1950. Later a bar was added, using local stone and glass salvaged from an offshore lighthouse, as well as an annex containing two floors of simply furnished guest bedrooms. Today the place functions as a family managed inn, set close to a white-sand beach and waters that are protected from ocean swells by an artificial reef. The place shows the wear and tear of the years, even though a windsurfing shop with the latest equipment has been added, along with a dive boat and dive master.

Sand Haven Beach Hotel & Restaurant. Sand Haven, Runaway, St. John's, Antigua, W.I. ☎ and fax **268/462-4491.** 14 rms. Winter, $50 single; $75 double; $100 triple; $130 family room for up to 6. Off-season, $40 single; $60 double; $85 triple; $95 family room. AE, MC, V.

Located on a secluded private beach in Dry Hill, this small hotel is a friend of the budget traveler. Although St. John's is only 3 miles away, the inn is in a secluded spot on its silvery stand of beachfront. It's the lazy life here, and you can see hotel patrons finding their favorite spot underneath the palms or ordering a cool rum punch at the beach bar. The hotel itself is flamboyantly painted in pink and turquoise, subdued with white. Each of the simply furnished rooms has a sea view, patio, or balcony, and is cooled by ceiling fans. The furnishings are standard, with stone floors and rugs. A TV and phone are available in the lounge. Its beachside restaurant, Spice of Life, serves regional specialties and fresh seafood.

Condos & Villas

Antigua Village. Dickenson Bay (P.O. Box 649, St. John's), Antigua, W.I. ☎ **800/223-1588** in the U.S., or 268/462-2930. Fax 268/462-0375. 65 studios and apts. A/C. Winter, $170–$195 studio for 2; $210–$245 one-bedroom apt for 2; $380–$440 two-bedroom apt for 4. Off-season, $95–$115 studio for 2; $115–$140 one-bedroom apt for 2; $210–$255 two-bedroom apt for 4. AE, MC, V.

Set on a peninsula 2 miles north of St. John's, Antigua Village is more of a self-contained condominium community than a holiday resort. The complex opens onto a popular beach and consists of two- and three-story red-roofed buildings. Many of the units are devoted to time-share arrangements. A freshwater pool and a minimarket are on the premises. You can use the neighboring tennis court, and there's an 18-hole golf course nearby, plus comprehensive water-sports facilities. The fairly simple apartments all have kitchenettes, patios or balconies, twin beds, and sofa beds in the living rooms.

Siboney Beach Club. Dickenson Bay (P.O. Box 222, St. John's), Antigua, W.I. ☎ **800/533-0234** in the U.S., or 268/462-0806. Fax 268/462-3356. 12 suites. A/C. Winter, $230–$290 suite for 2. Off-season, $130–$170 suite for 2. Tree house negotiable. Additional person $30 extra for adults, $20 extra for children 11 and under. AE, MC, V.

Owned by Australia-born Tony Johnson and his wife, Ann, the Siboney Beach Club is named after the Amerindian tribe who predated the Arawaks. Set north of St. John's on a thickly foliated acre of land fronting the mile-long white-sand beach of Dickenson Bay, the resort is shielded on the inland side by a tall, verdant hedge. The club's social center is the Coconut Grove restaurant (see "Where to Dine," below). The comfortable suites are in a three-story balconied building draped with bougainvillea and other vines. The suites have optional air-conditioning, fans, and louvered windows for natural ventilation, and TVs are available. All units have separate bedrooms, living rooms, and balconies or patios, plus tiny kitchens behind moveable shutters. There's also a tree house: a single room with a king-size bed and jungle decor perched high in a *Ficus benjamina* tree.

Where to Dine

In St. John's

Big Banana Holding Company. Redcliffe Quay. ☎ **268/462-2621.** Reservations not required. Main courses $7–$13. AE, DC, MC, V. Mon–Sat 8:30am–midnight. PIZZA.

The best pizza on the island is served in what used to be slave quarters, now amid the most stylish shopping and dining emporiums in town, a few steps from the Heritage Quay Jetty. The place is known locally as "The Hard Rock Café of Antigua." With its ceiling fans and laid-back atmosphere, you almost expect Sydney Greenstreet to stop in for a drink (called "dwinks" on the menu). The frothy libations, coconut or banana crush, are practically desserts. In addition to the zesty pizza, you can order overstuffed baked potatoes, pasta dishes, fresh fruit salad, or conch salad.

Hemingway's. Jardine Court, St. Mary's St. ☎ **268/462-2763.** Reservations not required. Main courses $10–$25. AE, MC, V. Mon–Sat 8:30am–11pm. WEST INDIAN/INTERNATIONAL.

Set on the second floor of a building in the heart of St. John's, and accented with intricate gingerbread painted in bright tropical colors, this charming and bustling cafe attracts a crowd of shoppers and sightseers. It's very busy when a cruise ship docks. From its upper verandas, you can see the landing dock and enjoy the sight of pedestrian traffic in the street below. Menu items include salads, sandwiches, burgers, sautéed fillets of fish, pastries, ice creams, and an array of brightly colored tropical drinks. This is a place for a convenient casual meal and great value rather than for serious gourmet fare.

✪ **Julians.** Church Lane and Corn Alley. ☎ **268/462-4766.** Reservations recommended. Main courses EC$48–EC$71 ($17.75–$26.25). AE, DISC, MC, V. Tues–Sun 7am–10pm. Closed June. CONTINENTAL.

Set within an antique, wood-sided, white-and-green-shuttered house, this restaurant, the island's best, has an English-style garden in back where clients can opt to dine if they want. There's no air-conditioning, but ceiling fans twirl above a black and white decor with lots of green plants and the inspired cuisine of Julian Waterer, the Essex (England)-born owner and chef who has earned lots of fans since he opened the place in January 1995. The menu reflects the most sophisticated cuisine on the island, and changes frequently according to the season and the inspiration of the owner. Perfectly prepared examples include a roulade of smoked salmon and asparagus, served with a tartare of fresh marinated salmon; breast of home-smoked duck with spicy Italian-style sausage layered on a bed of fresh endive and radicchio; escalope of fresh salmon on a bed of shredded leeks, served with a saffron and dill-flavored *beurre blanc* (white butter) sauce; a tenderloin of beef stuffed with a mousse of chicken livers and mushrooms, served on a fried crouton with Madeira sauce; and medallions of pork roasted with black, green, red and white peppercorns, on a bed of sautéed apples and presented with a reduction of red wine and port.

Around the Island

Admiral's Inn. In Nelson's Dockyard, English Harbour. ☎ **268/460-1027.** Reservations recommended, especially for dinner in high season. Main courses $11–$27. AE, MC, V. Daily 7:30–10am, noon–2:30pm, and 7–9:30pm. Closed Sept to mid-Oct. AMERICAN/CREOLE.

This historic building has already been recommended as a hotel (see "Where to Stay," above). At the restaurant, diners enjoy an 18th-century setting and can eat out on the terrace, if they wish, enjoying a view of the harbor. The favorite appetizer is pumpkin soup, which is followed by a choice of five or six main courses daily—perhaps local red snapper, grilled steak, or lobster. The menu changes every day and is scrawled on a blackboard. The food is generally good and home-style. It doesn't aspire to be much else, and that's precisely what its loyal fans like. Before dinner, have a drink at the bar, where you can read the names of sailors carved in wood more than a century ago. The service is agreeable, the value excellent, and the setting is heavy on atmosphere.

Coconut Grove. In the Siboney Beach Club, Dickenson Bay. ☎ **268/462-1538.** Reservations required for dinner. Main courses $9.25–$24.95. AE, MC, V. Daily 7–11am, 11:30am–3:30pm, and 5:30–10:30pm. INTERNATIONAL/SEAFOOD.

This restaurant features simple tables right on the beach set on a flagstone floor beneath a thatch roof. North of St. John's, in a coconut grove (of course) and cooled by sea breezes, the restaurant is one of the best on the island. Each day a tangy soup is prepared fresh from local ingredients. One appetizer is a seafood delight: scallops, shrimp, crab, lobster, and local fish with a mango-and-lime dressing. Lobster and shrimp dishes are strongly featured, and there's a catch of the day and a vegetarian specialty of the day. T-bone steak is a favorite, as is spicy Cajun chicken. Lighter fare is served at lunch. We hope that service will improve a bit by the time you visit.

Colombo's Restaurant. In the Galleon Beach Club, English Harbour. ☎ **268/460-1452.** Reservations recommended. Main courses $22–$32. AE, DC, MC, V. Daily 12:30–2:30pm and 7–10pm. Closed Sept–Oct 5. ITALIAN.

Colombo's serves up Italian food—the best on the island—on a Polynesian-style open-air terrace sheltered by a ceiling crafted from woven palm fronds. It's only a few steps across the flat sands to the water. Lunches in this sprawling place might include spaghetti marinara, lobster salad, and sandwiches. Dinners are more elaborate and include daily specials from a classic Italian inventory of veal scaloppini, veal pizzaiola, and lobster mornay. True, some dishes lack polish, but most selections are brimming with flavor. Meals can be accompanied by a wide assortment of French or Italian wines. Live music, including reggae, rock 'n' roll, jazz, and calypso, is presented on Wednesday night (no cover charge, but a two-drink minimum).

✪ **La Perruche.** English Harbour. ☎ **268/460-3040.** Reservations recommended. Main courses $18–$27. AE, MC, V. Mon–Sat 7–10pm. (Bar, Mon–Sat 6pm–midnight.) Closed Sept. CARIBBEAN/INTERNATIONAL.

One of the most consistently successful restaurants in English Harbour, La Perruche has a clearly signposted location near the entrance of Nelson's Dockyard. Although there's lots of pedestrian and vehicular traffic nearby, you'll be sheltered from the passersby by a high fence, a barrier of royal palms, and dozens of potted plants that almost create a miniature jungle. You'll dine al fresco in a setting whose cadre of chefs come and go. The place serves the best beef tenderloin on the island, as well as a superb version of blackened shrimp in a raspberry cream sauce. Game fish is a specialty, and includes wahoo, swordfish, dolphin, and tuna, any of which are accompanied by a choice of French-derived sauces (dill-herb is especially flavorful).

✪ **Le Bistro.** Hodges Bay. ☎ **268/462-3881.** Reservations required, especially in high season. Main courses EC$55–EC$80 ($20.35–$29.60). AE, MC, V. Tues–Sun 6:30–10:30pm. FRENCH.

This authentic bistro is one of the best on the island. Raffaele and Philippa Esposito run this little enclave of French cuisine on the north shore, 2 miles west of the airport on the road to Hodges Bay. Recognized for its superb fare by *Gourmet* and many other international magazines, it has an accomplished French chef whose specialties include maccheroni ziti Raffaele (named after one of the owners) made with cream, Parmesan, and mushrooms. Another good dish is côte de boeuf, a double rib of beef carved at the table and served with a béarnaise or bordelaise sauce. Yet a third, and especially delectable, main course is crisp roast duck with an aromatic mango sauce. For an appetizer, try the melon and shrimp salad marinated in a basil raspberry dressing.

Shirley Heights Lookout. Shirley Heights. ☎ **268/460-1785.** Reservations recommended. Main courses $15.75–$27. AE, DC, MC, V. Daily 9am–10pm. AMERICAN/SEAFOOD.

In the 1790s this was the lookout station for unfriendly ships heading toward English Harbour, site of a powder magazine constructed to strengthen Britain's position in this strategic location. Today this panoramic spot, directly east of English Harbour, is one of the most romantic on Antigua. Visitors sometimes prefer to be served on the stone battlements below the restaurant, although we'd rather dine under the angled rafters of the upstairs restaurant, where large, old-fashioned windows surround the room on all sides.

Specialties include pumpkin soup, grilled lobster in lime butter, garlic-flavored shrimp, and good desserts, such as banana flambé and carrot cake. It's not the world's grandest attempt at cuisine, and overcooking is the most frequent flaw, but it's a crowd-pleaser and a lot of fun, and what other restaurant can rival its view? Less expensive hamburgers and sandwiches are available in the bar downstairs.

A tradition with residents and visitors alike is Sunday at the Heights—the "end of the week" barbecue begins at 4pm and features six hours of nonstop entertainment, with a steel-band concert from 4 to 7pm and a reggae band from 7 to 10pm. However, avoid it when cruise-ship passengers take over. It's best at lunch.

Fun On & Off the Beach

BEACHES Beaches, beaches, and more beaches—Antigua has some 365 of them.

Note: Because of crime, it's unwise to go to any beach that appears to be deserted; you could be mugged in such a lonely setting. Increasingly, readers complain of vendors hustling everything from jewelry to T-shirts, disrupting their time on the beach. All beaches are public and open to all. Hotels can't restrict beach use, so be duly warned.

There's a lovely beach at **Pigeon Point,** in Falmouth Harbour, about a four-minute drive from the Admiral's Inn. The beach at **Dickenson Bay,** near the Rex Halcyon Cove Hotel, is also superior and a center for water sports; for a break, you can enjoy meals and drinks on the hotel's Warri Pier, built on stilts in the water. Chances are, however, you'll swim at your own hotel.

Other beaches are at the Curtain Bluff resort, with its long, white-sand **Carlisle Beach** set against a backdrop of coconut palms, and **Morris Bay,** which, in addition to its sandy strip of white sand, has waters attracting snorkelers, among others. The beach at **Long Bay** is on the somewhat-remote eastern coast, but the sands here are beautiful, and most visitors consider it worth the effort to get there. **Half Moon Bay** is famous in the Caribbean and attracts what used to be called "blue bloods"; it stretches for almost a mile. Site of such hotels as the Barrymore Beach, **Runaway Beach** is one of the most popular on Antigua, and because of its white sands it's worth fighting the crowds. **Five Islands** is actually a string of four remote beaches with brown sand and coral reefs located near the Hawksbill Hotel.

GOLF Antigua doesn't have the facilities of some of the other islands, but its premier course is good. The 18-hole, par-69 **Cedar Valley Golf Club,** Friar's Hill Road (☎ **268/462-0161**), is 3 miles east of St. John's, near the airport. The island's largest, with panoramic views of Antigua's northern coast, it was designed by the late Richard Aldridge to fit the contours of the area. Daily greens fees are $35 for 18 holes. Cart fees are also $35 for 18 holes, with club rentals going for $10.

PARASAILING This sport is gaining popularity on Antigua. Facilities are available during the day Monday to Saturday on the beach at **Dickenson Bay.** There are also facilities at the **Royal Antiguan Resort** (☎ **268/462-3732**) at Deep Bay, St. John's.

SAILING All major hotel desks can book a day cruise on the 108-foot "pirate ship," the ***Jolly Roger,*** Redcliffe Quay (☎ **268/462-2064**). For $50 you're taken sightseeing on a fun-filled day, with drinks and barbecued steak, chicken, or lobster. The *Jolly Roger* is the largest sailing ship in Antiguan waters. Lunch is combined with a snorkeling trip. There's dancing on the poop deck, and members of the crew teach passengers how to dance calypso. There are daily cruises, lasting 5½ hours from 9:30am to 3pm. There's also a Saturday night dinner cruise for $40, leaving Heritage Quay in St. John's at 7pm, returning at 10pm.

SCUBA DIVING, SNORKELING & OTHER WATER SPORTS Scuba diving is best arranged through **Dive Antigua**, at the Rex Halcyon Cove, Dickenson Bay (☎ **268/462-3483**), Antigua's most experienced dive operation. A resort course is offered for $85, with a two-tank dive costing the same. A six-dive package goes for $244, a 10-dive package for $306, with open water certification costing $475. All prices include equipment.

The **Long Bay Hotel,** on the northeastern coast of the island at Long Bay (☎ **268/463-2005**), is a good location for various water sports: swimming, sailing, waterskiing, and windsurfing. The hotel also has complete scuba facilities. Both beginning snorkelers and all divers are welcomed. You're taken on snorkeling trips by boat to Green Island and Great Bird Island (minimum of four). The shallow side of the double reef across Long Bay is ideal for the novice, and the whole area on the northeastern tip has many reefs of varying depths. A one-afternoon resort course costs $85, although certification, which could last four or five days, is $375.

TENNIS Tennis buffs will find courts at most of the major hotels, and some are lit for night games. We don't recommend playing tennis at noon—it's just too hot! If your hotel doesn't have a court, you can find them available at the previously recommended **Rex Halcyon Cove**, the **Cedar Valley Golf Club,** Friar's Hill, northeast of St. John's (☎ **268/462-0161**), and the **Royal Antiguan Resort,** Deep Bay (☎ **268/462-3732**); (the last two have eight courts each). If you're not a guest, you'll have to book a court and pay charges that vary from hotel to hotel. Guests of a hotel usually play free.

WINDSURFING Located at the Lord Nelson Beach Hotel, on Dutchman's Bay, **High Wind Centre** (☎ **268/462-3094**) offers windsurfing for the absolute beginner, the intermediate sailor, and the "Shredder," a hard-core windsurfer. The outlet guarantees to get beginners to enjoy the sport after a two-hour introductory lesson. A lesson costs $45, including free use of training equipment.

Seeing the Sights

ST. JOHN'S In the southern part of St. John's, the **market** is colorful and interesting, especially on Saturday morning. Vendors busy selling their fruits and vegetables bargain and gossip. The semiopen-air market lies at the lower end of Market Street.

Also in town, **St. John's Cathedral,** the Anglican cathedral between Long Street and Newgate Street at Church Lane (☎ **268/461-0082**), has had a disastrous history. Originally built in 1683, it was replaced by a stone building in 1745. That was destroyed by an earthquake in 1843. The present pitch-pine interior dates from 1847. The interior was being restored when, in 1973, the structure was badly damaged by another earthquake. The towers and the southern section have been restored.

The 3½-acre **Antigua and Barbuda Botanical Gardens,** at the corner of Nevis and Temple Streets (☎ **268/462-1007**), was established in 1893 in the Green Belt of St. John's, although the lack of rainfall here prevents the gardens from being as lush as on islands like Jamaica. As you enter the gardens you'll be struck by the majesty of an 80-year-old ficus tree, contrasted by the rolling lawns. The melodic sounds of tree frogs and birds emanate from a hollow filled with lianas draped from branches of trees in the rain forest. Tropical blossoms, herbal plants, ferns, dripping philodendrons, rare bromeliads, and a colorful carpet of flowers await the visitor. Open daily from 9am to 6pm; minimum donation of $2.

AROUND THE ISLAND After leaving St. John's, most visitors head southeast for 11 miles to ✪ **Nelson's Dockyard National Park** (☎ **268/460-1379**), one of the biggest attractions of the eastern Caribbean. The park's centerpiece is the restored Georgian naval dockyard, which was used by Admirals Nelson, Rodney, and Hood, and was the home of the British fleet during the Napoleonic Wars. From 1784 Nelson was the commander of the British navy in the Leeward Islands, and he made his headquarters at English Harbour. English ships used the harbor as a refuge from hurricanes as early as 1671.

The era of privateers, pirates, and great sea battles in the 18th century is recaptured in the dockyard's museum. Restored by the Friends of English Harbour, the dockyard is a sort of Caribbean Williamsburg. Its colonial naval buildings stand as they did when Nelson was here (1784–87). However, Nelson never lived at Admiral House—it was built in 1855. The house has been turned into a museum of nautical memorabilia. (For accommodations at English Harbour, see "Where to Stay," above.)

The park itself is worth exploring, filled with sandy beaches and tropical vegetation, including various species of cactus and mangroves. The latter provides shelter for a migrating colony of African cattle egrets. The park contains archaeological sites dating from well before the time of Christ. Nature trails have been cut through the park to expose the vegetation and coastal scenery. Tours of the dockyard are given, lasting 15 to 20 minutes, and tours along nature trails can last anywhere from 30 minutes to five hours. The cost is $2.50 per person to tour the dockyard; children 12 and under are admitted free. The dockyard and its museum are open daily from 8am to 6pm.

Another major attraction is the **Dow's Hill Interpretation Center** (☎ **268/460-1053**), just 2½ miles from the dockyard. The only one of its kind in the Caribbean, it offers multimedia presentations that cover six periods of the island's history, including the era of Amerindian hunters, the era of the British military, and the struggles connected with slavery. A belvedere opens onto a panoramic view of the park. Admission to the center, including the multimedia show, is $5 for adults and $3 for children 15 and under. The center is open daily from 9am to 5pm.

The footpath to **Fort Barclay** is located at the entrance to English Harbour, just outside the dockyard gate. The fort, a fine specimen of old-time military engineering, is about half a mile away.

If you're at English Harbour at sunset, head for **Shirley Heights,** directly to the east. It was named after General Shirley, governor of the Leeward Islands in 1781, who fortified the hills guarding the harbor. Some majestic Palladian arches, once part of the barracks, are still standing. The Block House, one of the main buildings, was put up as a stronghold in case of siege. The nearby Victorian cemetery contains an obelisk monument to the officers and men of the 54th Regiment.

On a low hill overlooking Nelson's Dockyard, **Clarence House** was built by English stonemasons to accommodate Prince William Henry, later known as the duke of Clarence, and even later known as William IV. The future king stayed here when he was in command of the *Pegasus* in 1787. At present it's the country home of the governor of Antigua and Barbuda and is open to visitors when His Excellency is not in residence. A caretaker will show you through (it's customary to tip, of course), and you'll see many pieces of furniture on loan from the National Trust. Princess Margaret and Lord Snowdon stayed here on their honeymoon.

On the way back, take ✪ **Fig Tree Drive,** a 20-some-mile circular drive across the main mountain range. It passes through lush tropical hills and fishing villages along the southern coast. You can pick up the road just outside Liberta, north of Falmouth. Winding through a rain forest, it passes thatched villages. Every hamlet has a church and lots of goats and children running about. But don't expect fig trees—*fig* is an Antiguan name for bananas.

About half a mile before reaching St. John's you come to **Fort James,** begun in 1704 as a main lookout post for the port and named after James II.

Other places on the island worth seeking out include the following:

Parham Church, overlooking Parham Town, was erected in 1840 in the Italian style. Richly adorned with stucco work, it was damaged by an earthquake in 1843. Much of the ceiling was destroyed and very little of the stucco work remains, but the octagonal structure is still worth a visit.

The **Potworks Dam,** holding back the largest artificial lake on Antigua, is surrounded by an area of great natural beauty. The dam has a capacity of a billion gallons of water and provides protection for Antigua in case of a drought.

Indian Town, one of Antigua's national parks, is at a northeastern point on the island. Over the centuries Atlantic breakers have lashed the rocks and carved a natural bridge known as Devil's Bridge. It's surrounded by numerous blowholes spouting surf.

Megaliths, at Greencastle Hill, reached by a long climb, are said to have been set up by human hands for the worship of a sun god and a moon goddess. Some experts believe, however, that the arrangement is an unusual geological formation, a volcanic rockfall.

The **Antigua Rum Distillery,** at Rat Island (☎ **268/462-1072**), turns out fine Cavalier rum. Check at the tourist office about arranging a visit. Established in 1932, the plant is next to Deep Water Harbour.

SHOPPING

Most of the shops are clustered on St. Mary's Street or High Street in St. John's. Some shops are open Monday to Saturday from 8:30am to noon and 1 to 4pm, but this rule varies greatly from store to store—Antiguan shopkeepers are an independent lot. Many of them close at noon on Thursday.

There are many duty-free items for sale, including English woolens and linens, and you can also purchase several specialized items made on Antigua, such as original pottery, local straw work, Antiguan rum, and silk-screened, hand-printed local designs on fabrics, as well as mammy bags, floppy foldable hats, and shell curios.

If you want an island-made bead necklace, don't bother to go shopping; just lie on the beach, anywhere, and some "bead lady" will find you.

If you're in St. John's on a Saturday morning, you can attend the **fruit and vegetable market** at the West Bus Station. Locally made handcrafts are also offered for sale. And the incredibly sweet and juicy Antiguan black pineapple is alone worth the trip into town.

Harmony Hall. In Brown's Bay Mill, near Freetown. ☎ **268/460-4120.** Follow the signs along the road to Freetown and Half Moon Bay.

This old plantation house and sugar mill overlooking Nonsuch Bay dates back to 1843. Much restored, it's ideal for a luncheon stopover or a shopping expedition. It displays an excellent selection of Caribbean arts and crafts. Lunch is served daily from noon to 4pm, featuring Green Island lobster, flying fish, and other specialties. Sunday is barbecue day.

Island Hopper. Jardine Court, St. Mary's St., St. John's. ☎ **268/462-2972.**

This shop has a range of gifts and clothing and specializes in products made in the Caribbean. The owner goes to some trouble to provide items not readily available elsewhere. The range is wide, including T-shirts, spices, coffees, handcrafts, and casual wear.

Quin Farara's Liquor Store. Long St. and Corn Alley, St. John's. ☎ **268/462-0463.**

Ever intent on overtaxing tourists to cover its inevitable deficits, the government has raised duty on liquor, and Antiguan alcohol isn't the bargain it once was. You can still buy liquor at discount prices, although because of heavy taxes liqueurs no longer offer much savings at all.

The Scent Shop. Lower High St., St. John's. ☎ **268/462-0303.**

This is the oldest and best perfume shop on the island. There's an array of crystal (Baccarat, Lalique, and Waterford) for sale, although the bulk of the store's income comes from exotic perfumes, some of which are not sold in any of the island's other stores.

Shoul's Chief Store. St. Mary's St. at Market St., St. John's. ☎ **268/462-1140.**

This all-purpose department store sells fabric, electrical appliances, souvenir items (more than 300 kinds), and general merchandise.

Shopping Centers

Most stores in these complexes are open all day Monday to Saturday.

HERITAGE QUAY Antigua's first shopping-and-entertainment complex is a multimillion-dollar center featuring some 40 duty-free shops and a vendors' arcade in which local artists and craftspeople display their wares. Restaurants in Heritage Quay offer a range of cuisine and views of St. John's Harbour; a food court serves visitors who prefer to feast on local specialties in an informal setting. You can start your shopping with any of these leading shops:

Colombian Emeralds (☎ **268/462-3462**) is the largest retailer of Colombian emeralds in the world, with branches throughout the Caribbean and The Bahamas. It offers an excellent variety of emeralds along with jewelry made from other precious stones.

Little Switzerland (☎ **268/462-3108**) is a name familiar to frequent travelers to the Caribbean. It sells the best selections of Swiss-made watches on Antigua, such as Rolex, Omega, and Cartier. It also displays china and crystal made by Royal Doulton and Baccarat. Little Switzerland has opened a perfume shop in Heritage Quay called **La Perfumery by Little Switzerland** (☎ **268/462-2601**).

"Sunsneakers," 51 Heritage Quay (☎ **268/462-4523**), was established in 1989 when duty-free shopping was introduced on Antigua on a large scale. The outlet has one of the largest selections of swimwear available in the Caribbean.

Island Arts, Upstairs, Heritage Quay (☎ **268/462-2787**), was founded by Nick Maley, a makeup artist who worked on *Star Wars* and *The Empire Strikes Back*. You can purchase one of his own fine-art reproductions, including the provocative *Windkissed & Sunswept*. Visitors are free to browse through everything from low-cost prints to works by artists exhibited in New York's Museum of Modern Art. You can also visit Nick's home and studio at Aiton Place, on Sandy Lane directly behind the Hodges Bay Club, 4 miles from St. John's. The residence is open Monday through

Saturday from 10am to 4pm, but it's always wise to call before going (☎ 345/461-6324).

REDCLIFFE QUAY This historic complex is the second best center for shopping (or dining) in St. John's. Once, Redcliffe Quay was a slave-trading quarter, but after the abolition of slavery the quay was filled with grog shops and merchants peddling various wares. Now it has been redeveloped and contains a number of the most interesting shops in town, some in former warehouses.

Caribelle Batik, Redcliffe Quay, St. John's (☎ 268/462-2972) is an outlet for the Romney Manor workshop on St. Kitts. The Caribelle label consists of batik and tie-dye items such as beach wraps, scarves, and a range of casual wear for both women and men. The Sensual Silk label is also found here; these items are 100% silk in Caribbean colors, ranging from dresses and separates to scarves.

A Thousand Flowers (**☎ 268/462-4264**) sells Indonesian batiks, crafted on the island into sundresses, knock-'em-dead shirts, sarongs, and rompers. Various accessories such as necklaces and earrings are also sold. Many of the garments are one-size-fits-all.

Jacaranda (**☎ 268/462-1888**) might tempt you with the art of local artists or place mats and prints by Jill Walker. The shop also stocks clothing, cookbooks, wood carvings, pottery, scrimshaw knives, herbs and spices as well as gels, soaps, and salts for the bath.

Base (**☎ 268/462-0920**), the brainchild of Steven Giles, an English designer, is one of the best-known companies in the Caribbean. It carries an intriguing line of casual comfort clothing in stripes, colors, and prints. The cotton and Lycra beachwear is eagerly sought out. The clothing is reasonable in price, catering to men, women, and children.

The Goldsmitty (**☎ 268/462-4601**) presents the designs of the well-known Hans Smit in precious stones and gold. The jewelry is all designed and made on the premises. Buyers can select from many one-of-a-kind creations. Black opal, imperial topaz, and other exotic gemstones are set in exquisite creations of 14- and 18-karat gold. The store is closed in September.

ANTIGUA AFTER DARK

Most nightlife revolves around the hotels, unless you want to roam Antigua at night looking for that hot local club. If you're going out for the night, make arrangements to have a taxi pick you up, otherwise you could be stranded in the wilds somewhere. Antigua has some of the best steel bands in the Caribbean.

The **Royal Casino,** in the Royal Antiguan Hotel, Deep Bay (**☎ 268/462-3733**), has American games, including blackjack, baccarat, roulette, craps, and slot machines. It's open daily from 9pm "until," and there's no cover.

BARBUDA

Known by the Spanish as Dulcina, sparsely populated Barbuda is part of the independent nation of Antigua and Barbuda. It's the last frontier of the Caribbean, even though today the island is home to two of the most expensive and exclusive resorts in the region (see below). Charted by Columbus in 1493, the island lies 26 miles to the north of Antigua. It's about 15 miles long by 5 miles wide and has a population of some 1,200 hardy souls, most of whom live around the unattractive village of Codrington.

Don't come here seeking lush, tropical scenery, as flat Barbuda consists of coral rock. There are no paved roads, few hotels, and only a handful of restaurants. There are pinkish-colored beaches, though, the most famous of which stretches for more than 17 miles. We prefer the sands north of Palmetto Point. The temperature seldom falls below an average of 75°F.

Getting There

The island is a 15-minute flight from Antigua's V. C. Bird Airport. Barbuda has two airfields: one at Codrington, the other a private facility, the Coco Point Airstrip, which lies some 8 miles from Codrington at the Coco Point Lodge.

To reach Barbuda from Antigua, you can contact **LIAT** (☎ **268/462-0701**), which operates two daily flights (usually around 8am and again around 4pm) from Antigua to Barbuda's Codrington Airport. The cost is EC$120 ($44.40) for a day return ticket or EC$130 ($48.10) if you're staying over.

Getting Around

Many locals rent small Suzuki four-wheel-drive **Jeeps,** which are the best way to get around the island. They meet incoming flights at Codrington Airport, and prices are negotiable. An Antiguan driver's license (see above) is needed if you plan to drive.

Where to Stay & Dine

Coco Point Lodge. Coco Point, Barbuda, W.I. ☎ **268/462-3816.** For reservations, contact Coco Point Lodge Reservations Office, 275 Madison Ave., Suite 1901, New York, NY 10016 (☎ 212/986-1416; fax 212/986-0901). 34 rms. Winter, $665–$1,060 double. Off-season, $585–$935 double. Rates are all-inclusive. Additional occupant of double room $175–$200 extra. No credit cards.

This is one of the most isolated and upscale hotels in the Caribbean. You don't just up and choose this place casually—it's a real escapist haven, and it takes some advance planning to get here. In the 1960s the Kelly family acquired a flat, sandy, 164-acre peninsula. Ever since, they've devoted their time, funds, and energy to building up a club that was so private that yacht owners who dropped in for a drink were often barred from the facilities. This is not a conventional resort; many of the guests have known each other for years. Either you'll fit in or you won't, but regardless, there's no denying the spectacular beauty of the natural setting.

Don't expect glitter: The resort is permeated with solid Yankee values, a lack of intrusive electronics (TV and phones are, to everyone's relief, absent from the bedrooms), and a real disdain for ostentation. The clientele has included well-known names and faces, all of whom appreciate the isolation. Each accommodation offers privacy and access to a perfect beach.

More than 90% of the overseas visitors arrive at the resort by a private aircraft, which meets incoming international flights at the Antigua airport. A team of congenial Barbudians is on hand to provide and procure whatever you want.

Facilities include tennis courts, the beach, lots of sailing craft and boats for virtually any waterborne experience, bars, and a dining room where the food is beautifully presented and prepared.

✪ **K-Club.** Barbuda, Antigua, W.I. ☎ **268/460-0304.** Fax 268/460-0305. 36 cottages, 9 suites, 1 villa. A/C MINIBAR TEL. Winter, $950–$1,100 cottage for 2; $1,600 suite; from $2,200 villa. Off-season, $750–$900 cottage for 2; $1,300 suite; from $2,100 villa. Children 11 and under not allowed. Rates include all meals. AE, DC, MC, V. Closed Sept–Nov 15.

The most interesting, and *superexpensive,* hotel to open recently in the Caribbean, the beachfront K-Club brings a chic Italian panache to one of the most far-flung backwaters of the Antilles. Located a 15-minute taxi ride from the airport and set on more than 200 acres, adjacent to the island's only other major hotel, it's the creative statement of Italy's Krizia Mariuccia Mandelli, whose sports and evening-wear empire has grossed a spectacular fortune.

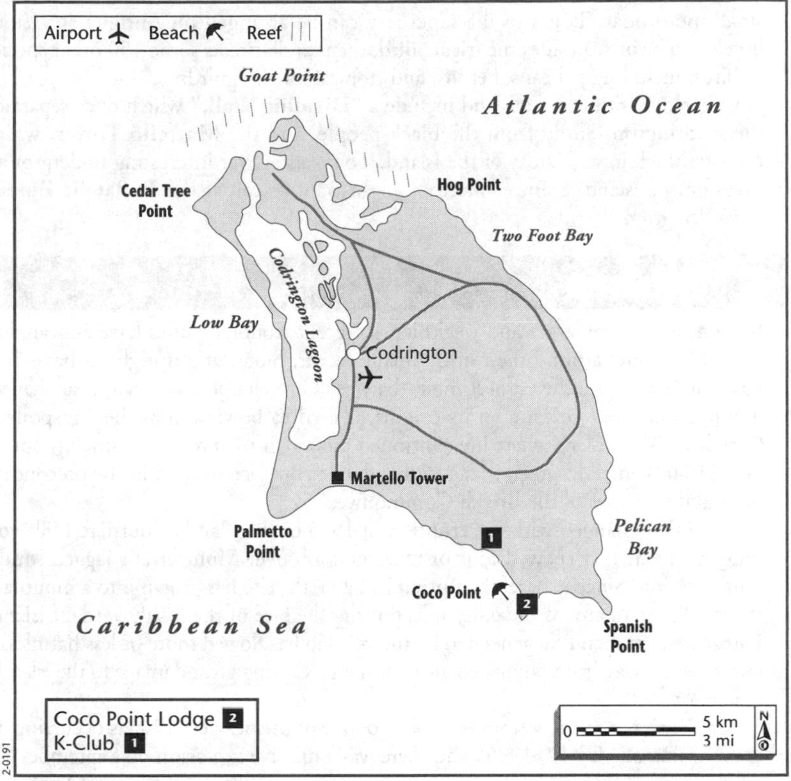

The resort's architectural style, conceived by Italian architect Gianni Gamondi, consists of cottages and a main clubhouse whose roof is supported by a forest of white columns. The resort's dominant color scheme is in the teal blue and white that are the designer's trademark. The furnishings include lots of Hamptons-style wicker and a stylish insouciance. The resort opened in 1990 when a planeload of glitterati, spearheaded by Giorgio Armani, headed for Barbuda en masse.

Dining/Entertainment: The all-inclusive rates provide for all meals (but no drinks or wine). The cuisine is fashioned after the Mediterranean kitchen, with an emphasis on Italian specialties and fresh pasta.

Services: Transportation from Codrington Airport.

Facilities: Two tennis courts, seawater swimming pool, waterskiing, snorkeling, Sunfish sailing, windsurfing, deep-sea fishing.

Exploring the Island

Hunters, anglers, and beachcombers are attracted to the island, as it has some fallow deer, guinea fowl, pigeons, and wild pigs. Those interested in fishing for bonefish and tarpon can negotiate with the owners of small boats who rent them out.

Visitors over just for the day usually head for **Wa'Omoni Beach Park,** where they can visit the frigate bird sanctuary, snorkel for lobster, and eat barbecue.

A most impressive sight, the **frigate bird sanctuary** is one of the largest in the world. Visitors can see the birds, *Fregata magnificens,* sitting on their eggs in the mangrove bushes. The mangroves stretch for miles in a long lagoon accessible only by small motorboat. Tours to the sanctuary can be arranged on Antigua at various hotels and resorts. Besides the frigate bird, the island attracts some 150 other species of birds, including pelicans, herons, and tropical mockingbirds.

Other curiosities of the island include a **"Dividing Wall,"** which once separated the Codrington family from the black people, and the **Martello Tower,** which predates the known history of the island. Tours also cover interesting underground caves on the island. Stamp collectors might want to call at the **Philatelic Bureau** in Codrington.

2 Montserrat

If Montserrat were larger and wealthier, its recent troubles would have appeared as part of headlines around the world. Small, decent, pious, and upright, it basks in a position 27 miles southwest of Antigua, between Guadeloupe and Nevis. Pear-shaped, mountainous, and volcanic in its origins, it used to be viewed as the "unspoiled" Caribbean isle, a place where life continued the way it used to be—a small (population 11,000) emerald-green island with a docile populace steeped in the preconceptions and priorities of the British Commonwealth.

All of that changed with the eruption in 1995 of the island's Soufrière Hills volcano, an event that spewed tons of rocks and ash over Montserrat's jagged south-central region. Since its fateful eruption in 1995, the site has grown into a mountain range taller than any of the older hills dotting the face of the lushly verdant island. Fortunately, molten lava generated by the volcano has flowed more or less harmlessly into the sea, away from populated areas, although causing great damage to the island's vegetation.

Ash continues to spew from the volcano, one of the heaviest ashfalls occurring on the morning of May 12, 1996. And there was a massive explosion on September 17, 1996, followed by earthquake activities that were especially worrisome in October of 1996. More of the same, it's feared, will probably follow. Volcano observers point to a frightening bulge in one side of the newly formed mountain, a bulge that might eventually be the site of a volcanic explosion. Motorists on the island have been warned to drive with due care and attention to slippery, ash-covered roads. Access routes to Plymouth, the once-thriving capital, are blocked by police barricades that allow only persons with urgent business inside. And all sites of public affairs and commercial enterprise, as well as every home on the eastern, western, and southern sides of the island have been relocated to the island's (relatively) stable northern area. Fortunately for the tattered shreds of tourism that remain in place, the island's northern tier, its officially designated "safe zone," was always known as the site of the best beaches and most of its tourist hotels.

If you opt to visit this once tranquil, once sleepy island, you'll gain insights into the effects of a radical, and strictly enforced, reconfiguration of the island's population zones. Expect a sojourn on an island caught in a major crisis, the lingering scent of sulfur and hints of impending doom, and few of the carefree and whimsical aspects that you might have hoped for from a Caribbean holiday.

Currently, it's anyone's guess as to the extent or duration of the crisis. But if things calm down and the homes and businesses of Plymouth are once again reclaimed by their former occupants, look for attempts to pick up the thread of an island culture that in the past has attracted such musical luminaries as Elton John, Paul McCartney, Sting, and Stevie Wonder. Regrettably, even the glory days of Montserrat's role in rock and roll ended in 1989 when Air Studios, a state-of-the-art recording studio on the island's northern tier, went bankrupt after its devastation by Hurricane Hugo.

Expect disruptions in your holiday, a limited roster of activities and touristic options (many of the hotels and restaurants, including all of those in Plymouth, are closed), and a sequestration of those geological oddities in the south and central parts of the island that have attracted nature lovers and hikers for decades. Instead, you'll be treated to views of a small, closely knit community as it struggles to relocate its primary places of business and government, and a population that's more or less coping gracefully under the strain.

Late-breaking news: Just as this edition went to the printer, another volcanic eruption occurred on June 25, killing at least nine people and temporarily closing the airstrip and the main pier. Little information was available before this book's press date; we strongly suggest that you call the tourist office for an update on the current situation before planning a trip.

GETTING THERE

At least 80% of passengers flying into Montserrat transfer through Antigua. (For information on getting to Antigua, see section 1 of this chapter.) From Antigua, two different airlines run a flotilla of small planes. **LIAT** (☎ **268/462-0701** on Antigua) operates daily flights to Montserrat on planes holding between 19 and 37 passengers. For information about these flights, call LIAT on Antigua or dial LIAT's Montserrat based sales representative, **Montserrat Aviation** (☎ **664/491-2533**). Throughout the year, LIAT offers four flights a day, each lasting from 12 to 20 minutes, to Montserrat from Antigua. Aircraft to this island's recently renamed W. H. Bramble Airport are rarely larger than a Dash-8 or a Twin Otter.

Because of the recent collapse of a local competitor, LIAT has very few rivals in the market of bringing visitors into tiny Montserrat, but some competitors do exist. Foremost among these is a charter outfit based in Antigua, **Carib Aviation** (☎ **268/462-3147** on Antigua), that can arrange charter flights from Antigua to fill in the gaps whenever LIAT flights aren't available or are sold out. A local travel agent that maintains a particularly good grip on alternative modes of transport in and out of Montserrat is **Carib World Travel,** Parliament Street, in Plymouth (at this writing, its temporary headquarters were within a private residence in the hamlet of Salem; ☎ **664/462-3147**).

Most passengers coming from the North American mainland find it cheaper and more convenient to allow larger carriers, such as **American** (☎ **800/433-7300**) or **BWIA** (☎ **800/327-7401**), to make bookings into Montserrat on the above-mentioned airlines as part of ongoing flights through Antigua from the North American mainland.

GETTING AROUND

BY TAXI & BUS Although the island contains 15 miles of surfaced roads, only those within the island's northern tier are currently accessible, and most of the island's vehicular traffic is limited to the route between the island's only airport and the designated "safe zone" in the northern tier. The typical taxi fare from the airport to any of the hotels in the northern tier, such as View Pointe, is EC$49 ($18.15). Sightseeing tours, when viable, cost around EC$30 ($11.10) per hour. The only regular bus service remaining on the island since the debut of volcanic activities are those that run from Corkhill, a once northerly suburb of Plymouth, and the island's northern tip. Fares cost EC$3 ($1.10) for as long as you want to ride in either direction.

BY RENTAL CAR None of the major U.S.-based car-rental companies offer an outlet on Montserrat, although you'll find a handful of private agencies. Before you rent, you'll be warned that volcanic ash, when spread over one of the island's roads, contributes to slippery driving conditions. You'll also be required to buy a local Montserrat driver's license for $12, which should accompany your valid U.S., British, Canadian, or other driver's license. These permits will usually be available from your car rental agent; if not, you can get one from a police officer or from the immigration department at the island's airport.

Most island agencies stock a battered roster of Toyotas, Sentras, Daihatsus, and Mazdas, and rent for between $25 and $35 a day, depending on their make and model. A collision-damage waiver costs from $9 to $11 per day, but even if you buy it, you'll still be liable for the cost of some of the repairs to your vehicle if you damage it, for any reason, during your tenure. Two of the island's leading agencies include the **Neville Bradshaw Agency,** P.O. Box 270, Plymouth (relocated to the northern suburb of Olveston since the crisis; ☎ **664/491-5270**); and **Montserrat Enterprises,** P.O. Box 58, Plymouth (also relocated to Olveston since the crisis; ☎ **664/491-2431**).

Be warned before you drive that since the eruption, there are only two gasoline stations on Montserrat, not enough to serve all of the gas-related needs of an island that made do with five stations before the shutdown of Plymouth. The foremost of these, Delta, lies on the northern outskirts of Plymouth; the other operates with limited hours from a position near the island's airport.

BY BIKE **Island Bikes,** Foxes Bay Road (☎ **664/491-5552**), offers an active way to see the lush scenery of Montserrat. You can ride on your own or ask Island Bikes to arrange a guide. Either way, you'll see Montserrat from a different perspective. The cost is $25 per day.

FAST FACTS: Montserrat

Currency Most Leeward Islands, including Montserrat, use the Eastern Caribbean dollar (EC$), although many hotel prices and many restaurants quote figures in U.S. dollars. Currently, the conversion rate is EC$2.70 to U.S.$1 or 37¢ in U.S. coinage to EC$1.

Drugstores The leading pharmacy on the island, **Lee's Pharmacy,** (☎ **664/491-3274**), fled from Plymouth and is operating in the island's northwestern hamlet of St. Peter's. Hours are Monday through Saturday from 9am to 6pm.

Electricity In honor of its British origins and mostly American clientele, Montserrat is one of the most electrically versatile islands in the Caribbean. Although the electrical current is officially 220-230 volts AC (60 cycles), the same as that used in Britain, most hotels are wired to accept 110-volt (North American) current as well. In theory, you might need to bring an adapter and transformer, but in actual practice, few American clients actually bother. If in doubt, check with your hotel before your arrival.

Hospitals After the debut of the crisis, Montserrat's largest hospital, the **Glendon Hospital** (☎ **664/491-2880**), moved from Plymouth into what was originally conceived as a school in St. John's. It maintains a 24-hour emergency room, and although many delicate medical procedures are performed on-site, some difficult cases opt to be evacuated to medical facilities on Antigua, Guadeloupe, or Miami.

Information Although th official address of the **Montserrat Tourist Board** remains on Marine Drive (P.O. Box 7), in Plymouth, Montserrat, B.W.I. (☎ **664/491-2230**), since the debut of the crisis the organization has relocated to

temporary headquarters at Mayfield Estates, Olveston, in the northern suburbs of the former capital. They're open Monday through Friday from 8am to 4pm.

Police Call ☎ **664/491-2555.**

Safety As in the Caymans and the British Virgins, crime is rare here. It would be wise, however, to take the usual precautions about safeguarding your valuables.

Taxes The government charges a hotel tax of 7% to 10%. In addition, it imposes an EC$25 ($9.25) departure tax when you leave the island.

Time Montserrat is on Atlantic standard time year-round: When it's 6am in Plymouth, it's 5am in New York or Miami. However, island clocks match those of the eastern zone on the mainland when summer's daylight saving time is in effect in the United States.

Tips and Service Hotels and restaurants add a 10% surcharge to your final tab to cover tips. If they don't, it's customary to tip 10% to 15%.

Weather The mean temperature of the island ranges from a high of 86.5° to a low of 73.5°F.

WHERE TO STAY

Because of volcanic activity, very few of Montserrat's already limited hotels are still operating. Since the number of rooms on the island is so limited, make sure you've nailed down an iron-clad reservation before you arrive.

Vue Pointe Hotel. P.O. Box 65, Old Towne, Montserrat, B.W.I. ☎ **800/235-0709** in the U.S., or 664/491-5210. Fax 664/491-4813. 40 rms. TV TEL. Winter, $170–$195 double; $225 triple. Off-season, $120–$135 double; $165 triple. MAP $40 per person extra. AE, DISC, MC, V.

This family-run cottage colony consists of hexagonal, shingle-roofed villas, plus some interconnected rooms. They're set on 5 acres of sloping land near a black-sand beach, just 11 miles from the Montserrat airport and about two minutes from the Montserrat Golf Club.

Most of the accommodations are constructed with natural lumber with open-beamed ceilings, and they're furnished with bamboo and modern pieces. Each has a private bath, a small refrigerator, a sitting-room area, and twin beds. A natural breeze sweeps through accommodations in lieu of air-conditioning. The staff members are unobtrusive and well trained.

Dining/Entertainment: The cuisine is the best on the island, and everybody shows up for the West Indian barbecue on Wednesday night. There are two attractive bars: one at the rambling main house; the other, called the Nest, at the water's edge. Dress is informal. Sometimes there's music and dancing to a steel band.

Services: Room service, laundry, baby-sitting.

Facilities: Freshwater swimming pool, dive shop, two tennis courts; fishing, sailing, and snorkeling can be arranged.

Condos & Villas

Belham Valley Hotel. P.O. Box 409, Old Towne, Montserrat, B.W.I. ☎ **664/491-5553.** 4 apts. TV TEL. Winter, $400 Jasmine studio apt; $500 one-bedroom apt; $500 Frangipani studio apt; $525 Mignonette two-bedroom apt. Off-season, $300 Jasmine studio; $375 one-bedroom apt; $375 Frangipani studio; $475 Mignonette unit. All rates are per week. AE, MC, V.

Despite the word *hotel* in the name, this establishment maintains and operates four apartment units, each with kitchen, which are rented on a weekly basis. These apartments lie on a hillside 4 miles north of Plymouth, overlooking Belham Valley, its river, and the golf course. The beach is about a seven-minute walk away, and in the evening you can also stroll over to the Vue Pointe Hotel. The Frangipani studio cottage, surrounded by tropical shrubs and coconut palms, can accommodate two guests and consists of a bedroom, living area, fully equipped kitchen, private bath, and a balcony facing the golf course and the sea. The Jasmine studio apartment also accommodates two and contains a large bed/living room, a small dinette, a private bath, a fully equipped kitchen, and a small private patio with views of the sea or mountains. Another apartment, the Mignonette, accommodates four guests and has two bedrooms, a bath, and a living area with kitchen, plus a big patio facing the golf course and sea. A fourth one-bedroom apartment sits above the Mignonette, offering the same view, with a large kitchen, living room, dining room, and even a balcony.

A Guest House

Providence Estate House. St. Peter's, Montserrat, W.I. ☎ **664/491-6476.** Fax 664/491-8476. 2 rms. TV. Winter, $77–$92 double. Off-season, $70–$85 double. Rates include breakfast. MC, V.

This B&B guest house is part of a turn-of-the-century plantation in the quiet countryside, about 20 minutes north of Plymouth. Several acres of gardens can be viewed from the large veranda that encloses the swimming pool. From the veranda, at an elevation of 500 feet, there's a panoramic 180° view of the Caribbean, including the islands of Nevis and Redonda, as well as much of the northern coastline of Montserrat. A full breakfast is served against this backdrop. The house became locally famous when Paul McCartney and his family rented it for several months some time ago. The guest rooms feature the original thick stone walls, heavy timbered ceilings, and tile floors. A kitchen is available on the veranda for drinks, snacks, and warm-up meals.

WHERE TO DINE

Many guests dine at their hotels. But since there are so few hotels and since many visitors rent condos and villas, a number of independent places exist, mainly cafes, although most have shut down because of volcanic activity. Some of these are tiny local spots with a loyal following. Often the appearance is a bit ramshackle, but good, simple food is served.

MODERATE

✪ **Belham Valley Restaurant.** Old Towne. ☎ **664/491-5553.** Reservations recommended, especially for dinner. Main courses $13–$30. AE, MC, V. Tues–Sun noon–2pm and 6:30–11pm. FRENCH/AMERICAN.

This place near the Vue Pointe Hotel, 4 miles north of Plymouth, is the premier restaurant of Montserrat. You can enjoy a creamy local pumpkin soup, prime steaks, or a combination of seafood served in a rich vermouth sauce. Look for some fresh inspiration to appear on the menu, perhaps fettuccine with seafood. A crowd pleaser is the spicy Montserrat conch fritters, and the kitchen always prepares Montserrat "mountain chicken" (frogs' legs), another favorite. Desserts are likely to include coconut-cream cheesecake, mango mousse, and fresh coconut pie. The setting is tropical, and the restaurant occupies a former private home on a hillside overlooking the Belham River and its valley. It's convenient for guests at the Montserrat Golf Course. In winter, live entertainment is offered Thursday to Saturday night.

Emerald Café. St. John's. ☎ **664/491-3821.** Main courses EC$8–EC$68 ($2.95–$25.20). Reservations recommended for dinner in winter. No credit cards. Daily 8am–11pm. CARIBBEAN/INTERNATIONAL.

Originally established in 1988, this was one of the first establishments to be relocated from unstable premises in Plymouth after the first volcanic activity in 1995. Its new location is in what was originally a private house, now enlarged to accommodate the business. Set on the main highway in St. John's, near the island's busiest gas station (the A&F Service Centre), it mingles aspects of a Red Cross canteen with that of a simple luncheonette and West Indian restaurant. Menu items include several styles of fish, lobster, tenderloin or sirloin steak, stewed beef or mutton, and barbecued spare ribs. Although you won't find the touches of comfort and glamour that were the norm here before its relocation, the establishment provides a worthwhile site for meeting local residents and hearing about the often bizarre situations the volcano has created.

Vue Pointe Restaurant. In the Vue Pointe Hotel, Old Towne. ☎ **664/491-5211.** Reservations recommended if you're not a hotel guest. Main courses EC$35–EC$55 ($12.95–$20.35). AE, MC, V. Daily 7am–11pm. FRENCH/CARIBBEAN.

Graciously elegant, this restaurant is surrounded by the lawns and shrubbery of the previously recommended Vue Pointe Hotel (4 miles north of Plymouth). It's the best-run restaurant on the island. The Wednesday-night barbecue, an island event, is enlivened by a steel band. The kitchen turns out "mountain chicken," fillet of kingfish, Creole-style red snapper, West Indian curried chicken with condiments, and filet of sole, and does each dish admirably well. Dessert might be lime cheesecake or a tropical fruit salad. In the winter, a Sunday beach barbecue is presented.

Hiking & Other Outdoor Pursuits

BEACHES Montserrat isn't known for its white sandy beaches. Most of its beaches are of volcanic black sand, and they lie on the northern rim of the island, which is not threatened by volcanic activity. The best beach is **Rendezvous Bay,** known for its dazzling white sand. The less popular **Carr's Bay, Little Bay,** and **Old Road Bay** are gray with rather drab-looking sands. Vue Pointe Hotel can arrange day sails to these beaches.

GOLF Constructed in 1964 and designed by Edmond Ault, the **Montserrat Golf Club,** Old Towne (☎ **664/491-5220**), has 18 tees but only 11 holes, which are combined in various configurations to create a conventional 18-hole game. Set on 100 acres in Belham Valley, it boasts some unusual layouts and features: The 11th hole, one of the course's most challenging, requires that players drive the ball across two branches of a stream know as the Belham River. And from the 6th and 7th holes, on clear days, you'll have a sweeping (and frankly, awesome) view over the steaming, and faraway, heights of one of the world's newest volcanoes. Clubs and pull carts can be rented, and there's a simple snack bar in the clubhouse serving sandwiches every day at lunchtime. Greens fees for a full day on the course are $30 per person.

HIKING The verdant hills and vales of Montserrat have attracted hikers since the island was first colonized by the British. Regrettably, some of the most unusual geological features lie within districts of the island that have been declared dangerous by local authorities because of their proximity to smoldering, ash-spewing volcanoes. The **Galway Soufrière Hike** and **Great Alps Falls,** until recently two of the premier geological sites in the Caribbean, aren't accessible at all until further notice.

Consequently, the Montserrat government has developed a network of panoramic, albeit less dramatic, hiking trails along the island's relatively safe northern tier. Foremost among these is a gentle uphill ramble from a clearly marked point just north of the hamlet of Salem to **The Cott.** Requiring 30 to 45 minutes each way, it presents sweeping views, elevations as high as 900 feet above the sea, and a visit to a ruined stone-built plantation house (more of a cottage, really), known as The Cott. Green and white signs indicate its location and the trails leading up to it.

Although you probably won't need a guide for this particular hike, Montserrat offers about a half-dozen government-trained guides who are willing to provide information about the status of more difficult climbs, including those within regions of the island presently designated as unfit or unsafe for hikers. For more information, contact the **Montserrat Tour Guides Association** (☎ **664/491-3160**).

SCUBA DIVING The colossal seismic changes that have affected the topography of southern Montserrat have also affected the safety and accessibility of offshore dive sites that, until recently, were superlative. Consequently, at this writing, dive experts list about 30 sites as safe and worthy of underwater exploration. All but a handful of these lie off the island's northwestern coast, near zones that are officially designated as safe from volcanic activity. Foremost among these are **Pinnacle (The Horn),** the underwater cone of an extinct volcano, a deepwater dive (from 65 to 300 feet below the waves) that's usually reserved for experts. Colorful sponges, huge brain corals, and cavernous basket sponges, large enough to conceal a fully equipped diver, are abundant, along with prodigious numbers of fish. Spear-fishing is illegal here. Other worthy sites include **Little Bay,** a relatively shallow dive that propels its participants into a cave filled with roosting and flying bats. Its entrance is open to the atmosphere only at some intervals throughout the day, depending on the tides. Other areas known for their abundant underwater life include **Virgin Island** and **Lime Kiln Bay.**

Sea Wolf Diving School. P.O. Box 289, Plymouth. ☎ **664/491-6859.**

This is the most professional and safety-conscious dive outfit on Montserrat, with a staff that has an intimate working knowledge of dive sites around the island. Headed by Wolf Krebs, former professor of anatomy at City College of New York, it's a PADI-registered school with a pair of dive boats, a policy of supervising only 10 divers at a time, and options that include dives designed for divers of all degrees of experience. At this writing, as a result of the volcanic crisis, the company operates out of the owner's private home in Woodlands. A snorkeling tour, lasting between 3 and 4 hours, costs from $25 to $35 per person, depending on the number of participants. Resort courses go for $70, including time spent in a swimming pool learning the basics of underwater breathing, plus time in the open water. A one-tank dive for experienced divers costs $50. Packages are available for stays on the island of a week or more, and the owners can arrange accommodation in private villas and guest houses throughout the island.

TENNIS Tennis buffs will find two asphalt courts at the previously recommended Vue Pointe Hotel, Old Towne. Residents play free, but nonresidents are charged EC$10 ($3.70) per hour. Two tennis courts are also available at the Montserrat Golf Club (see above) for those who pay court rental.

SEEING THE SIGHTS

The island is small, only 11 miles long and 7 miles across at its widest point. But seeing its former attractions is now a big problem. Virtually everything of geological or natural interest is off-limits or else covered in volcanic ash. For example, the former highest point, **Chances Peak,** which once rose to 3,000 feet, is now a minor bump (a local called it a "wart") and lies on the side of the massive, all-new volcano known as the **Soufrière Hills Volcano.** Naturally, this entire region is off-limits.

About a 15-minute drive from Plymouth, the ruined Fort St. George dates from the 18th century and can still be visited as it lies in a "safe zone." The fort is 1,184 feet above sea level and offers panoramic views. At yet another fortification, Bransby Point, you can see restored cannons. The early earthworks date from 1640 to 1660.

SHOPPING

There is no duty-free shopping, but some interesting locally made handcrafts are for sale. Straw goods and small ceramic souvenirs predominate, along with Sea Island cotton fabrics. Most shops are open Monday to Saturday from 8am to noon and 1 to 4pm, but they usually close at 12:30pm on Wednesday.

Carol's Corner, in the Vue Pointe Hotel, Old Towne (☎ **664/491-5210**), offers one of the best collections of Montserrat-related memorabilia on the island, including the famous stamps of Montserrat and copies of the difficult-to-obtain flag. There's also a collection of road maps, T-shirts, a selection of local jams and honey, and cosmetics and sundries as well.

MONTSERRAT AFTER DARK

Montserrat may be sleepy during the day, but it gets even quieter at night. The main center of activity is the Vue Pointe Hotel, Old Towne (☎ **664/491-5210**), where a steel band plays every Wednesday night, when you can order a barbecue dinner for EC$77 ($24.40) per person.

The **Village Place,** Salem (☎ **664/491-5202**), is for nostalgic rock buffs. If you weren't looking for it, you might think that its encircling hibiscus fences concealed a private house. Set north of Plymouth and directly east of Old Towne, it's one of the most popular night bars and most enduring restaurants on Montserrat. Serving endless rounds of beer and a lethal version of rum punch concocted by owner Andy Lawrence, it has been frequented by a number of legendary rockers, including Eric Clapton, Sting, and Mick Jagger. Elton John proposed to his wife here. Many visitors come just to drink, but if you want a meal, excellent fried chicken and barbecued spareribs are served by Andy's hardworking wife, Sonia. Sonia is an island legend for her "Impossible Pie"; its recipe is known only to her, although we know it requires patience, experience, and coconut juice. Snacks and main courses run from EC$2 to EC$35 (75¢ to $12.95). It's open Tuesday to Sunday from 6pm to very late.

3 St. Kitts

St. Kitts has become a resort mecca in recent years. Its major crop is sugar, a tradition dating from the 17th century. But tourism may overwhelm it in the years to come, as its southeastern peninsula, site of the best white-sand beaches, has been set aside for massive hotel and resort development. Most of the island's other beaches are of gray or black volcanic sand.

Far more active and lively than Nevis, its companion island, St. Kitts is still fairly sleepy itself. But go now before its lifestyle changes forever.

At some point during your visit you should eat sugar directly from the cane. Any farmer will sell you a huge stalk, and there are sugarcane plantations all over the island—just ask your taxi driver to take you to one. You strip off the hard exterior of the stalk, bite into it, chew on the tasty reeds, and swallow the juice. It's best with a glass of rum.

The Caribs, the early settlers, called the island Liamuiga, or "fertile isle." Its mountain ranges reach up to nearly 4,000 feet, and its interior contains virgin rain forests, alive with hummingbirds and wild green vervet monkeys. The monkeys were brought in as pets by the early French settlers and were turned loose in the forests when the island became British in 1783. These native African animals have proliferated and can be seen at the Estridge Estate Behavioral Research Institute. Another import, this one British, is the mongoose, brought in from India as an enemy of rats in the sugarcane fields. However, the mongooses and rats operate on different time cycles—the rats ravage while the mongooses sleep. Wild deer are found in the mountains.

Sugarcane climbs right up the slopes, and there are palm-lined beaches around the island. As you travel around St. Kitts, you'll notice ruins of old mills and plantation houses, as well as lots of trees and rich vegetation.

Once a British colony, St. Kitts was given self-government in 1967, and, along with Nevis, to which it's tied politically, it became a state in association with Britain. Anguilla, included in this associated state at the time, eventually broke away. On September 19, 1983, the Federation of St. Kitts and Nevis became a totally independent nation, complete with U.N. membership.

The capital, **Basseterre,** lies on the Caribbean shore near the southern end of the island, about a mile from Robert L. Bradshaw International Airport, where you'll land. With its white colonial houses with toothpick balconies, it looks like a Hollywood version of a West Indian port.

For decades St. Kitts and Nevis slumbered as backwaters of the Caribbean, but in recent years celebrities have been spotted here, almost for the first time. This doesn't mean, of course, that St. Kitts and Nevis are playgrounds for the rich and famous—not yet. But people who can go anywhere have selected St. Kitts and Nevis as their vacation choice, including Princess Di, James Michener, Oprah Winfrey, Sylvester Stallone, Barbara Mandrel, Danny Glover, Robert DeNiro, Michael J. Fox, and even

Gerald and Betty Ford. Sharon Stone herself has expressed interest in acquiring a getaway house here.

GETTING THERE

Dozens of daily flights on **American Airlines** (☎ **800/433-7300**) land in San Juan, Puerto Rico. From there, **American Eagle** (same phone) makes four daily nonstop flights into St. Kitts.

If you're already on St. Maarten and want to visit St. Kitts (with perhaps a side trip to Nevis), you can do so aboard one of the most remarkable little airlines in the Caribbean. Known by its nickname, **Winair** (Windward Islands Airways International; ☎ **809/465-2186**), it makes three flights a week from St. Maarten to St. Kitts, with easy connections to or from such other Dutch islands as Saba, St. Eustatius, and about a dozen other destinations throughout the Caribbean.

Another possibility involves transfers into St. Kitts or Nevis through Antigua, St. Maarten, or San Juan on the Antigua-based carrier, **LIAT** (☎ **268/465-2286**).

GETTING AROUND

BY TAXI Since most taxi drivers are also guides, this is the best means of getting around. You don't even have to find a driver at the airport—one will find you. Drivers also wait outside the major hotels. Before heading out, however, you must agree on the price—taxis aren't metered. Also, ask if the rates quoted to you are in U.S. dollars or the Eastern Caribbean dollar. To go from Robert L. Bradshaw International

Airport to Basseterre costs about EC$16 ($5.90); to Sandy Point, EC$36 ($13.30) and up.

BY RENTAL CAR The only U.S.-based car-rental firm maintaining a representative on St. Kitts is **Avis,** South Independence Square (☎ **800/331-2112** in the U.S., or 869/465-6507). It charges $45 to $50 per day, $270 to $300 per week, plus $10 per day for collision damage, with a $250 deductible. Nine-seat station vans are available for $70 per day or $240 per week. Tax is 5% extra, and a week's rental allows a seventh day for free. The company offers free delivery service to either the airport or to any of the island's hotels. Drivers must be between ages 25 and 75.

Delisle Walwyn & Co., Liverpool Row, Basseterre (☎ **869/465-8449**), is a local company offering cars and jeeps. This might be your best deal on the island.

Remember: *Driving is on the left!* You'll need a local driver's license, which can be obtained at the Traffic Department, on Cayon Street in Basseterre, for EC$40 ($14.80). Usually a member of the staff at your car-rental agency will drive you to the Traffic Department to get one.

FAST FACTS: St. Kitts

Banking Hours If you want to change your U.S. dollars into Eastern Caribbean dollars, you'll find banks open Monday to Thursday from 8am to noon and on Friday from 8am to noon and 3 to 5pm.

Currency The local currency is the **Eastern Caribbean dollar (EC$),** valued at about $2.70 to the U.S. dollar. Many prices, however, including those of hotels, are quoted in U.S. dollars. Always determine which "dollar" locals are talking about.

Customs You are allowed in duty free with your personal belongings. Sometimes luggage is subjected to a drug check.

Drugstores The **Skeritt's Drug Store,** Fort Street, Basseterre (☎ **869/465-2008**), is open Monday to Saturday from 8am to 6pm. When the pharmacy is closed, you can call for 24-hour prescription service at 869/465-2083.

Electricity St. Kitt's electricity is 230 volts AC (60 cycles), so you'll need an adapter and a transformer for U.S.-made appliances.

Emergencies Dial ☎ **911.**

Entry Requirements U.S. and Canadian citizens can enter with proof of citizenship, such as a voter registration card or birth certificate. British subjects need a passport, but not a visa.

Hospital In Basseterre, there's a 24-hour emergency room at **Joseph N. France General Hospital,** Buckley Site (☎ **869/465-2551**).

Information Tourist information is available from the tourist board's **Stateside offices** at 414 E. 75th St., New York, NY 10021 (☎ **800/582-6208** or 212/535-1234); 1464 Whippoorwill Way, Mountainside, NJ 07092 (☎ **908/232-6701**). In **Canada,** an office is at 365 Bay St., Suite 806, Toronto, ON, M5H 2V1 (☎ **416/368-6707**), and in the **United Kingdom** at 10 Kensington Court, London, W8 5DL (☎ **0171/376-0881**). **On the island,** the local tourist board operates at Pelican Mall, Bay Road in Basseterre (☎ **869/465-4040**), open Monday and Tuesday from 8am to 4:30pm and Wednesday through Friday from 8am to 4pm.

Language English is the language of the island and is spoken with a decided West Indian patois.

Police In an emergency, call ☎ **911.**

Safety This is still a fairly safe place to travel. Most crimes against tourists, and there aren't a lot, are robberies on Conaree Beach, so exercise the usual precautions. It would be wise to safeguard your valuables. Women should not go jogging alone along deserted roads.

Taxes The government imposes a 7% tax on rooms and meals, plus another EC$27 ($10) airport departure tax (but not to go to Nevis).

Telecommunications Telegrams and Telexes can be sent from **Skantel,** Cayon Street, Basseterre (☎ **869/465-1000**), Monday to Friday from 8am to 6pm, on Saturday from 7:30am to 1pm, and on Sunday and public holidays from 6 to 8pm. International telephone calls, including collect calls, can also be made from this office.

Time St. Kitts is on Atlantic standard time all year. This means that in winter when it's 6am in Basseterre, it's 5am in Miami or New York. When the U.S. goes on daylight saving time, St. Kitts and the East Coast mainland are on the same time.

Tipping Most hotels and restaurants add a service charge of 10% to cover tipping. If not, tip 10% to 15%.

Water The water on St. Kitts and Nevis is so good that Baron de Rothschild's chemists selected St. Kitts as their only site in the Caribbean to distill and produce CSR (Cane Sugar Rothschild), a pure sugarcane liqueur.

Weather St. Kitts lies in the tropics, and its warm climate is tempered by the trade winds. The average air temperature is 79°F, and the average water temperature is 80°F. Dry, mild weather is usually experienced from November to April; May to October it's hotter and rainier.

WHERE TO STAY

VERY EXPENSIVE

✪ **Golden Lemon.** Dieppe Bay, St. Kitts, W.I. ☎ **869/465-7260.** Fax 869/465-4019. 7 rms, 15 suites. A/C. Winter, $290–$365 double; from $435 suite. Off-season, $215–$260 double; from $340 suite. Rates include American breakfast. Four-night minimum stay required in winter. Honeymoon packages available. AE, DC, MC, V.

Arthur Leaman, one-time decorating editor of *House & Garden* magazine, has used his taste and background to create a hotel of great charm in this once-busy shipping port. The 1610 French manor house with an 18th-century Georgian upper story is set back from a coconut grove and a black volcanic-sand beach beyond St. Paul's, on the northwest coast of St. Kitts. Flanking the Great House are the Lemon Court and Lemon Grove Condominiums, where you can rent luxuriously furnished suites surrounded by manicured gardens. Most have private pools. The spacious rooms are furnished with antiques and always contain fresh flowers, but are not air-conditioned. Sophisticated and elegant describe both the Golden Lemon and its clientele. Children 15 and under are not accepted.

Dining/Entertainment: The Golden Lemon Restaurant serves a fine continental and Caribbean cuisine (see "Where to Dine," below).

Services: Massage, laundry, duty-free shopping.

Facilities: Swimming pool, tennis, snorkeling, rain-forest trips, horseback riding, scuba diving, day trips to other islands.

✪ **Ottley's Plantation Inn.** Ottley's (P.O. Box 345, Basseterre), St. Kitts, W.I. ☎ **800/772-3039** in the U.S., or 869/465-7234. Fax 869/465-4760. 15 rms. A/C. Winter, $330–$450 double. Off-season, $265–$325 double. Rates include MAP. Additional person $100–$120 extra. Wedding, honeymoon, and other packages available. AE, MC, V.

North of Basseterre on the east coast, beyond Hermitage Bay, Ottley's became one of the most desirable places to stay on the island shortly after it opened in 1989. It's 6 miles north of the airport. For those seeking charm and tranquility, it occupies a 35-acre site on a former West Indian plantation founded in the 18th century, near a rain forest. Nine rooms are in an 1832 Great House and six are divided among three cottages, with air-conditioning and overhead fans. One structure is called English cottage, in memory of a visit by Princess Margaret.

The innkeepers are Ruth and Art Keusch, who operated a chain of bookstores in the northeastern United States, and Nancy and Marty Lowell. The Great House contains a sitting room and library with an extensive collection of classic books and videos. Children 9 and under are "discouraged."

Dining/Entertainment: The plantation operates one of the best restaurants on the island, the Royal Palm (see "Where to Dine," below). There's a Sunday champagne brunch. With a day's advance notice, the kitchen will prepare a box lunch with directions on how to reach one of many secluded beaches on the southeastern peninsula.

Services: Room service for continental breakfast, laundry, baby-sitting, massage; daily shuttle to the beach, tennis, shops, golf course.

Facilities: Spring-fed, granite-tiled, 65-foot swimming pool in an old sugar factory; extensive tropical gardens and an on-site rain-forest ravine with walking trails.

Rawlins Plantation. P.O. Box 340, Mount Pleasant, St. Kitts, W.I. ☎ **800/346-5358** in the U.S., 869/465-6221, or 0171/730-7144 in London. Fax 869/465-4954. 10 rms. Winter, $390 double. Off-season, $275 double. Rates are MAP and include afternoon tea. AE, MC, V. Closed Sept–Oct.

This hotel near Dieppe Bay is situated among the remains of a muscovado sugar factory just outside St. Paul's, on the northeast coast, with a good sandy beach just a short drive away. The rather isolated former plantation is 350 feet above sea level and enjoys cooling breezes from both ocean and mountains. Behind the grounds the land rises to a rain forest and Mount Liamuiga.

A 17th-century windmill has been converted into a charming accommodation, complete with private bath and sitting room; and the boiling houses, which formerly housed caldrons of molasses, have been turned into a cool courtyard where guests dine amid flowers and tropical birds. Accommodations are pleasantly decorated cottages equipped with modern facilities. There is no air-conditioning, but ceiling fans and cross ventilation keep it cool.

Dining/Entertainment: A $25 West Indian buffet lunch is served daily. One critic called the food here "a mix of Kittitian, serious Cordon Bleu, and love and inspiration." In the evening elegant dinners are offered at a fixed price of $45, and reservations are required. Afternoon tea is also served and is included in the MAP rates.

Services: Free laundry.

Facilities: Spring-fed swimming pool, grass tennis court, croquet lawn.

The White House. P.O. Box 436, St. Peter's, St. Kitts, W.I. ☎ **800/223-1108** in the U.S. and Canada, or 869/465-8162. Fax 869/465-8275. 8 rms. Winter, $375 double. Off-season, $275 double. Rates are MAP and include afternoon tea. AE, MC, V. Closed July–Aug.

Small and special, the White House boasts a plantation Great House ambience. Set at the foot of Monkey Hill, overlooking Basseterre, it's directly west of Golden Rock Airport. The beach at Frigate Bay is a 10-minute ride away. Set in stone cottages, the guest rooms are bright and airy, with four-poster beds and Laura Ashley fabrics. Each one is individually decorated, and there's no air-conditioning except for ceiling fans and cross ventilation.

Dining/Entertainment: The menu changes daily, capitalizing on fresh fish in particular and locally grown ingredients. It's a zesty international cuisine with West Indian overtones. Since the hoteliers here own the Georgian House restaurant (see below), arrangements can be made for MAP to dine there as well.

Services: Room service, laundry, shuttle to the beach (15 minutes away).

Facilities: Swimming pool.

EXPENSIVE

Jack Tar Village St. Kitts Beach Resort & Casino. Frigate Bay (P.O. Box 406), St. Kitts, W.I. ☎ **800/999-9182** in the U.S., or 869/465-8651. Fax 869/465-1031. 241 rms, 3 suites. A/C TV TEL. Winter, $280–$310 double. Off-season, $190–$220 double. Suites $380 winter, $265 off-season. Rates include meals, golf fees, drinks, and most water sports. Children 5–12 sharing parents' room $60 extra in winter, nothing off-season. AE, MC, V.

The largest hotel on St. Kitts, and the showcase of the much-touted Frigate Bay development, is 1½ miles east of the airport. It's set on a flat, sandy isthmus between the sea and a saltwater lagoon. It seems a lot like a frenetic private country club, and it's almost completely self-contained. Each of the regular units has a patio or balcony and very simple tropical furniture. Most visitors prefer the second-floor rooms because of the higher ceilings. When you check in, ID tags are issued for security purposes.

Dining/Entertainment: The resort has two restaurants, serving a cuisine more bountiful than gourmet, a number of bars, and the island's only casino. Organized activities include Scrabble and shuffleboard tournaments, scuba lessons, and toga contests.

Services: Laundry, baby-sitting, an array of activities for kids.

Facilities: Two swimming pool areas (one for quiet reading, another for active sports), four tennis courts (two lit at night); golf course nearby.

MODERATE

Bird Rock Beach Hotel. P.O. Box 227, Basseterre, St. Kitts, W.I. ☎ **800/621-1270** in the U.S., or 869/465-8914. Fax 869/465-1675. 26 rms, 12 studios. A/C TV TEL. Winter, $140–$150 double; $240–$320 studio. Off-season, $75–$80 double; from $125–$170 studio. AE, MC, V.

Set on a secluded, half-moon-shaped beach 2 miles southeast of Basseterre, this small, white-sided resort is clean, uncomplicated, and easy-going. Views from the balconies of most of the bedrooms are either of the Bay of Basseterre and the capital or of the ocean stretching toward Nevis. Each of the studios contains a kitchen; all the units have private patios or balconies and rather bland furniture inspired by the tropics. There's a swimming pool with its own swim-up bar, a tennis court, a beachfront snack bar with a well-attended happy hour, and an evening restaurant with a well-prepared international cuisine.

Colony's Timothy Beach Resort. Frigate Bay (P.O. Box 1198, Basseterre), St. Kitts, W.I. ☎ **800/777-1700** in the U.S., or 869/465-8597. Fax 869/466-7085. 60 rms and suites. Winter, $195–$230 double; $165–$265 suite. Off-season, $65–$85 double; $95–$125 suite. AE, MC, V.

Located on a beach at the foot of a green mountain, this resort, a family favorite, is the only hotel on Caribbean Beach at Frigate Bay. It's located 3 miles east of Basseterre. Though short on island atmosphere, it opens onto one of the finest beaches on St. Kitts. Naturally the most sought-after units in this one- and two-bedroom condo complex are those opening directly onto the beach, with swimming, sailing, and water sports at your doorstep. There's also a swimming pool, and it's just a short drive from an 18-hole golf course. The rooms are furnished in a Caribbean motif, and the larger accommodations have kitchens.

Guests are booked in on the European plan (no meals), but they can patronize the increasingly popular Coconut Café, which features informal beachfront dining. Dinners at the cafe are particularly restful, and fresh grilled seafood is a specialty.

Frigate Bay Resort. P.O. Box 137, Frigate Bay, St. Kitts, W.I. ☎ **800/266-2185** in the U.S., or 869/465-8935. Fax 869/465-7050. 40 rms, 24 suites. A/C TV TEL. Winter, $123–$173 double; $263 one-bedroom suite; $373 two-bedroom suite. Off-season, $75–$107 double; $170 one-bedroom suite; $215 two-bedroom suite. MAP $37 per person extra. Honeymoon, dive, and golf packages available. AE, MC, V.

On a verdant hillside east of Basseterre, the Frigate Bay has standard rooms and condominium suites administered as hotel units for their absentee owners. The rooms are nicely furnished to the taste of the owners and painted in an array of pastel colors. They have cool tile floors, air-conditioning and ceiling fans, and private balconies. Many rooms have fully equipped kitchens with breakfast bars. The central core of the resort contains a large swimming pool and a cabana bar where you can enjoy a drink while partially immersed. The Garden Room Restaurant, overlooking the swimming pool and featuring its own swim-up bar, is open for three meals a day. An 18-hole golf course and tennis courts are within walking distance, and the beach is a four-minute walk from the hotel.

Ocean Terrace Inn. P.O. Box 65, Fortlands, St. Kitts, W.I. ☎ **800/524-0512** in the U.S., 800/267-7600 in Canada, 869/465-2754, or 0181/367-5175 in London. Fax 869/465-1057. 54 rms, efficiencies, and apts. A/C TV TEL. Winter, $116–$225 double; $165 efficiency for 2; $242–$346 one- or two-bedroom apt. Off-season, $101–$164 double; $138 efficiency; $177–$235 one- or two-bedroom apt. AE, DC, DISC, MC, V. Go west along Basseterre Bay Rd. past the Cenotaph.

The Ocean Terrace Inn is affectionately known as the "OTI" by its mainly business clients. If you want to be near Basseterre, it's the best hotel around the port. The OTI, with oceanfront verandas, commands a view of the harbor and the capital. It's so compact that a stay here is like a house party on a great liner. Terraced into a landscaped hillside above the edge of Basseterre, the hotel also has gardens and well-kept grounds.

All the handsomely decorated bedrooms have a light, tropical feel and overlook a well-planted terrace. In addition to its small, rather standard rooms in the hillside buildings, the hotel offers the Fisherman's Wharf and Village, a few steps from the nearby harbor. These apartments are filled with most of the comforts of home.

Dining/Entertainment: The flagstone-edged swimming pool has a row of underwater stools where you'll be served drinks while still immersed. Our favorite of the four bars is in the shadow of an elaborate aviary. For further details on the cuisine here, see "Where to Dine," below.

Services: Room service, laundry, baby-sitting.

Facilities: Two pools, Jacuzzi, water sports, scuba diving. Rain-forest safaris, historic-plantation tours, deep-sea fishing, snorkeling adventures, and island tours available through the hotel reception. A free shuttle hauls you to Turtle Beach, a 25-minute drive away.

WHERE TO DINE

EXPENSIVE

The Georgian House Restaurant. S. Independence Sq., Basseterre. ☎ **869/465-4049.** Reservations recommended. Main courses $20–$30. AE, MC, V. Mon–Sat 7–9:30pm. Closed July. INTERNATIONAL.

This restaurant occupies the most historic and notorious building on St. Kitts, but until it was taken over in 1995 by Janice and Malcolm Barber (English-born owners of the also-recommended White House Hotel), it languished in obscurity. It was erected "shortly after 1727" as the backdrop for the island's slave market, whose victims were purchased and sold in the square outside.

You'll find a genteel atmosphere inside, enhanced with crystal, Wedgwood porcelain, flickering candlelight, and the cuisine of Ms. Barber. In the 1980s this restaurant was known as the finest on St. Kitts. It closed but has now reopened, although perhaps never to regain its once-dominant reputation since there's so much more competition today. But it does now rank among the best, as reflected by such savory dishes as its black-bean cakes with shrimp and a zesty callalou soup. Filet steak you can get anywhere, but here it's served in an innovative mustard-pumpkin sauce. Grilled red snapper is appealing almost anywhere, but the chef does it especially well here, and, perhaps in an attempt to gild the lily, adds shrimp and flavors it with sesame. For dessert, the "banoffee cheesecake," made with caramel, bananas, and toffee, is a spectacular finish.

✪ **The Golden Lemon.** Dieppe Bay. ☎ **869/465-7260.** Reservations required. Fixed-price dinner $25–$50; Sun brunch $24. AE, DC, MC, V. Mon–Sat noon–3pm and 7–10:30pm, Sun noon–3pm (brunch) and 7–10:30pm. CONTINENTAL/CREOLE.

If you're touring St. Kitts, the best luncheon stop is at the Golden Lemon, a 17th-century house that's been converted into a fine hotel on the northern coast beyond St. Paul's. The food is very good, and the service is polite. Dinner is either served in an elegant, candlelit dining room, in the garden, or on the gallery. The cuisine features Creole, continental, and American dishes, with locally grown produce. Many of the recipes were created by the hotel's sophisticated owner (see previous recommendation). The menu changes daily, but is likely to include baked Cornish hen with ginger, fresh fish of the day, and Creole sirloin steak with a spicy rum sauce. Dress is casually chic.

The Patio. Frigate Bay Beach. ☎ **869/465-8666.** Reservations preferred. Main courses $26–$30. MC, V. Mon–Sat 7–9pm. Closed May 31–Dec 15. CARIBBEAN/INTERNATIONAL.

The Patio is at the private home of a Kittitian family, the Mallalieuses, six minutes southwest of the airport. Complimentary drinks are served in the flower garden just a few feet from the house. The family's high-ceilinged modern living room is transformed into a dining room with antique furniture, tablecloths, and kerosene lanterns. Meals include home-grown vegetables and a fresh seafood menu that changes nightly. Fresh lobster is cooked perfectly, never overdone, and the Black Angus beef is well flavored and tender. The orange-rum sauce certainly adds zest to the Long Island duckling, and the plantation roast loin of pork is spiked with ginger sauce for a tantalizing flavor. If you have any special menu requests, Peter Mallalieu will probably follow them; each dish is prepared to order. Dress is casual but elegant—no shorts, please.

✪ **The Royal Palm.** In Ottley's Plantation Inn, north of Basseterre, on the east coast. ☎ **869/465-7234.** Reservations required. Fixed-price 4-course dinner from $50; Sun champagne brunch $25. AE, MC, V. Mon–Sat noon–3pm, with dinner seating 7:30–8:30pm; Sun noon–2pm (brunch), with dinner seating 7:30–8:30pm. CARIBBEAN/FUSION.

Lying on the grounds of the previously recommended inn, the Royal Palm is an island favorite, serving the most creative cuisine on St. Kitts. It also has a picturesque setting: Gaze through the ancient stone arches to the ocean on one side and Mount Liamuiga and the inn's Great House on the other.

The restaurant is set beside the pool, and many diners prefer to visit it at night. The menu is changed daily, so you don't know what the inspiration of the moment will be. You might start with Brazilian gingered chicken soup or chili-flavored shrimp corn cakes, each equally tempting. The lobster quesadillas with local lobster, if featured, are worth crossing the island to sample. The dinner menu, wandering the globe for inspiration, is more elaborate, beginning perhaps with a white Cheddar and green chili bisque. The main courses tend to be impeccably prepared, especially the French roast of lamb or the breast of chicken Molyneux with almonds, country ham, mozzarella, and mushroom stuffing.

MODERATE

The Anchorage. Frigate Bay. ☎ **869/465-8235.** Main courses $13.50–$21.25. AE, MC, V. Mon–Thurs 11am–11pm, Fri–Sat 11am–midnight. WEST INDIAN/CONTINENTAL.

This isolated beachfront restaurant on the rolling acres of Frigate Bay isn't exactly famous for appearing in guidebooks. But when you're beaching it in the area or living in a condo nearby and don't want to cook dinner, it comes in handy. There's not much in the way of decor: In the shadow of a leafy tree, its tables are under a plain roof on a plain concrete floor. But if you're looking for that unspoiled beach restaurant, where everything is casual, you've come to the right joint. After a rum-based drink, you'll be ready to peruse the menu. At lunch you can order hamburgers or a dozen kinds of sandwiches along with fresh fish. If you return later, you may find lobster on the menu, either broiled or thermidor. The fresh catch of the day is prepared as you like it, or else you can order such old standbys as spareribs.

Ballahoo Restaurant. The Circus, Fort St., Basseterre. ☎ **869/465-4197.** Reservations recommended. Main courses EC$16–EC$55 ($5.90–$20.35). AE, MC, V. Daily 8am–10pm. CARIBBEAN.

Overlooking the town center's Circus Clock, the Ballahoo is about a block from the sea, on the second story of a traditional stone building. Its open-air dining area is one of the coolest places in town on a hot afternoon, thanks to the sea breezes. One of the best and most reliable dishes to order is Blue Parrot fish fillet. The chef also makes some of the best chili and baby back ribs in town. Seafood platters are served with a coconut salad and rice, and, for more elegant fare, there's Italian-style chicken breast topped with pesto tomatoes and cheese and served with a pasta and salad. The service is casual. Because of its central location, this restaurant draws the cruise-ship crowd.

Fisherman's Wharf Seafood Restaurant and Bar. Fortlands, Basseterre. ☎ **869/465-2754.** Reservations not required. Main courses $16–$26. AE, MC, V. Daily 6pm–midnight. SEAFOOD/CARIBBEAN.

At the west end of Basseterre Bay Road, the Fisherman's Wharf is between the sea and the white picket fence of the Ocean Terrace Inn. Near the busy buffet grill, hardworking chefs prepare fresh seafood. An employee will take your drink order, but you personally place your food orders at the buffet grill. It's a bit like eating at picnic tables, but the fresh fish selection is excellent, caught locally and grilled to order over St. Kitts chosha coals. Spicy conch chowder is a good starter; grilled lobster is an elegant main course choice, but you may prefer the grilled catch of the day, often snapper. Grilled swordfish steak is always a pleaser, as is the combination platter, which includes lobster, barbecued shrimp kebab, and calypso chicken breast.

Ocean Terrace Inn. Fortlands. ☎ **869/465-2754.** Reservations recommended. Main courses $15–$22; fixed-price 3-course lunch $15; fixed-price 4-course dinner $35. AE, DC, MC, V. Daily 7:30–9:30am, noon–2pm and 7:30–10:30pm. Drive west on Basseterre Bay Rd. to Fortlands. CARIBBEAN/INTERNATIONAL.

Some of the finest cuisine in Basseterre is found here, along with one of the best views, especially at night when the harbor is lit up. Dinner might include tasty fish cakes, accompanied by breaded carrot slices, creamed spinach, a stuffed potato, johnnycake, a cornmeal dumpling, and a green banana in a lime-butter sauce, topped off by a tropical fruit pie and coffee. The kitchen also prepares French or English dishes along with some flambé specialties, including Arawak chicken, chateaubriand, steak Diane, and veal Fantasia. The kitchen is best when preparing the real down-home dishes of the island instead of the blander international specialties. Some form of entertainment is often presented. Dining is on an open-air veranda.

StoneWalls. Princes Street. ☎ **869/465-5248.** Main courses $15–$22. AE, MC, V. Mon–Sat 5–11pm. CARIBBEAN/CAJUN.

Surrounded by ancient stone walls, this casual, open-air bar in a tropical garden in Basseterre's historical zone is cozy and casual. It's the type of Caribbean bar you think exists, but can rarely find. In a garden setting featuring banana, plantain, lime and bamboo trees, and climbing bougainvillea and elephant ears, Wendy and Garry Steckles present an innovative and constantly changing menu. The fare might be Cajun, with blackened snapper and a zesty gumbo, or an authentic, spicy Dhansak-style curry. Hot off-the-wok stir fries are served along with sizzling Jamaican-style jerk chicken. Appetizers might include piquant conch fritters. A small but carefully chosen wine list is available.

Turtle Beach Bar & Grill. Southeastern Peninsula. ☎ **869/469-9086.** Reservations recommended. Main courses $8.50–$18.50. AE, MC, V. Sun–Fri noon–5pm, Sat noon–5pm and 7:30–10pm. Follow the Kennedy Simmonds Highway over Basseterre's Southeastern Peninsula; then follow the signs. SEAFOOD.

Set directly on the sands above Turtle Beach, this airy, sun-flooded restaurant is downhill from the entrance of the previously recommended Ocean Terrace Inn. Many clients spend the hour before their meal swimming or snorkeling beside the offshore reef; others simply relax beneath the verandas or shade trees (hammocks are available), perhaps with a drink in hand. Scuba diving, ocean kayaking, windsurfing, and volleyball are available, and a flotilla of rental sailboats moor nearby. Menu specialties are familiar stuff, but prepared with an often scrumptious flavor. Typical dishes might be stuffed broiled lobster, conch fritters, barbecued swordfish steak, prawn salads, and barbecued honey-mustard spareribs.

INEXPENSIVE

Pisces Restaurant & Bar. Cayon St., Basseterre. ☎ **869/465-5032.** Reservations recommended for dinner. Main courses EC$16.50–EC$55 ($6.10–$20.35). No credit cards. Daily 7am–midnight. CARIBBEAN.

An immediate local favorite since it opened in 1993, Pisces lies on Cayon Street behind the Glimbara Guest House in Basseterre. The restaurant is owned and operated by Nerita Godfrey, or "Rita," as she's affectionately known on the island. She specializes in seafood such as lobster, shrimp, and whelk. Each day she prepares some local dish, perhaps bullfoot soup with dinner rolls or a "cookup" (saltfish, pigtail, pig snout, chicken, and red peas), which is traditionally served on Tuesday. Her barbecued spareribs and conch stew are justly praised. On Saturday locals visit to sample her "goatwater," a savory goat stew. Lamb chops, pork chops, shrimp fried rice, and her special chicken are favorites of those who don't want to go too local. Throughout the day you can order a cheap breakfast, sandwiches, and burgers (cheese, fish, and veggie).

BEACHES, WATER SPORTS & OUTDOOR PURSUITS

BEACHES Beaches are the primary concern of most visitors, who find the swimming best at the twin beaches of **Banana Bay** and **Cockleshell Bay, Conaree Beach** (2 miles from Basseterre), talcum-powder-fine **Frigate Bay** (north of Banana Bay), and **Friar's Bay** (a peninsula beach that opens onto both the Atlantic and the Caribbean). The narrow peninsula in the southeast that contains the island's salt ponds also boasts the best white-sand beaches. All beaches, even those that border hotels, are open to the public. However, if you use the beach facilities of a hotel, you must obtain permission first and will probably have to pay a small fee.

DIVING, SNORKELING & OTHER WATER SPORTS Some of the best diving spots include **Nagshead,** at the south tip of St. Kitts. This is an excellent shallow-water dive starting at 10 feet and extending to 70 feet. A variety of tropical fish, eaglerays, and lobster are found here. The site is ideal for certified divers. Another good spot for diving is **Booby Shoals,** lying between Cow 'n' Calf Rocks and Booby Island, off the coast of St. Kitts. Booby Shoals has abundant sea life, including nurse sharks, lobster, and stingrays. Dives are up to 30 feet in depth, ideal for both certified and resort divers.

A variety of activities are offered by **Pro-Divers,** at Turtle Beach (☎ **869/465-3223**). You can swim, float, paddle, or go on scuba-diving and snorkeling expeditions from there. A two-tank dive costs $50 with your own equipment or $60 without equipment. Night dives are $50. A PADI certification is available for $300, and a resort course costs $75. Snorkeling trips lasting three hours are offered for $35 per person, and also day trips to Nevis, costing $25 each.

GOLF The **Royal St. Kitts Golf Course,** Frigate Bay (☎ **869/465-8339**), is an 18-hole championship golf course that opened in 1976, covering 160 acres. It's bounded on the south by the Caribbean Sea and on the north by the Atlantic Ocean, featuring 10 water hazards. The course rating is 72 and can be 5,349, 6,033, 6,476, or 6,918 yards, depending on which tees are being used. It's open daily from 7am to 7pm, charging $35 for greens fees for 18 holes. Cart rentals cost $40 for 18 holes. A bar and restaurant on-site opens daily at 7am.

TENNIS To play tennis, you have to call one of the hotels and inquire if courts are free. The best courts are at the **Bird Rock Beach Hotel,** 2 miles southwest of Basseterre (☎ **869/465-8914**), and at **Golden Lemon,** Dieppe Bay (☎ **869/465-7260**), which is the best place on the island for lunch if you're touring.

SEEING THE SIGHTS

The British colonial town of **Basseterre** is built around a so-called **Circus,** the town's round square. A tall green Victorian clock stands in the center of the Circus. After Brimstone Hill Fortress, this **Berkeley Memorial Clock** is the most photographed landmark of St. Kitts. In the old days, wealthy plantation owners and their families used to promenade here.

At some point, try to visit the **marketplace.** Here, country people bring baskets brimming with mangos, guavas, soursop, mammy apples, and wild strawberries and cherries just picked in the fields, and tropical flowers abound.

Another major landmark is **Independence Square.** Once an active slave market, it's surrounded by private homes of Georgian architecture.

You can negotiate with a taxi driver to take you on a tour of the island for about $55 for a three-hour trip, and most drivers are well versed in the lore of the island. Lunch can be arranged either at the Rawlins Plantation Inn or the Golden Lemon.

For more information, call the **St. Kitts Taxi Association,** The Circus, Basseterre (☎ **869/465-4253** during the day, or 869/465-7818 at night).

The ✪ **Brimstone Hill Fortress** (☎ **869/465-6211**), 9 miles west of Basseterre, is the major stop on any tour of St. Kitts. This historic monument, among the largest and best preserved in the Caribbean, is a complex of bastions, barracks, and other structures ingeniously adapted to the top and upper slopes of a steep-sided 800-foot hill.

The fortress dates from 1690, when the British attempted to recapture Fort Charles from the French. In 1782 an invading force of 8,000 French troops bombarded the fortress for a month before its small garrison, supplemented by local militia, surrendered. The fortress was returned to the British the following year, and they embarked on an intense program of building and reconstruction that resulted in the imposing military complex that came to be known as "The Gibraltar of the West Indies."

Today the fortress is the centerpiece of a national park of nature trails and a diverse range of plant and animal life, including the **green vervet monkey.** It's also a photographer's paradise, with views of mountains, fields, and the Caribbean Sea. On a clear day, you can see six neighboring islands.

Visitors will enjoy self-guided tours among the many ruined or restored structures, including the barrack rooms at Fort George, which comprise an interesting museum. The gift shop stocks prints of rare maps and paintings of the Caribbean. Admission is $5, half price for children. The Brimstone Hill Fortress National Park is open every day from 9:30am to 5:30pm.

In the old days, a large tamarind tree in the hamlet of **Half-Way Tree** marked the boundary between the British-held sector and the French half, and you can visit the site.

It was near the hamlet of **Old Road Town** that Sir Thomas Warner landed with the first band of settlers and established the first permanent colony to the northwest at Sandy Point. Sir Thomas's grave is in the cemetery of St. Thomas Church.

A sign in the middle of Old Road Town points the way to **Carib Rock Drawings,** all the evidence that remains of the former inhabitants. The markings are on black boulders, and the pictographs date from prehistoric days.

Two commercial tours might interest you. Get your driver to take you to the **Sugar Factory,** which is best visited February to July, when you can see raw cane processed into bulk sugar. As mentioned, a very light liqueur, CSR, is now being produced at the factory, and it's enjoyed with a local grapefruit drink, "Ting." You don't need a reservation to visit the factory.

Guests are also allowed to visit the **Carib Beer Plant,** an English lager beer-processing house. Carib Beer is the best in the West Indies, if sales are any indication. At the end of the tour through the plant, visitors are given a cold Carib in the lounge. Check before heading there to see if it's open.

Most visitors to St. Kitts or Nevis like to spend at least one day on the neighboring island. **LIAT** provides three daily flights to and from Nevis at a cost of EC$60 ($22.20) per person one way. Make reservations at the LIAT office on Front Street in Basseterre (☎ **869/465-2286**) instead of at the airport.

If you'd rather not fly, the government passenger ferry **M.V. *Caribe Queen*** departs from each island between 7 and 7:30am on Monday, Tuesday, Wednesday, Friday, and Saturday, returning at 4 and 6pm (check the time at your hotel or the tourist office). The cost is $4 each way.

Into the Volcano

Mount Liamuiga was dubbed "Mount Misery" long ago, but it sputtered its last gasp around 1692. This dormant volcano on the northeast coast is today one of the major highlights for hikers on St. Kitts. The peak of the mountain often lies under a cloud cover.

The ascent to the volcano is usually made from the north end of St. Kitts at Belmont Estate. The trail winds through a rain forest and travels along deep ravines up to the rim of the crater at 2,625 feet. The actual peak is at 3,792 feet. Figure on 5 hours of rigorous hiking to complete the round-trip walk, with 10 hours required from hotel pick-up to return.

The caldera itself has a depth of some 400 feet from its rim to the crater floor. Many hikers climb or crawl down into the dormant volcano. However, the trail is steep and slippery, so be careful. At the crater floor is a tiny lake along with volcanic rocks and various vegetation.

Greg's Safaris, P.O. Box Basseterre (☎ **869/465-4121**), offers guided hikes to the crater for $60 per person (a minimum of four needed), including breakfast and a picnic at the crater's rim. The same outfit also offers half-day rain-forest explorations, also with a picnic, for $40 per person.

SHOPPING

The good buys here are in local handcrafts, including leather items made from goatskin, baskets, and coconut shells. Some good values are also to be found in clothing and fabrics, especially Sea Island cottons. Store hours vary, but are likely to be 8am to noon and 1 to 4pm Monday to Saturday.

If your time on the island is limited, head first for the **Pelican Shopping Mall,** which contains some two dozen shops. Opened in 1991, it also offers banking services, a restaurant, and a philatelic bureau. Some major retail outlets in the Caribbean, including Little Switzerland, have branches at this mall. But don't confine all your shopping here. Check out the offerings along the quaintly named **Liverpool Row,** which has some unusual merchandise. Fort Street is also worth traversing.

Ashburry's. The Circus/Liverpool Row, Basseterre. ☎ **869/465-8175.**

A local branch of a chain of luxury-goods stores based on St. Maarten, this well-respected emporium sells discounted luxury goods including fragrances, fine porcelain, crystal by Baccarat, handbags by Fendi, watches, and jewelry. Discounts range from 25% to 30% below what you might pay in retail stores in North America, although the selection is similar to dozens of equivalent stores throughout the Caribbean.

Cameron Gallery. 10 N. Independence Sq., Basseterre. ☎ **869/465-1617.**

Britisher Rosey Cameron-Smith displays her watercolors and limited-edition prints of scenes from St. Kitts and Nevis at this gallery. In her work, she makes an effort to capture the essence of true West Indian life. Rosey is well known on the island for her paintings of Kittitian Carnival clowns, and she also produces greeting cards, postcards, and calendars and displays the works of some 10 to 15 other artists.

Island Hopper. The Circus, Basseterre. ☎ **869/465-1640.**

In the Circus, below the popular Ballahoo Restaurant, Island Hopper is one of St. Kitts's most patronized shops. It has the biggest inventory of any store on the island. There's a lot of merchandise, both West Indian and international, on two different floors. Notice the all-silk, loose-fitting shift-style dresses from China, the array of batiks made on St. Kitts, and outfits suited for everything from formal to casual sportswear.

Kate Design. Mount Pleasant. ☎ **869/465-7740.**

Set in an impeccably restored West Indian house, on a hillside below the Rawlins Plantation (see "Where to Stay," above), this is the finest art gallery on St. Kitts. Virtually all the paintings on display are by English-born Kate Spencer, whose work is well known throughout North America and Europe. Her still lifes, portraits, and paintings of island scenes range in price from $200 to $3,000 and have received critical acclaim from several different sources. Also for sale are a series of Ms. Spencer's silk-screened scarves, each crafted from extra-heavy stone-washed silk, priced at $84 to $125 each.

Lemonaid. At the Golden Lemon, Dieppe Bay. ☎ **869/465-7260.**

This bazaar-style shop at the Golden Lemon (see "Where to Stay," above) specializes in local antiques, crafts, artwork, jewelry, and silverware, and carries a full line of elegant fragrances, plus spa products and skin-care lotions. Island clothes include those from John Warden's Island collection. The shop also sells Kisha batik fashions from Bali.

Little Switzerland. In the Pelican Shopping Mall, Basseterre. ☎ **869/465-9859.**

This is the most elaborate emporium of luxury goods on St. Kitts, with a medley of jewels, wristwatches, porcelain, and crystal specifically selected for North American tastes. Lots of business is conducted when cruise ships pull up to the nearby wharves. Prices are set at about 25% to 30% less than what you might have paid for equivalent goods in North America, but the true bargains appear during the promotional sales. These continue almost without a break throughout the year, and although the individual pieces of jewelry change from sale to sale, discounts remain constant at around 40%. Most items can be wrapped and shipped for an additional charge.

The Linen and Gold Shop. In the Pelican Mall, Bay Rd., Basseterre. ☎ **869/465-9766.**

There's a limited selection of gold and silver jewelry sold here, usually in bold modern designs, but the real appeal of this shop is the tablecloths and napery. Laboriously handcrafted in China from cotton and linen, they include everything from doilies to napkins to oversized tablecloths. The workmanship is as intricate as anything you'll find in the Caribbean.

The Palms. In the Palms Arcade, Basseterre. ☎ **869/465-2599.**

The Palms specializes in island "things," including handcrafts; larimar, sea opal, pottery, and amber jewelry; West Indies spices, teas, and perfumes; tropical clothes by Canadian designer John Warden; and Bali batiks by Kisha.

Romney Manor. Old Road, 10 miles west of Basseterre. ☎ **869/465-6253.**

This is the most unusual factory in St. Kitts. It was built around 1625 as a manor house for sugar baron Lord Romney, during the era when St. Kitts was the premier stronghold of British military might in the Caribbean. For years, it was used as the headquarters and manufacturing center for a local clothier, Caribelle batiks, whose tropical cotton wear sold widely to cruise-ship passengers and holiday-makers from at least three outlets in the eastern Caribbean.

In 1995, a tragic fire and the hurricanes completely gutted the historic building. Currently, the manor is being rebuilt, although construction is going slow. In the meanwhile, consider a stopover here at least to admire the five acres of lavish gardens, where 30 varieties of hibiscus, rare orchids, huge ferns, and a 250-year-old saman tree still draw horticultural enthusiasts. Entrance to the gardens is free.

Rosemary Lane Antiques. 7 Rosemary Lane. ☎ **869/465-5450.**

This little nugget is housed in an early 19th-century Caribbean building painted purple and white so it'll stand out. The owner, Robert Cramer, has a choice collection of Kittitian, Caribbean, and international antiques, including furniture, paintings, silver, china and glass. He'll ship anywhere in the world.

A Slice of the Lemon. Fort St., Basseterre. ☎ **869/465-2889.**

Decorated in lemony-orange sunshine colors, this store has the largest selection of perfumes on St. Kitts, but frankly, we're not sure that they're sold at the lowest prices available. A bottle of Chanel No. 5 was about $20 less on board our ship than it was here, so if you're in the market for an upscale scent, be aware of your prices before you buy. One room of this store functions as an outlet for Portmeirion English bone china.

ST. KITTS AFTER DARK

The **Ocean Terrace Inn's (O.T.I.) Fisherman's Wharf,** Fortlands (see "Where to Stay," above), has a live band every Friday night from 8 to 10pm and a disc jockey from 10pm. The **Turtle Beach Bar and Grill,** on the southeast peninsula, has a popular seafood buffet on Sunday with a live steel band from 12:30 to 3pm; on Saturday it's beach disco time. There's no cover charge at the inn's Fisherman's Wharf or Turtle Beach Bar and Grill.

If you're in the mood to gamble, St. Kitts's only casino is at the **Jack Tar Village,** Frigate Bay (☎ **869/465-8651**). It's open to all visitors, who can try their luck at roulette, blackjack, poker, craps, and slot machines. The casino is open daily from 10:30am to 2am. There's no cover charge.

4 Nevis

A local once said that the best reason to go to Nevis was to practice the fine art of *limin'*. To him, that meant doing nothing in particular. Limin' might still be the best reason to venture over to Nevis, a small volcanic island. Once here, you can stay at the lovely Four Seasons, or find lodging in one of the old plantation houses, now converted to inns, and experience the calm still found on Nevis. If you want to go to lie on the sands, head for reef-protected Pinney's Beach, a 3-mile strip of dark-gold sand set against a backdrop of palm trees, with panoramic views of St. Kitts.

Two miles south of St. Kitts, Nevis (*NEE-vis*) was sighted by Columbus in 1493. He called it Las Nieves, Spanish for "snows," because its mountains reminded him of the snow-capped range in the Pyrenees. When viewed from St. Kitts, the island appears like a perfect cone, rising gradually to a height of 3,232 feet. A saddle joins the tallest mountain to two smaller peaks, Saddle Hill (1,250 feet) in the south and Hurricane Hill (only 250 feet) in the north. Coral reefs rim the shoreline, and there's mile after mile of palm-shaded white-sand beaches.

Settled by the British in 1628, the volcanic island is famous as the birthplace of Alexander Hamilton, the American statesman who wrote many of the articles contained in the *Federalist Papers* and was Washington's secretary of the treasury. (He was killed by Aaron Burr in a duel.) Nevis is also the island on which Admiral Horatio Lord Nelson married a local woman, Frances Nisbet, in 1787. The historical facts are romanticized, but this episode is described in James Michener's best-seller *Caribbean.*

In the 18th century, Nevis, the "Queen of the Caribees," was the leading spa of the West Indies, made so by its hot mineral springs. Nevis was also once peppered with prosperous sugarcane estates, but they're gone now—many have been converted into some of the most intriguing hotels in the Caribbean. Sea Island cotton is the chief crop today.

As you drive around the island, through tiny villages such as Gingerland (named for the spice it used to export), you'll reach the heavily wooded slopes of Nevis Peak, which offers views of the neighboring islands. Nevis is an island of beauty and has remained relatively unspoiled. Its people, in the main, are descendants of African slaves.

On the Caribbean side, **Charlestown,** the capital of Nevis, was fashionable in the 18th century, when sugar planters were carried around in carriages and sedan chairs. Houses are of locally quarried volcanic stone, encircled by West Indian fretted verandas. A town of wide, quiet streets, this port only gets busy when its major link to the world, the ferry from St. Kitts, docks at the harbor.

GETTING THERE

BY PLANE You can fly to Nevis on **LIAT** (☎ **869/469-9333**), which offers regularly scheduled service to the island. Flights from St. Kitts and Antigua are usually nonstop, whereas flights from St. Thomas, St. Croix, San Juan, Barbados, and Caracas, Venezuela, usually require at least one stop before reaching Nevis. It's only a seven-minute hop from St. Kitts.

Nevis Express (☎ **869/469-9755**) operates a 16-flight daily shuttle service of six departures each way between St. Kitts and Nevis. A round-trip ticket from St. Kitts to Nevis costs $40. Call for reservations and information.

Any of North America's larger carriers, including **American Airlines** (☎ **800/433-7300**), can arrange ongoing passage to Nevis on LIAT through such hubs as Antigua, San Juan, or St. Maarten, connecting with your flight from North America.

The airport lies half a mile from Newcastle in the northern part of the island.

GETTING AROUND

BY TAXI Taxi drivers double as guides, and you'll find them waiting at the airport for the arrival of every plane. A taxi ride between Charlestown and Newcastle Airport costs EC$30 ($11.10); between Charlestown and Old Manor Estate, EC$26 ($9.60); and from Charlestown to Pinney's Beach, EC$10 ($3.70). Between 10pm and 6am, 50% is added to the prices for Charlestown trips.

BY FERRY You can also use the interisland ferry service from St. Kitts to Charlestown on Nevis aboard the government passenger ferry **M.V. *Caribe Queen.*** It departs from each island between 7 and 7:30am on Monday, Tuesday, Wednesday, Friday, and Saturday, returning at 4 and 6pm (check the time at your hotel or the tourist office). The cost is $4 each way.

BY RENTAL CAR If you're prepared to face the winding, rocky, potholed roads of Nevis, you can arrange for a rental car from a local firm through your hotel. Or you can check with **Skeete's Car Rental,** Newcastle Village, near the airport (☎ **869/469-9458**).

To drive on Nevis you must obtain a permit from the traffic department, which costs EC$30 ($11.10) and is valid for a year. Car-rental companies will handle this for you. Remember, *drive on the left side of the road.*

FAST FACTS: Nevis

Language, currency, and entry requirements have already been discussed in the St. Kitts section, earlier in this chapter. Most visitors will clear Customs on St. Kitts, so arrival on Nevis should not be complicated.

Banking Hours Banks are open Monday to Saturday from 8am to noon and most are also open on Friday from 3:30 to 5:30pm.

Drugstores Try **Evelyn's Drugstore,** Charlestown (☎ **869/469-5278**), open Monday to Friday from 8am to 5pm (closes at 4:30pm on Thursday), on Saturday from 8am to 7pm, and on Sunday for only one hour, from 7 to 8pm, to serve emergency needs.

Electricity As on St. Kitts, an electrical transformer and adapter will be needed for most U.S. and Canadian appliances as the electricity is 230 volts AC (60 cycles). However, check with your hotel to see if it has converted its voltage and outlets.

Emergencies For the police, call ☎ **911.**

Hospitals A 24-hour emergency room operates at **Alexandra Hospital** in Charlestown (☎ **869/469-5473**).

Information The best source is the Tourist Bureau on Main Street in Charlestown (☎ **869/469-1042**). For information before you go, refer to "Fast Facts: St. Kitts," in section 3 of this chapter.

Language English is the language of the island and is often accented with a lilting West Indian patois.

Post Office The post office, on Main Street in Charlestown, is open Monday to Wednesday and on Friday from 8am to 3pm, on Thursday from 8 to 11am, and on Saturday from 8am to noon.

Safety Although crime is rare here, protect your valuables and never leave them unguarded on the beach.

Taxes The government imposes a 7% tax on hotel bills, plus a departure tax of EC$27 ($10) per person. You don't have to pay the departure tax on Nevis if you're returning to St. Kitts.

Telecommunications Telegrams and telexes can be sent from the **Cable & Wireless office,** Main Street, Charlestown (☎ **869/469-5000**). International telephone calls, including collect calls, can also be made from the cable office. It's open Monday to Friday from 8am to 5pm, Saturday 8am to noon.

Time As with St. Kitts, Nevis is on Atlantic standard time year-round, which means it's usually one hour ahead of the U.S. East Coast, except when the mainland goes on daylight saving time; then clocks are the same.

Tipping A 10% service charge is added to your hotel bill. In restaurants it's customary to tip 10% to 15% of the tab.

Water In the 1700s, Lord Nelson regularly brought his fleet to Nevis just to collect water, and Nevis still boasts of having Nelson spring water.

WHERE TO STAY

VERY EXPENSIVE

✪ **Four Seasons Resort Nevis.** Pinney's Beach, Charlestown, Nevis, W.I. ☎ **800/332-3442** in the U.S., 800/268-6282 in Canada, or 869/469-1111. Fax 869/469-1112. 179 rms, 17 suites. A/C MINIBAR TV TEL. Winter, $575–$625 double; from $1,100 suite. Off-season, $220–$300 double; from $450 suite. MAP $80 per person extra. Up to 2 children stay free in parents' room. AE, DC, MC, V.

This hotel, run by the Toronto-based Four Seasons chain, is one of the Caribbean's world-class properties. It is hands-down the best hotel on Nevis. Located on the island's west coast, it's set in a palm grove beside Pinney's, the finest sandy beach on the island. On an island known for its small and intimate inns, this 1991 low-rise resort stands out as the largest and best-financed hotel on Nevis, with the most complete sports facilities (including a fabulous golf course). Designed in harmony with the surrounding landscapes, the accommodations offer rich but conservative mahogany furniture, touches of marble, carpeting, and wide patios or verandas overlooking the beach, the golf course, or Mount Nevis. Each contains all the amenities you'd expect, including hair dryers and bathrooms with double sinks. The public areas include rooms inspired by paneled libraries in London, complete with one of the few working fireplaces on Nevis.

Dining/Entertainment: Guests have the largest choice of bars and dining venues on Nevis. The resort's centerpiece is the plantation-inspired Great House, which contains the most formal restaurant of all, the Dining Room (see "Where to Dine," below). Other restaurants include the Grill Room (for steaks and barbecues), the Tap Room (similar to a British pub), the Pool Cabaña, the Ocean Terrace (drinks and light fare), and the most opulent watering hole on Nevis, the Library Bar.

Services: 24-hour room service, laundry, baby-sitting. Employees will arrange for diving, deep-sea fishing, boating, hiking, or shopping excursions. A flotilla of yachts is on hand to ferry hotel clients to and from the international airport on St. Kitts. There's also the Kids for All Seasons youth program, one of the most carefully planned programs in the Caribbean, and a supervised children's hour at 6pm daily in the Grill Room.

Facilities: Carved into the surrounding hills and valleys is a 18-hole Robert Trent Jones Jr.–designed golf course. The resort also boasts direct access to one of the finest beaches in the Caribbean, 10 tennis courts with three different surfaces, an on-site scuba department, massage facilities, health club, sauna, whirlpool, beauty salon, and two swimming pools.

✪ **Nisbet Plantation Beach Club.** Newcastle, St. James' Parish, Nevis, W.I. ☎ **800/742-6008** in the U.S. and Canada, or 869/469-9325. Fax 869/469-9864. 26 rms, 12 suites. Winter, $365 double; from $455 suite. Off-season, $255 double; from $295 suite. Rates include MAP. AE, DISC, MC, V. Turn left out of the airport and go 1 mile.

A respect for fine living prevails in this gracious estate house on a coconut plantation. This is the former home of Frances Nisbet, who married Lord Nelson at the age of 22. Although enamored of Miss Nisbet when he married her, Lord Nelson later fell in love with Lady Hamilton (as detailed in the classic film *That Hamilton Woman*).

The present main building was rebuilt on the foundations of the original 18th-century Great House. The ruins of a circular sugar mill stand at the entrance, covered with bougainvillea, hibiscus, and poinciana. Set in the palm grove are guest cottages consisting of superior and deluxe rooms with showers and covered verandas, and a series of deluxe suites and premier junior suites with private baths. All rooms come with king-size beds and are brightly decorated and beautifully appointed.

Dining/Entertainment: Breakfast and lunch are served at the Coconuts Beach and Poolside Restaurant, where a Thursday evening barbecue with a live band is served. Dinner is served inside the Great House. Local fish and lobster are featured, along with continental and American cuisine. Among the complimentary extras are afternoon tea and a rum-punch party.

Services: Laundry.

Facilities: Swimming pool, tennis court, snorkeling opportunities off the beach, 3 miles of beachcombing right in front of the hotel; scuba diving, sports fishing, sailing, horseback riding, ecorambles, mountain hiking, and golf at the Four Seasons can be arranged.

Romantik Montpelier Plantation Inn. St. John Figtree (P.O. Box 474), Montpelier, Nevis, W.I. ☎ **869/469-3462,** 416/484-4864 in Canada, 0181/367-5175 in England, or 212/599-8280 in New York City. Fax 869/469-2932. 17 rms, 1 two-bedroom suite. TEL. Winter, $280 double. Off-season, $180 double. Year-round, $330 suite. Rates include breakfast. Children under 8 not accepted in winter. MC, V. Closed mid-Aug through Sept.

One of the Plantation Inns of Nevis, the Montpelier stands in the hills, 700 feet high, with grandstand views of the ocean. It's owner-managed, and a house-party atmosphere prevails. Diana, Princess of Wales, made the inn her choice during a 1993 visit. Everything is done with style and grace. The 18th-century plantation is in the center of its own 100-acre estate, which contains 10 acres of ornamental gardens as a setting for the cottage rooms. Accommodations have ceiling fans and either one king-size bed or two double beds.

Dining/Entertainment: Montpelier focuses on the standards of its food, wine, and service. Much use is made of fresh local produce (see "Where to Dine," below). Breakfast is served in the garden room and dinner on a covered terrace overlooking the garden. In season, a steel or string band is brought in about every 10 days.

Services: Laundry, baby-sitting (evenings), room service (only for continental breakfast), complimentary transport to the inn's own private beach.

Facilities: Huge swimming pool with pool bar, hard tennis court, private beach 4 to 5 miles away but transportation provided, windsurfing, horseback riding, hiking, ecorambles.

EXPENSIVE

Golden Rock Estate. P.O. Box 493, Gingerland, Nevis, W.I. ☎ **869/469-3346.** Fax 869/469-2113. 14 rms, 1 suite. Winter, $255 double; $290 suite. Off-season, $180 double; $215 suite. Rates are MAP. Children under 2 stay free in parents' room. AE, MC, V.

This former sugar estate was built in 1815, high in the hills of Nevis. A 15-minute drive east of Charlestown, Golden Rock is one of the most charming and atmospheric inns in the Caribbean, set on 100 lushly tropical acres and fronted by a 25-acre garden. The original windmill, a stone tower, has been turned into a duplex honeymoon suite (or accommodations for a family of four), with a four-poster bed. Cottages are scattered about the garden, and each has four-poster king-size beds made of bamboo. Fabrics are island made, with tropical flower designs. In addition, the rooms have large porches with views of the sea.

There's access to one beach on the leeward side (part of Pinney's Beach) and another beach on the windward side (where there's surfing). The hotel also lies at the beginning of a rain-forest walk; it takes about three to four hours to follow the trail round-trip (the hotel provides a map).

Dining/Entertainment: Dinner is likely to be a West Indian meal served at the 175-year-old "long house." Saturday night from December to June there's a West Indian buffet, served plantation style, while a string band plays outside under the stars. Before dinner you can enjoy a drink in the hotel's bar. A separate facility at Pinney's Beach, the Old Fort, serves lobster, shrimp, grilled fish, and hamburgers with coconut-husk flavor; it's open daily during the winter season. Picnic lunches can be prepared in the hotel's kitchen.

Services: Laundry, baby-sitting, free round-trip shuttles to both beaches (with stops in Charlestown if requested).

Facilities: Freshwater swimming pool with a shady terrace (where tropical rum punches are served), tennis court, nature trail through the rain forest.

Hermitage Plantation. Hermitage Village, St. John's Parish, Nevis, W.I. ☎ **800/682-4025** in the U.S., or 869/469-3477. Fax 869/469-2481. 15 rms, 1 manor house. Winter, $260–$370 double. Off-season, $130–$220 double. Year-round, $600 manor house. MAP $50 per person extra. AE, MC, V. Proceed on the main island road 4 miles from Charlestown.

This much-photographed, frequently copied historians' delight is said to be the oldest all-wood house in the Antilles and was built amid the high-altitude plantations of Gingerland in 1740. Here, former Philadelphian Richard Lupinacci and his wife, Maureen, have assembled one of the best collections of antiques on Nevis. Wide-plank floors, intricate latticework, and high ceilings add to the hotel's beauty. The accommodations are in nine glamorous outbuildings designed like small plantation houses. Many contain huge four-poster beds, antique accessories, and colonial louvered windows. Gently sloping inland from the sea, the property is protected by rows of retaining walls. The most luxurious and expensive unit is a yellow manor house on a half acre of private gardens with its own ceramic-tile pool, two large bedrooms furnished with antique canopy beds, oversize baths with dressing rooms, a comfortable living room, dining room, full kitchen, and laundry.

Services: Laundry.

Facilities: Swimming pool, tennis court, thoroughbred stables. Complimentary beach transportation is provided; the best beach close by is a 15-minute drive away.

Mount Nevis Hotel & Beach Club. Newcastle (P.O. Box 494), Charlestown, Nevis, W.I. ☎ **800/75-NEVIS** in the U.S. and Canada, 869/469-9373, or 212/874-4276 in New York City. Fax 869/469-9375. 16 rms, 16 junior suites. A/C TV. Winter, $190–$215 double; $270 junior suite. Off-season, $130–$150 double; $190 junior suite. Rates include continental breakfast. Additional person $35 extra. AE, MC, V.

This family owned and run resort dating from 1989 is on the slopes of Mount Nevis, a five-minute drive southwest of Newcastle Airport. It's known for the quality of its accommodations, for its panoramic views, and for serving some of the best food on Nevis. Near the historic fishing village of Newcastle, it offers standard rooms and junior suites, the latter with fully equipped kitchens and space enough to accommodate at least four guests comfortably, making it an ideal family choice. The rooms have such amenities as VCRs and are furnished in a tropical motif, with wicker and colorful island prints.

Dining/Entertainment: The hotel's main restaurant is recommended separately (see "Where to Dine," below). Just a five-minute drive from the hotel, the Mount Nevis Beach Club offers a site on Newcastle Bay and features a beach pavilion, bar, PADI instructor, and restaurant. It pretty much introduced pizza to the island. The club is open November to June, daily from 10am to 10pm. Occasional entertainment is offered.

Services: Beach shuttle, room service (during mealtimes).

Facilities: Outdoor 60-foot swimming pool, water-sports program (with windsurfing, waterskiing, snorkeling, and deep-sea fishing at the beach club).

Old Manor Estate & Hotel. P.O. Box 70, Gingerland, Nevis, W.I. ☎ **800/892-7093** or 869/469-3445. Fax 869/469-3388. 13 rms. Winter, $195–$225 double. Off-season, $125–$185 double. MAP $37.50 per person extra. AE, MC, V.

East of Charlestown and north of Gingerland, at a cool and comfortable elevation of 800 feet, the Old Manor Estate & Hotel has an old-world grace, lying a 15- to 20-minute drive from Pinney's Beach, where the hotel operates its own beach bar and grill. When Nevis was originally colonized, the forested plot of land on which the hotel sits was granted to the Croney family in 1690 by the king of England. The estate thrived as a working sugar plantation until 1936. Today the stately ruins of its Great House, once described by British historians as "the best example of Georgian domestic architecture in the Caribbean," complement the hotel's outbuildings. The rusted flywheels of cane-crushing machines are scattered around the property. Since its acquisition by new owners in 1995, the hotel has been renovated and now has a far more cheerful, tropical appearance. The color scheme is green and light peach and blends beautifully with the cut stonework of the plantation buildings.

Each of the accommodations contains wide-plank floors of tropical hardwoods, reproduction furniture, and high ceilings.

The Cooperage dining room (see "Where to Dine," below) is among the best on the island. Facilities include a beach and town shuttle and a swimming pool.

Inexpensive

Hurricane Cove Bungalows. Oualie Beach, Nevis, W.I. ☎ **869/469-9462.** Fax 869/469-9462. 10 bungalows, 1 villa. Winter, $145 one-bedroom bungalow; $225–$265 two-bedroom bungalow; $395 three-bedroom villa. Off-season, $95 one-bedroom bungalow; $155–$195 two-bedroom bungalow; $225 three-bedroom villa. MC, V.

This cluster of self-contained bungalows is set on a hillside with a world-class view, a far better sight than the complex's rather ramshackle facade. It's located on the northernmost point of Nevis, a five-minute drive west of the airport. Each bungalow is wood-sided and vaguely Scandinavian in design, with a tile roof and a massive foundation that anchors it into the rocky hillside. No meals are served, but each bungalow contains a full kitchen, so guests can dine out every night or prepare meals themselves in their own kitchens or at a poolside barbecue grill. Each bungalow contains a queen-size bed, covered porch, and ceiling fan. There's a freshwater swimming pool built into the foundation of a 250-year-old fortification, and the beach lies at the bottom of a steep hillside. The three-bedroom villa has its own small but private pool.

Oualie Beach Club. Oualie Bay, Nevis, W.I. ☎ **869/469-9735.** Fax 869/469-9176. 18 rms, 4 studios. TV TEL. Winter, $175–$195 double; $255 studio. Off-season, $140–$155 double; $205 studio. AE, MC, V.

Set on low-lying flatlands adjacent to the white sands of the island's second-most-famous beach (Oualie Beach), this hotel contains four concrete outbuildings that offer a total of 22 accommodations. Each unit is clean and simple, with tiled floors, and the place is often fully booked several months in advance by European sun-worshipers. Eighteen rooms are air-conditioned, and many contain small, unstocked refrigerators; a few have kitchenettes. Set 5 miles east of Charlestown, on the island's relatively unpopulated north coast, the hotel was built in 1989. The resort's centerpiece is its well-recommended restaurant and bar, where doors open directly onto a view of the beach (see "Where to Dine," below).

WHERE TO DINE

VERY EXPENSIVE

✪ **The Dining Room.** In the Four Seasons Resort Nevis, Pinney's Beach. ☎ **869/469-1111.** Reservations recommended. Main courses $35–$45. AE, DC, MC, V. Tues–Sun 6:30–10pm. INTERNATIONAL/WEST INDIAN/ASIAN.

Set beneath a soaring, elaborately trussed ceiling, this is the largest and most formal dining room on Nevis, and the island's best and most super expensive restaurant. Decorated in a Caribbean interpretation of French Empire designs, it offers rows of beveled-glass windows on three sides, massive bouquets of flowers, hurricane lamps with candles, a fireplace, a collection of unusual paintings, and impeccable service.

The fusion cuisine, with lots of nouvelle touches, roams the world for inspiration. Only quality ingredients are used, and some dishes are low in fat and calories. You might opt to begin with a savory seafood gumbo or a Cuban black-bean soup with applewood-smoked bacon. The pan-seared salmon with a curried fruit relish is incomparably fragrant, although the grilled mahimahi with a wasabi-mango sauce would be an equally tempting alternative. Vegetarians also have options here, perhaps vegetable cannelloni gratiné with a purple-basil/tomato sauce. Dessert might be a flaming meringue "Mount Nevis." The service and the wine selection are the island's finest.

✪ **Miss June's.** Jones Bay. ☎ **869/469-5330.** Reservations required. Fixed-price meal $65 per person; off-season, $75 (Dec–Apr). MC, V. Three to 5 evenings a week, depending on business, beginning around 7:30pm. CARIBBEAN/INTERNATIONAL.

This charming dining venue is located in the private home of June Mestier, a Trinidad-born grande dame, and probably wouldn't exist if it had not been for an enthusiastic visit from Oprah Winfrey. On a recent trip, Oprah heard that Ms. Mestier was the finest cook on the island and arranged a private dinner; after being served an excellent meal, Oprah urged her to open a restaurant.

A dinner in Mestier's home requires advance reservations, and some visitors call before they even arrive on Nevis. The setting is midway between the Four Seasons Resort and the island's airport, in a house adorned with latticework and Victorian gingerbread. Guests at these dinner parties assemble for canapés and drinks in an airy living room, then sit down for soup and sherry. Fish and wine follow. All of this is followed with samples of about 20 buffet dishes that hail from Trinidad, New

Orleans, India, and the French isles. Ms. Mestier's comments on the food are one of the evening's most delightful aspects.

Seating is at tables holding 2 to 10 diners, and the silver and porcelain are quaintly elegant and charmingly mismatched. After the buffet, guests retire to a lounge for dessert and port. Many visitors find the meal to be one of the highlights of their visit to Nevis.

Expensive

Hermitage Plantation. Hermitage Village, St. John's Parish. ☎ **869/469-3477.** Reservations required. Dinner EC$94 ($34.80). AE, MC, V. Daily 8–10am, noon–3pm, and dinner at 8pm. Proceed south on the main island road from Charlestown. INTERNATIONAL.

At this restaurant you can combine an excellent dinner with a visit to the oldest house on Nevis, now one of the island's most unusual hotels (see "Where to Stay," above). Meals are served on the latticed porch of the main house, amid candles and good cheer. Maureen Lupinacci, who runs the place with her husband, Richard, combines continental recipes with local ingredients. Have a before-dinner drink in the colonial-style living room before you enjoy the likes of snapper steamed in banana leaves, carrot-and-tarragon soup, brown-bread ice cream, and a delectable version of rum soufflé. Many people turn up on Wednesday for the roast-pig dinner.

✪ **Mount Nevis Hotel Restaurant.** Newcastle. ☎ **869/469-9373.** Reservations recommended for dinner. Main courses $21–$29. AE, MC, V. Daily 8–10am, 11:30am–2:30pm, Mon–Sat 6:30–8:30pm. CARIBBEAN/CONTINENTAL.

This restaurant in the previously recommended hotel is a discovery, serving some of the finest cuisine on Nevis with menus that change every night. Just steps above the pool, the restaurant offers vistas of palm groves and the Caribbean Sea from its bar and dining terrace. You never know what's likely to be featured. A very smooth yet spicy conch chowder might get you going, or, equally as delectable, a coconut-fried lobster with a mango salsa providing that true island flavor. One soup, chilled gazpacho with papaya guacamole, might be a first for many diners. The standard fillet of salmon that occupies every menu in the Caribbean appears here with a novel twist, served with braised lentils, capers, and crispy shallots. And sliced loin of lamb is a fairly standard menu item, but here it's served with a christophene ratatouille. A worthy specialty is roast duck breast with a starfruit and red-onion confit. The lunch menu is more limited but still filled with some surprises—tannia fritters (instead of conch), for example. In addition to pita pockets and club sandwiches, you can even order a West Indian roti, the traditional Caribbean crepe.

Romantik Montpelier Plantation Inn. Montpelier. ☎ **869/469-3462.** Reservations recommended for lunch, required for dinner. Fixed-price 3-course dinner $55. MC, V. Daily 12:30–2pm and dinner at 8:15pm. Closed July–Sept. INTERNATIONAL.

This hotel, a mile off the main island road to Gingerland, provides some of the finest dining on the island. You dine by candlelight on the verandas of a grand old West Indian mansion, overlooking floodlit gardens, the lights of Charlestown, and the ocean. Lobster and fish are served the day the catch comes in, and the foreign and Nevisian chefs conspire to produce delectable tropical dishes. Menus might include Cajun prawns, fresh tuna salad, mussels Provençale, curried ackee, suckling pig, and soursop-and-orange mousse for dessert. There's one seating for dinner, so try to show up on time. An excellent and well-balanced wine list is available.

Moderate

✪ **The Cooperage.** In the Old Manor Estate, Gingerland. ☎ **869/469-3445.** Reservations recommended, especially for those not staying in the hotel. Main courses $13.50–$21. AE, MC, V. Daily 6:30am–9:30pm. INTERNATIONAL/CARIBBEAN.

Directly east of Charlestown and north of Gingerland, the Cooperage is set in a reconstructed 17th-century building where "coopers" once made barrels for the sugar mill. The dining room has a high, raftered ceiling and stone walls. The food doesn't even try to compete with that at the Four Seasons, but it's good and reliable. Some of the appetizers are those 1950s favorites: French onion soup or shrimp cocktail. For a main course you can order a 12-ounce New York strip steak or charcoal-grilled filet mignon with a béarnaise sauce. The grilled Caribbean lobster is also appealing, as is the Jamaican jerk pork or lamb loin chops. The menu harkens back to the days when appetites were more robust—main dishes are served with fresh vegetables of the day and your choice of twice-baked potato, rice, or pasta. Few leave hungry, especially after finishing with Old Manor's cheesecake, which has been sampled by all the movers and shakers on the island.

Oualie Beach Club. Oualie Bay. ☎ **869/469-9735.** Reservations recommended for dinner. Main courses $20–$30. AE, MC, V. Daily 7–10am, noon–4pm, and 6–11pm. INTERNATIONAL/NEVISIAN.

This restaurant is the centerpiece of the previously recommended Oualie Beach Club hotel, the only lodging adjacent to Oualie Beach. An airy, open-sided building with a pleasant staff and a setting a few steps from the ocean, it contains a bar area, a screened-in veranda, and a chalkboard menu containing the day's special. Depending on the catch that day, it might be broiled wahoo. The chef also prepares several lobster dishes, and the Creole conch stew is the island's best. Pastas also appear frequently on the menu, along with some fairly bland international dishes such as spinach-stuffed chicken breast. Every day, however, the chef prepares a creative menu with real Caribbean flair, so you may want to study it closely before ordering. Any of an array of brightly colored rum drinks is available, and you can get a reasonably priced breakfast or lunch here, too.

INEXPENSIVE

Eddy's. Main St., Charlestown. ☎ **869/496-5958.** Reservations not required. Dinner EC$28–EC$35 ($10.35–$13). AE, MC, V. Mon–Wed and Fri–Sat 11:45am–3pm and 7–9:30pm. INTERNATIONAL.

Set on the upper floor of a Nevisian house, this open-air, local restaurant offers an eagle's-eye view of street life in the island's capital. The balcony juts out over the pedestrian traffic below, and the clean and airy interior contains a tuckaway bar, lattices and gingerbread, and lots of tropical color. Menu items are posted on one of several signs and are among the best prepared in Charlestown. This is not a typical West Indian eatery; some of the dishes have real island flavor and sophistication. Begin perhaps with a roasted tomato soup with a tangy herbed yogurt or mixed greens with tannia-peanut fritters. Main dishes are likely to feature Eddy's fish cioppino with roasted-garlic mayonnaise croutons, his version of the classic Mediterranean fish stew. A juicy tandoori-sauced chicken marinated in yogurt and spices won our favor, as did the lime-glazed seafood kebabs with a black-bean salsa. Get Eddy to tell you about Tequila Sheila, his newer beach bar and restaurant.

Muriel's Cuisine. Upper Happyhill Dr., Charlestown. ☎ **869/469-5920.** Reservations recommended. Dinner EC$25–EC$55 ($9.25–$20.35). AE, MC, V. Daily 8–10am, 11:30am–4pm, and 7–10pm. WEST INDIAN.

This restaurant is in the back of a concrete building whose front is devoted to a store, Limetree. It's a six-minute walk from Charlestown's waterfront and set in an outlying neighborhood of low-rise commercial buildings. Head here for a slice of real island life, and for a West Indian cuisine that's typical of what the locals eat. Muriel's West Indian curries are the best in town, ranging from the simple goat or chicken to the more elaborate lobster. She also turns out some fabulous chicken or seafood rotis, or even a lobster Creole for those who want to get fancy. Her jerk pork or chicken would win the approval of a Jamaican, and her preparations of conch, stewed or curried, are worth the trip. If you want to go native all the way, ask for saltfish or goatwater stew. You can get a cheap breakfast or lunch here, too.

FUN ON & OFF THE BEACH

BEACHES The best beach on Nevis—in fact, one of the best beaches in the Caribbean—is the reef-protected ✪ **Pinney's Beach,** which has clear water, golden sands, and a gradual slope. It's just north of Charlestown on the west coast, 3 miles of uncrowded sand that culminate in a sleepy lagoon. It's best to bring your own sports equipment; while hotels are stocked with limited gear, it may be in use by other guests when you want it. You can go snorkeling or scuba diving among damselfish, tangs, grunts, blue-headed wrasses, and parrotfish, among other species.

BOAT CHARTERS & DEEP-SEA FISHING **Scuba Safaris,** an outfit that operates independently on the premises of the Oualie Beach Club (☎ **869/469-9518** or 809/469-9735), offers boat charters to Basseterre, Banana Bay, Cockleshell Bay, and other beaches, plus deep-sea fishing trips.

GOLF The **Four Seasons Golf Course,** Pinney's Beach (☎ **869/469-1111**), has one of the most challenging and visually dramatic golf courses in the world. Designed by Robert Trent Jones Jr. (who called it "the most scenic golf course I've ever designed"), this 18-hole championship golf course wraps around the resort and offers panoramic ocean and mountain views at every turn. From the first tee (which begins just steps from the well-accessorized Sports Pavilion), through the 660-yard, par-5, to the 18th green at the ocean's edge, the course is, in the words of one avid golfer, "reason enough to go to Nevis." Guests of the hotel pay $110 for 18 holes and nonguests are charged $135. Rental clubs are available, costing $40 for 18 holes.

HORSEBACK RIDING Horseback riding is available at the **Nisbet Plantation Beach Club,** Newcastle (☎ **869/469-9325**). You can ride English saddle, and the cost is $40 per person for 1½ hours. A guide takes you along mountain trails to visit sites of long-forgotten plantations.

MOUNTAIN CLIMBING Hikers can climb **Mount Nevis,** 3,232 feet up to the extinct volcanic crater, and enjoy a trek to the rain forest to watch for wild monkeys. This is strenuous and is recommended only to the stout of heart. Ask your hotel to pack a picnic lunch and arrange a guide (who will probably charge about $30 to $35 per person). The hike takes about 2½ hours and once at the summit you'll be rewarded with views of Antigua, Saba, Statia, St. Kitts, Guadeloupe, and Montserrat. Of course, you've got to reach that summit, which means scrambling up near-vertical sections of the trail requiring handholds on not-always-reliable vines and roots. It's definitely not for acrophobes! Guides can be arranged at the **Nevis Historical and Conservation Society,** based at the Museum of Nevis History on Main Street in Charlestown (☎ **869/469-5786**).

SNORKELING & DIVING For **snorkeling,** head for Pinney's Beach. You might also try the waters of Fort Ashby, where the settlement of Jamestown is said to have slid into the sea; legend has it that the church bells can still be heard and the undersea town can still be seen when conditions are just right. So far, no diver, to our knowledge, has ever found the conditions "just right."

For scuba divers, some of the best sites on Nevis include **Monkey Shoals,** 2 miles west of the Four Seasons. This is a beautiful reef starting at 40 feet, with dives up to 100 feet in depth. Angelfish, turtles, nurse sharks, and extensive soft coral can be found here. **The Caves** are on the south tip of Nevis, a 20-minute boat ride from the Four Seasons resort. A series of coral grottos with numerous squirrelfish, turtles, and needlefish make this an ideal dive for both certified and resort divers. **Champagne Garden,** a five-minute boat ride from the Four Seasons, gets its name from bubbles created from an underwater sulfur vent. Because of the warm water temperature, large numbers of tropical fish are found here. Finally, **Coral Garden,** 2 miles west of the Four Seasons, is another beautiful coral reef with schools of Atlantic spadefish and large seafans. The reef is at a maximum depth of 70 feet and is suitable for both certified and resort divers.

Scuba Safaris, Oualie Beach (☎ **869/469-9518** or 869/469-9735), on the island's north end, offers PADI scuba diving and snorkeling in an area rich in dive sites. It also offers resort and certification courses, dive packages, and equipment rental. A one-tank scuba dive costs $45; a two-tank dive, $80. Full certification courses cost $450 per person. Snorkeling trips cost $35 per person. Boat charters to Basseterre, Banana Bay, Cockleshell Bay, and other beaches are offered, as well as deep-sea fishing trips on request.

EXPLORING THE ISLAND

Negotiate with a taxi driver to take you around Nevis. The distance is only 20 miles, but you may find yourself taking a long time if you stop to see specific sights and talk to all the people who will want to talk to you. A 3½-hour sightseeing tour around the island will cost $75; the average taxi holds up to four people, so when the cost is sliced per passenger, it's a reasonable investment. No sightseeing bus companies operate on Nevis, but a number of individuals own buses that they use for taxi service. Call **All Seasons Streamline Tours** (☎ **869/469-5705** or 869/469-1138).

The major attraction is the **Museum of Nevis History,** located in the house where Alexander Hamilton was born, on Main Street in Charlestown (☎ **869/469-5786**), overlooking the bay. Hamilton was the illegitimate son of a Scotsman and Rachel Fawcett, a Nevisian of Huguenot ancestry. The family immigrated to St. Croix and from there Alexander made his way to the North American colonies where he became the first secretary of the U.S. Treasury. His picture, of course, appears on the U.S. $10 bill. The lava-stone house by the shore has been restored. The museum, dedicated to the history and culture of Nevis, houses the island's archives. The museum is open Monday to Friday from 8am to 4pm and on Saturday from 10am to noon. Admission is $2 for adults, $1 for children.

At Bath Village, about half a mile from Charlestown, stands the **Bath Hotel,** in serious disrepair, and its **Bath House,** which has been restored for use as a police garrison. Shortly after the Bath Hotel was completed on Nevis in 1778, its thermal baths attracted the elite from the United States, Canada, and Europe, who came to "take the waters." Temperatures rose as high as 108°F. They also drank and gambled in its casino with wealthy local residents who frequented the site. Some say that the Bath Hotel also housed a brothel for a short time. There are legends of entire plantation estates changing hands in the casino, as well as a fair share of bloody duels of honor.

Today the baths are in a stone and wood-sided outbuilding, a dim reminder of the site's earlier glamour. If you're interested in sampling the reputed health benefits of the waters, you'll be ushered down a flight of rough-sawed wooden steps to the reservoirs. Here, behind thin-walled partitions, five concrete-bottomed holding tanks contain shallow pools of the famous waters. No soap is allowed in the holding tanks, and no more than about 15 minutes of immersion is recommended, as serious health problems have resulted from too much time in the waters. The baths are open Monday to Friday from 8am to noon and 1 to 3:30pm and on Saturday from 8am to noon. Admission is free, although use of the baths costs $2.

The **Eden Brown Estate,** about 1½ miles from New River, is said to be haunted. Once it was the home of a wealthy planter, whose daughter was to be married, but her husband-to-be was killed in a duel at the prenuptial feast. The mansion was then closed forever and left to the ravages of nature. A gray solid stone still stands. Only the most adventurous come here on a moonlit night.

At one time, Sephardic Jews who came from Brazil made up a quarter of the island's population, and it's believed that Jews introduced sugar production into the Leewards. Outside the center of Charlestown, at the lower end of Government Road, the **Jewish Cemetery** has been restored and is the resting place of many of the early shopkeepers of Nevis. Most of the tombstones date from between 1690 and 1710.

An archaeological team from the United States believes that an old stone building in partial ruin on Nevis is probably the oldest **Jewish synagogue** in the Caribbean, according to historian Dr. Vincent K. Hubbar, a resident of the island and author of *Swords, Ships, and Sugar: A History of Nevis to 1900.* Preliminary findings in 1993 traced the building's history to one of the two oldest Jewish settlements in the West Indies, Hubbard noted, and current work at the site plus historic documents in England establish its existence prior to 1650.

The original function of the building site, located adjacent to the government administration building in Charlestown, has been long forgotten. However, because of Nevis's relatively large Jewish population in the 17th century and its well-known Jewish cemetery, many scholars and historians believed that a synagogue must have existed but didn't know exactly where.

The **Nevis Jockey Club** organizes and sponsors thoroughbred races every month. Local horses as well as some brought over from other islands fill out a typical five-race card. If you want to have a glimpse at what horse racing must have been like a century or more ago, you'll find the Nevis races a memorable experience. For information, contact Richard Lupinacci, a Jockey Club officer and owner and operator of the Hermitage Plantation (☎ **869/469-3477**).

SHOPPING

Normal store hours are Monday to Friday from 8am to noon and 1 to 4pm, but on Thursday some places close in the afternoon and on Saturday some stay open to 8pm. Most are closed Sunday.

Island Hopper. In the T.D.C. Shopping Mall, Main St., Charlestown. ☎ **869/469-5430.**

Hand-painted or tie-dyed cotton along with batik clothing are featured at this chain shop that also has locations on St. Kitts and Antigua. From beach wraps to souvenirs, a wide selection of products is available.

Nevis Handicraft Cooperative Society. Cotton House, Charlestown. ☎ **869/469-1746.**

In a stone building about 200 feet from the wharf, near the marketplace, this handcraft shop contains locally made gift items, including unusual objects of goatskin, local wines made from a variety of fruits grown on the island, hot-pepper sauce, guava cheese, jams, and jellies.

Nevis Philatelic Bureau. Head Post Office, Market St. (next to the public market), Charlestown. ☎ **869/469-5535.**

Those interested in stamp collecting can come here to see the wide range of colorful stamps. The postage stamps feature butterflies, shells, birds, and fish.

The Sandbox Tree. Evelyn's Villa, Charlestown. ☎ **869/469-5662.**

Housed in a clapboard house that was built in 1836, this gift shop is the most appealing on Nevis, with artwork from Haiti and Nevis, books for adults and children, hand-painted clothing, sheets, napkins, antique furniture, and spices, relishes, and exotic chutneys. It also sells 100% cotton hand–silk-screened fabrics and a complete line of clothing.

NEVIS AFTER DARK

Nightlife is not the major reason to visit Nevis. Summer nights are quiet but there's organized entertainment in winter, when steel bands often perform at the hotels (all of which are recommended above). Most action, if there is any, takes place at the **Four Seasons Resort** on Friday and Saturday nights. **Old Manor Estate** often brings in a steel band on Friday nights. On Saturday the action swings over to the **Golden Rock** where a string band enlivens the scene. Friday and Saturday nights can get raucous at **Eddy's** on Main Street (see previous recommendation) when West Indian buffets are presented and live bands entertain.

5 Anguilla

It's small, serene, secluded, and special, and if you look like Tom Cruise or Demi Moore and have millions in the bank, this place is for you. The northernmost of the Leeward Islands in the eastern Caribbean, 5 miles north of St. Maarten, Anguilla (rhymes with *vanilla*) is only 16 miles long, with 35 square miles in land area. Anguilla has very little rainfall, so its soil is unproductive, with mainly low foliage and sparse scrub vegetation, but the beaches of white coral sand around the island are reason enough to show up. Some 30 of them, shaded by sea grape trees, dot the coast of Anguilla.

The little island has a population of some 9,000 people, predominantly of African descent but also some of European, particularly Irish, ancestry. Most of the locals work in the tourist industry or in lobster fishing. Once part of the federation with St. Kitts and Nevis, Anguilla gained its independence from that association in 1980 and has since been a self-governing British possession.

Anguilla used to be for the adventurous. However, with the opening of some superdeluxe (and superexpensive) hotels in the 1980s, Anguilla was suddenly "discovered," and has become one of the most chic destinations in the Caribbean, rivaling or even surpassing St. Barts. Recently some more moderately priced hotels have opened, too. Not wanting to be spoiled by too much commercialization, Anguilla has controlled development, and most operations are small and informal.

GETTING THERE

BY PLANE Various airlines maintain more than 50 scheduled flights into Anguilla per week, not counting the many charter flights. Because there are no nonstop flights to Anguilla from mainland North America, visitors usually transfer through San Juan, Puerto Rico, or nearby St. Maarten. Some visitors also come in from St. Kitts, Antigua, and St. Thomas.

The most reliable service into Anguilla is offered by **American Eagle** (☎ **800/433-7300** in the U.S.), the commuter partner of American Airlines, which has two nonstop flights daily to Anguilla from its hub in San Juan. Carrying 44 to 46 passengers, flights leave at different times based on the seasons. Schedules are subject to change, so check with the airline or your travel agent.

From Dutch St. Maarten, **Winair** (Windward Islands Airways International; ☎ **800/813-4264**) offers one scheduled flight to Anguilla daily, usually on Twin Otters.

LIAT (☎ **809/465-2286**), not the most on-time airline, flies to Anguilla daily from Antigua and St. Kitts. On some days it might operate two or three flights to

Area Code Change Notice

Please note that within the year (at press time, the date had not been determined), the area code for Anguilla is changing from **809** to **264.** All of the Anguilla area codes in this book are listed as **809.**

Anguilla from either Antigua or St. Kitts. **Air Anguilla** (☎ **809/497-2643**) operates one scheduled flight daily from St. Thomas to Anguilla. It also operates charter flights from St. Maarten, Tortola (British Virgin Islands), and San Juan.

Tyden Air (☎ **809/497-2719**) offers daily flights between St. Maarten and Anguilla and also operates a charter service between San Juan and Anguilla. It maintains a kiosk at the St. Maarten airport.

Flying time from St. Maarten to Anguilla is seven minutes; from San Juan and Antigua, 50 minutes; and from St. Thomas and St. Kitts, 30 minutes.

BY FERRY Ferries run between the ports of Marigot Bay, French St. Martin, and Blowing Point, Anguilla, at approximately 30-minute intervals daily. The first ferry leaves St. Martin at 8am and the last at 7pm; from Blowing Point, the first ferry leaves at 7:30am and the last at 6:15pm. The one-way fare is $10. There's a $2 departure tax for those leaving by boat. No reservations are necessary. Schedules and fares, of course, are always subject to change.

GETTING AROUND

BY RENTAL CAR To explore the island in any detail, it's best to rent a car. Several rental agencies on the island can issue the mandatory Anguillan driver's licenses, which is valid for three months. These are also issued at police headquarters in the Valley and at ports of entry. You'll need a valid driver's license from your home country and pay a one-time fee of $6. Remember to *drive on the left!*

Most experienced visitors to Anguilla pay a taxi to carry them from the island's airport to their hotel, and then, the following day, arrange for a rental car to be delivered to wherever they're staying. Each of the island's car-rental companies delivers vehicles to anywhere on Anguilla for no extra charge, and each offers slight discounts for rentals of seven days or more.

Budget (☎ **800/527-0700** or 809/497-2217) and **Hertz** (☎ **800/654-3001** or 809/497-2934) operate on the island. Local firms include **Bennie & Sons, Blowing Point** (☎ **809/497-2788**); and **Connor's Car Rental,** c/o Maurice Connor, South Hill (☎ **809/497-6433**). Both agencies offer Jeeps as well as cars.

BY TAXI Typical taxi fares are as follows: from the airport to Cap Juluca, $18; to the Fountain Beach Hotel, $12; and to the Malliouhana Hotel, $14.

FAST FACTS: Anguilla

Banking Hours Banks are open Monday to Thursday from 8am to 3pm and on Friday from 8am to 5pm.

Currency The **Eastern Caribbean dollar (EC$)** is the official currency of Anguilla, although U.S. dollars are the actual "coin of the realm." The official exchange rate is about EC$2.70 to each U.S.$1 (EC$1 = 37¢ U.S.).

Customs Even for tourists, duties are levied on goods imported into the island at varying rates: from 5% on foodstuffs to 30% on luxury goods, wines, and liquors.

Documents All visitors must have an onward or return ticket. It is preferred that U.S. and Canadian citizens have a passport, even one that's expired (but not more than five years ago). In lieu of a passport, proof of identity is required—a photo ID with an original birth certificate, a voter registration card, or a driver's license. Citizens from the United Kingdom should have a valid passport.

Drugstores Go to the **Government Pharmacy** at the Princess Alexandra Hospital, Stoney Ground (☎ **809/497-2551**), open Monday to Friday from 8am to noon and 1 to 4pm and on Saturday from 10am to noon. In addition, **Paramount Pharmacy,** Water Swamp (☎ **809/497-2366**), has a 24-hour emergency service.

Electricity The electricity is 110 volts AC (60 cycles), so no transformers or adapters are necessary for U.S. appliances.

Hospitals For medical services, there's the **Princess Alexandra Hospital,** Stoney Ground (☎ **809/497-2551**), plus several district clinics.

Information Go to the **Anguilla Department of Tourism,** P.O. Box 1388, The Valley, Anguilla, B.W.I. (☎ **809/497-2759**). It's open Monday to Saturday from 8am to 5pm. In the United Kingdom, contact the **Anguilla Tourism Office,** 3 Epirus Rd., London SW6 7UI (☎ **0171/937-7725**).

Language English is spoken here, often with a West Indian accent.

Police You can reach the police at their headquarters in the Valley (☎ **809/497-2333**) or the substation at Sandy Ground (☎ **809/497-2354**). In an emergency, dial ☎ **911.**

Post Office The main **post office** is in the Valley (☎ **809/497-2528**). Collectors consider Anguilla's stamps valuable, and the post office also operates a philatelic bureau, open Monday to Friday from 8am to 3:30pm.

Safety Although crime is rare here, secure your valuables; never leave them in a parked car or unguarded on the beach. Anguilla is one of the safest destinations in the Caribbean, but you should take the usual precautions advised anywhere.

Taxes The government collects an 8% tax on rooms and a departure tax of $10 U.S. if you leave the island by air.

Telecommunications Telephone, cable, and Telex services are offered by **Cable & Wireless Ltd.,** Wallblake Road, The Valley (☎ **809/497-3100**), open Monday to Friday from 8am to 5pm and on Saturday from 9am to 1pm.

Time Anguilla is on Atlantic standard time year-round, which means it's usually one hour ahead of the U.S. East Coast. When the mainland goes on daylight saving time, the clocks are the same.

Weather The hottest months in Anguilla are July to October; the coolest, December to February. The mean monthly temperature is about 80°F.

WHERE TO STAY

Don't forget that an 8% government tax will be added to your hotel bill, plus 10% for service.

VERY EXPENSIVE

✪ **Cap Juluca.** Maunday's Bay (P.O. Box 240), Anguilla, B.W.I. ☎ **800/323-0139** in the U.S., 809/497-6666, or 212/425-4684 in New York City. Fax 809/497-6617. 85 rms, 13 suites. A/C TEL. Winter, $625–$770 double; from $1105 suite. Off-season, $350–$445 double; from $550 suite. MAP $75 per person extra. AE, MC, V.

This is one of the most boldly conceived and most luxurious oases in the Caribbean. Occupying a rolling 179-acre site along the southwestern coast on one of the island's best beaches, Cap Juluca caters to Hollywood stars and financial barons and offers some serious pampering at this hideout for the elite.

Accommodations are in villas evocative of Marrakesh, Morocco. Most have soaring domes, walled courtyards, labyrinthine staircases, and concealed swimming pools ringed with thick walls. Inside, a mixture of elegantly comfortable wicker furniture is offset with Moroccan accessories. Each unit faces one of the world's most perfect beaches.

Dining/Entertainment: Eclipse at Pimms (see "Where to Dine," below), is one of the island's finest restaurants, and the Pool Terrace provides a more casual alternative.

Services: Laundry, massage, concierge, golf carts from the guest rooms to the hotel's restaurants and bars.

Facilities: Water sports (including waterskiing, fishing, windsurfing, Sunfish sailing, and snorkeling), championship tennis court, large pool, fitness center.

Covecastles. Shoal Bay West (P.O. Box 248), Anguilla, B.W.I. ☎ **800/223-1108** in the U.S., or 809/497-6801. Fax 809/497-6051. 12 beach houses and villas. TV TEL. Winter, $595 beach house for 2, $795 beach house for 3 or 4; $795 villa for 2, $995 villa for 3 to 6. Off-season, $375 beach house for 2, $475 beach house for 3 or 4; $475 villa for 2, $675 villa for 3 to 6. AE. Closed Sept.

This resort on a lovely beach defines itself as something between a collection of private residences and a luxury hotel. Praised by *Architectural Digest,* it features modern structures designed in 1985 by award-winning architect Myron Goldfinger; it was later enlarged in 1988. The resort rooms are cooled by ceiling fans (not air-conditioning). The units include an interconnected row of town house-style beach houses and a handful of larger, fully detached villas. The design combines elements from North Africa, the Caribbean, and the futuristic theories of Le Corbusier.

Set amid the dunes and scrublands of the island's southwestern coast, at the edge of a white-sand beach, each of the deliberately stark buildings maximizes views of the sea. Each contains louvered doors and windows crafted from Brazilian walnut, terra-cotta tiles from the Dominican Republic, comfortably oversized rattan furniture, a fully equipped kitchen, and a hammock.

Dining/Entertainment: Candlelit dinners, prepared by the resort's French chef, are served overlooking the beach in an intimate private dining room, or en suite. At breakfast and lunch, meals are brought into your beach villa on request.

Services: Concierge, massage, car rental, baby-sitting.

Facilities: Sunfish sailboats, kayaks, bicycles, lit tennis court.

✪ **Malliouhana.** Meads Bay (P.O. Box 173), Anguilla, B.W.I. ☎ **800/835-0796** in the U.S., or 809/497-6111. Fax 809/497-6011. 35 rms, 19 suites. MINIBAR TEL. Winter, $480–$630 double; from $695 suite for 2. Off-season, $240–$290 double; from $395 suite. Seven-night minimum stay required Dec 18–Mar 5. No credit cards.

This glamorous hotel is one of the most discreetly elegant in the Caribbean, a cliff-side retreat that conjures up images of Positano in the tropics. It's even classier than Cap Juluca, although overly lavish, with typical 1980s overkill. Established in 1984 by the Anglo-French Roydon family, it occupies a rocky bluff jutting seaward between sandy beaches, in the southwest corner of the island beyond Long Bay and 8 miles west of the airport. Privacy is key at Malliouhana, where thick walls and shrubbery provide seclusion. The entire complex occupies 25 acres of sloping scrubland whose central core is landscaped into terraces and banks of flowers, pools, and fountains. At its edges sprawl almost 2 miles of white-sand beaches.

Public and private areas are beautifully landscaped, opening onto sea or garden views. A fine assemblage of Haitian art and decorations was chosen by the famed

"Boston Brahmin" decorator, Lawrence Carleton Peabody II. The spacious bedrooms and suites are distributed among the main buildings and outlying villas. Each room has tropical furnishings and wide private verandas, and the villas can be rented as a single unit or subdivided into three comfortable accommodations. Most of the rooms are air-conditioned.

Dining/Entertainment: The resort's restaurant is one of the most prestigious in the Caribbean (see "Where to Dine," below). Scattered over the premises are a handful of bars for drinking and snacking throughout the day.

Services: Room service (7am to 10pm), concierge, laundry, massage, tennis lessons from a qualified pro.

Facilities: Beauty salon, boutiques, TV room, library, water-sports center with instruction in practically everything, four tennis courts (three lit for night play), gym with resident instructor, swimming pools, state-of-the-art children's playground on Meads Bay Beach.

EXPENSIVE

Cinnamon Reef Resort. Little Harbour, Anguilla, B.W.I. ☎ **800/346-7084** in the U.S., or 809/497-2727. Fax 809/497-3727. 4 garden suites, 4 beach suites, 14 villa suites. MINIBAR TEL. Winter, $300 garden suite, $350 beach suite, $400 villa suite. Off-season, $175 garden suite, $225 beach suite, $250 villa suite. Rates include continental breakfast. Additional person $60 extra. MAP $50 per person extra. AE, DISC, MC, V. Closed Sept–Oct.

This small and intimate hotel lies 5 miles west of the airport on the southern coast. It sits astride a circular cove whose calm waters are the best on the island for windsurfing. The resort's Mediterranean-inspired 12-acre core is set on 30 acres of rolling scrubland. Because of its limited size, guests have the feeling of living in a pleasantly informal private estate. Accommodations are in unattached white stucco villas and garden suites. Each unit contains well-appointed bedrooms and dressing areas, ceiling fans, and spacious living rooms.

Dining/Entertainment: The Palm Court Restaurant and the bar area are the focal points (see "Where to Dine," below). The views over the veranda are of the reef-sheltered harbor. Some entertainment and occasional dancing is offered at night.

Services: Room service, laundry.

Facilities: Freshwater pool, hot tub and Jacuzzi, two championship tennis courts, beach sheltered by a reef, free sailboats, paddleboats, Windsurfers, kayaks, and snorkeling and fishing equipment; scuba diving can be arranged.

Sonesta Beach Resort Anguilla. Rendezvous Bay West, Anguilla, B.W.I. ☎ **800/SONESTA** or 809/497-6999. Fax 809/497-6899. 77 rms, 10 suites. A/C MINIBAR TV TEL. Winter, $290–$340 double; $390–$460 suite. Off-season, $170–$210 double; $250–$300 suite. MAP $60 per person extra. AE, MC, V.

Set at the edge of a 3-mile strip of beachfront, this hotel offers views of St. Martin's nearby mountains. In the 1980s, Arab investors commissioned architects to emulate a Moroccan palace beside an oasis. To create the Moorish motifs, teams of Moroccan artisans spent months on embellishments that included marble floors, intricate geometric mosaics, and imperial green tile roofs that glisten against the surrounding scrub-covered landscape.

Attempts were made to compete with some of the hyperexpensive hotels nearby (especially Cap Juluca and the Malliouhana). Despite the exotic decor (or perhaps because of it) the hotel never really attained the glamour or cachet of its neighbors. In 1995, after being damaged in that season's pair of back-to-back hurricanes, the property was sold to Sonesta, which poured money into its refurbishment, softening (some say weakening) aspects of the original Moorish design. Accommodations are scattered among a complex of buildings set either beside the beach or in a garden. Each room contains areas partially sheathed in Italian marble, a private patio, high ceilings capped with spinning ceiling fans, and "international" decors.

Dining/Entertainment: Continental cuisine is served in the Casablanca Restaurant and Bar. A bar, the Café Américain, borrows the Moorish theme (remember *Casablanca?*). The Seabreeze/Blue Parrot Grill serves food in an indoor/outdoor setting overlooking the pool and the sea. Complimentary tea is offered in the Library daily from 3 to 5pm.

Services: Massage, room service (7am to midnight), baby-sitting, concierge, valet, twice-daily maid service, children's programs ("Just Us Kids").

Facilities: One of the most exotic-looking swimming pools on Anguilla, health club with exercise machines overlooking the sea, two lit tennis courts, library, games room, wide array of land and water sports (some of them complimentary).

MODERATE

Fountain Beach Hotel. Shoal Bay Beach, Anguilla, B.W.I. ☎ **809/497-3491.** Fax 809/497-3493. 12 rms, 2 cottages. Winter, $150 double; $215 one-bedroom cottage; $315 two-bedroom cottage. Off-season, $100 double; $150 one-bedroom cottage; $250 two-bedroom cottage. MAP $35 per person extra. AE, DISC, MC, V.

Built right on the beach in 1989, this coral-colored resort was inspired by Mediterranean architecture. Surrounded by five acres of sloping and forested land on the island's underpopulated north coast, it's simple, with few amenities but with ample opportunities for reading, sunbathing, or just doing nothing. The bedrooms are large and airy, with ceramic-tile floors, sliding glass windows, and pastel color schemes. Each unit has an unstocked refrigerator, and some have kitchenettes. On the premises, in an annex at the edge of one of the island's best beaches, is a restaurant serving Italian cuisine and seafood.

La Sirena. Meads Bay (P.O. Box 200), Anguilla, B.W.I. ☎ **800/331-9358** in the U.S., 800/223-9815 in Canada, or 809/497-6827. Fax 809/497-6829. 20 rms, 5 villas. MINIBAR. Winter, $230–$295 double; $295–$410 two-bedroom villa; $495 three-bedroom villa. Off-season, $130–$180 double; $180–$240 two-bedroom villa; $280 three-bedroom villa. MAP $44 per person extra. AE, MC, V.

Built in 1989 on three acres of sandy soil, a four-minute walk from the beach, this resort is pleasant, intimate, and small scale (we found it almost a relief after the ultrasophisticated and chic ambience of Cap Juluca and Malliouhana). At least 80% of its clientele comes from either Switzerland or Germany, thanks to its Swiss ownership and its European marketing. The accommodations, arranged in two-story bougainvillea-draped wings, are large and airy, with rattan and wicker furnishings similar to those in some of the island's more expensive hostelries. Some have air-conditioning; all have ceiling fans and hair dryers. The hotel is not beside the beach; guests walk down through the garden and a sandy footpath to reach it. Once you get there, you'll find beach hats, umbrellas, and lounge chairs laid out for you.

Dining/Entertainment: The Top of the Palms restaurant, open only for dinner, is recommended separately (see "Where to Dine," below). Less formal is the Coconuts Café, for breakfast and lunch, specializing in pastas, sandwiches, and ice cream.

Services: Baby-sitting, laundry.

Facilities: Two freshwater swimming pools.

INEXPENSIVE

Easy Corner Villas. South Hill (P.O. Box 65), Anguilla, B.W.I. ☎ **800/223-9815** in the U.S., or 809/497-6433. Fax 809/497-6410. 12 apts. TV. Winter, $110–$160 one-bedroom apt; $195 two-bedroom apt; $240 three-bedroom apt. Off-season, $90–$125 one-bedroom apt; $155 two-bedroom apt; $250 three-bedroom apt. AE, MC, V.

On the main road west of the airport, the Easy Corner Villas are owned by Maurice E. Connor, the same entrepreneur who rents many of the cars on the island. The one-, two-, and three-bedroom apartment units are simply furnished and set on landscaped grounds with views of a good beach from their private porches. Each comes equipped with a kitchen, combination living and dining room, and large, airy living areas. Many have ceiling fans, and some are air-conditioned. Children over the age of 2 are welcome, and daily maid service is available at an extra charge.

ALL-INCLUSIVE RESORTS

Anguilla Great House & Beach Resort. Rendezvous Bay (P.O. Box 157), Anguilla, B.W.I. ☎ **800/583-9247** in the U.S. outside Florida, 407/994-5640 in Florida, or 809/497-6061. Fax 809/497-6019. 27 rms. Winter, $400–$440 double. Off-season, $330–$360 double. Rates are all-inclusive. Three-night minimum stay in winter. AE, DISC, MC, V.

Set on the white sands of Rendezvous Bay, near Anguilla's southernmost tip, this Anguillan-owned property is one of the few all-inclusive resorts on the island. It's designed around a central garden/courtyard with a view of the beach. The resort offers accommodations in colonial-inspired single-story units whose front verandas are connected like the wings of an old-fashioned plantation house. In most rooms, you get ceiling fans instead of air-conditioning, although some rooms have it. Most of the resort's social life revolves around an open-sided bar and restaurant where all food and beverages are included in the all-inclusive price. A freshwater swimming pool is on the premises. A water-sports program includes windsurfing, reef fishing, kayaking, snorkeling, and sailing.

Coccoloba MetaResort. Barnes Bay (P.O. Box 332), Anguilla, B.W.I. ☎ **800/727-7388** in the U.S., or 809/497-8178. Fax 809/497-8179. 12 suites, 42 villas. A/C MINIBAR TEL. All-inclusive: $195–$225 per person. Minimum stay 3 nights. AE, MC, V.

One of the island's most solidly comfortable resorts, Coccoloba is built on a rocky headland that juts seaward between two excellent beaches 7 miles west of the airport. Blasted by the hurricane winds of 1995, the resort was forced to close and make repairs, but it reopened as an all-inclusive resort, with unlimited à la carte dining for breakfast, lunch, and dinner. Encompassing 30 acres of seaside scrubland, it reminds many newcomers of a chic resort in the Mediterranean. Owned by a group of doctors from Reno, the resort has had an unstable management in the past, but we hope it will be operating smoothly at the time of your visit. Gaily striped parasols and awnings, an interconnected series of swimming pools, and a swim-up bar contribute to the holiday flavor. The resort's reception area lies in a soaring A-frame building. The accommodations ramble along a bluff above the sea, and most are in simple cottages with verandas and summer-inspired furniture.

Dining/Entertainment: The resort is justly proud of the Caribbean/Creole and French/American cuisine served in its major restaurant, the Pavilion. However, quantity sometimes takes precedence over quality. A pair of bars operate beside the pool and the beach.

Services: Room service (for continental breakfast only), laundry, massage, island tours.

Facilities: Freshwater pool and swim-up bar, health spa, two tennis courts (lit at night); deep-sea fishing, sunset-cruise trips, and waterskiing can be arranged.

The Mariners Cliffside Beach Resort. Road Bay (P.O. Box 139), Sandy Ground, Anguilla, B.W.I. ☎ **800/848-7938** in the U.S., or 809/497-2671. Fax 809/497-2901. 43 rms, 19 suites. A/C TV TEL. Winter, $220–$250 double; from $375 suite. Off-season, $140–$160 double; from $200 suite. For all-inclusive, add $70 per person extra to rates above. AE, DISC, MC, V.

This all-inclusive resort sits on 8½ acres beside an isolated beach whose access road winds between flowering shrubs and hillocks. Accommodations are in three two-story buildings and cottages delightfully embellished with West Indian gingerbread. All rooms have ceiling fans (some are air-conditioned), and a decor reminiscent of New England summer cottages in the 1930s prevails. It's also possible to stay here on EP rates (no meals), although most guests find the all-inclusive terms more favorable. The food often has zest, but much of it is fairly standard fare. The staff is very laid back.

Services: Room service, laundry.

Facilities: Swimming pool, tennis court lit at night, two Jacuzzis.

Condos & Villas

Vacation villas, which absentee owners rent out, are appearing more and more on the island. Several rental agencies have listings of these villas, which come in a vast range of prices. One of the best is **Anguilla Connection** (☎ **800/916-3336** in the U.S., or 809/497-4403; fax 809/497-4402). It's the only agency that offers 24-hour personalized service. Choices range from luxury in a secluded hideaway to condo-style living.

✪ **Carimar Beach Club.** Meads Bay (P.O. Box 327), Anguilla, B.W.I. ☎ **800/235-8667** or 809/497-6881. Fax 809/497-6071. 24 apts. Winter, $300–$350 one-bedroom apt; $400–$440 two-bedroom apt; $630 three-bedroom apt. Off-season, $130–$160 one-bedroom apt; $200–$230 two-bedroom apt; $325 three-bedroom apt. AE, MC, V.

Opening onto Meads Bay, west of the airport beyond Long Bay, this is the best of the island's small apartment hotels. Here you get the privacy of an apartment yet some of the comforts of a hotel, at excellent rates. The well-appointed units are in two-story Mediterranean-style villas, each with a large living room, dining area, and patio or balcony overlooking mile-long Meads Bay Beach. For dinner, if you want to splurge, you can go to the nearby super-priced Malliouhana or next door to Blanchards Restaurant. There are two tennis courts and complimentary snorkeling equipment.

WHERE TO DINE

VERY EXPENSIVE

✪ **Malliouhana Restaurant.** Meads Bay (8 miles west of the airport). ☎ **809/497-6111.** Reservations required. Main courses $28–$39. AE, MC, V. Daily 12:30–3:30pm and 7:30–10:30pm. FRENCH/CARIBBEAN.

This restaurant, with the Caribbean's most ambitious French menu, offers fluidly choreographed service, fine food, a 25,000-bottle wine cellar, and a glamorous clientele. Michel Rostang, the successful son of the legendary Jo Rostang, one of the most famous chefs of southern France, is often in charge. You'll dine in an open-sided pavilion built atop a rocky promontory jutting seaward. At night your candlelit table will be set with French crystal, Limoges china, and Christofle silver. There's lots of space between tables, an ocean view, and a splashing fountain.

The hors d'oeuvres selection is the finest on the island, including fresh goat-cheese terrine with sweet red peppers, and potted minced goose with mixed green salad and cornbread. There's also a fabulous lobster ravioli with carrots in lobster juice, or lemon-flavored fettuccine with a caviar cream. Main courses are likely to range from a perfectly prepared saddle of lamb with Sisteron flavored with shallots and garlic, to Bresse chicken roasted on a spit and served with a potato gratin. The fish dishes, including grilled snapper with baby leeks in a soya sauce, fillet of salmon grilled with fennel, or more simply the grilled catch of the day, are also popular with hard-core foodies. If we have a criticism, it's that some of the food served here seems a bit too heavy for the tropics.

EXPENSIVE

Barrel Stay Beach Bar & Restaurant. Sandy Ground. ☎ **809/497-2831.** Reservations recommended. Main courses $20–$40. AE, MC, V. Daily 11am–2:30pm and 6:30–9:30pm. FRENCH/CREOLE.

This restaurant sits beside the beach and has ample space for dining or drinking—there's an outdoor drink terrace and a smaller inner bar that sees most of its activity at night. Although many visitors find the restaurant pricey, it has a lot of fans. The fish soup served here in the French fashion is as good as any you'll find in Martinique. Conch Creole is a delight, and the fresh catch of the day prepared with a garlic sauce is almost always a sure bet. You're likely to find barbecued lobster on the menu or else a Black Angus steak. The well-heeled diners also go for the stuffed crab. A selection of expensive French wines is also available.

✪ **Blanchards.** Meads Bay. ☎ **809/497-6100.** Reservations recommended. Main courses $20–$45. AE, MC, V. Mon–Sat 6:30–9pm. INTERNATIONAL.

Bob and Melinda Blanchard, this restaurant's owners, have celebrated a love affair with Anguilla and the restaurant trade for about a decade. Founders of a successful salad dressing and condiment business in Vermont, their successes include earlier stints as restaurateurs in Anguilla and Aspen, Colorado. Missing Anguilla, they returned in 1995 to mastermind an eatery that's charming, low-key, and intensely fashionable, serving cuisine that's among the most creative and interesting on the island from a garden-swathed pavilion beside the sea, adjacent to the beach of the Hotel Malliouhana. Diners have included well-known figures from Hollywood, Broadway, and the worlds of art and fashion.

Behind very tall teal-blue shutters (which can be opened to the sea breezes), you're likely to find upscale, urbanized food with a Caribbean flair enhanced with spices from Spain, Asia, California, and the American Southwest. Dishes change according to the inspiration of chef Melinda but are likely to include Cajun grouper on a bed of onion marmalade; swordfish stuffed with leeks, dill, and fontina cheese; and jerk Jamaica-style chicken with bananas grilled and glazed with molasses and rum. It's unlikely that you'll ever order a bad dish here. Everything is elegantly casual, with a sense of theater provided by the media-hip clientele and the dramatic food.

✪ **Eclipse at Cap Juluca.** In the Cap Juluca, Maunday's Bay. ☎ **809/497-6666.** Reservations required. Main courses $28–$38. AE, MC, V. Daily 6:30–10pm. CALIFORNIAN/CARIBBEAN.

This pocket of posh, open only for dinner, is one of the most elegant restaurants on Anguilla and one of the finest in the Caribbean. Set among the archways and domes of Anguilla's most spectacular resort, Cap Juluca, it blends the finest culinary standards of the Old and New Worlds with fresh and exotic ingredients flown in regularly. Tables overlook the island's best beach and are lit with flickering candlelight.

The cuisine is under the direction of Bernard Erpicum and Serge Falesitch, famous for their Los Angeles restaurant, Eclipse, a longtime favorite of California connoisseurs and celebrities alike, including Cindy Crawford, Tom Cruise, Richard Gere, Anthony Hopkins, and Jane Fonda. The new Pimms, which previously had been the subject of numerous complaints from visitors, has bounced back with a California-Caribbean menu. Although the restaurant has dubbed its food with the corny title "Cuisine of the Sun," it does deliver an impressive roster of fresh-roasted Caribbean seafood specialties with an infusion of the flavors of Provence—olive oil, lemon, basil, tarragon, capers, and fennel.

Hibernia. Island Harbour. ☎ **809/497-4290.** Reservations required. Main courses $19.50–$33. AE, MC, V. May–July and Oct, Tues–Sat noon–2pm and 7–9pm. Closed Aug–Sept; dinner only Apr–Christmas. FRENCH/ASIAN.

Hibernia is a lovely little spot in a West Indian–style house with a veranda overlooking Scilly Cay, on the northeast corner of the island. Small and intimate, it contains only 10 tables. It's the personal statement of a French chef, Raoul Rodríguez, and Irish-born Mary Pat O'Hanlon. Local ingredients are used in the specialties, which sometimes have an Asian influence. Even the breads and ice cream are homemade. Soups and starters always inspire the imagination, especially the house specialty—a selection of smoked Caribbean fish with fresh ginger and sour cream. We are equally drawn to the Provençal tart made with eggplant, zucchini, and tomatoes. Our favorite dish is the fresh Anguillan rabbit terrine filled with apricots and marinated in aged rum. Another specialty is a kettle of filleted Caribbean fish cooked in a spicy Thai broth and served with wild rice.

KoalKeel Restaurant. The Valley. ☎ **809/497-2930.** Reservations recommended for dinner. Main courses $22–$28. AE, MC, V. Mon 7am–3pm, Tues–Sun 7am–11pm. Closed Sept to mid-Oct. CONTINENTAL/CARIBBEAN.

The setting for this restaurant is one of the few truly historic buildings on Anguilla, a dignified manor house originally built in 1790. Made of coral stone and clapboards, it's set on a hillside overlooking the island's administrative center, The Valley. The two-story dining area has an airy decor and sea views from its outdoor patio and second story.

Some of the menu items (slow-cooked lamb and rock-oven chicken with locally grown herbs) are cooked in the stone-sided, wood- and charcoal-burning oven (the KoalKeel) that was part of the original building. Grilled snapper with Creole sauce, lobster crêpes, lobster-studded pasta, and smoked grouper on a bed of leeks are deservedly popular bestsellers.

What should you drink to accompany all this local flavor? Le Dôme (a wine cellar and retail wine shop) stocks thousands of bottles of some of the most desirable wines on Anguilla, and the Old Rum Shop is an antique-studded outlet for "designer" rums (some of them vintage and very old). And if Viennese and French pastries are your thing, an upstairs tearoom (Le Petit Pâtissier) serves steaming pots of tea and deliciously fattening, freshly made pastries. All four of the entities in this building maintain the same hours as the KoalKeel.

Palm Court Restaurant. In the Cinnamon Reef Resort, Little Harbour. ☎ **809/497-2727.** Reservations recommended in winter. Main courses $22–$30. AE, MC, V. Daily 8–9:30am, noon–2:30pm, and 7–9:30pm. CARIBBEAN.

This restaurant in one of the finest small hotels on Anguilla has earned an excellent reputation. The tables are scattered before a sweeping view of a circular bay. Lunches are informal and feature Anguillan lobster or chicken salads; savory soups; seafood pasta made with grilled snapper, cream, and herbs; and sandwiches such as lobster clubs.

The real allure of the cuisine, however, appears at dinner, when the kitchen presents such tempting creations as jumbo shrimp with Thai chilis, a mixed grill of Caribbean seafood, and our favorite, a cumin- and coriander-dusted grouper with oven-roasted vegetables. Other good choices are the famous Anguillan lobster, charcoal-grilled and served with fresh angel-hair pasta, and baked Anguillan red snapper in red spices, served with a Key-lime fettuccine. If you don't want anything too fancy or Caribbean nouvelle, most of the meat and fish dishes can be simply grilled for you.

Top of the Palms. In La Sirena Hotel, Meads Bay. ☎ **809/497-6827.** Reservations recommended. Main courses $20–$35. AE, MC, V. Daily 7–9:30pm. FRENCH.

This restaurant on the second floor of the La Sirena Hotel is open to the cool ocean breezes and offers views over Meads Bay and the surrounding treetops. Menu specialties are prepared by a well-trained Swiss chef, Stephan Peterer. You might begin with conch fritters or quesadillas, then follow with filet of beef grilled the way you like it, or perhaps a choice of two types of fondue: bourguignonne or chinoise. If you want the fondues, you must call ahead by 5pm. Many fish dishes are regularly featured, including a fondue, Neptune that you cook for yourself, placing small pieces of lobster, fish, and shrimp onto a skewer and dipping them in a hot fish stock. The local lobster is grilled every night, and panfried grouper and steamed snapper also make regular appearances. The snapper is best when served with a touch of tarragon-and-lemongrass sauce. Homemade tropical fruit sorbets provide a smooth finish to a meal.

MODERATE

La Fontana. In the Fountain Beach Hotel, Shoal Bay Beach. ☎ **809/497-3492.** Reservations recommended for dinner. Main courses $17–$35. AE, MC, V. Daily noon–3pm and 6–10pm. NORTHERN ITALIAN.

This restaurant in the previously recommended Fountain Beach Hotel on the northern side of the island looks out over the western end of Shoal Bay Beach, whose waters washed ashore in 1995 and caused much devastation. Sheltered from the direct rays of the sun, but open to breezes at the sides, the restaurant combines ingredients from both Italy and the Caribbean. Italian wines, freshly baked breads, and an undeniable flair are part of the experience here. Since this place opened it has consistently served the island's finest Italian cuisine. The soups are homemade, and the pasta doesn't get any better than when it's served with lobster, shrimp, and calamari. Anguillan lobster also appears, marinated with fresh herbs and sautéed in white wine. The steak fiorentina has the evocative fragrances of Tuscany.

Lucy's Harbour View and Restaurant. South Hill. ☎ **809/497-6253.** Reservations recommended. Main courses $16–$30. AE, MC, V. Mon–Sat 11:30am–3:30pm and 7–10pm. Closed late Aug to late Oct. CARIBBEAN/INTERNATIONAL.

Not only does it boast the most attractive view on the island, but Lucy's also offers imaginatively prepared food. What makes it special is its owner, Lucy Halley, who lived in the French part of St. Martin and learned many secrets of the cuisine there. The 40-seat restaurant is in a converted home at the top of a steep hillside overlooking the salt ponds and houses of Sandy Ground. When you call or after you arrive, ask Lucy what she has in the larder, or tell her what kind of food you like. The menu usually contains homemade pumpkin soup, lobster salad, fresh Anguillan lobster (split and grilled), conch fritters, curried goat, kingfish, and T-bone steaks. The food has a real homemade taste with occasional imaginative flourishes. Dishes are usually served with fresh vegetables and bread pudding. This is a lively, fun, and very informal spot, painted in the signature green and white known throughout Anguilla as Lucy's trademark colors. Live entertainment is offered on Tuesday.

✪ **Mango's.** Barnes Bay. ☎ **809/497-6479.** Reservations required for dinner as far in advance as possible. Main courses $16–$30. AE, MC, V. Wed–Mon 6:30–9pm. Closed Aug–Oct. NEW AMERICAN.

In a pavilion set a few steps from the edge of the sea, on the northwestern part of the island, this is an alluring independent restaurant. It also has the healthiest cuisine of any of the island's top restaurants. Mango's specializes in serving the freshest obtainable fish, meat, and produce, all cooked on the grill with an absolute minimum of added fats or calories. All the breads and desserts, including the ice cream and sorbet, are made fresh daily on the premises. You might start with delectable lobster cakes with a homemade tartar sauce or a creamy conch chowder. For a main course, grilled local lobster is featured, as is spicy whole snapper. "Simply grilled" fish with lemon-and-herb butter is the preferred main dish. A reservation for dinner here in January and February is a hot ticket.

Paradise Café. Shoal Bay West End. ☎ **809/497-6010.** Reservations recommended. Main courses $12–$28. AE, MC, V. Tues–Sat noon–2pm and 7–9pm. MEDITERRANEAN/CARIBBEAN.

This restaurant is set right on the beach at Shoal Bay West End. Sea breezes tinkle the many wind chimes decorating the dining room. Attracting a clientele of movie stars, singers, politicians, the rich and famous, and some ordinary folks as well, it lies between the Blue Waters and Covecastles resorts. Diners enjoy a panoramic view of the islands of St. Martin and Saba.

On the lunch menu, you can order pumpkin soup, tempura calamari, a stir-fried scallop salad, or your basic grilled hamburger. The dinner menu is more elaborate, featuring various versions of focaccia or a quesadilla as an appetizer. Succulent pastas are regularly featured at night, including one made with local crayfish medallions.

You can also order such selections as a red Thai curry or grilled tenderloin with an onion confit. There's an originality about the food, and everything tastes like a personal creation by the chef. The fish dishes are uniformly enticing, especially the grilled whole snapper.

INEXPENSIVE

✪ **Ferryboat Inn.** Cul de Sac Rd., Blowing Point, Anguilla, B.W.I. ☎ **809/497-6613.** Reservations recommended. Main courses $9–$26. AE, MC, V. Mon–Sat noon–3pm and 7:30–10pm. Closed Tues in summer. Turn right just before the Blowing Point Ferry Terminal and travel 150 yards before making a left turn. CARIBBEAN/FRENCH.

Established by English-born John McClean and his Anguillan wife, Marjorie, and set directly on the beach (a short walk from the Blowing Point ferry pier), this restaurant comes well recommended; it's one of the best values on the island. Specialties are French onion soup, black-bean soup, some of the best lobster thermidor on the island (liberally laced with brandy, cream, and both Parmesan and gouda cheese), and scallop of veal Savoyard (with white wine and fresh cream), which is especially good. Don't miss the house's special planter's punch.

The McCleans also rent six one-bedroom apartments and one two-bedroom beach house. In winter, charges are $140 to $165 for an apartment, $225 for the beach house. Off-season rates are $70 to $85 for an apartment and $125 for the beach house.

Smitty's Restaurant. Island Harbour. ☎ **809/497-4300.** Reservations not required. Burgers and sandwiches $5–$8; platters $12–$20. No credit cards. Daily 10am–midnight. SEAFOOD/WEST INDIAN.

Set directly on the sands of a beach near Anguilla's northern tip, beneath sea grapes, palms, and a rickety lattice, this is a raffish hangout where the food is slowly prepared in the Caribbean style. Wiped out by a hurricane in 1995, it was forced to move but bounced back quickly. No one will mind if you spend an hour or two drinking a rum concoction at one of the battered wooden tables, but if you want something to eat, Smitty, the extroverted owner, or Seal, his wife, will prepare platters of ribs, chicken, fish, conch, steak, or lobster. Don't expect anything too fancy, just open-air informality and recorded reggae. The food is simple but savory, tasting its best when washed down with a beer or two. A steel band is brought in on Thursday, Friday, and Saturday.

BEACHES, WATER SPORTS & OTHER OUTDOOR PURSUITS

BEACHES Its beaches put Anguilla on the tourist map—there are no less than 39 of them, plus another half dozen or so on the outer cays. One of the most popular beaches is **Road Bay,** framed by the crescent-shaped village of Sandy Ground (the capital) and a large salt pond.

Sandy Isle is a tiny little islet with a few palms surrounded by a coral reef. It lies offshore from Road Bay. Once there, you'll find a beach bar and restaurant, plus free use of snorkeling gear and underwater cameras. **Sandy Island Enterprises** (☎ **809/497-5643**) has daily trips from the pier by Johnno's Beach Bar at Sandy Ground. The cost of a round-trip ticket is $8, and the first boat leaves at 10am. The last boat back (don't miss it) departs at 4pm. You can also go farther out to Prickly Pear Cay, which stretches like a sweeping arc all the way to a sand spit populated by sea birds and pelicans.

Other good beaches include **Shoal Bay** in the northeast, which, apart from its white silver sands, boasts some of Anguilla's best coral gardens, the habitat of hundreds of tiny iridescent fish. This 2-mile beach with its talcum-powder-soft sand is not only the best beach on Anguilla, but one of the best in the entire Caribbean Basin.

Rivaling Shoal Bay is **Rendezvous Bay** in the southwest, a long curving ribbon of pale gold sand stretching along a bay for 2½ miles. It's calmer, warmer, and shallower than Shoal Bay, which is on the Atlantic side.

Crocus Bay is a long, golden beach, where a fisher might take you in search of snapper or grouper, or ferry you to such wee islands as Little Scrub.

FISHING You can go out with the local fishers. Your hotel can make the arrangements for you, but you should bring your own tackle. Agree on the cost before setting out, however, as some misunderstandings have been reported.

Malliouhana, Meads Bay (☎ **809/497-6111**), has a 34-foot fishing cruiser, *Kyra,* that holds up to eight passengers at a time. It can be chartered for fishing parties. The cost is $400 for up to four hours, with a surcharge of another $100 for each additional hour. A box lunch can be packed for an additional charge, but all fishing gear is included.

SNORKELING & DIVING Most of the coastline of Anguilla is fringed by coral reefs, and the island's waters are rich in marine life; off the shore are sunken coral gardens and brilliantly colored fish. Conditions for scuba diving and snorkeling on the island are ideal. In addition, the government of Anguilla has systematically created artificial enlargements of the existing reef system, a first for the Caribbean. Never before have so many battered and outmoded ships been deliberately sunk in carefully designated places in efforts to enlarge the island's marine ecosystem. These artificial reefs act as nurseries for fish and lobster populations and also provide new sites for divers.

The Dive Shop, Sandy Ground (☎ **809/497-2020**), is a five-star PADI international training center and offers a complete line of PADI certification courses. They carry several lines of scuba equipment for sale or rental. A two-tank dive costs $75. Night dives go for $50.

TENNIS Most of the resorts have their own tennis courts (see "Where to Stay," above). **Malliouhana,** Meads Bay (☎ **809/497-6111**), has a pro-shop and four championship Laykold tennis courts with a year-round professional coach, Peter Burwash. Three courts are lit for night games. There are also two courts at **Cinnamon Reef,** Little Harbour (☎ **809/497-2727**).

WINDSURFING Many hotel and villa properties offer windsurfing to guests: Cap Juluca, the Cinnamon Reef Beach Club, Coccoloba, Fountain Beach, La Sirena, Malliouhana, the Mariners Cliffside Beach Resort, Shoal Bay Villas, and Rendezvous Bay. Water-sports facilities also offer windsurfing. The Mariners has windsurfing or Sunfish sailboats for $15 per half hour for rental or lessons, and $25 per hour for rental or lessons.

EXPLORING THE ISLAND

The best way to get an overview of the island is on a **taxi tour**. In about 2½ hours, a local driver (all of them are guides) will show you everything for $45. If you're visiting just for the day (as most sightseers do), you can be let off at your favorite beach after a look around, and then be picked up and returned to the airport in time to catch your flight back to wherever.

Boat trips can be arranged to **Sombrero Island,** 38 miles northwest of Anguilla. This mysterious island, with its lone lighthouse, is 400 yards wide at its broadest point and three-quarters of a mile in length. Phosphate miners abandoned it in 1890, and limestone rocks, now eroded, rise in cliffs around the island. The treeless, waterless terrain evokes a moonscape. Adventure seekers can sometimes arrange to go over on the supply boat serving the island on the 1st and the 16th of the month. A boat leaves Anguilla between 6 and 7am, returning at noon. Call Errol Carty (☎ **809/497-2564**) if you'd like to arrange such a trip, which is free.

One of Anguilla's most festive, and certainly most colorful, annual festivals is **Carnival,** held jointly under the auspices of the Ministries of Culture and of Tourism. Boat races are Anguilla's national sport, and during Carnival they form 60% of the celebration, in which the island's people display their culture, drama, creativity, and love of their land. The festival begins on the Friday before the first Monday in August and lasts a week. Carnival harks back to Emancipation Day, or "August Monday" as it's called, when all enslaved Africans were freed.

SHOPPING

Anguillan handcrafts are simple. Handcrafted mats are quite beautiful, and tablecloths and bedspreads are woven into spidery lace designs, but many of these are grabbed up by shops on neighboring islands and sold there at high prices. Baskets and mats are made from stripped corn husks and sisal rope. Model schooners and small pond boats are also for sale, as are gifts made of shells and wooden dolls.

Stamp collectors should head to the **Valley Post Office** (☎ **809/497-2528**).

The Boutique. In the Malliouhana Hotel, Meads Bay. ☎ **809/497-6111.**

The most interesting and upscale boutique on Anguilla lies in the island's premier hotel. Here you'll find jewelry, sportswear and casual beachwear for men and women, evening dresses, gift items, and bathing suits from La Perla, Gottex, and Canovas, plus Kaminsky Rafia hats.

Cheddie's Carving Shop. The Cove. ☎ **809/497-6027.**

Just before the Sonesta Beach Resort, this outlet showcases the work of Anguilla-born Cheddie Richardson, a self-taught carver whose unique pieces have attracted the notice of collectors of Caribbean art. Using mostly natural wood—mahogany, walnut, and driftwood—Cheddie also uses other Anguillan resources, including alabaster and coral. He makes bronze castings, too. His artwork mostly portrays wildlife: fish, dolphins, or birds. Each piece usually takes a week or so to complete, depending on size and amount of detail.

Devonish Art Gallery. George Hill Landing Mall. ☎ **809/497-2949.**

This gallery offers paintings by Anguillan, Caribbean, and international artists and also features the work of well-known proprietor-artist Courtney Devonish. The Devonish Gallery is housed in a historic Anguillan building, a reminder of a time when Anguilla grew cotton. Visitors might get to watch hand-made pottery production on Saturday.

New World Gallery. Old Factory Plaza, the Valley. ☎ **809/497-5950.**

This gallery features fine art, including exquisite pastels, paintings, and prints. New World also stocks an impressive range of exotic artifacts, textiles, and jewelry from around the globe.

Sunshine Shop. In South Hill. ☎ **809/497-6964.**

Opposite Connor's car-rental agency, this is easily identifiable by the "I-95 sign," as it's on I-95 West at the Blowing Point expressway exit. The shop stocks fine cotton wear, art, jewelry, and packable gift items. For men, there are unusual batik shirts and bathing briefs. The shop also sells shoes, belts, and hats. Look for a classic line of women's sportswear in linen.

ANGUILLA AFTER DARK

Nightlife on Anguilla is centered mainly at the various hotels, especially in winter, when they offer barbecues, West Indian parties, or singers and musicians. Calypso combo groups and other bands, both local and imported, are hired by the hotels.

The most intriguing cultural treat is a performance of the **Mayoumba Folkloric Theater** (☎ **809/497-6827**), playing at La Sirena on Meads Bay on Thursday night. Call for details before going. African drums and a string band will give you an insight into Antillean culture.

Johnno's Beach Bar, Sandy Ground (☎ **809/497-2728**), is a favorite of Michael J. Fox and other Hollywood types when they visit Anguilla. Open-air, with sunlight and sea winds wafting into its unpretentious premises, the club offers Beck's beer on the beach as well as barbecued spareribs, grilled chicken, or fresh fish. Try Johnno's popular drink of rum, crème de cacao, guavaberry liqueur, and guava nectar. Live entertainment is presented on Wednesday, Friday, Saturday, and Sunday from 8pm to 1am. A big Sunday barbecue begins at 11am and lasts "until the food runs out."

10 The Dutch Windwards in the Leewards

Sint Maarten, Sint Eustatius, and Saba, no more than dots on the map, have long been dubbed "The Dutch Windwards." This is confusing to the visitor, but it makes sense in the Netherlands. The Dutch-associated islands of Aruba, Bonaire, and Curaçao, just off the coast of South America, go by the name of "The Dutch Leewards" (covered in chapter 16). The three Windward Islands, along with Bonaire and Curaçao, form the Netherlands Antilles (Aruba is now a separate entity).

The Dutch Windwards were once inhabited by the Carib peoples, who lent their name both to the Caribbean and, after a bit of linguistic corruption, to cannibalism—the Caribs believed that one acquired the strength of a slain enemy by eating his flesh. Columbus, on his second voyage to America, is said to have sighted the group of small islands on the name day of San Martino (St. Martin of Tours), hence the present name of Sint ("Saint") Maarten.

Cooled by trade winds, the Windwards are comfortable to visit year-round. However, there's a history of unpredictable weather patterns during the hurricane season, so check the latest weather reports before you go.

1 St. Maarten

For an island with a big reputation for its restaurants, hotels, and energetic nightlife, St. Maarten is small—only 37 square miles, about half the area of Washington, D.C. An island divided between Holland and France, St. Maarten is the Dutch half. The other half, St. Martin, is French. Legend has it that a gin-drinking Dutchman and a wine-guzzling Frenchman walked around the island to see how much territory each could earmark for his country in one day; the Frenchman outwalked the Dutchman, but the canny Dutchman got the more valuable piece of property. (For more information on St. Martin, see chapter 12, "The French West Indies.")

Today, returning visitors who have been "off island" for a while are often surprised and shocked upon arriving in the St. Maarten greeting them today. No longer a sleepy Caribbean backwater, it has expanded like a boomtown in recent years. Many hotels and restaurants that sustained serious structural damage from Hurricane Luis in September 1995 have reopened with freshly renovated facilities, new and often better menus, and energized staffs (some proprietors were forced to renovate whether they liked it or not). A sense of freshness and rejuvenation now permeates the island.

In fact, you can live far more luxuriously on St. Maarten than you ever could before. Duty-free shopping has turned the island into a virtual mall, and the capital, Philipsburg, is often bustling with cruise-ship hordes. The nightlife is among the best in the Caribbean, with lively happy hours and casinos galore. Sunshine is pretty much guaranteed year-round on St. Maarten, so you can swim, snorkel, and sail on almost any day here. The island's 36 white-sand beaches remain unspoiled, and the clear turquoise waters are even more enticing.

Despite its natural beauty, much has been lost to the bulldozer on St. Maarten too. This is obviously not an island for people who don't like crowds, so if "getting away from it all" is your prerogative, we suggest that you head over to the nearby Dutch islands of St. Eustatius (Statia) and Saba. Nevertheless, in spite of its problems, including crime, occasional weather woes, traffic congestion, and corruption, St. Maarten continues to attract massive numbers of visitors who want a Caribbean island vacation with a splash of Las Vegas.

The divided island is the smallest territory in the world shared by two sovereign states. The only way you know you're crossing an international border is when you see the sign "Bienvenue Partie Française," attesting to the peaceful coexistence between the two nations. The island was officially split in 1648, and many visitors still ascend Mount Concordia, near the border, where the agreement was reached. Even so, St. Maarten changed hands 16 times before it became permanently Dutch.

St. Maarten lies 144 miles southeast of Puerto Rico. A lush island, rimmed with bays and beaches, it has a year-round temperature of 80°F. The Dutch capital, **Philipsburg,** curves like a toy village along Great Bay. The town lies on a narrow sand isthmus separating Great Bay and the Great Salt Pond. The capital was founded in 1763 by Commander John Philips, a Scot in Dutch employ. To protect Great Bay, Fort Amsterdam was built in 1737.

The main thoroughfare is busy **Front Street,** which stretches for about a mile and is lined with stores selling international merchandise, such as French designer fashions and Swedish crystal. More shops are along the little lanes, known as *steegijes,* that connect Front Street with Back Street, another shoppers' mart.

GETTING THERE

St. Maarten's **Queen Juliana International Airport** is the second busiest in the Caribbean, topped only by San Juan, Puerto Rico.

American Airlines (☎ **800/624-6262** in the U.S.) offers more options and more frequent service into St. Maarten than any other airline—one daily nonstop flight from both New York's JFK and Miami. Additional nonstop daily flights into St. Maarten are offered by American and its local affiliate **American Eagle** (same toll-free number) from San Juan, Puerto Rico. Ask for one of the airline's tour operators, because you can usually save money by booking your air travel and hotel accommodation at the same time.

ALM Antillean Airlines (☎ **800/327-7230** in the U.S.) offers nonstop and twice-daily direct service in winter to St. Maarten from the airline's home base on Curaçao. In the off-season, there are two flights on Wednesday and Friday plus one flight on Thursday and Sunday.

GETTING AROUND

BY TAXI Taxis are unmetered, but St. Maarten law requires drivers to have a list that details fares to major island destinations. A typical fare from Queen Juliana

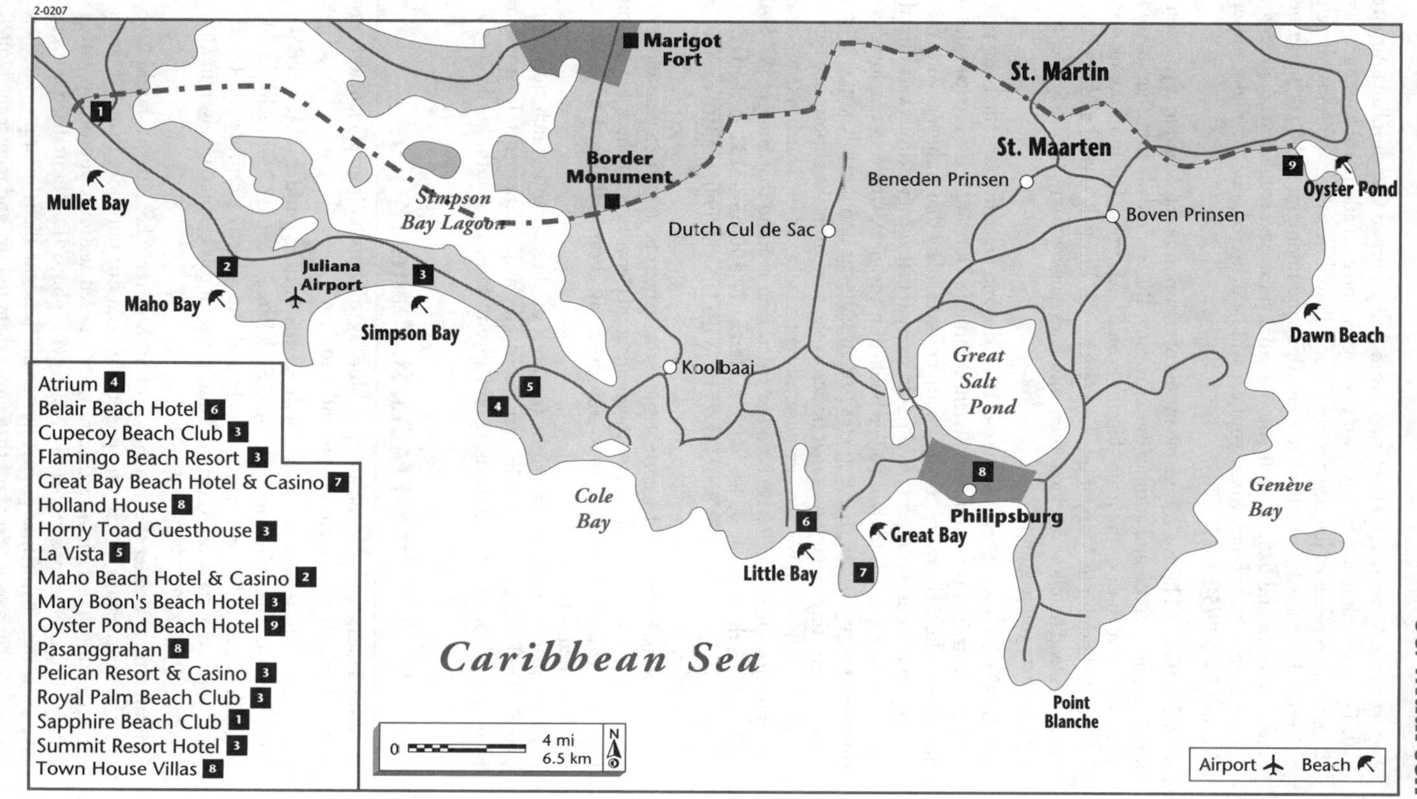
2-0207
Marigot Fort
St. Martin
St. Maarten
Border Monument
Simpson Bay Lagoon
Mullet Bay
Maho Bay
Juliana Airport
Simpson Bay
Dutch Cul de Sac
Beneden Prinsen
Boven Prinsen
Oyster Pond
Dawn Beach
Koolbaai
Great Salt Pond
Cole Bay
Little Bay
Great Bay
Philipsburg
Genève Bay
Point Blanche
Caribbean Sea
0
4 mi
6.5 km
N
Airport
Beach
Atrium 4
Belair Beach Hotel 6
Cupecoy Beach Club 3
Flamingo Beach Resort 3
Great Bay Beach Hotel & Casino 7
Holland House 8
Horny Toad Guesthouse 3
La Vista 5
Maho Beach Hotel & Casino 2
Mary Boon's Beach Hotel 3
Oyster Pond Beach Hotel 9
Pasanggrahan 8
Pelican Resort & Casino 3
Royal Palm Beach Club 3
Sapphire Beach Club 1
Summit Resort Hotel 3
Town House Villas 8

Airport to the Maho Beach Hotel is $5; from Philipsburg to Queen Juliana Airport, $10. There are minimum fares for two passengers, and each additional passenger pays $2 extra. Two pieces of luggage per person are allowed free; each additional piece is 50¢ extra. Fares are 25% higher between 10pm and midnight, and 50% higher between midnight and 6am. Even if you're renting a car, taxi regulations require you to take a cab to your hotel, where your car will be delivered. For late-night cab service, call ☎ **599/5-54317.**

BY MINIBUS This is a reasonable means of transport on St. Maarten if you don't mind inconveniences, and at times overcrowding. Buses run daily from 7am to midnight and serve most of the major locations on St. Maarten. The most popular run is from Philipsburg to Marigot on the French side. Privately owned and operated, minibuses tend to follow specific routes, with fares ranging from $1.15 to $2, depending on where you're going.

BY RENTAL CAR Because of the island's size and diversity, car rentals are practical, particularly if you want to experience both the Dutch and the French sides of the island. The taxi drivers' union strictly enforces a law that forbids anyone from picking up a car at the airport. As a result, every rental agency delivers cars directly to its customers' hotels (only if you've booked in advance), where an employee will complete the paperwork. If you prefer to rent your car upon arrival, you can head for one of the tiny rental kiosks that lie across the road from the airport, but beware of long lines. In recent years, policies against renting a car on the Dutch side to someone staying on the French have been less strict. Bear in mind that **Budget** (☎ **800/527-0700** in the U.S., or 599/5-54030), **Hertz** (☎ **800/654-3131** in the U.S., or 599/5-54314), and **Avis** (☎ **800/331-2112** in the U.S., or 599/5-44316) each maintain an office on both sides of the island.

All three major car-rental agencies require that renters be at least 25 years old. Your credit- or charge-card issuer may provide insurance coverage, so check before your trip; otherwise, it might be wise to buy the fairly cheap collision-damage waiver (CDW) when you rent.

Remember to **drive on the right** (on both the French and Dutch sides of the island). Traffic jams are common near the island's major settlements. International road signs are observed, and there are no Customs formalities at the border.

FAST FACTS: St. Maarten

Banking Hours Most banks are open Monday to Thursday from 8:30am to 1pm and on Friday from 8:30am to 1pm and 4 to 5pm.

Currency The legal tender is the **Netherlands Antilles guilder (NAf),** and the official rate at which the banks accept U.S. dollars is NAf 1.77 for each U.S.$1. Regardless, U.S. dollars are easily, willingly, and often eagerly accepted in the Dutch Windwards, especially St. Maarten. Thus, prices in this chapter are given in U.S. currency unless otherwise designated.

Documents To enter the Dutch side of St. Maarten, U.S. citizens should have proof of citizenship: a passport (preferably valid but not more than five years expired), an original birth certificate with a raised seal or a photocopy with a notary seal, or a voter's registration card with photo ID. Naturalized citizens may show their naturalization certificate, and resident aliens must provide their "green" card or a temporary card that allows them to leave and reenter the United States. British and Canadian visitors need valid passports, and all visitors must have a confirmed room reservation before their arrival, plus a return or ongoing ticket.

Electricity Dutch Sint Maarten uses the same voltage (110 volts AC; 60 cycles) with the same electrical configurations as the United States, so adapters and transformers are not necessary. However, on French St. Martin transformers and adapters are necessary. To simplify things, many hotels on both sides of the island have installed built-in sockets suitable for both the European and North American forms of electrical currents.

Emergencies Call the **police** at ☎ **599/5-22222** or an **ambulance** at ☎ **599/5-22111.**

Hospitals Go to the **Medical Center,** Welegen Road, Cay Hill (☎ **599/5-31111**).

Information Before you go, contact the **St. Maarten Tourist Office,** 675 Third Ave., Suite 1806, New York, NY 10017 (☎ **800/786-2278** or 212/953-2084). Once on the island, go to the **Tourist Information Bureau,** in the Imperial Building at 23 Walter Nisbeth Rd. (☎ **599/5-22337**), open Monday to Friday from 8am to noon and 1 to 5pm.

Language The language is officially Dutch, but most people speak English.

Safety Crime is on the rise on St. Maarten and, in fact, has become quite serious. If possible, avoid night driving—it's particularly unwise to drive on remote, unlit, back roads at night. Also, let that deserted, isolated beach remain so. You're safer in a crowd, although under no circumstances should you ever leave anything unguarded on the beach.

Taxes and Service A $5 departure tax is charged when you're leaving the island for St. Eustatius or Saba, and $10 is charged for international flights. A 5% government tax is added to hotel bills, and in general, hotels also add a 10% or 15% service charge. If service has not been added (unlikely), it's customary to tip around 15% in restaurants.

Telephone Neither Dutch St. Maarten nor French St. Martin is part of the 809 area code that applies to most of the Caribbean. To call Dutch St. Maarten from the United States, dial 011 (the international access code), then 599 (the country code for the Netherlands Antilles), and finally 5 (the area code for Dutch St. Maarten) followed by the five-digit local number.

To make a call within Dutch St. Maarten, you need only the five-digit local number. But if you're calling "long distance" from the Dutch side of the island to the French side of the island, dial "00," followed by 590 (the international access code for French St. Martin), followed by the six-digit local number. If you're on the French side of the island and want to call anyone on the Dutch side, you'll have to treat the call the same way you'd have handled a call to the Dutch side from the mainland of the United States: Dial "00," followed by 599, then 5, followed by the five-digit local number. Know in advance that calls between the French and Dutch sides are considered long-distance calls and are much, much more expensive than you might have imagined considering the relatively short distances involved.

Time St. Maarten operates on Atlantic standard time year-round. Thus in winter, when the United States is on standard time, if it's 6pm in Philipsburg it's 5pm in New York. During daylight saving time in the United States, the island and the U.S. East Coast are on the same time.

Weather The island has a year-round temperature of about 80°F.

WHERE TO STAY

A government tax of 5% and a 10% to 15% service charge are added to your hotel bill. Ask about this when you book a room to save yourself a shock when you check out.

EXPENSIVE

Atrium. Bill Foley Rd., Pelican Keys, Simpson Bay, St. Maarten, N.A. ☎ **599/5-42126.** Fax 599/5-42128. 90 studios and apts. A/C TV TEL. Winter, $180 studio; $260 one-bedroom apt. Off-season, $150 studio; $215 one-bedroom apt. AE, MC, V.

It's one of the newest hotels on St. Maarten, and one of the few that emerged almost unscathed from the twin hurricanes that demolished many hotels in 1995. Its secret, according to island engineers, derives from a structure of reinforced concrete and tempered sliding glass doors that bend before they break. The hotel rises nine floors above a beachfront within a five-minute walk of its much larger (and less upscale) sibling, the Pelican Resort, where guests must go for amenities like casinos, tennis, water sports, and fine dining. The Atrium does, however, maintain its own swimming pool, snack bar, and bar. The rooms boast views over the hills, the lagoon, and/or the sea; private balconies; and a simple, summery decor of peach and green, with lots of tile work and wicker. Each contains a kitchenette.

Belair Beach Hotel. Little Bay (P.O. Box 940), Philipsburg, St. Maarten, N.A. ☎ **800/622-7836** in the U.S., or 599/5-23362. Fax 599/5-25295. 72 suites. A/C TV TEL. Winter, $175–$335 one-bedroom suite for 2; $215–$375 two-bedroom suite for 3. Off-season, $195 one-bedroom suite for 2; $235 two-bedroom suite for 3. Children 17 and under stay free in parents' suite (subject to availability). AE, DC, DISC, MC, V.

One of the most surprising things about this breezy, oceanfront condo right on Little Bay Beach, a 10-minute taxi ride east of the airport, is the size of the accommodations: They're all suites. Each contains a large bedroom, two full baths with a tub and shower, a fully equipped kitchen, and a 21-foot terrace with a sweeping view of the sea. The suites were recently renovated, and are privately owned but rented to visitors when their owners are not on the island. Although the Belair Beach is expensive, many visitors to St. Maarten find that it's a good value, considering the amenities (especially the kitchen) and the family package rate.

Dining/Entertainment: The Sugar Bird Café serves breakfast, lunch, and dinner in a casual atmosphere. A grocery is on the premises.

Services: Laundry, baby-sitting, car-rental desk, activities desk.

Facilities: Beach with a seafront freshwater pool, two tennis courts, water sports.

Cupecoy Beach Club. Cupecoy Lowlands, Simpson Bay (P.O. Box 3007), Philipsburg, St. Maarten, N.A. ☎ **599/5-52243** or 599/5-52086. Fax 599/5-52243. 35 rms, 53 suites. A/C TV TEL. Winter, $175–$225 double; $250–$300 one-bedroom suite; $400–$500 two-bedroom suite; $550–$650 three-bedroom suite. Off-season, $125–$150 double; $175–$200 one-bedroom suite; $250–$300 two-bedroom suite; $350–$400 three-bedroom suite. AE, DISC, MC, V.

This place doesn't consider itself a hotel at all (technically, it's a cluster of condominiums whose units are rented out). Originally built in the 1970s, it consists of two all-white, Iberian-style buildings that rise above a low cliff beside Simpson Bay. Next to the 15th tee of the Mullet Bay Golf Course, Cupecoy is an elegant hotel, partly because of its individual furnishings, set on 4 acres of landscaped grounds. Although there's a pool and two bars, there are no organized activities here. Other than the friendly check-in service, a sense of anonymity prevails here. If you opt for a double room here, you'll be placed in the bedroom of what was originally configured as a suite. Doors are locked and unlocked to create a labyrinth of different floor plans.

The best thing about this place is that each room has a fully equipped kitchen, which allows guests to save on restaurant bills.

Flamingo Beach Resort. Pelican Key, Simpson Bay (P.O. Box 3035), St. Maarten, N.A. ☎ **599/5-43732.** Fax 011/599-5-43727. 51 units (about 40% of which are available for rentals). Winter $180–$240 studios or one-bedroom apts for up to 4 occupants, $20 for 5th and 6th. Off-season, $150–$190 studios or one-bedroom apts, $15 for 5th or 6th. AE, MC, V.

This peach-and-white, five-story time-share unit was originally built in the late 1980s as part of the sprawling Pelican Bay Resort and Condominium complex; however, in 1995, it split from Pelican Bay after investors (the same ones that manage the Royal Palm Beach Club) bought it. Most units are occupied by their owners, but around 40% of them are available as short-term rentals. This is an ideal place to stay if you shun large resort, prefer to cook some meals in-house, and cherish independence and privacy. Each unit—either a studio or one-bedroom apartment—contains a small porch and a full kitchen. At press time, the complex's swimming pool was still under construction, and almost all sports activities were arranged with outfitters off-premises.

Great Bay Beach Hotel and Casino. Front St. (P.O. Box 310), Philipsburg, St. Maarten, N.A. ☎ **800/223-0757** or 599/5-22446. Fax 599/5-23859. 285 rms, 10 suites. A/C TV TEL. Winter (all-inclusive), $330–$380 double; $405–$450 triple; $350–$410 suite for 2. Off-season (EP), $95–$130 double; $125–$160 triple; $115–$155 suite for 2. AE, DC, MC, V.

This deluxe all-inclusive resort is located at the southwestern corner of Great Bay. Within walking distance of Philipsburg, it's ideal for shopping excursions. The hotel received a $10 million renovation, followed by a second renovation after Hurricane Luis dropped in. It still lacks any real charm and is short on atmosphere. All guest rooms have been refurbished, and contain bland furniture, a terrace or patio, and a king-size bed or two full-size beds. The corner ocean rooms are the most expensive and the most preferred. The bathrooms have Valentino-designed tiles.

Dining/Entertainment: The hotel has a casino and nightclub, plus two dining areas, serving a standard international cuisine.

Services: Laundry, baby-sitting.

Facilities: One all-weather tennis court; two freshwater pools, which are infinitely preferred to the polluted water at the beach.

La Vista. Pelican Key Estates (P.O. Box 2086), Philipsburg, St. Maarten, N.A. ☎ **599/5-43005.** Fax 599/5-43010. 24 suites and cottages. A/C TV TEL. Winter, $300 junior suite; $350–$550 suite or cottage. Off-season, $220 junior suite; $260–$360 suite or cottage. AE, DC, MC, V.

La Vista, although not well known, offers large and handsomely furnished time-share suites and Antillean cottages. Each accommodation has a sea view and contains an equipped kitchenette, a spacious living and dining area, and a good-sized balcony. The resort is about a 10-minute drive west of Philipsburg, longer with traffic. It took a major hit from Hurricane Luis, but was restored in late 1995.

Dining/Entertainment: The complex features a lounge area, as well as an open-air restaurant, the Hideaway.

Services: Room service, laundry, baby-sitting.

Facilities: Freshwater swimming pool. Guests have use of the beach facilities at the adjacent Pelican Resort.

Maho Beach Hotel and Casino. Maho Bay, Philipsburg, St. Maarten, N.A. ☎ **599/5-52115.** Fax 599/5-53180. 600 rms, 35 suites. A/C TV TEL. Winter, $225–$375 double; $440–$590 suite. Off-season, $155–$250 double; $325–$460 suite. AE, DC, MC, V.

Separated into three distinct sections, each built over an eight-year period beginning in the mid-1980s, this megaresort is the largest hotel on the island. The hotel was massively renovated following hurricane damage in 1995. Set along the busy coastal road adjacent to a crescent-shaped beach, the hotel is unified by its trademark color scheme of pink and white. About a third of the rooms contain microwaves and refrigerators, and each has wicker furniture, Italian tiles, and plush upholstery. The hotel's only drawbacks are its very large size and the thundering noise of planes landing at the airport (two minutes away) several times a day.

Dining/Entertainment: Due to its size, the hotel contains 10 independently operated restaurants, more than any other hotel on the island. The Casino Royale, across the street, is the largest on the island. La Luna, an open-air disco, is an island hot spot.

Services: Laundry, baby-sitting.

Facilities: Four tennis courts, two outdoor swimming pools with a view of Maho Bay, health-club spa, duty-free shopping (70 boutiques), a beach with water sports at the bottom of the hill.

Pelican Resort & Casino. Simpson Bay (P.O. Box 431), Philipsburg, St. Maarten, N.A. ☎ **800/626-9637** in the U.S., or 599/5-42503. Fax 599/5-42133. 342 suites. A/C TV TEL. Winter, $114–$192 junior suite for 2, $204–$270 junior suite for 4; $306 one-bedroom suite for 2, $420 one-bedroom suite for 4; $445 two-bedroom suite for 4. Off-season, $95–$160 junior suite for 2, $170 junior suite for 4; $225 one-bedroom suite for 2, $255 one-bedroom suite for 4; $350 two-bedroom suite for 4. Seven-night minimum stay usually required in winter. AE, DC, MC, V.

The Pelican, built in 1979 on 12 acres of land near the airport, is the largest timeshare facility on St. Maarten, but it is dealing with bankruptcy problems. Although many of the suites are leased for predesignated periods throughout the year, others are rented as they become available by the on-site managers. Accommodations contain ceiling fans and full kitchens, and are arranged into village-style clusters separated from other units with lattices, hibiscus hedges, and bougainvillea. The furnishings are blandly international, in pastel colors, and most units contain a patio or veranda. Scattered around the property are a lily pond, many small waterways, and an orchid garden.

Dining/Entertainment: The Pelican Reef Restaurant is one of the island's best steak-and-seafood restaurants, with a waterfront ambience and an extensive wine list. The casual Crocodile Café offers good and reasonable fare. The Italian Connection delivers pizza and pasta and there's also a cozy bistro with a European-style menu. The hotel's casino is in a "gingerbread" historical building called the "Greathouse."

Services: Laundry, baby-sitting.

Facilities: Five tennis courts; six swimming pools; children's playground; 1,400 feet of ocean-front marina; L'Aqualine, a unique health and beauty center (see "A Revitalization Center" under "Beaches, Water Sports & Outdoor Pursuits," below). Water sports can be arranged.

✪ **Oyster Pond Beach Hotel.** Oyster Pond (P.O. Box 239), Philipsburg, St. Maarten, N.A. ☎ **599/5-22206.** Fax 599/5-25695. 20 rms, 20 suites. A/C TV TEL. Winter, $170–$275 double; $290–$310 suite. Off-season, $120–$175 double; $190–$200 suite. AE, DC, DISC, MC, V. Closed Sept.

At the end of a twisting, scenic road this elegant retreat is designed for vacationers who don't like overly commercialized megaresorts, like Maho Beach. However, in a year or so it will lose a great deal of intimacy itself, with the construction of 80 new two-bedroom suites. On a circular harbor on the eastern shore, near the French border, the fortresslike structure stands guard over a 35-acre protected marina and has a private, sandy half-moon beach. There's a central courtyard and an al fresco lobby, with white wicker and fine paintings. More than half the units are suites or duplexes, and most have a West Indian decor. The bedrooms have balconies overlooking the pond or sea. The most elegant and expensive accommodations are the tower suites.

Dining/Entertainment: Off the courtyard, and opening onto the sea, is a bar/ lounge, as warm and comfortable as a private home. The dining room is exceptional, and the chef turns out a well-prepared continental cuisine with some Creole dishes. All dining is à la carte.

Services: Laundry.

Facilities: Freshwater swimming pool (22 by 44 feet).

Royal Palm Beach Club. P.O. Box 3035, Airport Blvd., Simpson Bay. ☎ **599/5-43732.** Fax 599/5-43727. 140 two-bedroom apts., about 40% of which are available for rentals. A/C TV TEL. Winter, $360 for up to 6 occupants. Off-season, $240 for up to 6 occupants. AE, MC, V.

The beauty of renting here involves direct access to Simpson's Bay Beach. Each unit is more or less the same, with two bedrooms, two baths, cool off-white and gray ceramic tile floors, and simple, summery furniture that was for the most part re-furbished or replaced in 1996. Units occupy five different floors of a white-and-peach building and contain a foldaway bed in the living room, ceiling fans and air-conditioning. There's a swimming pool on the premises, but that's about it—you won't find any bars, restaurants, or communal spaces at this apartment complex. Most people rent here for the privacy and anonymity. The Flamingo Beach Resort (see above) is under the same management.

Sapphire Beach Club. 147 Lowlands, Cupecoy, St. Maarten, N.A. ☎ **599/5-52179.** Fax 599/5-52178. 100 units, about 40% of which are available for rentals. A/C TV TEL. Winter, $235 studio for up to 4, $285 one-bedroom apt for up to 6. Off season, $145 studio for up to 4, $175 one-bedroom apt for up to 6. AE, MC, V.

This seven-story, blue and white building, erected in 1993, is one of the newest condominium and time-share properties on St. Maarten. Set on a narrow strip of land, midway between Cupecoy Beach and the lagoon, near Mullet Bay, it features furnished studios and one-bedroom apartments that are fully equipped for a self-sufficient beachfront vacation. Each unit contains a kitchenette, VCR, and ceiling fans, and faces either the lagoon or the ocean. There's a swimming pool on the premises, as well as a bar, and a simple grill-style restaurant open daily for lunch. About half the rooms contain small Jacuzzis on a balcony. Clients can stock their private kitchens with food and other supplies from the in-house minimart.

Town House Villas. 175 Front St. (P.O. Box 347), Philipsburg, St. Maarten, N.A. ☎ **800/ 223-9815** in the U.S., 212/545-8469 in New York City, or 599/5-22898. Fax 599/5-22418. 11 apts. A/C TV. Winter, $300 apt for 1 to 4. Off-season, $150 all apts. No credit cards.

This group of duplex villas lies at the edge of the restaurant and shopping district of Philipsburg. At your doorstep is Great Bay Beach, dotted with palms—it's shut off from the main street by a rugged stone wall and a wrought-iron gate. The town houses are handsome and rather formal, with shingled mansard roofs. Each apartment has two large bedrooms and 1$^{1}/_{2}$ baths. There's a completely equipped kitchen, plus a raised dining area in the long and well-furnished living room, which, along with the price, makes this a good choice for families. Wide glass doors open onto ocean-view patios. You can enjoy a view of the bay from your living room or your terrace.

MODERATE

Holland House. Front St. (P.O. Box 393), Philipsburg, St. Maarten, N.A. ☎ **800/223-9815** in the U.S., or 599/5-22572. Fax 599/5-24673. 54 units, 6 suites. A/C TV TEL. Winter, $130–$175 for up to 3; $175–$205 suite. Off-season, $74–$114 for up to 3; $114–$144 suite. AE, DC, DISC, MC, V.

Located in the heart of town, this hotel rents cozy apartments decorated with furnishings from the Netherlands and the United States, with an emphasis on rattan. Units have exposure to the street or to the (polluted) beach, and each contains a tiny kitchenette, ideal for light cooking. You're right on the beach, where you can order drinks at the bar. An open-air dining terrace fronts Great Bay. The hotel is near all the major restaurants and shops of Philipsburg. Even if you're not staying here, you might want to call and reserve a table for dinner; this is one of the few hotels that serves authentic Dutch specialties at its restaurant, the Governor's Restaurant. International and Indonesian specialties are also featured.

Horny Toad Guesthouse. Simpson Bay (P.O. Box 3029), Philipsburg, St. Maarten, N.A. ☎ **800/417-9361,** ext. 3013, or 599/5-54323. Fax 599/5-53316. 8 rms. Winter, $180 double. Off-season, $98 double. Additional person $25–$40 extra. No credit cards.

Many guests consider it the most homey and welcoming guest house on St. Maarten. It's the well-maintained domain of a pair of expatriates from the snows of Maine, Earle and Betty Vaughn. Seven of its eight rooms are in an amply proportioned beachside house originally built in the 1950s as a private home by the island's former governor. The eighth room is in half of an octagonal "round house" known for its large windows and views of the sea. Each room has a kitchenette. The Vaughns' tenure here began in 1979 when they checked in as overnight guests. So charmed were they that they bought the place two years later. There's no swimming pool, no restaurant, and no organized activities of any kind, although the beach is a few steps away, and a pair of gas-fired barbecues act as excuses for impromptu get-togethers by resident guests (and owners). The only drawback is that the hotel is near the airport, though the roar of jumbo jets is heard only a few times a day for a few moments. Much of the infrastructure of this place was repaired and/or rebuilt (including the roofs and the decks) after the storms of 1995. Children seven and under are not encouraged, but families with children over seven often retreat here to avoid the megaresorts, and second-timers quickly become "part of the family."

Mary's Boon Beach Hotel. Simpson Bay (P.O. Box 2078), Philipsburg, St. Maarten, N.A. ☎ **599/5-54235.** Fax 599/5-53403. 14 rms. TV TEL. Winter, $125–$195 double. Off-season, $90–$125 double. MC, V.

Built in 1968 near the beach, this small-scale inn is like something out of a West Indies Hemingway story. The name is an amalgam of its founder (Mary Pomeroy) and her companion, Mr. Boon, although their legacy is dimly remembered since new owners, Karla and Mark Cleveland, took over in 1996. Everything about the place exudes an informal and relaxed hospitality. Each unit contains a kitchen of its own, there's an honor bar in the communal living room, and a garden blooms lushly whenever it isn't being massacred by a hurricane. Damage from the storms of 1995 instigated a renovation of much of the place that was sorely needed anyway. There's an on-site restaurant serving West Indian and international food, that's open every night for dinner except during October. The inn, however, stays open during that period. Don't expect luxury or opulence of any kind: The rooms are comfortable and outfitted with ceiling fans, rattan and wicker furniture, and louvered windows open to seafront breezes. All but four units are air-conditioned. Noise is sometimes bothersome from planes taking off from the nearby airport, but big airplanes are a factor only two or three times a day, and only land during daylight hours.

Pasanggrahan. 15 Front St. (P.O. Box 151), Philipsburg, St. Maarten, N.A. ☎ **599/5-23588.** Fax 599/5-22885. 30 rms. Winter, $128–$158 double. Off-season, $78–$95 double. AE, MC, V. Closed Sept.

Pasanggrahan is the Indonesian word for guest house, and this one is West Indian in style. A small, informal guest house, it's right on the busy, narrow main street of Philipsburg, toward the end of the mountain side of Front Street. It's set back under tall trees, with a white wooden veranda. The interior has peacock bamboo chairs, Indian spool tables, and a gilt-framed oil portrait of Queen Wilhelmina. So many guests asked to see the bedroom where the queen and her daughter, Juliana, stayed during World War II that the management turned it into the Sydney Greenstreet Bar. The renovated bedrooms have king-size beds and in some cases Saban bedspreads; some are in the main building, and others are in an adjoining annex. All rooms have ceiling fans, and all but six are air-conditioned. Set among the wild jungle of palms and shrubbery is the dining area, the Pasanggrahan Restaurant. The private beach is only 50 feet away.

Summit Resort Hotel. P.O. Box 456, Simpson Bay Lagoon, St. Maarten, N.A. ☎ **599/5-52150,** or 718/518-7470 in New York City. Fax 599/5-52615. 51 rms, 10 with kitchenette. A/C TV. Winter, $140 double without kitchen, $175 double with kitchen. Off-season, $95–$105 double without kitchen, $120–$130 double with kitchen. AE, MC, V.

This cluster of one- and two-story bungalows is adjacent to a lagoon, but within a 10-minute walk of Cupecoy Beach. The only drawback is its layout: The verandas of some rooms look over the lagoon; others overlook gardens or other verandas. The place is pleasant and uncomplicated. Other than treks to the swimming pool or the on-site restaurant, many visitors are self-sufficient. A shuttle bus will take you free to the beach (some visitors prefer to walk); it charges $5 for an excursion to Philipsburg and its shops and casinos. The accommodations have been undergoing a major renovation. Colors have been brightened with a tropical motif.

WHERE TO DINE

EXPENSIVE

Antoine's. 103 Front St., Philipsburg. ☎ **599/5-22964.** Reservations recommended, especially in winter. Main courses $17.75–$36. AE, MC, V. Daily 11:30am–10pm. FRENCH/CREOLE/ITALIAN.

Antoine's offers *la belle cuisine* in an atmospheric building by the sea. You can enjoy an apéritif in the bar while you peruse the menu. Antoine's has a certain sophistication and style, backed up by first-class service and an impressive wine list. Its Gallic specialties with Creole overtones are among the best on the island, ranking favorably with any of the better restaurants in the French zone. The Italian specialties, however, are better at Da Livio (see below). The cuisine is mainly old continental favorites. Gazpacho and vichyssoise appear on the menu, but we prefer to begin with the chef's savory kettle of fish soup. A quite good homemade pâté would also make a suitable opening. The menu is almost equally divided between meat and fish dishes. If featured, opt for the baked red snapper fillet, which is delicately flavored with white wine, lemon, shallots, and a butter sauce. Although the veal and beef dishes are shipped in frozen, they're thawed out and fashioned into rather delectable choices, especially the veal scaloppini with a mustard-and-cream sauce that was smooth and perfectly balanced.

✪ **Da Livio Ristorante.** 189 Front St., Philipsburg. ☎ **599/5-23363.** Reservations recommended for dinner. Main courses at lunch $16–$25; at dinner, $18–$30. AE, DC, MC, V. Mon–Sat noon–2pm and 6:30–10pm. ITALIAN.

This is the finest Italian dining in St. Maarten. The food here is consistently excellent, and the staff is graciousness itself (something rarely found on the island). The place is as Italian as they come, even if all the staff isn't. Bergamasco Livio himself hails from near Venice, and he purchases most of his ingredients from the best suppliers in his home country.

At the bottom of Front Street, with a panoramic view of the Great Bay, the restaurant sets a romantic mood in the evening with background music. Da Livio obviously adores Pavarotti. Since 1979, and in spite of hurricanes, Da Livio has been turning out the classics, offering daily specials with an emphasis on fresh pastas, fresh local fish, and such favorites as lobster and prime meats. Our favorite dish is their homemade manicotti della casa, filled with ricotta, spinach, and a zesty tomato sauce. For a main course, we suggest you tear into Fra Diavolo with linguine or else the tender and juicy veal chop with sage-flavored butter. Tony Bennett and even Eddie Murphy have sung the praises of these dishes. This is obviously a kitchen staff who cares, even going so far as to grow tomatoes in their own garden.

Indiana Beach. Simpson Bay. ☎ **599/5-42797.** Reservations recommended. Main courses $15–$20; breakfast buffet $6.95. AE, DISC, MC, V. Daily 7:30am–midnight. Closed Sept. CONTINENTAL.

One of the island's best choices for an al fresco meal, this place is at its most romantic during candlelit dinners. At night, seating choices range from intimate sheltered booths to outdoor tables set within sight and sound of the sea (it's on the road to the Pelican Resort & Casino). The fresh fish and other seafood specialties are your best bet. The lobster pasta is sublime; otherwise, the main dishes are all too familiar, though well prepared, including the filet mignon.

✪ **Le Perroquet.** 72 Airport Rd. ☎ **599/5-54339.** Reservations required. Main courses $18–$26. AE, DISC, MC, V. Tues–Sun 6–10pm. Closed June and Sept. FRENCH.

Only a short walk from the airport is the domain of M. Pierre Castagne, a French chef of exceptional ability. The St. Maarten version of the famed Chicago restaurant is in a typical West Indian house with shutters open to the trade winds blowing around Simpson Bay Lagoon. Monsieur Castagne offers such dishes as ostrich breast (yes, that's right) in a bordelaise sauce and fillet of boar, but you can also order more familiar fare, beginning with a savory fish soup or a fresh mâche salad, and moving on to a delectable mussels marinara, a savory duck with a Grand Marnier orange sauce, or a perfectly cooked red snapper in a garlic sauce. Some of the specialties are wheeled in on a table so you can make a visual selection—a nice touch.

✪ **Saratoga.** Simpson Bay Yacht Club, Airport Rd. ☎ **599/5-42421.** Reservations required. Main courses $16–$36. AE, MC, V. Mon–Sat 6:30–10:30pm. CONTEMPORARY AMERICAN.

This is the most creative and cutting-edge restaurant in St. Maarten—it's more closely aligned with trends you'd expect in Los Angeles or New York than in the Caribbean. The result is a burgeoning business that's both laid back and intensely choreographed at the same time. Thanks to the impressive quantities of varnished mahogany that line much of the interior, this restaurant, which resembles a Spanish colonial structure from the outside, is also one of the most beautiful restaurants on the island.

You might opt for a predinner drink ("ultramargaritas" and vodka martinis are the house specialties) in the bar. Seating is either inside or on a marina-side veranda, where the menu changes daily. There's always an artfully contrived low-fat or no-fat selection like onion-crusted salmon served on a compote of lentils and sweet corn. Yellowfin tuna might be grilled with basmati rice or wasabi-flavored butter and daikon leaves. Grilled salmon is sometimes served either orange flavored, wasabi-flavored, or ginger-flavored with flying fish caviar; and rack of venison is often featured with port or some other sauce owner and chef John Jackson (who hails, incidentally, from Saratoga Springs, New York) feels inspired to concoct on the night of your arrival.

Spartaco. Almond Grove Plantation Estate, Cole Bay. ☎ **599/5-45379.** Reservations recommended. Main courses $20–$24. AE, MC, V. Tues–Sun 6–11pm. Closed Sept–Oct. ITALIAN.

Spartaco is in a residential suburb midway between Philipsburg and the airport. The decor includes strong doses of 1930s art deco and some high-tech design. Guests sit in the main dining room or on a breeze-filled wraparound veranda. Season after season, Spartaco has continued to be the leader in Italian cuisine, and not the pizza and spaghetti selections too often passed off as Italian. Here you get the real thing, and that includes fresh black tagliolini (angel-hair pasta flavored with squid ink) served with shrimp, parsley, and garlic sauce. The swordfish Mediterranean is one of the most worthy dishes, composed of parsley, garlic, capers, and an olive oil that owner Spartaco Sargentoni imports from his relatives who produce it on a farm outside Florence. The antipasti, from squid and mussels to eggplant and carpaccio, make a fine beginning.

MODERATE

Chesterfields. Great Bay Marina, Philipsburg. ☎ **599/5-23484.** Reservations recommended. Lunch main courses $6.95–$13.95; dinner main courses $13.95–$16.95. No credit cards. Daily 5:30–10pm, Mon–Sat 11:30am–5pm, Sun 10:30am–2:30pm. AMERICAN/CARIBBEAN.

Just a few steps from Great Bay Marina, east of Philipsburg, this restaurant occupies a breezy veranda that's popular among yachties. Breakfasts are hearty and wholesome, and eye-opening entrees range from $2.99 to around $6—the seafood omelets are especially tasty. Besides dispensing bottled beer and mixed drinks from midmorning until long after sundown, the bar does a brisk lunch business too, serving platters of fish, grilled steaks and other meats, sandwiches, and salads. Dinners are more elaborate, and include yellowfin tuna or mahimahi, which can either be grilled and served with garlic butter, or panfried with a Creole sauce. Roasted duck is accompanied by banana-pineapple sauce, and has been a longtime favorite here. The Wednesday night special is prime rib, served with heaping portions of sautéed mushrooms.

La Rosa, Too. In the Maho Plaza Shopping Center. ☎ **599/5-53470.** Reservations recommended. Main courses $17.50–$25. AE, MC, V. Wed–Mon 6–11pm. ITALIAN.

La Rosa, Too is one of the most noteworthy Italian restaurants on Sint Maarten, a pink and terra-cotta enclave accented with Brazilian hardwoods and a southern Mediterranean flair. Menu specialties are often Sicilian, because of the origins of the likable owner, Guiseppe La Rosa. As you dine, water will cascade over a simulated tropical waterfall, distracting you from a view of passersby and shoppers at its shopping mall location. Menu items include two preparations of lobster, the more delectable of which (lobster cappriccio) is made with a 10-ounce tail with a dressing of cognac and mushrooms. Another version, rather oddly labeled as Caribbean style, includes a light mustard sauce. There's a full array of traditional Parmesan and marsala dishes (veal, jumbo shrimp, chicken), a worthy version of beef tenderloin, fusilli al pescatore (which everybody seems to like), and such fish dishes as snapper with a garlic-and-tomato sauce. The main dining room is air-conditioned, whereas the outdoor terrace is open to prevailing winds.

The Wajang Doll. 137 Front St., Philipsburg. ☎ **599/5-22687.** Reservations required. Dinner $18.90 for 14 dishes, $24.90 for 19 dishes. AE, MC, V. Mon–Sat 6:45–10pm. Closed Sept. INDONESIAN.

Housed in a wooden West Indian building on the main street of town, the Wajang Doll is the best Indonesian restaurant in the Caribbean. There's a low-slung front porch where you can watch the pedestrian traffic outside, and the big windows in back overlook the sea. The restaurant is best known for its 19-dish dinner, known as a *rijstaffel* (rice table). The cuisine varies from West Java to East Java, and the chef crushes his spices every day for maximum pungency, according to an ancient craft. The specialties include a spicy fried snapper in a chili sauce, marinated pork on a bamboo stick, and zestily flavored Javanese chicken dishes.

INEXPENSIVE

✪ **Cheri's Café.** 45 Cinnamon Grove, Shopping Centre, Maho Beach. ☎ **599/5-53361.** Reservations not accepted. Main courses $5.50–$16.75. No credit cards. Daily 11am–midnight. AMERICAN.

The island hot spot, Cheri's was winner of the *Caribbean Travel and Life* readers' pick for best bar in the West Indies. Known for its inexpensive food and live bands, it is by now an island institution, and has been ever since it opened in 1988. American expatriate Cheri Baston is the host of this open-air cafe serving some 400 meals a night.

The place is really only a roof without walls, and it's not on a beach. But people flock to it anyway, devouring 16-ounce steaks or a simple burger. You can also get really fresh grilled fish, dining under the canopy or on a terrace under the stars. Everybody from movie stars to rock bands, from high rollers at the casino to beach bums, comprises the clientele. Some come for the inexpensive food, others for the potent drinks, and some to dance to the music. The bartender's special is a frozen "Straw Hat" made with vodka, coconut, tequila, both pineapple and orange juice, and strawberry liqueur. Maybe even one more ingredient, we suspect, although nobody's talking.

✪ **Crocodile Express Café.** Casino Balcony, at the Pelican Resort & Casino, Simpson Bay. ☎ **599/5-42503,** ext. 1127. MC, V. Daily 7:30am–11pm. DELI/GRILL/AMERICAN.

Start the day overlooking Simpson Bay with extrathick French toast made with homemade bread, or order eggs any style. Otherwise, maybe lunch, or snacks in the afternoon? Many patrons file in for dinner as early as 6pm. Hearty deli fare includes well-stuffed sandwiches. At night you might prefer grilled local fish or tasty kebabs. A specialty is grilled chicken breast West Indian style, marinated in tropical fruit juices and served with grilled onions. Meals are followed by home-baked pies and other desserts, and drinks include fresh mango or frozen passion fruit.

Don Carlos Restaurant. Airport Rd., Simpson Bay. ☎ **599/5-53112.** Reservations not required. Main courses $10.50–$28.50. AE, DC, DISC, MC, V. Daily 7:30am–10pm. MEXICAN/CARIBBEAN/INTERNATIONAL.

This down-home restaurant is located just five minutes east of the airport, with a view of arriving and departing planes from the floor-to-ceiling windows surrounded by international flags. The place serves breakfast, lunch, and dinner, providing consistently decent fare at reasonable prices. Owners Shenny and Carl Wagner invite you for a drink in their Pancho Villa Bar before your meal in their hacienda-style dining room with a multilingual staff. Quantity, instead of quality, is the rule here, but diners seem to view this as a "fun" choice.

The Greenhouse. Bobby's Marina, Philipsburg. ☎ **599/5-22941.** Reservations not required. Main courses $9–$16. AE, MC, V. Daily 11am–1am. AMERICAN.

Open to a view of the harbor, off Front Street, the Greenhouse is filled with plants, as befits its name. As you dine, breezes filter through the open-air eatery. Lunches include the catch of the day, a wide selection of burgers, and conch chowder. Dinners might feature chunks of lobster in wine sauce or a whole red snapper. By no means does this place serve the best food on the island, but it's plentiful and a good value. Some patrons use it merely as a drinking venue. Happy hour from 4:30 to 7pm features half-price appetizers.

Lynette's. Simpson Bay Blvd. ☎ **599/5-52865.** Reservations recommended. Main courses $6.95–$25. AE, MC, V. Winter, daily 11:30am–10:30pm. Off-season, daily 6–10:30pm. WEST INDIAN.

This is the most noteworthy West Indian restaurant on St. Maarten. It's completely unpretentious, and rich in local flavors and understated charm. St. Maarten-born Lynette Felix, along with Clayton Felix, are the creative forces here, serving flavorful ethnic food from a location close to the airport. The setting is a concrete-sided, wood-trimmed building beside the highway, with a color scheme of pink, maroon, cream, and brown. The menu reads like a lexicon of tried-and-true Caribbean staples, including colombos (ragouts) of goat and chicken, stuffed crab backs, curried seafood, fillet of snapper with green plantains and Creole sauce or garlic butter. An ideal lunch might be a brimming bowlful of pumpkin (squash) soup followed by one of the main-course salads. The one made from herbed lobster, when available, is particularly succulent. The dishes here have true island flavor.

BEACHES, WATER SPORTS & OUTDOOR PURSUITS

BEACHES St. Maarten has 36 beautiful white-sand beaches, and it's comparatively easy to find a part of the beach for yourself. *Warning:* If it's too secluded, be careful. It's unwise to carry valuables to the beach; there have been reports of robberies on some remote beaches.

Regardless of where you stay, you're never far from the water. If you're a beach sampler, you can often use the changing facilities at some of the bigger resorts for a small fee. Nudists should head for the French side of the island, although the Dutch side is getting more liberal about such things.

On the west side of the island, west of the airport, **Mullet Bay Beach** is shaded by palm trees and can get crowded on weekends. Water-sports equipment rentals can be arranged through the hotel.

Great Bay Beach is preferred if you're staying along Front Street in Philipsburg. This mile-long beach is sandy, but since it borders the busy capital it may not be as clean as some of the more remote beaches. Immediately to the west, at the foot of Fort Amsterdam, **Little Bay Beach** looks like a Caribbean postcard, but it, too, can be overrun with hotel visitors.

Stretching the length of **Simpson Bay Village,** Simpson Bay Beach is shaped like a half moon with white sand. It's west of Philipsburg before you reach the airport. Water-sports-equipment rentals are available here.

North of the airport, **Maho Bay Beach,** at the Maho Beach Hotel and Casino, is shaded by palms and is ideal in many ways, if you don't mind the planes taking off and landing. Palms provide shade, and food and drink can be purchased at the hotel.

The sands are pearly white at **Oyster Pond Beach,** near the Oyster Pond Hotel northeast of Philipsburg. Bodysurfers like the rolling waves here. In the same location, **Dawn Beach** is noted for its underwater tropical beauty (reefs lie offshore).

DEEP-SEA FISHING **Pelican Watersports,** at the Pelican Resort and Casino, Simpson Bay (☎ **599/5-42640**), is set in the compound of one of the island's most comprehensive resorts. It's one of the few water-sports centers that survived more or less intact after the winds of 1995. Their 31-foot Blackfin is available for deep-sea-fishing expeditions priced at $425 for a half-day (8am to noon) and $725 for a full-day (8am to 4pm) excursion.

A subcontractor with which Pelican Watersports works in close cooperation is **Fun in the Sun,** Great Bay Marina (☎ **599/5-70210**). Its trio of boats (the 31-foot Blackfin mentioned above, as well as a 32-foot Prowler, and a third that departs from the Oyster Pond Marina) are among the most consistently busy on the island. The craft contain all the fishing equipment you'll need, and have upper decks for clear visibility of the depths. Each is suitable for up to six participants.

Know before you go that the crew of these boats (and of most other fishing craft on St. Maarten) is more bloodthirsty than you'd expect—they really want their passengers to catch a respectable amount of game fish. They sell, at substantial profits, whatever game fish their customers catch to local restaurants at the end of the day (although clients do receive a stack of fillets to take home for dinner), so if everybody agrees to it, they'll likely extend your time at sea if the fish are biting and the catch is good.

GOLF The **Mullet Bay Resort (☎ 599/5-52801,** ext. 1851) has an 18-hole course, one of the most challenging in the Caribbean, designed by Joseph Lee. Mullet Pond and Simpson Bay Lagoon provide both beauty and hazards. Greens fees are $105 for 18 holes.

HORSEBACK RIDING At **Crazy Acres,** Dr. J. H. Dela Fuente St., Cole Bay (**☎ 599/5-42793**), riding expeditions will invariably end on an isolated beach where the horses, with or without their riders, enjoy the cool waters in an after-ride romp. Two experienced escorts accompany a maximum of six people on the outings, which begin at 9:30am and 2:30pm Monday to Saturday and last 2½ hours. The price is $50 per person. Riders of all levels of experience are welcome, with the single provision that they wear bathing suits under their riding clothes for the grand finale on the beach. Reserve at least a day in advance. Riding lessons are available.

A REVITALIZATION CENTER **L'Aqualine,** at the Pelican Resort and Casino, Simpson Bay (**☎ 599/5-42426**), is a world-class European health, fitness, and beauty spa that offers services ranging from water aerobics to massages, and from cellulite therapy to body sculpting. Spa services include waxing, massages, medical pedicures, manicures, body peelings, facials, and beauty treatments. Facilities include eight separate treatment rooms, saunas, a steam room, and an ice-plunge and therapy pool. The center will send you full details. It's open Monday to Saturday from 9am to 6pm.

SAILING TO OTHER ISLANDS Experienced skippers make one-day voyages to St. Barts in the French West Indies and to Saba, another of the Dutch Windwards in the Leewards; they stop long enough for passengers to familiarize themselves with the island ports, shop, and have lunch. To arrange a trip, ask at your hotel or at the **St. Maarten Tourist Bureau,** 23 Walter Nisbeth Rd. in Philipsburg (**☎ 599/5-22337**).

If you'd like to see some of the other islands nearby, the best deal is offered by ***Voyager I*** and ***Voyager II.*** There are daily sails to St. Barts costing $50 round-trip or to Saba, going for $60 round-trip. Children under 12 ride for half price. These are good value trips well worth the time and money. For more details, call **Dockside Management** in Philipsburg (**☎ 599/5-24096**).

TENNIS You can try the courts at most of the large hotels. The best courts are at two previously recommended hotels, including the Oyster Pond Beach Hotel and the Maho Beach Hotel.

WATER SPORTS **Windsurfing** and **jet-skiing** are especially popular on St. Maarten. The unruffled waters of Simpson Bay Lagoon, the largest in the West Indies, are ideal for these sports, as well as for **waterskiing.**

St. Maarten's crystal-clear bays and the countless coves make for good **snorkeling** and **scuba diving.** Underwater visibility reportedly runs from 75 to 125 feet. The biggest attraction for scuba divers is the 1801 British man-of-war, HMS *Proselyte,* which came to a watery grave on a reef a mile off the coast. Most of the big resort hotels have facilities for scuba diving, and their staff can provide information about underwater tours, for photography as well as for night diving.

The best water sports, and the best value, are found at **Pelican Watersports,** Pelican Resort and Casino, Simpson Bay (☎ **599/5-42640**). Its PADI-instructed program features the most knowledgeable guides on the island, each one familiar with St. Maarten dive sites. Divers are taken out in custom-built 28- and 35-foot boats, and many return to claim that they've been led to some of the best reef diving in the Caribbean. A single-tank dive costs $45; a double-tank dive, $90. Snorkeling trips can also be arranged, as can trips to nearby islands, including Saba, Anguilla, and St. Barts.

CRUISES & TOURS

CRUISES A popular pastime is a day of picnicking, sailing, snorkeling, and sightseeing aboard one of several boats providing the service. The sleek sailboats usually pack large wicker hampers full of victuals and stretch tarpaulins over sections of the deck to protect sun-shy sailors. *Random Wind* is a sailing boat that operates in conjunction with **Fun in the Sun,** Great Bay Marina (☎ **599/5-70210**). It's a 47-foot traditional clipper making day trips that circumnavigate St. Maarten, carrying 15 passengers at a cost of $70. On Sunday a breakfast cruise is available at $30 per person, and dinner cruises (Wednesday only) cost $50. On Sunday Caribbean lunch cruises are also sold at $45 per head. Call for more information.

SIGHTSEEING TOURS The only outfits offering bus tours of the island are **Dutch Tours,** Cougar Road, 8 Unit One (☎ **599/5-23316**), and **St. Maarten Sightseeing Tours** (☎ **599/5-22753**), whose buses can accommodate between 22 and 52 people. They are only configured for large groups, and are very difficult to prearrange.

You can also hire a taxi driver as your guide; a 2½ hour tour of the entire island costs $30 for up to two passengers, and $7.50 for each additional passenger.

SHOPPING

St. Maarten is not only a free port, but there are no local sales taxes. Prices are sometimes lower here than anywhere else in the Caribbean except St. Thomas, with which it is locked in a head-to-head race. However, you must be familiar with the prices of what you're looking for to know what actually is a bargain. On some items we've priced (fine liqueurs, cigarettes, Irish linen, German cameras, French perfumes) we've found prices 30% to 50% lower than in the United States or Canada. Many well-known shops on Curaçao have branches here, in case you're not going on to the ABC islands (Aruba, Bonaire, and Curaçao).

Except for the boutiques at resort hotels, the main shopping area is in the center of Philipsburg. Most of the shops are on two leading streets, Front Street (called Voorstraat in Dutch), which is closer to the bay, and Back Street (Achterstraat), which runs parallel.

In general, the price marked on the merchandise is what you're supposed to pay. We're speaking of major retail outlets such as H. Stern, the jewelers, or Little Switzerland. At small, very personally run shops, where the owner is on site, some bargaining might be in order. Most shopkeepers will remind you that their merchandise is already discounted, sometimes considerably, and they might add, "We've got to make some profit, now don't we?"

Antillean Liquors. Queen Juliana Airport. ☎ **599/5-54267.**

This duty-free shop attracts the last-minute shopper. It has a complete assortment of liquor and liqueurs, as well as cigarettes and cigars. In general prices are lower here than in other stores on the island, and the selection is larger. Many bottles are priced anywhere from 30% to 50% lower than in the States. The only local product sold is an island liqueur called Guavaberry, which is made from rum (see the Guavaberry Company, below).

Caribbean Camera Centre. 79 Front St. ☎ **599/5-25259.**

The Caribbean Camera Centre has a wide range of merchandise, but it's always wise to know the prices charged back home. Cameras here may be among the lowest priced on St. Maarten; however, we've discovered better deals on St. Thomas if you're going there.

Colombian Emeralds International. Old St. ☎ **599/5-23933.**

Here you'll find stones ranging in style from collector to investment quality. Unmounted duty-free emeralds from Colombia, as well as emerald, gold, diamond, ruby, and sapphire jewelry, will tempt you. Prices here are approximately the same as in other outlets of this famous chain throughout the Caribbean, and if you're seriously shopping for emeralds, this is the place. There are some huckster fly-by-night vendors around the island pawning fakes off on unsuspecting tourists; Colombian Emeralds offers the genuine item.

Guavaberry Company. 10 Front St. ☎ **599/5-22965.**

This place sells the rare "island folk liqueur" of St. Maarten, which for centuries was made in private homes but is now available to everyone. Sold in square bottles, the product is made from rum that's given a unique flavor with rare, local berries usually grown in the hills in the center of the island. Don't confuse guavaberries with guavas—they're very different. The liqueur is aged and has a fruity, woody, almost bittersweet flavor. You can blend it with coconut for a unique guavaberry colada or pour a splash into a glass of icy champagne. Stop in at their shop and free-tasting house.

H. Stern Jewelers. 56 Front St. ☎ **599/5-23328.**

This is the Philipsburg branch of a worldwide firm that engages in mining, designing, manufacturing, exporting, and retailing jewelry in all price ranges. If you're looking for quality jewelry, sometimes at 25% off Stateside prices, H. Stern is the venue. Over the years we've made some good buys here in elegant watches. Unlike all that fake jewelry pedaled on St. Maarten and elsewhere, Stern gives guarantees that you might say are written in gold.

La Romana. Royal Palm Plaza, 61 Front St. ☎ **599/5-22181.**

Arguably the most interesting international specialty boutique on the island, this shop offers an excellent selection of the famous line of La Perla swimwear/beachwear for men and women, the La Perla fine lingerie collection, and the latest Fendi bags, luggage, accessories, and perfume. The management states that prices are sometimes up to 40% less than U.S. prices. Even if we lowered that to 25%, you'd still be getting a good bargain.

Little Europe. 80 Front St. (☎ **599/5-24371**).

This upscale purveyor of all the "finer things" in life is favored by cruise-ship passengers because its prices are inexpensive compared to North American boutiques. Inventory includes porcelain figurines by Hummel, jewelry, and watches by Concorde, Piaget, Corum, and Movado.

Little Switzerland. 42 Front St. ☎ **599/5-23530.**

These fine-quality European imports are made even more attractive by the prices charged here, often 25% or more lower than Stateside. Elegant famous-name watches, china, crystal, and jewelry are for sale, plus perfume and accessories. Little Switzerland has the best overall selection of these items of any shop in the Dutch side.

Old Street Shopping Center. With entrances on Front St. and Back St. ☎ **599/5-24712.**
The Old Street Shopping Center lies 170 yards east of the courthouse. Its lion's-head fountain is the most photographed spot on St. Maarten. Built in a West Indian-Dutch style, it features more than two dozen shops and boutiques, including branches of such famous stores as Colombian Emeralds. Dining facilities include the Philipsburg Grill and Ribs Co. and Pizza Hut. The stores are open Monday to Saturday from 9:30am to 6pm, but the Philipsburg Grill and Ribs Co. is open on Sunday if a cruise ship docks.

Shipwreck Shop. Front St. ☎ **599/5-22962.**
Here you'll find West Indian hammocks, beach towels, salad bowls, baskets, jewelry, T-shirts, postcards, books, and much more. It's also the home of wood carvings, native art, sea salt, cane sugar, and spices—in all, a treasure trove of Caribbean handcrafts. Indeed, the shop lives up to the promise of its name—all the items are things that might have washed up in a shipwreck. If you're looking for gifts or handcrafts in general, this might be your best bet, especially if funds are low.

Yellow House (Casa Amarilla). Wilhelminastraat. ☎ **599/5-23438.**
This shop is a branch of a century-old establishment on Curaçao. All kinds of perfumes and luxury items are sold, including Christian Dior cosmetics. Although primarily known for its cosmetics and perfumes, the store also carries a number of discounted luxury gift items as well.

ST. MAARTEN AFTER DARK

On the Dutch side of St. Maarten there are few real nightclubs. After-dark activities begin early here, as guests select their favorite nook for a sundowner, perhaps the garden patio of **Pasanggrahan** (see "Where to Stay," above).

Visitors watch for the legendary **"green flash,"** an atmospheric phenomenon described by Ernest Hemingway—it sometimes occurs in these latitudes just as the sun drops below the horizon. Each evening guests wait expectantly, and have been known to break into a round of applause at a particularly spectacular sunset.

Many hotels sponsor **beachside barbecues** (particularly in season) with steel bands, native music, and folk dancing. Outsiders are welcomed at most of these events, but call ahead to see if it's a private affair.

The most popular bar on the island is **Cheri's Café** (see "Where to Dine," above). For dancing and drinking, head to **Coconuts Night Club** in the Maho Beach Hotel and Casino, Maho Plaza (☎ **599/5-52115**). The club is open nightly from 9pm to 4am. Sometimes in season comedy acts are booked here. But since the venue is forever changing, it's always best to call ahead to see what's happening.

CASINOS

Most of the casinos are in the big hotels. The **Casino Royale,** at the Maho Beach Hotel on Maho Bay (☎ **599/5-52115**), opened in 1975. It has 16 blackjack tables, six roulette wheels, and three craps and three Caribbean stud-poker tables. The casino offers baccarat, mini-baccarat, and a large collection of more than 250 slot machines. It's open daily from 1pm to 4am. The Casino Royale Piano Bar is open nightly from 9:30pm, featuring the best of jazz, pop, and Caribbean music. There's no admission, and a snack buffet is complimentary.

A popular casino is at the previously recommended **Pelican Resort and Casino** (☎ **599/5-42503**), built to a Swiss design incorporating a panoramic view of Simpson Bay. The Las Vegas–style casino has two craps tables, three roulette tables, nine blackjack tables, two stud-poker tables, and 120 slot machines. It's open daily from 1pm to 3am.

The Roman-themed **Coliseum Casino,** on Front Street in Philipsburg (☎ **599/5-32102**), which opened in 1990, has taken several steps to attract gaming enthusiasts, especially "high rollers," and has the highest table limits ($1,000 maximum) on St. Maarten. Upon the management's approval, the Coliseum also offers credit lines for clients with a good credit rating at any U.S. casino. The Coliseum features about 225 slot machines, four blackjack tables, three poker tables, and two roulette wheels. The Coliseum is open daily from 11am to 3am.

2 St. Eustatius

Called "Statia," this Dutch-held island is just an 8-square-mile pinpoint in the Netherlands Antilles, still basking in its 18th-century heritage as the "Golden Rock." One of the true backwaters of the West Indies, it's just awakening to tourism.

It might be best to visit first on a day trip from St. Maarten to see if you'd like it for an extended stay. As Caribbean islands go, it's rather dull here, with no nightlife, and volcanic black-sand beaches aren't especially alluring. Some pleasant strips of beach exist on the Atlantic side, but the surf here is dangerous for swimming.

If you're a hiker or a diver, the outlook improves considerably. You can hike around the base of the Quill, an extinct volcano on the southern end of the island. Wandering through a tropical forest, you encounter wild orchids, philodendron, heliconia, anthurium, fruit trees, ferns, wildlife, and birds, with the inevitable oleander, hibiscus, and bougainvillea.

The island's reefs are covered with corals and enveloped by marine life. At one dive site, known as Crack in the Wall, or sometimes "the Grand Canyon," pinnacle coral shoots up from the floor of the ocean. Darting among the reefs are barracudas, eagle rays, black-tip sharks, and other large ocean fish.

Statia is located at a point 150 miles east of Puerto Rico, 38 miles south of St. Maarten, and 17 miles southeast of Saba. The two extinct volcanoes, the Quill and "Little Mountain," are linked by a sloping agricultural plain known as De Cultuurvlakte, where yams and sweet potatoes grow.

Overlooking the Caribbean on the western edge of the plain, **Oranjestad** (Orange City) is the capital and the only village, consisting of both an Upper and Lower Town, connected by stone-paved, dogleg Fort Road.

Statia was sighted by Columbus in 1493, on his second voyage, and the island was claimed for the Netherlands by Jan Snouck in 1640. The island's history was turbulent before it settled down to peaceful slumber under Dutch protection; from 1650 to 1816 Statia changed flags 22 times! Once the trading hub of the Caribbean, Statia was a thriving market, both for goods and for slaves.

Before the American Revolution the population of Statia did not exceed 1,200, most of whom were slaves engaged in raising sugarcane. When war came and Britain blockaded the North American coast, Europe's trade was diverted to the Caribbean. Dutch neutrality lured many traders, which led to the construction of 1½ miles of warehouses in Lower Town. The American revolutionaries obtained gunpowder and ammunition through Statia—perhaps one of the first places anywhere to recognize as a country the newly declared United States of America.

St. Eustatius

GETTING THERE

St. Eustatius can be reached from Dutch St. Maarten's Queen Juliana Airport via the 20-seat planes of **Windward Islands Airways International (Winair)** (☎ **599/5-52568** on St. Maarten). The five flights a day take only 20 minutes to hop the waters to Statia's Franklin Delano Roosevelt Airport. From here you can also make connections for flights to Saba or St. Kitts; two flights a day to Saba, and two a week to St. Kitts.

The little airline, launched in 1961, has an excellent safety record and has flown such passengers as David Rockefeller. Always reconfirm your return passage once you're on Statia.

GETTING AROUND

BY TAXI Taxis are your best bet. They meet all incoming flights, and on the way to the hotel your driver will offer himself as a guide during your stay on the island. Taxi rates are low, probably no more than $3.50 to $5 to your hotel from the airport. If you book a two- to three-hour tour (and in that time you should be able to cover all the sights on Statia), the cost is about $35 per vehicle.

BY RENTAL CAR **Avis** (☎ **800/331-1212** in the U.S., or 599/38-2421), offering unlimited mileage, is your best bet if you want to reserve a car in advance. Drivers must be 21 years old and present a valid license and credit or charge card. Avis is at the airport.

FAST FACTS: St. Eustatius

Banks Barclay's Bank, Wilhelminastraat, Oranjestad (☎ **599/38-2392**), the only bank on the island, is open Monday to Thursday from 8:30am to 3:30pm and on Friday from 8:30am to 12:30pm and 2 to 4:30pm. On weekends, most hotels will exchange money.

Currency The official unit of currency is the **Netherlands Antilles guilder (NAf),** at NAf 1.77 to each U.S.$1, but nearly all places will quote you prices in U.S. dollars.

Customs There are no Customs duties since the island is a free port.

Documents U.S. and Canadian citizens need proof of citizenship, such as a passport, voter registration card, or a birth certificate, along with an ongoing ticket. If you're using a birth certificate or voter registration card, you'll also need some photo ID. British subjects need a valid passport.

Electricity It's the same as in the United States, 100 volts AC (60 cycles).

Information The **Tourist Bureau** is at 3 Fort Oranjestraat (☎ **599/38-2433**), open Monday through Thursday from 8am to noon and 1 to 5pm, and Friday from 8am to noon and 1 to 4:30pm. The U.S.-based representative is **Classic Communications International,** P.O. Box 6322, Boca Raton, FL 33427 (☎ **800/722-2394** or 407/394-8580).

Language Dutch is the official language, but English is commonly spoken as well.

Medical Care A licensed physician is on duty at the **Queen Beatrix Medical Center,** 25 Princessweg in Oranjestad (☎ **599/38-2211**).

Safety Although crime is rare here, it's wise to secure your valuables and take the kind of discreet precautions you would anywhere. Don't leave valuables unguarded on the beach.

Taxes There's no departure tax if you're returning to the Dutch-held islands of St. Maarten or Saba; if you're going elsewhere, the tax is $10. Hotels on Statia collect a 7% government tax and a 5% electricity tax.

Telephone and Telegraph Ask at your hotel if you need to send a cable. St. Eustatius maintains a 24-hour-a-day telephone service—and sometimes it takes about that much time to get a call through!

Statia is not part of the 809 area code that applies to most of the Caribbean. To call Statia from the States, dial 011 (the international access code), then 599 (the country code for the Netherlands Antilles), and finally 3 (the area code for Statia) and the five-digit local number. To make a call within Statia, only the five-digit local number is necessary.

Time St. Eustatius operates on Atlantic standard time year-round. Thus in winter, when the United States is on standard time, if it's 6pm in Oranjestad it's 5pm in New York. During daylight saving time in the United States the island keeps the same time as the U.S. East Coast.

Tipping and Service Tipping is at the visitor's discretion, although most hotels, guest houses, and restaurants include a 10% service charge.

Water The water here is safe to drink.

Weather The average daytime temperature ranges from 78° to 82°F. The annual rainfall is only 45 inches.

WHERE TO STAY

Don't expect deluxe hotels or high-rises—Statia is strictly for escapists. Sometimes guests are placed in private homes. A 15% service charge and 7% government tax are added to hotel bills. The Talk of the Town bar and restaurant, listed under "Where to Dine," below, also rents rooms.

Airport View Apartments. Golden Rock, St. Eustatius, N.A. ☎ **599/38-2474.** Fax 599/38-2517. 9 apts. A/C TV TEL. $60 apt for 2. AE, MC, V.

This spotless but rawboned place has two locations: Most apartments are in the Golden Rock area near the airport and four others are in Upper Town, Oranjestad, Princessweg. The accommodations in the Golden Rock area all have compact refrigerators, coffeemakers, and private baths. They consist of five one-bed apartments for one or two people and four two-bed units for up to four guests. On the premises are a bar/restaurant and an outdoor patio with a swimming pool and barbecue facilities.

In Upper Town, the simple accommodations consist of two three-bedroom units holding up to nine guests and two two-bedroom apartments for up to four people. They all have kitchens, living rooms, cable television, dining rooms, and baths.

✪ **Golden Era Hotel.** Lower Town, St. Eustatius, N.A. ☎ **599/38-2345.** Fax 599/38-2545. 20 rms. Winter, $88 double; $104 triple. Off-season, $75 double; $90 triple. MAP $30 per person extra. AE, DC, MC, V.

Set directly on a rocky shoreline, this modern hotel is clean, serviceable, and comfortable, although quite basic. Built in stages between 1968 and 1975, the establishment, including its simply decorated bar and dining room, is operated by Hubert Lijfrock and Roy Hooker and is one of the best values on the island. Eight of the accommodations don't have a water view, but the remaining rooms offer a full or partial exposure to the sea; all are simple but spacious. Lunch and dinner are served daily. The fruit punch, with or without the rum, is delectable. The hotel also has a swimming pool.

La Maison sur la Plage. Zeelandia Beach, St. Eustatius, N.A. ☎ **599/38-2256.** Fax 599/38-2831. 5 two-bedroom cottages. TV. Winter, $95 double. Off-season, $75 double. Rates include continental breakfast. AE, DISC, MC, V.

On the Atlantic side of the island, fronting Zeelandia Beach, this beachfront hostelry lies only a mile from the airport. The waters of the Atlantic along the bordering 2-mile crescent of gray sand can have an undertow, so swimming is risky. The place is a strange little oasis in the desertlike town of Zeelandia, through which goats roam. Guests are housed in a series of sparsely furnished cottages, each with two somewhat musty bedrooms and a little private porch where a continental breakfast is served. The place is simply furnished and clean, with no air-conditioning. Facilities include a freshwater pool. Many visitors are drawn to the hotel's charming French restaurant.

Kings Well Resort. Oranje Bay, Oranjestad, St. Eustatius. ☎ **599/38-2538.** 8 rms. TV. Winter, $75–$112 double. Off-season, $65–$95 double. DISC, MC, V.

Set on the western or Caribbean side of the island, about a half mile north of Oranjestad, this simple, escapist hotel occupies about 2/3 of an acre of land that's perched on an oceanfront cliff, about 60 feet above the surf below. Construction began in 1994 and has progressed slowly ever since, contributing to the laid-back, no-frills atmosphere here. If you're looking for privacy and isolation, this is a good choice. Most views look out to the southwest, ensuring colorful sunsets that tend to be enhanced with drinks served from the resort's bar. Accommodations are deliberately understated. There's no swimming pool and few other facilities besides the bar and restaurant. The owners are German-born Win Piechutzki, who designed the layout and many of the doors and windows, and his American wife, Laura.

WHERE TO DINE

Kings Well Restaurant. Oranje Bay, Oranjestad. ☎ **599/38-2538.** Lunch platters $5–$22, dinner main courses $10–$22. DISC, MC, V. Daily 11:30am–2pm and 5–9:30pm. INTERNATIONAL.

It's more successful and more complete than the simple hotel in which its housed (see above). Set about a half mile north of Oranjestad, and perched on a cliff about 60 feet above the surf, it features wooden columns and panels, an open kitchen, and great sunset panoramas. Enjoy a fruity drink from the rustic bar before ordering lunch or dinner. Lunches feature deli-style sandwiches and a selection of platters from the dinner menu, which is more elaborate. Dishes might include grilled Colorado beefsteaks, fresh lobster, panfried grouper or snapper with parsley-butter sauce; plus a few German meat dishes like *Sauerbraten.*

L'Etoile. 6 Van Rheeweg, northeast of Upper Town. ☎ **599/38-2299.** Reservations required. Main courses $8.50–$30. AE, MC, V. Mon–Fri 9am–1pm and 5–9pm, Sat 9am–1pm and 5–10pm. CREOLE.

Caren Henríquez has had this second-floor restaurant with a few simple tables for some time. She is well known on Statia for her local cuisine, but you don't run into too many tourists here. Favored main dishes include the ubiquitous "goat water" (a stew), stewed whelks, mountain crab, and tasty spareribs. She also prepares Caribbean-style lobster. Caren is also known for her pastechis—deep-fried turnovers stuffed with meat. Expect a complete and very filling meal, almost the type you'd have received had Caren invited you over to her home for supper.

Talk of the Town Hotel. L. E. Sadlerweg, Golden Rock, St. Eustatius, N.A. ☎ **599/38-2236.** Reservations not required. Main courses NAf $21.50–$33.50 ($12.15–$19). AE, DISC, MC, V. Daily 7am–2pm and 5–9pm. (Bar stays open until 10:30pm.) AMERICAN/CREOLE.

At Golden Rock, a village in the center of the island, you get some of your best local food. Dishes are not spectacular, but they are well prepared and quite flavorful. Count on a soup of the day, or perhaps something more elegant, like shrimp cocktail or smoked salmon. Your best bet is usually fillet of snapper broiled in a white-wine sauce. The chef will also prepare a 12-ounce T-bone steak or sautéed chicken breast with green peas and a béarnaise sauce. Lunches are the usual: tuna salad sandwiches, burgers, or salads. Or else you can ask for chicken sate with a peanut-butter sauce.

The restaurant also rents 18 somewhat spartan motel-like bedrooms, each with private bath, phone, air-conditioning, and TV. Including breakfast, doubles range from $86 to $98 year-round.

BEACHES, WATER SPORTS & OUTDOOR PURSUITS

BEACHES Miles of golden-sand beaches are not the reason most visitors come to Statia. However, there are some, notably **Oranje Baai,** which have lots of black sand. It faces the Caribbean side of the island, off Lower Town. Other beaches include **Zeelandia** and **Lynch.** On the southwestern shore of Statia are the best volcanic beaches for swimming. Ask a taxi driver to take you to what he or she thinks is the best spot.

CRAB CATCHING We're perfectly serious. If you're interested, you can join Statians in a crab hunt. The Quill's crater is the breeding ground for these large crustaceans. At night they emerge from their holes to forage, and that's when they're caught. Either with flashlights or relying on moonlight, the "hunters" climb the Quill, catch a crab, and take the local delicacy home to prepare stuffed crab back.

HIKING This is the most popular sporting activity. Those with the stamina can climb the slopes of the Quill. The highest point on the island, the Quill's extinct volcanic cone harbors a crater filled with a dense tropical rain forest, containing towering kapok trees among other vegetation. A dozen or more species of wild orchids, some quite rare, grow here, and some 50 species of birdlife call it home, including the blue pigeon, a rare bird known to frequent the breadfruit and cottonwood trees here. Islanders once grew cocoa, coffee, and cinnamon in the crater's soil, but today bananas are the only crop. The tourist office will supply you with a list of a dozen trails with varying degrees of difficulty and can also arrange for you to go with a guide whose fee is $20 or more (that has to be negotiated, of course).

TENNIS Tennis can be played at the rather bleak **Community Center** on Rosemary Lane (☎ **599/38-2249**). The court has a concrete surface and is lit for night games. Changing rooms are available. The court fee is $2.80, and you must bring your own equipment.

WATER SPORTS On the Atlantic side of the island, at Concordia Bay, the **surfing** is best. However, there's no lifeguard protection.

Snorkeling is available through the Caribbean Sea to explore the remnants of an 18th-century man-of-war and the walls of warehouses, taverns, and ships that sank below the surface of Oranje Bay more than 200 years ago.

Dive Statia is a full PADI diving center on Fishermen's Beach in Lower Town (☎ **599/38-2435**), offering everything from beginning instruction to dive master certification. Its professional staff guides divers of all levels of experience to spectacular walls, untouched coral reefs, and historic shipwrecks. Dive Statia offers one- and two-tank boat dives, costing $40 to $75, including equipment. Night dives and snorkel trips are also available.

SEEING THE SIGHTS

Oranjestad stands on a cliff looking out on a beach and the island's calm anchorage, where in the 18th century you might have seen 200 vessels offshore. **Fort Oranje** was built in 1636 and restored in honor of the U.S. Bicentennial celebration of 1976. Perched atop the cliffs, its terraced rampart is lined with the old cannons.

St. Eustatius Historical Foundation Museum, Upper Town (☎ **599/38-2288**), is also called the de Graaff House in honor of its former tenant, Johannes de Graaff. After British Admiral Rodney sacked Statia for its tribute to the United States, he installed his own headquarters in this 18th-century house. Today a museum, the house stands in a garden, with a 20th-century wing crafted from 17th-century bricks. There are exhibits on the process of sugar refining, and shipping and commerce. Archeological artifacts from the colonial period and a pair of beautiful 18th-century antique furnished rooms are also on view. There's a section devoted to the pre-Columbian period. In the wing annex is a massive piece of needlework by an American, Catherine Mary Williams, showing the flowers of Statia. The museum is open Monday to Friday from 9am to 5pm and on Saturday and Sunday from 9am to noon; admission is $2 for adults, $1 for children.

A few steps away, a cluster of 18th-century buildings surrounding a quiet courtyard is called **Three Widows' Corner.**

Nearby are the ruins of the first **Dutch Reformed church.** To reach it, turn west from Three Widows' Corner onto Kerkweg. Tilting headstones record the names of the characters in the island's past. The St. Eustatius Historical Foundation recently completed restoration of the church. Visitors may climb to the top level of the tower and see the bay as lookouts did many years before.

Once Statia had a large colony of Jewish traders, and you can explore the ruins of **Honen Dalim,** the second Jewish synagogue in the western hemisphere. Built around 1740 and damaged by a hurricane in 1772, it fell into disuse at the dawn of the 19th century. The synagogue stands beside Synagogpad, a narrow lane whose entrance faces Madam Theatre on the square.

The walls of a *mikvah* (ritual bath) rise beside the **Jewish burial ground** on the edge of town. Most poignant is the memorial of David Haim Hezeciah de Lion, who died in 1760 at the age of 2 years, 8 months, 26 days; carved into the baroque surface is an angel releasing a tiny songbird from its cage.

SHOPPING

Mazinga Giftshop. Fort Oranje Straat, Upper Town. ☎ **599/38-2245.**

Here you'll find an array of souvenirs—T-shirts, liquor, costume jewelry, 14-karat-gold jewelry, cards, drugstore items, beachwear, children's books, handbags, Delft from Holland, and paperback romances. You may have seen more exciting stores in your life, but this is without parallel for Statia. The place keeps irregular hours.

ST. EUSTATIUS AFTER DARK

Las Vegas it isn't. Nightlife pickings here are among the slimmest in the Caribbean. Even though most visitors are satisfied by drinks and dinner, there are a few spots to wander after hours. Weekends are the best and busiest time to go out on Statia. Check to see if there's any action at **Talk of the Town** (see above), which often has live music on Sunday. **Exit Disco** (☎ **599/38-2543**) at the Stone Oven Restaurant, 16A Feaschweg, Upper Town, Oranjestad, often has dancing and local bands on weekends and you can also enjoy simple West Indian fare here. For local flavor try **Cool Corner** (☎ **599/38-2523**), across from the St. Eustatius Historical Foundation Museum, in the center of town. A lively crowd often gathers at **Franky's** (☎ **599/38-2575**), at Ruyterweg, also in the heart of town; it also serves basic West Indian fare.

3 Saba

An extinct volcano, with no beaches or flat land, cone-shaped Saba is 5 square miles of rock carpeted with such lush foliage as orchids, giant elephant ear, and Eucharist lilies. At its zenith, Mount Scenery, it measures 2,900 feet. Under the sea the volcanic walls that form Saba continue a sheer drop to great depths, making for some of the most panoramic dives in the Caribbean.

Unless you're a serious hiker or diver, you might confine your look at Saba to a day trip from St. Maarten (and flee as the sun sets). If you're a self-sufficient type who demands almost no artificial amusement, then sleepy Saba might be your hideaway.

Saba is 150 miles east of Puerto Rico and 90 miles east of St. Croix. Most visitors fly from St. Maarten, 28 miles to the north.

Sabans were known to take advantage of their special topography—they pelted invaders from above with rocks and boulders. Because of the English missionaries and Scottish seamen (from the remote Shetland Islands) who settled on the island, Saba has always been English-speaking. The official language, however, is Dutch. Also because of those early settlers from Europe, 60% of the population is Caucasian, many with red hair and freckled fair skin.

GETTING THERE

BY PLANE—You can leave New York's JFK airport in the morning and be at Captain's Quarters on Saba for dinner that night by taking a direct flight on either of the two airlines that currently fly from the United States to St. Maarten. From Queen Juliana Airport there, you can take the 12-minute hop to Saba on **Winair (Windward Islands Airways International; ☎ 599/5-52568** on St. Maarten).

Arriving by air from St. Maarten, travelers step from Winair's 20-passenger STOL (short takeoff and landing) plane onto the tarmac of the **Juancho Yrausquin Airport.** The airstrip is one of the shortest (if not *the* shortest) landing strips in the world, stretching only 1,312 feet along the aptly named Flat Point, one of the few level areas on the island.

Many guests at hotels on St. Maarten fly over to Saba on the morning flight, spend the day sightseeing, then return to St. Maarten on the afternoon flight. Winair connections can also be made on Saba to both St. Kitts and Statia.

GETTING AROUND

BY TAXI Taxis meet every flight. The cost of a two-hour tour is about $10 per person if there are at least four passengers making the trip.

BY RENTAL CAR None of the "big three" car-rental companies maintains a branch on Saba, partly because most visitors opt to get around by taxi. In the unlikely event that you should dare to drive a car on Saba, locally operated companies include **Johnson's Rental,** Windwardside (**☎ 599/4-62269**), renting about six Mazdas.

Some insurance is included in the rates, but you might be held partly responsible for any financial costs in the event of an accident. Because of the very narrow roads and dozens of cliffs, it's crucial to exercise caution when driving on Saba.

BY HITCHHIKING Hitchhiking has long been an acceptable means of transport on Saba, where everybody seemingly knows everybody else. On recent rounds, our taxi rushed a sick child to the plane and picked up an old man to take him up the hill because he'd fallen and hurt himself—all on our sightseeing tour! (We didn't mind.) By hitchhiking, you'll probably get to know everybody else, too.

ON FOOT The traditional means of getting around on Saba is still much in evidence. But we suggest that only the sturdy in heart and limb walk from the Bottom up to Windwardside. Many do, but you'd better have some shoes that grip the ground, particularly after a recent rain.

FAST FACTS: Saba

Banks The main bank on the island is Barclays, Windwardside (☎ **599/4-62216**), open Monday to Friday from 8:30am to 2pm.

Currency Saba, like the other islands of the Netherlands Antilles, uses the **Netherlands Antilles guilder (NAf),** valued at NAf 1.77 to U.S.$1. However, prices given here are in U.S. currency unless otherwise designated, since U.S. money is accepted by almost everybody here.

Customs You don't have to go through Customs when you land at Juancho E. Yrausquin Airport, as this is a free port.

Documents The government requires that all U.S. and Canadian citizens show proof of citizenship, such as a passport or voter registration card with photo ID. A return or ongoing ticket must also be provided. Britishers must have a valid passport.

Drugstore Try **The Pharmacy,** The Bottom (☎ **599/4-63289**), open Monday to Friday from 7:30am to 5:30pm.

Electricity Saba uses 110 volts AC (60 cycles), so most U.S.-made appliances don't need transformers or adapters.

Information The **Saba Tourist Board** is at Lambees Place in the heart of Windwardside (☎ **599/4-62231**). It's open Monday through Thursday from 8am to noon and 1 to 5pm, Friday 8am to noon and 1 to 4:30pm. Before you go, information can be obtained at the **Saba Tourist Office,** P.O. Box 6322, Boca Raton, FL 33427 (☎ **800/722-2394** or 407/394-8580).

Medical Care Saba's hospital complex is the **A. M. Edwards Medical Centre,** The Bottom (☎ **599/4-63289**).

Police Call ☎ **599/4-63237.**

Safety Crime on this island, where everyone knows everyone else, is practically nonexistent. But who knows? A tourist might rob you. It would be wise to safeguard your valuables.

Taxes The government imposes a 5% tourist tax on hotel rooms. If you're returning to St. Maarten or flying over to Statia, you must pay a $5 departure tax. If you're going anywhere else, however, a $10 tax is imposed.

Telephone and Telegraph Cables and international telephone calls can be placed at Antelecon, The Bottom (☎ **599/4-63211**).

Saba is not part of the 809 area code that applies to most of the Caribbean. To call Saba from the United States, dial 011 (the international access code), then 599 (the country code for the Netherlands Antilles), and finally 4 (the area code for all of Saba) and the five-digit local number. To make a call within Saba, only the five-digit local number is necessary.

Time Saba is on Atlantic standard time year-round, one hour earlier than eastern standard time. When the United States is on daylight saving time, clocks on Saba and the U.S. East Coast read the same.

WHERE TO STAY

If you've come here for a hotel on the beach, you've come to the wrong island. Saba's only beach, Wellsby Beach, is tiny and can be reached from most hotels by a $10 taxi ride.

Captain's Quarters. Windwardside, Saba, N.A. ☎ **599/4-62201,** or 212/289-6031 in New York. Fax 599/4-62377, or 212/289-1931 in New York. 12 rms. MINIBAR TV. Year-round, $170–$190 double. Additional person $35 extra. Rates include American breakfast. AE, DISC, MC, V.

A restored 1850s sea captain's house has been converted into a guest house where many visitors, including royalty and celebrities, spend hideaway holidays. Just off the village center of Windwardside, it's a complex of several guest houses surrounding the main house with its traditional verandas and covered porches. You make your way here by going down a narrow, steep lane. Thrust out toward the water is a freshwater swimming pool surrounded by a terrace, where you can sunbathe or order refreshments from an open-air bar.

The main house serves as library, sitting room, and kitchen on the first floor, with two private accommodations above (one is a "honeymoon" room). The house is furnished with antiques gathered from many ports of the world. About half the bedrooms contain four-poster beds, and each has a balcony overlooking the sea and Mount Scenery. Well-designed and cozy studio rooms are in the garden. Everything is a quaint reminder of New England.

Cottage Club. Windwardside, Saba, N.A. ☎ **599/4-62486.** Fax 599/4-62476. 10 studio apts. TV TEL. Nov 15-Mar, $115 double. Off-season, $84 double. $20 in any season for 3rd and 4th occupant. MC, V.

Small, intimate, and immersed in the architectural and aesthetic traditions of Saba, this hotel complex occupies about a half acre of steeply sloping and carefully landscaped terrain within a two-minute walk of the center of the island's capital. Only the lobby evokes a historic setting. Designed of local stone, and set at an altitude above the other buildings of the complex, it's the focal point for a collection of island antiques, lace curtains, and a round-sided swimming pool. Studio apartments each contain kitchenettes, a semi-private patio, ceiling fans, a living-room area, and a queen-size bed. They're housed within clapboard-sided replicas of antiques cottages—two units per cottage—with red roofs, green shutters, white walls, and yellow trim. Interiors are breezy, airy, and comfortable. There's no bar or restaurant on the premises, but residents can buy groceries at a nearby supermarket that will deliver supplies. The owners of the establishment are three Saban brothers (Gary, Mark, and Dean) whose extended families all seem to assist in maintaining the place.

Cranston's Antique Inn. The Bottom, Saba, N.A. ☎ **599/4-63203.** 6 rms. $57 double; $65 triple. AE, MC, V.

Everyone congregates for rum drinks and gossip on the front terrace of this inn, which has recently installed a swimming pool. Near the village roadway, Cranston's is on the west coast, north of Fort Bay. It's an old-fashioned house, from the 1830s, and every bedroom has antique four-poster beds. Mr. Cranston, the owner, will gladly rent you the same room where Queen Juliana once spent a holiday. Aside from the impressive wooden beds, the furnishings are mostly hit or miss. This place has never been known as the island style-setter.

Mr. Cranston has a good island cook, who makes use of locally grown spices. Local dishes are offered, such as goat meat, roast pork from island pigs, red snapper, and broiled grouper. Meals begin at $12 and are served on a covered terrace in the garden or inside. The house is within walking distance of Ladder Bay.

The Gate House. Hells Gate, Saba, N.A. ☎ **599/4-62416,** or 708/354-9641 (reservations only). Fax 599/4-62415. 6 rms. Winter, $95 double. Off-season, $75 double. Rates include continental breakfast. MC, V. Closed Sept.

Named for its position at the gateway to Saba, almost adjacent to the airport, this hotel sits on steep terrain that's about five minutes from the coast. Built in 1990, it consists of three two-story, cement-sided replicas of Saban townhouses surrounded by a wraparound veranda. There's also an oval-shaped pool on the premises. The red roofs, green shutters, and white walls evoke old Saba and inside floors are either wooden or tile. Your hosts are an American-Dutch couple, Jim Seigel and Manuela Doey, who devote much of their time and attention to running the popular in-house restaurant, which features staples like curried conch, coconut shrimp, and grilled flank steak (see "Where to Dine" below).

Juliana's Apartments. Windwardside, Saba, N.A. ☎ **599/4-62269.** Fax 599/4-62389. 9 rms, 1 apt, 1 cottage. Winter, $115 double; $135 apt or cottage. Off-season, $90 double; $115 apt or cottage. Additional person $20–$35 extra. Dive packages available. AE, MC, V.

Near Captain's Quarters, this hostelry is set on a hillside. Modern and immaculate, the comfortably furnished accommodations have balconies and radios; some come with a ceiling fan and TV. Juliana's offers a 2½-room apartment complete with kitchenette, and Flossie's Cottage, with a spacious living room, a dining room, a color TV, and a fully equipped kitchen. There's also a recreation room, a swimming pool, and a sun deck for lounging. The complex contains a simple restaurant, Tropics Café, that opens four nights a week for dinner.

Scout's Place. Windwardside, Saba, N.A. ☎ **599/4-62205.** Fax 599/4-62388. 15 rms, 14 with bath; 1 apt. $85 double; $100 apt for 2. Rates include continental breakfast. MC, V.

Right in the center of the village, Scout's Place is hidden from the street. Set on the ledge of a hill, the place is owned by Diana Medora, who makes guests feel right at home. With only 15 accommodations, it's still the second-largest inn on the island. The old house has a large open-walled dining room, where every table has a view of the sea. It's an informal place, with an individual decor that might include Surinam hand-carvings, peacock chairs in red-and-black wicker, and silver samovars. The rooms open onto a view of the sea. The apartment with kitchenette is suitable for up to five occupants; an extra person is charged $20.

✪ **Willards of Saba.** Booby Hill, Saba, N.A. ☎ **599/4-62498.** Fax 599/4-62482. 7 rms, 4 bungalows, 1 suite. Winter, $250 double; $300 bungalow for 2; $400 honeymoon suite. Off-season, discounts of around 20%. Additional person $45 extra. AE, DISC, MC, V.

Until Brad Willard arrived, Saba never had anything remotely related to posh. Willard is the great-grandson of Henry Augustus Willard, who built his namesake hotel in Washington, D.C. The Saba hotel opened in 1994 and became an immediate sell-out, attracting visitors who might not have set foot on the island before. Five of the accommodations are in a concrete building designed in the island's distinctive style of red roofs, white walls, and green shutters. The most spacious rooms are in the main lodge. Much care went into the design, making use of everything from cedar from the Northwest to original island paintings. No more than a dozen or so guests are ever found here at one time. Because of its position in a garden high on a hill overlooking the island's southwestern coastline, each accommodation has sweeping views and access to almost constant ocean breezes. From the swimming pool or hot tub, the inn's guests can look over the waters to at least five neighboring islands on a clear day. Corazon's restaurant and its bar are recommended in "Where to Dine," below. Facilities include tennis courts, hot tub/Jacuzzi, and the largest swimming pool on Saba.

WHERE TO DINE

Corazon. In Willards Hotel, Booby Hill. ☎ **599/4-62498.** Reservations required. Main courses $22.50–$35. AE, DISC, MC, V. Daily 11:30am–3pm and 7–9:30pm. ANTILLEAN/ASIAN.

Set in a previously recommended hotel, this restaurant features a breezy island decor, a sweeping, high-altitude view of the island's southeastern coastline, and some of the freshest fish and lobster on the island. Most of the catch featured on the "island-inspired" menu comes from the boats of local fisherfolk. Menu items change with the availability of the ingredients, although grouper, snapper Florentine, and lobster thermidor are usually featured on the menu, as are two recently sampled and truly savory dishes: pork loin covered with a champagne-and-caper sauce or beef with oyster sauce in the Chinese style. You can cool down with a crêpe stuffed with banana and jackfruit, then fried and served with homemade ice cream. The restaurant takes its name from Corazon de Johnson, manager and chef. Although born in the Philippines, she doesn't limit her culinary inspiration to her homeland, but roams the world for ideas for her fusion cuisine. There's a pleasant bar on the premises where you might enjoy a round of before-dinner drinks.

The Gate House. Hells Gate. ☎ **599-4-62416.** Reservations recommended. Set 3-course menus $20 per person. MC, V. Thurs–Tues 6:30–10:30pm. Closed Sept. CARIBBEAN.

Set on one of the upper floors of a previously recommended hotel, this place lies closer to the island's only airport than any other restaurant on Saba, and has become busier and more animated than the small, cement-sided hotel. Views of the coastline and the hotel's pool are sometimes interrupted by arriving and departing planes. The menu changes every night, depending on the availability of island ingredients and the chef's preferences. Staples include curried conch, coconut shrimp, and grilled flank steak, whereas panfried grouper, grilled mahimahi with jerk sauce, or grilled chicken with Creole sauce tend to come and go.

Saba Chinese Bar & Restaurant (Moo Goo Gai Pan). Windwardside. ☎ **599/4-62268.** Reservations not required. Main courses $5–$17. MC, V. Tues–Sun 11am–midnight. CHINESE.

Amid a cluster of residential buildings on a hillside above Windwardside, this place is operated by a family from Hong Kong. It offers some 120 dishes, an unpretentious decor of plastic tablecloths and folding chairs, and a cookery so popular that many residents claim this to be their most frequented restaurant. Meals include an array of Cantonese and Indonesian specialties—lobster Cantonese, Chinese chicken with mushrooms, sweet-and-sour fish, conch chop suey, several curry dishes, roast duck, and nasi goreng. If you've sampled the great Chinese restaurants of New York, San Francisco, and Hong Kong, you may find these dishes bland, but it's good change-of-pace fare.

Scout's Place. Windwardside. ☎ **599/4-62205.** Reservations required 2 to 3 hours in advance. Lunch $12; fixed-price dinner $16.50–$25. MC, V. Lunch daily at 12:30pm; dinner daily at 7:30pm. INTERNATIONAL.

This is a popular dining spot among day trippers to the island, but you should have your driver stop by early and make a reservation for lunch for you. Food at Scout's is simple, good, and filling, and the price is low too. Dinner is more elaborate, with tables placed on an open-sided terrace, the ideal spot for a drink at sundown. Fresh seafood is a specialty, as is curried goat. Even if you don't like the food, it's the best place on the island to catch up on the latest gossip, especially that spread among the expatriates.

WATER SPORTS & OUTDOOR ACTIVITIES

HIKING The island is as beautiful above the water as it is below. A favorite target for hikers is the top of **Mount Scenery,** a volcano that erupted 5,000 years ago. Allow half a day and take your time climbing the 1,064 sometimes-slippery concrete steps up to the cloud-reefed mountain. You'll pass along a nature reserve complete with a lush rain forest with palms, bromeliads, elephant ears, heliconia, mountain raspberries, lianas, and tree ferns. In her pumps, Queen Beatrix of the Netherlands climbed these steps and, upon reaching the summit, declared: "This is the smallest and highest place in my kingdom." One of the inns will pack you a picnic lunch. The higher you climb, the cooler it grows, about a drop of 1°F every 328 feet; on a hot day this can be an incentive. The peak is 2,855 feet high.

If you don't want to explore the natural attractions of the island on your own, the **Saba Tourist Office,** P.O. Box 527, Windwardside (☎ **559/4-62322**), can arrange tours of the island's tropical rain forests. James ("Jim") Johnson (☎ **599/4-63307**), a fit, fortyish Sabian guide, conducts most of these tours and knows the terrain better than anyone else on the island (he's sometimes difficult to reach, however). Johnson will point out orchids, golden heliconia, and other flora and fauna as well as the rock formations and bromeliads you're likely to see. Tours can accommodate one to eight hikers and usually last about half a day; depending on your particular route and number of participants, the cost can be anywhere from $50 to $100. Actual prices, of course, are negotiated.

WATER SPORTS Don't come to Saba for beaches: There's only one sand beach, and it's about 20 feet long. Sports here are mostly do-it-yourself. Visitors, such as John F. Kennedy Jr., enjoy the underwater scenery and dark, volcanic sands and coral formations.

Dive sites around Saba, all protected by the Saba Marine Park, have permanent moorings and range from shallow to deep. Divers see pinnacles, walls, ledges, overhangs, and reefs—all with abundant coral and sponge formations and a wide variety of both reef and pelagic marine life. There's also a fully operational recompression chamber/hyperbaric facility located in the Fort Bay harbor.

Saba Deep Dive Center, P.O. Box 22, Fort Bay, Saba, N.A. (☎ **599/4-63347**), is a full-service dive center that offers scuba diving, snorkeling, equipment rental/repair, and tank fills. Whether 1 diver or 20, novice or experienced, Mike Myers and his staff of NAUI/PADI/ACUC/CMAS instructors and dive masters make an effort to provide personalized service and great diving. The In Two Deep Restaurant and the Deep Boutique offer air-conditioned comfort, a view of the harbor area and the Caribbean Sea, good food and drink, and a wide selection of clothes, swimwear, lotions, and sunglasses. The restaurant is open for breakfast and lunch. A certification course goes for $375. A single-tank dive costs $45; a two-tank dive, $90. Night dives are $65. The center is open daily from 8am to 6pm, with Saturday-night dinners.

The Coral Gardens

Circling the entire island and including four offshore underwater mountains (seamounts), the **Saba Marine Park,** Fort Bay (☎ **599/4-63295**), preserves the island's coral reefs and marine life. The park is zoned for various pursuits. The all-purpose recreational zone includes Wells Bay Beach, Saba's only beach, but it's seasonal—it disappears with the winter seas, only to reappear in late spring. There are two anchorage zones for visiting yachts and Saba's only harbor. The five dive zones include a coastal area and four seamounts, a mile offshore. In these zones are more than two dozen marked and buoyed dive sites and a snorkeling trail. You plunge into a world of coral and sponges, swimming with parrotfish, doctorfish, and damselfish. The snorkel trail, however, is not for the neophyte. It can be approached from Wells Bay Beach but only from May to October. Depths of more than 1,500 feet are found between the island and the seamounts, which reach a minimum depth of 90 feet. There's a $3 per dive visitor fee and a $3 per person, per week, yacht visitor fee. Funds are also raised through souvenir sales and donations. The park office at Fort Bay is open Monday to Friday from 8am to 5pm; Saturday from 8am to noon, and Sunday from 10am to 2pm.

Sea Saba Dive Center, Windwardside (☎ **599/4-62246**), has nine experienced instructors eager to share their knowledge of Saba Marine Park: famous deep and medium-depth pinnacles, walls, spur-and-groove formations, and giant boulder gardens. Their two 40-foot uncrowded boats are best suited for a comfortable day on Saba's waters. Daily boat dives are made between 10am and 2pm, allowing a relaxing interval for snorkeling. Courses range from resort through dive master. Extra day and night dives can be arranged. A two-tank dive costs $90; package prices are available with advance booking, starting as low as $500 per person.

Saba Reef Divers, Fort Bay Harbour, Windwardside (☎ **599/4-62541**), a long-established dive center, was bought by a quartet of American-born divers and investors, Chuck and Nancy and Kathy and Curtis, in late 1996. They guide divers through the shoals, walls, shelves, reefs, pinnacles, and seamounts that surround the volcanic cone of the landmass of Saba, including the "Pinnacles" and Diamond Rock, where divers can spot barracuda, stingrays, grouper, and snapper lurking near its lush, sloping walls. Tent Reef, a long underwater fault crisscrossed with crevasses and drop-offs ranging from 40 to 130 feet, is another unusual option for adventurous divers. Their boat, the *Mama,* is a 40-foot vessel with plenty of shade. Packages are available; a single-tank dive costs around $50; a two-tank dive, around $85.

SEEING THE SIGHTS

Tidy white houses cling to the mountainside, and small family cemeteries adjoin each dwelling. Lace-curtained, gingerbread-trimmed cottages give a Disneyland aura.

The first Jeep arrived on Saba in 1947. Before that, Sabans went about on foot, climbing from village to village. Hundreds of steps had been chiseled out of the rock by the early Dutch settlers in 1640.

Engineers told them it was impossible, but Sabans built a single cross-island road by hand. Filled with hairpin turns, it zigzags from Fort Bay, where a deep-water pier accommodates large tenders from cruise ships, to a height of 1,600 feet. Along the way it has fortresslike supporting walls.

Past storybook villages, the road goes over the crest to **The Bottom.** Derived from the Dutch word *botte,* which means "bowl-shaped," this village is nestled on a plateau and surrounded by rocky volcanic domes. It occupies about the only bit of ground, 800 feet above the sea. It's also the official capital of Saba, a Dutch village of charm, with chimneys, gabled roofs, and gardens.

From The Bottom you can take a taxi up the hill to the mountain village of **Windwardside,** perched on the crest of two ravines at about 1,500 feet above sea level. This village of red-roofed houses, the second most important on Saba, is the site of the two biggest inns and most of the shops. From Windwardside you can climb steep steps cut in the rock to yet another village, **Hell's Gate,** teetering on the edge of a mountain. There's also a serpentine road from the airport to Hell's Gate, where you'll find the island's largest church. Only the most athletic climb from here to the lip of the volcanic crater.

SHOPPING

After lunch you can go for a stroll in Windwardside and stop at the boutiques, which often look like someone's living room—and sometimes they are. Most stores are open Monday to Saturday from 9am to noon and 2 to around 5:30pm; some are also open shorter hours on Sunday.

The traditional **drawn threadwork** of the island is famous. Sometimes this work, introduced by a local woman named Gertrude Johnson in the 1870s, is called Spanish work, because it was believed to have been perfected by nuns in Caracas. Selected threads are drawn and tied in a piece of linen to produce an ornamental pattern. It can be expensive if a quality linen has been used.

Try to go home with some **"Saba Spice,"** an aromatic blend of 150-proof cask rum, with such spices as fennel seed, cinnamon, cloves, and nutmeg, straight from someone's home brew. It's not for everyone (too sweet), but it will make an exotic bottle to show off at home.

Some streets in Windwardside have no names, but because it's so small shops are easy to find.

Around the Bend. At Scout's Place, Windwardside. ☎ **599/4-62519.**

Ex-Manhattanite Jean Macbeth runs this classy little boutique featuring gifts, oddments, and what she calls "pretties," all one-of-a kind. Charming locally made wooden Saba cottage wall plaques are sold along with magnets, switchplates, bright parrot and Toucan pinwheels, Caribbean perfumes, and spices. Naturally, there is a collection of hand-painted silk-screened T-shirts.

Saba Artisan Foundation. The Bottom. ☎ **599/4-63260.**

In recent years, the foundation has made a name for itself with its hand-screened resort fashions. The clothes are casual and colorful. Among the items sold are men's bush-jacket shirts, numerous styles of dresses and skirts, napkins, and place mats, as well as yard goods. Island motifs are used in many designs. Also popular are the famous Saba drawn-lace patterns. The fashions are designed, printed, sewn, and marketed by Sabans. Mail-order as well as wholesale-distributorship inquiries are invited.

Saba Tropical Arts. Windwardside ☎ **599/4-62373.**

This is the place to go to watch hand silk-screening, and perhaps even buy some wares. Designer Mieke Van Schadewijk has produced some catchy patterns, all of which are displayed at his workshop boutique.

11 Jamaica

Most visitors already have a mental image of this English-speaking nation before they arrive, picturing its boisterous culture of reggae and Rastafarianism, and its white sandy beaches, jungles, rivers, mountains, and clear waterfalls. Jamaica's art and cuisine are also remarkable.

Jamaica can be a tranquil and intriguing island, but there's no denying that it's plagued by crime, drugs, and muggings. There is also palpable racial tension here. But many visitors are unaffected; they're escorted from the airport to their heavily patrolled hotel grounds and venture out only on expensive organized tours. These vacationers are largely sheltered from the more unpredictable and sometimes dangerous side of Jamaica. Those who want to see "the real Jamaica," or at least to see the island in greater depth, had better be prepared for some hassle. Vendors on the beaches and in the markets can be particularly aggressive.

Most Jamaicans, in spite of economic hard times, have unrelenting good humor and genuinely welcome visitors to the island. Others, certainly a minority, harbor hostility toward tourists; many visitors vow never to return. Jamaica's appealing aspects have to be weighed against its poverty and problems, the legacy of a history of slavery and colonization common to the region, combined with more recent traumatic political upheavals, beginning in the 1970s.

Should you go? By all means, yes. Be prudent and cautious, just as if you were visiting New York, Miami, or Los Angeles. Jamaica is definitely worth it! The island has fine hotels and a zesty cuisine. It's well geared to couples who come to tie the knot or celebrate their honeymoon. As for sports, Jamaica boasts the best golf courses in the West Indies, and its landscape offers lots of outdoor activities like rafting and serious hiking. The island also has some of the finest diving waters in the world, with an average diving depth of 35 to 95 feet, and visibility of usually 60 to 120 feet. Most of the diving is done on coral reefs, which are protected by underwater parks where fish, shells, coral, and sponges are plentiful.

Jamaica lies 90 miles south of Cuba and is the third largest of the Caribbean islands, with some 4,400 square miles of predominantly green land, a mountain ridge peaking at 7,400 feet above sea level, and, on the north coast, many white-sand beaches with clear blue waters.

GETTING THERE

There are two **international airports** on Jamaica: Donald Sangster in Montego Bay (☎ **809/952-4001**) and Norman Manley in

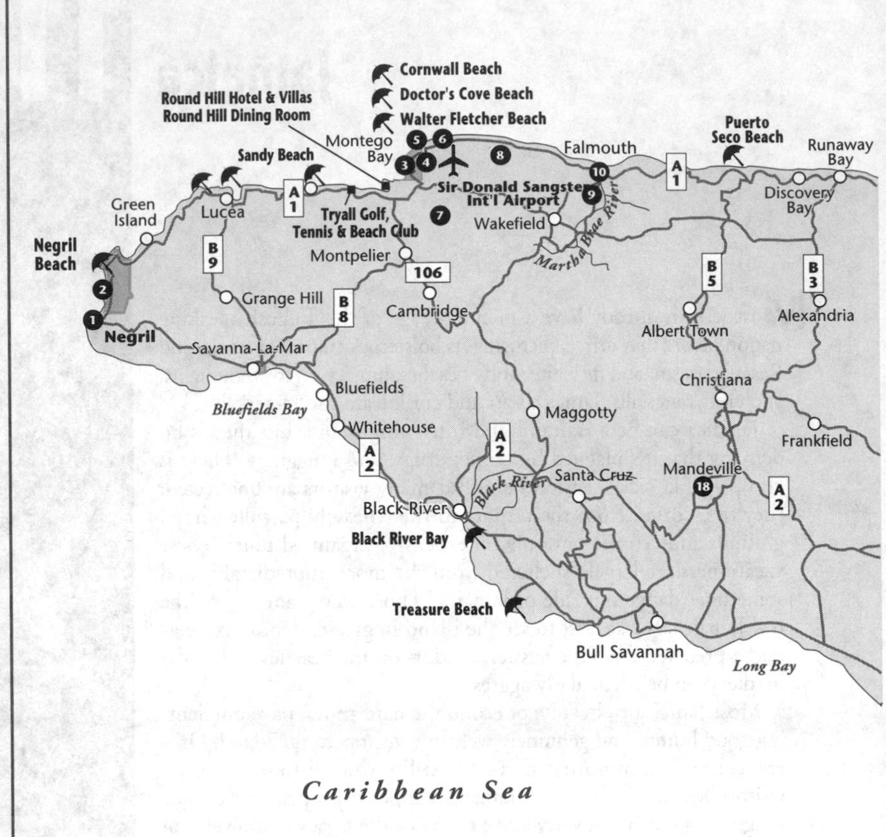

Kingston (☎ **809/924-8235**). The most popular flights to Jamaica are from New York and Miami. Remember to reconfirm all flights, going and returning, no later than 72 hours before departure. Flying time from Miami is 1¼ hours; from Los Angeles, 5½ hours; from Atlanta, 2½ hours; from Dallas, 3 hours; from Chicago and New York, 3½ hours; and from Toronto, 4 hours.

Some of the most convenient and popular service to Jamaica is provided by **American Airlines** (☎ **800/433-7300** in the U.S.) through its hubs in New York and Miami. Throughout the year, a daily nonstop flight departs from New York's Kennedy airport for Montego Bay, continuing on to Kingston. Return flights to New York from Jamaica usually depart from Montego Bay, touch down briefly in Kingston, then continue nonstop back to Kennedy. From Miami, at least two daily flights depart for Kingston and three daily flights for Montego Bay.

Air Jamaica (☎ **800/523-5585** in the U.S.), the national carrier, operates about 13 flights a week from New York's JFK, most of which stop at both Montego Bay and Kingston. They offer even more frequent flights from Miami. The airline has

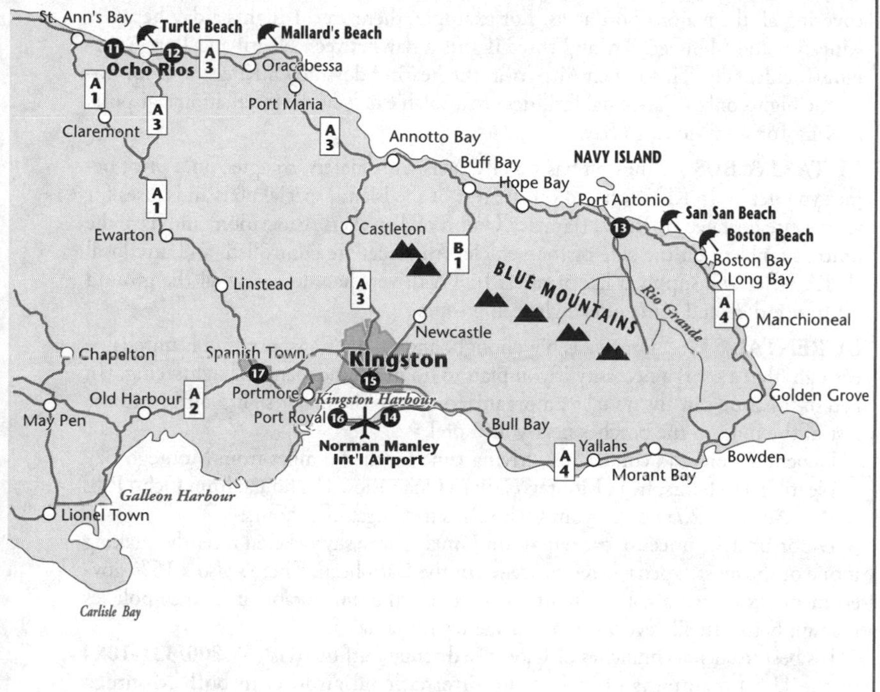

connecting service within Jamaica through its reservations network to a small independent airline, **Air Jamaica Express,** whose planes usually hold between 10 and 17 passengers. They fly from the island's international airports at Montego Bay and Kingston to small airports around the island, including Port Antonio, Boscobel (near Ocho Rios), Negril, and Tinson Pen (a tiny airport near Kingston).

Continental (☎ **800/525-0280** in the U.S.) offers nonstop service to Montego Bay from its hub in Newark, New Jersey, on Saturday and Sunday.

Air Canada (☎ **800/268-7240** in Canada or 800/776-3000 in the U.S.) flies to Jamaica from Toronto. In winter, service is daily; in off-season, flights are on Saturday and Sunday only. But all this is subject to change, depending on demand, so check with the airline.

In addition, **Northwest Airlines** (☎ **800/225-2525**) flies directly to Montego Bay from Minneapolis and Tampa.

British travelers usually take **British Airways** (☎ **800/247-9297**), which has three nonstop flights to Montego Bay and Kingston from London's Gatwick Airport.

GETTING AROUND

BY PLANE Most travelers enter the country via Montego Bay. If you want to fly elsewhere, you'll need to use the island's domestic air service, which is provided by Air Jamaica Express. Reservations are handled by **Air Jamaica** (☎ **809/923-8680**) in Kingston and Montego Bay (same phone for both cities), which has consolidated its reservation system. You can also reserve before you leave home through a travel agent or through Air Jamaica. Air Jamaica Express offers 30 scheduled flights daily, covering all the major resort areas. For example, there are 11 flights a day between Kingston and Montego Bay and three flights a day between Negril and Port Antonio. (Incidentally, Tinson Pen Airport in the heart of downtown Kingston is for domestic flights only.) Car-rental facilities are available only at the international airports at Kingston and Montego Bay.

BY TAXI & BUS Kingston has no city taxis with meters, so agree on a price before you get in. In Kingston and on the rest of the island, special taxis and buses for visitors are operated by JUTA (Jamaica Union of Travellers Association) and have the union's emblem on the side of the vehicle. All prices are controlled, and any local JUTA office will supply a list of rates. JUTA drivers handle nearly all the ground transportation, and some offer sightseeing tours.

BY RENTAL CAR Jamaica is big enough, and public transportation is unreliable enough, that a car is a necessity if you plan to do much independent sightseeing. (In lieu of this, you can always take an organized tour to the major sights and spend the rest of the time on the beaches near your hotel.)

Depending on road conditions, driving time for the 50 miles from Montego Bay to Negril is 1½ hours; from Montego Bay to Ocho Rios, 1½ hours; from Ocho Rios to Port Antonio, 2½ hours; from Ocho Rios to Kingston, 2 hours.

Unfortunately, prices of car rentals on Jamaica have skyrocketed recently, making it one of the most expensive rental scenes in the Caribbean. There's also a 15% government tax on rentals. Equally unfortunate are the unfavorable insurance policies that apply to virtually every car-rental agency on Jamaica.

It's best to stick to branches of U.S.-based rental outfits. **Avis** (☎ **800/331-1084** in the U.S.) maintains offices at the international airports in both Montego Bay (☎ **809/952-4543**) and Kingston (☎ **809/924-8013**). The company's least-expensive car requires a 24-hour advance booking. There's also **Budget Rent-a-Car** (☎ **809/952-3838** at the Montego Bay Airport, or 809/938-2189 in Kingston); with Budget, a daily collision-damage waiver costs another $15 and is mandatory. **Hertz** (☎ **800/654-3001** in the U.S.) operates branches at the airports at both Montego Bay (☎ **809/979-0438**) and Kingston (☎ **809/924-8028**).

Driving is on the left, and you should exercise more than your usual caution here because of the unfamiliar terrain. Be especially cautious at night. Speed limits in town are 30 m.p.h., and 50 m.p.h. outside towns. Gas is measured in the Imperial gallon (a British unit of measure that will give you 25% more than a U.S. gallon), and the charge is payable only in Jamaican dollars; most stations don't accept credit or charge cards. Your own valid driver's license from back home is acceptable for short-term visits to Jamaica.

BY BIKE & SCOOTER These can be rented in Montego Bay, and you'll need your valid driver's license. **Montego Honda/Bike Rentals,** 21 Gloucester Ave. (☎ **809/952-4984**), rents Hondas for $35 a day (24 hours), plus a $300 deposit. Scooters cost $35 per day. Deposits are refundable if the vehicles are returned in good shape. It's open daily from 7:30am to 5pm.

FAST FACTS: Jamaica

Banking Hours Banks islandwide are open Monday to Friday from 9am to 5pm.

Currency The unit of currency on Jamaica is the **Jamaican dollar,** and it uses the same symbol as the U.S. dollar ($). There is no fixed rate of exchange for the Jamaican dollar. Subject to market fluctuations, it's traded publicly. Visitors to Jamaica can pay for any goods in U.S. dollars. *Be careful!* Ask whether a price is being quoted in Jamaican or U.S. dollars.

In this guide we've generally followed the price-quotation policy of the establishment, whether in Jamaican dollars or U.S. dollars. The symbol "J$" denotes prices in Jamaican dollars; the conversion into U.S. dollars follows in parentheses. When dollar figures stand alone, they are always U.S. currency.

Jamaican currency is issued in banknotes of J$1, J$2, J$5, J$10, J$20, J$50, and J$100. Coins are 1¢, 5¢, 10¢, 20¢, 25¢, and 50¢. At press time (but subject to change), the exchange rate of Jamaican currency is J$35 to U.S.$1 (J$1 equals about 2.8¢ U.S.).

There are Bank of Jamaica exchange bureaus at both international airports (Montego Bay and Kingston), at cruise-ship piers, and in most hotels.

Customs Do *not* bring in or take out illegal drugs from Jamaica. Your luggage will be searched. Marijuana-sniffing police dogs are stationed at the airport. Otherwise, you can bring in most items intended for personal use.

Documents U.S. and Canadian residents do not need passports, but must have proof of citizenship (or permanent residency) and a return or ongoing ticket. In lieu of a passport, an original birth certificate or a certified copy, plus photo ID, will do. A voter registration card is acceptable in some cases, but only if you have a notarized affidavit of citizenship, plus photo ID. Always double-check, however, with the airline you're flying. Sometimes *it* won't accept a voter registration card. Other visitors, including British subjects, need passports, good for a maximum stay of six months.

Immigration cards, needed for bank transactions and currency exchange, are given to visitors at the airport arrivals desks.

Drugs You will almost certainly be approached by someone selling *ganja* (marijuana), and to be frank, that's why many travelers come here. However, we should warn you that drugs (including marijuana) are illegal, and imprisonment is the penalty for possession. Don't smoke pot openly in public. Of course, hundreds of visitors do and get away with it, but you may be the one who gets caught. You should even give a thought as to whether the person selling to you might be a police informant. And above all, don't even consider bringing marijuana back into the United States. There are drug-sniffing dogs stationed at the Jamaican airports and they *will* check your luggage. U.S. Customs agents, well aware of the drug situation on Jamaica, have also easily caught and arrested many who have tried to take a chance on bringing some home.

Drugstores In Montego Bay, try **McKenzie's Drug Store,** 16 Strand St. (☎ **809/952-2467**); in Ocho Rios, **Great House Pharmacy,** Brown's Plaza (☎ **809/974-2352**); and in Kingston, **Moodie's Pharmacy,** in the New Kingston Shopping Centre (☎ **809/926-4174**). Prescriptions are accepted by local pharmacies only if issued by a Jamaican doctor. Hotels have doctors on call. If you need any particular medicine or treatment, bring evidence, such as a letter from your own physician.

Electricity Most places have the standard 110 volts AC (60 cycles), as in the United States. However, some establishments operate on 220 volts AC (50 cycles). If your hotel is on a different current from your U.S.-made appliance, ask for a transformer and adapter.

Embassies Calling embassies or consulates in Jamaica is a challenge. Phones will ring and ring before being picked up, if they are answered at all. Extreme patience is needed to reach a live voice on the other end. The Embassy of the **United States** is at the Jamaica Mutual Life Centre, 2 Oxford Rd., Kingston 5 (☎ **809/929-4850**). The High Commission of **Canada** is in the Mutual Security Bank Building, 30–36 Knutsford Blvd., Kingston 5 (☎ **809/926-1500**), and there's a Canadian Consulate at 29 Gloucester Ave., Montego Bay (☎ **809/952-6198**). The High Commission of the **United Kingdom** is at 28 Trafalgar Rd., Kingston 10 (☎ **809/926-9050**).

Emergencies For the **police** and air rescue, dial ☎ **119;** to report a **fire** or call an **ambulance,** dial ☎ **110.**

Hospitals In Kingston, the **University Hospital** is at Mona (☎ **809/927-1620**); in Montego Bay, the **Cornwall Regional Hospital** is at Mount Salem (☎ **809/952-5100**); and in Port Antonio, the **Port Antonio General Hospital** is at Naylor's Hill (☎ **809/993-2646**).

Information Before you go, you can obtain information from the **Jamaica Tourist Board** at the following U.S. addresses: 500 N. Michigan Ave., Suite 1030, Chicago, IL 60611 (☎ **312/527-1296**); 1320 S. Dixie Hwy., Suite 1101, Coral Gables, FL 33146 (☎ **305/665-0557**); 3440 Wilshire Blvd., Suite 805, Los Angeles, CA 90010 (☎ **213/384-1123**); and 801 Second Ave., New York, NY 10017 (☎ **212/856-9727**). In Atlanta, information can be obtained on the phone by dialing **770/452-7799. In Canada,** contact 1 Eglinton Ave. E., Suite 616, Toronto, ON M4P 3A1 (☎ **416/482-7850**). Brits can call the **London** office: 1-2 Prince Consort Rd., London SW7 2BZ (☎ **0171/224-0505**).

Once on **Jamaica,** you'll find tourist board offices at 2 St. Lucia Ave., Kingston (☎ **809/929-9200**); Cornwall Beach, St. James, Montego Bay (☎ **809/952-4425**); Shop no. 29, Coral Seas Plaza, Negril, Westmoreland (☎ **809/957-4243**); in the Ocean Village Shopping Centre, Ocho Rios, St. Ann (☎ **809/974-2582**); in City Centre Plaza, Port Antonio (☎ **809/993-3051**); and in Hendriks Building, 2 High St., Black River (☎ **809/965-2074**).

Marriages You can get a marriage license after 24 hours' residence on the island and then marry as soon as it can be arranged. You'll need your birth certificate, and, where applicable, divorce documents or death certificates. All documents must be properly certified—ordinary photocopies will not be accepted. Most Jamaican hotels will make arrangements for your wedding and license. Otherwise, one of the offices of the Jamaica Tourist Board can assist you in meeting and making arrangements with a government marriage officer.

Nudity Nude bathing is allowed at a number of hotels, clubs, and beaches (especially in Negril), but only where there are signs stating SWIMSUITS OPTIONAL. Elsewhere, the law will not even allow topless sunbathing.

Safety Major hotels have security guards who protect the grounds, so most vacationers don't have any real problems. Under no circumstances should you accept an invitation to see "the real Jamaica" from some stranger you meet on the beach. Exercise caution when traveling around Jamaica. Safeguard your valuables, and never leave them unattended on a beach. Likewise, never leave luggage or other valuables in a car, or even the trunk of a car. The U.S. State Department has issued a travel advisory about crime rates in Kingston, so don't go walking around alone at night. Caution is also advisable in many north-coast tourist areas, especially remote houses and isolated villas that can't afford security.

Shopping Hours Hours vary widely, but as a general rule most establishments are open Monday to Friday from 8:30am to 4:30 or 5pm. Some shops are open on Saturday until noon.

Taxes The government imposes a 12% room tax. You'll be charged a J$400 ($11.20) departure tax at the airport, payable in either Jamaican or U.S. dollars. There's also a 15% government tax on rental cars and a 15% tax on all overseas telephone calls.

Time Jamaica is on eastern standard time year-round. However, when the United States is on daylight saving time, at 6am in Miami it's 5am in Kingston.

Tipping Tipping is customary. A general 10% or 15% is expected in hotels and restaurants on occasions when you would normally tip. Some places add a service charge to the bill. Tipping is not allowed in the all-inclusive hotels.

Water It's usually safe to drink piped-in water, islandwide, as it's filtered and chlorinated. But, as always, it's more prudent to drink bottled water if it's available.

Weather Expect temperatures around 80° to 90°F on the coast. Winter is a little cooler. In the mountains it can get as low as 40° F. There is generally a breeze, which in winter is noticeably cool. The rainy periods in general are October and November (although it can extend into December) and May and June. Normally rain comes in short, sharp showers; then the sun shines.

1 Montego Bay

Situated on the northwestern coast of the island, Montego Bay first attracted tourists in the 1940s when Doctor's Cave Beach became popular with wealthy vacationers who bathed in the warm water fed by mineral springs. It's now Jamaica's second-largest city.

Despite the large influx of visitors, it still retains its own identity as a thriving business and commercial center, and functions as the market town for most of western Jamaica. It has cruise-ship piers and a growing industrial center at the free port.

Since Montego Bay has its own airport, those who vacation here have little need to visit Kingston, the island's capital. You have everything you need in Mo Bay, the most cosmopolitan of Jamaica's resorts.

WHERE TO STAY

VERY EXPENSIVE

✪ **Half Moon Golf, Tennis & Beach Club.** Rose Hall (P.O. Box 80), Montego Bay, Jamaica, W.I. ☎ **800/626-0592** in the U.S., or 809/953-2211. Fax 809/953-2731. 418 rms, suites, and villas. A/C TV TEL. Winter, $330–$480 double; from $530 suite; from $1,650 villa. Off-season, $220–$280 double; from $320 suite; from $1,320 villa. MAP $65 per person extra. AE, DC, MC, V.

Located about 8 miles east of Montego Bay's city center and 6 miles from the international airport, this is a classic, and one of the 300 best hotels in the world, according to *Condé Nast Traveler*. The resort is set on a mile-long beach and has incredible sports facilities. From here, you can easily taxi into Montego Bay to sample the nightlife and shopping.

Montego Bay

2-0144

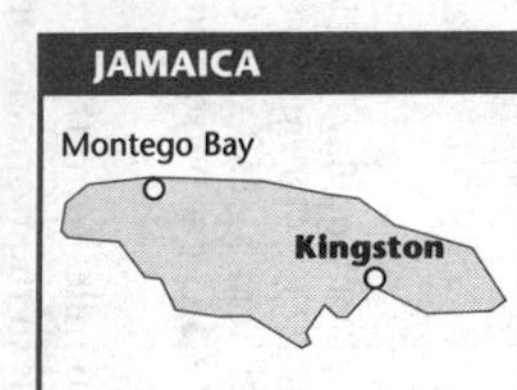

ACCOMMODATIONS

- Breezes Montego Bay 8
- Coral Cliff Hotel 11
- Coyaba 1
- Doctor's Cave Beach Hotel 7
- Half Moon Golf, Tennis & Beach Club 3
- Jack Tar Grand Montego Beach Resort 6
- Reading Reef Club 24
- Royal Court Hotel 15
- Sandals Inn, The 5
- Sandals Montego Bay 4
- Sandals Royal Jamaican 3
- Seacastles 3
- Sea Garden Beach Resort 3
- Vista Ambassador 19
- Wexford Court Hotel 10
- Winged Victory Hotel 9
- Wyndham Rose Hall Resort 3

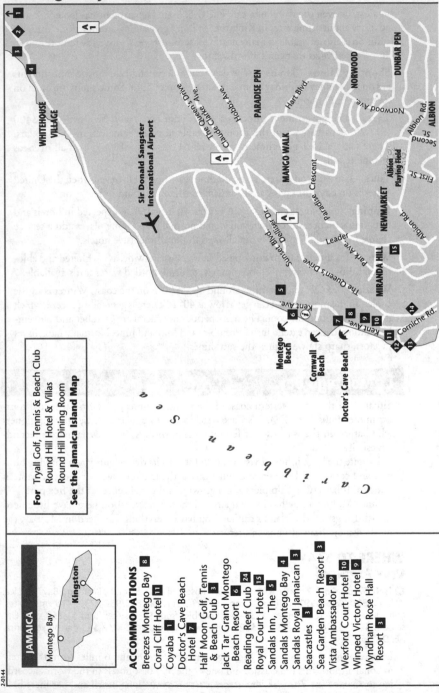

For Tryall Golf, Tennis & Beach Club
Round Hill Hotel & Villas
Round Hill Dining Room
See the Jamaica Island Map

Caribbean Sea

WHITEHOUSE VILLAGE
Sir Donald Sangster International Airport
A1
The Queen's Drive
Claude Clarke Ave.
Hobbs Ave.
PARADISE PEN
Sunset Blvd.
Delliser Dr.
MANGO WALK
Hart Blvd.
Montego Beach
Cornwall Beach
Doctor's Cave Beach
Kent Ave.
Paradise Crescent
Leader
Park Ave.
NORWOOD
Norwood Ave.
MIRANDA HILL
NEWMARKET
Albion Playing Field
DUNBAR PEN
Cornice Rd.
Albion Rd.
First St.
Second St.
ALBION

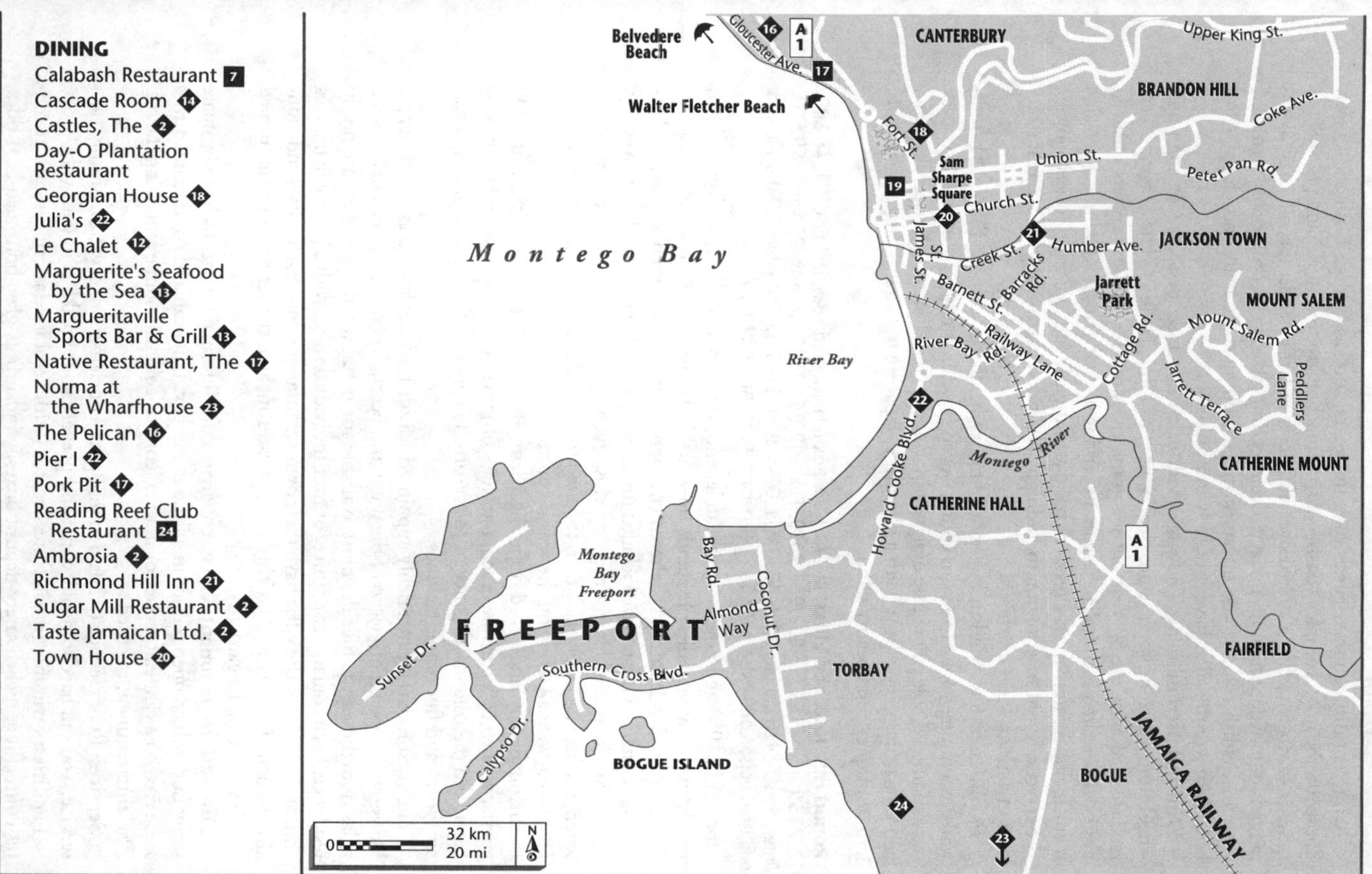
DINING
Calabash Restaurant 7
Cascade Room 14
Castles, The 2
Day-O Plantation Restaurant
Georgian House 18
Julia's 22
Le Chalet 12
Marguerite's Seafood by the Sea 13
Margueritaville Sports Bar & Grill 13
Native Restaurant, The 17
Norma at the Wharfhouse 23
The Pelican 16
Pier I 22
Pork Pit 17
Reading Reef Club Restaurant 24
Ambrosia 2
Richmond Hill Inn 21
Sugar Mill Restaurant 2
Taste Jamaican Ltd. 2
Town House 20
Belvedere Beach
Walter Fletcher Beach
Gloucester Ave.
CANTERBURY
Upper King St.
BRANDON HILL
Coke Ave.
Fort St.
Sam Sharpe Square
Union St.
Peter Pan Rd.
Church St.
JACKSON TOWN
Humber Ave.
Creek St.
St. James St.
Barnett St.
Barracks Rd.
Jarrett Park
MOUNT SALEM
Mount Salem Rd.
Montego Bay
River Bay
River Bay Rd.
Railway Lane
Cottage Rd.
Jarrett Terrace
Peddlers Lane
Montego River
CATHERINE MOUNT
Howard Cooke Blvd.
CATHERINE HALL
A1
Montego Bay Freeport
Bay Rd.
Coconut Dr.
Almond Way
FREEPORT
FAIRFIELD
Sunset Dr.
Southern Cross Blvd.
TORBAY
JAMAICA RAILWAY
Calypso Dr.
BOGUE ISLAND
BOGUE
0
32 km
20 mi
N

Attracting distinguished guests over the years, such as George Bush and Queen Elizabeth, the resort complex consists of spacious hotel rooms, suites, and private five- to seven-bedroom villas scattered over 400 acres of fertile landscape, all carefully arranged to provide maximum privacy. Each accommodation is comfortably furnished with an English colonial/Caribbean motif, including some mahogany four-poster beds. Many of the villas have private swimming pools.

Dining/Entertainment: The Sugar Mill restaurant is set beside a working water wheel from a bygone sugar estate (see "Where to Dine," below). The Seagrape Terrace (named after the 80-year-old sea grape trees on the property) offers meals al fresco. Il Giardino is an Italian restaurant serving a savory cuisine. Evening entertainment includes music from a resident band and nightly folklore and musical shows.

Services: Room service (7am to midnight), laundry, baby-sitting, massage, instruction in various water sports.

Facilities: Sailing, windsurfing, snorkeling, scuba diving, deep-sea fishing, 51 freshwater swimming pools, 13 tennis courts (seven floodlit at night), 4 lit squash courts, outstanding 18-hole golf course designed by Robert Trent Jones Sr., horseback riding, and sauna. Shopping village (with a pharmacy, Japanese restaurant, English-style pub, and boutiques), and beauty salon.

✪ **Round Hill Hotel and Villas.** Rte. A1 (P.O. Box 64), Montego Bay, Jamaica, W.I. ☎ **800/972-2159** in the U.S., or 809/956-7050. Fax 809/956-7505. 36 rms, 27 villas. A/C TEL. Winter, $330–$420 double; $520–$730 villa. Off-season, $190–$250 double; $280–$400 villa. Additional person $60 extra. MAP $65 per person extra. AE, DC, MC, V.

Opened in 1953 and now a Caribbean legend, this is one of the most distinguished hotels in the West Indies. It stands on a lushly landscaped 98-acre peninsula that slopes gracefully down to a sheltered cove where the elegant reception area and social center stand. Guests have included the Kennedys, Cole Porter, and more recently, Steven Spielberg and Harrison Ford. Most evenings are informal, except Saturday, when a jacket and tie or black tie is required for men. Likewise, it's preferred that tennis players wear all white on the tennis courts.

Surrounded by landscaped tropical gardens, Round Hill accommodates some 200 guests, who enjoy its private beach, the views of Jamaica's north shore and the mountains, and the colonial elegance of the resort. There are full spa services, lots of water sports, and fine tennis facilities.

The guest rooms are in a richly appointed seaside building known as the Pineapple House. Each opens onto views of the water and beach. There are also privately owned villas dotted over the hillside, most available for rental when the owners are not in residence. Each contains two, three, or four individual suites with a private living area and/or patio; 19 of the villas have their own swimming pools. Each villa is individually decorated, sometimes lavishly so, and rates include the services of a uniformed maid, a cook, and a gardener.

Dining/Entertainment: Guests congregate for informal luncheons in an intimate straw hut with an open terrace in a little sandy bay. Jamaican and continental dishes are served on a candlelit terrace or in the Georgian colonial room overlooking the sea. The entertainment is varied.

Services: Room service (7:30am to 9:30pm), concierge, laundry, baby-sitting, valet service. You can have someone come and prepare your breakfast in your villa.

Facilities: Swimming pool, fitness center (with aerobics classes), top-quality tennis courts (lit at night), safety-deposit boxes, windsurfing, glass-bottomed-boat rides, scuba diving, horseback riding, sailing, paddleboats, rubber-sided inflatable boats, waterskiing.

> ### Catch a Fire: Jamaica's Reggae Festivals
>
> Every August, Jamaica comes alive with the pulsating sounds of reggae during **Reggae Sunsplash,** the world's largest annual reggae festival. This week-long music extravaganza features some of the most prominent reggae groups and artists. In the past they have included Ziggy Marley, Cocoa Tea, and the Melody Makers. Sunsplash takes place at different venues; check with Jamaican tourist boards for the latest details.
>
> Some time during the second week of August, **Reggae Sunfest** takes place in Montego Bay. Usually this is a four-day musical event. Some of the biggest names in reggae, both from Jamaica and worldwide, usually perform. Many local hotels are fully booked for the festival, so advance reservations are necessary.
>
> The Jamaican Tourist Board's U.S. and Canadian offices can give you information about packages and group rates for the festivals and fill you in on other reggae concerts and events held throughout the year on Jamaica.

✪ **Tryall Golf, Tennis, and Beach Club.** St. James (P.O. Box 1206), Montego Bay, Jamaica, W.I. ☎ **800/238-5290** in the U.S., or 809/956-5660. Fax 809/956-5673. 47 rms, 48 villas. A/C TEL. Winter, $270–$490 double; $507–$1,592 villa. Off-season, $160–$260 double; $365–$750 villa. Additional person $70 extra in winter, $55 extra off-season. MAP $66 per person extra. AE, DC, MC, V.

With more spacious grounds than almost any other hotel on Jamaica, this stylish and upscale resort sits 12 miles west of town on the site of a 2,200-acre former sugar plantation. It doesn't have the fine beach that Half Moon does, nor the house-party atmosphere of Trident at Port Antonio, but it's noteworthy, nevertheless. Known as one of the grandest resorts of Jamaica, the property lies along a 1½-mile seafront and is presided over by a 162-year-old Georgian-style Great House. It's a top choice for vacationers who are serious about their golf game.

The accommodations are in either modern wings or luxurious villas scattered throughout the surrounding acreage. The bedrooms are decorated in cool pastels with an English colonial decor. All contain ceiling fans and air-conditioning, along with picture windows framing sea and mountain views. The resort's famous villas are set amid lush foliage and are designed for privacy. Each villa comes with a full-time staff, including a cook, maid, laundress, and gardener. All have private swimming pools.

Dining/Entertainment: The most formal of the resort's dining areas is in the Great House, where antiques evoke the plantation era. More casual meals are served in a beachside cafe. A resident band plays everything from reggae to slow-dance music every night during dinner. Afternoon tea is served in the Great House.

Services: Room service, baby-sitting, laundry, massage; lessons given in golf, tennis, and water sports.

Facilities: Championship 18-hole par-71 golf course (site of many world-class golf competitions and the pride of this elegant property), nine Laykold tennis courts, 2-mile jogging trail, swimming pool with a swim-up bar, windsurfing, snorkeling, deep-sea fishing, paddleboats, glass-bottom boats.

EXPENSIVE

✪ **Coyaba.** Little River Post Office, Montego Bay, Jamaica, W.I. ☎ **800/237-3237** or 809/953-9150. Fax 809/953-2244. 50 rms. A/C TV TEL. Winter, $220–$326 double. Off-season, $140–$198 double. All meals $65 per person extra. Children 11 and under get 50% discount. MC, V.

With only 50 rooms, and a graceful British colonial atmosphere, this is one of the newer, smaller, and more elegant all-inclusive resorts. It was established in 1994 by American/Jamaican-Chinese entrepreneurs, the Robertson family, and built from scratch at a cost of $4 million. Set on a lovely strip of beachfront, a 15-minute drive east of the center of Montego Bay, it's centered around an adaptation of a 19th-century Great House.

Accommodations in the main building overlook the garden; those in the pair of three-story outbuildings lie closer to the beach and are somewhat more expensive. The decor is British colonial, with traditional prints, expensive chintz fabrics, French doors leading onto private patios or verandas, carved mahogany furniture, and other reminders of the plantation age. The establishment, which welcomes children but hasn't yet built them any special facilities, is less rowdy and raucous than other Jamaican resorts geared to singles and young couples and prides itself on its peaceful and somewhat staid demeanor. The owners are usually on hand to ensure that the operation runs smoothly.

Dining/Entertainment: The hotel's main and most formal restaurant, the Vineyard, is open only for dinner, serving first-rate Jamaican and continental cuisine. Less upscale is Docks Caribbean Bar & Grill, where there's a daily salad bar from which you can create a full meal. There are also three bars scattered amid the grounds.

Services: Afternoon teas keep up the British colonial appearances, room service, massage, laundry, and nanny service for care and feeding of children.

Facilities: A tennis court lit at night, a rectangular swimming pool, exercise room, outdoor hot tub, watersports center, gift shop.

Wyndham Rose Hall Golf & Beach Resort. Rose Hall (P.O. Box 999), Montego Bay, Jamaica, W.I. ☎ **800/822-4200** in the U.S., or 809/953-2650. Fax 809/953-2617. 470 rms, 19 suites. A/C TEL. Winter, $185–$220 double; from $435 suite. Off-season, $130–$155 double; from $400 suite. MAP $50.60 per person extra. AE, DC, MC, V.

Wyndham Rose Hall sits at the bottom of a rolling 30-acre site along the north-coast highway 9 miles east of the airport. On a former sugar plantation that once covered 7,000 acres, the hotel abuts the 200-year-old home of the legendary "White Witch of Rose Hall," now a historic site, and has a thin strip of sandy beach. Although it's popular as a convention site, the hotel also caters to a family market (children are an important part of the clientele) and has serious golf and tennis facilities. The staff stays busy organizing games and social events. The seven-story H-shaped structure features a large and attractive lobby on the ground floor and, upstairs, guest rooms all have sea views and rather unremarkable furnishings. Most units have two queen-size beds, and each accommodation has a small private balcony. Although the rooms all have paintings by local artists depicting typical Caribbean scenes, what's missing here is real Jamaican style and ambience.

Dining/Entertainment: There are four restaurants, and it's never more than a short walk to one of the many bars scattered around the hotel property. Wednesday nights in season feature a poolside buffet and a Caribbean variety show with dancers, fire-eaters, and calypso and reggae performances.

Services: Room service (7am to 11pm), baby-sitting, laundry, massage. The "Kids Klub" has an array of supervised activities that's included in the rate.

Facilities: Three pools (one for wading that's suited to small children, two for swimming), complimentary sailboats, top-rated golf course meandering over part of the hotel grounds, tennis complex (with six lit all-weather Laykold courts) headed by pros who offer a complete tennis program, air-conditioned fitness center.

Moderate

✪ **Doctor's Cave Beach Hotel.** Gloucester Ave. (P.O. Box 94), Montego Bay, Jamaica, W.I. ☎ **809/952-4355.** Fax 809/952-5204. 78 rms, 12 suites. A/C TEL. Winter, $130–$140 double; $160 suite for 2. Off-season, $105–$115 double; $140 suite for 2. Additional person $30 extra. MAP $35 per person extra. AE, DC, MC, V.

Across the street from the well-known Doctor's Cave Beach in the bustle of the town's commercial zone, this three-story hostelry offers great value. It has its own gardens, a swimming pool, a Jacuzzi, and a small gymnasium, all set on four acres of tropical gardens. The rooms are simply but comfortably furnished, and suites have kitchenettes.

The two restaurants are the Coconut Grove, whose outdoor terrace is floodlit at night, and the less formal Greenhouse. In the Cascade Bar, where a waterfall tumbles down a stone wall, you can listen to a piano duo during cocktail hours.

Reading Reef Club. Rte. A1, on Bogue Lagoon, at the bottom of Long Hill (P.O. Box 225), Reading, Montego Bay, Jamaica, W.I. ☎ **800/315-0379** in the U.S., or 809/952-5909. Fax 809/952-7217. 30 rms, 4 suites. A/C TEL. Winter, $100–$165 double; $250 two-bedroom suite, $325 three-bedroom suite. Off-season, $75–$125 double; $200 two-bedroom suite, $250 three-bedroom suite. MAP $35 per person extra. AE, MC, V.

This pocket of posh was created by an American, JoAnne Rowe. A former fashion designer whose hobby is cooking, JoAnne has a sense of style and a flair for cuisine that are reflected in the hotel. Located on 2½ acres at the bottom of Long Hill Road, the hotel is a 15-minute drive west of Montego Bay, on a 350-foot sandy beach where people relax in comfort, unmolested by beach vendors. The complex of four buildings overlooks beautiful reefs once praised by Jacques Cousteau for their aquatic life.

The accommodations, which include two- and three-bedroom suites, open onto a sea view. All have air-conditioning and ceiling fans and a light Caribbean motif. The luxury rooms have minibars, and the two- and three-bedroom suites offer kitchenettes. See "Where to Dine," below, for details on the restaurant. There's also a bar/lounge and a beachside luncheon barbecue specializing in Jamaican (jerk) sausages, English sausages, and Tex-Mex food. Services include laundry, valet, and drivers for island tours. Guests also enjoy the freshwater swimming pool and free water sports, including snorkeling, windsurfing, and sailing in a 12-foot sailboat. Scuba diving costs extra.

Seacastles. Rte. A1, Rose Hall (P.O. Box 1), Montego Bay, St. James, Jamaica, W.I. ☎ **809/953-3250,** or 212/924-4209 for reservations. Fax 809/953-3062. 198 suites. A/C TEL. Winter, $130 suite for 2, $230 suite for 4, $335 suite for 6. Off-season, $110 suite for 2, $200 suite for 4, $290 suite for 6. Additional person $24 extra. MAP $35 per person extra. AE, MC, V.

Seacastles, one of the most architecturally dramatic hotels in the region, was built in 1991 along an isolated seafront 11 miles east of Montego Bay. Its development included at least a 50% participation by the Jamaican government, which helped to market many of the units as privately owned condominiums. The result is an airy, widely separated compound of postmodern buildings vaguely influenced by English colonial models. The resort contains only suites, each with kitchen or kitchenette, all scattered among a half dozen outbuildings ringed with greenery and capped with cedar-shingled roofs.

Lawns slope down to the beach, past arbors, gazebos, bars, and water-sports kiosks. The staff organizes activities like beer-drinking contests, volleyball on the beach, shows with staff and guests, bingo, and diving contests. The Castles Restaurant overlooks the graceful freshwater swimming pool; less formal meals and drinks are offered in the Clifftop Bar. Other amenities include laundry, baby-sitting, water-sports facilities, and a tour desk for island tours.

Wexford Court Hotel. Gloucester Ave. (P.O. Box 108), Montego Bay, Jamaica, W.I. ☎ **809/952-2854.** Fax 809/952-3637. 61 rms, 6 one-bedroom apts. A/C TV TEL. Winter, $120–$125 double; $130 apt. Off-season, $90–$95 double; $100 apt. MAP $25 per person extra. AE, DC, MC, V.

Stay here for economy, not style. About 10 minutes from downtown Mo Bay, near Doctor's Cave Beach, this hotel has a small pool and a patio (where calypso is enjoyed in season). The apartments have living/dining areas and kitchenettes, so you can cook for yourself. All the back-to-basics rooms have patios shaded by gables and Swiss chalet-style roofs.

The Wexford Grill includes a good selection of Jamaican dishes, such as chicken deep fried with honey. Guests can enjoy drinks in a bar nearby.

Winged Victory Hotel. 5 Queen's Dr., Montego Bay, Jamaica, W.I. ☎ **809/952-3892.** Fax 809/952-5986. 16 rms, 8 suites. A/C. Winter, $90–$100 double; $175–$225 suite. Off-season, $60–$80 double; $110–$150 suite. MAP $35 per person extra. AE, MC, V.

This tall and modern hotel on a hillside road in the Miranda Hill District of Montego Bay doesn't reveal its true beauty until you pass through its comfortable public rooms into a Mediterranean-style courtyard in back. There, urn-shaped balustrades enclose a terraced garden, a pool, and a veranda looking over the faraway crescent of Montego Bay. The veranda's best feature is the Calabash Restaurant. The dignified owner, Roma Chin Sue, added well furnished and comfortably appointed hotel rooms to her already well-known restaurant in 1985. All but five have a private balcony or veranda, along with an attractively eclectic decor that's part Chinese, part colonial, and part Iberian.

INEXPENSIVE

✪ **Coral Cliff Hotel.** 165 Gloucester Ave. (P.O. Box 253), Montego Bay, Jamaica, W.I. ☎ **809/952-4130.** Fax 809/952-6532. 32 rms. A/C TEL. Winter, $80–$90 double; $92–$112 triple. Off-season, $68–$80 double; $80–$90 triple. MC, V.

The Coral Cliff Hotel, a mile west of the center of town but only two minutes from Doctor's Cave Beach, is the best bargain in Montego Bay. The rates are extremely reasonable for what you get, including a luxurious swimming pool. The hotel grew from a colonial-style building that was once the private home of Harry M. Doubleday (of the famous publishing family). Many of the light, airy, and spacious bedrooms open onto balconies with a view of the sea.

The hotel's breeze-swept restaurant is appropriately called the Verandah Terrace, and it overlooks the bay. The food is good, featuring local produce and fresh seafood whenever available.

Royal Court Hotel. Sewell Ave. (P.O. Box 195), Montego Bay, Jamaica, W.I. ☎ **809/952-4531.** Fax 809/952-4532. 20 rms, 3 suites. A/C TEL. Winter, $90 double; $135 suite. Off-season, $70 double; $95 suite. AE, MC, V.

This hotel is clean and attractive, has a charming atmosphere, and is a good value. It's located on the hillside overlooking Montego Bay, above Gloucester Avenue and off Park Avenue. The rooms are furnished with bright, tasteful colors, and all have patios; the larger ones have fully equipped kitchenettes.

Meals are served in the Pool Bar and Eatery. Its restaurant, Leaf of Life, specializes in vegetarian food, among other selections. Free transportation is provided to the town, the beach, and the tennis club. Amenities and facilities include massage, gym, steam room, Jacuzzi, TV room, conference room, and a doctor on the premises.

All-Inclusive Resorts

Breezes Montego Bay. Gloucester Avenue, Montego Bay, Jamaica, W.I. ☎ **800/859-SUPER** or 809/940-1150. Fax 809/940-1160. 102 rms, 22 suites. A/C TV TEL. Winter, $1,598–$2,038 double; $2,418 suite for 2. Off-season, $1,298–$1,778 double; $2,158–$2,218 suite for 2. Rates are all-inclusive for 5 nights. AE, MC, V.

Built in 1995 in a boomerang-shaped five-story complex that encloses a swimming pool and a cluster of bars and boutiques, this is one of the newest members of Jamaica's SuperClub chain. Defined as "a sandbox for your inner child," it's the only major hotel set directly on the sands of Montego Bay's most popular public beach, Doctor's Cave. Guests here experience more of the street and beach life of Jamaica than those who stay at the more secluded resorts set off within compounds of their own. The venue is adult (no children under 16 are admitted) and indulgent, but without the emphasis on raucous partying that's the norm at Hedonism II (a member of the same SuperClub chain). Bedrooms are simply furnished and breezy, and overlook either the beach or the garden that separates the hotel from the traffic of Montego Bay's main commercial boulevard, Gloucester Avenue. Nonresidents can buy a "Day Pay" for $45, allowing them the same unlimited access to the bars and buffets.

Dining/Entertainment: Breakfast and informal lunches and dinners are served at Jimmy's Buffet, a dining terrace overlooking the swimming pool and the beach. A more formal, candlelit evening venue is available at Martino's, an Italian rooftop restaurant within the hotel. A poolside snack bar serves burgers and hot dogs throughout the day, and there are four bars, one with a live pianist, to quench your thirst.

Services: The staff works hard to provide group diversions, games, toga parties, mingle parties, "mixology" classes, steel bands, and reggae lessons.

Facilities: Freshwater swimming pool; rooftop Jacuzzi; a full range of water sports with instruction on how to use water skis, Hobie-Cats, and Windsurfers; a tennis court lit for night play; a fitness center with aerobics classes, water aerobics classes, and Nautilus equipment.

Jack Tar Grand Montego Beach Resort. Gloucester Ave. (P.O. Box 144), Montego Bay, Jamaica, W.I. ☎ **800/999-9182** in the U.S., or 809/952-4340. Fax 809/952-6633. 130 rms. A/C TV TEL. Winter, $300–$330 double; $435–$480 triple. Off-season, $200–$230 double; $285–$320 triple. Rates include all meals, drinks, activities, taxes, service, and airport transfers. Children 2–12 in parents' room charged $60 extra. AE, MC, V.

This is a very downscale version of an all-inclusive, make no mistake, but it does offer an affordable, worry-free beach vacation for families on a budget. (The Sandals Inn next door is far superior, even though it's Sandals' budget property.) This 3¼-acre beachfront resort encompasses a pair of buildings set two miles north of the commercial core of Montego Bay. Noted for its cheap, all-inclusive format, this is one of the smaller members of a chain known for generous (if not blue-chip) food and drink policies.

In 1996, the resort underwent a $4 million renovation, in which each of the bedrooms was upgraded. The guest units are modern but bland, and they sit a few steps from the beach, with a view of the water. Private balconies open directly onto Montego Bay. Guests practically live in their bathing suits.

Dining/Entertainment: Lunch is served at beachside or in the main dining room, and there is nightly entertainment. The international food isn't wildly creative or refined, but it's plentiful.

Services: Reggae dance lessons, massages.

Facilities: Freshwater pool, tennis clinic and tennis courts (for daytime), sauna, windsurfing, waterskiing, snorkeling, sailing.

The Sandals Inn (formerly Carlyle on the Bay). Kent Ave. (P.O. Box 412), Montego Bay, Jamaica, W.I. ☎ **800/SANDALS** in the U.S. and Canada, or 809/952-4140. Fax 809/952-6913. 52 rms. A/C TV TEL. Winter, $1,160–$1,300 double. Off-season, $1,080–$1,220 double. Rates are for 4 days/3 nights and include all meals, snacks, drinks, sports and entertainment activities, airport transfers, taxes, and tips. AE, MC, V.

The Sandals Inn is a couples-only (male and female) hotel built around a large pool and patio, with a beach a short walk across a busy highway. This is the least expensive, least glamorous, least spacious, and least attractive of the Sandals all-inclusive resorts scattered across Jamaica. But it's a trade-off: You don't get luxury, but you do get proximity to downtown Montego Bay, reasonable rates, and free day passes (including free transportation) to both of the Sandals resorts of Montego Bay.

Thirty-eight rooms open onto the swimming pool; all units contain king-size beds and hair dryers. There is now environmentally friendly linen service, so that sheets and towels are not changed unless you request it.

Dining/Entertainment: Food is served in bountiful portions in the resort's only dining room, and there's nightly entertainment. A specialty restaurant, Caryle, specializing in flambé dishes, breaks the routine of the main dining room.

Services: 24-hour room service, free round-trip airport transfers.

Facilities: Recreational and sports program, exercise room, saunas, Jacuzzi, tennis courts, swimming pool, room safes.

Sandals Montego Bay. Kent Ave. (P.O. Box 100), Montego Bay, Jamaica, W.I. ☎ **800/SANDALS** in the U.S. and Canada, or 809/952-5510. Fax 809/952-0816. 211 rms, 32 suites. A/C TV TEL. Winter, $1,380–$1,650 double; $1,790–$3,120 suite for 2. Off-season, $1,310–$1,560 double; $1,790–$2,940 suite for 2. Rates are for 4 days/3 nights and include all meals, drinks, activities, airport transfers, taxes, and tips. AE, MC, V.

Located five minutes northeast of the airport, this honeymoon haven next to Whitehouse Village is always booked solid (reserve as far ahead as possible). The 19-acre site is a couples-only (male and female), all-inclusive resort. Everything is covered in the price—that means all meals, snacks, nightly entertainment (including those notorious toga parties), unlimited drinks night or day at one of four bars, tips, and round-trip airport transfers and baggage handling from the Montego Bay airport. Lots of entertainment and sports facilities are available on the property, so many guests never leave.

In contrast to its somewhat more laid-back nearby counterpart (the Sandals Royal Jamaican), this resort offers many different activities for a clientele and staff who tend to be extroverted and gregarious; the Playmakers, as staff members are called, keep everybody amused and the joint jumping. If you want peace, quiet, and seclusion, it's probably not for you.

The accommodations are either in villas spread along 1,700 feet of white sandy beach or in the main house where all bedrooms face the sea and contain private balconies. Try to avoid booking into a room over the dining room; these don't have balconies and may be noisy. All units are well furnished, with king-size beds and hair dryers.

Dining/Entertainment: In addition to its main dining room, the resort has Tokyo Joe's, serving six-course Oriental meals; the Beach Grill; and the Oleander Deck, with "white glove service," featuring Jamaican and Caribbean cuisine. The Oleander offers the finest dining in the Sandals chain. Those who haven't tired themselves out can head for the late-night disco, which often has rum and reggae nights.

Services: Free shuttle bus to the resort's twin, the Sandals Royal Jamaican, whose facilities are open without charge to residents here.

Facilities: Waterskiing, snorkeling, sailing, scuba diving daily with a certification program (PADI or NAUI), windsurfing, paddleboats and a glass-bottom boat, two freshwater pools, three Jacuzzis, tennis (available day or night), fully equipped fitness center.

Sandals Royal Jamaican. Mahoe Bay (P.O. Box 167), Montego Bay, Jamaica, W.I. ☎ **800/SANDALS** in the U.S. and Canada, or 809/953-2231. Fax 809/953-2788. 176 rms, 14 suites. A/C TV TEL. Winter, $1,460–$1,650 per couple; $1,800–$2,020 suite for 2. Off-season, $1,350–$1,550 per couple; $1,780–$1,890 suite for 2. Rates are for 4 days/3 nights and include all meals, snacks, drinks, activities, airport transfers, taxes, and tips. AE, MC, V.

This all-inclusive, couples-only (male and female) resort is a reincarnation of a prestigious colonial-style Montego Bay hotel. The building lies on its own private beach (which, frankly, isn't as good as the one at the Sandals Montego Bay). Some of the British colonial atmosphere remains, as reflected by a formal tea in the afternoon, but there are modern touches as well, including a private island reached by boat where clothing is optional.

The spacious rooms range from standard to superior to deluxe. Even higher in price are the deluxe beachfront accommodations or a junior suite.

Dining/Entertainment: The Regency Suite and Deck is the Jamaican-inspired main dining room. Specialty restaurants include Bali Hai, an Indonesian restaurant built on the previously mentioned offshore island, and the Courtyard Grill, with such offerings as grilled sirloin, grilled snapper, and smoked marlin. There are four bars, plus food and drink available throughout the day. Live music by a local reggae band is presented.

Services: Laundry, massage, free shuttle bus to the resort's twin Sandals (whose facilities are available without charge to any resident). Weddings can be arranged (see "The Best Honeymoon Resorts," in chapter 1).

Facilities: Scuba diving, windsurfing, sailing, three tennis courts, swimming pool.

Sea Garden Beach Resort. Kent Ave. (P.O. Box 300), Montego Bay, Jamaica, W.I. ☎ **809/952-4780.** Fax 809/952-7543. 97 rms. A/C. Winter, $780–$840 per person double. Off-season, $660–$720 per person double. Rates are for 4 days/3 nights and include all meals, snacks, drinks, activities, airport transfers, taxes, and tips. AE, MC, V.

About five minutes from the noisy airport, this resort, one of the most lackluster of the all-inclusives, stands near some of the most popular public beaches. Designed in a British colonial style of neo-Victorian gingerbread, tall columns, and white lattices, it's airy and comfortable. The dining room, under a high arched ceiling and sheathed in mahogany, overlooks a flagstone-covered courtyard. The accommodations lie in sprawling motel-like units built around the pool in back. Each unit contains a private balcony or patio and simple mahogany furniture; most could stand to be spruced up a bit. Although this property competes with the all-inclusive Sandals, we think Sandals (and even Jack Tar) are superior. As for service, we know this is laid-back Jamaica, but there are limits! You need a lot of patience to stay here.

Dining/Entertainment: One main dining room is the venue for international meals. There are four bars, and a resident band plays six nights a week.

Services: Baby-sitting, laundry, free transportation to and from the airport.

Facilities: Two lit tennis courts, water sports (such as sailing, snorkeling, and windsurfing).

Vista Ambassador. Gloucester Ave. (P.O. Box 262), Montego Bay, Jamaica, W.I. ☎ **800/JAMAICA** in the U.S., or 809/952-4703. Fax 809/952-6810. 180 rms, 20 junior villa suites. A/C TEL. Winter, $1,450–$1,550 double; $1,750 junior villa suite. Off-season, $1,384–$1,496 double; $1,648 junior villa suite. Five-night package includes all meals, drinks, and airport transfers. Children 12 and under (one per adult) stay free in parents' room; children 13–17 are charged 30% of the adult rate. AE, MC, V.

Set on landscaped grounds adjacent to the Montego Bay Craft Market, this hotel was once known as Lifestyles. In 1995 it transformed itself into the first all-inclusive family resort in Jamaica. It's set on 10 acres of tropical gardens and offers panoramic views of Montego Bay and the Caribbean. Although it stands on a hillside with no beach of its own (it does have a swimming pool), it's only a five-minute walk from the white sands of Walter Fletcher Beach.

Contemporary tropical furnishings decorate the bedrooms, which can be adjusted to accommodate various family sizes, with standard and deluxe rooms as well as junior, one-bedroom, and two-bedroom villa suites. Each is equipped with a cable TV, safe, and ironing board. Each suite also has a private terrace with a Jacuzzi and wet bar.

Dining/Entertainment: The Island Verandah offers breakfast and casual dining, whereas the Blue Horizon is more elegant, featuring à la carte selections at dinner. There are three conveniently located lounges: Dolphins, a pool and juice bar; Expressions, a karaoke bar; and Rhapsody, a piano lounge.

Facilities: Spa and gym (with sauna, steam room, Jacuzzi, wet rooms, and many spa services, including massages, facials, body scrubs, and herbal wraps), adult swimming pool and children's pool, tennis court, private beach club.

WHERE TO DINE

The Montego Bay area has some of the finest (and most expensive) dining on the island. But if you're watching your wallet and don't have a delicate stomach, you'll find lots of terrific street food. On Kent Avenue you might try authentic jerk pork or seasoned spareribs grilled over charcoal fires and sold with extra-hot sauce; order a Red Stripe beer to go with it. Cooked shrimp are also sold on the streets of Mo Bay; they don't look it, but they're very spicy, so be warned. And if you have an efficiency unit with a kitchenette, you can buy fresh lobster or the catch of the day from Mo Bay fishers and make your own dinner.

EXPENSIVE

Georgian House. 2 Orange St. ☎ **809/952-0632.** Reservations recommended. Main courses $15–$33, lunch $5–$13. AE, MC, V. Mon–Fri noon–3pm; daily 6–11pm. The restaurant runs a private van service running round-trip from most hotels; ask when you reserve. INTERNATIONAL/JAMAICAN.

The landmark Georgian House, which includes a restaurant and an art gallery, brings grand cuisine and an elegant setting to the heart of town. The 18th-century buildings were constructed by an English gentleman for his mistress, or so it is said. You can select either the upstairs room, which is more formal, or the garden terrace, with its fountains, statues, lanterns, and cut-stone exterior.

You might begin with a traditional Jamaican appetizer such as ackee and bacon. Baked spiny lobster is another specialty, but ask that it not be overcooked. Continental dishes, such as tournedos Rossini, are also prepared with flair. The lunch menu is primarily Jamaican, but dinner offerings are broader in scope, with a variety of fresh seafood pastas and vegetarian choices. There's a fine wine list.

Julia's. Julia's Estate, Bogue Hill. ☎ **809/952-1772.** Reservations required. Fixed-price dinner $33–$45. AE, MC, V. Daily 5:30–10:30pm. Private van transportation provided; ask when you reserve. ITALIAN.

The winding jungle road you take to reach this place is part of the before-dinner entertainment. After a jolting ride to a setting high above the city and its bay, you pass through a walled-in park that long ago was the site of a private home built in 1840 for the duke of Sutherland. Today the focal point is a long, low-slung modern house with fresh decor and sweeping views. Raimondo and Julia Meglio, drawing on the cuisine of their native Italy, prepare chicken cacciatore, breaded cutlet Milanese with tomato sauce and mozzarella cheese, fillet of fresh fish with lime juice and butter, and 10 different kinds of pasta. Lobster, veal, and shrimp are also regularly featured. The food, although competently prepared with fresh ingredients whenever possible, can hardly compete with the view. The homemade breads and desserts, however, are always winning accompaniments.

✪ **Norma at the Wharfhouse.** Reading Rd. ☎ **809/979-2745.** Reservations recommended. Main courses $26–$32. MC, V. Thurs–Sun noon–3:30pm; Tues–Sun 6:30–10pm. Drive 15 minutes west of the town center along Rte. A1. NOUVELLE JAMAICAN.

Set in a coral-stone warehouse whose two-foot-thick walls are bound together with molasses and lime, this is the finest restaurant in Montego Bay. It's a favorite of many of Jamaica's visiting celebrities. Originally built in 1780, it was restored by Millicent Rogers, heiress of the Standard Oil fortune, and now serves as the north-shore domain of Norma Shirley, one of Jamaica's foremost restaurateurs. You can request a table either on the large pier built on stilts over the coral reef (where a view of Montego Bay glitters in the distance) or in an elegantly formal early 19th-century dining room illuminated only with flickering candles. Before or after dinner, drinks are served either in the restaurant or in an informal bar in a separate building, much favored by locals, the Wharf Rat.

Service in the restaurant is impeccable, and the food is praised throughout the island. Specialties include grilled deviled crab backs, smoked marlin with papaya sauce, chicken breast with callaloo, nuggets of lobster in a mild curry sauce, and chateaubriand larded with pâté in a peppercorn sauce. Many of the main dishes are served with a garlic sauce. Dessert might be a rum-and-raisin cheesecake or a piña-colada mousse. Each of these dishes is individually prepared and filled with flavor. This is the type of food you hope to find in Jamaica, but so rarely do.

Richmond Hill Inn. 45 Union St. ☎ **809/952-3859.** Reservations recommended. All main courses (including soup, salad, garlic bread, and dessert) $35. AE, MC, V. Daily 7:30am–10pm. Take a taxi (a 4-minute ride uphill, east of the town's main square), or ask the restaurant to have you picked up at your hotel. INTERNATIONAL/CONTINENTAL.

This plantation-style house was originally built in 1806 by owners of the Dewar's whiskey distillery, who happened to be distantly related to Annie Palmer, the "White Witch of Rose Hall." Today it's run by an Austrian family team, who prepare well-flavored food for an appreciative clientele. Dinners include a shrimp-and-lobster cocktail, an excellent house salad, different preparations of dolphin, breaded breast of chicken, surf and turf, Wiener schnitzel, filet mignon, and a choice of dessert cakes. Many of the dishes are of a relatively standard international style, but others, especially the lobster, are worth the trek up the hill.

Round Hill Dining Room. In the Round Hill Hotel and Villas, along Rte. A1, 8 miles west of the center of Montego Bay. ☎ **809/956-7050.** Reservations required. Main courses $18–$39. AE, DC, MC, V. Daily 12:30–2:30pm and 7–9:30pm. INTERNATIONAL.

The most prestigious dining room in Montego Bay, this place has attracted a smattering of celebrities with its simple but sophisticated surroundings. To reach the dining room, you'll have to pass through the resort's open-air reception area and proceed through a garden. Many visitors opt for a drink in the large and high-ceilinged bar area, designed by Ralph Lauren, before moving on to their dinner, which is served either on a terrace perched above the surf or (during inclement weather) under an open-sided breezeway.

Although many dishes are classic, the same recipes fed to Noël Coward or Cole Porter, other more innovative dishes reflect a taste of Jamaica. For example, shrimp and pasta Caribe is sautéed with chopped herbs, cream, and wine; and Rasta pasta is tossed with vegetables and basil. Caribbean veal is stuffed with spicy crabmeat and seared, and the catch of the day is served jerked, broiled, or steamed with butter, herbs, and ginger. Of course, you can also order more classic dishes, including rack of lamb or a medallion of lobster sautéed with cream and served over fettuccine. Afternoon tea and sandwiches are served daily at 4pm.

✪ **Sugar Mill Restaurant.** At the Half Moon Club, Half Moon Golf Course, Rose Hall, along Rte. A1. ☎ **809/953-2228.** Reservations required. Main courses $15–$33. AE, MC, V. Daily noon–3pm and 7–10pm. A minivan can be sent to most hotels to pick you up. INTERNATIONAL/CARIBBEAN.

This restaurant, near a stone ruin of what used to be a water wheel for a sugar plantation, is reached after a drive through rolling landscape. Guests dine by candlelight on an open terrace with a view of a pond, the water wheel, and plenty of greenery. You can also dine inside.

Although he came from Switzerland, it was in the Caribbean that chef Hans Schenk blossomed as a culinary artist. He has entertained everyone from the British royal family to Farouk, the former king of Egypt. Lunch can be a relatively simple affair, perhaps an ackee burger with bacon, preceded by Mama's pumpkin soup and followed with a homemade rum-and-raisin ice cream. Smoked north-coast marlin is a specialty. The chef makes the most elegant Jamaican bouillabaisse on the island and zesty jerk versions of pork, fish, or chicken. He also prepares the day's catch with considerable flair. On any given day you can ask the waiter what's cooking in the curry pot. Chances are, it will be a Jamaican specialty such as goat, full of flavor and served with island chutney. Top your meal with a cup of unbeatable Blue Mountain coffee.

MODERATE

Ambrosia. Across from the Wyndham Rose Hall Resort, Rose Hall. ☎ **809/953-2650.** Reservations recommended. Main courses $13–$29. AE, MC, V. Daily 6:30–10pm. MEDITERRANEAN.

This restaurant sits across from one of the largest hotels in Montego Bay. With its cedar-shingled design and trio of steeply pointed roofs, it has the air of a country club. Once you enter the courtyard, complete with a set of cannons, you find yourself in one of the loveliest restaurants in the area. You'll enjoy a sweeping view over the rolling lawns leading past the hotel and down to the sea, interrupted only by Doric columns. Not everything is ambrosia on the menu, but the cooks turn out a predictable array of good pasta and seafood dishes. Many of the flavors are Mediterranean, especially the shrimp scampi and other seafood dishes. The chefs handle the herb-crusted rack of lamb expertly, although it arrived frozen on the island from some faraway home.

Calabash Restaurant. In the Winged Victory Hotel, 5 Queen's Dr. ☎ **809/952-3892.** Reservations recommended. Main courses $6–$25. AE, MC, V. Daily noon–2:30pm and 6–10pm. INTERNATIONAL/JAMAICAN.

Perched on a hillside road in Montego Bay, 500 feet above the distant sea, this well-established restaurant has amused and entertained Peter O'Toole and Roger Moore, among others. It was originally built as a private villa by a doctor in the 1920s. More than 25 years ago owner Roma Chin Sue established the courtyard and elegantly simple eagle's-nest patio as a well-managed restaurant. The seafood, Jamaican classics, and international favorites include curried goat, lobster dishes, the house specialty of mixed seafood en coquille (served with a cheese-and-brandy sauce), and a year-round version of a Jamaican Christmas cake. Flavors are blended beautifully. Over the years the kitchen has been consistently good, and savvy locals keep returning.

Day-O Plantation Restaurant. Lot 1, Fairfield, P.O. Box 6, Granville P.O., Montego Bay. ☎ **809/952-1825.** Reservations required. Main courses $14–$28. AE, DC, DISC, MC, V. Tues–Sun 6:30–9:30pm (last order). Minivan service will pick up diners at any of the Montego Bay hotels, and return them after their meal. INTERNATIONAL/JAMAICAN.

This place was originally built in the 1920s as the home of the overseer of one of the region's largest sugar producers, the Barnett Plantation. Established as a restaurant in 1994, in a location an eight-minute drive west of town off the A-1 highway leading toward Negril, it occupies a long, indoor/outdoor dining room that's divided into two halves by a dance floor and a small stage. Here, the owner, Paul Hurlock, performs as a one-man band, singing and entertaining the crowd while his wife, Jennifer, and their three children manage the dining room and kitchen.

Every dish is permeated with Jamaican spices and a sense of tradition. Try the chicken made plantation-style, with dark red wine sauce and herbs; fillet of red snapper in Day-O style—with olives, white wine, tomatoes, and peppers—or, even better, there's one of the best versions of jerked snapper in Jamaica. We also like the grilled rock lobster with garlic butter sauce.

Marguerite's Seafood by the Sea and Margueritaville Sports Bar & Grill. Gloucester Ave. ☎ **809/952-4777.** Reservations recommended only for Marguerite's Seafood by the Sea. Main courses (in restaurant) $18–$35; platters, sandwiches, and snacks (in sports bar) $5–$20. AE, DC, MC, V. Restaurant daily 6–11pm; sports bar daily 10am–3am. INTERNATIONAL/SEAFOOD.

This two-in-one restaurant across from the Coral Cliff Hotel specializes in seafood served on a breeze-swept terrace overlooking the sea. There's also an air-conditioned lounge with an adjoining "Secret Garden." The chef specializes in exhibition cookery at a flambé grill. The menu is mainly devoted to seafood, including fresh fish. The cooks also turn out a number of innovative pastas and rather standard meat dishes. The changing dessert list is homemade, and a reasonable selection of wines is served. The sports bar and grill features a 110-foot Hydroslide, live music, satellite TV, water sports, a sundeck, a CD jukebox, and a display kitchen offering a straightforward menu of seafood, sandwiches, pasta, pizza, salads, and snacks—nothing fussy. Naturally, the bartenders specialize in margaritas.

Although a bit pricey, an interesting Jamaican experience is Combo at Lollypop on the Beach at Sandy Bay, Hanover, half a mile west of Tryall, held every Wednesday from 7:30 to 11pm (also on Saturday if the demand is heavy). Your $65 includes round-trip transport to the beach from Mo Bay hotels, a glass-bottom boat ride with a calypso band, a dinner of seafood and jerk meats, traditional dance groups performing Kumina, reggae, the basket dance, the bamboo dance, and the limbo, plus dancing on the beach. Children go for half price. For more information, call Lollypop on the Beach at ☎ 809/953-5314.

Pier 1. Howard Cooke Blvd. ☎ **809/952-2452.** Reservations not required. Main courses $15–$25. AE, MC, V. Mon–Fri 9:30am–11pm, Sat 1pm–midnight, Sun 4pm–midnight. A private minivan will pick you up and return you to your hotel. SEAFOOD.

Pier 1, one of the major dining and entertainment hubs of Mo Bay, was built on a landfill in the bay. Fisherfolk bring fresh lobster to the restaurant, which the chef prepares in a number of ways, including Creole style or curried. You might begin with one of the typically Jamaican soups such as conch chowder or red pea (which is actually red bean). At lunch the hamburgers are the juiciest in town, or you might find the quarter-decker steak sandwich with mushrooms equally tempting. The chef also prepares such famous island dishes as jerk pork and chicken, and Jamaican red snapper. (The jerk dishes, however, are better at the Pork Pit, reviewed below.) Finish your meal with a slice of moist rum cake. You can drink or dine on the ground floor, open to the sea breezes, but most guests seem to prefer the more formal second floor. Although this place remains a local favorite and its waterfront setting is appealing, service is very laid-back.

✪ **Reading Reef Club Restaurant.** On Bogue Lagoon, on Rte. A1 at the bottom of Long Hill Rd. (4 miles west of the town center). ☎ **809/952-5909.** Reservations required. Pastas $10–$11; main courses $5–$24. AE, MC, V. Daily 6:30am–11pm. ITALIAN/CONTINENTAL/CARIBBEAN.

There are those, and Lady Sarah Churchill was among them, who claim that the food served in this second-floor terrace overlooking the bay is the finest in Montego Bay. The menu is the creative statement of JoAnne Rowe, who has a passion for cooking and menu planning, a skill she perfected while entertaining prominent people in Montego Bay at her private dinner parties. Among her offerings are perfectly prepared scampi, imaginative pasta dishes, and a catch of the day, perhaps snapper, yellowtail, kingfish, or dolphin. She also imports quality New York sirloin steaks, but whenever possible likes to use local produce. Dinner might begin with Jamaican soup, such as pepperpot or pumpkin, and the restaurant is known for its lime pie. Lunches are low profile with a more limited menu. The restaurant opens onto beautiful Bogue Lagoon.

Town House. 16 Church St. ☎ **809/952-2660.** Reservations recommended. Main courses $14–$30. AE, DC, MC, V. Mon–Sat 11:30am–3:30pm; daily 6–10:30pm. Free limousine service to and from many area hotels. JAMAICAN/INTERNATIONAL.

Housed in a redbrick building dating from 1765, the Town House is a tranquil luncheon choice. It offers sandwiches and salads, or more elaborate fare if your appetite demands it. At night it's floodlit, with outdoor dining on a veranda overlooking an 18th-century parish church. You can also dine in what used to be the cellars, where old ship lanterns provide a warm light. Soups, which are increasingly ignored in many restaurants, are a specialty here. The pepper pot or pumpkin is a delectable opening to a meal. The chef offers a wide selection of main courses, including the local favorite, red snapper en papillote (wrapped in parchment paper). We're fond of the chef's large rack of barbecued spareribs, with the owners' special Tennessee sauce. Their pasta and steak dishes are also good, especially the homemade fettuccine with whole shrimp and the perfectly aged New York strip steak. The restaurant often attracts the rich and famous.

INEXPENSIVE

Le Chalet. 32 Gloucester Ave. ☎ **809/952-5240.** Main courses at lunch $2.25–$16; at dinner $4.50–$16. Mon–Sat noon–10pm, Sun 3:30–10pm. AE, MC, V. INTERNATIONAL/CHINESE/JAMAICAN.

Set in Montego Bay's "tourist strip," this high-ceilinged restaurant lies across Gloucester Avenue from the sea. The decor has that Howard Johnson's look, but this place offers great value. Food is served in copious and well-prepared portions, including a lunchtime selection of burgers, sandwiches, platters of barbecued ribs, and salads, and a more substantial selection of evening platters. Dinner options might include chicken platters, steaks, fresh fish, and lobster, which seems to taste best here if prepared with Jamaican curry. The staff is articulate and helpful, and proud of their straightforward and surprisingly well-prepared cuisine.

✪ **The Native Restaurant.** Gloucester Ave. ☎ **809/979-2769.** Reservations recommended. Main courses $9–$26. AE, MC, V. Daily 7:30am–10pm. JAMAICAN.

This restaurant continues to win converts as a self-termed "sis & bro" act, turning out dishes that Jamaican foodies love. Visitors have also discovered it. You might start with a tropical drink while selecting one of the international wines to go with your dinner. You know you're getting island flavor when faced with such appetizers as jerk reggae chicken, ackee and saltfish (an acquired taste), or perhaps smoked marlin. These can be followed by our favorite dish here, steamed fish. The cook will also serve you jerk or fried chicken, each filled with flavor. Lobster with garlic butter, although more costly, actually pales next to the curried shrimp. Perhaps the most tropical offering is "goat in a boat"—that is, in a pineapple shell. It's too fruity for our tastes, but you may like it. A more recent specialty is Boonoonoonoos, billed as "A Taste of Jamaica," a big platter with a little bit of everything, meats and several kinds of fish and vegetables. Although fresh desserts are prepared daily, you may choose instead just to have a Jamaican Blue Mountain coffee, which rounds the meal off nicely.

The Pelican. At the Pelican, Gloucester Ave. ☎ **809/952-3171.** Reservations recommended. Main courses $5–$23. AE, DC, MC, V. Daily 7am–11pm. JAMAICAN.

A Montego Bay landmark, the Pelican has been serving good food at reasonable prices for more than a quarter of a century. It's ideal for families. Many diners come here at lunch for well-stuffed sandwiches, juicy burgers, and barbecued chicken. You can also select from a wide array of Jamaican dishes, including stew peas and rice, curried goat, Caribbean fish, fried chicken, and curried lobster. A "meatless menu," including such dishes as a vegetable plate or vegetable chili, is also featured. Sirloin and seafood are also available, and the soda fountain serves old-fashioned sundaes with real whipped cream, making it a kiddies' favorite.

✪ **Pork Pit.** 27 Gloucester Ave., near Walter Fletcher Beach. ☎ **809/952-1046.** Reservations not required. One pound of jerk pork $10. No credit cards. Daily 11am–11:30pm. JAMAICAN.

The Pork Pit, an open-air gazebo right in the heart of Montego Bay, is the best place to go for the famous Jamaican jerk pork and jerk chicken. Many beach buffs come over here for a big lunch. Picnic tables encircle the building, and everything is open-air and informal. Half a pound of jerk meat, served with a baked yam or baked potato and a bottle of Red Stripe, is usually sufficient for a meal. The menu also includes steamed roast fish. Prices are very reasonable.

BEACHES, GOLF, RAFTING & OTHER OUTDOOR PURSUITS

BEACHES **Cornwall Beach** (☎ **809/952-3463**) is a long stretch of white-sand beach with dressing cabanas. Admission to the beach is $2 for adults and $1 for children, for the entire day. A bar and cafeteria offer refreshment daily from 9am to 5pm.

Across from the Doctor's Cave Beach Hotel, **Doctor's Cave Beach,** on Gloucester Avenue (☎ **809/952-2566**), helped launch Mo Bay as a resort in the 1940s. Admission to the beach is $2 for adults, $1 for children up to 12. Dressing rooms, chairs, umbrellas, and rafts are available from 8:30am to 5:30pm daily.

One of the premier beaches of Jamaica, **Walter Fletcher Beach,** in the heart of Mo Bay (☎ **809/952-5783**), is noted for its tranquil waters, which makes it a particular favorite for families with children. Changing rooms are available, as is lifeguard service. You can have lunch here in a restaurant. The beach is open daily from 9am to 5pm, with an admission charge of $1 for adults, 50¢ for children.

Frankly, you may want to skip all these public beaches entirely and head instead for the **Rose Hall Beach Club** (☎ **809/953-2323**), lying on the main road 11 miles east of Montego Bay. It's set on half a mile of secure, secluded white-sand beach with crystal-clear water. The club offers a full restaurant, two beach bars, a covered pavilion, an open-air dance area, showers, rest rooms, and changing facilities, plus beach volleyball courts, various beach games, and a full water-sports activities program. There's also live entertainment. Admission fees are $8 for adults and $5 for children. This beach club is far better equipped than any of the beaches previously recommended. The club is open daily from 10am to 6pm.

DEEP-SEA FISHING **Seaworld Resorts,** whose main office is at the Cariblue Hotel, Rose Hall Main Road (☎ **809/953-2180**), operates flying-bridge cruisers, with deck lines and outriggers, for fishing expeditions. A half-day fishing trip costs $330 for up to four participants.

DIVING & OTHER WATER SPORTS **Seaworld Resorts** (☎ **809/953-2180**; see above for address), operates scuba-diving excursions, plus many other water sports, including sailing and windsurfing. Its scuba dives plunge to offshore coral reefs, among the most spectacular in the Caribbean. There are three certified dive guides, one dive boat, and all the necessary equipment for either inexperienced or already-certified divers. Most dives begin at $35, $50 for night dives.

GOLF **Wyndham Rose Hall Golf & Beach Resort,** Rose Hall (☎ **809/953-2650**), has a noted course with an unusual and challenging seaside and mountain layout, built on the shores of the Caribbean. Its eighth hole skirts the water, then doglegs onto a promontory and a green thrusting 200 yards into the sea. The back nine are the most scenic and interesting, rising up steep slopes and falling into deep ravines on Mount Zion. The 10th fairway abuts the family burial grounds of the Barretts of Wimpole Street, and the 14th passes the vacation home of singer Johnny Cash. The 300-foot-high 13th tee offers a rare panoramic view of the sea and the roof of the hotel, and the 15th green is next to a 40-foot waterfall, once featured in a James Bond movie. A fully stocked pro shop, a clubhouse, and a professional staff are among the amenities. Nonresidents of the Wyndham pay $60 for 18 holes and $40 for 9 holes. Guests at the Wyndham are charged $50 for 18 holes, $40 for 9 holes. Mandatory cart rental costs $33 for 18 holes, and the use of a caddy (also mandatory) is another $12 for 18 holes.

The excellent course at the **Tryall** (☎ **809/956-5660**), 12 miles from Montego Bay, is so regal it's often been the site of major golf tournaments, including the Jamaica Classic Annual and the Johnnie Walker Tournament. For 18 holes, guests of Tryall are charged $40 in spring, summer, and fall, $60 in winter. Nonresidents of Tryall pay $75 from mid-April to mid-December and $150 in winter.

The **Half Moon,** at Rose Hall (☎ **809/953-2560**), features a championship course, designed by Robert Trent Jones Sr., which opened in 1961. The course has manicured and diversely shaped greens. For 18 holes nonresidents pay $95 year-round. Half Moon hotel guests receive a 50% discount. Carts in any season cost $30 for 18 holes, and caddies (mandatory in any season) are hired for $14 in any season.

The **Ironshore Golf & Country Club,** Ironshore, St. James, Montego Bay (☎ **809/953-2800**), another well-known 18-hole golf course with a 72 par, is privately owned. It is, however, open to all golfers who show up. Greens fees for 18 holes are $51.75.

HORSEBACK RIDING A good program for equestrians is offered at the **Rocky Point Riding Stables,** at the Half Moon Club, Rose Hall, Montego Bay (☎ **809/953-2286**). Housed in the most beautiful barn and stables in Jamaica, built in the colonial Caribbean style in 1992, it offers around 30 horses and a helpful staff. A

90-minute beach or mountain ride costs $50, whereas a 2½-hour combination ride (including treks along hillsides, forest trails, and beaches, and ending with a salt-water swim) goes for $70.

RAFTING **Mountain Valley Rafting,** 31 Gloucester Ave. (☎ **809/956-0020**), offers rafting excursions on the Great River, which depart from the Lethe Plantation, about 10 miles south of Montego Bay. Rafts are available for $36 for up to two participants. Trips last about an hour and operate daily from 8:30am to 4:30pm. The rafts are composed of bamboo trunks with a raised dais to sit on. In some cases, a small child can accompany two adults on the same raft, although due caution should be exercised if you choose to do this. Ask about pickup by taxi at the end of the rafting run to return you to your rented car. For $45 per person, a half-day experience will include transportation to and from your hotel, an hour's rafting, lunch, a garden tour of the Lethe property, and a taste of Jamaican liqueur.

TENNIS **Wyndham Rose Hall Golf & Beach Resort,** Rose Hall (☎ **809/953-2650**), outside Montego Bay, is an outstanding tennis resort, though it's not the equal of Half Moon or Tryall (see below). Wyndham offers six hard-surface courts, each lighted for night play. As a courtesy, nonresidents are sometimes invited to play for free, but permission has to be obtained from the manager. The resident pro charges $45 per hour for lessons, or $25 for 30 minutes.

Half Moon Golf, Tennis, and Beach Club, outside Montego Bay (☎ **809/953-2211**), has the finest tennis courts in the area, even outclassing Tryall (see below). Its 13 state-of-the-art courts, seven of which are lit for night games, attract tennis players from around the world. Lessons cost $25 per half hour, $45 per hour. Residents play free throughout the day or night. The pro shop, which accepts reservations for court times, is open daily from 7am to 8pm. If you want to play after those hours, you switch on the lights yourself. If you're not a guest of the hotel, you must purchase a day pass ($40 per person) at the front desk. It will allow you access to the resort's tennis courts, gym, sauna, Jacuzzi, pools, and beach facilities.

Tryall Golf, Tennis, and Beach Club, St. James (☎ **809/956-5660**), offers nine hard-surface courts, three lit for night play, near its Great House. Day games are free for residents; nonguests pay $25 per hour. All players are assessed $12 per hour for nighttime illumination. Four pros on-site provide lessons, costing $17 to $25 per half hour, or $25 to $40 per hour, depending on the rank of the pro.

SEEING THE SIGHTS

VISITING WITH THE BIRDIES

Rocklands Wildlife Station. Anchovy, St. James. ☎ **809/952-2009.** Admission J$320 ($8.95). Daily 2:30–5pm.

It's a unique experience to have a Jamaican doctor bird perch on your finger to drink syrup, to feed small doves and finches millet from your hand, and to watch dozens of other birds flying in for their evening meal. Don't take children five and under to this sanctuary, as they tend to bother the birds. Rocklands is about a mile outside Anchovy on the road from Montego Bay.

THE GREAT HOUSES

Occupied by plantation owners, the Great Houses of Jamaica were always built on high ground so that they overlooked the plantation itself and could see the next house in the distance. It was the custom for the owners to offer hospitality to travelers crossing the island by road; travelers were spotted by the lookout, and bed and food were given freely.

Barnett Estates and Bellfield Great House. Barnett Estates. ☎ **809/952-2382.** Admission $15. Daily 9:30am–5pm.

Once a totally private estate sprawled across 50,000 acres, this Great House has hosted everybody from President Kennedy to Churchill and even Queen Elizabeth II over the years. Now anybody who pays the entrance fee can come in and take a look. The domain of the Kerr-Jarret family during 300 years of high society, this was once the seat of a massive sugar plantation. At its center is the 18th-century Bellfield Great House (not as ornate as Rose Hall, see below). Restored in 1994, it is a grand example of Georgian architecture. Guides in costumes offer narrated tours of the property. After the tour, drop in to the old Sugar Mill Bar for a tall rum punch.

Greenwood Great House. On Rte. A1, 14 miles east of Montego Bay. ☎ **809/953-1077.** Admission $10 adults, $5 children. Daily 9am–6pm.

Some people find the 15-room Greenwood even more interesting than Rose Hall (see below). Erected on its hillside perch between 1780 and 1800, the Georgian-style building was the residence of Richard Barrett (cousin of poet Elizabeth Barrett Browning). Elizabeth Barrett Browning herself never visited Jamaica, but her family used to be one of the largest landholders here. An absentee planter who lived in England, her father once owned 84,000 acres and some 3,000 slaves. On display is the original library of the Barrett family, with rare books dating from 1697, along with oil paintings of the family, Wedgwood china, rare musical instruments, and a fine collection of antique furniture. The house today is privately owned but open to the public.

✪ **Rose Hall Great House.** Rose Hall Hwy., 9 miles east of Montego Bay. ☎ **809/953-2323.** Admission $15 adults, $10 children. Daily 9am–6pm.

The legendary Rose Hall is the most famous Great House on Jamaica and charges a very steep admission. The subject of at least a dozen gothic novels, Rose Hall was immortalized in the H. G. deLisser book *White Witch of Rosehall.* The house was built from 1778 to 1790 by John Palmer, a wealthy British planter. At its peak, this was a 6,600-acre plantation, with more than 2,000 slaves. However, it was Annie Palmer, wife of the builder's grandnephew, who became the focal point of fiction and fact. Called "Infamous Annie," she was said to have dabbled in witchcraft. She took slaves as lovers and then killed them off when they bored her. Servants called her "the Obeah woman" (*Obeah* is Jamaican for "voodoo"). Annie was said to have murdered several of her husbands while they slept and eventually suffered the same fate herself in a kind of poetic justice. Long in ruins, the house has now been restored and can be visited by the public. Annie's Pub is on the ground floor.

Organized Tours & Cruises

The **Croydon Plantation,** Catadupa, St. James (☎ **809/979-8267**), is a 25-mile ride from Montego Bay. It can be visited on a half-day tour from Montego Bay (or Negril) on Tuesday, Wednesday, and Friday. Included in the $45 price are round-trip transportation from your hotel, a tour of the plantation, a taste of tropical fruits in season, and a barbecued-chicken lunch. Most hotel desks can arrange this tour. The cost is $50 for adults, $22.50 for children 12 and under.

For a plantation tour, go on a **Hilton High Day Tour,** through Beach View Plaza (☎ **809/952-3343**). The tour includes round-trip transportation on a scenic drive through historic plantation areas. Your day starts at an old plantation house with a continental breakfast. You can roam the 100 acres of the plantation and visit the German village of Seaford town or St. Leonards village nearby. Calypso music is played throughout the day, and a Jamaican lunch is served at 1pm. The charge for the day is $50 per person for the plantation tour, breakfast, lunch, and transportation. There's an additional cost of $10 for 30 minutes of horseback riding. Tour days are Tuesday, Wednesday, Friday, and Sunday.

Day and evening cruises are offered aboard the *Calico,* a 55-foot gaff-rigged wooden ketch that sails from Margaritaville on the Montego Bay waterfront. An additional vessel, *Calico B,* also carries another 40 passengers per boat ride. You can be transported to and from your hotel for either cruise. The day voyage, which departs at 10am and returns at 3pm, provides a day of sailing, sunning, and snorkeling (with equipment supplied), plus a Jamaican buffet lunch served on the beach, all to the sound of reggae and other music. The cruise costs $50 per person and is offered daily. On the *Calico*'s evening voyage, which goes for $25 per person and is offered Wednesday to Saturday from 5 to 7pm, cocktails and wine are served as you sail through sunset. For information and reservations, call Capt. Bryan Langford, North Coast Cruises (☎ **809/952-5860**). A three-day notice is recommended.

SHOPPING

When you go shopping in Montego Bay, be prepared for aggressive vendors. Since selling a craft item may mean the difference between whether or not they put something in the stove that night, there's often a feverish attempt to peddle goods to potential customers, all of whom are viewed as rich. Therefore, prepare yourself for being pursued persistently.

Warning: Some so-called "duty-free" prices are actually lower than Stateside prices, but then the government hits you with a 10% "general consumption tax" on all items purchased. But you can still find good duty-free items here, including Swiss watches, Irish crystal, Italian handbags, Indian silks, and liquors and liqueurs. Appleton's rums are an excellent value. Tía Maria (coffee-flavored) and Rumona (rum-flavored) are the best liqueurs. Khus Khus is the local perfume. Jamaican arts and crafts are available throughout the resorts and at the Crafts Market (see below).

The main shopping areas are at **Montego Freeport,** within easy walking distance of the pier; **City Centre** (where most of the duty-free shops are, aside from those at the large hotels); and **Holiday Village Shopping Centre.**

The **Old Fort Craft Park,** a shopping complex with 180 vendors (all licensed by the Jamaica Tourist Board), fronts Howard Cooke Boulevard (up from Gloucester Avenue in the heart of Montego Bay, on the site of Fort Montego). A market with a varied assortment of handcrafts, it's grazing country for both souvenirs and more serious purchases. You'll see a selection of wall hangings, hand-woven straw items, and wood sculpture. You can even get your hair braided. Vendors can be very aggressive in trying to get you to buy something, so be prepared for major hassles. If you want some item, also be prepared for some serious negotiation. Persistent bargaining on your part will lead to substantial discounts.

At the **Crafts Market,** near Harbour Street in downtown Montego Bay, you can find the best selection of handmade souvenirs of Jamaica, including straw hats and bags, wooden platters, straw baskets, musical instruments, beads, carved objects, and toys. That "jipijapa" hat is important if you're going to be out in the island sun.

One of the newest and most intriguing places for shopping is a mall, **Half Moon Plaza,** set on the coastal road about 8 miles east of the commercial center of Montego Bay. This upscale minimall caters to the shopping and gastronomic needs of residents of one of the region's most elegant hotels, the Half Moon Club. On the premises are a bank and about 25 shops, each arranged around a central courtyard and selling a wide choice of carefully selected merchandise.

Arts & Crafts

Ambiente Art Gallery. 9 Fort St. ☎ **809/952-7919.**

This gallery is housed in a 100-year-old clapboard cottage set close to the road. The Austrian-born owner, Maria Hitchins, is one of the doyennes of the Montego Bay art scene. She has personally encouraged and developed scores of fine artworks and prints by local artists.

Blue Mountain Gems Workshop. At the Holiday Village Shopping Centre. ☎ **809/953-2338.**

Here you can take a tour of the workshops to see the process of jewelry creation, from raw stone to the finished product you can buy later. Wooden jewelry, local carvings, and one-of-a-kind ceramic figurines are also sold.

Neville Budhai Paintings. Budhai's Art Gallery, Reading Main Rd., Reading (5 miles east of town on the way to Negril). ☎ **809/979-2568.**

This is the art center of a distinguished artist, Neville Budhai, the president and co-founder of the Western Jamaica Society of Fine Arts. He has a distinct style and captures the special flavor of the island and its people in his artworks. The artist can sometimes be seen sketching or painting in Montego Bay or along the highways of rural Jamaica.

Things Jamaican. 44 Fort St. ☎ **809/952-5605.**

This is a showcase for the artisans of Jamaica. A wealth of products is displayed here, even food and drink, including rums and liqueurs along with jerk seasoning and orange-pepper jelly. Look for Busha Browne's fine Jamaican sauces, especially spicy chutneys or planters' spicy piquant sauce. Other items for sale are wood sculpture, salad bowls, trays, and hand-woven baskets.

Also look for reproductions of the Port Royal collection. Port Royal was buried by an earthquake and tidal wave in 1692. After resting underwater for 275 years, beautiful pewter items were recovered and are reproduced here. They include rat-tail spoons, a spoon with the heads of the monarchs William and Mary, and splay-footed lion rampant spoons. Many items were reproduced faithfully, right down to the pit marks and scratches.

Fashion

Jolie Madame Fashions. 30 City Centre Bldg. ☎ **809/952-3126.**

The racks of clothing for women and girls here might contain evening dresses, casual clothes, and beach attire. Many garments range from $25 to $200. Norma McLeod, the designer and founder, is always on hand to arrange to have garments custom-made.

Klass Kraft Leather Sandals. 44 Fort St. ☎ **809/952-5782.**

This store next door to Things Jamaican offers sandals and leather accessories made on location by a team of Jamaican craftspeople. All sandals cost less than $35.

Jewelry

Golden Nugget. 8 St. James Shopping Centre, Gloucester Ave. ☎ **809/952-7707.**

The Golden Nugget is a duty-free shop with an impressive collection of watches for both women and men and a fine assortment of jewelry, especially gold chains. The shop also carries leading brand-name cameras and a wide assortment of French perfumes.

MONTEGO BAY AFTER DARK

There's a lot more to do here at night than go to the discos, but the area certainly has those, too. Much of the entertainment is offered at the various hotels.

Pier 1, Howard Cooke Boulevard (☎ **809/952-2452**), already previewed as a dining option, might also be your choice for a night on the town. Friday night there's disco action from 10pm to 5am, with a J$100 ($2.80) cover charge, and cheap Red Stripe beer.

The **Cricket Club,** at the Wyndham Rose Hall (☎ **809/953-2650**), is more than just a sports bar. It's a place where people go to meet and mingle with an international crowd. Televised sports, karaoke sing-alongs, tournament darts, and backgammon are all part of the fun. The club is open daily from 7pm to 1am. There's no cover charge.

2 Negril

This once-sleepy village has turned into a tourist mecca, with visitors drawn to its beaches along three well-protected bays: Long Bay, Bloody Bay (now Negril Harbour), and Orange Bay. Negril became famous in the late 1960s when it attracted laid-back American and Canadian youths, who liked the idea of a place with no phones and no electricity; they rented modest digs in little houses on the West End where the local people extended their hospitality. But those days are long gone. Today more sophisticated hotels and all-inclusive resorts such as Hedonism II and Sandals Negril draw a better-heeled and less rowdy crowd, including Europeans.

On the western tip of the island, Negril is now famous for its Seven-Mile Beach. The town is 50 miles and about a two-hour drive from Montego Bay's airport, along a winding road and past ruins of sugar estates and Great Houses.

At some point you'll want to explore **Booby Key** (or Cay), a tiny islet off the Negril coast. Once it was featured in the Walt Disney film *20,000 Leagues Under the Sea,* but now it's overrun with nudists from Hedonism II.

Chances are, however, you'll stake out your own favorite spot along Negril's **Seven-Mile Beach.** You don't need to get up for anything, as somebody will be along to serve you. Perhaps it'll be the "banana lady," with a basket of fruit perched on her head. Maybe the "ice cream man" will set up a stand right under a coconut palm. Surely the "beer lady" will find you as she strolls along the beach with a carton of Jamaican beer on her head, and hordes of young men will peddle illegal ganja (marijuana) whether you smoke it or not.

There are really two Negrils: The West End is the site of many little local restaurants, and cottages that still receive visitors. The other Negril is on the east end, the first you approach on the road coming in from Montego Bay. Here are the upscale hotels, with some of the most panoramic beachfronts.

WHERE TO STAY

In addition to the following, the Café au Lait/Mirage Cottages (see "Where to Dine," below) has accommodations for rent.

EXPENSIVE

Poinciana Beach Resort. Norman Manley Blvd. (P.O. Box 44), Negril, Jamaica, W.I. ☎ **800/468-6728** in the U.S., or 809/957-4256. Fax 809/957-4229. 90 rms, 6 studios, 12 suites, 22 villas. A/C TV. Winter, $358–$396 double; $502–$548 studio for 2; $538–$576 suite for 2; $386–$430 villa for 2. Off-season, $310–$330 double; $394–$424 studio for 2; $420–$454 suite for 2; $336–$344 villa for 2. Rates are per person and include all meals. AE, MC, V.

Set on 6 acres of land, right on Seven-Mile Beach, this hotel and villa vacation resort attracts couples, singles, and families with a variety of accommodations and an extensive sports program. It's a mixture of both contemporary and colonial design, with tile floors, rattan and wood furnishings, and private balconies and ocean views. Superior rooms consist of one bedroom and bath and a private balcony or patio, and suites are furnished with a kitchenette and a large wraparound balcony. Some suites offer Jacuzzi-type tubs. Villas consist of one or two bedrooms, a living/dining area with kitchenette, and a private balcony or patio.

Dining/Entertainment: A poolside restaurant, the Captain's Table, serves three meals daily, with both Jamaican dishes and international specialties. Other dining choices include the Paradise Plum, with many innovative recipes, and the Starlight Terrace, offering fresh pastas and grilled selections under the stars. The Upper Deck Café serves after-dinner snacks, and at the Beach Bar a lively native band entertains five evenings a week during happy hour. Other evening entertainment is often staged, including a reggae/soca barbecue night on Saturday.

Services: Beauty salon, baby-sitting, children's program, massage.

Facilities: Two freshwater swimming pools, heated Jacuzzi, lawn and table tennis, 24-hour exercise gyms, water sports (including windsurfing, snorkeling, kayaks, glass-bottom-boat rides, Sunfish and Hobie cat sailing, and scuba diving).

Seasplash Resort. Norman Manley Blvd., Negril, Jamaica, W.I. ☎ **800/254-2786** in the U.S., or 809/957-4041. Fax 809/957-4049. 15 suites. A/C TV TEL. Winter, $199 suite for 2; $219 suite for 3; $239 suite for 4. Off-season, $135 suite for 2; $155 suite for 3; $175 suite for 4. Full board $57 per person extra. AE, MC, V.

Partly because of its small size, this beachfront resort often has a friendly, personable feeling. In deliberate contrast to the megaresorts nearby, it lies on a small but carefully landscaped sliver of beachfront land planted with tropical vegetation. The suites are spacious and stylishly decorated with wicker furniture and fresh pastel colors. All are the same size and contain the same amenities—a kitchenette, a balcony or patio, large closets, and either a king-size bed or twin beds—although those on the upper floor have higher ceilings and feel more spacious.

Dining/Entertainment: The resort contains two different restaurants, Calico Jack's (a simple lunchtime *bohîo*) and the more elaborate Tan-Ya's (see "Where to Dine," below). There's also a poolside bar.

Services: Baby-sitting, laundry, and room service.

Facilities: Guests have use of a small gym, a Jacuzzi, and a swimming pool.

MODERATE

✪ **Charela Inn.** Norman Manley Blvd. (P.O. Box 33), Negril, Jamaica, W.I. ☎ **809/957-4277.** Fax 809/957-4414. 39 rms. A/C TEL. Winter, $154–$187 double. Off-season, $105–$124 double. MAP $35 per person extra. Five-night minimum stay in winter. MC, V.

A seafront inn reminiscent of a Spanish hacienda, this place sits on the main beach strip on three acres of landscaped grounds. The building has an inner courtyard with a tropical garden and a round freshwater swimming pool opening onto one of the widest (250 feet) sandy beaches in Negril. The inn attracts a loyal following of visitors seeking a home away from home.

Its dining room faces both the sea and the garden and offers both an à la carte menu and a five-course fixed-price meal that's changed daily. Sunsets are toasted on open terraces facing the sea. Simplicity, a quiet kind of elegance, and excellent value for the money are the hallmarks of the inn. Sunset cruises, lasting 3½ hours, are offered, along with Sunfish sailing, windsurfing, and kayaking. On Thursday and Saturday nights there's live entertainment.

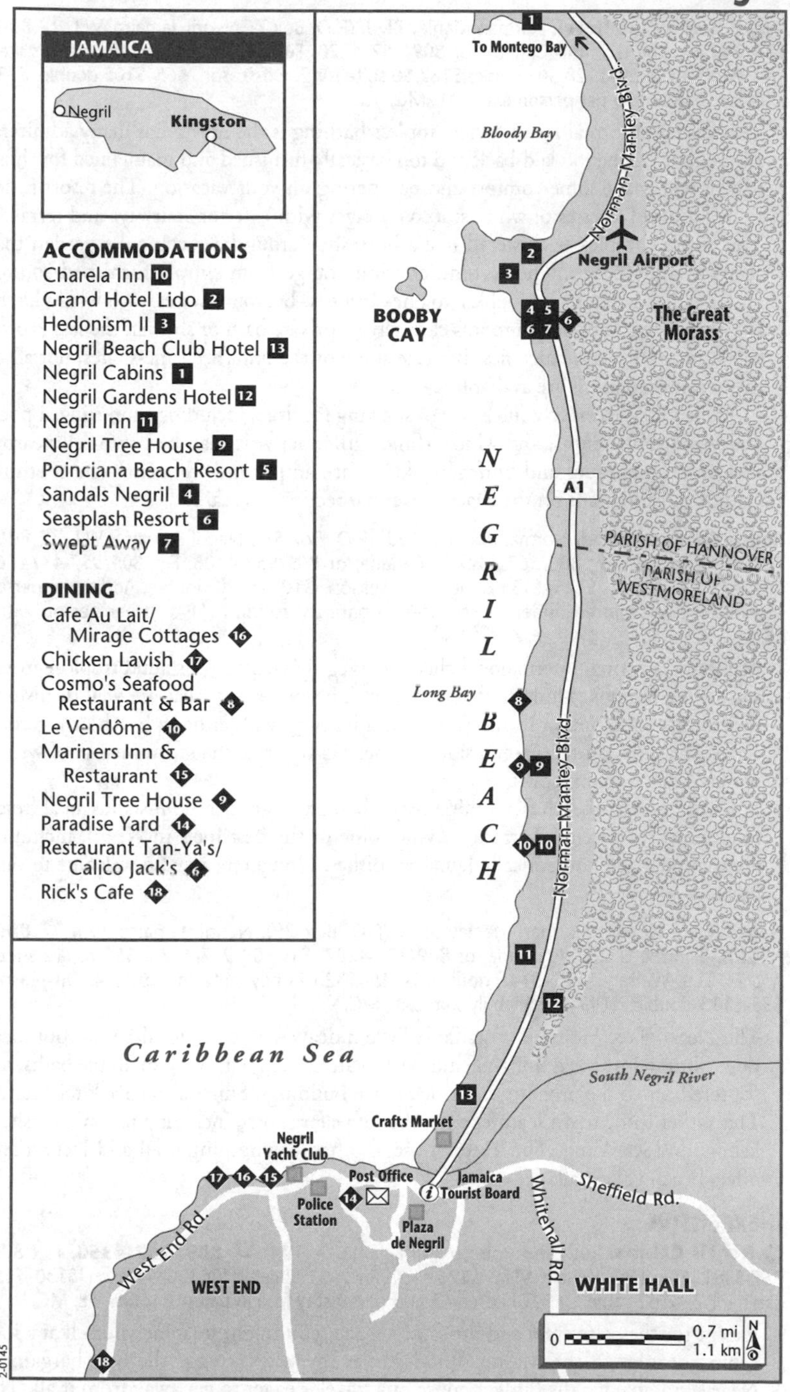
JAMAICA
Negril
Kingston
ACCOMMODATIONS
Charela Inn 10
Grand Hotel Lido 2
Hedonism II 3
Negril Beach Club Hotel 13
Negril Cabins 1
Negril Gardens Hotel 12
Negril Inn 11
Negril Tree House 9
Poinciana Beach Resort 5
Sandals Negril 4
Seasplash Resort 6
Swept Away 7
DINING
Cafe Au Lait/ Mirage Cottages 16
Chicken Lavish 17
Cosmo's Seafood Restaurant & Bar 8
Le Vendôme 10
Mariners Inn & Restaurant 15
Negril Tree House 9
Paradise Yard 14
Restaurant Tan-Ya's/ Calico Jack's 6
Rick's Cafe 18
To Montego Bay
Bloody Bay
Norman-Manley-Blvd.
Negril Airport
BOOBY CAY
The Great Morass
NEGRIL BEACH
A1
PARISH OF HANNOVER
PARISH OF WESTMORELAND
Long Bay
Norman-Manley-Blvd.
Caribbean Sea
South Negril River
Crafts Market
Negril Yacht Club
Post Office
Jamaica Tourist Board
Police Station
Plaza de Negril
Sheffield Rd.
Whitehall Rd.
West End Rd.
WEST END
WHITE HALL
0
0.7 mi
1.1 km
N
2-0145

Negril Beach Club Hotel. Norman Manley Blvd. (P.O. Box 7), Negril, Jamaica, W.I. ☎ **800/526-2422** in the U.S. and Canada, or 809/957-4220. Fax 809/957-4364. 47 rms, 6 suites. A/C. Winter, $94.50–$128.50 double; $167.50 suite for 2. Off-season, $65–$105 double; $135 suite for 2. MAP $30 per person extra. AE, MC, V.

This casual, informal resort, where topless bathing is the norm, has many admirers, although it will be too laid-back and too basically furnished and maintained for those of you who want some comfort and pampering on your vacation. The resort is designed around a series of white stucco cottages with exterior stairways and terraces. The entire complex is clustered like a horseshoe around a rectangular garden that abuts a sandy beach. The accommodations range from simply furnished rooms, rented either as singles or doubles, to one- and two-bedroom suites, each with a kitchenette. The well-appointed rooms each have a private bath or shower; the less expensive units don't have balconies. Because some of the units are time-shares, not all of the accommodations are available.

There's easy access to a full range of sporting facilities, including snorkeling, a pool, volleyball, table tennis, and windsurfing. Other activities can be organized nearby, and beach barbecues and buffet breakfasts are ample and frequent. The Seething Cauldron Restaurant on the beach serves barbecues and seafood.

Negril Gardens Hotel. Norman Manley Blvd. (P.O. Box 58), Negril, Jamaica, W.I. ☎ **800/752-6824** in the U.S., 800/567-5327 in Canada, or 809/957-4408. Fax 809/957-4374. 65 rms. A/C TV. Winter, $125–$135 double. Off-season, $105–$120 double. Additional person $30 extra; two children under 12 stay free in parents' room. MAP $40 per person extra. AE, MC, V.

Attracting a young, international clientele, Negril Gardens rests amid tropical greenery on the famous 7-mile stretch of beach. The two-story villas are well furnished, and rooms open onto a front veranda or a balcony with either a beach or a garden view. The units on the garden side are cheaper and face the swimming pool with a pool bar and a tennis court.

Directly on the beach is a Tahitian-style bar, and right behind it stands an al fresco restaurant, the Orchid Terrace, serving some of the best food in Negril, including international and authentically Jamaican dishes. Nonguests are also welcome to dine here.

Negril Tree House. Norman Manley Blvd. (P.O. Box 29), Negril, Jamaica, W.I. ☎ **800/NEGRIL-1** in the U.S. and Canada, or 809/957-4287. Fax 809/957-4386. 55 rms, 12 suites. A/C TV TEL. Winter, $115–$145 double; $245–$325 family suite for up to 4. Off-season, $85–$115 double; $145–$185 family suite. AE, MC, V.

The Negril Tree House is a desirable little hideaway with an ideal beachfront location. Simply furnished units, including 12 suites, each with very small tile baths, are scattered across the property in 11 octagonal buildings. Suites also have kitchenettes. This rather rustic resort features a number of water sports, including parasailing, snorkeling, and jet-skiing. The Tree House also has a swimming pool and Jacuzzi and offers beach volleyball.

INEXPENSIVE

✪ **Negril Cabins.** Ruthland Point, Negril, Jamaica, W.I. ☎ **809/957-4350.** Fax 809/957-5381. 50 cabins. Winter, $150–$176 cabin for 2; $192 cabin for 3. Off-season, $130–$154 cabin for 2; $162 cabin for 3. Children 12 and under stay free in parents' room. AE, MC, V.

Except for the palm trees and the sandy beach, you might imagine yourself at a log-cabin complex in the Maine Woods. In many ways, this is the best bargain in Negril, suitable for the budget-conscious traveler eager to get away from it all. The cabins are in a forest, across the road from a beach called Bloody Bay (where the infamous 18th-century pirate, Calico Jack, was captured by the British). The 9 acres of gardens are planted with royal palms, bull thatch, and a rare variety of mango tree.

The unadorned cabins are really small cottages, none more than two stories high, rising on stilts. Each timber cottage includes a balcony and some are air-conditioned. The bar and restaurant serve tropical punch, a medley of fresh Jamaican fruits, and flavorful but unpretentious Jamaican meals. A children's program is also available, and live entertainment is offered on some nights.

ALL-INCLUSIVE RESORTS

✪ **Grand Hotel Lido.** Bloody Bay (P.O. Box 88), Negril, Jamaica, W.I. ☎ **800/859-7873** in the U.S., 800/553-4320 in Canada, or 809/957-4010. Fax 809/957-4317. 182 junior suites, 18 one-bedroom suites. A/C MINIBAR TV TEL. Winter, $2,240–$3,420 suite for 2. Off-season, $1,900–$2,980 suite for 2. Rates are for the minimum stay of 4 days/3 nights and include all meals, snacks, drinks, entertainment, sports activities, airport transfers, taxes, and tips. AE, MC, V.

The grandest and most architecturally stylish hotel of its chain, the Grand Lido sits on a flat and lushly landscaped stretch of beachfront adjacent to Hedonism II. It's much more subdued than its neighbor. This is the most upscale and deliciously luxurious of the string of resorts known as Jamaica's SuperClubs. Each suite contains a stereo system, lots of space, and either a patio or a balcony that (except for a few) overlooks the beach. The smaller of the resort's two beaches is reserved for nudists. Only adults are welcome, but unlike many other all-inclusive resorts, especially Club Med, there's no resistance here to giving a room to a single occupant.

Dining/Entertainment: In addition to the cavernous and airy main dining room, there's a trio of restaurants, including one devoted to nouvelle cuisine, another to continental food, and a third to Italian pasta. Guests also enjoy an all-night disco, a piano bar, pool tables, and nine bars. Even after the four restaurants close, there are three different dining enclaves that remain open throughout the night, each with a bubbling Jacuzzi nearby.

Services: 24-hour room service, concierge, laundry, tour desk that arranges visits to other parts of Jamaica, instructors to teach tennis and sailing.

Facilities: Four tennis courts, two swimming pools, four Jacuzzis, gym/sauna/health club, two fine beaches lined with chaise lounges, and one of the most glamorous yachts in the West Indies, the M-Y *Zein,* given by Aristotle Onassis to Prince Rainier and Grace of Monaco as a wedding present.

Hedonism II. Negril Beach Rd. (P.O. Box 25), Negril, Jamaica, W.I. ☎ **800/859-7873** in the U.S., or 809/957-4200. Fax 809/957-4289. 280 rms. A/C. Winter, $1,398–$3,558 double. Off-season, $1,198–$3,098 double. Rates are for 4 days/3 nights and include all meals, drinks, activities, airport transfers, taxes, and tips. AE, MC, V.

Devoted to the pursuit of pleasure, Hedonism II packs the works into a one-package deal, including all the drinks and partying anyone could want. There's no tender of any sort, and tipping is not permitted. Of all the members of its chain, this is the most raucous. It's a meat market, deliberately inviting its mainly single guests to go wild for a week. To provide a sense of the ambience, we'll tell you that one manager boasted that the resort holds the record for the most people in a Jacuzzi at once. The rooms are stacked in two-story clusters dotted around a sloping 22-acre site about 2 miles east of the town center. Most of the guests, who must be at least 18 years of age, are Americans. Closed to the general public, this is not a couples-only resort;

singles are both accepted and encouraged. The hotel will find you a roommate if you'd like to book in on the double-occupancy rate.

On one section of this resort's beach, clothing is optional. It's called the "Nude" section; the other is known as "the Prude." The resort also has a secluded beach on nearby Booby Cay, where guests are taken twice a week for picnics.

Dining/Entertainment: Nightly entertainment is presented, along with a live band, a high-energy disco, and a piano bar. International cuisine is served in daily buffets. There's also a clothing-optional bar and grill.

Services: Massage.

Facilities: Sailing, snorkeling, waterskiing, scuba diving, windsurfing, glass-bottom boat, clothing-optional Jacuzzi, swimming pool, six tournament-class tennis courts (lit at night), two badminton courts, basketball court, two indoor squash courts, volleyball, table tennis, Nautilus and free-weight gyms, aerobics, indoor games room.

Negril Inn. Norman Manley Blvd. (P.O. Box 59), Negril, Jamaica, W.I. ☎ **809/957-4209.** Fax 809/957-4365. 46 rms. A/C. Winter, $280 double; $390 triple. Off-season, $220 double; $270 triple. Rates include all meals, drinks, activities, airport transfers, taxes, and tips. AE, MC, V.

Located about 3 miles east of the town center in the heart of the 7-mile beach stretch, this is one of the smallest all-inclusive resorts in Negril. Because of its size, the atmosphere is much more low-key than what you'll find at its larger competitors, such as Hedonism II. The resort, *not* confined to couples only, offers very simple but comfortably furnished guest rooms with private balconies, in a series of two-story structures in a garden setting. The helpful staff offers a host of activities, day and night. Children are not accepted in winter.

Dining/Entertainment: Included in the package are all meals, all alcoholic drinks (except champagne), and nightly entertainment (including a disco). Meals are consumed in the resort's only restaurant, although there are bars in the disco and beside the pool, and the food is pretty good.

Services: Room service (for breakfast only), laundry, round-trip transfers to and from the airport at Montego Bay, filtered water.

Facilities: Windsurfing, waterskiing, scuba diving, snorkeling, hydrosliding, aqua bikes, two floodlit tennis courts, Jacuzzi, piano room, Universal weight room, freshwater pool.

Sandals Negril. Rutland Point, Negril, Jamaica, W.I. ☎ **800/SANDALS** in the U.S. and Canada, or 809/957-4216. Fax 809/957-5338. 187 rms, 16 suites. A/C TV TEL. Winter, $1,660–$2,010 double; $2,250–$2,460 suite. Off-season, $1,550–$1,880 double; $2,080–$2,290 suite. Rates are for a minimum stay of 4 days/3 nights and include all meals, snacks, drinks, activities, airport transfers, taxes, and tips. AE, MC, V.

Sandals Negril is an all-inclusive, couples-only (male-female) resort, part of the expanding empire of the enterprising local businessman Gordon "Butch" Stewart, who pioneered similar operations in Montego Bay. If you're the wildest of raunchy party types, you'd be better off at Hedonism II—life isn't exactly subdued at Sandals, but it's tamer. The resort occupies some 13 acres of prime beachfront land a short drive east of Negril's center, on the main highway leading in from Montego Bay. It's about a 1½-hour drive (maybe more) from the Montego Bay airport.

The developers linked two older hotels into a unified whole, and most guests never leave the property. The crowd is usually convivial, informal, and young. There are five divisions of accommodations, rated standard, superior, deluxe, deluxe beachfront, and one-bedroom suite. The casually well-furnished rooms have a tropical motif, and hair dryers and radios. For a balcony and sea view, you have to pay the top rates.

Dining/Entertainment: Rates include all meals, even snacks, and unlimited drinks day and night at one of four bars (two of which are swim-up pool bars). Coconut

Cove is the main dining room, but guests can also elect to eat at one of the specialty rooms, including the Sundowner, offering white-glove service and a Jamaican cuisine, and the 4 C's, with low-calorie health food served beside the beach. Kimono offers a Japanese cuisine. Nightly entertainment, including theme parties, is also included.

Services: Laundry, massage.

Facilities: Three freshwater swimming pools, tennis courts for day or night, scuba diving, snorkeling, Sunfish sailing, windsurfing, canoeing, aerobics classes, glass-bottom boat, fitness center (with saunas and Universal exercise equipment).

✪ **Swept Away.** Norman Manley Blvd. (P.O. Box 77), Negril, Jamaica, W.I. ☎ **800/545-7937** in the U.S. and Canada, or 809/957-4061. Fax 809/957-4060. 134 suites. A/C TEL. Winter, $1,500–$1,620 per couple. Off-season, $1,380–$1,500 per couple. Rates are for 3 nights and include all meals, drinks, activities, airport transfers, taxes, and tips. AE, DC, MC, V.

Opened in 1990, this is one of the best-equipped hotels in Negril—it's certainly the one most conscious of both sports and relaxation. All-inclusive, it caters to male-female couples eager for an ambience with all possible diversions available but absolutely no organized schedule and no pressure to participate if you just want to relax. As a staff member told us (privately, of course), "We get the health and fitness nuts, and Sandals or Hedonism get the sex crazed." The resort occupies 20 flat and sandy acres, which straddle both sides of the highway leading in from Montego Bay.

The accommodations (the hotel defines them as "veranda suites" because of their large balconies) are in 26 two-story villas clustered together and accented with flowering shrubs and vines, a few steps from the 7-mile beachfront. Each accommodation contains a ceiling fan, a king-size bed, and (unless the vegetation obscures it) sea views. They're lovely, airy, and spacious.

Dining/Entertainment: The resort's social center is its international restaurant, Feathers, which lies inland, across the road from the sea. There's also an informal beachfront restaurant and bar, and four bars scattered throughout the property, including a "veggie bar."

Services: Room service (for continental breakfast only), laundry, tour desk for arranging visits to other parts of Jamaica.

Facilities: Racquetball, squash, and 10 lighted tennis courts; fully equipped gym; aerobics; yoga; massage; steam; sauna; whirlpool; billiards; bicycles; beachside swimming pool; scuba diving; windsurfing; reef snorkeling.

WHERE TO DINE

EXPENSIVE

Rick's Café. Lighthouse Rd. ☎ **809/957-0380.** Main courses $11–$28. MC, V. Daily 2–10pm. SEAFOOD/STEAK.

At sundown, everybody in Negril heads toward the lighthouse along the West End strip to Rick's Café, whether or not they want a meal. This laid-back cafe was made famous in the 70s as a hippie hangout, and ever since it's attracted the bronzed and the beautiful (and some who want to be), the best sunset-watching crowd this side of Key West. Here, the sunset is said to be the most glorious in Negril, and after a few fresh-fruit daiquiris (pineapple, banana, or papaya), you'll give no argument. Casual dress is the order of the day, and reggae and rock comprise the background music.

There are several Stateside specialties, including imported steaks along with a complete menu of blackened dishes (Cajun style). The fish is always fresh, including red snapper, fresh lobster, or grouper, and you might begin with the smoked marlin platter. The food is rather standard fare, and expensive for what you get, but that hardly keeps the crowds away. You can also buy plastic bar tokens at the door, which you can use instead of money, à la Club Med.

Moderate

Café au Lait/Mirage Cottages. Lighthouse Rd., West End, Negril, Jamaica, W.I. ☎ **809/957-4471.** Fax 809/957-4414. Main courses $9–$30. MC, V. Daily 5–11pm. FRENCH/JAMAICAN.

Daniel and Sylvia Grizzle, a Jamaican/French couple, prepare the cuisine as well as direct the smooth operation of this place, located 2 1/2 miles from the town center along the West End beach strip. Like the owners' marriage, the food is a successful blend of French mainland flair and Jamaican style and zest. The conch fritters or Jamaican patties are appropriately spicy to get you going. You can also order jerk pork here along with other spicy pork dishes. There are pizzas too, but you'll find better pies elsewhere. The fish, lobster, and shrimp dishes, however, are truly superb and well flavored. The wine list leans toward France, of course. If you like really sweet desserts, you may be attracted to the Jamaican desserts, including coconut pie and sweet-potato pudding.

Set in 4 1/2 acres of tropical gardens, the property flanks both sides of the road. The hotel has a total of seven units, four of which lie above the restaurant, located inland from the sea. Each of these has a small kitchenette. The other units are closer to the sea but don't have a kitchenette. All accommodations are priced the same: $110 double in winter, lowered to $66 double off-season.

Le Vendôme. In the Charela Inn, Negril Beach. ☎ **809/957-4277.** Reservations recommended for Sat dinner. Main courses $10–$29; fixed-price meal $22.50–$29.50; continental breakfast $4.50; English breakfast $8.50. MC, V. Daily 7:30am–10pm. JAMAICAN/FRENCH.

This place some 3 1/2 miles from the town center enjoys a good reputation. You don't have to be a hotel guest to sample the cuisine, which is, in the words of owners Daniel and Sylvia Grizzle (who also own the similar Café au Lait, above), a "dash of Jamaican spices" with a "pinch of French flair." Their wine and champagne are imported from France. You dine on a terra-cotta terrace, where you can enjoy a view of the palm-studded beach. You may want to order a homemade pâté, or perhaps a vegetable salad to begin with, and then follow with baked snapper, duckling à l'orange, or a seafood platter. You may have eaten better versions of these dishes at many other places, of course, yet the food is quite satisfying here, and there's rarely an unhappy customer.

Inexpensive

✪ **Chicken Lavish.** West End Rd. ☎ **809/957-4410.** Main courses $5–$13. AE, DISC, MC, V. Daily 10am–10pm. JAMAICAN.

Chicken Lavish, whose name we love, is the best of the cheap restaurants lining this West End beach strip. Just show up on the doorstep and see what's cooking. Curried goat is a specialty, as is fresh fried fish. The red snapper is caught in local waters. But the main reason we've recommended the place is because of its namesake dish. Ask the chef to make his special Jamaican chicken lavish. He'll tell you, and you may agree, that it's the best on the island. What to wear here? Dress as you would to clean up your backyard on a hot August day.

✪ **Cosmo's Seafood Restaurant & Bar.** Norman Manley Blvd. ☎ **809/957-4330.** Main courses J$150–J$500 ($4.20–$14). AE, MC, V. Daily 9am–10pm. SEAFOOD.

One of the best places to go for local seafood is centered around a Polynesian thatched *bohîo* open to the sea and bordering the main beachfront. This is the dining spot of Cosmo Brown, who entertains locals as well as visitors. You can order his famous conch soup, or conch in a number of other ways, including steamed or curried. He's also known for his savory kettle of curried goat, or you might order freshly caught seafood or fish, depending on what the catch turned up. It's a rustic joint, and the prices are among the most reasonable in town. Cosmo's cooking is right on target, and he doesn't charge a lot for it either.

Mariners Inn & Restaurant. West End Rd. ☎ **809/957-4348.** Pizzas J$120–J$300 ($3.35–$8.40); main courses J$120–J$300 ($3.35–$8.40). AE, MC, V. Daily 8am–10pm. JAMAICAN/AMERICAN.

Many guests escaping from their all-inclusive dining rooms head here, looking for some authentic Jamaican flavor. The bar is shaped like a boat, and there's an adjoining restaurant, entered through a tropical garden. As you drink or dine, the sea breezes waft in, adding to the relaxed experience. The one appetizer is a bacon-wrapped banana, not everybody's favorite way to begin a meal, but the food picks up considerably after that. The chef knows how to use curry effectively in the lobster and chicken dishes, and even the goat. The coq au vin (chicken in wine) has never been to France, so you're better off sticking to such dishes as panfried snapper or fried chicken.

Negril Tree House. Norman Manley Blvd. ☎ **809/957-4287.** Main courses $7–$23. AE, MC, V. Daily 7am–11pm. JAMAICAN.

This informal beachfront place takes its name from a mamee tree that grows through the main building of this resort hotel. Dining is on the second floor, but guests can come early and have a drink in the beachfront bar. This is a lively place both day and night. At lunch you can have a homemade soup, perhaps pepperpot, a sandwich, or else more elaborate fare, such as a typically Jamaican dish of escovitched fish (raw fish in a spicy marinade). Some of the produce comes from the owner's own farm in the country.

At night, Gail Y. Jackson, your hostess, offers her full repertoire of dishes, including a great lobster spaghetti. You might begin with a callaloo quiche and later follow with roast chicken (a specialty) or conch steak. Try the Tía Maria parfait for dessert. You can dine both inside and out.

✪ **Paradise Yard.** White Hall Rd. ☎ **809/957-4006.** Main courses J$175–J$450 ($4.90–$12.60). V. Daily 8am–10pm. JAMAICAN.

Set on the verdant flatlands of downtown Negril, near the police station and a 10-minute walk from the beach, this simple but welcoming restaurant lies on the Savanna-La-Mar side of the roundabout in Negril. It's one of the best buys in town. Meals, served either on the outdoor terrace or in an airy, comfortable interior, might include the house specialty, "Rasta Pasta" (red and green "dreadlocks pasta" with tomatoes, pepper, and ackee), pasta with lobster, curried chicken, Mexican enchiladas, and some of the best pumpkin soup on Jamaica. Meals are lustily flavored.

Restaurant Tan-Ya's/Calico Jack's. In the Seasplash Resort, Norman Manley Blvd. ☎ **809/957-4041.** Reservations recommended. Main courses $6–$26. AE, MC, V. Daily 11am–3pm and 6:30–10pm. JAMAICAN/INTERNATIONAL.

Set within the thick white walls of a previously recommended resort, these two restaurants provide well-prepared food and the charm of a small, family run resort. Informal and very affordable lunchtime food is served at Calico Jack's, whose tables are in an enlarged gazebo, near a bar and the resort's swimming pool. The resort's gastronomic showcase, however, is Tan-Ya's. Here, specialties include lemon-flavored shrimp, Tan-Ya's snapper with herb butter, three different preparations of lobster, smoked Jamaican lobster with a fruit salsa, and deviled crab backs sautéed in butter. On many nights these dishes are filled with flavor and well prepared; on some occasions they're slightly off the mark.

SCUBA DIVING

The **Negril Scuba Centre,** in the Negril Beach Club Hotel, Norman Manley Boulevard (☎ **800/818-2963** or 809/957-4425), is the most modern, best-equipped scuba facility in Negril. A professional staff of internationally certified scuba instructors and dive masters teach and guide divers to Negril's colorful coral reefs. Beginner's dive lessons are offered daily, as well as multiple-dive packages for certified divers. Full scuba certifications and specialty courses are also available.

A resort course, designed for first-time divers with basic swimming abilities, includes all instruction, equipment, a lecture on water and diving safety, and one open-water dive. It begins at 10am daily and ends at 2pm. Its price is $75. A one-tank dive costs $30 per dive plus $20 for equipment rental (not necessary if divers bring their own gear). More economical is a two-tank dive, which includes lunch. It costs $55, plus the (optional) $20 rental of all equipment. This organization is PADI-registered, although it accepts all recognized certification cards.

One of the best-recommended dive facilities in Negril is **Scuba World,** a PADI-approved five-star dive shop located on the premises of the Poinciana Beach Hotel (☎ **809/957-5221**), on Norman Manley Boulevard, near the Sandals Negril. It's open daily from 8am to 5pm and offers a four-day certification course for $300. A resort course for beginners costs $70, and a one-tank dive for already-certified divers costs $30, plus $20 for the rental of the necessary equipment. More than 20 dive sites, including coral reefs and caves, are located at Poinciana.

3 Falmouth

This port town lies on the north coast of Jamaica, only about 23 miles east of Montego Bay. The Trelawny Beach Hotel originally put it on the tourist map (though we no longer recommend staying here). The town itself is interesting but ramshackle. There's talk about fixing it up for visitors, but no one has done it yet. If you leave your car at Water Square, you can explore the town in about an hour. The present courthouse was reconstructed from the early 19th-century building, and fisherfolk still congregate on Seaboard Street. You'll pass the Customs Office and a parish church dating from the late 18th century. Later, you can go on a shopping expedition outside town to Caribatik.

WHERE TO STAY

✪ **Good Hope.** P.O. Box 50, Falmouth, Jamaica, W.I. ☎ **800/OUTPOST;** ☎ and fax 809/954-3289. 10 rms. Winter, $150–$250 double. Off-season, $100–$175 double. AE, MC, V.

The most romantic place to stay in the greater Montego Bay area isn't at any of the swank properties, but at this beautifully restored 1755 Georgian Great House in the mountains of Cockpit Country, 5 miles south of Falmouth and a beach. Set on a 2,000-acre plantation, the estate features lush gardens and country trails, horseback riding, tennis, and swimming. The Martha Brae River runs through the property. Like Strawberry Hill in Kingston, this place, too, is owned by the music impresario Chris Blackwell, who has exquisite taste. This is the closest you get to enjoying the rich life of the grand planters of long ago. It's like walking back into Georgian days, but with all the modern conveniences.

Don't despair as you traverse the unmarked potholed road getting there (call for directions). The house at the end is worth the effort to reach it. The main house is furnished with antiques, all evocative of the plantation era, and the former coach house with five rooms can be rented as a self-contained unit. In the rear is an antique guest house, ideal for a honeymoon with its wrought-iron canopy bed. One room is in this guest house; the other four are in the Great House. Six rooms are air-conditioned. All meals, including afternoon tea, are prepared in the classic Jamaican style and served in the main house. Even if you can't stay here, call and see if you can come for dinner.

WHERE TO DINE

✪ **Glistening Waters Inn and Marina.** Rock Falmouth (between Falmouth and the Trelawny Beach Hotel). ☎ **809/954-3229.** Reservations not required. Main courses $7–$22. AE, MC, V. Daily 10am–10pm. SEAFOOD.

Residents of Montego Bay often make the 28-mile drive out here, along Route A1, just to sample the ambience of old Jamaica. This well-recommended restaurant, with a veranda overlooking a lagoon, is housed in what was originally a private clubhouse of the aristocrats of nearby Trelawny. The furniture here may remind you of a stage set for *Night of the Iguana.* Menu items usually include local fish dishes, such as snapper or kingfish, served with bammy (a form of cassava bread). Other specialties include three different lobster dishes, three different preparations of shrimp, three different conch viands, fried rice, and pork served as chops or in a stew. The food is just what your mama would make (if she came from Jamaica).

The waters of the lagoon contain a rare form of phosphorescent microbe which, when the waters are agitated, glow in the dark. Ask about evening booze cruises, which cost $3 per person for diners. Departures are nightly at about 6:30pm.

RIVER RAFTING NEAR FALMOUTH

Rafting on the Martha Brae is an adventure. To reach the starting point from Falmouth, drive approximately 3 miles inland to **Martha Brae's Rafters Village** (☎ **809/952-0889**). The rafts are similar to those on the Río Grande, near Port Antonio, and cost $37 per raft, with two riders allowed on a raft, plus a small child if accompanied by an adult (but use precaution). The trips last 1 1/4 hours and operate daily from 9am to 4pm. You sit on a raised dais on bamboo logs. Along the way you can stop and order cool drinks or beer along the banks of the river. There's a bar, a restaurant, and a souvenir shop in the village. Call for more information.

SHOPPING

Two miles east of Falmouth on the north-coast road is **Caribatik Island Fabrics,** at Rock Wharf on the Luminous Lagoon (☎ **809/954-3314**). You'll recognize the place easily, as it has a huge sign painted across the building's side. This is the private living and work domain of Keith Chandler, who established the place with his late wife, Muriel, in 1970. Today the batiks created by Muriel Chandler before her death in 1990 are viewed as stylish and sensual garments by the chic boutiques in the States.

In the shop has a full range of fabrics, scarves, garments, and wall hangings, some patterned after such themes as Jamaica's "Doctor Bird" and various endangered animal species of the world. Muriel's gallery continues to sell a selection of her original batik paintings. Either Keith or a member of the staff will be glad to describe the intricate process of batiking during their open hours: 9am to 4pm Tuesday to Saturday. They're closed in September.

4 Runaway Bay

Once this resort was a mere western satellite of Ocho Rios. However, with the opening of some large resort hotels, plus a colony of smaller hostelries, Runaway Bay is now a destination in its own right.

This part of Jamaica's north coast has several distinctions: It was the first part of the island seen by Columbus, the site of the first Spanish settlement on the island, and the point of departure of the last Spaniards leaving Jamaica following their defeat by the British. Columbus landed at Discovery Bay on his second voyage of exploration in 1494, and in 1509 Spaniards established a settlement called Sevilla Nueva (New Seville) near what is now St. Ann's Bay, about 10 miles east of the present Runaway Bay village. Sevilla Nueva was later abandoned when the inhabitants moved to the southern part of the island.

Jamaica's most complete equestrian center is the **Chukka Cove Farm and Resort,** at Richmond Llandovery, St. Ann (☎ **809/972-2506**), located less than 4 miles east of Runaway Bay. A one-hour trail ride costs $30, and a two-hour mountain ride costs $40. The most popular ride is a three-hour beach jaunt where, after riding over trails to the sea, you can unpack your horse and swim in the surf. Refreshments are served as part of the $55 charge. A six-hour beach ride, complete with picnic lunch, goes for $130. Polo lessons are also available, costing $50 for 30 minutes.

WHERE TO STAY & DINE

EXPENSIVE

Breezes Runaway Bay. P.O. Box 58 (6 miles west of Ocho Rios), Runaway Bay, Jamaica, W.I. ☎ **800/859-7873** in the U.S., or 809/973-2436. Fax 809/973-2352. 234 rms, 4 suites. A/C TEL. Winter, $1,558–$1,618 double; $1,758 suite for 2. Off-season, $1,338–$1,418 double; $1,438–$1,478 suite for 2. Rates are all-inclusive for 3 nights. AE, DC, MC, V.

This stylish resort has had several identities since it was built. It operates on a price plan that includes three meals a day, all free drinks, and a galaxy of other benefits. Its long, low-lying clubhouse is approached by passing through a park filled with tropical trees and shrubbery. Inside the lobby is the best re-creation of the South Seas on Jamaica, with hanging wicker chairs and totemic columns. Each of the rooms has a view of a well-landscaped courtyard, with a private balcony overlooking the sea. Near the wide sandy beach is a minijungle with dangling hammocks, a swimming pool, and there's even a nearby nude beach. Children 15 and under are not accepted.

Dining/Entertainment: Live music emanates from the stylish Terrace every evening at 7pm, and a nightclub offers live shows six nights a week at 10pm. You dine either in the beachside restaurant or in the more formal Italian restaurant, Martino's.

Services: Reggae exercise classes held twice daily.

Facilities: Gym filled with Nautilus equipment, swimming pool, sports activities center (featuring scuba diving, windsurfing, and a golf school), 18-hole championship golf course.

FDR (Franklyn D. Resort). Main St. (P.O. Box 201), Runaway Bay, St. Ann, Jamaica, W.I. ☎ **800/654-1FDR** in the U.S., or 809/973-4591. Fax 809/973-3071. 76 suites. A/C TV TEL. Winter, $280 per person. Off-season, $266 per person. Rates include all meals, bar drinks, beer, cigarettes, sports, and entertainment. Children 15 and under stay free in parents' suite. AE, MC, V.

An all-inclusive resort on Route A1, 17 miles west of Ocho Rios, FDR is geared to families with children and is dedicated to including all meals and activities in a net price. The resort, named after its Jamaican-born owner and developer (Franklyn David Rance), is on six acres of flat, sandy land dotted with flowering shrubs and trees, on the main seaside highway. Each of the Mediterranean-inspired buildings has a terra-cotta roof, a loggia or outdoor terrace, Spanish marble in the bathroom, and a personal attendant whose cooking, cleaning, child-care, and miscellaneous services come with each of the units. Although neither its narrow beach nor its modest swimming pools are the most desirable on the island, many visitors appreciate the spacious units and the resort's wholehearted concern for visiting children. Each unit contains a kitchenette where, if you want, meals can be prepared by the personal attendant.

Dining/Entertainment: Two restaurants on the property serve free wine with lunch and dinner (and offer special children's meals), a piano bar provides music every evening, and a handful of bars keeps the drinks flowing whenever you're ready for them. Live music is provided nightly.

Services: A so-called "Girl Friday" baby-sits for free every day between 8am and 5pm, after which she can be hired privately for $3 an hour. There's a children's supervisor in attendance at "Kiddies' Centre" (where a computer center, a kiddies' disco, and even kiddies' dinners are regular features). Adults appreciate the scuba lessons, picnics, photography lessons, arts and crafts lessons, and donkey rides that keep the kids entertained.

Facilities: Water sports, illuminated tennis courts, satellite TV room, disco, exercise gym, free use of bicycles for getting around the neighborhood; free tours to Dunn's River Falls and Ocho Rios shopping are included.

MODERATE

✪ **Eaton Hall Beach Hotel.** Main St. (P.O. Box 112), Runaway Bay, St. Ann, Jamaica, W.I. ☎ **800/972-2158** in the U.S., or 809/973-3503. Fax 809/973-2432. 52 rms. A/C. Winter, $190–$220 double. Off-season, $160–$190 double. Rates include 3 meals a day, use of facilities, taxes, and tips. AE, DC, MC, V.

An original plantation Great House has been restored and turned into this small, affordable hotel of charm and character two blocks east of the main town square. A subterranean passage, now bricked up, leads from the living room to the coral cliffs behind the house. The property is a successful blending of old with new. Some of the bedrooms of the Great House open onto an arched portico, and four units in the main house front the sea. On each side of the hall are wings housing bedrooms with ocean views and furnished with tropical designs and older mahogany pieces. Some of the rooms have carved mahogany four-poster beds. Many of the accommodations are in a handful of modern villas set on a low and rocky ledge about six feet above the sea. Some rooms have phones. Children 11 and under are not accepted.

Dining/Entertainment: Entertainment, weekly floor shows, and a Jamaican buffet two or three times a week are also part of the all-inclusive plan. The one restaurant offers American, Jamaican, and continental foods, and there are two bars.

Services: Laundry.

Facilities: Sunfish sailing, snorkeling equipment, scuba diving.

INEXPENSIVE

✪ **Runaway H.E.A.R.T. Country Club.** Ricketts Ave. (off Main St.; P.O. Box 98), Runaway Bay, St. Ann, Jamaica, W.I. ☎ **809/973-2671.** Fax 809/973-2693. 20 rms. A/C TV TEL. Winter, $123 double. Off-season, $111 double. Rates include MAP. AE, MC, V.

The best-kept secret in Jamaica, this place is located on the main road, and it practically wins hands down as the bargain of the north coast. One of Jamaica's few training and service institutions, the club and its adjacent academy are operated by the government to provide a high level of training for young Jamaicans interested in the hotel trade. The hotel is well run; its professional staff includes trainees who are helpful and eager to please and offer perhaps the finest service of any hotel in the area.

The rooms are bright and airy and have either a king-size bed, a double bed, or twin beds. The accommodations open onto private balconies with views of well-manicured tropical gardens or vistas of the bay and golf course.

Dining/Entertainment: Guests enjoy having a drink in the piano bar (ever had a cucumber daiquiri?) before heading for the dining room, the Cardiff Hall Restaurant, which has a combination of Jamaican and continental dishes. Nonresidents can also enjoy dinner, served nightly from 7 to 10pm. The academy has won awards for some of its dishes, including "go-go banana chicken" and curried codfish.

Services: Laundry.

Facilities: Swimming pool, golf course.

A NEARBY ALL-INCLUSIVE

Braco Village Resort. Rio Bueno P.O., Trelawny, Jamaica. ☎ **800/654-1337** or 809/954-0000. Fax 809/954-0020-21. 172 rms, 6 suites. A/C TV TEL. Winter, $380–$450 double; $550–$600 suite. Off-season, $380–$430 double; $540 suite. Rates are all-inclusive. AE, DC, DISC, MC, V.

Established in 1995, this is one of the newest, and most historically evocative all-inclusive resorts in Jamaica. Set on 85 acres of land near Buena Vista, a 15-minute drive west of Runaway Bay, it was configured as a re-creation of a 19th-century Jamaican Victorian village set adjacent to an impressive stretch of prime beachfront. Meetings and entertainment are presented in a stately duplication of a courthouse, benches and flowering trees line the symmetrical borders of a town square, and meals are served within four separate venues inspired by an idealized version of Jamaica of long ago. Employees, most of whom come from the nearby hamlet of Rio Bueno, are encouraged to mingle with guests and share their personal and community stories. Here you get a more vivid insight into Jamaican life than would be possible at more cloistered and remote all-inclusive resorts. This is not a place for children: No one under 16 is allowed, and the venue is primarily adult, relaxed, and reasonably permissive.

Accommodations lie within 12 independent blocks of three-story buildings, each trimmed in colonial-style gingerbread and filled with wicker furniture. Each has a private patio or veranda, and throughout the entire resort, there's a predominant color scheme of pink and yellow. All units face the ocean, although blocks 1 through 6 are closer to the beachfront and blocks 5 and 6 face a strip of sand designated as a "clothing optional" area.

Dining/Entertainment: Four separate dining areas include a venue devoted to Jamaican cuisine, pizza and pasta, an international emporium called the Victorian Market, and a dinner-only upscale affair, the Susumber Tree, the only one to impose a dress code. At least three bars make getting a drink relatively easy.

Services: A staff who keeps conversations and good times rolling along.

Facilities: A soccer field where a local Jamaican team sometimes volunteers to play with (or against) aficionados from the village; a fitness center, a nine-hole golf course, disco, three fishing ponds, bike and jogging trails, four tennis courts, use of a glass-bottom boat for snorkeling tours, and one of the largest swimming pools in Jamaica.

SEEING THE SIGHTS

The **Columbus Park Museum,** on Queens Highway, in Discovery Bay (☎ **809/973-2135**), is a large, open area between the main coast road and the sea at Discovery Bay. You just pull off the road and then walk among the fantastic collection of exhibits; admission is free. There's everything from a canoe made of a solid piece of cottonwood (the way Arawaks did it more than five centuries ago), to a stone cross that was originally placed on the Barrett estate at Retreat (9 miles east of Montego

Bay) by Edward Barrett, brother of poet Elizabeth Barrett Browning. You'll see a tally, used to count bananas carried on men's heads from plantation to ship, as well as a planter's strongbox with a weighted lead base to prevent its theft. Other items are 18th-century cannons, a Spanish water cooler and calcifier, a fish pot made from bamboo, a corn husker, and a water wheel. Pimento trees, from which allspice is produced, dominate the park. Open daily from 9am to 5pm.

You can also visit the **Seville Great House,** Heritage Park (☎ **809/972-2191**), open daily from 9am to 5pm, charging $4 for admission. Built in 1745 by the English, the house contains a collection of artifacts once used by everybody from the Amerindians to African slaves. In all you're treated to an exhibit of five centuries worth of Jamaican history. Modest for a Great House, it has a wattle and daub construction. A small theater presents a 15-minute historical film about the house.

5 Ocho Rios

This north-coast resort is a two-hour drive east of Montego Bay or west of Port Antonio. Ocho Rios was once a small banana and fishing port, but tourism became the leading industry long ago. This resort, short on charm, is now Jamaica's cruise-ship capital. The bay is dominated on one side by a bauxite-loading terminal and on the other by a range of hotels with sandy beaches fringed by palm trees.

Ocho Rios and neighboring Port Antonio have long been associated with Sir Noël Coward (who invited the world to his doorstep) and Ian Fleming, creator of James Bond (see below for details about their homes here).

Frankly, unless you're a cruise passenger, you may want to stay away from the major attractions when a ship is in port. The duty-free shopping markets are overrun then, and the hustlers become more strident in pushing their crafts and junk souvenirs. Dunn's River Falls becomes almost impossible to visit at those times.

However, Ocho Rios has its own unique flavor and offers the usual range of sports, including a major fishing tournament every fall, in addition to a wide variety of accommodations.

WHERE TO STAY

VERY EXPENSIVE

✪ **Jamaica Inn.** Main St. (P.O. Box 1), Ocho Rios, Jamaica, W.I. ☎ **800/837-4608** in the U.S., or 809/974-2514. Fax 809/974-2449. 41 rms, 4 suites. A/C TEL. Winter (including all meals), $475–$525 double; from $575 suite for 2. Off-season (including MAP), $290–$325 double; from $325 suite for 2. AE, MC, V.

Built in 1950, the Jamaica Inn is a series of long, low, buildings set in a U shape near the sea, 1 1/2 miles east of town. It's an elegant anachronism, a true retro hotel, and has remained little changed in four decades, avoiding the brass and glitter of all-inclusives like Sandals. Lovely patios open onto the lawns, and the bedrooms are reached along garden paths. This gracious, family-run inn, long a Jamaican landmark, underwent a $4 million upgrade to all its rooms in 1993. The old charm, including the antique furniture, remains. The rooms open onto balconies. The White Suite here was a favorite of Winston Churchill. Over the years, many other celebrities have favored the inn with their patronage. Noël Coward, arriving with Katharine Hepburn or Claudette Colbert, was a regular, and Errol Flynn and Ian Fleming used to drop in from time to time. Close to the shore, the sea is almost too clear to make snorkeling an adventure, but farther out it's rewarding. Children 13 and under are not accepted.

Dining/Entertainment: The European-trained chef prepares both international and Jamaican dishes. The emphasis is on cuisine that uses fresh local produce. Men must wear a jacket and tie at night in winter.

Services: Room service, laundry.

Facilities: Swimming pool, wide champagne-colored sand beach, tennis, comfortable lounge with books, games room with cards and jigsaw puzzles; golf close by at the Upton Golf Course.

EXPENSIVE

High Hope Estate. Box 11, St. Ann's Bay, near Ocho Rios. ☎ **809/972-2277.** 6 rms. TEL. Year-round, $174–$270 double. Rates include breakfast. MC, V.

Because of the small size of this upscale hotel, your happiness, and the success of your holiday here, will depend a lot on whether your chemistry is right with the owner and the other guests. It's conceived as a tranquil private home that accepts paying guests, in the style of the British colonial world at its most rarefied. It was built for a socially prominent heiress, Kitty Spence, granddaughter of prairie-state populist William Jennings Bryan, and later served as the home and laboratory of a horticulturist who successfully bred 560 varieties of flowering hibiscus. Consequently, the estate's 40 acres, set 550 feet above the coast and 7 miles west of Ocho Rios, thrive with flowering plants and memories of such luminaries as Noël Coward, who used to play the grand piano that graces one of the public areas. There are absolutely no planned activities at this place. Basically, it's an upscale private home, the domain of U.S. entrepreneur Dennis Rapaport, whose staff is on hand to help with supervising children, maintaining the property, and preparing meals for anyone who gives advance notice. On the premises is a swimming pool, a tennis court, a communal TV room, and a semienclosed courtyard modeled on a 15th-century villa. There are sweeping views out over the Jamaican coastline; the nearest beach is a 10-minute ride away. You could rent the entire villa with a group of friends.

✪ **Plantation Inn.** Main St. (P.O. Box 2), Ocho Rios, Jamaica, W.I. ☎ **800/752-6824** in the U.S., 800/567-5327 in Canada, or 809/974-5601. Fax 809/974-5912. 61 rms, 15 suites, 2 villas. A/C TEL. Winter, $195–$270 double; $235–$310 triple; from $345 suite for 2. Off-season, $130–$175 double; $170–$190 triple; from $255 suite for 2. MAP $55 per person extra. AE, MC, V.

This hotel evokes an antebellum Southern mansion. At any moment, you expect Vivien Leigh as Scarlett to come rushing down to greet you. You'll drive up a sweeping driveway and enter through a colonnaded portico, set above the beach in gardens, $1^1/_2$ miles east of town. All bedrooms open off balconies and have their own patios overlooking the sea, where the hotel has a variety of water sports available. The double rooms are attractively decorated with chintz and comfortable furnishings, and there are also junior suites. Apart from the regular hotel, there are two units that provide lodgings: the Plantana Villa above the eastern beach sleeps two to six people; the Blue Shadow Villa on the west side accommodates up to eight guests.

Dining/Entertainment: There's an indoor dining room, but most of the action takes place under the tropical sky. You can have breakfast on your balcony and lunch is served outdoors. English tea is served on the terrace every afternoon.

Services: Room service, facials, massages, waxing.

Facilities: Two private beaches (36 steps down from the garden; seats on the way provide resting spots), jungle gym with exercise equipment, sauna, two tennis courts, snorkeling, Sunfish sailing, windsurfing, scuba diving, kayaking, glass-bottom boat; golf available at an 18-hole course a 15-minute drive away.

INEXPENSIVE

Hibiscus Lodge Hotel. 87 Main St. (P.O. Box 52), Ocho Rios, Jamaica, W.I. ☎ **809/974-2676.** Fax 809/974-1874. 27 rms. Winter, $92 double; $137.30 triple. Off-season, $80.75 double; $116.45 triple. Rates include breakfast. Tax and service extra. AE, CB, DC, MC, V.

The Hibiscus Lodge Hotel offers more value for your money than any resort in Ocho Rios. It's an intimate little inn with character and charm, perched precariously on a cliff side three blocks from the Ocho Rios Mall, along the shore. All bedrooms, either doubles or triples, have private baths, ceiling fans, and verandas opening to the sea. Singles can be rented for the double rate.

After a day spent swimming in a pool with a large sundeck suspended over the cliffs, guests can enjoy a drink in the unique swinging bar, which features swinging chairs. The 3-acre site also contains a Jacuzzi, a tennis court, and conference facilities. Dining at the Almond Tree (see "Where to Dine," below) is among the best at the resort. The Grotto is a piano bar open daily from 5pm to 2am.

ALL-INCLUSIVE RESORTS

Boscobel Beach. P.O. Box 63, Ocho Rios, Jamaica, W.I. ☎ **800/859-7873** in the U.S., or 809/975-7331. Fax 809/975-7370. 196 rms, 11 suites. A/C TV TEL. Winter, $1,778–$1,898 double; from $2,378 suite for 2. Off-season, $1,238–$1,678 double; from $1,858 suite for 2. Rates are for all-inclusive 3-day package. Two children 13 and under per paying adult stay free in parents' room; third child 13 and under $50 extra. AE, MC, V.

The best place on the island for families with children is outside Ocho Rios. Once this was one of Hugh Hefner's Playboy Clubs, and there was no sexier resort in all of Jamaica. But, with changing times, the playboys and their bunnies have long faded to make way for family fun. Boscobel Beach is now the most clearly marketed family resort in the Caribbean.

The name of this resort is old Spanish for "beautiful gardens by the sea," and it's that and more. Set on 14½ acres of prime seafront property, it stands 10 miles east of Ocho Rios. All the well-furnished and attractively decorated rooms are equipped with refrigerators. Some of them feature large balconies and sunken bathtubs. A series of 44 refurbished lanai rooms (these are smaller) open right onto the beach.

Dining/Entertainment: Dinner is offered in an open-air dining room (a special children's meal is served earlier). The Barbecue Pit is decorated with a children's theme and is promoted as a "kids only" restaurant. There are also five bars on the property, including one at the beach that serves snacks throughout the day. A disco opens at 11pm. Live local entertainment is a nightly feature.

Services: Transfers to and from the airport, transfers to the golf course, babysitting, laundry.

Facilities: Children's center and a mini-zoo, four tennis courts (lit for night play), fully equipped gym, exercise classes, aerobics, two Jacuzzis, reggae dance classes, windsurfing, sailing, waterskiing, scuba diving; golf nearby.

✪ **Ciboney Ocho Rios.** Main St. (P.O. Box 728), Ocho Rios, St. Ann, Jamaica, W.I. ☎ **800/333-3333** in the U.S. and Canada, or 809/974-1027. Fax 809/974-5838. 36 rms, 16 junior villa suites, 162 one-bedroom villa suites, 14 honeymoon villas, 26 two-bedroom villas. A/C MINIBAR TV TEL. $636–$666 double; $711 junior villa suite; $741 one-bedroom villa suite; $1,103 honeymoon villa; $711 two-bedroom villa for 4. Rates are per person for all-inclusive 3-night package. AE, DC, MC, V.

This all-inclusive Radisson Hotel franchise lies a 1½-mile drive southeast of town. It's set on 45 acres of a private estate dotted with red-tile villas. A Great House in the hills overlooks the Caribbean Sea. Across from the imposing gate near the entrance to the resort are the white sands of a private beach. All but a handful of the accommodations are in one-, two-, or three-bedroom villas, each of which offers a pool, fully equipped kitchen, and shaded terrace. Honeymoon villas have their own whirlpools. Thirty-six of the accommodations are traditional single or double rooms on the third floor of the Great House. Regardless of their location, accommodations are high-ceilinged, airy, and decorated in Caribbean colors. Throughout the property, a series of stone retaining walls frame the sloping grounds, which include carefully landscaped beds of flowering trees and vines. Children 15 and under are not accepted.

Dining/Entertainment: The Manor Restaurant & Bar offers both indoor and outdoor patio dining for dinner and entertainment, with classic Jamaican food. The Marketplace Restaurant has a contemporary menu of both American and Jamaican foods, and Alfresco Casa Nina, in a seaside setting, highlights Italian cuisine. Orchids is a restaurant developed in collaboration with the Culinary Institute of America, with a menu based on haute cuisine, as well as healthy food. Finally, late-night entertainment and dancing are featured at Nicole.

Services: Complimentary manicure and pedicure, choice of 25-minute massages.

Facilities: European-inspired beauty spa with its own health-and-fitness center, several different conference rooms, six tennis courts (lit for night play), beach club offering an array of water sports, two main swimming pools with swim-up bars (plus 90 other semiprivate swimming pools on the grounds), spa with 20 Jacuzzis; golf nearby.

Couples Ocho Rios. Tower Isle, along Rte. A3 (P.O. Box 330), Ocho Rios, Jamaica, W.I. ☎ **800/268-7537** in the U.S., or 809/975-4271. Fax 809/975-4439. 161 rms, 11 suites. A/C TEL. Winter, $1,550–$2,450 per couple. Off-season, $1,400–$2,210 per couple. Rates are for 3 nights and include all meals, drinks, cigarettes, activities, and airport transfers. AE, MC, V.

Don't come here alone—you won't get in! The management defines couples as "any *man and woman* in love," and this is a couples-only resort. Most visiting couples are married, and many are on their honeymoon; no one 17 or under is accepted. Everything is in pairs, even the chairs by the moon-drenched beach. Some couples slip away from the resort, which is an 18-minute drive (5 miles) east of town, to Couples' private island to bask in the buff. In general this is a classier operation than the more mass-market Sandals (the Dunn's River and the Ocho Rios versions).

Once you've paid the initial fee, you're free to use all the facilities. There will be no more bills. Even the cigarettes and whiskey are free. You get three meals a day, including all the wine you want; breakfast is bountiful. And tips aren't permitted.

The bedrooms have either a king-size bed or two doubles and pleasantly traditional furnishings. Each has a patio, fronting either the sea or the mountains. The hotel usually accepts bookings for a minimum of any 3 nights of the week, but most guests book in here on weekly terms. A 4-day stay is sometimes required at certain peak periods, such as over the Christmas holidays.

Dining/Entertainment: Dinners are five courses, and afterward there's dancing on the terrace every evening, with entertainment. Guests have a choice of four restaurants.

Services: Room service (for breakfast only), laundry.

Facilities: Five tennis courts (three lit at night), Nautilus gym, scuba diving, snorkeling, windsurfing, sailing, waterskiing.

✪ **The Enchanted Garden.** Eden Bower Rd. (P.O. Box 284), Ocho Rios, Jamaica, W.I. ☎ **800/847-2535** in the U.S., or 809/974-1400. Fax 809/974-5823. 58 rms, 55 suites. A/C TV TEL. Winter, $330–$370 double; from $440 suite for 2. Off-season, $270–$310 double; from $370 suite for 2. Rates include meals, snacks, and bar drinks; house wines at lunch and dinner; aerobics, yoga, and meditation classes; all nonmotorized water sports; entertainment; daily shuttle to private beach club; taxes; and round-trip transfers to airport at Montego Bay. AE, DC, MC, V.

This most verdant of Jamaican resorts sits on a secluded hilltop high above the commercial center of town. Owned and developed by Edward Seaga, former Jamaican prime minister, the land includes 20 acres of rare botanical specimens, nature trails, and 14 cascading waterfalls much loved by such former visitors as Mick Jagger. The resort's lobby is housed in a pink tower accented with white gingerbread; the interior sports marble floors, big windows, and enormous potted palms. Bisected by the Turtle River, whose 14 waterfalls are highlighted with garden paths and spotlights, the place is of particular interest to botanists and bird watchers.

The bedrooms have sturdy rattan furniture and are contained in eight different low-rise buildings set amid the resort's carefully conceived landscaping. Each has a private patio or balcony, and some contain kitchens.

Dining/Entertainment: The resort's restaurants serve continental food, plus Thai, Japanese, Indonesian, and regional Chinese cuisines. A Pasta Bar is designed like a treehouse amid a tropical forest. Guests may also dine at the Seaquarium, offering a cold buffet in a setting surrounded by tropical fish. A Beach Club is a minivan ride from the hotel. Annabella's nightclub provides a variety of after-dinner entertainment amid a decor like something out of the *Arabian Nights.*

Services: Daily transportation to the Beach Club, shuttle for shopping.

Facilities: Spa, beauty salon, swimming pool, two lighted tennis courts, walk-in aviary featuring hundreds of exotic birds (feeding time is every afternoon around 4pm), fitness center. There's also a Seaquarium with 15 aquariums for marine-life exotica.

Jamaica Grande Renaissance Resort. Main St. (P.O. Box 100), Ocho Rios, St. Ann, Jamaica. ☎ **800/HOTELS-1** in the U.S. and Canada, or 809/974-2201. Fax 809/974-2289. 705 rms, 15 suites. A/C TV TEL. Winter, $380–$400 double; from $920 suite. Off-season, $320–$340 double; from $680 suite. Rates include meals, drinks, and water sports. AE, DC, MC, V.

This is the largest hotel on Jamaica, a combination of two high-rise beachfront hostelries constructed in 1975 and 1976. The place is pure theatrics and special effects, like a Hollywood production, but is short on true Jamaican style. It seems to be meant to overwhelm guests. In 1993, an elaborate cluster of waterfalls and swimming pools were inserted into what had been parking lots between the towers, and the entire complex was unified into a coherent whole. Today the end result contains more beachfront than any other hotel in Ocho Rios and a comfortable array of public rooms (often filled with members of tour or conference groups). The standard bedrooms are tile-floored and furnished with Caribbean furniture. Each opens onto a private balcony.

Dining/Entertainment: The restaurants include the Dragon (Chinese) and L'Allegro (Italian), and the less formal Café Jamique and Mallard's Court (international). There's also a beachfront grill and a total of eight bars scattered throughout the premises. The hotel operates the Jamaic'N Me Crazy Disco and a casino, with only slot machines. Every Thursday the Jamaica Grande is transformed into a village for Jump Up Carnival, with Jamaican food, a live band, and shopping.

Services: Daily activities programs.

Facilities: Tennis courts lit for nighttime play, year-round children's program, a full range of water sports.

Sandals Dunn's River. Along Rte. A3 (P.O. Box 51), Ocho Rios, Jamaica, W.I. ☎ **800/SANDALS** in the U.S. and Canada, or 809/972-1610. Fax 809/972-1611. 246 rms, 10 suites. TV TEL. Winter, $1,680–$2,070 double; $2,210–$2,530 suite for 2. Off-season, $1,600–$1,960 double; $2,100–$2,400 suite for 2. Rates are for 4 days/3 nights (the minimum stay) and include all meals, unlimited wine and drinks, airport transfers, tax, and services. AE, MC, V.

Having been through various incarnations as the Jamaica Hilton and Eden II, this luxury, all-inclusive resort has now found its latest identity as a member of Jamaican entrepreneur Butch Stewart's rapidly expanding Sandals empire. Located on a wide sugary beach, this is the finest of the Sandals resorts, at least in the opinion of some guests who have sampled them all. Only male-female couples are allowed.

Set on the beachfront between Ocho Rios and St. Ann's Bay, the resort is very sports-oriented. It occupies 25 well-landscaped acres, offering attractively furnished and often quite spacious accommodations. All the rooms were reconstructed after the Sandals takeover and given an Italianate/Mediterranean motif. The guest rooms are scattered among the six-story main building, two lanai buildings, and a five-story west wing.

Dining/Entertainment: Before retreating to the disco, guests choose among several dining options. The International Room is elegant, with fabric-covered walls and rosewood furniture. West Indian Windies serves Caribbean specialties. D'Amore offers Italian cuisine, and Restaurant Teppanyaki serves Chinese, Polynesian, and Japanese dishes.

Services: Tours to Dunn's River Falls, shuttles to Sandals Ocho Rios, massages—all complimentary.

Facilities: Three Jacuzzis, two whirlpool baths, fitness center, jogging course, beach bar, pitch-and-putt golf course, one of the most spectacular swim-up bars on Jamaica in the lagoon-shaped pool; transport to the Sandals Golf and Country Club.

Sandals Ocho Rios. Main St. (P.O. Box 771), Ocho Rios, Jamaica, W.I. ☎ **800/SANDALS** in the U.S. and Canada, or 809/974-5691. Fax 809/974-5700. 237 rms. TV TEL. Winter, $1,470–$1,840 double. Off-season, $1,420–$1,740 double. Rates are for 4 days/3 nights and include all meals, snacks, unlimited wine and drinks, airport transfers, and the services and facilities listed below. AE, MC, V.

Another Jamaican addition to the ever-expanding couples-only empire of Gordon "Butch" Stewart, who pioneered similar properties in Montego Bay and Negril, Sandals Ocho Rios attracts a mix of coupled singles and married folk, including honeymooners. At times the place seems like a summer camp for grown-ups (or others who didn't quite grow up). The resort uses the same formula: one price per male-female couple, including everything. This is the most low-key of the Sandals resorts. Is it romantic? Most patrons think so, although we've encountered other couples here whose relationship didn't survive the three-night minimum stay.

On 13 well-landscaped acres a mile west of the town center, it offers comfortably furnished but uninspired rooms with either ocean or garden views, and there are some cottage units, too. All rooms are reasonably large, with king-size beds and hair dryers.

Dining/Entertainment: You can sip free drinks at an oceanside swim-up bar. Nightly theme parties and live entertainment take place in a modern amphitheater. A unique feature of the resort is an open-air disco. The resort's main dining room is St. Anne's, while Michelle's serves Italian food, and the Reef Terrace Grill does gourmet Jamaican cuisine and fresh seafood. If you want more man-sized grub and drinks, head for a new addition, the Arizona Steak House.

Services: Round-trip transfers from the airport, tours to Dunn's River Falls, massages, laundry.

Facilities: Three freshwater pools, private artificial beach, sporting equipment and instruction (including waterskiing, windsurfing, sailing, snorkeling, and scuba diving), paddleboats, kayaks, glass-bottom boat, Jacuzzi, saunas, fully equipped fitness center, two tennis courts.

✪ **Sans Souci Lido.** On Rte. A3 (P.O. Box 103), Ocho Rios, Jamaica, W.I. ☎ **800/859-7873** in the U.S., or 809/974-2353. Fax 809/974-2544. 12 rms, 90 suites, 9 penthouses. A/C MINIBAR TV TEL. Winter, $2,240 double; from $2,460 suite for 2; $3,420 penthouse for 2. Off-season, $1,800–$1,900 double; from $1,980 suite for 2; $2,880–$2,980 penthouse for 2. Rates are for all-inclusive 3-night package. AE, DC, MC, V.

If a cookie-cutter Sandals resort is the last thing you want in Jamaica, don your best resort finery and head for a classier joint: this one. Sans Souci is a pink cliff-side fantasy that recently completed a $7 million renovation, turning it into an all-inclusive Jamaica SuperClub. This is one of the finest spas in the Caribbean and has fabulous sports facilities. It's located 3 miles east of town on a forested plot of land whose rocky border abuts a good beach. A cliff-side elevator brings guests to an outdoor bar. There's a freshwater pool, a mineral bath big enough for an elephant, and a labyrinth of catwalks and bridges stretching over rocky chasms filled with surging water.

Each accommodation features a veranda or patio, copies of Chippendale furniture, plush upholstery, and subdued colonial elegance. Some contain Jacuzzis.

Dining/Entertainment: The resort offers guests the Casanova restaurant (see "Where to Dine," below). In addition, there's the Ristorante Palazzina by the beach. The Balloon Bar tries to bring back some 1920s style. There are also several terraces for drinking.

Services: Room service, laundry/valet, massages.

Facilities: Established in 1987, Charlie's Spa grew out of the hotel's mineral springs, frequented for medicinal benefits since the 1700s. Considered effective for treating certain skin disorders, arthritis, and rheumatism, the spa is the finest place on Jamaica for a health-and-fitness vacation, and one of the finest in the entire Caribbean. Sports lovers appreciate the hotel's three Laykold tennis courts (two lighted) and the nearby croquet lawn. Scuba diving, snorkeling, windsurfing, deep-sea fishing, and Sunfish and catamaran sailing are available at the beach. Guests can golf on an 18-hole course and watch polo matches while they take afternoon tea at the St. Ann Polo Club, Drax Hall.

WHERE TO DINE

EXPENSIVE

The Casanova. In the Sans Souci Lido, along Rte. A3, 3 miles east of Ocho Rios. ☎ **809/974-2353.** Nonresident evening pass of $75 per person includes dinner (Tues and Fri a beach buffet), entertainment, and drinks. AE, DC, MC, V. Daily 7–9:30pm. INTERNATIONAL.

The suave Casanova is one of the most elegant enclaves along the north coast, a super choice when you feel like dressing up and hitting the high spots. Meals are included for guests of course, but nonguests who purchase a pass (see above) can also dine here and be entertained as well. All drinks are included. Jazz wafting in from a lattice-roofed gazebo might accompany your meal.

In the late 1960s, Harry Cipriani (of Harry's Bar fame in Venice) taught the staff some of his culinary techniques, and a little more care seems to go into the cuisine here, as opposed to the mass-market chow-downs at some of the other all-inclusives. The pasta is made fresh daily, along with many of the other staples. Typical dishes include smoked chicken breast in a continental berry sauce as an appetizer, or a small vegetable mousse with a fontina cheese sauce. For your main course, you might prefer osso buco (braised veal shanks) or roast Cornish hen with citrus and mild spice. Desserts are sumptuous and might be followed by one of the house's four special coffees.

✪ **Plantation Inn Restaurant.** In the Plantation Inn, Main St. ☎ **809/974-5601.** Reservations required. Main courses $20–$35; three-course fixed-price $35. AE, DC, MC, V. Daily 7:30–10am, 12:30–1:30pm, 4:30–5:30pm (afternoon tea), and 7–10pm. JAMAICAN/CONTINENTAL.

You'll think you've arrived at Tara in *Gone With the Wind.* An evening here offers one of the most romantic experiences in Ocho Rios as you dine and dance by candlelight. The continental cuisine is spiced up a bit by Jamaican specialties. You're seated at beautifully laid tables with crisp linen, and after the dinner plates are cleared, a band plays for dancing. It's definitely the pampered life. The restaurant is divided into the indoor part (The Dining Room) and an outdoor section (Bougainvillea Terrace), with an annex, the Peacock Pavilion, a few steps away. Here, afternoon tea is served daily.

Appetizers are always spicy and tangy, our favorite being "Fire & Spice," which is a chicken and beef kebab with a ginger-pimiento sauce. For the main course, we always ask the chef to prepare a whole roast fish from the catch of the day. The always perfectly cooked fish is served boneless and seasoned with island herbs and spices. It's slowly roasted in the oven and presented with fresh country vegetables. Since the place attracts a lot of meat eaters, the chefs always prepare the classics, lamb chops Provençale and the like. The fixed-price menu featured every evening is also a good value. Opt for the banana cream pie for dessert, if featured—it's creamy and tasty.

Ruins Restaurant, Gift Shop, and Boutique. Turtle River, DaCosta Dr. ☎ **809/974-2442.** Reservations recommended. Main courses $12–$32. AE, DC, MC, V. Mon–Sat noon–2:30pm; daily 6–9:30pm. CHINESE/INTERNATIONAL/JAMAICAN.

Here you dine at the foot of waterfalls in the center of town. The falls are so inviting that they're a tourist attraction in their own right. In 1831 a British entrepreneur constructed a sugar mill on the site, using the powerful stream to drive his water wheels. Today, all that remains is a jumble of ruins, hence the restaurant's name. After you cross a covered bridge, perhaps stopping off for a drink at the bar in the outbuilding first, you find yourself in a fairyland where the only sounds come from the tree frogs, the falling water from about a dozen cascades, and the discreet clink of silver and china. Tables are set on a wooden deck leading all the way up to the pool at the foot of the falls, where moss and other vegetation line the stones at the base. At some point you may want to climb a flight of stairs to the top of the falls, where bobbing lanterns and the illuminated waters below afford one of the most delightful experiences on the island.

The only problem is that the setting is more dramatic than the cuisine. It's more "Chinese-American" than authentic regional Chinese—witness the several kinds of chow mein or chop suey and the sweet-and-sour pork. Lobster in a stir-fry is the house specialty. Dishes such as chicken Kiev try to justify the restaurant's "international" label, but that dish wouldn't be allowed out of the Russian Tea Room's kitchen in New York. Your best bet is to stick with the vegetarian dishes, which aren't bad.

MODERATE

✪ **Almond Tree Restaurant.** In the Hibiscus Lodge Hotel, 87 Main St. ☎ **809/974-2813.** Reservations recommended. Main courses $12.50–$36. AE, DC, MC, V. Daily 7am–2:30pm and 6–9:30pm. INTERNATIONAL.

The food, drink, reasonable prices, and casual cool keep them coming back night after night. Aptly, the Almond Tree is a two-tiered patio restaurant with a tree growing through its roof. It overlooks the Caribbean at the previously recommended resort (three blocks from the Ocho Rios Mall). Lobster thermidor is the most delectable item on the menu and lobster Almond Tree is a specialty, but we prefer the bouillabaisse (made with conch and lobster). Also excellent are the roast suckling pig, medallions of beef Anne Palmer, and a fondue bourguignonne. Jamaican plantation rice is a local specialty. The wine list offers a variety of vintages, including Spanish and Jamaican. Have an apéritif in the unique "swinging bar" (with swinging chairs, that is).

✪ **Evita's Italian Restaurant.** Eden Bower Rd. ☎ **809/974-2333.** Reservations recommended. Main courses $8.60–23.10. AE, MC, V. Daily 11am–11pm. ITALIAN.

Located a five-minute drive south of Ocho Rios, this restaurant is set in a hillside residential neighborhood with a panoramic view of the city's harbor. The premier Italian restaurant of Ocho Rios, this is also one of the most fun restaurants along the north coast of Jamaica. Its soul and artistic flair come from Eva Myers, the convivial former owner of some of the most legendary bars of Montego Bay. She established her culinary headquarters in this white, gingerbread-trimmed Jamaican house in 1990. An outdoor terrace offers additional seating and enhanced views. Even if the cuisine isn't as extraordinary as Evita claims, it's still pretty good. More than half the menu is devoted to pastas, and the selection includes almost every variety known in northern and southern Italy. If you don't want pasta, the fish dishes are excellent, especially the snapper stuffed with crabmeat and the lobster and scampi in a buttery white cream sauce. Italian (or other) wines by the bottle might accompany your menu choice. The restaurant lies a few steps from the Enchanted Garden, an all-inclusive resort.

INEXPENSIVE

Little Pub Restaurant. 59 Main St. ☎ **809/974-2324.** Reservations recommended. Main courses $13–$28. AE, MC, V. Daily 7am–midnight. JAMAICAN/INTERNATIONAL.

It's a bit contrived and a little too touristy for our tastes, but yet has undeniable appeal both for visitors and locals. Located in a redbrick courtyard with a fountain and a waterfall, this spot is surrounded by souvenir shops in the center of town. The indoor-outdoor pub's centerpiece is a restaurant in the dinner-theater style. Top local and international artists are featured, as are Jamaican musical plays. No one will mind if you just enjoy a drink while seated on one of the pub's barrel chairs. But if you want dinner, proceed to one of the linen-covered tables topped with fresh cut flowers and candles. Menu items include very familiar fare (too familiar, say some critics), and that means grilled kingfish, stewed snapper, barbecued chicken, and the inevitable and overpriced lobster. The cookery is competent, but it's all very casual here. Come for the convivial atmosphere rather than for the food.

Parkway Restaurant. 60 DaCosta Dr. ☎ **809/974-2667.** Main courses $8–$20. AE, MC, V. Daily 8am–11:30pm. JAMAICAN.

Come here to eat as Jamaicans eat. This popular spot in the commercial center of town couldn't be plainer or more unpretentious, but it's always packed. Local families and businessmen know they can get some of Ocho Rios's best-tasting and least expensive local dishes here. It's the local watering and drinking joint and is a bit disdainful of all those Sandals and Couples resorts with their contrived international food. Hungry diners are fed Jamaican-style chicken, curried goat, sirloin steak, and fillet of red snapper, and to top it off, banana cream pie. Lobster and fresh fish are usually featured. The food is straightforward, honest, and affordable.

Double V Jerk Centre. 109 Main St. ☎ **809/974-5998.** Jerk pork or chicken, J$300–J$460 ($8.40–$12.90) per pound. No credit cards. Mon–Sat 8:30am–1:30am. JERK/JAMAICAN.

When the moon is full and only the fiery taste of Jamaican jerk seasonings can ease your stomach growls, head here, and don't dress up. Set on Ocho Rios' main commercial boulevard, about a three-minute drive east of the town center, this place serves up the best jerked pork and chicken in town. Don't expect anything fancy. Just come for platters of meat that can be sold in quarter-pound or half-pound portions, depending on your appetite. Vegetables, salad, and fried breadfruit come with your main course, and everyone's preferred lubricant seems to be a frosty Red Stripe. Although lots of local office workers and shopkeepers come here at lunch, the place is especially lively after 10pm, when live music transforms it into the closest approximation of a singles bar in town.

BEACHES & SPORTS

BEACHES The most idyllic sands are found at the often-overcrowded **Mallards Beach,** shared by hotel guests and cruise-ship passengers, but locals may steer you to the white sands of **Turtle Beach** in the south.

GOLF **SuperClub's Runaway Golf Club,** at Runaway Bay near Ocho Rios on the north coast (☎ **809/973-2561**), charges no fee to guests who stay at any of Jamaica's affiliated SuperClubs. For nonguests, the price is $58 year-round. Players can rent carts and clubs.

The **Manchester Country Club,** Brumalia Road (☎ **809/962-2403**), is Jamaica's oldest golf course, but has only nine greens. Beautiful vistas unfold from 2,201 feet above sea level. Greens fees are $12.50, and caddy fees run $4 for 18 holes. The course has a clubhouse.

The Sandals Golf & Country Club (☎ **809/975-0119**), lying a 15-minute ride from the center of the resort, is a 6,500-yard course, known for its panoramic scenery some 700 feet above sea level. The 18-hole, par-71 course was designed by P. K. Saunders and opened in 1951 as the Upton Golf Club. Rolling terrain, lush vegetation, and flowers and fruit trees dominate the 120-acre course. A putting green and driving range are available for those who wish to hone their skills before challenging the course. Sandals guests play free; otherwise, the cost is $50 for 9 holes or $70 for 18 holes.

TENNIS **Ciboney Ocho Rios,** Main Street, Ocho Rios (☎ **809/974-1027**), focuses more on tennis than any other resort in the area. It offers three clay-surface and three hard-surface courts, all lit for nighttime play. Residents play free either day or night, but nonresidents must call and make arrangements with the manager. A pro on-site offers lessons for $15 an hour. Ciboney also sponsors twice-a-day clinics for both beginners and advanced players. Frequent guest tournaments are also staged, including handicapped doubles and mixed doubles.

SEEING THE SIGHTS

A pleasant drive south of Ocho Rios along Route A3 will take you inland through **Fern Gully.** This was originally a riverbed, but now the main road winds up some 700 feet among a profusion of wild ferns, a tall rain forest, hardwood trees, and lianas. There are hundreds of varieties of ferns, and roadside stands offer fruit and vegetables, carved-wood souvenirs, and basketwork. The road runs for about 4 miles, and then at the top of the hill you come to a right-hand turn onto a narrow road leading to Golden Grove.

Head west when you see the signs pointing to Lydford. You'll pass the remains of **Edinburgh Castle,** built in 1763, the lair of one of Jamaica's most infamous murderers, a Scot named Lewis Hutchinson, who used to shoot passersby and toss their bodies into a deep pit. The authorities got wind of his activities, and although he tried to escape by canoe, he was captured by the navy under the command of Admiral Rodney and was hanged. Rather proud of his achievements (evidence of at least 43 murders was found), he left £100 and instructions for a memorial to be built. It never was, but the castle ruins remain.

Continue north on Route A1 to **St. Ann's Bay,** the site of the first Spanish settlement on the island, where you can see the **statue of Christopher Columbus,** cast in his hometown of Genoa and erected near St. Ann's Hospital on the west side of town, close to the coast road. There are a number of Georgian buildings in the town—the **Court House** near the parish church, built in 1866, is the most interesting.

Brimmer Hall Estate. Port Maria, St. Mary's. ☎ **809/974-2244.** Tours $15. Tours given Thurs at 2pm.

Some 21 miles east of Ocho Rios, in the hills 2 miles from Port Maria, this 1817 estate is an ideal place to spend a day. You can relax beside the pool and sample a wide variety of brews and concoctions. The Plantation Tour Eating House offers typical Jamaican dishes for lunch, and there's a souvenir shop with a good selection of ceramics, art, straw goods, wood carvings, rums, liqueurs, and cigars. All this is on a working plantation where you're driven around in a tractor-drawn jitney to see the tropical fruit trees and coffee plants and learn from the knowledgeable guides about the various processes necessary to produce the fine fruits of the island.

Coyaba River Garden and Museum. Shaw Park Rd. ☎ **809/974-6235.** Admission $4.50 ages 13 and up, free for children 12 and under. Daily 8:30am–5pm. Take the Fern Gully–Kingston road, turn left at St. John's Anglican Church, and follow the signs to Coyaba, just half a mile farther.

A mile from the center of Ocho Rios, at an elevation of 420 feet, this park and museum were built on the grounds of the former Shaw Park plantation. The word *coyaba* comes from the Arawak name for paradise. Coyaba is a Spanish-style museum with a river and gardens filled with native flora, a cut-stone courtyard, fountains, and a crafts shop and bar. The museum boasts a collection of artifacts from the Arawak, Spanish, and English settlements in the area.

✪ **Dunn's River Falls.** On Rte. A3. ☎ **809/974-2857.** Admission $6 adults, $3 children 2–12, free for children under 2. Daily 9am–5pm (8am–5pm on cruise-ship arrival days). From St. Ann's Bay, follow Route A3 east back to Ocho Rios and you'll pass Dunn's River Falls; there's plenty of parking.

For a charge, you can relax on the beach or climb with a guide to the top of the 600-foot falls. You can splash in the waters at the bottom of the falls or drop into the cool pools higher up between the cascades of water. The beach restaurant provides snacks and drinks, and dressing rooms are available. If you're planning to climb the falls, wear old tennis shoes to protect your feet from the sharp rocks and to prevent slipping.

Firefly. Grants Pen, in St. Mary, 20 miles east of Ocho Rios above Oracabessa. ☎ **809/997-7201.** Admission $10. Daily 9am–5:30pm.

Firefly was the home of Sir Noël Coward and his longtime companion, Graham Payn, who, as executor of Coward's estate, donated it to the Jamaica National Heritage Trust. The recently restored house is more or less as it was on the day Sir Noël died in 1973. His Hawaiian print shirts still hang in the closet of his austere bedroom, with its mahogany four-poster. The library contains a collection of his books, and the living room is warm and comfortable, with big armchairs and two grand pianos (where he composed several famous tunes). When the Queen Mother was entertained here, the lobster mousse Coward was serving melted, so, with a style and flair that was the stuff of legend, he opened a can of pea soup instead. Guests were housed at Blue Harbour, a villa closer to Port Maria, and included Evelyn Waugh, Sir Winston Churchill, Errol Flynn, Laurence Olivier, Vivien Leigh, Claudette Colbert, Katharine Hepburn, and Mary Martin. Paintings by the noted playwright, actor, author, and composer adorn the walls. An open patio looks out over the pool and the sea, and across the lawn, on his plain, flat white marble gravestone is inscribed simply: "Sir Noël Coward, born December 16, 1899, died March 26, 1973."

Goldeneye. Oracabessa, 13 miles east of Ocho Rios. ☎ **809/974-5833.**

Noël Coward was a frequent guest of Ian Fleming's at Goldeneye, an estate made fashionable in the 1950s. It was here that the most famous secret agent in the world, 007, was born in 1952. Fleming built the house in 1946, and wrote each of the 13 original Bond books here. Through the large gates, with bronze pineapples on the top, came a host of international celebrities: Evelyn Waugh, Truman Capote, and Graham Greene, to name a few. The house was closed and dilapidated for some time after the writer's death, but its present owner, music publisher Christopher Blackwell, has restored the property. Although Fleming kept the place "just back to the basics," Blackwell sought the help of a designer to revamp the interior. Fleming's original desk, where 007 was born, remains, however. Unless you're a guest of the tenant, you aren't allowed to visit, as it's private property. However, all 007 fans in this part of the world like to go by, hoping for a look. Look for the Esso sign and take the narrow lane nearby going toward the sea. Since you can't go inside Goldeneye, you can settle for a swim on James Bond Beach.

Harmony Hall/The Garden Café. Tower Isles on Rte A3, 4 miles east of Ocho Rios. ☎ **809/975-4222.** Free admission. Gallery, Mon–Sat 10am–6pm, restaurant and cafe, daily 10am–10pm.

Harmony Hall was built near the end of the 19th century as the centerpiece of a sugar plantation. Today it has been restored and is now the focal point of an art gallery and restaurant that showcases the painting and sculpture of Jamaican artists as well as a tasteful array of arts and crafts. Among the featured gift items are Sharon McConnell's Starfish Oils, which contain natural additives harvested in Jamaica. The gallery shop also carries the "Reggae to Wear" line of sportswear, designed and made on Jamaica.

The Garden Café, which is also known as Alexander's after its co-owner, serves Jamaican cuisine as part of full evening meals priced at J$550 to J$900 ($15.40 to $25.20). The food is full of flavor with an authentic taste that may not be to everybody's liking. If you prefer to stop just for a cup of tea and a slice of homemade cake, it will cost about J$100 ($2.80).

Prospect Plantation. On Rte. A3, 3 miles east of Ocho Rios, in St. Ann. ☎ **809/994-1058.** Tours $12 adults, free for children 12 and under; one-hour horseback ride $20. Tours given Mon–Sat at 10:30am, 2pm, and 3:30pm; Sun at 11am, 1:30pm, and 3pm.

This working plantation adjoins the 18-hole Prospect Mini Golf Course. A visit to this property is an educational, relaxing, and enjoyable experience. On your leisurely ride by covered jitney through the scenic beauty of Prospect, you'll readily see why this section of Jamaica is called "the garden parish of the island." You can view the many trees planted by such visitors as Sir Winston Churchill, Dr. Henry Kissinger, Charlie Chaplin, Pierre Trudeau, Sir Noël Coward, and many others. You'll learn about and observe pimento (allspice), bananas, cassava, sugarcane, coffee, cocoa, coconut, pineapple, and the famous leucaena "Tree of Life." You'll see Jamaica's first hydroelectric plant and sample some of the exotic fruit and drinks.

Horseback riding is available on three scenic trails at Prospect. The rides vary from 1 to 2¼ hours. Advance booking of 1 hour is necessary to reserve horses.

SHOPPING

For many, Ocho Rios provides an introduction to shopping Jamaica style. After surviving the ordeal, some visitors may vow never to go shopping again. Literally hundreds of Jamaicans pour into Ocho Rios hoping to peddle something, often something they made, to cruise-ship passengers and other visitors. Be prepared for aggressive vendors. Pandemonium greets many an unwary shopper, who must also be prepared for some fierce haggling. Every vendor asks too much for an item at first, which gives them the leeway to "negotiate" until the price reaches a more realistic level. Is shopping fun in Ocho Rios? A resounding no. Do cruise-ship passengers and land visitors indulge in it anyway? A decided yes.

THE CENTERS & MALLS

There are seven main shopping plazas. We've listed them because they're here, not because we heartily recommend them. The originals are Ocean Village, Pineapple Place, and Coconut Grove. Newer ones include the New Ocho Rios Plaza, in the center of town, with some 60 shops. Island Plaza is another major shopping complex, as is the Mutual Security Plaza with some 30 shops. Opposite the New Ocho Rios Plaza is the Taj Mahal, with 26 duty-free stores.

Ocean Village Shopping Centre This shopping area contains numerous boutiques, food stores, a bank, sundries purveyors, travel agencies, service facilities, and what have you. The **Ocho Rios Pharmacy** (☎ **809/974-2398**) sells most proprietary brands, perfumes, and suntan lotions, among its many wares. You can call the shopping center at ☎ 809/974-2683.

Pineapple Place Shopping Centre Just east of Ocho Rios, this is a collection of shops in cedar-shingle-roofed cottages set amid tropical flowers.

Ocho Rios Craft Park This is a complex of some 150 stalls through which to browse. An eager seller will weave you a hat or a basket while you wait, or you can buy from the mixture of ready-made hats, hampers, handbags, place mats, and lampshades. Other stands stock hand-embroidered goods and will make small items while you wait. Wood carvers work on bowls, ashtrays, wooden-head carvings, and statues chipped from lignum vitae, and make cups from local bamboo.

Coconut Grove Shopping Plaza This collection of low-lying shops is linked by walkways and shrubs. The merchandise consists mainly of local craft items. Many of your fellow shoppers may be cruise-ship passengers.

Island Plaza This shopping complex is right in the heart of Ocho Rios. You can find some of the best Jamaican art here, all paintings by local artists. You can also purchase local handmade crafts (be prepared to do some haggling over price and quality), carvings, ceramics, even kitchenware, and most definitely the inevitable T-shirts.

SPECIALTY SHOPS

In general, the shopping is better in Montego Bay if you're going there. If not, wander the Ocho Rios crafts markets, although much of the merchandise has the same monotony. Among the places that deserve special mention are those listed below: **Casa dé Oro,** Soni's Mall, 19 Soni's Plaza (☎ **809/974-5392**), specializes in selling duty-free watches, fine jewelry, and the classic perfumes. **Swiss Stores,** in the

Ocean Village Shopping Centre (☎ **809/974-2519**), sells all the big names in Swiss watches, including Juvenia, Tissot, Omega, Rolex, Patek Philippe, and Piaget. And here, the Rolex watches are real, not those fakes touted by hustlers on the streets of Ocho Rios. The Swiss outlet also sells duty-free handcrafted jewelry, some of dubious taste but some really exquisite jewelry as well.

One of the best bets for shopping is **Soni's Plaza,** 50 Main Street, the address of all the shops recommended below. **Bollomongo** (☎ **809/974-7318**) has one of the island's widest selection of T-shirts, often in screen-printed designs. Bob Marley appears on many of them, and you can even get Bob Marley beach towels. Swimwear such as "Sharkbite," is also sold. **Chulani's** (☎ **809/974-2421**) sells a goodly assortment of quality watches and brand-name perfumes, although some of the leather bags might tempt you as well. Jewelry is set in a wide variety of 14-karat and 18-karat settings with diamonds, emeralds, rubies, and sapphires.

Gem Palace (☎ **809/974-2850**) is the place to go for diamond ring solitaires and tennis bracelets. The shop specializes in 14-karat gold chains and bracelets. **Taj Gift Centre** (☎ **809/974-9268**) has a little bit of everything: Blue Mountain coffee, film, Jamaican cigars, and hand-embroidered linen tablecloths. For something different, look for Jamaican jewelry made from hematite, a mountain stone.

Mohan's (☎ **809/974-9270**) offers one of the best selections of 14-karat and 18-karat gold chains, rings, bracelets, and earrings in Ocho Rios. Jewelry studded with precious gems such as diamonds and rubies are peddled here as well. **Soni's** (☎ **809/974-2303**) dazzles here with gold, but also cameras, French perfumes, watches, china and crystal, linen tablecloths, and even the standard Jamaican souvenirs. **Tajmahal** (☎ **809/974-6455**) beats most competition with its name-brand watches, jewelry, and fragrances. It also has Paloma Picasso leather wear and porcelain by Lladro.

If you'd like to avoid the hassle of the markets but still find some local handcrafts or art, head for **Beautiful Memories,** 9 Island Plaza (☎ **809/974-2374**), which has a limited but representative sampling of Jamaican art, as well as an exhibit of local crafts, pottery, woodwork, and hand-embroidered items.

OCHO RIOS AFTER DARK

Hotels often provide live entertainment to which nonresidents are invited. Ask at your hotel desk where "the action" is on any given night. Otherwise, you may want to look in on **Silks Discothèque,** in the Shaw Park Hotel, Cutlass Bay (☎ **809/974-2552**), which has a smallish dance floor and a sometimes-animated crowd of drinkers and dancers. If you're not a guest of the hotel, you can enter for an all-inclusive price of $25.

6 Port Antonio

Port Antonio is a verdant and sleepy seaport on the northeast coast of Jamaica, 63 miles northeast of Kingston. It has been called the Jamaica of 100 years ago. Port Antonio is the mecca of the titled and the wealthy, including European royalty and stars like Whoopi Goldberg, Peter O'Toole, and Tommy Tune.

This small, bustling town is like many on the island: clean but untidy, with sidewalks around a market filled with vendors; tin-roofed shacks competing with old Georgian and modern brick and concrete buildings. The market is a place to browse for local craftwork, spices, and fruits.

In other days visitors arrived by banana boat and stayed at the Titchfield Hotel (which burned down) in a lush, tropical, unspoiled part of the island. Captain Bligh landed here in 1793 with the first breadfruit plants, and Port Antonio claims that the ones grown in this area are the best on the island. Visitors still arrive by water, but now it's in cruise ships that moor close to Navy Island, and the passengers come ashore just for the day.

Navy Island and the long-gone Titchfield Hotel were owned for a short time by film star Errol Flynn. The story is that after suffering damage to his yacht, he put into Kingston for repairs, visited Port Antonio by motorbike, fell in love with the area, and in due course acquired Navy Island (some say he got it in a gambling game). Later, he either lost or sold it and bought a nearby plantation, Comfort Castle, still owned by his widow, Patrice Wymore Flynn, who spends most of her time there. He was much loved and admired by the Jamaicans and was totally integrated into the community. They still talk of him in Port Antonio—his reputation for womanizing and drinking lives on.

WHERE TO STAY

VERY EXPENSIVE

✪ **Trident Villas & Hotel.** Rte. A4 (P.O. Box 119), Port Antonio, Jamaica, W.I. ☎ **809/993-2602.** Fax 809/993-2960. 8 rms, 18 suites. A/C TV TEL . Winter, $385 double; $620 suite. Off-season, $220 double; $340 suite. Rates include MAP. AE, MC, V.

This elegant rendezvous of the rich and famous is about 2 1/2 miles east of Port Antonio along Allan Avenue, on the coast toward Frenchman's Cove. It's one of the most tasteful and refined hotels on the north shore. Sitting regally above jagged coral cliffs with a seaside panorama, it's the personal and creative statement of Earl Levy, scion of a prominent Kingston family. Nearby he has erected a multimillion-dollar replica of a European château, known as Trident Castle, which can be rented as one unit. Here, guests are grandly housed in eight large bedrooms beautifully furnished in plantation style.

The hotel's main building is furnished with antiques, and flowers decorate the lobby, which is cooled by sea breezes. Your accommodations will be a studio cottage or tower, reached by a pathway through the gardens. In a cottage, a large bedroom with ample sitting area opens onto a private patio with a view of the sea. All cottages and tower rooms have ceiling fans and plenty of storage space. Jugs of ice and water are constantly replenished. Solo travelers are accommodated in either junior or deluxe villa suites, whereas two or three guests are lodged in junior, deluxe villa, prime minister's, or imperial suites. There's a small private sand beach, and the gardens surround a pool and a gingerbread gazebo. Lounges, tables, chairs, and bar service add to your pleasure.

Dining/Entertainment: The main building has two patios, one covered, where breakfast and lunch are served. You can also have breakfast on your private patio, served by your own butler. At dinner, when men are required to wear jackets and ties, silver service, crystal, and Port Royal pewter sparkle on the tables. Dinner is a multicourse fixed-price meal, so if you have dietary restrictions, make your requirements known early.

Services: Room service, laundry, baby-sitting.

Facilities: Swimming pool, tennis, horseback riding, and such water sports as sailing and snorkeling.

EXPENSIVE

Fern Hill Club. Mile Gully Rd., San San (P.O. Box 100), Port Antonio, Jamaica, W.I. ☎ **809/993-3222.** Fax 809/993-7373. 31 units. A/C TV. Winter, $300 double; $330 suite for 2. Off-season, $209–$220 double; $231–$253 suite for 2. Rates are all-inclusive. AE, MC, V. Drive east along Allan Ave. and watch for the signs.

Attractive, airy, and panoramic, Fern Hill occupies 20 forested acres high above the coastline, attracting primarily a British and Canadian clientele. The accommodations come in a wide range of configurations, including standard rooms, junior suites, spa suites, and villas with cooking facilities. This is a far less elegant choice than its main competitor, Goblin Hill (see below). Technically classified as a private club, the establishment is comprised of a colonial-style clubhouse and three outlying villas, plus a comfortable annex at the bottom of the hill. The accommodations are highly private and attract many honeymooners. Many of the rooms are rather bland, and there is no air-conditioning.

Dining/Entertainment: There is the Blue Mahoe Bar and a patio for dining. The hotel restaurant offers an international menu (see "Where to Dine," below).

Services: A shuttle bus making daily trips down the steep hillside to the beach.

Facilities: Three swimming pools, tennis court.

Goblin Hill Villas at San San. San San (P.O. Box 26), Port Antonio, Jamaica, W.I. ☎ **809/993-3286,** or 809/925-8108 in Kingston for reservations. Fax 809/925-6248. 28 villas. Winter, $110–$195 one-bedroom villa; $185–$245 two-bedroom villa. Off-season, $90–$165 one-bedroom villa; $145–$195 two-bedroom villa. Rates include transfers and rental car. AE, MC, V.

This green and sun-washed hillside (once said to shelter goblins) is now filled with Georgian-style vacation homes on San San Estate. The swimming pool is surrounded by a vine-laced arbor, which lies just a stone's throw from an almost-impenetrable forest. A long flight of steps leads down to the crescent-shaped sands of San San beach. This beach is now private, but guests of the hotel receive a pass. The accommodations are town-house style, and some units have ceiling fans and king-size beds, but no phones or TVs. Housekeepers prepare and serve meals and attend to chores in the villas. There is also a restaurant and bar on the premises, serving a rather good international/Jamaican menu.

Facilities: Two Laykold tennis courts, beach, swimming pool. Dragon Bay, about a 5- to 10-minute drive away, offers a variety of water sports, including snorkeling, windsurfing, and scuba diving.

MODERATE

Jamaica Palace. Williamsfield (P.O. Box 277), Port Antonio, Jamaica, W.I. ☎ **800/423-4095** in the U.S., or 809/993-2021. Fax 809/993-3459. 21 rms, 52 junior suites, 6 full suites, 1 imperial suite. A/C TEL. Winter, $130–$160 double; $190–$325 suite. Off-season, $115–$145 double; $170–$290 suite. MAP $45 per person extra. MC, V. Head 1 mile east on Allan Ave.

Rising like a stately mansion from a hillock surrounded by five tropically landscaped acres, this hotel opened in 1989. Its owner, German-born Siglinde von Stephani-Fahmi, set out to combine the elegance of a European hotel with the relaxed atmosphere of a Jamaican resort. The public rooms are filled with furnishings and art from Europe, including a six-foot Baccarat crystal candelabrum and a pair of Italian ebony-and-ivory chairs from the 15th century. Outside, the Palace offers white marble columns, sun-filled patios and balconies, and an unusual 114-foot swimming pool shaped like the island of Jamaica.

Most accommodations are large, with 12½-foot ceilings and oversize marble bathrooms. Some, however, are rather small but still elegantly furnished. Suites are individually furnished with crystal chandeliers, Persian rugs, and original works of art. TV is available upon request.

Dining/Entertainment: Both continental and Jamaican food are served in the main dining room with its lighted "waterwall" sculpted from Jamaican cave stones. Men are requested to wear jackets and ties. There's also a poolside cafe with a barbecue area. Live dance music and calypso bands are featured.

Services: Room service, laundry, baby-sitting, massage facilities, fashion boutique (operated by Patrice Wymore Flynn, widow of Errol Flynn), complimentary shuttle service to private San San Beach to which hotel guests are admitted.

Facilities: Swimming pool.

Navy Island Marina Resort. Navy Island (P.O. Box 188), Port Antonio, Jamaica, W.I. ☎ **809/993-2667.** 1 rm, 9 villas. Year-round, $80 double; $100 double in one-bedroom villa, $140 triple in one-bedroom villa; $180 triple in two-bedroom villa, $200 quad in two-bedroom villa. Children under 12 free in parents' room. MC, V.

Jamaica's only private island getaway, this resort and marina is on that "bit of paradise" once owned by actor Errol Flynn. Today this cottage colony and yacht club is one of the best-kept travel secrets in the Caribbean. To reach the resort, you'll have to take a ferry from the dockyards of Port Antonio on West Street for a short ride across one of the most beautiful and convoluted harbors of Jamaica.

Each accommodation is designed as a studio cottage or villa branching out from the main club. Ceiling fans and trade winds keep the cottages cool, and mosquito netting over the beds adds a plantation touch.

One of the resort's beaches is a secluded clothing-optional stretch of sand known as Trembly Knee Cove. You can also explore the island, whose grounds are dotted with hybrid hibiscus, bougainvillea, and palms (many of which were originally ordered planted by Flynn himself).

Dining/Entertainment: At night, after enjoying drinks in the HMS *Bounty* Bar, guests can dine in the Navy Island Restaurant. A five-course dinner is served nightly.

Services: Free ferry service.

Facilities: Swimming pool, two beaches, water sports (including scuba diving and windsurfing).

WHERE TO DINE

All hotels welcome outside guests for dinner, but reservations are required.

Fern Hill Club. Mile Gully Rd. ☎ **809/993-3222.** Reservations recommended. Fixed-price meal $10 at lunch, $30 at dinner. AE, MC, V. Daily 7:30am–9:30pm. Head east on Allan Ave. INTERNATIONAL/JAMAICAN.

One of the finest dining spots in Port Antonio, this restaurant has a sweeping view of the rugged coastline. Sunset watching here is the best in the area. Well-prepared specialties are served: jerk chicken, jerk pork, grilled lobster, and Creole fish. Depending on who's in the kitchen at night, the food here can be quite satisfactory, though once in a while, especially off-season, the cuisine might be a bit of a letdown. The club is also a venue for entertainment, with a calypso band and piano music during the week, and disco music on weekends.

✪ **Trident Hotel Restaurant.** On Rte. A4. ☎ **809/993-2602.** Reservations required. Jackets and ties required for men. Fixed-price dinner $44. AE, MC, V. Daily 8am–4pm and 8–10pm. Head east on Allan Ave. INTERNATIONAL.

Trident Hotel Restaurant has long been sought out by travelers in search of fine cuisine on Jamaica. Part of the main hotel building, the restaurant has an air of elegance. The high-pitched wooden roof set on white stone walls holds several ceiling fans that gently stir the air. The antique tables are set with old china, English silver, and Port Royal pewter. The formally dressed waiters will help you choose your wine and whisper the name of each course as they serve it: Jamaican salad, coconut soup, dolphin (fish) with mayonnaise-and-mustard sauce, steak with broccoli and sautéed potatoes, and peach Melba and Blue Mountain coffee with Tía Maria, a Jamaican liqueur. The six-course dinner menu is changed every day. The cuisine is always fresh and prepared with first-class ingredients, though the setting and the white-gloved service are generally more memorable than the food. Tip at your discretion.

Yachtsman's Wharf. 16 West St. ☎ **809/993-3053.** Reservations not required. Main courses $6–$13. No credit cards. Daily 7:30am–10pm. INTERNATIONAL.

This restaurant beneath a thatch-covered roof is at the end of an industrial pier, near the departure point for ferries to Navy Island. The rustic bar and restaurant is a favorite of the expatriate yachting set. Crews from many of the ultraexpensive yachts have dined here and have pinned their ensigns on the roughly textured planks and posts. It opens for breakfast and stays open all day. Menu items include the usual array of tropical drinks, burgers, seafood ceviche, curried chicken, and ackee with saltfish. Main dishes include vegetables. Come here for the setting, the camaraderie, and the good times; the food is only secondary.

BEACHES & OUTDOOR PURSUITS

BEACHES Port Antonio has several white-sand beaches, including the famous **San San Beach,** which has recently gone private, although guests of certain hotels can be admitted with a pass (see above). Some beaches are free and others charge for the use of facilities. **Boston Beach** is free and often has light surfing; there are picnic tables as well as a restaurant and snack bar. Before heading to this beach, stop nearby and get the makings for a picnic lunch at the most famous center for peppery jerk pork and chicken in Jamaica, the **Boston Jerk Centre,** in rustic shacks east of Port Antonio and the Blue Lagoon.

Also free is **Fairy Hill Beach** (Winnifred), with no changing rooms or showers. **Frenchman's Cove Beach** attracts a chic crowd to its white-sand beach with its freshwater stream. Nonhotel guests are charged a fee.

Navy Island, once Errol Flynn's personal hideaway, is a fine choice for swimming (one beach is clothing optional) and snorkeling (at **Crusoe's Beach**). Take the boat from the Navy Island dock on West Street, across from the Exxon station. It's a seven-minute ride to the island, a one-way fare costing 30¢. The ferry runs 24 hours a day. The island is the setting for the Navy Island Marina Resort (see "Where to Stay," above).

DEEP-SEA FISHING Northern Jamaican waters are world renowned for their game fish, including dolphin, wahoo, blue and white marlin, sailfish, tarpon, Allison tuna, barracuda, and bonito. The Jamaica International Fishing Tournament and Jamaica International Blue Marlin Team Tournaments run concurrently at Port Antonio every September or October. Most major hotels from Port Antonio to Montego Bay have deep-sea-fishing facilities, and there are many charter boats.

A 30-foot-long **sport-fishing boat** (☎ **809/993-3086**) with a tournament rig is available for charter rental. Taking out up to six passengers at a time, it charges $150 per half day or $280 per day, with crew, bait, tackle, and soft drinks included. It docks at Port Antonio's International Marina, off West Palm Avenue, in the center of town. Call for bookings.

RAFTING Rafting started on the Río Grande as a means of transporting bananas from the plantations to the waiting freighters. In 1871 a Yankee skipper, Lorenzo Dow Baker, decided that a seat on one of the rafts was better than walking, but it was not until Errol Flynn arrived that the rafts became popular as a tourist attraction. Flynn used to hire the craft for his friends, and he encouraged the rafters to race down the Río Grande. Bets were placed on the winner. Now that bananas are transported by road, the raft skipper makes one or maybe two trips a day down the waterway. If you want to take a raft trip, **Río Grande Attractions Limited,** c/o Rafter's Restaurant, St. Margaret's Bay (☎ **809/993-2778**), can arrange it for you.

The rafts, some 33 feet long and only 4 feet wide, are propelled by stout bamboo poles. There's a raised double seat about two-thirds of the way back for the two passengers. The skipper stands in the front, trousers rolled up to his knees, the water washing his feet, and guides the craft down the lively river, about 8 miles between steep hills covered with coconut palms, banana plantations, and flowers, through limestone cliffs pitted with caves, through the "Tunnel of Love," a narrow cleft in the rocks, then on to wider, gentler water.

The day starts at the Rafter's Restaurant, west of Port Antonio, at Burlington on St. Margaret's Bay. Trips last 2 to 2½ hours and are offered from 8am to 4pm daily at a cost of $40 per raft, which is suitable for two people. From the Rafter's Restaurant, a fully insured driver will take you in your rented car to the starting point at Grants Level or Berrydale, where you board your raft. The trip ends at the Rafter's Restaurant, where you collect your car, which has been returned by the driver. If you feel like it, take a picnic lunch, but bring enough for the skipper, too, who will regale you with lively stories of life on the river.

EXPLORING THE SIGHTS

Athenry Gardens and Cave of Nonsuch. Portland. ☎ **809/993-3740.** Admission (including guide for gardens and cave) $5 adults, $2.50 children 11 and under. Daily 9am–5pm (last tour at 4:30pm). From Harbour St. in Port Antonio, turn south in front of the Anglican church onto Red Hassel Rd. and proceed approximately a mile to Breastworks community (fork in road); take the left fork, cross a narrow bridge, go immediately left after the bridge, and proceed approximately 3½ miles to the village of Nonsuch.

Twenty minutes from Port Antonio, it's an easy drive and an easy walk to see the stalagmites, stalactites, fossilized marine life, and evidence of Arawak civilization in Nonsuch. The cave is 1.5 million years old. From the Athenry Gardens, there are panoramic views over the island and the sea. The gardens are filled with coconut palms, flowers, and trees. Complete guided tours are given.

Crystal Springs. Buff Bay, Portland. ☎ **809/929-6280.** Admission J$100 ($2.80) adults, J$50 ($1.40) children. Daily 9am–5pm.

Crystal Springs is a tract of forested land whose borders were originally specified in 1655. Then it was attached to a nearby plantation whose Great House is now under separate (and private) ownership. Visitors, however, can trek through the organization's 156 acres of forest whose shelter is much beloved by bird- and wildlife. A simple restaurant is on the premises, as well as a series of cottages erected in the early 1990s. These are usually rented to visiting ornithologists who don't care for the amenities or distractions of a traditional resort.

Folly Great House. On the outskirts of Port Antonio on the way to Trident Village, going east along Rte. A4. Free admission.

This house was reputedly built in 1905 by Arthur Mitchell, an American millionaire, for his wife, Annie, daughter of Charles Tiffany, founder of the famous New York store. Sea water was used in the concrete mixtures of its foundations and mortar, and the house began to collapse only 11 years after they moved in. Because of the beautiful location, it's easy to see what a fine Great House it must have been. The house is currently being restored, largely through fund-raising efforts.

Somerset Falls. 8 miles west of Port Antonio, just past Hope Bay on Rte. A4. ☎ **809/926-2952.** Tour $3. Daily 9am–5pm.

Here the waters of the Daniels River pour down a deep gorge through a rain forest, with waterfalls and foaming cascades. You can take a short ride in an electric gondola to the hidden falls. A stop on the daily Grand Jamaica Tour from Ocho Rios, this is one of Jamaica's most historic sites; the falls were used by the Spanish before the English captured the island. At the falls, you can swim in the deep rock pools and buy sandwiches, light meals, soft drinks, beer, and liquor at the snack bar. The guided tour includes the gondola ride and a visit to both a cave and a freshwater fish farm.

7 Kingston

Kingston, the largest English-speaking city in the Caribbean, is the capital of Jamaica. It's home to a population of more than 650,000 people, including those living on the plains between Blue Mountain and the sea.

The buildings are a mixture of very modern, graceful, old, and just plain ramshackle. It's a busy city, as you might expect, with a natural harbor that's the seventh largest in the world. The University of the West Indies has its campus on the edge of the city. Kingston is Jamaica's cultural, industrial, financial, and political center.

WHERE TO STAY

Remember to ask if the 12% room tax is included in the rate quoted when you make your reservation. The rates listed below are year-round, unless otherwise noted. All leading hotels in security-conscious Kingston have guards.

✪ **Strawberry Hill.** Irish Town, Blue Mountains, Jamaica, W.I. ☎ **800/OUTPOST** or 809/944-8400. Fax 809/944-8408. 18 rms in one-, two-, and three-bedroom units. A/C. Winter (including continental breakfast), $306–$643 double. Off-season (without breakfast), $313–$490 double. AE, DC, MC, V. Guests are personally escorted to the hotel in a customized van or via a 7-minute helicopter ride. It's a 50-minute drive from the Kingston airport or 30 minutes via mountain roads from the center of the city.

The best place to stay in Kingston is *out* of Kingston. Strawberry Hill, in the Blue Mountains, lies 3,100 feet above the sea, overlooking this turbulent city, which seems far removed in this lush setting. A self-contained facility with its own power and water-purification system, Strawberry Hill has elaborate botanical gardens.

This cottage complex was built on the site of a Great House from the 1600s, which Hurricane Gilbert disposed of in 1988. The property was conceived by multimillionaire Chris Blackwell, the impresario who launched Bob Marley into reggae fame through Island Records. One former guest described this exclusive resort as a "home away from home for five-star Robinson Crusoes." Activities include coffee-plantation tours, hiking and mountain biking through the Blue Mountains, and even such spa services as massages.

Local craftspeople fashioned the cottages and furnished them in a classic plantation style, with canopied four-poster beds and louvered windows. In one case a doorway was carved with figures inspired by Madonna's book *Sex*.

Dining/Entertainment: The food is better than you'll find in Kingston, with such Jamaican dishes as curried cho-cho soup with grilled shrimp and fresh cilantro, or fresh grilled fish with jerk mango and sweet-pepper salsa. It's called "new Jamaican cuisine," and so it is.

Terra Nova Hotel. 17 Waterloo Rd., Kingston 10, Jamaica, W.I. ☎ **800/74-CHARMS** in the U.S. and Canada, or 809/926-2211. Fax 809/929-4933. 35 rms. A/C TV TEL. $165 double. AE, DC, MC, V.

This house is on the western edge of New Kingston, near West Kings House Road. Built in 1924 as a wedding present for a young bride, it has had a varied career. It

Climbing Blue Mountain

Jamaica has some of the most varied and unusual topography in the Caribbean, including a mountain range laced with rough rivers, streams, and waterfalls. The 192,000-acre **Blue Mountain–John Crow Mountain National Park** is maintained by the Jamaican government.

The mountainsides are covered with coffee fields, producing a blended version that's among the leading exports of Jamaica. But for the nature enthusiast, the mountains reveal an astonishingly complex series of ecosystems that change radically as you climb from sea level into the fog-shrouded peaks.

The most popular climb begins at Whitfield Hall, a high-altitude hostel and coffee estate about 6 miles from the hamlet of Mavis Bank. Reaching the summit of Blue Mountain Peak (3,000 feet above sea level) requires between five and six hours, each way. En route, hikers pass through acres of coffee plantations and forest, where temperatures are cooler (sometimes much cooler) than you might expect, and where high humidity encourages thick vegetation. Along the way, watch for an amazing array of bird life, including hummingbirds, many species of warblers, rufous-throated solitaires, yellow-bellied sapsuckers, and Greater Antillean pewees.

The best preparation against the wide ranges of temperature you'll encounter is to dress in layers and bring bottled water. If you opt for a 2am departure in anticipation of watching the sunrise from atop the peak, carry a flashlight as well. Sneakers are usually adequate, although many climbers bring their hiking boots to Jamaica solely in anticipation of their trek up Blue Mountain. Be aware that even during the "dry" season (from December to March), rainfall is common. During the "rainy" season (the rest of the year), these peaks can get up to 150 inches of rainfall a year, and fogs and mists are frequent.

Considering the social unrest in Jamaica and the tendency for hiking paths to be obscured by vegetation and tropical storms, it's a smart idea to hire a guide for your climb. We recommend **Sunventure Tours** (☎ **809/929-5694**) and **SENSE Adventures** (☎ **809/927-2097**). Depending on the time of departure (day or night) and the equipment that's included, the price of a guide for a trek up Blue Mountain ranges from $50 to $150 per person.

was once the family seat of the Myers rum dynasty and the birthplace and home of Christopher Blackwell, promoter of many Jamaican singers and musical groups, including Bob Marley and the Wailers. In 1959 the house was converted into a hotel, and, set in 2½ acres of gardens with a backdrop of greenery and mountains, it's now one of the best small Jamaican hotels, although the rooms are rather basic and not at all suited for those who want a resort ambience.

Most of the bedrooms are in a new wing. The Spanish-style El Dorado Room, with a marble floor, wide windows, and spotless linen, offers local and international food. Your à la carte breakfast is served on the coffee terrace, and there's a swimming pool at the front of the hotel, with a pool bar and grill.

In Nearby Port Royal

Morgan's Harbour Hotel & Beach Club. Port Royal, Kingston 1, Jamaica, W.I. ☎ **800/44-UTELL** in the U.S., or 809/967-8030. Fax 809/967-8073. 45 rms, 6 suites. A/C MINIBAR TV TEL. Year-round, $150 double; $170–$200 suite. AE, DC, MC, V. Take the public ferryboat that departs every 2 hours from near Victoria Pier on Ocean Blvd.; many visitors arrive by car or taxi, or else by the hotel's private boat from Victoria Pier.

The yachtie favorite, this hotel is in Port Royal, once believed to be the wickedest city on earth. Rebuilt after 1988's Hurricane Gilbert, Morgan's lies near the end of a long sandspit whose rocky and scrub-covered length shelters Kingston's harbor. On the premises is a 200-year-old redbrick building once used to melt pitch for His Majesty's navy, a swimming area defined by docks and buoys, and a series of wings whose eaves are accented with hints of gingerbread. Set on 22 acres of flat and rock-studded seashore, the resort contains a breezy waterfront restaurant called Henry Morgan's and a popular bar (where ghost stories about the old Port Royal seem especially lurid as the liquor flows on Friday night). Longtime residents quietly claim that the ghosts of soldiers killed by a long-ago earthquake are especially visible on hot and very calm days, when British formations seem to march out of the sea. The hotel also contains the largest marina facility in Kingston.

The hotel rents well-furnished bedrooms, each laid out in an 18th-century Chippendale-Jamaican motif. The Buccaneer Scuba Club is on-site, organizing dives to some of the 170-odd wrecks lying close to shore. Deep-sea-fishing charters and trips to outlying cays can also be arranged.

WHERE TO DINE

✪ **Blue Mountain Inn.** Gordon Town Rd. ☎ **809/927-1700.** Reservations required. Jackets required for men (ties optional). Dinner $18–$40, lunch $13–$20. AE, DC, MC, V. Mon–Fri noon–2pm; Mon–Sat 7–9:30pm. Head north on Old Hope Road into the mountains. CARIBBEAN/INTERNATIONAL.

About a 20-minute drive north from downtown Kingston is an 18th-century coffee plantation house set high on the slopes of Blue Mountain. Surrounded by trees and flowers, it rests on the bank of the Mammee River. On cold nights, log fires blaze, and the dining room gleams with silver and sparkling glass. The inn is one of Jamaica's most famous restaurants, not only for food but also for atmosphere and service. The effort of dressing up is worth it, and the cool night air justifies it; women are advised to take a wrap.

Ever since Olivia della Costa took over the restaurant in 1994, the cuisine has been considerably upgraded, especially the fresh seafood and vegetables from the gardens of Jamaica. It's not so old-fashioned in preparation any more, and menus change monthly. Top off your meal with one of the fresh fruit desserts or homemade ice creams.

SEEING THE SIGHTS

Even if you're staying at Ocho Rios or Port Antonio, you may want to visit Kingston for brief sightseeing and for trips to nearby Port Royal and Spanish Town.

IN TOWN One of the major attractions, **Devon House,** 26 Hope Rd. (☎ **809/929-7029**), was built in 1881 by George Stiebel, a Jamaican who became one of the first black millionaires in the Caribbean. He made his fortune mining in Latin America. A striking classical building, the house has been restored to its original beauty by the Jamaican National Trust. The grounds contain craft shops, boutiques, two restaurants, shops that sell the best ice cream in Jamaica (in exotic fruit flavors), and a bakery and pastry shop with Jamaican puddings and desserts. The main house also displays furniture of various periods and styles. Admission to the main house is $3, and it's open Tuesday to Saturday from 9:30am to 5pm. Admission to the grounds (the shops and restaurants) is free.

Almost next door to Devon House are the sentried gates of **Jamaica House,** residence of the prime minister, a fine, white-columned building set well back from the road.

Continuing along Hope Road, at the crossroads of Lady Musgrave and King's House roads, turn left and you'll see a gate on the left with its own personal traffic light. This leads to **King's House,** the official residence of the governor-general of Jamaica, the queen's representative on the island. The outside and front lawn of the gracious residence, set in 200 acres of well-tended parkland, is sometimes open to view Monday to Friday from 10am to 5pm. The secretarial offices are housed next door in an old wooden building set on brick arches. In front of the house is a gigantic banyan tree in whose roots, legend says, duppies (as ghosts are called in Jamaica) take refuge when they're not living in the cotton trees.

Between Old Hope and Mona roads, a short distance from the Botanical Gardens, is the **University of the West Indies (☎ 809/927-1660)**, built in 1948 on the Mona Sugar Estate. Ruins of old mills, storehouses, and aqueducts are juxtaposed with modern buildings on what must be the most beautifully situated campus in the world. The chapel, an old sugar-factory building, was transported stone by stone from Trelawny and rebuilt. The remains of the original sugar factory here are well preserved and give a good idea of how sugar was made in slave days.

The **National Library of Jamaica** (formerly the West India Reference Library), Institute of Jamaica, 12 East St. (**☎ 809/922-0620**), a storehouse of the history, culture, and traditions of Jamaica and the Caribbean, is the finest working library for West Indian studies in the world. It has the most comprehensive, up-to-date, and balanced collection of materials on the region, including books, newspapers, photographs, maps, and prints. Exhibits highlight different aspects of Jamaica and West Indian life. There's also a special exhibit of Arawak artifacts, including drawings, pictures, and diagrams of their life, plus flints and other artifacts that help you understand the early history of Jamaica. It's open Monday to Thursday from 9am to 5pm and on Friday from 9am to 4pm.

The **Bob Marley Museum** (formerly Tuff Gong Studio), 56 Hope Rd. (**☎ 809/927-9152**), is the most-visited sight in Kingston, but if you're not a Bob Marley fan it may not mean much to you. The clapboard house with its garden and high surrounding wall was the famous reggae singer's home and recording studio until his death. If you're interested, you can tour the singer's house and view assorted Marley memorabilia, and you might even catch a glimpse of his various children, who often frequent the grounds. The museum is open on Monday, Tuesday, Thursday, and Friday from 9:30am to 4:30pm and on Wednesday and Saturday from noon to 5:30pm. Admission is J$180 ($5.05) for adults, J$25 (70¢) for children 4 to 12, free for children 3 and under. It's reached by bus no. 70 or 75 from Halfway Tree, but take a cab to save yourself the hassle of dealing with Kingston public transport.

IN PORT ROYAL From West Beach Dock, Kingston, a ferry ride of 20 to 30 minutes will take you to Port Royal, which conjures up visions of swashbuckling pirates led by Henry Morgan, swilling grog in harbor taverns. This was once one of the largest trading centers of the New World, with a reputation for being the wickedest city on earth. Blackbeard stopped here regularly on his Caribbean trips. But the whole thing came to an end at 11:43am on June 7, 1692, when a third of the town disappeared underwater as the result of a devastating earthquake. Nowadays, Port Royal, with its memories of the past, has been designated by the government for redevelopment as a tourist destination.

Buccaneer Scuba Club, Morgan's Harbour, Port Royal, outside Kingston (**☎ 809/967-8030**), is one of Jamaica's leading dive and water sports operators. It offers a wide range of dive sites to accommodate various divers' tastes, from the incredible Texas Wreck to the unspoiled beauty of the Turtle Reef. PADI courses are also available. A wide array of water sports are offered, including waterskiing, body-boarding, ring-skiing, and even a banana boat ride. One-tank dives begin at $35, with a boat snorkeling trip costing $15, including equipment, for one hour.

As you drive along the Palisades, you arrive first at **St. Peter's Church.** It's usually closed, but you may persuade the caretaker, who lives opposite, to open it if you want to see the silver plate, said to be spoils captured by Henry Morgan from the cathedral in Panama. In the ill-kept graveyard is the tomb of Lewis Galdy, a Frenchman swallowed up and subsequently regurgitated by the 1692 earthquake.

Fort Charles (☎ 809/922-0620), the only one remaining of Port Royal's six forts, has withstood attack, earthquake, fire, and hurricane. Built in 1656 and later strengthened by Morgan for his own purposes, the fort was expanded and further armed in the 1700s, until its firepower boasted more than 100 cannons, covering both the land and the sea approaches. In 1779 Britain's naval hero, Horatio Lord Nelson, was commander of the fort and trod the wooden walkway inside the western parapet as he kept watch for the French invasion fleet. Scale models of the fort and ships of past eras are displayed. The fort is open daily from 9:30am to 4:30pm. There's an admission charge of $5.

Part of the complex, **Giddy House,** once the Royal Artillery storehouse, is another example of what the earth's movements can do. Walking across the tilted floor is an eerie and strangely disorienting experience.

IN SPANISH TOWN From 1662 to 1872 Spanish Town was the capital of the island. Originally founded by the Spaniards as Villa de la Vega, it was sacked by Cromwell's men in 1655, and all traces of Roman Catholicism were obliterated. The English cathedral, surprisingly retaining a Spanish name, **St. Jago de la Vega,** was built in 1666 and rebuilt after being destroyed by a hurricane in 1712. As you drive into the town from Kingston, the ancient cathedral, rebuilt in 1714, catches your eye with its brick tower and two-tiered wooden steeple, which was not added until 1831. Since the cathedral was built on the foundation and remains of the old Spanish church, it's half-English and half-Spanish, and displays two distinct styles: Romanesque and Gothic.

Of cruciform design and built mostly of brick, the cathedral is one of the most interesting buildings on the island. The black-and-white marble stones of the aisles are interspersed with ancient tombstones, and the walls are heavy with marble memorials that are almost a chronicle of Jamaica's history, dating back as far as 1662.

Beyond the cathedral, turn right and two blocks along you'll reach Constitution Street and the **Town Square.** This little square is surrounded by towering royal palms.

On the west side is old **King's House,** gutted by fire in 1925, although the facade has been restored. This was the residence of Jamaica's British governors until 1872 when the capital was transferred to Kingston. Many celebrated guests stayed here, among them Lord Nelson, Admiral Rodney, Captain Bligh of HMS *Bounty* fame, and William IV.

Beyond the house is the **Jamaica People's Museum of Craft & Technology,** Old King's House, Constitution Square (**☎ 809/922-0620**), open Monday to Thursday from 9am to 5pm and on Friday from 9am to 4pm. Admission is $4 for adults and $2 for children. The garden contains examples of old farm machinery, an old water mill wheel, a hand-turned sugar mill, a fire engine, and other items. An outbuilding displays a museum of crafts and technology, together with a number of smaller agricultural implements. In the small archaeological museum are old prints, models, and maps of the town's grid layout from the 1700s.

The streets around the old Town Square contain many fine Georgian town houses intermixed with tin-roofed shacks. Nearby is the **market,** so busy in the morning that you'll find it difficult, almost dangerous, to drive through. It provides, however, a bustling scene of Jamaican life.

8 Mandeville

The "English Town," Mandeville lies on a plateau more than 2,000 feet above the sea, in the tropical highlands. The commercial part of the town is small and is surrounded by a sprawling residential area popular with the large North American expatriate population (mostly involved with the bauxite-mining industry). Much cooler than the coastal resorts, it's a possible base from which to explore the entire island.

Shopping in the town is a pleasure, whether in the old center or in one of the modern complexes, such as Grove Court. The market in the center of town teems with life, particularly on weekends when the country folk bus into town for their weekly visit. The town has several interesting old buildings. The square-towered church built in 1820 has fine stained glass, and the little churchyard has an interesting history. The Court House, built in 1816, is a fine old Georgian stone-and-wood building with a pillared portico reached by a steep, sweeping double staircase. There's also Marshall's Pen, one of the Great Houses in Mandeville.

WHERE TO STAY

Hotel Astra. 62 Ward Ave., Mandeville, Jamaica, W.I. ☎ **809/962-3265.** 20 rms, 2 suites. TV TEL. $65 double; $150 suite. Rates include continental breakfast. AE, MC, V.

Our top choice for a stay in this area is the family-run Hotel Astra, operated by Diana McIntyre-Pike, known to her family and friends as Thunderbird. She's always coming to the rescue of guests, happily picking them up in her car and taking them around to see the sights. The rather spartan accommodations are mainly in two buildings.

Dining/Entertainment: The Country Fresh Restaurant offers excellent meals. Lunch or dinner is a choice of a homemade soup such as red pea or pumpkin, followed by local fish and chicken specialties. The kitchen is under the personal control of Diana, who is always collecting awards in Jamaican culinary competitions. A complete meal costs $10 to $20. Dinner is served from 6 to 9:30pm every day of the week.

Facilities: There's a pool and a sauna, and the inn offers therapeutic massages. You can also spend the afternoon at the Manchester Country Club, where tennis and golf are available. Horses can be provided for cross-country treks.

Mandeville Hotel. 4 Hotel St. (P.O. Box 78), Mandeville, Jamaica, W.I. ☎ **809/962-2138.** Fax 809/962-0700. 47 rms, 9 suites. TV TEL. $65–$125 double; from $95 suite. AE, MC, V.

This modern peach-colored hotel lies in the heart of Mandeville, across from the police station. It has an outdoor and indoor bar, a spacious lounge, and good food and service. The activities center mainly around the pool and the coffee shop, where substantial meals are served at moderate prices. There are attractive gardens, and golf and tennis can be played at the nearby Manchester Country Club.

WHERE TO DINE

Mandeville Hotel. 4 Hotel St. ☎ **809/962-2460.** Reservations recommended. Main courses J$250–J$350 ($7–$9.80). AE, MC, V. Daily 6:30am–9:30pm. JAMAICAN.

Close to the city center, near the police station, and popular with local businesspeople, the Mandeville Hotel offers a wide selection of sandwiches, plus milkshakes, tea, and coffee. In the restaurant the à la carte menu features Jamaican pepperpot soup, lobster thermidor, fresh snapper, and kingfish. Potatoes and vegetables are included in the main-dish prices. There is no pretension to the food at all. It's homemade and basic, almost like that served in the house of a typical Jamaican family. From the restaurant's dining room, you'll have a view of the hotel's pool and the green hills of central Jamaica.

SEEING THE SIGHTS

Mandeville is the sort of place where you can become well acquainted with the people and feel like part of the community.

One of the largest and driest **caves** on the island is at Oxford, about 9 miles northwest of Mandeville. Signs direct you to it after you leave Mile Gully, a village dominated by St. George's Church, some 175 years old.

Among the interesting attractions, **Marshall's Pen** is one of the Great Houses. A coffee plantation home some 200 years old, it has been restored and furnished in traditional style. In 1795 it was owned by one of the governors of Jamaica, the earl of Balcarres. It has been in the hands of the Sutton family since 1939; they farm the 300 acres and breed Jamaican Red Poll cattle. This is very much a private home and should be treated as such, although guided tours can be arranged. A contribution of $10 per person is requested. For information or an appointment to see the house, contact Ann or Robert Sutton, Marshall's Pen, Great House, P.O. Box 58, Mandeville, Jamaica, W.I. (☎ **809/904-5454**).

At **Marshall's Pen cattle estate and private nature reserve,** near Mandeville, guided birding tours of the scenic property and other outstanding birding spots on Jamaica may be arranged in advance for groups of bird watchers. Self-catering accommodation is sometimes available for bird watchers only, but arrangements must be made in advance. For further information, contact Ann or Robert Sutton, Marshall's Pen, P.O. Box 58, Mandeville, Jamaica, W.I. (☎ **809/904-5454**). Robert Sutton is co-author of *Birds of Jamaica*, a photographic field guide published by Cambridge University Press.

Milk River Mineral Bath, Milk River, Clarendon (☎ **809/924-9544**; fax 809/986-4962), lies 9 miles south of the Kingston-Mandeville highway. It boasts the world's most radioactive mineral waters, recommended for the treatment of arthritis, rheumatism, lumbago, neuralgia, sciatica, and liver disorders. These mineral-laden waters are available to guests of the Milk River Mineral Spa & Hotel, Milk River, Clarendon, Jamaica, West Indies, as well as to casual visitors to the enclosed baths or mineral swimming pool. The baths contain water at approximate body temperature (90°F) and are channeled into small tubs six feet square by three feet deep, each enclosed in a cubicle where participants undress. The cost of a bath is J$50 ($1.40) for adults and J$25 (70¢) for children. Baths usually last about 15 minutes (it isn't good to remain too long in the waters).

The restaurant offers fine Jamaican cuisine and health drinks in a relaxed old-world atmosphere. Some guests check into the adjacent hotel, where there are 25 rooms (17 with bath), many with air-conditioning, TV, and phone. Six of the rooms are in the main body of the hotel (a century-old Great House that was converted into a hotel in the 1930s). With MAP included, rates for rooms with bath are $102 double. Rates for rooms without bath are $96 double. AE, MC, V.

The French West Indies 12

It's France in the Caribbean, where Gallic charm meets tropical beauty. For most visitors, that's reason enough to come. A long way from Europe, France's "western border" is composed mainly of Guadeloupe and Martinique, with a scattering of tiny offshore archipelagos, such as the little Iles des Saintes.

Martinique is the northernmost of the Windwards, whereas butterfly shaped Guadeloupe is near the southern stretch of the Leewards. These are not colonies, as many visitors wrongly assume, but the westernmost *départements* of France, meaning that these *citoyens* are full-fledged French citizens, a status they have enjoyed since 1946.

Martinique has mountains dotted with lush vegetation, rain forests bursting with bamboo and breadfruit trees, and even a patch of desert in the south. But most visitors, including those from France, come just for the white-sand beaches.

In island boutiques you can purchase that Hermès scarf you've always wanted, certainly a bottle of Chanel perfume, or even some Baccarat crystal. For breakfast, freshly baked croissants will arrive on your plate. French cheeses are shipped in from Marseilles. The Creole cuisine is among the most distinctive in the West Indies.

Tropically forested Guadeloupe, Martinique's companion island, is less favored by visitors but still has plenty to offer. It has even better Creole restaurants, and its landscape is stippled with pineapple groves, banana plantations, and sugarcane fields. The surf pounds hard against the Atlantic coast, but the beaches on the west coast offer calmer seas.

Other satellites of the French West Indies include St. Martin (which shares an island with the Dutch-held St. Maarten; see chapter 10), St. Barthélemy, Marie-Galante, and La Désirade, a former leper colony.

The French West Indies serve some of the best food in the Caribbean, although one irate reader found it a "farcical version" of that offered in New Orleans. Don't be afraid if we've sent you to a dilapidated wooden shack. You may find the *New York Times* food editor here too, sampling a regional meal.

INFORMATION For more information on these islands before you leave home, contact the **French West Indies Tourist Board,** 444 Madison Ave., New York, NY 10022 (☎ **212/838-7800**). You can also contact branch offices of the **French National Tourist**

Office at 9454 Wilshire Blvd., Beverly Hills, CA 90212 (☎ **310/271-2358**), and 676 N. Michigan Ave., Chicago, IL 60611 (☎ **312/751-7800**). **In Canada,** visit 1981 Ave. McGill College, Suite 480, Montréal, PQ 113A ZW9 (☎ **514/288-4264**).

1 Martinique

With beautiful white-sand beaches and a culture full of French flair, Martinique is part of the Lesser Antilles and lies in the semitropical zone; its western shore faces the Caribbean and its eastern shore faces the more turbulent Atlantic. The surface of the island is only 420 square miles—50 miles at its longest and 21 miles at its widest point.

The ground is mountainous, especially in the rain-forested northern part where Mount Pelée, a volcano, rises to a height of 4,656 feet. In the center of the island the mountains are smaller, with Carbet Peak reaching a 3,960-foot summit. The high hills rising among the peaks or mountains are called *mornes.* The southern part of Martinique has only big hills, reaching peaks of 1,500 feet at Vauclin and 1,400 feet at Diamant. The irregular coastline of the island provides five bays, dozens of coves, and miles of sandy beaches. Almost a third of the island's year-round population of 360,000 lives in the capital and largest city, Fort-de-France.

The climate is relatively mild, with the average temperature in the 75° to 85°F range. At higher elevations it's considerably cooler. The island is cooled by a wind the French called *alizé,* and rain is frequent but doesn't last very long. From late August to November might be called the rainy season. April to September are the hottest months.

The early Carib peoples, who gave Columbus such a hostile reception, called Martinique "the island of flowers," and indeed it has remained so. The vegetation is lush and includes hibiscus, poinsettias, bougainvillea, coconut palms, and mango trees. Almost any fruit can sprout from Martinique's soil: pineapples, avocados, bananas, papayas, and custard apples.

Bird watchers are often pleased at the number of hummingbirds, and people also come to see the mountain whistler, the blackbird, and the mongoose. Multicolored butterflies flit through the island. After sunset, there's a permanent concert of grasshoppers, frogs, and crickets.

GETTING THERE

BY PLANE **Lamentin International Airport** lies outside the village of Lamentin, a 15-minute taxi ride east of Fort-de-France and a 40-minute taxi ride northeast of most of the resort hotels (on the Trois Islets peninsula). Most flights to Martinique and Guadeloupe require a transfer on a neighboring island, usually Puerto Rico, but occasionally Antigua. Direct or nonstop flights to the French islands from the U.S. mainland are rare: Air France (see below) offers only one weekly Sunday flight from Miami, and it stops at both islands.

American Airlines (☎ **800/433-7300**) flies from many North American cities into its busy hub in San Juan, and from there, transfers passengers to one of usually two daily **American Eagle** (same phone number) flights heading to both Martinique and Guadeloupe. Taking off late enough in the day to allow connections from virtually anywhere, the Eagle flights usually arrive at their destinations between 1 1/2 hours and 2 hours later. During the off-season, the evening flights to both islands are sometimes combined into a single flight, landing first at one island before continuing on to the next. Return flights to San Juan usually depart separately from both islands twice a day.

Martinique

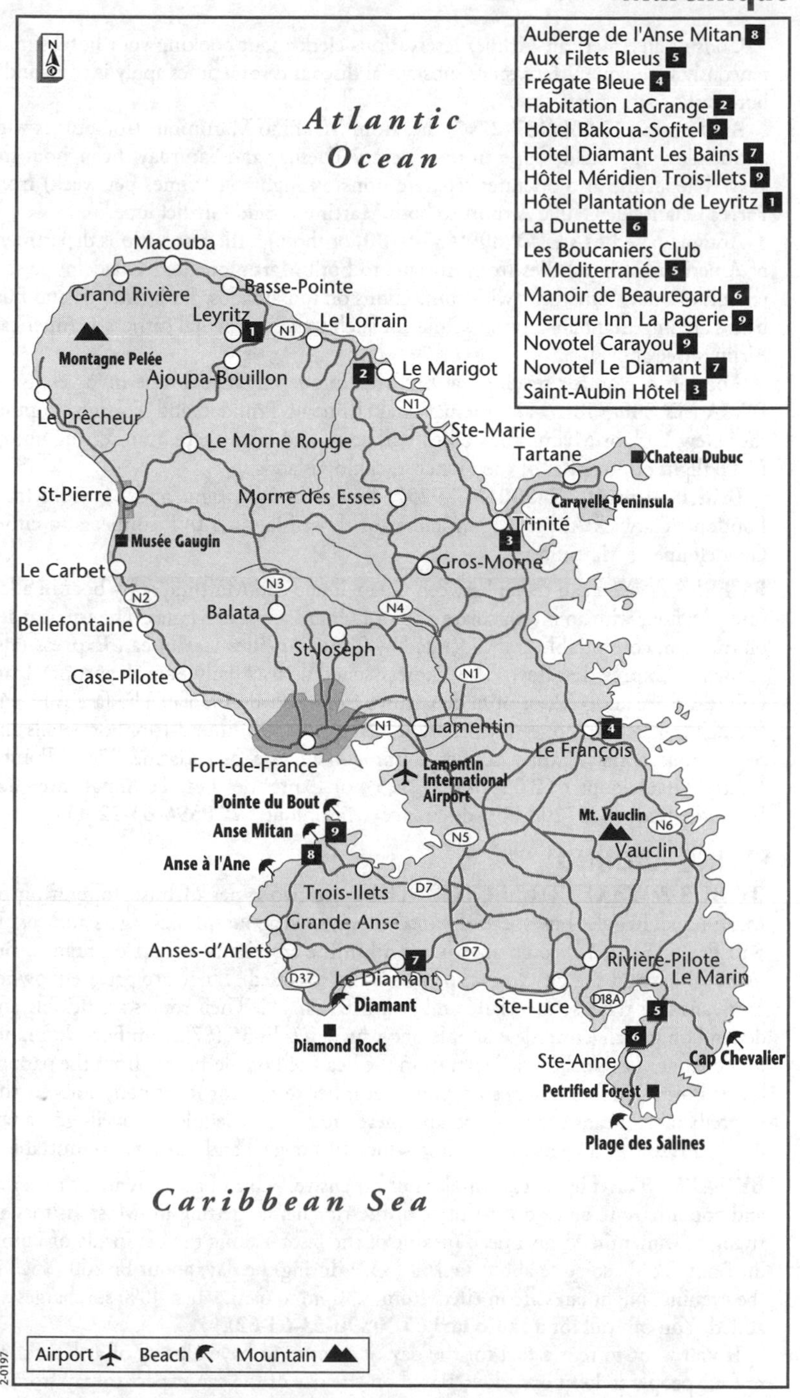

Auberge de l'Anse Mitan 8
Aux Filets Bleus 5
Frégate Bleue 4
Habitation LaGrange 2
Hotel Bakoua-Sofitel 9
Hotel Diamant Les Bains 7
Hôtel Méridien Trois-Ilets 9
Hôtel Plantation de Leyritz 1
La Dunette 6
Les Boucaniers Club Mediterranée 5
Manoir de Beauregard 6
Mercure Inn La Pagerie 9
Novotel Carayou 9
Novotel Le Diamant 7
Saint-Aubin Hôtel 3
Atlantic Ocean
Caribbean Sea
Macouba
Grand Rivière
Basse-Pointe
Leyritz
Le Lorrain
Montagne Pelée
Ajoupa-Bouillon
Le Marigot
Le Prêcheur
Ste-Marie
Le Morne Rouge
Tartane
Chateau Dubuc
Caravelle Peninsula
St-Pierre
Morne des Esses
Trinité
Musée Gaugin
Le Carbet
Gros-Morne
Balata
Bellefontaine
St-Joseph
Case-Pilote
Lamentin
Le François
Fort-de-France
Lamentin International Airport
Pointe du Bout
Anse Mitan
Anse à l'Ane
Mt. Vauclin
Vauclin
Trois-Ilets
Grande Anse
Anses-d'Arlets
Rivière-Pilote
Le Marin
Le Diamant
Diamant
Ste-Luce
Diamond Rock
Ste-Anne
Cap Chevalier
Petrified Forest
Plage des Salines
N1
N2
N3
N4
N5
N6
D7
D37
D18A
Airport
Beach
Mountain
2-0197

Consult an American Airlines reservations clerk about booking your hotel simultaneously with your airfare, since substantial discounts sometimes apply if you handle both tasks at the same time.

Air France (☎ **800/237-2747**) flies from Miami to Martinique (sometimes with a touchdown in Guadeloupe en route) every Tuesday and Saturday throughout the year. The airline also operates separate nonstop flights (10 times per week) from Paris's Charles de Gaulle Airport to both Martinique and Guadeloupe.

Antigua-based **LIAT** (☎ **809/462-0700,** or through the reservations department of American Airlines) flies from Antigua to both Martinique and Guadeloupe several times a day, sometimes with connections on to Barbados. Both Antigua and Barbados are important air-terminus links for such transcontinental carriers as American Airlines (see above).

Another option for reaching either Martinique or Guadeloupe involves flying **BWIA** (☎ **800/538-2942**), the national airline of Trinidad and Tobago, from either New York or Miami nonstop to Barbados, and from there, transferring onto a LIAT flight on to either of the French-speaking islands.

British Airways (☎ **800/247-9297**) flies to both Antigua and Barbados from London's Gatwick Airport. From either of those islands, LIAT connects to either Guadeloupe or Martinique.

BY FERRY You can travel between Guadeloupe and Martinique by boat in a leisurely $^{3}/_{4}$ hour with an intermediate stop in Dominica or Les Saintes. The trip is made on modern, comfortable craft operated by **Trans Antilles Caribbean Express** (also known as **Exprès des Iles**). The Express schedule lists daily 8am departures from Pointe-à-Pitre and 1, 2, or 3pm departures from Fort-de-France. The fare is Fr 345 (French francs) ($69) one-way per adult, or Fr 495 ($99) round-trip. For details and reservations, contact Exprès des Iles, 6 Immeuble Darse, quai Gatine, 97110 Pointe-à-Pitre, Guadeloupe (☎ **0596-82-12-45**), or Exprès des Iles, Terminal Inter-Iles, Bassin de Radoub, 97200 Fort-de-France, Martinique (☎ **0596-63-12-11**).

GETTING AROUND

BY BUS & TAXI COLLECTIF There are two types of buses operating on Martinique. Regular buses, called *grands busses,* hold about 40 passengers and cost Fr 5 to Fr 25 ($1 to $5) to go anywhere within the city limits of Fort-de-France. But to travel beyond the city limits, *taxis collectifs* are used. These are privately owned minivans that traverse the island and bear the sign TC. Their routes are flexible and depend on passenger need. A simple one-way fare is Fr 35 ($7) from Fort-de-France to Ste-Anne. Taxis collectifs depart from the heart of Fort-de-France from the parking lot of Pointe Simon. There's no phone number to call for information about this unpredictable means of transport, and there are no set schedules. Traveling in a taxi collectif is for the adventurous visitor—they're crowded and not very comfortable.

BY TAXI Travel by taxi is popular but expensive. Most of the cabs aren't metered, and you'll have to agree on the price of the ride before getting in. Most visitors arriving at Lamentin Airport head for one of the resorts along the peninsula of Pointe du Bout. To do so costs about Fr 160 ($32) during the day, about Fr 260 ($52) in the evening. Night fares are in effect from 7:30pm to 6am, when 40% surcharges are added. You can call for a **radio taxi** (☎ **0596-63-63-62**).

If you want to rent a taxi for the day, it's better to have a party of at least three or four people to keep costs low. Based on the size of the car, expect to pay from Fr 700 to Fr 850 ($140 to $170) and up for a five-hour tour, depending on the itinerary you negotiate with the driver.

BY RENTAL CAR The scattered nature of Martinique's geography makes renting a car especially tempting. Martinique has several local car-rental agencies, but clients have complained of mechanical difficulties and billing irregularities. We recommend renting from one of America's "big three" (Hertz, Budget, and Avis). You must be 21 and have a valid driver's license, such as one from the United States or Canada, to rent a car for up to 20 days. After that, an International Driver's License is required.

Budget has offices at rue Félix-Eboué, 12, in Fort-de-France (☎ **800/527-0700** in the U.S., or 0596-63-69-00); **Avis,** at rue Ernest-Deproge, 4, in Fort-de-France (☎ **800/331-2112** in the U.S., or 0596-51-11-70); and **Hertz,** at rue Ernest-Deproge, 24, in Fort-de-France (☎ **800/654-3001** or 0596-60-64-64). Although each of these rental companies also maintains a kiosk at Lamentin Airport with staffs willing to transport prospective renters to pickup depots a short drive away, prices are usually lower if you reserve a car in North America at least two business days before your arrival.

Remember that regardless of which company you choose, you'll be hit with a value-added tax (VAT) of 9.5% on top of the final car-rental bill. (VATs for some luxury goods, including jewelry, on Martinique can go as high as 14%.) Collision-damage waivers (CDWs), an excellent idea in a country where the populace drives somewhat recklessly, cost $11.60 to $20 per day, depending on the value of the car.

BY FERRY The least expensive way to go between quai d'Esnambuc in Fort-de-France and Pointe du Bout is by ferry (*vedette*), costing Fr 19 ($3.80) per passenger, round-trip (Fr 15 or $3 each way). Schedules for the ferryboats, which usually run every day from 6am to midnight, are printed in the free visitor's guide *Choubouloute,* which is distributed by the tourist office. However, if the weather is bad and/or the seas are rough, all ferryboat services may be canceled.

There is also a smaller ferryboat that runs between Fort-de-France and the small-scale, unpretentious beach resorts of Anse Mitan and Anse-à-l'Ane, both across the bay and home to many two- and three-star hotels and several modest and unassuming Creole restaurants. A boat departs daily from quai d'Esnambuc in Fort-de-France at 30-minute intervals every day between 6am and 6:30pm. The trip takes only about 15 minutes, but the fare is the same as that for the above-mentioned ferryboat for Pointe du Bout.

BY BICYCLE & MOTORBIKE You can rent motor scooters from **Funny,** rue Ernest-Deproge, 80, in Fort-de-France (☎ **0596-63-33-05**). The new 18-speed VTT (*velo tout terrain,* or all-terrain bike) is gradually making inroads from mainland France into the rugged countryside of Martinique, although there aren't many places to rent one. For tour information and possible rentals of these mountain bikes, as well as scooters, contact **Jacques-Henry Vartel,** VT Tilt, Anse Mitan (☎ **0596-66-01-01**). No driver's license is required to rent a motor scooter, only a valid piece of identification and a deposit of around Fr 1,500 ($300).

FAST FACTS: Martinique

Banking Hours Banks are open Monday to Friday from 7:30am to noon and 2:30 to 4pm.

Consulate The nearest U.S. consulate is on Barbados.

Currency The **French franc (Fr)** is the legal tender here. Prices in this chapter are in both U.S. dollars and French francs. At press time, 1 franc is worth about

20¢ (Fr 4.98 = U.S.$1). Banks give much better exchange rates than hotels, and there's a money-exchange service, **Change Caraïbes** (☎ **0596-42-17-11**) available at Lamentin Airport. Its downtown branch is at rue Ernest-Deproge, 4 (☎ **0596-73-06-16**).

Customs Items for personal use, such as tobacco, cameras, and film, are admitted without formalities or tax if not in excessive quantity.

Documents U.S. and Canadian citizens need proof of identity (a voter registration card or birth certificate, plus a photo ID, or a passport) for stays of less than 21 days. After that, a valid passport is required. A return or ongoing ticket is also necessary. British subjects need a valid passport.

Drugstores One of the most central is the **Pharmacie de la Paix,** at the corner of rue Perrinon and rue Victor-Schoelcher in Fort-de-France (☎ **0596-71-94-83**). It's open Monday to Friday from 7:15am to 6:15pm and on Saturday from 7:45am to 1pm.

Electricity Electricity here is 220 volts AC (50 cycles), the same as that used on the French mainland. However, check with your hotel to see if they have converted the electrical voltage and outlets in the bathrooms (some have). If they haven't, bring a transformer and an adapter for U.S. appliances.

Emergencies Call the **police** at ☎ **17,** report a **fire** at ☎ **18,** and summon an **ambulance** at ☎ **596/75-15-75.**

Hospitals There are 18 hospitals and clinics on the island, and a 24-hour emergency room at **Hôpital Pierre Zobda Quikman,** Châteauboeuf, right outside Fort-de-France (☎ **0596-55-20-00**).

Information The **Office Départemental du Tourisme** (tourist office) is on boulevard Alfassa in Fort-de-France, across the waterfront boulevard from the harbor (☎ **0596-63-79-60**), open Monday to Friday from 8am to 5pm and on Saturday from 8am to noon. The information desk at Lamentin Airport is open daily until the last flight comes in.

Languages French is spoken by almost everyone. The local Creole patois uses words borrowed from France, England, Spain, and Africa. In the wake of increased tourism, English is occasionally spoken in the major hotels, restaurants, and tourist organizations, but don't count on driving around the countryside and asking for directions in English.

Safety Crime is hardly rampant on Martinique, yet there are still those who prey on unsuspecting tourists. Follow the usual precautions here, especially in Fort-de-France and in the tourist-hotel belt of Pointe du Bout. It's wise to protect your valuables and never leave them unguarded on the beach.

Telephone Martinique is not part of the 809 area code that applies to most of the Caribbean. To call Martinique from the United States, dial 011 (the international access code), then 596 (the country code for the French West Indies), and finally the six-digit local number. To make a call within Martinique, only the six-digit local number is necessary. When making calls on island to another on-island place, you'll have to add a 0 to the country code, such as 0596 for Martinique, plus the six-digit local number—in all, 10 digits for calls made within the island.

Time Martinique is on Atlantic standard time year-round, one hour later than eastern time except when daylight saving time is in effect. Then Martinique time is the same as the East Coast of the United States.

Water Potable water is found throughout the island.

Weather The climate is relatively mild—the average temperature is in the 75° to 85°F range.

A PREVIEW OF BEACHES & WATER SPORTS AROUND THE ISLAND

BEACHES The beaches south of Fort-de-France are white; those on the northern part of the island have mostly gray sand. Outstanding in the south is the 1 1/2-mile-long **Plage des Salines,** near Ste-Anne, with palm trees and a long stretch of white sand, and the 2 1/2-mile-long **Diamant,** with the landmark Diamond Rock offshore. Swimming on the Atlantic coast is for experts only, except at **Cap Chevalier** and **Presqu'île de la Caravelle Nature Preserve.**

The clean white-sand beaches of **Pointe du Bout,** site of the major hotels of Martinique, were created by developers. However, to the south, the white-sand beaches at **Anse Mitan** have always been here welcoming visitors, including many snorkelers.

Incidentally, nudist beaches are not officially sanctioned, although topless sunbathing is widely practiced at the big hotels, often around their swimming pools. Public beaches rarely have changing cabins or showers. Some hotels charge nonguests for the use of changing and beach facilities, and request a deposit for towel rental.

DEEP-SEA FISHING Most hotels maintain a list of the yachts and skippers who will take groups out for a day of *la pêche à la ligne* on the wide blue sea. If yours doesn't offer such arrangements, you can call the staff at **Caribtours** (☎ **0596-66-02-56**). The cost of renting such a boat, in which all equipment is usually included, is around Fr 3,000 ($600) for a day's charter for up to six anglers. Most game fish tend to be most active very early in the morning, and many experienced fishermen claim that it's not worth fishing after 10am, so departures tend to leave before breakfast, around 6am. But note that this sport is in decline in waters around Martinique because of overfishing.

SAILING This is a big pastime around Martinique. It's also terribly expensive unless there are enough people in your party to share the cost. Not many travelers can or want to shell out the bucks for yacht charters, either crewed or bareboat.

If you want to see the waters around Martinique, it's better to go on one of the **sailboat excursions** in the bay of Fort-de-France and on the southeast coast of the island. Ask at your hotel desk what boats are taking passengers on cruises in Martinique waters. These vessels tend to change from season to season. On a smaller scale, many hotels (including the **Méridien** at Pointe du Bout) will rent Hobie cats and Sunfish to their guests, but only if you can demonstrate sailing competence.

SCUBA DIVING & SNORKELING Scuba divers come here to explore the St-Pierre shipwrecks sunk in the 1902 volcano eruption and the Diamond Rock caves and walls. Small scuba centers operate at many of the hotels, but one of the major centers (open to all) is **Bathy's Club** in Pointe du Bout's Hôtel Méridien (see the Pointe du Bout section for details).

Snorkeling equipment is usually available free to hotel guests, who quickly learn that coral, fish, and ferns abound in the waters around the Pointe du Bout hotels.

WATERSKIING & WINDSURFING Waterskiing is available at every beach near the large hotels. But windsurfing is the most popular sport in the French West Indies. Equipment and lessons are available at all hotel water-sports facilities, especially the **Hôtel Méridien** (see below) in Pointe du Bout.

AN OVERVIEW OF OUTDOOR PURSUITS AROUND THE ISLAND FOR LANDLUBBERS

CAMPING Camping is permitted in some places, including in the mountains and forests, and on many beaches. Check with the local mayor's office or property owner before setting up camp. Campsites are usually basic, although comfortable camps with cold showers and toilets are on the southeast coast at Macabou; at Ste-Luce, Le Marin, and Ste-Anne on the south coast; and Anse-à-l'Ane near Trois-Ilets. Contact the **Office National des Forêts** (☎ **0596-71-34-50**) for more information.

GOLF The only golf course on the island is the Robert Trent Jones–designed 18-hole **Golf de l'Impératrice-Joséphine** at Trois-Ilet, a five-minute drive from the leading resort area of Pointe du Bout and about 18 miles from Fort-de-France. See the Trois-Ilets section for details.

HIKING Inexpensive guided excursions for tourists are organized year-round by the personnel of the **Parc Naturel Régional de la Martinique,** Excollège Agricole de Tivoli, B.P. 437, 97200 Fort-de-France (☎ **0596-64-42-59**), and special excursions can be arranged for small groups.

The **Presqu'île de la Caravelle Nature Preserve,** a well-protected peninsula jutting into the Atlantic Ocean from the town of Trinité, has safe beaches and well-marked trails to the ruins of historic Château Debuc and through tropical wetlands.

Serious hiking excursions might include a climb up **Montagne Pelée** and the chance to explore the Gorges de la Falaise or the thick coastal rain forest between Grand' Rivière and Le Prêcheur. These are organized with local guides at certain times of the year by the park staff.

HORSEBACK RIDING The premier riding facility on Martinique, thriving since 1974, is **Ranch Jack,** Morne Habitué, Trois-Ilets. See the Trois-Ilets section below for details.

TENNIS Each large hotel has courts. Guests play free during the day, and night games usually require a surcharge of around Fr 15 ($3) per hour. Nonguests are faced with a playing-time charge of about Fr 50 ($10) per hour, although the tennis pros at Bathy's Club at the **Hôtel Méridien** (see below) in Pointe du Bout usually allow nonresidents to play for free if the courts are otherwise unoccupied, except at night, when the charge is almost always imposed.

Another good choice is to play at one of the three courts on the grounds of **Golf de l'Impératrice-Joséphine** at Trois-Ilets (see the Trois-Ilets section), a five-minute drive from the major hotels at Pointe du Bout. The setting here is one of the most beautiful on Martinique. The courts are open from 7am to 8pm daily, and you should reserve your court time in advance. It costs Fr 50 ($10) an hour to play (obtaining a racquet is a major hassle, so bring your own).

FORT-DE-FRANCE

With its iron-grillwork balconies overflowing with flowers, Fort-de-France, the largest town on Martinique, reminds us of a cross between New Orleans and a town on the French Riviera. It lies at the end of a large bay surrounded by evergreen hills.

The proud people of Martinique are even more fascinating than the town, although today the Creole women are likely to be seen in jeans instead of their traditional turbans and Empress Joséphine–style gowns, and they rarely wear those massive earrings that used to jounce and sway as they sauntered along.

Narrow streets climb up the steep hills where houses have been built to catch the overflow of the capital's more than 100,000 inhabitants.

Where to Stay

Rates are sometimes advertised in U.S. dollars, sometimes in French francs, and sometimes in a combination of both.

Don't stay in town if you want a hotel near a beach (see the hotels listed below for beach resorts). If you do opt to stay in Fort-de-France, you'll have to take a ferry boat to reach the beaches at Pointe du Bout (see below). The one exception to this is the Hotel La Batelière, which opens onto a small beach, but it's in the suburb of Schoelcher.

Hôtel La Batelière. 20 rue des Alizés, 97233 Schoelcher, Martinique, F.W.I. ☎ **0596-61-49-49.** Fax 0596-61-70-57. 197 rms, 5 duplexes, 2 suites. A/C TV TEL. Winter, Fr 1,815–Fr 2,115 ($363–$423) double; Fr 2,215–Fr 3,515 ($443–$703) duplex or suite. Off-season, Fr 845–Fr 1,365 ($169–$273) double; from Fr 1,815–Fr 3,515 ($363–$703) duplex or suite. Rates include buffet breakfast. AE, DC, MC, V.

This five-story, waterside, French-modern hotel isn't superglamourous, but it offers many social activities and dining choices, and is the best choice in the Fort-de-France area. It's a white stucco structure set back in a garden from a small beach that's sheltered from the waves by a breakwater. Each room has a wide glass door that opens onto your own water-view terrace.

Dining/Entertainment: In the Bleu Marine dining room, French, international, and Creole cuisine is served, and there's a beach restaurant (Le Sucrier) near the swimming pool. There's also a casino and disco.

Facilities: Tennis is free, except at night when there's a surcharge. On the premises are a swimming pool, a beauty salon, a barbershop, and a handful of boutiques.

Hôtel L'Impératrice. Place de la Savane, 15, rue de la Liberté, 97200 Fort-de-France, Martinique, F.W.I. ☎ **800/223-9815** in the U.S., or 0596-63-06-82. Fax 0596-72-66-30. 24 rms. A/C TV TEL. Fr 350–Fr 450 ($70–$90) double. Rates include breakfast. AE, DC, MC, V.

Favored by businesspeople, this stucco-sided, five-story hotel faces a landscaped mall in the heart of town, near the water's edge. L'Impératrice was originally built in the 1950s, renovated in 1994, and named in honor of one of Martinique's most famous exports (Joséphine). Its balconies overlook the traffic at the western edge of the sprawling promenade known as the Savane. The bedrooms are modern and functional, and many contain TVs. The front rooms tend to be noisy; yet, to compensate, windows overlook the life along the Savane. Don't expect outstanding service here. Almost no one on staff speaks English, and they all seem a bit jaded. But despite the confusion in the very noisy lobby, and the unremarkable decor of the simple bedrooms, you might end up enjoying the unpretentiousness of this place.

The hotel's restaurant, Le Joséphine, open daily for lunch and dinner, does a brisk business with local shoppers in town for the day. The more popular of the two lounges has large, white wickerwork chairs and an adjoining bar. Or you may prefer the second-floor bar, with its trademark colors of green and white.

Le Lafayette. 5 rue de la Liberté, 5, 97200 Fort-de-France, Martinique, F.W.I. ☎ **0596-73-80-50.** Fax 0596-60-97-75. 24 rms. A/C MINIBAR TV TEL. Apr–Oct, Fr 260 ($52) double (without breakfast); Nov–Mar, Fr 400 ($80) double, including buffet breakfast. Discounts offered for stays of 3 days or more. AE, DC, MC, V. Free parking at night, Fr 6 ($1.20) per hour during the day.

You'll enter this simple and modest downtown hotel, located right on La Savane, through rue Victor-Hugo; the reception hall is up a few terra-cotta steps. The dark-brown wooden doors are offset by soft beige walls. Japanese wall tapestries decorate the cramped and slightly dowdy bedrooms, and most rooms contain twin beds. The bathrooms are in pure white, and the overall impression is simple, neat, and unpretentious. The inn is the oldest continuously operating hotel in Martinique, originally built in the 1940s. There's no on-site restaurant, but several are within walking distance.

La Malmaison. 7 rue de la Liberté. ☎ **0596-63-90-85.** Fax 0596-60-03-93. 20 rms. A/C TV TEL. Fr 250–Fr 350 ($50–$70) double. AE, MC, V.

In a staid, 1940s-era building, with a Naugahyde-covered tavern (La Malmaison), this is a simple, unpretentious hotel whose rooms are oddly outfitted with a combination of modern and antique furniture. Some contain valuable four-poster beds crafted in the antique Creole style; others have modern 1960s-style headboards. The bathrooms are very basic. The place isn't special or enchanting, but it's decent, clean, and staffed with a watchdog-style crew who ensure tranquillity.

Where to Dine

Abri-Cotier. Pointe-Simon. ☎ **0596-63-66-46.** Main courses Fr 50–Fr 150 ($10–$30). AE, DC, MC, V. Daily noon–3pm and 7–11pm. (Bar service daily 10am–1am.) CREOLE.

It's little more than a wood-sided hut with Creole styling, with a wide veranda overlooking the harbor front and its parking lot. The management encourages cafe patrons to sit on the covered veranda and dining patrons to sit inside, at cramped tables arranged bistro style within the darkly paneled interior. Don't expect grand cuisine—it's simple local fare, but the service is fast and friendly. Menu items include a fricassée of shrimp, chicken with curry, rack of lamb, boudin Creole, and a brochette of seafood. Flavors are zesty, and no one puts on airs here. No one will mind if you simply opt for drinks.

✪ **Le Coq Hardi.** Rue Martin-Luther-King, 52. ☎ **0596-71-59-64.** Reservations recommended. Main courses Fr 100–Fr 170 ($20–$34). AE, MC, V. Wed 7–10:45pm, Thurs–Tues noon–1:45pm and 7:30–10:45pm. Closed Wed–Sat lunch (year-round) and Wed dinner (summer only). Take a taxi (a 2-minute ride) north from the main square (La Savane) of Fort-de-France. STEAKHOUSE.

This is the premier steakhouse on Martinique. If you ask a local for an atmospheric, charming spot in the center of town, they'll send you here. It's maintained by restaurateur Alphonse Sintive, who trained as a master butcher and charcutier before World War II on the French mainland. He can regale you with stories of his experiences in the French Foreign Legion in Indochina and Algeria. The juicy steaks and chops are imported from France by regular air shipments and grilled over a wood fire. Hearty eaters will appreciate the large portions. A specialty is tournedos Rossini with foie gras. One of the most generous and likable hosts on the island, Mr. Sintive usually offers a free after-dinner drink to anyone who mentions this guidebook.

La Fontane. Km 4, Route de Balata (Highway N3). ☎ **0596-64-28-70**. Reservations recommended. Fixed-price lunch Fr 100 ($20); main courses Fr 100–Fr 300 ($20–$60). MC, V. Tues–Sat noon–3pm and 7–10pm. FRENCH/CARIBBEAN.

Set within the verdant suburb of La Fontane, 2½ miles north of Fort-de-France, this restaurant occupies a century-old villa that the present owners have completely renovated. The setting is dotted with dowdy antiques. You can order well-seasoned dishes like crayfish au gratin, fresh fish fillets with coconut, lobster thermidor, Caribbean bouillabaisse *à la Fontane* (sliced fillet of lamb with mango), and a flavorful salad known locally as a *bambou de la Fontane* (fresh fish, crayfish, melon, tomato, and corn). The wine list is among the island's best.

La Mouina. Route de Redoute, 127. ☎ **0596-79-34-57.** Reservations recommended only at dinner Sat–Sun. Main courses Fr 95–Fr 210 ($19–$42). MC, V. Mon–Fri noon–2:30pm; Mon–Sat 7:30–9:30pm. FRENCH/CREOLE.

La Mouina, a Creole word for a meeting house, is a venerable restaurant established 16 years ago by members of the French-Swiss-Hungarian Karschesz family. Sitting next to the police station in the suburb of Redoute, about 1 1/2 miles north of Fort-de-France, this 60-year-old white colonial house is the culinary domain of one of the island's most experienced groups of chefs. You might begin with *crabes farcis* (stuffed crabs) or *escargots de Bourgogne,* then follow with tournedos Rossini, *rognon de veau entier grillé* (whole grilled kidneys), or duckling in orange sauce. The owners are particularly proud of their version of red snapper en papillotte. Ask at your hotel for good directions before setting out (or even better, take a taxi), because it's hard to find.

✪ **La Plantation.** In Martinique Cottages, Pays Mélé Jeanne-d'Arc, Lamentin. ☎ **0596-50-16-08.** Reservations required. Main courses Fr 95–Fr 190 ($19–$38). AE, DC, MC, V. Mon–Fri noon–2pm; Mon–Sat 7:30–9:30pm. FRENCH.

Near the airport, a 20-minute drive south of Fort-de-France, La Plantation is one of the finest restaurants on the island. In a small French Antillean hotel designed about 25 years ago to resemble a 19th-century private home, the restaurant is run by a hardworking brother-and-sister team, Jean-Marc and Peggy Arnaud. An imaginative cuisine is the aim of the chef, Laurent Maire, originally a native of Alsace-Lorraine, on the French mainland. The foie gras may have come from France, but the herbs flavoring it are Antillean. Foie gras appears again in a salade folle with lobster. We found the cream of sea urchin soup exceptional, and a traditional version of rack of lamb was perfectly cooked and herby. The chef is rightly proud of his signature dish, a soufflé of lobster served in the lobster's shell.

Seeing the Sights

At the center of the town lies a broad garden planted with many palms and mangos, **La Savane,** a handsome savannah with shops and cafes lining its sides. In the middle of this grand square stands a statue of Joséphine, "Napoléon's little Creole," made of white marble by Vital Debray. With the grace of a Greek goddess, the statue poses in a Regency gown and looks toward Trois-Ilets, where she was born.

If you like masquerades and dancing in the streets, you should be here in January or February to attend ✪ **carnival,** or "Vaval" as it's known here. The event of the year, carnival begins right after the New Year, as each village prepares costumes and floats. Weekend after weekend, frenzied celebrations take place, reaching fever pitch just before Lent.

Fort-de-France is the focal point for carnival, but the spirit permeates the whole island, as narrow streets are jammed with floats. On Ash Wednesday the streets of Fort-de-France are filled with *diablesses,* or she-devils (portrayed by members of both sexes). Costumed in black and white, they crowd the streets to form King Carnival's funeral procession. As devils cavort about and the rum flows, a funeral pyre is built at La Savane. When it's set on fire, the dancing of those "she-devils" becomes frantic (many are thoroughly drunk at this point). Long past dusk, the cortège takes the coffin to its burial, ending carnival until next year.

At any time of year, your next stop after La Savane should be the **St. Louis Roman Catholic Cathedral,** on rue Victor-Schoelcher, built in 1875. The religious centerpiece of the island, it's an extraordinary iron building, which someone once likened to "a sort of Catholic railway station." A number of the island's former governors are buried beneath the choir loft.

A statue in front of the Palais de Justice is of the island's second main historical figure, Victor Schoelcher (you'll see his name a lot on Martinique). As mentioned, he worked to free the slaves more than a century ago. The **Bibliothèque Schoelcher,**

Begin the Beguine

The sexy and rhythmic beguine was *not* an invention of Cole Porter. It's a dance of the islands—though exactly which island depends on whom you ask. Popular wisdom and the encyclopedia give the nod to Martinique. Guadeloupeans claim it for their own, and to watch them dance it might convince you of their claim. Of course, calypso and the merengue move rhythmically along too—these islanders are known for their dancing.

On Guadeloupe, the folkloric troupe **Ballets Guadeloupeans** makes frequent appearances at the big hotels, whirling and moving to the rhythms of island music in colorful costumes and well-choreographed routines. Some resorts, including the Club Med-Caravelle, use their weekly visit to set the theme for the evening with their restaurant, La Beguine, serving up a banquet of traditional island dishes to accompany the dance, music, and costumes.

Ask at your hotel where the Ballets Guadeloupeans will be appearing during your stay, as their schedule tends to vary as they tour the island. You can catch them as they rotate through the hotels Arawak, Salako, L'Auberge de le Vieille Tour, and Callinago as well as the Club Med-Caravelle. On the night of any of these performances, you can order a drink at the bar for Fr 30 ($6) and witness the show, or partake of a hotel buffet for Fr 250 ($50). Buffets usually start around 8pm, with the show beginning at 8:30pm. The troupe also performs on some cruise ships.

More famous than the dancers on Guadeloupe, however, is the touring group **Les Grands Ballets Martiniquais** on their sibling island. Everybody who goes to Martinique wants to see the show performed by this bouncy group of about two dozen dancers, along with musicians, singers, and choreographers. This most interesting program of folk dances in the Caribbean was launched in the early 1960s, and their performances of the traditional dances of Martinique have been acclaimed in both Europe and the States. With a swoosh of gaily striped skirts and clever acting, the dancers capture all the exuberance of the island's soul. The group has toured abroad with great success, but they perform best on their home ground, presenting tableaux that tell of jealous brides and faithless husbands, demanding overseers and toiling cane cutters. Dressed in traditional costumes, the island women and men dance the spirited mazurka, which was brought from the ballrooms of Europe, and, of course, the exotic beguine.

Les Grands Ballets Martiniquais perform Monday at the Hôtel Diamant-Novotel, Wednesday at the Novotel Carayou, Thursday at the Méridien Trois-Ilets, Friday at the Bakoua Beach, and Saturday at Hôtel La Batalière, but this, too, can vary, so check locally. In addition, the troupe gives mini-performances aboard visiting cruise ships. The cost of dinner and the show is usually Fr 200 ($40) per person. Most performances are at 8:30pm, with dinners at the hotels beginning at 7:30pm.

Whoever performs it for you, on whichever island, you'll soon realize that the beguine is more than a dance—it's a way of life. See it for yourself, or dance it, if you think you can.

rue de la Liberté, 21 (☎ **0596-70-26-67**), also honors this popular hero. Functioning today as the island's central government-funded library, the elaborate structure was first displayed at the Paris Exposition of 1889. Back then the Romanesque portal in red and blue, the Egyptian lotus-petal columns, even the turquoise tiles were imported piece by piece from Paris and reassembled here. Most of the books inside are in French, and it's one of the most stringently protected historic buildings in the

French West Indies. It's open Monday, Tuesday, and Thursday from 8:30am to 5:30pm, Wednesday and Friday from 8:30am to 5pm, and Saturday from 8:30am to noon.

Guarding the port is **Fort St-Louis,** built in the Vauban style on a rocky promontory. In addition, **Fort Tartenson** and **Fort Desaix** stand on hills overlooking the port.

The **Musée Départemental de la Martinique,** rue de la Liberté, 9 (☎ **0596-71-57-05**), the one bastion on Martinique that preserves its pre-Columbian past, has relics left from the early settlers, the Arawaks, and the Caribs. The museum faces La Savane and is open Monday to Friday from 8:30am to 5pm and on Saturday from 9am to noon, charging Fr 15 ($3) for adults, Fr 10 ($2) for students, and Fr 5 ($1) for children.

Sacre-Coeur de Balata Cathedral, at Balata, overlooking Fort-de-France, is a copy of the one looking down from Montmartre upon Paris—and this one is just as incongruous, maybe more so. It's reached by going along route de la Trace (route N3). Balata is 6 miles northwest of Fort-de-France.

A few minutes away on route RN3, the **Jardin de Balata (Balata Garden;** ☎ **0596-64-48-73**) is a tropical botanical park. The park was created by Jean-Philippe Thoze on land that the jungle was rapidly reclaiming around a Creole house that belonged to his grandmother. He has also restored the house, furnishing it with antiques and historic engravings. The garden contains flowers, shrubs, and trees growing in profusion and offering a vision of tropical splendor. Balata is open daily from 9am to 5pm. Admission is Fr 35 ($7) for adults and Fr 15 ($3) for children 7 to 12 years old; free for children under 6.

SHOPPING

Your best buys on Martinique are French luxury imports, such as perfumes, fashions, Vuitton luggage, Lalique crystal, or Limoges dinnerware. Sometimes (but don't count on it) prices are as much as 30% to 40% below those in the United States.

If you pay in dollars, store owners supposedly will give you a 20% discount; however, when you pay in dollars, the exchange rates vary considerably from store to store, and almost invariably they are far less favorable than the rate offered at one of the local banks. The net result is that you received a 20% discount, but then they take away from 9% to 15% on the dollar exchange, giving you a net savings of only 5% to 11%—not 20%. Actually, you're better off shopping in the smaller stores where prices are 8% to 12% lower on comparable items and paying in francs that you have exchanged at a local bank.

The main shopping street in town is **rue Victor-Hugo.** The other two leading shopping streets are **rue Schoelcher** and **rue St-Louis.** However, the most boutique-filled shopping streets are **rue Antione Siger, rue Lamartine,** and **rue Moreau de Jones.** Here you'll find the latest French design fashions. Facing the tourist office and alongside **quai d'Esnambuc** is an open market where you can purchase local handcrafts and souvenirs. Many of these are tacky, however.

Far more interesting is the display of vegetables and fruit at the **open-air stalls along rue Isambert.** It's full of local flavor and you can't help but smell the **fish market** alongside the Levassor River.

Gourmet chefs will find all sorts of spices in the open-air markets, or such goodies as tinned pâté or canned quail in the local *supermarchés.*

For the ubiquitous local fabric, madras, there are shops on every street with bolts and bolts of it, all colorful and inexpensive. So-called haute couture and resort wear are sold in many boutiques dotting downtown Fort-de-France.

Try to postpone your shopping trip if a cruise ship is in town, to avoid the stampede.

Cadet-Daniel. Rue Antoine-Siger, 72. ☎ **0596-71-41-48.**

Cadet-Daniel, which opened in 1840, offers the best buys in French china and crystal. It competes with Roger Albert. It's hard to say which store offers the better deal from year to year, so it pays to compare before you buy. Cadet-Daniel sells Christofle silver, Limoges china, and crystal from Daum, Baccarat, and Lalique. Because of the astronomical price increases of fine silver, porcelain, and crystal, the store now concentrates on 18-carat gold jewelry, crafted on Martinique into traditional Creole patterns.

La Case à Rhum. In the Galerie Marchande, rue de la Liberté, 5. ☎ **0596-73-73-20.**

Aficionados consider Martinique rum to be one of the world's finest distilled drinks. This shop is the best place for browsing, offering all the brands of rum manufactured on Martinique (at least 12), as well as several others famous for their age and taste. Bottles range in price from $6 to $1,000 for a connoisseur's delight—a bottle of rum distilled by the Bally Company in 1924 in the nearby hamlet of Carbet. They offer samples in small cups to prospective buyers. We suggest that you try Vieux Acajou, a dark, mellow Old Mahogany, or a blood-red brown liqueurlike rum bottled by Bally.

Centre des Métiers d'Art. Rue Ernest Deproges. ☎ **0596-70-25-01.**

This arts-and-crafts store is adjacent to the tourist office, fronting the town's waterfront. Inside, you'll find a mixture of valuable and worthless local handmade artifacts for sale, including bamboo, ceramics, painted fabrics, and patchwork quilts suitable for hanging. There's also a collection of original tapestries made by the store's charming owner, Yvonne Elima, which range in price from Fr 200 to Fr 1,500 ($40 to $300).

La Galleria. Route de Lamentin.

Set midway between Fort-de-France and the Lamentin Airport, this is the most upscale and elegant shopping complex on Martinique. On the premises are more than 60 different vendors. You'll find a handful of cafes and simple restaurants on-site to relieve your hunger pangs as you shop, as well as an outlet or two for the local pastries and sweets.

Galeries Lafayette. Rue Victor-Schoelcher, 10 (near the cathedral). ☎ **0596-71-38-66.**

This is a small-scale branch (a pale version) of what is the most famous department store in Paris, the world-class Galeries Lafayette. Specializing in fashion for men, women, and children, it also offers leather goods, jewelry, watches, and all the predictably famous names in French perfume and fashion. The store offers 20% off for purchases made with U.S. dollar traveler's checks or a credit or charge card.

Nouvelles Galeries. Rue Lamartine, 87. ☎ **0596-63-04-60.**

This is another of the capital's large department stores, stocked with a downscale assortment of housewares. Despite the many workaday items, it's also known for its toys, luggage, beauty accessories, china, crystal, and silver. Come here to look for occasional bargains. The emphasis is French with Caribbean overtones.

Paradise Island. Rue Ernest-Deproges, 20. ☎ **0596-63-93-63.**

Here you'll find the most stylish and upscale collection of T-shirts on Martinique, each displayed as a kind of couture-conscious art form. Whatever you like will probably be available in about a dozen different colors, and priced at Fr 49 to Fr 99 ($9.80 to $19.80) each.

Roger Albert. Rue Victor-Hugo, 7–9. ☎ **0596-71-71-71.**

This is by far the largest emporium of luxury goods on Martinique, a department store for locals and cruise-ship passengers. It's one of five different branches scattered throughout Martinique, although this, a short walk from the waterfront, is by far the busiest. You'll find wristwatches (both "fun" and expensive), perfumes, sportswear by LaCoste and Tacchini, Lladró and Limoges porcelain, and crystal by Swarovski and such other manufacturers as Daum and Lalique. For anyone with a non–French passport, there are reductions of 20% off what a local resident would pay, plus discounts of an additional 20%, depending on seasonal discounts and promotions. Even better, value-added tax is not added to the price of your purchases.

TROIS-ILETS

Marie-Josèphe-Rose Tascher de la Pagerié was born here in 1763. As Joséphine, she was to become the wife of Napoléon I and empress of France from 1804 to 1809. Six years older than Napoléon, she pretended that she'd lost her birth certificate so he wouldn't find out her true age. Although many historians call her ruthless and selfish, she is still revered by some on Martinique as an uncommonly gracious lady. Others have less kind words for her; because Napoléon is said by some historians to have "reinvented" slavery, they blame Joséphine's influence.

After 20 miles of driving south from Fort-de-France, you reach Trois-Ilets, a charming little village. One mile outside the hamlet, turn left to La Pagerie, where a small **museum** (☎ **0596-68-33-06**) of mementos relating to Joséphine has been installed in the former estate kitchen. Along with her childhood bed in the kitchen, you'll see a passionate letter from Napoléon. The collection was compiled by Dr. Robert Rose-Rosette. Here Joséphine gossiped with her slaves and played the guitar.

Still remaining are the partially restored ruins of the Pagerié sugar mill and the church (in the village itself) where she was christened in 1763. The plantation was destroyed in a hurricane. The museum is open Tuesday through Friday from 9am to 5:30pm and Saturday and Sunday from 9am to 1pm and 2:30 to 5:30pm, charging Fr 20 ($4) for admission.

A botanical garden, the **Parc des Floralies,** is adjacent to the golf course (see below), as is the museum devoted to Joséphine (see above).

Maison de la Canne, Pointe Vatable (☎ **0596-68-32-04**), stands on the road to Trois-Ilets. (From Fort-de-France, you can take a taxi or shuttle bus to La Marina, Pointe du Bout; from here, a bus heads for Pointe Vatable.) It was created in 1987 on the premises of an 18th-century distillery to house a permanent exhibition that tells the story of sugarcane and the sweeping role it played in the economic and cultural development of Martinique. Exhibits include models, tools, a miniature slave ship, an ancient plow tethered to life-size models of two oxen, and a restored carriage. Hostesses guide visitors through the exhibition. It's open Tuesday to Sunday from 9am to 5pm, charging an admission of Fr 15 ($3) for adults, Fr 5 ($1) for children 5 to 12 (free 4 and under).

OUTDOOR PURSUITS

GOLF In 1976, the famous golf course designer Robert Trent Jones Sr. visited Martinique and left behind the 18-hole **Golf de l'Impératrice-Joséphine** at Trois-Ilets (☎ **0596-68-32-81**), a five-minute drive from the leading resort area of Pointe du Bout and about 18 miles from Fort-de-France. The only golf course on

Martinique, the greens slope from the birthplace of Empress Joséphine (for whom it's named) across rolling hills with scenic vistas down to the sea. Amenities include a pro shop, a bar, a restaurant, and three tennis courts. Greens fees are Fr 270 ($54) per person for 18 holes. Residents of certain hotels (including the Bakoua, the Méridien, and the Novotel Le Diamant) receive discounted greens fees, Fr 230 ($46).

TENNIS Play on one of the three courts on the grounds of **Golf de l'Impératrice-Joséphine** at Trois-Ilets (☎ **0596-68-32-81**). The setting here is one of the most beautiful on Martinique. It costs Fr 50 ($10) per hour to play. No racquet rentals.

HORSEBACK RIDING The premier riding facility on Martinique is **Ranch Jack,** Morne Habitué, Trois-Ilets (☎ **0596-68-37-69**). It offers morning horseback rides for both experienced and novice riders, at a cost of Fr 340 ($68) per person for a 3½- to 4-hour ride. Jacques and Marlene Guinchard make daily promenades across the beaches and fields of Martinique, with a running explication of the history, fauna, and botany of the island. Cold drinks are included in the price, and transportation is usually free to and from the hotels of nearby Pointe du Bout. This is an ideal way to discover both botanical and geographical Martinique. Four to fifteen participants are needed to book a tour.

SHOPPING

Poterie de Trois-Ilets. Quartier Poterie, Trois-Ilets. ☎ **0596-68-03-44.**

At Christmastime, many of the island's traditional foie gras and pastries are presented in crocks made by Martinique's largest earthenware factories, the Poterie de Trois-Ilets. At least 90% of its production is devoted to brick-making. However, one small-scale offshoot of the company devotes itself to producing earth-toned stoneware and pottery whose colors and shapes have contributed to the folklore of Martinique. In theory, the studios are open Monday to Saturday from 7am to 4pm, but call before you set out to make sure they'll accept visitors.

POINTE DU BOUT

Pointe du Bout is a narrow peninsula across the bay from the busy capital of Fort-de-France. It's the most developed resort area of Martinique, with at least four of the island's largest hotels, an impressive marina, about a dozen tennis courts, swimming pools, and facilities for horseback riding and all kinds of water sports. There's also a handful of independent restaurants, a gambling casino, boutiques, and in nearby Trois-Ilets, a Robert Trent Jones–designed golf course (see above). Except for the hillside that contains the Hôtel Bakoua, most of the district is flat and verdant, with gardens and rigidly monitored parking zones. All the hotels listed below are near the clean, white sandy beaches of Pointe du Bout. Some of the smaller properties are convenient to the white sandy beaches of Anse Mitan.

GETTING THERE If you're driving from Fort-de-France, take Route 1, along which you'll cross the plain of Lamentin—the industrial area of Fort-de-France and the site of the international airport. Often the air is filled with the fragrance of caramel because of the large sugarcane factories in the surrounding area. After 20 miles, you reach Trois-Ilets, Joséphine's hometown. Three miles farther on your right, take Route D38 to Pointe du Bout.

For those who want to reach Pointe du Bout by sea, there's a **ferry service** (more fully described in "Getting Around"; see above) running all day long until midnight from the harbor front (quai d'Esnambuc) in downtown Fort-de-France. Round-trip fare is Fr 28 ($5.60).

Where to Stay

Expensive

Hôtel Bakoua-Sofitel. Pointe du Bout, 97229 Trois-Ilets, Martinique, F.W.I. ☎ **800/221-4542** in the U.S., 0596-66-02-02, or 0181/784-3433 in London. Fax 0596-66-00-41. 136 rms, 6 suites. A/C MINIBAR TV TEL. Winter, Fr 1,470–Fr 2,445 ($294–$489) double; from Fr 3,500 ($700) suite. Off-season, Fr 890–Fr 1,625 ($178–$325) double; from Fr 3,500 ($700) suite. Rates include continental breakfast. MAP Fr 210 ($42) per person extra. AE, DC, MC, V.

This famous and chic hotel has a long, glamorous history but surprisingly simple rooms. It's known for the beauty of its landscaping and its somewhat isolated hillside location. It's the only really upscale hotel on the island. Run by the Sofitel chain, it consists of three low-rise buildings in the center of a garden, plus another pair of bungalow-type buildings set directly on the beach. Rooms here are generally small, conservative, and modern. Celebrities, many of them French-speaking, often stay here. We'd choose this hotel over Hôtel Méridien (see below).

Dining/Entertainment: A dramatically engineered bar, crafted into a perfect circle out of exotic Caribbean hardwood, is one of the ideal rendezvous points of Pointe du Bout. The most upscale and elegant restaurant, Le Chateaubriand, serves French and Caribbean cuisine every night from 7 to 10pm. Other places to eat include La Sirene, a beachfront restaurant specializing in Caribbean cuisine.

Services: Concierge, laundry, baby-sitting, free twice-daily shuttle bus to the golf course.

Facilities: Swimming pool, active sports program (including a free golf lesson and a free scuba diving lesson), diving center, waterskiing, jet-skiing, golf, and horseback riding available nearby.

Hôtel Méridien Trois-Ilets. Pointe du Bout, Trois-Ilets (B.P. 894, 97245 Fort-de-France), Martinique, F.W.I. ☎ **800/543-4300** in the U.S. and Canada, or 0596-66-00-00. Fax 0596-66-00-74. 285 rms, 7 suites. A/C TV TEL. Winter, Fr 1,480–Fr 2,140 ($296–$428) double; Fr 2,100–Fr 4,000 ($420–$800) suite. Off-season, Fr 710 ($142) double; Fr 1,700–Fr 3,000 ($340–$600) suite. Rates include buffet breakfast. AE, MC, V.

This is the largest and (at seven stories) the tallest building in the resort community of Pointe du Bout, and offers extensive facilities. But despite its prominence, we definitely don't find it the most desirable place to stay locally—it needs renovations and some readers have complained about dingy rooms. At press time the bedrooms remained a patchwork of hasty repairs. In spite of that, many visitors wind up here, especially convention groups.

Owned and operated by Air France, the hotel has a slightly shabby reception area that opens onto the palm-fringed swimming pool, the waters of the bay, and the faraway lights of Fort-de-France. The hotel is slightly angled to follow the contours of the shoreline, so each bedroom overlooks either the Caribbean or the bay. Each unit contains a private balcony and conservatively modern furnishings with tropical accents.

Dining/Entertainment: La Capitane, the showcase restaurant at the hotel, is open to a view of the sea. The view, not its mess hall decor, is its best feature. Less expensive is Le Cocoterais, beside the beach. Regrettably, the once-proud casino was replaced several years ago with a staid cluster of slot machines. Around the huge block of rooms are a waterside garden, a 100-foot marina, and a cabana bar near the swimming pool. Every Thursday night the hotel hosts the Grands Ballets Martiniquais in a pavilion near the pool.

Services: Laundry, concierge, massage.

Facilities: Swimming pool; two tennis courts; sauna; hairdressing salon; extensive water sports facilities, including scuba diving (see entry below), sailing, snorkeling, waterskiing, and windsurfing.

Novotel Carayou. Pointe du Bout, 97229 Trois-Ilets, Martinique, F.W.I. ☎ **800/221-4542** in the U.S., or 0596-66-04-04. Fax 0596-66-00-57. 201 rms. A/C TV TEL. Winter, $232 double ($375 over Christmas). Off-season, $140 double. Rates include buffet American. Half board Fr 180 ($36) per person extra. AE, DC, MC, V.

A member of France's biggest hotel chain, the Accor Group, this hotel has always prided itself on its lush gardens and glamorous garden setting. Radically renovated in late 1994 and early 1995, it reopened with yellow-beige exterior walls and an almost completely rebuilt physical plant. The accommodations aren't the most attractive in the area, but they are housed in a series of three-story outbuildings, each encircled by large lawns dotted with coconut or palm trees and many flowering shrubs. The seaside rooms are the best.

Dining/Entertainment: There are three different dining areas, including a formal French and Creole restaurant and a beachfront grill for sandwiches and salads. Creole cookery is prepared with flair, especially the seafood items. One appealing bar, La Paillote, sports a view of the sea and many nautical accessories.

Services: 24-hour concierge, laundry.

Facilities: Swimming pool, a small beach, and water sports (including windsurfing, scuba diving, waterskiing, sailboat rentals, and snorkeling).

Moderate

Mercure Inn La Pagerie. Pointe du Bout, 97229 Trois-Ilets, Martinique, F.W.I. ☎ **800/221-4542** in the U.S., or 0596-66-05-30. Fax 0596-66-00-99. 98 units. A/C TV TEL. Winter, Fr 655–Fr 975 ($131–$195) double; Fr 845–Fr 1,180 ($169–$236) triple. Off-season, Fr 640 ($128) double; Fr 830 ($166) triple. Rates include buffet breakfast. AE, DC, MC, V.

The facilities here are relatively modest compared to those in some of the larger and more expensive hotels of Pointe du Bout, but its guests can compensate by visiting the many restaurants, bars, and sports facilities in the area. Set close to the gardens of the Hôtel Bakoua-Sofitel, a 16-mile drive from the airport, this moderately priced hotel offers private apartments, although walls are thin. The units are neat and uncomplicated, with tile floors. Each has a small refrigerator and a balcony with a view opening onto the bay, and about two-thirds contain tiny kitchenettes at no extra charge. The hotel has a small swimming pool and a tiny bar, open only in the evening, plus a bar and restaurant, L'Hibiscus. Guests usually walk the short distance to the Novotel Carayou, a nearby hotel (see above), for other facilities, including water sports and the beach.

Inexpensive

Auberge de l'Anse Mitan. Anse Mitan, 97229 Trois-Ilets, Martinique, F.W.I. ☎ **800/223-9815** in the U.S., or 0596-66-01-12. Fax 0596-66-01-05. 19 rms, 6 studios. A/C TEL. Winter, Fr 420 ($84) double; Fr 400 ($80) studio for 2. Off-season, Fr 330 ($66) double; Fr 300 ($60) studio for 2. Rates for doubles include breakfast (studios don't). AE, DC, MC, V.

Many guests like the location of this place—at the isolated end of a road whose more commercial side is laden with restaurants and bustling nighttime activity. The hotel was originally built in 1933, but it has been renovated several times since then by the hospitable Athanase family. What you see today is a three-story concrete-box-type structure filled with wicker furniture. Six of the units are studios with kitchens and TVs; all have private showers. You don't get a lot that's special here, but the price is right.

Where to Dine

In the words of one longtime expatriate, "We have some really crummy restaurants in Pointe du Bout." Here's the pick of the litter.

Pignon sur Mer. Anse-à-l'Ane. ☎ **0596-68-38-37.** Reservations not necessary. Main courses Fr 75–Fr 175 ($15–$35). AE, MC, V. Tues–Sat 12:15–4pm, Tues–Sun 7–9:30pm. CREOLE.

Simple and unpretentious, this is a small-scale Creole restaurant containing about 15 tables, set within a rustically dilapidated building beside the sea (it's a 12-minute drive from Pointe du Bout). Menu items are island-inspired, and might include *delices du Pignon,* a platter of shellfish, or whatever grilled fish or shellfish was hauled in that day. *Lambi* (conch), shrimp, and crayfish are almost always available.

Le Poisson d'Or. L'Anse Mitan. ☎ **0596-66-01-80.** Reservations recommended. Main courses Fr 60–Fr 165 ($12–$33); set menu Fr 100 ($20). AE, MC, V. Tues–Sun noon–2:30pm and 7–10pm. Closed July. CREOLE.

Its location near the entrance of the resort community of Pointe du Bout makes it easy to find. There's no view of the sea and the traffic runs close to the edge of the veranda and terrace, but the reasonable prices and the complete change of pace make up for that. The rustic dining room offers such menu items as grilled fish, grilled conch, grilled seafood, scallops sautéed in white wine, poached local fish, and flan. These dishes are ordinary, of course, but they're prepared with a certain flair and served with style, and visitors are warmly welcomed.

Villa Creole. Anse Mitan. ☎ **0596-66-05-53.** Reservations recommended. Set menus Fr 160–Fr 250 ($32–$50); main courses Fr 90–Fr 150 ($18–$30). MC, V. Tues–Sat noon–2pm; Tues–Sun 7–10:30pm. CREOLE.

This restaurant, which lies within a three or four-minute drive from the hotels of Pointe du Bout, has thrived since the late 1970s, offering a colorful, small-scale respite from the island's high-rise resorts. Set within a simple but well-maintained Creole house, with no particular views other than the small garden that surrounds it, the restaurant serves fairly priced set-price menus that offer a selection of such staples as *accras de morue* (beignets of codfish); *boudin creole* (blood sausage); and *un féroce* (a local form of pâté concocted from fresh avocados, pulverized codfish, and manioc flour). Especially flavorful is the *filet de vivaneau* (red snapper) prepared either with tomato sauce or grilled "facon Villa Creole." Owner Guy Bruère-Dawson, a singer and guitarist, entertains as you dine.

Playing in the Water

DIVING The Hôtel Méridien's **Bathy's Club** (☎ **0596-66-00-00**) is one of the major scuba centers for Pointe du Bout and welcomes anyone who shows up. Daily dive trips, depending on demand, leave from the Hôtel Méridien's pier. Prices include equipment rental, transportation, guide, and drinks on board. Dives are conducted twice daily, from 8am to noon and 2 to 6pm, and full-day charters can be arranged. The dive shop on the Méridien's beach stocks everything from weight belts and tanks to partial wetsuits and underwater cameras. Dives cost Fr 290 ($58) per person. Initial instruction is offered for beginners, free if they're residents of the Hôtel Méridien.

WINDSURFING The most popular sport in the French West Indies, equipment and lessons are available at all hotel water-sports facilities, especially the **Hôtel Méridien,** Pointe du Bout (☎ **0596-66-00-00**), where 30-minute lessons cost Fr 60 to Fr 100 ($12 to $20). Board rentals are only Fr 100 ($20) per hour.

Shopping

You'll find that the Marina complex has a number of interesting boutiques. Several sell handcrafts and curios from Martinique. They're sometimes of good quality, and are quite expensive, regrettably, particularly if you purchase some of the batiks of natural silk and the enameled jewel boxes.

La Belle Matadore. Immeuble Vermeil-Marina, Pointe du Bout. ☎ **0596-66-04-88.**

The owner of this shop, Martinique-born Marie-Josée Ravenel, has carefully researched the history and traditions associated with the island's jewelry. Virtually all the merchandise sold here derives from models developed during slave days by the *matadores* (prostitutes), midwives, and slaves. Designs are vivid and bold, and for the most part crafted on the island from 18-karat gold. Set midway between the La Pagerie Hôtel and the Hôtel Méridien, the store carries baubles that range in price from Fr 60 ($12) for a pendant shaped like the island of Martinique to around Fr 12,000 ($2,400) for a gold necklace.

THE SOUTH LOOP

We now leave Pointe du Bout and head south for more sun and beaches. Resort centers here include Le Diamant and Sainte-Anne.

From Trois-Ilets, you can follow a small curved road that brings you to **Anse-à-l'Ane, Grande Anse,** and **Anses d'Arlets.** At any of these places are small beaches, quite safe and usually not crowded. At Anses d'Arlets the scenery is beautiful. Fishing boats draw up on the beach, and the nets are spread out to dry in the sun. From Anses d'Arlets, Route D37 takes you to Diamant. The road is panoramic.

Le Diamant

Set on the island's southwestern coastline, this village offers a good beach, which is open to the prevailing southern winds. The village is named after one of Martinique's best-known geological oddities, *Le Rocher du Diamant,* or **Diamond Rock,** a barren offshore island that juts upward from the sea to a height of 573 feet. Sometimes referred to as the Gibraltar of the Caribbean, it figured prominently in a daring British-led invasion in 1804, when British mariners carried a formidable amount of ammunition and 110 sailors to the top. Here, despite frequent artillery bombardments from the French-held coastline, the garrison held out for 18 months, completely dominating the passageway between the rock and the coastline of Martinique. Intrepid foreigners sometimes visit Diamond Rock, but the access across the strong currents of the channel is risky.

Diamond Beach, on the Martinique "mainland," offers a sandy bottom, verdant groves of swaying palms, and many different surf and bathing possibilities. The entire district has developed in recent years into a resort, scattered with about 10 hotels, which consist of simple clusters of low-rise buildings with good landscaping and access to this beach.

Where to Stay & Dine

Hotel Diamant Les Bains. 97223 Le Diamant, Martinique. F.W.I. ☎ **800/322-2223** or 0596-76-40-14. Fax 0596-76-27-00. 4 rms, 20 bungalows. A/C TV TEL. Winter, Fr 500 ($100) double; Fr 600 ($120) bungalow. Off-season, Fr 300–Fr 380 ($60–$76) double; Fr 350–Fr 450 ($70–$90) bungalow. Rates include continental breakfast. MAP Fr 110 ($22) per person extra. MC, V. Closed 10 days in June, and Sept 1 to mid-Oct.

Capably managed by resident owners Hubert and Marie-Yvonne Andrieu, this is a simple, unpretentious, family-style hotel. Twenty of its 24 accommodations are in outlying motel-style bungalows set either in a garden or beside the beach; the others are in the resort's main building containing the dining and drinking facilities. Two rooms are outfitted for travelers with disabilities. From the edge of the resort's swimming pool you can enjoy a view of the offshore island of Diamond Rock. Most accommodations have white tile floors, small refrigerators, and built-in furniture made from polished fruitwoods.

The main building, whose bedrooms are lined along an upper deck, houses the restaurant, where Mr. Andrieu works as the chef. Full meals are served at lunch and dinner every day of the week except Wednesday. A fixed-price meal might include classic Creole specialties such as crab salad, spicy black pudding, and a fish blaff. Dessert might be a coconut flan. The cuisine is for the most part Creole, with some French dishes thrown in. Locally caught fish often appears on the menu.

Novotel Le Diamant. 97223 Le Diamant, Martinique, F.W.I. ☎ **800/221-4542** in the U.S., or 0596-76-42-42. Fax 0596-76-22-87. 181 rms, 6 suites. A/C TV TEL. Winter, $230–$375 double; $322–$468 suite. Off-season, $150–$168 double; $244–$263 suite. Rates include breakfast. AE, CB, DC, MC, V.

On 6 acres of forested land, 2 miles outside the village and 18 miles south of Fort-de-France, the Novotel resort is in one of the most beautiful districts on Martinique—on a rock-bordered peninsula that was famous as an 18th-century stronghold of the (eventually defeated) English. A low-rise building fitted into the landscaping around it, this hotel is known for a particularly difficult staff. It's the ultimate in laissez-faire management—guests, often tour groups from France, are basically left to fend for themselves.

From many of the bedrooms, the views are more evocative of the South Pacific than of the Caribbean. Units face either the pool or the coast, with its view of Diamond Rock, and are tropical in their decor. The reception opens onto a large pool that you traverse via a Chinese-style wooden bridge to get to the dining facilities. These include Le Flamboyant (dinner only, and the most formal), La Cabana du Pêcheur (dinner), Les Alizés (for lunch), and a poolside cafe. Outside the hotel, the neighboring beaches aren't too crowded because they aren't too good. Lawns and gardens, as well as tennis courts, surround the hotel. Water sports are also offered. The trip from the airport in a taxi should take about 40 minutes.

SAINTE-ANNE

As you follow the road south to Trois Rivières, you'll come to **Sainte-Luce,** one of the island's most charming villages. Beaches of varying quality surround the town, and it's the site of the Forêt Montravail. Continuing, you'll reach Rivière-Pilote, quite a large town, and **Le Marin,** at the bottom of a bay of the same name.

From Le Marin, a 5-mile drive brings you to Sainte-Anne, at the extreme southern tip of Martinique. This is a sleepy little village, with white-sand beaches. It opens onto views of the Sainte Lucia Canal, and nearby is the site of the Petrified Savannah Forest. The French call it **Savane des Pétrifications.** It's a field of petrified volcanic boulders in the shape of logs. The eerie, desertlike no-man's-land is studded with cacti. The region is so barren you'll not want to linger long.

After passing Le Marin, you reach **Vauclin,** a fishing port and market town that is pre-Columbus. If you have time, stop in at the 18th-century **Chapel of the Holy Virgin.** Visitors like to make an excursion to **Mount Vauclin,** the highest point in southern Martinique. Here they are rewarded with one of the most beautiful views in the West Indies.

Where to Stay

Les Boucaniers (Buccaneer's Creek) Club Mediterranée. Point Marin, 97227 Sainte-Anne, Martinique, F.W.I. ☎ **800/CLUB-MED** in the U.S., or 0596-76-76-13. Fax 0596-76-72-02. 313 rms. A/C. Winter, Fr 875–Fr 1,575 ($175–$315) per person double per week. Off-season, 25%–30% discount. Single occupancy (any season) 20%–30% more and only if space available. Rates include all meals and sports. AE, MC, V.

Set on a peaceful cove at the southernmost tip of Martinique, about a 50-minute drive from the airport, this all-inclusive resort is designed as a series of scattered outbuildings reminiscent of a Creole village. The club is on the 48-acre site of a former pirate's hideaway at Buccaneer's Creek, amid a forest of coconut palms. The small, spartan accommodations are in bungalows with twin beds and private shower baths. Although many Club Meds welcome children, this particular club does not accept children 11 and under, and is more geared toward single guests or couples, some of whom like the au naturel beach nearby. The emphasis is often on group activities.

Dining/Entertainment: In a domed two-level building in the heart of the resort, you'll find an amusement center, theater, dance floor, and bar. A walk along rue du Port (the main street of Club Med) leads to Tour du Port, a bar that overlooks the sailboat fleet anchored in the marina. The resort contains a communal dining room (Le Grand Restaurant) and a well-recommended, less formal restaurant (La Maison Creole) specializing in Antillean cuisine. Meals are served at long tables whose seating plans are conducive to meeting other guests (even if you don't want to). The disco stays open until the wee hours.

Services: Social director, massage.

Facilities: Sailing, waterskiing, snorkeling; part of the beach is reserved for nude sunbathing.

La Dunette. 97227 Sainte-Anne, Martinique, F.W.I. ☎ **0596-76-73-90.** Fax 0596-76-76-05. 18 rms. A/C TV TEL. Winter, Fr 600–Fr 700 ($120–$140) double. Off-season, Fr 400 ($80) double. Rates include continental breakfast. MC, V.

An unpretentious seaside inn with a simple, summery decor, the hotel is accented with a garden filled with flowers and tropical plants. It's a motel-like stucco structure set directly beside the sea, and it appeals to those who appreciate simplicity and isolation from the more developed resort areas of Martinique (it lies near the Club Med and the white-sand beaches of the Salines). The furnishings are casual and modern. Some of the rooms are quite small, and they were last completely renovated in 1993.

Drinks are served every night on the terrace above the sea. The in-house restaurant, open daily for lunch and dinner, is better than average, thanks to the culinary finesse of Tanzania-born owner Gerard Kambona. Main courses include a succulent version of red snapper stuffed with sea urchins, or a wide selection of fresh shellfish. Water sports and excursions can be arranged for you, but this place usually attracts do-it-yourself types.

Manoir de Beauregard. Chemins des Salines, 97227 Ste-Anne, Martinique, F.W.I. ☎ **0596-76-73-40.** Fax 0596-76-93-24. 11 rms. A/C TEL. Winter, Fr 900–Fr 1,100 ($180–$220) double; Fr 1,100–Fr 1,300 ($220–$260) triple. Off-season, Fr 750–Fr 800 ($150–$160) double; Fr 850–Fr 900 ($170–$180) triple. AE, MC, V.

One of the most venerable and historic hotels on Martinique lies within the massive walls of a manor house that once administered many acres of surrounding sugarcane fields. It was originally built between 1720 and 1800 by a prominent French family. Located within a five-minute walk south of Ste-Anne, it almost resembles a medieval church. A tragic fire in 1990 completely gutted the building's interior and led to four years of restoration. Today, there are three bedrooms on the upper floors of the original house, and another eight within a modern, less inspired one-story annex, built a few steps from the main house in 1975. Rooms within the annex, although not as dignified, have access to a private patio and antique West Indian beds. A truly superb beach, Plage des Salines, lies within a five-minute drive to the south, and a slightly less appealing beach, Plage de Sainte-Anne, is within a 15-minute walk.

Dining/Entertainment: Menu items are conservative, traditional, and similar to the tried-and-true Creole cuisine that flourished at this place throughout the early 20th century. Examples include codfish fritters, boudin Creole, grilled fish in Creole sauce, curries, and fresh lobster.

Where to Dine

Aux Filets Bleus. Point Marin, Sainte-Anne. ☎ **0596-76-73-42.** Reservations required. Fixed-price meal Fr 59–Fr 240 ($11.80–$48). MC, V. Daily noon–3:30pm and 7–10:30pm. CREOLE/ FRENCH.

Set on a flat area close to the beach, a 30-minute drive south of the airport, this stylish restaurant might remind you of the south of France. It's flanked by canopies and separated from the road by a hedge. Once you've entered, the seaside al fresco dining room and its terrace make you forget everything but the sound of the waves. (You can go for a swim before or after your meal.) What appears to be a glass-covered reflecting pool set into the floor is actually a lobster tank, one of only a few on the island.

Specialties include bouillabaisse de la mer; three types of fish covered with a tomato-and-onion sauce; crabmeat salad with a coulis of tomato, basil, and olive oil; and salade "filets bleus," with fresh crayfish, hearts of palm, avocados, fresh tomatoes, and a whisky-laden cocktail sauce. The chef pleases most palates with his *pavé de daurade aux senteurs des îles* (whitefish with a coriander-and-fennel sauce). He gains extra points for using local ingredients whenever possible.

THE NORTH LOOP

As we swing north from Fort-de-France, our main targets are Le Carbet, St-Pierre, Montagne Pelée, and Leyritz. However, we'll sandwich in many stopovers along the way.

From Fort-de-France there are three ways to head north to Montagne Pelée. The first way is to follow Route N4 up to St-Joseph. There you take the left fork for 3 miles after St-Joseph and turn onto Route D15 toward Marigot.

Another way to Montagne Pelée is to take Route N3 through the vegetation-rich *mornes* (hills) until you reach Le Morne Rouge. This road is known as "route de la Trace" and is now the center of the Parc Naturel de la Martinique.

Yet a third route to reach Montagne Pelée is to follow Route N2 along the coast. This is the route we'll follow, and the order in which we'll list the towns along the way. Near Fort-de-France, the first town you reach is **Schoelcher.** Farther along Route N2 you reach **Case-Pilote,** and then Bellefontaine. This portion, along the most frequented tourist route in Martinique—that is, Fort-de-France to St-Pierre—is very reminiscent of the way the French Riviera used to look. **Bellefontaine** is a small fishing village, with boats stretched along the beach. Note the many houses also built in the shape of boats.

LE CARBET

Leaving Bellefontaine, a 5-mile drive north will deliver you to Le Carbet. Columbus landed here in 1502, and the first French settlers arrived in 1635. In 1887 Gauguin lived here for four months before going on to Tahiti. You can stop for a swim at an Olympic-size pool set into the hills, or watch the locals scrubbing clothes in a stream. The town lies on the bus route from Fort-de-France to St-Pierre.

The **Centre d'Art Musée Paul-Gauguin,** Anse Turin, Le Carbet (☎ **0596-78-22-66**), is near the beach, represented in the artist's paintings, *Bord de Mer*. The landscape has not changed in 100 years. The museum, housed in a five-room building, commemorates the French artist's stay on Martinique in 1887, with books, prints, letters, and other memorabilia. There are also paintings by René Corail, sculpture by Hector Charpentier, and examples of the artwork of Zaffanella. Of special interest are faïence mosaics made of pieces of colored volcanic rock (formed in 1902 when the fires of Montagne Pelée devastated St-Pierre). The museum is open daily from 9am to 5pm, charging an admission of Fr 15 ($3).

ST-PIERRE

At the beginning of this century, St-Pierre was known as the "Little Paris of the West Indies." With 30,000 inhabitants, it was the cultural and economic capital of Martinique. On May 7, 1902, the citizens read in their daily newspaper that "Montagne Pelée does not present any more risk to the population than Vesuvius does to the Neapolitans."

However, on May 8, at 8am, the southwest side of Montagne Pelée exploded with fire and lava. At 8:02am all 30,000 inhabitants were dead—that is, all except one. A convict in his underground cell was saved by the thickness of the walls. When islanders reached the site, the convict was paroled and left Martinique to tour in Barnum and Bailey's circus.

St-Pierre never recovered its past splendor. Now it could be called the Pompeii of the West Indies. Ruins of the church, the theater, and some other buildings can be seen along the coast. A 50-passenger **submarine,** operated by the Companie de la Baie de St-Pierre, 76 rue Victor-Hugo, St-Pierre (☎ **0596-78-28-28**), enables visitors to explore the underwater wrecks of the ships destroyed in 1902 by the eruption of the volcano (until 1994 the wrecks had been accessible only to scuba divers). The cost of the submarine exploration is considerable, but worth it to many: Fr 450 ($90) for adults and Fr 225 ($45) for children.

One of the best ways to get an overview of St-Pierre involves riding a rubber-wheeled "train," the **CV *Paris Express*** (☎ **0596-78-31-41**), which departs on tours from the base of the Musée Volcanologique. Tours cost Fr 50 ($10) for adults, and Fr 25 ($5) for children and run Monday through Friday from 10:30am to 1pm and 2:30 to 7pm. In theory, tours depart about once an hour, but they only leave when there are enough people to justify a trip.

At the **Musée Volcanologique,** rue Victor-Hugo, St-Pierre (☎ **0596-78-10-32**), pictures and relics dug from the debris allow you to trace the story of what happened to St-Pierre. Dug from the lava is a clock that stopped at the exact moment the volcano erupted. The museum is open daily from 9am to 5pm, with an admission of Fr 15 ($3), free for children 7 and under.

High-speed quadrimarans bring visitors by water from Fort-de-France to St-Pierre.

LE PRÊCHEUR

From St-Pierre, you can continue along the coast north to Le Prêcheur. Once the home of Madame de Maintenon, the mistress of Louis XIV, it's the last village along the northern coast of Martinique. Here you can see hot springs of volcanic origin and the **Tombeau des Caraïbes (Tomb of the Caribs),** where, according to legend, the collective suicide of many West Indian natives took place after they returned from a fishing expedition and found their homes pillaged by the French.

MONTAGNE PELÉE

A panoramic and winding road (Route N2) takes you through a tropical rain forest. The curves are of the hairpin variety, and the road is not always kept in good shape. However, you're rewarded with tropical flowers, baby ferns, plumed bamboo, and valleys so deeply green you'll think you're wearing cheap sunglasses.

The village of **Morne Rouge,** right at the foot of Montagne Pelée, is a popular vacation spot for Martiniquais. From there on, a narrow and unreliable road brings you to a level of 2,500 feet above sea level, 1,600 feet under the round summit of the volcano that destroyed St-Pierre. Montagne Pelée itself rises 4,575 feet above sea level.

If you're a trained mountain climber and you don't mind four or five hours of hiking, you can scale the peak. Realize that this is a mountain, that rain is frequent, and that temperatures drop very low. Tropical growth often hides deep crevices in the earth, and there are other dangers. So if you're really serious about this climb, you should hire an experienced guide. The park service maintains more than 100 miles of trails, which reward the determination of the rugged and the physically fit who toil to the peak's beautiful panoramas. Although the hikes up from Grand-Rivière or Le Prêcheur are generally the less arduous of the three options leading to the top, most visitors opt for departures from Morne Rouge, a landlocked village set to the south of the summit, because it doesn't take as long to finish the trip. It's steeper, rockier, and more exhausting, but you can make it in just 2½ hours versus the five hours it takes from the other two towns. There are no facilities other than these villages, so it's vital to bring water and food with you. Your arduous journey will be rewarded at the summit with sweeping views over the sea and panoramas that sometimes stretch as far as mountainous Domenica to the south. As for the volcano, its deathly eruption in 1902 apparently satisfied it—at least for the time being!

Upon your descent from Montagne Pelée, drive down to **Ajoupa-Bouillon,** one of the most beautiful towns on Martinique. Abounding in flowers and shrubbery with bright yellow and red leaves, this little village is the site of the remarkable **Gorges de la Falaise.** These are minicanyons on the Falaise River up which one can travel to reach a waterfall. Ajoupa-Boullion also makes a good lunch stop.

Where to Dine

Le Fromagter. Route de Fonds-St-Denis, St-Pierre. ☎ **0596-78-19-07.** Reservations recommended. Fixed-price menus Fr 100–Fr 150 ($20–$30); main courses Fr 78–Fr 130 ($15.60–$26). AE, DC, DISC, MC, V. Daily noon–3pm, Fri–Sat 7:30–midnight. CREOLE/FRENCH.

Set about a half mile uphill (east) of the center of St-Pierre, this indoor-outdoor villa, owned by the René family, welcomes diners with humor and charm that's half–French, half-Martiniquais. It has a sweeping view of the town, and resembles a covered open-air pavilion. Menu items include marinated octopus, grilled conch or lobster, curried goat or chicken, and whatever grilled fish is available that day. Evenings (Friday and Saturday nights only), focus more aggressively on grilled lobster and steaks, and include some kind of live entertainment, usually a pianist or guitarist.

LEYRITZ

Continue east toward the coast, toward the town of Basse-Pointe in northeastern Martinique. A mile before Basse-Pointe, turn left and follow a road that goes deep into sugarcane country to Leyritz, where you'll find one of the best-restored plantations on Martinique, and perhaps stop by for lunch.

Where to Stay & Dine

✪ **Hôtel Plantation de Leyritz.** 97218 Basse-Pointe, Martinique, F.W.I. ☎ **0596-78-53-92.** Fax 0596-78-92-44. 67 rms. A/C TV TEL. Winter, Fr 670–Fr 825 ($134–$165) double. Off-season, Fr 495 ($99) double. Rates include continental breakfast. AE, MC, V.

This hotel, which offers spa facilities, occupies the site of a structure erected in 1700 by Bordeaux-born Michel de Leyritz. Sprawled over flat, partially wooded terrain (part of which still functions as a working banana plantation), a half-hour drive from the nearest beach (Anse à Zerot, in Sainte-Marie), it was the site of the "swimming pool summit meeting" in 1974 between Presidents Gerald Ford and Valéry Giscard d'Estaing. Today, instead of politicians, you're likely to meet a daytime stampede of cruise-ship passengers touring the island during their brief time ashore. The resort includes 16 acres of tropical gardens, and at the core is a stone-sided 18th-century Great House. From the grounds, the view sweeps across the Atlantic and takes in fearsome Montagne Pelée. The owners have kept the best of the old, including the rugged stone walls (20 inches thick), the beamed ceilings, and the tile and flagstone floors.

The setting is historic, cozy, and curiously barren, although it contains mahogany tables, overstuffed sofas, and gilt mirrors. About half the accommodations lie in a network of small outbuildings scattered around the property; others are in a newer annex adjacent to the spa. Don't expect well-polished luxury—that's not the style here. All rooms and public areas here were renovated in 1992.

Dining/Entertainment: The dining room is in a rum distillery, incorporating the fresh spring water running down from the hillside. Eating here is dramatic (and more intimate without the daytime crowds) at night, and the cuisine is authentically Creole. Tour-bus crowds predominate at lunch, which costs Fr 105 to Fr 120 ($21 to $24). Lunch might be grilled chicken covered in coconut-milk sauce, along with *ouassous* (a freshwater crayfish that comes in an herb sauce), sautéed breadfruit, and sautéed bananas. Dinner is more elaborate, with both French and Creole dishes, including duck with pineapple, a colombo of lamb, and *boudin* (blood pudding) Creole. Dinners are fixed-price affairs, costing Fr 105 to Fr 120 ($21 to $24) each. Lunch is served from 12:30 to 3pm and dinner is from 7:30 to 9pm daily.

Services: Laundry, concierge.

Facilities: Outdoor swimming pool, tennis court.

BASSE-POINTE

At the northernmost point on the island, Basse-Pointe is a land of pineapple and banana plantation fields, covering the Atlantic-side slopes of Mount Pelée volcano.

Where to Dine

Chez Mally Edjam. Route de la Côte Atlantique. ☎ **0596-78-51-18.** Reservations required. Main courses Fr 65–Fr 180 ($13–$36); fixed-price menu Fr 65 ($13). AE, MC, V. Daily noon–3pm; dinner by special arrangement only. Closed mid-July to mid-Aug. FRENCH/CREOLE.

This local legend operates from a modest house beside the main road in the center of town, 36 miles from Fort-de-France. Appreciating its exotic but genteel charm, many visitors prefer to drive all the way from Pointe du Bout to dine here, instead of at the Leyritz Plantation. You sit at one of a handful of tables on the side porch, unless you prefer a seat in the somewhat more formal dining room.

Grandmotherly Mally Edjam (assisted to an ever-increasing degree by her younger, France-born friend, Martine Hugé) is busy in the kitchen turning out her Creole delicacies. Both women know how to prepare all the dishes for which the island is known: stuffed land crab with a hot seasoning, small pieces of conch in a tart shell, and a classic *colombo de porc* (the Creole version of pork curry). Equally delectable are the lobster vinaigrette, the papaya soufflé (which must be ordered in advance), and the highly original confitures, which are tiny portions of fresh island fruits, such as pineapple and guava, that have been preserved in a vanilla syrup.

Grand' Rivière

After Basse-Pointe, the town you reach on your northward trek is Grand' Rivière. From here you must turn back, but before doing so you may want to stop at a good restaurant right at the entrance to the town.

Where to Dine

Yva Chez Vava. Boulevard de Gaulle. ☎ **0596-55-72-72.** Reservations recommended. Main courses Fr 60–Fr 140 ($12–$28); set menu Fr 80 ($16). AE, DC, MC, V. Daily noon–6pm. FRENCH/CREOLE.

Directly west of Basse-Pointe, in a low-slung building painted the peachy-orange of a papaw fruit, Yva Chez Vava is a combination private home and restaurant. It represents the hard labor of three generations of Creole women. Infused with a simple country-inn style, it was established in 1979 by a well-remembered, long-departed matron, Vava, whose daughter, Yva, is now assisted by her own daughter, Rosy. Local family recipes are the mainstay of this modest bistro. À la carte menu items include Creole soup, lobster, and various colombos or curries. Local delicacies have changed little since the days of Joséphine and her sugar fortune, and include *z'habitants* (crayfish), *vivaneau* (red snapper), *tazard* (kingfish), and *accras de morue* (cod fritters).

Le Marigot

After passing back through Basse-Pointe and Le Lorraine, you come to a small village that was relatively ignored by tourists until hotelier Jean-Louis de Lucy used France's tax-shelter laws to restore a landmark plantation (see below) and turn it into one of the finest hotels on the island. True, the nearest good beach is at Trinité, about a 30-minute drive from the hotel, but guests of the Habitation LaGrange don't seem to mind.

Where to Stay & Dine

Habitation LaGrange. 97225 Le Marigot, Martinique, F.W.I. ☎ **0596-53-60-60.** Fax 0596-53-50-58. (For reservations, contact Caribbean Inns, P.O. Box 7411, Hilton Head Island, SC 29983; 800/633-7411 in the U.S.) 11 rms, 1 suite. A/C MINIBAR TEL. Winter, Fr 2,300–Fr 2,600 ($460–$520) double; Fr 2,900 ($580) suite. Off-season, Fr 1,400 ($280) double; Fr 1,900 ($380) suite. Rates include breakfast. Half board Fr 250 ($50) per person extra. AE, MC, V.

One of the more unusual and historic properties of Martinique, this hotel lies in isolation about a mile north of the village of Le Marigot. It's set on 6 acres of land whose edges are engulfed by acres of banana fields. About 1½ miles inland from the coast, it was originally built in 1928 as part of the last sugar plantation and rum distillery on Martinique. Today the ruins of that distillery rise a short distance from the Louisiana-style main house.

Rooms are either in the main house or in a comfortable annex, which was erected in 1990. Each accommodation is different, and each contains antique or reproduction furniture crafted from mahogany, baldaquin-style beds, and accessories steeped in the French colonial style. Each unit has a veranda or patio, and ample vistas over a tropical landscape of gardens and faraway banana groves. As a conscious effort to preserve the calm and quiet, none contains a TV set or radio.

Dining/Entertainment: Meals are prepared in the Creole style by local chefs and served in an open-sided pavilion, the Ajoupa. Fixed-price lunches or dinners cost Fr 300 ($60) for three courses without wine.

Services: Concierge (who can arrange car or boat rentals and sports activities around the island), pickup service available from the airport (on request).

Facilities: Swimming pool, tennis court.

Sainte-Marie

Heading south along the coastal road, you'll pass Le Marigot en route to a sightseeing stop in the little town of Sainte-Marie. The **Musée du Rhum Saint-James,** Route de l'Union at the Saint James Distillery (☎ **0596-69-30-02**), displays engravings, antique tools and machines, and other exhibits tracing the history of sugarcane and rum from 1765 to the present. When inventories of rum are low and the distillery is functioning (February 1 to July 30), guided tours of both the museum and its distillery are offered. Tours depart four times a day, at 90-minute intervals (10am, 11:30am, 1pm, and 2:30pm), cost Fr 20 ($4) per person, and include a session of rum-tasting. Admission to the museum (open daily from 9am to 6pm, regardless of whether the distillery is functioning) is free. Samples of rum are available for purchase on-site.

From here you can head out the north end of town and loop inland a bit for a stopover at Morne-des-Esses, or continue heading south straight to Trinité.

Morne-des-Esses

This is the *vannerie* (basket-making) capital of Martinique, and you can pick up a sturdy straw food basket in any of the small shops in the village. You also might want to stop for a Creole lunch at Le Colibri restaurant.

Where to Dine

✪ **Le Colibri (The Hummingbird).** Allée du Colibri. ☎ **0596-69-91-95.** Reservations not required. Main courses Fr 110–Fr 240 ($22–$48). AE, DC, MC, V. Daily noon–3pm and 7–11pm. CREOLE.

One of the longest-running restaurants on the island, Le Colibri was established by owner Mme Clotilde Paladino, who is assisted now by her daughters. It's located in the heart of town near the post office. If the terrace fills up with weekenders from Fort-de-France, you'll be seated on another smaller veranda where you can survey the cooking. The place is decidedly informal with first-class, typically Creole cookery. You might begin with a calalou soup with crab or a sea-urchin tart. We recommend a *buisson d'écrevisses* (a stew of freshwater crayfish), stuffed pigeon, chicken with coconut, crabmeat-stuffed avocado, and roast suckling pig. For dessert, try a coconut flan. French wines accompany most meals.

Trinité

If you're in Morne-des-Esses, continue south then turn east, or from Ste-Marie head south along the coastal route (N1), to reach Trinité. The town is the gateway to the Carvalle peninsula, where the **Presqu'île de la Caravelle Nature Preserve** offers excellent hiking and one of the only safe beaches for swimming on the Atlantic coast. It would hardly merit actually stopping here were it not for the Saint-Aubin Hôtel.

Where to Stay

✪ **Saint-Aubin Hôtel.** 97220 Trinité, Martinique, F.W.I. ☎ **0596-69-34-77.** Fax 0596-69-41-14. 15 rms. A/C TEL. Winter, Fr 480–Fr 580 ($96–$116) double. Off-season, Fr 370–Fr 470 ($74–$94) double. Rates include continental breakfast. AE, MC, V.

A former restaurant owner, Normandy-born Guy Forêt, has sunk his fortune into restoring this three-story Victorian house and turning it into one of the loveliest inns in the Caribbean. The house was originally built in 1920 of brick and poured concrete to replace a much older plantation house. It was named after the uninhabited offshore islet of Saint-Aubin, visible from the hotel. Painted a vivid pink, and with fancy gingerbread, it sits on a hillside above sugarcane fields and Trinité's bay,

19 miles from Fort-de-France, and 2 miles from the seaside village of Trinité itself. There are 800 yards of public beach, plus a swimming pool on the grounds. All rooms sport wall-to-wall carpeting and modern furniture, all with a view of the garden or the sea.

After dinner you can relax on the veranda on the first and second floors. The hotel restaurant and bar are reserved for the use of hotel guests. Meals are served only at dinnertime, never at lunch, Monday through Saturday. A fixed-price meal is offered for Fr 135 ($27) per person. Menu items might include a salad with avocado vinaigrette, codfish fritters, stingray à l'étouffée, Creole black pudding, grilled fresh fish, or a more sophisticated daube of tuna, stuffed crab, or fish poached in court bouillon.

Le François

Continuing your exploration of the east coast of Martinique, you can stop over in Le François to visit the **Musée Rhum Clement** at the Domaine de l'Acajou (☎ **0596-54-62-07**), about 1½ miles south of the village center. It's open daily from 9am to 6pm, charging an admission of Fr 38 ($7.60). The distillery lies in the cellar of an 18th-century mansion with period furnishings, whose premises form part of the museum. The house commemorates the summit meeting of Presidents Mitterand and Bush in 1992. Exhibits in the cellars include a testimonial to Christopher Columbus as well as exhibits tracing the institution of slavery in the islands. The museum is located in a botanical park and you could easily spend two or three hours exploring the exhibits and grounds.

Where to Stay

Frégate Bleue. Route de Vauclin, Le François 97240, F.W.I. ☎ **800/633-7411** or 0596-54-54-66. Fax 0596-54-78-48. 7 rms with kitchenette. Winter, $200–$225 double. Off-season, $120–$140 double. Extra person $20. AE, MC, V.

This is the closest thing to a European B&B on the island. It's a calm and quiet place with touches of personal, old-fashioned charm. It's not the place for vacationers looking for nightlife and lots of activities—it's for escapists who don't mind the 10-minute drive to the beaches of St–François or the prevailing sense of isolation. Much of this ambience is the work of owner Madame Yveline de Lucy de Fossarieu, an experienced veteran of the hotel industry. Her house is a five-minute drive inland from the sea, and it overlooks several chains of deserted offshore islands (including Les Ilets de St–François and Les Ilets de l'Imperatrice).

Breakfast is served *en famille,* and three nights a week, Mme de Fossarieu (who speaks perfect English) prepares an evening meal, served to whomever requests it in advance, for around $28 per person.

2 Guadeloupe

"The time is near, I believe, when thousands of American tourists will come to spend the winter among the beautiful countryside and friendly people of Guadeloupe." So Theodore Roosevelt accurately predicted on February 21, 1916. Guadeloupe isn't the same place it was when the Rough Rider rode through, but the natural beauty he observed is still here.

Guadeloupe is part of the Lesser Antilles, about 200 miles north of Martinique, closer to the United States than to its cousin island. Guadeloupe is formed by two different islands, separated by a narrow seawater channel known as the Rivière Salée. **Grande-Terre,** the eastern island, is typical of the charm of the Antilles, with its rolling hills and sugar plantations. **Basse-Terre,** to the west, is a rugged mountainous island, dominated by the 4,800-foot volcano, La Soufrière, which is still alive. Its mountains are covered with tropical forests, impenetrable in many places. Bananas grown on plantations are the main crop. The island is ringed by beautiful beaches, which have attracted much tourism.

GETTING THERE

Most flights into Guadeloupe are tied in with air connections to Martinique. See "Getting There" in the Martinique section, earlier in this chapter. Passengers originating in Toronto usually fly **Air Canada** to Miami, then transfer to flights on such other airlines as **Air France** on to Guadeloupe. There are no direct flights from anywhere in Canada to either Guadeloupe or Martinique.

GETTING AROUND

BY RENTAL CAR Having a car enables you to circumnavigate Basse-Terre, which is one of the loveliest drives in the Caribbean.

Car-rental kiosks at the airport are usually open to meet international flights. Rental rates at local companies might appear lower, depending on the agency, but several readers have complained of mechanical problems and billing irregularities, and difficulties in resolving insurance disputes in the event of accidents. So we recommend reserving a car in advance through North America's largest car-rental companies: **Hertz** (☎ **800/654-3001**), **Avis** (☎ **800/331-2112**), and **Budget** (☎ **800/527-0700**), each of which is represented on the island and has its headquarters at the airport. Local phone numbers for the offices are Avis, ☎ **0590-21-13-54;** Budget, ☎ **0590-82-95-58;** and Hertz, ☎ **0590-21-09-35.**

In addition to the rental rates, you'll have to pay a one-time airport surcharge of $12 and VAT (value-added tax) of 9.5%. Prices are usually 20% to 25% lower between March and early December.

As in France, **driving is on the right-hand side of the road,** and there are several gas stations along the island's main routes. Because of the distance between gas stations away from the capital, try not to let your gas gauge fall below the halfway mark.

BY TAXI You'll find taxis when you arrive at the airport, but no limousines or buses. From 9pm until 7am, cabbies are legally entitled to charge you 40% more. In practice, either day or night, they charge you whatever they think the market will bear, although technically fares are regulated by the government. Always agree on the price before getting in. Approximate fares are Fr 120 ($24) from the airport to Gosier hotels, or Fr 70 ($14) from the airport to Pointe-à-Pitre. **Radio taxis** can be called at ☎ **0590-82-99-88.**

If you're traveling with more than two people, it's possible to sightsee by taxi. Usually the concierge at your hotel will help you make this arrangement. Fares are usually negotiated.

BY BUS Buses link almost every hamlet to Pointe-à-Pitre. However, you may need to know some French to use the system. From Pointe-à-Pitre you can catch one of these jitney vans, either at the Gare Routière de Bergevin if you're going to Basse-Terre, or the Gare Routière de Mortenol if Grande-Terre is your destination. Service is daily from 5:30am to 7:30pm. The fare from the airport to the Pointe-à-Pitre terminal on rue Peynier is Fr 7 ($1.40).

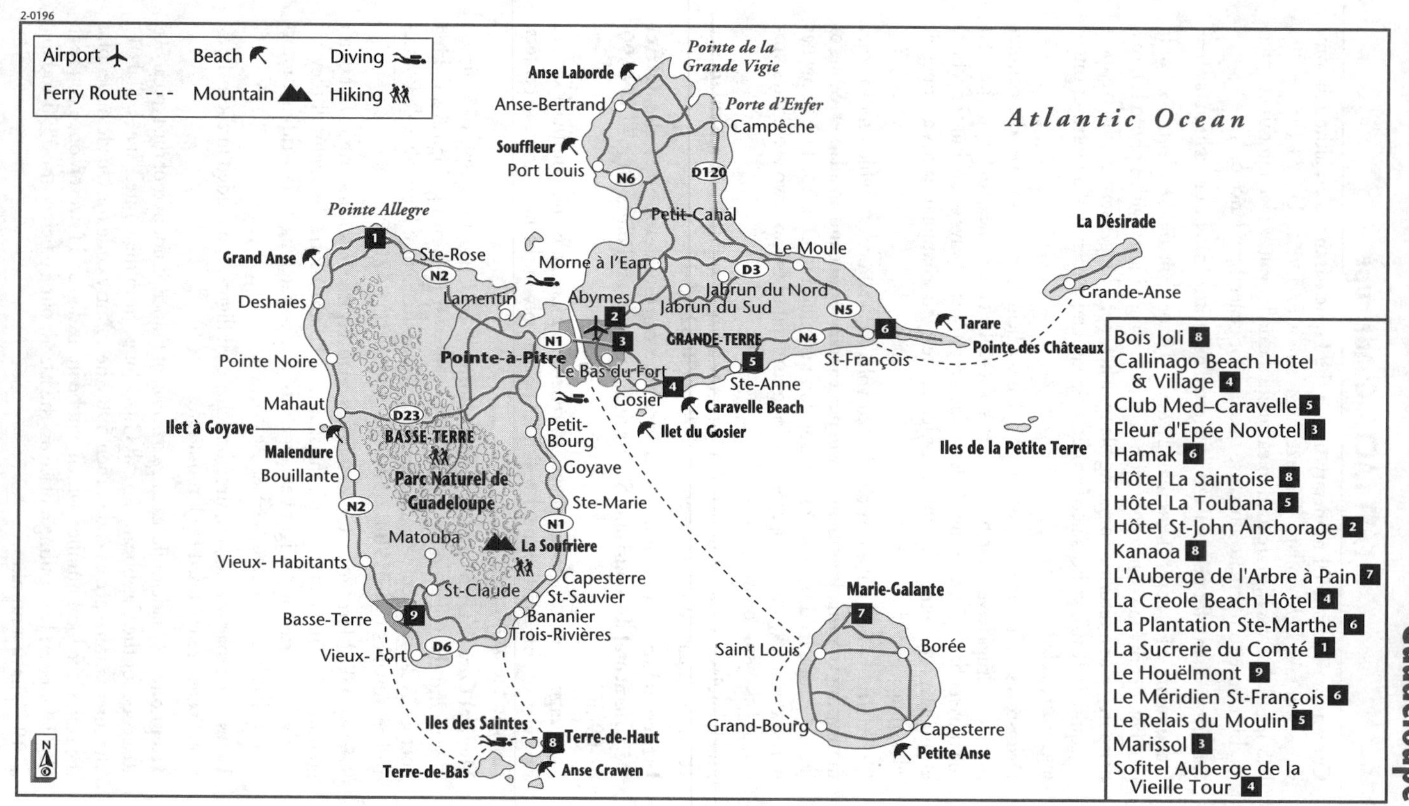

2-0196
Airport
Beach
Diving
Ferry Route
Mountain
Hiking
Atlantic Ocean
Pointe de la Grande Vigie
Anse Laborde
Anse-Bertrand
Porte d'Enfer
Campêche
Souffleur
Port Louis
N6
D120
Petit-Canal
Pointe Allegre
Grand Anse
Ste-Rose
N2
Morne à l'Eau
Le Moule
D3
Jabrun du Nord
Jabrun du Sud
Deshaies
Lamentin
Abymes
N5
N1
Pointe-à-Pitre
GRANDE-TERRE
N4
Pointe Noire
Le Bas du Fort
Ste-Anne
St-François
Tarare
Pointe des Châteaux
La Désirade
Grande-Anse
Gosier
Caravelle Beach
Ilet du Gosier
Mahaut
D23
Ilet à Goyave
Malendure
BASSE-TERRE
Petit-Bourg
Bouillante
Parc Naturel de Guadeloupe
Goyave
Ste-Marie
N1
Matouba
La Soufrière
Iles de la Petite Terre
Vieux- Habitants
Capesterre
St-Claude
St-Sauvier
Bananier
Trois-Rivières
Basse-Terre
Vieux- Fort
D6
Marie-Galante
Saint Louis
Borée
Grand-Bourg
Capesterre
Petite Anse
Iles des Saintes
Terre-de-Haut
Terre-de-Bas
Anse Crawen
Bois Joli 8
Callinago Beach Hotel & Village 4
Club Med–Caravelle 5
Fleur d'Epée Novotel 3
Hamak 6
Hôtel La Saintoise 8
Hôtel La Toubana 5
Hôtel St-John Anchorage 2
Kanaoa 8
L'Auberge de l'Arbre à Pain 7
La Creole Beach Hôtel 4
La Plantation Ste-Marthe 6
La Sucrerie du Comté 1
Le Houëlmont 9
Le Méridien St-François 6
Le Relais du Moulin 5
Marissol 3
Sofitel Auberge de la Vieille Tour 4

FAST FACTS: Guadeloupe

Currency The official monetary unit is the **French franc (Fr),** although some shops will take U.S. dollars. The exchange rate is Fr 4.98 to U.S.$1 (Fr 1 = 20¢ U.S.), and this was the rate used to calculate the dollar values given in this chapter. As this is sure to fluctuate a bit, use this rate for general guidance only.

Customs Items for personal use "in limited quantities" can be brought in tax free.

Documents For stays of less than 21 days, U.S. or Canadian residents need only proof of identity (a voter registration card or birth certificate with a photo ID, or a passport), plus a return or ongoing plane ticket. For a longer stay, a valid passport is required. British visitors need a valid passport and evidence of a return or ongoing airline ticket.

Drugstores The pharmacies carry French medicines, and most over-the-counter American drugs have French equivalents. Prescribed medicines can be purchased if the traveler has a prescription. At least one drugstore is always open, but the schedule is always changing. The tourist office can tell you what pharmacies are open at what time.

Electricity The local electricity is 220 volts AC (50 cycles), which means that those using U.S.-made appliances will need a transformer and an adapter. Some of the big resorts lend these to guests, but don't count on it. One hotel we know has only six in stock, and a long, long waiting list (and of the six, two are always broken!). Take your own.

Emergencies Call the **police** at **17,** report a **fire** or summon an **ambulance** at **18.** If the situation is less urgent, call ☎ **0590-82-13-17.**

Information The major tourist office on Guadeloupe is the **Office Départemental du Tourisme,** Square de la Banque, 5, in Pointe-à-Pitre (☎ **0590-82-09-30**).

Language The official language is French, and Creole is the unofficial second language. As on Martinique, English is spoken only in the major tourist centers, rarely in the countryside.

Medical Care There are five modern hospitals on Guadeloupe, plus 23 clinics. Hotels and the Guadeloupe tourist office can assist in locating English-speaking doctors. A 24-hour emergency room operates at the Centre Hôpitalier de Pointe-à-Pitre, Abymes (☎ **0590-82-98-80** or 0590-83-59-57).

Safety Like Martinique, Guadeloupe is relatively free of serious crime. But don't go wandering alone at night on the streets of Pointe-à-Pitre; by nightfall they are relatively deserted and might be dangerous. Purse-snatching by fast-riding motorcyclists has been reported, so exercise caution.

Taxes A departure tax, required on scheduled flights, is included in the airfares. Hotel taxes are included in all room rates.

Telephone Guadeloupe, as a *département* of France, is not part of the typical 809 area code for the Caribbean. To call Guadeloupe from the United States, dial 011 (the international access code), then 590 (the country code for Guadeloupe, plus the rest of the local number, which will be in six digits). However, once you're in Guadeloupe and are calling a place on the island, put a 0 before the 0590 and dial all 10 digits of a number.

Time Guadeloupe is on Atlantic standard time year-round, one hour ahead of eastern standard time (when it's 6am in New York, it's 7am on Guadeloupe). When daylight saving time is in effect in the States, clocks in New York and Guadeloupe show the same time.

Tips and Service Hotels and restaurants usually add a 10% to 15% service charge, and most taxi drivers who own their own cars do not expect a tip.

POINTE-À-PITRE

The port and chief city of Guadeloupe, Pointe-à-Pitre lies on Grande-Terre. Unfortunately, it doesn't have the old-world charm of Fort-de-France on Martinique, and what beauty it does possess is often hidden behind closed doors.

Having been burned and rebuilt so many times, the port now lacks character. Modern apartments and condominiums form a high-rise backdrop over jerry-built shacks and industrial suburbs. The rather narrow streets are jammed during the day with a colorful crowd that creates a permanent traffic jam. However, at sunset the town becomes quiet again and almost deserted. The only raffish charm left is around the waterfront, where you expect to see Bogie or Sydney Greenstreet sipping rum at a cafe table.

The real point of interest in Pointe-à-Pitre is **shopping.** It's best to visit the town in the morning—you can easily cover it in half a day—taking in the waterfront and outdoor market (the latter is livelier in the early hours).

The town center is **place de la Victoire,** a park shaded by palm trees and poincianas. Here you'll see some old sandbox trees said to have been planted by Victor Hugues, the mulatto who organized a revolutionary army of both whites and blacks to establish a dictatorship. In this square he kept a guillotine busy, and the death-dealing instrument stood here (but not in use) until modern times.

With the recent completion of the **Centre St-John-Perse,** a $20 million project that had been on the drawing boards for many years, the waterfront of Pointe-à-Pitre has been transformed from a bastion of old warehouses and cruise-terminal buildings into an architectural complex comprising a hotel, 3 restaurants, 80 shops and boutiques, a bank, and the expanded headquarters of Guadeloupe's Port Authority.

Named for Saint-John Perse, the 20th-century poet and Nobel Laureate who was born just a few blocks away, the center is designed in contemporary French Caribbean style, which blends with the traditional architecture of Pointe-à-Pitre. It offers an array of French Caribbean attractions: duty-free shops selling Guadeloupean rum and French perfume; small tropical gardens planted around the complex; and a location near the open-air markets and small shops. For brochures and maps, the Guadeloupe tourist office is just minutes away.

WHERE TO STAY

Hôtel St-John Anchorage. Centre Saint-John-Perse at the harbor front side of rue Frébaut. ☎ **0590-82-51-57.** Fax 0590-82-52-61. 44 rms. A/C TV TEL. Fr 462–Fr 512 ($92.40–$102.40) double. Rates include continental breakfast. MC, V.

Stay here only if you want to be in the capital and don't have convenient transportation to go elsewhere. To reach a beach, you'll have to travel 2 miles to the east to Le Bas du Fort and the Gosier area (see below). This hotel rises four stories above a harbor-front location, near the quays. The bedrooms are clean and simple, furnished with locally crafted mahogany pieces. Very few have views over the sea. Once you check in, the lax staff might just leave you alone until the end of your stay. There's a simple coffee shop/cafe on the street level.

WHERE TO DINE

Le Big Steak House. 2 rue Delgrès at Quai Lardenoy. ☎ **0590-82-12-44.** Main courses Fr 85–Fr 125 ($17–$25). AE, MC, V. Mon–Sat noon–3pm. STEAKS/SEAFOOD.

Virtually every shopkeeper and office worker in Pointe-à-Pitre is familiar with this two-fisted, well-managed restaurant, since it offers some of the best midday meals in town. Adjacent to the piers, this place is ideal for cruise-ship day-trippers. Decorated with wood paneling and Wild West accents, this steakhouse imports its meats twice a week from the mainland of France, and prepares them any way you prefer, usually with your choice of five different sauces. Anyone who wants more than one sauce as a garnish is cheerfully obliged—you can order a sauce of mustard, shallots, peppercorns, and chives. Fish culled from local waters is also popular, and includes red snapper cooked en papillote, or grilled daurade with Creole sauce. As you'd expect, there's a wide array of French wines.

Shopping

Frankly, we suggest that you skip a shopping tour of Pointe-à-Pitre if you're going on to Fort-de-France on Martinique, as you'll find far more merchandise there, and perhaps better service. If you're not, however, we recommend the shops below, some of which line **rue Frébault.**

Your best buys will be anything French—perfumes from Chanel, silk scarves from Hermès, cosmetics from Dior, crystal from Lalique and Baccarat. We've found (but not often) some of these items discounted as much as 30% below U.S. or Canadian prices. Shops, which most often will accept U.S. dollars, give these discounts only to purchases made by traveler's check. Purchases are duty free if brought directly from store to airplane. In addition to the places below, there are also duty-free shops at Raizet airport selling liquor, rums, perfumes, crystal, and cigarettes.

When cruise ships are in port, many eager shopkeepers stay open longer than usual, even on weekends.

One of the best places to buy French perfumes, at prices often lower than those charged in Paris, is **Phoenicia,** 8 rue Frébault (☎ **0590-83-50-36**). The shop also has a good selection of imported cosmetics. U.S. traveler's checks will get you further discounts.

Roséblеu, 5 rue Frébault (☎ **0590-82-93-44**), sells fine crystal, fine porcelain, and tableware from all the grand chic names of Europe's leading porcelain manufacturers. These include Christofle, Kosta Buda, and Villeroy & Bosch, always at prices 20% less than on the French mainland.

Vendôme, 8–10 rue Frébault (☎ **0590-83-42-84**), has imported fashions for both men and women, as well as a large selection of gifts and perfumes, including the big names. Usually you can find someone who speaks English to sell you a Cardin watch.

Tim-Tim, 15 rue Henri-IV (☎ **0590-83-48-71**), is for nostalgia buffs. In the local Creole patois, Tim-Tim translates as "once upon a time." This little antique shop is run by the famous French author André Schwarz-Bart and his Guadeloupean wife, Simone, also a writer. They have assembled a sometimes-whimsical collection of Creole furnishings, baskets, madras table linens, and even dolls and maps.

Distillerie Bellevue, rue Bellevue-Damoiseau, 97160 Le Moule (☎ **0590-23-55-55**), caters to those who like to purchase "the essence of the island" wherever they shop. On Guadeloupe that essence is *rhum agricole,* a pure rum that's fermented from sugarcane juice. Once this rum was available in great abundance but now only two distilleries still process it. Savvy locals say the rum here (whose brand name is Rhum Damoiseau) is the only rum you can drink without suffering a hangover. You're allowed to taste the product.

If you're adventurous, you may want to seek out some native goods in little shops along the backstreets of Pointe-à-Pitre. Collector's items are the straw hats or **salacos** made in Les Saintes islands. They look like Chinese coolie hats and are often made of split bamboo. Native **doudou dolls** are also popular gift items.

Open-air stalls surround the **covered market** (*Marché Couvert*) at the corner of rue Frébault and rue Thiers. Here you can discover the many fruits, spices, and vegetables that are enjoyable just to view if not to taste. In madras turbans, local Creole women make deals over their strings of fire-red pimientos. The bright fabrics they wear compete with the rich tones of oranges, papayas, bananas, mangos, and pineapples, and the sounds of an African-accented French fill the air.

Moving On

Saint-John Perse once wrote about the fine times sailors had in Pointe-à-Pitre, as a stopover on the famous route du Rhum. But since that day is long gone, you may not want to linger; you can take a different route instead, this one to the "South Riviera," from Pointe-à-Pitre to Pointe des Châteaux. Hotels recommended below grew up on Grande-Terre because of the long stretches of sand lying between Bas-du-Fort and Gosier (see below). These beaches, however, are not spectacular—they're often narrow and artificial.

LE BAS DU FORT

The first tourist complex, just 2 miles east of Pointe-à-Pitre, is called Le Bas du Fort, near Gosier.

The **Aquarium de la Guadeloupe,** place Creole, Marina Bas-du-Fort (☎ **0590-90-92-38**), is rated as one of the three most important of France and is the largest and most modern in the Caribbean. Just off the main highway near Bas-du-Fort Marina, it's home to tropical fish, coral, underwater plants, and huge sharks and other sea creatures. The exhibits are all clearly labeled. Open daily from 9am to 7pm. Admission is Fr 38 ($7.60) for adults, Fr 20 ($4) for children 6 to 12, and free for kids 5 and under.

Where to Stay

Fleur d'Epée Novotel. Le Bas du Fort, 97190 Gosier, Guadeloupe, F.W.I. ☎ **800/221-4542** in the U.S., or 0590-90-40-00. Fax 0590/90-99-07. 190 rms. A/C TV TEL. Winter, Fr 845–Fr 1,590 ($169–$318) double. Off-season, Fr 795 ($159) double. Rates include continental breakfast. AE, DC, MC, V.

This is Guadeloupe's most prominent branch of the successful French hotel chain. Even though the hotel has a rather laid-back staff and is architecturally undistinguished, it's still popular with young people from the French mainland who turn up here in bikini-clad droves. Most recently renovated in early 1996, it stands beside a pair of crescent-shaped bays whose narrow, cramped white sands are shaded by palms and sea-grape trees. Geared for the resort-lovers, the hotel has only three floors; each bedroom is a well-scrubbed, modern, tiled enclave with private bath and a simple motel-style floor plan.

There's a breeze-filled restaurant, Le Jardin des Tropiques, on the premises, as well as about a dozen indoor/outdoor restaurants within walking distance, many with views of the beach.

Marissol. Le Bas du Fort, 97190 Gosier, Guadeloupe, F.W.I. ☎ **800/221-4542** in the U.S., or 0590-90-84-44. Fax 0590-90-83-32. 195 rms. A/C TV TEL. Winter, Fr 1,080–Fr 1,435 ($216–$287) double. Off-season, Fr 740 ($148) double. Rates include continental breakfast. AE, DC, MC, V.

This secluded bungalow colony of two- and three-story structures sits near the entrance to the touristic complex of Bas du Fort. They were originally built in 1975, and partially renovated in 1991, but those renovators need to make another visit. The Marissol is set away from the main road and occupies the ground between a secondary route and the shoreline. In a setting of banana trees and lawns, it offers rooms either in bungalows or in the two-story wings of the main building, which open onto a view of the grounds or the water. The furnishings are sober and modern (nothing special), the floors are tiled, the baths have a separate toilet, and all units have either twin or double beds.

Dining/Entertainment: Lack of interest from the dining public forced this hotel to close its deluxe restaurant, Le Grand Baie, focusing instead on its moderately priced bistro, Sicali, an open grill lying halfway between the beach and the pool. Next to the pool is a circular bar. The in-house disco is Diapasen, open only to hotel guests and their guests, and only in winter on Friday and Saturday.

Services: Laundry, massage, baby-sitting, concierge.

Facilities: Small artificial beach, large swimming pool, beauty and fitness center, water-sports kiosk (featuring windsurfing, sailing, and snorkeling). Scuba diving can be arranged.

GOSIER

Some of the biggest and most important hotels of Guadeloupe are found at Gosier, with its nearly 5 miles of sandy but narrow beach, stretching east from Pointe-à-Pitre. All the hotels below are in easy proximity to the sands below.

For an excursion, you can climb to **Fort Fleur-d'Epée,** dating from the 18th century. Its dungeons and battlements are testaments to the ferocious fighting between the French and British armies in 1794. The well-preserved ruins command the crown of a hill. From there you'll have good views over the bay of Pointe-à-Pitre, and on a clear day you can see the neighboring offshore islands of Marie-Galante and Iles des Saintes.

WHERE TO STAY

Callinago Beach Hotel and Village. Pointe de la Verdure, 35, Gosier, Guadeloupe, F.W.I. ☎ **0590-84-25-25.** Fax 0590-84-24-90. 40 rms, 115 studios and duplex apts. A/C MINIBAR TV TEL. Winter, Fr 634–Fr 1,122 ($126.80–$224.40) double (with breakfast included); Fr 506–Fr 1,047 ($101.20–$209.40) studio for 2; Fr 888–Fr 1,513 ($177.60–$302.60) two-bedroom duplex apt for 4–6. Off-season, Fr 610 ($122) double (with breakfast included); Fr 486 ($97.20) studio for 2; Fr 851 ($170.20) two-bedroom duplex apt for 4–6. American buffet breakfast Fr 75 ($15) extra for apt occupants. AE, CB, MC, V.

Named after a Carib military hero, and reminiscent of a small resort along the Mediterranean, this hotel stands on the Gosier beachfront about 2 miles east of Pointe-à-Pitre. The rooms are housed in pink-and-white stucco buildings and contain private baths and balconies. Most of the accommodations, however, are in a separate compound designed somewhat like a small village. It holds a series of spacious studios and duplex apartments with modern furnishings, a bathroom, and a complete kitchen. A sliding glass wall opens onto a small private balcony overlooking Gosier Bay. Each of the duplexes, suitable for two or six occupants, contains a spiral staircase that leads to an upstairs bedroom, with a private bath and another small terrace.

Dining/Entertainment: Although studio and apartment residents can prepare their meals in their own kitchens, there's a Creole/French restaurant, Le Tomaly, on the premises that serves breakfast and dinner. A less formal restaurant, Le Sucrier, serves lunch with a view of the pool.

Services: Room service (for breakfast only, and only for residents of the hotel, not the apartments), laundry, baby-sitting.

Facilities: Beach, freshwater swimming pool, two tennis courts, market selling food supplies; waterskiing, sailing, snorkeling, pedal boating, and windsurfing available at an extra charge.

La Creole Beach Hôtel. Pointe de la Verdure, 97190 Gosier, Guadeloupe, F.W.I. ☎ **800/322-2223** or 0590-90-46-46. Fax 0590-90-46-66. 315 rms, 6 duplexes. A/C MINIBAR TV TEL. Winter, Fr 1,125–Fr 1,386 ($225–$277.20) double; Fr 1,600 ($320) duplex. Off-season, Fr 746–Fr 840 ($149.20–$168) double; Fr 1,500 ($300) duplex. Rates include continental breakfast in rooms, Fr 81 ($16.20) per person extra in duplex. AE, DC, MC, V.

Sporting one of the most pleasing designs of any accommodation in Gosier (half New Orleans and half colonial), La Creole stands alongside two beaches in a setting of lawns, trees, hibiscus, and bougainvillea. Renovated in 1989, with partial improvements completed in 1994, the bedrooms are traditional in tone, with dark-wood pieces and carpeted floors. Your balcony will be large enough to be a breakfast spot or a perch for your sundowner. The place attracts both families and young couples, often from France.

Dining/Entertainment: The hotel restaurant, Les Alizés attractively decorated with plants, serves many local specials along with a more familiar international cuisine. During the day guests enjoy drinks at the poolside bar or a lunch at the beach snack bar. Another restaurant, Le Zawag, lies just on the rocks by the sea, offering fresh fish and seafood along with lobster.

Services: Laundry, baby-sitting.

Facilities: Swimming pool, tennis courts, scuba diving, waterskiing, sailboat rentals, deep-sea fishing.

Sofitel Auberge de la Vieille Tour. Montauban, 97190 Grosier, Guadeloupe, F.W.I. ☎ **800/221-4542** or 0590-84-23-23. Fax 0590-84-33-43. 163 rms, 10 duplex suites. A/C MINIBAR TV TEL. Winter, $137–$527 double; $564–$640 duplex suite (2–4). Off-season, $128–$179 double; $300–$400 duplex suite (2–4). Rates include breakfast. AE, DC, MC, V.

Though it became a Sofitel in 1995, this place grew from a family inn that was originally built around the shadow of an old sugar mill. Today, the former mill's stone-sided tower serves as the resort's reception area. Despite some improvements Sofitel has made to the place since its takeover, the personal service and attention to detail are not particularly noticeable. If you don't mind the relative anonymity of a chain hotel, the hotel is appropriate for guests who don't expect a lot of pampering and are adept at creating their own good times regardless of the setting.

The older bedrooms are relatively short on charm, and some contain vestiges of battered and ill-equipped kitchens that most guests use only for storing cold drinks. The better-maintained units, none of which ever contained kitchens, lie within La Résidence, a series of town house–style accommodations set near the pool. Some of the units have balconies that overlook the gardens or the small semi-private and often rather crowded beach.

Dining/Entertainment: The resort contains two restaurants, the Zagaya for Creole dishes, and the Ajoupa, an informal restaurant that's open most days only at lunch, except for a Thursday night gala buffet and barbecue.

Services: Laundry, concierge.

Facilities: Water sports are available from a booth set up on the hotel's small and narrow beach (including snorkeling, sailing, and windsurfing), tennis court lit at night, swimming pool.

WHERE TO DINE

La Chaubette. Route de Ste-Anne. ☎ **0590-84-14-29.** Reservations recommended. Main courses Fr 50–Fr 80 ($10–$16). AE, MC, V. Mon–Sat noon–8pm (last order), Sun by reservation only. CREOLE.

This is a "front porch" Creole restaurant with lots of local color and raffish charm. About a 12-minute ride east of Pointe-à-Pitre, it might remind you of a roadside inn, with its red-checked tablecloths and bamboo curtains. Mme Gitane Chavalin has dispensed food, drink, and good cheer since 1972, and she's known in the area for her Creole recipes and sense of humor. She uses the fish and produce of her island whenever possible. When it's available, her langouste is peerless, as is her hog's-head cheese with a minced-onion vinaigrette. Begin your meal here with a rum punch, made with white rum and served with a lime wedge and sugar. But don't have too much—it's lethal, and you won't be able to get through the rest of dinner. Finish with coconut ice cream or a banana flaming with rum.

Chez Violetta. Perinette Gosier. ☎ **0590-84-10-34.** Reservations not required. Main courses Fr 55–Fr 140 ($11–$28); fixed-price meal Fr 80–Fr 200 ($16–$40). AE, DC, MC, V. Daily noon–3:30pm and 7:30–11pm. FRENCH/CREOLE.

At the far-eastern end of Gosier village, en route to Ste-Anne, this is the most formally decorated of all the Creole restaurants on the island. The decor combines elements of the French colonial world, art deco, and a color scheme of burgundy and white. In spite of its neocolonial trappings, this was the domain of a high priestess of Creole cookery. Her name was Violetta Chaville, and her skill became a legend on the island. Today her polite and well-mannered brother, Josef Galaya, carries on in her tradition. What's missing is her personality and style. But she must have recorded her recipes before she passed on, as the same dishes and the same flavor and taste are still found here.

On the à la carte menu, try stuffed crabs, blaff of seafood, and fresh fish of the day (perhaps red snapper). For an appetizer, ask for cod fritters or beignets called accra. The classic blood sausage, boudin, is also served here. In addition, the chef does a fine conch ragout, superb in texture and flavor; it's best when served with hot chiles grown on Guadeloupe. On occasion, he'll even prepare a brochette of shark, if available. Fresh pineapple makes an ideal dessert, or you can try the banana cake.

La Verandah. In the Hôtel/Résidence Canella Beach, Pointe de la Verdure, Gosier. ☎ **0590-90-44-00.** Reservations recommended. Main courses Fr 70–Fr 120 ($14–$24). AE, DC, MC, V. Daily noon–2pm and 7–10pm. FRENCH/CREOLE.

Set on the grounds of a hotel and apartment complex in Gosier, this restaurant, operated by a French-speaking emigré from South India, Bernard Sinniamourd, is decorated in tones of pink and white, with lots of potted palms. It's an indoor/outdoor place that prides itself on a creative menu that includes such dishes as grilled marlin with tamarind sauce, spicy Indian-style lamb, and a soupière of scallops with freshwater crayfish.

STE-ANNE

About 9 miles east of Gosier, little Ste-Anne is a sugar town and a resort offering many fine beaches and lodgings. In many ways it's the most charming village of Guadeloupe, with its town hall in pastel colors, its church, and its principal square, place de la Victoire, where a statue of Schoelcher commemorates the abolition of slavery in 1848.

WHERE TO STAY & DINE

Club Med—Caravelle. 97180 Ste-Anne, Guadeloupe, F.W.I. ☎ **800/CLUB-MED** in the U.S., or 0590-85-49-50. Fax 0590-85-49-70. 329 rms. A/C TEL. Winter, Fr 900–Fr 1,560 ($180–$312) per person per week double. 25%–30% discount in the off-season. Rates include all-you-can-eat meals, with unlimited wine at lunch and dinner, plus use of all sports facilities, with expert instruction and equipment. Children 4–12 are charged 75% of the adult rate; children 3 and under not accepted. Single supplement 20%–40% above the per person double rate. AE, MC, V. A free hotel shuttle meets passengers at the airport.

Ste-Anne's best-known resort is Club Med—Caravelle, covering 45 acres along a peninsula dotted with palm trees. Its beach is one of the finest in the French West Indies. The rooms tend to be small, as are the baths.

Note that during the summer (but a bit less so during the winter) this resort markets itself almost exclusively to a French clientele through its sales outlets in Paris. Though North Americans are welcome, almost all midsummer activities here are conducted in French.

Dining/Entertainment: When it comes to dining here, the emphasis is on quantity, not quality. The breakfast and lunch buffet tables groan with French, continental, and Creole food. Dinner is served in the main dining room, which has been enlarged and remodeled into a series of small, comfortable sections, or in the candlelit and more romantic La Beguine annex restaurant. There's a weekly folklore night when the dinner features specialties of the region, along with a performance by the Guadeloupe folklore ballet. Also in the evening, guests gather around the bar and dance floor. Afterward you can dance at the midnight disco.

Services: Laundry. Children 4 and over are welcome, but special supervision and "child-amusing" programs are in place only at specific times of the year, usually during school vacations.

Facilities: Beach, windsurfing, sailing, snorkeling trips (leaving daily from the dock), sea excursions to explore the island's coastline, six tennis courts, archery, calisthenics, volleyball, basketball, table tennis.

Hôtel La Toubana. Durivage (B.P. 63), 97180 Ste-Anne, Guadeloupe, F.W.I. ☎ **800/322-2223** or 0590-88-25-78. Fax 0590-88-38-90. 32 bungalows. A/C TEL. Winter, Fr 960–Fr 1,460 ($192–$292) bungalow for 2. Off-season, Fr 680–Fr 812 ($136–$162.40) bungalow for 2. Rates include breakfast. AE, CB, DC, MC, V.

Built on 4 acres of sloping land close to the beach, Hôtel La Toubana is centered around a low-lying stone building on a rocky cliff overlooking the bay and Ste-Anne Beach. Many guests come here just for the view, which on a clear day encompasses Marie-Galante, Dominica, La Désirade, and the Iles des Saintes, but you'll quickly learn that there's far more to this charming place than just a panorama. The red-roofed bungalows lie scattered among the tropical shrubs along the adjacent hillsides (*toubana* is the Arawak word for "small house"). Each unit contains a kitchenette.

Dining/Entertainment: The hotel restaurant, Le Baobab, which was renovated and enlarged in 1995, offers both indoor and al fresco dining in a position overlooking the swimming pool.

Services: Laundry, baby-sitting.

Facilities: Beach (a five-minute walk on a path carved into the cliff side), tennis court. Deep-sea fishing and other water sports can be arranged.

Le Relais du Moulin. Châteaubrun, 97180 Ste-Anne, Guadeloupe, F.W.I. ☎ **0590-88-23-96.** Fax 0590-88-03-92. 20 bungalows, plus 20 duplex apts. A/C MINIBAR TEL. Winter, Fr 720 ($144) double occupancy of bungalow or duplex without kitchen; Fr 810 ($162) double occupancy of duplex with kitchen. Off-season, Fr 470 ($94) double occupancy of duplex or bungalow without kitchen; Fr 536 ($107.20) double occupancy of duplex with kitchen. Rates include continental breakfast. AE, DC. MC, V.

The 19th-century stone tower that juts boldly above the hilly countryside on the outskirts of Ste-Anne and serves as the centerpiece of this hotel was originally built as the headquarters of a prosperous sugar plantation. About half the units here are private bungalows with red roofs and white walls. The remainder are duplex apartments, each with a kitchenette and upgraded plumbing facilities, grouped into connected clusters of four, whose white exterior walls are covered with trumpet vines and bougainvillea. Each unit has a private bath, terrace with a hammock, and refrigerator, but many are extremely small.

Dining/Entertainment: The resort contains two different eating areas, one of which lies near the swimming pool (Le Restaurant). Another (Le Courcelle) is in an indoor area with a *faux* half-timbered look, serving lunch only.

Facilities: Because the resort lies inland and requires a car or taxi to reach the nearest beach, most clients congregate around the resort's swimming pool. There is also a set of rentable bicycles on-site to ride over to the beach at Ste-Anne, 10 minutes away.

ST–FRANÇOIS

Continuing east from Ste-Anne, you'll notice many old round towers named for Father Labat, the Dominican founder of the sugarcane industry. These towers were once used as mills to grind the cane. St–François, 25 miles east of Pointe-à-Pitre, used to be a sleepy fishing village, known for its native Creole restaurants. Then Air France discovered it and opened a Méridien hotel with a casino. That was followed by the promotional activities of J. F. Rozan, a native who invested heavily to make St–François a jet-set resort. Now the once-sleepy village has first-class accommodations, as well as an airport available to private jets, a golf course, and a marina.

WHERE TO STAY

Hamak. 97118 St–François, Guadeloupe, F.W.I. ☎ **800/221-4542** in the U.S., or 0590-88-59-99. Fax 0590-88-41-92. 56 suites. A/C MINIBAR TV TEL. Winter, Fr 1,600–Fr 2,900 ($320–$580) suite for 2. Off-season, Fr 900–Fr 2,000 ($180–$400) suite for 2. Rates include continental breakfast. AE, MC, V.

One of the most prestigious and stylish in Guadeloupe, this resort lies 25 miles east of Pointe-à-Pitre and a quarter of a mile from the Méridien. Its private white-sand beach along the saltwater lagoon and its proximity to golf and a tiny airport once made it the most popular place on the island for jet setters. Despite its sometimes illustrious clientele, it maintains a simple and unpretentious style of management, with few dress-code restrictions and a friendly, open-handed approach to newcomers. Spread on a 250-acre estate, about half of which is devoted to the island's only golf course, the accommodations are in villas. Each has two individual tropical suites with twin beds opening onto a walled garden patio where you can sunbathe au naturel. The beige-sided bungalows house two visitors comfortably, although some readers have found the rooms cramped and simple for the price.

Dining/Entertainment: Hamak maintains a day bar and a night bar, and a dining room that opens onto views of both the beach and the garden. Outsiders can dine here if they reserve in advance.

Services: Room service, laundry, baby-sitting.

Facilities: The island's top golf course, the Robert Trent Jones–designed Golf Municipale de St–François, lies a short walk from the hotel. On the premises of the hotel are tennis courts, a private beach, and facilities for windsurfing and other water sports. There's no swimming pool, but few clients seem to mind, in view of the nearby beach.

✪ **La Plantation Ste-Marthe.** 97118 St–François, Guadeloupe, F.W.I. ☎ **800/223-5695** or 0590-93-11-11. Fax 0590-88-72-47. 96 rms, 24 duplex suites. A/C MINIBAR TV TEL. Winter, Fr 1,000–Fr 1,200 ($200–$240) double; Fr 1,200–Fr 1,400 ($240–$280) duplex suite for 2. Off-season, Fr 800 ($160) double; Fr 1,000 ($200) duplex suite for 2. Rates include breakfast. AE, MC, V.

Built on the site of a 19th-century sugar plantation in 1992, this is one of Guadeloupe's newest major hotels. Although the manor house that once stood on the premises is now in ruins, vestiges of the site's original function are still visible in the stables, the ruined rum distillery, and the molasses factory whose crumbling walls still evoke a sense of the French colonial empire. All buildings that are associated with a vacation, however, are new, scattered amid the vegetation of a landscaped garden whose centerpiece is a large swimming pool. Beach-goers are shuttled to and from the nearby seacoast by minivan.

Accommodations are in a quartet of three-story buildings, the architecture of which was inspired by the Creole buildings of Louisiana. Each unit has lots of exposed wood and boldly patterned tiles, and a large terrace or balcony that many visitors end up using as an extension of their living quarters. The duplex suites feature a sleeping loft designed in a style that might remind you of a big-city apartment. The furnishings are modernized versions of antique French designs, with lots of woven cane.

Dining/Entertainment: The hotel's main restaurant, La Vallée d'Or, has an ambitious menu based on modern French cuisine. A buffet only restaurant, Chan-Kan-La (from the Creole, meaning sugarcane field) opened in 1996. The premises also contain two bars: one by the reception area, another (which features a live pianist every evening) in the restaurant.

Services: Concierge, baby-sitting, minivan transfers to and from the beach (La Plage du Lagon).

Facilities: Two tennis courts, one of the largest swimming pools on the island, health club, water sports.

Le Méridien St–François. 97118 St–François, Guadeloupe, F.W.I. ☎ **800/543-4300** in the U.S., or 0590-88-51-00. Fax 0590-88-40-71. 249 rms, 16 suites. A/C TV TEL. Winter, Fr 1,500–Fr 1,800 ($300–$360) double; from Fr 3,000 ($600) suite. Off-season, Fr 870 ($174) double; from Fr 1,500 ($300) suite. Rates include continental breakfast. AE, DC, MC, V.

At five stories, this is one of the tallest buildings in St–François. It stands alongside one of the best beaches on Guadeloupe on 150 acres of land at the southernmost tip of the island, a 10-minute walk from the village of St–François. The climate, quite dry here, is refreshed by trade winds. Rooms, renovated in the early 1990s, each overlook the sea or the Robert Trent Jones–designed golf course. Each contains many amenities and furnishings inspired by a modern style combined with Creole overtones.

Dining/Entertainment: Guests dine at Balaou, a terraced restaurant with an evening buffet and an à la carte lunch. Other dining choices include the Casa Zomar, serving lunch only, the Bambou snack bar for sandwiches and salads, and the Lele Bar.

Services: Room service (breakfast only), massage, baby-sitting, laundry.

Facilities: Swimming pool, two tennis courts, Windsurfers, small airport for anyone wanting to charter flights to such neighboring islands as La Désirade; golf available for an extra charge at the course next door (call ☎ 0590-88-41-87 for information), nearby marina, access to additional water sports.

WHERE TO DINE

La Louisiane. Quartier Ste-Marthe, outside St–François. ☎ **0590-88-44-34.** Main courses Fr 70–Fr 300 ($14–$60). MC, V. Tues–Sun noon–2:30pm and 6–10pm. Closed 2 weeks in Sept. FRENCH/CARIBBEAN.

The oldest building in the neighborhood (about 1½ miles east of St–François), this century-old former plantation house is sheltered from the road by trees and shrubbery. French owners Daniel and Muriel Hugon have brought some of the best cuisine of their native regions, Provence and the Vosges. Savor the fillet of swordfish with wine sauce or the shark meat with saffron sauce. What really won us over were the scallops in a ginger-and-lime sauce. They were stupendously tasteful, more so than the fillet of red snapper with a basil-flavored cream sauce that you can find throughout the French West Indies. The chef proved himself again with the marmite du pêcheur, loaded with fresh lobster and whitefish, everything set off with the golden saffron flavoring. The restaurant evokes the France of long ago, in an environment streaming with Caribbean sunlight and vegetation.

Restaurant Les Oiseaux. Anse des Rochers. ☎ **0590-88-56-92.** Reservations recommended. Main courses Fr 85–Fr 180 ($17–$36)). MC, V. Mon–Sat 7–10pm, Sun noon–2:30pm. FRENCH/ ANTILLEAN.

The best imitation of a Provençal farmhouse on the island stands on a seaside road about 3 1/2 miles west of St–François. It rests on a scrub-covered landscape whose focal point is the sea and the island of Marie-Galante. The walled-in front garden frames a stone-sided, low-slung building that produces an aroma of a southern French and Antillean cuisine worth the detour.

This is the domain of Arthur Rollé and his French-born wife, Claudette. Together they serve dishes like fish mousse, Creole-style beef, a cassolette of seafood, and a fillet en croûte with red-wine sauce. Try also the marmite Robinson, inspired by Robinson Crusoe, a delectable fondue of fish and vegetables that you cook for yourself in a combination of bubbling coconut and corn oil. Dessert might be a composite of four exotic sherbets or a crêpe.

When the Five-Iron Calls

Guadeloupe's only golf course is the well-known **Golf de St–François** (☎ **0590-88-41-81**), opposite the Hôtel Méridien. The golf course runs alongside an 800-acre lagoon where windsurfing, waterskiing, and sailing prevail. The course, designed by Robert Trent Jones, is a challenging 6,755-yard, par-71 course, with water traps on 6 of the 18 holes, not to mention massive bunkers, prevailing trade winds, and a particularly fiendish 400-yard, par-4 ninth hole. The par-5 sixth is the toughest hole on the course; its 450 yards must be negotiated in the constant easterly winds. Greens fees are Fr 250 ($50) per day per person, which allows a full day of playing time. You can rent clubs for Fr 100 ($20) a day; a cart costs Fr 220 ($44) for 18 holes.

POINTE DES CHATEAUX

Seven miles east of St–François is Pointe des Châteaux, the easternmost tip of Grand-Terre, where the Atlantic meets the Caribbean. Here, where crashing waves sound around you, you'll see a cliff sculpted by the sea into castlelike formations, the erosion typical of France's Brittany coast. The view from here is panoramic. At the top is a cross erected in the 19th century.

You might want to walk to **Pointe des Colibris,** the extreme end of Guadeloupe. From here you'll have a view of the northeastern sector of the island, and to the east a look at La Désirade, another island that has the appearance of a huge vessel anchored far away. Among the coved beaches found around here, **Pointe Tarare** is the *au naturel* one.

LE MOULE

To go back to Pointe-à-Pitre from Pointe des Châteaux, you can use an alternative route, Route N5 from St–François. After a 9-mile drive, you reach the village of Le Moule, which was founded at the end of the 17th century, and known long before Pointe-à-Pitre. It used to be a major shipping port for sugar. Now a tiny coastal fishing village, it never regained its importance after it was devastated in the hurricane of 1928, like so many other villages of Grand-Terre. Because of its more than 10-mile-long, crescent-shaped beach, it's become quite a vacation spot, with several hotels along the beaches.

Specialties of this Guadeloupian village are palourdes, the clams that thrive in the semisalty mouths of freshwater rivers. Known for being more tender and less "rubbery" than saltwater clams, they often, even when fresh, have a distinct sulfur taste not unlike that of overpoached eggs. Local gastronomes prepare them with saffron and aged rum or cognac.

Nearby, the sea unearthed some skulls, grim reminders of the fierce battles fought among the Caribs, French, and English. It's called the "Beach of Skulls and Bones."

The **Edgar Clerc Archeological Museum Le Moule,** Parc de la Rosette, Le Moule (☎ **0590-23-57-57**), shows one of the largest collections of Amerindian artifacts in the Caribbean, including a collection of both Carib and Arawak relics gathered from Guadeloupe and the neighboring islands of the Lesser Antilles. The museum is open Monday to Friday from 9am to 12:30pm and 2 to 5:30pm, and on Saturday and Sunday from 9am to 12:30pm and 2 to 6:30pm. Admission costs Fr 10 ($2). The museum lies 3 miles from Le Moule toward Campêche.

To return to Pointe-à-Pitre, we suggest that you use Route D3 toward Abymes. The road winds around as you plunge deeply into Grand-Terre. As a curiosity, about halfway along the way, a road will bring you to **Jabrun du Nord** and **Jabrun du Sud.** These two villages are inhabited by Caucasians with blond hair, said to be survivors of aristocrats slaughtered during the revolution. Those members of their families who escaped found safety by hiding out in Les Grands Fonds. The most important family here is named Matignon, and they gave their name to the colony known as "les Blancs Matignon." These citizens are said to be related to Prince Rainier of Monaco.

Pointe-à-Pitre lies only 10 miles from Les Grands Fonds.

A DRIVING TOUR NORTH FROM POINTE-A-PITRE

From Pointe-à-Pitre, head northeast toward Abymes, passing next through Morne à l'Eau; you'll reach **Petit Canal** after 13 miles. This is Guadeloupe's sugarcane country, and a sweet smell fills the air.

PORT LOUIS

Continuing northwest along the coast from Petit Canal, you come to Port Louis, well known for its beach, La Plage du Souffleur, which we find best in the spring, when the brilliant white sand is contrasted by the flaming red poinciana. During the week the beach is an especially quiet spot. The little port town is asleep under a heavy sun, but it has some good restaurants.

Where to Dine

Le Poisson d'Or. Rue Sadi-Carnot, 2, Port Louis. ☎ **0590-22-88-63.** Reservations required. Main courses Fr 75–Fr 150 ($15–$30); fixed-price meal Fr 85–Fr 150 ($17–$30). MC, V. Daily 11:30am–3pm; dinner by reservation only. Drive northwest from Petit Canal along the coastal road. CREOLE.

You'll enter this green-and-white Antillean house by walking down a narrow corridor and emerging into a rustic dining room lined with varnished pine. Despite the simple setting, which was badly damaged during the hurricanes of 1995, the food is well prepared and satisfying. Don't even think of coming here at night without an advance reservation—you might find the place locked up and empty. The establishment's true virtue, however, is evident during the lunch hour, when, depending on the season, owner-chef Esther Madel is likely to shelter a mixture of local residents and French visitors. Try the stuffed crabs, the court bouillon, the boudin of conch, or octopus fricassée, and top it off with homemade coconut ice cream.

Anse Bertrand

About 5 miles from Port Louis lies Anse Bertrand, the northernmost village of Guadeloupe. What is now a fishing village was the last refuge of the Carib tribes, and a reserve was once created here. Everything now, however, is sleepy.

Where to Dine

✪ **Le Château de Feuilles.** Campêche, Anse Bertrand. ☎ **0590-22-30-30.** Reservations required, especially in summer when meals are prepared only in anticipation of your arrival. Main courses Fr 110–Fr 165 ($22–$33). MC, V. Winter, Tues–Sun 11:30am–4pm; at night, at least 15 diners must reserve before they will open. Closed June. FRENCH/CARIBBEAN.

Set inland from the sea, amid 8 rolling acres of greenery and blossoming flowers, this gastronomic hideaway is owned and run by a Norman-born couple, Jean-Pierre and Martine Dubost, whose main goal in moving to this outpost was to escape the detrimental effects of civilization. To reach their place, which is 9 miles from Le Moule, near the eastern tip of Grande-Terre, motorists must pass the ruins of La Mahaudière, an 18th-century sugar mill. A gifted chef making maximum use of local ingredients, Monsieur Dubost prepares pâté of warm sea urchins, sautéed conch with Creole sauce, a cassolette of crayfish, gigot of shark with fresh pasta and saffron sauce, and a traditional version of magret of duckling with fresh sugarcane. One unusual taste sensation is a *pavé of tazar* (a local fish) served with a fresh garlic sauce. On our most recent visit to Guadeloupe, we had our finest meal at this restaurant.

✪ **Chez Prudence (Folie Plage).** Anse Laborde, 97121 Anse Bertrand, Guadeloupe, F.W.I. ☎ **0590-22-11-17.** Reservations recommended. Main courses Fr 70–Fr 153 ($14–$30.60); fixed-price meal Fr 100–Fr 160 ($20–$32). AE, MC, V. Daily noon–3pm and 7–10pm. CREOLE.

About a mile north of Anse Bertrand at Anse Laborde, this place is owned by Prudence Marcelin, a *cuisinière patronne* who enjoys much local acclaim for her Creole cookery. She draws people from all over the island, especially on Sunday when this place is its most crowded. Island children frolic in the establishment's saltwater pool, and in between courses diners can shop for handcrafts, clothes, and souvenirs sold by a handful of nearby vendors. Her court bouillon is excellent, as are both her goat and chicken (curried) colombo. Virtually every matriarch on the island makes a colombo, but this one is particularly spicy and palate-tempting. The *palourdes* (clams) are superb, and she makes a zesty sauce to serve with fish. The place is relaxed and casual.

She also rents half a dozen very basic motel-style bungalows priced at Fr 250 ($50) for single or double occupancy, for overnight stays.

Continuing the Tour to the Northern Tip

From Anse Bertrand, you can drive along a gravel road heading for **Pointe de la Grande Vigie,** the northernmost tip of the island, which you reach after 4 miles of what we hope will be cautious driving. Park your car and walk carefully along a narrow lane that will bring you to the northernmost rock of Guadeloupe. The view of the sweeping Atlantic from the top of rocky cliffs is remarkable—you stand about 280 feet above the sea.

Afterward, a 4-mile drive south on quite a good road will bring you to the **Porte d'Enfer** or "gateway to hell," where the sea rushes violently against two narrow cliffs.

After this awesome experience in the remote part of the island, you can head back, going either to Morne à l'Eau or Le Moule before connecting to the road taking you back to Pointe-à-Pitre.

AROUND BASSE-TERRE

Leaving Pointe-à-Pitre by Route N1, you can explore the lesser windward coast. Here you'll find views as panoramic as those along the corniche along the French Riviera, but without the heavy traffic and crowds. After 1 1/2 miles you cross the Rivière Salée at Pont de la Gabarre. This narrow strait separates the two islands that form Guadeloupe. For the next 4 miles the road runs straight through sugarcane fields.

At the sign, on a main crossing, turn right on Route N2 toward **Baie Mahault.** Don't confuse this with the town of Mahault, which is a different entity on Basse-Terre's westernmost coast. Leaving that town, head northwest to **Lamentin.** This village was settled by *corsairs* (pirates) at the beginning of the 18th century. Scattered about are some colonial mansions.

STE-ROSE

From Lamentin, you can drive for 6 1/2 miles to Ste-Rose, where you'll find several good beaches. On your left, a small road leads to **Sofaia,** from which you'll have a panoramic view over the coast and forest preserve. The locals claim that a sulfur spring here has curative powers.

Where to Stay

La Sucrerie du Comté. Comté de Lohéac, 97115 Ste-Rose, Guadeloupe, F.W.I. ☎ **800/528-1234** or 0590-28-60-17. Fax 0590-28-65-63. 52 rms. A/C. Winter, Fr 550 ($110) double. Off-season, Fr 440 ($88) double. Rates include breakfast. MAP Fr 135 ($27) per person extra. AE, MC, V.

Although you'll see the ruins of a 19th-century sugar factory (including a rusting locomotive) on the 8 acres of forested land overlooking the sea, most of the resort is modern (it opened in 1991). Accommodations are in 26 rectangular, pink-toned bungalows, each cramped but cozy, each with chunky and rustic handmade furniture and a bay window overlooking either the sea or a garden. (Each bungalow contains two units, both with ceiling fans; none has a TV or telephone.) Scuba diving, snorkeling, and fishing can be arranged. Partial renovations were made on this place in 1993, when its ownership changed. There's a restaurant on-site, open daily for lunch and dinner, and a bar set beneath a veranda-style roof near a swimming pool. The nearest major beach is Grand'Anse, a 10- to 15-minute drive from the hotel, but there's a small, unnamed beach lying within a 10-minute walk, although the swimming isn't very good.

Where to Dine

Restaurant Clara. Ste-Rose. ☎ **0590-28-72-99.** Reservations recommended. Main courses Fr 60–Fr 140 ($12–$28). MC, V. Mon–Tues and Thurs–Sat noon–2:30pm and 7–10pm, Sun noon–2:30pm. CREOLE.

On the waterfront near the center of town is the culinary statement of Clara Lesueur and her talented and charming semiretired mother, Justine. Clara lived for 12 years in Paris as a member of an experimental jazz dance troupe, but she returned to Guadeloupe, her home, and set up her breeze-cooled restaurant, which she rebuilt in 1990 after hurricane damage. Try for a table on the open patio, where palm trees complement the color scheme.

Clara and Justine artfully meld the French style of fine dining with authentic, spicy Creole cookery. Specialties include *ouassous* (freshwater crayfish), brochette of swordfish, *palourdes* (small clams), several different preparations of conch, sea-urchin omelets, and *crabes farcis* (red-orange crabs with a spicy filling). The "sauce chien" that's served with many of the dishes is a blend of hot peppers, garlic, lime juice, and "secret things." The house drink is made with six local fruits and ample quantities of rum. Your dessert sherbet might be guava, soursop, or passionfruit.

DESHAIES/GRAND ANSE

A few miles farther along, you reach Pointe Allegre, the northernmost point of Basse-Terre. At **Clugny Beach,** you'll be at the site where the first settler landed on Guadeloupe.

A couple of miles farther will bring you to **Grand Anse,** one of the best beaches on Guadeloupe. It's very large and still secluded, sheltered by many tropical trees.

At **Deshaies,** snorkeling and fishing are popular pastimes. The narrow road winds up and down and has a corniche look to it, with the blue sea underneath, the view of green mountains studded with colorful hamlets.

Nine miles from Deshaies, **Pointe Noire** comes into view. Its name comes from black volcanic rocks. Look for the odd polychrome cenotaph in town.

ROUTE DE LA TRAVERSÉE

Four miles from Pointe Noire, you reach **Mahaut.** On your left begins the ✪ **route de la Traversée,** the Transcoastal Highway. This is the best way to explore the scenic wonders of **Parc Naturel de Guadeloupe,** passing through a tropical forest as you travel between the capital, Basse-Terre, and Pointe-à-Pitre.

To preserve the Parc Naturel, Guadeloupe has set aside 74,100 acres, about one-fifth of its entire terrain. Reached by modern roads, this is a huge tract of mountains, tropical forests, and panoramic scenery.

The park is home to a variety of tame animals, including Titi (a raccoon adopted as its official mascot), and such birds as the wood pigeon, turtledove, and thrush. Small exhibition huts, devoted to the volcano, the forest, or to coffee, sugarcane, and rum, are scattered throughout the park.

The Parc Naturel has no gates, no opening or closing hours, and no admission fee.

From Mahaut, you climb slowly in a setting of giant ferns and luxuriant vegetation. Four miles after the fork, you reach **Les Deux Mamelles (The Two Breasts),** where you can park your car and go for a hike. Some of the trails are for experts only; others, such as the Pigeon Trail, will bring you to a summit of about 2,600 feet where the view is impressive. Expect to spend at least 3 hours going each way. Halfway along the trail you can stop at Forest House. From that point, many lanes, all signposted, branch off on trails that will last anywhere from 20 minutes to 2 hours. Try to find the **Chute de l'Ecrevisse,** the "Crayfish Waterfall," a little pond of very cold water at the end of a 1/4-mile path.

After the hike, the main road descends toward Versailles, a hamlet about 5 miles from Pointe-à-Pitre.

However, before taking this route, while still traveling between Pointe Noire and Mahaut on the west coast, you might consider the following luncheon stop.

Where to Dine

Chez Vaneau. Mahaut/Pointe Noire. ☎ **0590-98-01-71.** Reservations not required. Main courses Fr 60–Fr 150 ($12–$30). AE, MC, V. Daily noon–5pm; Mon–Wed and Fri–Sat 7pm–midnight. Closed Thurs and Sun night. CREOLE.

Set in an isolated pocket of forest about 18 miles north of Pointe Noire, far from any of its neighbors, Chez Vaneau offers a wide, breeze-filled veranda overlooking a gully, the sight of local neighbors playing cards beside a blaring TV set. Steaming Creole specialties come from the kitchen. This is the well-established domain of Vaneau Desbonnes, who is assisted by his wife, Marie-Gracieuse, and their children. Specialties include oysters with a piquant sauce, crayfish bisque, ragout of goat, fricassée of conch, different preparations of octopus, and roast pork. In 1995 they installed a salt-water tank for the storage of lobsters, which are now featured heavily on their menu.

BOUILLANTE

If you don't take the route de la Traversée at this time but wish to continue exploring the west coast, you can head south from Mahaut until you reach the village of Bouillante, which is exciting for only one reason: You might encounter part-time resident and former French film star Brigitte Bardot.

Try not to miss seeing the small island called **Ilet à Goyave** or **Ilet du Pigeon.** Jacques Cousteau often explored the silent depths around it.

Facing the islet is the best choice for a luncheon on the whole island. After a meal at La Touna, you can explore the area surrounding the village of Bouillante, known for its thermal springs. In some places if you scratch the ground for only a few inches you'll feel the heat.

Where to Dine Near Bouillante

Chez Loulouse. Malendure Plage. ☎ **0590-98-70-34.** Reservations not necessary at lunch, required for dinner. Main courses Fr 80–Fr 160 ($16–$32). AE, MC, V. Daily noon–3:30pm and 7–10pm. CREOLE.

A worthy choice for an informal and colorful lunch is Chez Loulouse, a staunchly matriarchal establishment with plenty of charm. It sits beside the sands of the well-known beach, opposite Pigeon Island. Many guests like to sip rum punch on the panoramic veranda. A quieter oasis is the equally colorful dining room inside, just past the bar. Here, beneath a ceiling of palm fronds, is a wraparound series of Creole murals that seem to go well with the reggae music emanating loudly from the bar.

This is the creation of one of the most visible and charming Creole matrons on this end of the island, Mme Loulouse Paisley-Carbon. Assisted by her children, she offers house-style Caribbean lobster, spicy versions of conch, octopus, accras, gratin of christophine (squash), and savory colombos (curries) of chicken or pork. At nighttime, you'll probably experience some pressure to arrive with a group of at least four diners; an unpleasant and sometimes impractical demand that makes this place much more appealing for lunch than it is at dinnertime.

La Touna. Malendure. ☎ **0590-98-70-10.** Reservations recommended on Sun. Main courses Fr 60–Fr 200 ($12–$40). MC, V. Tues–Sat noon–3pm and 7–9:30pm, Sun noon–3pm. Closed Sept 15–Oct 8. In the village of Mahaut, turn left on Rte. 2 and drive south. SEAFOOD/CREOLE.

Built on a narrow strip of sand between the road and the sea, this restaurant specializes in seafood. Most of the tables are on a side veranda whose ceiling is covered with palm fronds. Many prefer to have a drink (the fruit-based rum drinks are among the best in the area) before dinner in the sunken bar whose encircling banquettes give the impression of a ship's cabin. The decor is French colonial and suitably blasé—you might feel like you're in a low-rent restaurant in the south of France. The smoked swordfish mousse is a smooth way to start, or go with the savory calamari Provençale. Local crabs and sea urchins are filled with a spicy stuffing. For dinner, you might try kingfish au poivre or other platters of fish and shellfish from Caribbean waters.

VIEUX HABITANTS

The winding coast road brings you to Vieux Habitants (Old Settlers), one of the oldest villages on the island, founded in 1636. The name comes from the people who settled it. After serving in the employment of the West Indies Company, they retired here. But they preferred to call themselves inhabitants, so as not to be confused with slaves.

BASSE-TERRE

Another 10 miles of winding roads bring you to Basse-Terre, the seat of the government of Guadeloupe. The town lies between the water and La Soufrière, the volcano. Founded in 1634, it's the oldest town on the island and still has a lot of charm; its market squares are shaded by tamarind and palm trees.

The town suffered heavy destruction at the hands of British troops in 1691 and again in 1702. It was also the center of fierce fighting during the French Revolution, when the political changes that swept across Europe caused explosive tensions on Guadeloupe. As it did in France, the guillotine claimed many lives on Guadeloupe during the infamous Reign of Terror.

In spite of the town's history, there isn't much to see in Basse-Terre except for a 17th-century cathedral and Fort St-Charles, which has guarded the city (not always well) since it was established.

Where to Stay & Dine

Le Houëlmont. Rue de la République, 34, 97120 Basse-Terre, Guadeloupe, F.W.I. ☎ **0590-81-35-96.** Reservations recommended. Main courses Fr 75–Fr 200 ($15–$40); fixed-price meal Fr 95 ($19). MC, V. Mon–Sat noon–3pm and 7–10:30pm. INTERNATIONAL.

Set in the monumental heart of town, near the bus station, across a boulevard from a massive government building called the Conseil Général, is the oldest and best-established restaurant in the island capital, Le Houëlmont. The restaurant is named after an extinct volcano that can be viewed from the windows of the dining room. After climbing a flight of stairs to the paneled second story, diners enjoy a sweeping view over the hillside sloping down to the sea one block away. Madame Boulon, the longtime owner, who remembers the Guadeloupe of very, very long ago, serves meals to many of the island's government bureaucrats. Specialties include a medley of Creole food, such as accras, court bouillon of fish, grilled fish, steaks, shellfish, and blood sausage, plus French and international dishes. Everything is familiar, nothing is innovative, and locals want to keep it that way.

It's also possible to rent one of the eight bedrooms here, each with private bath and air-conditioning (some units contain TVs). Year-round, doubles cost Fr 280 to Fr 300 ($56 to $60).

LA SOUFRIÈRE

The big attraction of Basse-Terre is the famous sulfur-puffing La Soufrière volcano, which is still alive, but dormant—for the moment at least. Rising to a height of some 4,800 feet, it's flanked by banana plantations and lush foliage.

After leaving the capital at Basse-Terre, you can drive to **St-Claude,** a suburb, 4 miles up the mountainside at a height of 1,900 feet. It has an elegant reputation for its perfect climate and tropical gardens.

Instead of going to St-Claude, you can head for **Matouba,** in a country of clear mountain spring water. The only sound you're likely to hear at this idyllic place is of birds and the running water of dozens of springs. The village was settled long ago by Hindus.

From St-Claude, you can begin the climb up the narrow, winding road the Guadeloupeans say leads to hell—that is, **La Soufrière.** The road ends at a parking area at La Savane à Mulets, at an altitude of 3,300 feet. This is the ultimate point to be reached by car. Hikers are able to climb right to the mouth of the volcano.

However, in 1975 the appearance of ashes, mud, billowing smoke, and earthquakelike tremors proved that the old beast was still alive.

In the resettlement process that followed the eruption, 75,000 inhabitants were relocated to safer terrain in Grande-Terre. No deaths were reported, but the inhabitants of Basse-Terre still keep a watchful eye on the smoking giant.

Even in the parking lot, you can feel the heat of the volcano merely by touching the ground. Steam emerges from fumaroles and sulfurous fumes from the volcano's "burps." Of course, fumes come from its pit and mud cauldrons as well.

Where to Dine En Route

Chez Paul de Matouba. Rivière Rouge. ☎ **0590-80-29-20.** Reservations not required. Main courses Fr 50–Fr 130 ($10–$26); fixed-price meal Fr 100 ($20). No credit cards. Daily noon–4pm. Follow the clearly marked signs; it's beside a gully close to the center of the village. CREOLE/INTERNATIONAL.

You'll find good food in this family-run restaurant, which sits beside the banks of the small Rivière Rouge (Red River). The dining room on the second floor is enclosed by windows, allowing you to drink in the surrounding dark-green foliage of the mountains. The cookery is Creole, and crayfish dishes are the specialty. However, because of the influence of the region's early settlers, East Indian meals are also available. By all means, drink the mineral or spring water of Matouba. What one diner called "an honest meal" might include stuffed crab, colombo (curried) chicken, as well as an array of French, Creole, and Hindu specialties. You're likely to find the place overcrowded in the winter season with the tour-bus crowd.

The Windward Coast

From Basse-Terre to Pointe-à-Pitre, the road follows the east coast, called the Windward Coast. The country here is richer and greener than elsewhere on the island.

To reach **Trois Rivières** you have a choice of two routes: One goes along the coastline, coming eventually to Vieux Fort, from which you can see Les Saintes archipelago. The other heads across the hills, Monts Caraïbes.

Near the pier in Trois Rivières you'll see the pre-Columbian petroglyphs carved by the original inhabitants, the Arawaks. They're called merely Roches Gravées, or "carved rocks." In this archeological park, the rock engravings are of animal and human figures, dating most likely from A.D. 300 or 400. You'll also see specimens of plants, including cocoa, pimento, and banana, that the Arawaks cultivated long before the Europeans set foot on Guadeloupe. From Trois Rivières, you can take boats to Les Saintes.

After leaving Trois Rivières, you continue on Route 1. Passing through the village of Banaier, you turn on your left at Anse Saint-Sauveur to reach the famous **Chutes du Carbet,** a trio of waterfalls. The road to two of them is a narrow, winding one, along many steep hills, passing through banana plantations as you move deeper into a tropical forest.

After 3 miles, a lane, suitable only for hikers, brings you to Zombie Pool. Half a mile farther along, a fork to the left takes you to Grand Etang, or large pool. At a point 6 miles from the main road, a parking area is available and you'll have to walk the rest of the way on an uneasy trail toward the second fall, Le Carbet. Expect to spend around 20 to 30 minutes, depending on how slippery the lane is. Then you'll be at the foot of this second fall where the water drops from 230 feet. The waters here average 70°F, which is pretty warm for a mountain spring.

The first fall is the most impressive, but it takes two hours of rough hiking to get there. The third fall is reached from Capesterre on the main road by climbing to

Routhiers. This fall is less impressive in height, only 70 feet. When the Carbet water runs out of La Soufrière, it's almost boiling.

After Capesterre, you can go along for 4½ miles to see the statue of the first visitor who landed on Guadeloupe, which stands in the town square of Ste-Marie. That visitor was Christopher Columbus, who anchored a quarter of a mile from Ste-Marie on November 4, 1493. In the journal of his second voyage he wrote, "We arrived, seeing ahead of us a large mountain which seemed to want to rise up to the sky, in the middle of which was a peak higher than all the rest of the mountains from which flowed a living stream."

However, when the Caribs started shooting arrows at him, he left quickly.

After Ste-Marie, you pass through Goyave, then Petit-Bourg, seeing on your left the route de la Traversée before reaching Pointe-à-Pitre. You'll have just completed the most fascinating scenic tour Guadeloupe has to offer.

BEACHES, WATER SPORTS & OUTDOOR PURSUITS AROUND THE ISLAND

BEACHES Chances are, your hotel will be right on a beach or will lie no more than 20 minutes from a good one. There are lots of natural beaches dotting the island from the surf-brushed dark-sand beaches of western Basse-Terre to the long stretches of white sand encircling Grande-Terre. Public beaches are generally free, but some charge for parking. Unlike hotel beaches, they have few facilities. Hotels welcome nonguests, but charge for changing facilities, beach chairs, and towels.

Sunday is family day at the beach. Topless sunbathing is common at hotels, less so on village beaches. Nudist beaches also exist at **Ilet du Gosier,** off the shore of Gosier, site of many leading hotels, and at **Plage de Tarare,** which lies near the tip of Grand-Terre at Pointe des Châteaux, site of many local restaurants.

Guadeloupe's best beaches are **Caravelle Beach,** a long, reef-protected stretch of sand outside Ste-Anne, about 9 miles from Gosier. On Basse-Terre, one of the best beaches is **Grande Anse,** a palm-sheltered beach north of Deshaies on the northwest coast. Other good beaches are found on the offshore islands, Iles des Saintes and Marie-Galante (see below).

DEEP-SEA FISHING The season for barracuda and kingfish is January to May. For tuna, dolphin, and bonito, it's December to March. Hotels will recommend deep-sea-fishing boats. At Marina Bas-du-Fort, **Caraïbe Pêche** (☎ **0590-90-97-51**) charters Jeanneaus and Merry Fishers for half-day and full-day outings.

GOLF Guadeloupe's only golf course is the well-known **Golf de St–François** (☎ **0590-88-41-87**) at St–François, opposite the Hôtel Méridien, about 22 miles east of Raizet Airport. The course, designed by Robert Trent Jones, runs alongside an 800-acre lagoon (see "When the Five Iron Calls" in the St–François section, above, for details).

HIKING The **Parc Naturel de Guadeloupe** is the best hiking grounds in the Caribbean (see the touring notes on *route de la Traversée* in "Around Basse-Terre," above). Marked trails cut through the deep foliage of rain forests until you come upon a waterfall or a cool mountain pool. The big excursion country, of course, is around the volcano, La Soufrière. Hiking brochures are available from the tourist office. Hotel tour desks can arrange this activity. For information about this and other hikes within the national park, contact Organisation des Guides de Montagne de la Caraïbe, Maison Forestière, Matouba (☎ **0590-94-29-11**).

Warning: Hikers may experience heavy downpours. The annual precipitation on the higher slopes is 250 inches per year, so be prepared.

SAILING Sailboats of varying sizes, crewed or bareboat, are plentiful. Information can be secured at any hotel desk. Sunfish sailing can be arranged at almost every beachfront hotel.

SCUBA DIVING Scuba divers are drawn more to the waters off Guadeloupe than to any other point in the French-speaking islands. The allure is the relatively calm seas and the **Cousteau Underwater Reserve,** a kind of French national park with many intriguing dive sites, where the underwater environment is rigidly protected. Jacques Cousteau described the waters off Guadeloupe's Pigeon Island as "one of the world's 10 best diving spots." During a typical dive, sergeant majors become visible at a depth of 30 feet, spiny sea urchins and green parrotfish at 60 feet, and magnificent stands of finger, black, brain, and star coral at 80 feet. Despite the violent churning of the water caused by the 1995 hurricanes, and the destruction of some branch coral, the reserve is still one of the most desirable underwater sites in the French-speaking world.

The most popular dive sites include Aquarium, Piscine, Jardin de Corail, Pointe Carrangue, Pointe Barracuda, and Jardin Japonais. Although scattered around the periphery of the island, many are in the bay of Petit Cul-de-Sac Marin, south of Rivière Salée, the channel that separates the two halves of Guadeloupe. North of the Salée is another bay, Grand Cul-de-Sac Marin, where the small islets of Fajou and Caret also boast fine diving.

Centre International de la Plongée (C.I.P.), B.P. 4, Lieu-Dit Poirier, Malendure Plage, 97125 Pigeon, Bouillante, Guadeloupe, F.W.I. (☎ **0590-98-81-72**), is acknowledged as the most professional dive operation on the island. In a wood-sided house on Malendure Plage, close to a well-known restaurant, Chez Loulouse, it's well-positioned at the edge of the Cousteau Underwater Reserve. Dive boats depart three times a day, usually at 10am, 12:30pm, and 3pm. Certified divers pay Fr 200 ($40) for a one-tank dive. What the Americans usually refer to as a "resort course" for first-time divers (the French refer to it as a *baptème*) costs Fr 230 ($46) and is conducted one-on-one with an instructor. Packages of 6 or 12 dives are offered for Fr 1,000 and Fr 1,800 ($200 and $360) respectively, with inexperienced divers paying a supplement of Fr 500 ($100) for their initial certification (it includes insurance). A miniresort, **Le Jardin Tropicale** (☎ **0590-98-77-23**), patronized almost exclusively by dive enthusiasts from France, lies adjacent to this school.

TENNIS All the large resort hotels have tennis courts, many of which they light at night. The noonday sun is often too hot for most players. If you're a guest, tennis is free at most of these hotels, but you'll be charged for night play.

If your hotel doesn't have a court, consider an outing to **Le Relais du Moulin,** Châteaubrun, near Ste-Anne (☎ **0590-88-23-96**).

WINDSURFING & WATERSKIING Windsurfing is the hottest sport on Guadeloupe today, and it's available with lessons at all the major beach hotels, at a cost of Fr 130 ($26) and up. Most seaside hotels can arrange waterskiing at around Fr 125 ($25) for 15 minutes' boating time.

GUADELOUPE AFTER DARK

Guadeloupeans claim that the beguine was invented here, not on Martinique, and they dance it as if it truly was their own (see the "Begin the Beguine" box in the Martinique section). Ask at your hotel where the folkloric **Ballets Guadeloupeans** will be appearing. This troupe makes frequent appearances at the big hotels, although they don't enjoy the fame of the Ballets Martiniquais, the troupe on the neighbor island already described.

The **Casino de la Marina,** avenue de l'Europe (☎ **0590-88-41-44**), stands near the Hotel Méridien at St–François. It's open Sunday to Thursday from noon to 3am and on Friday and Saturday from noon to 4am to those age 18 or above with ID—a driver's license or valid passport. Once inside, you can play American roulette and blackjack. Dress is casual. Admission is Fr 69 ($13.80).

Another casino, **Gosier-les-Bains,** is in the resort community of Gosier (Bas du Fort), on the grounds of the Hôtel Arawak (☎ **0590-84-79-68**). Entrance costs Fr 69 ($13.80), and an ID card with a photo, or a passport, is required for admission. Although dress tends to be casually elegant, coat and tie are not required. The casino is open Sunday through Thursday from 7:30pm to 3am and on Friday and Saturday from 7:30pm to 4am. One area containing slot machines is open daily from 10am to 4am. The most popular games are blackjack, roulette, and chemin-de-fer.

A SIDE TRIP TO THE ILES DES SAINTES

A cluster of eight islands off the southern coast of Guadeloupe, the Iles des Saintes are certainly off the beaten track. The two main islands and six rocks are Terre-de-Haut, Terre-de-Bas, Ilet-à-Cabrit, La Coche, Les Augustins, Grand Ilet, Le Redonde, and Le Pâté. Only Terre-de-Haut ("land above"), and to a lesser extent Terre-de-Bas ("land below"), attract visitors.

If you're planning a trip here, **Terre-de-Haut** is the most interesting Saint to call upon: It's the only one with facilities for overnight guests.

Some claim that Les Saintes has one of the nicest bays in the world, a mini-Rio de Janeiro with a sugarloaf. The isles, just 6 miles from the main island, were discovered by Columbus on November 4, 1493, who named them "Los Santos."

The history of Les Saintes is very much the history of Guadeloupe itself. In years past, the islands have been heavily fortified, as they were Guadeloupe's Gibraltar. The climate is very dry, and until the desalination plant opened, water was often rationed.

The population of Terre-de-Haut is mainly Caucasian, all fisherfolk or sailors and their families who are descended from Breton corsairs (pirates). The very skilled sailors maneuver large boats called *saintois* and wear coolielike headgear called a *salaco,* which looks like a small parasol. If you want to take a photograph of these sailors, please make a polite request and make it in French, otherwise they won't understand. Visitors often like to buy these hats (if they can find them) for themselves.

Terre-de-Haut is a place for discovery and lovers of nature, many of whom stake out their exhibitionistic space on the nude beach at Anse Crawen.

GETTING THERE

BY PLANE The fastest way to get there is by plane. The "airport" is a truncated landing strip that accommodates nothing larger than 20-passenger propeller planes. **Air Guadeloupe** (☎ **0590-82-47-00** on Guadeloupe, or 0590-99-51-23 on Terre-de-Haut) has two round-trip flights daily from Pointe-à-Pitre, which take 15 minutes and cost around Fr 150 ($30) per person, round-trip.

BY FERRY Most islanders reach Terre-de-Haut via one of the several ferryboats that travel from Guadeloupe every day. Most visitors opt for one of the two boats that depart daily from Pointe-à-Pitre's Gare Maritime des Iles, on quai Gatine, across the street from the well-known open-air market. The trip is 60 minutes each way, and costs Fr 180 ($36) for round-trip passage. The most popular departure time for Terre-de-Haut from Pointe-à-Pitre is 8am, Monday through Saturday, and at 7am on Sunday, with return trips every afternoon at 3:45pm. Be at the terminal at least

privacy, families might be interested in renting one of them. Food served dining room is based on conservative and relatively uninspired Creole traditio Blandin, the France-born owner, can arrange for waterskiing, sailing, boat some of the islets or rocks that form Les Saintes, and snorkeling. In winter, ho ervations are suggested at least six months in advance.

Hôtel La Saintoise. Place de la Mairie, 97137 Terre-de-Haut, Les Saintes, Guadeloupe ☎ **800/423-4433** or 0590-99-52-50. 8 rms. A/C. Year-round, Fr 360 ($72) double include continental breakfast. MC, V.

Originally built in the 1960s, La Saintoise is a modern, two-story building se the almond trees and poinciana of the town's main square, near the ferryboat The inn places tables and chairs on the sidewalk, where you can sit and observe action there is. The *menu de jour* costs Fr 80 ($16), and is served whenever the lackadaisical staff thinks there's enough interest. The owner welcomes guests shows them through the uncluttered lobby to one of the second-floor bedrooms, of which is outfitted with a tile bath and modest furnishings. This aura is that French Caribbean inn where simplicity rules.

Kanaoa. 97137 Terre-de-Haut, Les Saintes, Guadeloupe, F.W.I. ☎ **800/221-4542** or 0 99-51-36. Fax 0590-99-55-04. 19 rms, 3 bungalows with kitchenette. A/C TEL. Winter, Fr ($120) double; Fr 700–Fr 800 ($140–$160) bungalow for 2. Off-season, Fr 350 ($70) dou Fr 450 ($90) bungalow for 2. Rates include continental breakfast. MC, V.

Named after the log canoes used by the Arawaks, this modern concrete struct 1¼ miles from the airport on a little beach at Pointe Coquelet, north of the center, is utterly plain. Originally built in the 1970s

SAILING Sailboats of varying sizes, crewed or bareboat, are plentiful. Information can be secured at any hotel desk. Sunfish sailing can be arranged at almost every beachfront hotel.

SCUBA DIVING Scuba divers are drawn more to the waters off Guadeloupe than to any other point in the French-speaking islands. The allure is the relatively calm seas and the **Cousteau Underwater Reserve,** a kind of French national park with many intriguing dive sites, where the underwater environment is rigidly protected. Jacques Cousteau described the waters off Guadeloupe's Pigeon Island as "one of the world's 10 best diving spots." During a typical dive, sergeant majors become visible at a depth of 30 feet, spiny sea urchins and green parrotfish at 60 feet, and magnificent stands of finger, black, brain, and star coral at 80 feet. Despite the violent churning of the water caused by the 1995 hurricanes, and the destruction of some branch coral, the reserve is still one of the most desirable underwater sites in the French-speaking world.

The most popular dive sites include Aquarium, Piscine, Jardin de Corail, Pointe Carrangue, Pointe Barracuda, and Jardin Japonais. Although scattered around the periphery of the island, many are in the bay of Petit Cul-de-Sac Marin, south of Rivière Salée, the channel that separates the two halves of Guadeloupe. North of the Salée is another bay, Grand Cul-de-Sac Marin, where the small islets of Fajou and Caret also boast fine diving.

Centre International de la Plongée (C.I.P.), B.P. 4, Lieu-Dit Poirier, Malendure Plage, 97125 Pigeon, Bouillante, Guadeloupe, F.W.I. (☎ **0590-98-81-72**), is acknowledged as the most professional dive operation on the island. In a wood-sided house on Malendure Plage, close to a well-known restaurant, Chez Loulouse, it's well-positioned at the edge of the Cousteau Underwater Reserve. Dive boats depart three times a day, usually at 10am, 12:30pm, and 3pm. Certified divers pay Fr 200 ($40) for a one-tank dive. What the Americans usually refer to as a "resort course" for first-time divers (the French refer to it as a *baptème)* costs Fr 230 ($46) and is conducted one-on-one with an instructor. Packages of 6 or 12 dives are offered for Fr 1,000 and Fr 1,800 ($200 and $360) respectively, with inexperienced divers paying a supplement of Fr 500 ($100) for their initial certification (it includes insurance). A miniresort, **Le Jardin Tropicale** (☎ **0590-98-77-23**), patronized almost exclusively by dive enthusiasts from France, lies adjacent to this school.

TENNIS All the large resort hotels have tennis courts, many of which they light at night. The noonday sun is often too hot for most players. If you're a guest, tennis is free at most of these hotels, but you'll be charged for night play.

If your hotel doesn't have a court, consider an outing to **Le Relais du Moulin,** Châteaubrun, near Ste-Anne (☎ **0590-88-23-96**).

WINDSURFING & WATERSKIING Windsurfing is the hottest sport on Guadeloupe today, and it's available with lessons at all the major beach hotels, at a cost of Fr 130 ($26) and up. Most seaside hotels can arrange waterskiing at around Fr 125 ($25) for 15 minutes' boating time.

GUADELOUPE AFTER DARK

Guadeloupeans claim that the beguine was invented here, not on Martinique, and they dance it as if it truly was their own (see the "Begin the Beguine" box in the Martinique section). Ask at your hotel where the folkloric **Ballets Guadeloupeans** will be appearing. This troupe makes frequent appearances at the big hotels, although they don't enjoy the fame of the Ballets Martiniquais, the troupe on the neighbor island already described.

The **Casino de la Marina,** avenue de l'Europe (☎ **0590-88-41-44**), stands near the Hotel Méridien at St–François. It's open Sunday to Thursday from noon to 3am and on Friday and Saturday from noon to 4am to those age 18 or above with ID—a driver's license or valid passport. Once inside, you can play American roulette and blackjack. Dress is casual. Admission is Fr 69 ($13.80).

Another casino, **Gosier-les-Bains,** is in the resort community of Gosier (Bas du Fort), on the grounds of the Hôtel Arawak (☎ **0590-84-79-68**). Entrance costs Fr 69 ($13.80), and an ID card with a photo, or a passport, is required for admission. Although dress tends to be casually elegant, coat and tie are not required. The casino is open Sunday through Thursday from 7:30pm to 3am and on Friday and Saturday from 7:30pm to 4am. One area containing slot machines is open daily from 10am to 4am. The most popular games are blackjack, roulette, and chemin-de-fer.

A SIDE TRIP TO THE ILES DES SAINTES

A cluster of eight islands off the southern coast of Guadeloupe, the Iles des Saintes are certainly off the beaten track. The two main islands and six rocks are Terre-de-Haut, Terre-de-Bas, Ilet-à-Cabrit, La Coche, Les Augustins, Grand Ilet, Le Redonde, and Le Pâté. Only Terre-de-Haut ("land above"), and to a lesser extent Terre-de-Bas ("land below"), attract visitors.

If you're planning a trip here, **Terre-de-Haut** is the most interesting Saint to call upon: It's the only one with facilities for overnight guests.

Some claim that Les Saintes has one of the nicest bays in the world, a mini-Rio de Janeiro with a sugarloaf. The isles, just 6 miles from the main island, were discovered by Columbus on November 4, 1493, who named them "Los Santos."

The history of Les Saintes is very much the history of Guadeloupe itself. In years past, the islands have been heavily fortified, as they were Guadeloupe's Gibraltar. The climate is very dry, and until the desalination plant opened, water was often rationed.

The population of Terre-de-Haut is mainly Caucasian, all fisherfolk or sailors and their families who are descended from Breton corsairs (pirates). The very skilled sailors maneuver large boats called *saintois* and wear coolielike headgear called a *salaco,* which looks like a small parasol. If you want to take a photograph of these sailors, please make a polite request and make it in French, otherwise they won't understand. Visitors often like to buy these hats (if they can find them) for themselves.

Terre-de-Haut is a place for discovery and lovers of nature, many of whom stake out their exhibitionistic space on the nude beach at Anse Crawen.

GETTING THERE

BY PLANE The fastest way to get there is by plane. The "airport" is a truncated landing strip that accommodates nothing larger than 20-passenger propeller planes. **Air Guadeloupe** (☎ **0590-82-47-00** on Guadeloupe, or 0590-99-51-23 on Terre-de-Haut) has two round-trip flights daily from Pointe-à-Pitre, which take 15 minutes and cost around Fr 150 ($30) per person, round-trip.

BY FERRY Most islanders reach Terre-de-Haut via one of the several ferryboats that travel from Guadeloupe every day. Most visitors opt for one of the two boats that depart daily from Pointe-à-Pitre's Gare Maritime des Iles, on quai Gatine, across the street from the well-known open-air market. The trip is 60 minutes each way, and costs Fr 180 ($36) for round-trip passage. The most popular departure time for Terre-de-Haut from Pointe-à-Pitre is 8am, Monday through Saturday, and at 7am on Sunday, with return trips every afternoon at 3:45pm. Be at the terminal at least

15 minutes before departure. Pointe-à-Pitre is not the only departure point for Terre-de-Haut: Other ferryboats (two per day) also depart from Trois Rivières, and one additional ferryboat leaves every day from the island's capital of Basse-Terre. Transit from either of these last two cities requires 25 minutes each way, and costs Fr 100 ($20) for the round-trip passage.

For more information and last-minute departure schedules, contact **Frères Brudey** (☎ **0590-82-12-99**) or **Trans Antilles Express** Gare Maritime, quai Gatine, Pointe-à-Pitre (☎ **0590-83-12-45**).

Getting Around

On an island that doesn't have a single car-rental agency, you get about by walking or renting a **bike** or **motor scooter** from a hotel or in town near the pier.

There are also minibuses called **Taxis de I'lle** (12 in all), which can carry up to six (and sometimes up to eight) passengers.

Where to Stay

Bois Joli. 97137 Terre-de-Haut, Les Saintes, Guadeloupe, F.W.I. ☎ **800/322-2223** in the U.S., or 0590-99-52-53. Fax 0590-99-55-05. 22 rms, 8 bungalows. A/C TEL. Winter, Fr 905 ($181) double; Fr 1,280 ($256) bungalow for 2. Off-season, Fr 785 ($157) double; Fr 1,155 ($231) bungalow for 2. Rates include MAP. MC, V.

On the western part of the island, 2 miles from the village, this hotel overlooks a fine beach. Renovated in 1996, Bois Joli is a stucco structure set on a palm-studded rise of a slope. The accommodations include bedrooms in the main house and eight bungalows (two of which have kitchenettes) on the hillside. Bungalows with kitchens don't cost more than those without. Bold-patterned fabrics are used on the beds, and the rooms have modern but bland furnishings. All but two of the units are air-conditioned, with various combinations of shower and bath arrangements. Most rooms have private phones. Because of the bungalows' isolation and increased sense of privacy, families might be interested in renting one of them. Food served in the dining room is based on conservative and relatively uninspired Creole traditions. Mr. Blandin, the France-born owner, can arrange for waterskiing, sailing, boat trips to some of the islets or rocks that form Les Saintes, and snorkeling. In winter, hotel reservations are suggested at least six months in advance.

Hôtel La Saintoise. Place de la Mairie, 97137 Terre-de-Haut, Les Saintes, Guadeloupe, F.W.I. ☎ **800/423-4433** or 0590-99-52-50. 8 rms. A/C. Year-round, Fr 360 ($72) double. Rates include continental breakfast. MC, V.

Originally built in the 1960s, La Saintoise is a modern, two-story building set near the almond trees and poinciana of the town's main square, near the ferryboat dock. The inn places tables and chairs on the sidewalk, where you can sit and observe what action there is. The *menu de jour* costs Fr 80 ($16), and is served whenever the rather lackadaisical staff thinks there's enough interest. The owner welcomes guests and shows them through the uncluttered lobby to one of the second-floor bedrooms, each of which is outfitted with a tile bath and modest furnishings. This aura is that of a French Caribbean inn where simplicity rules.

Kanaoa. 97137 Terre-de-Haut, Les Saintes, Guadeloupe, F.W.I. ☎ **800/221-4542** or 0590-99-51-36. Fax 0590-99-55-04. 19 rms, 3 bungalows with kitchenette. A/C TEL. Winter, Fr 600 ($120) double; Fr 700–Fr 800 ($140–$160) bungalow for 2. Off-season, Fr 350 ($70) double; Fr 450 ($90) bungalow for 2. Rates include continental breakfast. MC, V.

Named after the log canoes used by the Arawaks, this modern concrete structure 1¼ miles from the airport on a little beach at Pointe Coquelet, north of the town center, is utterly plain. Originally built in the 1970s, and renovated in 1995, the accommodations have private showers and rather Spartan furnishings; five have views of the sea and Anse Mire cove. A very limited amount of English is spoken, and the staff might not be able to respond to many of your needs. Despite that, the hotel exerts a powerful allure on escapists of all sorts. A garden with its own swimming pool is near the hotel, and a restaurant serves breakfast, lunch, and dinner on the premises.

Where to Dine

Les Amandiers. Place de la Mairie. ☎ **0590-99-50-06.** Reservations recommended. Fixed-price menus Fr 65–Fr 85 ($13–$17). AE, MC, V. Daily 8am–3pm and 6:30–9:30pm. CREOLE.

Across from the town hall on the main square of Le Bourg is the most traditional Creole bistro on Terre-de-Haut. Monsieur and Madame Charlot Brudey are your hosts in this beige-painted building whose upper balconies sport tables and chairs for open-air dining. *Lambi* (conch) is prepared either in a fricassée or a colombo, a savory curry stew. Also available is a court bouillon of fish, a gâteau (terrine) of fish, and a seemingly endless supply of grilled crayfish. You'll find an intriguing collection of stews, concocted from fish, bananas, and christophine (chayote, to many readers), as well as a complicated dish identified as gâteau de raie ("cake of stingray"). A knowledge of French would be helpful around here.

Chez Jeannine (Le Casse-Croûte). Fond-de-Curé, Terre-de-Haut. ☎ **0590-99-53-37.** Reservations recommended for large groups only. Fixed-price meal Fr 70 ($14) for 3 courses. AE, MC, V. Mon–Sat 9–10am, noon–3pm, and 7–10pm. CREOLE.

The creative statement of Mme Jeannine Bairtran and her children, this restaurant is in a simple Creole house decorated with modern Caribbean accessories. It's a three-minute walk south of the town center. Only one fixed-price meal, the components of which vary from day to day, is served. It might include avocado stuffed with crabmeat, a gâteau de poissons (literally "fish cake"), and several different curry-enhanced stews (including one made with goat). Crayfish and grilled fish (the ubiquitous catch of the day) appear daily on the menu. Local vegetables are used. The ambience is that of a Creole bistro—in other words, a hut with nautical trappings and bright tablecloths.

Exploring the Island

On Terre-de-Haut, the main settlement is at **Le Bourg,** a single street that follows the curve of the fishing harbor. A charming but sleepy hamlet, it has little houses with red or blue doorways, balconies, and Victorian gingerbread gewgaws. Donkeys are the beasts of burden, and everywhere you look are fish nets drying in the sunshine. You can also explore the ruins of **Fort Napoléon,** which is left over from those 17th-century wars, including the naval encounter known in European history books as "The Battle of the Saints." You can see the barracks and prison cells, as well as the drawbridge and art museum. Occasionally you'll spot an iguana scurrying up the ramparts. Directly across the bay, atop Ilet-à-Cabrit, sits the fort named in honor of empress Joséphine.

You might also get a sailor to take you on his boat to the other main island, Terre-de-Bas, which has no accommodations. Or you can stay on Terre-de-Haut and hike to **Le Grand Souffleur** with its beautiful cliffs, and to **Le Chameau,** the highest point on the island, rising to a peak of 1,000 feet.

Scuba-diving centers are not limited to mainland Guadeloupe. The underwater world off Les Saintes has attracted deep-sea divers as renowned as Jacques Cousteau, but even the less experienced may explore its challenging depths and multicolored reefs. Intriguing underwater grottoes found near Fort Napoléon on Terre-de-Haut are also explored.

SHOPPING

Few come here to shop, but there is one offbeat choice at **Kaz an Nou Gallery** at Terre-de-Haut (☎ **0590-99-52-290**), where a local artist, Pascal Fay, makes carved wooden house facades, all candy colored and trimmed in gingerbread. Naturally, they are in miniature. The most popular reproduction graces the cover of the best-selling picture book, *Caribbean Style.* Mr. Fay will point the way to the real house a few blocks away, which has become a sightseeing attraction all on its own because of the book's popularity. The "houses" measure about 16 inches by 13 inches and sell for $100 to $400 each. His gallery ("Our House" in English) is open daily from 9am to noon and 2 to 6pm.

A SIDE TRIP TO MARIE-GALANTE

This tiny offshore dependency of Guadeloupe is an almost-perfect circle of about 60 square miles. Almost exclusively French-speaking, it lies 20 miles south of Guadeloupe's Grand-Terre and is full of rustic charm. Here you return to the Caribbean of yesteryear.

Columbus noticed it before he did Guadeloupe, on November 3, 1493. He named it for his own vessel, but didn't land here. In fact, it was 150 years later that the first European came ashore.

The first French governor of the island was Constant d'Aubigné, father of the marquise de Maintenon. Several captains from the West Indies Company attempted settlement, but none succeeded. In 1674 Marie-Galante was given to the Crown, and from that point on its history was closely linked to Guadeloupe.

However, after 1816 the island settled down to a quiet slumber. You could hear the sugarcane growing on the plantations—and that was about it. Many windmills were built to crush the cane, and lots of tropical fruits were grown.

Now, some 8,000 inhabitants live here and make their living from sugar and rum, the latter said to be the best in the Caribbean. The island's climate is rather dry, and there are many good beaches. One of these stretches of sand covers at least 5 miles, brilliantly white. However, swimming can be dangerous in some places. The best beach is at **Petite Anse,** 6½ miles from **Grand-Bourg,** the main town, with an 1845 baroque church. A beach secret likely to be overlooked by the day-trippers from Guadeloupe? Try **Anse Canot,** a beach-lover's dream, north of St-Louis, with its hidden coves. You can visit the 18th-century Grand Anse rum distillery and the historic fishing hamlet of Vieux Fort.

GETTING THERE & GETTING AROUND

Air Guadeloupe (☎ **0590-82-47-00** on Guadeloupe, or 0590-97-82-21 on Marie-Galante) will bring you to the island in just 20 minutes from Pointe-à-Pitre, landing at Les Basse Airport on Marie-Galante, about 2 miles from Grand-Bourg. Round-trip passage costs Fr 400 ($80).

Antilles Trans Express (Exprès des Iles), Gare Maritime, quai Gatine, Pointe-à-Pitre (☎ **0590-83-12-45** or 0590-91-13-43), operates boat service to the island with three daily round-trips between Pointe-à-Pitre and Grand-Bourg. The round-trip costs Fr 160 ($32). Departures from Pointe-à-Pitre are daily at 8am, 12:45pm, and 5pm, with returns from Grand-Bourg at 6am, 9am, and 3:45pm.

A limited number of **taxis** are available at the airport, but the price should be negotiated before you drive off.

WHERE TO STAY & DINE

There are only a few little accommodations on the island, which, even if they aren't very up-to-date in amenities, are clean and hearty, and often fully booked throughout the winter. The greetings are friendly, but they may be bewildering if you speak no French. Even if you do, be prepared for some very unusual phraseology and grammar.

L'Auberge de l'Arbre à Pain. Rue Jeanne-d'Arc, 32, 97112 Grand-Bourg, Marie-Galante, Guadeloupe, F.W.I. ☎ **0590-97-73-69.** 7 rms. A/C. Fr 250 ($50) double. V. At the harbor, take the first street going toward the church.

Set behind a clapboard facade close to the street, a five-minute stroll from the harbor front, this establishment was named after the half dozen breadfruit trees (*les arbres à pain*) that shelter it from the sun. Guests will find simple but respectable accommodations here, and lots of emphasis on the activities taking place in the kitchen. It thrived as a restaurant long before its owners ever decided to accept overnight guests. Each room has uncomplicated furnishings, a private bath, and easy access to nearby beaches.

Meals at the popular restaurant are served daily from noon to 2pm and 7 to 11pm. Main courses cost Fr 65 to Fr 100 ($13 to $20) and include a selection of fresh fish and shellfish. Usually whatever's available includes a court bouillon of fish, grilled fish, a soufflé of sea urchins, soufflé de clams, grilled lobster, a coquette (deep-fried stew) of christophene, and meat dishes. No reservations are required for the restaurant (everyone seems to just drop in). Because the bedrooms are usually in demand throughout the winter, advance reservations for overnight stays are virtually essential.

A SIDE TRIP TO LA DESIRADE

The ubiquitous Columbus spotted this *terre désirée* or "sought-after land" after his Atlantic crossing in 1493. Named La Désirade, the island is less than 7 miles long, about 1 1/2 miles wide, and has a single potholed road running along its length. It lies just 5 miles off the eastern tip of Guadeloupe proper.

The island has fewer than 1,700 inhabitants, including the descendants of Europeans exiled here by royal command. Tourism has hardly touched the place, except for "day-trippers" from Guadeloupe. There are almost no accommodations here, with the exception of one or two barely recommendable places.

Grande Anse is the main hamlet, with a small church with a presbytery and flower garden, plus the homes of the local inhabitants. **Le Souffleur** is a boat-building village, and at **Baie Mahault** are the ruins of an old leper colony (including a barely recognizable chapel) from the early 18th century.

The best **beaches** are Souffleur, a tranquil oasis near the Le Souffleur, and Baie Mahault, a small beach that's quintessential Caribbean.

GETTING THERE & GETTING AROUND

From Pointe-à-Pitre, **Air Guadeloupe** (☎ **0590-82-47-00**) offers flights to La Désirade from Guadeloupe's Le Raizet Airport three times a week on aircraft containing between 9 and 19 passengers. The round-trip cost is Fr 380 ($76) per person, and trip time is between 15 to 20 minutes each way. Unless a respectable number of passengers shows up for the flight, Air Guadeloupe might cancel it, leaving passengers to fend for themselves and find other means of transport. As a result, some visitors opt to charter a three-passenger plane, suitable for daytime flights only, from **Ailes Guadeloupiennes** (☎ **0590-83-02-65**) for a one-way fare of Fr 600 ($120), the cost of which is divided among the three passengers.

Because of the infrequency of flights and the expense, most passengers opt for transit to La Désirade by **ferryboat,** which leaves St–François every day at 8am and 5pm (and sometimes at 3pm as well, depending on the season) from the wharves at St–François, near Guadeloupe's eastern tip. Returns from La Désirade for St–François include a daily departure every day at 3pm, allowing convenient access for day-trippers. Trip time is around 50 minutes each way, depending on conditions at sea. Round-trip passage on the ferryboat costs Fr 120 ($24) per person.

If you'd like to spend the night, call **L'Oasis** at ☎ **0590-20-02-12** or **Le Mirage** (☎ **0590-20-01-08;** fax 0590-20-07-45). Both are at Beauséjour, half a mile from the airport.

On La Désirade, three or four **minibuses** run between the airport and the towns. To get around, you might negotiate with a local driver. **Bicycles** are also available.

Most visitors opt to spend only a day on Désirade, sunning, or perhaps touring the island's barren expanses. There are, however, a handful of exceptionally simple guest houses charging around Fr 300 ($60) for overnight accommodations for two. Don't expect anything grand.

3 St. Martin

"Why French St. Martin?" you may ask. It hardly has the attractions of St. Thomas, Puerto Rico, or Jamaica. There are no dazzling sights, no spectacular nightlife. Even the sports scene on St. Martin isn't as well organized as on many Caribbean islands, although the Dutch side has golf and other diversions.

Most people visit St. Martin just to relax on its many white-sand beaches. Mostly they come to sample "France in the tropics" on the smallest island in the world to be divided between two sovereign states (France and the Netherlands). France got the larger, northern part, with 21 of the total 37 square miles. The Dutch even spell the name of the island differently: Sint Maarten (see chapter 10 for information on the Dutch half).

French St. Martin not only has some of the best cuisine in the Caribbean, but it is filled with an extraordinary number of bistros and restaurants. It has a distinctly French air. Policemen, for example wear képis. The towns have names like Colombier and Orléans, the streets are *rues,* and the French flag flies over the *gendarmerie* in Marigot, the capital. Its advocates cite it as distinctly more sophisticated, prosperous, stylish, and cosmopolitan than its neighboring *départements d'outre-mer,* Guadeloupe and Martinique.

Don't come here to escape the crowds, however. From a sleepy backwater in Caribbean tourism in 1970, the place has boomed, with a year-round population of 11,000, plus thousands of visitors, often tour groups and conventioneers arriving weekly.

The island, both the French and the Dutch sides, is almost completely devoid of racial tensions, although crime, usually muggings and robberies of visitors, is on the rise.

Both French St. Martin and Dutch Sint Maarten are highly touted for their shopping bargains. Sometimes you can pick up French or Dutch imports at discounted prices, but other goods, like electronics, are cheaper on the U.S. mainland.

There's complete freedom of movement between the two halves of the island. If you arrive on the Dutch side and clear Customs here, there'll be no red-tape formalities when crossing over to the French side—either for shopping, a hotel, or certainly for dining, as it has the best food (with some notable exceptions).

French St. Martin is governed from Guadeloupe and has direct representation in the government in Paris. Lying between Guadeloupe and Puerto Rico, the tiny island has been half French, half Dutch since 1648.

The principal town on the French side is **Marigot,** the seat of the subprefect and municipal council. Visitors come here not only for shopping, as the island is a free port, but also to enjoy the excellent cookery in the Creole bistros.

Marigot is not quite the same size as its counterpart, Philipsburg, in the Dutch sector. It has none of the frenzied pace of Philipsburg, which is often overrun with cruise-ship passengers. In fact, Marigot looks like a French village transplanted to the Caribbean. If you climb the hill over this tiny port, you'll be rewarded with a view from the old fort there.

About 20 minutes by car beyond Marigot is **Grand-Case,** a small fishing village that's an outpost of French civilization with many good restaurants and a few places to stay.

GETTING THERE

Most arrivals are at the Dutch-controlled **Queen Juliana International Airport,** St. Maarten. For a more detailed description of transportation on that side of the island, see "Getting There" for St. Maarten in chapter 10.

If you're coming from St. Barts, however, **Air Guadeloupe** (☎ **0590-27-61-90** on St. Barts, or 0590-87-10-36 on St. Martin) maintains 10-minute flights (two or three a day) into French St. Martin's **Espérance Airport** in Grand-Case (☎ **0590-87-10-36**). The cost of a one-way flight between St. Barts and French St. Martin is about Fr 256 ($51.20) per person.

GETTING AROUND

BY BUS It's cheapest to get around on one of the island's buses, which are operated by a sometimes-motley crew of local drivers, with a widely divergent armada of privately owned minivans and minibuses. They run daily from 6am until midnight. One departs from Grand-Case for Marigot every 20 minutes. There's a departure every hour from Marigot to the Dutch side. A sample bus fare from Marigot to Grand-Case is between $1.50 and $2. Because they're sometimes difficult for a newcomer to spot, the best way to identify one is to ask a local resident.

BY TAXI For visitors, the most common means of transport is a taxi. A **Taxi Service & Information Center** operates at the port of Marigot (☎ **0590-87-56-54**). Always agree on the rate before getting into an unmetered cab. Taxi fares from Marigot to Grand-Case, from Juliana Airport to Marigot, and from Juliana Airport to La Samanna are all about $10 for two passengers, plus a supplement of about $1 for each suitcase or valise. These fares are in effect from 7am to 10pm; after that, they go up by 25% until midnight, rising by 50% after midnight.

You can also book two-hour sightseeing trips around the island, either through the organization listed above or at any hotel desk. The cost is $45 for one or two passengers, plus $10 for each additional person.

BY RENTAL CAR The division of the island into dual political zones used to make car rentals on St. Martin rather complicated. In past years, car-rental companies were unwilling to rent one of their cars to clients staying on the opposite side of the border, preferring that clients in hotels on the French side rent only from agencies on the French side. Fortunately, those rivalries no longer seem to exist, as rental companies on both sides of the Dutch–French border are now cooperating more fully with one another.

Because there are virtually no restrictions about which side of the island you rent your car on, you might opt to pick your car up at the Juliana Airport, on the Dutch side, after you land, and navigate your way alone across the island to your French-speaking hotel. Some visitors, however, opt to pay for a taxi to take them and their luggage directly to their hotel, recover from their jet lag, and then contact any of the three rental agencies listed below. Depending on circumstances, any of them will either arrange for a car to be brought directly to your hotel, or for a minivan to transport you without charge to a depot where the cars are stored. That depot might lie on either the French or the Dutch side, depending on the location of your hotel and the renting outfit's inventory of cars. Unlike in years past, once a car is rented, no one seems to mind whether you drop it off on the French or the Dutch side of the island on the day of your departure. Prices are usually somewhat less expensive for clients who reserve their cars several days in advance before leaving home.

Each of the largest North American car-rental companies—**Avis** (☎ **800/331-1084** or 0590-87-50-60), **Budget** (☎ **800/527-0700** or 0590-87-38-22), and **Hertz** (☎ **800/654-3001** or 0590-87-73-01)—maintains at least one branch on both the French and Dutch sides of the island. (For more information on this, see "Getting Around" for St. Maarten in chapter 10.) All three charge roughly equivalent rates, which are usually similar to rates at branches of the same company on the Dutch side. Occasionally, additional discounts are granted for membership in organizations such as the AAA or AARP.

Most of the companies require that renters be at least 25 years or older, and each charges between $11 and $20 a day for a collision-damage waiver (CDW). Even if you buy the waiver, you'll sometimes still be responsible for $400 to $600 worth of collision damage to your car. Use of certain types of credit or charge cards sometimes eliminates the need to pay for a CDW; check with your card issuer. Once you reach the French side of St. Martin, call for delivery of your car.

Regardless of how you negotiate your car rental, you'll probably use very little gasoline driving around the flat, scrub-covered landscapes of the island. One tank of gas should last an entire week.

FAST FACTS: St. Martin

Banking Hours Banks are generally open Monday to Friday from 8:30am to 1pm and 2 to 4 or 5pm. Most banks have ATMs in their vestibules that work in ways similar to U.S.-based banks (you'll need a valid credit card and a PIN number, of course).

Currency The currency, officially at least, is the **French franc (Fr),** yet U.S. dollars seem to be preferred wherever you go. Canadians should convert their money into U.S. dollars and not into francs. The current exchange rate is Fr 4.98 to U.S.$1 (Fr 1 = 20¢ U.S.), but check the most up-to-date quotation at the time of your visit.

Documents U.S. and Canadian citizens should have either a passport, a voter registration card, or a birth certificate, plus an ongoing or a return ticket. With a birth certificate or voter registration card, you'll also need photo ID. British subjects need a valid passport.

Electricity Officially, the electricity is 220 volts AC (50 cycles), enough to blow out the motor of any appliances made for use in North America. Some hotels have altered the voltage and outlets in their bathrooms to a voltage compatible with U.S. appliances, so check with an employee before you actually plug something in, or ask before your arrival. If you discover that your appliance is not compatible with the hotel's voltage, don't always rely on the hotel to provide the necessary hardware; bring your own transformer and adapter if you plan to use U.S.-made appliances.

Information The tourist board, called the **Office du Tourisme,** is at the port de Marigot, 97150 Marigot, St. Martin, F.W.I. (☎ **0590-87-57-21**).

Language English is widely spoken on St. Martin, although this is a French possession. A patois is spoken only by a small segment of the local populace.

Medical Care Hotels will assist visitors in contacting English-speaking doctors. In a medical emergency, dial ☎ **18.** The local hospital is Hospital de Marigot in Marigot (☎ **0590-29-57-57** or 0590-29-57-48).

Safety The crime wave hitting Dutch-held St. Maarten also plagues French St. Martin. Travel with extreme caution here, especially at night. Avoid driving at night along the Lowlands road. Armed patrols have helped the situation somewhat, but hotel safes should be used to guard your valuables. You can reach the **police** by calling ☎ **17** or **0590-87-50-10.** In case of **fire,** dial ☎ **13.**

Tax There is no departure tax imposed for departures from Espérance Airport on the French side. However, for departures from Juliana Airport on the Dutch side, a departure tax of between $12 and $15 is assessed, depending on the destination. This tax is not included in the price of most airline tickets.

Telephone French St. Martin is linked to the Guadeloupe telephone system, which is *not* a part of the 809 area code that applies to most of the Caribbean. To call French St. Martin from the United States, dial 011 (the international access code), then 590 (the country code for Guadeloupe), and then the six-digit local number.

To make a call within French St. Martin, a 10-digit local number is necessary; no codes are needed unless you're calling "long distance" to the Dutch side of the island, in which case dial 19-5-99-5 and the five-digit Dutch number. To call French St. Martin from the Dutch side, dial 00, 0590, and the six-digit local number. Local critics of this inefficient and expensive system complain that calling from the French to the Dutch side of the island, a distance of only a few miles, is the equivalent of dialing Holland from within the borders of mainland France, and vice versa. Part of this is because of the fact that all calls are actually routed to Guadeloupe before being transferred back to the island's Dutch side. Such calls will usually be more (sometimes much more) expensive than you might have thought.

Time St. Martin operates on Atlantic standard time year-round, one hour ahead of eastern standard time, which means that the only time the U.S. East Coast and St. Martin are in step is during the daylight saving time of summer.

Tips and Service Your hotel is likely to add a 10% to 15% service charge to your bill to cover tipping. Likewise, most restaurant bills include the service charge.

Water The water of St. Martin is safe to drink. In fact, most hotels serve desalinated water.

WHERE TO STAY

Hotels on French St. Martin add a 10% service charge and a *taxe de séjour*. This visitors' tax on hotel rooms differs from hotel to hotel, depending on its classification, but the minimum is $3 a day.

VERY EXPENSIVE

Le Méridien L'Habitation/Le Domaine. Anse Marcel (B.P. 581, 97106 Marigot), St. Martin, F.W.I. ☎ **800/543-4300** in the U.S., or 0590-87-67-00. Fax 0590-87-30-38. 314 rms, 82 suites. A/C MINIBAR TV TEL. Winter, $450–$560 double; from $590 suite. Off-season, $160–$220 double; from $240 suite. AE, DC, MC, V. Closed Sept.

Since its expansion in 1992, this has become the largest resort complex on the French side of St. Martin, and one of its most heavily promoted, often attracting French-speaking tour groups. It's tucked under Pigeon Pea Hill, opening onto one of the tiny

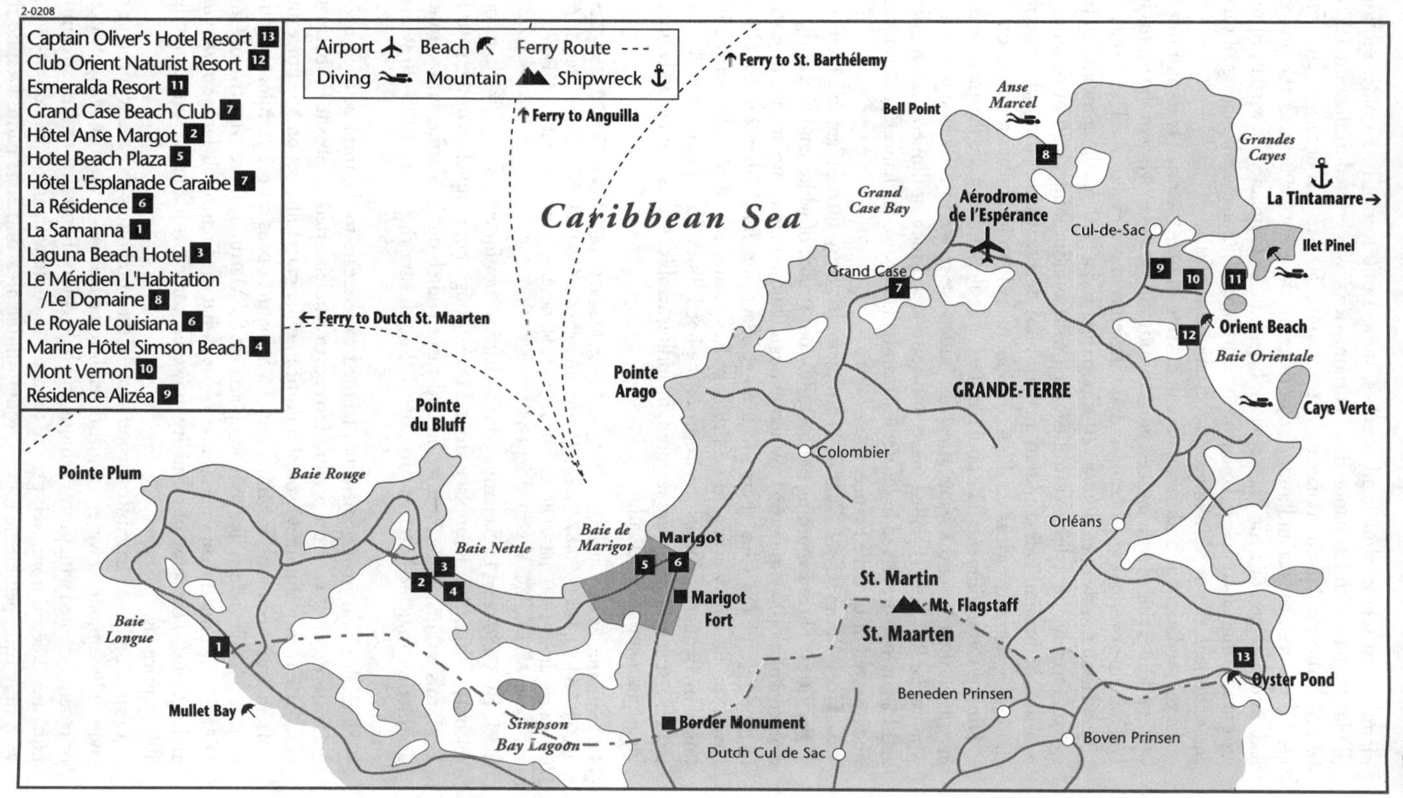

2-0208
Captain Oliver's Hotel Resort 13
Club Orient Naturist Resort 12
Esmeralda Resort 11
Grand Case Beach Club 7
Hôtel Anse Margot 2
Hotel Beach Plaza 5
Hôtel L'Esplanade Caraïbe 7
La Résidence 6
La Samanna 1
Laguna Beach Hotel 3
Le Méridien L'Habitation /Le Domaine 8
Le Royale Louisiana 6
Marine Hôtel Simson Beach 4
Mont Vernon 10
Résidence Alizéa 9
Airport
Beach
Ferry Route
Diving
Mountain
Shipwreck
Ferry to St. Barthélemy
Ferry to Anguilla
Ferry to Dutch St. Maarten
Caribbean Sea
Bell Point
Anse Marcel
Grandes Cayes
La Tintamarre
Ilet Pinel
Grand Case Bay
Aérodrome de l'Espérance
Cul-de-Sac
Grand Case
Orient Beach
Baie Orientale
Caye Verte
GRANDE-TERRE
Pointe Arago
Pointe du Bluff
Colombier
Pointe Plum
Baie Rouge
Orléans
Baie de Marigot
Marigot
Baie Nettle
St. Martin
Marigot Fort
Mt. Flagstaff
St. Maarten
Baie Longue
Oyster Pond
Beneden Prinsen
Mullet Bay
Border Monument
Boven Prinsen
Simpson Bay Lagoon
Dutch Cul de Sac

island's most scenic white-sand beaches, some 1,600 feet of it. Its older section (L'Habitation), with less panoramic bedroom views, was erected in the mid-1980s by a consortium of French insurance companies on a 150-acre tract of rugged scrubland nestled between the sea and a mountain ridge. In the early 1990s, after the project had been purchased by Air France, work began on Le Domaine, a few steps to the west of the original complex. Today both resorts are fully integrated, sharing all their entertainment, dining, drinking, and recreational facilities.

Accommodations at both resorts are in a string of neo-Victorian two- and three-story buildings ringed with lattices, gingerbread, and verandas. Most of the rooms in Le Domaine overlook the ocean, and are therefore more expensive. The rooms in L'Habitation mostly open onto a 120-slip marina and a garden. All rooms and suites are comfortably and stylishly furnished, each with soundproofing, balcony or terrace, two-sink bathroom, radio, and an airy, tropical decor, which, along with special children's programs such as the Pirates' Club, make it an ideal place for families.

Dining/Entertainment: The pool bar (Le Carbet) resembles a tile-sheathed gazebo on stilts at the edge of the water. Breakfast buffets are served in Le Balaou restaurant, whereas Le BBQ offers grilled meats and seafood at lunch or dinner. Pastas, grills, and Italian food are served in La Veranda, an Italian bistro. An haute Caribbean cuisine is served in La Belle France.

Services: Room service (7am to 11pm), laundry, baby-sitting (7am to 11pm).

Facilities: Three swimming pools, 1,600-foot stretch of white-sand beach, nightclub complex, 100-slip marina. When enough children are in attendance to justify its expense, a Pirates' Club offers a wide range of activities for children 2 to 14. Guests have complimentary access to Le Privilege Resort and Spa, a complex on the hill linked by frequent minibus service from the hotel. Both fitness training and European spa-style treatments are featured, including aerobics classes, tennis, body building, squash, and racquetball.

✪ **La Samanna.** Baie Longue (B.P. 4077), 97064 St. Martin CEDEX, F.W.I. ☎ **800/854-2252** or 0590-87-64-00. Fax 0590-87-87-86. 36 rms, 46 suites. A/C MINIBAR TV TEL. Winter, $575–$700 double; from $800 suite. Off-season, $250–$550 double; from $650 suite. MAP $75 per person extra. AE, DC, MC, V. Closed Sept–Oct.

Sleek, chic, and sexy, La Samanna admits that it's "not for everyone." Off-the-record celebrity visits are commonplace around here, though not as much as in the past. In 1995, this was one of the most seriously damaged hotels on St. Martin, with so much destruction that the hotel was forced to close during the entire 1995–96 winter season.

Since then, the management has labored to re-create to the form beloved by so many devotees. If you're a person devoted to wholehearted, unabashed sybaritism (and have plenty of money) you should fit in quite gracefully. Set on 55 choice and isolated acres northwest of Mullet Bay, La Samanna opens onto $1^1/_2$ miles of white-sand beach. The resort, like so many places on St. Martin, is more evocative of Côte D'Azur or Morocco than the Caribbean—it's what the French call *intime, tranquille,* and *informel.* That sense of formality, however, comes with a hefty, sometimes disabling, price tag.

Owned by Dallas-based Rosewood Hotels, the hotel offers an eclectic mélange of styles. Throughout, however, furniture tends to be Haitian-made mahogany, wicker, or rattan, accented with puffy cushions and bold colors. Regardless of their size, most units are screened from their private terrace and come with ample bedrooms—each with fully equipped kitchen, living room, dining area, and large patio. Despite the resort's prestige, some clients complain that service and staff attitude aren't commensurate with the expensive rates.

Dining/Entertainment: Dining is al fresco with a French cuisine. You eat on a candlelit terrace overlooking Baie Longue. After dinner, the bar becomes a disco. At the poolside grill, waiters serve food, St-Tropez style, on the beach.

Services: 24-hour room service, laundry, baby-sitting, massages; a hotel driver meets all guests at the airport.

Facilities: Fitness and activity center with daily aerobics classes, outdoor swimming pool, waterskiing, three tennis courts, library, sailboat rentals, shopping boutique. Ironically, although many of La Samanna's buildings were damaged during the 1995 hurricanes, the storms enlarged its adjoining beach with tons of fresh sand.

EXPENSIVE

Captain Oliver's Hotel Resort. Oyster Pond (B.P. 645), 97150 St. Martin, F.W.I. ☎ **0590-87-40-26.** Fax 0590-87-40-84. 50 junior suites. A/C MINIBAR TV TEL. Winter, $218–$350 junior suite for 2. Off-season, $155–$245 junior suite for 2. Rates include continental breakfast. AE, DC, MC, V.

This hotel is named for Oliver Lange, who was a Paris restaurateur for nearly a quarter of a century before coming here. At the French–Dutch border 10 miles east of Queen Juliana Airport, this hotel is near the prestigious Oyster Pond Hotel on the Dutch side. Lange constructed pink bungalows in a labyrinth of outlying cottages, with a bit of gingerbread and connected with boardwalks. High on a hill, the cottages command panoramic views, and from the large terraces you can gaze over to St. Barts. After the hurricanes of 1995, great time and money was spent on upgrading the compound. Each unit is furnished in white rattan and decorated with local prints. The accommodations come with kitchenettes, marble-trimmed baths, double sinks, large double closets, and many amenities. Each junior suite has two beds, plus a sofa bed, which makes them perfect for families.

Dining/Entertainment: See Captain Oliver Restaurant in "Where to Dine," below. A pool bar is open daily from noon to midnight, and a breakfast room and snack bar, the Dinghy Duck, whose canvas roof was replaced with a sturdier version after the hurricane, serves daily from 7am to midnight.

Services: Room service (7am to 10:30pm), laundry, baby-sitting.

Facilities: Scuba-diving facilities, outdoor swimming pool, private taxi boat to nearby beach, shopping boutiques.

Esmeralda Resort. Parc de la Baie Orientale (B.P. 5141), 97150 St. Martin, F.W.I. ☎ **800/221-4542** or 0590-87-36-36. Fax 0590-87-35-18. 55 rms, 10 suites. A/C TV TEL. Winter, $400–$450 double; from $500 suite. Off-season, $180–$210 double; from $300 suite. Rates include continental breakfast. AE, MC, V.

Originally conceived as a site for a single private villa, and then for a semiprivate club, this hillside housing development, like something in Arizona, is a 25-minute taxi ride northeast of Queen Juliana Airport. Opening onto Orient Beach, the Esmeralda blossomed into a full-scale resort in the early 1990s, offering views over Orient Bay and a decidedly French focus. During the 1995 hurricanes, it was among the least severely damaged of the hotels on the island, and since repairs were activated almost instantly after the storm's end, it survived the debacle better than most. Up to a maximum of four separate vaguely Spanish mission–style accommodations are in each of 18 tile-roofed villas whose interior doors can be locked or unlocked as needed to create a variety of different-size units. Each of the units contains a kitchenette, bathroom, private terrace, and a private entrance. Each of the three to five units in each villa shares a communal swimming pool for a feeling similar to that of a private club.

Dining/Entertainment: The resort's bar and grill (Le Coco Beach) lies close to the nearby beach. There's also an impressive, relatively upscale restaurant, L'Astrolabe, for more formal dining. The hotel also maintains cooperative relationships with several local beach bars, any of which allows guests of Esmeralda to sign for food and drinks throughout the day and evening.

Services: Room service for breakfast and dinner, laundry, baby-sitting, massage.

Facilities: 17 swimming pools, 2 tennis courts, day and night scuba diving, snorkeling, horseback riding, waterskiing.

Grand Case Beach Club. Grand-Case, 97150 St. Martin, F.W.I. ☎ **800/447-7462** in the U.S. and Canada, or 0590-87-51-87. Fax 0590-87-59-93. 32 studios, 39 suites. A/C TV TEL. Winter, $200–$270 studio; $270–$320 suite. Off-season, $130–$185 studio; $170–$195 suite. AE, MC, V. Closed Sept.

This restored condo complex lies directly on the sands of Grand Case Beach, within a quintet of motel-like buildings with white trim. Accommodations contain a private patio or balcony, a kitchenette, a mostly white and rather simple decor, and views of either the garden or the sea. Due to its position in a garden that's awfully close to the level of the waves, the hotel's buildings tend to suffer heavy damage during storms. As such, after its original construction in 1977, the entire hotel received an almost complete overhaul after the hurricanes of 1995. Everything here is extremely informal. It's the kind of place where you don't need much more than a bathing suit.

Dining/Entertainment: Although there's a bar and a simple, summery restaurant on the premises (it was the last of the hotel's components to be rebuilt), many guests prepare their meals in their kitchenettes.

Services: Laundry, baby-sitting.

Facilities: A beach and a nearby swimming pool; a beach boutique; water-sports facilities, including waterskiing, snorkeling, and sailing; free use of St. Martin's first artificial-grass tennis courts; car-rental facilities.

Hôtel Anse Margot. Baie Nettlé (B.P. 4071, 97150 Marigot), St. Martin, F.W.I. ☎ **0590-87-92-01.** Fax 0590-87-92-13. 57 rms, 38 suites. A/C TV TEL. Winter, Fr 1,020–Fr 1,600 ($204–$320) double; Fr 1,420–Fr 2,080 ($284–$416) suite. Off-season, Fr 840–Fr 1,000 ($168–$200) double; Fr 1,240–Fr 1,420 ($248–$284) suite. Rates include buffet breakfast. AE, DC, MC, V.

This French-owned resort, just west of Marigot, consists of eight pastel-colored buildings. Built in 1988, and renovated in 1996, they sit on a narrow strip of scrub-covered sand that separates the ocean from the largest of the island's saltwater lagoons. It suffered very little damage, less than almost any other hotel on the island, during the 1995 hurricanes. Each of the multistory buildings is embellished with ornate balconies and gingerbread in a stylized version of colonial Creole architecture. The bedrooms are furnished in a French Antillean decor of pastel floral colors, and the many amenities include a small refrigerator set on an outdoor terrace or balcony.

Dining/Entertainment: The resort's social center rises like a well-designed miniature temple, with a pair of swimming pools flanking it on either side. After dark, a pianist performs live music, which might include Piaf or jazz. A French cuisine is served in the hotel's restaurant, Entre Deux Mers.

Services: Room service (available during normal meal hours), laundry, baby-sitting.

Facilities: Scuba diving, two outdoor swimming pools, two Jacuzzis, waterskiing, sailboat rentals, shopping boutiques. Nettlé Beach across from the hotel is best for swimming, and there's a beach along Simpson Bay that's possible for sunbathing (not swimming).

Hotel Beach Plaza. Baie de Marigot, 97150 St. Martin. ☎ **0590-87-87-00.** 140 rms, 4 suites. A/C MINIBAR TV TEL. Winter, $203–$275 double; $380–$438 suite. Off-season, $160–$190 double; $291 suite. Rates include buffet breakfast. AE, MC, V.

Set closer to Marigot than many of its middle-bracket competitors in Baie Nettlé, this three-story hotel lies within a cluster of buildings mostly composed of condominiums. Built in 1996, and painted in shades of blue and white, it's set midway between the open sea and the lagoon, and as such, all rooms have balconies with water views. Color schemes inside are pure white accented with varnished, dark-tinted woods, and each contains a writing desk and simple, beach-inspired furniture. There's a water-sports kiosk for sailing, windsurfing, snorkeling, and scuba, plus a swimming pool that's visible from the windows of Le Corsaire, the only restaurant. The hotel has two bars, one beside the pool, another with a resident pianist. The congenial staff is rightfully proud of the hotel's position as a worthy competitor among the more deeply entrenched properties nearby.

Hôtel L'Esplanade Caraïbe. (B.P. 5007), Grand-Case, 97150 St. Martin. ☎ **800/633-7411** or 0590-87-06-55. Fax 0590-87-29-15. 24 suites. A/C TV TEL. Winter, $240 suite for 2; $280–$320 suite for 4. Off-season, $150 suite for 2; $170–$200 suite for 4. Extra person $40–$60. AE, MC, V.

Although the hamlet of Grand-Case has always been known as a potpourri of many different restaurants, its hotel choices were rather limited. In 1992 this changed with the construction of an elegant collection of suites on a steeply sloping hillside above the town's approach road from Marigot. Covered with cascades of bougainvillea, and accented with a vaguely Hispanic overlay of white walls, hand-painted tiles, and cream-colored roofs, the resort's various elements are connected by a network of concrete stairs that add to the layout's drama.

The resort has a swimming pool, a series of terraced gardens, and access to a beach that you'll reach after descending a winding, stair-dotted pathway after a six-minute walk. Views from the bedrooms and their terraces are always angled out toward the sea. The only on-site dining option is a snack bar (breakfast, lunch, and all-day drinks) beside the pool. Each of the accommodations contains a kitchen with a large refrigerator and up-to-date cookware. The rooms have a blue, green, and white color scheme with lots of exposed mahogany and wicker furniture.

Mont Vernon. Baie Orientale Chevrise (B.P. 1174, 97062 Marigot), St. Martin, F.W.I. ☎ **800/233-0888** in the U.S. or 0590-87-62-00. Fax 0590-87-37-27. 394 suites. A/C TV TEL. Winter, Fr 1,290–Fr 1,730 ($258–$346) junior suite for 2; Fr 2,115–Fr 2,280 ($423–$456) suite for 2. Off-season, Fr 640–Fr 765 ($128–$153) junior suite for 2; Fr 1,195 ($239) suite for 2. Extra person Fr 390 ($78) per day. Rates include buffet breakfast. Children under 12 stay free in their parents' suite. AE, MC, V.

Opened in 1989, this resort complex with a lacy gingerbread architecture offers junior suites and two-room suites, with twin or king-size beds and private balconies opening onto the water. Each suite has a number of amenities, such as a refrigerator. It's a favorite among package-tour groups, especially those originating in France. The hotel suffered severe damage from the 1995 hurricanes, but was completely rebuilt and reconfigured in 1996.

Dining/Entertainment: There's a 200-seat main restaurant, Le Creole; a 50-seat main bar and patio; an 80-seat beach bar; and a 100-seat pool snack bar with a barbecue, called Le Sloop. French, Italian, and Creole cuisine are offered.

Services: Laundry, baby-sitting, massage.

Facilities: Duty-free shopping arcade, large swimming pool with sun deck, tennis courts, archery, water-sports center where deep-sea fishing can be arranged.

MODERATE

Club Orient Naturist Resort. Baie Orientale, 97150 St. Martin, F.W.I. ☎ **800/828-9356** or 0590-87-33-85. Fax 0590-87-33-76. 34 studios, 30 mini-suites, 36 chalets. A/C. Winter, $198 studio for 2; $238 mini-suite for 2; $288–$340 chalet for 2. Off-season, $135 studio for 2; $155 mini-suite for 2; $165–$195 chalet for 2. AE, DC, MC, V.

Isolated from the rest of St. Martin, this is the only resort in the French West Indies that's committed to the creation of a safe and socially acceptable environment for nudists. Established in the late 1970s, by a Dutch-born family, and completely rebuilt after its devastation by hurricanes in 1995, it welcomes a European and North American clientele. There's a great beach here and a restaurant, the Papagayo, where you can dine al fresco, literally. However, most guests opt to cook their meals in-house, as each unit has its own kitchenette (there's an on-site mini-market). Accommodations, set in red pine chalets imported from Finland, are utterly plain and basic and most have porches. There's no pool on the premises, but the chalets are right on the beach.

Laguna Beach Hotel. 97150 Baie Nettlé, St. Martin, F.W.I. ☎ **0590-87-91-75.** Fax 0590-87-81-65. 63 rms. A/C TV TEL. Winter, $150–$182 double. Off-season, $118 double. AE, MC, V.

On the road between Marigot and the Lowlands, the Laguna Beach Hotel, which opened in 1988, and was renovated in 1996, offers simple, reasonably priced accommodations in a pair of two-level buildings. Neither is as glamorous as those at Anse Margot, although that hardly matters to the beach aficionados who spend most of their time outside at Laguna Beach. The rooms, for the most part, are uncomplicated and comfortable, and include terraces, private safes, refrigerators, and hair dryers. There's a central freshwater swimming pool and three tennis courts, and a dining room that's open to the breezes. The public rooms are furnished in part with rattan and decorated with Haitian art. Laundry service and baby-sitting are available.

Marine Hôtel Simson Beach. Baie Nettlé (B.P. 172, 97150 Marigot), St. Martin, F.W.I. ☎ **800/221-4542** or 0590-87-54-54. Fax 0590-87-92-11. 120 studios, 45 duplexes. A/C TV TEL. Winter, $159–$183 studio for 2; $207–$241 duplex. Off-season, $129 studio for 2; $170 duplex. Rates include buffet breakfast. AE, DC, MC, V.

One of the most stylish hotels in its price bracket on the French side of the island is operated by the French hotel conglomerate Accor. It's good value for the money, especially because of the kitchenettes perched on the outside balconies. The Marine occupies a flat, sandy stretch of land between a saltwater lagoon and the beach, 5 miles west of Queen Juliana Airport. French travelers on "le budget" flock to this place. Decorated throughout in ocean-inspired pastels, it was designed with five three-story buildings, each evocative of a large, many-balconied Antillean house. In its center, two swimming pools serve as the focal point for a bar built out over the lagoon, an indoor/outdoor restaurant, and a flagstone terrace that hosts steel bands and cocktail parties in the evening. In addition to the kitchenette, each unit offers ceiling fans and simple, durable wicker furniture. The most desirable accommodations, on the third (top) floor, contain sloping ceilings sheltering sleeping lofts as well as two bathrooms. Laundry and baby-sitting are available. There's also a restaurant whose Creole name (La Vi Bo Kaye) translates as "Life at Home."

La Résidence. Rue du Général-de-Gaulle (B.P. 679), 97150 Marigot, St. Martin, F.W.I. ☎ **800/423-4433** or 0590-87-70-37. Fax 0590-87-90-44. 16 rms. A/C MINIBAR TV TEL. Winter, $102–$122 double. Off-season, $92–$98 double. Rates include continental breakfast. AE, DISC, MC, V.

In the commercial center of town, La Résidence has a concrete facade enlivened with neo-Victorian gingerbread fretwork and a street level devoted to some of the capital's most upscale shops. Because of its location close to virtually everything, it's favored by business travelers from, among other places, Miami and Guadeloupe, who don't particularly care about the hotel's distance from a beach (the closest one is a 10-minute cab ride or a 20-minute walk). The bedrooms are arranged around a landscaped central courtyard with a fish-shaped fountain. A bar with a soaring tent serves drinks to clients relaxing on wicker and bentwood furniture. Each of the bedrooms contains minimalist decor, and all but a few have sleeping lofts and a duplex design of mahogany-trimmed stairs and balustrades. Room service is available. The hotel is known for its French and Creole restaurant, offering a reasonably priced set menu. Lunch and dinner are served in a series of small curtained gazebos, divided by tropical plants that grow from a garden below. Such dishes are served as stuffed sea crab with Creole sauce and fillet of duck with peaches.

Résidence Alizéa. 97150 Mont Vernon, St. Martin, F.W.I. ☎ **0590-87-33-42.** Fax 0590-87-41-15. 18 rms, 8 bungalows. A/C TV TEL. Winter, $185 double; $265 bungalow. Off-season, $126 double; $186 bungalow. Rates include continental breakfast. AE, MC, V. After passing through Grand-Case, turn left and follow the signs along the cul-de-sac.

On the northeastern end of the island, this is the smallest hotel in a district with some of the biggest resorts. The inn opens onto a panoramic vista of Orient Bay. A swimming pool is on the premises, but the beach is just a five-minute hike through fields and across a road. Each accommodation was renovated after the damages of the hurricane in 1995, and all contain a kitchenette set on an open-air veranda, a light and airy collection of wooden furniture, and a color scheme of Caribbean pastels.

There are no facilities for lunch in the hotel, because of the five simple beachfront restaurants nearby. Dinner, however, can be ordered at the hotel restaurant, Le Mango.

Inexpensive

Le Royale Louisiana. 4 Rue du Général-de-Gaulle, 97150 Marigot, St. Martin, F.W.I. ☎ **0590-87-86-51.** Fax 0590-87-96-49. 54 rms, 14 duplexes. A/C TV TEL. Winter, Fr 440–Fr 490 ($88–$98) double; Fr 610–Fr 690 ($122–$138) duplex. Off-season, Fr 410 ($82) double; Fr 640 ($128) duplex. Rates include continental breakfast. AE, DC, MC, V.

Occupying a prominent position in the center of Marigot, this hotel appeals to business travelers and holiday-makers who aren't particularly concerned about its lack of a swimming pool and its inconvenient distance from a beach (the closest beach is a 10-minute taxi ride away, or a 20-minute walk). Designed in a hip-roofed French-colonial Louisiana style, its rambling balconies are accented with ornate balustrades. Each accommodation contains big sunny windows and modern furniture. The standard rooms have either king- or queen-size beds. The duplexes, ideal for families, have a bedroom and bath on the upper level and a sitting room with a fold-out sofa on the lower floor. A simple menu of breakfasts and lunchtime salads and sandwiches is served in the hotel's restaurant. There's a bar on the premises, and a simple restaurant serving breakfast, lunch, and snack-style dinners. Its major drawback is its blasé and not particularly cooperative staff.

Where to Dine

In Baie Longue

La Samanna. Baie Longue. ☎ **0590-87-51-22.** Reservations required for dinner, not for lunch. Main courses Fr 275–Fr 425 ($55–$85). AE, DC, MC, V. Daily 12:30–2:30pm and 7–9:30pm. Closed Sept–Oct. FRENCH.

Even though you may not be staying at La Samanna, you might want to make a reservation to enjoy a meal at this sometimes chillingly upscale dining terrace. Judges of this cuisine have declared it among the best in the Caribbean, saying it emulates the finest world-class restaurants in Paris. The high prices reflect the establishment's stylish image. Innovatively prepared and impeccably presented, dishes are likely to include the likes of lobster risotto, a hot and cold array of California foie gras, and Norwegian salmon with a sauce of red flame seedless grapes. Many dishes are a modernized version of the cuisine of Provence, priced at levels higher than you'd find even in that expensive region of France. The Dover sole and the oysters are flown in fresh from France, and the steaks are imported from New York. The al fresco dining terrace's parapet overlooks the sea, with dinner served by candlelight. Each table is set with Rosenthal china, lit by lamps from the *Orient Express,* and, at lunch, adorned with local flowers. Lunches, where a theatrically prepared steak tartare is a favorite, are slightly less expensive than dinners. La Samanna's underground, air-conditioned wine cellar houses more than 25,000 bottles from elite vineyards around the world.

In & Around Marigot

Very Expensive

✪ **La Vie en Rose.** Boulevard de France at rue de la République. ☎ **0590-87-54-42.** Reservations required, especially in winter and as far in advance as possible. Main courses $25–$40. AE, MC, V. Daily 11:30am–2:30pm and 6:30–10pm. Closed Sun off-season. FRENCH.

The dining room in this balconied second-floor restaurant evokes the nostalgia of the 1920s, with ceiling fans and candlelight. If you don't like the parlor, you can sit at one of the tables on a little veranda overlooking the harbor, provided you requested one when you made a reservation. Even though the menu is classic French, it nevertheless has Caribbean flavors, exemplified by the medallions of lobster with a lime sauce. Lobster also appears with the filet mignon, prepared in a Nantua sauce. The boneless breast of duck on a bed of raspberry sauce is definitely French, but here it's served with fried bananas. French visitors seem more willing to pay astronomical prices for these "vittles" than do Americans.

Expensive

La Maison sur le Port. Rue de la République. ☎ **0590-87-56-38.** Reservations recommended. Main courses $17–$20; fixed-price dinner $22. AE, MC, V. Mon–Sat noon–2:30pm and daily 6–10:30pm. FRENCH.

The staff welcomes people to enjoy their French cuisine in a refined atmosphere and elegant surroundings, with a view of three waterfalls in the garden. Overall, this is a rather grand, rather Parisian, and rather upscale choice. The tables are dressed with snowy tablecloths and Limoges china. At lunch, when you're seated on the covered terrace, you can choose from a number of salads as well as fish and meat courses. Dinner choices include fresh fish, such as snapper, salmon, or fresh-caught swordfish with coconut sauce; and fillet of lamb, veal, or steak, each with a light sauce. Duck has always been a specialty, as has bouillabaisse. The cookery is grounded firmly in France, but there are Caribbean twists and flavors, which come as delightful surprises. You can order from a wine list with an extensive selection of imported French products at moderate prices. Many guests come here at sundown to enjoy the harbor view.

Le Mini Club. Rue de la Liberté. ☎ **0590-87-50-69.** Reservations required. Main courses Fr 90–Fr 160 ($18–$32); Wed and Sat dinner buffet Fr 200 ($40). AE, MC, V. Daily noon–3pm and 6–11pm. FRENCH/CREOLE.

After you climb a flight of wooden stairs, you'll find yourself in an environment like a tree house built among coconut palms. Suspended on a wooden deck above the sands of the beach, this establishment is filled with Haitian murals and grass carpeting. It's not the best, and certainly not the most innovative restaurant on the island, but it has many fans because it uses quality ingredients and prepares every dish exceedingly well. The specialties include lobster soufflé (made for two or four people), an array of fish and vegetable terrines, red snapper with Creole sauce, sweetbreads in puff pastry, and many kinds of salad. Dessert might be bananas flambéed with cognac. Lavish buffets are held every Wednesday and Saturday night, with unlimited wine included. The restaurant is along the seafront at Marigot.

Moderate

✪ **La Brasserie de Marigot.** Rue du Général-de-Gaulle, 11. ☎ **0590-87-94-43.** Reservations not required. Main courses Fr 50–Fr 88 ($10–$17.60). AE, MC, V. Mon–Sat 7am–10pm, Sun 9am–4pm. FRENCH/CARIBBEAN.

This is where the real French eat. Opened in a former bank, it has a marble-and-brass decor, a sort of retro 1950s style with green leather banquettes. Meals include pot-au-feu, choucroûte (sauerkraut garni), blanquette de veau, even chicken on a spit and steak tartare, all those good dishes that the French enjoyed at blue-collar bistros "between the wars." Naturally, you can order interesting terrines here, and wine is sold by the glass, carafe, or bottle. The kitchen also prepares a handful of Caribbean dishes such as red snapper in lobster sauce. The brasserie, located in the center of town, is air-conditioned, with sidewalk tables overlooking the pedestrian traffic outside. It also features the most glamorous "take-out" service on St. Martin. For good food at good prices, this is an excellent choice.

In & Around Grand-Case

Before the 1995 hurricanes, this isolated beach town, a scant mile-long brush stroke of Antillean houses, had the greatest concentration of restaurants in the Caribbean. They lined the seafront, a virtual movie set of the colonial Caribbean. Tragically, most of the buildings on the "more desirable" (that is, the seafront) side of the street were demolished by the pounding waves of the hurricanes of 1995. The most upscale of them rebuilt, whereas the less prosperous have simply closed their doors forever and moved on, sometimes to greener pastures back in France. Here's a short list of the best in business now.

Expensive

✪ **L'Auberge Gourmande.** 89 Boulevard de Grand-Case. ☎ **0590-87-73-37.** Reservations required. Main courses $17–$28. AE, MC, V. Winter, Thurs–Tues, with seatings at 7 or 9pm. Off-season, Thurs–Tues 6–10pm (seatings any time). FRENCH.

This restaurant is in a century-old French Antillean house. Philippe Cassan, the chef, is assisted by his wife, Christine, who also has much experience in running restaurants. If you appreciate good French food and a family ambience, along with professional service, this is the place for you. Begin with vichyssoise, onion soup, or perhaps the mussel soup flavored with orange. No one pretends that the cuisine is the finest on the island, but it's honest and straightforward. Rarely is a dish overcooked or underseasoned, and the place has a raffish nautical atmosphere that many diners seek when dining out in the West Indies. Among their classic dishes are pork tenderloin with an old-fashioned mustard sauce, and a fillet of beef with either a blue cheese or black pepper sauce. This is excellent, as is the duck breast with a honey-and-lemon sauce. For dessert, try the profiteroles. Ask about *le service au vin,* which allows you to taste several wines throughout the course of your meal.

✪ **Le Cottage.** Grand Case. ☎ **0590-29-03-30.** Reservations recommended. Main courses $12–$19. AE, DC, MC, V. Daily 7–10:30pm Closed Aug. FRENCH/CREOLE.

Set within what looks like a private house on the landward side of the main road running through Grand Case, this restaurant benefits from the cuisine of a talented young chef (Pascal Ostronzec) whose earlier credits included stints at some of the most glamorous restaurants in France. It's one of the few restaurants in the Caribbean where a wine steward will recommend a different type of French wine for each of the courses you order. Menu items include both rustic *cuisine du terroir* (gratin of confit of pork jowls served with a traditional garnish), and dishes more closely linked to Creole traditions (a *croustillant* of blood sausage served with fried potatoes and honey-flavored vinaigrette). You may also choose *l'aiguillette* of duckling served with spiced coconut and pink whortleberries, a mille-feuille of artichoke hearts, or rack of lamb with olive oil and five spices.

Hévéa. Boulevard de Grand-Case. ☎ **0590-87-56-85.** Reservations required. Main courses $22–$32; menu Creole (featuring West Indian items) $35. MC, V. Daily 6:30–11pm. FRENCH.

Normandy-born restaurateurs (a team headed by Annick Grasset) own this place, the most obviously French of any restaurant in Grand-Case. After storm damage in 1995, they reopened with Louis XV chairs, candlelight, and a sense of formality. There are fewer than a dozen tables, so advance reservations are usually very important. The Caesar salad remains the best on the island. Opinion continues to be divided whether they do meat or fish dishes better. In honor of their homeland, there is a classically prepared *magret de canard* (duckling), with a mushroom-flavored wine sauce. A deservedly popular specialty, *escalope de veau Vallée de l'Auge,* is a Norman dish of veal with Calvados and cream sauce. You might also try the terrine of duck or else foie gras maison. To remind you you're in the West Indies, there's also a platter of smoked Caribbean fish.

Il Nettuno. 70 Boulevard de Grand-Case. ☎ **0590-87-77-38.** Reservations recommended. Pastas $14–$20; main courses $18–$24; lunch platters $12–$15. AE, MC, V. Daily noon–2:30pm and 6–10:30pm. Closed 3 weeks June and Sept. ITALIAN/SEAFOOD.

In a clapboard-sided house, this is a well-run place with lots of zest and Italian panache. On the main street of Grand-Case, close to the main pier, this is one of the most interesting Italian restaurants on either side of the island. Its interior is painted in shades of pink and draped with fish nets, Chianti bottles, and memorabilia of the Washington Redskins (its French-Italian owner lived in the U.S. capital for a time, and considers it his "home team"). You judge an Italian restaurant by its pastas, and we asked the waiter to bring us "the chef's pride." Agnolotti stuffed with ricotta and porcini mushrooms was the delectable result. Companions at our table were equally pleased with the chef's penne with salmon or the ravioli stuffed with spinach and ricotta. The saltimbocca is as good as you'd expect in Rome, and fresh fish includes mahimahi, tuna, and swordfish; there's also a choice of traditional Italian veal and chicken dishes. Fish can be blackened, grilled, or fried, and served with a choice of sauces that usually includes a version made with saffron.

Rainbow. Grand Case. ☎ **0590-87-55-80.** Reservations recommended. Lunch main courses $12–$15; dinner main courses $20–$30. AE, MC, V. Dec–May only, Mon–Sat noon–2pm; Oct–Aug Mon–Sat 6:30–10:30pm. Closed Sept. CARIBBEAN/CONTINENTAL.

The staff and owners here are a bit blasé; you might get the idea that they'd rather be sailing than preparing your meal. But, don't be turned off by their attitude. You'll be pleasantly surprised by a delectable platter of tuna, snapper, mahimahi, or lobster, if you can stand the wait. The blue-and-white dining room is in a 70-year-old Creole house on the seaward side of Grand Case's main road. For lunch, there's burgers and salads, along with the more upscale entrees served at night. Dinners include a fricassée of shrimp with scallops and Caribbean chutney; grilled swordfish; or a very French version of *magret* of duckling. Remain patient—the inconvenience will most likely be worth the effort.

Le Tastevin. Grand Case. ☎ **0590-87-55-45.** Reservations recommended. Lunch main courses $8–$29; dinner main courses $22–$31. AE, MC, V. Daily noon–2:15pm and 6–10pm. FRENCH.

Few other restaurants in Grand Case respect the traditional tenets of French *cuisine bourgeoise* as carefully as this one. Set in an open-sided pavilion, a former guest house originally built around 1915, the dining area is less than 10 feet from the water and is adorned with masses of potted palms. Menu items include Dover sole with garlic-flavored snails served on a bed of leeks, and dishes with more Caribbean flair like scallops and shrimp served with a lobster cream sauce; crispy salmon rolls with curry; veal cutlets in a mustard and pepper sauce; and breaded rack of lamb with tropical herbs. Dessert might feature a chocolate-coconut mousse cake garnished with rum-enhanced *crème anglaise.* All wines are from France and the selection is extensive, including an impressive collection of Burgundies.

In Colombier

La Rhumerie. Colombier. ☎ **0590-87-56-98.** Reservations required. Main courses Fr 80–Fr 250 ($16–$50). MC, V. Fri–Wed 7–10pm. Closed Sept–Oct. FRENCH/CREOLE.

Minutes from Marigot, in the tiny hamlet of Colombier, this restaurant is run by West Indies–born owner Francillette Le Moine, who is continuing a tradition established by her late husband, Yannick. They transformed this brown-and-white private home in a country setting into a restaurant that includes traditional French dishes. The mood is airy, stylish, relaxed, and outdoorsy. In addition to the mainland *cuisine bourgeoise* (escargot and onion soup gratiné), she serves West Indian dishes such as stuffed crab back, curried goat, a salad of coffre (a local fish), conch in fresh herbs, and *poulet boucanne* Creole (home-smoked chicken with baked green papayas and christophine au gratin). This is the food you might be served if you were invited to dinner at the home of an Antillean family.

In Oyster Pond

Captain Oliver Restaurant. In Captain Oliver's Hotel Resort. ☎ **0590-87-30-00.** Reservations recommended. Main courses $12–$22. AE, DC, MC, V. Daily noon–10:30pm. FRENCH/CREOLE.

Partially built on piers above the bay, this restaurant is located at the Dutch border. Captain Oliver is reached from either Marigot or Philipsburg along a twisting and much-potholed road. Once there, in a wood-sheathed setting overlooking some very expensive yachts, you'll find West Indian conch, "fish soup of the captain," a fisher's platter, tuna steak grilled with caper sauce, and fresh grilled lobster. This place has been known to island gourmets since it opened in 1983.

Beaches, Water Sports & Outdoor Pursuits

BEACHES The island as a whole has 36 white-sand beaches, some of whose forms were altered during the 1995 hurricanes. But the same forces that built the beaches originally have rebuilt them two years later. If you're a beach lover, don't despair: Zoologists were thrilled after the storms to find some of the best seashells they'd ever known on St. Martin. Shells available only in the deepest waters emerged in abundance on the altered beaches, and will continue to emerge through natural processes.

The hotels, for the most part, have grabbed up the choicest sands. Usually for a small fee nonguests can use hotel beaches and changing facilities. Top rating on St. Martin goes to **Baie Longue,** a long, beautiful beach that's rarely overcrowded. Chic and very expensive La Samanna (see "Where to Stay," above) opens onto this beachfront, one of the few on the island that grew rather than diminished in size. Unfortunately, drop-offs after the storm have made swimming here more hazardous than in prestorm days (though this is eventually being corrected by the forces of natural erosion). Baie Longue lies to the north of Cupecoy Beach, reached by taking the Lowlands road. Don't leave any valuables in your car, as many break-ins have been reported along this occasionally dangerous stretch of highway. If you continue north along the highway, you reach the approach to another long and popular stretch of sand and jagged coral, **Baie Rouge.** Snorkelers are drawn to the rock formations at both ends of this beach, even more of which were exposed through the erosion of the 1995 storms. There are no changing facilities, but, for some, that doesn't matter as they prefer to get their suntan au naturel.

Topless sunbathing is practiced commonly at the beaches on the French side. The nudist resort is **Club Orient Naturist Resort** (☎ **0590-87-33-85**), which was badly damaged in 1995 but rebuilt (see "Where to Stay" above for separate listing). Don't think, however, that you have to head to any particular beach for a glimpse of some flesh: Nude or monokini (as opposed to bikini) is relatively common throughout St. Martin, even though total nudity is not officially endorsed.

Ilet Pinel, a tiny island off St. Martin, is perfect for beach recluses. You can get here by negotiating with a passing fisher to provide transport back and forth. Stripped of some sand in 1995, it's slowly rebuilding itself.

Beyond the sprawling Mullet Beach Resort on the Dutch side, **Cupecoy Bay Beach** lies just north of the Dutch–French border. On the western side of the island, it's a string of three white-sand beaches set against a backdrop of caves and sandstone cliffs that provide morning shade. The beach doesn't have facilities but is very popular. One section of the beach is "clothing optional." The storm, unfortunately, unearthed some rocky parts that sunbathers find uncomfortable.

On the north side of the island, to the west of Espérance Airport, **Grand-Case Beach** is small but select, despite the deposit upon its sand of many tons of storm debris after the 1995 hurricanes. By the time of your visit, the sands will once again be white and clean.

For a description of beaches on the Dutch side, see "Beaches, Water Sports & Outdoor Pursuits" in section 1 on St. Maarten in chapter 10.

SCUBA DIVING Scuba diving is excellent around St. Martin, with reef, wreck, night, cave, and drift diving; the depth of dives is 20 to 70 feet. Off the northeastern coast on the French side, dive sites include Ilet Pinel, for shallow diving; Green Key, a barrier reef; Flat Island, for sheltered coves and geologic faults; and Tintamarre, known for its shipwreck. To the north, Anse Marcel and neighboring Anguilla are good choices. Most hotels will arrange for scuba excursions on request. The island's premier dive operation is **Marine Time,** whose offices are based in the same building as L'Aventure, Chemin du Port, 97150 Marigot (☎ **0590-87-20-28**). Operated from in front of The Market Dock in downtown Marigot by England-born Philip Baumann and his Mauritius-born colleague, Corine Mazurier, it offers morning and afternoon dives in deep and shallow water, wreck dives, and reef dives at a cost of $45 per dive. A resort course for first-time divers with reasonable swimming skills costs $75 and includes 60 to 90 minutes of instruction in a swimming pool, then a one-tank dive above a coral reef. Full PADI certification costs $350 to $550 depending on the equipment used and past diving experience and requires five days.

You can also try **Blue Ocean Watersport & Dive Center,** BP 4079, Baie Nettlé, St. Martin (☎ **0590-87-89-73**). A certified dive costs $45, including equipment. A PADI certification course is available for $350, and takes five days. Three dives are offered for $120, five dives for $175.

SNORKELING The calm waters ringing the shallow reefs and tiny coves found throughout the island make it a snorkeler's heaven. The waters off the northeastern shores of St. Martin have been classified as a regional underwater nature reserve, **Réserve Sous-Marine Régionale.** The area, comprising Flat Island (also known as Tintamarre), Pinel Islet, Green Key, and Petite Clef, is thus protected by official government decree. The use of harpoons is strictly forbidden. Snorkeling can be enjoyed individually or on sailing trips. Equipment can be rented at almost any hotel.

One of the best-recommended sites for snorkeling lies on the beachfront of the Grand-Case Beach Club, where **Under the Waves** (☎ **0590-87-51-87**) operates as a beachfront gift shop and clothing store, a source of information for island activities, and a departure point for hour-long snorkeling trips to St. Martin's offshore reefs. The preferred snorkeling spot is in the reefs surrounding Creole Rock, an offshore clump of reef-ringed boulders that are rich in underwater fauna. Michigan-born Maria Welch operates hour-long, supervised boat rides, with snorkeling gear included, to the rock, priced at $25 per person. Reservations are recommended.

TENNIS Tennis buffs heading for French St. Martin can play at most hotels. The **Méridien L'Habitation** has six courts, all lit for night play. The Omnisport (artificial grass) court at **Grand Anse Beach Club** is also lit. There are three unlit courts at the exclusive **La Samanna.**

WATERSKIING & PARASAILING Most beachfront hotels have facilities for waterskiing as well as parasailing. Waterskiing averages $40 per half hour, and parasailing costs about $25 to $30 a ride.

WINDSURFING Most windsurfers congregate on the adjoining beaches near Grand Case, including Orient Beach and Coconut Grove Beach, and to a lesser extent, Dawn Beach.

Three recommendable outfits on these beaches that are known for the quality of their instruction include: **Bikini Beach Watersports** (☎ **0590-87-43-25**), **Kon Tiki Watersports** (☎ **0590-87-46-89**), and **Tropical Wave** (☎ **0590-87-37-25**). The latter, an outfit operated by American-born Pat Turner, is one of the island's leading sales agents for Mistral windsurfers. Boards rent for around $15 an hour, instruction goes for around $32 an hour.

SHOPPING

Many day-trippers come over to Marigot from the Dutch side just to look at the collection of French-inspired boutiques and shopping arcades. Because it's a duty-free port, you'll find some of the best shopping in the Caribbean. There's a wide selection of European merchandise, much of it geared to the luxury trade, including crystal, perfumes, jewelry, and fashions, sometimes at 25% to 50% less than in the United States and Canada. There are also fine liqueurs, cognacs, and cigars. Whether you're seeking jewelry, perfume, or St-Tropez bikinis, you'll find it in one of the boutiques along rue de la République and rue de la Liberté in Marigot. Look especially for French luxury items, such as Lalique crystal, Vuitton bags (the real item, not the fake seen worldwide), and Chanel perfume.

Prices are often quoted in U.S. dollars, and salespeople frequently speak English. Credit and charge cards and traveler's checks are generally accepted. When cruise ships are in port on Sunday and holidays, some of the larger shops open.

IN MARIGOT

At harborside in Marigot there's a frisky **morning market** with vendors selling spices, fruit, shells, and local handcrafts. Shops here tend to be rather upscale, stocking mostly luxury items inspired by French fashions and tastes, catering to clients of the small but choice cruise ships that make a habit of docking offshore, especially in midwinter. One of the few fortunate legacies of Hurricanes Luis and Marilyn was the improvement and regeneration of Marigot's harbor front shops.

At **Port La Royale,** the bustling center of everything, mornings are even more alive: Schooners unload produce from the neighboring islands, boats board guests for picnics on deserted beaches, a brigantine sets out on a sightseeing sail, and the owners of a dozen different little dining spots are getting ready for the lunch crowd. The largest shopping arcade on St. Martin, it has many boutiques, some of which come and go with great rapidity.

Another shopping complex, the **Galerie Périgourdine,** facing the post office, is also a cluster of boutiques. Here you might pick up some designer wear for both men and women, including items from the collection of Ted Lapidus.

Act III. 3 rue du Gen'l de Gaulle. ☎ **0590-29-28-43.**

This shop is known for carrying expensive and/or chic brand-name women's clothing. Designers include as Versace, Christian Lacroix, Cerruti, and Gaultier. Expect a bit of Gallic attitude and high prices.

Gingerbread & Mahogany Gallery. 4-14 Marina Royale. ☎ **0590-87-73-21.**

Owner Simone Seitre scours Haiti four times a year to secure the best works of a cross section of Haitian artists, both the "old master" and the talented amateur. One of the most knowledgeable purveyors of Haitian art in the Caribbean, this pan-European has promoted Haitian art at exhibits around the world. Even if you're not in the market for an expensive piece of art (the paintings come in all price ranges), you'll find dozens of charming and inexpensive handcrafts. The little gallery is a bit hard to find (on a narrow alleyway at the marina), but it's worth the search.

Havane. Port La Royale. ☎ **0590-87-70-39.**

Havane offers exclusive collections of French clothing, in both sports and high-fashion designs for men. This is the leading choice for French designer fashions on the island, and sometimes you get discounts, depending on how willing they are to move the merchandise.

Lipstick. Port La Royale, Ave. Kennedy. ☎ **0590-87-73-24.**

This is the leading purveyor of women's cosmetics and skin-care products on French St. Martin, with a beauty parlor one floor above street level that's devoted to an intelligent and tasteful use of the store's impressive inventories. For sale are virtually every conceivable cosmetic or beauty aid made by such manufacturers as Chanel, Lancôme, Guerlain, Yves St. Laurent, Dior, and an emerging brand from Japan known as Chiseido. Hair removals, massages, manicures, pedicures, facials, and hair styling are available upstairs. The outfit maintains another outlet a few storefronts away (Lipstick, rue de la République, ☎ **0590-87-53-92**) that sells the cosmetics but that does not contain any of the beauty treatment facilities.

Maneks. No. 24 rue de la République. ☎ **0590-87-54-91.**

This place has a little bit of everything: video cameras, electronics, household appliances, liquors, gifts, souvenirs, Kodak film, watches, T-shirts, sunglasses, and pearls from Majorca. The shop also carries beach accessories. The staff even sells Cuban cigars, but these will have to be smoked abroad, as they can't be brought back into the United States.

Oro de Sol Jewelers. Rue de la République. ☎ **0590-87-56-51.**

This well-stocked store, one of the most upscale jewelry stores on St. Martin, has one of the most imaginative selections, including an array of gold watches by Bulgari, Cartier, Ebel, Patek Philippe, and the like, and high-fashion jewelry studded with precious stones.

La Romana. Rue de la République. ☎ **0590-87-88-16.**

In the heart of Marigot, this specialty boutique retails the latest collections of La Perla and Fendi. La Perla lines include swimwear, resort wear for day and evening, perfume, and lingerie. The Fendi collection of bags, luggage, and accessories is one of the largest in the Caribbean.

In Orleans

Roland Richardson. Orléans. ☎ **0590-87-32-24.**

Local artist Roland Richardson welcomes visitors to his beautiful small gallery located on the waterfront in Marigot. A native of St. Martin, Mr. Richardson is recognized today as one of the Caribbean's premier artists. His work encompasses oil, watercolor, pastel, charcoal, and etching. Often referred to as a "modern-day Gauguin," he is a gifted Impressionist painter known for his landscape, portraiture, and colorful still life paintings. His work has been exhibited in more than 70 one-man and group exhibitions in museums, major trade centers, and fine art galleries around the world and is included in many fine private and public collections. Gallery hours are Monday through Friday, 10am to 6pm, Saturday, 9am to 2pm; the gallery is closed on Sunday. Special appointments are available.

ST. MARTIN AFTER DARK

Some St. Martin hotels have dinner-dancing, piano-lounge music, and even discos. But the most popular after-dark pastime is leisurely dining.

Club l'Aventure, rue de la République, in Marigot (☎ **0590-87-01-97**), is still the most talked-about, most stylish, and most popular nightclub on the island's French side. Designed in a waterfront format that evokes an upscale yacht club, it contains two restaurants, one for pizza and snacks, and a more formal venue on its street level, where meals cost around $25 per person. Upstairs is a high-energy multicultural disco, where even 40-year-olds feel comfortable mingling with the island's young and energetic. Entrance is $5, and drinks begin at $5 each. It's open Monday through Saturday from 10:30pm until the management decides to close sometime in the wee hours.

4 St. Barthélemy

For luxury with minimum hassle, although at a high price tag, St. Barts is rivaled only by Anguilla. It's the ultimate in sophistication in the tropics: chic, rich, and very Parisian. Forget such things as historical sights or ambitious water-sports programs here, and come for the relaxation, the ultimate comfort, the French cuisine, and the white-sand beaches.

New friends call it "St. Barts," whereas old-time visitors prefer "St. Barths." Either way, it's short for St. Barthélemy, named by its discoverer Columbus in 1493 and pronounced *San Bar-te-le-MEE.* The uppermost corner of the French West Indies, it's the only Caribbean island with a touch of Sweden.

For the most part, St. Bartians are descendants of Breton and Norman fisherfolk. Many are of French and Swedish ancestry, the latter showing in their fair skin, blond hair, and blue eyes. The mostly Caucasian population is small, about 3,500 living in some 8 square miles, 15 miles southeast of St. Martin and 140 miles north of Guadeloupe.

Occasionally you'll see St. Bartians dressed in the provincial costumes of Normandy, and when you hear them speak Norman French, you'll think you're back in the old country, except for the temperature. In little Corossol, more than anywhere else, people follow traditions brought from 17th-century France. You might see elderly women wearing the starched white bonnets, at least on special occasions. This headgear, brought from Brittany, was called *quichenotte,* a corruption of "kiss-me-not," and served as protection from the close attentions of English or Swedish men on the island. The bonneted women can also be spotted at local celebrations, particularly on August 25, St. Louis's Day. Many of these women are camera-shy, but they offer their homemade baskets and hats for sale to visitors.

For a long time the island was a paradise for a few millionaires, such as David Rockefeller, who has a hideaway on the northwest shore, and Edmond de Rothschild, who occupies some fabulous acres at the "other end" of the island. The Biddles of Philadelphia are in the middle. Nowadays, however, St. Barts is developing a broader base of tourism as it opens more hotels. Nevertheless, the island continues as a celebrity favorite in the Caribbean, attracting the likes of Tom Cruise, Harrison Ford, and Mikhail Baryshnikov. It also attracts a lot of star-seeking paparazzi, who not only stalk celebrities at their private villas, but also at the beach, including Grand Saline beach, where Brad Pitt was photographed bathing in the nude (which is common and legal at this beach). In February, the island guest list reads like a roster from *Lifestyles of the Rich and Famous.*

The island's capital is **Gustavia,** named after a Swedish king. It's St. Barts's only town and seaport. A sheltered harbor, it has the appearance of a little dollhouse-scale port.

GETTING THERE

BY PLANE From the United States, the principal gateways are St. Maarten (see chapter 10), St. Thomas (see chapter 6), and Guadeloupe (see section 2 of this chapter). At any of these islands, you can connect to St. Barts via interisland carriers.

It's just a 10-minute flight from Queen Juliana Airport on Dutch-held St. Maarten. From St. Maarten, your best bet is **Windward Islands Airways International (Winair)** (**☎ 0590-27-61-01**), which will fly you to St. Barts in the morning (the first of its 10 daily flights departs at 7am) and return you to St. Maarten around 5pm. Flights cannot depart from or land on St. Barts after sundown. Round-trip passage costs $106 per person.

If you're on Guadeloupe, you can fly **Air Guadeloupe** (**☎ 0590-27-61-90**); trip time is 45 minutes and flights depart four or five times a day from Pointe-à Pitre's Le Raizet Airport. Round-trip passage from Guadeloupe to St. Barts costs Fr 1,002 ($200.40), or Fr 567 ($113.40) one-way. Air Guadeloupe also offers regular service, about three flights a day, to St. Barts from the small Espérance Airport on the French side of St. Martin. One-way transit costs Fr 256 ($51.20).

Air St. Thomas (**☎ 800/522-3084**) offers two flights a day to St. Barts from both San Juan and St. Thomas. However, flyers complain that the airline's schedule is unpredictable.

The makeshift landing strip on St. Barts has been the butt of many jokes. It's short and accommodates only small aircraft; the biggest plane it can land is a 19-seat STOL (short takeoff and landing craft). In addition, no landings or departures are permitted after dark, so plan your arrival accordingly.

St. Barthélemy

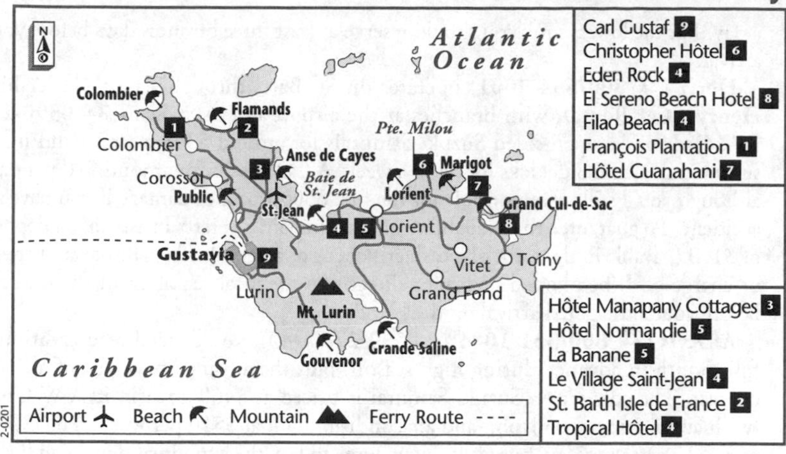

Note: Always reconfirm your return flight from St. Barts with one of the secondary carriers recommended above. If you don't, you'll find your reservation has been canceled. Also, don't check your luggage all the way through to St. Barts or you may not see it for a few days. Check your bags to your gateway destination (whatever island you're connecting through, most often Dutch St. Maarten), then take your luggage to your carrier and recheck your bags to St. Barts.

BY BOAT OR FERRY There is a variety of services between St. Maarten and St. Barts, but schedules vary with the season, so it's best to check on the spot. Contact the offices of such vessels as ***White Octopus*** (☎ **599/5-23170**), a motorized catamaran that departs from St. Maarten six days a week at 9am, arriving on St. Barts 90 minutes later. It docks, depending on the day of the week, at Bobby's Marina on the Dutch side. The vessel departs from St. Barts at 3:30pm and arrives back at St. Maarten at 5pm. The price is $50 for the round-trip, plus $5 departure tax. Call for more information. A roughly equivalent service, charging equivalent fares, on a smaller boat that's more affected by rough seas than the *White Octopus,* is offered by the ***Gustavia Express,*** a catamaran (☎ **0590-27-77-24**).

GETTING AROUND

BY TAXI Taxis meet all flights and are not super-expensive, mostly because destinations aren't far from one another. Dial ☎ **0590-27-66-31** for taxi service. A typical rate, St-Jean to Cul-de-Sac, is Fr 75 ($15). Night fares are 20% higher, as are fares on Sunday and holidays.

BY RENTAL CAR The hilly terrain, and the sense of adventure of the residents, combine to form a car-rental situation unique in the Caribbean. Never have we seen as many open-sided Mini-Mokes and Suzuki Samurais as we have on St. Barts. Painted in vivid colors, they're fast, fun, and very windy. You'll enjoy driving one too, as long as you're handy with a stick shift and don't care about your coiffure.

Budget Rent-a-Car (☎ **800/527-0700** or 0590-27-66-30) offers the least stringent terms for its midwinter rentals, and some of the most favorable prices. It rents Mitsubishi Mini-Mokes for around $420 a week, with unlimited mileage included. A collision-damage waiver (CDW; in French, *une assurance tous-risques*), absolving renters of all but $150 of responsibility in the event of an accident, costs around $10 a day. For the lowest rate, you should reserve at least three business days before your arrival.

Hertz (☎ **800/654-3001**) operates on St. Barts through a local dealership, **Henry's Car Rental,** with branches at the airport and in St-Jean (☎ **0590-27-71-14**). It offers open-sided Suzuki Samurais for around $348 a week, and more substantial Suzuki Sidekicks for $450 a week. A CDW sells for around $10 per day, although you'll still be responsible for the first $500 worth of damage if you have an accident. To guarantee the availability of a car in winter, Hertz insists that a deposit of $100 (payable in the form of a cashier's check or a debit held against a valid credit or charge card) be phoned or mailed directly to the local rental agent three weeks before your anticipated arrival on the island.

At **Avis** (☎ **800/331-1084** or 0590-27-71-43), you'll need a reservation a full month in advance during high season, plus the advance payment of a $100 deposit. The company's Suzuki Samurai is priced at $460 a week; its VW Golfs (with automatic transmission and air-conditioning), at $510 per week. The CDW costs $10 extra per day, but even if you agree to buy the extra insurance, you'll still be liable for the first $500 worth of damage to your rented vehicle in the event of an accident.

Gas is extra. Tanks hold enough to get you to one of the island's two gas stations. Never drive with less than half a tank of gas; you might regret it if you do, especially since the Shell station near the airport is closed from noon on Saturday until Monday morning. (Fortunately, the pumps here are automated, and accept VISA cards, a fact that might allow you to avoid running out of gas over a long weekend.) The island's only other gas station is a Shell station near L'Orient. All valid foreign driver's licenses are honored. Honk your horn furiously while going around the island's blind corners, a practice that avoids many sideswiped fenders.

BY MOTORBIKE & SCOOTER Denis Dufau operates **Rent Some Fun,** rue Gambetta (☎ **0590-27-70-59**), as well as **Boutique Harley Davidson,** at the Aéroport St-Jean (☎ **0590-27-54-83**). Both maintain the same inventories of machines and charge equivalent prices for rentals. A helmet is provided, and potential bikers must either leave an imprint of a valid credit card (MC or V), or pay a $200 cash deposit. Rental fees vary from $26 to $34 a day, depending on the size of the bike. A valid driver's license is required.

BY SIGHTSEEING TOUR Group tours are scaled to the island's size: eight passengers per minibus. If you go by private taxi, of course, it's more expensive. An hour-long tour by minibus costs about $40 for three or $50 for up to eight; prices, naturally, have to be negotiated. The local tourist office can arrange private tours, as can most hotel desks.

FAST FACTS: St. Barthélemy

Banks The two best-established banks are both in Gustavia and are both open Monday to Friday. The Banque Française Commerciale, rue du Général-de-Gaulle (☎ **0590-27-62-62**), is open from 8am to 12:30pm and 2 to 4:30pm. The Banque Nationale de Paris, rue du Bord-de-Mer (☎ **0590-27-63-70**), is open from 8am to noon and 2 to 3:30pm.

Currency The official monetary unit is the **French franc (Fr),** but most stores and restaurants prefer payment in U.S. dollars. Most hotels also quote their rates in American currency at a discount from the rates quoted in francs. For your reference, at press time the current exchange rate is Fr 4.98 to U.S.$1 (Fr 1 = 20¢ U.S.), and this is the rate that was used to convert prices in this chapter. As this is sure to fluctuate a bit, use this rate for general guidance only.

Customs You are allowed to bring in items for personal use, including tobacco, cameras, and film.

Documents If you're flying in, you'll need to present your return or ongoing ticket. U.S. and Canadian citizens need only photo identification or a passport. Visitors from Britain must have a valid passport.

Drugstores The Pharmacie de Saint-Barth is on Quai de la République (☎ **0590-27-61-82**) in Gustavia. It's open Monday to Saturday from 8am to 8pm.

Electricity The electricity is 200 volts AC (50 cycles); therefore, U.S.-made appliances require adapter plugs and transformers.

Emergencies Dial ☎ **16** for **police** or **medical** emergencies, ☎ **18** for **fire** emergencies.

Information Go to the **Office du Tourisme,** in the Town Hall, quai du Général-de-Gaulle, in Gustavia (☎ **0590-27-87-27**).

Medical Care St. Barts is not the greatest place to find yourself in a medical emergency. Except for holiday-making doctors escaping their own practices in other parts of the world, it has only 7 resident doctors and about 16 on-call specialists. The island's only hospital, and only emergency facilities, are about 1/4 mile north of Gustavia, the Hôpital de Bruyn, rue Jean-Bart (☎ **0590-27-60-35**). Serious medical cases are often flown out to St. Martin, Martinique, Miami, or wherever the accident victim or his/her family specifies.

Safety Although crime is rare here, it would be wise to protect your valuables. Don't leave them unguarded on the beach or in parked cars, even if locked in the trunk.

Taxes An airport departure tax of Fr 30 ($6) is assessed. Hotels don't add a room tax (though they usually levy a service charge of 10% to 15%).

Telephone St. Barts is linked to the Guadeloupe telephone system, which is *not* part of the 809 area code that applies to parts of the Caribbean. To call St. Barts from the United States, dial 011 (the international access code), then 590 (the country code for Guadeloupe), and finally the six-digit local number. To make a call within St. Barts dial all 10 digits of the phone codes listed throughout this chapter.

Time When standard time is in effect in the United States and Canada, St. Barts is one hour ahead of the U.S. East Coast. Thus, when it's 7pm on St. Barts, it's only 6pm in New York or Toronto. When daylight saving time is in effect in the United States, clocks in New York and St. Barts show the same time.

Weather The climate of St. Barts is ideal: It's dry with an average temperature of 72° to 86°F.

WHERE TO STAY

With the exception of a few of the really expensive hotels, most places here are homey, comfortable, and casual. Everything is small, as tiny St. Barts is hardly in the mainstream of tourism. In March it's often hard to stay on St. Barts unless you've made reservations far in advance. Accommodations throughout the island, with some exceptions, tend to be exceptionally expensive, and a service charge of between 10% and 15% is usually added to your bill. Some hotels quote their rates in U.S. dollars, others in French francs.

St. Barts has a sizable number of villas, beach houses, and apartments for rent by the week or month. Villas are dotted around the island's hills—very few are on the beach. Instead of an oceanfront bedroom, you get a panoramic view. One of the best agencies to contact for villa, apartment, or condo rentals is **St. Barth Properties,** 2 Master Dr., Franklin, MA 02038 (☎ **800/421-3396** in the U.S. and Canada, or 508/528-7727). Here, Peg Walsh, a long-time aficionado of St. Barts, will let you know what's available; she can also make arrangements for car rentals and air travel to St. Barts, and when you arrive, she can book baby-sitters and restaurant reservations. Sometimes, for example, you can rent a one-room "studio" villa away from the beach for $875 per week off-season, rising to $32,000 per week for a minipalace at Christmas. Yes, that $32,000 is right, but it's for a very unusual, antique-furnished luxury home. Most rentals are far cheaper, beginning around $2,500 a week. In addition to villas, Ms. Walsh can also arrange accommodations in all categories of St. Barts's hotels.

VERY EXPENSIVE

La Banane. 97133 L'Orient, St. Barthélemy, F.W.I. ☎ **0590-27-68-25.** Fax 0590-27-68-44. 9 rms. A/C MINIBAR TV TEL. Winter, $340–$500 double. Off-season, $170–$190 double. MAP Fr 225 ($49.50) extra. AE, MC, V.

About a mile from the airport, on the outskirts of the village of L'Orient, is this small, intimate, and well-furnished hotel. It's filled with some of the most stylish antiques on the island. Set on a flat, low-lying, and somewhat steamy landscape, the hotel grounds are richly planted with bananas, flowering shrubs, and palms. It's about a three-minute walk from the beach. Our favorite accommodation contains a large mahogany four-poster bed whose trim was made from a little-known Central and South American wood called angelique. The other units are less spacious, but each has some Haitian art, a mixture of antique and modern designs, a refrigerator, a private terrace, and louvered windows overlooking the garden. Some units are air-conditioned. Frankly, this is a very French, rather blasé setting where the staff seems happiest if you quietly enjoy your holiday and basically leave them alone.

Dining/Entertainment: There's a small, informal restaurant where a French/Caribbean cuisine is prepared using fresh local ingredients. Meals cost between Fr 150 and Fr 175 ($30 and $35) per person, without wine, and prepared in a French Caribbean style. Dinner might include grilled snapper with herbs and citrus sauce, steak au poivre, or sautéed calamari.

Services: Room service.

Facilities: Two freshwater pools; beach nearby.

✪ **Carl Gustaf.** Rue des Normands, 97099 Gustavia, St. Barthélemy, F.W.I. ☎ **800/322-2223** in the U.S., or 0590-27-82-83. Fax 0590-27-82-37. 14 suites. A/C MINIBAR TV TEL. Winter, $770–$990 one-bedroom suite; $1,050–$1,270 two-bedroom suite. Off-season, $490 one-bedroom suite; $690 two-bedroom suite. Rates include continental breakfast. AE, MC, V.

The most glamorous hotel in Gustavia rises above the town's harbor from its position on a steep hillside. Each accommodation is in one of a dozen pink, blue, or green, red-roofed villas whose facilities include a private kitchenette, two phones, fax machines, two stereo systems, a private terrace, a private pool, two color TVs, and comfortably plush rattan furniture. Access to each building is via a central staircase, which tests the stamina of even the most active of guests. The wood-frame units are angled for maximum views of the boats bobbing far below in the bay and panoramic sunsets. The mood is French, not unlike what you'd find on the coast of Provence.

Dining/Entertainment: There's a restaurant set on the uppermost level of the hotel, and a small but charming bar. The cuisine is French and Creole. Often a well-known chef from Paris appears in winter. There's also a sunset bar with live music, featuring a different cocktail every day.

Services: 24-hour room service, concierge, massage.

Facilities: Sauna, exercise room, two yachts that can be privately chartered (at a rate of $1,500 to $1,600 a day for up to 10 participants) for excursions. Beach facilities are within a 10-minute walk.

Christopher Hôtel. Pointe Milou (B.P. 571), 97098 St. Barthélemy, F.W.I. ☎ **800/221-4542** in the U.S., or 0590-27-63-63. Fax 0590-27-92-92. 40 rms, 1 suite. A/C MINIBAR TV TEL. Winter, $340–$500 double; from $610 suite. Off-season, $225–$280 double; $450 suite. Rates include American breakfast. One child under 12 (limit of 2) can stay free in parents' room. AE, DC, MC, V. Closed Sept–Oct 15.

On a dramatic promontory above the ocean, this is a full-service hotel offering views of St. Martin and nearby islets. It required major renovations in 1995 following hurricane damage. Built and managed by Sofitel, the luxury division of the Paris-based hotel giant Accor, it offers a French-colonial decor and a low-rise design that incorporates four slate-roofed, white-sided buildings arranged in a semicircle above a rocky coastline. Although the hotel is not adjacent to a sandy beach, clients usually drive about 10 minutes to reach Plage de l'Orient. Most of the resort's activities revolve around the swimming pool. Each room has a veranda or balcony overlooking the sea, a ceiling fan, and in some instances, a semiprivate garden.

Dining/Entertainment: Breakfast and gourmet French dinners are served at L'Orchidée, whereas lunch is a poolside affair, featuring platters, light snacks, and low-calorie or dietetic meals.

Services: Room service (7am to 9:30pm), a concierge who can arrange horseback riding, scuba diving, or deep-sea fishing.

Facilities: The resort's swimming pool, a 4,500-square-foot pair of interconnected ovals with a bridge, is the largest on the island. Nearby, a fitness center/health club offers nutritional counseling, massage, and relaxation therapy.

✪ **Filao Beach.** Baie de St-Jean (B.P. 667), 97099 St. Barthélemy, F.W.I. ☎ **0590-27-64-84.** Fax 0590-27-62-24. 30 rms. A/C MINIBAR TV TEL. Winter, Fr 1,800–Fr 3,500 ($360–$700) double. Off-season, Fr 1,000–Fr 2,200 ($200–$440) double. Rates include continental breakfast and airport transfers. AE, DC, MC, V. Closed Aug 31–Oct 16.

This white stucco bungalow hotel is set on 4 flat acres, four minutes from the airport, next to one of the island's most important beaches, the oh-so-chic St. Jean Bay Beach. Established in 1982, and permeated with a sense of Gallic nostalgia and style, this is one of the few Relais & Châteaux hotels in the Caribbean. Each room is named after a château in France. Although the staff is charming and the setting is supremely comfortable, the hotel simply isn't able to maintain the standards of a Relais & Châteaux property in France. The bedrooms, many of which suggest a nice motel room, were renovated in 1994, then refitted with new floor tiles and upholsteries after the hurricanes of 1995. All rooms are modern and fitted with large closets, private safes, ceiling fans, and sun-flooded terraces, where you can enjoy a leisurely breakfast. Some units are subject to traffic noise. Critics maintain that despite the management's efforts, the place has a subtle dowdiness that prevents it from being one of St. Barts's avidly sought-ought hotels.

Dining/Entertainment: A bar and restaurant, open only for lunch, overlooks St. Jean Beach and serves both French and international cuisine. Guests have to dine out at night at one of the island's other restaurants.

Services: Laundry and baby-sitting can be arranged.

Facilities: Freshwater swimming pool; scuba diving, snorkeling, windsurfing, and waterskiing can be arranged.

Hôtel Guanahani. 97098 Anse de Grand Cul-de-Sac, St. Barthélemy, F.W.I. ☎ **800/223-6800** in the U.S., or 0590-27-66-60. Fax 0590-27-70-70. 53 rms, 22 suites. A/C MINIBAR TV TEL. Winter, $395–$640 double; $735–$965 suite. Off-season, $230–$345 double; $505–$640 suite. Rates include continental breakfast. AE, DC, MC, V. Closed Sept.

The Hôtel Guanahani, isolated in the northeast part of the island, has been the largest hotel on the island ever since its much-publicized opening in 1986. Much of its charm is also the root of much of its inconvenience: On its own peninsula, it's spread over 7 steeply sloping acres dotted with a network of 50 Lilliputian cottages trimmed in gingerbread and painted in playland versions of bold tropical colors. Don't consider this place if you're immobile, wheelchair-bound, or hate puffing up and down steep altitudes. If that's not a problem, the views over the sea from each unit are broad and sweeping, and the exercise you'll get might contribute to your overall health. Most units, at least those on the resort's upper slopes, are self-contained in their own individual cottages. Those closer to the beach (which were damaged but quickly repaired after the 1995 storms) sometimes configure two accommodations into the same bungalow. Regardless of the layout, each contains a private patio, a refrigerator, ceiling fans, and a radio.

Dining/Entertainment: The Guanahani has two restaurants. The more formal is a Provençal/Italian hideaway, Bartolomeo (see "Where to Dine," below). Indigo is the more casual poolside cafe.

Services: Room service, laundry, baby-sitting, massages.

Facilities: Two freshwater swimming pools and a Jacuzzi with a good view of Grand Cul-de-Sac, two hard-surface tennis courts (lit at night), a private white-sand beach on a reef-protected bay, fitness center, water sports (some at an additional charge).

✪ **Hôtel Manapany Cottages.** Anse des Cayes (B.P. 114), 97133 St. Barthélemy, F.W.I. ☎ **800/847-4249** in the U.S., or 0590-27-66-55. Fax 0590-27-75-28. 46 units. A/C TV TEL. Winter, $410–$615 double; $845 junior suite; $1,250–$1,450 cottage. Off-season, $195–$385 double; $295–$345 suite; $350–$630 cottage. Rates include continental breakfast. AE, DC, MC, V.

The Hôtel Manapany climbs a steep, well-landscaped hillside on the northwestern side of the island, a 10-minute taxi ride north of the airport. Although Hurricane Luis widened the beach in 1995, it's still not too good for swimming. This is one of the most stylish hotels on St. Barts. It's small, intimate, and accommodating. The name, translated from Malagese, means "small paradise." Accommodations were designed as a mini-village of gingerbread-trimmed Antillean cottages, set either on a steeply sloping hillside or beside the sea. Each has a red roof contrasting sharply with the verdant vegetation and rambling verandas open to the sea. Living is a combination of indoor/outdoor, since bedrooms are air-conditioned behind sliding glass doors. Most occupants spend more time in their open-sided living rooms, enjoying the trade winds. Units can be reconfigured depending on your needs. For example, an entire cottage can be rented, or it can be subdivided with a junior suite created, or else a double room shut off from the layout of the rest of the cottage. The furnishings include both white-painted rattan and Caribbean colonial pieces carved into chunky patterns from mahogany and imported from the Dominican Republic. Mosquito netting covers most of the four-poster beds for a romantic style. The accommodations include large-screen TVs with in-house video movies, ceiling fans, a tile bath, and a kitchenette.

Dining/Entertainment: The restaurant, Ouanalao, is a crescent-shaped terrace overlooking the sea, featuring casual Italian dining with light lunches and candlelit romantic dinners. More formal meals are served in an elegant raftered dining room, overlooking the swimming pool and the resort's gardens. The Ouanaloa is open throughout the year.

Services: Concierge, room service, laundry, baby-sitting.

Facilities: Small-scale spa facility for massages and stress reduction.

St. Barth Isle de France. 97133 Anse des Flamands, St. Barthélemy, F.W.I. ☎ **800/322-2233** in the U.S., or 0590-27-61-81. Fax 0590-27-86-83. 18 rms, 3 beach junior suites, 18 bungalows. A/C MINIBAR TV TEL. Winter, $620 double; $780 suite; $420–$590 bungalow. Off-season, $470 double; $640 suite; $300–$440 bungalow. Rates include continental breakfast. AE, DC, MC, V.

Set adjacent to one of the island's finest and prettiest beaches, this resort opened in 1992 but was devastated by Hurricane Luis in 1995, which led to massive renovations. Centered around a re-creation of a colonial plantation house, the hotel is small, family run, and completely isolated from a chain-hotel mentality, with unusually spacious bedrooms for St. Barts. Each contains a private safe, a coffeemaker, and an individual decor with antique mahogany furniture and engravings collected from neighboring islands.

Dining/Entertainment: The restaurant, La Case de L'Isle, is on the beachside opening onto views of Baie de Flamands. Jean Claude DuFour, whose experience is mainly with the fabled Trois Gros restaurant family of France, has tremendously upgraded the cuisine here, blending haute cuisine overtones with Caribbean products. Try his red mullets flavored with basil or fillet of lamb in a parsley cream sauce.

Facilities: Air-conditioned squash court, direct access to an excellent beach, two swimming pools a few steps from the beach, tennis court, exercise room, gift shop.

Expensive

Eden Rock. 97133 St-Jean, St. Barthélemy, F.W.I. ☎ **0590-27-72-94.** Fax 0590-27-88-37. 14 rms. A/C MINIBAR TEL. Winter, $350–$600 double. Off-season, $240–$500 double. Rates include continental breakfast. AE, MC, V.

When the quartzite promontory this hotel sits on was purchased many years ago by the island's former mayor, Rémy de Haenen, the seller was an old woman who laughed at him for paying too many francs for it. Today it's part of the island lore, and the single most spectacular building site on St. Barts, flanked by two perfect beaches. The building capping its pinnacle looks like an idealized version of a Provençal farmhouse set amid a landscape of rocks, scrub, and pines. Offering some of the best panoramas on the island, it's surrounded on three sides by the waters of St. Jean Bay, allowing views from the terra-cotta terrace of frigatebirds wheeling and diving for fish in the turquoise waters below. In 1995 the building was sold to English expatriates David Matthews and family, who emptied the contents of their manor house in Nottinghamshire to fill it. Regrettably, shortly after the transfer of title, Hurricane Luis struck in full fury, delaying the opening of the new entity for a few months and requiring repairs to the terraces and wraparound decks. Today, the stone house contains a collection of French antiques and paintings left over from the de Haenen family, and English antiques and paintings imported by the new owners. Each of the half-dozen bedrooms has a sea view, air-conditioning or ceiling fan, and a stylish decor for an upscale and sophisticated clientele. By the time you arrive, some new beachfront units may have been added.

Dining/Entertainment: The hotel has a bar and a well-known restaurant, the Eden Roc. Lunches feature barbecue-style meals. Dinners are much more elaborate, focusing on French nouvelle and classic food.

François Plantation. 97133 Colombier, St. Barthélemy, F.W.I. ☎ **800/233-5695** in the U.S., or 0590-27-78-82. Fax 0590-27-61-26. 12 bungalows. A/C MINIBAR TV TEL. Winter, $300–$450 bungalow for 2. Off-season, $240–$280 bungalow for 2. Rates include American breakfast and free use of a rental car in summer only. AE, MC, V. Closed Aug 15–Oct 20.

This complex, 2 miles northwest of Gustavia and a 10-minute ride from the airport, re-creates the plantation era, standing on a steep hill with panoramic views of the beach below. The management skillfully compensates for its position inland from the beach by including, during off-season only, the use of a Mini-Moke or equivalent car in the rate. Newly arrived clients drive themselves from the airport to the hotel, then enjoy maximum independence during their stay. The resort consists of a tropical garden, a central administrative center, and 12 bungalows, each decorated in an elegant West Indian style, with reproduction antique four-poster beds. Each has a ceiling fan and safe. Eight of the units open onto sea views, whereas others look out over a garden. The owners are Françoise and François (you heard right) Beret, longtime residents of St. Barts.

Dining/Entertainment: The hotel has an exceptional restaurant, La Route des Epices, featuring food that's more exotic than many of its competitors.

Services: Laundry.

Facilities: Swimming pool with a view over the sea several hundred feet below.

El Sereno Beach Hôtel. Grand Cul-de-Sac (B.P. 19), 97133 St. Barthélemy, F.W.I. ☎ **800/221-4542** in the U.S., or 0590-27-64-80. Fax 0590-27-75-47. 18 rms, 14 suites, 9 villas with kitchenette. A/C MINIBAR TV TEL. Winter, $320 double; $580 suite; $180–$280 villa for 2; $220–$320 villa for 3; $260–$360 villa for 4. Off-season, $200 double; $440 suite; $180 villa for 2; $220 villa for 3; $260 villa for 4. Rates for rooms and suites include continental breakfast, $12 extra for occupants of the villas. AE, DC, MC, V. Closed Sept–Oct 15.

Sereno's low-slung pastel facade and its isolated location (4 miles east of Gustavia) create the aura of St-Tropez in the Antilles. A lot of the Riviera crowd is attracted to it, partly because of its location on a good beach with calm waters. More of the units overlook the gardens than the sea, although in view of their relaxed informality and comfort, no one seems to mind. Each unit contains two beds, an individual safe, and a refrigerator. Video movies are available. The villas are gracefully isolated from the rest of the compound, and each contains its own kitchenette for Robinson Crusoe–style living à la Française.

Dining/Entertainment: The feeling is a bit like a private compound, whose social center is an open-air bar and poolside restaurant, the West Indies Café, recommended separately.

Facilities: Freshwater pool, in the center of which is a verdant island.

MODERATE

Tropical Hôtel. St-Jean (B.P. 147), 97095 St. Barthélemy, F.W.I. ☎ **800/223-9815** or 0590-27-64-87. Fax 0590-27-81-74. 20 rms. A/C TV TEL. Winter, Fr 1,080–Fr 1,250 ($216–$250) double. Off-season, Fr 670–Fr 730 ($134–$146) double. Rates include continental breakfast. AE, MC, V.

Small and unpretentious, with a facade that looks like a postcard of a Caribbean colonial inn, this hotel is composed of scattered bungalows trimmed in gingerbread. It's a restful, calm, and relatively uneventful place. Originally built in 1981, and partially renovated after the hurricanes of 1995, it's perched on a hillside about 50 yards above St. Jean Beach (a mile from the airport and a mile and a half from Gustavia). Each room contains a private shower, king-size bed, tile floor, and a refrigerator to cool your tropical drinks. Nine come with a sea view and balcony, and 11 contain a porch opening onto a garden that's so lush it looks like a miniature jungle.

There's a hospitality center, where guests read, listen to music, or order drinks at a paneled bar surrounded by antiques. The freshwater swimming pool is small, but water sports are available on the beach. Breakfast is served on the poolside terrace.

✪ **Le Village Saint-Jean.** Baie de Saint-Jean (B.P. 623), 97098 St. Barthélemy CEDEX, F.W.I. ☎ **800/651-8366** in the U.S., or 0590-27-61-39. Fax 0590-27-77-96. 6 rms, 20 cottages, 4 suites. A/C TEL. Winter, $140 double; $160–$315 one-bedroom cottage; $420–$430 two-bedroom cottage; $260–$350 suite. Off-season, $89 double; $110–$220 one-bedroom cottage; $280 two-bedroom cottage; $165–$200 suite. Room rates include continental breakfast, Fr 58 ($11.60) extra for occupants of cottages and the suite. AE, CB, MC, V.

Over the years, this cottage colony hideaway, 1 mile from the airport toward St-Jean, has attracted a distinguished clientele, including food critic Craig Claiborne. Lying in the most central part of St. Barts, a five-minute drive uphill from Plage de Saint-Jean, it offers one of the best values on this high-priced resort island. Its stone-and-wood cottages contain kitchens, sun decks or gardens, terrace living rooms, balconies, and ceiling fans. Although the rate structure is modest compared to other places on the island, don't be surprised to see a media headliner here; after all, some of them like to save money too.

The complex has a well-managed restaurant and bar, Le Patio, with a sprawling terrace on a platform above the sloping terrain. The hotel's swimming pool has two decks overlooking the bay, cascading water, and a Jacuzzi. Founded in the early 1960s, this was the first inn of its kind on St. Barts, and it's still administered by the Charneau family.

INEXPENSIVE

Hôtel Normandie. 97133 L'Orient, St. Barthélemy, F.W.I. ☎ **0590-27-61-66.** Fax 0590-27-98-83. 8 rms. A/C. Winter, Fr 350–Fr 420 ($70–$84) double. Off-season, Fr 320–Fr 350 ($64–$70) double. No credit cards.

Modest, unassuming, and completely without chic, this is what the French call an *auberge antillaise.* Set near the intersection of two major roads, about 100 yards from the sands of L'Orient Beach and 3 miles east of the airport, it offers motel-inspired bedrooms of casual comfort, the more expensive of which are larger, lie adjacent to the hotel's modest-size swimming pool, and contain TV sets. The less expensive, smaller rooms are next to the highway and lack a TV. A family-owned hotel, it contains virtually no facilities other than the clean but somewhat-dreary accommodations. It's one of the least expensive places to stay on St. Barts.

WHERE TO DINE

IN GUSTAVIA

Expensive

Au Port. Rue Sadi-Carnot. ☎ **0590-27-62-36.** Reservations recommended, especially for veranda tables. Main courses Fr 78–Fr 125 ($15.60–$25); menu Creole Fr 190 ($38). AE, MC, V. Daily 6:30–10pm. Closed Sept–Oct. FRENCH/CREOLE.

In the center of town at the waterfront, this restaurant has a narrow veranda jutting above the road. You climb a steep flight of stairs to reach its second-floor dining room, where the neocolonial decor includes different sailboat maquettes and antiquities. You might begin with a fish terrine with a herb sauce, crab and conch ravioli in a rich fish stock, or perhaps a gizzard and duck-liver salad with passion sauce. The owner, Alain Bunel, prepares excellent fish and meat dishes, including mahimahi with crunchy cabbage and Creole oils; cassolette with vegetables; jumbo prawn colombo served with spicy rice; chicken leg with morels; and fillet of duck with wine sauce.

✪ **La Mandala.** Rue Courbet. ☎ **0590-27-96-96.** Reservations recommended. Main courses Fr 90–Fr 140 ($18–$28); set-price dinner Fr 180 ($36). Mon 7–11pm, Tues–Sun noon–2pm and 7–11pm. DC, MC, V. MEDITERRANEAN/CARIBBEAN.

Established shortly after the hurricanes of 1995, this is one of the most exciting restaurants on St. Barts. It occupies the premises of a house on the steepest street in Gustavia, high above the harbor. If you drive your own car up to the entrance, a valet will park it for you. Its name derives from the Mandala, symbol of Buddhist harmony, whose design of a square within a circle is duplicated by the position of the dining deck above a swimming pool visible from above. A specialty here is Spanish-style tapas, which some diners consider an important before-dinner adjunct to their meal. The owners and chefs are partners Kiki and Boubou (Christophe Barjetta and Olivier Megnin), whose nicknames disguise their formidable training at some of the grandest restaurants of France. Menu items include conch in puff pastry, goat cheese and fresh green salad, an array of pastas whose ingredients change every week, fillet of beef with Roquefort sauce, and jumbo shrimp with ginger sauce. All main courses are accompanied by at least four local vegetables, including a gratin of green papaya and puree of sweet potatoes. Lunches are simpler than dinners and focus on set menus featuring exotic salads, quiches, and seafood.

Le Sapotillier. Rue Sadi-Carnot. ☎ **0590-27-60-28.** Reservations required. Main courses Fr 120–Fr 210 ($24–$42); fixed-price menu Fr 250 ($50). AE, MC, V. Daily 6:30–10:30pm. Closed May to mid-Oct. FRENCH/SEAFOOD.

This West Indian house beside the less frequented part of Gustavia's harbor is the domain of Austrian-born Adam Rajner, who runs one of the best-known restaurants in Gustavia. Le Sapotillier is near the top of the list for every visiting gourmet. Named after a gnarled and wind-blown sapodilla tree in the restaurant's courtyard, the restaurant offers diners a choice of seating locations. They include a candlelit patio or a table in a clapboard-covered Antillean bungalow that was transported from the outlying village of Corossol.

Mr. Rajner, in the best tradition of European innkeeping, pays strict attention to the quality and presentation of his food. Your meal might begin with a hot goat-cheese salad with a hazelnut-oil dressing or homemade duck-liver pâté, perhaps homemade fish soup. Among the more interesting meat dishes, a whole young pigeon on spinach is served, as is a fillet of young lamb with ratatouille. A couscous is made with large spicy shrimp, or you might order steamed stingray with a horseradish sauce. A casserole of sea scallops and prawns is flavored with balsamic vinegar and served with Creole sauce.

Moderate

L'Escale. La Pointe. ☎ **0590-27-81-06.** Reservations required in season. Main courses Fr 80–Fr 180 ($16–$36). MC, V. Daily noon–2pm and 6:30pm–midnight. Closed Sept 15–Oct 15. FRENCH/ITALIAN.

Some villa owners cite L'Escale, a hip, sometimes raucous, and always irreverent hang-out for the raffish and wealthy, as their favorite restaurant on the island. It's set in a simple, industrial-looking building on the relatively unglamorous south side of Gustavia's harbor, adjacent to dozens of moored yachts. You can dine lightly and inexpensively here or spend a lot of money, depending on your menu selections and appetite. Typical fare might include one of their excellent salads, a pizza which emerges from a wood-burning oven, or a pasta dish. A perennial favorite is steak tartare, whose ingredients are presented and prepared before the gaze of the clients, fillet of beef pizzaiola, carpaccio, and a dramatically flambéed fruits. The food is hearty and full of flavor. The chef doesn't try to compete with the grand cuisine of the island's more fabled restaurants.

L'Iguane. Carré d'Or, quai de la République. ☎ **0590-27-88-46.** Reservations recommended for dinner. Continental breakfast Fr 38 ($7.60); sushi Fr 14–Fr 28 ($2.80–$5.60) per piece; main courses Fr 110–Fr 300 ($22–$60). AE, MC, V. Mon–Sat 8am–midnight. Closed Sept–Oct. JAPANESE/INTERNATIONAL.

Set adjacent to three upscale shops, this restaurant offers an international menu that includes sushi, American breakfasts, and California-style sandwiches and salads. The walls are ocher and blue, and the lighting fixtures are filtered to flatter even the most weather-beaten skin. The sometimes-glamorous clients all seem to be watching their waistlines. The ambience grows more Asian as the evening progresses. Sushi is the main allure here, served ultra-fresh from whatever fishing boat happens to have deposited its catch nearby on the day of your arrival.

In the St-Jean Beach Area

✪ **Le Patio.** Village St-Jean. ☎ **0590-27-70-67.** Reservations required. Main courses Fr 115–Fr 145 ($23–$29). CB, MC, V. Thurs–Tues 6:30–10pm. Closed mid-June to late July. ITALIAN/PIZZA.

Le Patio has a deserved reputation for offering some of the best food values on the island and some of the best panoramic views. The restaurant features a northern Italian cuisine, along with pizza and some French dishes. Menu items that are consistently appealing include spaghetti with lobster, one of the most appealing platters of antipasti on the island (loaded with "Italianized" versions of local fish and island vegetable), and such fish as yellowtail snapper cooked in parchment with locally grown herbs and spices. The homemade pizza and pasta dishes include the chef's selection of the day. They also feature "selections of the week," which might feature grilled local fish in a sauce chien (hot) or escalope parmigiana. The restaurant is 1 mile from the airport toward St-Jean.

✪ **Vincent Adam.** Carenage de St-Jean. ☎ **0590-27-93-22.** Reservations recommended, especially in winter. Set menus Fr 190–Fr 240 ($38–$48). AE, MC, V. Daily 6:30–10pm. CONTINENTAL/CARIBBEAN.

Set within a 50-year-old converted Creole house, high in the hills above the bay of St. Jean, this is one of the finest restaurants in St. Barts. Expect to sit in one of two indoor/outdoor dining areas where groves of banana plants frame a sweeping view of the seacoast below. Ironically, the restaurant's namesake is no longer associated with the restaurant, but the new owner, Gilles Malfroid, retains the name purely for PR purposes. The innovative menu changes every Friday night, and might include items like mille-feuille of foie gras and potatoes; fillet of lamb in puff pastry with a duxelle of mushrooms; or a Provence-derived *barigoule* of red snapper and shrimp cooked on a brochette and served on a bed of artichoke hearts and herbs. The set menu priced at Fr 240 ($48) features different preparations of lobster, served both as an appetizer and as a main course. All wines are from France.

At Morne Lurin

Santa Fe Restaurant. Morne Lurin. ☎ **0590-27-61-04.** Reservations not required. Burgers Fr 25–Fr 50 ($5–$10); meal platters Fr 60–Fr 100 ($12–$20). No credit cards. Mon–Tues and Thurs–Sat noon–2pm and 5–10pm, Sun 5–10pm. Closed lunch Apr–Oct. AMERICAN.

Set inland from the sea, atop one of the highest elevations on the island, this burger house and sports bar has carved out a formidable niche for itself with the island's English-speaking clientele. Named after a romantic song popular at the time of its establishment in 1966 (and having nothing to do with the city in New Mexico), it features wide-screen TVs that show things like the American Super Bowl to as many as 450 viewers. After the hurricanes of 1995, its roof, wraparound decks, and bar tops were completely rebuilt of teakwood, and a more nautical flair was introduced. You can take in the view of the surrounding landscapes for free, but most clients stop for one of the well-recommended hamburger, steak, shrimp, or barbecued-chicken dishes. Frankly, this place made its original reputation on its burgers, cheeseburgers, and fresh-made fries, which some diners compare to the best available in the States.

At Colombier

✪ **La Route des Epices.** In the François Plantation, Colombier. ☎ **0590-27-78-82.** Reservations required. Main courses Fr 175–Fr 280 ($35–$56). AE, MC, V. Daily 6:30–10pm. Closed Aug 1–Oct 15. FRENCH.

In 1995 Françoise and François Beret decided to initiate a cuisine that many diners consider an enjoyable departure from the ubiquitous French/Creole. Their dining room, adapted from part of the old plantation that stood here, makes it a point to flavor many dishes with spices not usually seen in the French repertoire. Exact components change frequently, but might include boeuf de coutancie (a "core" of entrecôte prepared in the traditional style); an aromatic, highly spicy version of fish soup; a stir-fry of jumbo shrimp with lime-and-ginger sauce; or local red snapper roasted in its own skin and served with vinegar-marinated algae pods and cumin. Food items are as cerebral as they are satisfying. The wine, the service, and the quality of ingredients used in the dishes presented are top-notch.

Anse du Grand Cul-de-Sac

Bartolomeo. In the Hôtel Guanahani, Anse du Grand Cul-de-Sac. ☎ **0590-27-66-60.** Reservations required, especially for nonhotel guests. Main courses Fr 115–Fr 170 ($23–$34). AE, DC, MC, V. Sun–Fri 7:30–10pm. Closed Sept. PROVENÇAL/NORTHERN ITALIAN.

This is the deluxe dining choice for one of the most exclusive and expensive hotels on the island, in spite of the fact you may have to dine to loud American R&B. The menu selection changes frequently, but always includes a varied and lengthy array of gastronomic specialty dishes, interestingly spiced, sauced, and served. The casual but elegant restaurant also offers an outside terrace for drinks and dinner (it was rebuilt and improved after the devastating damage of Hurricane Luis in 1995). Piano entertainment is provided. The food seems to vary every winter, although it's always first class. Everything depends on the chef, who changes annually, imported from France or wherever. Typical dishes, however, are likely to include lobster minestrone, crisp salmon filled with sesame seeds and cumin, or duck flavored with honey and lemon.

Grande Saline

Le Tamarin. Plage de Saline. ☎ **0590-27-72-12.** Reservations required for dinner. Main courses Fr 100–Fr 170 ($20–$34). MC, V. Nov 1–June 15 and July 15–Aug 30, daily 12:30–3pm and Thurs–Sat 7–9:30pm. Closed other months. FRENCH/CREOLE.

One of the island's genuinely offbeat sites for a meal is Le Tamarin, a deliberately informal bistro that caters to a clientele from the nearby Plage de Saline. Lunch is the more popular and animated meal here, and most customers dine in bikinis and bathing suits. It's isolated amid rocky hills and forests east of Gustavia, within a low-slung cottage whose eaves are accented with gingerbread. Inside, teak-and-bamboo motif prevails. If you have to wait, you can order an apéritif in one of the hammocks stretched under a tamarind tree (hence the name of the restaurant). Fresh fish is invariably featured, but meat dishes and poultry also are cooked well. Service can be hectic, but if you're in a rush you shouldn't be here. It's for a lazy afternoon on the beach.

Grand Cul-de-Sac

Club Lafayette. Grand Cul-de-Sac. ☎ **0590-27-62-51.** Reservations recommended. Main courses Fr 210–Fr 365 ($42–$73). AE, MC, V. Daily noon–4pm. Closed May–Nov. FRENCH/CREOLE.

No one would ever dream of coming here for dinner, as the pale-pink wood-sided house it occupies closes down completely after dark. Come here instead for a sun-flooded, wine-soaked lunch in the sun amid beach-loving clients who shrug at the idea that their *maillots de bain* are revealing. Lunching here, at a cove on the eastern end of the island, east of Marigot, is like taking a meal at your own private beach club—and a very expensive beach club at that. After a dip in the ocean or pool, you can order a planteur in the shade of a sea grape, and later proceed to lunch itself: a Roquefort-and-walnut salad, charcoal-grilled langouste, émincée of crayfish with a choice of three sauces (beurre blanc or "white butter," pepper, or provençal), magret of duck stuffed with foie gras, or grilled fresh fish. In other words, this is no hamburger fast-food beach joint. Afterward, have a refreshing citrus-flavored sherbet.

✪ **West Indies Café.** In Sereno Beach Hôtel. ☎ **0590-27-64-80.** Reservations recommended. Main courses Fr 75–Fr 200 ($15–$40). AE, MC, V. Daily noon–3pm and 7:30–10pm. Closed Sept–Oct 15. FRENCH/INTERNATIONAL.

Four miles east of Gustavia, one of the most endearing restaurants on the island is shaded from the sun by a wooden roof like a giant parasol. The restaurant offers a 360° open-air view overlooking a lagoon and a swimming pool. The menu is deliberately geared to have a midmarket price range, though the attention to food might make you think that prices should be considerably higher. The best items on the menu are grilled lobster and the grilled tuna steak. The eggplant mousse and fish tartare are also excellent.

Vitet

Hostellerie des Trois Forces. Vitet. ☎ **0590-27-61-25.** Reservations required. Main courses Fr 55–Fr 200 ($11–$40). AE, MC, V. Mon–Sat noon–3pm and 6–10pm. FRENCH/CREOLE/VEGETARIAN.

Isolated from the bulk of St. Barts's tourism, this restaurant is located midway up the island's highest mountain (Morne Vitet). The place has a resident astrologer, a French provincial decor, terraces accented with gingerbread, and food that in 1995 won its owner/chef an award from France's prestigious Confrérie de la Marmite d'Or. The heart and soul of the place is Hubert de la Motte, who arrived from Brittany with his wife to create a hotel where happiness, good food, comfort, and conversation are a way of life. Even if you don't stay here, you might want to drive out for a meal. The setting is a compound of pastel-colored, gingerbread-trimmed cottages, each named after a different sign of the zodiac, in a high-altitude setting of bucolic charm. Although the same menu is available throughout the day and evening, dinners are more formal than lunches, and might include fish pâté, beef shish kebab with curry sauce, grilled fresh lobster, veal kidneys flambé with cognac, a cassolette of snails, and such desserts as crêpes Suzette flambé. "Each dish takes time," in the words of the owner, because it's prepared fresh. Count on a leisurely meal and a well-informed host who has spent years studying astrology.

PUBLIC

Maya's. Public. ☎ **0590-27-75-73.** Reservations required. Main courses Fr 150–Fr 260 ($30–$52). AE, MC, V. Mon–Sat 6–11pm. Closed June to mid-Oct. CREOLE.

It's the most surprising restaurant on St. Barts, because of its artful simplicity and glamorous clients. A much-rebuilt green-and-white Antillian house with almost no architectural charm, it attracts crowds of luminaries from the worlds of media, fashion, and entertainment between New York and Hollywood. This is the kind of place you might find on Martinique, because that's where its French-Creole chef, Maya Beuzelin-Gurley, is from. Assisted by her Massachusetts-born husband, Randy Gurley, it stresses "clean, simple" food with few adornments other than its freshness and a flavorful sprinkling of island herbs and lime juice. You might begin with the salad of tomatoes, arugula, and endive, then follow with grilled fish in sauce chien (hot) or a grilled fillet of beef. She also prepares what she calls "sailor's chicken," a marinated version prepared with fresh chives, lime juice, and hot peppers, and coconut tarts. Almost no cream is used in any dish, a fact that makes the place beloved by the fashion models and actors who hang out here. You'll find the place directly west of Gustavia, close to the island's densest collection of factories and warehouses. Views face west and south, ensuring glorious sunset-watching.

WHERE TO FIND PICNIC FARE

The island is so expensive that many visitors opt to consume at least one of their meals from take-out delis, perhaps a "gourmet lunch to go" package. The most centrally located of the island's epicurean delis is **La Rôtisserie,** rue Oskar-II (☎ **0590-27-63-13**), which is proud of its endoxrsement by Fauchon, the world-famous food store in Paris. There are bottles of wine, crocks of mustard, pâté, herbs, and exotic oils and vinegars that are always on display, as well as an assortment of take-out (and very French) platters sold by the gram. *Plats du jour* cost around Fr 40 to Fr 45 ($8 to $9) for a portion suitable for one diner, and change every day. Set on a narrow street behind the eastern edge of Gustavia's harbor, the place is open Monday to Saturday from 7am to 7pm and on Sunday from 7am to 1pm. American Express, MasterCard, and Visa are accepted.

BEACHES, WATER SPORTS & OUTDOOR PURSUITS

BEACHES There are 14 white-sand beaches on St. Barts. Few are ever crowded, even in winter; all are public and free; and each rapidly regained whatever sand it had lost during the devastating hurricanes of 1995. Nudism is officially prohibited, but topless is quite common. The most famous beach is **St-Jean,** which is actually two beaches divided by the Eden Rock promontory. It offers water sports, beach restaurants, and a few hotels, as well as some shady areas. **Flamands,** to the west, is a very wide beach with a few small hotels and some areas shaded by lantana palms. For beaches with hotels, restaurants, and water sports, **Grand Cul-de-Sac,** on the northeast shore, fits the bill. This is a narrow beach protected by a reef.

Gouverneur, a beach on the south, can be reached by driving through Gustavia and up to Lurin. Turn at the Santa Fe Bar Restaurant (see "Where to Dine," above) and head down a narrow road. The beach is gorgeous, but wear lots of sunscreen as there's no shade. **Saline,** to the east of Gouverneur, is reached by driving up the road from the commercial center in St-Jean; a short walk over the sand dune and you're there. Like Gouverneur, Saline offers some waves, but again there's no shade. **Lorient,** on the north shore, is quiet and calm, with shady areas. **Marigot,** also on the north shore, is narrow but offers good swimming and snorkeling. **Colombier** is a beach difficult to get to but well worth the effort, despite the fact that it lost some of its sand in 1995 during Hurricane Luis. It can only be reached by boat or by taking a rugged goat path from Petite Anse past Flamands, a 30-minute walk. Shade and snorkeling are found there, and you can pack a lunch and spend the day.

FISHING People who like fishing are fond of the waters around St. Barts. From March to July, they catch dolphin (the fish, not the mammal); in September, wahoo. Atlantic bonito, barracuda, and marlin also turn up with frequency. **Marine Service,** quai du Yacht-Club in Gustavia (☎ **0590-27-70-34**), rents a 30-foot cabin cruiser, which was created for big-game fishing, for Fr 2,600 to Fr 4,100 ($520 to $820) for the boat. The rate is for four hours, with captain and first mate. The outfitter also offers shore fishing on a 20-foot day cruiser. Right off St. Barts's shores, fishers are successful in catching tuna, barracuda, and other fish. A three-hour tour costs Fr 1,500 ($300) for the entire boat.

TENNIS It's mainly for hotel guests. There are courts at the **Hôtel Manapany Cottages** (☎ **0590-27-66-55**). Use of the court is free to residents both day and night. Nonresidents pay Fr 80 ($16) per hour during daylight, Fr 150 ($30) for nighttime illumination.

WATERSKIING Because of the shape of the coastline, skiers must remain at least 80 yards from shore on the windward side of the island and 110 yards off on the leeward side.

You can make arrangements through **Marine Service,** quai du Yacht-Club in Gustavia (☎ **0590-27-70-34**). The cost is about Fr 210 ($42) per half hour.

WATER SPORTS **Marine Service,** quai du Yacht-Club in Gustavia (☎ **0590-27-70-34**), is the most complete water-sports facility on the island. It operates from a one-story building set directly on the water at the edge of a marina, on the opposite side of the harbor from the more congested part of Gustavia. The outfit offers a series of **dives,** including exploration for beginners (as well as for certified divers), night dives, PADI certification (within three days), and dives to the wreck of the *Non-stop,* a 210-foot yacht sunk during Hurricane Hugo. An Aquascope for 10 passengers is available for a one-hour trip among tropical fish and colorful flora to the wreck *Non-stop.* The rate is Fr 175 ($35) per person. One of the most interesting half-day trips goes to Colombier Beach or Fourchue Island, the best for snorkeling (see below). Trips are daily from 9am to 12:30pm and 1 to 5pm.

Ile Fourchue (Forked Island) is a popular rendezvous point for boats and snorkelers. Named for its configuration, with rocky peaks separated by valleys, Ile Fourchue is horseshoe-shaped, with a protected anchorage. Its only permanent residents are goats, but a few ruins bear witness to the fact that it was once the home of a Breton who lived a Robinson Crusoe–style life here for many years. Another attraction is **Colombier Beach** (see "Beaches," above). A full day's excursion to both Ile Fourchue and Colombier costs Fr 480 ($96) per person, with lunch included. A half-day excursion to Colombier goes for Fr 290 ($58) per person, including a French picnic. Each cruise features an open bar.

WINDSURFING Windsurfing is one of the most popular sports. Try **St. Barth Wind School** near the Tom Beach Hotel on Plage de St-Jean (☎ **0590-27-71-22**). It's open daily from 9am to 5pm. Windsurfing generally costs Fr 100 to Fr 120 ($20 to $24) per hour, and professional instructors are on hand.

SHOPPING

You don't pay any duty on St. Barts, so it's a good place to buy liquor and French perfumes, at some of the lowest prices in the Caribbean. Perfume, for example, is cheaper on St. Barts than it is in France itself. Champagne is cheaper than in Epernay, France. St. Barts is the only completely free-trading port in the world, with the exception of French St. Martin and Dutch St. Maarten. The only trouble is, selections are limited. However, you'll find good buys in sportswear, crystal, porcelain, watches, and other luxuries.

If you're in the market for some island crafts, try to find those fine straw hats St. Bartians like to wear. *Vogue* once featured this high-crown head wear in its fashion pages. They also have some interesting block-printed resort clothes in cotton.

La Boutique. Rue du Général-de-Gaulle, 8. ☎ **0590-27-51-66.**

Tucked off a courtyard that's adjacent to one of the main streets of Gustavia, this shop sells shirts and blouses with hand-painted references to the flora and fauna of St. Barts. Suitable as something both men or women might wear to a "casually elegant" onboard cocktail party, they sell for between $10 and $50 each. Also available are what might be the most elegant beach towels in the world, each a thirsty mass of terry cloth embroidered in gold letters with yachty-looking references to St. Barts.

Le Comptoir du Cigare. Rue du Général-de-Gaulle, 6. ☎ **0590-27-50-62.**

Very few shops in the Caribbean are as elegant and upscale as this one, and of the few that exist, this might be the only one designed exclusively for the tastes of gentlemen. It was established in 1994 by Patrick Gerthofer, as a branch of his cigar and cognac emporium based in Bordeaux, France. Elegantly sheathed in exotic hardwood, and enhanced with a glass-sided, walk-in humidor for the storage of thousands of cigars, it caters to the December-to-April crowd of super-upscale villa and yacht owners who flock to St. Barts. Cigars hail from Cuba and the Dominican Republic; the connoisseur-quality rums come from Martinique, Cuba, and Haiti. Cuban cigars, however, cannot be brought into the United States so you must smoke them abroad. There's also a worthy collection of silver ornaments suitable for adorning the desk of a CEO; artisan-quality Panama hats from Ecuador; and the most beautiful collection of cigar boxes and humidors in the Caribbean. Accessories are by Davidoff, DuPont, and Dunhill.

Diamond Genesis/Kornérupine. Rue du Général-de-Gaulle, 12/Les Suites du Roi-Oskar-II. ☎ **0590-27-68-11.**

Established in 1984 by a third-generation descendent of a French jeweler, this well-recommended gold, gemstone, and diamond shop maintains an inventory of ornaments whose design is strongly influenced by French and European tastes. Although the price of objects here can go as high as $60,000, a particularly appealing best-seller is an 18-karat-gold depiction of St. Barts, which sells for around $20. It's one of the few shops on the island where jewelry is handcrafted on the premises, in this case, from an atelier that's visible from the establishment's showroom. You can also peruse the selection of watches by Corum and Jaeger Lecoultre (both of which are available only through this store), and Brietling and Tag Heuer.

Gianni Versace. Carré d'Or, quai de la République. ☎ **0590-27-99-30.**

The garments here are tasteful, often crafted with what observers of the fashion scene describe as absolutely perfect taste.

Laurent Eiffel. Rue du Géneral de Gaulle. ☎ **0590-27-54-02.**

Despite the elegance of this store, and the tact of its employees, nothing sold here is original, as everything is either "inspired by" or crafted "in imitation of" designer models that usually cost 10 times as much. Look for belts, bags, and accessories that were originally launched by Prada, Hermès, Gucci, and Chanel, sold at prices much less than what you'd have paid in Paris. One of the few objects specifically advertised as a direct copy of a designer model is the "Kelly" purse, made famous by Grace Kelly around the time of her marriage to Ranier. Originally crafted by Hermès, its copyright expired, in accordance with French law, after 30 years and is now more or less in the public domain.

Little Switzerland. Rue de la France. ☎ **0590-27-64-66.**

It's the largest purveyor of luxury goods on St. Barts, a glittering tribute to the good life of conspicuous consumption. The entire second floor is devoted to perfumes and crystal, the street level to jewelry and a densely packed inventory of all kinds of watches. Prices are usually 25% to 30% less than equivalent retail goods sold on the North American mainland, and since the island is a duty-free port, some good buys can be had. Smart shoppers immediately ask what sales promotions are in effect at the time of their visit, which create discounts of 15% to 20% less than equivalent prices Stateside.

La Maison de Free Mousse. Carré d'Or, quai de la République. ☎ **0590-27-63-39.**

It shares the same courtyard as Versace and Lauren, which together form an awesomely chic minimall on the northern edge of Gustavia's harbor front. Inside is a cornucopia of exotic handcrafts imported from virtually everywhere (Mexico, Brazil, Central Africa, Thailand, Italy, Bali, or the Philippines). Anything you buy can be shipped.

Plein Sud. Galerie du Commerce, St-Jean. ☎ **0590-27-98-75.**

If there's a model in town, or an heiress who's trying to look like one, chances are that she'll head immediately for what everyone says is the most stylish women's clothing boutique on St. Barts. Don't expect sportswear, tennis dresses, or beachwear here. The look is casually elegant to formally elegant, the allure is Parisian, and both the taste level and the prices are high.

Polo Ralph Lauren. Carré d'Or, quai de la République. ☎ **0590-27-90-06.**

Predictably upscale, this branch of the worldwide arbiter of good taste does a thriving business close to the northern edge of Gustavia's harbor front. You'll find the designer's line of home products, sportswear for men and women, and a more elegant line of clothing (women only) for evening and gala wear.

Taxi-Brousse (Push-Taxi). Rue Lafayette, near the corner of rue du Port (no phone).

It's charming, tricultural, and endlessly hip, run by a pair of French/Danish entrepreneurs (Dominique Gauthier and his associate, Nina) who have skillfully managed to combine the best of Hollywood with the French-speaking Caribbean. The beachwear is among the most innovative on the island, featuring sunglasses (by Revo), bathing suits (by Jam's World), and psychedelic T-shirts (by Banana Moon) that no self-respecting Hawaiian beachgoer would ever be without. There's also an original assortment of dresses whose crumpled "I just had time to throw this together" look has proved enormously popular as an après-nudist cover-up at certain beaches. Many of the garments here cost less than $20 each, including lots of stylish souvenir ware unique to St. Barts.

ST. BARTS AFTER DARK

Most guests consider a French Creole dinner under the stars near the sea enough of a nocturnal adventure. After that, there isn't a lot of excitement.

In Gustavia, the most popular gathering place is **Le Select,** rue de la France (☎ **0590-27-86-87**), apparently named after its more famous granddaddy in the Montparnasse section of Paris. It's utterly simple, and a game of dominoes might be under way as you walk in. In the open-air cafe garden, near the port, tables are placed outside on the gravel. At the outdoor grill, Jimmy Buffet found inspiration for "Cheeseburger in Paradise." Need we say more? You never know who might show up here, perhaps Mick Jagger. Beer begins at Fr 14 ($2.80), and the place is open Monday to Saturday from 10am to 11pm. The locals like it a lot, and outsiders are welcomed but not necessarily embraced until they get to know you a bit. If you want to spread a rumor and have it travel fast across the island, start it here.

La Cantina, rue du Bord-de-Mer (☎ **0590-27-55-66**), is one of the more charming watering holes in Gustavia, lying along the waterfront. It was established by an expatriate from St-Tropez, Olivier Magnan. Part of its offbeat allure stems from its "Côte d'Azur in the 1970s" mood (before it was ruined by tour operators). The decor includes artifacts from Mexico. The menu, whose prices are printed in both dollars and francs, is set up like something aboard a cruise ship, and is very, very simple, featuring only sandwiches, salads, and drinks. Don't expect gourmet fare, but come to check out the scenery and sociology from this portside perch in the heart of Gustavia. Salads and platters range from $3.50 to $10, and it's open daily from 8:30am to 11pm.

Bar de l'Oubli, rue de la République, 5 (☎ **0590-27-70-06**), occupies the most prominent corner in Gustavia, at the intersection of streets that are so well known that most local residents don't even know their names—they refer to it simply as "Centre-Ville." The setting is hip and Gallic, the color scheme is marine blue and white, and the Rolling Stones might be blasting recorded music over a repertoire of sandwiches and salads. It's open daily from 8am (when breakfast is served to clients recovering from various stages of their hangovers) to 11pm.

13

The British Windwards

The British Windwards are made up of four main islands—St. Lucia, St. Vincent, Grenada, and Dominica—along with a scattering of isles or spits of land known as the Grenadines. Truly far-out islands, the Grenadines are a chain stretching from St. Vincent to Grenada. Some people group Barbados and Trinidad and Tobago in the British Windwards, but we have preferred to treat these independent island nations separately in later chapters.

Topped by mountains and bursting with greenery, the British Windward islands are far enough off the tourist circuit to be something of an adventure. At some of the more remote oases, you'll have the sand crabs, iguanas, and sea birds all to yourself.

For the most part, the islands are small and volcanic in origin. There's little or no industry, except for tourism.

1 Dominica

The meager beaches aren't worth the effort to get here, but the landscape and rivers are. Nature lovers who visit Dominica experience a wild Caribbean setting, as well as the rural life that has largely disappeared on the more developed islands. Dominica is, after all, one of the poorest and least developed islands in the Caribbean, where many of its citizens make a subsistence living from fishing or living off the land. Come to Dominica for the beauties of nature more than *la dolce vita.*

Hiking and mountain climbing are good reasons to visit Dominica, and the flora is extremely lush and often rare. Covered by a dense tropical rain forest that blankets its mountain slopes, including cloud-wreathed Morne Diablotin at 4,747 feet, it has vegetation unique in the West Indies.

Untamed, unspoiled Dominica (pronounced *Dom-in-EE-ka*) is known for clear rivers, waterfalls, hot springs, and boiling lakes. According to myth, it has 365 "rivers," one for each day of the year. This is the most rugged of the Caribbean islands.

With a population of 71,000, Dominica lies in the eastern Caribbean, between Guadeloupe to the north and Martinique to the south. English is the official language, but a French patois is widely spoken. The Caribs, the indigenous people of the Caribbean, live as a community on the northeast of the island. The art of traditional basketry is still practiced by the Carib community, whose numbers have dwindled to 3,000.

The mountainous island is 29 miles long and 16 miles wide, with a total land area of 290 square miles, much of which has never been seen by explorers.

Because of the pristine coral reefs, dramatic drop-offs, and shipwrecks found in the crystal-clear waters (with visibility of 100-plus feet), scuba diving is becoming increasingly popular, particularly off the west coast, site of Dominica's two dive operations.

Yearly rainfall varies from 50 inches along the dry west coast to as much as 350 inches in the tropical rain forests of the mountainous interior, where downpours are not uncommon.

Clothing is casual, including light summer wear for most of the year. However, take along walking shoes for those trips into the mountains and a sweater for cooler evenings. Locals, who are rather conservative, frown on bikinis and swimwear when worn on the streets of the capital city, **Roseau,** or in the villages.

National Day celebrations on November 3 commemorate Columbus's discovery in 1493 and independence in 1978. Cultural celebrations of Dominica's traditional dance, music, song, and storytelling begin in mid-October and continue to Community Day, November 4, when people undertake community-based projects.

GETTING THERE

BY PLANE There are two airports on Dominica, neither of which is large enough to handle a jet; therefore, there are no direct flights from North America. The **Melville Hall Airport** is on the northeastern coast of the island, almost diagonally across the island from the capital, Roseau, on the southwestern coast. Should you land at Melville Hall, there's a 1½-hour taxi ride into Roseau, a tour across the island through the forest and coastal villages. The fare from Melville Hall to Roseau is $17 per person, and drivers have the right to gather up at least four passengers in their cabs. By private taxi the cost could be $50.

The newer **Canefield Airport** is about a 15-minute taxi ride to the north of Roseau. The 2,000-foot airstrip accommodates smaller planes than those that can land at Melville Hall. From here, the typical taxi fare into town is $8. There's also a public bus (with an *H* that precedes the number on the license plate). Charges are only $2 per person. They come every 20 minutes and hold between 15 and 18 passengers.

For many Americans, the easiest way to reach Dominica is to take the daily **American Eagle** (☎ **800/433-7300**) flight from San Juan. From Antigua, you can take one of the five daily **LIAT** (☎ **809/448-0275** or 809/448-2422) flights to Dominica. Another possibility would be to fly via St. Maarten. From there, LIAT offers one nonstop flight daily and two other daily flights with intermediary stops. It's also possible to fly to Guadeloupe (see "Getting There" in section 2 of chapter 12) and make a connection to Dominica on **Air Guadeloupe** (☎ **809/448-2181**). This airline has two flights a day to Dominica except on Sunday when there is no morning flight (flight time is 30 minutes). If you're in Fort-de-France on Martinique, you can take a LIAT flight to Dominica.

Many experienced Dominica visitors flying in from neighboring islands resort to chartering a small plane from **Mustique Airways** (☎ **809/458-4380**) or **Air Anguilla** (☎ **809/497-2643**), either of which can arrange a special expedition to Dominica from almost anywhere in the central or southern Caribbean.

BY BOAT The **Caribbean Express** (☎ **596/60-12-38**, or 809/448-2181 on Dominica), sailing from the French West Indies (see chapter 12), runs between Guadeloupe in the north to Martinique in the south, and Dominica is a port of call along the way. Call for exact schedules. Departures are twice a week.

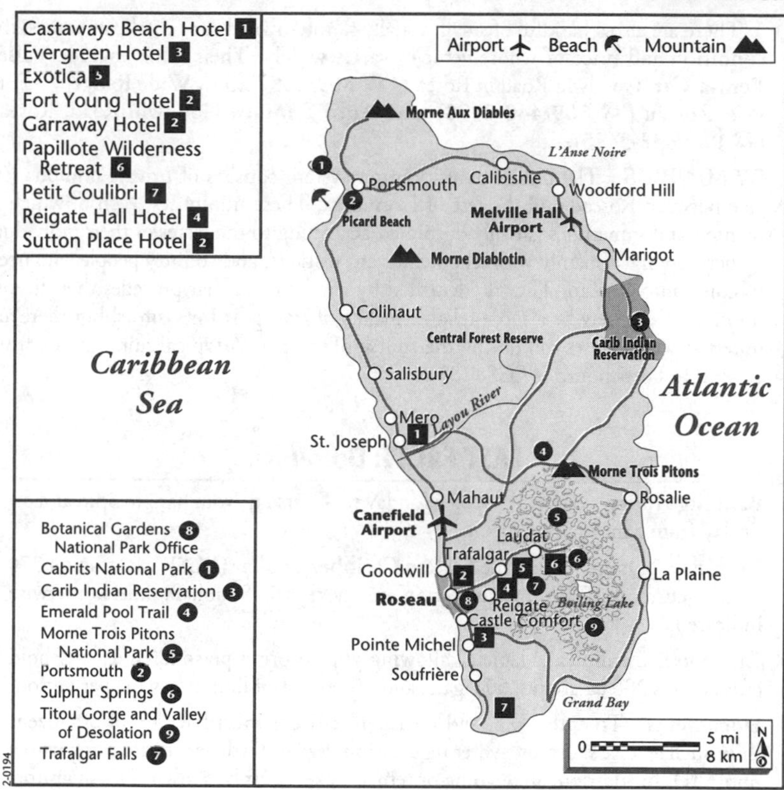

In addition, ***Madikera*** is a car-ferry sailing from Pointe-à-Pitre to Roseau five to seven times a week, depending on demand. For information about schedules, contact **Trois Pitons Travel,** 5 Great Marlborough St. in Roseau (☎ **809/448-6977**).

GETTING AROUND

The capital of Dominica is Roseau, and many of the places to stay are found here or very close by.

BY TAXI At either the Melville Hall or Canefield Airport, you can rent a taxi. Prices are regulated by the government (see "Getting There," above). If you want to see the island by taxi, rates are about $18 per car for each hour of touring, and as many as four passengers can go along at the same time.

BY RENTAL CAR If you rent a car, a fee of EC$30 ($11.10) is charged to obtain a driver's license, which is available at the airports. There are 310 miles of newly paved roads, and only in a few areas is a four-wheel-drive necessary. *Driving is on the left.*

Most U.S. vacationers reserve their car in advance from the local representative of **Budget Rent-a-Car,** headquartered near the island's major airport on the Main Highway, Canefield (☎ **800/527-0700** or 809/449-2080). Another option is the local office of **Avis,** 4 High St. in Roseau (☎ **800/331-1212** or 809/448-2481), although we've found the service here poor.

There are also a handful of small, usually family-owned car-rental companies, the condition and price of whose vehicles varies widely. Their ranks include **Valley Rent-a-Car,** Goodwill Road in Roseau (☎ **809/448-3233**); **Wide Range,** 79 Bath Rd., Roseau (☎ **809/448-2198**); and **Auto Rentals,** Goodwill Road, Roseau (☎ **809/448-3425**).

BY MINIBUS The public transportation system consists of private minibus service between Roseau and the rest of Dominica. These minibuses, each of which is painted and sometimes garishly decorated according to the tastes of their individual owners, are filled mainly with schoolchildren, workers, and country people who need to come into Roseau. They're identified by the letter *H* that precedes their license number. Taxis may be a more reliable means of transport for visitors, but there are hotels at which buses call during the course of the day. A typical minibus fare from Roseau to Portsmouth is EC$8 ($3).

FAST FACTS: Dominica

Banking Hours Banks are open Monday to Thursday from 8am to 3pm and on Friday from 8am to 5pm.

Currency Dominica uses the **Eastern Caribbean dollar (EC$),** worth about 37¢ in U.S. currency. Prices in this section are given in U.S. dollars unless otherwise indicated.

Customs Dominica is lenient, allowing you to bring personal and household effects, plus 200 cigarettes, 50 cigars, and 40 ounces of liquor or wine per person.

Documents To enter, U.S. and Canadian citizens must have proof of citizenship, such as a passport, or a voter registration card or birth certificate along with a photo ID. In addition, an ongoing or return ticket must be shown. British visitors should have a valid passport.

Drugstores The island's best-stocked drugstore is **Jolly's Pharmacy,** with two branches in Roseau at 37 Great George St., and at 12 King George V St. Both branches share the same phone number and hours (☎ **8098/448-3388**). They're open Monday to Thursday from 8am to 4:30pm, Friday from 8am to 5pm, and Saturday from 8am to 1:30pm.

Electricity The electricity is 220–240 volts AC (50 cycles), so both adapters and transformers are necessary for U.S.-made appliances. It's advisable to take a flashlight with you to Dominica, in case of power outages.

Emergencies Call the police, report a fire, or summon an ambulance by dialing ☎ **999.**

Hospitals The island hospital is **Princess Margaret Hospital,** Federation Drive, Goodwill (☎ **809/448-2231**). However, those with serious medical complications may want to forgo a visit to Dominica, as island medical facilities are often inadequate.

Information The **Dominica Tourist Information Office** is on the Old Market Plaza, Roseau, with administrative offices at the National Development Corporation offices, Valley Road (☎ **809/448-2186**); it's open on Monday from 8am to 5pm and Tuesday to Friday from 8am to 4pm. Also, there are information bureaus at Melville Hall Airport (☎ **809/445-7051**) and Canefield Airport (☎ **809/449-1242**). Before you go, you can contact the **Dominica Tourist Office** at 10 E. 21st St., Suite 600, New York, NY 10010 (☎ **212/475-7542**). In Canada, information is available at the **High Commission for the Eastern Caribbean States,** 112 Kent St., Suite 1610, Ottawa, ON K1P 5P2 (☎ **613/236-8952**), and in England at the **Caribbean Tourism Organization,** Vigilant House, 120 Wilton Rd., London SW1V 1JZ (☎ **0171/233-8382**).

Language English is the official language. Locals often speak a Creole-French patois.

Safety Although crime is rare here, you should still safeguard your valuables. Never leave them unattended on the beach or left alone in a locked car.

Taxes A 10% government room tax is added to every hotel accommodation bill, plus a 3% tax on alcoholic drinks and food items. Anyone who remains on Dominica for more than 24 hours must pay a $10 (U.S.) departure tax.

Telecommunications Dominica maintains phone, telegraph, teletype, Telex, and telefax connections with the rest of the world. International direct dialing (IDD) is available, as well as U.S. direct service through AT&T. To call Dominica from another island within the Caribbean's 809 area code, just dial the seven-digit local number.

Time Dominica is on Atlantic standard time, one hour ahead of eastern standard time in the United States. Dominica does not observe daylight saving time, so when the United States changes to daylight time, clocks in Dominica and the U.S. East Coast tell the same time.

Tipping Most hotels and restaurants add a 10% service charge to all bills. Where this charge has not been included, tipping is up to you.

Water The water is drinkable from the taps and in the high mountain country. Pollution is hardly a problem here.

Weather Daytime temperatures average between 70° and 85°F. Nights are much cooler, especially in the mountains. The rainy season is June to October, when there can be warnings of hurricane activity. Regrettably, Dominica lies in the "hurricane path," and fierce storms have taken their toll on the island over the years.

WHERE TO STAY

The government imposes a 10% tax on hotel rooms and a 3% tax on beverages and food, which will be added to your hotel bill. Unless otherwise noted, the rates given below are year-round.

IN ROSEAU & CASTLE COMFORT

Evergreen Hotel. P.O. Box 309, Castle Comfort, Dominica, W.I. ☎ **809/448-3288.** Fax 809/448-6800. 22 rms. A/C TV TEL. $103–$118 double; $128–$143 triple. Rates include full breakfast. AE, DC, MC, V.

Built in 1986, this pleasant family-run hotel looks a bit like a Swiss chalet from the outside, although once inside you're greeted with a new open-air restaurant with bright jungle prints, crystal teardrop chandeliers, and an art deco bar. Rooms are better in the newer annex, even though it is sterile looking, than they are in the main building. A few of the rooms have access to wraparound tile-floored verandas; all have stone accents. It sits amid a cluster of other hotels about a mile south of Roseau. A stony beach is visible a few steps beyond the garden. Inside and out, the airy, spacious, comfortably modern place is trimmed with local gommier wood.

Mena Winston, the Dominican-born owner, assists in preparing your meals, which are well done and cost $20 to $25. Laundry service and scuba diving can be arranged. The hotel has added a swimming pool.

Fort Young Hotel. Victoria St. (P.O. Box 519), Roseau, Dominica, W.I. ☎ **800/223-1588** in the U.S., 800/531-6767 in Canada, or 809/448-5000. Fax 809/448-5006. 30 rms, 3 suites. A/C TV TEL. $125–$135 double; $140–$160 suite. AE, MC, V.

Occupying a cliff-side setting, this hotel grew from the ruins of the 1770 Fort Young, once the island's major military installation. Traces of its former historic role remain, including cannons at the entrance. The hotel was upgraded and renovated in 1995. Once a domain of business travelers to Roseau, it is attracting more and more tourists, drawn to its comfortable bedrooms with ceiling fans and balconies. Here you are elevated far above the "mosquito line" so you can actually sit out and enjoy the balmy Caribbean air without being attacked by these pests, the curse of the West Indies. The most desirable units open onto the sea, and they're worth the extra $10 you pay for them. The modern hotel's core is surrounded by the historic walls of the old fort. There's also an outdoor pool and laundry service, and the hotel staff can arrange tours for you. The restaurant, Marquis de Bouille, a candlelit room with stone walls and a ceiling of wood rafters, is better than ever. An Indian chef not only draws upon his homeland for inspiration, but is an expert at island dishes. Much of his repertoire evokes a continental flair.

Garraway Hotel. Place Heritage, The Bayfront (P.O. Box 789), Roseau, Dominica, W.I. ☎ **809/449-8800.** Fax 809/449-8807. 20 rms, 11 suites. A/C TV TEL. $130 double; $140–$170 suite. AE, DC, MC, V.

This hotel opened in 1994 adjacent to the home of its owners, the Garraway family, who cater largely to a business clientele, although it's a perfectly acceptable choice for leisure travelers as well. If you normally book into a Ramada wherever you go, this would be the closest thing you could find on Dominica. It offers spacious bedrooms in seashell colors, usually with views stretching all the way to Dominica's southernmost tip. The bedrooms are outfitted with rattan furniture and pastel-colored fabrics with flowered prints. The higher you go on the upper floors, the more colorful the views of the rooftops of Roseau. Don't faint right away, but Dominica now has a hotel with an elevator. Some locals like to visit just to ride up in it, but Garraway rises only five floors. Public rooms are given an authentic island touch with art work and locally made vetiver mats.

On the premises is a restaurant, the Balisier (recommended separately in "Where to Dine," below), and, adjacent to the sea, the Pavement Café. Room service and laundry service are available, and baby-sitting can be arranged.

Reigate Hall Hotel. Mountain Rd. (P.O. Box 200), Reigate, Dominica, W.I. ☎ **809/448-4031.** Fax 809/448-4034. 17 rms, 2 suites. A/C TEL. $75 double; $150–$180 suite. Rates include breakfast. AE, MC, V.

On a steep hillside about a mile east of Roseau, this hotel was originally built in the 18th century as a plantation house. Before increasing competition from such properties as Sutton Place Hotel, it was once the finest hotel on the island. Regrettably, the hotel isn't what it was in terms of maintenance and service, although it still has its admirers, particularly those drawn to its lofty setting with panoramic views. Some parts of the original structure are left, but the building has been substantially altered. The hotel has a comfortably airy design of hardwood floors and exposed stone. The guest rooms curve around the sides of a rectangular swimming pool and offer ocean vistas. The hotel has an outdoor tennis court, a good restaurant (see "Where to Dine," below), laundry, baby-sitting, and room service.

✪ **Sutton Place Hotel.** 25 Old St., Roseau, Dominica, W.I. ☎ **809/449-8700.** Fax 809/448-3045. 5 rms, 3 suites. A/C TV TEL. Year-round, $95–$135 double. AE, DISC, MC, V.

If former visitors Alec Waugh, Noël Coward, or Princess Margaret were to show up today, chances are they would head for this little retreat created by the Harris family. A small historic property in the center of town, it was once a 1930s guest house run by "Mother" Harris, a matriarch who became a local legend. Destroyed by Hurricane David in 1979, the new Sutton Place was rebuilt in a traditional Caribbean style by the same Harris family who continue the old traditions, but in far greater style. Rooms are tastefully furnished with antique-style pieces including four-poster beds, swing-arm brass desk lamps, and teak bathroom furnishings. The staircase and floors of the suites are laid with a fine hardwood, Tauroniro from South America. Suites contain fully equipped kitchenettes. Stylized floral arrangements, exotic prints, and luxurious fabrics add up to upscale styling. The cellar, housing a bar, is the only part of the original structure that survived the hurricane. The restaurant is now one of the choice places to dine in Roseau, with a Creole/International menu that also embraces some dishes from Italy, China, and India. The nearest beach is about a mile or so away.

ALONG THE BEACHFRONT

Castaways Beach Hotel. P.O. Box 5, Mero, Dominica, W.I. ☎ **800/322-2233** in the U.S., or 809/449-6244. Fax 809/449-6246. 26 rms. $96 double; $120 triple. MAP $30 per person extra. AE, MC, V.

The island's first major resort along the coast lies some 11 miles north of Roseau, 8 miles north of Canefield Airport. It's a favorite with divers. Nestled between the tropical forest and a mile-long black-sand beach and bordered on the inland side by huge tamarind trees, the hotel has rooms shaded by tall coconut palms. The beach was eroded during the 1995 hurricane season but for the most part has come back. Each of the spacious accommodations has a private bath or shower and is filled with simple, island-made contemporary furniture. Some of the somewhat musty rooms are air-conditioned, costing $10 a day extra; others are cooled by ceiling fans. Many units also contain a phone and TV. Overall many of the rooms show years of wear and tear, but the young diver crowd doesn't seem to mind.

The hotel dining room is reviewed separately (see "Where to Dine," below). On the beach is an open-air bar thatched with palmetto fronds. Water sports can be arranged through the reception desk, as can guided excursions to the island's principal sights. There's a dive shop on the premises. Room service is available from 8am to 5pm.

AT SALISBURY

Lauro Club. Salisbury (P.O. Box 483, Roseau), Dominica, W.I. ☎ **809/449-6602.** Fax 809/449-6603. 10 apts. $84–$122 double; $123–$144 triple; $135–$160 quad. Off-season, $65–$85 double; $95–$110 triple; $105–$120 quad. AE, DC, MC, V.

Built in 1991, a short walk uphill from the island's west coast, this rustic villa complex lies about half a mile from the town of Salisbury (pop. 2,000), midway between Roseau and Portsmouth. Owned and operated by a married pair of Swiss expatriates (Roland and Laurence Pralong), it's a simple but neat compound of white-sided concrete buildings with either green, red, or gray roofs. This is a small, nonresorty hotel with few amenities and definitely an escapist mood favored by Europeans. There are few diversions other than the beach and the local botany. The studios come two to a cottage, but the one-bedroom units stand alone. None have a TV or telephone, but each has a covered veranda, flower-patterned draperies and upholstery, and views of the water. Although the sea is nearby, it takes a five-minute walk and a climb down a long, serpentine staircase to get to a beach that's suitable for swimming. On the premises is a restaurant (the Lauro Club), serving Creole and international dishes. Table tennis, scuba diving, snorkeling, and guided tours of Dominica are available through the reception desk.

In the Rain Forest

Papillote Wilderness Retreat. Trafalgar Falls Rd. (P.O. Box 2287), Roseau, Dominica, W.I. ☎ **809/448-2287.** Fax 809/448-2285. 7 rms, 1 suite, 1 cottage. Year-round, $80 double; $90 suite; $175 two-bedroom cottage w/ kitchenette for 6. MAP $30 per person. AE, DISC, MC, V. Closed Sept.

This hotel and restaurant is run by the Jean-Baptistes: Cuthbert (who handles the restaurant) and his wife, Anne Grey (who was once a marine scientist). Their place, 4 miles east of Roseau, stands right in the middle of Papillote Forest, in the foothills of Morne Macaque. In this remote setting, they have created a unique rain-forest resort; you can lead an Adam and Eve life here, surrounded by exotic fruits, flowers, and herb gardens.

The weather isn't always sunny, since this part of the jungle is known for its downpours, but the rain keeps the orchids, begonias, and brilliantly colored bromeliads lush. The 12 acres of sloping and forested land are covered with a labyrinth of stone walls and trails, beside which flows a network of freshwater streams, a few of which come from hot mineral springs. Natural hot mineral baths are available, and you'll be directed to a secluded waterfall where you can swim in the river. Regrettably, the bedrooms, although clean and reasonably comfortable, are hardly the equal of the lush setting. Rooms are a bit dark and have a slight musty feeling: This is rustic living indeed. Some readers have complained of noise from the chief hydroelectric plant nearby. So it's not a complete paradise here, but almost. The Jean-Baptistes also run a boutique in which they sell Dominican products, including appliquéd quilts made by local artisans. Even if you don't stay here, it's an experience just to dine in the dappled shade of breadfruit and fern trees (see "Where to Dine," below).

Near Soufrière

✪ **Petit Coulibri.** (P.O. Box 3331), Petit Coulibri Estate, near Soufrière, Dominica, W.I. ☎ **809/446-3150.** Fax 809/446-3150. 2 studios, 3 two-bedroom cottages. Winter, $90 studio; $200 cottage. Off-season, $90 studio; $160 cottage. AE, DISC, MC, V.

After a lot of publicity in travel magazines, this escapist Shangri-la with "Florida efficiency" but Dominican botany is emerging as a famous local spot and makes for an exceptional and affordable vacation experience. That is, if you can get to it. This aerie is reached only after a bumpy 10-minute drive from Soufrière by four-wheel drive. But once you arrive at this solar-powered little gem, it's worth the effort. U.S. expats Loye and Barney Barnard have created a trio of two-bedroom cottages, each with large verandas and a kitchen, plus two small, rather basic-looking studios, each with a big bedroom and small veranda. The Barnards built cottages out of stone and wood and added artful decorative touches, including stained glass. Dominican crafts help create a homey island ambience. The cottages aren't air-conditioned at this high an elevation where nights are cool. Supplies can be gathered in Roseau, although shopping is very basic. The hotel will also stock your kitchen if asked. Even better is to enjoy a home-cooked breakfast for $10 or a delectable dinner for $25 prepared by the owners. There's also a pool overlooking a 1,000-foot-drop and a view over the Martinique Channel.

At Morne Anglais

Exotica. Morne Anglais (P.O. Box 109), Roseau, Dominica, W.I. ☎ **809/448-8839** or 809/448-8849. Fax 809/448-8829. 8 cottages. Year-round, $172.50 double; $195.50 triple; $218 quad. AE, DISC, MC, V.

In 1995, one of Dominica's best-known couples, Fae and Altherton Martin, erected this cluster of cottages on the western slope of Morne Anglais in the southern half of the island. It's a tropical setting, with some 38 different flowers and fruit trees on this 4-acre organic farm. This is called an "agro-eco" resort. The cottages are constructed from hardwoods, cured pine, and stone to blend into their natural surroundings. Once you finally reach the place after a harrowing ride, you can enjoy the cool mountain breezes at 1,600 feet above sea level at a point some 5 miles from Roseau. The best swimming is in a nearby river, a five-minute walk away. Guests can prepare their own meals or else dine on the grounds at the Sugar Apple Café, enjoying such delights as steamed local fish or apricot-glazed chicken with savory rice. Accommodations are tastefully furnished and comfortable, with a private porch, spacious living room, kitchen, and dinette, along with a large bedroom with two double beds and a private bath.

WHERE TO DINE

It's customary to dine at your hotel, although Dominica has a string of independent eateries. Dress is casual. If you're going out in the evening, always call to make sure your dining choice is actually open. You'll also have to arrange transportation there and back because of the bad lighting and awful roads.

IN ROSEAU

Balisier. In the Garraway Hotel, Place Heritage, The Bayfront. ☎ **809/449-8800.** Reservations recommended. Main courses EC$35–EC$75 ($12.95–$27.75); lunch EC$30–EC$75 ($11.10–$27.75), Fri lunch buffet EC$40 ($14.80). AE, MC, V. Daily noon–2:30pm and 6:30–10pm. CREOLE/INTERNATIONAL.

Named after a small red flower that thrives in the jungles of Dominica, this restaurant occupies the ground floor of the hotel and was designed to maximize the views over Roseau's harbor. We highly recommend the food, which might include shrimp mousse; chicken Garraway (breast of chicken stuffed with plantain and sweet corn); loin of pork with pineapple, mushrooms, and onions; and a choice of steak, vegetarian, or lobster dishes. Favorite local dishes include crab backs and Creole-style mountain chicken (frogs' legs). Any of these might be followed with a slice of homemade coconut-cream pie. Lunches are simpler than dinners and might include West Indian curries, fish Creole, or several kinds of salad.

✪ **Guiyave.** 15 Cork St. ☎ **809/448-2930.** Reservations recommended. Main courses EC$25–EC$45 ($9.25–$16.65). AE, MC, V. Mon–Fri 8am–3pm, Sat 9am–2:30pm. CREOLE.

This airy restaurant occupies the second floor of a wood-frame West Indian house. Rows of tables almost completely fill the narrow balcony overlooking the street outside. You can enjoy a drink at the stand-up bar on the second floor. The establishment is open only for breakfast and lunch. Specialties include different preparations of conch and rabbit, octopus and lobster, spareribs, chicken, crab backs, and mountain chicken. The dishes have true island flavor, and fresh ingredients are used whenever possible. On Saturday they prepare rotis, souse (or rustic pork stew), and "goat water," a spicy meat stew. The place is known for its juices, including refreshing glasses of soursop, tamarind, sorrel, cherry, and strawberry juice. One part of the establishment is a pâtisserie specializing in French pastries. This place has excellent value for the money.

✪ **La Robe Creole.** 3 Victoria St. ☎ **809/448-2896.** Reservations required. Main courses $20–$25. DISC, MC, V. Mon–Sat noon–9:30pm. CREOLE/SEAFOOD.

The best independent restaurant in the capital, La Robe Creole sits on the second floor of a colonial house, beside a sunny plaza on a slope above the sea. The staff, dressed in madras Creole costumes, serves food in a long and narrow dining room capped with heavy beams and filled with relics from the 19th century. You can enjoy pumpkin-pimiento soup, callaloo with cream of coconut soup, crab backs (in season), pizzas, mountain chicken in beer batter, and shrimp in coconut with garlic sauce. The food is in the spicy Creole style. One patron found the cuisine "seductive." For dessert, try banana or coconut cake or ice cream.

A street-level section of the restaurant, **The Mouse Hole,** is a good place for food on the run. You can take out freshly made sandwiches and salads, and light meals start at $6. They make good Trinidad-inspired rotis here—wheat pancakes wrapped around beef, chicken, or vegetables. On Dominica, these rotis are often flavored with curry. The Mouse Hole is open Monday to Saturday from 8am to 9:30pm.

Orchard Restaurant. 31 King George St. ☎ **809/448-3051.** Reservations not necessary. Main courses EC$20–EC$50 ($7.40–$18.50); snacks in fast-food restaurant EC$3–EC$9 ($1.10–$3.35). AE, MC, V accepted only in restaurant. Restaurant Mon–Fri 10am–9pm; snack bar Mon–Sat 8am–6pm. CREOLE.

This clean, wood-lined oasis of calm lies on a busy street in the capital. It contains both a fast-food outlet dispensing sandwiches, rotis, hot pies, and chicken wings, as well as a more substantial restaurant that's favored by island businesspeople and foreign visitors. Within a simple but tidy setting that's clean and decent, you can order such menu items as mountain chicken (frogs' legs), callaloo soup with crabmeat, coconut shrimp, black pudding, blood sausage, several pumpkin dishes, and breadfruit puffs. Friday night features barbecued meat dishes. The menu is familiar fare on Dominica, but the kitchen manages to put a unique stamp on all dishes, especially its lambi (conch) concoctions. When available, lobster is featured. The food is hearty, and there's not a lot of subtlety; but if you want home cooking, island style, you'll get that and a smile too.

Reigate Hall Restaurant. In the Reigate Hall Hotel, Mountain Rd. ☎ **809/448-4031.** Reservations recommended, especially if you're not a hotel guest. Main courses $15–$28. AE, MC, V. Daily 1–3pm and 7–10:30pm. FRENCH/CREOLE.

Reigate Hall lies only a mile east of the center of Roseau, but it seems so much farther because of the tortuous road leading up to it. On the second story of the hotel, the restaurant is an intimately lit enclave of polished tropical hardwoods and exposed stone. A spillway splashing water onto a water wheel adds an old-fashioned accent. Menu items are French or Creole and might include fish soup, beef curry, coq au vin, prawns in garlic sauce, seafood au gratin, fish Creole, and mountain chicken (frogs' legs) in a champagne sauce. The local Creole cookery wins out over the French-inspired cuisine. Come here more for the view and the ambience than the high-quality cookery, which isn't as good as it used to be.

World of Food Restaurant and Bar. In Vena's Hotel, 48 Cork St. ☎ **809/448-3286.** Reservations not required. Main courses EC$25–EC$58 ($9.25–$21.45). No credit cards. Daily 7:30am–10:30pm. CREOLE.

If you want to reach the restaurant without passing through Vena's Hotel (which is really a guest house), its entrance is on Field's Lane. In the 1930s, the garden containing this restaurant belonged to a well-known female novelist, Jean Rhys. Today it's the patio for one of the most charming Creole restaurants in Roseau. Some say that its owner, Vena McDougal, is the best Creole cook in town. You can have a drink at the stone-walled building at the far end of the garden if you want, but many guests select one of the tables in the shadow of a large mango tree. Specialties include steamed fish or fish steak, curried goat, chicken-filled roti, black pudding, mountain chicken (frogs' legs), breadfruit puffs, crab backs, conch, and tee-tee-ree (fried fish cakes). She also makes the best rum punches on the island.

ALONG THE BEACHFRONT

The Almond Tree. In the Castaways Beach Hotel, Mero. ☎ **809/449-6244.** Reservations not required. Main courses EC$25–EC$75 ($9.25–$27.75). AE, MC, V. Daily seatings at noon, 2pm, and 6:30pm. CREOLE.

If you're touring north along the coast, consider stopping in for a meal at the Castaways, 11 miles north of Roseau. In this resort setting, nonguests are welcome to eat in the waterfront hotel dining room. Patrons dress in casual resort wear and enjoy the hospitality of the staff. Here you get the standard cuisine for which Dominica is known, including crapaud, or mountain chicken (frogs' legs). You can also get lambi (conch), as well as island crab mixed with a savory Creole stuffing. Fish and pork dishes are also served. All dishes are garnished with the fruits and vegetables of Dominica's rich soil, including passion fruit. Before dining, try a rum punch in the lounge or beach bar. The service is very laid-back, and you can find better versions of many of these Creole dishes elsewhere; but if you're on this part of the island, a meal here should be generally satisfying.

IN THE RAIN FOREST

Papillote Wilderness Retreat. Trafalgar Falls Rd. ☎ **809/448-2287.** Reservations recommended for lunch, required for dinner. Main courses EC$25–EC$40 ($9.25–$14.80); fixed-price dinner EC$50 ($18.50). AE, DISC, MC, V. Daily 7:30am–10pm; dinner served at 7:30pm. CREOLE/CARIBBEAN.

Previously recommended for its lodgings, Papillote is an alluring "Garden of Eden" type of restaurant. It would certainly be Tarzan's favorite. Even if you're not staying here, come by taxi for lunch; it's only 4 miles east of Roseau. For dinner, you'll need to make arrangements. Amid nature trails laced with exotic flowers, century-old trees, and filtered sunlight, you dine overlooking rivers and mountains. The array of healthful food includes flying fish and truly delectable freshwater prawns known as bookh. Mountain chicken (frogs' legs) appears in season, as does kingfish. Breadfruit or dasheen puffs merit a try if you've never ordered them, and tropical salads are flavor filled. Favorite dishes here include "the seafood symphony" and chicken rain forest (sautéed with orange, papaya, and banana, and wrapped in a banana leaf). Sturdy walking shoes and a bathing suit are often called for. Near the dining terrace is a Jacuzzi-size pool, which is constantly filled with the mineral-rich waters of a hot spring. Nonguests may use the pool for EC$5 ($1.85).

EXPLORING "JUNGLE JIM" COUNTRY

BEACHES If you're a true beach buff and you demand great beaches as part of your Caribbean vacation, you should wing over to another island. Dominica has some of the worst beaches in the Caribbean. There are some beaches in the northwest part of the island, around Portsmouth, and there are also secluded beaches in the northeast, along with panoramic coastal scenery. But these are all hard to reach, and you might settle instead for a freshwater swimming pool or river swimming.

The finest beach, lying on the northwestern coast, is **Picard.** It stretches for about 2 miles, a strip of grayish sand with palm trees in the background. The previously recommended Castaways Beach Hotel opens onto this beach. Snorkelers like it a lot, and some visitors windsurf here, too. The finest swimming, however, is along the banks of the **Layou River.**

HIKING Serious hikers find Dominica a major challenge. Guides should be used for all unmarked trails. You can arrange for a guide by going to the office of the

Dominica National Park in the Botanical Gardens in Roseau (☎ **809/448-2732**) or the Dominica Tourist Board.

Wild and untamed Dominica offers very experienced and physically fit hikers some of the most bizarre geological oddities in the Caribbean. Sights include scalding lava covered with a hot, thin, and not-very-stable crust; a boiling lake where mountain streams turn to vapor as they come into contact with super-heated volcanic fissures; and a barren wasteland known as the Valley of Desolation.

All these attractions are in the 17,000 heavily forested acres of the ✪ **Morne Trois Pitons National Park,** in the island's south-central region. You should go with a guide—they're in plentiful supply, waiting for your business in the village of Laudat. Few markers appear en route, but the trek, which includes a real assortment of geological oddities, stretches 6 miles in both directions from Laudat to the Boiling Lake. Hikers bring their lunch and walk cautiously, particularly in districts peppered with bubbling hot springs. Regardless of where you turn, you'll run into streams and waterfalls, the inevitable result of an island whose mountaintops receive up to 400 inches of rainfall a year. Winds on the summits are strong enough to have pushed one recreational climber to her death several years ago, so be careful. Ferns, orchids, trees, and epiphytes create a tangle of underbrush, and insect, bird, and reptilian life is profuse.

During your trek, pay a visit to the **Titou Gorge,** a deep and very narrow ravine whose depths were created as lava floes cooled and contracted. En route, there might be views of rare Sisserou and Jacquot parrots, monkeys, and vines whose growth seems to increase visibly on an hourly basis. The hill treks of Dominica have been described as "sometimes easy, sometimes hellish," and if it should happen to rain during your climb (and it rains very frequently on Dominica), your path is likely to become very slippery. But botanists and geologists agree with the assessment of experienced hikers, that climbs through the jungles of Dominica are the most rewarding in the Caribbean.

Locals warn that to proceed along the island's badly marked trails into areas that can be physically treacherous is not a good idea, and climbing alone or even in pairs is not advisable. Forestry officials recommend **Ken's Hinterland Adventure Tours & Taxi Service,** in Roseau (☎ **809/448-4850**). Depending on their destination and the attractions they feature, treks cost $100 to around $150 for up to four participants and require five to eight hours round-trip. Transportation from Roseau in a minivan to the starting point of your hill climb is usually included in the price.

SCUBA DIVING Diving holidays in Dominica are becoming more and more important. The underwater terrain is spectacular, extending into the ocean. Most of the diving is on the southwestern end of the island, with its dramatic drop-offs, walls, and pinnacles. These volcanic formations are interwoven with cuts, arches, ledges, and overhangs. A myriad of sponges, gorgonians, and corals cloak these ledges. An abundance of invertebrates, reef school fish, and unusual sea creatures such as sea horses, frog-fish, batfish, and flying gunards attract the underwater photographer. You can discover diving on the island with **Dive Dominica,** in the Castle Comfort Diving Lodge, (P.O. Box 2253, Roseau) Castle Comfort, Dominica, W.I. (☎ **800/544-7631** or 809/448-2188). Open-water certification (both NAUI and PADI) instruction is given, costing $400 for five or six days of instruction. Two diving catamarans (45 and 33 feet long, respectively), plus a handful of other, smaller boats that are used for groups of divers, get you to the dive sites in relative comfort. The dive outfit is closely linked to its on-site hotel, a 15-room lodge where at least 90% of the clientele check in as part of the outfit's dive packages. A seven-night dive package, double occupancy, where breakfasts and dinners are included as part of the price, along with five two-tank dives and one night dive, begins at $906 per person. The same package, geared to inexperienced divers not yet certified by PADI or NAUI, costs $605 per person, onto which is added the $400 certification fee described immediately above. All rooms in the lodge are air-conditioned, and about half have TV and a telephone. On the premises is a bar (for residents and their guests only), a swimming pool, and a Jacuzzi.

Divers from all over the world patronize the **Dive Centre,** at the Anchorage Hotel in Castle Comfort (☎ **809/448-2188**). A fully qualified PADI and NAUI staff awaits divers there. A single-tank dive costs $45; a double-tank dive, $70; and a one-tank night dive, $50. A unique whale and dolphin watch from 2pm to sunset is a popular feature, where all participants are actively engaged in trying to sight the far-away plumes of pods of whales, herds of dolphins, and even schools of flying fish. The price for a 3½-hour experience of communal straining to catch sight of the animals is $50 per person. On the way home (and not before), rum punches are served. Celebrity participants of this experience in the past have included author Peter Benchley. With a pool, classrooms, a private dock, a mini-flotilla of dive boats, and a well-trained and alert staff, this is the most complete dive resort on Dominica.

SEEING THE PRIMORDIAL SIGHTS

Those making day trips to Dominica from other Caribbean islands will want to see the ✪ **Carib Indian Reservation,** in the northeast. In 1903 Britain got the Caribs to agree to live on 3,700 acres of land. Hence, this is the last remaining turf of the once-hostile tribe for whom the Caribbean was named. Their look is Mongolian, and they are no longer "pure-blooded," as they have married outside their tribe. Today they survive by fishing, growing food, and weaving baskets and vertiver grass mats, which they sell to the outside world. They still make dugout canoes, too.

It's like going back in time when you explore ✪ **Morne Trois Pitons National Park,** a primordial rain forest. Mists rise gently over lush, dark-green growth, drifting up to blue-green peaks that have earned Dominica the title "Switzerland of the Caribbean." Framed by banks of giant ferns, rivers rush and tumble. Trees sprout orchids, and everything seems blanketed with some type of growth. Green sunlight filters down through trees, and roaring waterfalls create a blue mist.

One of the best starting points for a visit to the park is the village of Laudat, 7 miles from Roseau. Exploring the heart of Dominica is for serious botanists and only the most skilled hikers, who should never penetrate unmarked trails without a very experienced guide.

Deep in the park is the **Emerald Pool Trail,** a half-mile nature trail that forms a circuit loop on a footpath passing through the forest to a pool with a beautiful waterfall. Downpours are frequent in the rain forest, and at high elevations cold winds blow. It lies 3½ miles northeast of Pont Casse.

Five miles up from the **Roseau River Valley,** in the south-central sector of Dominica, **Trafalgar Falls** can be reached after you drive through the village of Trafalgar. There, however, you have to approach on foot, as the slopes are too steep for vehicles. After a 20-minute walk past growths of ginger plants and vanilla orchids, you arrive at the base, where a trio of falls converge into a rock-strewn pool.

The **Sulphur Springs,** and the Boiling Lake east of Roseau as well, are evidence of the island's volcanic past. Jeeps or Land Rovers can get quite close. This seemingly bubbling pool of gray mud sometimes belches smelly sulfurous fumes—the odor is like a rotten egg. Only the very fit should attempt the six-hour round-trip to **Boiling Lake,** the world's second-largest boiling lake. Go only with an experienced guide, as, according to reports, some tourists lost their lives in the **Valley of Desolation;** they stumbled and fell into the boiling waters.

Finally, **Titou Gorge** is a deep and narrow gorge where it's possible to swim under a waterfall. Later you can get warm again in a hot sulfur spring close by. Again, a visit here is best attempted only with an experienced guide (arranged at the tourist office). The guide will transport you to the gorge and will know if swimming is dangerous, which it can be after heavy rainfall.

On the northwestern coast, **Portsmouth** is Dominica's second-largest settlement. Once here, you can row up the Indian River in native canoes, visit the ruins of old Fort Shirley in Cabrits National Park, and bathe at Sandy Beach on Douglas Bay and Prince Rupert Bay.

Cabrits National Park, on the northwestern coast, 2 miles south of Douglas Bay (☎ **809/448-2401,** ext. 415), is a 1,313-acre protected site containing mountain scenery, tropical forests, swampland, volcanic sand beaches, coral reefs, and the ruins of a fortified 18th-century garrison of British, then French construction. The park's land area is a panoramic promontory formed by twin peaks of extinct volcanoes, overlooking beaches, with Douglas Bay on one side and Prince Rupert Bay across the headland. Part of Douglas Bay forms the marine section of the park. Fort Shirley, the large garrison last used as a military post in 1854, is being wrested from encroaching vegetation. A small museum highlights the natural and historic aspects of the park. The name Cabrits comes from the Spanish-Portuguese-French word for goat because of the animals left here by early sailors to provide fresh meat on future visits.

SHOPPING

Store hours are usually 8am to 5pm Monday to Friday and 9am to 1pm on Saturday. In Roseau, the **Old Market Plaza,** of historical significance as a former slave-trading market and more recently the site of a Wednesday-, Friday-, and Saturday-morning vegetable market, now houses three craft shops, each specializing in coconut, straw, and Carib craft products.

Tropicrafts Island Mats, 41 Queen Mary St. and Turkey Lane (☎ **809/448-2747**), offers the well-known grass rugs handmade and woven in several intricate patterns at Tropicrafts' factory. They also sell handmade bags, shopping bags, and place mats, all appliquéd by hand. The handmade dolls are popular with doll collectors. The Dominican vertiver-grass mats are known throughout the world, and you can watch the weaving process during store hours. There's another outlet on Bay Street opposite Burroughs Square in Portsmouth (☎ **809/445-5956**).

Caribana, 31 Cork St. (☎ **809/448-7340**), displays Dominica's art, craft, and culture. This is the latest manifestation of the old Caribana Handicrafts, established by the late Iris Joseph, who is credited with creating the straw-weaving industry on the island. Caribana is operated by her granddaughter. The staff is usually pleased to explain the dyeing processes that turns the straw into one of three different earth tones. When straw is buried in the earth, it turns from brown to black, depending on how long it's buried; when it's soaked in saffron, it turns yellow; and when it's boiled with the bark of a tang tree, it turns purple.

DOMINICA AFTER DARK

It's not very lively, but there is some evening activity. A couple of the major hotels, such as the **Castaways Beach Hotel** (☎ **809/449-6244**) and **Reigate Hall Hotel** (☎ **809/448-4031**), have entertainment on weekends, usually a combo or "jing ping" (traditional local music). In the winter season, the Castaways sponsors a weekend barbecue on the beach with live music. The **Anchorage Hotel** at Castle Comfort (☎ **809/448-2638**) also has live entertainment and a good buffet on Thursday. Call for details.

The Warehouse, Checkhall Estate (☎ **809/449-1303**), a five-minute drive north of Roseau, adjacent to Canefield Airport, is the island's major disco, a social magnet open on Saturday for the island's night owls and disco lovers. It's owned and operated by Rosie and Cleve Royer, who converted a 200-year-old stone building once used to store rum. Recorded disco, reggae, and other music is played at loud volumes from 11pm to 4am. Admission is EC$10 ($3.70), and beer costs EC$4 ($1.50).

If you're seeking more action, such as it is, head for **Wykie's Tropical Bar,** 51 Old St. (☎ **809/448-8015**), in Roseau. This is little more than a cramped hole in the wall, yet curiously enough it draws the movers and shakers of the island. Happy hour on Friday is the time to show up. You might be offered some black pudding or stewed chicken to go with your local tropical drink. A home-grown calypso band is likely to entertain. You'll definitely hear some "jing ping."

The Dominica Club, 49 High St. (☎ **809/448-29925**), in Roseau, is a final choice. They have two tennis courts, a lively bar, and live music on Wednesday night and Saturday afternoon.

2 St. Lucia

In very recent years St. Lucia (pronounced *LOO-sha*), second largest of the Windward Islands, has become one of the most popular destinations in the Caribbean, with some of its finest resorts. The heaviest tourist development is concentrated in the northwest, between the capital of Castries and the northern end of the island, where there's a string of white-sand beaches.

The rest of the island remains relatively unspoiled, a checkerboard of green-mantled mountains, valleys, banana plantations, a bubbling volcano, wild orchids, and fishing villages. There's a hint of the South Pacific about it and a mixed French and British heritage.

A mountainous island of some 240 square miles, St. Lucia has about 120,000 inhabitants. The capital, **Castries,** is built on the southern shore of a large harbor surrounded by hills. The approach to the airport is very impressive.

Native son Derek Walcott was born in Castries. His father was an unpublished poet who died when Walcott was just a year old, and his mother was a former headmistress at the Methodist school on St. Lucia. In 1992 Walcott won the Nobel Prize for literature. He prefers, however, not to tout the charms of St. Lucia and told the press, "I don't want everyone to go there and overrun the place." His warning has come too late.

GETTING THERE

BY PLANE You'll probably have to change planes somewhere else in the Caribbean to get to St. Lucia. Both **American Airlines** and **American Eagle** serve each of the island's two airports with nonstop flights from the airline's hub in San Juan. The airline offers two daily nonstop flights from San Juan into Vigie Airport and one daily nonstop flight from San Juan into the more remote and isolated Hewanorra Airport. Connections from all parts of the North American mainland to the airline's enormous hub in San Juan are frequent and convenient.

Air Canada (☎ **800/268-7240** in Canada, or 800/776-3000 in the U.S.) has a nonstop flight to St. Lucia that departs year-round on Saturday from Toronto.

LIAT (☎ **758/462-3142**) has small planes flying from many points throughout the Caribbean into Vigie Airport, near Castries. Points of origin include such islands as Barbados, Antigua, St. Thomas, Sint Maarten, and Martinique. The airline also offers less frequent service into Hewanorra Airport, mostly from St. Vincent and points to the south. Know in advance that LIAT flights tend to island-hop en route to St. Lucia, although some visitors consider this part of their Caribbean adventure.

British Airways (☎ **800/247-9297**) offers three flights a week from London's Gatwick Airport to St. Lucia's Hewanorra airport. All these touch down briefly on Antigua before continuing to St. Lucia. Service is available on Tuesday, Friday, and Sunday.

The island maintains two separate airports whose different locations cause endless confusion to most newcomers. Most international long-distance flights land at **Hewanorra International Airport** in the south, 45 miles from Castries. If you fly in here and you're booked into a hotel in the north, you'll have to spend about an hour and a half going along the potholed East Coast Highway. The average taxi ride costs $50 for up to four passengers.

Flights from other parts of the Caribbean usually land at the somewhat-antiquated **Vigie Field,** in the island's northeast, whose location just outside Castries affords much more convenient access to the capital and most of the island's hotels.

GETTING AROUND

BY TAXI Taxis are ubiquitous on the island, and most drivers are eager to please. The drivers have to be quite experienced to cope with the narrow, hilly, switchback roads outside the capital. Special programs have trained them to serve as guides. Their cars are unmetered, but tariffs for all standard trips are fixed by the government. Always determine if the driver is quoting a rate in U.S. dollars or Eastern Caribbean dollars (EC$).

BY RENTAL CAR First, *remember to drive on the left,* and try to avoid some of the island's more obvious potholes. You'll need a St. Lucia driver's license, which can easily be purchased at either airport when you arrive or at the car-rental kiosks when you pick up your car. Present a valid driver's license from home to the counter attendant or government official and pay a fee of $12.

All three of the big U.S.-based car-rental companies maintain offices on St. Lucia: **Budget** (☎ **800/527-0700** or 758/452-0233), **Avis** (☎ **800/331-2112** or 758/452-2046), and **Hertz** (☎ **800/654-3001** or 758/452-0679). All three companies maintain offices at (or will deliver cars to) both of the island's airports. Each also has an office in Castries and, in some cases, at some of the island's major hotels.

Drive carefully and honk your horn while going around the island's blind hairpin turns.

BY LOCAL BUS Minibuses (with names like "Lucian Love") and jitneys connect Castries with such main towns as Soufrière and Vieux Fort. They're generally overcrowded and often filled with produce on the way to market. At least they're cheap, unlike taxis. Buses for Cap Estate, in the northern part of the island, leave from Jeremy Street in Castries, near the market. Buses going to Vieux Fort and Soufrière leave from Bridge Street in front of the department store.

FAST FACTS: St. Lucia

Banking Hours Banks are open Monday to Thursday from 8am to 1pm and on Friday from 8am to noon and 3 to 5pm.

Currency The official monetary unit is the **Eastern Caribbean dollar (EC$).** It's about 37¢ in U.S. currency. Most of the prices quoted in this section will be in American dollars, as they are accepted by nearly all hotels, restaurants, and shops.

Customs At either airport, Customs may be a hassle if there's the slightest suspicion, regardless of how ill-founded, that you're carrying illegal drugs.

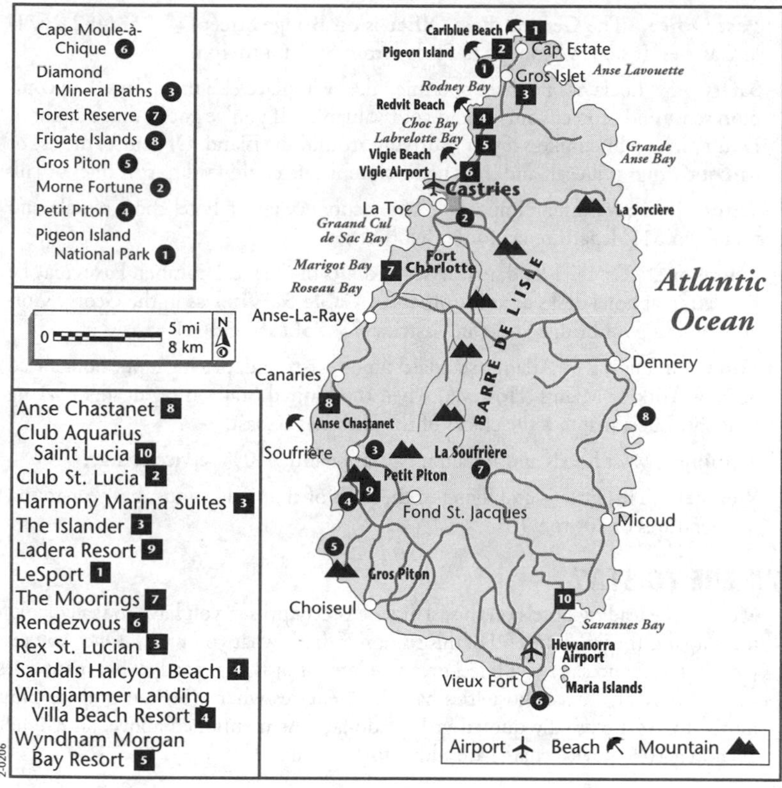

Documents U.S., British, and Canadian citizens need a valid passport, plus an ongoing or return ticket.

Drugstore The best is **William Pharmacy,** Williams Building, Bridge Street, in Castries (☎ **809/452-3173**), open Monday to Saturday from 8am to 4:30pm.

Electricity Visitors from the U.S. will need to bring an adapter and transformer, as St. Lucia runs on 220–230 volts AC (50 cycles).

Emergency Call the police at ☎ **999.**

Hospitals There are 24-hour emergency rooms at **St. Jude's Hospital,** Vieux Fort (☎ **758/454-6041**), and **Victoria Hospital,** Hospital Road, Castries (☎ **758/452-2421**).

Information The **St. Lucia Tourist Board** is at Point Seraphine, Castries (☎ **758/452-4094**); in the **United States,** the office is at 820 Second Ave., New York, NY 10017 (☎ **800/456-3984** or 212/867-2950). In **Canada,** information is available at 130 Spadina Ave, Suite 703, Toronto, ON M52 2L4 (☎ **416/703-0141**). In the **United Kingdom,** information is available at 421A Finchley Rd., London NW3 6HJ (☎ **0171/431-3675**).

Language With its mixed French and British heritage, St. Lucia has interesting speech patterns. Although English is the official tongue, St. Lucians probably don't speak it the way you do. Islanders also speak a French-Creole patois, similar to that heard on Martinique.

Post Office The **General Post Office** is on Bridge Street (☎ **758/452-2671**) in Castries. It's open Monday to Friday from 8:30am to 4pm.

Safety St. Lucia has its share of crime, like everyplace else these days. Use common sense and protect yourself and your valuables. If you've got it, don't flaunt it! Don't pick up hitchhikers if you're driving around the island. Of course, the use of narcotic drugs is illegal, and their possession or sale could lead to stiff fines or jail.

Taxes The government imposes an 8% occupancy tax on hotel-room rentals, and there's an $11 departure tax for both airports.

Telephone On the island, dial all seven digits of the local number. Faxes may be handed in at hotel desks or at the offices of **Cable & Wireless** in the George Gordon Building on Bridge Street in Castries (☎ **758/452-3301**).

Time St. Lucia is on Atlantic standard time year-round, placing it one hour ahead of New York or Miami. However, when the United States is on daylight saving time, St. Lucia matches the clocks of the U.S. East Coast.

Tipping Most hotels and restaurants simply add a 10% service charge.

Weather This little island, lying in the path of the trade winds, has year-round temperatures of 70° to 90°F.

WHERE TO STAY

Most of the leading hotels on this island are pretty pricey; you have to really look for the bargains (begin at the end of this section if that's what you want). Once you reach your hotel, chances are you'll feel pretty isolated, but that's exactly what many guests want. Many St. Lucian hostelries have kitchenettes where you can prepare simple meals. Prices are usually quoted in U.S. dollars. As mentioned above, an 8% hotel tax and a 10% service charge are added to your bill.

VERY EXPENSIVE

✪ **Ladera Resort.** P.O. Box 225, Soufrière, St. Lucia, W.I. ☎ **800/738-4752** in the U.S. and Canada, or 758/459-7323. Fax 758/459-5156. 13 suites, 6 villas. Winter, $330–$450 suite; $475–$650 villa. Off-season, $195–$350 suite; $295–$525 villa. Extra person $25–$50. MAP $40 per person extra. Minimum stay 7 nights Dec 18–Jan 4. AE, DISC, MC, V.

The Ladera is upscale in the extreme, a frequent retreat for the rich and famous who seek total privacy. Outside the town of Soufrière, in the southern tier of St. Lucia, this luxury hideaway is perched on a hillside 1,000 feet above sea level, 15 to 20 minutes from a good beach. It's sandwiched between the Pitons, opening onto the Caribbean Sea. The villas and suites all have walls that fold back completely to expose the Pitons framed by the Caribbean Sea.

Villas and suites are constructed of tropical hardwoods, stone, and tile and are furnished with 19th-century French furniture, wicker, and accessories built by local craftspeople. All units are decorated with local artwork and have indoor gardens. Certain villas and suites have plunge pools as well. To get in here in winter, reserve four months in advance.

Dining/Entertainment: The Dasheene Restaurant & Bar offers fine dining, specializing in a local Creole and continental cuisine. The seafood is caught fresh daily and is most often preferred grilled. Guests enjoy high tea in Ladera's botanical garden.

Services: Shuttle service to the beach at Anse de Pitons, complimentary transportation to and from the town of Soufrière and Hewanorra International Airport.

Facilities: Large swimming pool and deck lying below the restaurant and bar with a view of the Pitons (used in the filming of the movie *Superman II*), horseback riding, scuba-diving and snorkel trips, sailboating, fishing charters.

EXPENSIVE

✪ **Anse Chastanet.** Anse Chastanet Beach (P.O. Box 7000, Soufrière), St. Lucia, W.I. ☎ **800/223-1108** in the U.S., or 758/459-7000. Fax 758/459-7700. 48 rms. Winter, $385–$630 double; $465–$780 triple. Off-season, $276–$530 double; $377–$690 triple. Rates include MAP. AE, MC, V.

One of the few places that merits the cliché "tropical paradise," this is not only St. Lucia's premier dive resort but also an exceptional Caribbean inn. It offers warm service, excellent food, a beach location, and first-class facilities. It lies 18 miles north of Hewanorra International Airport (a 50-minute taxi ride), 2 miles north of Soufrière on a forested hill, a 103-step climb above palm-fringed Anse Chastanet Beach. You're surrounded by coffee trees, mangos, papayas, banana plants, breadfruit, grapefruit, coconut palms, flamboyants, and hibiscus. The core of the house is a main building decorated in a typical island style, with a relaxing bar and dining room.

Guests can stay on the beach in spacious accommodations styled like West Indian plantation villas. Other units, constructed like octagonal gazebos and cooled by ceiling fans, have views of the Pitons, St. Lucia's famous twin peaks. Each accommodation is large and comfortably appointed with locally made furniture crafted from island woods.

Dining/Entertainment: You can dine or drink on a wind-cooled terrace, built like a tree house over the tropical landscape, in the Pitons Bar and Restaurant. Even if you're not a guest of the hotel, consider a stop at the beachside restaurant, Trou au Diable, offering a West Indian cuisine and a barbecue grill, plus a twice weekly Creole dinner buffet.

Services: Laundry, baby-sitting, transfers from the airport (available with advance notification).

Facilities: Five-star PADI dive operation, waterskiing, sailboat rentals.

✪ **Windjammer Landing Villa Beach Resort.** Labrelotte Bay (P.O. Box 1504, Castrles), St. Lucia, W.I. ☎ **800/743-9609** in the U.S., 800/267-7600 in Canada, 800/373-742 in the United Kingdom, or 758/452-0913. Fax 758/452-0907. 38 suites, 90 villas. A/C TEL. Winter, $200–$310 suite for 2; $295–$395 villa for 2, $455–$590 villa for 4, $525–$670 villa for 6. Off-season, $150–$205 suite for 2; $225–$295 villa for 2, $375–$385 villa for 4, $445–$460 villa for six. MAP $54 per person extra. Additional person $45 extra. AE, DC, MC, V.

The Windjammer is set on 55 tropical acres north of Reduit Beach, about a 15-minute drive from the capital. It's a quiet, luxurious retreat, one of the most glamorous in the West Indies. The resort was designed with a vaguely Moorish motif heavily influenced by Caribbean themes; pastel colors predominate. It's composed of a cluster of white villas climbing a forested hillside above a desirable beach. This is an all-suite or all-villa resort (the larger villas have private plunge pools), making it a good choice for families or anyone who likes a lot of space. The roomy interiors offer separate living and dining rooms, fully equipped kitchens, ceiling fans, cassette players, clocks, and VCRs upon request. All bedrooms adjoin private baths and open onto sun terraces.

Dining/Entertainment: A housekeeper/cook arrives daily, or you can choose from the Windjammer's bevy of restaurants and two bars. Some of the island's best food is served at Windjammer's restaurants, including the Conch & Bandshell, Ernestine

Hummingway's Caribbean Cuisine, Papa Don's, and Embers Barbecue. Another restaurant, Jammer's, is a trilevel waterfront choice with a continental cuisine and a nautical setting.

Services: The "Golden Family Plan" features a personal nanny for five days, supervised children's activities, a kiddies' cocktail party, and a villa food pack (soft drinks, cereals, whatever) on arrival.

Facilities: These are all complimentary and are available upon request. Water sports, horseback riding, greens fees, and tennis; largest freshwater pool on the island, with built-in waterfalls; guests are taken out on the 44-foot cabin cruiser *Columbus.* Fitness center, children's program, health and beauty club.

ALL-INCLUSIVE RESORTS

Club Aquarius Saint Lucia. Savannes Bay, St. Lucia, W.I. ☎ **800/CLUB-MED** in the U.S., or 758/454-6546. Fax 758/454-6017. 256 rms. A/C. Winter, $700–$980 per person double. Off-season, $455–$700 per person double. Rates are per week and include all meals and use of most facilities. Special packages for children 11 and under.

In 1996, Club Med's only property on St. Lucia was reconfigured into a more downscale resort modeled on the Club Aquarius subsidiary of Club Med. Patterned after similar models in Europe, and the only one of its kind in the western hemisphere, it modifies the all-inclusive Club Med format into a venue where individual amenities and activities can be selected on an à la carte basis rather than individually. The result makes for cheaper prices with greater freedom for clients (and the many families with children toward whom the new venue is aimed) to delete activities from their daily agenda that otherwise would have added to the cost.

Club Aquarius lies remotely on 95 acres of black-sand beach on the southeast coast at the southernmost tip of St. Lucia. It opens onto Savannes Bay and is located just five minutes from the international airport at Hewanorra. Completely refurbished, the club offers beachside living in four-story buildings in a coconut grove. The rooms tend to be small, the furnishings standard. This club caters to children and has separate children's facilities. Solo travelers, on the other hand, will find better grazing grounds at such properties as Anse Chastanet.

Dining/Entertainment: There's an open-air bar and a dance and theater area in the heart of the complex. Rather standard meals are served in the second-floor dining room with a panoramic view, and guests enjoy unlimited wine at lunch and dinner. The food, however, is not of the standard of other Club Meds in the Caribbean—fewer choices and much more basic.

Service: Laundry, baby-sitting.

Facilities: Tennis, archery, volleyball, basketball, soccer, a swimming pool, practice golf, windsurfing, and aerobics are included in the price. Scuba diving, horseback riding, and 18-hole golf are extra.

Club St. Lucia. Smugglers Village (P.O. Box 915), St. Lucia, W.I. ☎ **758/450-0551.** Fax 758/450-0281. 372 rms, 16 suites. Winter, $308–$386 double; $364 suite for 2. Off-season, $254–$330 double; $320 suite for 2. Rates include all meals, drinks, and use of facilities. AE, DC, MC, V.

The most economical but also the least luxurious all-inclusive resort on the island sits in Cap Estate on a 50-acre site, an area near LeSPORT. It's 8 miles north of Vigie Airport at the northern tip of the island. Very sports- and entertainment-oriented, the hotel opens onto a curved bay where smugglers used to bring in brandies, cognacs, and cigars from Martinique. The club's core is a wooden building with decks from which you can look down on a free-form pool. The accommodations are in simple bungalows scattered over landscaped grounds and feature one king-size bed or two twin beds, air-conditioning and/or ceiling fans, and patios or terraces. Your fellow guests are likely to be vacationing Brits, Germans, or Swiss.

Dining/Entertainment: The all-inclusive package is an impressive one, offering all meals, even snacks, along with unlimited beer, wine, and mixed drinks both day and night. Guests have a choice of dining in the club's regular restaurant, Lakatan, or of sampling the seafood at Lambi's. The food is standard resort fare, but you'll never go hungry here. A pizza parlor is one of the attractions. To break the monotony, guests are often transported to a restaurant, the Great House, where they receive a discount on meals ordered. This restaurant at Cap Estate offers a view of Anse Becune Bay and Martinique. Other activities include free movies and nightly entertainment.

Services: Laundry, baby-sitting, shuttle bus to Rodney Bay and Reduit Beach.

Facilities: Day or night tennis, unlimited water sports (waterskiing, Sunfish sailing, windsurfing, snorkeling, and pedal boats), three swimming pools, two beaches, children's Mini Club with a playground and a supervised activities program.

LeSPORT. P.O. Box 437, Cariblue Beach, St. Lucia, W.I. ☎ **800/544-2883** in the U.S. and Canada, or 758/450-8551. Fax 758/450-0368. 100 rms, 2 suites. A/C TEL. Winter, $530–$580 double; $670 suite. Off-season, $450–$500 double; $590 suite. Children 6–15 50% discount, $15 per day 5 or younger. AE, MC, V.

LeSPORT cares for your body with first-class pampering and isn't a hotel for jocks as the name suggests. It's set on a 1,500-acre estate at the northernmost tip of the island. You're an 8-mile run from Castries, and guests seem to prefer this isolation.

The resort makes a promise faithfully kept: Everything "you do, see, enjoy, drink, eat, and feel" is included in the price. That means not only accommodations, three meals a day, all refreshments, and bar drinks, but also use of all sports equipment, facilities, and instruction, plus airport transfers. The bedrooms all overlook the sea and have hair dryers. The resort offers a full fitness program and a selection of relaxation classes, such as stress management, tai chi, and yoga.

Dining/Entertainment: Breakfast and lunch are buffet style. Dinner offers a choice between a lighter fixed-price menu or an à la carte menu. Nonhotel guests are welcome to dine here, and meals are served in an open-air restaurant overlooking the Caribbean. The food served here is arguably the best of that offered by the all-inclusive resorts. Live entertainment is provided, and a piano bar is popular until late at night.

Services: Room service (for breakfast), transfers to and from the airport; laundry, baby-sitting, and salon available at additional charge.

Facilities: Full program of daily scuba diving, windsurfing, waterskiing, snorkeling, sailing, pool swimming, use of a floodlit tennis court, fencing, archery, and riding; emphasis on European body tonics based on thalassotherapy, involving sea-water massage, thermal jet baths, toning, and beauty treatments for both sexes; rather basic exercise room.

Rendezvous. P.O. Box 190, Malabar Beach, St. Lucia, W.I. ☎ **800/544-2883** in the U.S. and Canada, or 758/452-4211. Fax 758/452-9639. 89 rms, 11 suites. A/C TEL. Winter, $370–$430 double; $445–$510 suite for 2. Off-season, $395–$420 double; $435–$475 suite for 2. Rates are all-inclusive. AE, MC, V.

On Malabar Beach, Rendezvous (formerly Couples, St. Lucia) is an unusual hotel, where all meals, drinks, entertainment, and most incidental expenses are included in the initial price. There are several price categories, depending on the season and the accommodation; top prices are charged for oceanfront luxury suites for two. The resort lies in a 7-acre tropical garden north of Vigie Field, near Castries. The center of the complex is under a gridwork of peaked terra-cotta tile ceilings. Set on the edge of a beach bordered by palm trees, the hotel has a garden centered around a 150-year-old samaan tree. No children are allowed, and only couples are accepted.

Dining/Entertainment: A classical colonial-style dining room called the Trysting Place is highlighted by polished brass chandeliers. The Pasta Terrace is an informal open-air restaurant featuring pastas as well as traditional favorites. For live entertainment six nights a week, guests frequent the Piano Bar.

Services: A member of the staff will meet your plane at the airport.

Facilities: Two freshwater outdoor swimming pools, swim-up bar at the free-form pool with landscaped island, fitness center, sauna, scuba-diving facilities, waterskiing, tennis courts, catamaran cruises, windsurfing, sailing, beach volleyball, fitness classes, bicycle tours.

Sandals Halcyon Beach. Choc Bay (P.O. Box GM 910, Castries), St. Lucia, W.I. ☎ **800/ SANDALS** or 758/453-0222. Fax 758/451-8435. 170 rms. TV TEL. Winter, $1,725–$2,165 per person double. Off-season, $1,640–$2,075 per person double. Rates are per week and all-inclusive. AE, MC, V.

Within walking distance of Palm Beach, this is the smaller of the two Sandals properties on St. Lucia (see below), and this one has fewer facilities. Many cost-conscious guests select this 22-acre resort with the understanding that free 15-minute minibus transfers are offered between it and its larger twin, Sandals St. Lucia. The combination allows for some savings, plus free access to the nine-hole golf course and enlarged amenities of the larger resort. Only male-female couples are welcome at this resort. It's a 15-minute drive northeast of Castries and contains three pools (one with a swim-up bar) and a piano bar, plus a wide array of water sports and diversionary activities. All food, drink, and diversions are included in one all-inclusive price. The food is copious, but not of the highest quality. The best place to dine here is the Pier Restaurant, a West Indian–style restaurant atop a 150-foot pier.

Sandals St. Lucia at La Toc. La Toc Rd. (P.O. Box 399, Castries), St. Lucia, W.I. ☎ **800/ SANDALS** in the U.S. and Canada, or 758/452-3081. Fax 758/452-1012. 219 rms, 54 suites. A/C TV TEL. Winter, $1,860–$2,355 per person double; $2,500–$3,525 per person suite. Off-season, $1,760–$2,230 per person double; $2,365–$2,840 per person suite. Rates are per week and all-inclusive. AE, DC, MC, V.

The Jamaica-based Sandals opened this clone on a forested 155-acre site that slopes steeply down to the sea. The hotel is a 10-minute drive west of Castries on the island's northwestern coast. Centered around a gazebo-capped swimming pool that incorporates an artificial waterfall, a swim-up bar, and a dining pavilion, the resort offers larger-than-expected bedrooms where each unit contains a king-size four-poster bed with a mahogany headboard, a balcony or patio, a safe, a hair dryer, and a pastel-colored tropical decor. Only couples (male-female) without children are admitted. The minimum stay in any season is three nights/four days.

Dining/Entertainment: The resort contains five food outlets, which are infinitely superior to the cuisine served at Sandals Halcyon Beach (see above). French food is offered in the resort's most upscale eatery, La Toc. Japanese food is served at Kimonos, where food is cooked on a heated table top, teppanyaki style. There's also the main dining room for continental food, and Les Pitons, serving St. Lucian specialties. The Arizona Restaurant, as befits its name, offers the cuisine of the American Southwest. After dark, guests gravitate to Jaime's, the nightclub/disco, or to Herbie's Piano Bar.

Services: Massage, hairdresser/manicure, currency exchange, tour desk.

Facilities: Nine-hole golf course, five tennis courts (lit for night play), health club, a series of "neighborhood Jacuzzis" that appear unexpectedly in different areas of the resort.

Wyndham Morgan Bay Resort. Choc Bay (P.O. Box 2167, Gros Islet), St. Lucia, W.I. ☎ **800/822-4200** in the U.S., or 758/450-2511. Fax 758/450-1050. 238 rms, 2 suites. A/C TV TEL. Winter, $430–$500 double. Off-season, $340–$400 double. Year–round, $550 suite for 2. Rates are all-inclusive. In winter, children 13–18 staying in parents' room $70, children 3–12 $50, children under 3 free; off-season, children 17 and under stay free in parents' room. AE, DC, DISC, MC, V.

Set a 10-minute drive north of Castries, on 45 landscaped acres partially shaded with trees and flowering shrubs, this all-inclusive resort draws more Europeans than Americans. Opened in 1992 and operated by the Wyndham chain, it offers accommodations in six different annexes. The accommodations contain marble-trimmed bathrooms and are outfitted with patios or verandas and furniture crafted from rattan or wicker. Unlike some other all-inclusive hostelries on the island, this one welcomes children.

Dining/Entertainment: The resort's premier restaurant is the Trade Winds, with candlelit meals served in a setting overlooking the garden. You can also dine at the snack bar and grill, Palm Grill, which overlooks the beach and offers a nightly buffet dinner, often a theme night. The cuisine is resort standard, nothing more. Local musicians, steel bands, and calypso singers often perform live in the Sundowner Bar.

Services: Car-rental kiosk on-site, tour desk, Kids Club (for ages 5 to 12).

Facilities: A heart-shaped freshwater swimming pool, four tennis courts (two lit for night play), fitness center (with saunas, Jacuzzis, and steam room), archery, croquet, water sports, day-care center outfitted like a summer camp for children of guests; the beach is small with murky water.

MODERATE

✪ **Harmony Suites.** Rodney Bay Lagoon (P.O. Box 155, Castries), St. Lucia, W.I. ☎ **758/452-0336.** Fax 758/452-8677. 30 one-bedroom suites. A/C TV TEL. Winter, $100–$125 suite for 2. Off-season, $75–$100 suite for 2. MAP $45 per person extra. Additional person $20. AE, MC, V.

Between 1992 and 1993 this set of two-story buildings, a short walk from one of the island's finest beaches at Reduit, was renovated and upgraded. Originally built in 1980, the complex now offers well-maintained accommodations at reasonable rates. Eight of the suites contain kitchenettes, ideal for families on a budget, and come complete with coffeemakers, refrigerators, and a wet bar. The suites sit adjacent to a saltwater lagoon where boats find refuge from the rough waters of the open sea. Each of the units offers a patio or balcony with views of moored yachts, the lagoon, and surrounding hills. The suites are decorated in rattan, wicker, and florals. All suites, except the VIP/honeymoon units (eight of these) have sofa sleepers folding out to make a double bed in the living room. The VIP suites feature a double Jacuzzi, a four-poster queen-size bed on a pedestal, and a sundeck, bidet, and white rattan furnishings. The restaurant, the Mortar & Pestle, is recommended separately (see "Where to Dine," below).

✪ **The Islander.** Rodney Bay (P.O. Box 907, Castries), St. Lucia, W.I. ☎ **800/223-9815** in the U.S., 800/468-0023 in Canada, 212/545-8469 in New York City, or 758/452-8757. Fax 758/452-0958. 40 rms, 20 studios, 4 two-bedroom apts. A/C TV TEL. Winter, $120 double; $130 studio for 2; $240 apt for 6. Off-season, $85 double; $90 studio for 2; $175 apt for 6. MAP $28 per person extra. Additional person $25 extra in winter, $20 extra off-season. AE, DC, DISC, MC, V.

North of Castries, near the St. Lucian Hotel and Reduit Beach, this affordable and well-recommended hotel has an entrance festooned with hanging flowers. A brightly painted fishing boat serves as a buffet table near the pool, and there's a spacious covered bar area perfect for socializing with the owner, Greg Glace. Twenty of the accommodations are studios, with kitchenette and private bath or shower, while the rooms have private showers and small bars with minirefrigerators; the studios are slightly more expensive. Four two-bedroom apartments are in an annex across the street. Overlooking a grassy courtyard sheltered with vines and flowers, all rooms also have radios. A network of walkways leads to a convivial restaurant. Guests can walk the few hundred feet to the beach or take a courtesy bus, a three-minute ride.

The Moorings. Marigot Bay (P.O. Box 101, Castries), St. Lucia, W.I. ☎ **800/437-7880** in the U.S., or 758/451-4357. Fax 758/451-4353. 16 one-bedroom cottages. Winter, $135 cottage for 2. Off-season, $85 cottage for 2. MAP $41 per person extra. Additional person $15 extra. AE, MC, V.

Operated by a company famous for chartering yachts, this resort lies at the southern edge of a symmetrically shaped lagoon that author James Michener described as "the most beautiful bay in the Caribbean." The resort consists of a wood-sided, heavily timbered main building and a series of veranda-fronted accommodations that extend over a steeply sloping hillside above the bay. A ferryboat makes frequent runs across the bay to a neighboring resort, Marigot Beach Club.

Well known in yachting circles for the safe haven provided by Marigot Bay, the Moorings offers an opportunity to relax and read amid the palm and banana groves and to swim and sail. The decor is inspired by the West Indies, with lots of rattan, pastel colors, and open-sided patios. All rooms have king-size beds.

Dining/Entertainment: The Hurricane Hole is recommended separately (see "Where to Dine," below).

Services: Laundry, baby-sitting.

Facilities: Swimming pool, base for the Moorings Yacht Charter fleet.

Rex St. Lucian. P.O. Box 512, Reduit Beach, St. Lucia, W.I. ☎ **800/255-5859** in the U.S., 305/471-6170 in Miami, 0181/741-5333 in London, or 758/452-8351. Fax 758/452-8331. 120 rms. TEL. Winter, $175–$192 double; $234–$259 triple. Off-season, $140–$157 double; $199–$225 triple. MAP $46 per person extra. AE, DC, MC, V.

Some 6½ miles north of Castries, the St. Lucian not only has one of the best water-sports programs on the island, but it also opens onto the most panoramic beachfront, Reduit Beach. In 1996, Rex St. Lucian was subdivided, and its former second half became the Rex Papillon, one of St. Lucia's less favored all-inclusive resorts. Rex St. Lucian has well-landscaped grounds, with swaying palms, latticed breezeways, and flowering shrubs. The bedrooms are a bit tired after hosting too many tour groups, but this is an action-oriented hotel where guests spend little time in the rooms anyway. Almost all units are air-conditioned. Some guests find the activities and food here so rich and varied that they never leave the grounds, although we recommend that you do.

Dining/Entertainment: There is a choice of bars and restaurants, including food from the Far East offered at The Oriental and barbecues and more casual dining at the all-day outdoor covered restaurant, Mariners. The Admirals Lounge features live entertainment.

Services: Room service, laundry, baby-sitting, doctor on 24-hour call.

Facilities: Beach and lots of water sports, including scuba diving and windsurfing (nonresidents can also participate; see "Beaches and Outdoor Activities," below).

WHERE TO DINE

As virtually every hotel on St. Lucia seems to be going all-inclusive, the independent restaurants have had to sail through rough waters. But there are quite a few, nevertheless, of varying quality. The big problem about dining out at night, as on nearly all Caribbean islands, is getting to that special hideaway and back again with adequate transportation across the dark, potholed roads.

In Castries

Green Parrot. Red Tape Lane, Morne Fortune, St. Lucia, W.I. ☎ **758/452-3399.** Reservations recommended. Fixed-price dinner EC$90–EC$110 ($33.30–$40.70). AE, MC, V. Daily 7am–midnight. EUROPEAN/WEST INDIAN.

About 1½ miles east of the center, the Green Parrot overlooks Castries Harbour and remains the local hot spot for both visitors, expats, and locals. It takes about 12 minutes to walk from downtown, but the effort is worth it. This elegant place is the home of its chef, Harry, who had many years of training in prestigious restaurants and hotels in London, including Claridges. Guests take their time and make an evening of it. Many enjoy a before-dinner drink in the Victorian-style salon. You might like to try a Grass Parrot (made from coconut cream, crème de menthe, bananas, white rum, and sugar).

The price of a meal in the English-colonial dining room usually includes entertainment: Harry is not only a cook but also an entertainer of some note. Folkloric shows (with limbo dancers and fire eaters, followed by music for dancing) are presented on Wednesday and Saturday, whereas Tuesday is a barbecue and Monday is ladies' night, when any woman wearing a flower in her hair and accompanied by a man in a coat and tie receives a free dinner.

All this may sound gimmicky, but the food doesn't suffer because of all the activity. There's an emphasis on St. Lucian specialties and using home-grown produce when it's available. Try the christophine au gratin (a Caribbean squash with cheese) or the Creole soup made with callaloo and pumpkin. There are also five kinds of curry with chutney, as well as a selection of omelets and sandwiches at lunchtime. Steak Pussy Galore is a specialty. Lunch is à la carte.

The Green Parrot also offers some of the island's least expensive lodging; rooms come with air-conditioning and telephone. In winter, doubles are $110, lowered in off-season to $80.

Jimmie's. Vigie Cove Marina. ☎ **758/452-5142.** Reservations not accepted. Main courses EC$37.50–EC$65 ($13.90–$24.05). AE, MC, V. Mon–Sat 9am–10:30pm. Closed mid-July to Aug. CREOLE.

Near Vigie Field, with a view of Castries Harbour and the Morne, Jimmie's is known for its fresh fish menu and tasty Creole cookery. Jimmie is a native St. Lucian, and after training in England, he returned to his homeland to open this spot, which is popular with visitors and locals alike. St. Lucia divides into two camps: those who like to go for a night out at the Green Parrot and those who prefer to patronize Jimmie's. Both are equally fun. The bar is a prime rendezvous point. Guests like the open-air terrace dining and the good-tasting dishes that are just like mama made (provided your mother came from the islands and learned secret Creole spices). Fish is the item to order here, and it's prepared in any number of ways, including Jimmie's special, a Caribbean seafood risotto seasoned with fresh herbs. Conch is made according to Jimmie's secret recipe, which he claims is a known aphrodisiac. Lobster is classic, but for something truly delectable try octopus Helen, cooked from an old St. Lucian recipe. Nearly a dozen banana desserts are featured; St. Lucians call bananas "figs."

San Antoine. Morne Fortune. ☎ **758/452-4660.** Reservations recommended. Main courses EC$50–EC$100 ($18.50–$37). AE, MC, V. Mon–Fri 11:30am–2:30pm and 6:30–10:30pm, Sat 6:30–10:30pm. CONTINENTAL/WEST INDIAN.

Constructed in the 19th century as a Great House, this restaurant lies up the Morne and offers vistas over the capital and the water. Sometime in the 1920s it was turned into the first hotel on St. Lucia by Aubrey Davidson-Houston, the British portrait painter whose subjects have included W. Somerset Maugham. However, in 1970 it was destroyed by fire. When it was restored in 1984, whatever could be retained, including the original stonework, was given a new lease on life, cleaned, and repaired.

You might begin with the classic callaloo soup of the island, then follow with fettuccine Alfredo, or perhaps fresh fish en papillote. Lobster thermidor might also be featured. Frankly, many visitors have found the view and ambience far more stunning than the cuisine, but if you order grilled fish and fresh vegetables, you should have a most satisfying meal.

At Marigot Bay

Café Paradis. At the Marigot Beach Club. ☎ **758/451-4974.** Reservations recommended. Main courses $8–$30; nightly barbecue $15. AE, MC, V. Daily 8am–10:30pm. FRENCH/ INTERNATIONAL.

This is a culinary showplace, the proud domain of a French-trained chef who was eager to escape to the Caribbean. With extended hours, the restaurant derives some of its income from its award-winning rum punches. A view of the water beckons from the restaurant's veranda. Lunch items include rotis, brochettes, burgers, salads, and grilled fish platters—nothing imaginative here. The menu at dinner is enhanced with a choice of daily specials that vary according to the ingredients. Rack of lamb and lobster, prepared in about four different ways, are upscale staples. The linguine with king prawns and scallops is one of the best dishes on the menu. The best deal here is the nightly barbecue where for one price you get a soup or salad, a choice of baby back ribs, chicken, or steak, plus dessert. The barbecue starts at 6:30pm.

To reach the place, you'll have to take a ferryboat across Marigot Bay. Attached by a cable to either end of Marigot Bay, it makes the short run from its origin at the Moorings Marigot Bay Resort about every 10 minutes throughout the day and evening. Show a staff member the return half of your ferryboat ticket and you'll receive a $1 discount off your food or bar tab.

Hurricane Hole. In the Moorings, Marigot Bay. ☎ **758/451-4357.** Reservations recommended for nonguests. Main courses EC$17.50–EC$28 ($6.50–$10.35). AE, MC, V. Daily 7:30–10am, noon–2:30pm, and 6:30–10pm. INTERNATIONAL/ST. LUCIAN.

Cozy, candlelit, and nautical, this is the restaurant of the Marigot Bay Resort, which charters yachts to clients from around the hemisphere. The congenial bar does a brisk business before dinner, when the Marigot Hurricane (rum, banana, grenadine, and apricot brandy) is especially popular. Ceiling fans spin languidly as you peruse the menu, which is geared in part to surf-and-turf fans, although many dishes have genuine island flavor, especially at dinner. The callaloo soup with crab is given added zest by okra, although we're equally fond of the pumpkin soup blended with herbs and cream. A stuffed crab back is an alluring appetizer, followed by the freshest available fish of the day, which can be served in any number of ways, although we prefer au natural with herbs, fresh butter, lemon, and garlic. Meats and poultry range from a spicy Indian curried chicken to smoked pork chops that are grilled to perfection.

In the Soufrière Area

Chez Camilla Guest House & Restaurant. 7 Bridge St., Soufrière, St. Lucia, W.I. ☎ **758/459-5379.** Main courses $9–$29. AE, MC, V. Mon–Sat 8am–10pm. WEST INDIAN.

Set one block inland from the waterfront, one floor above street level, this is a clean and decent Caribbean-style restaurant with simple, unpretentious food. It's operated by a local matriarch, Camilla Alcindor, who will welcome you for coffee, a soda, or Perrier, or for full-fledged dinners that include Caribbean fish Creole, lobster thermidor, and prime loin of beef with garlic sauce. The food is straightforward but with good flavor. Opt for the fish and shellfish instead of the beef, although the chicken curry is a savory choice as well. Lunches are considerably less elaborate and include an array of sandwiches, cold salads, omelets, and burgers. Our favorite tables are the pair that sit on a balcony overlooking the energetic activities in the street below. Otherwise, the inside tables can get a bit steamy on a hot night, as there's no air-conditioning. This is the only really good place to eat in the village of Soufrière itself. In addition to serving good food, Camilla invites you to stay at her guest house, which has seven bedrooms, two kitchens, and a living room. In winter, rooms run $35 for a single, $65 for a double, $85 for a triple, and $135 for a family of six. Off-season, rates are $30 for a single, $50 for a double, $75 for a triple, and $115 for a family of six. Residents at Chez Camilla can cook their own meals in the establishment's fully modern kitchen, make arrangements for the maid to prepare meals for them, or eat at Camilla's Restaurant at a 10% discount.

✪ **Dasheene Restaurant & Bar.** In the Ladera Resort, between Gros and Petit Piton. ☎ **758/459-733.** Reservations recommended. Main courses EC$51–EC$70 ($18.85–$25.90). AE, MC, V. Daily 8–10am, 11:30am–2:30pm, and 6:30–9pm. CARIBBEAN/CALIFORNIAN.

One of the most widely heralded restaurants in St. Lucia, definitely the one with the most dramatic setting, this hideaway features the best of the Caribbean/Creole kitchen with the innovative cookery of California as an added inspiration. This small mountaintop retreat offers some of the most refined and certainly the most creative cuisine in St. Lucia. Begin with a garden salad made with locally grown greens or else christophene and coconut soup. We're especially fond of the chilled Creole seafood soup, which is reminiscent of gazpacho. In terms of main dishes, the chef has a special flair for seafood pasta or marinated sirloin steak, and chicken appears stuffed with bread crumbs, sweet peppers, and onions. But the best bet is the catch of the day, likely to be kingfish or red snapper, which is grilled to perfection. The chocolate soufflé flambée for dessert makes the night out all the more festive.

The Still. Soufrière. ☎ **758/459 7224.** Reservations not required. Main courses $10–$30. AE, V. Daily 8am–5pm. CREOLE.

The first thing you'll see as you drive up the hill from the harbor is a very old rum distillery set on a platform of thick timbers, the home of this restaurant less than a mile east of Soufrière. The site is a working cocoa and citrus plantation that has been in the same St. Lucian family for four generations. The front blossoms with avocado and breadfruit trees, and a mahogany forest is a few steps away. The bar near the front veranda is furnished with tables cut from cross sections of mahogany tree trunks. A more formal and spacious dining room is nearby. St. Lucian specialties are served here, depending on what's fresh at the market that day. Try to avoid the place when it's overrun with cruise-ship passengers or tour groups. There are far better restaurants on St. Lucia, but if it's lunchtime and you're near Diamond Falls, you don't have a lot of choices.

In Rodney Bay

The Bistro (On the Waterfront). Rodney Bay. ☎ **758/452-9494.** Reservations recommended. Main courses EC$25–EC$64 ($9.25–$23.70). AE, MC, V. Fri–Wed 5:30–10:30pm. Closed Thurs. SEAFOOD/INTERNATIONAL.

Operated by Nick and Pat Bowden, a husband-and-wife team of English expatriates, this always-popular restaurant was designed as a long, thin veranda; it offers more waterfront tables than any other restaurant on the island. The bistro features a comfortable bar area. The owners may be English but their place has a decidedly French cafe atmosphere. Many of the owners of the luxury yachts moored alongside the restaurant dine here, knowing that the Bowdens provide the freshest ingredients available. Look to the chalkboards for daily specials. Our favorite appetizer is lambi (conch) au gratin, chopped finely and baked in a creamy sauce with cheese. The seafood bisque with such items as lobster and shrimp is excellent, as are any of the homemade pastas, including a Cajun cannelloni with chicken and a spicy Italian sauce. In honor of the owners' origins, pub grub such as shepherd's pie is still featured. Here's your chance to sample a traditional hot-and-spicy West Indian "pepperpot," with beef, lamb, and chicken. Potato-crusted snapper in a tomato-basil sauce is a sublime inspiration.

Capone's. Reduit Beach, Rodney Bay. ☎ **758/452-0284.** Reservations required. Main courses EC$30–EC$40 ($11.10–$14.80). AE, MC, V. Tues–Sun 6:30–10:30pm. ITALIAN.

Capone's could have been inspired by *Some Like It Hot.* Actually, this is a rendition of a Miami Beach speakeasy from the 1930s. North of Reduit Beach, near the lagoon, it's brightly lit at night.

At the entrance is a self-service pizza parlor that also serves burgers and well-stuffed pita-bread sandwiches daily from 11am to 1pm. However, we recommend that you go into the back for a really superb Italian meal, beginning with a drink, perhaps "Prohibition Punch" or a "St. Valentine's Day Massacre," served by "gangster" barmen, who will later present the check in a violin case. A player piano enlivens the atmosphere. If you feel all this atmosphere is a little too cute and gimmicky to serve really good food, be assured that the dishes here are well prepared with fresh, quality ingredients. Naturally, the "Little Caesar" salad leads off many a meal. The creamy lasagna is a special favorite. The safest bet is the fresh local charcoal-grilled fish or some of the best steaks on the island. Another good specialty is the flame-grilled chicken breast with Dijon mustard, including ham and cream cheese. Finish with an Italian espresso.

The Charthouse. Reduit Beach, Rodney Bay. ☎ **758/452-8115.** Reservations recommended. Main courses $12–$34. AE, MC, V. Mon–Sat 6–10:30pm. AMERICAN/CREOLE.

In a large building with a skylit ceiling and mahogany bar, the Charthouse is one of the oldest restaurants in the area. It's built several feet above the bobbing yachts of the lagoon, without walls, to allow an optimal view of the water. The restaurant serves simple, honest, good food in large portions. With its helpful staff, virtually unchanged since its inception, the Charthouse continues to enjoy its reputation as one of the island's most popular dining venues. The specialties might include callaloo soup, St. Lucian crab backs, "meat-falling-off-the-bone" baby back spareribs, and fresh local lobster (from September to April you can often witness the live lobster being delivered from the boat at around 5pm). If you fancy a well-cooked charcoal-broiled steak, you'll see why this dish made the restaurant famous. Of course, traditionalists always visit the Charthouse for one reason only—its roast prime rib of beef, which is never better on St. Lucia than here.

✪ **The Lime.** Rodney Bay. ☎ **758/452-0761.** Reservations recommended for dinner. Main courses EC$29–EC$70 ($10.75–$25.90). MC, V. Wed–Mon 11am–2pm and 6:30–11pm. Closed mid-June to July 7. AMERICAN/CREOLE.

The Lime stands north of Reduit Beach in an area that's known as restaurant row. Some of these places are rather expensive, but the Lime continues to keep its prices low, its food good and plentiful, and its service among the finest on the island. Both locals and visitors come here for "limin'," or hanging out. West Indian in feeling and open-air in setting, the Lime features a "lime special" drink in honor of its namesake.

Specialties include stuffed crab backs and fish steak Creole, and it also serves shrimp, steaks, lamb and pork chops, and roti. The steaks are done over a charcoal grill. Nothing is fancy, nothing is innovative, and nothing is nouvelle—just like the savvy local foodies like it. It's cheaper than the more touristy Capone's.

The Mortar & Pestle. In the Harmony Marina Suites, Rodney Bay Lagoon. ☎ **758/452-8756.** Reservations recommended, especially for dinner. Main courses EC$45–EC$85 ($16.65–$31.45). AE, MC, V. Daily 7am–3pm and 7–11pm. CARIBBEAN/INTERNATIONAL.

Set on the waterfront of Rodney Bay Lagoon, in a previously recommended hotel, this restaurant offers indoor-outdoor dining with a view of the boats moored at the nearby marina. The restaurant serves select recipes from the various islands of the southern Caribbean, with their rich medley of African, British, French, Spanish, Portuguese, Dutch, Indian, Chinese, and even Amerindian influences. To get you going, try the rich and creamy conch chowder, followed by crab farci (a delicious stuffed crab in the shell). Trinidad rule Jol (salt codfish with tomatoes, onions, peppers, and lime juice, with pepper sauce), an unusual dish and an acquired taste for some, is also available. To sample something truly regional, try the Barbados souse, with marinated pieces of lean cooked pork, or the frogs' legs from Dominica. All the good stuff is here, including Jamaican ackee and saltfish or Guyana Casareep pepperpot, an Amerindian specialty with beef, pork, and salt meats simmered slowly in Casareep syrup, cloves, star anise, cinnamon, and chili. Music by a steel band or some other local band sometimes accompanies the meals.

In Gros Islet

Great House. Cap Estate. ☎ **758/450-0450.** Reservations recommended. Main courses EC$35–EC$58 ($12.95–$21.45). AE, DC, DISC, MC, V. Daily 7–10:30pm. FRENCH/CREOLE.

Built on the foundation stones of the original plantation house of Cap Estate, this restaurant lies under a canopy of ampeche and cedar trees. The inviting ambience extends to the formal dining room, which opens onto a tranquil patio overlooking the sea. French cuisine is served here with Caribbean flair. The service, food, and wine are first rate. The menu is adjusted frequently so that only the freshest of ingredients are used. Begin with a chilled avocado and orange soup or else stuffed squid with ratatouille "caviar." Creatively prepared main courses include a breadnut-crusted Banga Mary with sweet potato chips and a pineapple relish (this is a freshwater fish from Guyana, similar to trout). To go local, try the St. Lucian beef, chicken, and pork pepperpot. For dessert, the coconut cheesecake with a tropical fruit topping is without equal.

Beaches & Outdoor Activities

BEACHES Since most of the island hotels are built right on the beach, you won't have far to go for swimming. All beaches are open to the public, even those along hotel properties. However, if you use any of the hotel's beach equipment, you must pay for it, of course. We prefer the beaches along the western coast because a rough surf on the windward side makes swimming there potentially dangerous.

Leading beaches include **Pigeon Island,** off the northern shore, with white sand and picnic facilities. **Vigie Beach,** north of Castries Harbour, is one of the most popular on St. Lucia. It has fine sands, often a light beige in color. But for a novelty, you might try the black volcanic sand at Soufrière. The beach here is called **La Toc.**

Just north of Soufrière is that beach connoisseur's delight, the white sands of **Anse Chastanet,** set at the foothills of lush, green mountains. While here, you might want to patronize the facilities of the previously recommended Anse Chastanet Hotel. **Reduit Beach** with its fine brown sands lies between Choc Bay and Pigeon Point.

DEEP-SEA FISHING The waters around St. Lucia are known for their game fish, including blue marlin, sailfish, mako sharks, and barracuda, with tuna and kingfish among the edible catches. Most hotels can arrange fishing expeditions. Call **Mako Watersports** (☎ **758/452-0412**) or **Captain Mike's** (☎ **758/452-7044**) for information about fishing trips.

GOLF St. Lucia has a 9-hole golf course at the **Cap Estate Golf Club,** at the northern end of the island (☎ **758/450-8523**). Greens fees are $27 for 18 holes, $21 for 9 holes, and there are no caddies. Hours are 8am to sunset daily. Another 9-hole course is now called **St. Lucia Sandals** (☎ **758/452-3081**), although preference is given to the guests of that all-inclusive hotel.

HORSEBACK RIDING North of Castries, you can rent a horse at **Cas-En-Bas;** to make arrangements, call René Trim (☎ **758/450-8273**). The cost is $30 for one hour; a two-hour ride costs $45. Ask about a picnic trip to the Atlantic, with a barbecue lunch and drink included, for $55. Departures on horseback are at 8:30am, 10am, 2pm, and 4pm. Nonriders can be included; they are transported to the site in a bus and pay nothing.

SCUBA DIVING In Soufrière, **Scuba St. Lucia,** in the Anse Chastanet Hotel (☎ **758/459-7000**), offers one of the world's top dive locations at a five-star PADI dive center. At the southern end of Anse Chastanet's 1/4-mile-long, soft, secluded beach, it offers premier diving and comprehensive facilities for divers of all levels. Some of the most spectacular coral reefs of St. Lucia, many only 10 to 20 feet below the surface of the water, lie a short distance from the beach and provide shelter for many marine denizens and a backdrop for schools of reef fish.

Many professional PADI instructors offer four dive programs a day. Photographic equipment is available for rent (film can be processed on the premises), and instruction is offered in picture taking, the price depending on the time and equipment involved. Experienced divers can rent the equipment they need on a per item basis. The packages include tanks, backpacks, and weight belts. PADI certification courses are available. A two- to three-hour introductory lesson costs $75 and includes a short theory session, equipment familiarization, development of skills in shallow water, a tour of the reef, and all equipment. Single dives cost $30. Hours are 8am to 5:45pm daily.

Rosemond Trench Divers, at the Marigot Beach Club, Marigot Bay (☎ **758/451-4761**), is set adjacent to the waters of the most famous bay on St. Lucia. The outfit takes both novices and experienced divers to shallow reefs or to some of the most challenging trenches in the Caribbean. A resort course designed for novices (it includes theory, a practice dive in sheltered waters, and one dive above a reef) costs $75. A one-tank dive for certified divers, with all equipment included, costs $50; a two-tank dive goes for $70, with night dives costing $65. They also have a six-dive package for $190, plus a 10-dive package for $300.

TENNIS The best place for tennis on the island is the **St. Lucia Racquet Club,** adjacent to Club St. Lucia (☎ **758/450-0551**). It opened in 1991 and quickly became one of the best tennis facilities in the Lesser Antilles. Its seven courts are maintained in state-of-the-art condition, and there's also a good pro shop on-site. You must reserve 24 hours in advance. Guests of the hotel play for free; non-guests are charged $10 a day. To rent a tennis racquet costs $6 per hour.

WATER SPORTS Unless you're interested in scuba (in which case you should head for the facilities at the Anse Chastenet Hotel), the best all-around water-sports center is **St. Lucian Watersports,** at the Rex St. Lucian Hotel (☎ **758/452-8351**). Waterskiing costs $8 for a 10-minute ride. Windsurfers can be rented for $12 to $19

Rare Birds & Other Critters

The fertile volcanic soil of St. Lucia sustains a rich diversity of bird and animal life. Some of the richest troves for ornithologists are in protected precincts off the St. Lucian coast, in either of two national parks, Frigate Islands Nature Reserve and the Maria Islands Nature Reserve.

The **Frigate Islands** are a cluster of rocks a short distance offshore from Praslin Bay, midway up St. Lucia's eastern coastline. Barren except for tall grasses that seem to thrive in the salt spray, the islands were named after the scissor-tailed frigate birds (*Fregata magnificens*), which breed here every year between May and July. Then, large colonies of the graceful birds fly in well-choreographed formations over islands that you can only visit under the closely supervised permission of government authorities. Many visitors believe that the best way to admire the Frigate Islands (and to respect their fragile ecosystems) is to walk along the nature trail that the St. Lucian government has hacked along the cliff top of the St. Lucian mainland, about 150 feet inland from the shoreline. Even without binoculars, you'll be able to see the frigates wheeling overhead. You'll also enjoy eagle's-eye views of the unusual geology of the St. Lucian coast, which includes sea caves, dry ravines, a waterfall (which flows only during rainy season), and a strip of mangrove swamp.

The **Maria Islands** are larger and more arid and are almost constantly exposed to salt-laden winds blowing up from the equator. Set to the east of the island's southernmost tip, off the town of Vieux Fort, they contain a strictly protected biodiversity. The approximately 30 acres of cactus-dotted land comprising the two largest islands (Maria Major and Maria Minor) are home to more than 120 species of plants, lizards, butterflies, and snakes that are believed to be extinct in other parts of the world. These include the large ground lizard (*Zandolite*) and the nocturnal, nonvenomous kouwes (*Dromicus ornatus*) snake.

The Marias are also a bird refuge, populated by such species as the sooty tern, the bridled tern, the Caribbean martin, the red-billed tropicbird, and the brown noddy, which usually builds its nest under the protective thorns of prickly pear cactus.

If permission is granted, visitors will set foot in either park as part of a group that arrives by boat under the supervision of a qualified guide. The cost is $55 per person for the Frigates and $70 per person for the Marias, for guided tours that last a full day and include lunch. These must be arranged through the staff of the **St. Lucia National Trust** (**☎ 758/452-5005**), who will supply further details.

an hour; lessons cost $38 per person for a three-hour course. Snorkeling is free for guests of the hotel; nonresidents pay $25, including equipment.

SEEING THE SIGHTS: FISHING PORTS, A VOLCANO & MINERAL BATHS

Lovely little towns, beautiful beaches and bays, mineral baths, banana plantations—St. Lucia has all this and more. You can even visit a volcano.

Most hotel front desks will make arrangements for tours that take in all the major sights of St. Lucia. For example, **Sunlink Tours,** Reduit Beach Avenue (**☎ 758/452-8232**), offers many island tours, including full-day boat trips along the west coast of Soufrière, the Pitons, and the volcano for $75 per person. Plantation tours go for $55, and Jeep safaris can be arranged for $70. One of the most popular jaunts is a rain-forest ramble for $55, and there's also a daily shopping tour for $15. The company has tour desks and/or representatives at most of the major hotels.

CASTRIES The capital city has grown up around its harbor, which occupies the crater of an extinct volcano. Charter captains and the yachting set drift in here, and large cruise-ship wharves welcome vessels from around the world. Because it has been hit by several devastating fires (most recently in 1948) that destroyed almost all the old buildings, the town today has a look of newness, with glass-and-concrete (or steel) buildings replacing the French colonial or Victorian look typical of many West Indian capitals.

The **Saturday-morning market** in the old tin-roofed building on Jeremy Street in Castries is our favorite "people-watching" site on the island. The country women dress up in their traditional garb and cotton headdresses; the number of knotted points on top reveals their marital status (ask one of the locals to explain it to you). The luscious fresh fruits and vegetables of St. Lucia are sold as weather-beaten men sit close by playing *warrie*, a fast game using pebbles on a carved board. You can also pick up such St. Lucian handcrafts as baskets and unglazed pottery.

Government House is a late Victorian building. A Roman Catholic cathedral stands on Columbus Square, which has a few restored buildings.

Beyond Government House lies **Morne Fortune,** which means "Hill of Good Luck," even though no one had much luck here, certainly not the battling French and British fighting for Fort Charlotte. The barracks and guard rooms changed nationalities many times. You can visit the 18th-century barracks to view the military cemetery, a small museum, the old powder magazine, and the "Four Apostles Battery" (a quartet of grim muzzle-loading cannons). The view of the harbor of Castries is panoramic: You can see north to Pigeon Island or south to the Pitons. To reach Morne Fortune, head east on Bridge Street.

PIGEON ISLAND NATIONAL LANDMARK St. Lucia's first national park was originally an island flanked by the Caribbean on one side and the Atlantic on the other. It's now joined to the mainland island by a causeway. On its west coast are two white-sand beaches. There's also a restaurant, Jambe de Bois, named after a wooden-legged pirate who once used the island as a hideout for his men.

Pigeon Island offers an **Interpretation Centre,** equipped with artifacts and a multimedia display on local history, ranging from the Amerindian occupation of A.D. 1000 to the Battle of the Saints, when Admiral Rodney's fleet set out from Pigeon Island and defeated Admiral De Grasse in 1782. The Captain's Cellar Olde English Pub lies under the center and is evocative of an 18th-century English bar.

Pigeon Island, only 44 acres in size, got its name from the red-neck pigeon or ramier that once made this island home. It's ideal for picnics, weddings, and nature walks. The park is open daily from 9am to 5pm, charging an entrance fee of EC$10 ($3.70). For more information, call the **St. Lucia National Trust** (**☎ 758/452-5005**).

MARIGOT BAY Movie crews, including those for Rex Harrison's *Dr. Doolittle* and Sophia Loren's *Fire Power,* have used this bay, one of the most beautiful in the Caribbean, for background shots. Lying 8 miles south of Castries, it's narrow yet navigable by yachts of any size. Here Admiral Rodney camouflaged his ships with palm leaves while lying in wait for French frigates. The shore, lined with palm trees, remains relatively unspoiled, but some building sites have been sold. Again, it's a delightful spot for a picnic if you didn't take your food basket to Pigeon Island.

SOUFRIÈRE This little fishing port, St. Lucia's second-largest settlement, is dominated by two pointed hills called ✪ **Petit Piton and Gros Piton.** These two hills,

"The Pitons," have become the very symbol of St. Lucia. They are two volcanic cones rising to 2,460 and 2,619 feet. Formed of lava and rock, and once actively volcanic, they are now clothed in green vegetation. Their sheer rise from the sea makes them a landmark visible for miles around, and waves crash around their bases. It's recommended that you only attempt to climb Gros Piton, but to do so requires the permission of the Forest and Lands Department (☎ **758/450-2231**) and a knowledgeable guide.

Near Soufrière lies the famous "drive-in" volcano, ✪ **Mount Soufrière.** It's a rocky lunar landscape of bubbling mud and craters seething with fuming sulfur. You literally drive your car into an old (millions of years) crater and walk between the sulfur springs and pools of hissing steam. A local guide is usually waiting beside them, shrouded in sulfurous fumes that are said to have medicinal properties. For a fee, he'll point out the blackened waters, among the few of their kind in the Caribbean. If you do hire a guide, agree, then doubly agree, on what that fee will be.

Nearby are the ✪ **Diamond Mineral Baths** (☎ **758/452-4759**), surrounded by a tropical arboretum. Constructed in 1784 on the orders of Louis XVI, whose doctors told him that these waters were similar in mineral content to the waters at Aix-les-Bains, they were intended to provide recuperative effects for French soldiers fighting in the West Indies. Later destroyed, they were rebuilt after World War II. They have an average temperature of 106°F and lie near one of the geological attractions of the island, a waterfall that changes colors (from yellow to black to green to gray) several times a day. For EC$5 ($1.85), you can bathe and try out the recuperative effects for yourself.

From Soufrière in the southwest, the road winds toward Fond St-Jacques where you'll have a good view of mountains and villages as you cut through St. Lucia's Cape Moule-à-Chique tropical rain forest. You'll also see the Barre de l'Isle divide.

SHOPPING

Most of the shopping is in Castries, where the principal streets are William Peter Boulevard and Bridge Street. Many stores will sell you goods at duty-free prices (providing you don't take the merchandise with you but have it delivered to the airport or cruise dock). There are some good (but not remarkable) buys in bone china, jewelry, perfume, watches, liquor, and crystal. Souvenir items include bags and mats, local pottery, and straw hats—again, nothing remarkable.

POINTE SERAPHINE

Built for the cruise-ship passenger, Pointe Seraphine, in Castries, has the best collection of shops on the island, together with offices for car rentals, organized taxi service (for sightseeing), a bureau de change, a Philatelic Bureau, an Information Centre, and international telephones. Cruise ships berth right at the shopping center. Under red roofs in a Spanish-style setting, the complex requires that you present a cruise pass or an airline ticket to the shopkeeper when purchasing goods. Visitors can take away their purchases, except liquor and tobacco, which will be delivered to the airport. All shops in the complex keep the same hours. The center is open in winter, Monday to Friday from 8am to 5pm and on Saturday from 8am to 2pm; off-season, Monday to Saturday from 9am to 4pm. It's also open when cruise ships are in port.

Benneton. Pointe Seraphine. ☎ **758/452-7685.**

All the sportswear here was sewn in either Italy or Spain, and any of these pieces would be appropriate for a cruise wardrobe. In addition to T-shirts, tennis shirts, and shorts, there's an assortment of women's pants suits, men's business suits, and children's wear. Prices are about 20% lower than Stateside.

Colombian Emeralds. Pointe Seraphine. ☎ **758/453-7721.**

Colombian Emeralds's major competitor in this mall is Little Switzerland, and although it doesn't even try to stock the porcelain, crystal, perfume, and luggage of its larger rival, its selection of watches and gemstones is more diverse. There are two adjoining buildings, one of which sells only gold chains (14- and 18-karat) and wristwatches; the other features a sophisticated array of precious and semiprecious stones that would tempt a Turkish vizier. Chains range from $85 to $1,100, wristwatches cost $90 to $14,000, and gemstones, set in twinkling and tempting settings, are often reasonable in price. Of special value are the wristwatches, which sometimes sell for up to 40% less than equivalent retail prices in North America.

Images. Pointe Seraphine. ☎ **758/452-6883.**

Images operates two shops within Castries' wharf-side shopping mall, but the more interesting of them sells the most exhaustive collection of enameled Indian jewelry on St. Lucia. Laboriously handcrafted with lots of exotic swirls, the ornaments (necklaces, bracelets, and earrings) range in price from $10 to $60. Also worthwhile are India-made evening bags lavishly adorned with sequins (a bargain at $24 each), and bags by Ted Lapidus. A few steps away, the establishment's second store specializes in perfumes that cost around 20% less than equivalent goods sold retail in North America. Most fragrances are from France and the States, although the perfume shop sells some locally made essences as well.

The Land Shop. Pointe Seraphine. ☎ **758/452-7488.**

This store specializes in elegant handbags, garment bags, and briefcases. Some come with the English-made labels affixed. Others are made by relatively obscure manufacturers in Colombia whose quality is nonetheless very high. Prices are at least 25% less than equivalent items sold in North America, and your purchases are, like everything else in the complex, tax-free. Also available is a selection of shoes, although the inventory for women is more varied and interesting than the choices for men. Bags and briefcases range from $79 to $550.

Little Switzerland. Pointe Seraphine. ☎ **758/451-6799.**

Its inventory includes a broad-based but predictable array of luxury goods. Prices of the porcelain, crystal, wristwatches, and jewelry are usually around 25% less than those of equivalent goods bought on the North American mainland, but wise shoppers are usually alert to the special promotions (with savings of up to 40% below Stateside retail prices) that influence the prices. Various special promotions could be in effect at the time of your visit.

Elsewhere on the Island

Gablewoods Mall, on Gros Islet Highway, 2 miles north of Castries, contains three restaurants and one of the densest concentrations of shops on the island. The best clothing and sundry shop is **Top Banana** (☎ **758/451-6389**). Inventory includes beachwear, scuba and snorkeling equipment, gifts, inflatable rafts, and casual resort wear. Other branches of this store can be found at both the Rex St. Lucian Hotel and the Windjammer Hotel.

Bagshaws. La Toc. ☎ **809/451-9249.**

Just outside Castries, this is the leading island hand-printer of silk-screen designs. An American, Sydney Bagshaw, founded the operation in the mid-1960s, and today it's operated by his daughter-in-law, Alice Bagshaw. The family has devoted their considerable skills to turning out a high-quality line of fabric as colorful as the Caribbean. The birds (look for the St. Lucia parrot), butterflies, and flowers of St. Lucia are incorporated into their original designs. The highlights are an extensive household line in vibrant prints on linen, as well as clothing and beachwear for both men and women, and the best T-shirt collection on St. Lucia. At La Toc Studios, the printing process can be viewed seven days a week.

There are **four other retail outlets:** in the Pointe Seraphine duty-free shopping mall (☎ **758/452-7570**), in Marigot Bay (☎ **758/451-4378**), in Rodney Bay (☎ **758/452-9435**), and at the "Best of St. Lucia" at Hewanorra International Airport, Vieux Fort (☎ **758/454-7784**).

Caribelle Batik. Howelton House, Old Victoria Rd., The Morne. ☎ **758/452-3785.**

In this workshop, just a five-minute drive from Castries, you can watch St. Lucian artists creating intricate patterns and colors through the ancient art of batik. You can also purchase batik in cotton, rayon, and silk, made up in casual and beach clothing, plus wall hangings and other gift items. Drinks are served in the Dyehouse Bar and Terrace in the renovated Victorian-era building.

Eudovic Art Studio. Goodlands, Morne Fortune. ☎ **758/452-2747.**

Vincent Joseph Eudovic is a master artist and wood carver whose sculptures have gained increasing fame. He usually carves his imaginative free-form sculptures from local tree roots, such as teak, mahogany, and red cedar. Some of his carvings are from Laurier Cannelle trees, which have disappeared from the island, although their roots often remain in a well-preserved state. Native to St. Lucia, he teaches pupils the art of wood carving. Much of the work of his pupils is on display in the main studio. However, ask to be taken to his private studio, where you'll see his own remarkable creations.

Noah's Arkade. Jeremie St. ☎ **758/452-2523.**

Many of the Caribbean handcrafts and gifts here are routine tourist items, yet you'll often find something interesting if you browse around. They sell local straw place mats, baskets, and rugs, wall hangings, maracas, shell necklaces, locally made bowls, dolls dressed in banana leaves, and warri boards. Branches are found at Hewanorra International Airport and the Pointe Seraphine duty-free shopping mall.

Sea Island Cotton Shop. Gablewoods Mall, Castries. ☎ **758/452-3674.**

Catering almost exclusively to tourists, this is the largest shop in the center of Castries. It carries T-shirts, Sunny Caribbee herbs and spices, hand-painted souvenirs, and beach- and swimwear. There are other locations at the Rex St. Lucian Hotel, the Windjammer Landing Villa Beach Resort, and Pointe Seraphine.

ST. LUCIA AFTER DARK

There isn't much except the entertainment offered by hotels. In the winter months, at least one hotel offers a steel band or calypso music every night of the week. Otherwise, check to see what's happening at **Capone's** (☎ **758/452-0284**) and **The Green Parrot** (☎ **758/452-3167**).

Indies, at Rodney Bay (☎ **758/452-0727**), is a split-floor, soundproof dance club with a large wooden dancing area and stage. There's also a trio of bars, with smoking and no-smoking sections. The DJs keep the joint jumping, with both West Indian and international sounds, often American. Surprise entertainment is occasionally featured to spice up the party. The action gets going Wednesday, Friday, and

Saturday from 11pm. There's a cover charge of EC$20 ($7.40). Indies has opened a new bar around the side of the building called the Back Door, featuring alternative music and reggae. A sort of rock and sports bar, it serves snacks until 3am.

The Lime (see "Where to Dine," above) also operates **The Late Lime Night Club,** offering entertainment Wednesday to Saturday, beginning at 10pm and lasting until the crowd folds. Jazz, reggae, country/western—it's all here, even easy-listening music on Sunday. Wednesday, Friday, and Saturday are disco nights. Admission is EC$15 ($5.55).

3 St. Vincent

One of the major Windward Islands, sleepy St. Vincent is only now awakening to tourism, which hasn't yet reached massive dimensions the way it has on nearby St. Lucia. Sailors and the yachting set have long known of St. Vincent and its satellite bays and beaches in the Grenadines, and until recently it was a well-kept vacation secret.

Visit St. Vincent for its botanical beauty and the Grenadines for the best sailing waters in the Caribbean. Don't come for nightlife, grand cuisine, and fabled beaches. There are some white-sand beaches near Kingstown on St. Vincent, but most of the other beaches ringing the island are of black sand. The yachting crowd seems to view St. Vincent merely as a launching pad for the 60-mile string of the Grenadines, but the island still has a few attractions that make it worth exploring on its own.

Unspoiled by the fallout that mass tourism sometimes brings, the people actually treat visitors like human beings: Met with courtesy, they respond with courtesy. British customs predominate, along with traces of Gallic cultural influences, but all with a distinct West Indian flair.

GETTING THERE

In the eastern Caribbean, St. Vincent—the "gateway to the Grenadines" (see section 4, later in this chapter)—lies 100 miles west of Barbados, where most visitors from North America fly first and then make connections that will take them on to St. Vincent's **E. T. Joshua Airport** and the Grenadines. For details on getting to Barbados from North America, see chapter 14. However, the transfer through Barbados is no longer necessary, as **American Eagle** (☎ **800/433-7300**) has one flight daily from San Juan, so getting here is more convenient than ever before.

If you decide to visit St. Vincent once you are already in Barbados, you can fly **LIAT** (☎ **809/457-1821**) here, as that never-on-time airline offers five flights daily, plus two flights daily from Trinidad to St. Vincent.

Air Martinique (☎ **809/458-4528**) runs twice-daily service between Martinique, St. Lucia, St. Vincent, and Union Island.

Increasing numbers of visitors to St. Vincent prefer the dependable service of one of the best charter airlines in the Caribbean, **Mustique Airways.** For reservations, contact Mustique Airways/Grenadine Travel Company (☎ **809/458-4380**), or their representative at the Mustique Airport (☎ **809/458-4621**). The airline makes frequent runs from St. Vincent to the major airports of the Grenadines. With advance warning, Mustique Airways will arrange specially chartered (and reasonably priced) transport for you and your party to and from many of the surrounding islands (including Grenada, Aruba, St. Lucia, Antigua, Barbados, Trinidad, and any other in the southern Caribbean). The price of these chartered flights is less than you might expect and often matches the fares on conventional Caribbean airlines. Currently the airline owns seven small aircraft, none of which carries more than nine passengers.

St. Vincent & the Grenadines

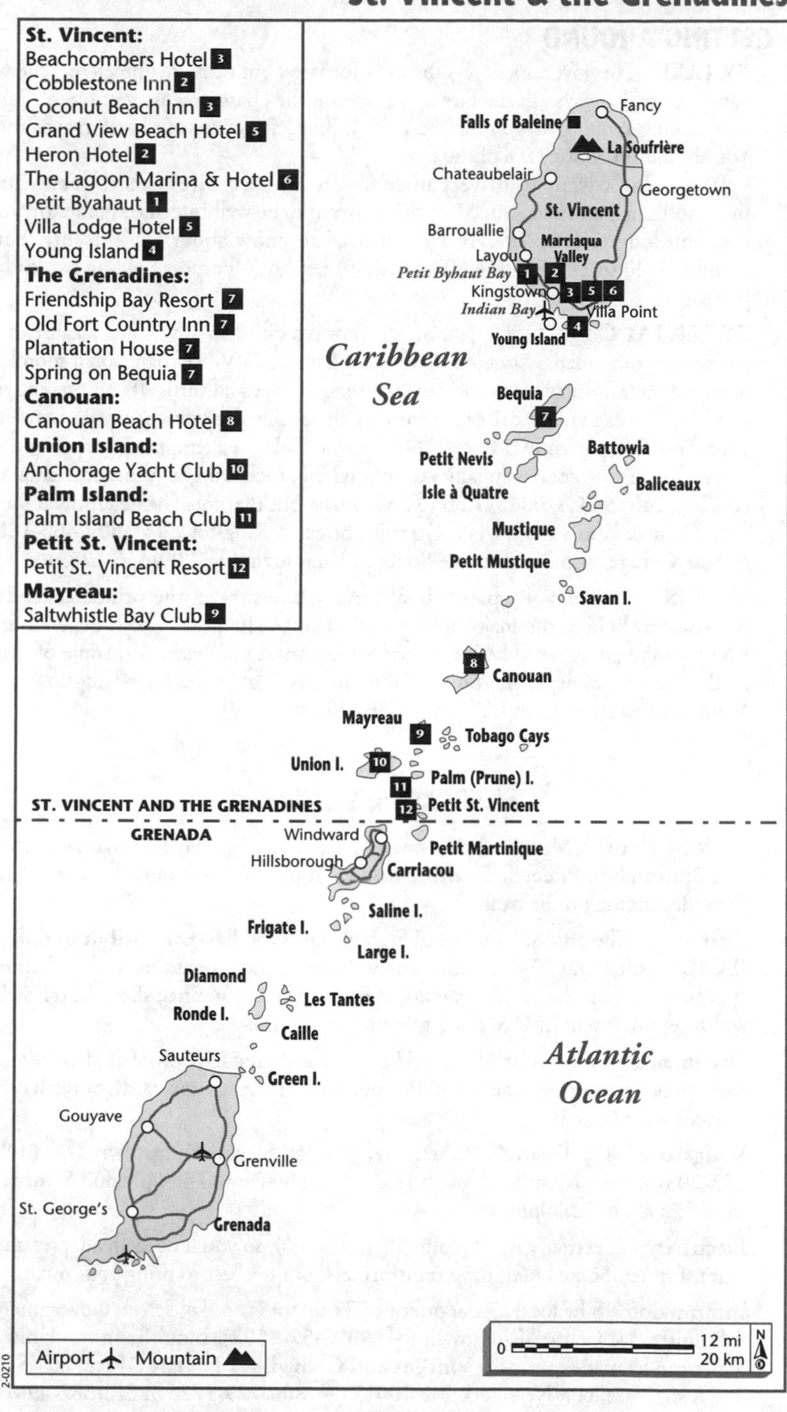

St. Vincent:
Beachcombers Hotel 3
Cobblestone Inn 2
Coconut Beach Inn 3
Grand View Beach Hotel 5
Heron Hotel 2
The Lagoon Marina & Hotel 6
Petit Byahaut 1
Villa Lodge Hotel 5
Young Island 4
The Grenadines:
Friendship Bay Resort 7
Old Fort Country Inn 7
Plantation House 7
Spring on Bequia 7
Canouan:
Canouan Beach Hotel 8
Union Island:
Anchorage Yacht Club 10
Palm Island:
Palm Island Beach Club 11
Petit St. Vincent:
Petit St. Vincent Resort 12
Mayreau:
Saltwhistle Bay Club 9
Fancy
Falls of Baleine
La Soufrière
Chateaubelair
Georgetown
St. Vincent
Barrouallie
Marriaqua Valley
Layou
Petit Byhaut Bay
Kingstown
Indian Bay
Villa Point
Young Island
Caribbean Sea
Bequia
Battowia
Petit Nevis
Baliceaux
Isle à Quatre
Mustique
Petit Mustique
Savan I.
Canouan
Mayreau
Tobago Cays
Union I.
Palm (Prune) I.
ST. VINCENT AND THE GRENADINES
Petit St. Vincent
GRENADA
Windward
Petit Martinique
Hillsborough
Carriacou
Saline I.
Frigate I.
Large I.
Diamond
Les Tantes
Ronde I.
Caille
Sauteurs
Green I.
Atlantic Ocean
Gouyave
Grenville
St. George's
Grenada
Airport
Mountain
0
12 mi
20 km
N
2-0210

GETTING AROUND

BY TAXI The government sets the rates for fares, but taxis are unmetered; the wise passenger will always ask the fare and agree on the charge before getting in. Figure on spending about $7 to go from the E. T. Joshua Airport to your hotel, maybe more. You should tip about 12% of the fare.

If you don't want to drive yourself, you can also hire taxis to take you to the island's major attractions. Most drivers seem to be well-informed guides (it won't take you long to learn everything you need to know about St. Vincent). You'll spend EC$40 to EC$50 ($14.80 to $18.50) per hour for a car holding two to four passengers.

BY RENTAL CAR Driving on St. Vincent is a bit of an adventure because of the narrow, twisting roads. *Drive on the left.* To drive like a Vincentian, you'll soon learn to sound your horn a lot as you make the sharp curves and turns. If you present your valid U.S. or Canadian driver's license at the police department on Bay Street in Kingstown and pay an EC$40 ($14.80) fee, you'll obtain a temporary permit to drive.

The major car-rental companies do not have branches on St. Vincent. Rental cars cost EC$140 to EC$200 ($51.80 to $74) a day, but that must be determined on the spot. Contact **Kim's Rentals,** on Grenville Street in Kingstown (☎ **809/456-1884**), or **Star Garage,** also on Grenville Street in Kingstown (☎ **809/456-1743**).

BY BUS Flamboyantly painted "al fresco" buses travel the principal roads of St. Vincent, linking the major towns and villages. The price is low, depending on where you're going, and the experience will connect you with the people of the island. The central departure point is the bus terminal at the New Kingstown Fish Market. Fares range from EC$1 to EC$6 (40¢ to $2.20).

FAST FACTS: St. Vincent

Banking Hours Most banks are open Monday to Thursday from 8am to either 1 or 3pm and on Friday from either 8am to 5pm or from 8am to 1pm and 3 to 5pm, depending on the bank.

Currency The official currency of St. Vincent is the **Eastern Caribbean dollar (EC$),** worth about 37¢ in U.S. money. Most of the quotations in this chapter appear in the U.S. dollars unless marked EC$. Most restaurants, shops, and hotels will accept payment in U.S. dollars or traveler's checks.

Documents British, Canadian, or U.S. citizens should have proof of identity and a return or ongoing airplane ticket. Passports, voter registration cards, or birth certificates are sufficient.

Drugstore Try **Deane's Pharmacy,** Halifax Street, Kingstown (☎ **809/457-2056**), open Monday through Friday from 8:30am to 4:30pm and Saturday from 8:30am to 12:30pm.

Electricity Electricity is 220 volts AC (50 cycles), so you'll need an adapter and a transformer. Some hotels have transformers, but it's best to bring your own.

Information The local **Department of Tourism** is on Bay Street, Government Administrative Centre, Kingstown (☎ **809/457-1502**). Inquiries in the United States can be made to the **St. Vincent and Grenadines Tourist Office,** 801 Second Ave., 21st Floor, New York, NY 10017 (☎ **800/729-1726** or 212/687-4981), or 6505 Cove Creek Place, Dallas, TX 75240 (☎ **800/235-3029** or 214/239-6451).

Language English is the official language.

Medical Care There are two hospitals on St. Vincent, **Kingstown General Hospital,** Kingstown (☎ **809/456-1185**), and **Medical Associates Clinic,** Kingstown (☎ **809/457-2598**).

Post Office The **General Post Office,** on Halifax Street in Kingstown (☎ **809/456-1111**), is open Monday to Friday from 8:30am to 3pm and on Saturday from 8:30 to 11:30am. There are sub-post offices in 56 districts throughout the country, including offices on the Grenadine islands of Bequia, Mustique, Canouan, Mayreau, and Union Island.

Safety St. Vincent and its neighboring islands of the Grenadines are still safe islands to visit. In Kingstown, the capital of St. Vincent, chances are you'll encounter little serious crime. However, take the usual precautions and never leave valuables unguarded.

Taxes The government imposes an airport departure tax of EC$20 ($7.40) per person. A 7% government occupancy tax is charged for all hotel accommodations.

Time Both St. Vincent and the Grenadines operate on Atlantic standard time year-round: When it's 6am on St. Vincent, it's 5am in Miami. During daylight saving time in the United States, St. Vincent keeps the same time as the U.S. East Coast.

Tipping Hotels and restaurants add a 10% to 15% service charge.

Weather The climate of St. Vincent is pleasantly cooled by the trade winds all year. The tropical temperature is in the 78° to 82°F range. The rainy season is May to November.

WHERE TO STAY

Don't expect high-rise resorts here; everything is kept small. The places are comfortable, not fancy, and you usually get a lot of personal attention from the staff. Most hotels and restaurants add a 7% government tax and a 10% to 15% service charge to your bill; ask about this when you register.

VERY EXPENSIVE

Young Island. P.O. Box 211, Young Island, St. Vincent, W.I. ☎ **800/223-1108** in the U.S. and Canada, or 809/458-4826. Fax 809/457-4567. 30 cottages. Winter, $430–$640 cottage for 2. Off-season, $275–$485 cottage for 2. Rates are MAP. Additional person $90 extra. "Lovers' packages" available. AE, MC, V.

This 32-acre resort, which might have attracted Gauguin, is supposedly where a Carib tribal chieftain kept his harem. It lies just 200 yards off the south shore of St. Vincent, to which it's linked by a ferry from the pier right on Villa Beach, a five-minute ride. Wood and stone bungalows are set in a tropical garden, and the beach is of brilliant white sand. Hammocks are hung under thatched roofs.

You're housed in Tahitian cottages (all for couples) with a bamboo decor and outdoor showers. Floors are of tile and terrazzo, covered with rush rugs. Many guests, however, have complained of hearing "domestic noises" in the rooms adjoining them. Ask about package rates, under the category of "young lovers"; these are bargain deals offered during off-season periods.

Dining/Entertainment: Food and service are not always of a high standard, in spite of the longtime fame of this hotel. Dining is by candlelight, and dress is informal. Sometimes a steel band plays for dancing after dinner, and you're serenaded by strolling singers. On some nights the hotel transports guests over to its other island, Fort Duvemette, for a cocktail party.

Services: Room service (for breakfast), baby-sitting.

Facilities: Swimming pool (modeled on a tropical lagoon and set in landscaped grounds) and a saltwater lagoonlike pool (at the far end of the beach, where you can hear parrots and macaws chattering), tennis court (lit for night games), Carib canoes and Sailfish. All water sports (such as scuba diving and waterskiing) are available.

EXPENSIVE

Grand View Beach Hotel. P.O. Box 173, Villa Point, St. Vincent, W.I. ☎ **800/223-6510** in the U.S., or 809/458-4811. Fax 809/457-4174. 17 rms, 2 honeymoon suites. MINIBAR TV TEL. Winter, $210 double; from $270 suite. Off-season, $130 double; from $190 suite. MAP $35 per person extra. AE, DC, MC, V.

Owner-manager F. A. (Tony) Sardine named this place well: The "grand view" promised is of islets, bays, yachts, Young Island, headlands, lagoons, and sailing craft. Villa Point lies just 5 minutes from the airport and 10 minutes from Kingstown. On well-manicured grounds, this resort is set on 8 acres of gardens. The converted plantation house is a large, white, two-story mansion. Twelve rooms are air-conditioned.

Dining/Entertainment: The West Indian fare served here is average.

Services: Room service, laundry, baby-sitting.

Facilities: Swimming pool, tennis and squash courts, fitness club with a range of exercise options and sauna and massage.

MODERATE

The Lagoon Marina & Hotel. P.O. Box 133, Blue Lagoon, St. Vincent, W.I. ☎ **800/74-CHARMS;** ☎ & fax 809/458-4308. 19 rms. Winter, $95–$100 double. Off-season, $80–$90 double. AE, MC, V.

A two-story grouping of rambling modern buildings crafted from local wood and stone, this hotel lies 4 miles from the airport on the main island road, opening onto a narrow, curved black-sand beach. There's a pleasantly breezy bar with open walls and lots of exposed planking, often filled with seafaring folk. As you relax, you'll overlook a moored armada of boats tied up at a nearby marina. A two-tiered swimming pool, terraced into a nearby hillside, offers two lagoon-shaped places to swim. Snorkeling, windsurfing, and daily departures on sailboats to Mustique and Bequia can be arranged through the hotel. Each of the high-ceilinged accommodations has a balcony, and about half the rooms are air-conditioned. Room service and laundry are available.

Villa Lodge Hotel. P.O. Box 1191, Villa Point, St. Vincent, W.I. ☎ **800/742-4276** in the U.S., or 809/458-4641. Fax 809/457-4468. 10 rms. A/C TV TEL. Winter, $115 double; $125 triple; $135 quad. Off-season, $105 double; $115 triple; $125 quad. AE, MC, V.

Set on the side of a residential hillside a few minutes southeast of the center of Kingstown and the E. T. Joshua Airport, this place is a favorite of visiting businesspeople. Because of its access to a beach and its well-mannered staff, it evokes the feeling of a modern villa. It's ringed with tropical, flowering trees and shrubs growing in the gardens. The air-conditioned rooms have ceiling fans, king-size beds, minirefrigerators, hair dryers, and comfortable rattan and local mahogany furniture. The hotel also rents eight apartments in its Breezeville Apartments complex, charging year-round prices of $120 for a double, $130 for a triple, and $140 for a quad.

Dining/Entertainment: There's a wood-sheathed bar on the second floor with a view of Young Island and the Grenadines, and a dining room where good food is served, usually from a fixed-price menu. There's also a bar and restaurant down by the pool.

Services: Room service, laundry, baby-sitting.
Facilities: Swimming pool.

INEXPENSIVE

✪ **Beachcombers Hotel.** P.O. Box 126, Villa Beach, St. Vincent, W.I. ☎ **809/458-4283.** Fax 809/458-4385. 14 rms. TEL. $75–$80 double. AE, MC, V.

This relative newcomer, established by Richard and Flora Gunn, immediately became a far more inviting choice than the traditional budget favorites, Heron and Cobblestone. Right on the beach, adjacent to Sunset Shores, it is set in a tropical garden. A pair of chaletlike buildings house the accommodations, which are tastefully decorated with private baths. They're cooled by ceiling fans, and each has a patio. The standard of cleanliness and maintenance is the finest on the island. Try for rooms 1, 2, or 3, as they are not only the best but open onto the water. Some of the units have small kitchenettes. The hotel has a health spa (Mrs. Gunn is a massage and beauty therapist). And, astonishingly for a B&B, the Beachcombers offers a steam room, Turkish bath, sauna, and even facials, aromatherapy, and reflexology. The Beachbar & Restaurant, a favorite gathering place for locals, fronts an open terrace and serves an excellent cuisine. Daughter Cheryl, who mastered her cookery skills in England, is the chef.

Cobblestone Inn. P.O. Box 867, Kingstown, St. Vincent, W.I. ☎ **809/456-1937.** Fax 809/456-1938. 19 rms. A/C TEL. $72 double. Rates include continental breakfast. AE, DC, DISC, MC, V.

The Cobblestone is conveniently close to town; however, you'll have to drive about 3 miles to get to the nearest beach. Originally built as a warehouse for sugar and arrowroot in 1814, the core of this historic hotel is made of stone and brick. Today it's one of the most famous hotels on St. Vincent, known for its labyrinth of passages, arches, and upper hallways. To reach the reception area, you pass from the waterfront through a stone tunnel into a chiseled courtyard. At the top of a stone staircase you are shown to one of the simple old-fashioned bedrooms. The rooms in back are rather dark, but aren't as noisy as those up front. Some units have TVs, and others have windows opening over the rooftops of town. Meals are served on a third-floor aerie high above the hotel's central courtyard; there's also an adjacent bar with rows of windows and rattan tables.

Coconut Beach Inn. P.O. Box 355, Indian Bay, St. Vincent, W.I. ☎ **809/457-4900.** Fax 809/457-4900. 10 rms. $45–$65 double. Rates include full breakfast with the $65 room. AE, MC, V.

This owner-occupied inn, restaurant, and bar lies five minutes (2 miles) south of the airport and a five-minute drive from Kingstown. The hotel, which grew out of a villa constructed in the 1930s by one of the region's noted eccentrics, lies across the channel from the much more expensive Young Island. Its seaside setting makes it a good choice for swimming and sunbathing. Island tours, such as sailing the Grenadines, can be arranged, as can diving, snorkeling, and mountain climbing. Each unit is furnished in a straightforward modern style, although the bedrooms vary widely from one another. A beach bar at water's edge serves tropical drinks, and an open-air restaurant opens onto a view of Indian Bay and features West Indian and Vincentian cooking. Steaks, Cornish game hens, and hamburgers round out the fare.

Heron Hotel. P.O. Box 226, Kingstown, St. Vincent, W.I. ☎ **809/457-1631.** Fax 809/457-1189. 12 rms. A/C TEL. $56.50–$62.50 double. Rates include full breakfast. MC, V.

This enduring favorite is for people who like a 1950s-style guest house with a lot of West Indian flavor. It sits in a bustling location in town. The hotel is in a wood-frame warehouse that a century ago stored vast quantities of copra (dried coconut) before it was shipped to Europe. You can always read quietly in the elegantly sparse living room. American and Creole meals are served beneath the soaring ceiling of a room whose view encompasses a private courtyard encircled by some of the simple but comfortable accommodations. Room 15 is particularly spacious.

Petit Byahaut. Petit Byahaut Bay, St. Vincent, W.I. ☎ **809/457-7008.** Fax 809/457-7008. 6 tents. $125–$155 per person per day or $595–$750 per person for 5 days/5 nights. Rates include all meals, snorkeling, beach items, sailboats, kayaks, and boat trips. Scuba packages available. MC, V.

This adventurous accommodation attracts snorkelers, scuba divers, hikers, and nature lovers. It lies 4½ miles north of Kingstown on the leeward coast and is accessible only by boat. It accepts no more than 14 guests at a time. They're housed in roomy tents with freshwater showers and large roofed decks. A house-party atmosphere prevails. Opening onto a horseshoe-shaped bay, the complex stands in a 50-acre private valley. Foliage between the tents provides privacy. A seaside bar and restaurant offer wholesome meals. Picnics are prepared during the day, and dinner is by candlelight. The snorkeling and scuba diving right off the beach are excellent, and water-sports equipment is provided.

WHERE TO DINE

Most guests eat at their hotels on the Modified American Plan (half board), and many Vincentian hostelries serve authentic West Indian cuisine. There are also a few independent restaurants, but not many.

Basil's Bar & Restaurant. Bay St., Kingstown. ☎ **809/457-2713.** Reservations recommended. Main courses EC$35–EC$55 ($12.95–$20.35); lunch buffet EC$30 ($11.10). AE, MC, V. Daily 8–11:30am, noon–2pm, and 7–10pm. SEAFOOD/INTERNATIONAL.

This brick-lined enclave is a less famous annex of the legendary Basil's Beach Bar on Mustique. It lies in the early 19th-century walls of an old sugar warehouse, on the waterfront in Kingstown beneath the previously recommended Cobblestone Inn. The air-conditioned interior is accented with exposed stone and brick, soaring arches, and a rambling mahogany bar, which remains open throughout the day. The food is quite creditable, but nowhere near as good as that enjoyed by Princess Margaret or Mick Jagger at Basil's other bar on Mustique. The menu could include lobster salad, shrimp in garlic butter, sandwiches, hamburgers, and barbecued chicken. Dinners feature grilled lobster, escargots, shrimp cocktail, grilled red snapper, and grilled filet mignon, all fairly standard dishes of the international repertoire. You can order meals here throughout the day and late into the evening—until the last satisfied customer leaves.

Bounty. Egmont St., Kingstown. ☎ **809/456-1776.** Snacks and sandwiches EC$3.85–EC$6 ($1.40–$2.20); main courses EC$10–EC$13 ($3.70–$4.80). No credit cards. Mon–Fri 8am–5pm, Sat 8am–1:30pm. AMERICAN/WEST INDIAN.

In the redbrick Troutman Building, in the center of Kingstown, you'll find the extremely affordable Bounty serving the local workers (the true power-lunch venue is Basil's, recommended above). A friendly local staff greets you, and people who work nearby frequent the place, making it their second home. Fill up on pastries of all kinds, rotis, hot dogs, hamburgers, and sandwiches, along with homemade soups. Fish and chips are also served, along with quiche and pizza. The cookery is just as simple as the surroundings. The interesting collection of drinks includes passion fruit and golden apple.

Dolphins Bar & Restaurant. Villa Beach. ☎ **809/457-4337.** Reservations required for dinner, recommended for lunch. Main courses $18–$40. AE, MC, V. Daily 10am–2am. CARIBBEAN.

Between the French Restaurant and Lime N' Pub, this restaurant specializes in fresh local ingredients, and handles them well. The staff is rather inexperienced, however, and not always helpful. A barbecue pit in the garden is busy all day. Don't come here for the decor, but to enjoy the fresh fish of the day—probably kingfish or snapper. Lobster frequently appears on the menu, as do conch and shrimp. One local food writer kept trying to get a recipe for a dish, only to be told, "Caribbean, Caribbean, Caribbean!" A soca band plays on Friday nights when the place becomes quite festive.

✪ **French Restaurant.** Villa Beach. ☎ **809/458-4972.** Reservations recommended. Main courses EC$40–EC$80 ($14.80–$29.60); lunch EC$8–EC$25 ($2.95–$9.25). AE, MC, V. Daily noon–2pm and 7–9:30pm. Closed Sept. FRENCH/SEAFOOD.

In a clapboard house 2 miles from the airport, near the pier where the ferry from Young Island docks, this is one of the most consistently good restaurants on the island. It offers a long, semishadowed bar, which you pass on your way to the rear veranda. Here, overlooking the moored yachts off the coast of Young Island, you can enjoy well-seasoned, Gallic-inspired food. Surrounded with vine-laced lattices, you may order seafood casserole or curried conch, shrimp in garlic sauce, or fresh fish in a ginger and peppercorn sauce. You can also order lobster fresh from a tank. Lunch is simpler and cheaper, with fresh fish, seafood kebabs, grilled cheesy steak, and spicy pineapple conch. The staff is inexperienced, but the food makes up for that.

Juliette's Restaurant. Egmont St., Kingstown. ☎ **809/457-1645.** Reservations not required. Rotis and sandwiches EC$3–EC$5 ($1.10–$1.85); fixed-price menus EC$10–EC$12 ($3.70–$4.45). No credit cards. Mon–Fri 8:30am–4:30pm, Sat 8:30am–2pm. WEST INDIAN.

Set amid the capital's cluster of administrative buildings, across from the National Commercial Bank, this restaurant dispenses more lunches to office workers than any other establishment in town. They do not serve breakfast, although they open early, and only offer snacks or lunch-type items in the morning. Meals are served in a clean and respectable dining area headed by a 27-year veteran of the restaurant trade, Juliette Campbell. (Ms. Campbell's husband is the island's well-known attorney general.) Menu items include soups, curried mutton, an array of fish, stewed chicken, stewed beef, and sandwiches. Many of the platters are garnished with fried plantains and rice. This is the type of cuisine you are likely to be served in a decent family-style boarding house in St. Vincent.

Lime N' Pub Restaurant. Opposite Young Island at Villa. ☎ **809/458-4227.** Main courses EC$30–EC$100 ($11.10–$37). AE, DC, MC, V. Daily noon–midnight. WEST INDIAN/INTERNATIONAL/INDIAN.

This is one of the island's most popular restaurants, opposite the superexpensive Young Island Hotel, right on Young Island Channel. It's the most congenial pub on the island, with a wide selection of pub grub, including pizzas. There's even a live lobster pond. A local band enlivens the atmosphere a few times every week in winter. In the more formalized section of this indoor and al fresco restaurant, you can partake of some good-tasting West Indian food, along with some dishes from India or the international kitchen. The rotis win high praise, but we gravitate to the fresh fish and lobster dishes instead. Coconut shrimp is generally excellent. Service is among the most hospitable on the island.

Rooftop Restaurant & Bar. Bay St., Kingstown. ☎ **809/457-2845.** Reservations not required for lunch, recommended for dinner. Main courses EC$25–EC$50 ($9.25–$18.50); lunch platters EC$18 ($6.70). AE, DISC, MC, V. Mon–Sat 8:30–10am, 11:30am–2pm, and 7–10pm. WEST INDIAN/INTERNATIONAL.

This restaurant does a thriving business because of its well-prepared food and its location three stories above the center of Kingstown. After you climb some flights of stairs, you'll see a bar near the entrance, an indoor area decorated in earth tones, and a patio open to the prevailing breezes. Lunches stress traditional Creole recipes using fresh fish, chicken, mutton, beef, and goat. Dinners are more international and include lobster, an excellent snapper with lemon-butter and garlic sauce, steaks with onions and mushrooms, and several savory preparations of pork. Every Wednesday and Friday a karaoke sing-along is featured, and on Saturday evening it's family night, with a barbecue along with a steel band in attendance after 6pm. In addition, 60 different drinks are featured at the bar.

FUN ON & OFF THE BEACH

BEACHES All beaches on St. Vincent are public, and many of the best ones border hotel properties, which you can patronize for drinks or luncheons. Most of the resorts are in the south, where the beaches have white or golden-yellow sand. However, many of the beaches in the north have sands with a lava ash color. The safest swimming is on the leeward beaches; the surf on the windward beaches is often rough and can be quite dangerous.

Some of the best beaches are the white sands of **Villa Beach** and the black sands of **Buccament Bay** or **Questelle's Bay,** all west-coast sites.

FISHING It's best to go to a local fisher for advice if you're interested in this sport, which your hotel can also arrange for you. The government of St. Vincent doesn't require visitors to take out a license. If you arrange things in time, it's sometimes possible to accompany the fisher on a trip, perhaps 4 or 5 miles from shore. A modest fee should suffice. The fishing fleet leaves from the leeward coast at Barrouallie. They've been known to return to shore with everything from a 6-inch redfish to a 20-foot pilot whale.

HIKING The best hikes are the **Vermont Nature Trails,** if you don't want to face Soufrière, which blows its volcanic top on occasions. These marked trails (get a map at the tourist office) take you through a rain forest in the middle of the island. You'll pass long-ago plantations that nature has reclaimed and enter a "Jungle Jim" world of tropical fruit trees. If it's your lucky day, you might even see the rare St. Vincent parrot with its flamboyant plumage. Wear good hiking shoes and your anti-mosquito cologne. You can stop in at **T&M Ltd.** in Kingstown (☎ **809/456-1616**) to get directions and the provisions for a picnic, everything from pâté to French cheese.

SAILING & YACHTING St. Vincent and the Grenadines are one of the great sailing centers of the Caribbean. Here you can obtain yachts that are fully provisioned if you want to go bareboating. If you're a well-heeled novice, you can hire a captain and a crew. Any hotel can recommend charter yachts.

SNORKELING & SCUBA DIVING The best area for snorkeling and scuba diving is the Villa/Young Island section on the southern end of the island.

Dive St. Vincent, on the Young Island Cut (☎ **809/457-4928**), has been owned and operated by a transplanted Texan, Bill Tewes, for more than 10 years. The oldest and best dive company in the country, Dive St. Vincent now has two additional dive shops: Dive Canouan, at the Tamarind Beach Hotel on Canouan Island, and Grenadines Dive, at the Sunny Grenadines Hotel on Union Island. The shops have a total of six instructors and three dive masters, as well as seven dive boats. The chain of dive shops allows visitors to dive or be certified with a consistency of quality while sailing throughout St. Vincent and the Grenadines. All shops offer dive/snorkel trips as well as sightseeing day trips and dive instruction. Single-tank dives cost $50 and two-tank dives go for $90, including all equipment and instructors and/or dive master guides. Dive packages are also available.

TENNIS **Young Island** and the **Grand View Beach Hotel** (see "Where to Stay," above) have tennis courts.

AN UNFORGETTABLE HIKE UP A VOLCANO

Exploring St. Vincent's hot volcano, **La Soufrière,** is an intriguing adventure. As you travel the island, you can't miss its cloud-capped splendor. This volcano has occasionally captured the attention of the world. The most recent eruption was in 1979, when the volcano spewed ashes, lava, and hot mud that covered the vegetation on its slopes and forced thousands of Vincentians to flee its fury. Belching rocks and black curling smoke filled the blue Caribbean sky. Jets of steam spouted 20,000 feet into the air. About 17,000 people were evacuated from a 10-mile ring around the volcano.

Fortunately, the eruption was in the sparsely settled northern part of the island. The volcano lies away from most of the tourism and commercial centers of St. Vincent, and even if it should erupt again, volcanologists don't consider it a danger to visitors lodged at beachside hotels along the leeward coast. The last major eruption of the volcano occurred in 1902, when 2,000 people were killed. Before its 1979 eruption, the volcano had been quiet since 1972. The activity that year produced a 324-foot-long island of lava rock jutting up from the water of Crater Lake.

At the rim of the crater you'll be rewarded with one of the most panoramic views in the Caribbean. That is, if the wind doesn't blow too hard and make you topple over into the crater itself! Extreme caution is emphasized. Looking inside, you can see the steam rising from the crater. The trail back down is much easier, we assure you.

Even if you're an experienced hiker, don't attempt to explore the volcano without a guide. Also, wear suitable hiking clothes and be sure that you're in the best of health before making the arduous journey. The easiest route is the 3-mile-long eastern route leaving from Rabacca. Some people attempt this on their own. The more arduous trail, longer by half a mile, is the western trail from Chateaubelair, which definitely requires a guide. The round-trip to the crater takes about five hours.

The **St. Vincent Forestry Headquarters,** in the village of Campden Park, about 3 miles from Kingstown along the west coast (☎ **809/457-8594**), offers a pamphlet giving hiking data to La Soufrière. It's open Monday to Friday from 8am to noon and 1 to 4pm. **Hazeco Tours** (☎ **809/457-8634**) offers guided hikes up to La Soufrière, costing $100 per couple, including lunch.

SEEING THE SIGHTS

Special events include the week-long **Carnival** in early July, one of the largest in the eastern Caribbean, with steel-band and calypso competitions, along with the crowning of the king and queen of the carnival.

KINGSTOWN Lush and tropical, the capital isn't as architecturally fascinating as St. George's on Grenada. Some English-style houses do exist, many of them looking as if they belonged in Penzance, Cornwall, instead of the Caribbean. However, you can still meet old-timers if you stroll on Upper Bay Street. White-haired and bearded, they can be seen loading their boats with produce grown on the mountain, before heading to some secluded beach in the Grenadines. This is a chief port and gateway to the Grenadines, and you can also view the small boats and yachts that have dropped anchor here. The place is a magnet for charter sailors.

At the top of a winding road on the north side of Kingstown, **Fort Charlotte** (☎ **809/456-1165**) was built on Johnson Point around the time of the American Revolution, enclosing one side of the bay. The ruins aren't much to inspect; the reason to come here is the view. The fort sits atop a steep promontory some 640 feet above the sea. From its citadel, you'll have a commanding sweep of the leeward shores to the north, Kingstown to the south, and the Grenadines beyond. On a clear day you can even see Grenada. Three cannons used to fight off French troops are still in place. You'll see a series of oil murals depicting the history of black Caribs. Admission is free, and it's open 24 hours.

The second major sight is the ✪ **Botanic Gardens,** on the north side of Kingstown (☎ **809/457-1003**). Founded in 1765 by Governor George Melville, they are the oldest botanic gardens in the West Indies. In this Windward Eden, you'll see 20 acres of such tropical exotics as teak, almond, cinnamon, nutmeg, cannonball, and mahogany; some of the trees are more than two centuries old. One of the breadfruit trees was reputedly among those original seedlings brought to this island by Captain Bligh in 1793. There's also a large *Spachea perforata* (the Soufrière tree), a species believed to be unique to St. Vincent and not found in the wild since 1812. The gardens are open daily from 6am to 6pm. Admission is free.

✪ THE LEEWARD HIGHWAY The leeward or west side of the island has the most dramatic scenery. North of Kingstown, you rise into lofty terrain before descending to the water again. There are views in all directions. On your right you'll pass the Aqueduct Golf Course before reaching Layou. If you want to play golf, check its status, as it has sporadic hours. Here you can see the massive **Carib Rock,** with a human face carving dating back to A.D. 600. This is one of the finest petroglyphs in the Caribbean.

Continuing north you reach **Barrouallie,** where there's a Carib stone altar. Even if you're not into fishing, you might want to spend some time in this whaling village, where some still occasionally set out in brightly painted boats armed with harpoons, Moby Dick style, to seek the elusive whale. But environmentalists should note that while Barrouallie may be one of the last few outposts in the world where such whale-hunting is carried on, Vincentians point out that it doesn't endanger an already endangered species since so few are caught each year. If one is caught, it's an occasion for festivities.

The leeward highway continues to **Chateaubelair,** the end of the line. Here you can swim at the attractive **Richmond Beach** before heading back to Kingstown. In the distance, the volcano, La Soufrière, looms menacingly in the mountains.

The adventurous set out from here to see the **Falls of Baleine,** 7½ miles north of Richmond Beach on the northern tip of the island, accessible only by boat. Baleine is a freshwater falls that comes from a stream in the volcanic hills. If you're interested in making the trip, check with the tourist office in Kingstown for tour information.

THE WINDWARD HIGHWAY This road runs along the eastern Atlantic coast from Kingstown. Waves pound the surf, and panoramic seascapes are all along the rocky shores. If you want to go swimming along this often-dangerous coast, stick to the sandy spots, as they offer safer shores. Along this road you'll pass coconut and banana plantations and fields of arrowroot.

North of Georgetown lies the **Rabacca Dry River,** which shows the flow of lava from the volcano when it erupted at the beginning of the 20th century. The journey from Kingstown to here is only 24 miles, but it will seem like much longer. For those who want to go the final 11 miles along a rugged road to **Fancy,** the northern tip of the island, a Land Rover, Jeep, or Moke will be needed.

MARRIQUA VALLEY Sometimes known as the Mesopotamia Valley, this area is one of the lushest cultivated valleys in the eastern Caribbean. Surrounded by mountain ridges, the drive takes you through a landscape planted with nutmeg, cocoa, coconut, breadfruit, and bananas. The road begins at Vigie Highway, to the east of the E. T. Joshua Airport runway. At Montréal you'll come upon natural mineral springs. Only rugged vehicles should make this trip.

Around Kingstown, you can also enjoy the **Queen's Drive,** a scenic loop into the high hills to the east of the capital. From here, the view is panoramic over Kingstown and its yacht-clogged harbor to the Grenadines in the distance.

SHOPPING

You don't come to St. Vincent to shop, but once here, you might pick up some of the Sea Island cotton fabrics and clothing that are specialties here. In addition, Vincentian artisans make pottery, jewelry, and baskets that have souvenir value at least.

Since Kingstown consists of about 12 small blocks, you can walk and browse and see about everything in a morning's shopping jaunt. Try to be in town for the colorful, noisy **Friday-morning market.** You might not purchase anything, but you'll surely enjoy the riot of color.

Juliette's Fashions. Back St. ☎ **809/456-1143.**

Owned and operated by the same entrepreneur who runs Juliette's Restaurant, this is the best-stocked and most glamorous women's clothing store on St. Vincent, but that's not saying a lot. Beneficiary of its owner's frequent buying trips to Miami and New York, it's one of the few outlets on the island to sell semiformal evening wear.

Noah's Arkade. Bay St., Kingstown. ☎ **809/457-1513.**

Noah's sells gifts from the West Indies, including wood carvings, T-shirts, and a wide range of books and souvenirs. Noah's has shops at the Frangipani Hotel in Bequia.

St. Vincent Handcraft Centre. Frenches Gate, Kingstown. ☎ **809/457-2516.**

Set in an early 19th-century cotton factory, on the northern outskirts of Kingstown, this well-recommended shop stockpiles the island's largest displays of macramé, pottery, textiles, metalwork jewelry, as well as grass mats and baskets. Some of the goods are made by artisans who labor on-site.

St. Vincent Philatelic Services. Bonadie's Building, Bay St., Kingstown. ☎ **809/457-1911.**

This is the largest operating bureau in the Caribbean, and its issues are highly acclaimed by stamp collectors around the world. Stamp enthusiasts can visit or order by mail.

Sprott Brothers. Homeworks, Bay St. ☎ **809/457-1121.**

At this department store you can buy clothing designed by Vincentians, along with an array of fabrics, linens, and silk-screened T-shirts, and even Caribbean-made furniture. In fact, there's a little bit of everything here.

Y. de Lima. Bay and Egmont Sts., Kingstown. ☎ **809/457-1681.**

The familiar Y. de Lima is well stocked with cameras, stereo equipment, toys, clocks, binoculars, and jewelry, the best selection on the island. Paragon bone china is sold, along with a selection of gift items. Caribbean gold and silver jewelry are also featured.

ST. VINCENT AFTER DARK

The focus is mainly on the hotels, and activities are likely to include nighttime barbecues and dancing to steel bands. In season, at least one hotel seems to have something planned every night during the week. Beer is extremely cheap at all the places noted below.

The Aquatic Club. Adjacent to the departure point of the ferryboat from St. Vincent to Young Island. ☎ **809/458-4205.**

During party nights when it rocks and rolls (usually Wednesday, Saturday, and Sunday), this is the loudest, most raucous, and most animated nightspot on St. Vincent, a source of giddy fun to its fans and a sore bone of contention to nearby hotel guests who claim they can't sleep because of the noise. On these nights, things heat up by 11pm and continue until as late as 3am. The other nights of the week the place functions just as a bar, with a spate of recorded music, but without the high-volume live bands that keep the three-times-per-week parties jumping. Centered around an open-sided veranda and an outdoor deck, the place is open every night from 9pm to 2 or 3am, and there's always a cover charge of between EC$5 and EC$20 ($1.85 and $7.40).

The Attic. In the Kentucky Bldg., at Melville and Back Sts., Kingstown. ☎ **809/457-2558.** Cover EC$5–EC$50 ($1.90–$18.50), depending on the entertainment.

The air-conditioned Attic features jazz and easy-listening music. Music is live only on Friday and Saturday; Tuesday and Thursday it's recorded. Wednesday is karaoke night. Fish and burgers are available.

Touch Entertainment Centre (TEC). Back St., Kingstown. ☎ **809/457-1825.**

Opposite Kentucky Fried Chicken on the top floor of the Cambridge Building, this is the best-known nightspot in the region. With advanced lighting, it's a soundproof (from the outside), air-conditioned environment, popular with tourists. Every Wednesday night in summer is disco night, especially for the young and restless. Friday and Sunday nights the club has a house party with a DJ. Surprisingly, they are not open on Saturday night.

4 The Grenadines

South of St. Vincent, this small chain of islands extends for more than 40 miles and offers the finest yachting area in the eastern Caribbean. The islands are strung like a necklace of precious stones and have such romantic-sounding names as Bequia, Mustique, Canouan, and Petit St. Vincent. We'll explore Union and Palm Islands, and Mayreau as well.

A few of the islands have accommodations, which we'll visit, but many are so small and so completely undeveloped that they attract only beachcombers and stray boaters.

Populated by the descendants of African slaves and administered by St. Vincent, the Grenadines collectively add up to a land mass of 30 square miles. These bits of land, often dots on nautical charts, may lack natural resources, yet they're blessed with white-sand beaches, coral reefs, and their own kind of sleepy beauty. If you don't spend the night in the Grenadines, you should at least go over for the day to visit one of them and enjoy a picnic lunch (which your hotel will pack for you) on one of the long stretches of beach.

GETTING THERE

BY PLANE Four of the Grenadines—Bequia, Mustique, Union Island, and Canouan—have small airports, the landing spots for flights on **Mustique Airways** (☎ **809/458-4380** on St. Vincent). Its planes are technically charters, although flights depart St. Vincent for Bequia on Monday, Wednesday, Friday, and Sunday at 8am. The cost is EC$80 ($29.60) round-trip.

BY BOAT The ideal way to go, of course, is to rent your own yacht, as many wealthy visitors do. But a far less expensive method of transport is to go on a mail, cargo, or passenger boat as the locals do, but you'll need time and patience. However, boats do run on schedules. The **government mail boat,** MV *Baracuda,* leaves St. Vincent on Monday and Thursday at 10:30am, stops at Bequia, Canouan, and Mayreau, and arrives at Union Island at about 3:45pm. On Tuesday and Friday, the boat leaves Union Island at about 6:30am, stops at Mayreau and Canouan, reaches Bequia at about 10:45am, and makes port at St. Vincent at noon. One-way fares from St. Vincent are: to Bequia, EC$10 ($3.70) Monday to Friday and EC$12 ($4.45) on weekends; to Canouan, EC$13 ($4.80); to Mayreau, EC$15 ($5.55); and to Union Island, EC$20 ($7.40).

You can also reach Bequia Monday through Saturday on the *Admiral I* and *II.* For information on these sea trips, inquire at the **Tourist Board,** Bay Street, in Kingstown (☎ **809/457-1502**).

BEQUIA

Only 7 square miles of land, Bequia (pronounced *BECK-wee*) is the largest of the Grenadines. It's the northernmost island in the Grenadines (only 9 miles south of St. Vincent), offering quiet lagoons, reefs, and long stretches of nearly deserted beaches. Descended from seafarers and other early adventurers, its population of some 6,000 will give you a friendly greeting if you pass them along the road. Of the inhabitants, 10% are of Scottish ancestry, who live mostly in the Mount Pleasant region. A feeling of relaxation and informality prevails on Bequia. There's a small airport, and you can also travel here by boat (see "Getting There," above).

GETTING AROUND **Rental cars,** owned by local people, are available at the port, and you can hire a **taxi** at the dock to take you around or to your hotel if you're spending the night. Taxis are reasonably priced, but an even better bet are the so-called **dollar cabs,** which take you anywhere on the island for a small fee. They don't seem to have a regular schedule—you just flag one down. Before going to your hotel, drop in at the circular **Tourist Information Centre** (you'll see it right on the beach). Here you can ask for a driver who's familiar with the attractions of the island (all of them are). You should negotiate the fare in advance.

WHERE TO STAY

✪ **Friendship Bay Resort.** Friendship Cove (P.O. Box 9), Bequia, The Grenadines, St. Vincent, W.I. ☎ **809/458-3222.** Fax 809/458-3840. 27 rms, 1 suite. Winter, $150–$225 double; $300–$350 suite. Off-season, $110–$150 double; $200 suite. Rates include continental breakfast. MAP $25 per person extra. MC, V.

In this beachfront resort, the well-decorated rooms offer private verandas and lie nestled in 12 acres of tropical gardens. The complex, an excellent lodging value, stands on a sloping hillside above a crescent of one of the best beaches on the island, at Friendship Cove, with its white sands. Guests have a view of the sea and neighboring islands. Brightly colored curtains, bedspreads, handmade wall hangings, and grass rugs decorate the rooms, which are cooled by the trade winds. The owners have added a beach bar with swinging chairs in Caribbean style, and they offer "jump-ups" on Saturday nights in winter, with music provided by a band. The food is good too, with many island specialties on the menu. You can enjoy water sports and tennis here or take boat excursions.

Old Fort Country Inn. Mount Pleasant, Bequia, The Grenadines, St. Vincent, W.I. ☎ **809/458-3440.** Fax 809/457-3340. 6 rms. Winter, $240 double. Off-season, $210 double. Rates include MAP. AE, MC, V. Closed Aug–Sept.

A special hideaway has been created from the ruins of a French-built plantation house commanding the best views on Bequia. At a point 450 feet above the sea, the climate is excellent, with no mosquitoes. Historical dates list the property from 1756 (it may be older), and the 3-foot-thick walls are made from cobblestones. In the reconstruction, the owner matched the original style by using the old stones with exposed ceiling beams and rafters, creating a medieval feel. The resort sits on 30 tropical acres. The atmospheric restaurant holds eight tables, serving four- or five-course dinners. The fine cuisine offers Creole and Mediterranean specialties, including a whole barbecued fish. Dinner is served nightly at 7:30pm. The owners recently built a 15-by-30-foot freshwater pool, with views of the ocean on three sides. There are also nature trails on the property. The nearest beach is a 10-minute hike from the hotel, but is part of the property.

✪ **Plantation House.** Admiralty Bay (P.O. Box 16), Bequia, The Grenadines, St. Vincent, W.I. ☎ **809/458-3425.** Fax 809/458-3612. 27 units. A/C MINIBAR TV TEL. Winter, $389–$426 double. Off-season, $253–$307 double. Rates include MAP. AE, MC, V.

Completely renovated in 1989, the Plantation House lies on Admiralty Bay, just a five-minute walk from the center of town along the beach. The informal hotel has a "new Caribbean style," and it's the most luxurious place to stay on the island. The accommodations consist of 17 West Indian "superior" cottages, painted in peach and white, each with its own private porch, plus luxury beachfront units with fans and five deluxe rooms with air-conditioning in the main house. Bedrooms are furnished and decorated in a fresh-looking Caribbean style, with color and textures such as bamboo and flower prints. The facilities include a dining room, a bar, a beach-bar grill, and a kidney-shaped beachside pool, all set in 10 acres of tropical gardens. There is hotel bar service on the beach. The cuisine is excellent, and barbecues, tennis, and scuba diving are offered. See "Where to Dine," below.

Spring on Bequia. Spring Bay, Bequia, The Grenadines, St. Vincent, W.I. ☎ **809/458-3414,** or 612/823-1202 in Minneapolis. Fax 809/457-3305. 10 rms. Winter, $120–$205 double. Apr 15–June 15 and Nov–Dec 14, $70–$140 double. MAP $40 per person extra. AE, DC, DISC, MC, V. Closed June 16–Oct.

In the late 1960s the Frank Lloyd Wright design of this hotel won an award from the American Institute of Architects. Fashioned from beautifully textured honey-colored stone, it has a flattened hip roof inspired by the old plantation houses of Martinique. Constructed on the 18th-century foundations of a West Indian homestead, it sits in the middle of 28 acres of hillside orchards, producing oranges, grapefruit, bananas, breadfruit, plums, and mangos. Because of the almost-constant blossoming of one crop or another, you always get the feeling of springtime (hence the name of the establishment). Candy Leslie, the Minnesota-born owner, will welcome you. From the main building's stone bar and open-air dining room, you might hear the bellowing of a herd of cows. On the premises is a swimming pool and a tennis court. Each of the units is ringed with stone and contains Japanese-style screens to filter the sun. The sandy beach is a three-minute walk away through a coconut grove, but it's too shallow for good swimming.

Where to Dine

The food is good and healthy here—lobster, chicken, and steaks from such fish as dolphin, kingfish, and grouper, plus tropical fruits, fried plantains, and coconut and guava puddings made fresh daily. Even the beach bars are kept spotless.

Frangipani. In the Hotel Frangipani, Port Elizabeth. ☎ **809/458-3255.** Reservations required for dinner. Main courses EC$20–EC$50 ($7.40–$18.50); fixed-price meal EC$42–EC$80 ($15.50–$29.60); Thurs barbecue EC$65 ($24.10). AE, MC, V. Daily 7:30am–5pm and 7–9pm. Closed Sept to mid-Oct. CARIBBEAN.

This waterside dining room is one of the best restaurants on the island (although we give the nod to the food at Plantation House). The yachting crowd often comes ashore to dine here. With the exception of the juicy steaks imported for barbecues, only local food is used in the succulent specialties. Lunches, served throughout the day, include sandwiches, salads, and seafood platters. Dinner specialties feature conch chowder, baked chicken with rice-and-coconut stuffing, lobster, and an array of fresh fish. A fixed-price menu is available, or you can order à la carte. A Thursday-night barbecue with a steel band is an island event.

Friendship Bay Resort. Port Elizabeth. ☎ **809/458-3222.** Reservations required for dinner. Main courses EC$32–EC$75 ($11.85–$27.75); lunch EC$18–EC$45 ($6.65–$16.65). MC, V. Daily noon–3pm and 7:30–10pm. Closed Sept–Oct 15. INTERNATIONAL/WEST INDIAN.

You'll find this friendly dining room in the previously recommended hotel. Guests dine in a candlelit room high above a sweeping expanse of seafront on a hillside rich with the scent of frangipani and hibiscus. Lunch is served at the beach bar, but dinner is more elaborate. It might include grilled lobster in season, curried beef, grilled or broiled fish (served Creole style with a spicy sauce), shrimp curry, and charcoal-grilled steak flambé. Dishes are flavorful and well prepared. An island highlight is the Friday and Saturday night jump-up and barbecue.

✪ **Plantation House.** Admiralty Bay. ☎ **809/458-3425.** Main courses EC$45–EC$50 ($16.65–$18.50). AE, MC, V. Daily 7–10pm. CREOLE/INTERNATIONAL.

The premier dining spot on the island is in this previously recommended hotel. Although informal, evenings here are the most elegant on Bequia. The service is first rate, as is the food. Many visit just for lunch. Of course salads, cold dishes, and burgers are available, even a quiche of the day, but you can also order the poached catch of the day in a white-wine sauce or the pasta of the day. A more romantic aura prevails in the evening. The chef emphasizes fresh ingredients, a blend of some of the finest of European cookery along with West Indian spice and flair. Try the chicken cordon bleu with mousseline potatoes, christophene in cheese sauce, and buttered pumpkin, or the roast breast of duck with orange sauce. Curried conch is a local specialty.

Whaleboner Inn. Admiralty Bay, Port Elizabeth. ☎ **809/458-3233.** Reservations required for dinner. Dinner $20–$30. AE, MC, V. Daily 8am–10:30pm. CARIBBEAN/SEAFOOD.

An enduring favorite, the Whaleboner is still going strong, serving dishes with the most authentic island flavor on Bequia. It's next to the Hotel Frangipani, directly south of Port Elizabeth. Inside, the bar is carved from the jawbone of a giant whale, and the bar stools are made from the vertebrae. Dinner is only served from 7 to 10:30pm, although the bar often stays open later, depending on the crowd. The owners offer the best pizza on the island, along with a selection of fish and chips or well-made sandwiches for lunch. At night you may want one of the wholesome dinners prepared by a West Indian cook, including a choice of lobster, fish, chicken, or steak. We prefer the curried-conch dinner beginning with the callaloo soup. Favored by the yachting set, the restaurant has full bar service.

Exploring the Island

Obviously, the secluded beaches are tops on everyone's list of Bequia's attractions. As you walk along the beaches, especially near Port Elizabeth, you'll see craftspeople building boats by hand, a method they learned from their ancestors. Whalers sometimes still set out from here in wooden boats with hand harpoons, just as they do from a port village on St. Vincent.

Dive Bequia, Gingerbread House, Admiralty Bay (P.O. Box 16), Bequia, St. Vincent, W.I. (☎ **809/458-3504**), specializes in diving and snorkeling. Scuba dives cost $50 for one, $85 for two in the same day, and $400 for a 10-dive package. Introductory lessons go for $15 each per person. A four-dive open-water certification course is $400. A snorkeling trip is $15 per person. These prices include all the necessary equipment.

The main harbor village, **Port Elizabeth** is known for its safe anchorage, Admiralty Bay. The bay was a haven in the 17th century for the British, French, and Spanish navies, as well as for pirates. Descendants of Captain Kydd (aka Kidd) still live on the island. Today the yachting set anchors here, often bringing a kind of excitement to the locals.

Frankly, after you leave Port Elizabeth there aren't many sights, and you'll probably have your driver, booked for the day, drop you off for a long, leisurely lunch and some time on a beach. However, you'll pass a fort with a harbor view and drive on to Industry Estates, which has a Beach House restaurant serving a fair lunch. At **Paget Farm,** you can wander into an old whaling village and maybe inspect a few jawbones leftover from the catches of yesterday.

At Moonhole, there's a vacation and retirement community built into the cliffs as practically a free-form sculpture. These are private homes, of course, and you're not to enter without permission. For a final look at Bequia, head up an 800-foot hill that the local people call **"The Mountain."** From that perch, you'll have a 360° view of St. Vincent and the Grenadines to the south.

Shopping

This is not a particularly good reason to come to Bequia, but there are some interesting stores.

The Crab Hole. Next door to the Plantation House, Admiralty Bay. ☎ **809/458-3290.**

At shops scattered along the water you can buy hand-screened cotton made by Bequians. The best of these is the Crab Hole, where they invite guests to visit their silk-screen factory in back. Later you can make purchases at their shop in front, including sterling-silver and 14-karat-gold jewelry.

Noah's Arkade. In the Frangipani Hotel, Port Elizabeth. ☎ **809/458-3424.**

Island entrepreneur Lavinia Gunn sells Vincentian and Bequian batiks, scarves, hats, T-shirts, and a scattering of pottery. There are also dolls, place mats, baskets, and homemade jellies concocted from grapefruit, mango, and guava, plus West Indian cookbooks and books on tropical flowers and reef fish. This place stands a few steps from the terrace bar of the Frangipani Hotel.

Sargeant's Model Boatshop Bequia. Front St., Port Elizabeth. ☎ **809/458-3344.**

Anyone on the island can show you the way to the workshops of Sargeant's Model Boatshop Bequia, lying west of the pier past the oil-storage facility. Sought out by yacht owners looking for a scale-model reproduction of their favorite vessel, Lawson Sargeant is the self-taught wood carver who established this business. The models are carved from a soft local wood called gumwood, then painted in brilliant colors of red, green, gray, or blue, whatever your fancy dictates. When a scale model of the royal family's yacht, *Britannia,* was commissioned in 1985, it required five weeks of work and meticulous blueprints and cost $10,000. You can pick up a model of a Bequia whaling boat for much less. The Sargeant family usually keeps 100 model boats in many shapes and sizes in inventory.

MUSTIQUE

This island of luxury villas, which someone once called "Georgian West Indian," is so remote and small it almost deserves to be unknown, and it would be if it weren't for Princess Margaret and other world-class celebrities who have cottages here.

The island is privately owned by a consortium of businesspeople. When word of Princess Margaret's retreat splashed on front pages in London, it was owned by beer baron Colin Tennant, a millionaire Scottish nobleman (now known as Lord Glenconner). After Princess Margaret, a host of celebrities followed, including Truman Capote, Paul Newman, Mick Jagger, Raquel Welch, Richard Avedon, and Prince Andrew.

The island is only 3 miles long and 1 mile wide, and it has only one major hotel (see below). It's located 15 miles south of St. Vincent. After settling in, you'll find many good white-sand beaches against a backdrop of luxuriant foliage. Our favorite is **Macaroni Beach,** where the water is turquoise.

On the northern reef of Mustique lies the wreck of the French liner *Antilles,* which ran aground on the Pillories in 1971. Today its massive hulk, now gutted, can be seen cracked and rusting a few yards offshore, an eerie sight.

If you wish to tour the small island, you can rent a Mini-Moke to see some of the most elegant homes in the Caribbean. To stay on Mustique, you can even rent Les Jolies Eaux (Pretty Waters)—that is, if you can afford it. This is the Caribbean home of Princess Margaret. A five-bedroom/five-bath house, it has a large swimming pool, naturally. Accommodating 10 guests, it's available only when Her Royal Highness is not in residence. If you rent it, the princess will require references.

GETTING THERE & GETTING AROUND The best way to go to Mustique is by air charter on **Mustique Airways** (☎ **809/458-4380** in St. Vincent), which maintains two daily commuter flights between St. Vincent and Mustique. Flights depart St. Vincent daily at 7:30am and 4:30pm and land on Mustique about 10 minutes later. Flights then head immediately back to St. Vincent. Chartered planes arrive on Mustique on the small airstrip in the middle of the bird sanctuary. The airport closes at dusk because there are no landing lights. The cost is EC$110 ($40.70), and there's no discount for same-day returns.

Once here, you can call **Michael's Taxi** (☎ **809/458-4621,** ext. 448). But chances are, someone at the Cotton House will already have seen you land.

WHERE TO STAY

✪ **The Cotton House.** Mustique, The Grenadines, St. Vincent, W.I. ☎ **800/826-2809** in the U.S., or 809/456-4777. Fax 809/456-5887. 20 rms and suites. MINIBAR TEL. Winter, $740–$1,090 double. Off-season, $490–$890 double. Rates are inclusive. AE, MC, V.

The Caribbean's most exclusive hotel, once operated as a private club, is as casually elegant and palpably British as its clientele. The 18th-century main house is built of coral and stone and was painstakingly restored, rebuilt, and redecorated by Oliver Messel, uncle by marriage to Princess Margaret. The entire property was again renovated in 1996. The design of the hotel is characterized by arched louvered doors and cedar shutters. The antique loggia sets the style, and the decor includes everything from Lady Bateman's steamer trunks to a scallop-shell fountain on a quartz base. Guests sit here and enjoy their sundowners, perhaps after a game on the tennis court or a swim in the pool surrounded by Messel's "Roman ruins." Some of the rooms were also originally designed by Messel. Units are in two fully restored Georgian houses, a trio of cottages, a newer block of four rooms, and a five-room beach house, all of which open onto windswept balconies or patios.

Dining/Entertainment: The hotel enjoys an outstanding reputation for its West Indian/continental food and service. Nonguests are welcome to dine here, but must reserve. The hotel also has three bars. You might find Mick Jagger at one of them.

Services: Room service, laundry, baby-sitting.

Facilities: Two tennis courts, deep-sea fishing, sailboats, horseback riding. Guests go between two beaches, each lying only a couple of minutes walk away—Endeavour Bay, on the leeward side, with calmer waters, and L'Ansecoy, on the other side. Jagger owns a Japanese-style villa opening onto this beach.

✪ **Firefly.** Mustique, The Grenadines, St. Vincent, W.I. ☎ **809/456-3414.** Fax 809/456-3514. 4 rms. Year-round, $250 double. Rates include full breakfast. AE, MC, V.

Firefly, which used to be the island's only budget hostelry, has been upgraded by its new owner, Elizabeth Clayton, from Sussex, England. The rooms overlook Britannia Bay and the Lower Grenadines, and Basil's Bar is only five minutes away, as is a good white-sand beach. The rooms have an airy openness and contain four-poster beds. All the bathrooms have been overhauled and have antique pedestal sinks and showers. One room has a bathtub protruding out into the trees. The most sumptuous room is the Garden Room, a private suite unique in the Grenadines. Separate from the main house, it has its own large balcony and views over the garden to the ocean. The hotel restaurant specializes in authentic Caribbean dishes, and the bar affords the island's best sunset views.

Where to Dine

Basil's Beach Bar. 13 Britannia Bay. ☎ **809/458-4621.** Reservations not required. Main courses EC$45–EC$85 ($16.70–$31.45). AE, MC, V. Daily 11am–7pm and 7:30–10:30pm. (Bar, daily 8am "until very late.") SEAFOOD.

Nobody ever goes to this island of indigenous farmers and fisherfolk without spending a night drinking at Basil's, a South Seas–type place more authentic than any reproduction in an old Dorothy Lamour flick. It's the gathering place for yachters, as well as owners of those luxurious villas. Who knows who might be at the next table? Maybe Princess Margaret, Spike Lee, Mick Jagger, Jerry Hall, David Bowie, Stephen Segal, or Michael Caine, or an array of fashion models, princes, filmmakers, and most definitely royal photographer Lord Lichfield. The bar, but mainly its owner, has received a lot of newspaper publicity. Its greeter, Basil S. Charles, is a 6-foot, 4-inch heavily muscled charmer whom *Esquire* magazine called "the island's most famous product after its sandy beaches."

Some people come here to drink and see the panoramic view, but Basil's is also, by reputation, one of the finest seafood restaurants in the Caribbean. Both lunch and dinner are served daily at this establishment built on piers above the sea. You can dine under the open-air sunscreens or with the sun blazing down on you. On Wednesday night in winter you can "jump-up" at a barbecue. A boutique is also on the premises. On nights when there's a live band, there's a EC$15 ($5.55) cover charge.

CANOUAN

In the shape of a half circle, Canouan is surrounded by coral reefs and blue lagoons. The island is only $3^1/_2$ miles by $1^1/_2$ miles in size and is visited mainly by those who want to enjoy its splendid long beaches. Canouan has a population of fewer than 2,000 people, many of whom fish for a living and reside in **Retreat Village,** the island's only hamlet.

The governing island, St. Vincent, lies 14 miles to the north, and Grenada is 20 miles to the south. Canouan rises from its sandy beaches to the 800-foot-high peak of Mount Royal in the north. Here you'll find unspoiled forests of white cedar.

GETTING THERE You can reach Canouan only by air by taking a charter flight on **Mustique Airways** (☎ **809/458-4380** in St. Vincent). The cost from St. Vincent to Canouan is EC$110 ($40.70) per airplane each way; the aircraft carries only nine passengers. You can also reach Canouan from St. Vincent by boat (see "Getting There," in the introduction to the Grenadines, above).

WHERE TO STAY

Canouan Beach Hotel. South Glossy Bay, Canouan, St. Vincent, W.I. (c/o Mr. Joe Nadal, Manager, Canouan Beach Hotel, Canouan Post Office, St. Vincent, W.I.). ☎ **809/458-8888.** Fax 809/458-8875. 32 rms. A/C. Winter, $183–$210 per person double. Off-season, $146–$168 per person double. Rates are all-inclusive, except for alcohol. MC, V. Guests fly to Barbados, where a chartered plane from Mustique Airways flies guests on to Canouan (the hotel will arrange this in advance of your arrival); the price is $110 per person each way from Barbados to Canouan; from the airport, take a taxi, a 5-minute ride.

Until 1996 this was the only resort on an island with nothing but sandy beaches and a sweltering scrub-covered landscape. Opened in 1984 and set on 7 acres of glaringly white beachfront, it does a thriving business with escapist Europeans (primarily French, German, and English) in search of few distractions and a life patterned on Gauguin. The location is about $^1/_8$ mile from the island's airport, on a periwinkle-dotted peninsula jutting out between the Atlantic and the Caribbean. Don't expect to find a lot to do other than sleep, swim, sunbathe, snorkel, sail, and reminisce about the people and things you left behind. The resort's social center lies beneath the sun-screen of a mahogany-trussed parapet whose sides are open, like virtually everything else here, to views of the water. A pair of lush but uninhabited islands lie offshore. Snorkeling, windsurfing, small sailboats, and a catamaran are available without charge to guests. All water sports, dining (usually in the form of buffet lunches and barbecue-style suppers), and soft drinks are included in the all-inclusive price (but there are extra charges for alcohol). Accommodations are in stone-sided buildings with sliding glass doors and uncomplicated furnishings. The resort's predominant organized activity involves a 36-foot catamaran, which departs on seaborne excursions six afternoons a week.

UNION ISLAND

Midway between Grenada and St. Vincent, Union Island is the southernmost of the Grenadines. It's known for its dramatic 900-foot peak, Mount Parnassus, which yachting people can often see from miles away. For those cruising in the area, Union is the port of entry for St. Vincent. Yachters are required to check with Customs upon entry.

Perhaps you'll sail into Union on a night when the locals are having a "big drum" dance, in which costumed islanders dance and chant to the beat of drums made of goatskin.

GETTING THERE The island is reached either by chartered or scheduled aircraft, by cargo boat, by private yacht, or by mail boat (see "Getting There" in section 3 on

St. Vincent and at the beginning of this section). **Air Martinique** (☎ **809/458-4528**) flies to Union Island from both Martinique and St. Vincent, and **LIAT** (☎ **809/457-1821**) flies here from St. Vincent.

Where to Stay & Dine

Anchorage Yacht Club. Clifton, Union Island, The Grenadines, St. Vincent, W.I. ☎ **809/458-8221.** Fax 809/458-8365. 6 rms, 3 bungalows, 3 apts. A/C. Winter, $110 double; $150 bungalow or apt. Off-season, $90 double; $140 bungalow or apt. Rates include continental breakfast. Additional person $35 extra. 7% tax extra. MC, V.

This club occupies a prominent position a few steps from the bumpy airplane landing strip that services at least two nearby resorts (Petit St. Vincent and Palm Island) and about a half dozen small islands nearby. As such, something of an airline hub aura permeates the place as passengers shuttle between their airplanes, boats, and the establishment's bar and restaurant. Although at least two other hotels are nearby, this is the most important. It combines a threefold function as a hotel, a restaurant, and a bar, with (under different management) a busy marine-service facility in the same scrubby, concrete-sided compound. Each of the bedrooms is set between a pair of airy verandas and has white tile floors and simple, somewhat-sunbleached modern furniture. The most popular units are the bungalows and cabañas beside the beach.

The yachting club meets in the wood-and-stone bar, where you can order meals for EC$80 ($29.60) and up. The menu might include fish soup, a wide array of fresh fish, and Creole versions of lamb, pork, and beef. Try the mango daiquiri. The bar is open all day and into the night, but meals are served daily: breakfast from 7 to 10am, lunch from noon to 2:30pm, and dinner from 7 to 10:30pm.

PALM ISLAND

Is this island a resort or is the resort the island? Casual elegance and privacy prevail on these 130 acres in the southern Grenadines. Surrounded by five white-sand beaches, the island is sometimes called "Prune," so one can easily understand the more appealing name change. A little islet in the sun, it offers complete peace and quiet with plenty of sea, sand, sun, and sailing.

GETTING THERE To get to Palm Island, you must first fly to Union Island (see "Getting There" in section 3 on St. Vincent for details). From Union Island, a hotel launch will take you to Palm Island.

Where to Stay & Dine

Palm Island Beach Club. Palm Island, The Grenadines, St. Vincent, W.I. ☎ **800/999-PALM** in the U.S., or 809/458-8824. Fax 809/458-8804. 24 rms. Winter, $290–$365 double. Off-season, $270 double. Rates include all meals, afternoon tea, tennis, use of snorkeling gear, and airport transfers. AE, DISC, MC, V.

This place is the fulfillment of John and Mary Caldwell's long-cherished wish to establish a hotel on an idyllic and isolated island. That dream came true, and in time such celebs as Ted Kennedy, Barbra Streisand, Donald Trump, and Françoise Sagan showed up. John is nicknamed "Coconut Johnny" because of his hobby of planting palms. At Prune Island, he planted hundreds upon hundreds of trees until its name was changed to Palm Island. An adventurer, this Texan once set out to sail by himself across the Pacific, coming to rest off the coast of Fiji. He made it to Australia, where he constructed his own ketch, *Outward Bound,* loaded his family aboard, and took off again. Eventually he made it to the Grenadines, where he operated a charter business. His exploits, including getting embroiled in a hurricane, were documented in the autobiographical book *Desperate Voyage,* an account of his 106-day, 8,500-mile journey at sea.

He eventually built this cottage colony with enough room for 50 guests spaced under palms on the white-sand beach. Accommodations are in the Beach Club duplex cottages or in one of the villas, which are built of stone and wood, with louvered walls as well as sliding glass doors that open onto terraces. All rooms are superior, with ceiling fans, window screens, rattan furniture, beach lounges, private showers, small refrigerators, and outdoor walled patios on the oceanfront.

Dining is in a South Seas–style pavilion where the food is good and plentiful. The nautically oriented guests like to have tall drinks at the Sunset Beach Bar or at the nearby Yacht Club Bar and Restaurant. There are barbecues twice a week, calypso on Wednesday, and a Saturday evening "jump-up." Sailboats and scuba equipment are available for rental, and snorkeling gear, table tennis, and Sunfish sailing are offered free. Guests can also make day sails to Tobago Cays and Mayreau on a 37-foot CSY yacht.

PETIT ST. VINCENT

A private island 4 miles from Union in the southern Grenadines, this speck of land is rimmed with white-sand beaches. On 113 acres, it's an out-of-this-world corner of the Caribbean that's only for self-sufficient types who want to escape from just about everything.

GETTING THERE The easiest way to get to Petit St. Vincent is to fly to Union Island via St. Vincent (see "Getting There" in section 3 on St. Vincent for details). Make arrangements with the hotel to have its "PVS boat" pick you up on Union Island.

WHERE TO STAY & DINE

Petit St. Vincent Resort. Petit St. Vincent, The Grenadines, St. Vincent, W.I. ☎ **800/654-9326** in the U.S., or 809/458-8801. Fax 809/458-8428. 22 cottages. MINIBAR. Winter, $600–$700 cottage for 2. Off-season, $470 cottage for 2. Rates are all-inclusive. AE, V (personal checks accepted and preferred). Closed Sept–Oct.

The Petit St. Vincent Resort has a nautical chic. It was conceived by Hazen Richardson, who had to do everything from planting trees to laying cables. Open to the trade winds, this self-contained cottage colony was designed by a Swedish architect, Arne Hasselquist, who used purpleheart wood and the local stone, called blue bitch (yes, that's right), for the walls. This is the only place to stay on the island, and if you don't like it and want to check out, you'd better have a yacht waiting. But we think you'll be pleased.

The cottages are built on a hillside or set close to the beach, in a 113-acre setting. The cottages open onto big outdoor patios, all with views. Each is cooled by trade winds and paddle-style ceiling fans. Wicker and rattan along with khuskhus rugs set the Caribbean tone of the place. When you need something, write out your request, place it in a slot in a bamboo flagpole, and run up the yellow flag. One of the waiters will arrive on a motorized cart to collect your order.

To make reservations, contact **Petit St. Vincent,** P.O. Box 12506, Cincinnati, OH 45212 (☎ **800/654-9326** or 513/242-1333).

Facilities: Tennis court, a fitness trail, and watersports center with snorkeling gear, Sunfish, Hobie Cats, and windsurfing equipment.

MAYREAU

A tiny cay, 1½ square miles of land in the Grenadines, Mayreau is a privately owned island shared by a hotel and a little hilltop village of about 170 inhabitants. It's on the route of the mail boat that plies the seas to and from St. Vincent, visiting also

Canouan and Union Island. It's completely sleepy unless a cruise ship should anchor offshore and hustle its passengers over for a lobster barbecue on the beach.

Where to Stay & Dine

Saltwhistle Bay Club. Mayreau, The Grenadines, St. Vincent, W.I. ☎ **809/458-8444.** Fax 809/458-8944. 10 rms. Winter, $450 double. Off-season, $300 double. Rates are MAP. Children under 18 granted 50% discounts. AE, V. Closed Sept–Oct. Take the private hotel launch from the airport on Union Island, costing $50 per person round-trip.

This is a last frontier for people seeking a tropical island paradise. The accommodations were built by local craftspeople, using local stone, floor tiles, and such tropical woods as purpleheart and greenheart. All units are cooled by ceiling fans. Slightly less formal and less expensive than the Petit St. Vincent Resort on Petit St. Vincent (see above), to which it's frequently compared, the place caters to escapists with money.

The dining room at the hotel is made up of circular stone booths topped by thatch canopies, and you can enjoy seafood fresh from the waters around Mayreau: lobster, curried conch, and grouper. Guests can get acquainted at the bar. By day you can go snorkeling, fishing, windsurfing, cruising on a yacht, or just lolling in one of the hammocks strung among the trees in the 20-acre tropical garden, perhaps taking a swim along the expanse of white-sand beaches that curve along both the leeward and windward sides of the island. One of the enjoyable excursions available is a "Robinson Crusoe" picnic on a little uninhabited island nearby. Scuba divers will be glad to know that there's a shipwreck to explore, a 1912 gunboat lying in 40 feet of water a few hundred feet offshore.

5 Grenada

Its political troubles long over, this sleepy island offers fairly friendly people and the lovely and popular white sands of Grand Anse Beach. Exploring its lush interior, especially Grand Etang National Park, is also worthwhile. Crisscrossed by nature trails and filled with dozens of secluded coves and sandy beaches, Grenada has moved beyond the 1980s and is a safe and secure place to visit. It's not necessarily for the serious party person and definitely not for those seeking action at the casino. Instead, it attracts visitors who like snorkeling, sailing, fishing, and doing nothing more invigorating than lolling on a beach under the sun.

The "Spice Island," Grenada is an independent three-island nation that includes Carriacou, the largest of the Grenadines, and Petite Martinique. Grenada is imbued with the fragrance of various spices and exotic fruits. It has more spices per square mile than any other place in the world—cloves, cinnamon, mace, cocoa, tonka beans, ginger, and a third of the world's supply of nutmeg. "Drop a few seeds anywhere," the locals will tell you, "and you have an instant garden." The central area is like a jungle of palms, oleander, bougainvillea, purple and red hibiscus, crimson anthurium, bananas, breadfruit, birdsong, ferns, and palms.

Beefed up by financial aid from the United States, Grenada has revived a sagging tourist industry. Following the election of Nicholas Braithwaite as prime minister in 1990, the present government of Grenada is regarded as U.S.-friendly. Much improvement to the island, including a workable phone system and better roads, has been made with the benefit of U.S. aid.

Getting There

The **Point Salines International Airport** lies at the southwestern toe of Grenada. The airport not only makes it possible for jumbo jets to land, but it also makes most of the major hotels accessible in only 5 to 15 minutes by taxi.

American Airlines (☎ **800/433-7300**) offers a daily morning flight from Kennedy in New York to San Juan, with connections to Grenada. If you live in many cities of the southeast, such as Atlanta, the better connection is via Miami.

BWIA (☎ **800/538-2942**) has nonstop service from New York's Kennedy Airport on Thursday and Sunday. The rest of the week they fly from Kennedy to Grenada with stopovers in either Antigua, St. Lucia, or Barbados.

LIAT (☎ **809/462-0700**) also has scheduled service between Barbados and Grenada, as well as to the smaller neighboring island of Carriacou (see below). There are at least four flights daily between Barbados and Grenada, although flights are sometimes canceled with little notice. We've often spent hours and hours waiting in the Barbados airport for a plane. Through either LIAT or BWIA, you can connect on Barbados with several international airlines, including British Airways, Air Canada, American Airlines, and Air France.

In addition, **British Airways** (☎ **800/247-9297**) flies to Grenada every Thursday and Saturday from London's Gatwick Airport, making a single stop at Antigua en route.

GETTING AROUND

BY TAXI Rates are set by the government. Most arriving visitors take a cab at the Point Salines International Airport to one of the hotels near St. George's, at a cost of about $10. Add 33¹/₃% to the fare from 6pm to 6am. You can also use most taxi drivers as a guide for a day's sightseeing, and the cost can be divided among three or four passengers. The price can be negotiated, depending on what you want to do.

BY RENTAL CAR First, remember to *drive on the left.* A U.S., British, or Canadian driver's license is valid on Grenada; however, you must obtain a local permit, costing EC$30 ($11.10), before getting onto the roads. These permits can be obtained either from the car-rental companies or from the traffic department at The Carenage in St. George's.

Among the major U.S.-based car-rental firms, **Avis** (☎ **800/331-2112** or 473/440-3936) operates out of a Shell gasoline station on Lagoon Road, on the southern outskirts of Saint George's. Avis will agree to meet you at the airport, but requires at least 24-hour notice before its toll-free reservations service will guarantee availability. **Budget Rent-a-Car,** Lemarquis Complex Grand Anse (☎ **473/444-2277**), is also represented on Grenada.

A word of warning about local drivers: There's such a thing as Grenadian driving machismo; the drivers take blind corners with abandon. An extraordinary number of accidents are reported in the lively local paper. Gird yourself with nerves of steel, and be extra-alert for children and roadside pedestrians while driving at night. Many foreign visitors, in fact, find any night driving hazardous.

BY BUS Minivans, charging EC$1 to EC$6 (40¢ to $2.20), are the cheapest way to get around. The most popular run is between St. George's and Grand Anse Beach. Most minivans depart from Market Square or from the Esplanade area of St. George's.

FAST FACTS: Grenada

Banks In St. George's, the capital, **Barclays** is at Church and Halifax streets (☎ **473/440-3232**); **Scotiabank,** on Halifax Street (☎ **473/440-3274**); the **National Commercial Bank** (NCB), at the corner of Halifax and Hillsborough streets (☎ **473/440-3566**); the **Grenada Bank of Commerce,** at the corner of Halifax and Cross streets (☎ **473/440-3521**); and the **Grenada Cooperative Bank,** on Church Street (☎ **473/440-2111**).

Currency The official currency is the **Eastern Caribbean dollar (EC$),** worth about 37¢. Always determine which dollars, EC or U.S., you're talking about when someone on Grenada quotes you a price.

Documents Proof of citizenship is needed to enter the country. A passport is preferred, but a birth certificate or voter registration card is accepted for American, British, and Canadian citizens, providing they also have photo ID.

Electricity Electricity is supplied on the island by Grenada Electricity Services. It's 220–240 volts AC (50 cycles), so transformers and adapters will be needed for U.S.-made appliances.

Embassies and High Commissions Grenada, unlike many of its neighbors, has a **U.S. Embassy** at Point Salines at St. George's (☎ **473/444-1173**). It also has a **British High Commission,** on Church Street, St. George's (☎ **473/440-3536**).

Emergencies Dial ☎ **911** to summon the police, report a fire, or call an ambulance.

Information Go to the **Grenada Board of Tourism,** The Carenage, in St. George's (☎ **473/440-2279**), open Monday to Friday from 8am to 4pm. Maps, guides, and general information are available. In the United States, the **Grenada Tourist Office** is at 820 Second Ave., Suite 900D, New York, NY 10017 (☎ **800/927-9554** or 212/687-9554). In Canada, contact the **Grenada Board of Tourism,** 439 University Ave., Suite 920, Toronto, ON M5G 1Y8 (☎ **416/595-1339**); and in London, contact the **Grenada Board of Tourism,** 1 Collingham Gardens, London, SW5 0HW (☎ **0171/370-5164**).

Language English is commonly spoken on this island of some 100,000 people because of the long years of British influence. However, now and then you'll hear people speaking in a French-African patois handed down from long ago.

Medical Care There is a general hospital, **St. George's Hospital** (☎ **473/440-2051**), with an X-ray department and operating theater. Private doctors and nurses are available on call.

Pharmacies Try **Gittens Pharmacy,** Halifax Street, St. George's (☎ **473/440-2165**), open Monday, Tuesday, Wednesday, and Friday from 8am to 6pm, Thursday from 8am to 5pm, and Saturday from 8am to 3pm.

Post Office The **General Post Office** is at The Pier, St. George's, open Monday to Friday from 8am to 3:30pm.

Safety Crime is on the rise on Grenada. Don't go walking on the beach at night. In fact, it's unwise to go walking anywhere after dark; take a taxi to where you're going. Tourists have been attacked by locals holding machetes at their throats while they were robbed. The island is generally safe during the day if the usual precautions are taken.

Taxes A 10% VAT (value-added tax) is imposed on food and beverages, and there's an 8% room tax. Upon leaving Grenada, you must fill out an immigration card and pay a departure tax of EC$35 ($13).

Telecommunications International telephone service is available 24 hours a day from pay phones. Public telegraph, Telex, and fax services are also provided from The Carenage offices of **Grenada Telecommunications** (Grentel) in St. George's (☎ **473/440-1000** for all Grentel offices), open Monday to Friday from 7:30am to 6pm, on Saturday from 7:30am to 1pm, and on Sunday and holidays from 10am

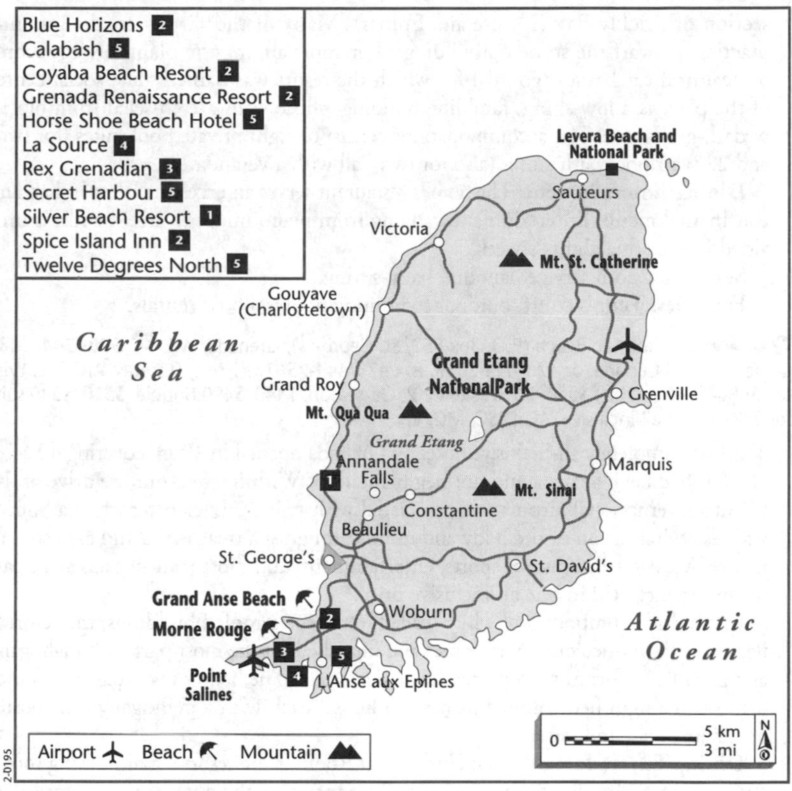

to noon. To call another number on Grenada, dial all seven digits, as the island is divided among four telephone exchanges: 440, 442, 443, and 444. The most commonly used is 440.

Tipping A 10% service charge is added to most restaurant and hotel bills.

Weather Grenada has two distinct seasons, dry and rainy. The dry season is from January to May; the rest of the year is the rainy season, although the rainfall doesn't last long. The average temperature is 80°F. Because of constant trade winds, there's little humidity.

WHERE TO STAY

Your hotel or inn will probably add a service charge of 10% to your bill—ask in advance about this. Also, there's an 8% government tax on rooms.

VERY EXPENSIVE

✪ **Calabash.** L'Anse aux Epines (P.O. Box 382, St. George's), Grenada, W.I. ☎ **800/528-5835** in the U.S. and Canada, or 473/444-4334. Fax 473/444-5050. 30 suites. A/C MINIBAR TEL. Winter, $350–$495 suite for 2. Off-season, $235–$320 suite for 2. MAP $35 per person extra. Additional person $100–$160 extra in winter, $95–$115 extra off-season. Children 12 and under welcome in summer and charged $35 a day, including all meals, in rooms with their parents. Only children 13 and over are welcome in winter. AE, MC, V.

Built in the early 1960s, the Calabash is today the most prestigious hotel on Grenada. Five miles south of St. George's and only minutes from the Point Salines International Airport, it occupies a landscaped 8-acre beach plotted along an isolated section of Prickly Bay (L'Anse aux Epines). Many of the shrubs on the grounds practically dwarf the stone outbuildings. Foremost among the plants are the scores of beautiful calabashes (gourds) for which the resort was named. The social center of the place is a low-slung, rambling building whose walls are chiseled from blocks of dark-gray stone. The accommodations consist of eight private pool suites (for two) and 22 whirlpool bath suites (also for two), all with a veranda.

Dining/Entertainment: The hotel's restaurant serves an excellent West Indian and continental menu. Entertainment, ranging from piano music to steel bands, is provided four or five nights a week.

Services: Room service, laundry, baby-sitting.

Facilities: Tennis court, outdoor swimming pool, sailboat rentals.

✪ **La Source.** Pink Gin Beach (P.O. Box 852, St. George's), Grenada, W.I. ☎ **800/544-2883** in the U.S. and Canada, or 473/444-2556. Fax 473/444-2561. 91 rms, 9 suites. A/C TEL. Winter, $480–$560 double; $550–$610 suite for 2. Off-season, $440–$490 double; $510–$540 suite for 2. Rates are all-inclusive. AE, DISC, MC, V.

The first completely all-inclusive hotel on Grenada opened in 1993, covering 40 acres of what had been a cocoa and nutmeg plantation. Within a five-minute drive of the island's international airport and associated with two St. Lucian resorts, La Source stresses revitalization of the body and mind through spa treatments and exposure to nature. Meals, drinks, water sports, entertainment, and most (but not all) spa treatments are included in one all-inclusive price.

In a hillside compound of white-walled, terra-cotta-roofed buildings, the resort is floored with multicolored marble tiles and furnished for the most part with mahogany and greenheart furniture imported from Venezuela. The bedrooms evoke accommodations in a dignified colonial plantation house, each with a mahogany four-poster bed, hair dryer, and radio.

Dining/Entertainment: The plush Great Room is the resort's main dining room, serving one of the island's best cuisines. Less formal is the open-sided Terrace Restaurant. Live piano music is presented during the cocktail hour in one bar, whereas a small stage in the other offers live bands for dancing.

Services: Concierge; instruction in such pastimes as fencing, windsurfing, calypso dancing, and weight training.

Facilities: Two free-form swimming pools, two white-sand beaches separated from one another by a rocky knoll, and a nonregulation "mashie" golf course, with very short distances between the holes (outings to a regulation nine-hole golf course in the area can be arranged). The Oasis offers massages, saunas, land and water aerobics classes, yoga, stress-management treatments, and salt loofah rubs.

✪ **Spice Island Inn.** Grand Anse (P.O. Box 6, St. George's), Grenada, W.I. ☎ **800/223-9815** in the U.S., 212/251-1800 in New York City, or 473/444-4258. Fax 473/444-4807. 56 suites. A/C MINIBAR TEL. Winter, $375–$725 suite for 2; $455–$825 suite for 3. Off-season, $295–$550 suite for 2; $380–$650 suite for 3. Rates are MAP. AE, MC, V.

On an estate overlooking the Caribbean, this inn is built along 1,200 feet of Grand Anse beach, directly north of the airport. The main house, reserved for dining and dancing, has a tropical aura and lots of nice touches, showing that taste went into the design. Some 32 units are beach suites, and these are preferred. Second-floor suites have terraces overlooking the ocean and the garden. And 17 units have their own private plunge pools where guests can go skinny-dipping. The furnishings in the rooms are not elaborate, with outdoorsy-type pieces such as wicker chairs or rattan. The bathrooms are the largest and most luxurious on Grenada, with fluffy white towels (enough to please Frank Sinatra during his road days) and Jacuzzis.

Dining/Entertainment: Chefs not only prepare an international cuisine, but also deftly turn out good Grenadian food, including soursop ice cream (nutmeg is also a specialty), breadfruit vichyssoise, and Caribbean lobster. Sometimes a combo plays for dancing.

Services: Room service for all three meals.

Facilities: Beach, private swimming pools, fitness center, day and night tennis. Bikes, nonmotorized water sports, and greens fees for the Grenada Golf Course are complimentary.

EXPENSIVE

Grenada Renaissance Resort. P.O. Box 441, Grand Anse Beach, Grenada, W.I. ☎ **800/HOTELS-1** in the U.S., or 473/444-4371. Fax 473/444-4800. 184 rms, 2 suites. A/C TV TEL. Winter, $188–$256 double; from $376–$384 suite. Off-season, $129–$183 double; $376 suite. MAP $53 per person extra. AE, DC, DISC, MC, V.

Renovated in 1991, but still short on island atmosphere, this hotel stands on a desirable stretch of white sandy beachfront 3 miles north of the airport. The cedar-shingled facade might have been inspired by an 18th-century plantation house. Any comparison with another century, however, ends when visitors see the interior. Guests register beneath the octagonal roof of the entrance hall, then are ushered between a pair of manicured formal gardens to their (often-small) rooms, which are tiled and furnished with mahogany pieces. Each has a balcony or patio. The beach-view rooms are the most desirable, of course.

Dining/Entertainment: Guests or nonguests can dine in or out of doors in the Terrace Restaurant, which has a passable international cuisine. Entertainment is usually offered at night.

Services: Room service, laundry, baby-sitting.

Facilities: Beach, swimming pool, fitness center, tennis courts, water-sports kiosk (renting snorkeling and scuba-diving equipment, sailboats, Windsurfers, sailfish, and Jet Skis).

Rex Grenadian. Point Salines (P.O. Box 893, St. George's), Grenada, W.I. ☎ **473/444-3333.** Fax 473/444-1111. 192 rms, 20 suites. TEL. Winter, $175–$260 double; $280–$360 suite. Off-season, $115–$200 double; $220–$300 suite. MAP $49 per person extra. AE, CB, DC, MC, V.

Opened late in 1993, this is the largest and most important hotel on the island but not the best. It's a convention group favorite, set on 12 rocky, partially forested acres that slope steeply down to a pair of white-sand beaches. The hotel is about a quarter of a mile from the island's international airport. Each of the wintergreen and pale-blue units is configured differently from its neighbors, and each is outfitted in rattan, wicker, and muted tropical fabrics. Eighty-four of the accommodations offer ocean views, but not all are air-conditioned. Adjacent to the accommodations is a 2-acre artificial lake strewn with islands that are connected to the "mainland" with footbridges and paddle boats.

Dining/Entertainment: Drinking and dining options include the International, specializing in buffets with foods from around the world, and the far better Oriental, for Asian cuisine. In the evening the Tamarind Lounge offers cabaret singing and disco music.

Services: Room service, baby-sitting, laundry.

Facilities: Water-sports options include scuba, snorkeling, sailing, and deep-sea fishing; other diversions can be arranged. There's a fitness center in an outlying annex (the Pavilion), two beaches, and the most dramatic swimming pool on the island. Graced with a water cascade and its own bar and restaurant, it was drilled and blasted

directly into the volcanic rock of a stony promontory jutting out toward the open ocean.

✪ **Secret Harbour.** Mount Hartman Bay, L'Anse aux Epines (P.O. Box 11, St. George's), Grenada, W.I. ☎ **800/437-7880** in the U.S. and Canada, or 473/444-4439. Fax 473/444-4819. 20 suites. A/C TEL. Winter, $230 suite for 2, $245 suite for 3, $265 suite for 4. Off-season, $130 suite for 2, $145 suite for 3, $165 suite for 4. MAP $41 per person extra. Additional person $20 extra. No children under 12 accepted. AE, MC, V.

Seen from the water of Mount Hartman Bay, Secret Harbour reminds one of a Mediterranean complex on Spain's Costa del Sol—a tasteful one, that is, with white stucco arches, red-tile roofs, and wrought-iron light fixtures. From all over Grenada, including some island plantation homes, antiques were purchased, restored, and installed here. The bathrooms are also luxurious, with sunken tubs lined with Italian tiles. Each of the suites has a dressing room, living area, and patio overlooking the water. Steps lead down to the beach. Units also have small refrigerators.

Secret Harbour is a favorite of the yachting set. While many guests stay at the hotel, others stay on yachts anchored off the property. Owned by the Moorings, an international hotel and yacht-charter company based in Clearwater, Florida, Secret Harbour is located about 20 minutes from Point Salines International Airport and 15 minutes from St. George's.

Dining/Entertainment: The antique-filled Mariners Restaurant features a good international menu, often prepared with fresh produce from Grenada. Guests enjoy the lobby/bar/terrace in the evening, savoring the tranquillity—there's no loud, aggressive entertainment. The restaurant overlooks Mount Hartman Bay.

Services: Room service, laundry.

Facilities: Marina, wide range of water sports (including snorkeling and windsurfing), sailing, and boating programs (including bareboat charters and "Learn to Cruise" lessons), tennis court, swimming pool, a good beach.

Twelve Degrees North. L'Anse aux Epines (P.O. Box 241, St. George's), Grenada, W.I. ☎ **473/444-4580** (call collect to make reservations). Fax 473/444-4580. 8 apts. Winter, $195 one-bedroom apt for 2, $300 two-bedroom apt for 4. Off-season, $130 one-bedroom apt for 2, $225 two-bedroom apt for 4. MC, V. Additional person $60–$70 extra. No children under 15.

On a very private beach, this complex is operated by Joseph Gaylord, a former commercial real-estate broker from New York, who greets visitors in front of a large flame tree on his front lawn. He owns this cluster of spotlessly clean efficiency apartments 3 miles east of the airport at Point Salines.

Many of the staff members have been with Mr. Gaylord since he opened the place many years ago. They'll cook breakfast, prepare lunch (perhaps pumpkin soup and flying fish), do the cleaning and laundry, and fix regional specialties for dinner (which you heat up for yourself later). A grass-roofed beach bar faces the water. Each unit (two with two bedrooms and six with one bedroom) comes with an individual uniformed housekeeper/cook, who arrives at 8 o'clock each morning to perform the thousand small kindnesses that make Twelve Degrees North a favorite lair for repeat guests from America and Europe. Each unit is equipped with an efficiency kitchen with a 16-cubic-foot refrigerator. The large beds can be separated or pushed together. The owner prefers to rent by the week because, as he says, "a few days aren't enough to get to know Grenada."

Facilities: Beach, double-seat kayak, swimming pool, snorkeling equipment, tennis court, two Sunfish—all free.

Moderate

Blue Horizons Cottage Hotel. P.O. Box 41, Grand Anse, Grenada, W.I. ☎ **800/223-9815** in the U.S. and Canada, or 473/444-4316. Fax 473/444-2815. 32 cottages. A/C TV TEL. Winter, $160–$180 cottage for 2. Off-season, $110–$120 cottage for 2. Extra person $35–$50. AE, DC, DISC, MC, V.

Co-owners Royston and Arnold Hopkin purchased this place from a bankrupt estate and transformed the neglected property into one of the finest on the island. Grand Anse Beach is only a five-minute walk away. The units are spread throughout a flowering garden of 6¼ acres. Rates depend on the category of the cottage: superior or deluxe. Each has an efficiency kitchen and comfortable solid-mahogany furniture. Children are welcome, and they can watch the 21 varieties of native birds said to inhabit the grounds.

Guests who prefer to cook in their rooms can buy supplies from a Food Fair at Grand Anse, a 10-minute walk away. On the grounds is one of the best restaurants on the island, La Belle Creole (see "Where to Dine," below). Lunch is served around a pool bar. Laundry, baby-sitting, and room service are provided.

Coyaba Beach Resort. Grand Anse Beach (P.O. Box 336, St. George's), Grenada, W.I. ☎ **473/444-4129.** Fax 473/444-4808. 70 rms. A/C TV TEL. Winter, $175 double. Off-season, $100 double. MAP $35 per person extra. Additional person $40 extra in winter, $20 extra off-season. AE, DC, MC, V.

On a 5½-acre site on Grand Anse Beach next to the medical school, this resort, whose name means "heaven" in Arawak, is 6 miles from St. George's and 3 miles north of Point Salines International Airport. Opened in 1987, the hotel has views of the town and of St. George's harbor. All units have double beds, plus verandas and patios, spacious baths, and hair dryers. For persons with disabilities, this is the best choice on the island. Three of the rooms are wheelchair accessible, and widened doors and wheelchair ramps have made the hotel more user friendly. Laundry service is available, as are room service and baby-sitting. The hotel offers two open-air restaurants, the main dining room, Pepperpot, and a less formal eatery at poolside. There are two bars as well, one at poolside. Activities include tennis on a Laykold court, volleyball, and water sports offered by Grand Anse Aquatics on the premises.

✪ **Horse Shoe Beach Hotel.** L'Anse aux Epines (P.O. Box 174, St. George's), Grenada, W.I. ☎ **473/444-4244,** or 718/726-8600 in New York City. Fax 473/444-4844. 4 rms, 6 suites, 12 villas. A/C TEL. Winter, $100 double; $130–$150 suite for 2; $130 villa for 2. Off-season, $80 double; $110–$115 suite for 2; $100 villa for 2. MAP $40 per person extra. Additional person $20 extra in winter, $15 extra off-season. AE, DISC, MC, V.

This small Mediterranean-style hotel with vintage charm, one of the island's best values, is set on a gentle slope on the south coast of the island 3 miles east of the airport. To get to the beach, you'll stroll down the carefully landscaped hillside. Guests can also be transported to Grand Anse Beach. Constructed on a small promontory, the complex captures the sea breezes at night, and you'll hear the rustling sound of wind blowing through the acres of tropical gardens. The doorway to the Spanish stucco building is almost hidden by the foliage. The Grenadian-Iberian dining room and red-tile lounge has cozy nooks and original oil paintings. The restaurant frames views of the beach and swimming pool, as well as of the gardens. Guests are so well coddled here that they keep returning to the appealing rooms furnished with antiques from old island-family houses.

A dozen accommodations are in six terra-cotta–roofed villas. Each shares a kitchenette with its neighbor, and each has a canopied four-poster bed and a private terrace.

In the main building are six suites, more modern in concept and slightly larger than the outlying villas.

WHERE TO DINE

EXPENSIVE

✪ **Canboulay.** Morne Rouge. ☎ **473/444-4401.** Reservations recommended. Four-course fixed-price meal (in winter) EC$80–EC$100 ($29.60–$37); main courses (off-season) EC$38–EC$55 ($14.10–$20.40) at dinner. AE, DC, MC, V. Mon–Fri 11:30am–2:30pm and Mon–Sat 6:30–9:30pm. CARIBBEAN.

This restaurant has a gracious West Indian formality and an elegant Caribbean-colonial decor. It offers some of the most unusual Antillean food on Grenada. Set on a hilltop with a view of Grand Anse Beach, it occupies a clapboard house painted in vibrant Caribbean colors. Menu items are more original at night than at lunchtime. Throughout the winter the only evening option available is a fixed-price menu. Specialties include coconut crêpes stuffed with crabmeat and served with callaloo relish, cornmeal baked or fried in coconut milk (the result is a traditional starch known as "coo coo"), blackened flying fish, fried conch served with a local citrus sauce, grilled or baked chicken with a sauce of tomatoes and local herbs, and many kinds of steak. The owners are Erik and Gina-Lee Johnson, who are sorcerers in the kitchen.

✪ **Coconut's Beach Restaurant.** Grand Anse Beach. ☎ **473/444-4644.** Reservations recommended. Main courses EC$35–EC$75 ($13–$27.80); lunch platters EC$15–EC$35 ($5.60–$13). AE, DISC, MC, V. Daily noon–10pm. Closed Mon off-season. FRENCH/CREOLE.

Raffish and informal, the restaurant occupies a pink-and-green clapboard house set directly on the sands of the beach, about a 1/2 mile north of St. George's. In the dining room you can watch the staff at work in the exposed kitchen. They'll definitely be making a callaloo soup, cooked here with local herbs and blended to a creamy smoothness. The kitchen specializes in various kinds of lobster, including one made with spaghetti, although the lobster stir-fry with ginger chili is more imaginative. Fish predominates, including a catch of the day served with mango chutney and curried conch West Indian style. Chicken and meats are also savory, especially breast of chicken cooked in local herbs and lime juice.

Warning: Because of the restaurant's close proximity to at least four major hotels, many people opt to walk along the beach to reach it. Don't! Tourists have been attacked by machete-carrying local druggies who've robbed them and threatened their lives. Even though it might be only a short ride, take a taxi to the door instead.

✪ **La Belle Creole.** At Blue Horizons, Grand Anse Beach. ☎ **473/444-4316.** Reservations required for non-hotel guests. Main courses $25–$30; 5-course dinner $35–$40. AE, DC, DISC, MC, V. Daily 12:30–2pm and 7–9pm. CREOLE/SEAFOOD.

One of the best restaurants on Grenada, a five-minute walk from Grand Anse Beach, is run by Arnold and Royston Hopkin, sons of "Mama" Audrey Hopkin, long considered the best cook on the island if you're seeking West Indian specialties. In the restaurant, archways frame views of the mountains and the beach.

Lunch, which can be taken poolside, features soup and chicken, fish, or lobster salad. Dinner can be a fixed-price menu, with a variety of choices from continental recipes with West Indian substitutions for ingredients not available on the island. The chefs prepare one of the most creative cuisines on the island, as exemplified by their choice of appetizers and soups. To get you going, try chilled conch mousse if it's featured; it's tasty and smoothly delectable in every way, as is the christophene vichyssoise, which has a velvety texture. The lobster Creole is a classic and it's served in a shell, but even better is the spicy ginger pork chops with local seasonings, heightened with a touch of white wine. Another longtime favorite of ours is the deviled fish with curry and local seasonings. Three local vegetables fresh from the lush countryside are served with each meal. Desserts, however, are nothing special.

MODERATE

Bird's Nest. Grand Anse. ☎ **473/444-4264.** Reservations recommended. Main courses EC$24–EC$55 ($8.90–$20.35). AE, MC, V. Daily 9am–11pm. CHINESE/CREOLE.

For a change of pace, we suggest the Bird's Nest, in its own building with three palm trees at the entrance. It's 3 miles north of the airport, opposite the Grenada Renaissance. This family business offers Chinese food, mainly Szechuan and Cantonese, along with seafood and Caribbean cuisine. You'll see the familiar shrimp egg rolls along with eight different chow meins. Sweet-and-sour fish is a favorite, and daily specials are posted. The best items are those made with Caribbean lobster. A takeout service is also available. This may not be the world's greatest Chinese restaurant, and some dishes are short on flavor, but it's generally satisfying and is something different. Sandwiches can be ordered for lunch.

✪ **Morne Fendue.** St. Patrick's. ☎ **473/442-9330.** Reservations required. Fixed-price lunch EC$45 ($16.45). No credit cards. Mon–Sat 12:30–3pm. CREOLE.

As you're touring north from the beach at Grand Anse, one place is especially memorable: Betty Mascoll's Morne Fendue, 25 miles north of St. George's. This 1912 plantation house, constructed the year she was born, is her ancestral home. It was built of chiseled river rocks held together with a mixture of lime and molasses, as was the custom in that day. Mrs. Mascoll and her loyal staff, two of whom have been with her for many, many years, always need time to prepare for the arrival of guests, so it's imperative to call ahead. This may be your last chance to enjoy food from old-time recipes (many now fading from cultural memory). You dine as perhaps an upper-class family did back in 1922. Lunch is likely to include a yam and sweet-potato casserole or curried chicken with lots of island-grown spices. You get all of Grandmother's favorites, including fritters made of tannia (a starchy tuber) and corn coo coo (resembling spoonbread). The most popular local vegetable is curried christophone with a taste of squash. The most famous dish is Betty's legendary pepperpot stew, which may have been simmering for decades. Pork and oxtail are included in this savory brew, and they've been tenderized by the juice of grated cassava. Because this is very much a private home, tipping should be done with the greatest tact. Nonetheless, the hardworking cook and maid seem genuinely appreciative of a gratuity. Mrs. Mascoll is now in her 80s and struggling to continue her long tradition of hospitality, but her delicious and affordable food still make dining here a worthwhile and unforgettable experience.

The Nutmeg. The Carenage, St. George's. ☎ **473/440-2539.** Main courses EC$18–EC$55 ($6.65–$20.35). AE, DISC, MC, V. Mon–Sat 8am–11pm, Sun 2–11pm. SEAFOOD/CREOLE.

Right on the harbor, the Nutmeg is over the Sea Change Shop where you can pick up paperbacks and souvenirs. Since the mid-1960s it has been a hangout for the yachting set and a favorite with just about everybody, both expatriates living on the island and visitors. It's suitable for a snack or a full-fledged dinner, and its drinks are very good. Try one of the Grenadian rum punches made with Angostura bitters, grated nutmeg, rum, lime juice, and syrup. An informal atmosphere prevails as you're served your fillet of fish with potato croquettes and string beans. There's always fresh fish and usually callaloo soup. Lambi (that ubiquitous conch) is also done very well here. We think this place's lobster thermidor is the best in town. There's a small wine list with some California and German selections, and you can drop in for just a glass of beer to enjoy the sea view. Sometimes, however, you'll be asked to share a table.

The Red Crab. L'Anse aux Epines. ☎ **473/444-4424.** Reservations required in winter. Main courses EC$30–EC$93.50 ($11.10–$34.60). AE, DISC, MC, V. Mon–Sat 11am–2pm and 6–10:30pm. WEST INDIAN/INTERNATIONAL.

The Red Crab, a popular place with visitors and locals alike, is only a short taxi ride from the major hotels. Patrons can dine inside or under the starry night. The place is especially popular with students from the medical college, although we don't know how they can afford some of the prices. The beefsteaks are Grenada's finest, especially the peppersteak. Other specialties include local lobster tail; lambi (conch); locally caught fish such as snapper, dolphin, and grouper; and even garlic shrimp, though other island chefs prepare better versions of these seafood dishes. Dessert might be a homemade cheesecake. It's not sublime cuisine, but go here for the convivial atmosphere and the good times.

✪ **Rudolf's.** The Carenage, St. George's. ☎ **473/440-2241.** Reservations recommended. Main courses EC$19.50–EC$55 ($7.20–$20.40). MC, V. Mon–Sat 10am–midnight. INTERNATIONAL.

This longtime favorite restaurant, an excellent value for your money, overlooks a deep, U-shaped harbor lined with commercial establishments in St. George's. On the north center of the Carenage, it's a good spot for drinks in the late afternoon if you want to join the yachting machismo set and their lethal rum drinks. Rudolf (from the Styria district of Austria) is very charming, and his restaurant is the most solid choice in St. George's. It does a busy lunch business and has a hardworking and genteel staff. Ceiling fans cool patrons off at midday. The ceiling is sheathed in a layer of corrugated egg cartons, which adds an unconventional, appealing touch and also muffles the noise from the sometimes very crowded bar area. The food is well prepared and the menu is the most extensive on the island. The steaks are the best in the capital. Conch is prepared in four different ways, as are shrimp and octopus. Flying fish and dolphin deserve the most praise, and they, too, are prepared in several different ways. On occasion wild game such as rabbit stew or duck is prepared, and even possum (manicou) stew. There's even a classic Wiener schnitzel—again, the best in town—in honor of the chef's origins.

Spice Island Inn. Grand Anse Beach. ☎ **473/444-4258.** Reservations required for nonguests. Fixed-price dinner $40. AE, DC, MC, V. Daily 7:30–9:30am, 12:30–2:30pm, and 7–9:30pm. CREOLE/SEAFOOD.

Want to dine on an uncrowded beachfront in the full outdoors, with a parapet over your head to protect you from sudden tropical showers? The parapet here, built of imported pine and cedar, looks like a Le Corbusier rooftop. Some of the best hotel food on the island is found here in a winning setting. At this inn, located directly north of the airport, the view is of one of the best beaches in the Caribbean—miles of white sand sprouting an occasional grove of sea grape or almond trees. You can eat lunch in a swimsuit. Dinner menus change frequently and can be cooked to your specifications. Local seafood is featured on the constantly changing menu. The best buffet on the island, a real Grenadian spread, is served on Wednesday with live entertainment. Friday is barbecue night when a steel band entertains, and on Saturday seafood is the specialty.

INEXPENSIVE

Delicious Landing. The Carenage. ☎ **473/440-9747.** Main courses EC$15–EC$28 ($5.55–$10.35). MC, V. Mon–Sat 8am–11pm. INTERNATIONAL/WEST INDIAN.

This place was originally built as a warehouse at the extreme tip of the northern edge of the Carenage, but when someone added a waterfront veranda to the boxy, unimaginative building, it was immediately transformed into the most desirable perch along the waterfront. The place is best suited for a midday pick-me-up, with or without alcohol, partly because of the cool breezes that blow in off the port. Cocktails include U.S. bombers, mango daiquiris, and an especially potent concoction the owners refer to as "navy grog." Menu items include such West Indian dishes as lambi (conch) chowder, sandwiches, and the most popular dish on the menu, lobster pando, a form of ragout. We wouldn't say it's the best cookery in town, but it's quite competent, and you get good value here.

✪ **Mamma's.** Lagoon Rd., St. George's. ☎ **473/440-1459.** Reservations required a day in advance. Fixed-price meal EC$45 ($16.65). No credit cards. Daily 8am–midnight. CREOLE.

On the road leading to Grenada Yacht Services, Mamma's is a trip unto itself: No one else captures the authentic taste of Grenada in the very special way that Mamma's does. Serving copious meals, this Mamma became particularly famous during the U.S. intervention in Grenada, as U.S. servicepeople adopted her as their own island mama. Mamma (alias Insley Wardally) is now deceased, but her daughter, Cleo, carries on.

Meals, we were told, come in two sizes: "the usual" and "the special." But we were later told that "the usual" and "the special" were the same. Either way, meals include such dishes as callaloo soup with coconut cream, shredded cold crab with lime juice, freshwater crayfish, fried conch, and a casserole of cooked bananas, yams, and dasheen, along with ripe baked plantain, and rotis made of curry and yellow chickpeas, followed by sugar-apple ice cream. Mamma's seafoods are likely to include crab backs, octopus in a hot-and-spicy sauce, and even turtle steak, although the latter could be an endangered species. Mamma is also known for her "wild meats," including armadillo, opossum, monkey (yes, that's right), game birds, and even the endangered iguana. Gourmets flock to this restaurant to sample these delicacies, and the unusual menu has been widely written about in U.S. media. However, "wild things" are only available when Cleo can obtain them. The specialty drink of the house is rum punch—the ingredients are a secret. Dinner here must be reserved a day in advance so you'll be sure of having a choice of 20 to 25 different foods from Grenada.

Portofino. The Carenage, St. George's. ☎ **473/440-3986.** Reservations recommended. Pastas and pizzas EC$16–EC$40 ($5.90–$14.80); main courses EC$25–EC$59 ($9.25–$21.85). AE, MC, V. Mon–Sat 11am–11pm, Sun 6–11pm. ITALIAN/SEAFOOD.

The venue is spartan and simple, with hints of Italy's Portofino. It's not nearly as substantial as Rudolf's, farther down The Carenage, but still it's not a bad choice, with fine, unpretentious food like pastas, veal, chicken, and Italian-style beef. The restaurant serves the best pizzas in the capital, Italian-style antipasti such as eggplant Parmesan, and a good bowl of minestrone. However, the fish and meat dishes are more ordinary, although the catch of the day, served with pasta and fresh vegetables, is usually available, as are shrimp and lobster. The finest pasta dish is the linguine with fresh fish. They also cater to vegetarians with choices like vegetarian lasagna. Live jazz is presented every Friday night, and on Sunday night a festival of Caribbean music is presented, along with candlelight dining and dancing. There's no cover.

BEACHES, WATER SPORTS & OTHER OUTDOOR PURSUITS

BEACHES One of the best beaches in the Caribbean is ✪ **Grand Anse,** 2 miles of sugar-white sands extending into deep waters far offshore. Most of Grenada's best hotels are within walking distance of Grand Anse. You can also take off and discover dozens more beaches on your own, as they're all public.

DEEP-SEA FISHING Fishers come here from November to March in pursuit of both blue and white marlin, yellowfin tuna, wahoo, sailfish, and other catches. Most of the bigger hotels have a sports desk that will arrange fishing trips for you. The

Annual Game Fishing Tournament, held in January, attracts a number of regional and international participants.

Havadu is a 32-foot ocean-going pirogue, available for deep-sea-fishing excursions and snorkeling. Various prices depend on the size of the group. For more information, contact **Best of Grenada,** The Carenage (☎ **473/440-4386**).

GOLF At the **Grenada Golf Course and Country Club,** Woodlands (☎ **473/444-4128**), you'll find a nine-hole course, with greens fees of $12 for nine holes. The course is open Monday to Saturday from 8am to sunset and on Sunday from 8am to noon. The course offers a view of both the Caribbean Sea and the Atlantic.

SCUBA DIVING & SNORKELING Along with many other water sports, Grenada offers the diver an underwater world rich in submarine gardens, exotic fish, and coral formations, sometimes with underwater visibility stretching to 120 feet. Off the coast is the wreck of the ocean liner *Bianca C,* which is nearly 600 feet long. Novice divers might want to stick to the west coast of Grenada, while more experienced divers might search out the sights along the rougher Atlantic side.

Daddy Vic's Watersports, in the Grenada Renaissance, Grand Anse Beach (☎ **473/444-4371,** ext. 638), is directly on the sands. The premier dive outfit on the island, it offers night dives or a two-tank dive for $45, and PADI instructors will offer an open-water certification program for $350 per person.

In addition, this is the best center for other water sports, offering snorkeling trips for $18 (1½ to 2 hours) or windsurfing with board rentals for $16 per hour. Sunfish rentals are $16 per half hour, parasailing is $30 per 10 minutes, jet-skiing $44 per half hour, and waterskiing is $15 per run. Even deep-sea-fishing arrangements can be made.

Giving the center serious competition is **Grand Anse Aquatics,** at the previously recommended Coyaba Beach Resort on Grand Anse Beach (☎ **473/444-4129**). A Canadian-run place, it's welcoming and inviting to divers, and there's a PADI instructor on-site. The dive boat is well equipped with well-maintained gear. Diving instruction and scuba diving and snorkeling jaunts to panoramic reefs and shipwrecks teaming with marine life are offered. A single dive costs $40, a resort course, $55, and a night dive, also $55. A snorkeling trip can be arranged for just $18.

If you'd rather strike out on your own, take a drive to Woburn and negotiate with a fisher for a ride to **Glovers Island,** an old whaling station, and snorkel away. Glovers Island is an uninhabited rock spit a few hundred yards offshore from the hamlet of Woburn.

Warning: Divers should know that Grenada doesn't have a decompression chamber. If you should get the bends, you'll have to take an excruciatingly painful air trip to Trinidad.

SAILING Two large "party boats," designed for 120 and 250 passengers, respectively, operate out of St. George's harbor. The ***Rhum Runner*** and ***Rhum Runner II,*** c/o Best of Grenada, P.O. Box 188, St. George's (☎ **473/440-4FUN**) make shuttle-style trips, three times a day, with lots of emphasis on strong liquor, steel-band music, and good times. Four-hour daytime tours, conducted every morning and afternoon, coincide with the arrival of cruise ships, but will carry independent travelers if space is available. Rides cost $20 per person and include snorkeling stops at reefs and beaches along the way. Evening tours are much more frequently attended by island locals and are more bare-boned, louder, and usually less restrained. They cost $7.50 per person. Regardless of when you take it, your cruise will include rum, reggae music, and lots of hoopla.

TENNIS Tennis, like cricket and football, is a popular everyday sport on Grenada. Guests at the Secret Harbour, Grenada Renaissance, Calabash, Coyaba Beach Resort, and Twelve Degrees North can avail themselves of those well-kept courts.

EXPLORING THE ISLAND: FROM TROPICAL WATERFALLS TO A SPECTACULAR RAIN FOREST

Carnival time on Grenada is the second weekend of August, with colorful parades, music, and dancing. The festivities begin on a Friday, continuing practically nonstop to Tuesday. Steel bands and calypso groups perform at Queen's Park. Jouvert, one of the highlights of the festival, begins at 5am on Monday with a parade of Djab Djab/Djab Molassi, devil-costumed figures daubed with a black substance. (*Be warned:* Don't wear your good clothes to attend this event—you may get sticky from close body contact.) The carnival finale, a gigantic "jump-up," ends with a parade of bands from Tanteen through The Carenage into town.

ST. GEORGE'S The capital city of Grenada, St. George's is one of the most attractive ports in the West Indies. Its landlocked inner harbor is actually the deep crater of a long-dead volcano, or so one is told.

In the town you'll see some of the most charming Georgian colonial buildings in the Caribbean, still standing in spite of a devastating hurricane in 1955. The streets are mostly steep and narrow, which enhances the attractiveness of the ballast bricks, wrought-iron balconies, and red tiles of the sloping roofs. Many of the pastel warehouses date from the 18th century. Frangipani and flamboyant trees add to the palette of color.

The port, which some have compared to Portofino, Italy, is flanked by old forts and bold headlands. Among the town's attractions is a pink 18th-century Anglican **church,** on Church Street, and the **Market Square,** where colorfully attired farm women offer even more colorful produce for sale.

Fort George, on Church Street, built by the French, stands at the entrance to the bay, with subterranean passageways and old guardrooms and cells.

Hounded by spice peddlers and taxi drivers trying to drum up business, people stroll along the waterfront of **The Carenage** or relax on its Pedestrian Plaza, with seats and hanging planters providing shade from the sun.

On this side of town, the **Grenada National Museum,** at the corner of Young and Monckton streets (☎ **473/440-3725**), is set in the foundations of an old French army barracks and prison built in 1704. Small but interesting, it houses finds from archaeological digs (including petroglyphs), native fauna, the first telegraph installed on the island, a rum still, and memorabilia depicting Grenada's history. The most comprehensive exhibit traces the native culture of Grenada. One of the exhibits shows two bathtubs—the wooden barrel used by the fort's prisoners and the carved marble tub used by Joséphine Bonaparte during her adolescence on Martinique. The museum is open Monday to Friday from 9am to 4:30pm and on Saturday from 10am to 1pm. Admission is EC$5 ($1.85).

An afternoon tour of St. George's and its environs takes you into the mountains northeast of the capital. After a 15-minute drive, you reach ✪ **Annandale Falls,** a tropical wonderland, where a cascade about 50 feet high falls into a basin. The overall beauty is almost Tahitian, and you can have a picnic surrounded by liana vines, elephant ears, and other tropical flora and spices. The **Annandale Falls Centre** (☎ **473/440-2452**) houses gift items, handcrafts, and samples of the indigenous spices of Grenada. Nearby, an improved trail leads to the falls where you can enjoy a refreshing swim. Swimmers can use the changing cubicles at the falls for free. The center is open daily from 8am to 4pm.

AROUND THE ISLAND The next day you can head north out of St. George's along the western coast, taking in beaches, spice plantations, and the fishing villages that are so typical of Grenada.

You'll pass through **Gouyave,** a spice town, the center of the nutmeg and mace industry. Both spices are produced from a single fruit. Before reaching the village, you can stop at the Dougaldston Estate, where you'll witness the processing of nutmeg and mace.

Proceeding along the coast, you reach **Sauteurs,** at the northern tip of Grenada. This is the third-largest town on the island. It was from this great cliff that the Caribs leaped to their deaths instead of facing enslavement by the French.

To the east of Sauteurs is the palm-lined **Levera Beach,** an idyllic strip of sand where the Atlantic meets the Caribbean. This is an ideal spot for a picnic lunch, but swimming can sometimes be dangerous. On the distant horizon you'll see some of the Grenadines.

Opened in 1994, the 450-acre **Levera National Park** has several white-sand beaches for swimming and snorkeling, although the surf is rough here where the Atlantic meets the Caribbean. It's also a hiker's paradise. Offshore are coral reefs and seagrass beds. The park contains a mangrove swamp, a lake, and a bird sanctuary; perhaps you'll see a rare tropical parrot. The interpretation center (☎ **473/442-1018**) is open Monday to Friday from 8am to 4pm, on Saturday from 10am to 4pm, and on Sunday from 10am to 5pm.

Heading down the east coast of Grenada, you reach **Grenville,** the island's second city. If possible, pass through here on a Saturday morning when you'll enjoy the hubbub of the native fruit-and-vegetable market. There's also a fish market along the waterfront. A nutmeg factory here welcomes visitors.

From Grenville, you can cut inland into the heart of Grenada. Here you're in a world of luxuriant foliage, passing through nutmeg, banana, and cocoa plantations. In the center of the island, reached along the major interior road between Grenville and St. George's, is **Grand Etang National Park,** containing the island's spectacular rain forest, which has been made more accessible by hiking trails. Beginning at the park's forest center, the Morne LeBaye Trail affords a short hike along which you can see clear to the 2,309-foot Mount Sinai and the east coast. Down the **Grand Etang Road** trails lead to the 2,373-foot summit of Mount Qua Qua and the Ridge and Lake Circle Trail, taking hikers on a 30-minute trek along Grand Etang Lake, the crater of an extinct volcano lying in the midst of a forest preserve and bird sanctuary. Among the birds you're likely to see are the yellow-billed cuckoo and the emerald-throated hummingbird. The park is also a playground for Mona monkeys. Covering 13 acres, the water is a cobalt blue. All three trails offer the opportunity to see a wide variety of Grenada's flora and fauna. Guides for the park trails are available, but arrangements must be made in advance. After a rainfall, the trails can be very slippery; hikers should wear sneakers or jogging shoes and carry drinking water as well. Much of the rain falls on Grenada between June and November. The park's **Grand Etang Interpretation (Nature) Centre** (☎ **473/442-7425**), on the shores of Grand Etang Lake, is open Monday through Friday from 8am to 4pm, featuring a video show about the park. Admission is $1.

You'll then begin your descent from the mountains. Along the way you'll pass hanging carpets of mountain ferns. Going through the tiny hamlets of Snug Corner and Beaulieu, you eventually come back to the capital.

On yet another day, you can drive south from St. George's to the beaches and resorts spread along the already much-mentioned **Grand Anse,** which is among the most beautiful beaches in the West Indies. Water taxis can also take you from The Carenage in St. George's to Grand Anse.

Point Salines, where the airport is located, is at the southwestern tip of the island, where a lighthouse stood for 56 years. However, a sculpture of the lighthouse has been constructed on the grounds just outside the airport terminal building. A panoramic view ranging from the northwestern side of Grenada to the green hills in the east to the undulating plains in the south can be seen from a nearby hill.

Along the way you'll pass through the village of **Woburn,** which was featured in the film *Island in the Sun,* and go through the sugar belt of **Woodlands,** with its tiny sugarcane factory.

SHOPPING

Everybody who visits Grenada comes home with a basket of spices, better than any you're likely to find in your local supermarket. These hand-woven panniers of palm leaf or straw are full of items grown on the island, including the inevitable nutmeg, as well as mace, cloves, cinnamon, bay leaf, vanilla, and ginger. The local stores also sell a lot of luxury imports, mainly from England, at prices that are almost (not quite) duty free. Of course, Grenada is no grand merchandise mart of the Caribbean like St. Thomas and Sint Maarten, but you may locate some local handcrafts, gifts, and even art; wherever you go you'll be besieged by spice vendors.

Bon Voyage. The Carenage. ☎ **473/440-4217.**

This is the island's leading purveyor of diamonds, precious stones, and gold and silver jewelry, plus china and crystal that includes such world-renowned names as Wedgwood, Aynsley, Blue Delft, Royal Doulton, Royal Brierley, and Coalport. Of course, if you're going on to Aruba, Sint Maarten, or St. Thomas, you may want to wait and make serious purchases there. Bon Voyage also sells sunglasses, scarves, and accessories.

Creation Arts & Crafts. The Carenage. ☎ **473/440-0570.**

This is one of the only stores on Grenada selling handcrafts from off-island, which in this case includes Venezuela, St. Maarten, and Cuba. You'll have to wander and drag answers out of the lethargic staff. The inventory includes Cuban cigars and cigarettes, cinnamon-scented soaps and wooden bowls, painted masks made from calabash, and sculptures of birds crafted by Grenadian artisans, plus casual wear. U.S. citizens, of course, must consume the Cuban cigars and cigarettes while abroad and not attempt to bring them back into the United States.

Gift Remembered. Cross St., St. George's. ☎ **473/440-2482.**

In the center of town a block from the water, Gift Remembered sells handcrafts, straw articles, jewelry, batiks, film, beach wear, postcards, high-quality T-shirts, books, and wood carvings. It's mainly for a sort of aimless shopping, but could come in handy if you promised to bring some remembrance back from the islands for a niece, nephew, or friend.

Imagine. Grand Anse Shopping Centre. ☎ **473/444-4028.**

If you're in the Grand Anse Beach area and would like to break up your time in the sun with some handcraft purchases, this is your best bet nearby. The resort wear isn't the most fashionable we've ever seen, but it's ideal if you're seeking some minor gift item. It offers excellent value in Caribbean handcrafts, all made of natural materials—dolls, ceramics, and straw items.

Sea Change Bookstore. The Carenage. ☎ **473/440-3402.**

It's cramped, it's crowded, and the staff here might remind you of the dissatisfied teachers who used to punish you during elementary school. But despite these drawbacks, it's the largest repository of British and American newspapers on Grenada, piled untidily on overflowing shelves but pretty recent. There's also a collection of paperback books, island souvenirs, postcards, and film.

Spice Island Perfumes. The Carenage. ☎ **473/440-2006.**

Here's a little gem, a virtual treasure trove of perfumes made from the natural extracts of all those herbs and spices grown on Grenada. If you're a collector of exotic scents, this is your store. At least you'll smell different from everybody else. The workshop produces and sells perfumes, potpourri, and teas made from the locally grown flowers and spices. If you like, they'll spray you with a number of desired scents, including island flower, spice, frangipani, jasmine, patchouli, and wild orchid. The shop stands near the harbor entrance, close to the Ministry of Tourism and the public library.

Tikal. Young St., St. George's. ☎ **473/440-2310.**

This early 18th-century brick building is off The Carenage, next to the museum. You'll find an array of tastefully chosen handcrafts from around the world, as well as the finest selection of crafts made on Grenada, including batiks, ceramics, wood carvings, paintings, straw work, and clothing. The owner, Jeanne Fisher, is the designer of the local crafts.

Yellow Poui Art Gallery. Cross St., St. George's. ☎ **473/440-3001.**

A two-minute walk from Market Square, this is the most interesting shop for souvenirs and artistic items. Here you can see oil paintings and watercolors, sculpture, prints, photography, rare antique maps, engravings, and woodcuts, with prices beginning at $10 and going up. There's also a comprehensive display of newly acquired works from Grenada, the Caribbean area, and other sources, shown in three rooms.

GRENADA AFTER DARK

Regular evening entertainment is provided by the resort hotels and includes steel bands, calypso, reggae, folk dancing, and limbo—even crab racing. Ask at your hotel desk to find out what's happening at the time of your visit.

Cat Bam, Grand Anse Beach (☎ **473/444-2050**), offers dancing and dining and stays open late (at least until 3am on Friday and Saturday). Next to the Coyaba Beach Resort, it sells Carib beer and rotis on its open terrace. You can also try **Boatyard,** Prickly Bay, L'Anse aux Epines (☎ **473/444-4662**), down by the Marina. The time to show up is Friday night after 11pm when a local DJ spins dance music until dawn. You should also consider the **Beachside Terrace** at the Flamboyant Hotel, Grand Anse (☎ **473/444-4247**), a laid-back spot featuring crab races on Monday nights (you can bet on your favorites), a live steel band on Wednesday, and, our favorite, a beach barbecue with live calypso music on Friday nights. **Le Sucrier,** Sugar Mill, Grand Anse (☎ **473/444-1068**), has comedy acts, golden oldies, and a disco scene, but only Wednesday through Saturday nights. A young local crowd, both visitors and residents, shows up any time after 9pm.

For those seeking culture, the 200-seat **Marryshow Folk Theatre,** Herbert Blaize Street near Bain Alley, St. George's (☎ **473/440-2451**), offers performances of

Grenadian, American, and European folk music, drama, and West Indian interpretative folk dance. This is a project of the University of the West Indies School of Continuing Studies. Check with the Marryshow Theatre or the tourist office to see what's on. Tickets cost EC$15 to EC$20 ($5.60 to $7.40).

The island's most popular nightspot is **Fantazia 2001,** at the Gem Holiday Beach Resort, Morne Rouge Bay, St. George's (☎ **473/444-2288**). It's air-conditioned, with state-of-the-art equipment, good acoustics, and fantastic disco lights, and plays the best in regional and international sounds. Theme nights are frequent, ranging from "Oldie Goldies" to reggae nights. Live shows are presented on Friday and Saturday. Admission to the club costs EC$10 to EC$35 ($3.70 to $12.95) per person, depending on the entertainment.

A SIDE TRIP TO CARRIACOU

Largest of the Grenadines, Carriacou, "land of many reefs," is populated by about 8,000 inhabitants, mainly of African descent, who are scattered over its 13 square miles of mountains, plains, and white-sand beaches. There's also a Scottish colony, and you'll see such names as MacFarland. In the hamlet of Windward, on the east coast, villagers of mixed Scottish and African descent carry on the tradition of building wooden schooners. Large skeletons of boats in various stages of readiness line the beach where workers labor with the most rudimentary of tools, building the West Indian trade schooner fleet. If you stop for a visit, a master boatbuilder will let you climb the ladder and peer inside the shell, and will explain which wood came from which island and why the boat was designed in its particular way. Much of the population, according to reputation, is involved in smuggling; otherwise, they're sailors, fishers, shipwrights, and farmers.

GETTING THERE The fastest way to go is on a 19-seat plane, which takes just 25 minutes from the Point Salines International Airport on Grenada to Carriacou's **Lauriston Airport. LIAT** (☎ **809/462-0700**) makes the short takeoff and landing (STOL) flight in about 20 minutes. There are five flights a day from Grenada. It's also possible to fly **Airlines of Carriacou** (☎ **473/444-3549**), which has daily scheduled service not only to Carriacou but to St. Vincent and the Grenadines. There are two flights per day on both Monday and Friday. For reservations, you can contact a travel agent, LIAT, or Airlines of Carriacou itself at the Point Salines airport.

Boats leave from Grenada for Carriacou at 9am on Tuesday, Wednesday, Friday, Saturday, and Sunday, charging $7.50 for a one-way ticket or $12 round-trip. On Sunday there's a round-trip excursion boat. Otherwise, boats return from Carriacou to Grenada on Monday and Thursday. In addition, there is express boat service between Grenada and Carriacou, taking 1½ to 2 hours, as opposed to the 3 hours for the regular service. This express boat offers two round-trips on Monday, Tuesday, Thursday, and Friday, plus one round-trip on Saturday. The cost is EC$40 ($14.80) one-way or EC$75 ($27.75) round-trip. The tourist office will have the latest details. From Hillsborough, you can sail on to Petit Martinique (see below). Carriacou has good places to stay; Petit Martinique does not.

ESSENTIALS For information about the island, go to the **Carriacou Board of Tourism** in Hillsborough (☎ **473/443-7948**), open Monday to Friday from 8am to noon and 1 to 4pm.

WHERE TO STAY & DINE

Caribbee Inn at Prospect. Prospect, Carriacou, Grenada, W.I. ☎ **473/443-7380.** Fax 473/443-8142. 2 rms, 8 suites. Winter, $120 double; $200 suite. Off-season, $90 double; $150 suite. MAP $40 per person extra. DISC, MC, V.

Set in the rolling hills at the northern edge of the island, on a road best suited for donkeys, this inn stands in its own secluded cove with a view of a scattering of offshore islands. On the border of a national park, the inn has its own 10 acres of tropical gardens, where you can see wild parrots and hike the nature trails. On the premises are a small library and a cultivated garden with a small swimming pool. Each accommodation is cooled by trade winds. The hotel's restaurant serves a combination of French and Creole cuisine (also to nonguests who phone ahead) every evening at a single sitting, around 7pm, for a fixed price of around $40. It's the best meal on the island. Hiking, snorkeling, and boating are among the several popular daytime activities.

Cassada Bay Hotel. Belmont, Carriacou, Grenada, W.I. ☎ **473/443-7494.** Fax 473/443-7672. 16 cabins. Winter, $95 cabin for 2. Off-season, $75 cabin for 2. Rates include American breakfast. MC, V.

Formerly a research study center for a university marine-biology department, this property has been converted into a comfortable, secluded hotel. It occupies a prime hillside with panoramic views of uninhabited islands. Two cabins are made of rough-cut timber and have all-white paneled rooms with simple furniture, double bedrooms, living rooms, and verandas, all serviced by a maid. The bedrooms have insect screens, louvered windows, and ceiling fans. The restaurant serves traditional West Indian food, and there's an open-air bar terrace where you can watch the sun go down (with a rum punch made with local limes and flavored with freshly ground nutmeg). The area is ideal for beach buffs and snorkelers, and local boats take picnic-bound passengers for trips to nearby islands. There are two dive operations within easy reach, and jeep rentals can be arranged. It's a five-minute ride from the airport.

Silver Beach Resort. Silver Beach, Beauséjour Bay, Carriacou, Grenada, W.I. ☎ **800/223-9815** in the U.S., 212/545-8469 in New York City, or 473/443-7337. Fax 473/443-7165. 10 rms, 6 cottages. Winter, $95–$105 double; $85 cottage. Off-season, $80–$95 double; $65 cottage. AE, MC, V.

This small hotel is about a five-minute walk north of Hillsborough, on a mile-long white-sand beach. The accommodations include spacious cottages, with bedrooms, living rooms, fully equipped kitchenettes, and patios; there are also bedrooms, each with a sea view from its own patio. The charges include gas, electricity, linen, cutlery, and crockery. The bar and dining pavilion are found between the cottages and the beach. At dinner you can sample some good Carriacouan dishes prepared by local cooks, including lobster, conch, and fresh fish. Locally grown vegetables and fruits are also served. Fishing, snorkeling, scuba diving, windsurfing, and boating to nearby islands can be arranged, including trips to World's End Reef in the Tobago Cays. Tennis is also available.

Exploring the Island Time Forgot

The best time to visit Carriacou is in August during its **regatta,** which was begun by J. Linton Rigg in 1965. The work boats and schooners (for which the Grenadines are famous), as well as miniature "sailboats" propelled by hand, join the festivities. Banana boats docking at the pier are filled with people rather than bananas, and sailors from Bequia and Union Island camp on tiny Jack-a-Dan and Sandy Isle, only 20 minutes away by outboard motor from Hillsborough. The people of the Grenadines try their luck at the greased pole, foot, and, of course, sailing races. Music fills the air day and night, and impromptu parties are held. At the three-day celebration, Big Drum dancers perform in the Market Square.

The **Big Drum dance** is part of the heritage of Carriacou brought from Africa and nurtured here more purely than perhaps on any other Caribbean island. The "Go

Tambo," or Big Drum, is an integral part of such traditional events as stone feasts (marking the setting of a tombstone) and the accompanying rites. The feast, called *saraca,* and setting of the tombstone may take place as long as 20 years after a death. Another event involving the Big Drum and saracas is the *maroon.* This can involve a dream interpretation, but it seems actually to be just a regular festivity, held in various places during the dry season, with dancing and feasting. A boat launching may also be accompanied by the Big Drum and the saraca and usually draws crowds of participants.

The **Carriacou Parang Festival** is usually held on the weekend closest to December 25. The festival serves to maintain the indigenous culture of the people of Carriacou. Bands are formed out of guitar, cuatro, bass drum, and violin players.

Hillsborough is the chief port and administrative center, handling the commerce of the little island, which mainly grows limes and cotton. The capital bustles on Monday when the produce arrives, then settles down again until "mail day" on Saturday. The capital is nestled in a mile-long crescent of white sand.

The **Carriacou Museum,** on Paterson Street in Hillsborough (☎ **473/443-8288**), opposite Grentel, has a display of Amerindian artifacts, European china, glass shards, and exhibits of African culture. In two small rooms, it preserves the history of Carriacou, which parallels that of its neighbor island, Grenada. It's open Monday to Friday from 9:30am to 3:45pm and on Saturday from 10am to 2pm. Admission is EC$5 ($1.85) per person.

The largest and only inhabited island near Carriacou is 486-acre **Petite Martinique** (that's "pitty," not "petite"), with a population of about 600. The chief occupation, officially, is building and sailing fishing boats, but it's also infamous as the reputed center of the smuggling trade among the islands, dealing in cigarettes and liquor from St. Barts's and St. Maarten's duty-free ports.

Forgotten by time, this little island suddenly became prominent in the news in the autumn of 1996 when it was announced that the U.S. government planned to build a base here for the Grenada Coast Guard. The dockside site is intended to strengthen drug interdiction efforts in the Caribbean. In spite of strong local objection, plans are moving ahead to build the base.

Islanders claim the American "gift" looks suspiciously like a Trojan horse. They fear that this is just an American effort to gain a permanent foothold here where even the authority of Grenada's government seems weak. Actually, Petite Martinique would be the first of a series of such bases throughout the Caribbean, with other Coast Guard operations slated for Barbuda, Nevis, St. Vincent, Tobago, and St. Lucia.

14 Barbados

Bajans like to think of their island as "England in the tropics," but endless pink- and white-sand beaches are what really put Barbados on the map. Rich in tradition, Barbados has a grand array of hotels (many of them superexpensive). Although it doesn't offer casinos, it has more than beach life for travelers interested in learning about the local culture and more sightseeing attractions than most islands of the West Indies.

Afternoon tea remains a tradition at many places, cricket is still the national sport, and many Bajans speak with a British accent. Crime has been on the rise in recent years, although Barbados is still viewed as a safe destination. The difference between the haves and the have-nots doesn't cause the sometimes-violent clash here that it does on some other islands, such as Jamaica.

Don't rule out Barbados if you're seeking a peaceful island getaway. Although the south coast is known for its nightlife and the west-coast beach strip is completely built up, some of the island remains undeveloped. The east coast is fairly tranquil, and you can often be alone here (but since it faces the Atlantic, the waters aren't as calm as they are on the Caribbean side). Many escapists, especially Canadians seeking a low-cost place to stay in the winter, don't seem to mind the Atlantic waters at all.

Because it's so built up with hotels and condos, Barbados offers more package deals than most islands. You can often get a steal in the off-season, which lasts from April until mid-December. You don't necessarily have to pay the rack rate (walk-in rate for individual bookings) at hotels if you'll take the time to shop around. Barbados is filled with bargains, especially along its southern coast directly below Bridgetown. This strip of beachfront isn't the most glamorous, but it's the most reasonable in price.

GETTING THERE

More than 20 daily flights arrive on Barbados from all over the world. **Grantley Adams International Airport** is on Highway 7, on the southern tip of the island at Long Bay, between Oistins and The Crane (a village). From North America, the four major gateways to Barbados are New York, Miami, Toronto, and San Juan. Flying time to Barbados from New York is $4^1/_2$ hours, from Miami it's $3^1/_2$ hours, from Toronto it's 5 hours, and from San Juan, $1^1/_2$ hours.

American Airlines (☎ **800/433-7300**) has dozens of connections passing through San Juan plus a daily nonstop flight from New York's JFK to Barbados and one from Miami to Barbados. U.S. passengers who do fly through San Juan can usually speed through U.S. Customs clearance in San Juan on their return flight rather than in their home cities, saving time and inconvenience.

Travelers via New York and Miami can opt for nonstop flights offered daily by **BWIA** (☎ **800/538-2942**), the national airline of Trinidad and Tobago. BWIA also offers many flights from Barbados to Trinidad.

Canadians sometimes select nonstop flights to Barbados from Toronto. **Air Canada** (☎ **800/776-3000** in the U.S., or 800/268-7240 in Canada) offers the most nonstop scheduled service from Canada to Barbados, with convenient evening departures. There are seven flights per week from Toronto in winter, plus one Sunday flight from Montréal year-round. In summer, when demand slackens, there are less flights from Toronto.

Barbados is a major hub of the Caribbean-based airline known as **LIAT** (☎ **246/434-5428** for reservations, or 809/428-0986 at the Barbados airport), which provides generally poor service from Barbados to a handful of neighboring islands, including St. Vincent in the Grenadines, Antigua, and Dominica.

British Airways (☎ **800/247-9297**) offers nonstop service to Barbados from both of London's major airports (Heathrow and Gatwick).

GETTING AROUND

BY TAXI Taxis aren't metered, but rates are fixed by the government. Taxis on the island are identified by the letter *Z* on their license plates. One to five passengers can be transported at the same time and can share the fare. Overcharging is infrequent; most drivers have a reputation for courtesy and honesty. Taxis are plentiful, and drivers will produce a list of standard rates, which is $16 per hour.

BY RENTAL CAR If you don't mind *driving on the left,* you may find a rental car ideal on Barbados. A temporary permit is needed if you don't have an International Driver's License. The rental agencies listed below will all issue you a visitor's permit, or you can go to the police desk upon your arrival at the airport. You're charged a registration fee of BD$10 ($5), and you must have your own license. The speed limit is 20 m.p.h. inside city limits, 30 m.p.h. elsewhere on the island. No taxes apply to car rentals on Barbados.

None of the major U.S.-based car-rental companies maintains an affiliate on Barbados, but a host of local companies rent vehicles, many of which are in bad shape. Except in the peak midwinter season, cars are usually readily available without a prior reservation.

Most renters pay for a taxi from the airport to their hotel and then call for the delivery of a rental car. This is especially advisable because of frequent delays at airport counters.

Many local car-rental companies continue to draw serious complaints from readers, both for overcharging and for the condition of the rental vehicle. Proceed very carefully with rentals on this island. Check out the insurance and liability issues carefully when you rent.

The island's most frequently recommended car-rental firm is **National Car Rentals,** Bush Hall, Main Road, St. Michael (☎ **246/426-0603**), which offers a wide selection of all-Japanese cars (note that it's not affiliated with the U.S. chain of the same name). Located near the island's national stadium (the only one on the island), it lies 3 miles northeast of Bridgetown. Cars will be delivered to almost any location on the

Barbados

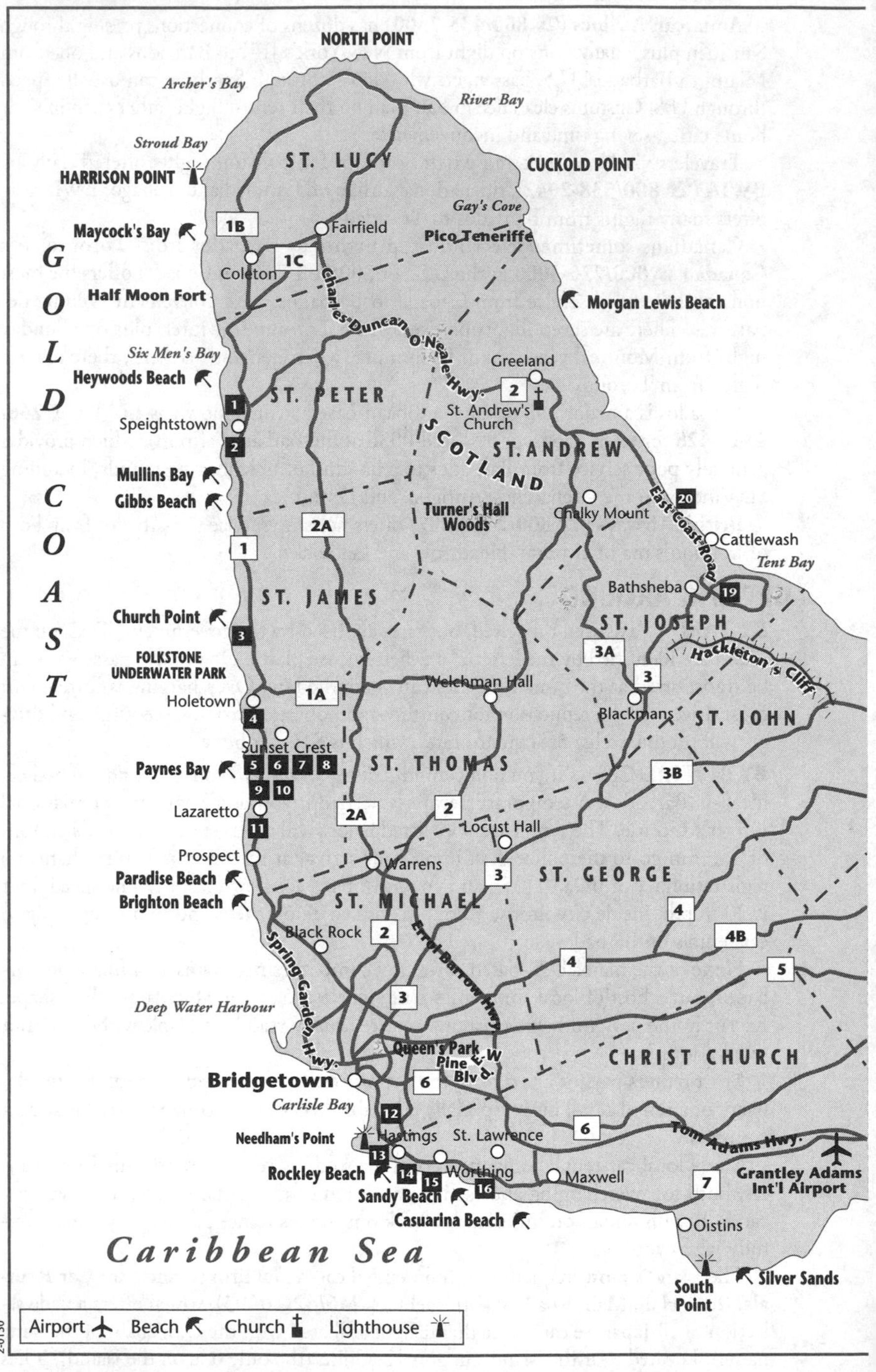

NORTH POINT
Archer's Bay
River Bay
Stroud Bay
HARRISON POINT
ST. LUCY
CUCKOLD POINT
Gay's Cove
1B
Maycock's Bay
Fairfield
Pico Teneriffe
Coleton
1C
Half Moon Fort
Morgan Lewis Beach
Charles Duncan O'Neale Hwy.
G O L D C O A S T
Six Men's Bay
Heywoods Beach
Greeland
ST. PETER
St. Andrew's Church
Speightstown
SCOTLAND
ST. ANDREW
Mullins Bay
Gibbs Beach
Chalky Mount
East Coast Road
Turner's Hall Woods
Cattlewash
Tent Bay
Bathsheba
ST. JAMES
Church Point
ST. JOSEPH
Hackleton's Cliff
FOLKSTONE UNDERWATER PARK
Welchman Hall
Holetown
Blackmans
ST. JOHN
Sunset Crest
Paynes Bay
ST. THOMAS
Lazaretto
Locust Hall
Prospect
Warrens
ST. GEORGE
Paradise Beach
Brighton Beach
ST. MICHAEL
Black Rock
Spring Garden Hwy.
Errol Barrow Hwy.
Deep Water Harbour
Queen's Park
Pine Blv d.
E. W.
CHRIST CHURCH
Bridgetown
Carlisle Bay
Needham's Point
Hastings
St. Lawrence
Tom Adams Hwy.
Rockley Beach
Worthing
Maxwell
Grantley Adams Int'l Airport
Sandy Beach
Casuarina Beach
Oistins
Caribbean Sea
South Point
Silver Sands
Airport
Beach
Church
Lighthouse
2-0150

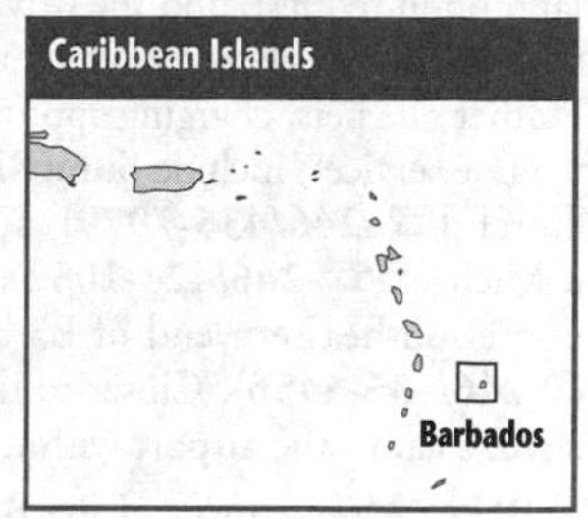

Atlantic Ocean

Almond Beach Club 5
Almond Beach Village 1
Bagshot House Hotel 16
Barbados Hilton 13
Casuarina Beach Club 16
Cobblers Cove Hotel 2
Coconut Creek Club 6
Colony Club 3
Coral Reef Club 3
Crane Beach Hotel 17
The Crystal Cove 11
Divi Southwinds Beach Resort 16
The Edgewater Inn 19
Fairholme 17
Glitter Bay 3
Grand Barbados Beach Resort 12
Kingsley Club 20
Ocean View 14
Royal Pavilion 3
Sandpiper Inn 4
Sam Lord's Castle 18
Sandy Beach Hotel 16
Sandy Lane 7
Settlers Beach 3
Southern Palms 16
Tamarind Cove 10
Traveller's Palm 9
Treasure Beach 8
Woodville 15

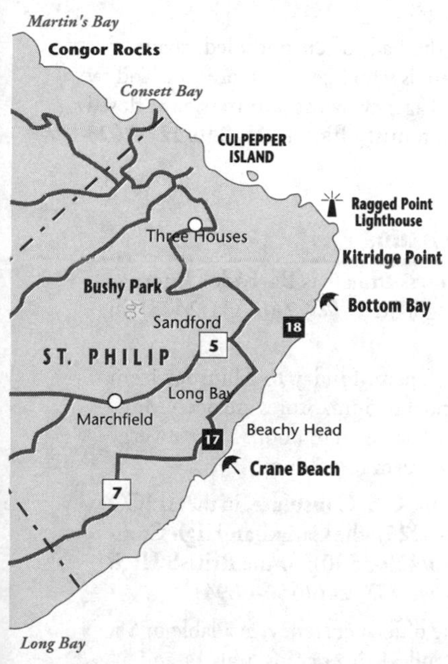

0 3 km 1.9 mi N

island upon request, and the driver who delivers it will carry the necessary forms for the Bajan driver's license, which may be purchased for $5.

Other safe bets, charging approximately the same prices and offering approximately the same services, include **Sunny Isle Motors,** Dayton, Worthing Main Road, Christ Church (☎ **246/435-7979**), and **P&S Car Rentals,** Pleasant View, Cave Hill, St. Michael (☎ **246/424-2052**). One company conveniently close to hotels on the remote southeastern end of Barbados is **Stoutes Car Rentals,** Kirtons, St. Philip (☎ **246/435-4456**). Closer to the airport than its competitors, it can theoretically deliver a car to the airport within 10 minutes of a call placed when you arrive.

BY BUS Unlike most of the British Windwards, Barbados has a reliable bus system fanning out from Bridgetown to almost every part of the island. On most major routes, there are buses running every 20 minutes or so. Bus fares are BD$1.50 (75¢) wherever you go. Exact change is required.

The nationally owned **buses** of Barbados are blue with yellow stripes. They're not numbered, but their destinations are marked on the front. Departures are from Bridgetown, leaving from Fairchild Street for the south and east; from Lower Green and the Princess Alice Highway for the north going along the west coast. Call the Barbados Tourist Board (☎ **246/436-6820**) for bus schedules and information.

Privately operated **minibuses** run shorter distances and travel more frequently. They are bright yellow, with their destinations displayed on the bottom-left corner of the windshield. Minibuses in Bridgetown are boarded at River Road, Temple Yard, and Probyn Street. They, too, cost BD$1.50 (75¢).

BY SCOOTER OR BICYCLE In spite of the bad, often potholed, roads, this could be a viable option for some adventurous souls who like to explore an island by scooter or bike. The trouble is in finding a rental agency. Most outfitters have closed down, finding it unprofitable. You can call the tourist office at ☎ **246/427-2623** to see if a rental agency has opened.

FAST FACTS: Barbados

American Express The island's American Express affiliate is **Barbados International Travel Services,** Horizon House, McGregor Street (☎ **246/431-2423**), in the heart of Bridgetown.

Business Hours Most banks on Barbados are open Monday to Thursday from 9am to 3pm and on Friday from 9am to 1pm and 3 to 5pm. Stores are open Monday to Friday from 8am to 4pm and on Saturday from 8am to noon. Most government offices are open Monday to Friday from 8:30am to 4:30pm.

Consulates and High Commissions Contact the **U.S. Consulate,** in the ALICO Building, Cheapside, Bridgetown (☎ **246/431-0225**); the **Canadian High Commission,** Bishop Court, Hill Pine Road (☎ **246/429-3550**); or the **British High Commission,** Lower Collymore Rock, St. Michael (☎ **246/436-6694**).

Currency The **Barbados dollar (BD$)** is the official currency, available in $5, $10, $20, and $100 notes, as well as 10¢, 25¢, and $1 silver coins, plus 1¢ and 5¢ copper coins. The Bajan dollar is worth 50¢ in U.S. currency. Unless otherwise specified, currency quotations in this chapter are in U.S. dollars. Most stores take traveler's checks or U.S. dollars. However, it's best to convert your money at banks and pay in Bajan dollars.

Dentist **Dr. Derek Golding,** with two other colleagues, maintains one of the busiest practices on Barbados. Located at the Beckwith Shopping Mall in Bridgetown (☎ **246/426-3001**), he accepts most of the emergency dental problems from the many cruise ships that dock off Barbados. This practice will accept any emergency and often remains open late for last-minute problems. Otherwise, hours are Monday through Saturday from 8:30am to 4pm. All members of this dental team received their training in the United States, Britain, Canada, or New Zealand.

Doctor Your hotel might have a list of doctors on call, although some of the best recommended are **Dr. J. D. Gibling** (☎ **246/432-1772**) and **Dr. Adrian Lorde** or his colleague **Dr. Ahmed Mohamad** (☎ **246/424-8236**), any of whom will pay house calls to patients unable or unwilling to leave their hotel rooms.

Documents A U.S. or Canadian citizen coming directly from North America to Barbados for a period not exceeding three months must have proof of identity and national status, such as a passport, which is always preferred. However, a birth certificate (either an original or a certified copy) is also acceptable, provided it's backed up with photo ID. For stays longer than three months, a passport is required. An ongoing or return ticket is also necessary. British subjects need a valid passport.

Electricity The electricity is 110 volts AC (50 cycles), so at most places you can use your U.S.-made appliances.

Emergencies In an **emergency,** call ☎ **119.** Other important numbers include the police at ☎ **112,** the **fire** department at ☎ **113,** and an **ambulance** at ☎ **115.**

Hospitals The **Queen Elizabeth Hospital** is on Martinsdale Road in St. Michael (☎ **246/436-6450**). There are several private clinics as well; one of the most expensive and best recommended is the **Bayview Hospital,** St. Paul's Avenue, Bayville, St. Michael (☎ **246/436-5446**).

Information The **Barbados Tourism Authority** is on Harbour Road (P.O. Box 242), Bridgetown, Barbados, W.I. (☎ **246/427-2623**); call or write for information. **In the United States,** you can obtain information before you go at the following offices: 800 Second Ave., New York, NY 10017 (☎ **212/986-6516**) or 3440 Wilshire Blvd., Suite 1215, Los Angeles, CA 90010 (☎ **800/221-9831** or 213/380-2198). **In Canada,** there is no longer an office in Montréal, but you can call **800/268-9122** for information. **In the United Kingdom,** the Barbados Tourism Authority is at 263 Tottenham Court Rd., London W1P 9AA (☎ **0171/636-9448**).

Language The Barbadians, or Bajans, as they're called, speak English, but with their own island lilt.

Safety Crimes against tourists used to be rare, but the U.S. State Department reports rising crime, such as purse snatching, pickpocketing, armed robbery, and even sexual assault upon women. The department advises that you not leave cash or valuables in your hotel room, beware of purse snatchers when walking, exercise caution when walking on the beach or visiting tourist attractions, and be wary of driving in isolated areas of Barbados.

Taxes When you leave, you'll have to pay a BD$25 ($12.50) departure tax. A 7½% government sales tax is added to hotel bills.

Tipping Most hotels and restaurants add at least a 10% service charge to your bill.

Water Barbados has a pure water supply. It's pumped from underground sources in the coral rock that covers six-sevenths of the island, and it's safe to drink.

Weather Daytime temperatures are in the 75° to 85°F range throughout the year.

1 Where to Stay

Per square inch, Barbados has the best hotels in the Caribbean. Many are small and personally run. Most of our recommendations are on fashionable St. James Beach. The biggest news on the hotel scene is the projected opening of one of Jamaican entrepreneur Butch Stewart's new Sandals resorts on the west coast. This long-delayed project will be called—you guessed it—**Sandals Barbados.** For more information and details, call ☎ **800/SANDALS.**

Now here's the bad news: Because Barbados is so popular with charter groups, hotels often are extremely expensive in high season. Many hotels will also insist that you take their meal plans if you're there in the winter.

But Barbados does have some bargains, and we've surveyed the best of these as well. You'll have to head south from Bridgetown to such places as Hastings and Worthing for the best buys, which are often self-contained efficiencies or studio apartments where you can do your own cooking.

Prices cited in this section, unless otherwise indicated, are in U.S. dollars. the government hotel tax of 7½% and a 10% service charge will be added to your final bill.

ON THE WEST COAST

VERY EXPENSIVE

✪ **Cobblers Cove Hotel.** Road View, St. Peter, Barbados, W.I. ☎ **800/890-6060** in the U.S., 800/424-5500 in Canada, 0181/367-5175 in London, or 246/422-2291. Fax 246/422-2291. 40 suites. A/C MINIBAR TEL. Winter, $520–$850 standard suite; $1,250 Camelot suite, $1,300 Colleton suite. Off-season, $340–$480 standard suite for 2; $760 Camelot suite, $780 Colleton suite. Rates include MAP. AE, MC, V. Closed late Sept to mid-Oct.

One of the small, exclusive hotels of Barbados, Cobblers Cove (a former mansion) is built like a fort, with a mock-medieval style. The home, now a member of Relais & Châteaux, was erected over the site of a former British fort that used to protect vessels going into the harbor at nearby Speightstown, a 10-minute walk away. Today, after an exhaustive overhaul, the hotel is a favorite honeymoon retreat, offering first-class suites housed in 10 Iberian-style villas placed throughout the gardens.

Overlooking a white-sand beach, each unit has a spacious living room, a private balcony or patio, and a kitchenette. Two of the most exclusive accommodations you can rent on all of Barbados are the Camelot and Colleton suites on the rooftop of the original mansion; they're beautifully decorated and offer panoramic views of both the beach and the garden. Meals can be delivered to your suite so you can dine in privacy. The resort contains many acres of well-developed tropical gardens and lawns.

Dining/Entertainment: The open-air dining room overlooks the sea. The cuisine has won many awards and has an emphasis on Caribbean specialties from the sea—say, a fish of the day grilled or poached with Bajan seasoning, or shrimp flavored with ginger. Nearby is the resort's social center, the bar.

Services: Laundry, baby-sitting, arrangements for island tours, car rentals.

Facilities: Complimentary tennis day or night, swimming pool, water sports (including waterskiing, Sunfish sailing, snorkeling, and windsurfing).

Coral Reef Club. St. James Beach, Barbados, W.I. ☎ **800/223-1108** or 246/422-2372. Fax 246/422-1776. 69 units. A/C TEL. Winter, $435–$645 double; $970 two-bedroom suite for 2, $1,095 two-bedroom suite for 4. Off-season, $300–$355 double; $435 two-bedroom suite for 2, $630 two-bedroom suite for 4. Children under 12 not accepted in February. Rates include MAP. AE, MC, V.

Family owned and managed, this small luxury hotel has set standards that are hard for competitors to match. It's one of the best and most respected establishments on the island. Set on elegantly landscaped, flat land beside a good beach, the hotel is about a five-minute drive north of Holetown. A collection of veranda-fronted private accommodations surrounds a main building and clubhouse. This contains the reception area, a reading room, a dining area and bar, and a quartet of deluxe bedrooms on the second floor. The accommodations are scattered about a dozen landscaped acres, fronting a long strip of white-sand beach, ideal for swimming. They open onto private patios, and some of the rooms have separate dressing rooms. Not all are in cottages. Some, not in the main building, are in small coral-stone wings in the gardens. Rental units here vary greatly.

Dining/Entertainment: You can enjoy lunch in an open-air area. Dining in the evening is in a room with three sides open to ocean views. A first-class chef runs the kitchen. There's a weekly folklore show and barbecue every Thursday and a Bajan buffet on Monday evening, featuring an array of food, along with whole baked fish and lots of local entertainment.

Services: Room service (during restaurant hours), laundry, massage, hair salon, a helpful reception staff.

Facilities: Freshwater swimming pool, tennis court (floodlit at night), water sports (including windsurfing, snorkeling, scuba diving, and use of a minifleet of small sailboats).

Glitter Bay. Porters, St. James, Barbados, W.I. ☎ **800/223-1818** in the U.S., or 246/422-5555. Fax 246/422-3940. 83 rms and suites. A/C MINIBAR TEL. Winter, $415–$445 double; $510–$585 one-bedroom suite for 2, $925–$1,150 two-bedroom suite for 4. Off-season, $215–$300 double; $250–$365 one-bedroom suite for 2, $465–$710 two-bedroom suite for 4. MAP $60 per person extra. Children under 12 are charged $40 per day when sharing a suite with their parents. AE, DC, MC, V.

This carefully maintained resort, managed by Princess Hotels International, has discreet charm and Mediterranean style, although it isn't as sophisticated and alluring as its next-door sibling, the Royal Pavilion (see below). But with its cottage-like suites with kitchenettes, it's a favored choice for families (well-to-do families, that is). Built in 1981 by a small Barbados-based hotel chain (the Pemberton Group), it lies on a 10-acre plot of manicured lowlands near a sandy beachfront a mile north of Holetown and offers a wide array of sports facilities. In the 1930s, this property was owned by Sir Edward Cunard of shipbuilding fame. The parties he gave here in the Great House were so famous that it helped make Barbados synonymous with glitter and glamour back in England. The accommodations are in a white minivillage of Iberian inspiration, whose patios, thick beams, and red terra-cotta tiles surround a garden with a swimming pool, an artificial waterfall, and a simulated lagoon. Most units contain art, built-in furniture, louvered doors, and spacious outdoor patios or balconies ringed with shrubbery. The larger units have small kitchenettes, and some of the biggest accommodations are suitable for four to six people.

Dining/Entertainment: The hotel's social center is the Piperade Restaurant, beneath a terra-cotta roof and amid a garden. Offering American and international cuisine, it contains its own bar. The Sunset Beach Bar is a popular rendezvous spot. Sheltered by shrubbery and tropical trees, guests can dance on an outdoor patio and enjoy local entertainment, such as a steel band or calypso.

Services: 24-hour room service, concierge, laundry, baby-sitting, business services, limousine service.

Facilities: Fitness and massage center, two tennis courts (complimentary for guests day and night), aerobics classes, and complimentary water sports (including waterskiing, windsurfing, snorkeling, and catamaran sailing), two swimming pools (one a shallow children's pool); golf at nearby Royal Westmoreland (a Pemberton associated company); horseback riding, scuba diving, and motorboating can be arranged.

✪ **Royal Pavilion.** Porters, St. James, Barbados, W.I. ☎ **800/223-1818** in the U.S., or 246/422-5555. Fax 246/422-3940. 72 junior suites, 3 villas. A/C MINIBAR TEL. Winter, $510–$585 suite for 2; $995–$1,125 villa for 4, $1,500–$1,690 villa for 6. Off-season, $250–$365 suite for 2; $470–$720 villa for 4, $715–$1,070 villa for 6. MAP $60 per person extra. AE, DC, MC, V.

A spectacular place to stay, this hotel is a mile north of Holeton and sits next door to Glitter Bay, part of the same chain, whose gardens it shares. The lush resort was built on the site of the former Miramar Hotel, which was radically redesigned in 1987, transformed into a pink-walled structure with lily ponds and splashing fountains. British grace and Bajan hospitality blend in this property, which became one of the finest resorts on Barbados the moment it opened. We find it far superior to the more famous Sandy Lane (see below).

The architects created a California-hacienda style for their 72 waterfront junior suites and a villa consisting of three suites in 8 acres of landscaped gardens. Guests staying here can visit the drinking, dining, and sports facilities at Glitter Bay (and vice versa). Children 11 and under are not accepted in winter.

Dining/Entertainment: There are two oceanfront restaurants. Tabora's serves breakfast and lunch. The more formal Palm Terrace, set below the seaside columns of an open-air loggia, is open only for dinner. Both restaurants offer an à la carte menu of Caribbean and international fare. On Wednesday night there's an international buffet.

Services: 24-hour room service, concierge, laundry, baby-sitting, business service, limousine service.

Facilities: Freshwater swimming pool overlooking the ocean, massage center, fitness center at Glitter Bay, two tennis courts (complimentary for guests day and night), water-sports program (including complimentary snorkeling, waterskiing, sailing, and windsurfing), duty-free shops, beauty shop with hairdresser. Guests also enjoy privileged tee times at the nearby Royal Westmoreland.

Sandy Lane. St. James, Barbados, W.I. ☎ **800/225-5843** in the U.S. and Canada, or 246/432-1311. Fax 246/432-2954. 90 rms, 30 suites. A/C MINIBAR TEL. Winter, $800–$1,000 double; from $1,150 suite. Off-season, $525–$580 double; from $630 suite. Rates include breakfast. AE, DC, DISC, MC, V.

If you have to ask about the rates, you can't afford it. The last remaining outpost of British colonialism on Barbados, this place is stiffly formal and very British, the ideal choice if Prince Charles should visit (though Di would look elsewhere). The world created here has been called "more Evelyn Waugh than Beatrix Potter." In the 1960s, it set the standards for style and elegance, but, in spite of a massive overhaul, we've found that its former glory just never returned.

Originally established in 1961, on the 380-acre site of a bankrupt sugar plantation less than a mile south of Holetown, this hotel still attracts many of the biggest names in Britain. In 1991, after a period of much-publicized decline, the hotel received a multimillion-dollar infusion of cash from the Forte chain, its present owners. Today the place offers well-furnished suites and rooms, a private white-sand beach, and one of the most prestigious golf courses on Barbados. The buildings are made of cut coral, with shingle roofs, baronial arches, high ceilings, and a porte-cochère—in all, the grounds resemble a lavish estate with tall gates, a driveway, and ornamental steps. All rooms and suites have refrigerators.

Dining/Entertainment: You can order a cool salad at the pool at lunch and later enjoy a continental-style candlelight dinner. Buffet tables are frequent, as is regular entertainment, such as calypso. You can also dine on Italian cuisine in the Seashell

Restaurant or munch on club sandwiches and hamburgers at either the Oasis Beach Bar or an informal bar/restaurant beside the golf course. Scattered in various corners of the place, you'll find five different bars. Live entertainment (usually from a dance band) is presented nightly, and a Bajan floor show and cabaret is presented once a week.

Services: 24-hour room service, baby-sitting, laundry and dry cleaning, concierge, valet.

Facilities: The otherwise dreary swimming pool is surrounded by Italianate gardens, Roman fountains, and colonnaded verandas; the overall effect is one of neo-Palladian grandeur. There's also an outstanding 18-hole golf course, five all-weather tennis courts (four lit for night play), water sports (including scuba diving, windsurfing, sailboat rentals, and snorkeling), bikes for rent, and an activities center for children 2 to 12. Although we've seen better gyms, the winning touch is the chilled eucalyptus-scented towels you're handed after a workout.

Settlers Beach. St. James, Barbados, W.I. ☎ **246/432-0840.** Fax 246/432-2174. 22 villas. A/C TEL. Winter, $450–$600 villa for 2–5. Off-season, $225–$250 villa for 2–5. Children 17 and under stay free in parents' room. MAP $50 per person extra. AE, MC, V.

This seaside collection of comfortable two-story villas is located on 4 acres of beachfront property 8 miles from Bridgetown, north of Holetown. Each unit has two bedrooms, two bathrooms, a spacious tile-floored lounge and dining room, and a fully equipped kitchen. The apartments are decorated in sunny colors, and all units were last refurbished in 1995. This resort, squeezed between larger properties, appeals to those who are independent and don't want to be coddled. This property is, frankly, dated, but it must be doing something right because it has lots of repeat clients, attracting American families in summer and English visitors in winter.

Dining/Entertainment: The independently run restaurant has won awards and is one of the finest on the island. A bar lies nearby.

Services: Room service (8am to 9pm), laundry, baby-sitting.

Facilities: Swimming pool, two nearby tennis courts, sandy beach.

Treasure Beach. Payne's Bay, St. James, Barbados, W.I. ☎ **800/223-6510** in the U.S., 800/424-5500 in Canada, or 246/432-1346. Fax 246/432-1094. 30 suites. A/C TEL. Winter, $420–$550 one-bedroom suite for 2, $1,200 superior luxury suite. Off-season, $155–$235 one-bedroom suite for 2, $550 superior luxury suite. MAP $45 per person extra. AE, DC, DISC, MC, V.

Set on about an acre of sandy beachfront land, this hotel is a minivillage of two-story buildings arranged into a horseshoe pattern around a pool and garden. Treasure Beach has a loyal following. It's small but choice, known for its well-prepared food and the comfort and style of its amenities. The atmosphere is both intimate and relaxed, with personalized service a mark of the well-trained staff. The hotel is set on small grounds in St. James in the glittery hotel belt of Barbados, about half a mile south of Holetown. The accommodations are furnished in a tropical motif and open onto private balconies or patios. (The baths are a little cramped.) The clientele is about evenly divided between North American and British clients. Children 11 and under are accepted only on special request.

Dining/Entertainment: Even if you aren't staying here, try to sample some of the culinary specialties at the Treasure Beach Restaurant, including freshly caught seafood and favorites from the Bajan culinary repertoire.

Services: Room service (7:30am to 9:30pm), valet and laundry service, safety-deposit boxes, receptionist available to arrange for car rentals and island tours.

Facilities: Rental of sailboats, swimming pool that's too small; access to nearby golf and tennis courts.

EXPENSIVE

Almond Beach Club. Vauxhall, St. James, Barbados, W.I. ☎ **800/4-ALMOND** in the U.S., or 246/432-7840. Fax 246/432-2115. 95 rms, 65 suites. A/C TV TEL. Winter, $450–$500 double; $525–$540 suite for 2. Off-season, $365–$380 double; $395–$425 suite for 2. Rates include all meals. Children under 16 not accepted. AE, MC, V.

Set on flat and sandy beach about a two-minute walk from its more famous neighbor, Sandy Lane, this hotel lies on the island's west coast, south of Holetown. The narrow beach here is less than ideal. An overhauled property, this was the first of Barbados's all-inclusive resorts, established in 1991 as part of a $2 million refurbishment. The accommodations are spread among seven low-rise, three-story buildings (no elevators). Pool-view units open onto three freshwater swimming pools and the gardens, planted with frangipani trees and palms; beachfront units open onto the Caribbean. Island motifs, tropical fabrics, and tile floors dominate the room decor.

Dining/Entertainment: The all-inclusive program offers a dine-around option, allowing guests to consume one lunch and one dinner per week-long stay at one of three neighboring hotels. On the premises is a continental restaurant (the Almond Beach), a West Indian/Bajan restaurant (Enid's), and a beachfront snack bar. The Rum Shop Bar evokes 19th-century colonial days and offers a sampling of virtually every kind of distilled rum on Barbados. There's lively nightly entertainment until 2am, including jazz bands, steel-drum bands, Bajan folk dancing, and contemporary music, as well as piano bar entertainment.

Services: Laundry, baby-sitting, guest services department (organizing island tours).

Facilities: Three freshwater swimming pools, tennis and squash courts, fitness center with sauna, fishing, windsurfing, waterskiing, reef fishing, kayaking, and "banana boating."

Almond Beach Village. Speightstown (15 miles north of Bridgetown along Hwy. 2A), St. Peter, Barbados, W.I. ☎ **800/4-ALMOND** in the U.S., or 246/422-4900. Fax 246/422-1581. 288 rms, 23 suites. A/C TV TEL. Dec–Apr, $450–$500 double; $525–$570 suite. May–Nov, $365–$380 double; $395–$450 suite. Rates are all-inclusive. AE, MC, V.

Set near a string of more expensive hotels (referred to as the island's Gold Coast), this hotel occupies the site of a 19th-century sugarcane plantation. In 1994, it was acquired by the largest industrial conglomerate on Barbados (Barbados Shipping and Trading) and benefited from a $13 million renovation. Today it's the most desirable all-inclusive resort on the island (with all meals, drinks, and most sports included in one net price) and a good choice for families.

On 30 acres of tropically landscaped gardens and prime beachfront, its relatively isolated position makes leaving the premises awkward, although that doesn't seem to bother guests who check in here on all-inclusive plans. Accommodations are clustered into seven different compounds to create something akin to a miniature, self-contained village. Exchange privileges are available with its all-inclusive twin, the Almond Beach Club (see above).

Dining/Entertainment: Four different restaurants add diversity to the dining options. A specialty Italian restaurant, La Smarita, is the most formal of the lot. The main dining room is the Horizons. Least formal is Enid's, for Bajan food. Other choices are the Reef, a burger-and-hot-dog joint, and a more formal seafood venue where you can dine by candlelight at nighttime.

Services: Laundry facilities, baby-sitting, room services. The resort offers one of the best children's programs on the island: It has a club just for children (with videos, Nintendo, computer lab, books, and board games), two children's playgrounds, kiddies' pool, activity center, pool and beach games, nature walks, water sports, treasure hunts, story time, arts and crafts, and evening entertainment.

Facilities: Five floodlit tennis courts, a nine-hole par-3 golf course (too easy for professionals but well tuned for beginners), two air-conditioned squash courts.

Coconut Creek Club. Derricks, St. James, Barbados, W.I. ☎ **246/432-0803.** Fax 246/438-4697. 53 rms. A/C TEL. Winter, $186–$210 double. Off-season, $140–$179 double. Rates include MAP. AE, MC, V.

Small, intimate, and known as an escape for publicity-shy European celebrities, this is an elegantly informal and landscaped retreat on the west coast, about a mile south of Holetown. Completely renovated in 1995, it resembles an exclusive country retreat in Devon, England. About half the rather small accommodations lie atop a low bluff overlooking what might be the two most secluded beaches on the island's west coast. Many of the bedrooms are built on the low cliff edge overlooking the ocean, whereas others open onto the pool or the flat, tropical garden. Each bedroom has a veranda or balcony where breakfast can be served. The baths are cramped.

Dining/Entertainment: The establishment's only restaurant, Cricketers, was modeled after an upscale English pub. Bajan buffets and barbecues are served on the restaurant's vine-covered open pergola, overlooking the gardens and the sea. The inn's food has been praised by *Gourmet* magazine. There's dancing to West Indian calypso and steel bands almost every night. Clients on the MAP are encouraged to dine at the restaurants connected to this chain's three other properties—the Crystal Cove Hotel, the Tamarind Cove Hotel, and the Colony Club—for no additional charge.

Services: Room service (7:30am to 10pm), baby-sitting, arrangements for island tours and rental cars.

Facilities: Freshwater swimming pool, complimentary water sports (including waterskiing, windsurfing, snorkeling, and Hobie Cat sailing); scuba diving can be arranged for an extra charge; tennis available nearby.

Colony Club. Porters, St. James Beach, Barbados, W.I. ☎ **246/422-2335.** Fax 246/422-0667. 64 rms, 34 junior suites. A/C TEL. Winter, $225–$267 double; $267–$299 suite. Off-season, $167–$192 double; $192–$210 suite. Rates include MAP. AE, DC, MC, V.

Originally established by an English expatriate in the 1950s, this discreetly elegant hotel is on the island's western coast. It caters mainly to Brits. Set behind an entrance lined with Australian pines, it occupies a site a mile north of Holetown, beside one of the island's best beaches. A complex of restored rooms looks out over shaded verandas and landscaped grounds. About a third of the rooms lie beside the sea; the others are scattered throughout the gardens. On 7 acres of tropical gardens, the grounds contain free-form lagoon rock pools. The rooms and suites are all air-conditioned with bath, shower, phone, radio, and bar. All have either a patio or a balcony, with some extending up to the lagoon rock pools. Some rooms look a bit dowdy; others are up-to-date and spiffy. Your verdict on this resort is likely to be shaped by your room assignment.

Dining/Entertainment: Set between the beachside freshwater pool and the main building is the open-sided Laguna Restaurant. The Orchids Room, the hotel's formal restaurant, offers an international cuisine. The dance floor, on an "island" in the middle of the pool, is accessed by a footbridge. There's nightly entertainment.

Services: Room service (7:30am to 9:30pm), laundry, baby-sitting, arrangements for outings and excursions.

Facilities: Four freshwater swimming pools, hairdressing/beauty salon, complimentary water sports, chauffeured speedboat and catamaran rides, air-conditioned fitness center, two floodlit tennis courts.

The Crystal Cove. Fitt's Village, St. James, Barbados, W.I. ☎ **800/223-6510** or 246/432-2683. Fax 246/424-0996. 56 rms, 32 suites. A/C TEL. Winter, $210–$221 double; $237–$273 junior suite for 2, $265–$285 one-bedroom suite for 2. Off-season, $155–$161 double; $179–$192 junior suite for 2, $186–$198 one-bedroom suite for 2. Rates include MAP. AE, MC, V.

This was once known as the Barbados Beach Village, but now it's the Crystal Cove, and is much better than before. Set on a 4-acre beachfront site at Fitt's Village, 4 miles north of Bridgetown along the west coast, it's a member of the Barbados-based St. James Beach Hotels, which owns some of the best properties on the island, including the Colony Club, Coconut Creek, and Tamarind Cove. Guests have access to the other hotels' combined facilities, and a water taxi is provided for transportation among the different properties. This, in fact, is one of the major reasons we recommend the Crystal Cove; if you want a change of scene, you can visit the next venue of the St. James group.

If you don't like the food, you can prepare your own, as more than two dozen units have kitchenettes. The rooms are either standard, somewhat like a motel, or more upscale, with living areas separate from the bedrooms. Most of them have high ceilings as well.

Dining/Entertainment: There are two restaurants. You might not drive across the island to sample the food, but it's above average. Entertainment is provided most nights.

Facilities: The hotel has a beach, but be warned of the treacherous pilings and a lot of offshore rocks. There are also three swimming pools and two tennis courts.

The Sandpiper. Holetown, St. James, Barbados, W.I. ☎ **800/223-1108** or 246/422-2251. Fax 246/422-1776. 22 rms, 24 suites. A/C TEL. Winter, $310–$370 double; $440–$740 suite. Off-season, $185 double; $235–$340 suite. MAP $50 per person extra. Children not accepted in Feb. AE, MC, V.

The Sandpiper has more of a South Seas look than most of the hotels of Barbados. Affiliated with the Coral Reef Club (see above), it's a self-contained, intimate resort near the water. The resort maintains a Bajan flavor and stands in a small grove of coconut palms and flowering trees right on the beach, a three-minute walk north of Holetown. A cluster of rustic-chic units surrounds the swimming pool, and some have a fine sea view. The rooms open onto little terraces that stretch along the second story, where you can order drinks or have breakfast. Each unit contains a small refrigerator.

Dining/Entertainment: Dining is under a wooden ceiling, and the cuisine is both continental and West Indian. Once a week in winter, big buffets are spread out for you, with white-capped chefs in attendance. There are two bars, one of which sits a few paces from the surf.

Services: Room service (7am to 10:30pm), laundry, baby-sitting.

Facilities: Swimming pool, two lighted tennis courts.

Tamarind Cove. Paynes Bay, St. James Beach (P.O. Box 429, Bridgetown), Barbados, W.I. ☎ **246/432-1332.** Fax 246/432-6317. 59 rms, 107 suites. A/C TEL. Winter, $222–$233 double; $261–$323 junior suite for 2, $279–$311 one-bedroom suite for 2. Off-season, $165–$171 double; $186–$216 junior suite for 2, $198–$214 one-bedroom suite for 2. Rates include MAP. AE, DC, MC, V.

This is the flagship of a British-based hotel chain (St. James Beach Properties) and a major challenger to the Coral Reef/Sandpiper properties, attracting somewhat the same upmarket clientele. In 1990, an $8 million restoration expanded it into one of the most noteworthy hotels on Barbados. In 1995, a new south wing, with some

49 luxurious rooms and suites, some with private plunge pools, was added, along with a freshwater swimming pool with a beachfront terrace.

Designed in an Iberian style, with pale-pink walls and red terra-cotta roofs, it occupies a desirable site beside St. James Beach 1 1/2 miles south of Holetown. The stylish and comfortable accommodations are in a series of hacienda-style buildings interspersed with vegetation. Each unit has a patio or balcony overlooking the gardens or ocean.

Dining/Entertainment: In addition to an informal beachfront eatery, Tamarind contains two elegant restaurants, the more memorable of which is Neptune's, specializing in sophisticated seafood dishes. The Flamingo is the main restaurant. A handful of bars are scattered throughout the property, and there's some kind of musical entertainment every night.

Services: Room service, baby-sitting, laundry, massage, concierge staff.

Facilities: Immediately adjacent white-sand beach, four freshwater swimming pools, complimentary water sports (including waterskiing, windsurfing, catamaran sailing, and snorkeling); golf, tennis, horseback riding, and polo available nearby.

INEXPENSIVE

Traveller's Palm. 265 Palm Ave., Sunset Crest, St. James, Barbados, W.I. ☎ **246/432-7722.** 16 apts. A/C. Winter, $75 apt for 2. Off-season, $50 apt for 2. MC, V.

Designed for those who want to be independent, this is a choice collection of simply furnished one-bedroom apartments with fully equipped kitchens, a 5-minute drive south of Holetown. Stay here only for reasons of economy, and don't expect too much. The apartments have living- and dining-room areas, as well as patios where you can have breakfast or a candlelit dinner you've prepared yourself (no meals are served here). The slightly worn apartments are filled with bright but fading colors, and they open onto a lawn with a swimming pool. There's maid service. A handful of beaches are within a 10-minute walk.

SOUTH OF BRIDGETOWN

Barbados Hilton. Needham's Point (P.O. Box 510), St. Michael, Barbados, W.I. ☎ **800/HILTONS** in the U.S., 800/268-9275 in Canada, or 246/426-0200. Fax 246/436-8946. 182 rms, 2 suites. A/C MINIBAR TV TEL. Winter, $262–$285 double; $520 suite. Off-season, $216–$236 double; $402 suite. MAP $42 per person extra. AE, DC, DISC, MC, V.

On more than 14 acres of landscaped gardens, this is a self-contained six-story resort, although it lies on the heavily populated southern edge of Bridgetown near an oil refinery whose smell sometimes drifts over its very good white-sand beach. It's the favorite of commercial travelers and conventioneers. Built in 1966 and overhauled and redecorated several times since then, it occupies the rugged peninsula where in the 18th century the English navy built Fort Charles. The Hilton's architecture incorporates bleached coral interspersed with jutting balconies and wide expanses of glass. The bedrooms are arranged around a central courtyard filled with tropical gardens, and vines cascade from the skylit roof. Each of the comfortable units has a balcony with a view of Carlisle Bay on the north side or the Atlantic on the south. Several kinds of water sports are offered on the nearby beach, whose outermost edge is protected from storm damage by a massive breakwater of giant rocks. The Hilton isn't in the island's top ranks, and it looks a bit worn and tired, but it's often packed every night.

Dining/Entertainment: The Verandah restaurant, whose backdrop is a row of diminutive clapboard Bajan houses, serves lackluster island and international specialties. The hotel has a gaming room with slot machines and both a beachfront daytime bar and snack restaurant and a nighttime bar.

Services: Room service (7am to midnight), laundry, massage.

Facilities: Four tennis courts (lit at night), 1,000-foot-wide artificial beach, in-house sauna and health club; access to horseback riding and golf.

Grand Barbados Beach Resort. Aquatic Gap, Bay St. (P.O. Box 639), Bridgetown, St. Michael, Barbados, W.I. ☎ **246/426-0890.** Fax 246/429-2400. 128 rms, 5 suites. A/C MINIBAR TV TEL. Winter, $245–$275 double; $500–$650 suite. Off-season, $145–$190 double; $300–$350 suite. MAP $47 per person extra. AE, DC, DISC, MC, V.

On scenic Carlisle Bay, opening onto a white-sand beach, this well-designed eight-story resort incorporates an older hostelry dating from 1969 that was massively overhauled in 1986. Like the Hilton, it is close to an oil refinery. Set on 4 acres of grounds, it offers well-furnished but often small bedrooms with many amenities, including a minisafe and eight-channel satellite TV. The storage space for luggage is inadequate. The two top floors are devoted to executive rooms, including a lounge where a complimentary continental breakfast is served. The hotel is about a mile southeast of Bridgetown.

Dining/Entertainment: At the end of a 260-foot historic pier is the Schooner Restaurant, specializing in seafood and buffet lunches. Pier One is an informal al fresco dining area. It's also the hotel's entertainment center, where live shows are often presented.

Services: Room service (7am to 11pm), exercise room, laundry, activity coordinator arranging tours and rentals.

Facilities: Water sports, a tiny outdoor swimming pool, Jacuzzi, sauna, Sunfish sailing, free use of the hotel's fitness center; complimentary day/night tennis nearby; complimentary glass-bottom boat rides; sports, such as golf, waterskiing, and horseback riding, can be arranged.

ON THE SOUTH COAST

MODERATE

Divi Southwinds Beach Resort. St. Lawrence Gap, Christ Church, Barbados, W.I. ☎ **800/367-3484** or 246/428-7181. Fax 246/428-4674. 33 studios, 127 suites. A/C TV TEL. Winter, $185–$200 studio for 2; $205–$230 one-bedroom suite for 2. Off-season, $110–$125 studio for 2; $140–$155 one-bedroom suite for 2. MAP $42 per person extra. AE, MC, V.

Midway between Bridgetown and the hamlet of Oistins, this resort was created when two distinctly different complexes were combined. Scattered over sandy flatlands of about 20 acres, the resorts were built in 1975 and 1986, respectively. Each enjoys a loyal clientele, often young families. The showplace of the present resort is the newer (inland) buildings consisting of one- and two-bedroom suites with full kitchens. This section looks like a connected series of town houses, with wooden balconies and views of a large L-shaped swimming pool. From these buildings, visitors need only cross through two groves of palm trees and a narrow lane to reach a white-sand beach. The older, more modest, plainly furnished, but fully renovated units lie directly on the beachfront, ringed with palm trees, near an oval swimming pool of their own.

Dining/Entertainment: The Aquarius Restaurant, which rises above the largest of the resort's swimming pools, is the resort's main dining and drinking emporium. The food is standard. A snack/drink bar lies beside the beach, near the older units.

Services: Laundry, island tours.

Facilities: Three swimming pools (one a wading pool reserved for children), sailboat rentals, snorkeling equipment, putting green, hair salon.

Sandy Beach Hotel. Worthing, Christ Church, Barbados, W.I. ☎ **246/435-8000.** Fax 246/435-8053. 89 rms and suites. A/C TV TEL. Winter, $120 double; $205 one-bedroom suite, $305 two-bedroom suite. Off-season, $85 double; $125 one-bedroom suite, $170 two-bedroom suite.

MAP $40 per adult extra. Additional person $30 extra in winter, $25 extra off-season. Children 11 and under stay free in parents' room. AE, MC, V.

Definitely not to be confused with Sandy Lane, this hotel, originally established in 1980 and renovated in 1994, is an unexciting but thoroughly reliable choice. It rests on 2 acres of beachfront land, 4 miles southeast of Bridgetown. The Barbadian-owned property rises around its architectural centerpiece, a soaring cone-shaped structure known as a *palapa.* Suitable for families with children, the resort contains standard motel-like double rooms, one- and two-bedroom suites, as well as 16 honeymoon suites with queen-size beds and completely private patios. All the simply decorated and spacious accommodations have fully equipped kitchenettes and private balconies or patios, and all the furniture at this informal place is locally made. Facilities for persons with disabilities are provided in some of the ground-floor suites.

Dining/Entertainment: Kolors, specializing in seafood and steaks, is under the palapa and opens onto a view of the sea and swimming pool. Every Monday, when outsiders are welcome, the resort sponsors a rum-punch party and a Bajan buffet. Entertainment is presented three nights a week.

Services: Room service (7:30am to 9:30pm), laundry, dry cleaning, activities desk to arrange island tours.

Facilities: Swimming pool with tropical waterfall, children's play area, wading pool. Water sports, which cost extra, include three-hour snorkeling trips, windsurfing, paddleboats, Sailfish, scuba lessons, and use of air mattresses, snorkels, fins, and masks.

Southern Palms. St. Lawrence, Christ Church, Barbados, W.I. ☎ **800/424-5500** in the U.S., or 246/428-7171. Fax 246/428-7175. 72 rms, 20 suites. A/C TV TEL. Winter, $185–$220 double; $270 suite. Off-season, $112–$140 double; $162 suite. MAP $40 per person extra. AE, DC, MC, V.

A seafront club with a distinct personality and great value, the Southern Palms lies on the 1,000-foot stretch of Pink Beach of Barbados, midway between the airport and Bridgetown. The core of the resort is a pink-and-white manor house built in the Dutch style, with a garden-level colonnade of arches. Spread along the sands are multiarched two- and three-story buildings. Italian fountains and statues add to the Mediterranean feeling. In its more modern block, an eclectic mixture of rooms includes some with kitchenettes, some facing the ocean, others opening onto the garden, and some with penthouse luxury. Each room is a double, and the suites have small kitchenettes. The decor is the standard motel-like tropical motif. A cluster of buildings, the drinking and dining facilities, link the accommodations together.

Dining/Entertainment: The Khus-Khus Bar and Restaurant serves both a West Indian and a continental cuisine. A local orchestra often entertains with merengue and steel-band music.

Services: Room service (7:30am to 9:30pm), laundry, tour desk.

Facilities: Terrace for sunning, two beachside freshwater swimming pools, sailboat rentals arranged, two tennis courts; snorkeling and scuba diving available.

Inexpensive

Bagshot House Hotel. St. Lawrence, Christ Church, Barbados, W.I. ☎ **246/435-6956.** Fax 246/435-2889. 16 rms. A/C TEL. Winter, $120 double. Off-season, $80 double. Rates include breakfast. AE, CB, DC, DISC, MC, V.

Renovated in 1995, this small, affordable, family-managed hotel has flowering vines tumbling over the railing of its balconies and an old-fashioned, unhurried kind of charm. The hotel was named after the early 19th-century manor house that once stood on this site. In front, a white-sand beach stretches out before you. Some of the well-kept, recently renovated rooms boast views of the water. A sunbathing deck, which doubles as a kind of living room for the resort, is perched at the edge of a lagoon. A deck-side lounge is decorated with paintings by local artists, and a restaurant, Sand Dollar, is on the premises (see "Where to Dine," later in this chapter).

Casuarina Beach Club. St. Lawrence Gap, Christ Church, Barbados, W.I. ☎ **800/223-9815** in the U.S., or 246/428-3600. Fax 246/428-1970. 123 studios, 20 one-bedroom suites, 14 two-bedroom suites. A/C TEL. Winter, $165–$180 studio for 2; $195 one-bedroom suite, $330 two-bedroom suite. Off-season, $90–$100 studio for 2; $120 one-bedroom suite, $180 two-bedroom suite. MAP $32 per person extra. Children 11 and under stay free in parents' room. AE, DISC, MC, V.

Set on a 900-foot coral sand beach, this unpretentious resort is low slung and Mediterranean in styling. This place is designed for those who prefer to cook for themselves. Family run, it also caters to families with reasonably priced suites offering kitchenettes. It's the best of the south-coast resorts. You'll approach this resort, located midway between Bridgetown and Oistins, through a forest of palm trees swaying above a well-maintained lawn. Originally established in 1981, with substantial additions and improvements completed in 1991, the resort is pleasant, although the staff could afford to be a lot friendlier. Designed with red-tile roofs and white walls, the main building has a series of arched windows leading onto verandas. To get to your accommodations, you pass through the outlying reception building and beside the pair of swimming pools. These are separated from the wide sandy beach by a lawn area dotted with casuarina and bougainvillea. On the premises is an octagonal roofed open-air bar and restaurant, two floodlit tennis courts, and a fitness room. The front desk can arrange most seaside activities through outside agencies. Each accommodation is equipped with a ceiling fan and rattan furniture, and each suite contains a kitchenette for preparing snacks and meals.

Fairholme. Maxwell, Christ Church, Barbados, W.I. ☎ **246/428-9425.** 11 rms, 20 studios. Winter, $33 double; $55 studio. Off-season, $28 double; $35 studio. No credit cards.

Fairholme is a converted plantation house that has been enlarged during the past 20 years with a handful of connected annexes. The main house and its original gardens are just off a major road, 6 miles southeast of Bridgetown. The hotel is a five-minute walk to the beach and across from its neighbor hotel, the Sea Breeze, which has a waterfront cafe and bar that Fairholme guests are allowed to use. The older part has 11 double rooms, each of which has a living-room area and a patio overlooking an orchard and swimming pool. Beside the pool is a lawn for sunbathing. More recently added are 20 Spanish-style studio apartments, all with balcony or patio, high cathedral ceilings, dark beams, and traditional furnishings. The restaurant has a reputation for home-cooking; wholesome food, nothing fancy, but the ingredients are fresh. Air-conditioning, which is only available in the studios, is coin-operated: At the reception desk, you buy a brass token for $3 that you insert into your air-conditioner for around eight hours of cooling-off time.

Woodville Beach Hotel. Hastings, Christ Church, Barbados, W.I. ☎ **246/435-6694.** Fax 246/435-9211. 36 studios and apts. TEL. Winter, $98–$115 studio; $125 one-bedroom apt, $172 two-bedroom apt. Off-season, $65–$76 studio; $86 one-bedroom apt, $125 two-bedroom apt. AE, MC, V.

These apartments, last renovated in 1995, represent one of the best bargains on Barbados and are ideal for families on a budget holiday. Set directly on a rocky shoreline 2½ miles southeast of Bridgetown, the hotel is in the heart of the village of Hastings, on slightly less than an acre of land. The U-shaped apartment complex is built around a pool terrace overlooking the sea. Functional and minimalist in decor, it is nevertheless clean and comfortable. The kitchenettes in each accommodation are fully equipped, and a variety of rental units are offered. All have balconies or decks, and some units contain air-conditioning. There are supermarkets, stores, and banks within easy walking distance. Although a handful of athletic guests attempt to swim off the nearby rocks, most opt for a five-minute walk to the white sands of nearby Rockley (Accra) Beach. A small restaurant is open on the property, serving American and Bajan fare.

ON THE EAST COAST

MODERATE

Crane Beach Hotel. Crane Bay, St. Philip, Barbados, W.I. ☎ **800/223-6510** or 246/423-6220. Fax 246/423-5343. 14 rms, 4 suites. TEL. Winter, $180 double; $250–$295 one-bedroom suite, $450 two-bedroom suite. Off-season, $100 double; $140–$175 one-bedroom suite, $260 two-bedroom suite. MAP $40 per person extra. Honeymoon packages available. AE, MC, V.

Near the easternmost end of the island, this remote hilltop hostelry stands on a cliff overlooking the Atlantic. Crane Beach was called by one writer "the most beautiful spot on earth." At least Prince Andrew thought so when he built his clearly visible house on a nearby cliff. The location may be beautiful, but the hotel leaves much to be desired. Time-share units are hawked in the lobby, and the housekeeping appears lax. Rubberneckers, who pay an entrance fee to enter the property and patronize the area around the pool and the bar, often disturb the tranquillity. In other words, it's not for everybody, but yet is one of the most famous hostelries in the southern Caribbean. Located near Marriott's Sam Lord's Castle resorts, the hotel opens onto one of the most scenic beaches on Barbados and is reached by walking down some 200 steps. At times the water can be too rough for swimming. Canopied beds and antique furnishings grace many of the bedrooms, and the views are often panoramic. Some of the units have kitchenettes, but only one has air-conditioning, which is reserved for guests in dire need of it. The hotel is about 14 miles from Bridgetown and a 15-minute drive from the airport.

Dining/Entertainment: Many visitors for the day head here just to have a drink on the panoramic terrace or to order a meal. An international cuisine is served with West Indian flair. At night the tables are candlelit. The Sunday brunch is a well-attended event.

Services: Room service, baby-sitting, laundry.

Facilities: The Roman-style swimming pool with columns, separating the main house from the dining room, has been used as a backdrop for more fashion layouts than any other place in the Caribbean. The resort also has tennis courts.

✪ **Sam Lord's Castle Resorts.** Long Bay, St. Philip, Barbados, W.I. ☎ **246/423-7350.** Fax 246/423-6361. 234 rms. A/C MINIBAR TV TEL. Winter, $225–$275 double. Off-season, $115–$145 double. MAP $50 in winter, $40 off-season per person extra. AE, DC, DISC, MC, V.

In spite of its name, this is no castle but a Great House built in 1820 by one of Barbados's most notorious scoundrels. According to legend, Samuel Hall Lord (the "Regency Rascal") constructed the estate with money acquired by luring ships to wreck on the jagged but hard-to-detect rocks of Cobbler's Reef.

The Great House, near the easternmost end of the island, a 15-minute drive northeast of the airport, was built in the pirate's more mellow "golden years." Craftspeople were imported from England to reproduce sections of the queen's castle at Windsor. The decor includes the dubiously acquired but nonetheless beautiful art of Reynolds, Raeburn, and Chippendale.

Amid 72 landscaped acres, the estate has a wide, lengthy private sandy beach edged by tall coconut trees. Only seven rooms are in the Main House, and these are stylishly decorated with antique furnishings. Three rooms have canopied beds. The rest of the accommodations are in cottages and wings, either two or four floors high, and there are some rather tacky motel rooms with a faux-castle theme. (Some of these units evoke southwest Miami in the 1950s—no great compliment.) For privacy's sake and to get more light, try to avoid the ground-floor units if possible. The best (and most expensive) accommodations are in structures 7, 8, and 9.

Dining/Entertainment: Three meals a day are served in the Wanderer Restaurant, and you can order a hamburger at the Oceanus Café, right on the beach. There are many bars as well. A fiesta night in the hotel's Bajan Village is offered once a week, as is a shipwreck barbecue and beach party with a steel-drum band, a limbo show, and fire-eaters on South Beach.

Services: Beauty/barber shop, laundry, baby-sitting, concierge to arrange island tours and whatever. The staff often seems more concerned with the demands of the group traffic than for the individual traveler (the hotel is a favorite for conventions).

Facilities: Three swimming pools, exercise room, shuffleboard, table tennis, library; sailing, horseback riding, snorkeling, fishing, and other activities can be arranged.

INEXPENSIVE

✪ **Kingsley Club.** Cattlewash-on-Sea, near Bathsheba, St. Joseph, Barbados, W.I. ☎ **246/433-9422.** Fax 246/433-9226. 8 rms. Winter, $101 double. Off-season, $84 double. Rates include breakfast. AE, MC, V. Take Hwy. 3 north of Bathsheba.

This little West Indian inn, an exceptionally affordable gem, is far removed from the bustle of the tourist-ridden west coast, and is often a favorite stopover for Bajans themselves. In the foothills of Bathsheba, opening onto the often-turbulent Atlantic, the Kingsley Club lies on the northeast coast. A historic inn, it offers simply furnished and very modest but clean and comfortable bedrooms. At night, you can sit back and enjoy a rum punch made from an old planter's recipe. The club enjoys a reputation for good cooking, and its Bajan food will be recommended later for those traveling to the east coast just for the day. Cattlewash Beach is one of the longest, widest, and least crowded on Barbados. But be aware that swimming here can be extremely dangerous.

2 Where to Dine

ON THE WEST COAST

EXPENSIVE

✪ **Bagatelle Restaurant.** Hwy. 2A, St. Thomas. ☎ **246/421-6767.** Reservations recommended. Lunch $12; fixed-price dinner $45. AE, MC, V. Mon–Sat 11am–2:30pm and 7–9:30pm. Cut inland near Paynes Bay north of Bridgetown, 3 miles from both Sunset Crest and the Sandy Lane Hotel. FRENCH/CARIBBEAN.

This restaurant is housed in one of the most historic and impressive buildings on the island. Set a 15-minute drive north of Bridgetown, and originally built in 1645 as the residence of the island's first governor (Lord Willoughby), it lies in 5 acres of forest. The sylvan retreat is in the cool uplands, just south of the island's center, and retains the charm of its original buildings.

The Bagatelle is one of the island's finest and most elegant choices for French cuisine with a Caribbean flair. Candles and lanterns illuminate the old archways and the ancient trees. The service is the best we found on Barbados. Try the homemade duck-liver pâté, deviled Caribbean crab backs, or smoked flying-fish mousse with horseradish mayonnaise. The beef Wellington Bagatelle style with a chasseur sauce is a favorite, as is the crisp roast duckling with an orange-and-brandy sauce. The local catch of the day, perhaps the most popular item on the menu, can be prepared grilled, barbecued, or in the style of Baxters Road (that is, spicily seasoned and sautéed in deep oil). A different list of homemade desserts is featured nightly, and coffee can be served on the terrace. Cruise-ship passengers can take advantage of its light lunches before their ships sail at sunset.

✪ **Carambola.** Derricks, St. James. ☎ **246/432-0832.** Reservations recommended. Main courses $21–$47. AE, MC, V. Mon–Sat 6:30–9:30pm. Closed Aug. FRENCH/CARIBBEAN/ASIAN.

Built beside the road that runs along the island's western coastline, this restaurant sits atop a 20-foot seaside cliff 1 1/2 miles south of Holetown. Carambola offers one of the most panoramic dining terraces in the Caribbean. However, you'll have to go early for dinner to see the view, since Carambola doesn't serve lunch. The prize-winning cuisine is creative and good, with modern French-inspired touches. The dishes may be French or continental, but they definitely have Caribbean flair and flavor, as exemplified by the fillet of swordfish or dolphin often served. A selection of savory vegetarian dishes is offered as well, and a crowd-pleasing favorite is the chicken stuffed with crab. To head to the Far East, select the spicy Thai pork tenderloin, and try to save room for one of the luscious desserts such as the lime mousse. The impressive wine list features mostly French vintages.

✪ **The Cliff.** Hwy. 1, Derrick, St. James. ☎ **246/432-1922.** Reservations recommended. Main courses $21–$48. AE, MC, V. Mon–Sat 6:30–10pm. INTERNATIONAL/CARIBBEAN.

Built atop a coral cliff, this open-air restaurant has a four-level dining room crafted with terra-cotta tiles and coral stone. It rests above a 10-foot cliff adjacent to the Coconut Creek Hotel, on the island's Gold Coast. Despite the fact that the English/Bajan partners who own it don't consider it exclusive, posh, or even particularly formal, it has attracted Prince Andrew and assorted titled and bejeweled clients of the nearby upscale hotels. No one will mind, despite all this, if you wear well-tailored shorts; the place really is surprisingly low key. The food here was accurately praised by Frommer's reader and gourmet Dr. Stephen C. Bandy of Princeton, New Jersey, who wrote: "The Cliff offers a menu of the highest quality: the best cuts of meat, the freshest and most interesting vegetables and greens I have ever eaten on the island, and dessert confections that would not be looked down on in New York restaurants like Bouley and Lespinasse." How right he is! Menu items include grilled snapper drizzled in three types of coriander sauce (cream-based, oil-based, and vinaigrette style), accompanied with garlic-infused mashed potatoes, and Thai-style curried shrimp. Sushi is presented (when available) as a starter, complete with wasabi and portions of fresh local tuna, scallops, and snapper. As you dine, watch for manta rays, which glide through the illuminated waters below. The seas are usually calm enough to spot them, and a sighting is considered a sign of good luck.

Hudson's Brasserie. Summerland Great House, Prospect (between Batts Rock and Tamarind Cove), St. James. ☎ **246/424-2424.** Reservations recommended, especially in winter. Main courses $15–$32. AE, MC, V. Wed–Mon 7–10:30pm. Closed June. ASIAN/INTERNATIONAL.

The decor is evocative of an old-fashioned plantation house, with tall ceilings, crystal chandeliers, and a balcony for sundowners. The most impressive room (reserved for groups and wedding receptions) is lined with Bajan antiques or antique reproductions.

The food is taken seriously. It is, in fact, among the stellar dining choices on the island. Try the sesame prawn pâté, sweet-and-sour shrimp, or Creole fish soup. Other courses include crispy aromatic duck and a dish inspired by the cuisine of India: tikka makhani, a creamy and spicy chicken cooked slowly in a tandoor and served with stir-fried vegetables. The chef also serves a U.S. tenderloin perfectly charbroiled the way you like it. For dessert, perhaps profiteroles with chocolate sauce and an old-fashioned English syllabub are the best choices.

La Maison. Holetown, St. James. ☎ **246/432-1156.** Reservations recommended. Main courses $22.50–$40. MC, V. Tues–Sun 6:30–9:30pm. FRENCH/CARIBBEAN.

Located on the beach south of Holetown and open on two sides to the sea and to a flowering courtyard (whose centerpiece is a mermaid-capped fountain), this restaurant derives most of its decor from the exposed coral of the walls and the intricate ceiling, crafted from a Guyanan hardwood called greenheart. The award-winning cuisine is served with quiet dignity. Most diners are won over by the taste and flavor of the menu. The intriguing appetizers are likely to include blackened flyingfish fillets set on a sweet-potato salad. Main courses feature such exotica as barracuda steamed with passion fruit or a trio of flying fish prepared in three different ways. If you don't want anything too unusual, try the broiled chicken breast stuffed with sun-dried tomatoes or the grilled sirloin with cracked peppercorns. The restaurant even knows how to do the simpler dishes well. Desserts aren't neglected either, and a delectable one is spicy tropical fruits in phyllo pastry with cinnamon ice cream.

✪ **Neptune's.** In the Tamarind Cove Beach Resort, Paynes Bay, St. James. ☎ **246/432-1332.** Reservations recommended. Main courses $25–$45. AE, DC, MC, V. Wed–Sun 6:30–10pm. Closed Tues off-season. SEAFOOD.

This is the best seafood restaurant on Barbados and one of the island's most expensive culinary selections, with management virtually insisting that every food and beverage tab exceed $60 per person. Located south of Holetown, in one of the island's top resorts, it abandons the standard tropical Caribbean motif found in most of the island's other restaurants. Instead, you'll find a stylish octagonal room sheathed in faux malachite, whose emerald-green tones reflect the colors of an illuminated aquarium in the room's center. Service is impeccable.

Appetizers range from Bajan fish terrine to fresh local fish set in a champagne jelly scented with peppercorns. Another delectable choice is the kebab of scallops on a bed of confit leeks or the chef's blackened snapper. Neptune's catch is a selection of island fish, often served in a light orange sauce flavored with herbs. You can also order that island favorite, fillet of red snapper, or splurge on lobster medallions in a red-pepper sauce. Chicken is served Caribbean style, in a mango sauce wrapped in phyllo pastry and baked. The dessert menu is one of the most elaborate on Barbados, ranging from a classical tiramisu to a coconut-and-mango parfait or a trio of rich chocolate mousses.

✪ **Olives Bar & Bistro.** Second St. at the corner of Hwy. 1, Holetown. ☎ **246/432-2112.** Reservations recommended. Main courses $12.50–$30. AE, MC, V. Daily 6:30–10:30pm. MEDITERRANEAN/CARIBBEAN.

Established in 1994 by a couple from New Zealand, this restaurant is named for the only oil used in preparing the cuisine. Additionally, olives are the only snack served in the bar, where there's a welcome rowdiness. The street-level dining room (no-smoking/air-conditioned) spills out from its original coral-stone walls and scrubbed-pine floorboards into a pleasant garden. The cuisine celebrates the warm-weather climates of southern Europe and the Antilles, and does so exceedingly well. Even some local chefs like to dine here on their nights off. The best items include yellowfin tuna, marinated and seared rare and served on a bed of roast-garlic mashed potatoes with grilled ratatouille. You can also order roast lamb flavored with honey, garlic, and fresh herbs. More Caribbean in its flavors is a jerk tenderloin of pork. For dessert, try the toffee and walnut tart or else the Creole bread and butter pudding. Next door is a sandwich bar serving light luncheon fare Monday through Friday from 8am to 4pm.

The Orchid Room. In the Colony Club Hotel, Porters, St. James. ☎ **246/422-2335.** Reservations recommended. Main courses $17.50–$42.50. DC, MC, V. Winter daily 6:30–10pm. Closed 1 or 2 days a week off-season (call for times). CARIBBEAN/FRENCH.

The Orchid Room blends a plantation-house ambience with velvet-glove service and culinary finesse. It's even won the approval of the earl of Bradford, head of the Master Chefs of Great Britain, who found his last meal here "beautifully presented and perfectly prepared." Beneath sparkling chandeliers and surrounded by period furnishings, main courses are served with a dash of showmanship as silver domes are removed to reveal their treasures.

The chef brings Gallic flair to his creations, which are composed mostly of local ingredients. The appetizers are likely to include a salad of lobster with mango, delicate but full flavored. Goat cheese is set on a sweet-potato pancake and scattered with walnuts. Your soup may be pumpkin with smoked salmon. The main courses are varied, ranging from grilled dorado laid on a puree of eggplant and potato and dressed with lime and olive oil to Washington state lamb fillet gift-wrapped in a cornmeal crepe with a deeply reduced Cabernet Sauvignon sauce.

The Palm Terrace. In the Royal Pavilion Hotel, Porters (between Sunset Crest and Gibbs Beach), St. James. ☎ **246/422-4444.** Reservations required. Main courses $25–$45. AE, DC, DISC, MC, V. Daily 7–9:30pm. CARIBBEAN/FRENCH.

In an elegant setting on a pink-marble terrace, this dramatic restaurant opens onto the oceanfront. The Palm Terrace has a French chef who oversees a Bajan staff. Together they turn out some of the more delectable cuisine offered at any west coast hotel. To the sounds of music, with the trade winds sweeping in, you can sample such dishes as chicken-liver parfait served with a pear chutney and walnut brioche as an appetizer, or perhaps smoked fish tacos and black beans with a chili-pepper sauce. The pastas are generally excellent, or you may prefer grilled red snapper with roast garlic. We were recently won over by the Thai green chicken curry. Each evening the chef prepares a prime roast carved at your table.

MODERATE

Château Créole. Porters, St. James. ☎ **246/422-4116.** Reservations recommended. Main courses $14–$31. AE, MC, V. Mon–Sat 6:30–9pm (last seating). BAJAN/CREOLE.

This stucco-and-tile house is 2 miles north of Holetown in a tropical garden dotted with a trio of gazebos. After passing under an arbor, you'll be invited to order a drink, served on one of the flowered banquettes that fill various parts of the house. Go here for zesty dishes packed with island flavors. Specialties include Creole dishes such as stuffed crab backs, which are so well done here that they prove the gastronomic potential of this often mishandled dish. Begin, perhaps, with red-bean soup or a succulent version of fish chowder before moving on to main courses. The chef manages to come up with such simple dishes as baked whitefish stuffed with crabmeat and gives them artistry with the fine use of fresh herbs. For a real taste of Barbados, try the chicken with fresh mangos seasoned with ginger. Meals are served on the rear terrace, al fresco style, by candlelight.

✪ **The Fathoms.** Paynes Bay, St. James. ☎ **246/432-2568.** Reservations recommended for dinner. Main courses $16–$29. AE, DISC, MC, V. Daily noon–3pm and 6:30–10pm (last order). INTERNATIONAL.

Located in a red-roofed stucco house close to the surf of the island's western coastline, this pleasant restaurant serves meals on an outdoor terrace shaded by a mahogany tree and in an interior decorated with accents of terra-cotta, wood, and pottery.

The restaurant offers a fairly ambitious menu and does itself proud with appetizers like shrimp and crab étouffé, herbed conch cakes, or blackened shrimp with mango. For a main dish, try the caramelized barracuda, grilled pork medallions, or Dorado fish Hunan, which has zesty and winning flavors. Upstairs is a Santa Fe–style tapas bar, primarily for drinks, wines, and finger foods. A pool table and board games help you pass the evening away. This attractive watering hole is open daily from 5pm until the crowd finally departs.

Koko's. Prospect, St. James. ☎ **246/424-4557.** Reservations recommended. Main courses $8–$22. MC, V. Daily 6:30–10pm. Closed Mon May–Nov. BAJAN.

Koko's is an award-winning restaurant, known for its excellent Caribbean cookery, a kind of Bajan *cuisine moderne.* The location alone is appealing: It's in a charming once-private house, built on coral blocks on a terrace overlooking the sea. You might begin with a homemade local soup, perhaps pepperpot, made with "roots of the Caribbean," or conch fritters with a hot dip. Shrimp and crab fritters are also served with a fiery dip. Main dishes include the chef's "ketch of de day," as well as barracuda teriyaki, roast pork calypso, or steamed or panfried flying fish. Each dessert is homemade and luscious. This place is not for your typical surf-and-turf diner; if you're seeking authentic island flavors, you'll find them here.

✪ **Nico's Champagne & Wine Bar.** Derrick's, St. James. ☎ **246/432-6386.** Reservations recommended. Main courses $19–$30. AE, MC, V. Mon–Sat 11:30am–10:30pm. INTERNATIONAL.

Set on the landward side of a road that bisects some of the most expensive residential real estate on Barbados (the west coast), this is a great value, an informal bistro inspired by the wine bars of London. In a 19th-century building originally constructed in the 1800s as the headquarters for a plantation, it does a thriving business from its air-conditioned bar area. About a dozen kinds of wine are sold by the glass. Meals are served at tables protected with a shed-style roof in the garden out back. The food is flavorful and designed to accompany the wine: Examples include deep-fried Camembert with passion fruit sauce, chicken breasts stuffed with crab, red snapper, and some of the best lobster (grilled simply and served with garlic butter) on Barbados. Chris Millward and Cheryl Wiltshire, your hosts, seem to have devoted a lot of care and attention to what you eat and drink.

Raffles. First St., Holetown. ☎ **246/432-6557.** Reservations recommended. Main courses BD$40–BD$55 ($20–$27.50). AE, DC, MC, V. Thurs–Tues 6–10pm (last order). CARIBBEAN.

Located amid the weather-beaten buildings along the main street of Holetown, this cozy enclave has a relatively unusual list of gastronomic specialties. A decor of faux leopard skin and safari-derived artifacts adds to the exotic atmosphere. The food here has been called "decadent," but that's meant as an allusion to its rich, zesty, and spicy dishes. The appetite-rousing appetizers include herb-flavored shrimp set on a bed of local greens. Tourists who order that old wives' favorite, Bajan saltfish cakes, often ask for a second helping, proof of the chef's talent. Other Caribbean specialties include Jamaican ackee and saltfish, which is perhaps an acquired taste but nonetheless well-prepared here. To go all the way to Africa, ask for babouttie, which is ground and heavily curried beef baked in custard and served with sliced bananas. If all that is too much, barbecued pork and tenderloin steaks also appear on the menu. The place is also known for its changing array of local fish—dolphin, barracuda, kingfish, the inevitable flying fish, and sea trout—prepared in any of at least three different methods, including blackened, grilled, or sautéed.

SPEIGHTSTOWN

Mango's. 2 West End, Queen St. ☎ **246/422-0704.** Reservations recommended. Main courses $12–$28. MC, V. Sun–Fri 6–10pm. INTERNATIONAL.

Speightstown was never noted for its dining choices until the opening of this restaurant and bar overlooking the water. Run by a couple from Montréal, Gail and Pierre Spenard, the restaurant offers entertainment on some nights and features daily specials. It's best known for its seafood, and the owners buy the catch of the day directly from the fisher's boats. The food is exceedingly good, and the seasonings don't overpower the flavor of the main ingredient, as they do at many Bajan restaurants. Seasonal market-fresh ingredients are used to good advantage. Grilled lobster with lime butter and white wine is also featured. If you don't want fish, opt for the 8-ounce U.S. of A. tenderloin steak cooked to perfection or the fall-off-the-bone barbecued baby back ribs. Appetizers might be anything from an intriguing green peppercorn pâté to pumpkin soup. Top the meal off with a passion fruit cheesecake or a starfruit torte.

SOUTH OF BRIDGETOWN

Brown Sugar. Aquatic Gap, St. Michael. ☎ **246/426-7684.** Reservations recommended. Main courses $14–$35; buffet lunch $17.50. AE, DC, DISC, MC, V. Sun–Fri noon–2:30pm and 6–9:30pm, Sat 6–9:30pm (last order). BAJAN.

Hidden behind lush foliage, Brown Sugar is an al fresco restaurant in a turn-of-the-century bungalow. The ceiling is latticed, with slow-turning fans, and there's an open veranda for dining by candlelight amid lots of hanging plants. The chefs prepare some of the tastiest Bajan specialties on the island. Among the soups, we suggest hot gun-go-pea soup (pigeon peas cooked in chicken broth and seasoned with fresh coconut milk, herbs, and a touch of white wine). Of the main dishes, Creole broiled pepper chicken is popular, or perhaps you'd like stuffed crab backs. Conch fritters and garlic pork are especially spicy options. A selection of locally grown vegetables is also offered. For dessert, we recommend the Bajan bread pudding with rum sauce. The restaurant is known for its good-value lunches, which are served buffet style to local businesspeople.

ON THE SOUTH COAST

EXPENSIVE

Josef's. St. Lawrence Gap. ☎ **246/435-6541.** Reservations recommended. Main courses $20–$28. AE, DC, MC, V. Mon–Fri noon–2:30pm and 6:30–10pm, Sat 6:30–10pm. CARIBBEAN/CONTINENTAL.

Set in the garden of a pink-and-white Bajan house, between the road and the sea, this is one of the island's veteran upscale restaurants. Since the menu is roughly equivalent at lunch and dinner, you'll save a bit of money by opting for a midday, rather than an evening, meal. Swedish specialties include meatballs in traditional gravy and Swedish-style steak. More tropical dishes include garlic shrimp, jerk shrimp, blackened kingfish, seafood crepes, and curried chicken. Fillet Marco Polo is made from strips of filleted beef steak floating in a pool of red-wine sauce. Although some of the Swedish fare seems heavy for the tropics, the chef can show a lighter touch. The cookery is characterized by rural good sense rather than citified refinements.

MODERATE

✪ **David's Place.** St. Lawrence Main Rd., Worthing, Christ Church. ☎ **246/435-9755.** Reservations recommended. Main courses $12–$40. AE, DISC, MC, V. Tues–Sun 6–10pm. BAJAN.

Owner-operators David and Darla Trotman promise that in their restaurant you'll sample "Barbadian dining at its best," and they deliver on that promise, and at reasonable prices, too. The establishment is south of Bridgetown between Rockley Beach and Worthing, in an old-fashioned seaside house on St. Lawrence Bay. The tables are positioned so that diners get a view of the Caribbean. Everybody's favorite, pumpkin or cucumber soup, might get you going, or you can select the more prosaic fish cakes or even pickled chicken wings. If you're afraid to venture to Baxter's Road at night, you can order Baxter's road chicken here. It's seasoned the Bajan way, that is, marinated in lime, salt, and herbs, then deep-fried. Pepperpot is a hot-and-spicy dish with beef, salt pork, chicken, and lamb. Fish steak, the best item to order, might be dolphin, kingfish, barracuda, shark, or red snapper. It's served in a white-wine sauce or deep-fried the Bajan way. Desserts are equally good: Here, at last, is a restaurant that offers that old drugstore favorite of the 1940s and 1950s, a banana split, or you might opt instead for the coconut cream pie or the carrot cake in rum sauce.

✪ **Ile de France.** In the Windsor Arms Hotel, Hastings, Christ Church. ☎ **246/435-6869.** Reservations recommended. Main courses $18–$37.50. MC, V. Tues–Sun 6:30–9:30pm (last order). CLASSIC FRENCH.

A 12-minute drive southeast of the center of Bridgetown, this restaurant presents the finest and most authentic French cuisine on Barbados. Place yourself in the capable hands of Michel and Martine Gramaglia, two French-born expatriates who handle their kitchen and dining room with an enviable savoir-faire. Meals are served on a candlelit outdoor terrace overlooking a manicured garden, beside one of the oldest and most venerable hotels on the island, which is currently closed. Ingredients are either flown in from France (or Martinique) or obtained fresh on Barbados. Specialties might include escargots de Bourgogne, a flavorful version of fish soup with lobster, or a marinade of three fish whose exact composition depends on the catch of the day. Other dishes include tournedos with a béarnaise sauce, rack of lamb, catch of the day, shrimp, and roast lobster. For dessert, try the tart tatin, crème brulée, or banana terrine. The atmosphere is charming and traditional.

Luigi's Restaurant. Dover Woods, St. Lawrence Gap, Christ Church. ☎ **246/428-9218.** Reservations recommended. Main courses $11.50–$21.50. MC, V. Daily 6–10:30pm (last order). ITALIAN.

Since 1963 this open-air Italian trattoria has operated in a green-and-white building built as a private house. The feeling is contemporary, airy, and comfortable. Pizzas are offered as appetizers, along with more classic choices such as half a dozen escargots or a Caesar salad (when available). Half orders of many pastas are also available as starters. The baked pastas, such as a creamy lasagna, are delectable, and you can also order the fresh fish or veal special of the day, among other dishes. For dessert, try the zabaglione and one of the wide selections of coffee, ranging from Italian to Russian or Turkish.

Pisces. St. Lawrence Gap, Christ Church. ☎ **246/435-6564.** Reservations recommended. Main courses $15–$33. AE, DC, MC, V. Daily 6–9:30pm (last order). From Bridgetown, take Hwy. 7 south for about 4 miles; then turn right at the sign toward St. Lawrence Gap. BAJAN.

Pisces offers al fresco dining at water's edge. A beautiful restaurant with a tropical decor, it primarily serves a Caribbean seafood menu. You might begin with one of the soups, perhaps split pea or pumpkin. Other savory appetizers include flying fish Florentine and octopus salad. Seafood lovers enjoy the Pisces platter, consisting of charcoal-broiled dolphin, fried flying fish, broiled kingfish, and butter-fried prawns. You might also be drawn to seasonal Caribbean fish, which can be broiled, blackened, or panfried before it's served with lime-herb butter. Another seasonal delight is snapper Caribe, which is stuffed with shrimp, tomato, and herbs, then baked and served with a white-wine sauce. A limited but good selection of poultry and meat is offered, including roast pork Barbados with a traditional Bajan stuffing. New restaurants come and go on Barbados, but this old favorite still hangs in.

Sand Dollar. In Bagshot House Hotel, St. Lawrence Coast Rd., Christ Church. ☎ **246/435-6956.** Reservations recommended. Lunch main courses $10–$20; dinner main courses $15–$32. AE, DC, MC, V. Daily 11am–2:30pm and 6–10:30pm. INTERNATIONAL.

The hotel that contains this restaurant has featured some kind of restaurant since it was originally established in the early 1940s, and as such, the location has become something of a staple in the minds of many long-time island residents. Housed in a pink-walled hotel and opening onto a masonry terrace that extends almost to the edge of the water, it's less formal than it was in years past, with a modern outlook stemming from a complete renovation in 1996. Menu items include a well-seasoned peppersteak, jerk chicken, brochettes of jerk shrimp, chicken with a honey rosemary sauce, and different versions of steak and lobster. Lunches feature a roster of sandwiches and salads that aren't available at dinner and always a special sandwich of the day, including a succulent version made with lobster salad. No one will object if you wear shorts, but bathing suits aren't allowed.

Witch Doctor. St. Lawrence Gap, Christ Church. ☎ **246/435-6581.** Reservations recommended. Main courses $11–$30. MC, V. Daily 6:15–10pm. BAJAN/AFRICAN.

The Witch Doctor hides behind a screen of thick foliage in the heart of the southern coast. The decor, in honor of its name, features African and island wood carvings of witch doctors. The place purveys a fascinating cuisine with some unusual concoctions that are tasty and well prepared, a big change from a lot of the bland hotel fare. For an appetizer, try the split-pea-and-pumpkin soup, or maybe the cold, lime-soused ceviche. Chef's specialties include various flambé dishes such as steak, shrimp Creole, fried flying fish, and chicken piri-piri (inspired by Mozambique). At a sidewalk bar, you can order from the restaurant's appetizer menu and also request vegetable lasagne, small pizzas, and shrimp.

INEXPENSIVE

The Ship Inn. St. Lawrence Gap, Christ Church. ☎ **246/435-6961.** Reservations recommended for the Captain's Carvery only. Main courses $8–$13; all-you-can-eat carvery meal $10.50 at lunch, $20 at dinner, plus $7.50 for appetizer and dessert. AE, MC, V. Daily noon–3pm and 6–10:30pm. ENGLISH PUB/BAJAN.

South of Bridgetown between Rockley Beach and Worthing, the Ship Inn is a traditional English-style pub with an attractive, rustic decor of nautical memorabilia. As an alternative, patrons may wish to drink and enjoy a tropical atmosphere in a garden bar. Many guests come for darts and to meet friends, and certainly to listen to the live music presented nightly by some of the island's top bands (see "Barbados After Dark," later in this chapter). The Ship Inn serves substantial bar food, such as homemade steak-and-kidney pie, shepherd's pie, and chicken, shrimp, and fish dishes. For more formal dining, visit the Captain's Carvery, where you can have your fill of succulent cuts of prime roasts on a nighttime buffet table and an array of traditional Bajan food (fillets of flying fish, for example). Diners can enjoy their repast in a tropical garden. Patrons come here for the big, filling, and hearty portions and the drinks, not for the refined cuisine. After dinner, guests can listen to top local bands performing in the pub at no extra charge.

T.G.I. Boomers. St. Lawrence Gap, Christ Church. ☎ **246/428-8439.** Reservations not required. Main courses $9–$22.50; lunch specials $8–$12.50. AE, DISC, MC, V. Daily 8am–10pm. AMERICAN/BAJAN.

Four miles south of Bridgetown near Rockley Beach along Highway 7, T.G.I. Boomers offers some of the best bargain meals on the island. An American/Bajan operation, it has an active bar and a row of tables where food is served, usually along with frothy pastel-colored drinks. The cook prepares a special catch of the day, and the fish is served with soup or salad, rice or baked potato, and a vegetable. You can always count on seafood, steaks, and hamburgers. For lunch, try a daily Bajan special or a jumbo sandwich. Most folks come here for a belt-busting good time with tried-and-true dishes that never go out of favor. Be sure to try one of the 16-ounce daiquiris.

On the East Coast

✪ **Atlantis Hotel.** Bathsheba, St. Joseph. ☎ **246/433-9445.** Reservations required for the Sun buffet and the 7pm dinner, recommended at all other times. Two-course fixed-price lunch $11.50; set dinner $15; Sun buffet $17.25. AE. Daily 11:30am–3pm and at 7pm (and don't be late). BAJAN.

An insight into the old-fashioned Barbados of several years ago, the run-down Atlantis Hotel is often filled with both Bajans and visitors. It's located between Cattlewash-on-Sea and Tent Bay on the east (Atlantic) coast. In the sunny, breeze-filled interior, with a sweeping view of the turbulent ocean, Enid I. Maxwell has been welcoming visitors from all over the world ever since she opened the place in 1945. Her copious buffets are one of the best food values on the island. From loaded tables, you can sample such Bajan foods as pumpkin fritters, peas and rice, macaroni and cheese, chow mein, souse, and/or a Bajan pepperpot. No one ever leaves here hungry, and no one has thought of adding anything new to the repertoire since World War II ended.

Café Calabash. St. Nicholas Abbey, on the St. Peter/St. Lucy border. ☎ **246/422-8725.** Creole lunch, snacks, traditional English teas $4–$15. No credit cards. Mon–Fri 10am–4pm. BAJAN/AFTERNOON TEA.

On the site of a Jacobean plantation Great House, this is the most romantic place in Barbados to have afternoon tea or else to stop in for a Bajan lunch of Creole fare. It was created by Nick Hudson, a restaurateur who became famous island wide when he operated the restaurant La Cage aux Folles, in 1997. Now you can eat or drink at one of the premier tourist attractions of Barbados. The cafe looks out onto one of the few remaining virgin rain forests in the Caribbean. A typical menu might include Bajan fish cakes, pepperpot stew, jerked pork chops, pickled bread fruit, and vegetarian samosas, followed by delectable desserts such as Key lime or coconut meringue pie.

Kingsley Club. Cattlewash-on-Sea, St. Joseph (1/4 mile northeast of Bathsheba, about 15 miles from Bridgetown). ☎ **246/433-9422.** Reservations required for dinner, recommended for lunch. Main courses $8–$19; fixed-price 4-course meal $25–$35. AE, DISC, MC, V. Daily 11am–3pm and 6–7:30pm (last order). BAJAN.

A historic inn amid the rolling hills of the northeastern coast of Barbados in an area called the Scotland district, the Kingsley Club also serves some of the best Bajan food on the island in a turn-of-the-century house cooled by Atlantic breezes. You're invited to "come tuck in" and enjoy your fill of split-pea-and-pumpkin soup, dolphin meunière, or planters fried chicken, followed by one of their homemade desserts, perhaps coconut meringue pie. The cuisine always struck us as what a Bajan might prepare for dinner.

3 Beaches, Water Sports & Other Outdoor Pursuits

You've probably come to swim and sunbathe, and both are far preferable on the western coast in the clear, buoyant waters of the Caribbean, although you may also want to visit the surf-pounded Atlantic coast in the east, which is better for the views than for swimming.

BEACHES

Bajans will tell you that their island has a beach for every day of the year. If you're only visiting for a short time, however, you'll probably be happy with the ones that are easy to find. They're all open to the public—even those in front of the big resort hotels and private homes—and the government requires that there be access to all beaches, via roads along the property line or through the hotel entrance. The beaches on the west, the so-called **Gold Coast,** are the most popular.

WEST COAST Waters are calm here. Major beaches include **Paynes Bay,** which is accessed from the Coach House. This is a good beach for water sports, especially snorkeling. There's also a parking area. The beach can get rather crowded, however, but the beautiful bay somehow makes it seem worth the effort to get here.

Directly south of Payne's Bay, at Fresh Water Bay, are three of the best west-coast beaches: **Brighton Beach, Brandon's Beach,** and **Paradise Beach.**

Church Point lies north of St. James Church, opening onto Heron Bay, site of the Colony Club Hotel. This is one of the most scenic bays on Barbados and the swimming is ideal. The beach can get overcrowded, however. There are some shade trees when you've had enough sun. You can also order drinks at the beach terrace operated by the Colony Club.

Mullins Beach, a final west-coast selection, is also recommended. Its blue waters are glassy and attract snorkelers. There's parking on the main road. Again, the beach has some shady areas. At the Mullins Beach Bar, you can order that rum drink.

SOUTH COAST Beaches here include **Casuarina Beach,** with access from Maxwell Coast Road, going across the property of the Casuarina Beach Hotel. This is one of the wider beaches of Barbados, and we've noticed that it's swept by trade winds even on the hottest days of August. Windsurfers are especially fond of this one. Food and drink can be ordered at the hotel.

Silver Sands Beach, to the east of Oistins, is near the southernmost point of Barbados, directly east of South Point Lighthouse and near the Silver Rock Hotel. This white-sand beach is a favorite with many Bajans (who probably want to keep it a secret from as many tourists as possible). Drinks are sold at the Silver Rock Bar.

Sandy Beach, reached from the parking lot on the Worthing main road, has tranquil waters opening onto a lagoon, the epitome of Caribbean charm. This is a family favorite, with lots of screaming and yelling on the weekends especially. Food and drink are sold here.

SOUTHEAST COAST The southeast coast is the site of the big waves, especially at **Crane Beach,** the white-sand beach set against a backdrop of palms that you've probably seen in all the travel magazines. The beach is spectacular, as Prince Andrew, who has a house overlooking the beach, might agree. It offers excellent body surfing, but at times the waters might be too rough for all but the strongest swimmers. The beach is set against cliffs, and the Crane Beach Hotel towers above it. This is ocean swimming, not the calm Caribbean, so take precautions.

Bottom Bay, north of Sam Lord's Castle Resorts, is one of our all-time Bajan favorites. You park on the top of a cliff, then walk down steps to this much-photographed tropical beach with its grove of coconut palms. There's even a cave. The sand is brilliantly white against the aquamarine sea, a picture-postcard perfect beach paradise.

EAST COAST (ON THE ATLANTIC) There are miles and miles of uncrowded beaches along the east coast, but this is the Atlantic side and swimming here is potentially dangerous. Many visitors like to visit the beaches here, especially those in the **Bathsheba/Cattlewash** areas, for their rugged grandeur. Waves are extremely high on these beaches, and the bottom tends to be rocky. The currents are also unpredictable. Otherwise, the beaches are ideal for strolling if you don't go into the water.

WATER SPORTS

SNORKELING & SCUBA DIVING The clear waters off Barbados have a visibility of more than 100 feet most of the year. More than 50 varieties of fish are found on the shallow inside reefs. On night dives, sleeping fish, night anemones, lobsters, moray eels, and octopuses can be seen. On a mile-long coral reef two minutes by boat from **Sandy Beach,** sea fans, corals, gorgonias, and reef fish are plentiful. *J.R.*, a dredge barge sunk as an artificial reef in 1983, is popular with beginners for its coral, fish life, and 20-foot depth. The *Berwyn,* a coral-encrusted tugboat that sank in Carlisle Bay in 1916, attracts photographers because of its variety of reef fish, shallow depth, good light, and visibility.

The **Asta Reef,** with a drop of 80 feet, has coral, sea fans, and reef fish in abundance. It's the site of a Barbados wreck sunk in 1986 as an artificial reef. **Dottins,** the most beautiful reef on the west coast, stretches 5 miles from Holetown to Bridgetown and has numerous dive sites at an average depth of 40 feet and drop-offs of 100 feet. The SS *Stavronika,* a Greek freighter, is a popular dive site for advanced divers. Crippled by fire in 1976, the 360-foot freighter was sunk 1/4 mile off the west coast to become an artificial reef in **Folkestone Underwater Park.** The mast is at 40 feet, the deck at 80 feet, and the keel at 140 feet. It's encrusted with coral.

The Dive Shop, Pebbles Beach, Aquatic Gap, St. Michael (☎ **246/426-9947**), offers some of the best scuba diving on Barbados, charging $48 for a one-tank dive and $70 for a two-tank dive. Every day, three dive trips go out to the nearby reefs and wrecks. In addition, snorkeling trips and equipment rentals are possible. Visitors with reasonable swimming skills who have never dived before can sign up for a resort course. Priced at $60, it includes pool training, safety instructions, and a one-tank open-water dive. The establishment is NAUI- and PADI-certified. It's open daily from 9am to 5pm.

DEEP-SEA FISHING The fishing is first-rate in the waters around Barbados, where fishers pursue dolphin, marlin, wahoo, barracuda, and sailfish, to name only the most popular catches. There's also an occasional cobia.

The Dive Shop (see above; ☎ **246/426-9947**) can arrange half-day charters for one to six people (all equipment and drinks included), costing $350 per boat. Under the same arrangement, the whole-day jaunt goes for $700.

WINDSURFING Experts say that the windsurfing off Barbados is as good as any this side of Hawaii. Judging from the crowds of 20- to 35-year-olds who flock here, it's true. Windsurfing on Barbados has turned into a very big business between November and April. Thousands of windsurfers from all over the world now come here from as far away as Finland, Argentina, and Japan. The shifting of the trade winds between November and May and the shallow offshore reef off **Silver Sands** create unique conditions of wind and wave swells. This allows windsurfers to reach speeds of up to 50 knots and do complete loops off the waves. Silver Sands is rated the best spot in the Caribbean for advanced windsurfing (skill rating five to six). In other words, one needs skills similar to those of a professional downhill skier to master these conditions.

An outfit set up to handle the demand from the hordes of international windsurfers is **Barbados Windsurfing Club,** which maintains two branches on the island. Beginners and intermediates usually opt for the branch in Oistins (☎ **246/428-7277**), where winds are constant but where the sea is generally flat and calm. Advanced intermediates and expert windsurfers usually select the branch adjacent to the Silver Sands Hotel, in Christ Church (☎ **246/428-6001**), where stronger winds and higher waves allow surfers to combine aspects of windsurfing with the conventional surfing known in Hawaii. The boards and equipment used by both branches of this outfit are provided by the Germany-based Club Mistral. Lessons at either branch cost between $40 and $55 per hour, depending on how many people are in your class. Equipment rents for between $25 and $35 per hour or $55 to $65 per half-day, depending on where and what you rent. Budgeteers usually opt for the Oistins branch, as prices are less expensive that at the Silver Sands branch.

OTHER SPORTS

GOLF The **Royal Westmoreland Golf & Country Club,** Westmoreland, St. James (☎ **246/422-4653**), is the island's premier golf course, a title once held by Sandy Lane. Built in 1994 by Robert Trent Jones Jr., this $30 million, 27-hole course is spread across 500 acres overlooking the Gold Coast of the island's western edge. It's part of a private residential community and can only be played by guests of the Royal Pavilion, Glitter Bay, Colony Club, Tamarind Cove, Coral Reef, Crystal Cove, Cobblers Cove, Sandpiper Inn, and Sandy Lane. It costs $60 for 9 holes, or $110 for 18 holes, including a cart.

Open to all is the 18-hole championship golf course of the **Sandy Lane Hotel,** St. James (☎ **246/432-1311**), on the west coast. Greens fees are $100 in winter and $75 in summer for 18 holes, or $65 in winter and $45 in summer for 9 holes. Carts and caddies are available.

HIKING The **Barbados National Trust** (☎ **246/426-2421**) offers Sunday morning hikes throughout the year. The program gives participants an opportunity to learn about the natural beauty of Barbados. It attracts more than 300 participants weekly. Led by young Bajans and members of the National Trust, the hikes cover a different area of the island each week. Tour escorts give brief talks on various aspects of the hikes, such as geography, history, geology, and agriculture. The hikes, free and open to participants of all ages, are divided into fast, medium, and slow categories. All the hikes leave promptly at 6am; each is about 5 miles long and takes about three hours to complete. There are also hikes at 3:30pm and 5:30pm, the latter conducted only if it is a moonlit night. For information or transportation, contact the Barbados National Trust.

HORSEBACK RIDING A different view of Barbados is offered by the **Caribbean International Riding Centre** (☎ **246/422-7433**), Cleland Plantation, Farley Hill, St. Andrew. With nearly 40 horses, Mrs. Roachford or one of her daughters offers a variety of trail rides for all levels of experience. The various rides range from the 1-hour trek for $30 to a 2½-hour jaunt for $65. You ride through some of the most panoramic parts of Barbados, especially the hilly terrain of the Scotland district. Wild ducks and water lilies, with the rhythm of the Atlantic as background music, are some of nature's sights viewed along the way.

TENNIS **Sandy Lane,** St. James (☎ **246/432-1311**), places more emphasis on tennis than any other resort on Barbados, with two pros on hand, along with five courts and an open-door policy to nonguests. Two of the five well-maintained courts are lit for night games. One of the courts simulates the feel of grass, whereas the other four are hard-surfaced. Court no. 1 is the most frequently used because it's adjacent to the clubhouse, bar, and restaurant. It's advised to play early or late, although the courts are wide open during the hot times between 10am and 3pm. Court rentals are

$20 per hour, or $10 per half hour. Lessons with a pro cost $25 per half hour or $50 per hour.

The **Barbados Hilton,** Needham's Point (☎ **246/426-0200**), maintains four hard-surface courts, each of which is lit for night play. The Hilton's courts are not nearly as clubby or gracious as those of Sandy Lane, but they're closer to Bridgetown and more convenient for many visitors. Guests play for free, while nonresidents pay $20 per half hour. All players at night are charged $10 per half hour for illumination of the courts.

4 Exploring the Island

TOURS & CRUISES

Barbados is worth exploring, either in your own car or with a taxi-driver guide. Unlike on so many islands of the Caribbean, the roads are fair and quite passable. They are, however, poorly signposted, and newcomers invariably get lost, not only once, but several times. If you get lost, the people in the countryside are generally helpful.

TAXI TOURS Nearly all Bajan taxi drivers are familiar with the entire island and like to show it off to visitors. If you can afford it, touring by taxi is far more preferable to taking a standardized bus tour. The average day tour by taxi costs $50, but, of course, that figure has to be negotiated in advance.

ORGANIZED SIGHTSEEING TOURS Instead of a private taxi, you can also book a tour with **Bajan Tours,** Glenayre, Locust Hall, St. George (☎ **246/437-9389**), a locally owned and operated tour company. The best bet for the first-timer is the Exclusive Island Tour, costing $56 per person, with departures between 8:30 and 9am, with a return from 3:30 to 4pm daily. It covers all the highlights of the island, including the Barbados Wildlife Reserve, the Chalky Mount Potteries, and the rugged east coast.

On Friday, for the same price, the outfit conducts a Heritage Tour, mainly of the island's major plantations and museums. And Monday through Friday it offers an Eco Tour, which takes in the natural beauty of the island. It, too, costs $56 and leaves at the same time as the above two tours. A full buffet lunch is included in all tours.

CRUISES Largest of the coastal cruising vessels, the *Bajan Queen* is modeled after a Mississippi riverboat and is the only cruise ship offering table seating and dining on local fare produced fresh from the onboard galley. There's also cover available in case of too much sun or rain. The *Bajan Queen* becomes a showboat by night, with local bands providing music for dancing under the stars. You're treated to a dinner of roast chicken, barbecued steak, and seasoned flying fish with a buffet of fresh side dishes and salads. Cruises are usually sold out, so you should book early to avoid disappointment. Each cruise costs BD$110 ($55) and includes transportation to and from your hotel. For reservations, contact **Jolly Roger Cruises,** Shallow Draft, Bridgetown Harbour (☎ **246/436-6424**). Cruises are on Wednesday from 6 to 10pm and on Saturday from 5 to 9pm.

The same company also owns two motorized replicas of pirate frigates, the *Jolly Roger I* and the *Jolly Roger II.* One or both of these, depending on demand, departs five mornings a week for daytime snorkeling cruises from 10am to 2pm. Included in the price of BD$123 ($61.50) is an all-you-can-eat buffet, complimentary drinks, and free use of snorkeling equipment, which requires a $20 refundable deposit. There's an onboard boutique on both of these boats. For information, call Jolly Roger Cruises or visit the berth at Bridgetown Harbour. They also operate a fourth boat, *Excellent,* a catamaran running on Monday, Wednesday, and Friday from 9am to

2pm and on Sunday from 10am to 3pm. The price of $55 includes a continental breakfast, a lunch buffet, free drinks, and free snorkeling gear (no deposit), plus inflatable water mattresses. Since it's a catamaran, there are less people, making the ambience more intimate.

Limbo Lady Sailing Cruises, 78 Old Chancery Lane, Christ Church (☎ **246/420-5418**) is another touring option. Patrick Gonsalves skippers the classic 44-foot CSY yacht, *Limbo Lady,* and his wife, Yvonne, a singer and guitarist, serenades you on a sunset cruise. Daily lunch cruises are also available, with a stop for swimming and snorkeling (equipment provided). Both lunch and sunset cruises offer a complimentary open bar and transportation to and from your hotel. Lunch cruises lasting 4½ hours cost $63, and 3-hour sunset cruises, including a glass of champagne, go for $52. Moonlight dinner cruises can also be arranged as well as private charters, both local and to neighboring islands (call for more information).

SUBMERGED SIGHTSEEING You no longer have to be an experienced diver to see what lives 150 feet below the surface of the sea around Barbados. Now all visitors can view the sea's wonders on sightseeing submarines. The air-conditioned submersibles seat 28 to 48 passengers and make several dives daily from 9am to 6pm. Passengers are transported aboard a ferry boat from the Careenage in downtown Bridgetown to the submarine site, about a mile from the west coast of Barbados. The ride offers a view of the west coast of the island.

The submarines have viewing ports allowing you to see a rainbow of colors, tropical fish, plants, and even a shipwreck that lies upright and intact below the surface. You're taken aboard either *Atlantic I* or *III* on two different trips, beginning with the Odyssey, which is a dive onto a reef where professional divers leave the vessel and perform a 15-minute dive show for the viewing passengers, costing $84.50 for adults or $42.25 for children. The Expedition costs $73.50 for adults and $36.25 for children. For reservations, contact **Atlantis Submarines (Barbados),** Shallow Draught, Bridgetown (☎ **246/436-8929**). It's also possible to go cruising over one of the shore reefs to observe marine life. You sit in air-conditioned comfort aboard the *Atlantis Seatrec,* a semi-submersible boat, which gives you a chance to get a snorkeler's view of the reef through large viewing windows. You can also relax on deck as you take in the scenic coastline. The tour costs $29.50 for adults; children 4 to 12 are charged half fare (not suitable for those 3 or under). A second *Seatrec* tour explores wreckage sites. Divers go down with video cameras to three different wrecks on Carlisle Bay, and the video is transmitted to TV monitors aboard the vessel. The price is the same as for the first tour. For reservations, call the number above.

EXPLORING BRIDGETOWN

Often hot and traffic clogged, the capital, Bridgetown, merits no more than a morning's shopping jaunt (see section 5 of this chapter for a rundown of the best stores).

Since some half million visitors arrive on Barbados by cruise ship each year, the government has opened a $6 million **cruise-ship terminal** for them. It offers a variety of shopping options, including 20 duty-free shops, 13 local retail stores, and scads of vendors. Many of the stores stock the arts and crafts of Barbados, and cruise passengers can choose among a range of other products, including jewelry, liquor, china, crystal, electronics, perfume, and leather goods. Some shops sell Barbadian wood carvings and art, as well as locally made fashions. The interior was designed to re-create an island street scene, with some storefronts appearing as traditional chattel houses in brilliant island colors with street lights, tropical landscaping, benches, and pushcarts.

Begin your tour at **The Careenage** (the French word for turning vessels on their side for cleaning). This was a haven for the clipper ship, and even though today it doesn't have the color of yesteryear, it's still worth exploring.

At **Trafalgar Square,** the long tradition of British colonization is immortalized. The monument here, honoring Lord Nelson, was executed by Sir Richard Westmacott and erected in 1813. The **Public Buildings** on the square are of the great, gray Victorian/gothic variety that you might expect to find in London. The east wing contains the meeting halls of the Senate and the House of Assembly, with some stained-glass windows representing the sovereigns of England. Look for the "Great Protector" himself, Oliver Cromwell.

Behind the Financial Building, **St. Michael's Cathedral,** east of Trafalgar Square, is the symbol of the Church of England. This Anglican church was built in 1655, but was completely destroyed in a 1780 hurricane. Reconstructed in 1789, it was again damaged by a hurricane in 1831, but was not completely demolished as before. George Washington is said to have worshipped here on his Barbados visit.

The **Synagogue,** Synagogue Lane (☎ **246/432-0840**), is one of the oldest in the western hemisphere and is surrounded by a burial ground of early Jewish settlers. The present building dates from 1833. It was constructed on the site of an even older synagogue, erected by Jews from Brazil in 1654. Sometime in the early 20th century the synagogue was deconsecrated, and the structure has since served various roles. In 1983 the government of Barbados seized the deteriorating building, intending to raze it and build a courthouse on the site. An outcry went up from the small Jewish community on the island; money was raised for its restoration, and the building was saved and is now part of the National Trust of Barbados and a synagogue once again. It's open Monday to Friday from 8am to 4:30pm.

First made popular in 1870, **cricket** is the national pastime on Barbados. Matches can last from one to five days. If you'd like to see a local match, watch for announcements in the newspapers or ask at the Tourist Board, on Harbour Road (☎ **246/427-2623**). From Bridgetown, you can hail a taxi if you don't have a car and visit **Garrison Savannah,** just south of the capital, which is a frequent venue for cricket matches and horse races.

The **Barbados Museum,** St. Ann's Garrison, St. Michael (☎ **246/427-0201**), is housed in a former military prison. In the exhibition "In Search of Bim," extensive collections show the island's development from prehistoric to modern times. "Born of the Sea" gives fascinating glimpses into the natural environment. There are also fine collections of West Indian maps, decorative arts, and fine arts. The museum sells a variety of quality publications, reproductions (maps, cards, prints), and handcrafts. Its Museum Café is a good place for a snack or light lunch. The museum is open Monday to Saturday from 9am to 5pm and on Sunday from 2 to 6pm. Admission is $5 for adults, $2.50 for children.

Nearby, the russet-red **St. Ann's Fort,** on the fringe of the Savannah, garrisoned British soldiers in 1694. The fort wasn't completed until 1703. The Clock House survived the hurricane of 1831.

HEADING INLAND TO STROLL THROUGH TROPICAL GARDENS & TAKE A SPECTACULAR CAVE TOUR

Take Highway 2 from Bridgetown and follow it to **Welchman Hall Gully,** in St. Thomas (☎ **246/438-6671**), a lush tropical garden owned by the Barbados National Trust. You'll see some specimens of plants that were here when the English settlers landed in 1627. Many of the plants are labeled—clove, nutmeg, tree fern, and cocoa, among others—and occasionally you'll spot a wild monkey. You'll also see breadfruit trees that are claimed to have descended from the seedlings brought ashore by Captain Bligh, of *Bounty* fame. Admission is $5, half price for children 6 to 12, and kids 5 and under enter free. It's open daily from 9am to 5pm.

Also at Welchman Hall, St. Thomas, **Harrison's Cave** (☎ **246/438-6640**) is the number-one tourist attraction of Barbados. Visitors can view a beautiful underground world from aboard an electric tram and trailer. During the tour, visitors see bubbling streams, tumbling cascades, and deep pools, which are subtly lit, while all around stalactites hang overhead like icicles, and stalagmites rise from the floor. Visitors may disembark and get a closer look at this natural phenomenon at the Rotunda Room and the Cascade Pool. Tours are conducted daily from 9am to 4pm (closed Good Friday, Easter Sunday, and Christmas Day). You should reserve by phone. Admission is $8.75 for adults and $4.35 for children.

The **Flower Forest,** Richmond Plantation, St. Joseph (☎ **246/433-8152**), on an old sugar plantation, stands 850 feet above sea level near the western edge of the "Scotland district," a mile from Harrison's Cave. Set in one of the most scenic parts of Barbados, it's more than just a botanical garden; it's where people and nature came together to create something beautiful. After viewing the grounds, visitors can purchase handcrafts at Best of Barbados. It's open daily from 9am to 5pm, and admission is $7 for adults and $3.50 for children 5 to 16 (free 4 and under).

HISTORIC SIGHTS IN ST. MICHAEL & ST. GEORGE PARISHES

Tyrol Cot Heritage Village. Codrington Hill, St. Michael. ☎ **246/424-2074.** Admission $5 adults, $2.50 children. Mon–Fri 9am–5pm.

If you arrived at the airport, you'll recognize the name of Sir Grantley Adams, the leader of the Bajan movement for independence from Britain. This was once his home, and his wife, Lady Adams, lived in the house until her death in 1990. Once you had to wrangle a highly prized invitation to visit, but it's now open to all who pay admission. It was built sometime in the mid-1850s from coral stone in a Palladian style. The grounds have been turned into a museum of Bajan life, including small chattel houses where potters and artists work.

Francia Plantation. St. George, Barbados. ☎ **246/429-0474.** Admission $4.50. Mon–Fri 10am–4pm. On the ABC Highway, turn east onto Hwy. 4 at the Norman Niles Roundabout (follow the signs to Gun Hill); after going 1/2 mile, turn left onto Hwy. X (follow the signs to Gun Hill); after another mile, turn right at the Shell gas station and follow Hwy. X past St. George's Parish Church and up the hill for a mile, turning left at the sign to Francia.

A fine family home, this house stands on a wooded hillside overlooking the St. George Valley and is still owned and occupied by descendants of the original owner. You can explore several rooms, including the dining room with family silver and an 18th-century James McCabe bracket clock. On the walls are antique maps and prints, including a map of the West Indies printed in 1522.

Gun Hill Signal Station. Hwy. 4. ☎ **246/429-1358.** Admission $4 adults, $2 children 13 and under. Mon–Sat 9am–5pm. Take Hwy. 3 from Bridgetown and then go inland from Hwy. 4 toward St. George Church.

One of two such stations owned and operated by the Barbados National Trust, the Gun Hill Signal Station is strategically placed on the highland of St. George and commands a panoramic view from the east to the west. Built in 1818, it was the finest of a chain of signal stations and was also used as an outpost for the British army stationed here at the time. The old military cookhouse has been restored and houses a snack bar and gift shop.

A MEMORABLE DRIVE AROUND THE ISLAND

If you can afford it, the ideal way to take this tour is with a local taxi driver, who will generally negotiate a fair rate. Of course, you can tour on your own, although you'll have to rent an expensive car. Locals know the roads, which are often unmarked; visitors don't. If you do explore on your own, you can count on getting lost, at least several times. Although there are lots of signs, highway authorities will often leave you stranded at strategic junctions, and it's very easy to take a wrong turn if you don't know the way. Even people who live on Barbados often get confused. No clear, concise map of Barbados has yet been devised. Maps only help you with general directions; when you're looking for the route to a specific destination, they can often be most unhelpful.

That having been said, know that part of the fun of exploring Barbados is the discovery of the island. So if you do get lost a few times and miss an attraction or two, that's no great harm. The tour we've outlined below can be done in a day.

After leaving Bridgetown (see above), head south along Highway 7, passing through the resorts of Hastings, Rockley, Worthing, and St. Lawrence.

After going through Worthing, and providing you can find this madly, badly marked road, turn right along **St. Lawrence Gap,** which is the restaurant row of Barbados, including such well-known places as the Witch Doctor and the Ship Inn. There are also several budget- and medium-priced hotels located along this strip, which is generally lively both day and night.

At the end of St. Lawrence Gap, resume your journey along Highway 7 by taking a right turn. You'll bypass the town of **Oistins,** a former shipping port that today is a fishing village. Here the Charter of Barbados was signed at the Mermaid in 1652, as the island surrendered to Commonwealth forces. The Mermaid Inn, incidentally, was owned by a cousin of John Turner, who built the House of the Seven Gables in Salem, Massachusetts.

At the sign, take a left for Providence and the Grantley Adams Airport, a continuation of Highway 7. You'll pass the airport on your right. After bypassing the airport, follow the signs to Sam Lord's Castle Resorts. At the hamlet of Spencers, leave Highway 7 and turn onto Rock Hall Road, going through the villages of St. Martins and Heddings until you come to the remote hilltop **Crane Beach Hotel** (☎ **246/423-6220**). Everyone touring the south coast stops here for the view of the Atlantic, and its much-photographed Roman-style swimming pool is beloved by all visiting cruise-ship passengers. There are two different entrance fees, costing $2.50 or $10. The $2.50 fee lets you hang out at the bar and is applied to your bar tab. A $10 pool package gives you greater access to the hotel's facilities, and $5 of this fee is applied to your bar tab.

After leaving the hotel, follow Crane Road east. Turn right at the sign and continue to the end of the road and **Sam Lord's Castle Resorts.** Although this is a hotel, it's also one of the major sightseeing attractions of Barbados; you can stop for a bite here if you didn't already stop at the Crane Beach Hotel. Built by slaves in 1820, and furnished in part with Regency pieces, the house is like a Georgian plantation mansion. Take note of the ornate ceilings, said to be the finest example of stucco work in the western hemisphere. At the entrance to the hotel are shops selling handcrafts and souvenirs. If you're not a guest, you'll have to pay BD$10 ($5) to enter.

After leaving Sam Lord's Castle, take a right onto Long Bay Road and continue east. Go right via the village of Wellhouse and continue along the main road, which skirts the coastline but doesn't touch the coast. On your right you'll see the **Ragged Point Lighthouse.** Turn right down a narrow road to the easternmost point of

Barbados. Built in 1885, the lighthouse stands on a rugged cliff. Since that time, its beacon has warned ships approaching the dangerous reef, called the Cobblers. The view from here is panoramic.

After leaving the lighthouse, continue straight along Marley Vale Road (don't expect proper signs). At the sign to Bayfield, go right and pass Three Houses Park. Take a right at the sign to Bridgetown onto Thickets Road. Take a right again at the sign to Bathsheba. When you come to another signpost, turn left toward Bathsheba and follow the signs to **Codrington College,** which opened in 1745. A cabbage-palm-lined avenue leads to old coral-block buildings. Today the college is a training school for men and women from the entire Caribbean to enter the ordained ministry of the Anglican church. The college is under the auspices of the Dioceses of the West Indies. Entrance is $2.50.

After leaving the college, go right, then take the next left up the steep Coach Hill Road, where you'll see excellent views of the east coast and the lighthouse just visited. At the top of the hill, continue right and follow the signs to **St. John's Church,** perched on the edge of a cliff opening on the east coast some 825 feet above sea level. The church dates from 1836 and in its graveyard in the rear rests a descendant of Emperor Constantine the Great, whose family was driven from the throne in Constantinople (Istanbul) by the Turks. Ferdinando Paleologus, the royal relative, died on Barbados in 1678.

After leaving the church, go left and then take the next right onto Gall Hill Road. Stay on this road until you reach Four Roads Junction, go along Wakefield Road, and at the sign, turn left and then take the next right by **Villa Nova,** in St. John, which is currently closed to the public. Built in 1834 as a fine sugar plantation Great House, it's surrounded by 6 1/2 acres of landscaped gardens and trees. Its most famous association was with Sir Anthony Eden, former prime minister of Great Britain, who purchased it from the Bajan government in 1965. In 1966 the earl and countess of Avon entertained Queen Elizabeth and Prince Philip at the Great House. It has since been sold to private owners.

After leaving Villa Nova, turn left and pass through the hamlet of Venture. At the next intersection, continue left until you see the sign pointing right toward Easy Hall, another east coast hamlet. At the next sign, pointing toward Flower Forest (described earlier in this section), go left along Buckden House Road. Take the next right and head down Highway 3, a steep, curvy road toward the ocean.

Turn right toward Bathsheba, and follow the signs to the **Andromeda Botanic Gardens,** Bathsheba, St. Joseph (☎ **246/433-9261**). On a cliff overlooking Bathsheba on the rugged east coast, limestone boulders make for a natural 8-acre rock-garden setting, where thousands of orchids are in bloom every day of the year along with hundreds of hibiscus and heliconia. Many varieties of ferns, begonias, and other species grow here in splendid profusion. One section, a palm garden, has more than 100 species. A simple guide helps visitors to identify many of the plants. On the grounds you'll occasionally see frogs, herons, lizards, humming birds, and sometimes a mongoose or a monkey. With an admission of BD$10 ($5) for adults, BD$5 ($2.50) for children, the gardens are open daily from 9am to 5pm; children 5 and under enter free.

After leaving the gardens, turn right and follow the signs to the **Atlantis Hotel,** Bathsheba, St. Joseph Parish (☎ **246/433-9445**), one of the oldest hotels on Barbados, where Enid Maxwell has been serving her favorite Bajan dishes, including flying fish and pickled breadfruit, for longer than she cares to remember. Tattered but respectable, this hotel was once a villa built by a wealthy planter in 1882. It's directly on the coast, just south of the "Scotland District."

Now continue north along the coast road to the town of **Bathsheba,** where ocean rollers break, forming cascades of white foam. This place has been called "Cornwall in miniature." Today the old fishing village is a favorite low-cost resort for Bajans, although the waters of the Atlantic Ocean are dangerous for swimmers.

The trail north from Bathsheba takes you along the **East Coast Road,** which runs for many miles, opening onto dramatic views of the Atlantic. Chalky Mount rises from the beach to a height of 500 feet, forming a trio of peaks, and a little to the south, Barclays Park is a 15-acre natural wonder presented as a gift to the people of Barbados by the British banking family. There's a snack bar and a place to picnic here.

Farther north is the **Morgan Lewis Sugar Windmill,** in St. Andrew (☎ **246/426-2421**). This is typical of the wind-driven mills that crushed the juice from the sugarcane from the 17th to the 19th century, producing the sugar that made Barbados Britain's most valuable possession in the Americas. It was from Barbados sugarcane that rum was first produced. Admission is $2.50 for adults, $1.25 children 13 and under, and it's open Monday to Friday from 9am to 5pm. Before coming here, however, check to see if it has reopened.

Climb Morgan Lewis Hill to reach one of the panoramic sights of Barbados, **Cherry Tree Hill,** on Highway 1, which offers magnificent views. You can look right down the eastern shore past Bathsheba to the lighthouse at Ragged Point. The place is about 850 feet above sea level, and from it you can see out over the Scotland district. The cherry trees from which the hill got its name no longer stand here, having given way to mahogany.

On Cherry Tree Hill, signs point the way to **St. Nicholas Abbey** (☎ **246/422-8725**), a Jacobean plantation Great House and sugarcane fields that have been around since about 1650. It was never an abbey—around 1820 an ambitious owner simply christened it as such. More than 200 acres are still cultivated each year. The structure, at least the ground floor, is open to the public Monday to Friday from 10am to 3:30pm, charging an admission of $5; children 12 and under enter free. The house is believed to be one of three Jacobean houses in the western hemisphere and is characterized by curved gables. Lt.-Col. Stephen Cave, the owner, is descended from the family that purchased the sugar plantation and Great House in 1810. You can lunch or take afternoon tea here (see Café Calabash in "Where to Dine," above).

After leaving the abbey, follow the road to Diamond Corner, where you go left. Take another left onto the Charles Duncan O'Neal Highway to Farley Hill National Park, in northern St. Peter Parish. Farley Hill House was used as a backdrop for the 1957 film *Island in the Sun,* starring Harry Belafonte. Unfortunately, it was gutted by fire. The park, dedicated by Queen Elizabeth in 1966, is open daily from 8:30am to 6pm. You pay a vehicular entrance fee of $1.50 for cars. After disembarking in the parking area, you can walk the grounds and enjoy the tropical flowers and lush vegetation.

Across the road from the park lies the **Barbados Wildlife Reserve** (☎ **246/422-8826**), an operation set in a mahogany forest that's run by the Barbados Primate Research Center in St. Peter. From 10am to 5pm daily, for an admission charge of BD$20 ($10) for adults (half price for children 12 and under), you can stroll through what is primarily a monkey sanctuary and an arboretum. Aside from the uncaged monkeys, you can see wild hares, deer, tortoises, otters, wallabies (which were brought into Barbados), and a variety of tropical birds. Another attraction of the Wildlife Reserve is the **Grenade Hall Signal Station & Forest.** The signal station, which has been renovated from the original built in 1819, offers the most panoramic view of the east, west, and north coasts. Housed in the signal station are archaeological findings accompanied by a recorded commentary. Next to the signal station are 5 acres of indigenous woodland of whitewood, inkberry, liana vines, and other species. The forest is open to the public daily from 10am to 5pm.

From Farley Hill Park and the Wildlife Reserve, backtrack to the junction of Highways 1 and 2. From here, head west along Highway 1 and follow the signs to **Speightstown,** which was founded around 1635 and for a time was a whaling port. The "second city" of Barbados, the town has some colonial buildings constructed after the devastating hurricane of 1831. The parish church, rebuilt in a half-Grecian style after the hurricane, is one of the places of interest.

After exploring Speightstown, if you have time, turn left toward the **Gold Coast,** the protected western shoreline that opens onto the gentler Caribbean. Along the shoreline of the parishes of St. James and St. Peter are the island's plushest hotels.

On Highway 1, directly north of Holetown, lies **St. James Church,** an Anglican church rebuilt in 1872 on the site of the early settlers' church of 1660. On the southern porch is an old bell bearing the inscription "God Bless King William, 1696," one stop on a 1982 visit by Ronald and Nancy Reagan that is still fondly recalled by locals.

Continue south on Highway 1 to **Holetown,** the main center of the west coast; it takes its name from the town of Hole on the Thames River. The first English settlers landed here in the winter of 1627. An obelisk marks the spot where the *Olive Blossom* landed the first Europeans. The monument, for some reason, lists the date erroneously as 1605. After Holetown, Highway 1 continues south taking you back to Bridgetown.

EXPLORING THE GREEN HILLS

Unless visitors make special efforts to explore the lush interior of this former British colony, most of their time on Barbados might be confined to the island's densely populated coastal plain. But much of Barbados's true beauty can only be appreciated through treks, tours, or hill climbs through such rarely visited parishes as St. Thomas and St. George (both of which are landlocked) and the Atlantic coast parishes of St. Andrews and St. John (where the rough surf of the Atlantic usually discourages the embarkation of sailing vessels). Until recently, most visitors were requested to restrict their sightseeing in these relatively undeveloped parishes to the sides of the highways and roads. But a locally owned tour operator, **Highland Outdoor Tours,** Canefield, St. Thomas Parish (☎ **246/438-8069**), conducts a series of tours across privately owned land. With its verdant, rolling hills and many dramatic rock outcroppings, much of the terrain might remind you of a windswept but balmy version of Scotland.

You'll have the option of conducting your tour on horseback, on foot, or as a passenger in a tractor-drawn jitney. Horseback rides and walking tours last anywhere from two to five hours. As you traverse what used to be some of the most productive sugar plantations in the British Empire, your guide will describe the geology, architecture, and historical references you'll see en route.

All tours depart from the Highland Outdoor Tour Center in the parish of St. Thomas (in north-central Barbados). Transportation to and from your hotel is included in the price of horseback tours (from $25), hiking tours (from $50), and tractor-drawn jitney tours (from $25). Mountain bike tours start at $32.50.

5 Shopping

On Barbados you might find duty-free merchandise at prices 20% to 40% lower than in the United States and Canada. But, of course, you've got to be a smart shopper to spot bargains and also be familiar with prices back in your hometown. Duty-free shops have two prices listed on items of merchandise, the local retail price and the local retail price less the government-imposed tax.

Some of the best duty-free buys include cameras (Leica, Rolex, and Fuji), watches (Omega, Piaget, Seiko), crystal (Waterford and Lalique), gold (especially jewelry), bone china (Wedgwood and Royal Doulton), cosmetics and perfumes, and liquor (including locally produced Barbados rum and liqueurs), along with tobacco products and cashmere sweaters, tweeds, and sportswear from Britain. If you purchase items made on Barbados, you don't have to pay duty.

The outstanding item in Barbados handcrafts is black-coral jewelry. Clay pottery is another Bajan craft. We recommend a visit to **Chalky Mount Potteries,** where this special craft originated. Potters turn out different products, some based on designs that are centuries old. The potteries (signposted) are found north of Bathsheba on the east coast in the parish of St. Joseph, near Barclay's Park. In shops across the island, you'll also find a selection of locally made vases, pots, pottery mugs, glazed plates, and ornaments.

Wall hangings are made from local grasses and dried flowers, and island craftspeople also turn out straw mats, baskets, and bags with raffia embroidery. Still in its infant stage, leather work is also found on Barbados, particularly handbags, belts, and sandals.

Cruise passengers generally head for the **Bridgetown Cruise Terminal** at Bridgetown Harbour, which has some 20 duty-free shops, 13 local and regional merchandise shops, and several vendors.

Articrafts. Broad St., Bridgetown. ☎ **246/427-5767.**

Here John and Rosyln Watson have assembled one of the most impressive displays of Bajan arts and crafts on the island. Roslyn's woven wall hangings are decorated with objects from the island, including sea fans and coral. They make a distinctive handcrafted design. Straw work, handbags, and bamboo items are also sold.

Best of Barbados. In the Southern Palms, St. Lawrence Gap, Christ Church. ☎ **246/420-8040.**

Part of an islandwide chain of 12 stores, Best of Barbados sells only products designed and/or made on Barbados. It's the best shop on the island for local products. It was established in 1975 by an English-born painter, Jill Walker, whose prints are best-sellers. They sell coasters, mats, T-shirts, pottery, dolls and games, and cookbooks, among other items. This tasteful shop is around the corner from the entrance to Southern Palms.

A more convenient location might be the outlet in Bridgetown at Mall 34, Broad Street (☎ **246/436-1416**).

Cave Shepherd. Broad St., Bridgetown. ☎ **246/431-2121.**

The best place to shop for tax-free merchandise on Barbados is Cave Shepherd, which has branches at Sunset Crest in Holetown, Da Costas Mall, Grantley Adams International Airport, and the Bridgetown Cruise Terminal. If your time is limited and you want a preview of what's for sale on Barbados, try this outlet. It has the widest selection of goods islandwide. Cave Shepherd is the largest department store on Barbados and one of the most modern in the Caribbean. The store offers perfumes, cosmetics from the world's leading houses, fine full-lead crystal and English bone china, cameras, gold and silver jewelry, swimwear, leather goods, men's designer clothing, handcrafts, T-shirts, and souvenirs. More than 70 brands of liqueurs are sold as well as other spirits. After you finish shopping, relax on the top floor in the cool comfort of the Ideal Restaurant. You can also patronize the Balcony, overlooking Broad Street and serving vegetarian dishes with a salad bar and beer garden as well.

Colours of De Caribbean. The Waterfront Marina, Bridgetown. ☎ **246/436-8522.**

Next to the Waterfront Café, on the Careenage, this unique store has a very individualized collection of tropical clothing, all made in the West Indies, and jewelry and decorative objects. Original hand-painted and batiked clothing may hold the most interest.

Cotton Days. Bay St., St. Michael. ☎ **246/427-7191.**

Boutiques abound on Barbados, and Cotton Days is the best known and most stylish. It inventories a wide array of casually elegant one-of-a-kind garments suitable for cool nights and hot climes. The collection has been called wearable art. For inspiration, the in-house designers turn to the flora and fauna of the island and the underwater world. The sales staff is skilled at selecting whimsical accessories to accompany the dresses, blouses, and shifts sold here. Magazines such as *Vogue* and *Glamour* have praised this collection.

Earthworks Pottery/The Potter's House Gallery. Edgehill Heights 2, St. Thomas Parish. ☎ **246/425-0223.**

Some serious shoppers consider this one of the artistic highlights of Barbados. Deep in the island's central highlands, its modern building was erected in the 1970s by Canadian-born Goldie Spieler. Trained as an art teacher and ceramic artist, Ms. Spieler and her son, David, create whimsical plates, cups, saucers, and bowls whose blue and green colors emulate the color of the Bajan sea and sky. Some fans claim that a breakfast of corn flakes in a cerulean-blue porringer on a snowy Stateside morning re-creates the warmth of a Caribbean holiday. Many objects are decorated with the Antillean-inspired swirls and zigzags and can be shipped virtually anywhere. On the premises is the studio where the objects are crafted and a showroom that sells the output of at least half a dozen other island potters. Prices range from $3 to $400.

The Great House Gallery. At the Bagatelle Restaurant, Hwy. 2A, St. Thomas. ☎ **246/421-6767.**

On the airy upper floor of one of the most historic Great Houses on Barbados, this art gallery combines an inventory of artworks with West Indian graciousness. Pieces are displayed on high white walls amid the reflected glow of an antique mahogany floor: oils and watercolors by Caribbean, Latin American, and British artists priced at $10 to $2,000. Among them are the award-winning works of the owners themselves.

Harrison's. 1 Broad St., Bridgetown. ☎ **246/431-5500.**

In addition to this main shop, Harrison's has 14 branch stores, all selling a wide variety of duty-free merchandise, including china, crystal, jewelry, leather goods, and perfumes—all at fair prices. We've been able to find good buys here in the range of Baccarat, Lalique, Royal Doulton, and Waterford crystal. They also sell some state-of-the-art leather products handcrafted in Colombia. Harrison's is the major competitor to Cave Shepherd on the island, but we'd give the edge to Cave Shepherd.

Little Switzerland. In the Da Costas Mall, Broad St., Bridgetown. ☎ **246/431-0029.**

At this outlet you'll find a wide selection of fragrances and cosmetics from such famous houses as Giorgio, Chanel, Guerlain, Yves St. Laurent, La Prairie, and more. Fine china and crystal from European manufacturers such as Lladró are also sold, as is an array of goodies from Waterford, Lalique, Swarovski, Baccarat, and others. The shop also specializes in watches and jewelry, offering a wide range of 14- and 18-karat-gold jewelry, with both precious and semiprecious stones. Watches include Rolex, Swatch, Omega, Raymond Weil, Tag Heuer, Ebel, and others. The store also stocks the distinctive Mont Blanc pens.

Mall 34. Broad St., Bridgetown. ☎ **246/435-8800.**

One of Bridgetown's most modern shopping complexes offers duty-free shopping in air-conditioned comfort at several outlets. You can find watches, clocks, china, jewelry, crystal, linens, sweaters, and liquor, together with souvenir items and tropical fashions.

Pelican Village. Princess Alice Hwy., Bridgetown. ☎ **246/427-5350.**

While in Bridgetown, go down to the Pelican Village on Princess Alice Highway leading down to the city's Deep Water Harbour. A collection of island-made crafts and souvenirs is sold here in a tiny colony of thatch-roofed shops, and you can wander from one to another. Sometimes you can see craftspeople at work. Some of the shops here are gimmicky and repetitive, although interesting items can be found.

The Shell Gallery. Carlton House, St. James. ☎ **246/422-2593.**

For the shell collector, this is the best collection in the West Indies. Shells for sale come from all over the world. The outlet features the shell art of Maureen Edghill, who is considered the finest artist in this field. She founded this unique gallery in 1975. Also offered are hand-painted chinaware, shell jewelry, local pottery and ceramics, and batik and papier-mâché artwork depicting shells and aquatic life.

Walker's Caribbean World. St. Lawrence Gap. ☎ **246/428-1183.**

Close to the Southern Palms, this outlet offers many locally made items for sale, as well as handcrafts from the Caribbean Basin. Here you can buy the famous Jill Walker prints. There's also a gallery devoted to tropical prints.

6 Barbados After Dark

Most of the big resort hotels feature entertainment nightly, often steel band dance music and occasional Bajan floor shows. Sometimes beach barbecues are staged.

Beach Club. Sunset Crest, St. James. ☎ **246/432-1309.** No cover Sun–Fri; free Sat for diners, $10 for nondiners.

This bar and restaurant serves as a social focal point for Sunset Crest, with many island residents happily hobnobbing with their friends and colleagues. Happy hour at the Beach Bar is from 5 to 6pm nightly, when drinks are half price. Fish fries, barbecues, or buffets are offered from 7 to 10pm daily, priced at $10 to $12.50. There's live entertainment most nights, including bands and amateur talent shows.

Coach House. Paynes Bay, St. James. ☎ **246/432-1163.** Cover from $5 (as soon as you pay it, you'll be given coupons worth $3 for drinks at the bar).

The Coach House, named after a pair of antique coaches that sometimes stand outside, is a green-and-white house said to be 200 years old. The atmosphere is a Bajan version of an English pub, with an outdoor garden bar. Businesspeople and habitués of nearby beaches come here to order Bajan buffet lunches, served Monday to Friday from noon to 3pm. The price is $11 for an all-you-can-eat lunchtime assortment that includes local vegetables and salads prepared fresh daily. If you visit from 6 to 10:30pm, you can order bar meals, including flying-fish burgers, priced at $8 and up. Live music is presented most nights, featuring everything from steel bands to jazz,

The Joints Are Still Jumping at Dawn: Where to Find the Best Local Watering Holes

For the most authentic Bajan evening possible, head for Baxters Road in Bridgetown, where there's always something cooking on Friday and Saturday after 11pm. In fact, if you stick around until dawn, the party's still going strong. The street is safer than it looks because Bajans come here to have fun, not to make trouble. The entertainment tends to be spontaneous. Some old-time visitors have compared Baxters Road to the backstreets of New Orleans in the 1930s. If you fall in love with the place, you can "caf crawl" up and down the street, where nearly every bar is run by a Bajan mama. Each place has its own atmosphere.

The most popular "caf" on Baxters Road is **Enid's** (she has a phone, "but it doesn't work"), a little ramshackle establishment where Bajans come to devour fried chicken at 3 in the morning. Her place is open daily from 8:30pm to 8:30am, when the last satisfied customer departs into the blazing morning sun and Enid heads home to get some sleep before the new night begins. Stop in for a Banks beer.

pop, and rock. The pub is on the main Bridgetown-Holetown road, just south of Sandy Lane, about 6 miles north of Bridgetown. Live music and an attentive crowd assemble together here nightly from 9pm on.

Harbour Lights. Marine's Villa, Upper Bay St., about a mile southeast of Bridgetown. ☎ **246/436-7225.** Cover $6–$15, Wed and Fri.

This is the most popular weekend venue for dancing, drinking, and flirting on all of Barbados. In a modern seafront building whose oceanfront patio allows dancers the chance to cool off, the place plays reggae, soca, and just about anything else that happens to be popular in the Caribbean at the time. No one under 18 is admitted. Grilled meats and hamburgers are available from a barbecue pit/kiosk on the premises. It's open till the wee hours every night. Monday is beach party night, costing $39 including transportation to and from your hotel, a barbecue buffet, free drinks, and a live band.

John Moore Bar. On the waterfront, Weston, St. James Parish. ☎ **246/422-2258.**

This is the most atmospheric and least pretentious bar on Barbados. Although its namesake (John Moore) died in 1987, the place is owned and managed by Mr. Lamont (Breedy) Addison, whose tenure here began as a teenager. If you think this bar functions only as a watering hole, think again: It's the nerve center in this waterfront town, filled throughout the day and evening with the widest and most congenial group of residents in the neighborhood. Most visitors opt for a rum punch or beer, but if you're hungry, platters of local fish can be prepared, after a moderate delay.

✪ **Plantation Restaurant and Garden Theatre.** Main Rd. (Hwy. 7), St. Lawrence, Christ Church. ☎ **246/428-5048.** Cover (including unlimited drinks) $52.50 for dinner, the show, and transport; $25 for the show only.

This is the island's most prominent showcase for evening dinner theater and Caribbean cabaret. Dinner and a show are presented every Wednesday and Friday. Dinner is served at 6:30pm, and a show, *Plantation Tropical Spectacular II,* is presented at 8pm. The show involves plenty of exotic costumes and lots of reggae, calypso, limbo, and Caribbean exoticism. Reserve in advance.

1627 and All That. Sherbourne Centre, St. Michael. ☎ **246/428-1627.** Cover $50.

Nothing else on Barbados so effectively combines music with entertainment and dancing. It's the most interesting place on Barbados to visit on a Thursday night. The entertainment combines a cocktail hour, a large buffet of Bajan food, and a historic and cultural presentation. The site, Sherbourne Centre, is a conference facility. The ticket includes transportation to and from your hotel. Dinner is served at 7pm, with show time at 8pm, concluding at 9:30pm.

The Ship Inn. St. Lawrence Gap, Christ Church. ☎ **246/435-6961.** Cover $5 after 9pm.

Previously recommended as a restaurant, this inn is now among the leading entertainment centers on the south coast. The pub is the hot spot. Top local bands perform every night of the week, and patrons gather to listen to live reggae, calypso, and Top 40 music. The entrance fee to the Ship Inn complex is redeemable in food or drink at any of the other bars or restaurants in the complex. That means that guests are actually only paying $2 for the live entertainment.

Waterfront Café. Cavan's Lane, The Careenage, Bridgetown. ☎ **246/427-0093.** No cover.

By anyone's estimate, this is the busiest, most interesting, and most animated nighttime watering hole in Bridgetown. In a turn-of-the-century warehouse originally built to store bananas and freeze fish, it welcomes both diners and drinkers to its reverberating walls for Creole food, beer, and pastel-colored drinks. Live music (reggae, ragtime, rock 'n' roll, or jazz) is presented Tuesday to Saturday from 8 to 11:30pm. Careenage Coffee, laced with various after-dinner potions, is an enduring favorite. Food is served Monday to Saturday from 10am to midnight.

Trinidad & Tobago 15

Trinidad, birthplace of the calypso and the steel pan, used to be visited only by business travelers in Port-of-Spain. The island was more interested in its oil, natural gas, and steel industries than in tourism. But all that has changed now. Trinidad is a serious vacation destination, with a spruced-up capital and a renovated airport.

The island's sophistication and cultural mélange, which is far greater than that of any other island in the southern Caribbean, is also a factor in increased visitor volume in Trinidad.

Conversely, Tobago, its sibling island, is just as drowsy as ever, and that's its charm. Through the years the country has been peopled by immigrants from almost every corner of the world: Africa, the Middle East, Europe, India, China, and the Americas. It's against such a background that the island has become the fascinating mixture of cultures, races, and creeds that it is today.

Trinidad, which is about the size of Delaware, and its neighbor island, tiny Tobago, 20 miles to the northeast, together form a nation popularly known as "T&T." South African Bishop Desmond Tutu once dubbed it "The Rainbow Country," for its abundance of floral growth and the diversity of its population. The islands are the southernmost outposts of the West Indies. Trinidad lies only 7 miles from the Paria Peninsula of Venezuela, to which it was once connected in prehistoric times.

The Spanish settled the island, making their first permanent settlement in 1592 and holding onto it longer than they did any of their other real estate in the Caribbean. The English captured Trinidad in 1797, and it remained British until the two-island nation declared its independence in 1962. The British influence is still clearly visible today, from the strong presence of the British dialect to the islanders' fondness for cricket.

FAST FACTS: Trinidad & Tobago

Banking Hours Most banks are open Monday to Thursday from 8am to 2pm and on Friday from 9am to noon and 3 to 5pm.

Currency The **Trinidad and Tobago dollar (TT$)** is loosely pegged to the U.S. dollar at an exchange rate of about TT$6 = U.S.$1 (TT$1 = 16.6¢ U.S.). Ask what currency is being referred to when rates are quoted. We've used a combination of both in this chapter, depending on the establishment. U.S. and Canadian dollars are accepted in exchange for payment, particularly in Port-of-Spain. However, you'll do better by converting your Canadian or U.S. dollars into local currency. British pounds should be converted into the local currency. Unless otherwise specified, dollar quotations appearing in this chapter are in U.S. currency.

Customs Readers have reported long delays in clearing Customs on Trinidad. Personal effects are duty free, and visitors may bring in 200 cigarettes or 50 cigars plus 1 quart of "spirits."

Documents Visitors arriving in Trinidad and Tobago should have an ongoing or return ticket from their point of embarkation. A visa is not required for tourist/business stays for less than two months. You'll be asked to fill out an immigration card upon your arrival, and the carbon copy of this should be saved, as it must be returned to immigration officials when you depart. Citizens of the United States, Britain, and Canada need passports to enter Trinidad and Tobago.

Electricity The electricity is either 110 or 230 volts AC (60 cycles), so ask when making your hotel reservations if you'll need transformers and/or adapters.

Embassies and High Commissions In Port-of-Spain on Trinidad, the **U.S. Embassy** is at 7–9 Marli St., 15 Queen's Park West (☎ **868/622-6371**); the **Canadian High Commission** is at Maple House, 3 Sweet Briar Rd., St. Clair (☎ **868/622-6232**); and the **British High Commission** is at 19 St. Clair Ave., St. Clair (☎ **868/622-2748**).

Emergencies Call the **police** at ☎ **999.** To report a **fire** or summon an **ambulance,** dial ☎ **990.**

Information Before you go, write or call the **Trinidad & Tobago Tourism Development Authority** at 10–14 Philip St., Port-of-Spain, Trinidad, W.I. (☎ **868/623-1932**).

Language English is the official language, although you'll hear it spoken with many different accents, including British. Hindi, Chinese, French, and Spanish are also spoken.

Safety As a general rule, Tobago is safer than its larger neighbor, Trinidad. Crime does exist, but it's not of raging dimensions. If you can, avoid the downtown streets of Port-of-Spain at night, especially those around Independence Square, where muggings have been reported. Evening jaunts down Wilson Street and the Market of Scarborough are also discouraged. Visitors are open prey for pickpockets during Carnival time, so be alert during large street parties. It would also be wise to safeguard your valuables and never leave them unattended at the beach or even in a locked car.

Taxes The government imposes a 15% value-added tax (VAT) on room rates. It also imposes a departure tax of TT$75 ($12) on every passenger more than 5 years old.

Time Trinidad and Tobago time is the same as the U.S. East Coast. But when the States go on daylight saving time, Trinidad and Tobago does not; then, when it's 6am in Miami, it's 7am in T&T.

Tipping The big hotels and restaurants add a 10% to 15% service charge to your final tab.

Weather Trinidad has a tropical climate all year, with constant trade winds maintaining mean temperatures of 84°F during the day, 74° at night, with a range of

Area Code Change Notice

During the summer of 1997, the area code in Trinidad and Tobago changed from 809 to 868. This change is reflected in the phone numbers given throughout chapter 15.

70° to 90°F. The rainy season runs from May to November, but it shouldn't deter you from visiting; the rain usually lasts no more than two hours before the sun comes out again. However, carry along plenty of insect repellent if you come then.

1 Trinidad

Trinidad is completely different from the other islands of the Caribbean, and that forms part of its charm and appeal. The island itself is 50 miles long and 40 miles wide. The limbo was born here, as was calypso, and steel-drum music (in the late 1930s, African musicians began beating on pots, pans, and car parts during the Carnival). Visitors in increasing numbers are drawn to this island of many rhythms.

Trinidad is not for everyone, though. Because Port-of-Spain is one of the most bustling commercial centers in the Caribbean, more business travelers than vacationers are drawn here, but still, tourism is on the rise. The island has beaches, but most of them are far away from the capital. The city itself is hot, humid, and slightly on the dirty side (though it's being cleaned up), whereas the hilly suburbs are as charming as a southern city set in a tropical paradise. Pastel-colored homes that exhibit a Victorian architectural influence are complemented by intricately landscaped lawns boasting tropical foliage.

Although Port-of-Spain, with its shopping centers, fast-paced food joints, contemporary hotels, and energetic nightlife, draws mixed reviews from readers, the countryside is calmer. Far removed from the traffic jams of the capital, you can explore the lush fauna and flora of the island by foot, Jeep, moped, or bike.

Part of the island's appeal lies in its pleasant inhabitants, who are fervent conversationalists with inquisitive minds and plenty of opinions. There's little racial tension, if any, here. Its polyglot population includes Syrians, Chinese, Americans, Europeans, East Indians, Parsees, Madrasis, Venezuelans, and the last of the original Amerindians, the early settlers of the island. You'll also find Hindustanis, Javanese, Lebanese, African descendants, and Creole mixtures. In all, there are about 1.2 million inhabitants, whose language is English, although you may hear speech in a strange argot, Trinibagianese.

Port-of-Spain, in the northwestern corner of the island, is the capital, with the largest concentration of the population, about 120,000. With the opening of its $2 million cruise-ship complex in the port, Trinidad now has become a major port of call for Caribbean cruise lines. A shopper's haven for everything from Irish linens to Japanese cameras, the upscale stores along Frederick Street are much frequented by cruisers. And along with the more costly souvenirs, to the delight of visitors, local crafts and produce are also freely displayed throughout town.

One of the most industrialized nations in the Caribbean, and the third-largest exporter of oil in the western hemisphere, Trinidad is also blessed with the huge 114-acre Pitch Lake from which comes most of the world's asphalt. Further, it's also the home of Angostura Bitters, the recipe for which is a guarded secret.

GETTING THERE

From North America, Trinidad is one of the most distant islands in the Caribbean. Because of the legendary toughness of Trinidadian Customs, it's preferable to arrive during the day (presumably when your stamina might be at its peak) if you can schedule it.

Trinidad is the transfer point for many passengers heading on to the beaches of Tobago. For information about getting to Tobago, refer to section 2 of this chapter.

Most passengers from eastern North America fly **American Airlines** (☎ **800/433-7300**), which has connections through New York. American also offers a daily nonstop flight to Trinidad from Miami, which is especially useful for transfers from the Midwest and the West Coast.

From New York, **BWIA** (☎ **800/538-2942**) offers one to three daily flights into Port-of-Spain, depending on the day of the week and the season. Several of these are nonstop; most of them touch down en route, usually on Barbados or Antigua, before continuing without a change of planes to Trinidad, the airline's home base.

From Miami, BWIA offers a daily nonstop flight to Port-of-Spain, departing every afternoon and arriving on Trinidad in the early evening. Port-of-Spain is also serviced by as many as two additional flights per day, touching down on Barbados, Antigua, Grenada, and St. Lucia.

Air Canada (☎ **800/268-7240** in Canada, or 800/776-3000 in the U.S.) doesn't fly to Trinidad, but offers flights four or five times a week to Barbados, from which connecting flights are possible into Port-of-Spain.

GETTING AROUND

BY TAXI There are only unmetered taxis on Trinidad, and they're identified by their license plates, beginning with the letter *H.* There are also "pirate taxis" as well—private cars that cruise around and pick up passengers like a regular taxi. Maxi Taxis or vans can also be hailed on the street. A taxi ride from Piarco Airport into Port-of-Spain generally costs about $20.

To avoid the anxiety of driving, you can rent taxis and local drivers for your sightseeing jaunts. Although it costs more, it alleviates the hassles of badly marked (or unmarked roads) and contact with the sometimes-bizarre local driving patterns; if a rented taxi and driver is too expensive, you can take an organized tour. Most drivers will serve as guides. Their rates, however, are based on route distances, so get an overall quotation and agree on the actual fare before setting off. All fares are subject to 50% increases after midnight.

BY RENTAL CAR Since the island is one of the world's largest exporters of asphalt, Trinidad's some 4,500 miles of roads are well paved. However, outback roads should be avoided during the rainy season as they're often narrow, twisting, and prone to washouts. Inquire about conditions, particularly if you're headed for the north coast.

The fierce traffic jams of Port-of-Spain are legendary, and night driving anywhere on the island is rather hazardous.

If you're brave enough to set out on a venture via rental car, arm yourself with a good map and beware: The car will probably have a right-hand-mounted steering wheel, hence, **you'll drive on the left.** Visitors with a valid International Driver's License or a license from the United States, Canada, France, or the United Kingdom may drive without extra documentation for up to three months.

The major U.S.-based car-rental firms currently have no franchises on the island, so you have to make arrangements with a local firm (go over the terms and

insurance agreements carefully). Count on spending about $40 to $60 per day or more, with unlimited mileage included.

One of the island's leading local car-rental firms is **Bacchus Taxi & Car Rental Service,** 37 Tragarete Rd., Port-of-Spain (☎ **868/622-5588**), which does not take reservations. You have to inquire if cars are available upon your arrival. Others include: **Auto Rental,** Piarco Airport (☎ **868/669-2277**), and **Singh's Auto Rental,** 7–9 Wrightson Rd., Port-of-Spain (☎ **868/625-4247**).

BY BUS All the cities of Trinidad are linked by regular bus service from Port-of-Spain. Fares are low (about 50¢ for runs within the capital). However, the old buses are likely to be very overcrowded. Always try to avoid them at rush hours. And beware of pickpockets.

ESSENTIALS

Medical care is sometimes limited, and physicians and health-care facilities expect immediate cash payment for medical services. Don't expect to pay with a credit or charge card. Medical insurance from the United States is not always valid outside the country, but supplemental medical insurance with specific overseas coverage is available. Contact the U.S. Embassy for updates. The **Port-of-Spain General Hospital** is on Charlotte Street (☎ **868/623-2951**).

As for **banks,** the **Bank of Nova Scotia** has an office on Park Street at Richmond Street, Port-of-Spain (☎ **868/625-3566** or 868/625-5222). **Citibank** has offices at

12 Queen's Park East, Port-of-Spain (☎ **868/625-1046** or 868/625-1049) and at 18–30 High St., San Fernando (☎ **868/652-3691** or 868/652-3293).

The main **post office** is on Wrightson Road, Port-of-Spain, and is open Monday to Friday from 8am to 4pm. You can send a cable or fax at the offices of **Textel,** 1 Edward St., Port-of-Spain (☎ **868/625-4431**).

WHERE TO STAY

The number of hotels is limited, and don't expect your Port-of-Spain room to open directly on a white-sand beach—the nearest beach is a long, costly taxi ride away. Don't forget that a 15% government tax and a 10% service charge will be added to your hotel and restaurant bills. All hotels raise their rates during Carnival.

EXPENSIVE

✪ **Trinidad Hilton.** Lady Young Rd. (P.O. Box 442), Port-of-Spain, Trinidad, W.I. ☎ **800/HILTONS** in the U.S. and Canada, or 868/624-3211. Fax 868/624-4485. 394 rms, 25 suites. A/C TV TEL. $183–$225 double; from $300 suite. Rates include breakfast. AE, DC, MC, V.

This is the most dramatic and architecturally sophisticated hotel on Trinidad. Because of its position on some of the steepest terrain in Port-of-Spain, the building's lobby lies on its uppermost floor and the rooms are staggered in rocky but verdant terraces that sweep down the hillside. Its location just above Queen's Park Savannah provides most of its rooms with a view of the sea and mountains.

The hotel offers a wide range of accommodations that get cheaper the higher up they're situated. The more expensive rooms, on the Executive Floor, have upgraded services and amenities and complimentary continental breakfast. Regardless of their comfort levels, all units have balconies and a neutral international decor.

Dining/Entertainment: The main dining room, La Boucan (see "Where to Dine," below), contains museum-quality murals by Geoffrey Holder, one of the island's best-known artists. Less formal are the Pool Terrace and the Gazebo Bar, both of which serve Caribbean and international food and colorful drinks in sunny settings. Live music is played Saturday night in the Carnival Bar from 5pm to 1am and *The Taste of Trinidad,* a lively musical show, is offered on Monday night, along with a buffet, for $17.35.

Services: Room service (6am to 11:30pm), concierge, baby-sitting, travel agency, laundry.

Facilities: Olympic-size swimming pool, pharmacy, bank, two all-weather tennis courts (lit at night), arcade with boutiques, business center, fitness center.

MODERATE

Trinidad Holiday Inn. Wrightson Rd. At London Rd. (P.O. Box 1017), Port-of-Spain, Trinidad, W.I. ☎ **800/HOLIDAY** in the U.S. and Canada, or 868/625-3361. Fax 868/625-4166. 235 rms, 9 suites. A/C TV TEL. $110 double; from $185 suite. AE, MC, V.

Originally built during the 1960s in an international but bland modern style and proud of its role as the second-largest hotel on Trinidad, the Holiday Inn lies on the northern perimeter of the city's commercial zone, a five-minute walk from the center. It's a favorite with business travelers. The recently renovated bedrooms contain private balconies along with two double beds. The hotel has added two executive floors and such room amenities as trouser pressers, magnifying mirrors, hair dryers, mahogany furniture, and brass lamps. Rooms are tastefully decorated in Caribbean pastels.

Dining/Entertainment: The main dining room, the Olympia Restaurant, is adorned with Roman-style pillars, with plants cascading over the top. La Ronde Restaurant, with a classical French decor, is the only revolving restaurant in the

Caribbean and serves an international cuisine. A bar just above the lobby offers taped island music.

Services: Room service, laundry, baby-sitting.

Facilities: Hair salon, gift shops, full gym, exotic pool with "sunken" bar (open 24 hours), a pool for children, business center.

INEXPENSIVE

Asa Wright Nature Centre and Lodge. Spring Hill Estate, Arima, Trinidad, W.I. ☎ **800/426-7781** in the U.S., or 868/667-4655. Fax 868/667-4655. 23 rms. Winter, $105 double. Off-season, $80 double. Rates include all meals, afternoon tea, and a welcoming rum punch. No credit cards.

There really isn't anything else like it in the Caribbean. Known to bird watchers throughout the world, this center sits on 196 acres of protected land at an elevation of 1,200 feet in the rain-forested northern mountain range of Trinidad, 10 miles north of Arima, beside Blanchisseuse Road. Hummingbirds, toucans, bellbirds, manakins, several varieties of tanagers, and the rare oilbird are all on the property. Back-to-basics accommodations are available in the lodge's self-contained rooms, in guest bedrooms in the 1908 Edwardian main house, or in one of the cottages built on elevated ground above the main house; all have private baths but no air-conditioning, TV, or phones.

Guided tours are available on the nature center's grounds, which contain several well-maintained trails, including a natural pool with a waterfall in which guests can swim in lieu of a beach that involves a 90-minute drive to the coast. Summer seminars are conducted with expert instructors in natural history, ornithology, and nature photography. The minimum age is 14 years if accompanied by an adult or 17 if unaccompanied.

For more information or to make reservations, call the above toll-free number or write Caligo Ventures, 156 Bedford Rd., Armonk, NY 10504.

✪ **Chaconia Inn.** 106 Saddle Rd. (P.O. Box 3340), Maraval, Trinidad, W.I. ☎ **868/628-8603.** Fax 868/628-3214. 27 rms, 4 apts. A/C TV TEL. $65–$95 double; $110–$120 two-bedroom apt. MAP $30 per person extra. Tax 20% extra. AE, DC, MC, V.

This place offers great value for your money. Named for the country's scarlet national flower, the low-rise Chaconia is a miniature self-contained resort 3 miles north of Port-of-Spain. In the cool mountain residential valley of Maraval, it's about 10 miles from Maracas Beach. The buildings are simple, and the furnishings are in a contemporary motel idiom. You'll be housed in one of three different types of accommodations, including two-bedroom apartments, superior rooms, and standard rooms. All are equipped with private baths and TVs, and the superior rooms and apartments also have kitchenette facilities. The hotel restaurant (referred to as the Lounge) is recommended separately (see "Where to Dine," below).

Kapok Hotel and Restaurant. 16–18 Cotton Hill, St. Clair, Trinidad, W.I. ☎ **800/344-1212** or 868/622-6441. Fax 868/622-9677. 71 rms, 6 suites. A/C TV TEL. $89–$92 double; $130–$143 suite. AE, DC, MC, V.

The Kapok, a modern but unpretentious nine-floor hotel located in the residential suburb of St. Clair, is now part of the Golden Tulip Hotel chain. It has been run by the Chan family for several years and is an efficient, well-maintained operation. Located a minute's drive and just north from the city's biggest park, the Savannah, the Kapok also lies near the zoo and Presidential Palace and away from the worst traffic of the city. From its lounge, you'll have a panoramic view not only of the Savannah, but also of the Gulf of Paria. Guests who prefer small to medium-size hotels feel at home here and appreciate the slick neatness, the comfortably appointed wicker-furnished bedrooms, and the rooftop restaurant serving Chinese and Polynesian food. In the back is an expanded pool area with a waterfall, garden, menagerie, and sundeck. The well-furnished, spacious rooms have private baths.

Normandie Hotel and Restaurant. 10 Nook Ave., St. Ann's (P.O. Box 851), Port-of-Spain, Trinidad, W.I. ☎ **868/624-1181.** Fax 868/624-0108. 53 units: 12 studios, 16 superior rms (doubles), 25 standard rms (singles or doubles). A/C TV TEL. $72–$87 double; $97 loft studio for 3. Children 11 and under stay free in parents' room. AE, DC, MC, V.

Originally built in the 1930s by two French brothers on the site of an old coconut plantation, this was already a well-established hotel when its owners modernized it in 1986. It rises around a banyan- and banana-filled courtyard that surrounds a swimming pool accented with a jet of water. Inside, each room has a balcony or patio. The beds in some rooms are set onto minilofts arranged in a small-scale but serviceable duplex format. The cheaper rooms here have drawn fire from readers, especially for the noisy air-conditioning.

Calm and cosmopolitan, the hotel sits 3½ miles northwest of the city center, next to one of the best art galleries on Trinidad, a skylight-covered shopping center, an attractive restaurant (La Fantasie), the botanical gardens of Port-of-Spain, and the official residence of the prime minister of Trinidad and Tobago. In addition, brunch, lunch, or tea can be ordered in the hotel's cafe, and the Cascade Club offers entertainment on Friday and Saturday nights.

Valley Vue Hotel. Ariapita Rd., St. Ann's, Trinidad, W.I. ☎ **86824-0940.** Fax 868/627-8046. 56 rms, 12 suites. A/C MINIBAR TV TEL. $80–$100 double; $120 suite for 2. AE, DC, MC, V.

Originally built in 1986, this modern hotel is a favorite with business travelers. It's about 5 miles northwest of the center of Port-of-Spain. With a vaguely English kind of decor, it has lots of wicker furniture and touches of marble in its floors and walls. Each of the pleasant bedrooms contains two telephones, a balcony, and comfortably unpretentious furniture. Because of the view, deluxe doubles cost as much as suites. On the premises is an oval swimming pool with a "swim-through" bar and a water slide, two squash courts, gym, and an airy restaurant, the Skyview, serving American-Creole cuisine.

WHERE TO DINE

The food probably should be better than it is, considering all the different culinary backgrounds that shaped the island, including West Indian, Chinese, French, and Indian.

Stick to local specials such as stuffed crabs or chip-chip (tiny clamlike shellfish), but skip the armadillo or opossum stewpots. Spicy Indian rotis filled with vegetables or ground meat seem to be everyone's favorite lunch, and the drink of choice is a fresh rum punch flavored with the natively produced Angostura Bitters. Except for a few fancy places, dress tends to be very casual.

MODERATE

✪ **La Boucan.** In the Trinidad Hilton, Lady Young Rd. ☎ **868/624-3211.** Reservations required. Jacket required for men. Main courses TT$59–TT$125 ($21); lunch buffet TT66 ($11). AE, DC, MC, V. Mon–Sat noon–2:30pm and 7–11:30pm. INTERNATIONAL.

The finest hotel restaurant on Trinidad, with some of the most lavish buffets, this establishment satisfies the eye as well as the palate. Taking its name from the smoking process by which pirates and buccaneers used to preserve meat for long voyages, La Boucan incorporates this smoky flavor into many of its West Indian dishes.

Against one of its longest walls stretches a graceful mural by Geoffrey Holder, one of the most famous artists of the Caribbean. (Born on Trinidad, although living in New York most of his life, he painted this mural to honor the social gatherings that used to take place in Port-of-Spain's central park, the Savannah.)

Not all dishes reflect the nurturing and refinement they should, but most diners are satisfied with the results. Typical dishes include sirloin or tenderloin steaks; a daily selection of fish (usually grouper or snapper), which is grilled, poached, or panfried according to your wishes and served with herb-butter sauce; baked snapper in a crab crust; lamb curry; and Creole-style shrimp. The desserts are sumptuous. Live music from a piano (and on weekends from a dance band) provides entertainment.

La Fantasie. In the Normandie Hotel and Restaurant, 10 Nook Ave., St. Ann's Village. ☎ **868/624-1181,** ext. 2306. Reservations recommended. Main courses TT$40–TT$100 ($7–$17). AE, DC, MC, V. Daily noon–2pm and 6–10pm. FRENCH/CREOLE.

Off Queen's Park Savannah, and named after the 18th-century plantation that once stood here, La Fantasie is loaded with style and features a tempting modern Creole cuisine. Many of the dishes are given a light touch as opposed to the usually heavy, deep-fried food, a sort of *cuisine nouvelle Creole*. That alone would make it a winning choice. Since fresh ingredients are used and deftly handled, no false notes jar the senses. However, you're not exactly pampered here, and service has drawn complaints from readers.

The changing menu might include filet mignon with a tamarind-flavored sauce, chicken curry, locally caught Trinidadian salmon in a wine-based sauce with sultana raisins and bananas, and shrimp with Creole sauce in a pastry shell flavored with cheese. "Fish walk up the hill" is grilled fish with chopped herbs. Meals might follow with a Trinidadian fruitcake with a rum-flavored custard.

The Lounge. In the Chaconia Inn, 106 Saddle Rd., Maraval. ☎ **868/628-8603.** Reservations recommended. Main courses TT$30–TT$160 ($5–$27). AE, DC, MC, V. Daily 7am–10pm. INTERNATIONAL.

On the street level of a previously recommended hotel, this conservatively decorated, modern dining room offers international cuisine to a busy crowd of lunch and dinner clients, most of whom appreciate its straightforward cuisine. It may not be innovative, but everything is market fresh. Menu items include several different preparations of fish, steak, shrimp, pork, and pasta dishes, as well as salads and a small choice of vegetarian dishes. On Saturday night the facilities are supplemented by those of the Roof Garden Restaurant, on the hotel's uppermost floor, where barbecued meals are featured once a week.

Rafters. 6A Warner St., Newtown. ☎ **868/628-9258.** Reservations recommended. Main courses TT$35–TT$125 ($6–$21); buffets from TT$95 ($16). AE, DC, MC, V. Mon–Thurs 11:30am–midnight, Fri 11am–3am, Sat 7pm–2am. SEAFOOD.

Rafters is a good-value dining choice housed in a century-old grocery shop in the central business district of a suburb of Port-of-Spain, a short walk off the Savannah. Wednesday to Saturday there are buffets, and you can also order from an à la carte menu devoted mainly to local seafood items. The food is more plentiful than refined, but a very good value. Buffets begin at 7pm. On Wednesday through Saturday there are carvery buffets. On the regular menu, house specialties include seafood Creole. You can also order U.S. choice beef steaks. In the lounge, a snack-and-sandwich menu is offered daily in a relaxed atmosphere, attracting folks of all ages and occupations.

✪ **Solimar.** 6 Nook Ave. (opposite the Normandie Hotel and Restaurant, 3 1/2 miles northwest of the city center), St. Ann's. ☎ **868/624-6267.** Reservations recommended. Main courses

TT$52–TT$175 ($9–$29). AE, MC, V. Mar–Nov, Tues–Sat 6:30–10:30pm, Dec–Feb, Mon–Sat 6:30–10:30pm. Tentative closings occur 1 week in mid-May and 2 weeks in mid-Aug (exact dates vary). INTERNATIONAL.

By some estimates, this restaurant offers the most creative cuisine and most original format in Trinidad and Tobago. Established by an English-born chef (Joe Brown) who worked for many years in the kitchens of Hilton hotels around the world, it occupies a garden-style building whose open walls are cooled by ceiling fans. As you dine, you'll hear the sound of an artificial waterfall that cascades into a series of fish ponds.

The menu, which changes every six weeks, presents local ingredients inspired by the cuisines of the world. The chefs know some parts of the world better than others, but the results are usually very convincing, with tasty results. Dishes might include an English-inspired combination of grilled breast of chicken and jumbo shrimp dressed with a lobster sauce, and a Sri Lankan dish of herb-flavored chicken vindaloo. The restaurant's double-chocolate mousse is the highlight of any meal here.

Tiki Village. In the Kapok Hotel, 16–18 Cotton Hill, St. Clair. ☎ **868/622-6441.** Reservations recommended, especially for dinner. Main courses $6.50–$15; buffets $6.75–$8.50. AE, DC, MC, V. Daily 11:30am–7pm with dinner seatings at 7:30 and 9pm. POLYNESIAN/CHINESE.

The Tiki Village, with a South Seas theme, perches on the top floor of a previously recommended hotel and has a panoramic view of the nearby Queen's Park Savannah. Decorated in a medley of sunset colors, the restaurant prides itself on an assortment of hors d'oeuvres (which arrives flaming at your table) known as a Polynesian delight. Consider it the Trader Vic's of Trinidad. Though we've rarely had anything here we'd call superb, the egg roll is among the best we've ever ordered in the West Indies. Among the main courses, we'd recommend the Hawaiian luau fish: a whole fish coated with water-chestnut flour and fried crisply before it's engulfed in a sweet-and-pungent sauce. Chicken provincial is boneless cubes sautéed in a black-bean sauce. Desserts include a Polynesian cheesecake, followed by Chinese tea. Especially charming is the assortment of dim sum on Saturday and Sunday.

INEXPENSIVE

Monsoon. 72 Tragarete Rd., Port-of-Spain. ☎ **868/628-7684.** Reservations recommended. Main courses TT$14–TT$42 ($2–$7). AE, MC, V. Mon–Sat 11am–10pm. INDIAN.

At this restaurant where East and West Indian cuisines combine, the walls are adorned with framed hand-painted fabrics from India and Trinidad. The house specialty is curry, including chicken, lamb, vegetables, duck, pork, fish, shrimp, and conch. These curries are served with a chickpea mixture, chutney, and potatoes. Other items are *dhalpuri,* a flat bread (spread with ground peas) that's wrapped around meats and vegetables, and *paratha,* a flaky bread cooked on an open grill and served as a staple (much like potatoes or rice) with meats and vegetables. For the best bargain, visit Wednesday evening when an authentic Indian buffet is showcased for TT$65 ($11), including breads, appetizers, soups, rice, vegetables, coffee, desserts, and meat or seafood entrees.

Restaurant Singho. Long Circular Mall, Level 3, Port-of-Spain. ☎ **868/628-2077.** Main courses TT$18–TT$60 ($3–$9.95). AE, MC, V. Daily 11am–11pm. CHINESE.

This restaurant contains an almost mystically illuminated bar and aquarium. The restaurant is on the second floor of one of the capital's largest shopping malls, midway between the commercial center of Port-of-Spain and the Queen's Park Savannah. It's better than your typical chop suey and chow mein joint, and many of its dishes are quite tasty and spicy. For Trinidad, this cuisine of the Orient isn't bad. À la carte dishes include shrimp with oyster sauce, shark-fin soup, stewed or curried beef, almond pork, and spareribs with black-bean sauce. The take-away service is one of the best known in town.

✪ **Veni Mangé.** 67A Ariapata Ave. ☎ **868/624-4597.** Reservations recommended. Main courses $5–$10. AE, MC, V. Daily 7–10am and 11:30am–3pm. Wed 7:30–10pm. Fri open for bar service only, 3pm–midnight. CREOLE.

Originally built in the 1930s and set about a mile west of Port-of-Spain's center, Veni Mangé (whose name translates as "come and eat") is painted in coral tones and has louvered windows on hinges that ventilate the masses of potted plants. It was established by two of the best-known women in Trinidad, Allyson Hennessy and her sister, Rosemary Hezekiah. Allyson, the Julia Child of Trinidad, hosts a daily television talk show that's broadcast throughout Trinidad. Best described as a new generation of Creole women, both Allyson and Rosemary (whose parents were English/Venezuelan and African-Caribbean/Chinese) entertain with their humor and charm.

Start with the bartender's special, a coral-colored fruit punch, which is a rich, luscious mixture of papaya, guava, orange, and passion fruit juices. On some days they do an authentic callaloo soup, which, according to Trinidadian legend, can make a man propose marriage. Save room for one of the main courses, such as curried crab or West Indian hotpot (a variety of meat cooked Creole style), perhaps a vegetable lentil loaf. The helpings are large, and if you still have room, order their pineapple upside-down cake, unless you prefer a homemade version of soursop ice cream or a coconut mousse.

Dinner is served only on Wednesday nights and is something of a social event among regulars. On Friday, the bar buzzes, but no formal food is served; only snacks and finger foods, "cutters," are served.

BEACHES & OTHER OUTDOOR PURSUITS

For golf and tennis holidays, we recommend that you try another island.

BEACHES Trinidad isn't thought of as beach country, yet it has more beach frontage than any other island in the West Indies. The only problem is that most of its beaches are undeveloped and found in distant, remote places, far removed from Port-of-Spain. The closest of the better beaches, **Maracas** (on the North Coast Road), is a full 18 miles from Port-of-Spain. Tobago (see below) has lovely, inviting, and more accessible beaches.

GOLF The oldest golf club on the island, **St. Andrew's Golf Course,** Moka Estate (☎ **868/629-2314**), is in Maraval, about 2 miles from Port-of-Spain. This 18-hole course has been internationally acclaimed ever since it hosted the 1976 Hoerman Cup Golf Tournament. There's a full-service clubhouse on the premises. Greens fees are $30. Open Monday to Friday from 7am to 7:30pm and on Saturday and Sunday from 6:30am to 8:30pm.

TENNIS The **Trinidad Hilton,** Lady Young Road (☎ **868/624-3211**), has the best courts on the island. These are two chevron courts lit for night pay. At the **Trinidad Country Club,** Champs-Elysees, Maraval (☎ **868/622-3470**), six courts are available, and they're lit at night. You have to become a member to play, but a cost of temporary membership is only TT$69 ($11). There are public courts in Port-of-Spain on the grounds of the Prince's Building (ask at your hotel for directions to these).

EXPLORING THE ISLAND

ORGANIZED TOURS Sightseeing tours are offered by **The Travel Centre,** Uptown Mall, Edward Street, Port-of-Spain (☎ **868/623-5096**), in late-model sedans, with a trained driver-guide. Prices are quoted on a seat-in-car basis. Private arrangements will cost more.

A daily city tour, lasting two hours and costing $22 per person for two, but $16 per person for three or more, will take you past (but not inside) the main points of interest of Port-of-Spain: Whitehall, the President's House, Queen's Park Savannah, the Botanical Gardens, the National Museum and Art Gallery, the Emperor Valley Zoo, cathedrals, a mosque, temples, and through the commercial and residential centers, then to Lady Young Lookout for a view of the city.

You'll see tropical splendor at its best on a Port-of-Spain/Maracas Bay/Saddle Road jaunt leaving at 1pm daily, lasting 3¹/₂ hours. The tour begins with a drive around Port-of-Spain, passing the main points of interest listed above and then going on through the mountain scenery over the "Saddle" of the northern range to Maracas Bay, a popular beach. You return via Saddle Road, Santa Cruz Valley, the village of San Juan, and the Lady Young Road for the view of Port-of-Spain.

An Island Circle Tour is a 9- to 10-hour journey that includes a lunch stop (the tour price doesn't include lunch) and a welcome drink. Leaving at 9am daily, your car goes south along the west coast with a view of the Gulf of Paria, across the central plains, through Pointe-à-Pierre and San Fernando, and on eastward into rolling country overlooking sugarcane fields. Then you go down into the coconut plantations along the 14-mile-long Mayaro Beach for a swim and lunch before returning along Manzanilla Beach and back to the city. The cost is $75 per person for two or $55 per person for three or more.

An especially interesting trip is to the Caroni Swamp and Bird Sanctuary, a four-hour trek by car and flat-bottomed boat into the sanctuary where you'll see rich Trinidad bird life. The tour guides recommend long pants and long-sleeved, casual attire along with lots of insect repellent. The cost is $45 per person for two or $30 per person for three or more.

PORT-OF-SPAIN One of the busiest harbors in the Caribbean, Trinidad's capital, Port-of-Spain, can be explored on foot. Start out at ✪ **Queen's Park Savannah,** on the northern edge of the city. Called "The Savannah," it consists of 199 acres, complete with soccer, cricket, and rugby fields, and vendors hawking coconut water. What is now the park was once a sugar plantation until it was swept by a fire in 1808 that destroyed hundreds of homes.

Among the Savannah's outstanding buildings is the pink-and-blue ✪ **Queen's Royal College,** containing a clock tower with Westminster chimes. Today a school for boys, it stands on Maraval Road at the corner of St. Clair Avenue. On the same road, the family home of the Roodal clan is affectionately called **"the gingerbread house"** by Trinidadians. It was built in the baroque style of the French Second Empire.

In contrast, the family residence of the Strollmeyers was built in 1905 and is a copy of a German Rhenish castle. Nearby stands **Whitehall,** which was once a private mansion but today has been turned into the office of the prime minister of Trinidad and Tobago. In the Moorish style, it was erected in 1905 and served as the U.S. Army headquarters in World War II. These houses, including Hayes Court, the residence of the Anglican bishop of Trinidad, and others form what is known as **"the magnificent seven"** big mansions standing in a row.

On the south side of the Memorial Park, a short distance from the Savannah and within walking distance of the major hotels, stands the **National Museum and Art Gallery,** 117 Frederick St. (☎ **868/623-5941**), open Tuesday to Saturday from 10am to 6pm. The museum contains a representative exhibition of Trinidad artists, including an entire gallery devoted to Jean Michel Cazabon (1813–88), permanent collections of artifacts giving a general overview of the island's history and culture, Amerindian archaeology, British historical documents, and a small natural-history exhibition including geology, corals, and insect collections. There's also a large display filled with costumes dedicated to the colorful culture of Carnival.

At the southern end of Frederick Street, the main artery of Port-of-Spain's shopping district, stands **Woodford Square.** The gaudy **Red House,** a large neo-Renaissance structure built in 1906, is the seat of the government of Trinidad and Tobago. Nearby stands **Holy Trinity Cathedral,** whose gothic look may remind you of the churches of England. Inside, search out the marble monument to Sir Ralph Woodford made by the sculptor of Chantry.

Another of the town's important landmarks is **Independence Square,** dating from Spanish days. Now mainly a parking lot, it stretches across the southern part of the capital from the **Cathedral of the Immaculate Conception** to Wrightson Road. The Roman Catholic church was built in 1815 in the neo-Gothic style and consecrated in 1832.

The cathedral has an outlet that leads to the **Central Market,** on Beetham Highway on the outskirts of Port-of-Spain. Here you can see all the spices and fruits for which Trinidad is known. It's one of the island's most colorful sights, made all the more so by the wide diversity of people who sell their wares here.

At the north of the Savannah, the **Royal Botanical Gardens** (**☎ 868/622-4221**) cover 70 acres and are open daily from 6am to 6pm. Once part of a sugar plantation, the park is filled with flowering plants, shrubs, and rare and beautiful trees, including an orchid house. Seek out also the raw beef tree: An incision made in its bark is said to resemble rare bleeding roast beef. Licensed guides will take you through and explain the luxuriant foliage to you. In the gardens is the **President's House,** official residence of the president of Trinidad and Tobago. Victorian in style, it was built in 1875.

Part of the gardens is the **Emperor Valley Zoo** (**☎ 868/622-3530**), in St. Clair, which shows a good selection of the fauna of Trinidad as well as some of the usual exotic animals from around the world. The star attractions are a family of mandrills, a reptile house, and open bird parks. You can take shady jungle walks through tropical vegetation. Adults pay TT$4 ($1), children 3 to 12 are charged TT$2 (50¢), and children under 3 are admitted free. It's open daily from 9:30am to 6pm.

AROUND THE ISLAND For one of the most popular attractions in the area, the **Asa Wright Nature Centre,** see "Where to Stay," above.

On a peak 1,100 feet above Port-of-Spain, **Fort George** was built by Governor Sir Thomas Hislop in 1804 as a signal station in the days of the sailing ships. Once it could be reached only by hikers, but today it's accessible by an asphalt road. From its citadel, you can see the mountains of Venezuela. Locals refer to the climb up the winding road as "traveling up to heaven," since nature's bounty is at its greatest along this route. The drive is only 10 miles, but to play it safe, allow about two hours.

Enhanced by the blue and purple hues of the sky at sunset, clouds of scarlet ibis, the national bird of Trinidad and Tobago, fly in from their feeding grounds to roost at the ✪ **Caroni Bird Sanctuary** (**☎ 868/645-1305**). The 40-square-mile sanctuary is a big mangrove swamp interlaced with waterways and framed by mangrove trees. The setting couldn't be more idyllic, with blue, mauve, and white lilies, oysters growing on mangrove roots, and caimans resting on mudbanks. The sanctuary lies abut a half-hour drive (7 miles) south of Port-of-Spain.

Visitors are taken on a launch through these swamps to see the birds (bring along some insect repellent). For your exploration of this wonderland, the most reliable tour operator is **James Meddoo,** Bamboo Grove Settlement, 1 Butler Highway

(☎ **868/662-7356**). Meddoo has toured the swamps for some 25 years. His tour leaves daily at 4pm, lasting 2½ hours and costing $10 per person.

The ✪ **Pitch Lake** lies on the west coast of Trinidad with the village of Le Brea on its north shore. To reach the Pitch Lake from Port-of-Spain, take the Solomon Hocoy Highway. It's about a two-hour drive, depending on traffic (which can be heavy around Port-of-Spain). At Le Brea, you'll find some bars and restaurants.

One of the wonders of the world, with a surface like elephant skin, the lake is 300 feet deep at its center. It's possible to walk on its rough side, but we don't recommend that you proceed far. Legend has it that the lake devoured a tribe of Chayma Amerindians, punishing them for eating hummingbirds in which the souls of their ancestors reposed. The bitumen mined here has been used for paving highways throughout the world. This lake was formed millions of years ago, and it's believed that at one time it was a huge mud volcano into which muddy asphaltic oil seeped. Churned up and down by underground gases, the oil and mud eventually formed asphalt. According to legend, Sir Walter Raleigh discovered the lake in 1595 and used the asphalt to caulk his ships. Some say that no matter how much is dug out, the lake is fully replenished in a day, but actually the level of the lake drops at the rate of about 6 inches a year. A tour of 120 miles around the lake lasts five hours.

The ✪ **Saddle** is a humped pass on a ridge dividing the Maraval Valley and the Santa Cruz Valley. Along this circular run you'll see the luxuriant growth of the island, as reflected by grapefruit, papaya, cassava, and cocoa. Leaving Port-of-Spain by Saddle Road, going past the Trinidad Country Club, you pass through Maraval Village with its St. Andrew's Golf Course. The road rises to cross the ridge at the spot from which the Saddle gets its name. After going over the hump, you descend through Santa Cruz Valley, rich with giant bamboo, into San Juan and back to the capital along Eastern Main Road or via Beetham Highway. You'll see panoramic views in every direction. This tour takes about two hours and covers 18 miles.

Nearly all cruise-ship passengers are hauled along Trinidad's "Skyline Highway," the **North Coast Road.** Starting at the Saddle, it winds for 7 miles across the Northern Range and down to Maracas Bay. At one point, 100 feet above the Caribbean, you'll see on a clear day as far away as Venezuela in the west or Tobago in the east, a sweep of some 100 miles.

Most visitors take this route to ✪ **Maracas Beach,** the most splendid on Trinidad. Enclosed by mountains, it has the expected charm of a Caribbean fantasy: white sands, swaying coconut palms, and crystal-clear water.

SHOPPING

One of the large bazaars of the Caribbean, Port-of-Spain has luxury items from all over the globe, including Irish linens, English china, Scandinavian crystal, French perfumes, Swiss watches, and Japanese cameras. Even more interesting are the Asian bazaars, where you can pick up items in brass. Reflecting the island's culture are calypso shirts (or dresses), sisal goods, woodwork, cascadura bracelets, silver jewelry in local motifs, and saris. For souvenir items, visitors often like to bring back figurines of limbo dancers, carnival masqueraders, or calypso singers.

Art Creators and Suppliers. Apt. 402, Aldegonda Park, 7 St. Ann's Rd., St. Ann's. ☎ **868/624-4369.**

It's in a banal apartment complex, but the paintings and sculptures sold inside are among the finest in the Caribbean. Karen De Lima Rosa Foster and Stella Beaubrun, the creative forces behind the gallery, are recognized for their knowledge of Trinidadian art. The works sold here are fairly priced samples of the best on Trinidad.

Among the artistic giants are Glasgow, Robert Mackie, Boscoe Holder, Sundiata, Keith Ward, Jackie Hinkson, and many others.

Gallery 1-2-3-4. 10 Nook Ave., St. Anne's Village. ☎ **868/625-5502.**

More iconoclastic and less conservative than any other gallery on the island, this art center displays its paintings in a space of minimalist walls and careful lighting. The gallery opened in 1985 and since then has attracted the attention of the art world because of its wide selection of Caribbean artists.

The Market. 10 Nook Ave., St. Ann's. ☎ **868/624-1181.**

One of the most fashionable shopping complexes on Trinidad contains some 20 boutiques that represent some of the best jewelers, designers, and art dealers on the island. At this complex, you'll find a wide assortment of merchandise to buy, including clothing, cosmetics, bags, shoes, china, decorative tableware, handcrafts, and designer jewelry and accessories. The complex forms an interconnected bridge among three previously recommended establishments: the Normandie Hotel and Restaurant, the restaurant La Fantasie, and a top-notch art emporium, Gallery 1-2-3-4.

Stecher's. 27 Frederick St. ☎ **868/623-5912.**

For those luxury items we mentioned above, visit Stecher's, which sells crystal, watches, jewelry, perfumes, Georg Jensen silver, Lladró, Wedgwood, Royal Doulton, Royal Albert, Aynsley, Hutschenreuther china, and other in-bond items that can be delivered to Piarco International Airport upon your departure. If you don't want to go downtown, you'll find branches at Long Circular Mall and West Mall, in residential areas of Port-of-Spain. You can also pay a last-minute call at their three tax-free airport branches—one outlet for famous perfumes, another for sunglasses, Cartier watches, lighters and pens, leather goods, Swarovski crystal, and local ceramics. A third branch sells tobacco and liquor. There's also a branch at the Cruise Ship Complex at the Port-of-Spain docks.

Y. De Lima. 83 Queen St. And 23 Frederick St. ☎ **868/623-1364.**

This is another good store for duty-free cameras and watches, but its main focus is local jewelry. Its third-floor workroom will make whatever you want in jewelry or bronze work. You may emerge with anything from steel-drum earrings to a hibiscus-blossom broach.

TRINIDAD AFTER DARK

Chaconia Inn. 106 Saddle Rd., Maraval. ☎ **868/628-8603.** No cover.

This place becomes a hot spot on Saturday night when a DJ enlivens the atmosphere. Open 24 hours, seven days a week.

Mascamp Pub. French St. at Ariapata Ave., on the western outskirts of Port-of-Spain. ☎ **868/623-3745.** Cover $2–$5.

This is the only venue on Trinidad where calypso music from the island's greatest bands is presented continually throughout the year. Many similar places offer this music only during Carnival. Set on the western outskirts of Port-of-Spain, it promotes a rootsy, sometimes raucous, and generally high-energy format that's recommended only to adventurous readers who happen to love live musical performances with an ethnic slant.

Although simple lunches are served here every weekday from 11am to around 3pm, for a cost of about $7, the place is far more recommendable (and exciting) as a nightspot. Live music begins every night at 9pm and continues until as late as 4am, but calypso and its modern variations are the almost exclusive format every Friday, Saturday, and Sunday.

Trinidad Hilton. Lady Young Rd., Port-of-Spain. ☎ **868/624-3211.** Cover (including a buffet dinner with grills) TT$105 ($17).

The Hilton stages a Poolside Fiesta show, which happens every Monday night, with a folkloric performance beginning at 9pm and continuing live until 11pm. It features lots of live music, calypso, a steel band, and limbo. It's the most spectacular on Trinidad.

2 Tobago

Dubbed "the land of the hummingbird," Tobago lies 20 miles northeast of Trinidad, to which it's connected by frequent flights. It has long been known as a honeymooner's paradise. The physical beauty of Tobago is stunning, with its forests of breadfruit, mango, cocoa, and citrus, through which a chartreuse-colored iguana will suddenly dart.

Unlike bustling Trinidad, Tobago is sleepy, and Trinidadians come here, especially on weekends, to enjoy its wide sandy beaches. The legendary home of Daniel Defoe's Robinson Crusoe, Tobago is only 27 miles long and 7½ miles wide. The people are hospitable, and their villages are so tiny they seem to blend with the landscape.

Tobago's idyllic natural beauty makes it one of the greatest escapes in the Caribbean. It's for those who like a generous dose of sand, sun, and solitude in a mellow atmosphere.

Fish-shaped Tobago was probably sighted by Columbus in 1498 when he charted Trinidad, but the island was so tiny he paid no attention to it in his log. For the next 100 years it lay almost unexplored. In 1628 when Charles I of England gave it to one of his nobles, the earl of Pembroke, the maritime countries of Europe suddenly showed a belated interest. From then on, Tobago was fought over no fewer than 31 times by the Spanish, French, Dutch, and English, as well as marauding pirates and privateers.

After 1803 the island settled down to enjoy a sugar monopoly unbroken for decades. Great Houses were built, and in London it used to be said of a wealthy man that he was "as rich as a Tobago planter." The island's economy collapsed in 1884, and Tobago entered an acute depression. The ruling monopoly, Gillespie Brothers, declared itself bankrupt and went out of business. The British government made Tobago a ward of Trinidad in 1889, and sugar was never revived.

The island's villagelike capital lies on the southern coast and provides a scenic setting with its bay surrounded by a mountainside. **Scarborough,** which is also the main port, is a rather plain town, however. The local market, the Gun Bridge, the Powder Magazine, and Fort King George will provide a good day's worth of entertainment. Most of the shops are clustered in streets around the market.

GETTING THERE

BY PLANE A recently established Trinidad-based airline, **Air Caribbean** (☎ **868/623-2500**), maintains popular shuttle flights between Trinidad and Tobago, departing from Port-of-Spain every two hours daily between 6am and 8pm. The final return to Trinidad departs from Tobago daily at 9pm. A round-trip ticket costs $50. Because the beaches of Tobago are a favorite of vacationing Trinidadians, shuttle flights on any airline between the two islands are almost always crowded, and on

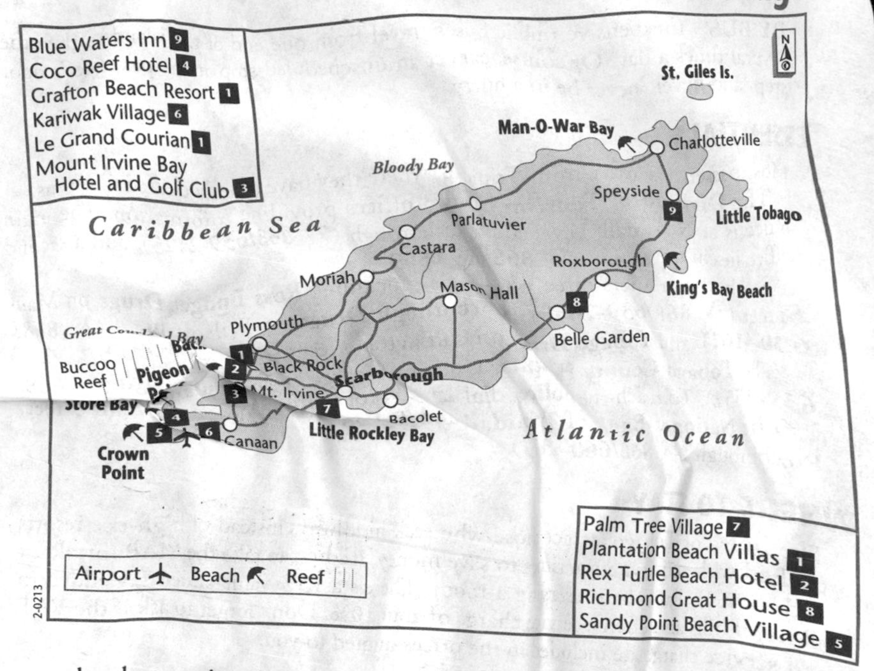

weekends, sometimes impossibly overbooked. Air Caribbean, however, operates extra flights on Friday, Sunday, and public holidays to meet traffic demands.

LIAT (☎ **868/462-0701**) maintains one daily flight from Trinidad to Tobago, but you can only fly to Tobago on LIAT if you flew into Trinidad on this airline from some other island. If you'd like to skip Trinidad completely, you can book a LIAT flight with direct service to Tobago from either Barbados or Grenada.

Tobago's small airport lies at Crown Point, near the island's southwestern tip.

BY BOAT It's possible to travel between Trinidad and Tobago by ferry service managed and operated by the **Port Authority of Trinidad and Tobago** (☎ **868/625-3055** in Port-of-Spain or 868/639-2181 in Scarborough, Tobago). Call for departure times and more details. Ferries leave once a day (trip time is five hours). The round-trip fare is TT$60 ($10) in tourist class and TT$50 ($8) in economy class. Cabins are also available for TT$160 ($27).

GETTING AROUND

BY TAXI From the airport to your hotel, take an unmetered taxi, which will cost $8 to $32, depending on the location of your hotel. You can also arrange (or have your hotel do it for you) a sightseeing tour by taxi. Rates must be negotiated on an individual basis.

BY RENTAL CAR Contact **Tobago Travel,** Store Bay Road, Milford (☎ **868/639-8778**), where the average cost of a vehicle begins at $52 per day, with unlimited mileage, collision damage coverage, value-added tax, and comprehensive insurance, plus delivery if you're housed in a hotel near the airport. An international driver's license or your valid license from home entitles you to drive on the roads of Tobago. **Don't forget to drive on the left.**

BY BUS Inexpensive public buses travel from one end of the island to the other several times a day. Of course, expect an unscheduled stop at any passenger's doorstep, and never, never be in a hurry.

ESSENTIALS

Most passengers arrive from Trinidad, where they have already cleared Customs.

The **Division of Tourism** has two offices providing information. The main office is at NIB Mall, Level 3, in Scarborough (☎ **868/639-2125**), and a second office lies in the airport (☎ **868/639-0509**).

Scarborough offers three **pharmacies,** including **Ross Budget Drugs** on Main Street (☎ **868/639-2658**), **Scarborough Drugs** on Wilson Road (☎ **868/639-4161**), and **Tobago Drugs** on Carrington Street (☎ **868/639-3930**).

The **Tobago County Hospital** is on Fort George Street, Scarborough (☎ **868/639-2551**). To reach the **police,** dial ☎ **999;** for a **fire** [illegible] **ambulance,** [illegible]

The **National Bank of Trinidad and Tobago** has an office on Main Street, Roxborough (☎ **868/660-4311**).

WHERE TO STAY

The hotels of Tobago attract those who seek hideaways instead of high-rise resorts packed with activity. Sometimes to save money, it's best to take the MAP (breakfast and dinner) plan when reserving a room. There's a 15% value-added tax added to all hotel bills and often a service charge of abut 10%. Don't forget to ask if the VAT and service charge are included in the prices quoted to you.

VERY EXPENSIVE

✪ **Le Grand Courlan.** Black Rock (P.O. Box 25, Scarborough), Tobago, W.I. ☎ **800/468-3750** in the U.S., 800/424-5500 in Canada , or 868/639-9667. Fax 868/639-9292. 60 rms, 10 suites. A/C MINIBAR TV TEL. Winter, $250–$295 double; $425–$475 suite. Off-season, $200–$225 double; $375 suite. Extra person $50. MAP $57 per person extra. Children 4 and under stay and dine free. AE, DC, MC, V.

Operated by the same owners as the Grafton Beach Resort, this pricey hotel is definitely five star and definitely deluxe, something Tobago has rarely seen. It opened in the autumn of 1995 and was named for the bay on which it sits on the western edge of the island, 5 miles from Crown International Airport. Constructed of stone and teak harvested from farms on Trinidad, the hotel is furnished with handcrafted mahogany pieces and decorated with original artwork. It was constructed to fit in with its natural surroundings and enjoys the privilege of a soft sandy beach at its doorstep, everything set against a backdrop of bougainvillea, white frangipani, and hibiscus.

The floors are covered with Italian porcelain tile, and the ceilings are made from Guyana hardwood. The bedrooms are handsomely tropical and spacious and have two phones, room service, bathrobes, a king-size bed, and large balconies.

Dining/Entertainment: The hotel offers a Mediterranean-style bistro, plus an international à la carte restaurant. The food is among the best on the island—in fact, among the best in the Caribbean. There's also nightly entertainment. The hotel also operates a health-food bar.

Services: Laundry, room service.

Facilities: The spa specializes in cell therapy, first made famous by movie stars on a pilgrimage to Switzerland. It has a koi pond and aerobics and offers consultations in nutrition, fitness coaching, and ozone-and-steam detoxing, even fresh fruit facials and full-body compression "release" massages. There's also a floodlit tennis court, plus an 80-foot swimming pool and beach cabanas. Water sports can be arranged at the diving center.

EXPENSIVE

✪ **Coco Reef Hotel.** Coconut Beach (P.O. Box 434), Tobago, W.I. ☎ **800/221-1294** or 868/639-8571. Fax 868/639-8574. 129 rms, 10 suites, 6 villas. A/C MINIBAR TV TEL. Winter, $198–$220 double; from $350 suite or villa. Off-season, $198–$220 double; from $319 suite or villa. AE, DC, DISC, MC, V.

Set on the eastern shore of Tobago, close to the airport, this hotel represents the radical 1995 renovation and upgrading of a dilapidated property, the Crown Reef. With a certain South Florida pizzazz, it's the largest hotel on the island, boasting lots of facilities and surrounded by 10 acres of grassy, sloping terrain. Its concrete walls (painted to mimic the peachy-pink color of local papaw fruits) and red roofs were inspired by the eclectic architecture of nearby Trinidad. Most accommodations are in the two- and three-story main core, although about a half-dozen cottages (management calls them villas) are scattered over the surrounding terrain. The designer incorporated a number of environmentally friendly features, including the use of recycled materials. The bedrooms are spacious and airy, filled with wicker furniture imported from the Dominican Republic, big baths with white tiles, and balcony trim as intricate as Belgian lace. The complex stands near a trio of the island's best beaches, including Store Bay, Pigeon Point, and Coconut Beach itself, the latter just steps from your room or suite.

Dining/Entertainment: Tamara's Restaurant, the resort's most formal, is open for breakfast, lunch, and dinner. Bachanals is simpler, suitable for sun-flooded lunches and light dinners. Lobster's Cocktail Bar serves drinks and snacks.

Services: Spa services include aerobics, massage, weight-loss regimes, and exercise areas.

Facilities: Sailing, waterskiing, snorkeling, scuba diving, and windsurfing, plus deep-sea fishing, horseback riding, and tennis.

Grafton Beach Resort. Black Rock (P.O. Box 25, Scarborough), Tobago, W.I. ☎ **800/223-6510** in the U.S., 800/424-5500 in Canada, or 868/639-0191. Fax 868/639-0030. 112 rms, 2 suites. A/C MINIBAR TV TEL. Winter, $252 double; from $450 suite. Off-season, $162 double; from $300 suite. Rates include buffet breakfast. 10% service and 10% tax extra. AE, DC, MC, V.

The most action-oriented resort on the island, this luxurious complex of low-rise stone-and-stucco buildings lies on 5 acres. It's 4 miles south of Scarborough, between a hill and the pale-dotted stretch of a white-sand beach, 4 miles from the airport, on Grafton Road. The clientele is mainly from Europe. Each well-furnished accommodation contains a ceiling fan and a sliding glass door opening onto a balcony. In addition to such amenities as a hair dryer, rooms often contain teak furnishings and terra-cotta tiles along with marble baths.

Dining/Entertainment: The resort's swimming pool, traversed by an ornamental bridge, is ringed with cafe/restaurant tables, and there are several different bars including a swim-up bar. Both a regional and an international cuisine are served in the Ocean View and Neptunes restaurants. Limbo dancing and calypso, or some other form of entertainment, are featured nightly.

Services: 18-hour room service, laundry, baby-sitting, massages.

Facilities: Two squash courts, gym, dive shop, outdoor swimming pool; access to a nearby golf course.

Mount Irvine Bay Hotel and Golf Club. Mount Irvine (P.O. Box 222, Scarborough), Tobago, W.I. ☎ **800/74-CHARMS** in the U.S., or 868/639-8871. Fax 868/639-8800. 107 rms, 51 cottages, 5 suites. A/C TV TEL. Winter, $235 double; $390 cottage; $720 one-bedroom suite; $1,000 two-bedroom suite. Off-season, $165 double; $320 cottage; $510 one-bedroom suite; $720 two-bedroom suite. AE, DC, MC, V.

Originally established in 1972 on the grounds of an 18th-century sugar plantation, this 16-acre resort is part of a recreational complex that totals more than 150 acres. It's about a 5-mile drive northwest of the airport. Most of the acreage is devoted to the Mount Irvine Golf Course, one of the finest in the Caribbean. The remainder is filled with sprawling lawns and tropical gardens, in the center of which rise the ruins of a stone sugar mill and a luxurious oval swimming pool. The grounds slope down to a good sandy beach. On the hill leading to the beach are the newer and better-maintained cottage suites covered with heliconia. Most accommodations are in the main building, a two-story hacienda-inspired wing of rather large but rather standard guest rooms, each of which opens toward a view of green lawns and flowering shrubbery.

Dining/Entertainment: The hotel features three restaurants, including the Sugar Mill (see below). The hotel also offers dining at Le Beau Rivage at the golf course, and at the Jacaranda, which has a high standard of international cuisine. There's dancing about every evening, and calypso singers are often brought in to entertain guests.

Services: Room service (7am to 10pm), baby-sitting, laundry, massage.

Facilities: Tennis courts, swimming pool with swim-up bar, beauty salon, barbershop, boat rentals, Windsurfers and snorkeling equipment available at the beach. Guests become temporary members of the golf club (see "Enjoying Tobago's Magnificent Beaches & Outdoor Pursuits," below), and their greens fees are discounted by 30%.

Plantation Beach Villas. Stonehaven Bay, Black Rock (P.O. Box 435, Scarborough), Tobago, W.I. ☎ **868/639-0455** or 868/639-9377. Fax 868/639-7297. 6 villas. A/C TEL. Winter, $450 villa for 2 to 4; $510 villa for 5 or 6. Off-season, $297 villa for 2 to 4; $370 villa for 5 or 6. AE, DC, MC, V.

This is a pink-sided compound of two-story villas set near the island's southwestern tip, on a forested hillside adjacent to Tobago's nature reserve. Its verdant setting and cool, white-painted verandas evoke the age of British colonization. Each villa contains three bedrooms (each with its own balcony), a fully equipped kitchen (including microwave, dishwasher, and coffeemaker), white-tiled floors, a 40-foot teak-floored veranda, and a somewhat more narrow veranda servicing the bedrooms of the second floor. Furnishings include four-poster beds and solid wood antique replicas. There's a washing machine and dryer in each unit, plus a gas-fired barbecue on each veranda. The swimming pool and beach bar are set in tropical gardens a few steps from Stonehaven Beach, where the great leatherback turtles return to lay eggs each year between April and June. The price includes a housekeeper, and the management will arrange a local cook or baby-sitter, plus water sports, car rentals, and day trips.

Moderate

Blue Waters Inn. Batteaux Bay, Speyside, Tobago, W.I. ☎ **800/742-4276** in the U.S., or 868/660-4341. Fax 868/660-5195. 38 rms, 4 efficiencies, 3 one- or two-bedroom bungalows. Winter, $121 double; $150 one-bedroom efficiency, $248 two-bedroom efficiency; $275 one-bedroom bungalow, $400 two-bedroom bungalow. Off-season, $85 double; $110 one-bedroom efficiency, $185 two-bedroom efficiency; $175 one-bedroom bungalow, $260 two-bedroom bungalow. Extra person $20. AE, MC, V.

Attracting nature-lovers, this property on the northeastern coast of Tobago is nestled along the shore of Batteaux Bay, where a private 1,000-foot-long beach beckons guests. Family-owned and managed, the inn is about 24 miles from the airport and 20 miles from Scarborough. From the airport, it's a 1 1/4-hour drive along narrow, winding country roads. Part of the charm of the Blue Waters Inn is that the entrance almost appears to drop over a cliff. This is a rustic retreat that's so natural birds might actually fly through the open windows of the driftwood-adorned dining room. It's a very informal place, so leave your fancy resort wear at home.

Extending onto acres of tropical rain forests with myriad exotic birds, butterflies, and other wildlife, the inn now offers several newly renovated units with kitchenettes. Two of the rooms are wheelchair accessible, and a dive shop is a full-service PADI outfitter. All the basic no-frills rooms have a private shower and ceiling fan; several are air-conditioned as well. Families may want to rent the units with cooking facilities, which are suitable for two adults and two children.

The Fish Pot, appropriately named by the proprietor, Mrs. Judy MacLean, offers local seafood and international dishes. Children get a 50% reduction on meals. Guests can dine and then retire to the Shipwreck Bar for Caribbean cocktails without ever leaving the premises. Fishing, tennis, windsurfing, kayaking, and skin diving can be arranged, as can boat trips (including glass-bottom boats) to Little Tobago.

✪ **Kariwak Village.** Local Road, Store Bay (P.O. Box 27, Scarborough), Tobago, W.I. ☎ **868/639-8545.** Fax 868/639-8441. 24 rms. A/C TEL. Winter, $90 double. Off-season, $60 double. MAP $25 per person extra. AE, DC, DISC, MC, V.

A self-contained cluster of cottages evoking the South Pacific, this complex is about a six-minute walk from the beach on the island's western shoreline, a two-minute drive from the airport. The name is a combination of the two native tribes that originally inhabited Tobago, the Caribs and the Arawaks. During its construction in 1982, the builders made much use of Tobago's palm fronds, raw teak, coral stone, and bamboo. The bedrooms are very basic, but clean and comfortable.

Live entertainment is provided on Friday and Saturday year-round. The food served in the Village Restaurant is among the best on the island, and you may want to come here for a meal even if you aren't staying here. A fixed-price meal, either à la carte or in the form of one of the weekend buffets, ranges from $20 to $24 per person.

Palm Tree Village. Milford Rd., Little Rockley Bay, Milford (P.O. Box 327, Scarborough), Tobago, W.I. ☎ **868/639-4347.** Fax 868/639-4180. 20 rms, 18 villas. A/C TV TEL. Winter, $120 double; $165–$200 villa. Off-season, $75 double; $165 villa. Children 12 and under stay free in parents' room. Breakfast included in double room. AE, MC, V.

Favored by families with children, this hotel and villa complex is not set on particularly attractive grounds. It occupies 5½ acres of rough terrain on the shore of a rather skimpy beach on the island's southwestern coast. Opened in 1991, it's arranged into a dignified compound of cream-colored, tile-roofed buildings adjacent to a narrow beach and a pair of swimming pools. Each unit opens onto a view of the ocean and has either a patio or a balcony and a collection of simple furniture. All are comfortably furnished and contain TV and a safe; the villas also have a fully equipped kitchen. The small hotel rooms are half the price of cottages. On Friday night there's entertainment in the beachfront bar and restaurant, the Carambeau. Facilities include a pool bar, a fitness center, a beach bar, a piano room, horseback riding, and a daily minivan shuttle from the hotel to four of Tobago's most popular beaches.

Rex Turtle Beach Hotel. Courtland Bay (P.O. Box 201, Scarborough), Tobago, W.I. ☎ **868/639-2851.** Fax 868/639-1495. 125 rms. A/C TV TEL. Winter, $140 double; $193 triple. Off-season, $110 double; $151 triple. MAP $45 per person extra. AE, MC, V.

Standing directly on a mile of sandy beach on Courland Bay, this hotel sits on the leeward shore in the midst of a 600-acre coconut plantation. It's 8 miles from the airport and 5 miles from Scarborough. The entrance loggia is a long covered terrace where you can enjoy the relaxed, casual lifestyle while seated on sofas and armchairs with a tall fruit-and-rum drink. Lunches are served around the garden pool or at the beach. There is different entertainment nightly, and a steel band is brought in on weekends. If you don't want the beach, you can swim in a freshwater pool. Fishing can be arranged, as can snorkeling at Buccoo Reef. A water-sports shop is on the premises.

The accommodations lie in an interconnected series of white two-story bungalows, between beds of hibiscus and oleander. All rooms are oceanfront and have a bathroom with both tub and shower, a patio or balcony, and smartly tailored furnishings. Rooms on the second floor have sloped open-beamed ceilings, with white walls and shuttered doors.

INEXPENSIVE

Richmond Great House. Belle Garden, Tobago, W.I. ☎ & fax **868/660-4467.** 7 rms, 3 suites. Winter, $135–$155 double; $175–$205 suite for 2. Off-season, $120–$135 double; $155–$180 suite for 2. Rates include MAP. MC, V.

One of the most charming and affordable accommodations on the island is an 18th-century Great House set on 6 acres, part of a cocoa- and coconut-growing estate. Near Richmond Beach, it's owned by Dr. Hollis R. Lynch, who is a Tobago-born professor of African history at Columbia. As befits his profession, he has decorated the mansion with African art along with a collection of island antiques. Guests are free to explore the garden and grounds and to enjoy the pool and the barbecue. It's not a bad choice for families. On the premises are two 19th-century tombs containing the remains of the original English founders of the plantation. All accommodations have a private bathroom and an individualized decor. The hotel lies on the southern (windward) coast of Tobago, and the airport is within a 45-minute drive. Both a regional and an international cuisine are served. Since it's such a small place, the cook asks guests about their culinary preferences.

Sandy Point Beach Village. Crown Point, Tobago, W.I. ☎ **868/639-8533.** Fax 868/639-8496. 9 studios, 35 suites and apts. A/C TV TEL. Winter, $60 double studio; $70 double suite; $80 two-bedroom apartment. Off-season, $35 double studio; $45 double studio; $55 two-bedroom apartment. MAP $15 per person extra. Additional adult $10 extra; children 11 and under sharing parents' room $5 extra. MC, V.

Built in two different sections in 1977 and 1991, this miniature vacation village somewhat resembles a Riviera condominium development. All but six of the units (those at poolside) contain a kitchenette. It's just a three-minute run from the airport, but its shoreside position on the island's southwestern coast makes it seem remote. Airport noise, however, can be a problem. The little village of peaked and gabled roofs is landscaped all the way down to the sandy beach, where there's a rustic Steak Hut, which serves meals throughout the day and evening. The units are fully equipped, and each opens onto a patio, toward the sea, or onto a covered loggia. The studios contain living and dining areas with Jamaican wicker furniture, plus satellite color TV. Some of the studios have a rustic open stairway leading to a loft room with bunk beds, although there's a twin-bedded room on the lower level as well. On the premises are two different swimming pools, plus a small gym and a disco in the basement.

WHERE TO DINE

EXPENSIVE

✪ **Le Beau Rivage.** In the Mount Irvine Bay Hotel, Tobago Golf Course, Buccoo Bay. ☎ **868/639-8871.** Reservations required. Main courses $16–$28. AE, DC, MC, V. Daily 7–10pm. FRENCH/CARIBBEAN.

Run by the hotel, this restaurant resides in a former golf clubhouse five minutes northwest of the airport. From its windows you'll have a sweeping view of one of Tobago's most historic inlets, Mount Irvine Bay. The food is more competent than exciting, but still quite good. Menu choices vary daily, but might include combinations of local ingredients with continental inspirations of *cuisine moderne,* including grilled Caribbean lobster, grilled fillet of red snapper in a tomato puree, and rack of lamb. Dessert might include a fresh fruit salad, coconut pie, coconut tart, or a fresh mango flan floating on a coulis of tropical fruits.

MODERATE

✪ **The Blue Crab.** Robinson St., Scarborough. ☎ **868/639-2737.** Reservations recommended. Main courses $17–$25; lunch $12–$20. AE, MC, V. Daily 11:30am–3:30pm and 7–10pm. CARIBBEAN/INTERNATIONAL.

One of our favorite restaurants in the capital, adjacent to the town's only Methodist church, this family-run spot occupies an Edwardian-era house with an oversize veranda. This is the domain of the Sardinha family, who returned to their native country after a sojourn in New York. They make the most of local ingredients and regional spices. Dinners might not always be available; when they are served, the menu is dictated by whatever is available that day in the marketplace. The food is homemade and good. Menu items include fresh conch, stuffed crab backs, shrimp, an array of Creole meat dishes grilled over coconut husks, flying fish in a mild curry-flavored batter, shrimp with garlic butter or cream, and a vegetable-laced rice dish of the day. Lobster sometimes appears on the menu.

Kiskadee Restaurant. In the Rex Turtle Beach Hotel, Courland Bay. ☎ **868/639-2851.** Reservations recommended for those not staying in the hotel. Main courses TT$65–TT$90 ($11–$15). AE, DC, DISC, MC, V. Daily 7:30–10am, 1–2:30pm, and 7–9:30pm. CREOLE/CARIBBEAN.

Five miles from Scarborough, the Kiskadee is casual. Its tables sit on an outdoor veranda whose edges overlook a tropical garden and the sea. Specialties include the catch of the day, steamed, baked, or grilled. The kitchen will also make a curry of the catch of the day. Other courses include baked chicken, sirloin steak, or lobster thermidor. The kitchen doesn't exactly extend itself in preparing these dishes, but flavors are zesty and spicy, and most diners leave having satisfied their tastes and appetites.

Old Donkey Cart House. Bacolet St., Scarborough, Tobago, W.I. ☎ **868/639-3551.** Reservations required. Main courses TT$50–TT$90 ($8–$15). AE, MC, V. Daily 8am–11pm. INTERNATIONAL.

An unusual and noteworthy restaurant occupies a green-and-white Edwardian house about half a mile south of Scarborough. Its entrepreneurial owner, Gloria Jones-Knapp, was once a fashion model in Europe. "Born, bred, and dragged up" on Tobago, she is today the island's leading authority on selected European wines that she purchases with her husband. These selections include Italian, French, Austrian, and German. Her restaurant also serves freshly made fruit drinks laced with the local rum. You get the standards here—grilled steaks, stir-fried shrimp, stuffed crab back, homemade pasta, shrimp and crabmeat cocktail, fresh fish, beef Stroganoff, salads, homemade garlic bread, and callaloo soup with crab. Dining can be enjoyed either in the palm garden or on the verandas of the Hibiscus Bar while seated in rattan chairs.

If you're interested, ask about the apartment suites for rent, costing $76 to $120 daily, double occupancy, including breakfast and taxes.

The Steak Hut. In the Sandy Point Beach Village, Crown Point. ☎ **868/639-8533.** Reservations recommended. Main courses TT$75–TT$95 ($12–$16). AE, MC, V. Daily 7–11:15am, 11:30am–5pm, and 7–9:15pm. STEAK.

On the island's southwestern side, the Steak Hut serves the best beef on the island, specializing in U.S. sirloin, T-bone, porterhouse, and tenderloin. The location, near the beach and swimming pool of this previously recommended hotel, is ideal, especially in the evening. The seafront restaurant also features local fish steaks: shark, flying fish, grouper, dolphin, barracuda, and kingfish. A steel band plays Saturday night.

Sugar Mill Restaurant. In the Mount Irvine Bay Hotel, Buccoo Bay. ☎ **868/639-8871.** Reservations required for those not staying at the hotel. Main courses TT$35–TT$45 ($6–$7); fixed-price meal TT$140 ($23). AE, DC, MC, V. Daily 7–10am, noon–3pm, and 7–10pm. INTERNATIONAL.

About a 5-mile drive northwest of the island's airport, this restaurant has at its core a 200-year-old sugar mill. Open-air, breezy, casually elegant, and permeated with the scent from nearby jasmine, this is the best restaurant on Tobago.

Lunch includes everything from salads and sandwiches to lamb chops Provençale or sirloin steak. Dinner might include lobster bisque, a carbonade of beef, shrimp Newburg with rice pilaf, marinated grilled chicken, lobster sautéed in ginger, and fillet of dolphin. Meals are usually accompanied by live music and entertainment, at least in season.

INEXPENSIVE

Jemma's Seaview Kitchen. Speyside. ☎ **868/660-4066.** Reservations recommended. Main courses TT$55–TT$110 ($9–$18). No credit cards. Sun–Thurs 9am–9pm, Fri 9am–5pm. TOBAGONIAN.

A short walk north of the hamlet of Speyside, on Tobago's northeastern coast, this is one of the very few restaurants in the Caribbean designed as a tree house. Although the simple kitchen is firmly anchored to the shoreline, the dining area is set on a platform nailed to the massive branches of a 200-year-old almond tree that leans out over the water. Some 50 tables are available on a wooden deck that provides a rooflike structure for shelter from the rain.

The establishment's owner is Mrs. Jemma Sealey, whose charming staff provides meals where soup or salad is included in the price of a main course. Lunch platters include shrimp, fish, and chicken, whereas dinners feature more elaborate portions of each of those, as well as steaks, curried lamb, grilled or curried kingfish, lamb chops, and lobster served grilled or thermidor style. No liquor is served (only fresh orange or pineapple juice).

ENJOYING TOBAGO'S MAGNIFICENT BEACHES & OUTDOOR PURSUITS

BEACHES On Tobago sands you can still feel like Robinson Crusoe in a solitary cove—at least for most of the week before the Trinidadians fly over to sample the sands on a Saturday.

A good beach, **Back Bay,** is within an eight-minute walk of the Mount Irvine Bay Hotel. Along the way you'll pass a coconut plantation and an old cannon emplacement. Sometimes there can be dangerous currents here, but you can always enjoy exploring Rocky Point with its brilliantly colored parrot fish.

Try also **Man-O-War Bay,** one of the finest natural harbors in the West Indies, at the opposite end of the island. Once there, you'll come to a long sandy beach, and you can also enjoy a picnic at a government-run rest house.

The finest for last: **Pigeon Point,** on the island's northwestern coast, is the best-known bathing area with a long coral beach. Thatched shelters provide changing rooms, as well as tables and benches for picnics.

BOATING The **Rex Turtle Beach Hotel,** Courland Bay (☎ **868/639-2851**), rents Aqua-finn sailboats and is a registered Mistral Sailing Centre.

GOLF Tobago is the proud possessor of an 18-hole, 6,800-yard golf course at Mount Irvine. Called the **Tobago Golf Club** (☎ **868/639-8871**), it covers 150 breeze-swept acres and was featured in the *Wonderful World of Golf* TV series. Even beginners agree the course is friendly to golfers. As a guest of the Mount Irvine Bay Hotel, you're granted temporary membership, use of the clubhouse and facilities, and a 30% discount on greens fees. All serious golfers should stay at the Mount Irvine. Nonresidents pay $40 for 18 holes, $25 for 9 holes.

TENNIS The **Rex Turtle Beach Hotel** (☎ **868/639-2851**) has courts. The best courts, however, are at the **Mount Irvine Bay Hotel** (☎ **868/639-8871**), where two good courts are available free to guests. Night tennis costs $5.

WATER SPORTS—SNORKLING, DIVING & MORE The unspoiled reefs off Tobago teem with a great variety of marine life. Divers can swim through rocky canyons 60 to 130 feet deep, and underwater photographers can shoot pictures they won't find anywhere else. Snorkeling over the celebrated Buccoo Reef is one of the specialties of Tobago. Hotels arrange for their guests to visit this underwater wonderland.

The **Rex Turtle Beach Hotel,** Courland Bay (☎ **868/639-2851**), is the best equipped for water sports. Sailing and windsurfing are available free, and waterskiing is offered at reasonable rates.

Dive Tobago, Pigeon Point (P.O. Box 53, Scarborough), Tobago, W.I. (☎ **868/639-0202**), is the oldest and most established dive operation on Tobago, operated by Jay Young. It offers easy resort courses, single dives, and dive packages. Equipment is available to rent. It caters to the beginner as well as to the experienced diver. A basic resort course, taking half a day and ending in a 30-foot dive, costs $55. Young is a certified PADI instructor.

Tobago Dive Experience, at the Turtle Beach Hotel, Black Rock (☎ **868/639-7034**), offers scuba dives, snorkeling, and boat trips. All dives are guided, with a boat following. Exciting drift dives are available for experienced divers. Manta rays are frequently seen five minutes from the shore, and there is rich marine life with zonal compaction. A one-tank dive costs $35 with no equipment or $42 with equipment.

Man Friday Diving, Charlotteville (☎ **868/660-4676**), is a Danish-owned dive center with certified PADI instructors along with PADI dive masters. The location is right on the beach of Man-O-War Bay at the northernmost tip of Tobago. With more than 40 different dive sites, they're always able to find suitable locations for diving, no matter what the water conditions are. Guided boat trips for certified divers go out twice a day except Sundays, at 9:30am and at 2pm. A resort course costs $75; a PADI open-water certification, $375. A one-tank dive costs $35, with a night dive going for $50. The outfitter also rents single or double kayaks.

EXPLORING THE ISLAND

In Tobago's capital, **Scarborough,** you can visit the local market Monday to Saturday morning and listen to the sounds of a Creole patois. Scarborough's stores have a limited range of merchandise, more to tempt the browser than the serious shopper.

The town need claim your attention only briefly before you climb up the hill to **Fort King George,** about 430 feet above the town. Built by the English in 1779, it was later captured by the French. After that it jockeyed back and forth among various conquerors until nature decided to end it all in 1847, blowing off the roofs of its buildings. The cannons still mounted had a 3-mile range, and one is believed to have come from one of the ships of Sir Francis Drake (you can still see a replica of the *Tudor Rose*). One building used to house a powder magazine, and you can see the ruins of a military hospital. Artifacts are displayed in a gallery on the grounds.

If you'd like to get a close-up view of Tobago's exotic and often rare tropical birds, as well as a range of other island wildlife and lush tropical flora, naturalist-led field trips are the perfect answer. The trips lead you to forest trails and coconut plantations, along rivers and past waterfalls. Each trip lasts about two to three hours, so you can take at least two per day if you like. One excursion goes to two nearby islands. The price per trip is $42 to $55 per person. For details, contact **Pat Turpin,** Man-O-War Bay Cottages, Charlotteville (☎ **868/660-4327**).

From Scarborough, you can drive northwest to **Plymouth,** Tobago's other town. Perched on a point at Plymouth is **Fort James,** which dates from 1768 when it was built by the British as a barracks. Now it's mainly in ruins.

From Speyside, you can make arrangements with a local fisher to go to **Little Tobago,** a 450-acre offshore island where a bird sanctuary attracts ornithologists. Threatened with extinction in New Guinea many birds, perhaps 50 species in all, were brought over to this little island in the early part of this century.

Off Pigeon Point lies **Buccoo Reef,** where sea gardens of coral and hundreds of fish can be seen in waist-deep water. This is the natural aquarium of Tobago. Nearly all the major hotels arrange boat trips to these acres of submarine gardens, which offer the best scuba diving and snorkeling. Even nonswimmers can wade knee-deep in the waters. Remember to protect your head and body from the tropical heat and to guard your feet against the sharp coral.

After about half an hour at the reef, passengers reboard their boats and go over to **Nylon Pool,** with its crystal-clear waters. Here in this white-sand bottom, about a mile offshore, you can enjoy water only three or four feet deep. After a swim, you'll be returned to the Buccoo Village jetty in time for a goat and crab race.

Cotton House Fashion Studio, Old Windward Road, in Bacolet (☎ **868/639-2727**), is one of the island's best choices for "hands-on" appreciation of the fine art of batik. Batik is an Indonesian tradition where melted wax, brushed onto fabric, resists dyes on certain parts of the cloth, thereby creating unusual colors and designs. This outlet contains one of the largest collections of batik clothing and wall hangings on Tobago. Dying techniques are demonstrated to clients, who can try their skills at the art form free.

TOBAGO AFTER DARK

Your best bet for entertainment is at the **Mount Irvine Bay Hotel** (☎ **868/639-8871**), where you might find some disco action or a steel band performing. The **Rex Turtle Beach Hotel** (☎ **868/639-2851**) is the place to be on Wednesday night, when it stages a Caribbean buffet dinner with cultural entertainment and dancing. You get real West Indian flavor here. Every Saturday night a steel band is brought in to entertain at a barbecue dinner from 7 to 10pm.

The Dutch Leewards

16

Cactus fences surround pastel-washed houses, divi-divi trees with their windblown look stud the barren countryside, free-form boulders are scattered about, and on occasion you'll come across an abandoned gold mine. Formerly Dutch possessions, the so-called "ABC" group of islands—Aruba, Bonaire, and Curaçao—lie just off the northern coast of Venezuela. The islands have a widely diversified population, many of whom speak Papiamento, a language made up of Spanish, Portuguese, Dutch, African, and English elements. Dutch is the official tongue.

Duty-free shopping and gambling are promoted by the governments on all three islands. Curaçao has the most conspicuously Dutch atmosphere, with a significant number of 18th-century buildings lining its streets. Curaçao, along with Aruba, boasts highly developed tourist centers, whereas Bonaire attracts the most dedicated scuba divers. Someone once said that there are more flamingos than people on Bonaire. Aruba, meanwhile, has superior beaches and a greater selection of hotel accommodations.

The canny Dutch emerged from the European power struggle in the West Indies with these tiny specks of land, arid and for all appearances inconsequential. But they proceeded to turn these ugly-duckling properties into some of the most valuable real estate in the Caribbean, and while they have developed into thriving upscale resorts, these spotless islands have still managed to retain old-world charm and are clean and thriving.

On January 1, 1986, Aruba became a separate entity within the Kingdom of the Netherlands under a political arrangement called Status Aparte. Before that date, it was a member of the Netherlands Antilles. The Kingdom of the Netherlands, with Aruba's new status, has three separate components: the Netherlands, the Netherlands Antilles, and Aruba. The government of the Netherlands is responsible for the defense and foreign affairs of the kingdom, but other government tasks are carried out by each island country for itself.

In addition to Bonaire and Curaçao, the Netherlands Antilles encompasses Saba, St. Eustatius (Statia), and St. Maarten, already discussed in chapter 10, "The Dutch Windwards in the Leewards."

1 Aruba

Forget lush vegetation on Aruba—that's impossible with only 17 inches of rainfall annually. Aruba is dry and sunny almost year-round, with clean, exhilarating air like that found in the desert of Palm Springs, California. Its own Palm Beach, one of the best in the world, draws tourists in droves, as do its glittering casinos. Aruba is for vacationers who prefer to complement a sun-drenched body with an elegant evening gown rather than to don pajamas and spend the night absorbed in a popular novel.

Aruba is not a chic address like St. Barts or Anguilla, but honeymooners, sun worshippers, snorkelers, sailors, and weekend gamblers find that it suits their needs just fine. As you lie back along the 7-mile stretch of white-sand beach, enjoying an 82°F daytime temperature, you're not harassed by locals peddling wares you don't want. There is almost no racial tension, and, chances are, you won't get mugged. Trade winds keep the island from becoming uncomfortably hot, and there's very low humidity.

Aruba stands outside the hurricane path. Its coastline on the leeward side is smooth and serene, with white-sand beaches; but on the eastern coast, the windward side, the look is rugged and wild, typical of the windswept Atlantic.

Many visitors come here for the annual pre-Lenten Carnival, a month-long festival with events day and night. With music, dancing, parades, costumes, and "jump-ups" (Caribbean hoe-downs), Carnival is the highlight of Aruba's winter season.

Today Aruba stands as one of the most popular Caribbean destinations with more than a dozen resort hotels populating its once-uninhabited beaches. A recent moratorium on hotel construction has halted the building of newer resorts, so at least for a while, visitors should take advantage of what the island presently offers: pleasant accommodations and an activity-packed safe haven.

GETTING THERE

On **American Airlines** (☎ **800/433-7300**), Aruba-bound passengers can catch a daily nonstop 4½-hour flight from New York's JFK Airport. American also offers two flights daily from its hub in San Juan, Puerto Rico, and one daily trip from Miami. This last flight enables vacationers from Chicago, Los Angeles, San Francisco, and Seattle to fly directly to Aruba via the American Airlines Miami hub.

American's lowest fare is included in its "land package," whereby prearranged and prepaid accommodations at selected hotels (recommended in this guide) are booked at the same time as the airfare through American's tour department. Contact an American Airlines reservations clerk or a travel agent for details.

For clients who prefer to make their own hotel arrangements, American offers its least expensive tickets to those who can reserve at least 14 days in advance. Weekday travel (Monday to Thursday) is usually cheaper than travel in any direction on a Friday, Saturday, or Sunday.

ALM (☎ **800/327-7230**) has good connections into Aruba from certain parts of the United States. There are direct flights to Aruba from Fort Lauderdale on Thursday and Sunday but check carefully with the airline as these face seasonal adjustments. Flights leave Miami daily for Aruba going via Curaçao. There is a direct flight to Aruba from Atlanta on Sunday, plus a flight from Atlanta via Curaçao on Saturday.

Tiny **Air Aruba** (☎ **800/88-ARUBA**), the country's national carrier, boasts Newark (New Jersey), Baltimore, Tampa, and Miami as North American gateways. Air Aruba offers daily nonstop flights from Miami, daily flights from Newark,

0
12.4 mi
20 km
N
California Lighthouse
Malmok Beach
California Sand Dunes
Fisherman's Hut Beach
Palm Beach
Eagle Beach
Manchebo Beach
Divi Beach
Druif Bay
Oranjestad
Noord
Altovista Chapel
Bushiribana
Natural Bridge
Casibari
Ayó
Queen Beatrix Airport
Santa Cruz
Hooiberg
Caribbean Sea
Spanish Lagoon
Fontein Cave
Boca Prins
Guadarikiri Cave
Huliba Cave
Caribbean Sea
Savaneta
Boca Grandi
Sint Nicolas (San Nicolas)
Grapefield Beach
Rodgers Beach
Seroe Colorado
Baby Beach
Hotels:
Americana Aruba Beach Resort & Casino 4
Aruba Marriott Resort & Stellaris Casino 1
Aruba Palm Beach Resort and Casino 7
Aruba Sonesta Resorts at Seaport Village 12
Bucuti Beach 9
Caribbean Palm Village Resort 13
Divi Aruba Beach Resort 10
Hyatt Regency Aruba 3
Radisson Aruba Caribbean Resort & Casino 6
Tamarijn Aruba Beach Resort 11
Wyndham Hotel & Resort 5
Condos & Time-Share Properties:
Amsterdam Manor Beach Resort 8
La Cabana All Suite Beach Resort & Casino 8
Playa Linda Beach Resort 2
Airport
Beach
Lighthouse
2-0190

twice-weekly (Saturday and Sunday) nonstop flights from Baltimore, and five weekly flights from Tampa. Air Aruba also has links to Bonaire and Curaçao.

Air Canada (☎ **800/363-5440** in Canada, 800/776-3000 in the U.S.) has good connections from such cities as Toronto and Québec to Miami. Once in Miami, Canadians and other passengers can fly Air Aruba to the island.

GETTING AROUND

BY BUS Aruba has an excellent bus service, with a round-trip fare between the beach hotels and Oranjestad of $1.75. Bus schedules are available at the Arubus Office at the central bus station on Zoutmanstraat. Your hotel reception desk will also know the approximate times the buses pass by where you're staying. There's regular daily service from 6am to midnight. Try to have exact change. For bus schedules and information, call the **Aruba Tourism Authority** at ☎ **297/8-23777.**

BY TAXI On Aruba, the taxis are unmetered but rates are fixed, so tell the driver your destination and ask the fare before getting in. The main office is on Sands Street between the bowling center and Taco Bell. A **dispatch office** is located at Bosabao (☎ **297/8-22116**). A ride from the airport to most of the hotels, including those at Palm Beach, costs about $8 to $14 per car, and a maximum of four passengers is allowed. Some of the local people don't tip, but it's good to give something extra, especially if the driver has helped you with luggage. Additionally, since it's next to impossible to locate a taxi on some parts of the island, when traveling to a remote area or restaurant, it's a good idea to ask the taxi driver to return to pick you up at a certain time.

You'll also usually find the English-speaking drivers willing tour guides. Most of them seem well informed about their island and are eager to share it with you. A one-hour tour (and you don't need much more than that) is offered at $35 per hour for a maximum of four passengers.

BY RENTAL CAR Unlike most Caribbean islands, Aruba makes it easy to rent a car and explore independently. The roads connecting the major tourist attractions are excellent, and a valid U.S. or Canadian driver's license is accepted by each of the major car-rental companies and is sufficient to drive on Aruba. Most of the big hotels have desks that will rent cars to you. Ask them a day in advance and you'll have a better chance of getting the car you want.

Three major U.S. car-rental companies maintain offices on Aruba, and a quick comparison of prices before you leave the United States will reveal current price differences. Many of the companies have both airport branches and kiosks at the major hotels. No taxes are imposed on car rentals on Aruba, but insurance can be tricky. Even with the purchase of a collision-damage waiver, a driver is still responsible for between $300 and $500 worth of damage. Rental rates (subject to change) range between $35 and $70 per day at the following agencies: **Budget Rent-a-Car,** Kolibristraat 1 (☎ **800/472-3325** in the U.S., or 297/8-28600); **Hertz,** L. G. Smith Blvd. 142 (☎ **800/654-3001** in the U.S., or 297/8-24545), and **Avis,** Kolibristraat 14 (☎ **800/331-1084** in the U.S., or 297/8-28787). Budget requires that renters be at least 25; Avis, 23; and Hertz, 21.

BY MOTORCYCLE & MOPED Since the roads of Aruba are good and the terrain is flat, many visitors prefer this form of transport. Mopeds and motorcycles cost an average of $37 to $40 per day at **George's Scooter Rental,** L. G. Smith Blvd. 136, Oranjestad (☎ **297/8-25975**). **Nelson Motorcycle Rental,** Gasparito 10A, Noord (☎ **297/8-66801**), rents scooters for $25 and motorcycles for $44 to $89.

FAST FACTS: Aruba

Banking Hours Banks are open Monday to Friday from 8am to noon and 1:30 to 3:45pm.

Currency The currency is the **Aruba florin (AFl),** which is divided into 100 cents. Silver coins are in denominations of 5, 10, 25, and 50 cents and 1 and 2¹/₂ florins. The 50-cent piece, the square "yotin," is Aruba's best-known coin. The current exchange rate is AFl 1.77 to U.S.$1 (AFl 1 is worth about 56¢). U.S. dollars, traveler's checks, and major credit and charge cards are widely accepted throughout the island. Unless otherwise stated, prices quoted in this chapter are in U.S. dollars.

Documents To enter Aruba, U.S., British, and Canadian citizens may submit a valid passport or a birth certificate (or, for U.S. citizens only, a voter registration card with a photo ID).

Electricity The electricity is 110 volts AC (60 cycles), the same as in the United States. Adapters and transformers are not needed for U.S. and Canadian appliances.

Emergencies For the **police,** dial ☎ **11100.** For a **medical emergency,** dial ☎ **74300.** For the **fire department,** call ☎ **115.**

Information For information, go to the **Aruba Tourism Authority,** L. G. Smith Blvd. 172, Oranjestad (☎ **297/8-23777**). Before leaving home, you can also contact the Aruba Tourism Authority at the following locations: 1000 Harbor Blvd., Weehawken, NJ 07087 (☎ **800/TO-ARUBA**); 2344 Salzedo St., Miami, FL 33144 (☎ **305/567-2720**); 199 14th St. NE, Suite 2008, Atlanta, GA 30309 (☎ **404/892-7822**); or 86 Bloor St. W., Suite 204, Toronto, ON M5S 1M5, Canada (☎ **416/975-1950**).

Language The official language is Dutch, but nearly everybody speaks English. The language of the street is often Papiamento. Spanish is also widely spoken.

Medical Care The **Horacio Oduber Hospital** is on L. G. Smith Boulevard, near the Alhambra Casino (☎ **297/8-74300**). It's a modern building with excellent medical facilities open 24 hours a day. Hotels also have doctors on call, and there are good dental facilities as well (make appointments through your hotel).

Safety Aruba is one of the Caribbean's safer destinations, in spite of its numerous hotels and gambling casinos. Of course, pickpockets and purse-snatchers are around, but not in great numbers. However, it's always wise to guard your valuables. Never leave them unattended on the beach or even in a locked car.

Taxes and Service The government of Aruba imposes a 6.66% room tax, as well as a $20 airport departure tax. At your hotel, you'll have an 11% to 15% service charge added to charges for room, food, and beverages.

Telephones Aruba is not part of the 809 area code that applies to most of the Caribbean. To call Aruba from the United States, dial 011 (the international access code), then 297 (the country code for Aruba), and then 8 (the area code) and the five-digit local number.

Once on Aruba, to call another number on the island, only the five-digit local number is necessary. Hotels charge astronomical rates even for local calls, so be selective to avoid costly phone charges.

Time Aruba is on Atlantic standard time year-round, so most of the year Aruba is one hour ahead of eastern time (when it's 10am on Aruba, it's 9am in New York). When daylight saving time is in effect in the United States, clocks in New York and Aruba show the same time.

Water The water, which comes from the world's second-largest desalination plant, is pure.

Weather Dry and sunny, Aruba has a median temperature of 81 °F. As mentioned, the cool trade winds, extremely moderate rainfall, and absence of tropical storms or hurricanes make it likely that your stay will be sunny and incredibly hot, even in winter.

WHERE TO STAY

Most of Aruba's hotels are of the resort variety, bustling and self-contained. There's a tremendous dearth of family or budget hotels. Guest houses are few and tend to be booked up early in winter by faithful returning visitors. In season, it's imperative to make reservations well in advance; don't ever arrive expecting to find a room on the spot—you must have an address to give Immigration when you arrive on Aruba. Don't forget to ask if the 6.66% room tax and service charge are included in the rates quoted when you make your reservation.

HOTELS

Very Expensive

Americana Aruba Beach Resort & Casino. J. E. Irausquin Blvd. 83 (P.O. Box 218), Oranjestad, Aruba. ☎ **800/447-7462** in the U.S., 212/661-4540 in New York City, or 297/8-64500. 419 rms, 14 suites. A/C MINIBAR TV TEL. Winter, $390–$440 double; from $580 suite. Off-season, $290–$310 double; from $380 suite. Rates are all-inclusive. AE, DC, MC, V.

Rising high above Palm Beach, this hotel underwent a $25 million renovation that was completed in 1990. Still, it's not nearly as glamorous as some of its competitors. The cloverleaf-shaped pool is creatively designed with a waterfall at one end and two Jacuzzis whirling about in its center. This hostelry is clean, well managed, and popular, attracting families and repeat guests, along with an array of tour groups, mostly from the United States and Canada. Occupying twin towers separated by a garden, the hotel was originally built in the early 1970s and, even after its refurbishment, still seems to need constant renewal. Each of the bedrooms is comfortably furnished with conservatively contemporary white bamboo and bleached-wood furniture in tropical colors of blue, green, and peach. Cable television with remote control and built-in hair dryers are among the room amenities.

Dining/Entertainment: Le Petit Café is the establishment's most formal restaurant. Other choices include the Trade Winds. Our favorite spot for a quiet drink is Jardin Brezilien, a second-floor veranda filled with plants and wicker settees overlooking the splashing fountains of the resort's swimming pool. The hotel's nightclub, the Showroom, offers star-spangled Las Vegas–style revues. There's also an in-house casino.

Services: Room service, laundry, massages, baby-sitting.

Facilities: White strip of palm-dotted beach, lagoon-shaped pool, two tennis courts, health club, adventure club for ages 4 to 13, water-sports center on the hotel's beach.

Aruba Marriott Resort & Stellaris Casino. Palm Beach, Aruba. ☎ **800/223-6388** in the U.S. and Canada, or 297/8-69000. Fax 297/8-60649. 413 rms, 15 suites. A/C MINIBAR TV TEL. Winter, $300–$500 double; $900 suite. Off-season, $195–$350 double; $250–$550 suite. MAP $60 per person extra. Additional person $40 extra. 11% service and tax extra. AE, DC, MC, V.

Opened in 1995, this luxury high-rise resort has proved heavy competition for the Hyatt, although the Hyatt is still the premier choice. On 600 feet of sandy beachfront on the northwestern coast of Aruba, this five-star hotel offers the most spacious accommodations on the island. All its oversize guest rooms have private balconies opening onto the sea, along with such extras as refrigerators and safety-deposit boxes. The hotel is 7 miles from the airport.

Dining/Entertainment: Restaurant options include casual dining at La Vista; Tuscany, for an Italian specialty cuisine; or al fresco lunches at a beach bar and grill. Guests gather for sundowners at the casino lounge, later trying their luck in the casino.

Services: Baby-sitting, laundry, room service.

Facilities: Free-form pool with cascading waterfalls, state-of-the-art health club, beauty clinic; nearby golf and tennis. Red Sail Sports arranges most activities on the beach, everything from boat rentals such as kayaks to waterskiing and parasailing.

Divi Aruba Beach Resort. J. E. Irausquin Blvd. 45, Oranjestad, Aruba. ☎ **800/554-2008** in the U.S., or 297/8-23300. Fax 297/8-31940. 202 rms, 1 suite. A/C TV TEL. Winter, $450–$560 double; $800 suite. Off-season, $340–$410 double; $560 suite. Rates are all-inclusive. AE, DC, MC, V.

On the largest beach on the island, this casual, comfortable DHC-managed resort is one of the island's friendliest oases, but certainly not the best hotel. The beach is more alluring than the hotel. The philosophy at this popular low-rise hotel remains "barefoot elegance," and guests are free to dash through the lobby in their bathing suits. The main section has 90 standard guest rooms, 20 beachfront lanai rooms, and 40 garden bungalows that overlook individual courtyards. The Divi Dos, as they're called, contain luxury rooms and a bridal suite, all with mini-refrigerators and Jacuzzi bathtubs. The recently redecorated rooms literally glow in yellow, green, and creamy white. Special packages include champagne breakfast, photo albums, beach towels, and fruit baskets. The hotel is north of Oranjestad, and about 6 miles northwest of the airport.

Dining/Entertainment: Meals are served on the casual Pelican Terrace or in the Red Parrot dining room. All year, dancing and special theme nights, including Tuesday's Carnival and Saturday's Beach Barbecue Fiesta, add to the nightly festivities. The Alhambra Casino stands across the road from the resort.

Services: Laundry, baby-sitting.

Facilities: Two freshwater swimming pools, tennis court, water-sports center.

✪ **Hyatt Regency Aruba.** L. G. Smith Blvd. 85, Palm Beach, Aruba. ☎ **800/233-1234** in the U.S. and Canada, or 297/8-61234. Fax 297/8-61682. 354 rms, 18 suites. A/C MINIBAR TV TEL. Winter, $365–$425 double; $490 Regency Club double; from $680 suite. Off-season, $195–$235 double; $295 Regency Club double; from $390 suite. MAP $65 per person extra. AE, DC, MC, V.

The most glamorous resort on Aruba lies on 12 landscaped beachfront acres about 2 miles north of Oranjestad. Built in the early 1990s at a cost exceeding $57 million, it offers a series of public rooms reminiscent of a large-scale Latin American hacienda, with soaring ceilings and a facade with art deco touches. The finest gardens on Aruba are dotted with waterfalls and reflecting pools, exotic birds, and stonework. The bedrooms are luxurious in their appointments, filled with many amenities, including original artworks commissioned from around the Americas. Guests in the hotel's 29 Regency Club rooms, located on the ninth floor, receive the special features of a private concierge, upgraded linens, and other amenities. For families, they offer a Camp Hyatt program for children as well as a teen program.

Dining/Entertainment: Situated throughout the property are several restaurants and lounges, including the indoor/outdoor Ruinas del Mar restaurant, with decor reminiscent of Aruba's gold-mining past. Fashioned out of native island stone, it's positioned on the edge of the lagoon and offers scenic ocean views; the cuisine is Mediterranean. For more casual dining, the beachfront Palms Restaurant presents an open-air Caribbean-style seafood grill. Other dining choices include the Olé Restaurant, serving Spanish tapas with singing waiters and other live entertainment, and Café Piccolo, an Italian-style cafe and bistro. The Casino Copacabana with its entertainment and gaming tables evokes the Côte d'Azur.

Services: 24-hour room service, laundry, massages, baby-sitting.

Facilities: A $2.5 million multilevel pool complex and lagoon (with waterfalls, tropical gardens, and slides), health and fitness facilities (including exercise room, saunas, massage, steam rooms, outdoor whirlpool, and aerobics sundeck), two tennis courts (lit at night); scuba diving can be arranged. Supervised activities and special programs for children 3 to 15 on weekends and holidays in summer. Teen program (ages 13 to 17), including Jeep excursions, snorkeling trips, "Rock Out" barbecues, dances, and sunset sails.

Radisson Aruba Caribbean Resort & Casino. J. E. Irausquin Blvd. 81, Palm Beach, Aruba. ☎ **800/333-3333** or 297/8-66555. Fax 297/8-63260. 367 rms, 19 one- and two-bedroom suites. A/C MINIBAR TV TEL. Winter, $235–$385 double; $500–$575 one-bedroom suite; $850–$950 two-bedroom suite. Off-season, $170–$260 double; $375–$400 one-bedroom suite; $600–$650 two-bedroom suite. AE, DC, DISC, MC, V.

Elizabeth Taylor and Eddie Fisher have long gone, but the queen of the Netherlands still checks in on occasion. The first high-rise ever built on Aruba, the hotel was rescued by a massive overhaul that came none too soon. Fronting 1,500 feet of sands along Palm Beach, the Radisson rises eight floors above the strip. The massive lobby has been pulled together more attractively, and the bedrooms are well appointed, with individual climate controls. Decoration is in a contemporary island style, and the most desirable rooms are those with full ocean views. Rooms accessible to travelers with disabilities are also available. Each guest room has a private balcony or shower.

Dining/Entertainment: The signature restaurant, Bistro 81, serves a Caribbean-influenced French cuisine, whereas Watapana offers lighter fare and colorful island dishes. Carnival nights or theme nights are often featured at the Sunset Grill. Casino games occupy many a guest's evening.

Services: Room service, laundry, baby-sitting.

Facilities: Olympic-size pool, exercise room, four lighted tennis courts, a wide assortment of water sports.

Tamarijn Aruba Beach Resort. J. E. Irausquin Blvd. 41, Palm Beach, Aruba. ☎ **800/554-2008** in the U.S., or 297/8-24150. Fax 297/8-31940. 236 rms. A/C TV TEL. Winter, $410 double. Off-season, $300 double. Rates are all-inclusive. AE, DC, MC, V.

This resort enjoys one of the longest beachfronts on Aruba. A favorite of honeymooners, it's a sprawling mixture of Dutch-style two-story units, resembling a collection of connected waterfront town houses. The narrow strip of sandy turf between the accommodations and the beach is planted with almond, palm, and sea grape trees. Each of the sunny rooms contains a radio and big glass doors that slide open to receive beach breezes. All rooms have a beachfront view, a patio or balcony, air-conditioning, cable TV, and safe-deposit boxes. A 1990 redecoration brought these once-basic accommodations up to par. Guests can ride to the Alhambra Casino and the Divi Aruba Beach Hotel in free carts. The hotel is 6 miles northwest of the airport.

Dining/Entertainment: There's a choice of five dining outlets, but the cuisine is only standard. At one end of the long and narrow property, the open-air Bunker Bar is perched on stilts above a lopsided fortification remaining intact from World War II. On the premises are several drinking spots, including the Palm Court, the Cunucu Terrace, and the Pizza Bar. The two-story Coconuts Bar offers a panoramic view.

Services: Laundry, baby-sitting. Electric carts transport visitors to the Alhambra Casino and the Divi Aruba Beach Resort, where admission to the casino and use of the facilities are free.

Facilities: Swimming pool, two hard-surface tennis courts (lit at night), water sports (including scuba diving and waterskiing).

Wyndham Hotel & Resort. J. E. Irausquin Blvd., Palm Beach, Aruba. ☎ **800/WYNDHAM** or 297/8-64466. Fax 297/8-68217. 444 rms, 80 suites. A/C MINIBAR TV TEL. Winter, $275–$375 double; $475–$2,000 suite. Off-season, $175–$195 double; $385–$1,300 suite. Package rates available. AE, DC, MC, V.

Originally built in the 1970s, this 14-story skyscraper rises beside a white-sand beach in a cluster of other high-rise hotels north of Oranjestad. Reopened as a Hilton in the early 1990s, and currently under Wyndham Hotels & Resorts, after millions of dollars' worth of renovations its lobby is sheathed in layers of stucco tinted in desert-inspired colors of terra-cotta and cerulean blue. Each of the bedrooms offers a balcony, an ocean view, comfortable furniture designed in Caribbean themes, and lots of electronic amenities.

Dining/Entertainment: The Casablanca Casino occupies a large room near the lobby. Rick's Cabaret Lounge and the Baci Café, serving an Italian cuisine, is adjacent to the Casablanca Casino. A touch of exotica is created in the Pago Pago, which serves a "touristy" Polynesian cuisine. The Café Royale, which hosts dinner shows, is for nighttime diversions.

Services: Room service (7am to 11pm), laundry, baby-sitting, concierge.

Facilities: State-of-the-art health club, water-sports facilities, one tennis court, free-form Olympic-size swimming pool (on three different levels, with waters rippled by waterspouts and fountains).

Expensive

Aruba Palm Beach Resort and Casino. J. E. Irausquin Blvd. 79, Oranjestad, Aruba. ☎ **800/345-2782** in the U.S. and Canada, or 297/8-63900. Fax 297/8-61941. 176 rms, 20 cabanas, 4 suites. A/C TV TEL. Winter, $194–$220 double; $225–$248 cabana; $250–$275 suite. Off-season, $125–$194 double; $145 cabana; $175 suite. MAP $41.98 per person extra. Additional adult $20 extra. Children stay free in parents' room. AE, DC, MC, V.

Formerly a Sheraton, this seashell-pink high-rise palace stands in a choice location, in a beachside palm grove 6 miles north of the airport. Accented with coral stone and Moorish arches both inside and out, the place is sleek, stylish, and comfortable, with a polite staff and rooms that benefited from a complete overhaul in 1996. Every unit has quality and character, with a walk-in closet, cable TV, and a tiny balcony; all overlook either the ocean, the pool, or the gardens. Other amenities include small refrigerators.

Dining/Entertainment: You can enjoy the Las Vegas–inspired Palm Casino, nightly entertainment in the Oasis Lounge, fine dining in the Palm Garden Café, or cozy outdoor dining in the nautically inspired Seawatch Restaurant, which features U.S. beef and seafood. The Players Club offers live music until 3am.

Services: Room service, laundry, baby-sitting, beauty salon.

Facilities: Olympic-size freshwater swimming pool (the best on the island for swimming laps), children's pool, three tennis courts, an array of shops; excursions include scuba diving and windsurfing.

Aruba Sonesta Resorts at Seaport Village. L. G. Smith Blvd. 9, Oranjestad, Aruba. ☎ **800/SONESTA** in the U.S. and Canada, or 297/8-36000. Fax 297/8-34389. 285 rms, 15 suites (Aruba Sonesta Resort & Casino); 250 one-bedroom suites (Aruba Sonesta Suites & Casino). A/C MINIBAR TV TEL. Winter, $240–$330 double; $400–$495 suite; $300–$400 one-bedroom suite. Off-season, $145–$235 double; $305–$400 suite; $205–$305 one-bedroom suite. Additional person $30 extra. Children 11 and under stay free in parents' room. AE, MC, V.

This is a two-in-one resort, located in the Seaport Village Complex (the island's largest shopping and entertainment facility). It's next to two marinas and a recreational park. It's the only major resort at Oranjestad Harbor, and is the only one on Aruba boasting a private island and six beaches. The first resort, Aruba Sonesta Resort & Casino, is adjacent to the Seaport Mall with an outdoor pool and terrace, whereas Aruba Sonesta Suites & Casino is a time-share resort catering to upscale yachties. Each of the latter accommodations come with a fully equipped kitchenette and open onto a sand beach, although there are two outdoor free-form pools. The accommodations in both complexes are contemporary in style, with lots of rattan and floral prints. Each unit has a small balcony.

Dining/Entertainment: For a recommendation of the top restaurant, L'Escale, see "Where to Dine," below. The restaurant is connected to the most luxurious casino on the island, and the only one operating 24 hours. Local entertainment is presented in the Crystal Lounge.

Services: Room service (7am to 1am), laundry, baby-sitting.

Facilities: Swimming pool, tennis courts, gym on 40-acre offshore island, with many different water sports, plus a restaurant and bar, along with six beaches and tennis courts. Year-round program of counselor-supervised activities for children 5 to 12.

✪ **Bucuti Beach.** Eagle Beach, Aruba. ☎ **800/223-1108,** 800/528-1234, or 297/8-31100. Fax 297/8-28161. 63 rms. A/C MINIBAR TV TEL. Winter, $200–$260 double; $210–$270 triple. Off-season, $120–$160 double; $130–$170 triple. Tax and 11% service extra. AE, DC, MC, V.

Although affiliated with Best Western, this little hotel has its own personality. It opens onto one of the Caribbean's best beaches. The bedrooms, each fronting the sands, are spacious and well furnished. At this owner-managed resort, you get personal service and a kind of European charm. The accommodations contain two queen-size beds or one king-size bed, plus a sofa suitable for sleeping. The most expensive units have two queen-size beds and an oceanfront balcony or terrace. Amenities in the rooms include safety-deposit boxes, microwave ovens, refrigerators, ceiling fans, designer toiletries, and hair dryers.

Across from the Alhambra Bazaar and Casino, the hotel operates the newly remodeled Pirates' Nest Restaurant, specializing in good steaks and fresh seafood, inside a replica of a 17th-century Dutch galleon. Theme nights at the restaurant range all the way from Indonesia to Italy. The resort enjoys heavy patronage from Europeans and garners a large repeat business, so it must be doing something right. Recent renovations added a fitness center and expanded veranda at the Pirates' Nest.

Moderate

Caribbean Palm Village Resort. Noord 43-E, Aruba. ☎ **297/8-627000.** Fax 297/8-62380. 114 rms, 58 one-bedroom suites, 56 two-bedroom suites. A/C TV TEL. Winter, $160–$170 double; $215–$225 one-bedroom suite; $280–$305 two-bedroom suite. Off-season, $90–$100 double; $115–$125 one-bedroom suite; $155–$165 two-bedroom suite. Service and tax extra. Honeymoon packages available. AE, DC, MC, V.

The place doesn't have a beachfront, and this is cited as one of its major drawbacks, but there are pools for all ages, and public beaches are within a minute's drive. The price, in pricey Aruba, is right too. It's in the village of Noord in the Palm Beach district, half a mile from the beach and 7 miles from the airport. It's the site of Aruba's only five-star Italian restaurant (Valentino's; see "Where to Dine," below). In the Spanish style, the resort offers handsomely decorated and streamlined bedrooms, along with one- and two-bedroom suites in a tropical garden setting. Suites come with full kitchen facilities. All rooms, although air-conditioned, contain ceiling fans, plus queen- or king-size beds, with a pull-out sofa and private safe.

CONDOS & TIME-SHARE PROPERTIES

Time-sharing and condos have become a major vacation investment on Aruba. Even if you're not interested for yourself, you may want to consider renting a unit as a one-time vacationer.

Amsterdam Manor Beach Resort. J. E. Irausquin Blvd. 252 (P.O. Box 1302), Oranjestad, Aruba. ☎ **297/8-71492.** Fax 297/8-71463. 73 units. A/C TV TEL. Winter, $160–$310 unit for 1 or 2. Off-season, $100–$230 unit for 1 or 2. Additional person $20 extra. AE, DC, MC, V.

Opened in 1991, this hotel sports one of the most interesting facades on the island. Inspired by the connected rows of canal-front houses in Amsterdam, it lies amid an arid landscape across the street from Eagle Beach. Owned by a trio of Dutch investors, it has a series of inner courtyards, a vivid sense of colonial Dutch life, a swimming pool fed by a pair of splashing waterfalls, and a simple bar and restaurant. More than in any other hotel on the island, the accommodations draw from 19th-century Dutch models, and contain pinewood furniture, country-rustic colors of dull reds, blues, and greens, and in some cases, high ceilings leading to gable-capped peaks. Units contain fully equipped kitchens, and come as studios and one- or two-bedroom apartments. The accommodations are especially suitable for families, with babysitting, use of washer/dryers, and a children's playground.

La Cabana All Suite Beach Resort & Casino. J. E. Irausquin Blvd. 250 (P.O. Box 4273), Oranjestad, Aruba. ☎ **800/835-7193** in the U.S. and Canada, or 297/8-79000. Fax 297/8-75474. 803 studios and suites. A/C TV TEL. Winter, $215–$245 studio; $265–$310 one-bedroom suite; $465–$550 two-bedroom suite; $715–$855 three-bedroom suite. Off-season, $115–$135 studio; $145–$185 one-bedroom suite; $250–$310 two-bedroom suite; $395–$485 three-bedroom suite. AE, DC, MC, V.

Originally conceived in 1991 as a 441-unit all-suite resort, this establishment was almost doubled in size in 1993 when another 362 grand suites were built on the flatlands in back. Today, La Cabana is the largest and most ambitiously marketed hotel on Aruba (and also the third-largest hotel in the Caribbean). It caters to a clientele who appreciate all the facilities of a private apartment in their hotel accommodation. The centerpiece of the older section is a free-form pool sunk into a landscaped courtyard, with a water slide, a poolside bar, and an outdoor cafe. The four-story, pink-sided accommodations in the newer section are angled around a lavishly landscaped courtyard of their own, in the center of which are two pools with an artificial waterfall.

Regardless of their location, the studios and suites are carefully engineered cocoons of pink or blue, each with richly furnished kitchens and a patio or veranda, and, in all cases, whirlpools, minisafes, and alarm clocks. Ground-floor rooms afford less privacy. Suites can be combined through connecting doors to create accommodations suitable for up to 10 occupants.

Dining/Entertainment: In a separate outbuilding, the hotel maintains its Royal Cabana Casino, the third largest in The Bahamas–Caribbean region. The Tropicana Theater features Las Vegas–style glitter and entertainment. Scattered around the premises are four different bars, snack kiosks, and restaurants, specializing in either Italian cuisine, steaks, or seafood. Different bars cater to cravings for frozen yogurt, chocolates, espresso, or tropical drinks. Buffet-style barbecues or Mexican barbecues are featured during the several-times-a-week theme parties.

Services: The hotel provides an on-site child-care center, the Club Cabana Nana, which supervises and amuses children 5 to 12 for a cost of $80 a week including lunch and a T-shirt; it's open daily except Saturday. There's also an intricately scheduled array of daily activities (beach tennis, aerobics, billiards for kids, etc.).

Facilities: Health club (with squash and racquetball courts), a limited array of spa treatments and a beauty-care center, five tennis courts (illuminated for night play), water-sports facilities and an information desk for all water sports, including scuba, windsurfing, sailing, and snorkeling.

Playa Linda Beach Resort. J. E. Irausquin Blvd. 87, Palm Beach (P.O. Box 1010, Oranjestad), Aruba. ☎ **297/8-61000.** Fax 297/8-63479. 194 studios and one- and two-bedroom suites (maximum, 5 people). A/C TV TEL. Winter, $220 studio for 1 to 4; $330 one-bedroom suite; $650 two-bedroom suite. Off-season, $170 studio for 1 or 2; $220 one-bedroom suite; $420 two-bedroom suite. Rates include continental breakfast. Additional person $30 extra. AE, DC, V.

Designed in an M-shape of receding balconies, this salmon-colored time-share complex sits amid tropical foliage on a desirable stretch of white-sand beachfront. The units offer kitchens and private verandas, and contain foldaway couch beds suitable for children. Amenities and facilities at Playa Linda include a large lagoon-shaped swimming pool, outdoor whirlpool baths, tennis courts, access to an 18-hole professional golf course, and a shopping arcade featuring a beauty parlor, perfumery, and souvenir and gift shop. The Linda Vista Restaurant serves international food. Laundry and baby-sitting are available. The hotel is 6 miles northwest of the airport.

WHERE TO DINE

Sometimes, at least on off-season package deals, visitors on the MAP (breakfast and dinner) are allowed to dine around on an exchange plan with other hotels.

IN ORANJESTAD

Expensive

✪ **Chez Mathilde.** Havenstraat 23. ☎ **297/8-34968.** Reservations recommended. Main courses $18.50–$32. AE, DC, MC, V. Mon–Sat 11:30am–2:30pm and 6–11pm, Sun 6–11pm. FRENCH.

Oranjestad's *restaurant français* is expensive, but most satisfied customers agree that it's worth the price, especially those diners who order the chef's bouillabaisse, made with more than a dozen different sea creatures. Other well-recommended dishes include rack of lamb chops with fine French herbs, a juicy grilled veal chop topped with a slice of goose-liver fillet, and fillet of red snapper topped with a blend of onions, tomatoes, green peppers, fresh herbs, and a dash of rum baked in parchment paper. Not only do you get distinguished food and service, including a haute-cuisine classic French repertoire, but you enjoy your repast in an elegant setting. The structure housing the restaurant was built in the 1800s, and it has been preserved more or less as it was originally. The intimate dining rooms contain beautifully set tables and a restrained but romantic decor. Enjoy an apéritif while you peruse the comparatively large wine list. Live piano music enhances the total experience. The restaurant is near the Sonesta hotel complex, a five-minute drive north of the airport.

✪ **L'Escale.** In the Aruba Sonesta Resort & Casino at Seaport Village, L. G. Smith Blvd. 82. ☎ **297/8-36000.** Reservations recommended in winter. Main courses $22–$32.50. AE, DC, DISC, MC, V. Daily 6:30–11pm; Sun 10am–2pm. FRENCH/INTERNATIONAL.

Although it offers direct access to Oranjestad's bustling Crystal Casino, this restaurant is calm, elegant, and peaceful, thanks to a raised bar area that separates it from the action nearby. Designed in a French Empire style, it offers panoramic views of the harbor front, formal service, and well-prepared cuisine. There are some savvy locals who prefer this to Chez Mathilde (see above) and, in fact, claim that Escale is the best on Aruba. We think it's a toss-up between the two. The meals, in spite of a reliance on imported foodstuffs, are perfectly cooked. The ingredients are of high quality and are skillfully handled by the chefs.

Diners enjoy the sounds of a Hungarian string orchestra. Menu choices might include Singapore shrimp with a spicy curry sauce, lobster bisque, Thai salad on a nest of egg noodles, or a variety of Aruban seafood. One specialty that's interesting is veal topped with crabmeat and served with green asparagus and a béarnaise sauce.

Gasparito. Gasparito 3. ☎ **297/8-67144.** Reservations recommended. Main courses $17.50–$37.50. AE, DISC, MC, V. Mon–Sat 5–11pm. ARUBAN/INTERNATIONAL.

This bright, upbeat restaurant is set in a traditional Aruban-style house with yellow walls adorned with local art. The atmosphere is lively and the food varied. The chef brings in top-quality ingredients that he fashions into dishes with zest, flair, and consummate skill. Diners can enjoy such dishes as baked chicken stuffed with a peach, filet mignon served with either sautéed mushroom or black-pepper sauce, or a variety of keshi yena (Dutch cheese stuffed with a choice of beef, chicken, or seafood). The menu also features an array of fresh seafood, including lobster served with a garlic-butter sauce or sautéed with onions, green peppers, tomatoes, and a multitude of spices. If there's any room left at the end of the meal, you can finish with a bowl of ice cream served with bananas and cinnamon or a warm slice of homemade pound cake.

Moderate

La Dolce Vita. Palm Beach 39. ☎ **297/8-65241.** Reservations recommended, especially in winter. Main courses $11.95–$28.95. AE, DISC, MC, V. Thurs–Tues 6–11pm. ITALIAN.

Since 1980 La Dolce Vita has been among the most acclaimed Italian restaurants on Aruba. It wasn't long before it was discovered by the food and wine critics of such prestigious Stateside magazines as *Gourmet.* In an arid neighborhood inland from the sea, it's a rustic-style restaurant ringed with a cactus garden. Menu items are creatively Italian, and include most of the usual favorites as well as a scattering of unusual dishes. A meal might include slices of veal served Parmesan style, with marsala sauce, cordon bleu style, la Florio (with artichokes), or la Bartolucci (with ricotta, spinach, and mozzarella). Snapper can be prepared in three ways: simmered with clams and mussels, broiled with lemon or wine, or stuffed with pulverized shrimp. Also available is a stewpot of fish, and linguine with either red or white clam sauce. Finish with an espresso, a zabaglione, or perhaps some Italian ice cream.

The Waterfront Crabhouse. Seaport Market, L. G. Smith Blvd. ☎ **297/8-36767.** Reservations recommended. Main courses $13.95–$24.95; continental breakfast $5.95; lunch from $12. AE, MC, V. Daily 8–11am, noon–4:30pm, and 5:30–10:30pm. SEAFOOD/STEAK.

Set at the end of a shopping mall in downtown Oranjestad, this restaurant overlooks a manicured lawn. Amid painted murals and rattan furniture, and tables placed both indoors and on a garden terrace, you can enjoy well-prepared seafood. Menu items include such appetizers as stuffed clams and fried squid with a marinara sauce, and linguine with white or red clam sauce, which can be ordered on the side or as a main course. The chef lists "crabs, crabs, crabs" as his specialty, including garlic crabs, Alaskan crab legs, and (in season) soft-shell crabs. Other items include stuffed Maine lobster and some of the best steaks on island. Blackened Cajun shrimp is cooked over an open fire, as are a wide range of other fish dishes, including yellowfin tuna and swordfish. Ecologists will appreciate the fact that all fish served are caught with a hook-and-line, never with drift nets.

Inexpensive

✪ **Boonoonoonoos.** Wilhelminastraat 18. ☎ **297/8-31888.** Reservations recommended for dinner in winter. Main courses $15.75–$33.75. AE, DC, MC, V. Mon–Sat 11:30am–10:30pm, Sun 4–10:30pm. CARIBBEAN/INTERNATIONAL.

Named after the legendary beach parties of Jamaica (Boonoonoonoos), this restaurant in an old-fashioned Aruban house on the capital's main shopping street celebrates the widely divergent traditions of Caribbean cuisine and is a great value for your money. It offers a confectionery decor of blues, greens, and pinks, a bar outfitted with rows of hard-bottomed benches, and a crew of waiters in carnival-colored shirts. Even if you're not visiting the rest of the Caribbean, you can go on a culinary tour by wandering across the menu. Try, for example, an appetizer known as ajaka, an Aruban dish seasoned with chicken and wrapped in banana leaves. Soups also make good appetizers, including a local callaloo soup and a homemade fish soup. For a main dish, the most popular is actually Aruban: keshi yena (Aruban chicken casserole). You can also order Jamaican jerk ribs, based on a recipe dating back three centuries. You might also try a Bajan pepperpot or Trinidad-style curried chicken. A small section of the menu is devoted to French cuisine, including filet mignon and Dover sole meunière. This place continues to draw mixed reactions from readers, everything from raves to attacks. Slow service seems to be one of the major complaints.

NEAR PALM BEACH

Moderate

Chalet Suisse. J. E. Irausquin Blvd. 246. ☎ **297/8-75054.** Reservations recommended. Main courses $14–$25. AE, DC, MC, V. Mon–Sat 6–10:30pm. SWISS/INTERNATIONAL.

Designed like an alpine chalet, and set beside the highway close to La Cabana Hotel, this restaurant is the closest replica of an old-fashioned Swiss dining room in the entire Caribbean. In deliberate contrast to the arid scrublands that surround it, the restaurant is an air-conditioned refuge of thick plaster walls, pinewood panels, and a sense of *gemütlichkeit* (well-being). Menu items include a lobster bisque, Dutch pea soup, beef Stroganoff, a pasta of the day, Wiener schnitzel, roast duckling with orange sauce, red snapper with Creole sauce, and an array of high-calorie desserts. The food is what you'd find in a quality roadside inn along a ski trail in Switzerland. It isn't bad, although the cuisine strikes many diners as heavy for the tropics.

De Olde Molen (The Old Mill). L. G. Smith Blvd. 330, Palm Beach. ☎ **297/8-62060.** Reservations recommended. Main courses $15–$30. AE, DC, MC, V. Mon–Sat 6–11pm. INTERNATIONAL.

This landmark structure is just across the street from the Wyndham and within walking distance of a number of other Palm Beach hotels. The windmill housing the restaurant was built in Holland in 1804, but it was torn down, shipped to Aruba, and reconstructed piece by piece, a gift of the queen of the Netherlands. Since 1960, it has been a tourist-focused destination for dinner. An international and regional cuisine is served, including thick Dutch split-pea soup, chateaubriand for two people, veal cordon bleu, shrimp Provençal, and red snapper arubiano (with a Creole sauce). You might want to finish your meal with an Irish coffee. Although the windmill setting may seem gimmicky to some, the cuisine is basically noteworthy, although we've found some dishes too heavy for a hot night. Don't come here expecting something adventurous or something different from your visit last year. The tried and the true reign supreme.

✪ **Mi Cushina.** In the La Quinta Beach Resort, J. E. Irausquin Blvd. 228. ☎ **297/8-72222.** Reservations recommended. Main courses $12–$30. AE, DC, MC, V. Tues-Sun noon–2pm and 6–10pm. ARUBAN/INTERNATIONAL.

For years in another and far more remote location, this little restaurant was known for serving some of the most authentic Aruban dishes on the island, maintaining a local tradition when nearly all other places had gone international. The world used to come to its door, but it was difficult to reach, especially at night. Mi Cushina decided to move right into the heart of the "hotel belt," to make itself more accessible. The decor isn't as quaint as it used to be, and the prices are a lot higher (still an excellent value), but the old recipes were brought along to the new location. Yes, you'll still find conch stir-fry, stewed goat, and slices of fish cooked Aruban style on the new menu, but it also caters to a more international palate with its offering of such dishes as lobster thermidor and filet mignon. You can find better versions of those international dishes at other restaurants nearby, but here you can order some of the island's best funchi (cornmeal), a fried concoction that accompanies many dishes, along with pan bati (a pancake), and other local fare.

The Old Cunucu House. Palm Beach 150. ☎ **297/8-61666.** Reservations recommended. Main courses $15.95–$31.95. AE, DC, DISC, MC, V. Mon–Sat 6–10pm. ARUBAN/INTERNATIONAL.

When it was originally constructed as a private house in the 1920s, this was the only building in the neighborhood. Today it retains its original decor of very thick plaster-coated walls, ultra-simple furniture, and tile floors. Many visitors appreciate a before-dinner drink under a shed-style roof in front, where chairs and tables overlook a well-kept garden studded with desert plants. The restaurant maintains a warm, traditional feeling, and focuses on local and international recipes, including fish soup, fried squid, coconut fried shrimp, and broiled swordfish. Several dishes are served with funchi (cornmeal) and pan bati (a local pancake). The chef is skilled, knowing how to embroider a traditional repertoire. He uses first-class ingredients. Calypso bands provide entertainment every Saturday night.

At or Near Noord

Expensive

✪ **Valentino's.** In the Caribbean Palm Village, Noord 43-E. ☎ **297/8-62700.** Reservations recommended. Main courses $17.95–$29.95. AE, DC, MC, V. Mon–Sat 6–11pm. ITALIAN.

This is the most elegant Italian restaurant on Aruba. Nestled in the central courtyard of an upscale condominium complex, it offers the option of an apéritif near the entrance, then invites guests to climb a flight of stairs to reach the peak-ceilinged dining room. Here, amid a color scheme of soft pinks and grays, you'll have a glassed-in view of a well-designed kitchen, views over the palms and pools of the condominium complex, and the attentions of the youthful but well-trained staff, who hail from around the world. The prices are a bit high, but the tastes usually excite the palate so you forgive them. It's a cozy, comfortable place. Menu items might include chicken Parmesan, veal scaloppini, tenderloin peppersteak, rack of lamb in rosemary sauce with mint jelly, and a selection of fish dishes.

Moderate

The Buccaneer. Gasparito 11-C. ☎ **297/8-66172.** Reservations not accepted. Main courses $12–$23. AE, MC, V. Mon–Sat 5:30–10pm. SEAFOOD/INTERNATIONAL.

In a rustic-looking building near the hamlet of Noord, close to many of the island's biggest high-rise hotels, this is one of the most reasonably priced and popular seafood restaurants on Aruba. Inside, you'll find a decor of varnished pine, nautical accessories, and bubbling aquariums. Menu items include crabmeat cocktail, escargots, shrimp in Pernod sauce, lobster thermidor, and a land-and-sea platter containing portions of fish, shrimp, and tenderloin. A simple dessert menu contains peach

Melba. The food is hearty and truly delicious. A spacious bar area is a good place to linger over drinks.

La Paloma. Noord 39. ☎ **297/8-74611.** Reservations recommended. Main courses $10–$26. AE, MC, V. Wed–Mon 6–11pm. ITALIAN/INTERNATIONAL.

Established in 1983, this was one of the first restaurants along a road that later sprouted with less-desirable competitors. A 10-minute drive north of Oranjestad, it contains a semicircular bar area and a crowded but convivial dining area filled with bamboo and rattan furniture. The place is often packed with both visitors and locals seeking a fun-loving, casual atmosphere. The food selections never really test the ability of the chefs, who've made each dish thousands of times, but they're good, decent, and uncomplicated. Choices include linguine scampi marinara, lobster Provençal, red snapper en papillotte, a seafood platter, a 12-ounce filet mignon, and a 14-ounce strip loin steak.

Papiamento. Washington 61. ☎ **297/8-64544.** Reservations recommended, especially on weekends. Main courses $20–$35. AE, MC, V. Tues–Sun 6:30–10:30pm. CONTINENTAL.

One of the most popular independent restaurants on Aruba occupies a stone farmhouse in a cozy, intimate, romantic setting. Transformed into a stylish hideaway, and named after Aruba's distinctive patois, it boasts a collection of modern paintings, and such old-world touches as massive brass chandeliers. Fresh meat or seafood is served raw on sizzling marble slabs so that your dinner is cooked in front of you the way you like. Meals might include chicken Parmesan, snapper Provençal, lamb chops, snapper, filet mignon, surf and turf, lobster, sirloin, and a combination platter of shrimp and scallops. All this uncomplicated bistro fare sits well with most diners. After dining here many times, we've had only one disappointing meal. Perhaps it was the chef's night off.

At Tierra del Sol

Expensive

Ventanas del Mar. In the Clubhouse of the Tierra del Sol Golf Course, Malmokweg. ☎ **297/8-67800.** Reservations recommended for dinner. Lunch sandwiches, salads, and platters $9–$32; dinner main courses $17–$32. AE, MC, V. Daily 6am–10am, 11am–3pm, and 6–10:30pm. INTERNATIONAL.

Until 1995, the land this high-ceilinged restaurant now occupies was nothing more than a sunblasted, arid sand dune dotted with rocks and scrub. Since its transformation into an emerald-colored oasis favored by golfers, the popularity of its showcase restaurant has soared. You'll dine near windows whose views sweep out over the coastline and the sea, within a comfortably contemporary decor that's especially soothing considering the sometimes blistering heat outside. Lunches are less formal than dinners and feature sandwiches and salads in addition to the steaks and grilled fish featured at dinner. Evening meals focus instead on heaping, two-fisted platters of filet mignon with lobster, panfried oysters, prime rib, veal chops, grilled garlic shrimp, and sautéed grouper. There's a bar with golfing memorabilia on the premises that remains open throughout the afternoon.

East of Oranjestad

Moderate

Brisas del Mar. Savaneta 222A. ☎ **297/8-47718.** Reservations required. Main courses $11–$32. AE, MC, V. Mon 6:30–9:30pm, Tues-Sun noon–2:30pm and 6:30–9:30pm. SEAFOOD.

A 15-minute drive east of Oranjestad, near the police station, Brisas del Mar is like a place you might encounter in some outpost in Australia. Here, in very simple surroundings right at water's edge, Lucia Rasmijn opened this little hut with an air-conditioned bar in front of which the locals gather to drink the day away. The place is often jammed on weekends with many of the same local people, who come here to drink and dance. In back the tables are open to the sea breezes, and nearby you can see the catch of the day, perhaps wahoo, being sliced up and sold to local buyers. Specialties include mixed seafood platter, baby shark, and broiled lobster; you can order meat and poultry dishes as well, including tenderloin steak and broiled chicken. Don't expect subtlety of cuisine. This is the type of food Arubans enjoyed back in the 1950s, and nothing much has changed since then.

Charlie's Bar and Restaurant. B. v/d Veen Zeppenveldstraat 56 (Main St.), San Nicolas. ☎ **297/8-45086.** Daily soup $4.75; main courses $15–$18. No credit cards. Mon–Sat noon–9:30pm. (Bar, Mon–Sat noon–10pm.) SEAFOOD/INTERNATIONAL.

Charlie's is the best reason to visit San Nicolas. The bar dates from 1941 and is the most overly decorated in the West Indies, sporting an array of memorabilia and local souvenirs. Where roustabouts and roughnecks once brawled, you'll now find tables filled with contented tourists admiring thousands of pennants, banners, and trophies dangling from the high ceiling. Two-fisted drinks are still served, but the menu has improved since the good old days, when San Nicolas was one of the toughest towns in the Caribbean. You can now enjoy freshly made soup, grilled scampi, Creole-style squid, and churrasco. Sirloin steak and red snapper are usually featured. Even so, most patrons come here for the good times and the brew, not necessarily for the food, although it isn't bad. Charlie's is a 25-minute drive east of Oranjestad.

BEACHES, WATER SPORTS & OUTDOOR PURSUITS

BEACHES The western and southern shore, called the **Turquoise Coast,** attracts sun seekers to Aruba. **Palm Beach** and **Eagle Beach** (the latter closer to Oranjestad) are the best beaches. No hotel along the strip owns the beaches, all of which are open to the public (if you use any of the hotel's facilities, however, you'll be charged, of course). You can also spread your towel on **Manchebo Beach** or **Druif Bay Beach**—in fact, anywhere along 7 miles of uninterrupted sugar-white sands. In total contrast to the leeward side, the north or windward shore is rugged and wild.

CRUISES Visitors interested in combining a boat ride with a few hours of snorkeling should contact **De Palm Tours,** which has offices in eight of the island's hotels and its main office at L. G. Smith Blvd. 142, in Oranjestad (☎ **297/8-24400**). De Palm Tours offers a one-hour glass-bottom-boat cruise that visits two coral reefs and the German shipwreck *Antilla* daily except Sunday and Thursday. The cost is $17.50 per person.

DEEP-SEA FISHING In the deep waters off the coast of Aruba you can test your skill and wits against the big ones—wahoo, marlin, tuna, bonito, and sailfish. **De Palm Tours,** L. G. Smith Blvd. 142, in Oranjestad (☎ **297/8-24400**), takes out a maximum of six people (four of whom can fish at the same time) on one of its four boats, which range in length from 29 to 38 feet. Half-day tours, with all equipment included, begin at $250 for two people and $270 for six. The prices are doubled for full-day trips. Boats leave from the docks in Oranjestad. De Palm maintains 11 branches, most of which are in Aruba's major hotels.

GOLF Visitors can play at the Aruba Golf Club, Golfweg 82 (☎ **297/8-42006**), near San Nicolas on the southeastern end of the island. Although it has only 10 greens, they are played from different tees to simulate 18-hole play. Twenty-five different sand traps add an extra challenge. Greens fees are $10 for 18 holes and $7.50 for 9 holes. The course is open daily from 7:30am to 5pm, although anyone wishing to play 18 holes must begin the rounds before 1:30pm. Golf carts and clubs can be rented on-site in the pro shop. There's an air-conditioned restaurant and changing rooms with showers on the premises.

Aruba's long-awaited **Tierra del Sol Golf Course** (☎ **297/8-67800**) opened in 1995. Designed by Robert Trent Jones Jr., the course is on the northwest coast, near the California Lighthouse. The 18-hole, par-71, 6,811-yard golf course was designed to combine the beauty of the island's indigenous flora, such as the swaying divi-divi tree, with lush greens. Facilities include a restaurant and lounge in the clubhouse and two swimming pools. The course is managed by Golf Hyatt. In winter, greens fees are $120, including golf cart, or $72 after 3pm. Off-season, greens fees are $85, or $57 after 3pm. The course is open daily from 6am to 7pm.

TENNIS Most of the island's beachfront hotels have tennis courts, often swept by trade winds, and some have top pros on hand to give instruction. Many of the courts can also be lit for night games. We don't advise playing in Aruba's hot noonday sun. Some hotels restrict their courts to use by guests.

The best tennis is at the **Aruba Racket Club** (☎ **297/8-60215**), the island's first world-class tennis facility, with eight courts, an exhibition center court, a pro shop, a swimming pool, an aerobics center, a fitness center, and a shopping center. The club is open Monday through Saturday from 8am to 11pm and on Sunday from 8am to 6pm. Rates are $10 per hour per court, with lessons going for $35 per hour. The location is part of the Tierra del Sol complex on Aruba's northwest coast, near the California Lighthouse.

WATER SPORTS You can snorkel in rather shallow waters, and scuba divers find stunning marine life with endless varieties of coral as well as tropical fish in infinite hues; at some points visibility is up to 90 feet. The goal of most divers is the German freighter *Antilla,* which was scuttled in the early years of World War II off the northwestern tip of Aruba, not too far from Palm Beach.

Red Sails Sports, Palm Beach (☎ **297/8-61603**), is the best water-sports center on the island. The center has an extensive variety of activities, including sailing, windsurfing, waterskiing, and scuba diving. Red Sail dive packages include shipwreck dives as well as exploration of marine reefs all in one day. Guests are first given a poolside resort course in which Red Sail's certified instructors teach procedures that ensure safety during dives. For those who wish to become certified, full PADI certification can be achieved in as little as four days. One-tank dives cost $35 and up.

Divi Winds Center, J. E. Irausquin Blvd. 41 (☎ **297/8-23300,** ext. 623), near the Tamarind Aruba Beach Resort, is the windsurfing headquarters of the island. Equipment is made by Fanatic and is rented for $18 per hour or $35 per half day and $50 all day. The resort is on the quiet (Caribbean) side of the island and doesn't face the fierce Atlantic waves. Sunfish lessons can also be arranged, and snorkeling gear can be rented.

SEEING THE SIGHTS

The capital of Aruba, **Oranjestad,** attracts shoppers rather than sightseers. The bustling city has a very Caribbean flavor, and it's part Spanish, part Dutch in architecture. Cutting in from the airport, the main thoroughfare, Lloyd G. Smith Boulevard, goes along the waterfront and on to Palm Beach, changing its name along the way to J. E. Irausquin Boulevard. But most visitors cross it heading for Caya G. F. Betico Croes and the best duty-free shopping.

After a shopping trip, you might return to the harbor where fishing boats and schooners, many from Venezuela, are moored. Nearly all newcomers to Aruba like to take a picture of the **Schooner Harbor.** Not only does it have colorful boats docked along the quay, but boat people display their wares in open stalls. The local patois predominates. A little farther along, at the **fish market,** fresh fish are sold directly from the boats. Also on the sea side of Oranjestad, **Wilhelmina Park** was named after Queen Wilhelmina of the Netherlands. A tropical garden has been planted along the water, and there's a sculpture of the Queen Mother.

Aside from shopping, the major attractions of Aruba are ✪ **Eagle Beach** and ✪ **Palm Beach,** among the finest in the Caribbean. Most of Aruba's high-rise hotels are stretched in a Las Vegas–strip style along these pure-white sand stretches on the leeward coast.

Out in the Country

If you can lift yourselves from the sands for one afternoon, you might like to drive into the ***cunucu,*** which in Papiamento means "the countryside." Here Arubans live in very modest but colorful pastel-washed houses decorated with tropical plants, which require expensive desalinated water to grow. Of course, all visitors venturing into the center of Aruba want to see the strangely shaped divi-divi tree with its trade-wind-blown coiffure.

Aruba is studded with rocks, and the most impressive ones are those found at **Ayo** and **Casibari,** northeast of Hooiberg. These stacks of diorite boulders are the size of buildings. The rocks, weighing several thousand tons, are a puzzle to geologists. Ancient Amerindian drawings appear on the rocks at Ayo. At Casibari, you can climb the boulder-strewn terrain to the top for a panoramic view of the island or look at rocks nature has carved into seats or likenesses of prehistoric birds and animals. You might want to pay special attention to the unusual species of lizards and cacti on the island. Casibari is open daily from 9am to 5pm. No admission is charged. There's a lodge at Casibari where you can buy souvenirs, snacks, soft drinks, and beer.

Guides can also point out drawings on the walls and ceiling of the **Caves of Canashito,** south of Hooiberg. While here, you may get to see the giant green parakeets.

Hooiberg is affectionately known as "The Haystack." It's Aruba's most outstanding landmark, and anybody with the stamina can take the steps all the way to the top of this 541-foot-high hill. One Aruban jogs up there every morning. From its location in the center of the island you can see Venezuela on a clear day.

On the jagged, windswept northern coast, the **Natural Bridge** has been carved out of the coral rock by the relentless surf. In a little cafe overlooking the coast you can order snacks. Here you'll also find a souvenir shop with a large selection of trinkets, T-shirts, and wall hangings, all for reasonable prices.

You turn inland for the short trip to **Pirate's Castle** at Bushiribana, which stands on a cliff on the island's windward coast. This is actually a deserted gold mill from the island's now-defunct industry. Another gold mill is in the old ghost town on the west coast, Balashi.

You can continue to the village of Noord, known for its **St. Anne's Church,** which has a hand-carved, 17th-century Dutch altar.

East to San Nicolas

Driving along the highway toward the island's southernmost section, more or less paralleling the south coast of Aruba, you may want to stop at the **Spaans Lagoen** (Spanish Lagoon), where legend says pirates used to hide out as they waited to plunder rich cargo ships in the Caribbean. Today this is an ideal place for snorkeling, and you can picnic at tables under the mangrove trees.

On to the east, you'll pass an area called **Savaneta,** where some of the most ancient traces of human habitation have been unearthed. You'll see along here the first oil tanks marking the position of the Lago Oil & Transport Company, the Exxon subsidiary around which the town of San Nicolas developed. A "company town" until the refinery was closed in 1985, San Nicolas, 12 miles from Oranjestad, is called the Aruba Sunrise Side, and tourism has become its main economic engine. In the area are caves with Arawak artwork on the walls and a modern innovation, a PGA-approved golf course with sand "greens" and cactus traps.

Boca Grandi, on the windward side of the island, is a favorite windsurfing location; if you prefer quieter waters, you'll find them at **Baby Beach and Rodgers Beach,** on Aruba's leeward side. Overlooking the latter two beaches is **Seroe Colorado (Colorado Point),** from which it's possible to see the coastline of Venezuela as well as the pounding surf on the windward side. You can climb down the cliffs, and perhaps spot an iguana here and there; protected by law, the once-endangered saurians now proliferate in peace.

Other sights in the San Nicolas area are the **Guadarikiri Cave** and **Fontein Cave,** where you can see the wall drawings, plus the **Huliba** and **Tunnel of Love caves,** with guides and refreshment stands. Guadarikiri Cave is a haven for wild parrots.

An Underwater Journey

One of the island's most diverting pastimes involves an underwater journey on one of the world's few passenger submarines, operated by ✪ **Atlantis Submarines,** Seaport Village Marina (opposite the Sonesta), Oranjestad (☎ **800/253-0493** or 297/8-36090). The underwater ride offers one of the Caribbean's best opportunities for nondivers to witness firsthand the life of a coral reef, with fewer obstacles and dangers than posed by a scuba expedition. Carrying 46 passengers to a depth of up to 150 feet, the ride provides all the thrills of an underwater dive without ever getting wet. In 1995 an old Danish fishing vessel was sunk to create a fascinating view for divers and submariners. The submarine organizes departures from the Oranjestad harbor front every hour on the hour, Tuesday to Sunday from 10am to 2pm (there are no departures on Monday). Each tour includes a 25-minute transit by catamaran to Barcadera Reef, 2 miles southeast of Aruba, a site chosen for the huge variety of its underwater flora and fauna. At the reef, participants are transferred to the submarine for a one-hour underwater lecture and tour.

Allow two hours for the complete experience. The cost is $69 for adults and $29 for children 4 to 14 (no children under 4 are admitted). Advance reservations are essential, either through the concierge of one of the island's hotels or via the telephone number listed above. In either event, a staff member will ask for a credit- or charge-card number (and give you a confirmation number) to hold the booking for you. To prove your bravery, *Atlantis's* passengers will receive an official dive certificate.

A Sightseeing Tour

De Palm Tours, L. G. Smith Blvd. 142, Oranjestad (☎ **297/8-24400**), has desks at all the major hotels. Its latest attraction is De Palm Island, a complete entertainment facility built on a private island just five minutes by ferry from Aruba. Their tours include a wide range of activities, featuring snorkeling, beach barbecues, and folklore shows. Its office is open Monday to Saturday from 8:30am to noon and 1 to 5pm. The cost of their organized jaunts range upward from $17.50, depending on what activity you select.

SHOPPING

Aruba manages to compress six continents into the ½-mile-long Caya G. F. Betico Croes, the main shopping street of Oranjestad. While this is not technically a free port, the duty is so low (3.3%) that articles are attractively priced—and Aruba has no sales tax. You'll find the usual array of Swiss watches; German and Japanese cameras; jewelry; liquor; English bone china and porcelain; Dutch, Swedish, and Danish silver and pewter; French perfume; British woolens; Indonesian specialties; and Madeira embroidery. Delft blue pottery is an especially good buy. More good buys include Dutch cheese (Edam and Gouda), as well as Dutch chocolate and English cigarettes in the airport departure area.

Philatelists interested in the wealth of colorful and artistic stamps issued in honor of the changed governmental status of Aruba can purchase a complete assortment, as well as other special issues, at the post office in Oranjestad.

Shopping Centers

Alhambra Moonlight Shopping Center. Adjacent to the Alhambra Casino, L. G. Smith Blvd. ☎ **297/8-35000.**

This is a blend of international shops, outdoor marketplaces, and cafes and restaurants. Merchandise ranges from fine jewelry, chocolates, and perfume to imported craft items, leather goods, clothing, and lingerie.

Seaport Village. L. G. Smith Blvd. 92. ☎ **297/8-36000.**

Comprising Seaport Village Mall, the Crystal Casino, and the Aruba Sonesta Resort & Casino, this complex is landmarked by the Crystal Tower and is located across from the harbor at the "entrance" of the center of downtown, only a five-minute drive from the cruise terminal. Here are more than 130 stores and boutiques, carrying a wide selection of merchandise to meet everyone's taste and budget—fashions, gifts, souvenirs, sporting goods, liquors, and fragrances. Top brands are featured, such as Gucci, Escada, Polo/Ralph Lauren, Givenchy, Paloma Picasso, Lancôme, Baccarat, Lalique, Fendi, Movado, Valentino, Christofle, and many others known internationally.

One of the shops, the **Boulevard Book & Drugstore** (☎ **297/8-27358**), has a complete range of goods from the latest paperback books to cosmetics, candies, gifts, toys, high-quality T-shirts and sweatshirts, swimwear, sportswear, and souvenirs. You can also buy stamps, road maps, current magazines, and newspapers.

Specialty Shops

Artistic Boutique. Caya G. F. Betico Croes 25. ☎ **297/8-23142.**

This boutique carries 14- and 18-karat fine-gold jewelry set with precious or semi-precious stones, as well as porcelain figurines from well-known companies. It also sells Oriental antiques, handmade dhurries and rugs, and a wide variety of Madeira fine linens and organdy tablecloths. Its collections of Indonesian imports is the best on the island. If you want something made locally, ask to see the selection of Aruban hand-embroidered linens. You'll find none more exquisitely crafted on the entire island.

Aruba Trading Company. Caya G. F. Betico Croes 14. ☎ **297/8-22602.**

Come here for Aruba's finest selection of perfume. The company also offers a complete range of other items: cosmetics, shoes, clothing for men and women, liquor, and cigarettes (the last two purchases can be delivered to your plane). We'll let you in on a secret: Brand-name perfumes are often discounted here, but you'll have to search the store carefully to find the good buys.

D'Orsy's. In the Oranjestad Strada Complex II. ☎ **297/8-31233.**

At this parfumerie, Ralph Lauren's Safari fragrance is the best-selling item. But many other fragrances are also sold, including Lancôme, Cartier, Tiffany, and Estée Lauder.

Although the selection is fairly standard, the merchandise is first rate, and the prices are somewhat less than on other islands such as Curaçao.

Gandelman Jewelers. Main St. 5A. ☎ **297/8-32121.**

Gandelman offers an extensive collection of fine gold jewelry and famous-name timepieces at duty-free prices. Go here if you're in the market for a Swatch watch. Prices are reasonable, and they're the real thing, not those imitations being hawked along the waterfront. For collectors of gold bracelets, this is also the venue. There are branch stores in the Americana Aruba Hotel, Airport Departure Hall, Wyndham Hotel, Royal Plaza, and Hyatt Regency Aruba.

Jewelers Corner. In the Seaport Village Mall. ☎ **297/8-36045.**

This popular international jewelry store is found at Sonesta's Seaport Village Mall near the center of Oranjestad. It carries a complete line of rings, earrings, and bracelets.

Les Accessories. In the Seaport Village Mall. ☎ **297/8-37965.**

Agatha Brown, an award-winning American designer, operates this shop, featuring her exclusive designs. Her high-fashion designer sportswear collection is produced in Chile, reflecting her distinctive taste and style. She also offers assorted designer collections of swimwear, sportswear, and evening wear. The men's department features Oscar de la Renta and Hubert ties of Italy.

Little Switzerland Jewelers. Caya G. F. Betico Croes 47. ☎ **297/8-21192.**

Famous for its duty-free 14- and 18-karat-gold jewelry and watches, Little Switzerland also carries a big variety of famous-name Swiss watches. Over the years we've gotten some very good buys here in their Omega and Rado watches, which are usually discounted handsomely from Stateside prices. Consider this a venue for fine tableware, Baccarat crystal, Lladró figurines, and Swarovski silver as well. This Curaçao-based store, with branches throughout the Caribbean, stands for dependability. It's not one of the fly-by-night operations peddling jewelry on Aruba. There are branches at most of the large hotels on Aruba.

New Amsterdam Store. Caya G. F. Betico Croes 50. ☎ **297/8-21152.**

Aruba's leading department store is best for linens, with its selection of napkins, place mats, and embroidered tablecloths from as far as China. It has an extensive line of other merchandise as well, from Delft blue pottery to beachwear and boutique items, along with assorted gift items, porcelain figures by Hummel, European and American women's wear, and leather bags and shoes.

Penha. Caya G. F. Betico Croes 11–13. ☎ **297/8-24161.**

Penha offers one of the largest selections of top-name perfumes and cosmetics on the island. Long a household name on Aruba, it's one of the most dependable stores around, right up there with Gandelman and Little Switzerland in the sense that it stands by the merchandise it sells. Prices are usually lower than in the States. Of course, you must know your hometown prices before you'll spot what's a bargain here and what's not.

ARUBA AFTER DARK

THE CLUB & BAR SCENE

Nongamblers or those who grow tired of the casinos can patronize hotels' cocktail lounges and supper clubs. You don't have to be a guest of a hotel to see the shows, but you should make a reservation. Tables at the big shows, especially in season, are likely to be booked early in the day. Usually you can go to one of the major hotel supper clubs and just order drinks.

The Alhambra. L. G. Smith Blvd. 47. ☎ **297/8-35000.**

Like a neon-swathed moghul's palace, this complex of buildings and courtyards designed like an 18th-century Dutch village contains about a dozen shops selling souvenirs, leather goods, jewelry, and beachwear. From the outside the complex looks Moorish, with serpentine mahogany columns, arches, and domes; the desert setting of Aruba seems appropriate. On the premises you'll find one of the busiest casinos on Aruba (open from 10am till very late at night).

CASINOS

The casinos of the big hotels along Palm Beach are the liveliest nighttime destinations, and they stay open as long as business demands, often into the wee hours. In plush gaming parlors, guests try their luck at roulette, craps, blackjack, and of course, the one-armed bandits. The **Americana Aruba Beach Resort** (☎ **297/8-24500**) opens daily at noon for slots, blackjack, and roulette, and at 8pm for all games. The **Holiday Inn Aruba Beach Resort** (☎ **297/8-67777**) wins the prize for all-around action. Its casino doors are open from 9am to 4am. The **Aruba Palm Beach Resort & Casino** (☎ **297/8-63900**) opens its slots at 9am and its other games at 1pm; it stays open until 2am.

The **Casino Masquerade,** at the Radisson Aruba Caribbean Resort & Casino, J. E. Irausquin Blvd. 81, Palm Beach (☎ **297/8-66555**), is one of the newest casinos on Aruba. In the center of the high-rise hotel area, it sits on the lower-level lobby of the hotel and is open from 10am to 4am daily. It offers blackjack, single deck, roulette, Caribbean stud, craps, and "Let It Ride."

One of the island's best casinos is the **Crystal Casino** at the Aruba Sonesta Resort & Casino at Seaport Village (☎ **297/8-36000**), open daily from 8am to 4am. The 14,000-square-foot casino offers 11 blackjack tables, 270 slot machines, 4 roulette tables, 3 Caribbean stud-poker tables, 2 craps tables, 1 minibaccarat table, and 3 baccarat tables. The casino evokes European casinos with its luxurious furnishings, ornate moldings, marble, and crystal chandeliers.

Visitors have a tendency to flock to the newest casinos on the island, and these include those at the **Wyndham Hotel and Resort** (☎ **297/8-64466**) and at the **Hyatt Regency Aruba** (☎ **297/8-61234**). But outdrawing them all is the **Royal Cabana Casino,** at the previously recommended La Cabana All Suite Beach Resort & Casino (☎ **297/8-79000**). It's known for its multitheme three-in-one restaurant, but mainly for its showcase cabaret theater and nightclub, which features everything from Las Vegas–style revues to female impersonators to comedy series on the weekend. You should call to find out what's happening here at the time of your visit and to reserve a table if the action interests you. The largest casino on Aruba, it offers 33 tables and games, plus 320 slot machines.

2 Bonaire

Untrampled by hordes of tourists, unspoiled Bonaire is only gently touched by development. Although it boasts attractions ranging from bird watching to doing nothing, Bonaire is a scuba diver's delight. It also offers some of the Caribbean's best snorkeling. This sleepy island is devoid of the glitzy diversions of Aruba. Instead, powdery white sands and turquoise waters beckon.

Bonaire is a bird watcher's haven, where obtrusive flamingos nearly outnumber the sparse human population. There are more than 190 different species—not only the flamingo, but also the big-billed pelican, as well as parrots, snipes, terns, parakeets, herons, and hummingbirds. A pair of binoculars is an absolute necessity.

Bonaireans zealously treasure their precious environment and will go to great lengths to protect it. Even though they eagerly seek tourism, they aren't interested in creating "another Aruba," with its high-rise hotel blocks. Spearfishing isn't allowed in its waters, nor is the taking or destruction of any coral or other living animal from the sea. Unlike some islands, Bonaire isn't just surrounded by coral reefs—it is the reef, sitting on the dry, sunny top of an underwater mountain. Its shores are thick with rainbow-hued fish.

Bonaire is close to the coast of Latin America, known for many generations as the Spanish Main. It's just 50 miles north of Venezuela. Part of the Netherlands Antilles (an autonomous part of the Netherlands), Bonaire has a population of about 10,000. Its name is Amerindian for "low country." The capital is **Kralendijk.** It's most often reached from its neighbor island of Curaçao, 30 miles to the west. Like Curaçao, it's desertlike, with a dry and brilliant atmosphere. Often it's visited by "day-trippers," who rush through here in pursuit of the shy, elusive flamingo.

Boomerang-shaped Bonaire comprises about 112 square miles, making it the second largest of the ABC Dutch-affiliated grouping. Its northern sector is hilly, tapering up to Mount Brandaris, all of 788 feet. However, the southern half, flat as a flapjack, is given over to bays, reefs, beaches, and a salt lake that attracts the flamingos.

The big annual event is the **October Sailing Regatta,** a five-day festival of racing sponsored by the local tourist bureau. Now an international affair, the event attracts sailors and spectators from around the world, as a flotilla of sailboats and yachts anchor in Kralendijk Bay. If you're planning to visit during regatta days, make sure you have an iron-clad hotel reservation.

GETTING THERE

ALM (☎ 800/327-7230) is one of your best bets for flying to Bonaire. The airline flies from Miami on Wednesday and Saturday and from Atlanta on Saturday and Sunday. It also flies from Newark, New Jersey, via Curaçao on Wednesday and Saturday. **Air Aruba (☎ 800/882-7822)** has links from Newark also, going via Aruba and touching down on Bonaire Thursday through Sunday.

Convenient for many travelers are the daily **American Airlines (☎ 800/433-7300)** flights to Curaçao from Miami. These depart late enough in the day (11am departure) to allow easy transfers from almost anywhere on North America's East Coast. They reach Curaçao early enough (2:40pm arrival) to allow immediate transfers on to Bonaire. These are usually accomplished on any of ALM's four or five daily nonstop flights between Curaçao (ALM's corporate headquarters) and Bonaire.

Other routings to Bonaire are possible on any of American's daily nonstop flights to Aruba through American's hubs in New York, Miami, and San Juan, Puerto Rico. Once on Aruba, ALM will transfer passengers on to Bonaire, usually after a brief touchdown (or change of equipment) on Curaçao. Although these transfers are somewhat complicated, American will set up any of them and will also offer reduced rates at some Bonairean hotels if you book your reservation simultaneously with your air passage.

GETTING AROUND

Even though the island is flat, renting Mopeds or motor scooters is not always a good idea. The roads are often unpaved, pitted, and peppered with rocks. Touring

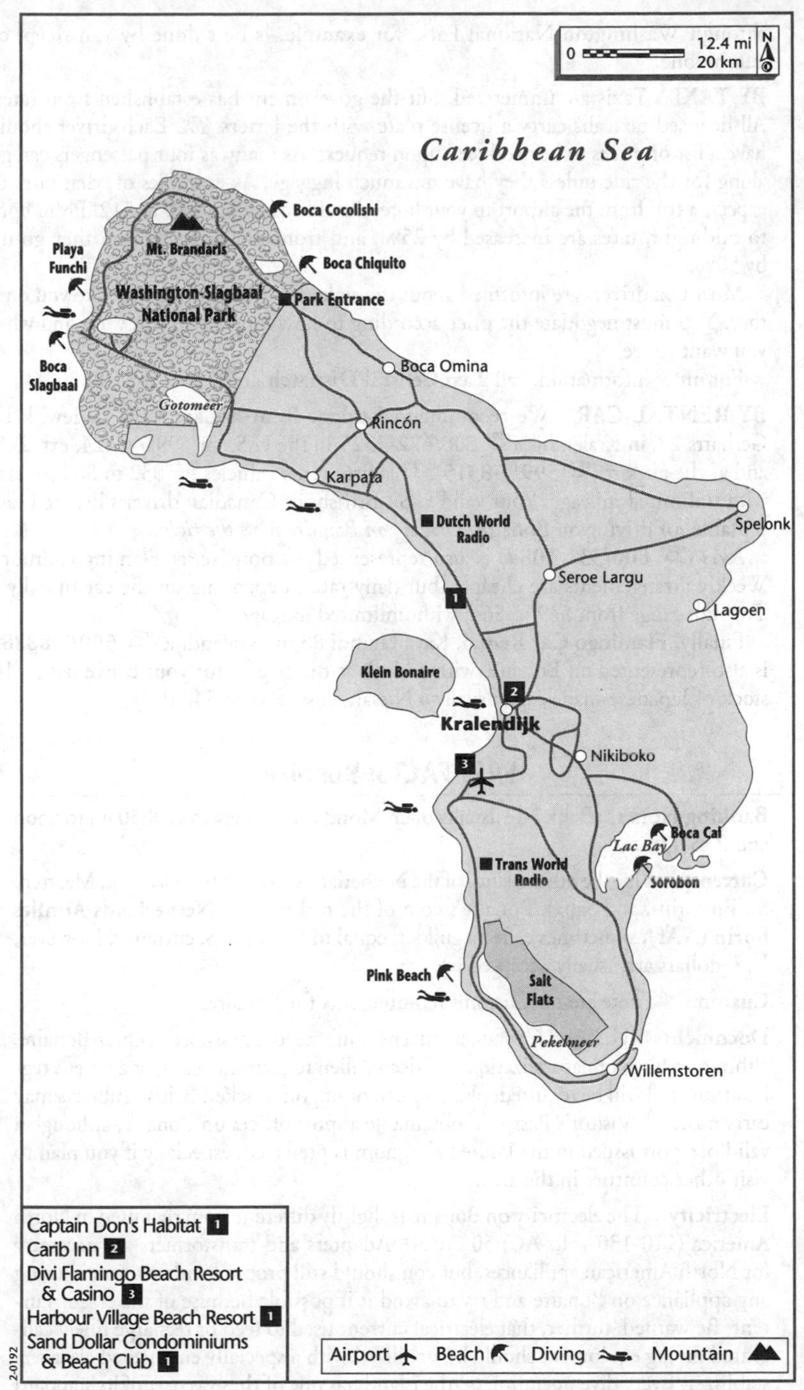
0
12.4 mi
20 km
N
Caribbean Sea
Boca Cocolishi
Mt. Brandaris
Playa Funchi
Boca Chiquito
Washington-Slagbaai National Park
Park Entrance
Boca Slagbaai
Boca Omina
Gotomeer
Rincón
Karpata
Spelonk
Dutch World Radio
Seroe Largu
Lagoen
Klein Bonaire
Kralendijk
Nikiboko
Boca Cai
Lac Bay
Trans World Radio
Sorobon
Pink Beach
Salt Flats
Pekelmeer
Willemstoren
Captain Don's Habitat 1
Carib Inn 2
Divi Flamingo Beach Resort & Casino 3
Harbour Village Beach Resort 1
Sand Dollar Condominiums & Beach Club 1
Airport
Beach
Diving
Mountain
2-0192

through Washington National Park, for example, is best done by van, Jeep, or automobile.

BY TAXI Taxis are unmetered, but the government has established fixed rates. All licensed taxicabs carry a license plate with the letters *TX.* Each driver should have a list of prices to be produced upon request. As many as four passengers can go along for the ride unless they have too much luggage. As examples of what rates to expect, a trip from the airport to your hotel should cost about $10 to $12. From 8pm to midnight, fares are increased by 25%, and from midnight to 6am they go up by 50%.

Most taxi drivers are informed about the sights of Bonaire and will take you on a tour. You must negotiate the price according to how long a trip you want and what you want to see.

For more information, call **Taxi Central Dispatch** at ☎ **599/7-8100.**

BY RENTAL CAR We recommend **Budget Rent-a-Car,** Kaya Lodewijk D. Gerharts 22, in Kralendijk (☎ **800/472-3325** in the U.S., or 599/7-7424, ext. 225) and at the airport (☎ **599/7-8315**). This firm rents vehicles for $32 to $62 per day with unlimited mileage. Your valid U.S., British, or Canadian driver's license is acceptable for driving on Bonaire. *Driving on Bonaire is on the right.*

Avis (☎ **800/331-1084**) is also represented on Bonaire, at Flamingo Airport. Weekly arrangements are cheaper, but daily rates, depending on the car (usually a Toyota), range from $39 to $64, with unlimited mileage.

Finally, **Flamingo Car Rental,** Kaya Grandi 86, in Kralendijk (☎ **599/7-8888**), is also represented on Bonaire, with a kiosk at the airport for your convenience. Its stock of Japanese-made cars, usually a Nissan, costs $38 to $40 daily.

FAST FACTS: Bonaire

Banking Hours Banks are usually open Monday to Friday from 8:30am to noon and 2 to 4pm.

Currency Like the other islands of the Netherlands Antilles (Curaçao, St. Maarten, St. Eustatius, and Saba), Bonaire's coin of the realm is the **Netherlands Antilles florin (NAf),** sometimes called a guilder, equal to 56¢ in U.S. currency. However, U.S. dollars are usually accepted.

Customs There are no Customs requirements for Bonaire.

Documents U.S. and Canadian citizens don't need a passport to enter Bonaire, although a birth or naturalization certificate, alien registration card, or a voter's registration card will be required, plus a return or ongoing ticket. British subjects may carry a British Visitor's Passport, obtainable at post offices on Bonaire, although a valid passport issued in the United Kingdom is preferred, especially if you plan to visit other countries in the area.

Electricity The electricity on Bonaire is slightly different from that used in North America (110-130 volts AC; 50 cycles). Adapters and transformers are necessary for North American appliances, but you should still proceed with caution in using any appliance on Bonaire and try to avoid it if possible because of the erratic current. Be warned, further, that electrical current used to feed or recharge finely calibrated diving equipment should be stabilized with a specially engineered electrical stabilizer. Every dive operation on the island has one of these as part of its standard equipment for visiting divers to use.

Emergencies For the **police,** dial ☎ **11,** or 599/7-8004 for non-life-threatening situations; for an **ambulance,** dial ☎ **599/7-8900.**

Information For tourist information on Bonaire, go to the **Bonaire Government Tourist Bureau,** Kaya Libertad Simon Bolivar 12, Kralendijk (☎ **599/7-8322**), open Monday to Friday from 7:30am to noon and 1:30 to 5pm. Before you go, you can contact the **Bonaire Government Tourist Office at Adams Unlimited,** 10 Rockefeller Plaza, Suite 900, New York, NY 10020 (☎ **800/U-BONAIR** or 212/956-5911), open Monday to Friday from 9am to 5pm.

Language English is widely spoken, but you'll hear Dutch, Spanish, and Papiamento.

Medical Care The St. Francis Hospital is in Kralendijk (☎ **599/7-8900**). A plane on standby at the airport takes seriously ill patients to Curaçao for treatment.

Safety "Safe, safe Bonaire" might be the island's motto in this crime-infested world. But remember, any place that attracts tourists also attracts people who prey on them. Safeguard your valuables.

Taxes and Service The government requires a $5.50 per person daily room tax on all hotel rooms. Most hotels and guest houses add a 10% service charge in lieu of tipping. Restaurants generally add a service charge of 15% to the bill, plus a 6% tax on all meals. Upon leaving Bonaire, you'll be charged an airport departure tax of $10, so don't spend every penny. There's also an interisland departure tax of $5.75.

Telephones Bonaire is not a part of the 809 area code that applies to most of the Caribbean. To call Bonaire from the United States, dial 011 (the international access code), then 599 (the country code for Bonaire), and then 7 (the area code) and the four-digit local number.

Once on Bonaire, to call another number on the island only the four-digit local number is necessary.

Time Bonaire is on Atlantic standard time year-round, one hour ahead of eastern standard time (when it's noon on Bonaire, it's 11am in Miami). When daylight saving time is in effect in the United States, clocks in Miami and on Bonaire show the same time.

Water Drinking water is pure and safe. It comes from distilled seawater.

Weather Bonaire is known for its climate, with temperatures hovering at 82°F. The water temperature averages 80°F. It's warmest in August and September, coolest in January and February. The average rainfall is 22 inches, and December to March are the rainiest months.

WHERE TO STAY

Hotels, all facing the sea, are low-key, personally run operations where everybody gets to know everybody else rather fast.

Reminder: Taxes and service charges are seldom included in the prices you're quoted, so ask about them when making your reservations.

VERY EXPENSIVE

✪ **Harbour Village Beach Resort.** Kaya Gobernador N. Debrot, Playa Lechi (P.O. Box 312), Bonaire, N.A. ☎ **800/424-0004** in the U.S. and Canada, or 599/7-7500. Fax 599/7-7507. 30 rms, 40 suites. A/C TV TEL. Year-round, $275–$395 double; $425–$695 suite. Rates include breakfast. Dinner $40 per person extra. AE, DC, MC, V.

Conceived by one of the largest land developers in Venezuela, this complex, the most stylish on the island, is designed like an Iberian village, opening onto a sandy beach. One of the most upscale resorts in the Caribbean, it has brought a pocket of posh to Bonaire for those divers who don't want the more laid-back atmosphere of Captain Don's Habitat. Accommodations are in a cluster of Dutch Caribbean–style villas painted in pastels and roofed in red tile with terraced balconies. Guests rooms have island-style ceiling fans in addition to air-conditioning.

Dining/Entertainment: Kasa Coral Dining Terrace offers breakfast and dinner, featuring an international menu and, on many evenings, live music. Our favorite restaurant, however, is La Balandra Bar and Grill, a gazebolike structure set beside a massive pier jutting seaward beside the beach. Here, an octagonal bar area ringed with tables and flanked by an open grill and salad bar is open to the sea view and breezes. A marina bar and grill, Captain Wook's, overlooks a 60-slip marina, offering a menu consisting of grill specialties.

Services: The only hotel on Bonaire to offer room service (7 to 10am), laundry and dry cleaning, baby-sitting, wake-up service, pickup at the airport (10 minutes from the resort).

Facilities: Swimming pool, scuba-diving shop (with state-of-the-art diving and underwater photographic equipment), four tennis courts, fitness center, bicycles. In 1995 a full-service European spa opened, offering a full range of beauty treatments, fitness equipment, and massage.

EXPENSIVE

Captain Don's Habitat. Kaya Gobernador N. Debrot 103, Pier 7, Bonaire, N.A. ☎ **599/7-8290.** Fax 599/7-8240. (For all reservations and business arrangements, contact Captain Don's Habitat, 903 South America Way, Miami, FL 33132; ☎ 800/327-6709; fax 305/371-2337.) 62 units. A/C. Winter, $996–$1,324 double. Off-season, $764–$973 double. Rates are for 8 days/7 nights and include breakfast, airport transfers, tax, service, equipment, and 6 guided dives. AE, MC, V.

Built on a coral bluff overlooking the sea about five minutes north of Kralendijk, this is a unique diving, snorkeling, and nature-oriented resort, with an air of congenial informality. The staff is devoted to diving. Habitat and its accompanying dive shop are the creation of Capt. Don Stewart, Caribbean pioneer and "caretaker of the reefs." A former Californian, he sailed his schooner from San Francisco through the Panama Canal, arriving on a reef off Bonaire in 1962 and has been here ever since. Called the "godfather of diving" on the island, Captain Don was instrumental in the formation of the Bonaire Marine Park, whereby the entire island became a protected reef. The captain still shows up once or twice a week and he's got some tall tales to tell.

More than 90% of the clients coming here opt for one of the packages that combine a number of dives with accommodations (ranging from standard double rooms to oceanfront villas). The most popular arrangement is the eight-day/seven-night package.

Dining/Entertainment: This resort has an oceanfront restaurant and two seaside bars. A casual, laid-back crowd gathers for meals at Rum Runners, the social hub. Theme nights are staged weekly, which divert guests from the rather standard fare served here.

Services: Laundry, baby-sitting.

Facilities: Boutique, ocean-bordering pool, complete diving program.

MODERATE

Divi Flamingo Beach Resort & Casino. J. A. Abraham Blvd., Bonaire, N.A. ☎ **800/367-3484** in the U.S., 919/419-3484 in Chapel Hill, N.C., 0800/373742 in the U.K., or 599/

7-8285. Fax 599/7-8238. 100 rms, 40 studios. A/C. Mid-Dec to Mar, $125–$185 double; from $195 studio. Apr to mid-Dec, $84–$115 double; from $125 studio. MAP $42 per person extra. Rates about 10% higher between Christmas and New Year's. Several inclusive packages offered. AE, MC, V.

This beachfront resort, with its comfortable but rather worn bedrooms, was once a gone-to-seed hotel with a cluster of flimsy wooden bungalows that had been used to intern German prisoners in World War II. With foresight and taste, the owners turned it into a resort, offering individual cottages and seafront rooms with private balconies resting on piers above the surf, so you can stand out and watch rainbow-hued tropical fish in the water below.

The resort's original rooms were supplemented in 1986 with the addition of time-sharing units, forming Club Flamingo. These are the newest and best rooms. Each of the units is rentable by the day or week. The accommodations in both sections are spacious and sunny, with ceiling fans and a selection of Mexican accessories. The newer units are clustered into a green-and-white neo-Victorian pavilion facing its own curving swimming pool. Each contains a kitchenette with carved cupboards and cabinets of pickled hardwoods. Both sections benefit from the social hostesses, the water-sports facilities, and the proximity of a good dive operation and a beautiful beach. A pair of restaurants, the Chibi-Chibi and the Calabase Terrace, provide satisfying but unspectacular meals.

Sand Dollar Condominiums & Beach Club. Kaya Gobernador N. Debrot 79, Bonaire, N.A. ☎ **800/288-4773** in the U.S., or 599/7-8738. Fax 599/7-8760. 85 units. A/C TV. Winter, $165 studio for 2; $215 one-bedroom apt; $250 two-bedroom apt; $360 three-bedroom apt. Off-season, $155 studio for 2; $180 one-bedroom apt; $200 two-bedroom apt; $310 three-bedroom apt. MAP $38.50 per person extra. AE, MC, V.

On the beachfront, just 1½ miles north of Kralendijk and 3 miles north of the airport, the Sand Dollar, with its fun-time, upbeat atmosphere, offers studios and one-, two-, and three-bedroom apartments with all the style, comfort, and convenience of a full-service hotel. A kind of European design is blended with a Caribbean motif. All accommodations are equipped with electric ranges, ovens, dishwashers, refrigerators, custom cabinets, and modern furnishings, with decks or balconies facing the ocean. The resort mainly attracts diving aficionados.

Dining/Entertainment: On the grounds is the Green Parrot Restaurant and Bar (see "Where to Dine," below).

Facilities: Two lighted tennis courts, freshwater swimming pool with bar and cabana, Sand Dollar Dive and Photo (see "Beaches, Water Sports & Outdoor Pursuits," below). The minuscule beach is engulfed at high tide.

INEXPENSIVE

✪ **Carib Inn.** J. A. Abraham Blvd. (P.O. Box 68), Kralendijk, Bonaire, N.A. ☎ **599/7-8819.** Fax 599/7-5295. 10 studio, efficiency, and 1- , 2- , or 3-bedroom apts. A/C TV. Winter, $89 studio; $99 efficiency; $119 one-bedroom apt; $139 two-bedroom apt; $159 three-bedroom apt. Off-season, $79 studio; $89 efficiency; $109 one-bedroom apt; $129 two-bedroom apt; $149 three-bedroom apt. AE, MC, V.

On the water, and owned and managed by American diver Bruce Bowker, this is the most intimate little dive resort on Bonaire. Dedicated scuba divers are drawn to the Carib Inn's five-star PADI dive facility. The inn remains one of Bonaire's best values. Eight of its 10 units have kitchens where guests can prepare their own meals. All units are equipped with refrigerators, and maid service is provided daily. Accommodations are furnished simply in tropical rattan pieces. There's no restaurant or bar, although Richard's Waterfront Dining is close at hand (see "Where to Dine," below). Repeat guests are likely to book this place far in advance in winter.

Coastal Reef Diving

One of the richest reef communities in the entire West Indies, Bonaire has plunging walls that descend to a sand bottom at 130 or so feet. The reefs are home to various coral formations that grow at different depths, ranging from the knobby brain coral at 3 feet to staghorn and elkhorn up to about 10 feet deeper, and gorgonians, giant brain, and others all the way to 40 to 83 feet. Swarms of rainbow-hued tropical fish inhabit the reefs, and the deep reef slope is home to a range of basket sponges, groupers, and moray eels. Most of the diving is done on the leeward side where the ocean is lake flat. There are more than 40 dive sites on sharply sloping reefs.

The waters off the coast of Bonaire received an additional attraction in 1984. A rust-bottomed general cargo ship, 80 feet long, was confiscated by the police along with its contraband cargo, about 25,000 pounds of marijuana. Known as the *Hilma Hooker* (familiarly dubbed "The Hooker" by everyone on the island), it sank unclaimed (obviously) and without fanfare one calm day in 90 feet of water. Lying just off the southern shore near the capital, its wreck is now a popular dive site.

The ✪ **Bonaire Marine Park** was created to protect the coral-reef ecosystem off Bonaire. The park incorporates the entire coastline of Bonaire and neighboring Klein Bonaire. Scuba diving and snorkeling are all popular here. The park is policed, and services and facilities include a Visitor Information Center at the Karpata Ecological Center, lectures, slide presentations, films, and permanent dive-site moorings.

Visitors are asked to respect the marine environment and to refrain from activities that may damage it, including sitting or walking on the coral. All marine life is completely protected. This means there's no fishing or collecting fish, shells, or corals—dead or alive. Spearfishing is forbidden, as is anchoring; all craft must use permanent moorings, except for emergency stops (boats shorter than 12 feet may use a stone anchor). Most recreational activity in the marine park takes place on the island's leeward side and among the reefs surrounding uninhabited Klein Bonaire.

Bonaire has a unique program for divers in that the major hotels offer personalized, close-up encounters with the island's fish and other marine life under the expertise of Bonaire's dive guides.

WHERE TO DINE

EXPENSIVE

Chez Truus. Kaya Hellmund 5. ☎ **599/7-8617.** Reservations recommended. Main courses $8.70–$21.30. AE, MC, V. Wed–Mon 6:30–10pm. INTERNATIONAL.

This sea-bordering bistro near the Divi Flamingo is in one of the island's oldest houses. Intimate tables and candlelight create a romantic ambience in the main restaurant, although you can dine less formally outside on the terrace overlooking the harbor. The menu always features the catch of the day as well as steak dishes. Sample a rather delectable duck breast, followed by one of the homemade desserts. Finish off with one of their rich, Cuban-style coffees. Flavors are precisely defined, although nearly all ingredients have to be imported.

Chibi-Chibi. In the Divi Flamingo Beach Resort & Casino, J. A. Abraham Blvd. ☎ **599/7-8285.** Reservations recommended. Main courses $14.25–$20.25. AE, MC, V. Daily 6–10pm. CONTINENTAL.

On the sea on the periphery of Kralendijk, this restaurant is named after the yellow-breasted tropical birds that can be observed from your dining table. An imposing

Dive I and **Dive II,** at opposite ends of the beachfront of the Divi Flamingo Beach Resort & Casino, J. A. Abraham Boulevard (☎ **599/7-8285**), north of Kralendijk, are among the island's most complete scuba facilities. They're open Monday to Saturday from 8:30am to noon and 1:30 to 5pm. Both operate out of well-stocked beachfront buildings, rent diving equipment, charge the same prices, and offer the same type of expeditions. A resort course for first-time divers costs $88; for experienced divers, a one-tank dive goes for $38.50.

Captain Don's Habitat Dive Shop, Kaya Gobernador N. Debrot 103 (☎ **599/7-8290**), is a PADI five-star training facility. The open-air, full-service dive shop includes a classroom, photo/video lab, camera-rental facility, equipment repair, and compressor rooms grouped around spacious seafront patios. Habitat's slogan is "Diving Freedom," and divers can take their tanks and dive anywhere any time of day or night, most often along "The Pike," half a mile of protected reef right in front of the property. The highly qualified staff is there to assist and advise but not to police or dictate dive plans. Diving packages include boat dives, unlimited offshore diving (24 hours a day), unlimited air, tanks, backpack, weights, and belt. Some dive packages also include accommodations and meals (see "Where to Stay," above).

At the **Bonaire Scuba Center,** in the Black Durgon Inn, Playa Lechi (☎ **599/7-5736**), some of the island's best diving is available from the doorstep of this seven-room inn. A living reef just 50 feet from shore quickly drops to 150 feet. Snorkeling is also possible from the property. The center caters to both novice and advanced divers and offers both resort and certification courses.

Sand Dollar Dive and Photo, at the Sand Dollar Condominium & Beach Club, Kaya Gobernador N. Debrot (☎ **599/7-5252**), is open daily from 8:30am to 5:30pm. It offers dive packages, PADI and NAUI instruction, and equipment rental and repairs; boat and shore trips with an instructor are available by appointment. The photo shop offers underwater photo and video shoots, PADI specialty courses by appointment, E-6 processing, print developing, and equipment rental and repair.

two-tier structure, the restaurant is perched over a coral-encrusted sea bottom, and you can see schools of multicolored fish in the illuminated waters. The chef prepares a continental menu, which also includes Antillean onion soup, veal piccata, fettuccine Flamingo, keshi yena (Edam cheese stuffed with meat and then baked), and some of the freshest fish on the island. In spite of the rather standard food, this place has a devoted following.

Den Laman Restaurant. Kaya Gobernador N. Debrot 77. ☎ **599/7-8955.** Reservations not required. Main courses $12–$31. AE, MC, V. Wed–Mon 6-11pm. Closed Sept 1–22. SEAFOOD.

Located between the Sunset Beach Hotel and the Sand Dollar Condominiums & Beach Club, Den Laman serves the best seafood on Bonaire. An excellent beginning is the fish soup (the chef's special). The fresh fish of the day depends on what was caught, of course. Perhaps you'll order conch Flamingo, a local favorite, or lobster from the tank. Other dishes include grouper Creole and New York sirloin steak. When it's featured, we always go for the red snapper meunière. It's easy to spend $35 here, but it's also possible to dine for less. Meals are served on a breezy seaside terrace, and a 6,000-gallon aquarium complements the decor.

MODERATE

Mona Lisa. Kaya Grandi 15. ☎ **599/7-8718.** Reservations recommended. Main courses $14.50–$23. AE, MC, V. Mon–Fri noon–2pm and 6–10pm. FRENCH/INTERNATIONAL.

A local favorite, this is one of the best places in town for food with a homemade taste. The prices are some of the best around, considering the quality of the food served and the generous portions. Although many regulars just come to patronize the Dutch bar and catch up on the latest gossip, the old-fashioned dining room deserves serious attention. On the main street of town, in an old building, guests enjoy the fresh fish of the day (often wahoo) or such meat dishes as a leg of lamb fillet, tournedos, and sirloin steak. The most ordered appetizers are onion soup, smoked fish, and shrimp cocktail. It's known for serving the freshest vegetables on an island where nearly everything is imported.

✪ **Richard's Waterfront Dining.** J. A. Abraham Blvd. 60. ☎ **599/7-5263.** Reservations recommended for groups of 6 or more. Main courses $12.50–$19.90. DC, MC, V. Tues–Sun 6:30–10:30pm. STEAK/SEAFOOD.

On the airport side of Kralendijk, within walking distance of the Divi Flamingo, this restaurant has a large covered terrace. Reasonable in price, it's also the preferred favorite of many locals who have sampled every restaurant on the island. Boston-born Richard Beady and his partner, Mario, from Aruba, operate a welcoming oasis and begin happy hour at 5pm, one hour before dinner. Gathered around the coral bar, guests speculate on the offerings that night, which appear on a chalkboard menu. You're likely to be offered grilled wahoo or the fresh catch of the day, filet mignon béarnaise, U.S. sirloin with green-peppercorn sauce, or scampi. It's best to begin with the fish soup, if featured. Pastas are also an item here. On a recent visit, we had our best meal on Bonaire at this restaurant. The menu is wisely kept small so that dishes every night can be given the attention they deserve. The style of the kitchen is to deliver all the natural goodness of a dish without overwhelming it with sauces or too many seasonings. The fact that all diners are welcomed with such a warm hospitality contributes to the enjoyment of an evening. Seating is on a first-come, first-served basis.

Zeezicht Restaurant. Kaya Corsow 10. ☎ **599/7-8434.** Reservations not required. Main courses $8–$26. AE, MC, V. Daily 9am–11pm. INTERNATIONAL.

This is the best place in the capital to go for a sundowner. You join the old salts or the people who live on boats to watch the sun go down, and you try to see the "green flash" that Hemingway wrote about. Pronounced *Zay-zict* and meaning "sea view," this place has long been popular for its excellent local cookery. A two-story operation, the restaurant offers a small *rijstaffel* (an Indonesian banquet) as well as fresh fish from the nearby fish market. Lobster is occasionally featured, and there's always steak. Go here for local specialties, items such as conch stew or goat curry. You can also order basic Stateside fare, but even these dishes reflect an Antillean touch. We've enjoyed far better Indonesian specialties than those served here. Nevertheless, it's an enduring local favorite and has a lot of fans.

INEXPENSIVE

Beefeaters. Kaya Grandi 12. ☎ **599/7-7776.** Reservations recommended. Main courses $10–$21. AE, DISC, MC, V. Daily 4–10pm. INTERNATIONAL.

Don't interpret the name of this place as a sign that this is a steak-and-ale joint. It isn't. In fact, it offers greater numbers of vegetarian platters (at least five) than any other restaurant on Bonaire. It was established in the mid-1970s by an English expatriate ("Beefeater" Richard Dove) who was joined later by his German-born wife, Brigitte Kley, and their Dutch-born manager, Jeanette. Together, they maintain a garden-style restaurant that's permeated with European mystique, subtle flavors, and replicas of the Tudor-era guards that appear on ads for English gin. Unless it rains, which in Bonaire is rare, you'll pass through a trio of indoor dining rooms to find a seat in the artfully lit garden. Here, near a convivial bar area, you can enjoy such dishes as spinach or seafood crepes; seafood pasta; Curaçaon goat meat stew; the catch of the day garnished with crabmeat, mussels, and fruit sauce; and a well-seasoned array of curry dishes (pork, shrimp, fish, and lamb). What should you do if you stumble in accidentally thinking the place is just a steakhouse? Order either the T-bone or fillet steak. They're very good.

China Garden. Kaya Grandi 47. ☎ **599/7-8480.** Reservations recommended. Main courses $6–$12. AE, MC, V. Wed–Mon 11:30am–2pm and 4:30–10pm. ASIAN.

Good-tasting Eastern dishes, with some Indonesian specialties, are served to West Indians and visitors in this restored Bonairean mansion between the Divi Flamingo and Sunset Beach hotels. Portions are enormous, and prices are low considering what you get. The chefs from Hong Kong also cook Chinese, American, and local dishes, including a variety of curries ranging from beef to lobster. The menu also offers seafood dishes prepared in a variety of styles, including lobster in black-bean sauce. Special culinary features include a Java rijstaffel and the nasi goreng special. We don't want to oversell this place, as you'll find far better Chinese dining elsewhere in the Caribbean, especially Puerto Rico, than you'll get here. A lot of the Cantonese fare is on the bland side. However, there's a warmth and conviviality about the place, and the reasonable prices are a find in Bonaire. The place is air-conditioned and seats 60 guests.

Green Parrot Restaurant. In the Sand Dollar Condominium & Beach Club, Kaya Gobernador N. Debrot 79. ☎ **599/7-8738.** Reservations recommended. Main courses $8–$28.50; lunch $4.85–$9.25. AE, MC, V. Daily 8–10:30am and 11am–10pm. CONTINENTAL.

Set on a breezy pier, this place is part of the previously recommended resort, a 15-minute drive from the airport. It serves burgers, pasta, sandwiches, and seafood dishes. You can gaze at the waves, enjoy a frozen tropical fruit drink, and watch the sunset. On Saturday night there's a barbecue buffet with entertainment. The food consistently ranks among the best on the island, especially the charcoal-grilled fish (based on the catch of the day). You might also try the barbecued chicken and ribs, and various U.S. beef cuts (from T-bone to filet mignon), as well as garlic shrimp and the highly favored onion strings (like an onion loaf). Go here for the fun and the good times, and when you're in the mood for familiar fare and don't want to dine too experimentally.

BEACHES, WATER SPORTS & OUTDOOR PURSUITS

The true beauty on Bonaire is under the sea, where visibility is 100 feet 365 days of the year, and the water temperatures range from 78° to 82°F. Many dive sites can be reached directly from the beach, and sailing is another favored pastime. The bird watching is among the best in the Caribbean, and for beachcombers there are acres and acres of driftwood, found along the shore from the salt flats to Lac.

BEACHES Bonaire has some of the whitest sand beaches in the West Indies. The major hotels have beaches, but you may want to wander down to the southeast coast for a swim at the "clothes-optional" **Sorobon** or **Boca Cai** on Lac Bay. In the north, you may want to swim at **Playa Funchi,** on the coastline of Washington/Slagbaai National Park.

BIRD WATCHING Bonaire is home to 190 species of birds, 80 of which are indigenous to the island. But most famous are its flamingos, which can number 15,000 during the mating season. For great places to bring your binoculars, see "Seeing the Sights," below.

BOATING Every visitor to Bonaire wants to take a trip to uninhabited Klein Bonaire. The **Flamingo Beach Hotel** (☎ **599/7-8285**) and **Sunset Beach Hotel** at Playa Lechi (☎ **599/7-5300**) offer trips daily. You'll be left in the morning for a day of snorkeling, beachcombing, and picnicking, then be picked up later that afternoon. Other hotels will also arrange a trip to the islet for you, perhaps including a barbecue.

FISHING The island's offshore fishing grounds offer some of the best fishing in the Caribbean. A good day's catch might include mackerel, tuna, wahoo, dolphin, blue marlin, Amber Jack, grouper, sailfish, or snapper. Bonaire is also one of the best-kept secrets of bonefishing enthusiasts.

Your best bet is Chris Morkos, **Piscatur Fishing Supplies,** Kaya Herman 4, Playa Pabao (☎ **599/7-8774**). A native Bonairean, he has been fishing almost since he was born. A maximum of six people are taken out on a 42-foot boat with a guide and captain, at a cost of $350 for a half day or $500 for a whole day, including all tackle and bait. Reef fishing is another popular sport, in boats averaging 15 and 19 feet. A maximum of two people can go out for a half day at $200 or a whole day at $300. For the same price, a maximum of four people can fish for bonefish and tarpon on the island's large salt flats.

HORSEBACK RIDING Spend part of a day or all day at one of Bonaire's fine horse ranches, where private lessons and trail rides are available. You can usually arrange a day in the saddle through your hotel.

MOUNTAIN BIKING Biking on Bonaire can be a rewarding experience; you can explore more than 186 miles of trails and dirt roads where you can venture off the beaten path to enjoy the scenery and contrasting geography. Check with your hotel about arranging a trip.

SCUBA DIVING Bonaire is internationally known for its beautiful reefs and dive sites, and many hotels cater almost exclusively to scuba divers. See the above box, "Coastal Reef Diving," for details, descriptions of dive sites, and outfitters.

SEA KAYAKING Paddle the protected waters of Lac Bay, or head for the miles of flats and mangroves in the south (the island's nursery) where baby fish and wildlife can be viewed. Kayak rentals are available at **Bonaire Windsurfing,** Lac Bay (☎ **599/7-5363**), for $15 per hour or $25 per half day.

SNORKELING Snorkeling equipment can be rented at such previously recommended establishments as **Harbour Village Beach Resort,** the **Carib Inn,** or at any of the scuba centers (see the "Coastal Reef Diving" box, above), including **Sand Dollar Dive and Photo, Bonaire Scuba Center,** or **Captain Don's Habitat Dive Shop.**

TENNIS The **Sunset Beach Hotel** at Playa Lechi (☎ **599/7-5300**) has two good tennis courts, illuminated for night play. Use of the courts is free to both hotel guests and non-guests during the day, although any night games will incur a small charge for illumination. A tennis instructor is available, and racquets and balls can be borrowed without charge.

In addition, there are two courts at the **Sand Dollar Condominium & Beach Club** and **Divi Flamingo Beach Resort** (see "Where to Stay," above); all the courts are lit for night play.

WINDSURFING Consistent conditions, enjoyed by windsurfers with a wide range of skill levels, make the shallow, calm waters of Lac Bay the island's home to the sport. Call **Bonaire Windsurfing** (☎ **599/7-5363**) for details.

SEEING THE SIGHTS

KRALENDIJK

The capital, Kralendijk, means "coral dike" and is pronounced *KROLL-en-dike,* although most denizens refer to it as *Playa,* Spanish for "beach." A dollhouse town of some 2,500 residents, it's small, neat, pretty, Dutch-clean, and just a bit dull. Its stucco buildings are painted pink and orange, with an occasional lime green. The capital's jetty is lined with island sloops and fishing boats.

Kralendijk nestles in a bay on the west coast, opposite **Klein Bonaire,** or Little Bonaire, an uninhabited, low-lying islet a 10-minute boat ride from the capital.

The main street of town leads along the beachfront on the harbor. A Protestant church was built in 1834, and St. Bernard's Roman Catholic Church has some stained-glass windows.

At **Fort Oranje** you'll see a lone cannon dating from the days of Napoleon. If possible, try to get up early to see the **Fish Market** on the waterfront, where you'll see a variety of strange and brilliantly colored fish.

THE TOUR NORTH

The road north is one of the most beautiful stretches in the Antilles, with turquoise waters on your left and coral cliffs on your right. You can stop at several points along this road where you'll find paved paths for strolling or bicycling.

After leaving Kralendijk and passing the Sunset Beach Hotel and the desalination plant, you'll come to **Radio Nederland Wereld Omroep (Dutch World Radio).** It's a 13-tower, 300,000-watter. Opposite the transmitting station is a lovers' promenade, built by nature and an ideal spot for a picnic.

Continuing, you'll pass the storage tanks of the Bonaire Petroleum Corporation, the road heading to **Gotomeer,** the island's inland sector, with a saltwater lake. Several flamingos prefer this spot to the salt flats in the south.

Down the hill the road leads to a section called **"Dos Pos"** or two wells, which has palm trees and vegetation in contrast to the rest of the island, where only the drought-resistant kibraacha and divi-divi trees, tilted before the constant wind, can grow, along with forests of cacti.

Bonaire's oldest village is **Rincón.** Slaves who used to work in the salt flats in the south once lived here. There are a couple of bars and the Rincón Ice Cream Parlour makes homemade ice cream in a variety of interesting flavors. Above the bright roofs of the village is the crest of a hill called Para Mira or "stop and look."

A side path outside Rincón takes you to some Arawak inscriptions supposedly 500 years old. The petroglyph designs are in pink-red dye. At nearby **Boca Onima,** you'll find grotesque grottoes of coral.

Before going back to the capital, you might take a short bypass to **Seroe Largu,** which has a good view of Kralendijk and the sea. Lovers frequent the spot at night.

Washington/Slagbaai National Park (☎ **599/7-8444**) is concerned with the conservation of the island's fauna, flora, and landscape, and is a changing vista highlighted by desertlike terrain, secluded beaches, caverns, and a bird sanctuary. Occupying 15,000 acres of Bonaire's northwesternmost territory, the park was once plantation land, producing divi-divi, aloe, and charcoal. It was purchased by the Netherlands Antilles government, and since 1967 part of the land, formerly the

Washington plantation, has been a wildlife sanctuary. The southern part of the park, the Slagbaai plantation, was added in 1978.

You can see the park in a few hours, although it takes days to appreciate it fully. Touring the park is easy, with two routes: a 15-mile "short" route, marked by green arrows, and a 22-mile "long" route, marked by yellow arrows. The roads are well marked and safe, but somewhat rugged, although they're gradually being improved. Tickets cost $5 for adults and $1 for children 11 and under, and can be purchased at the gate. The park is open daily except holidays from 8am to 5pm. No one is allowed to enter after 3pm because there isn't enough time left to explore before closing.

Whichever route you take, there are a few important stops you should make. Just past the gate is **Salina Mathijs,** a salt flat that's home to flamingos during the rainy season. Beyond the salt flat on the road to the right is **Boca Chikitu,** a white-sand beach and bay. A few miles up the beach lies **Boca Cocolishi,** a two-part black-sand beach. Many a couple has raved about the romantic memories of this beach, perfect for picnics, privacy, and seclusion. Its deep, rough seaward side and calm, shallow basin are separated by a ridge of calcareous algae. The basin and the beach were formed by small pieces of coral, mollusks and their shells (*cocolishi* means "shells"), thus the "black sand." The basin itself has no current, so it's perfect for snorkeling close to shore, where hermit crabs scuttle through the shallow water and black sands.

The main road leads to **Boca Bartol,** a bay full of living and dead elkhorn coral, seafans, and reef fish. A popular watering hole good for bird watching is **Poosdi Mangel. Wajaca** is a remote reef, perfect for divers and home to the island's most exciting sea creatures, including turtles, octopuses, and trigger-fish. Immediately inland towers 788-foot **Mount Brandaris,** Bonaire's highest peak, at whose foot is **Bronswinkel Well,** a watering spot for pigeons and parakeets. Some 130 species of birds live in the park, many with such exotic names as banana quit and black-faced grassquit. Bonaire has few mammals, but you'll see goats and donkeys, perhaps even a wild bull.

Heading South

Leaving the capital again, you pass the **Trans World Radio antennas,** towering 500 feet in the air, transmitting with 810,000 watts. This is one of the hemisphere's most powerful medium-wave radio stations, the loudest voice in Christendom and the most powerful nongovernmental broadcast station in the world. It sends out interdenominational Gospel messages and hymns in 20 languages to places as far away as Eastern Europe and the Middle East.

Later, you come on the ✪ **salt flats,** where the brilliantly colored pink flamingos live. Bonaire shelters the largest accessible nesting and breeding grounds in the world. The flamingos build high mud mounds to hold their eggs. The best time to see the birds is in spring when they're usually nesting and tending their young. The salt flats were once worked by slaves, and the government has rebuilt some primitive stone huts, bare shelters little more than waist high. The slaves slept in these huts, and returned to their homes in Rincón in the north on weekends. The centuries-old salt pans have been reactivated by the International Salt Company. Near the salt pans you'll see some 30-foot obelisks in white, blue, and orange built in 1838 to help mariners locate their proper anchorages.

Farther down the coast is the island's oldest lighthouse, **Willemstoren,** built in 1837. Still farther along, **Sorobon Beach** and **Boca Cai** come into view. They're at landlocked Lac Bay, which is ideal for swimming and snorkeling. Conch shells are stacked up on the beach. The water here is so vivid and clear you can see coral 65 to 120 feet down in the reef-protected waters.

A Sightseeing Tour

Bonaire Sightseeing Tours (☎ **599/7-8778**) transports you on tours of the island, both north and south, taking in the flamingos, slave huts, conch shells, Goto Lake, the Amerindian inscriptions, and other sights. Each of these tours lasts two hours and costs $17 per person. You can also take a half-day "City and Country Tour," lasting three hours and costing from $22 per person, allowing you to see the entire northern section and the southern part as far as the slave huts.

Shopping

Kralendijk features an assortment of goods, including gemstone jewelry, wood, leather, sterling, ceramics, liquors, and tobacco priced 25% to 50% less than in the United States and Canada. Prices are often quoted in U.S. dollars, and major credit and charge cards and traveler's checks are usually accepted. Walk along Kaya Grandi in Kralendijk to sample the merchandise.

Ki Bo Ke Pakus ("What Do You Want"). In the Divi Flamingo Beach Resort & Casino, J. A. Abraham Blvd. ☎ **599/7-8239.**

This place has some of the most popular merchandise on the island—T-shirts, handbags, locally made jewelry, beach wear, and Delft blue items.

Littman Jewelers. Kaya Grandi 35. ☎ **599/7-8160.**

Steve and Esther Littman have restored this old house to its original state. The shop sells Tag Heuer dive watches and also carries Daum French crystal and Lladró Spanish porcelain. Next door, the Littmans have a shop called **Littman's Gifts,** selling standard and hand-painted T-shirts, plus sandals, hats, Gottex swimsuits, gift items, costume jewelry, and toys.

Things Bonaire. At the Sunset Beach Hotel. ☎ **599/7-8190.**

This shop carries many gift items, including sunglasses, postcards, and locally made shell and driftwood items. They also carry men's and women's swimsuits, shorts, T-shirts, beach towels, guayaberas, caps, hats, and visors.

United Colors of Benetton. Kaya Grandi 49. ☎ **599/7-5107.**

This worldwide chain with its multicolored clothing and controversial (to some) ads has invaded Bonaire. Directly imported from Italy, the clothing is often priced 30% lower than in Europe or the United States, or so they claim.

Bonaire After Dark

Underwater **slide shows** provide entertainment for both divers and nondivers in the evening. The best shows are at **Captain Don's Habitat** (☎ **599/7-8290**) (see "Beaches, Water Sports & Outdoor Pursuits," above).

Divi Flamingo Beach Resort & Casino. J. A. Abraham Blvd. ☎ **599/7-8285.**

A casino opened here in 1984 in a former residence adjoining the property. Promoted as "The World's First Barefoot Casino," it offers blackjack, roulette, poker, wheel of fortune, video games, and slot machines. Gambling on the island is regulated by the government. Entrance is free. Open Monday to Saturday from 8pm to 2am.

Fantasy Disco. Kaya L. Z. Gerharts 1 at Kaya Grandi. ☎ **599/7-7345.** Cover $6.

Set near the heart of town, within a landlocked, two-story modern building that seems to encourage clients to wander from one level to the next, this is the island's busiest, most popular, and most deeply entrenched disco. The musical theme will vary, depending on the night of the week, focusing on either merengue, reggae, or

American style rock 'n' roll, depending on what the DJ's in the mood for that night. Wednesday night is ladies' night, when females drink for reduced prices.

Karel's Beach Bar. On the waterfront. ☎ **599/7-8434.**

Almost Tahitian in its high-ceilinged, open-walled design, this popular bar is perched above the sea on stilts. You can sit at the long rectangular bar with many of the island's dive and boating professionals or select a table near the balustrades overlooking the illuminated surf. On weekends, local bands entertain. Drinks begin at $4 each. Open daily 11am to 2am.

3 Curaçao

Just 35 miles north of the coast of Venezuela, Curaçao, the "C" of the Dutch ABC islands of the Caribbean, is the most populous of the Netherlands Antilles. It attracts visitors because of its distinctive culture, warm people, duty-free shopping, lively casinos, and water sports. Fleets of tankers head out from its harbor to bring refined oil to all parts of the world.

A self-governing part of the Netherlands, Curaçao was discovered not by Columbus, but by two of his lieutenants, Alonso de Ojeda and Amerigo Vespucci, in 1499. The Spaniards exterminated all but 75 members of a branch of the peaceful Arawaks. However, they in turn were ousted by the Dutch in 1634, who also had to fight off French and English invasions.

The Dutch made the island a tropical Holland in miniature. Pieter Stuyvesant, stomping on his pegleg, ruled Curaçao in 1644. The island was turned into a Dutch Gibraltar, bristling with forts. Thick ramparts guarded the harbor's narrow entrance; the hilltop forts (many now converted into restaurants) protected the coastal approaches.

In this century it remained sleepy until 1915, when the Royal Dutch/Shell Company built one of the world's largest oil refineries to process crude from Venezuela. Workers from some 50 countries poured onto the island, turning Curaçao into a polyglot, cosmopolitan community.

The largest of the Netherlands Antilles, Curaçao is 37 miles long and 7 miles across at its widest point. Because of all that early Dutch building, Curaçao is the most important island architecturally in the entire West Indies, with more European flavor than anywhere else. After leaving the capital, **Willemstad,** you plunge into a strange, desertlike countryside that evokes the American Southwest. The relatively arid landscape is studded with three-pronged cactus, spiny-leafed aloes, and divi-divi trees, with their windblown foliage. Classic Dutch-style windmills are scattered in and around Willemstad and in parts of the countryside. These standard farm models pump water from wells to irrigate vegetation.

Curaçao, together with Bonaire, St. Maarten, St. Eustatius, and Saba, is in the Kingdom of the Netherlands as part of the Netherlands Antilles. Curaçao has its own governmental authority, relying on the Netherlands only for defense and foreign affairs. Its population of 171,000 represents more than 50 nationalities.

GETTING THERE

The air routes to **Curaçao International Airport,** Plaza Margareth Abraham (☎ **599/9-682288**), are still firmly linked to those leading to nearby Aruba. In recent years, however, developments at such airlines as American (see below) have initiated direct or nonstop routings into Curaçao from such international hubs as Miami.

American Airlines (☎ **800/433-7300**) offers one daily nonstop flight to Curaçao from its hub in Miami, which departs late enough in the day (10:45am) to permit

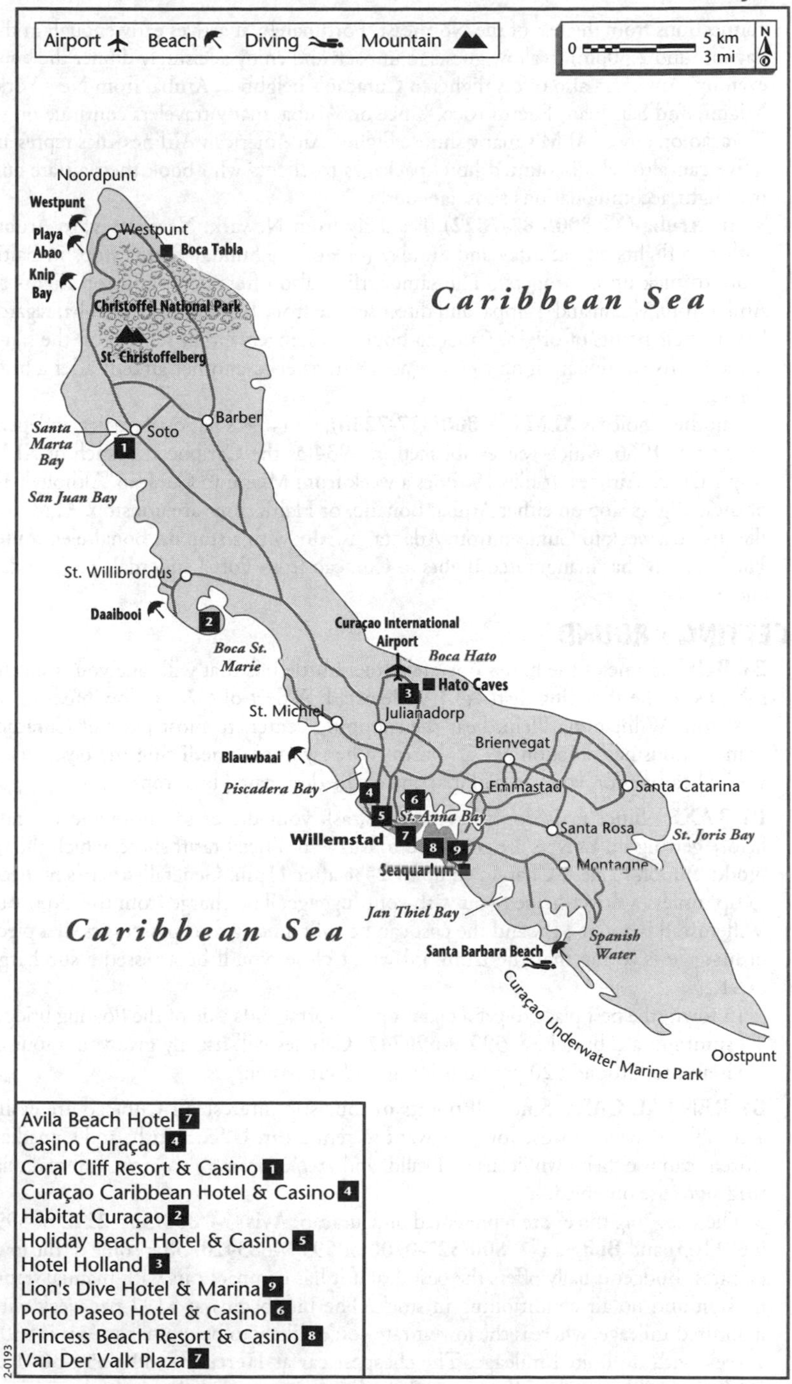

Airport
Beach
Diving
Mountain
0
5 km
3 mi
N
Noordpunt
Westpunt
Playa Abao
Knip Bay
Westpunt
Boca Tabla
Christoffel National Park
St. Christoffelberg
Caribbean Sea
Barber
Santa Marta Bay
Soto
San Juan Bay
St. Willibrordus
Daaibooi
Boca St. Marie
Curaçao International Airport
Boca Hato
Hato Caves
St. Michiel
Julianadorp
Brienvegat
Blauwbaai
Piscadera Bay
Emmastad
Santa Catarina
St. Anna Bay
Willemstad
Santa Rosa
St. Joris Bay
Seaquarium
Montagne
Jan Thiel Bay
Caribbean Sea
Santa Barbara Beach
Spanish Water
Curaçao Underwater Marine Park
Oostpunt
Avila Beach Hotel 7
Casino Curaçao 4
Coral Cliff Resort & Casino 1
Curaçao Caribbean Hotel & Casino 4
Habitat Curaçao 2
Holiday Beach Hotel & Casino 5
Hotel Holland 3
Lion's Dive Hotel & Marina 9
Porto Paseo Hotel & Casino 6
Princess Beach Resort & Casino 8
Van Der Valk Plaza 7
2-0193

connections from the rest of the Northeast. Fortunately, it arrives early enough in the day (around 2:30pm) to allow guests to unpack and enjoy a leisurely dinner the same evening. American also offers flights to Curaçao's neighbor, Aruba, from New York, Miami, and San Juan, Puerto Rico. Once on Aruba, many travelers continue on to Curaçao on any of ALM's many shuttle flights. An American Airlines sales representative can also sell discounted hotel packages to clients who book their airfare and overnight accommodations simultaneously.

Air Aruba (☎ **800/882-7822**) flies daily from Newark, New Jersey, to Aruba, with two flights on Saturday and Sunday (one of the Sunday flights stops in Baltimore to pick up passengers). The same airline also offers daily nonstop flights to Aruba from Miami and Tampa, and direct service from Baltimore. On Aruba, regardless of their points of origin, Curaçao-bound passengers either remain on the same plane for its continuation on to Curaçao, or transfer to another aircraft after a brief delay.

Another choice is **ALM** (☎ **800/327-7230**), Curaçao's national carrier, independent since 1966, which was established in 1934 as the Caribbean branch of KLM Royal Dutch Airlines. It flies 15 times a week from Miami to Curaçao. Although 10 of these flights stop on either Aruba, Bonaire, or Haiti, three are nonstop. ALM also flies twice a week to Curaçao from Atlanta, usually with a stop on Bonaire en route. Finally, ALM has inaugurated flights to Curaçao from Fort Lauderdale on Tuesday and Sunday.

GETTING AROUND

BY BUS Some of the hotels operate a free shuttle bus that will take you from the suburbs to the shopping district of Willemstad. A fleet of DAF yellow buses operates from Wilhelmina Plein, near the shopping center, to most parts of Curaçao. Some limousines function as "C" buses. When you see one listing the destination you're heading for, you can hail it at any of the designated bus stops.

BY TAXI Since taxis don't have meters, ask your driver to quote you the rate before getting in. Drivers are supposed to carry an official tariff sheet, which they'll produce upon request. Charges go up by 25% after 11pm. Generally there's no need to tip, unless a driver helped you with your luggage. The charge from the airport to Willemstad is about $15, and the cost can be split among four passengers. If a piece of luggage is so big that the trunk lid won't close, you'll be assessed a surcharge of $1.

In town, the best place to get a taxi is on the Otrabanda side of the floating bridge. To summon a cab, call ☎ **599/9-690747.** Cabbies will usually give you a tour of the island for around $20 per hour for up to four passengers.

BY RENTAL CAR Since all points of touristic interest on Curaçao are easily accessible by paved roads, you may want to rent a car. U.S., British, and Canadian citizens can use their own licenses, if valid, and *traffic moves on the right.* International road signs are observed.

The U.S. "big three" are represented on Curaçao. **Avis** (☎ **800/331-2112** or 599/9-681163) and **Budget** (☎ **800/527-0700** or 599/9-683420) offer some of the lowest rates. Budget usually offers the best deal if it has compact cars with manual transmission and no air-conditioning in stock. The rate begins at $192 per week with unlimited mileage, whereas the lowest rate you're likely to be quoted at Avis is $308 a week with unlimited mileage. The cheapest car at **Hertz** (☎ **800/654-3001** or 599/9-681182) rents for $283 per week, and represents especially good value because it includes air-conditioning. A renter's membership in certain organizations, such as AAA, or access to a corporate account, might reduce the prices a bit.

At Budget and Hertz, renters must be 25 years old, although at Budget, renters aged 23 or 24 could pay a $3 daily supplement and circumvent that rule. Avis requires a minimum age of only 21. Purchase of a collision-damage waiver (priced at $10 a day at all three companies for their least expensive cars) reduces a renter's liability in case of an accident to between $280 and $300. Some credit and charge cards will cover this insurance themselves; check directly with the issuer of the card for details. At least a week before your anticipated arrival on Curaçao, you should phone all three companies for a comparison of their latest prices and promotional offerings. In almost every case, rentals are cheaper for clients who reserve their car from North America before their departure.

FAST FACTS: Curaçao

Banks Banking hours are Monday to Friday from 8:30am to noon and 1:30 to 4:30pm. However, the Banco Popular and the Bank of America remain open during the lunch hour, doing business Monday to Friday from 9am to 3pm.

Currency While Canadian and U.S. dollars are accepted for purchases on the island, the official currency is the **Netherlands Antilles florin (NAf),** also called a guilder, which is divided into 100 NA (Netherlands Antillean) cents. The exchange rate is U.S.$1 to NAf1.77 (or 56¢ U.S. equals NAf1). Shops, hotels, and restaurants usually accept most major U.S. and Canadian credit and charge cards.

Documents To enter Curaçao, U.S. or Canadian citizens need proof of citizenship, such as a birth certificate or a passport, along with a return or continuing airline ticket out of the country. British subjects need a valid passport.

Electricity The electricity is 110-130 volts AC (50 cycles), the same as in North America, although many hotels will have transformers if your appliances happen to be European.

Information For tourist information on Curaçao, go to the **Curaçao Tourist Board,** Pietermaai (☎ **599/9-616000**). **In the United States,** contact the Curaçao Tourist Board at 400 Madison Ave., Suite 311, New York, NY 10017 (☎ **800/270-3350** or 212/683-7660); or 330 Biscayne Blvd., Suite 330, Miami, FL 33132 (☎ **305/374-5811**).

Language Dutch, Spanish, and English are spoken on Curaçao, along with Papiamento, a language that combines the three major tongues with Amerindian and African dialects.

Medical Care Medical facilities are well equipped, and the 534-bed St. Elisabeth Hospital, Breedestraat 193 (☎ **599/9-624900**), near Otrabanda in Willemstad, is one of the most up-to-date facilities in the Caribbean.

Police The police emergency number is ☎ **114** or 444444.

Safety While Curaçao is not plagued with crime, it would be wise to safeguard your valuables.

Taxes and Service Curaçao levies a room tax of 7% on accommodations, and most hotels add 12% for room service. There's a departure tax of $12.50 for international flights, or $5.65 for interisland flights.

Telephones Curaçao is not part of the 809 area code that applies to most of the Caribbean. To call Curaçao from the United States, dial 011 (the international access code), then 599 (the country code for Curaçao), and then 9 (the area code) and the local number (the number of digits in the local number varies).

Once on Curaçao, to call another number on the island only the local number is necessary; to make calls to an off-island destination, dial 021 and then the area code and number.

Time Curaçao is on Atlantic standard time year-round, one hour ahead of eastern standard time and the same as eastern daylight saving time.

Water The water comes from a modern desalination plant and is safe to drink.

Weather Curaçao has an average temperature of 81°F. Trade winds keep the island fairly cool, and it's flat and arid, with an average rainfall of only 22 inches per year.

WHERE TO STAY

Your hotel will be in Willemstad or in one of the suburbs, which lie only 10 to 15 minutes from the shopping center. The bigger hotels often have free shuttle buses running into town, and most of them have their own beaches and pools.

Curaçao is a bustling commercial center, and the downtown hotels often fill up fast with business travelers and visitors from neighboring countries such as Venezuela on a shopping holiday. Therefore, reservations are always important.

When making reservations, ask if the 7% room tax and 12% service charge are included in the price you're quoted.

VERY EXPENSIVE

✪ **Sonesta Beach Hotel & Casino Curaçao.** Piscadera Bay (P.O. Box 6003, Willemstad), Curaçao, N.A. ☎ **800/766-3782** in the U.S., or 599/9-368800. Fax 599/9-627502. 214 rms, 34 suites. A/C MINIBAR TV TEL. Winter, $255–$330 double; from $365 suite. Off-season, $180–$245 double; from $275 suite. MAP $60 per person extra. Additional person $40 extra. AE, DC, MC, V.

This is the most glamorous and most visible hotel on the island. Operated by Boston-based Sonesta Hotels, a chain known for the original artworks throughout its hotels, it opened in 1992. It's set beside the longest and most popular beach on Curaçao, 10 minutes from both the airport and the capital of Willemstad. The architects arranged it into a low-lying cluster of three-story buildings whose distinctive shape and ocher color were adapted from traditional Dutch colonial architecture. The open-sided lobby was designed for maximum views of the resort's beach and the many fountains on the property. Scattered throughout the property are unusual, often monumental, artworks by local and international artists, and a collection of unfussy, overstuffed furniture.

Each of the accommodations offers tropical accessories, a view of the ocean, and color schemes of fuchsia and turquoise whose cool tones contrast with the glaring sunlight outside.

Dining/Entertainment: The Palm Café, an American and Caribbean restaurant, is an open-air resting point serving breakfast and lunch. Every Wednesday, the Palm Café hosts a limbo/fire-eating show. The Emerald Bar & Grill serves grilled continental specialties and light appetizers in an atmosphere similar to that of an upscale private club. The Portofino, open for dinner only, features northern Italian specialties in an airy setting inspired by a resort along the Mediterranean. There's also an in-house casino, with at least five kinds of gambling-related activities.

Services: Room service (6am to midnight), concierge, massage, children's program for kids 5 to 12.

Facilities: Two tennis courts lit at night, lagoon-shaped swimming pool with swim-up bar, two open-air Jacuzzis patterned on Roman models, duty-free shopping arcade, a variety of land and water sports, the largest hotel beach on the island.

EXPENSIVE

✪ Avila Beach Hotel. Penstraat 130 (P.O. Box 791), Willemstad, Curaçao, N.A. ☎ **599/9-614377.** Fax 599/9-611493. 80 rms, 7 suites. TV TEL. Winter, $118–$208 double; $280 suite. Off-season, $105–$170 double; $240 suite. MAP $50 per person extra. AE, DC, MC, V.

This historic hotel consists of a beautifully restored 200-year-old mansion and a large extension, called La Belle Alliance, completed in 1992, which added 40 deluxe rooms and seven suites. All the new rooms have air-conditioning, television, private bathrooms with tub, minirefrigerator, and a balcony with an ocean view, and some also contain a kitchenette. The rooms in the main mansion are rather basic and small, but have charm. The hostelry lies on the shore road leading east out of the city from the shopping center. It's the only beachfront hotel in Willemstad proper, set on its own private beach. The core of the hotel remains the historic mansion, which was built by the English governor of Curaçao during the British occupation of the island at the time of the Napoleonic wars. The mansion was converted into a hotel in 1949, and today attracts the royals of the Netherlands.

Dining/Entertainment: The hotel offers two restaurants: the Belle Terrace, a romantic open-air restaurant at the seaside shaded by huge trees. They feature a full à la carte menu (see "Where to Dine," below). Blues, an elevated restaurant/bar at the end of the pier, provides facilities for small informal parties, catering to a crowd with a taste for jazz, swing, and, of course, blues. Antillean nights with local cuisine and live music are featured, as are Saturday-night barbecues.

Services: Baby-sitting, laundry.

Facilities: Tennis court (available daytime and evening), year-round ocean swimming from private sandy beach, terrace overlooking the ocean.

Curaçao Caribbean Hotel & Casino. Piscadera Bay, John F. Kennedy Blvd. (P.O. Box 2133, Willemstad), Curaçao, N.A. ☎ **599/9-625000.** Fax 599/9-625846. 181 rms, 15 suites. A/C TV TEL. Winter, $150–$160 double; $160–$170 triple; $170–$180 quad. Off-season, $120–$130 double; $130–$140 triple; $140–$150 quad. Suites from $275 year-round. AE, DC, MC, V.

This five-story resort on the outskirts of Willemstad opens onto a tiny beach. It has a free bus service to take you shopping in town. A self-contained concrete complex, it's set among rocky bluffs with all rooms either on the ocean or a garden. Glass-enclosed elevators clinging to the exterior walls of the hotel offer a panoramic view as you're whisked to your room. The bedrooms have baths with big towels, traditional furnishings, and private balconies. Many of the regular rooms are dull, in spite of refurbishing since 1994. However, for business or other travelers, the hotel offers an Executive Floor, with amenities such as direct-dial telephones, fax machines, and secretarial services.

Dining/Entertainment: The hotel offers several restaurants and two bars. The wide-open lower lounge area, giving everyone a trade-wind-swept view of Piscadera Bay, is the most impressive. Furnished in wicker, the Pisca Terrace bar and restaurant opens onto an eight-pointed-star-shaped pool and the ruins of a fort two centuries old. You can enjoy a buffet breakfast on this terrace. Other dining choices include La Garuda, serving Indonesian food, Pirates Restaurant for seafood, the Buccaneer for both seafood and international specialties, and the Coco Steak House. Mexican nights are popular, as are Antillean nights with folklore shows. Of course, the casino is a major attraction.

Services: Room service (7am to 11pm), laundry, baby-sitting, free bus service to town.

Facilities: The Seascape, a dive shop offering the best water-sports program on the island (including skin diving, sailing, deep-sea fishing, and sea Jeeps), two Grasstex tennis courts (lit at night), well-stocked shopping complex.

Habitat Curaçao. Rif St. Marie, Curaçao, N.A. ☎ **599/9-607263.** Fax 305/371-2337. 56 junior suites, 20 two-bedroom cottages. A/C. Winter, $513–$939 per person suite; $495–$720 per person cottage. Off-season, $360–$610 per person suite; $377–$492 per person cottage. Rates include buffet breakfast, airport transfers, 2-tank boat dive daily, unlimited 24-hour shore diving on 5-day and 4-night package. AE, DC, MC, V.

The diving legend of the ABC Islands, Captain Don Stewart, longtime operator of Captain Don's Habitat on Bonaire, has invaded Curaçao. About 20 minutes from Willemstad, this new oceanfront resort provides environmentally sensitive dive vacations. Facilities include a PADI five-star instruction center, offering dive courses from the novice to instructor levels. There's also a swimming pool, and the resort, set in manicured gardens, opens onto a private beach. Accommodations include junior suites which are fully air-conditioned and tastefully furnished with two queen-size beds, a fully equipped kitchenette, a large balcony or patio, and a full bath. Cottages, each consisting of two bedrooms, are also air-conditioned, with a living room, kitchen, bath, and large patio.

Princess Beach Resort & Casino. Dr. Martin Luther King Blvd., Willemstad, Curaçao, N.A. ☎ **800/327-3286** in the U.S. and Canada, or 599/9-367888. Fax 599/9-614131. 341 rms, 8 suites. A/C MINIBAR TV TEL. Winter, $200–$275 double; from $300 suite. Off-season, $145–$195 double; from $210 suite. MAP $50 per person extra. AE, DC, MC, V.

This island's largest resort is a modern, low-rise condominium-style beachfront resort in front of the Curaçao Underwater Park and close to the Seaquarium (a complimentary shuttle ride away from Willemstad). This high-energy hotel has the only half-kilometer-long beach on the island. Many people assume that it's operated by the Princess Cruise Line because of its name; actually, it's a Holiday Inn Crowne Plaza Resort. The hotel is Sonesta's only serious rival on the island, but we give the edge to Sonesta for superior amenities. Many of the refurbished bedrooms look out over the beach, and all have hair dryers and either balconies or patios shielded by tropical plants. The most modern rooms and the most sought-after are in a wing completed in 1993.

Dining/Entertainment: The hotel has an outdoor dining area, plus an air-conditioned gourmet restaurant featuring an international dinner menu. A casino, the best in Curaçao, and nightly entertainment are added features.

Services: Room service, laundry, dry cleaning, baby-sitting.

Facilities: Docking facilities for deep-sea fishing, windsurfing center, two tennis courts, two freshwater pools (one with a swim-up bar), and, in the vicinity, a nine-hole golf course.

MODERATE

Coral Cliff Resort & Casino. Santa Martha Bay (P.O. Box 3782), Curaçao, N.A. ☎ **599/9-641610.** Fax 599/9-641781. 55 units. A/C TV TEL. Winter, $150 double. Off-season, $135 double. MAP $28 per person extra. AE, MC, V.

On the western part of the island, this resort is surrounded and isolated by 18 acres of grounds, cliffs, mountains, and bays. Renovated in 1994, it offers rooms overlooking the Caribbean Sea. This is not a plushly decorated place—in fact, it's rather rustic, with wood beams. Tourists from the Netherlands view it as an offbeat Antillean retreat; others seeking first-class accommodations may find the rooms a bit austere and ready for some rejuvenation. The location is on a natural beach attracting scuba divers and snorkelers. Scuba and other water-sports equipment is available at the hotel's beachside water-sports center, and other facilities include day and night tennis, minigolf, volleyball, and a children's playground, or they can arrange for horseback riding or waterskiing.

The hotel staff will pick you up at the airport, and provide complimentary shuttle service into town, as well as laundry and baby-sitting on request. Guests can relax at the beach bar and have a drink as they watch the sun set over the open-air Cliffhanger Bar. Later, they go to the open-air Terrace Restaurant, overlooking the water, for international-style but sometimes rather bland meals. A small and lackluster casino also overlooks the sea.

Holiday Beach Hotel & Casino. Pater Euwensweg 31 (P.O. Box 2178), Willemstad, Curaçao, N.A. ☎ **599/9-625400.** Fax 599/9-624397. 200 rms. A/C TV TEL. Winter, $150–$165 double. Off-season, $110–$120 double. MAP $33 per person extra. AE, DC, MC, V.

Along a sandy beach dotted with palm trees, this four-story establishment, no longer a Holiday Inn, sits near a grassy peninsula jutting out to sea about a mile from the capital. It boasts all the facilities of a resort hotel, a crescent-shaped beach against a backdrop of palms, and exceptionally reasonable rates. The main part of the complex houses the Casino Royale, one of the largest casinos on the island, and the premises contain a handful of tennis courts. Local entertainment is offered in the hotel's nightclub.

The sleeping quarters are in two four-story wings, centering around a U-shaped garden with a large freshwater swimming pool. The 30-year-old bedrooms have recently been refurbished, opening onto private balconies. A few open onto the water; others face the parking lot or pool. Wall-to-wall carpeting and big tile baths are just two of the comforts. Laundry, baby-sitting, and room service are available. A water-sports concession operates on the grounds, and there's also a supervised children's program.

Lion's Dive Hotel & Marina. Bapor Kibrá, Willemstad, Curaçao, N.A. ☎ **599/9-618100.** Fax 599/9-618200. 72 rms. A/C TV TEL. Winter, $145 double. Off-season, $125 double. AE, DC, MC, V.

On the island's largest white-sand beach, a 30-minute taxi ride southeast of the airport, this complete dive resort features programs supervised by the Underwater Curaçao staff. Each of its comfortable but routinely standard accommodations has a sea view, as well as a balcony or terrace, and two queen-size beds, plus a safety-deposit box. Other facilities include a freshwater pool and a restaurant specializing in steak and seafood. There's also a beach bar and restaurant open for lunch and dinner. Introductory dives and resort and certification courses are offered, and on the premises is a fully equipped rental dive shop. Seven boat dives are conducted daily. Waterskiing, windsurfing, and sailing can also be arranged. Massage facilities are available, as are laundry and baby-sitting services. The hotel also has a health club and fitness center, Body Beach. A seaquariam complex includes marine life encounters.

INEXPENSIVE

Hotel Holland. F. D. Rooseveltweg 524, Curaçao, N.A. ☎ **599/9-688044.** Fax 599/9-688114. 40 rms, 5 suites. A/C TV TEL. $79 double; from $117 suite. AE, DC, MC, V.

A five-minute drive from the airport, the affordable Hotel Holland contains the Flying Dutchman Bar, which is a popular gathering place, plus a small casino that opened in 1991. For a few brief minutes of every day, you can see airplanes landing from your perch at the edge of the poolside terrace, the Cockpit Restaurant, where well-prepared meals are served during good weather. The rather basic but clean accommodations have VCRs, refrigerators, and balconies. Laundry and baby-sitting are available, and dive packages can be arranged. As for service and a helpful staff? On our recent visit, they couldn't even tell us when their restaurant was open.

✪ **Porto Paseo Hotel & Casino.** De Rouvilleweg 47, Willemstad, Curaçao, N.A. ☎ **599/9-627878.** Fax 599/9-627969. 43 rms, 1 suite, 2 one-bedroom apts with kitchenette, 1 two-bedroom apt without kitchenette. Year-round rates, $95 single or double, including breakfast; $125 suite for 2, including breakfast; $110 one-bedroom apt, without breakfast; $140 two-bedroom apt, without breakfast. AE, MC, V.

Set on the Otrabanda side of Willemstad's harbor front, this is one of the capital's most beautiful and stylish restorations of a historic building, and one of the island's best hotel values. Completed in 1992, it incorporates what was originally constructed in the 1870s as the island's first hospital with a sprawling, pancake-flat garden and clusters of modern, low-rise buildings that each contain between four and five accommodations. One of the centerpieces of the estate is a flagstone-covered courtyard illuminated with streetlamps, and a simple brasserie, the Bon Bini, which is only open for lunch. (In the evening, many clients walk the short distance to E Gai, recommended separately.) On the premises is a casino, a bar with views over Santa Ana bay, a collection of ornamental birds that include cockatoos, and a sense of Dutch colonial life of long ago. Bedrooms are severely dignified, airy, and comfortable.

Van Der Valk Plaza. Plaza Pier (P.O. Box 813), Willemstad, Curaçao, N.A. ☎ **800/447-7462** or 599/9-612500. Fax 599/9-616543. 236 rms, 18 suites. A/C TV TEL. Winter, $91–$124 double; from $141 suite. Off-season, $57–$95 double; $118 suite. Rates include American breakfast. AE, MC, V.

Standing guard over the Punda side of St. Anna Bay, the Plaza is nestled in the ramparts of an 18th-century waterside fort on the eastern tip of the entrance to the harbor, a 20-minute drive south of the airport. In fact, it's one of the harbor's two "lighthouses." The hotel has to carry marine collision insurance, the only hostelry in the Caribbean with that distinction. Since it's hardly on a beachfront, it often attracts more business clients than tourists. However, for vacationers who want to be within walking distance of the heart of town, this would be a suitable choice. The original part of the hotel followed the style of the arcaded fort. However, now there's a tower of rooms stacked 12 stories high. Each of the bedrooms, your own crow's nest, is comfortably furnished and contains a personal safe, although the room decor strikes many as garish. All is forgiven, however, because of the view of the passing ships. The pool, with a bar and suntanning area, is placed inches from the parapet of the fort. In the hotel's Waterfort Grill, you can order American and continental dishes. Tournesol is a more formal and panoramic dining view, within the penthouse level of the hotel, serving a French cuisine Tuesday through Sunday nights. The hotel offers laundry, baby-sitting, and room service (from 7:30am to 11pm), and has a small casino. It also operates a diving shop and a diving school.

WHERE TO DINE

EXPENSIVE

✪ **Bistro Le Clochard.** Riffort, on the Otrabanda side of the pontoon bridge. ☎ **599/9-625666.** Reservations recommended. Main courses $21.30–$29.30. AE, MC, V. Mon–Fri noon–2pm and 6:30–10:45pm, Sat 6:30–10:45pm. (Harborside Terrace, Mon–Sat 6–11pm.) FRENCH/SWISS.

Bistro Le Clochard has been snugly fitted into the northwestern corner of the grim ramparts of Fort Rif, at the gateway to the harbor. Its entrance is marked with a canopy, which leads to a series of rooms, each built under the 19th-century vaulting of the old Dutch fort. Several tables have a view of the Caribbean Sea. More panoramic is the establishment's outdoor terrace (the Harborside Terrace), built directly at the edge of the water, with a view over the harbor and the sparkling lights of the nearby town.

To begin, you might order bouillabaisse *à notre façon,* a fresh local fish soup. Among the alpine specialties are raclette (melted Swiss cheese served with boiled potato, onions, and pickles) and a fondue bourguignonne. Of course, critics say that food such as this is best served at a ski resort in the Alps. One section of the menu is called "Romancing the Stone." The stone is heated in the oven and remains at a constant temperature. It's brought directly to the table, and, without using oil or fat, your choice from the menu is cooked on the stone—tournedos, sirloin, T-bone, boneless chicken breast, or fresh fish. Heavy or light, the food is consistently reliable and good, although we wish the prices weren't so high.

Legends. Orionweig 12, Salina. ☎ **599/9-618222.** Reservations recommended. Main courses $16.50. Mon–Fri noon–2pm and 7–10pm; Sat 7–10pm. INTERNATIONAL.

This *très-intime* spot, with only eight tables, offers a cuisine that ranks among the island's best. It's the domain of an Italian chef with much European experience. His menu is international, although it leans heavily toward French and Italian cuisine. The location is east of the harbor. Prices are a bit high, but there is value here in that every dish is freshly prepared and is made with quality ingredients. The service is flawless. The pricing scheme is unique on the island: All appetizers, including the smoked salmon or the savory kettle of snails, go for just one price. Each main course is also priced the same. You might feast off the catch of the day (usually red snapper), which is generally perfectly cooked and not allowed to dry out. Nearly everything is imported, but handled deftly by the kitchen staff, especially the beef tenderloin, the Norwegian salmon, the veal, or scampi. Desserts are quite luscious, evoking some of the best in Italy, including cheesecake or tiramisu.

Fort Nassau. Near Point Juliana. ☎ **599/9-613086.** Reservations recommended. Main courses $20.50–$27.10. AE, DC, MC, V. Mon–Fri noon–2pm and 6:30–11pm, Sat–Sun 6:30–11pm. INTERNATIONAL.

This restored restaurant and bar is built on a hilltop overlooking Willemstad in the ruins of a buttressed fort dating from 1796. It has retained an 18th-century decor. From the Battery Terrace, a 360° panorama of the sea, the harbor, and Willemstad unfolds. You'll even have a faraway view of the island's vast oil refinery. A signal tower on the cliff sends out beacons to approaching ships. You can visit the fashionably decorated bar just to have a drink and watch the sunset; happy hour is 6 to 7pm Monday through Friday.

Queen Beatrix and Crown Prince Claus have dined here, and rumor has it they were more captivated by the view than by the food. Some of the more imaginative dishes on the menu perhaps should never have been conjured up. However, we were impressed with the goat cheese in puff pastry and a cold terrine with layers of salmon and sole. The cream of mustard (yes, that's right) soup seems an acquired taste. Opt for the breast of duck with sun-dried tomatoes and basil, or even a well-prepared steak. The restaurant is a five-minute drive from Willemstad.

La Pergola. In the Waterfront Arches. Waterfort Straat. ☎ **599/9-613482.** Reservations recommended. Main courses $20–$50. AE, MC, V. Mon–Sat noon–2pm, daily 6:30–10:30pm. ITALIAN.

Of the quintet of restaurants nestled into the weather-beaten core of the island's oldest fort, this is the only one focusing on the cuisine and traditions of Italy. The kitchen and one of the three dining areas are in the cellar, whereas two others benefit from streaming sunlight and a view over the seafront. As the name implies, decoration is enhanced with a replica of a pergola evocative of the Renaissance. Menu items change virtually every day, and are as authentic to Italian (non-Americanized) traditions as anything else in Curaçao. Examples include gnocchi of chicken, fettuccine Julio Cesare (with ham, cream, and mushrooms), a succulent version of *grigliata mista,* carpaccio della Pergola, seafood salad, and a topnotch version of exotic mushrooms, in season, garnished with Parmesan cheese and parsley. Looking for an unusual form of pasta? Ask for *maltagliata* (pasta cut at random angles and lengths) served with either Gorgonzola sauce or Genoan-style pesto. This restaurant has thrived here for more than a decade.

Wine Cellar. Ooststraat/Concordiastraat. ☎ **599/9-612178.** Reservations required. Main courses $18–$35. AE, DC, MC, V. Tues–Fri noon–2pm and 6pm–midnight, Sat–Sun 6pm–midnight. INTERNATIONAL.

Opposite the cathedral in the center of town is the domain of Nico and Angela Cornelisse and their son, Ivo, who offer one of the most extensive wine lists on the island. The Victorian atmosphere is reminiscent of an old-fashioned Dutch home. The kitchen turns out an excellent lobster salad and a sole meunière in a butter-and-herb sauce. You might also try, if featured, fresh red snapper or U.S. tenderloin of beef with goat cheese sauce. Game dishes are imported throughout the year from Holland and are likely to include venison roasted with mushrooms, hare, or roast goose. After years of dining here, we have found the food commendable in every way—dishes are flavorful and hearty, although there are selections for lighter appetites. Of course, the food never matches the impressive and large wine list. Our greatest disappointment in this restaurant always occurs when the check is presented. One hopes you'll have won at the casino that day.

MODERATE

Belle Terrace. In the Avila Beach Hotel, Penstraat 130. ☎ **599/9-614377.** Reservations required. Main courses $15–$34; *menu dégustation* $27 for 2 courses, $32 for 3 courses. AE, DC, MC, V. Daily 7–10:30pm (Wed and Sat, barbecue). INTERNATIONAL/DANISH.

You'll discover this open-air restaurant in a 200-year-old mansion on the beachfront of Willemstad. It offers superb dining in a relaxed and informal atmosphere. The Schooner Bar, where you can enjoy a rum punch, is shaped like a weather-beaten ship's prow looking out to sea. The restaurant, sheltered by an arbor of flamboyant branches, features Scandinavian, continental, and local cuisine with such specialties as pickled herring, smoked salmon, barracuda, and a Danish lunch platter. Local dishes, such as keshi yena (baked Gouda cheese with a spicy meat filling), are on the menu. On Saturday night the chef has a beef-tenderloin barbecue and a help-yourself salad bar. Fish is always fresh at Belle Terrace, and the chef prepares a seafood platter to perfection: grilled, poached, or meunière. Desserts include Danish pastry and cakes, as well as a large selection of homemade ice creams.

From the airport, follow the signs to Punda. Turn left after the second traffic light in town. Stay on the right side of that road (Plaza Smeets) and go straight ahead. If you keep to the right side of the road you'll enter Penstraat, where you'll find the Avila Beach Hotel on the right-hand side.

Fort Waakzaamheid Bistro. Seru di Domi, Otrabanda. ☎ **599/9-623633.** Reservations recommended. Main courses $18–$22; 3-course "early bird" dinner (at 7pm) $14.30. AE, MC, V. Wed–Mon 5–10pm. (Bar, open until 1am, later on weekends.) INTERNATIONAL.

Captain Bligh, of *Bounty* fame, captured this old fort in 1804 and laid siege to Willemstad for almost a month. A stone-and-hardwood tavern and restaurant have been created in the fort, which opens onto a view of Otrabanda and the harbor entrance. The atmosphere is that of a country tavern. Try to arrive in time to watch the panoramic sunset. You can visit just for a drink or munchies. Otherwise, stick around for dinner, enjoying mainly steaks and barbecued fish along with generous helpings from the salad bar. This fort is often patronized by those wishing to escape the hordes who occasionally descend on Fort Nassau (see above). This is not a venue for overly elaborate cuisine. Your best bet might be the fresh fish, perhaps Curaçao snapper. Prime rib, garlic shrimp (a bit overcooked for our taste), and a notable conch platter are likely to be offered.

Pisces Seafood. Caracasbaaiweg 476. ☎ **599/9-672181.** Reservations recommended. Main courses $15–$30. AE, DC, MC, V. Fri–Wed 6–10pm. CREOLE/SEAFOOD.

This West Indian restaurant may be difficult to find, as it's on a flat industrial coastline near a marina and an oil refinery, about 20 minutes from the capital on the island's southernmost tip. There has been a restaurant here since the 1930s, when sailors and workers from the oil refinery came for home-cooked meals. Today the simple frame building offers seating near the rough-hewn bar or in a breeze-swept inner room. Pisces serves combinations of seafood that depend on the catch of the day. Main courses, served with rice, vegetables, and plantains, might include sopi, "seacat" (squid), mula (similar to kingfish), red snapper, or any of these served, if you wish, in copious quantities for two or more people in the Pisces platter. Shrimp and conch are each prepared three different ways: with garlic, with curry, or Creole style. Essentially, this place offers food the way the locals used to eat long before the cruise ships started arriving and the sprawling resorts opened. It's simple, straightforward, affordable, and often quite good.

Rijstaffel Restaurant Indonesia and Holland Club Bar. Mercuriusstraat 13, Salinja. ☎ **599/9-612999.** Reservations recommended. Main courses $12.70–$21.20; rijstaffel $22 for 16 dishes, $24.30 for 20 dishes, $37.15 for 25 dishes; all-vegetarian rijstaffel $21 for 16 dishes. AE, DC, MC, V. Mon–Sat noon–2pm and 6–9:30pm, Sun 6–9:30pm. INDONESIAN.

This is the best place on the island to sample the Indonesian rijstaffel, the traditional "rice table" with all the zesty side dishes. You must ask a taxi to take you to this villa in the suburbs near Salinja, near the Princess Beach Resort & Casino southeast of Willemstad. At lunchtime, the selection of dishes is more modest, but for dinner, Javanese cooks prepare the specialty of the house, a rijstaffel consisting of 16, 20, or 25 dishes. There's even an all-vegetarian rijstaffel. Warming trays are placed on your table, and the service is buffet style. It's best to go with a party so that all of you can share in the feast. The food is spicy, with a lot of flavor, and you can season your plate with peppers rated hot, very hot, and palate-melting. It's a good change of pace when you can't face another serving of steak and lobster tail.

INEXPENSIVE

The Cockpit. In the Hotel Holland, F. D. Rooseveltweg 524. ☎ **599/9-688044.** Reservations required. Main courses $10–$25. AE, DC, MC, V. 7am–10pm. DUTCH/INTERNATIONAL.

The decor of this restaurant has an aeronautical flavor: the nose of an airplane cockpit is the main decorative focal point. Located on the scrub-bordered road leading to the airport, a few minutes from the landing strips, the Cockpit serves up international cuisine with an emphasis on Dutch and Antillean specialties. Guests enjoy such dishes as fresh fish in season (served Curaçao style), Dutch-style steak, Caribbean curried chicken, split-pea soup, and various pasta dishes such as the shrimp linguine della mama served in a lobster sauce and topped with melted cheese. All dishes are accompanied by fresh vegetables and Dutch-style potatoes. No one pretends that the food is gourmet fare; it's robust, hearty, and filled with good country flavor, nothing else. On some occasions nothing else will do, and happily this place is also one of the best dining values on this island where food prices often climb to dizzy heights. Guests can enjoy their meals outside around the pool or in the cockpit-inspired dining room.

E Gai. Klipstraat 10. ☎ **599/9-627878,** ext. 216. Reservations recommended. Main courses $7–$15. AE, DC, MC, V. Daily 10am–11pm. CURAÇAON.

More than any other restaurant on the island, this one emphasizes the cuisine, architecture, and traditions of Curaçao. It's housed in what was originally built in 1862 as the home of a wealthy colonial, and derived its name (Papiamento for "the rooster") from an incident in 1879 when a rooster in a tree on the property soiled the uniform of the island's governor, whose residence at the time lay nearby. The vengeful and tyrannical governor ordered that the bird be imprisoned in the island's jail, an event that survives as a legend to this day. For years after that, the site was the home of a pair of sisters who baked buttercakes for a living. In 1996, the house was transformed into a citadel of civic pride, whose goal seems to be the conversion of ordinary folk into connoisseurs of Curaçaon cuisine. In a pair of dining rooms accented with linen tablecloths, or on an outdoor terrace, you can enjoy dishes that include *sopa di banana* (banana soup); *cabrito* (roasted goat); *papaya soba* (roasted papaya stuffed with minced beef or pork); *balchi di pesca* (fish stew with Creole sauce); and *tournedos Otrabanda* (tenderloin steak with rum and black-pepper sauce).

Golden Star. Socratesstraat 2. ☎ **599/9-654795.** Reservations not required. Main courses $7.50–$25.70. AE, DC, MC, V. Daily 9am–1am. CREOLE.

The best (and one of the cheapest) place to go on the island for *criollo,* or local food, is inland from the coast road leading southeast from St. Anna Bay, at the corner of Dr. Hugenholtzweg and Dr. Maalweg, southeast of Willemstad. Comparable to a roadside diner, the air-conditioned restaurant is very simple, but it boasts a varied menu of very tasty Antillean dishes, such as *carco stoba* (conch stew), *bestia chiki* (goat-meat stew), *bakijauw* (salted cod), and *concomber stoba* (stewed meat and marble-size spiny cucumbers). Other specialties include *kiwa* (criollo shrimp) and *sopi carni* (meat stew). Everything is served with a side order of funchi, the cornmeal staple. The restaurant's clientele is dominated mostly by locals, but it's not unusual for an occasional tourist to drop in. The place is almost deliberately tacky, just the way its devotees like it.

Pinocchio. Schottegatweg 82, Salinja. ☎ **599/9-376784.** Reservations not required. Main courses $12.30–$21.50. AE, DC, MC, V. Mon–Sat 10am–10pm, Sun 6–10pm. INTERNATIONAL.

Set in the suburb of Salinja, a short drive south of Willemstad, this plant-filled restaurant caters to couples and families. Decorated in a tropical medley of bright colors, it maintains an active bar area. Menu items are simple and flavorful, including burgers, sandwiches, salads, steaks, fish dishes, buffalo-style chicken wings, and pita pockets filled, Lebanese style, with spiced lamb (*shoarma*). Go here when you're on the run and want something simple, plain, and fast.

BEACHES, WATER SPORTS & OUTDOOR PURSUITS

BEACHES Its beaches are not as good as Aruba's 7-mile strip of sand, but Curaçao does have some 38 of them, ranging from hotel sands to secluded coves. About 30 minutes from town, in the Willibrordus area on the west side of Curaçao, **Daaibooi** is a good beach. It's free, but there are no changing facilities. A good private beach on the eastern side of the island is **Santa Barbara Beach,** on land owned by a mining company. It's between the open sea and the island's primary water-sports and recreational area known as Spanish Water. On the same land are Table Mountain, a remarkable landmark, and an old phosphate mine. The natural beach has pure-white sand and calm water. A buoy line protects swimmers from boats. Rest rooms, changing rooms, a snack bar, and a terrace are among the amenities. You can rent water bicycles and small motorboats. The beach, open daily from 8am to 6pm, has access to the Curaçao Underwater Park.

Blauwbaai (Blue Bay) is the largest and most frequented beach on Curaçao, with enough white sand for everybody. Along with showers and changing facilities, there are plenty of shady places to retreat from the noonday sun. To reach it, follow the road that goes past the Holiday Beach Hotel, heading in the direction of Juliandorp. Follow the sign that tells you to bear left for Blauwbaai and the fishing village of San Michiel.

Other beaches include: **Westpunt,** known for the gigantic cliffs that frame it and the Sunday divers who jump from the cliffs into the ocean below. This public beach is located on the northwestern tip of the island. **Knip Bay,** just south of Westpunt, is a beach at the foot of beautiful turquoise waters. On weekends, live music and dancing make it a lively place. Changing facilities and refreshments are available. **Playa Abao,** with crystal turquoise water, is a beach at the northern tip of the island.

A word of caution to swimmers: The sea water remains an almost-constant 76°F year-round, with good underwater visibility, but beware of stepping on the spines of the sea urchins that sometimes abound in these waters. To give temporary first aid for an embedded urchin's spine, try the local remedies of vinegar or lime juice, or as the natives advise, a burning match if you're tough. While the urchin spines are not fatal, they can cause several days of real discomfort.

BOATING TOURS **Taber Tours,** Dokweg (☎ **599/9-376637**), offers a handful of seagoing tours, such as an eight-hour snorkel/barbecue trip to Port Marie, which includes round-trip transportation to excellent reef sites, use of snorkeling equipment, and a barbecue, for a cost of $60 per person. No children 9 and under are allowed.

A less ambitious tour involves a sunset cruise on which wine, cheese, and French bread are served. The two-hour sailing trip leaves at dusk on Saturday only, for a cost of $30 per adult and $20 for children 11 and under.

Travelers looking for a seagoing experience similar to the sailing days of yore should book a trip on the ***Insulinde,*** Handelskade (☎ **599/9-601340;** beware, this is a cellular phone so the connection might be muffled). This 120-foot traditionally rigged sail clipper is available for day trips and chartering. Every Thursday (or by special arrangement), the ship sails north from its berth beside Willemstad's main pier to the island's northwestern shore. Here, at Porto Marie (also referred to as Boca St. Marie), guests disembark onto the white sands of a beach, beside a private beach house. Included in the $55 per person charge is lunch and free use of snorkeling equipment. Advance reservations are necessary. Outbound transit is by sail; the return is by the ship's engines. Departure from the pier is at 9am every Thursday; return to the pier is around 6pm the same day. Longer trips to Bonaire or Venezuela are also possible.

GOLF The **Curaçao Golf and Squash Club,** Wilhelminalaan, in Emmastad (☎ **599/9-373590**), is your best bet. Greens fees are $20, and both clubs and carts can be rented upon demand. The nine-hole course (the only one on the island) is open to nonmembers only in the morning, daily except Thursday from 8am to noon. Afternoon tee-offs are reserved for members and for tournaments. Thursday hours for nonmembers are 10am until sundown.

TENNIS There are tennis courts at the Curaçao Caribbean Hotel & Casino, Princess Beach Resort & Casino, and Holiday Beach Hotel & Casino.

WATER SPORTS Most hotels offer their own water-sports programs. However, if your hotel isn't equipped, we suggest that you head for one of the most complete water-sports facilities on Curaçao, **Seascape Dive and Watersports,** at the Curaçao Caribbean Hotel (☎ **599/9-625905**). Specializing in snorkeling and scuba diving to reefs and underwater wrecks, it operates from a hexagonal kiosk set on stilts above the water, just offshore from the hotel's beach.

Open from 8am to 5pm daily, the company offers snorkeling excursions for $25 per person in an underwater park offshore from the hotel, waterskiing for $50 per half hour, and rental of Jet-Skis for $50 per half hour. A Sunfish can be rented for $20, and an introductory scuba lesson, conducted by a competent dive instructor with PADI certification, goes for $45; four-dive packages cost $124. Bottom fishing, with all equipment included, aboard a 38-foot Delta suitable for up to six passengers, costs $180 for a half day and $300 for a full day.

One trip enthusiastically endorsed by some visitors departs from the hotel at 7am (when participation warrants). The destination is Little Curaçao, midway between Curaçao and Bonaire. Swimwear is skimpy once you get to the sugar-white sands of the island. Fishing, snorkeling, and the acquisition of a "topless tan" are highlights. The price is $70 per person, and the excursion lasts all day.

They can also arrange deep-sea fishing for $336 for a half-day tour carrying a maximum of six people, $560 for a full-day tour. Drinks and equipment are included, but you'll have to get your hotel to pack your lunch.

Underwater Curaçao, in Bapor Kibrá (☎ **599/9-618131**), has a complete PADI-accredited underwater-sports program. A fully stocked modern dive shop has retail and rental equipment. Individual dives and dive packages are offered, costing $33 per dive for experienced divers. An introductory dive for novices is priced at $65, and a snorkel trip costs only $20, including equipment.

Scuba divers and snorkelers can expect spectacular scenery in waters with visibility often exceeding 100 feet at the **Curaçao Underwater Park,** which stretches along 12½ miles of Curaçao's southern coastline. Although the park technically begins at Princess Beach and extends all the way to East Point, the island's most southeasterly tip, some scuba aficionados and island dive operators are aware of other, excellent dive sites outside the official boundaries of this park. Lying beneath the surface of the water are steep walls, at least two shallow wrecks, gardens of soft corals, and more than 30 species of hard corals. Although access from shore is possible at Jan Thiel Bay and Santa Barbara Beach, most people visit the park by boat. For easy and safe mooring, the park has 16 mooring buoys, placed at the best dive and snorkel sites. A snorkel trail with underwater interpretive markers is laid out just east of the Princess Beach Resort & Casino and is accessible from shore. Spearfishing, anchoring in the coral, and taking anything from the reefs, except photographs, are strictly prohibited.

SEEING THE SIGHTS

Most cruise-ship passengers see only Willemstad—or, more accurately, the shops—but you may want to get out into the *cunucu,* or countryside, and explore the towering cacti and rolling hills topped by *landhuizen* (plantation houses) built more than three centuries ago.

WILLEMSTAD

Willemstad was originally founded as Santa Ana by the Spanish in the 1500s. Dutch traders found a vast natural harbor, a perfect hideaway along the Spanish Main, and they renamed it Willemstad in the 17th century. Not only is Willemstad the capital of Curaçao, it's also the seat of government for the Netherlands Antilles. Today it boasts rows of pastel-colored, red-roofed town houses in the downtown area.

The city grew up on both sides of the canal. Today it's divided into **Punda** (Old World Dutch ambience and the best shopping) and **Otrabanda** ("the other side," the contemporary side). Both sections are connected by the **Queen Emma Pontoon**

Bridge, a pedestrian walkway. Powered by a diesel engine, it swings open many times every day to let ships from all over the globe pass in and out of the harbor.

The view from the bridge is of the old **gabled houses** in harmonized pastel shades. The bright colors, according to legend, are a holdover from the time when one of the island's early governors is said to have had eye trouble and flat white gave him headaches.

The colonial-style architecture, reflecting the Dutch influence, gives the town a "storybook" look. The houses, built three or four stories high, are crowned by "step" gables and roofed with orange Spanish tiles. Hemmed in by the sea, a tiny canal, and an inlet, the streets are narrow, and they're crosshatched by still narrower alleyways.

Except for the pastel colors, Willemstad may remind you of old Amsterdam. It has one of the most intriguing townscapes in the Caribbean. Don't let the colors deceive you. The city can be rather dirty, in spite of its fairy-tale appearance.

A **statue of Pedro Luis Brion** dominates the square known as Brionplein right at the Otrabanda end of the pontoon bridge. Born in Curaçao in 1782, he became the island's favorite son and best-known war hero. Under Simón Bolívar, he was an admiral of the fleet and fought for the independence of Venezuela and Colombia.

In addition to the pontoon bridge, the **Queen Juliana Bridge** opened to vehicular traffic in 1973. Spanning the harbor, it rises 195 feet, which makes it the highest bridge in the Caribbean and one of the tallest in the world.

The Waterfront originally guarded the mouth of the canal on the eastern or Punda side, but now it has been incorporated into the Van Der Valk Plaza Hotel. The task of standing guard has been taken over by **Fort Amsterdam,** site of the Governor's Palace and the 1769 Dutch Reformed church. The church still has a British cannonball embedded in it. The arches leading to the fort were tunneled under the official residence of the governor.

A corner of the fort stands at the intersection of Breedestraat and Handelskade, the starting point for a plunge into the island's major shopping district.

A few minutes' walk from the pontoon bridge, at the north end of Handelskade, is the **Floating Market,** where scores of schooners tie up alongside the canal, a few yards from the main shopping section. Docked boats arrive from Venezuela and Colombia, as well as other West Indian islands, to sell tropical fruits and vegetables—a little bit of everything, in fact. The modern market under its vast concrete cap has not replaced this unique shopping expedition, which is fun to watch. Either arrive early or stay late to view the panoramic scene.

At some point save time to visit the **Waterfort Arches,** stretching for a quarter mile. They rise 30 feet high and are built of barrel-vaulted 17th-century stone set against the sea. Waterfort offers a chance to explore boutiques, have film developed fast, cash a traveler's check, or else purchase fruit-flavored ice cream. You can walk through to a breezy terrace on the sea for a local Amstel beer or a choice of restaurants. At night the grand buildings and cobbled walkways are illuminated.

Between the I. H. (Sha) Capriles Kade and Fort Amsterdam, at the corner of Columbusstraat and Hanchi di Snoa, stands the **Mikve Israel-Emanuel Synagogue** (**☎ 599/9-611633**), one of the oldest synagogue buildings in the western hemisphere. Consecrated on the eve of Passover in 1732, it antedates the first U.S. synagogue (in Newport, Rhode Island) by 31 years and houses the oldest Jewish congregation in the New World, dating from 1651. A fine example of Dutch colonial architecture, covering about a square block in the heart of Willemstad, it was built in a Spanish-style walled courtyard, with four large portals. Sand covers the sanctuary floor following a Portuguese Sephardic custom, representing the desert where Israelites camped when the Jews passed from slavery to freedom. The *theba* (pulpit) is in the center, and the congregation surrounds it. The highlight of the east wall is the Holy Ark, rising 17 feet, and a raised banca, canopied in mahogany, is on the north wall.

Joaño d'Illan led the first Jewish settlers (13 families) to the island in 1651, almost half a century after their expulsion from Portugal by the Inquisition. The settlers came via Amsterdam to Curaçao. The first Jew to arrive on Curaçao (although he stayed less than a year) was Samuel Coheno, an interpreter for the Dutch naval commander, Johan van Walbeck, who wrested Curaçao from the Spaniards in 1634.

The synagogue has services on Friday at 6:30pm and Saturday at 10am, as well as similar holiday service times. Visitors are welcome to all services, with appropriate dress required.

Adjacent to the synagogue courtyard is the **Jewish Cultural Historical Museum,** Kuiperstraat 26–28, housed in two buildings dating back to 1728. They were originally the rabbi's residence and the bathhouse. The 2½-centuries-old mikvah, or bath for religious purification purposes, was in constant use until around 1850 when this practice was discontinued and the buildings sold. They have been re-acquired through the Foundation for the Preservation of Historic Monuments and turned into the present museum. On display are a great many ritual, ceremonial, and cultural objects, many of which date back to the 17th and 18th centuries and are still in use by the congregation for holidays and events.

The synagogue and museum are open to visitors Monday to Friday from 9 to 11:45am and 2:30 to 4:45pm; if there's a cruise ship in port, also on Sunday from 9am to noon. There's a $2 entrance fee to the museum.

West of Willemstad

You can walk to the **Curaçao Museum,** Van Leeuwenhoekstraat (☎ **599/9-626051**), from the Queen Emma Pontoon Bridge. The tiny museum was built in 1853 by the Royal Dutch Army Corps of Engineers as a military quarantine hospital for yellow fever victims and was carefully restored in 1946–48 as a fine example of 19th-century Dutch architecture. Equipped with paintings, objets d'art, and antique furniture made in the 19th century by local cabinetmakers, it re-creates the atmosphere of an era gone by. The museum contains a large collection from the Caiquetio tribes, the early inhabitants described by Amerigo Vespucci as 7-foot-tall giants. In the gardens are specimens of the island's trees and plants. There's also a reconstruction of a traditional music pavilion in the garden where Curaçao musicians give regular performances. It's open Monday to Friday from 9am to noon and 2 to 5pm, and on Sunday from 10am to 4pm. Admission is $2.50 for adults, $1.25 for children 13 and under.

The **Curaçao Underwater Marine Park** (☎ **599/9-624242**), established in 1983 with the financial aid of the World Wildlife Fund, stretches from the Princess Beach Resort & Casino to the east point of the island, a strip of about 12½ miles of untouched coral reefs. For information on snorkeling, scuba diving, and trips in a glass-bottom boat to view the park, see "Beaches, Water Sports & Outdoor Pursuits," above.

The **Country House Museum,** Doktorstuin 27 (☎ **599/9-642742**), is located 12 miles west of Willemstad. This is a small-scale restoration of a 19th-century manor house that boasts thick stone walls, a thatched roof, and artifacts that represent the old-fashioned methods of agriculture and fishing. It's open Tuesday to Friday from 8am to 4pm, and Saturday and Sunday from 8am to 6pm. Admission is $1.50.

En route to Westpunt, you'll come across a seaside cavern known as **Boca Tabla,** one of many such grottoes on this rugged, uninhabited northwest coast.

In the Westpunt area, a 45-minute ride from Punda in Willemstad, **Playa Forti** is a stark region characterized by soaring hills and towering cacti, along with 200-year-old Dutch land houses, the former mansions that housed slave owners.

Out toward the western tip of Curaçao, a high-wire fence surrounds the entrance to the 4,500-acre **Christoffel National Park** in Savonet (☎ **599/9-640363**), about a 45-minute drive from the capital. A macadam road gives way to dirt, surrounded on all sides by abundant cactus and bromeliads. In the higher regions you can spot rare orchids. Rising from flat, arid countryside, 1,230-foot-high St. Christoffelberg is the highest point in the Dutch Leewards. Donkeys, wild goats, iguanas, the Curaçao deer, and many species of birds thrive in this preserve, and there are some Arawak paintings on a coral cliff near the two caves. A folk legend surrounds Piedra di Monton, a rock heap accumulated by African slaves who worked on the former plantations. According to the legend passed down through the generations, any worker would be able to climb to the top of the rockpile, jump off, and fly back home across the Atlantic. If, however, the slave had at any time in his life tasted a grain of salt, the magic would not work and he would crash to his death below.

The park has 20 miles of one-way trail-like roads, with lots of flora and fauna along the way. The shortest trail is about 5 miles long, and because of the rough terrain, takes about 40 minutes to drive through. Various walking trails are available also. One of them will take you to the top of St. Christoffelberg in about 1 1/2 hours. (Come early in the morning when it isn't so hot.) The park is open Monday to Saturday from 8am to 4pm and on Sunday from 6am to 3pm. Admission is $9 for both adults and children. The park also has a museum with varying exhibitions year-round set in an old storehouse left over from plantation days. Phone to arrange a guided tour. Next door, the park has opened the **National Park Shete Boka** (Seven Bays). It's a turtle sanctuary and contains a cave with pounding waves off the choppy north coast. Admission to this park is $1.50 per person.

NORTH & EAST OF WILLEMSTAD

Just northeast of the capital, **Fort Nassau** was completed in 1797 and christened by the Dutch as Fort Republic. Built high on a hill overlooking the harbor entrance to the south and St. Anna Bay to the north, it was fortified as a second line of defense in case the Waterfront gave way. When the British invaded in 1807, they renamed it Fort George in honor of their own king. Later, when the Dutch regained control, they renamed it Orange Nassau in honor of the Dutch royal family. Today diners have replaced soldiers (see "Where to Dine," above).

Along the coast to the southeast of town, the oddly shaped **Octagon House** on Penstraat was where the liberator, Simón Bolívar, used to visit his two sisters during the wars for Venezuelan independence. This landmark used to be a museum, but it's now closed.

In the area, the **Amstel Brewery** (☎ **599/9-612944**) allows visitors to tour its plant where Curaçao beer is brewed from desalinated seawater. Tours are given only on Tuesday and Thursday at 9:30am.

In addition, the **Curaçao Liqueur Distillery,** in the Salinja area (☎ **599/9-613526**), offers a chance to visit and taste at Chobolobo, the 17th-century landhuis where the famous Curaçao liqueur is made. The cordial, named after the region where it originated, is a distillate of dried peel of a particular strain of orange found only on Curaçao. Several herbs are added to give it an aromatic bouquet. It's made by a secret formula handed down through generations. One of the rewards of a visit here is a free snifter of the liqueur, offered Monday to Friday from 8am to noon and 1 to 5pm.

On Schottegatweg West, northwest of Willemstad, past the oil refineries, lies the **Beth Haim Cemetery,** the oldest Caucasian burial site still in use in the western hemisphere. Meaning "House of Life," the cemetery was consecrated before 1659. On about 3 acres are some 2,500 graves. The carving on some of the 17th- and 18th-century tombstones is exceptional.

Landhuis Brievengat, Brienvengat (☎ **599/9-378344**), gives visitors a chance to visit a Dutch version of an 18th-century West Indian plantation house. This stately building, in a scrub-dotted landscape on the eastern side of the island, contains a few antiques, high ceilings, and a gallery facing two entrance towers, said to have been used to imprison slaves. The plantation was originally used for the cultivation of aloe and cattle, but an 1877 hurricane caused the plantation to cease operation. The building was pulled down, but around 1925 the remains of the structure were donated to the Society for the Preservation of Monuments, which rebuilt and restored it. It's open daily from 9:30am to noon and 3 to 6pm; admission is $1.

The **Hato Caves,** F. D. Rooseveltweg (☎ **599/9-680379**), have been called "mystical." Every hour, professional local guides take visitors through this Curaçao world of stalagmites and stalactites, found in the highest limestone terrace of the island. Actually, they were once old coral reefs, which were formed when the ocean water fell and the land mass was lifted up over the years. Over thousands of years, limestone formations were created, some mirrored in an underground lake. After crossing the lake, you enter the "Cathedral," an underground cavern. The largest hall of the cave is called La Ventana or "The Window." Also displayed are samples of ancient Indian petroglyph drawings. The caves are open Tuesday to Sunday from 10am to 5pm, charging $6.25 for adults and $4.50 for children 4 to 11 (free for kids 3 and under).

The **Curaçao Seaquarium,** off Dr. Martin Luther King Boulevard at a site called Bapor Kibrá (☎ **599/9-616666**), has more than 400 species of fish, crabs, anemones, sponges, and coral displayed and growing in a natural environment. A rustic boardwalk connects the low-lying hexagonal buildings comprising the Seaquarium complex, which sits near a point where the *Oranje Nassau* hit the rocks and sank in 1906 (the name of the site, Bapor Kibrá, means "sunken ship"). Located a few minutes' walk along the rocky coast from the Princess Beach Resort & Casino, the Seaquarium is open daily from 8:30am to 11pm. Admission to the Seaquarium is $13.25 for adults, $7.50 for children 14 and under.

A special feature of the aquarium is a "shark and animal encounter." Divers, snorkelers, and experienced swimmers are able to feed, film, and photograph sharks, which are separated from them by a large window with feeding holes. In the Animal-Encounter section, swimmers are able to swim among stingrays, lobsters, tarpons, parrotfish, and other marine life, feeding and photographing these creatures in a controlled environment where safety is always a consideration. For the nonswimmer, a 46-foot semisubmarine (underwater observatory) is in the middle. Sharks as well as other species are "called" to the windows of the semisubmarine for a close-up view. The Animal Encounters exhibit allows you to interact with stingrays, angelfish, tarpon, and grouper. The Seaquarium is also home to Curaçao's only full-facility, palm-shaded, white-sand beach.

The newest attraction at the Seaquarium is the *Seaworld Explorer,* a semi-submersible submarine that departs daily at 4:30pm on hour-long journeys into the deep. You're taken on a tour of submerged wrecks off the shores of Curaçao and are treated to close encounters of coral reefs with their rainbow-hued tropical fish. The *Explorer* has a barge top that submerges only 5 or so feet under the water, but the submerged section has wide glass windows allowing passengers underwater views, which can extend for 110 feet or so. Reservations must be made a day in advance by calling ☎ **599/9-628986.** Adults pay $30.75; children 11 and under are charged $20.15.

Sightseeing Tours

Taber Tours, Dokweg (☎ **599/9-376637**), offers several tours, both day and night, to points of interest on Curaçao. The tour through Willemstad, to the Curaçao Liqueur distillery, through the residential area and the Bloempot shopping center, and to the Curaçao Museum (admission fee included in the tour price) costs $12.50 for adults, $6.25 for children 11 and under.

The easiest way to go exploring is to take a 1¼-hour trolley tour, visiting the highlights of Willemstad. The open-sided cars, pulled by a silent "locomotive," make two tours each week—Monday at 11am and Wednesday at 4pm. The tour begins at Fort Amsterdam near the Queen Emma Pontoon Bridge. The cost is $15 for adults or $10 for children 2 to 12 (free 1 and under). Call ☎ **599/9-628833** for more information.

Shopping

Curaçao is a shopper's paradise. Some 200 shops line the major shopping malls of such streets as Heerenstraat and Breedestraat. Right in the heart of Willemstad, the Punda shopping area is a five-block district. Most stores are open Monday to Saturday from 8am to noon and 2 to 6pm (some, from 8am to 6pm). When cruise ships are in port, stores are also open for a few hours on Sunday and holidays. To avoid the cruise-ship crowds, do your shopping in the morning.

Look for good buys in French perfumes, Dutch Delft blue souvenirs, finely woven Italian silks, Japanese and German cameras, jewelry, silver, Swiss watches, linens, leather goods, liquor, and island-made rum and liqueurs, especially Curaçao liqueur, some of which has a distinctive blue color. The island is famous for its 5-pound "wheels" of Gouda or Edam cheese. It also sells wooden shoes, although we're not sure what you'd do with them. Some of its stores also stock some good buys in intricate lacework imported from Portugal, China, and everywhere between. If you're a street shopper and want something colorful for a back bathroom, consider one of the wood carvings or flamboyant paintings from Haiti or the Dominican Republic. Both are hawked by street vendors at any of the main plazas.

Incidentally, Curaçao is not technically a free port, but its prices are often inexpensive because of its low import duty.

Benetton. Madurostraat 4. ☎ **599/9-614619.**

This member of a worldwide casual sportswear chain based in Italy has invaded Curaçao with all its many colors. In July you can stock up on winter wear, and in December make summer purchases. Some items are marked down by about 20% off Stateside prices.

Bert Knubben Black Koral Art Studio. In the Princess Beach Resort & Casino, Dr. Martin Luther King Blvd. ☎ **599/9-367888.**

Bert Knubben is a name synonymous with craftsmanship and quality. Although collection of black coral has been made illegal by the Curaçao government, an exception was made for Bert, a diver who has been harvesting corals from the sea and fashioning them into the fine jewelry and objets d'art for more than 35 years. The jewelry is finished with 14-karat gold. Collectors avidly seek out this type of coral, not only because of the craftsmanship in the work, but because it's becoming increasingly rare and may one day not be offered for sale at all. The black coral jewelry is rivaled only by Bernard I. Passman's "Black Coral and . . ." shops in George Town in the Cayman Islands and in Charlotte Amalie on St. Thomas.

Boolchand's. Heerenstraat 4B, Punda. ☎ **599/9-612262.**

In business since 1930, Boolchand's stands for reliability in electronic equipment. Electronics are a good buy in Curaçao because the local government has declared that these can be sold duty free.

Gandelman Jewelers. Breedestraat 35, Punda. ☎ **599/9-611854.**

This is the island's best and most reliable choice for the jewelry collector. The store is well stocked with a large selection of fine jewelry, often exquisitely designed, and set with diamonds, rubies, emeralds, sapphires, and other gemstones. Of course, these items are sold all around the world; if you want something local, ask to see their selection of Curaçaoan gold pieces. They come in a vast selection of modern settings and designs, some of them worthy of an award. Here you'll find timepieces by Piaget, Corum, Concord, Baume & Mercier, Tag Heuer, Gucci, Swiss Army, Fendi, Swatch, and many others. Exclusive here is the unique line of Prima Classe leather goods with the world map. Gandelman Jewelers has eight other stores in the Dutch Caribbean.

Obra Di Man. Bargestraat 57. ☎ **599/9-612413.**

Some shoppers ignore the jewelry and camera stores (merchandise available almost anywhere) and seek out local crafts instead. The best selection for authentic local handcraft items, especially handmade dolls, is Obra Di Man. Most of the dolls here represent island folkloric characters. These dolls are authentic: You won't find *Made in Korea* pasted on them. The store also sells hand-screened fabrics, black coral jewelry, and souvenirs of your Curaçao visit. You can also purchase posters of Curaçao's architecture.

Palais Hindu. Heerenstraat 17. ☎ **599/9-616897.**

To satisfy your audio and video needs, Palais Hindu sells a wide range of video and cassette recorders. It also stocks a lot of photographic equipment, along with cameras and watches. Go here only if you didn't find what you were looking for at Boolchand's, a store that has the upper hand in similar merchandise.

Penha & Sons. Heerenstraat 1. ☎ **599/9-612266.**

In the oldest building in town, constructed in 1708, this traditional outlet has a history dating from 1865. It has long been known for its perfumes and brand-name clothes, one of the finest collections in the ABC islands. It's the distributor of such names as Boucheron, Calvin Klein, Yves Saint Laurent, and other perfumes and cosmetics of Elizabeth Arden, Clinique, Clarins, and Estée Lauder, among others. The collection of merchandise at this prestigious store is quite varied—Hummel figurines and Delft blue souvenirs. Their men's and women's boutiques feature travel and sportswear. The firm has 10 other stores in the Caribbean.

The Yellow House (La Casa Amarilla). Breedestraat 46. ☎ **599/9-613222.**

Housed in a yellow-and-white 19th-century building, and operating since 1887, this place sells an intriguing collection of perfume from all over the world, and is an agent of Christian Dior, Guerlain, Cartier, and Van Cleef & Arpels. It has the widest and best selection of perfume on Curaçao, although it isn't a "cut-rate" discount house. There's also an impressive array of cosmetics.

CURAÇAO AFTER DARK

Most of the action spins around the island's **casinos:** at the Sonesta Beach Hotel & Casino Curaçao, the Curaçao Caribbean Hotel & Casino, the Holiday Beach Hotel & Casino, and the Princess Beach Resort & Casino—all hotels previously recommended. The Emerald Casino at the Sonesta is especially popular, designed to resemble an open-air courtyard. It features 143 slot machines, 6 blackjack tables, 2 roulette wheels, 2 Caribbean stud poker tables, 1 craps table, 1 baccarat table, and 1 minibaccarat table. The casino at the Princess Beach Hotel is the liveliest on the island. These hotel gaming houses usually start their action at 2pm, and some of them remain open until 4am. The Princess Beach serves complimentary drinks.

The historic **Landhuis Brievengat** (see "Seeing the Sights," above), in addition to being a museum with island artifacts, is also the site of Wednesday and Friday night rijsttafel parties. They begin at 7pm, require an admission fee of $8 (which includes the first drink), and feature heaping portions of rijsttafel that begin at $16 each. Although the Landhuis itself is not directly connected with the dancing and drinking, there's a platform set up amid the flamboyant trees nearby, and two bands that alternate with one another to provide a happy ambience. It's wise to phone before going, but the event, especially on Friday nights, is very popular.

The landlocked, flat, and somewhat dusty neighborhood of **Salinja** is now the nightlife capital of Curaçao, with many drinking and dancing outlets. Among the best of them are:

Club Façade. Lindbergweg 8. ☎ **599/9-614640.** Cover $10.

In the Salinja district, this is one of the most popular discos on the island. Spread over several different levels of a modern building, it has a huge bar and three dance floors, and is sometimes filled with balloons. There's live music daily. Open Wednesday to Sunday from 8pm to 3am.

Club Safari. Lindbergweg, Salinja. ☎ **599/9-655453.** Cover $6–$7.

In a sprawling and much-renovated low-slung building set inland from the coast, in the heart of the Salinja district, this is the leading and most attractive disco on Curaçao. The jungle motif is enhanced with masses of coconut palms, a dance floor where rhythms seem to pulsate out of the floor, and a copious bar area where more than a usual number of drinks seem to be tinted blue. Although hours vary with the season and according to the number of foreign visitors on island, it's usually open Wednesday to Sunday from 9:30pm to 2am.

Index of Hotels and Resorts